Fodor's 2014

ITALY

WELCOME TO ITALY

Italy is the kind of destination that travelers return to over and over. They come for awe-inspiring art and architecture that influenced Western civilization, and stunning historical ruins—as well as for some of the world's best food and wine. Also beckoning irresistibly are Italy's sun-kissed olive groves and vineyards, the sparkling waters of Lake Como and the Mediterranean, and atmospheric monasteries, castles, and farmhouses. And if you seek vibrant cities with renowned museums, restaurants, and shopping opportunities, Rome, Florence, and Milan await.

TOP REASONS TO GO

★ **Food:** Italy is a pasta lover's paradise; but don't forget the pizza and the gelato.

★ **Romance:** Whether you're strolling atmospheric Venice or sipping wine, Italy enchants.

★ **History:** The ruins of ancient Pompeii and the leaning tower of Pisa breathe antiquity.

★ **Art:** The big hitters—Botticelli, Michelangelo, Raphael, Caravaggio, and more.

★ **Shopping:** Few things say quality or style like "made in Italy."

★ **Stunning landscapes:** Tuscany, the Amalfi Coast, the Cinque Terre, to name just a few.

Fodor's ITALY 2014

Publisher: Amanda D'Acierno, *Senior Vice President*

Editorial: Arabella Bowen, *Executive Editorial Director*; Linda Cabasin, *Editorial Director*

Design: Fabrizio La Rocca, *Vice President, Creative Director*; Tina Malaney, *Associate Art Director*; Chie Ushio, *Senior Designer*; Ann McBride, *Production Designer*

Photography: Melanie Marin, *Associate Director of Photography*; Jessica Parkhill and Jennifer Romains, *Researchers*

Maps: Rebecca Baer, *Map Editor*; David Lindroth and Mark Stroud (Moon Street Cartography) *Cartographers*

Production: Linda Schmidt, *Managing Editor*; Evangelos Vasilakis, *Associate Managing Editor*; Angela L. McLean, *Senior Production Manager*

Sales: Jacqueline Lebow, *Sales Director*

Marketing & Publicity: Heather Dalton, *Marketing Director*; Katherine Fleming, *Senior Publicist*

Business & Operations: Susan Livingston, *Vice President, Strategic Business Planning*; Sue Daulton, *Vice President, Operations*

Fodors.com: Megan Bell, *Executive Director, Revenue & Business Development*; Yasmin Marinaro, *Senior Director, Marketing & Partnerships*

Writers: Lynda Albertson, Nicole Arriaga, Martin Wilmot Bennett, Peter Blackman, Erica Firpo, Fergal Kavanagh, Dana Klitzberg, Bruce Leimsidor, Megan McCaffrey-Guerrera, Patricia Rucidlo, Amanda Ruggeri, Margaret Stenhouse, Mark Walters, Jonathan Willcocks

Editors: Stephen Brewer, Robert I. C. Fisher, Jess Moss, Penny Phenix, Caroline Trefler

Production Editor: Jennifer DePrima

ISBN 978-0-7704-3231-7

ISSN 0361–977X

SPECIAL SALES

This book is available at special discounts for bulk purchases for sales promotions or premiums. For more information, e-mail specialmarkets@randomhouse.com

PRINTED IN CHINA

10 9 8 7 6 5 4 3 2 1

CONTENTS

Fodor's Features

NORTHERN ITALY

MAPS

ABOUT THIS GUIDE

Fodor's Recommendations

Everything in this guide is worth doing—we don't cover what isn't—but exceptional sights, hotels, and restaurants are recognized with additional accolades. **Fodor's Choice★** indicates our top recommendations; and **Best Bets** call attention to notable hotels and restaurants in various categories. Care to nominate a new place? Visit Fodors.com/contact-us.

Trip Costs

We list prices wherever possible to help you budget well. Hotel and restaurant price categories from **$** to **$$$$** are noted alongside each recommendation. For hotels, we include the lowest cost of a standard double room in high season. For restaurants, we cite the average cost of a meal. The meal includes three courses: *primo* (usually pasta or an appetizer), *secondo* (meat or fish main course), and *dolce* (dessert). For attractions, we always list adult admission fees; discounts are usually available for children, students, and senior citizens.

Hotels

Our local writers vet every hotel to recommend the best overnights in each price category, from budget to expensive. Unless otherwise specified, you can expect private bath, phone, and TV in your room. For expanded hotel reviews, facilities, and deals visit Fodors.com.

Restaurants

Unless we state otherwise, restaurants are open for lunch and dinner daily. We mention dress code only when there's a specific requirement and reservations only when they're essential or not accepted. To make restaurant reservations, visit Fodors.com.

Top Picks
★ Fodor's Choice

Listings
✉ Address
✉ Branch address
☎ Telephone
🖷 Fax
⊕ Website
✉ E-mail
🎫 Admission fee
☉ Open/closed times
Ⓜ Subway
⊹ Directions or Map coordinates

Hotels & Restaurants
🏨 Hotel
↩ Number of rooms
🍴 Meal plans
✗ Restaurant
✍ Reservations
👔 Dress code
⊟ No credit cards
Ⓢ Price

Other
⇨ See also
☞ Take note
⛳ Golf facilities

Credit Cards

The hotels and restaurants in this guide typically accept credit cards. If not, we'll say so.

EXPERIENCE
ITALY

ITALY TODAY

... is eating well

The old joke says that three-quarters of the food and wine served in Italy is good... and the rest is amazing. In some sense, that's still true, and the "good" 75% has gotten even better.

Those pundits would claim that ingredients that in the past were available only to the wealthy can now be found even in the remotest parts of the country at reasonable prices. Dishes originally conceived to make the most of inferior cuts of meat or the least flavorful part of vegetables are now made with the best.

But there's increasing evidence—pause, gesture, exclamation—that many Italians would say that the food in Italy is getting worse. There's a proliferation of fast food, and increasing tourism has allowed many restaurants to lower their standards while raising their prices. This is true not only in Rome, but in most other tourist centers as well. Also, economic developments have brought women into the workplace and people don't go home for lunch prepared by mamma anymore. Accordingly, the standard that young people are exposed to has changed, and not for the better.

The good news is Italy is home to one of the world's greatest cuisines, and its traditional favorites still put meat on bones and smiles on faces. Italian restaurateurs seem determined to make the most of the country's reputation for good food. Though quaint family-run trattorias with checkered tablecloths, traditional dishes, and informal atmosphere are still common but on the decline, nearly every town has a newer eatery with matching flatware, a proper wine list, and an innovative menu.

The same is true of Italian wine. A generation ago, the omnipresent straw-basket Chianti was a mainstay of pizzerias around the world, but the wine inside was often watery and insipid. Today, through investment and experimentation, Italy's winemakers are figuring out how to get the most from their gorgeous vineyards. It's fair to say that Italy now produces more types of high-quality wine from more different grape varieties than any other country in the world.

... is passionate about soccer

Soccer stands without rival as the national sport of Italy, but recent years have seen some changes to the beautiful game. On the positive side, Italy won its fourth World Cup in 2006, giving the country more world titles than any other this side of Brazil. The game is still played at a high level and its teams do well in international tournaments. In the past few years, however, soccer lovers have had to come to terms with a series of unwelcome developments, including more violence around the stadia (which keeps children away), rigged referee selections to favor some major teams, and, worst of all, match-fixing at all levels (and throughout Europe) financed by betting consortia in Asia. More games in the schedule and dwindling fan bases mean fewer people are seen at the stadium. Still, the fans can't stop watching the game on television.

... is getting older

Italy's population is the oldest in Europe (worldwide, only Japan's is older)—the result of its low birth rate, relatively strict immigration standards, and one of the highest life expectancy rates in the world. As of 2012, the median Italian was 43.8 years old (compared to 37.1 in the U.S.) and the number keeps rising.

The result is a remarkably stable population: the number of Italian residents

barely rises most years, and, according to the most recent estimates, is projected to start contracting by 2020. But the situation is putting a strain on the country's pension system and on families, because elderly family members are likely to live with their children or grandchildren in a country where retirement homes are rare.

The trend also has an impact in other areas, including politics (where older politicians are eager to promote policies aimed at older voters), the popular culture (where everything from fashion to television programming takes older consumers into consideration), and a kind of far-reaching nostalgia. Thanks to a long collective memory, it's common to hear even younger Italians celebrate or rue something that happened 50 or 60 years earlier as if it had just taken place.

... lives with a black-market economy

Nobody knows how big Italy's black-market economy is, though experts all agree it's massive. Estimates place it at anywhere from a fourth to a half of the official, legal economy.

Put another way, if the highest estimates are correct, Italy's black market is about as large as the entire economy of Switzerland or Indonesia. If the estimated black-market figures were added to the official GDP, Italy would likely leapfrog France and the U.K. to become the world's fifth-largest economy.

The presence of the black market isn't obvious to the casual observer, but whenever a customer isn't given a printed receipt in a store or restaurant, tobacco without a tax seal is bought from a street seller, or a product or service is exchanged for another product or service, that means the transaction goes unrecorded, unreported, and untaxed. But that's all penny-ante stuff compared to what many professionals evade by neglecting to declare all they earn.

... has a growing parks system

Italy boasts 25 national parks covering a total of around 1.5 million hectares (58,000 square miles), or about 5% of the entire surface area of the country—more than twice as much as 25 years ago. And a new park is added or an existing park is expanded every few months.

Part of the reason for the expansion has been a growing environmental movement in Italy, which has lobbied the government to annex undeveloped land for parks, thus protecting against development. But the trend is a boon for visitors and nature lovers, who can enjoy huge expanses of unspoiled territory.

... is staying home in August

Italy used to be the best example of Europe's famous August exodus—where city dwellers would spend most of the month at the seaside or in the mountains, leaving the cities nearly deserted. Today the phenomenon continues, but is much less prevalent, as economic pressures have forced companies to keep operating through August. As a result, vacations are more staggered and vacationers' plans are often more modest.

The loss of shared vacation time for Italian workers can be a boon to visitors, both because in August there's more room at the seaside and in the mountains, and because cities have taken to promoting local events designed to appeal to residents who are staying put. These days, summers in Italy boast a plethora of outdoor concerts and plays; longer restaurant and museum hours; and food, wine, and culture fairs.

WHAT'S NEW

Steeped in history and tradition, and bearing a lustrous patina of antiquity, Italy luxuriates in the illusion that change comes slowly—or maybe not at all—in the *Bel Paese*. Despite the ravages of war and urban renewal, Italians have skillfully retained so much of the past that it seems the historical centers of many Italian cities would be easily recognizable to residents of 350 years ago. The present and the past merge seamlessly. Tiny cars and whining scooters in Italian cities and towns maneuver without missing a beat through narrow cobblestone streets designed for horses and carriages.

The Hot, the Hip, and the New

The pervasiveness of the past also makes us forget that Italy, not by breaking with tradition but rather by continuing it, has been in the forefront of creating major monuments of today's style. By creating everything from skyscrapers to sports cars, raincoats to coffee pots, contemporary Italian designers and architects have infused beauty into the everyday lives of people around the world. In so doing, they have proved themselves to be true sons and daughters of the Renaissance, heirs to Brunelleschi and Leonardo, who bound together the ideas of beauty and functionality.

Despite Italy's ties to the past, "modern" and "Italian design" have become almost synonymous. Perhaps because Italy, or more exactly, Milan has become the epicenter of the fashion and design world, Italians seem to be more obsessed with fashion and with the "new" than other Europeans are. While you'll easily be able to buy your choice of a classic suit or dress for business wear, for casual wear you'll have to look hard for a sweater or shirt that's not in the very latest season's color or cut. And be forewarned: there's zero tolerance for even slightly worn or frayed clothing.

After Berlusconi

Visitors also tend to forget that Italy is one of Europe's newest countries, having been unified only in 1861. Prior to that, Italy had been divided into myriad states, some at times independent and glorious, but most for centuries under the domination of Spain, France, Austria, or the Papacy. Many Italians still identify with their region or city more strongly than with the Italian nation, and local cultural and even linguistic differences have been maintained.

The variety and contrasts that Italian regionalism produces makes Italy a fascinating place to visit, but it weakens Italians' commitment to developing a viable nation-state. The centuries-long period of foreign domination may also explain the weakness in Italy of the democratic social and political institutions now taken for granted in many other west European countries, contributing to Italy's frequent episodes of political instability.

The idea that Italy really can't govern itself—shared even by many Italians—and the weakness of its political institutions came home to roost in the most recent change of government. Like a disturbing dream from the past, it was foreign powers, not Italians, who indirectly, but quite clearly, forced the elected (but corrupt and inept) Italian government from power.

In late 2011 it was understood by European leaders that the government of Silvio Berlusconi had led Italy into a fiscally chaotic situation that seriously threatened the economic stability of the European Union. Previously, over the course of several months, the EU had pressed Mr. Berlusconi to institute the painful but necessary

fiscal and labor market reforms to rebuild confidence in the Italian economy and stimulate growth.

Finally, facing increasingly severe expressions of lack of confidence in Italy from international financial markets, the EU, through threats of withdrawal of fiscal support, which would have plunged Italy into extreme economic chaos, caused Parliament to deliver a vote of no confidence, thus forcing Berlusconi from power. The Italian President appointed an unelected technocrat prime minister, Mario Monti, to initiate and carry through far-reaching reforms that imply a substantial restructuring of Italian society. At this writing, the EU is satisfied with the job Mr. Monti is doing, but he's encountering fierce resistance from Berlusconi's allies in Parliament and from broad sectors of the Italian populace.

How to Handle Immigration

Italians have long enjoyed a reputation for being a friendly and hospitable people, but lately that situation seems to have changed. Until quite recently, more Italians left than immigrants arrived, but with growing Italian prosperity, unaccustomed numbers of refugees (and people simply looking for a better material life) began arriving from across the Mediterranean and from Eastern Europe. Although Italy still has a lower percentage of foreign-born residents than most western European countries (and the increased immigration has had no effect either on crime or the unemployment rate), the Berlusconi government was able to politicize the issue and manipulate public opinion against immigrants. Italy has subsequently been rated as the most xenophobic country in Europe, and its government strongly

condemned by the human rights body of the European Union.

But Italian friendliness and hospitality haven't totally disappeared; even those who complain about immigrants will contribute generously to charities assisting them, and incidents of violence against immigrants are much less frequent in Italy than in other European countries.

A Secular State? Well, Maybe . . .

Rome is still the spiritual home of the world's 1.1 billion Catholics, but, as in other European countries, church attendance in Italy has been eroding since the 1950s, and today fewer than one in five Italians attend church regularly. Although religion is assumed to maintain a powerful hold on Italian life, with the Church regularly weighing in on political and social issues, the Church was powerless to dampen the well-publicized sexual excesses of Mr. Berlusconi, and its voice was ignored when opposing the anti-immigrant and xenophobic measures of his government.

While the Church has been able to silence any serious discussion of legalization of same-sex relationships, it's been less effective in doing the same with issues that concern the personal interests of large numbers of Italians. Divorce, although complicated, is possible in Italy; so is legal abortion.

Although the Italian Constitution proclaims that Italy is a secular state, a crucifix still adorns courts and schoolrooms, and if you're unlucky enough to land in jail, a statue of the Madonna is likely to greet you as you enter. The Italian courts have ruled that these are cultural, and not religious, symbols.

WHAT'S WHERE

1 **Rome.** Italy's capital is one of the great cities of Europe. It's a large, busy metropolis that lives in the here and now, yet there's no other place on earth where you'll encounter such powerful evocations of a long and spectacular past, from the Colosseum to the dome of St. Peter's.

2 **Northern Italy.** The prosperous north has Italy's most sophisticated culture and its most diverse landscape. **Venice** is a rare jewel of a city, while **Milan** and **Turin** are centers of commerce and style. Along the country's northern border, the mountain peaks of the **Dolomites** and **Valle d'Aosta** attract skiers in winter and hikers in summer, while the **Lake District** and the coastline of the **Riviera** are classic summertime playgrounds. Food here is also exceptional, from the French-influenced cuisine of **Piedmont** to Italian classics prepared with unrivaled skill in **Emilia-Romagna.**

3 **Central Italy.** No place better epitomizes the greatness of the Renaissance than

Florence, where there's a masterpiece around every corner, from Michelangelo's *David* to Botticelli's *Venus.* Elsewhere, the central regions of **Tuscany** and **Umbria** are characterized by midsize cities and small hilltop towns, each with its own rich history and art treasures. Highlights include the walled city of **Lucca; Pisa** and its Leaning Tower; **Siena,** home of the Palio; and **Assisi,** the city of St. Francis. In between, the gorgeous countryside produces some of Italy's finest wine.

4 **Southern Italy.** The region of **Campania** is a popular place both to unwind—on the pint-size island of **Capri** or in the resort towns of the **Amalfi Coast**—and to explore the past—at the archaeological ruins of **Pompeii, Herculaneum,** and **Paestum.** In the middle of everything is the vibrant, chaotic city of **Naples.** Farther south, in the off-the-beaten-path regions of **Puglia, Basilicata,** and **Calabria,** you'll find attractive beaches, mysterious ancient dwellings, and the charming town of **Lecce.** Across a narrow strait from Calabria is **Sicily.** Baroque church–hopping could be a sport on the cacophonous streets of **Palermo** and **Siracusa,** while one of the world's best-preserved Greek ruins stand amid the almond groves of **Agrigento.**

Elevation	
15,577	4,748
10,825	3,300
9,840	3,000
8,860	2,700
7,875	2,400
6,900	2,100
5,900	1,800
4,920	1,500
3,940	1,200
2,920	900
1,970	600
980	300
490	150
250	75
100	30
feet	meters

ITALY PLANNER

Getting Here

The major gateways to Italy are Rome's Aeroporto Leonardo da Vinci (FCO), better known as Fiumicino, and Milan's Aeroporto Malpensa (MXP). There are some direct flights to secondary airports, primarily Venice and Pisa, but to fly into most other Italian cities you need to make connections at Fiumicino, Malpensa, or another European hub. You can also take the FS airport train to Rome's Termini station or a bus to Milan's central train station (Centrale) and catch a train to any other location in Italy. It'll take about one hour to get from either Fiumicino or Malpensa to the train station.

Italy's airports all have restaurants and snack bars, and there's Internet access and at least one nearby hotel. Ramped-up security measures may include random baggage inspection and bomb-detection dogs. In the case of Florence and Pisa, the city centers are only a 15-minute taxi ride away.

For further information about getting where you want to go, see "Getting Here" at the beginning of each section of this book and the similar sections found under many town headings.

What to Pack

In summer, stick with light clothing, as things can get steamy in June, July, and August. But throw in a sweater in case of cool evenings, especially if you're headed for the mountains and/or islands. Sunglasses, a hat, and sunblock are essential. Brief summer afternoon thunderstorms are common in inland cities, so an umbrella will come in handy. In winter, bring a coat, gloves, hats, scarves, and boots. In winter, weather is generally milder than it is in the northern and central United States, but central heating may not be up to your standards, and interiors can be cold and damp; take wools or flannel rather than sheer fabrics. Bring sturdy shoes for winter and comfortable walking shoes in any season.

As a rule, Italians dress exceptionally well. They don't usually wear shorts. Men aren't required to wear ties or jackets anywhere, except in some of the grander hotel dining rooms and top-level restaurants, but are expected to look reasonably sharp—and they do. Formal wear is the exception rather than the rule at the opera nowadays, though people in expensive seats usually do get dressed up.

A certain modesty of dress (no bare shoulders or knees) is expected in churches, and strictly enforced in many.

For sightseeing, **pack a pair of binoculars**; they'll help you get a good look at painted ceilings and domes. If you stay in budget hotels, **take your own soap.** Many such hotels don't provide it, or they give guests only one tiny bar per room.

Restaurants: The Basics

A full meal in Italy has traditionally consisted of five courses, and every menu you encounter will still be organized along some version of this five-course plan.

■ First up is the *antipasto* (appetizer), often consisting of cured meats or marinated vegetables. Next to appear is the *primo,* usually pasta or soup, and after that the *secondo,* a meat or fish course with, perhaps, a *contorno* (vegetable dish) on the side. A simple *dolce* (dessert) rounds out the meal.

■ This, you've probably noticed, is a lot of food. Italians have noticed as well—a full, five-course meal is reserved for special occasions. Instead, meals are a mix-and-match affair: a primo and a secondo, or an antipasto and a primo, or a secondo and a contorno. In our reviews, the quoted prices are for meals consisting of a primo, secondo, and dolce.

■ The crucial rule of restaurant dining is that you should order at least two courses. It's a common mistake for tourists to order only a secondo, thinking they're getting a "main course" complete with side dishes. What they wind up with is one lonely piece of meat.

Hotels: The Basics

Hotels in Italy are usually well maintained, but in some respects they won't match what you find at comparably priced U.S. lodgings. Keep the following points in mind as you set your expectations, and you're likely to have a good experience:

■ First and foremost, rooms are usually smaller, particularly in cities. If you're truly cramped, ask for another room, but don't expect things to be spacious. A "double bed" is commonly two singles pushed together.

■ In the bathroom, tubs aren't a given—request one if it's essential. In budget places, showers sometimes use a drain in the middle of the bathroom floor. Most hotels have satellite TV, but there are fewer channels than in the United States, and only one or two will be in English.

■ Don't expect wall-to-wall carpeting. Particularly outside the cities, tile floors are the norm.

Speaking the Language

In most cities and many towns you won't have a hard time finding locals who speak at least rudimentary English. Odds are if the person you want to talk with doesn't know English, there will be someone within earshot who can help translate. The farther south you travel, the fewer English speakers you'll encounter, but if nothing else someone at your hotel will know a few words. No matter where in Italy you're going, if you learn some common phrases in Italian, your effort will be appreciated.

Driving in Italy

Americans tend to be well schooled in defensive-driving techniques. Many Italians aren't. When you hit the road, don't be surprised to encounter tailgating and high-risk passing. Your best response is to take the same safety-first approach you use at home. On the upside, most of Italy's roads are very well maintained. Note that wearing a seat belt and having your lights on at all times are required by law. Having a vehicle in Italian cities is almost always a liability, but outside the cities it's often crucial. An effective strategy is to start and end your Italian itinerary in major cities, car-free, and to pick up wheels for countryside touring in between.

ITALY
TOP ATTRACTIONS

The Vatican
(A) The home of the Catholic Church, a tiny independent state tucked within central Rome, holds some of the city's most spectacular sights, including St. Peter's Basilica, the Vatican Museums, and Michelangelo's Sistine Chapel ceiling. (⇨ *Chapter 1.*)

Ancient Rome
(B) The Colosseum and the Roman Forum are remarkable ruins from Rome's ancient past. Sitting above it all is the Campidoglio, with a piazza designed by Michelangelo and museums containing one of the world's finest collections of ancient art. (⇨ *Chapter 1.*)

Venice's Grand Canal
A trip down Venice's "Main Street," whether by water bus or gondola, is a signature Italian experience. (⇨ *Chapter 3.*)

Palladio's Villas and Palazzi
The 16th-century genius Andrea Palladio is one of the most influential figures in the history of architecture. You can visit his creations in his hometown of Vicenza, in and around Venice, and outside Treviso. (⇨ *Chapter 4.*)

Ravenna's Mosaics
This town off the Adriatic, once the capital of the Western Roman Empire and seat of the Byzantine Empire in the West, is home to 5th- and 6th-century mosaics that rank among the greatest art treasures in Italy. (⇨ *Chapter 9.*)

Galleria degli Uffizi, Florence
The Uffizi—Renaissance art's hall of fame—contains masterpieces by Leonardo, Michelangelo, Raphael, Botticelli, Caravaggio, and dozens of other luminaries. (⇨ *Chapter 10.*)

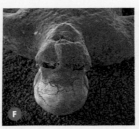

Duomo, Florence
(C) The massive dome of Florence's Cathedral of Santa Maria del Fiore (aka the Duomo) is one of the world's great feats of engineering. (⇨ *Chapter 10.*)

Piazza del Campo, Siena
(D) Siena is Tuscany's classic medieval hill town, and its heart is the Piazza del Campo, the beautiful, one-of-a-kind town square. (⇨ *Chapter 11.*)

Basilica di San Francesco, Assisi
(E) The giant basilica—made up of two churches, one built on top of the other—honors St. Francis with its remarkable fresco cycles. (⇨ *Chapter 12.*)

Palazzo Ducale, Urbino
No other building better exemplifies the principles and ideals of the Renaissance than this palace in the Marches region, east of Umbria. (⇨ *Chapter 12.*)

The Ruins of Pompeii
(F) When Vesuvius erupted in AD 79, its fallout froze the town of Pompeii in time. Walking its streets brings antiquity to life. (⇨ *Chapter 13.*)

Ravello, on the Amalfi Coast
(G) Nowhere else better captures the essence of the gorgeous Amalfi Coast than Ravello. Perched high above the Tyrrhenian Sea, it's the place to go for your blissful *la dolce vita* moment. (⇨ *Chapter 13.*)

Lecce, Puglia
With its lavish Baroque architecture and engaging street life, Lecce takes the prize for the most appealing town in Italy's deep south. (⇨ *Chapter 14.*)

Valle dei Templi, Sicily
(H) The Greek influence in Sicily dates to ancient days, as is borne out by these well-preserved temple ruins. (⇨ *Chapter 15.*)

TOP EXPERIENCES

Il Dolce Far Niente

"The sweetness of doing nothing" has long been an art form in Italy. This is a country in which life's pleasures are warmly celebrated, not guiltily indulged.

Of course, doing "nothing" doesn't really mean nothing. It means doing things differently: lingering over a glass of wine for the better part of an evening as you watch the sun slowly set; savoring a slow and flirtatious evening *passeggiata* (stroll) along the main street of a little town; and making a commitment—however temporary—to thinking that there's nowhere that you have to be next, and no other time but the magical present.

In the quiet, stunningly positioned hilltop village **Ravello** above the Amalfi Coast (⇨ *Chapter 13*), it's easy to achieve such a state of mind. The same holds true for **Bellagio,** on Lake Como (⇨ *Chapter 6*), where you can meander through stately gardens, dance on the wharf, or just watch the boats float by in the shadow of the Alps.

And there's still nothing more romantic than a **gondola ride** along Venice's canals (⇨ *Chapter 3*), your escorted trip to nowhere, watched over by Gothic palaces with delicately arched eyebrows.

Driving the Back Roads

If you associate Italian roads with unruly motorists and endless traffic snarls, you're only partly right. Along the rural back roads, things are more relaxed.

You might stop on a lark to take a picture of a crumbling farmhouse, have a coffee in a time-frozen hill town, or enjoy an epic lunch at a rustic *agriturismo* inaccessible to public transportation. Driving, in short, is the best way to see Italy.

Among the countless beautiful drives, these are three of the most memorable: the legendary mountain ascent on **SS48, the Grande Strada delle Dolomiti** (⇨ *Chapter 5*), takes you through the heart of the Dolomites, the famous Passo di Sella, and into the Val Gardena, passing unforgettable, craggy-peaked views. Every time the A1 Autostrada tunnels through the mountains, the smaller **SS1, Via Aurelia** (⇨ *Chapter 8*), stays out on the jagged coastline of the Italian Riviera, passing terraced vineyards, cliff-hanging villages, and shimmering seas. **SS222, the Strada Chiantigiana** (⇨ *Chapter 11*), between Florence and Siena, meanders through classic Tuscan landscapes. Be aware that Italian roads are often poorly marked. It helps to know a little geography, as many signs indicate the town the road leads to, but not what the road number is.

Hiking the Hills

Even if you don't fancy yourself a disciple of Reinhold Messner (the favorite son of the Dolomites and the first man to reach the peak of Everest without oxygen), you'll find great summer hiking aplenty all over Italy.

The **Vie Ferrate (Iron Paths)** are reinforced trails through the mountains of Trentino–Alto Adige (⇨ *Chapter 5*), once forged by the Italian and Austro-Hungarian armies; they're a great way to get off the beaten path in the Dolomites.

The **Cinque Terre**—five cliff-clinging villages along the Italian Riviera (⇨ *Chapter 8*)—are spectacular, and they're all connected by hiking trails with memorable views of the towns, the rocks, and the Ligurian Sea.

In Umbria (⇨ *Chapter 12*) you can hike the **Paths of St. Francis** outside Assisi.

An easy half-hour walk takes you from the town of Cannara to Pian d'Arca, site of St. Francis's sermon to the birds; with a bit more effort you can make the walk from Assisi to the Eremo delle Carceri, and from here to the summit of Monte Subasio, which has views for miles in every direction.

Tasting the Wine

When it comes to wine making, the Italian Renaissance is happening right now: from tip to toe, vintners are challenging themselves to produce wines of ever-higher quality. You can taste the fruits of their labor at wine bars and restaurants throughout the country, and in many areas you can visit the vineyards as well.

For touring guidance in the northeastern region of the Veneto, see **Traveling the Wine Roads** (⇨ *Chapter 4*). For the lowdown on Italy's "King of Wines," see **On the Trail of Barolo** (⇨ *Chapter 7*). And for a full primer on the wines of Tuscany, see **Grape Escapes** (⇨ *Chapter 11*).

Picking up Some Italian Style

"Made in Italy" is synonymous with style, quality, and craftsmanship, whether it refers to high fashion or Maserati automobiles.

Every region has its specialties: Venice is known for glassware, lace, and velvet; Milan and Como for silk; and the Dolomites and the mountains of Calabria and Sicily for hand-carved wooden objects.

Bologna and Parma are the places for hams and cheeses; Modena for balsamic vinegar; Florence for straw goods, gold jewelry, leather, and paper products (including beautiful handmade notebooks); Assisi for embroidery; and Deruta, Gubbio, Vietri, and many towns in Puglia and Sicily for ceramics.

In Milan, Italy's fashion capital, the streets of the **Quadrilatero** district (⇨ *Chapter 6*) are where to go for serious shopping—or just for taking in the chic scene. Rome's **Piazza di Spagna** (⇨ *Chapter 1*) is another mecca for high-fashion shopping, and a few steps away is the Via del Corso, with more than a mile of stores of all varieties.

To be overwhelmed by the aromas of Emilia-Romagna's legendary food, head to **Tamburini** in Bologna (⇨ *Chapter 9*), where you can get vacuum-packed delicacies to take home with you.

Church or Museum?

Few images are more identifiable with Italy than the country's great churches, amazing works of architecture that often took centuries to build. The name Duomo (derived from the Latin for "house," *domus*, and the root of the English "dome") is used to refer to the principal church of a town or city. Generally speaking, the bigger the city, the more splendid its duomo.

Still, impressive churches inhabit some unlikely places—in the Umbrian hill towns of **Assisi** and **Orvieto,** for example (⇨ *Chapter 12*).

In Venice the Byzantine-influenced **Basilica di San Marco** (⇨ *Chapter 3*) is a testament to the city's East-meets-West character. **Milan's Duomo** (⇨ *Chapter 6*) is the largest, most imposing Gothic cathedral in Italy. The spectacular dome of **Florence's Duomo** (⇨ *Chapter 10*) is a work of engineering genius. The **Basilica di San Pietro** in Rome (⇨ *Chapter 1*) has all the grandeur you'd expect from the seat of the Catholic Church. And Italy's classical past is on display at **Siracusa's Duomo** (⇨ *Chapter 15*), which incorporates the columns of a 6th-century-BC Greek temple.

QUINTESSENTIAL ITALY

Il Caffè (Coffee)

The Italian day begins and ends with coffee, and more cups of coffee punctuate the time in between. To live like the Italians do, drink as they drink, standing at the counter or sitting at an outdoor table of the corner bar. (In Italy, a "bar" is a coffee bar.) A primer: *caffè* means coffee, and Italian standard issue is what Americans call espresso—short, strong, and usually taken very sweet. *Cappuccino* is a foamy half-and-half of espresso and steamed milk; cocoa powder *(cacao)* on top is acceptable, and sometimes cinnamon, too.

If you're thinking of having a cappuccino for dessert, think again—most Italians drink only caffè or caffè *macchiato* (with a spot of steamed milk) after lunchtime. Confused? Homesick? Order caffè *americano* for a reasonable facsimile of good-old filtered joe. Note that you usually pay for your coffee first, then take your receipt to the counter and tell the barista your order.

Il Calcio (Soccer)

Imagine the most rabid American football fans—the ones who paint their faces on game day and sleep in pajamas emblazoned with the logo of their favorite team. Throw in a dose of melodrama along the lines of a tear-jerking soap opera. Ratchet up the intensity by a factor of 10, and you'll start to get a sense of how Italians feel about their national game, soccer—known in the mother tongue as *calcio*. On Sunday afternoons throughout the long September-to-May season, stadiums are packed throughout Italy.

Those who don't get to games in person tend to congregate around television sets in restaurants and bars, rooting for the home team with a passion that feels like a last vestige of the days when the country was a series of warring medieval city-states. How calcio mania affects your stay in Italy depends on how eager you are to get involved. At the very least, you may notice

If you want to get a sense of contemporary Italian culture and indulge in some of its pleasures, start by familiarizing yourself with the rituals of daily life. These are a few highlights—things you can take part in with relative ease.

an eerie Sunday-afternoon quiet on the city streets, or erratic restaurant service around the same time, accompanied by cheers and groans from a neighboring room.

If you want a memorable, truly Italian experience, attend a game yourself. Availability of tickets may depend on the current fortunes of the local team, but they often can be acquired with help from your hotel concierge.

Il Gelato (Ice Cream)

During warmer months, gelato—the Italian equivalent of ice cream—is a national obsession. It's considered a snack rather than a dessert, bought at stands and shops in piazzas and on street corners, and consumed on foot, usually at a leisurely stroll.

Gelato is softer, less creamy, and more intensely flavored than its American counterpart.

It comes in simple flavors that capture the essence of the main ingredient. (You won't find Chunky Monkey or Cookies 'n' Cream.) Standard choices include pistachio, *nocciola* (hazelnut), caffè, and numerous fresh-fruit varieties. Quality varies; the surest sign that you've hit on a good spot is a line at the counter.

La Passeggiata (Strolling)

A favorite Italian pastime is the passeggiata (literally, the promenade). In the late afternoon and early evening, especially on weekends, couples, families, and packs of teenagers stroll the main streets and piazzas of Italy's towns.

It's a ritual of exchanged news and gossip, window-shopping, flirting, and gelato-eating that adds up to a uniquely Italian experience. To join in, simply hit the streets for a bit of wandering. You may feel more like an observer than a participant, until you realize that observing is what la passeggiata is all about.

MAKING THE MOST OF YOUR EUROS

Below are suggestions for ways to save money on your trip, courtesy of the Travel Talk Forums at Fodors.com.

Transportation

"For regional and IC trains just wait until Italy to buy your ticket—about same price but for ES or AV or high-speed trains you can save some dough by booking weeks ahead of time at *www.trenitalia. com* though that can still be a very very frustrating site to actually get to work— attested to by many many posts on Fodors expressing problems with getting it to work." —PalenQ

"Instead of taking the Leonardo Express from Fiumicino to Termini in Rome, take the FR1 to whichever station is most convenient for you. The FR1 departs every 15 minutes (instead of every 30 minutes for the Express), costs only €8 (instead of €14 for the Express), and avoids the hullabaloo of Termini." —Therese

Food and Drink

"Buy snacks and bottled water in bulk at a neighborhood supermarket at the beginning of your stay and keep them cool in your apartment or hotel fridge. Grab a bottle when leaving in the AM and that way avoid buying expensive water or snacks near tourist attractions, where prices are much higher. Save your euros for espresso or gelato." —cruisinred

"Bars always have two different prices: If you have your coffee at the counter it's cheaper than when a waiter serves it at a table (*servizio al tavolo*)." —quokka

"Visit wine fill-up shops in Italy; get table wine from the cask for 2–3 euros a liter. In Rome we would get them filled at the Testaccio market . . . I will usually ask at the local bar where I go for my coffee." —susanna

Sights

"The small cities can be less expensive but still fabulous. We were just in Assisi—all the sites were free, a delicious dinner for two with wine was 22 euros, and our hotel was reasonable at 65 euros per night." —rosetravels

"For the art lover on a budget: Most of the art I saw in Rome is free. Where else can you see countless Caravaggios, two Michelangelos, and even more Berninis for the cost of the wear and tear on the soles of your shoes?" —amyb

"One way to save on the expense of guided tours is to register online at Sound Guides (www.sound-guides.com) and download the various free self-guided tours to your iPod or MP3 player." —monicapileggi

Lodging

"Go off-season—March or November have better air prices and also accommodations, particularly if you stay in apartments, which you can rent for much less off-season (and plan some meals in-house—make the noon meal your biggest of the day, then have a small dinner in the apartment)." —bobthenavigator

"Everyone talks about going in the off season and mentions November or March. But in Florence at least, July is a shoulder season. I got a hotel room for half to a third the cost of the same room during the high season." —isabel

"We try to book apartments whenever we can and in Tuscany we rent farm houses. Especially if you are traveling with more than 2 persons these are usually much more reasonable." —caroltis

A GREAT ITINERARY

ROME, FLORENCE, VENICE, AND HIGHLIGHTS IN BETWEEN

This itinerary is designed for maximum impact. Think of it as rough draft for you to revise according to your own interests and time constraints.

Day 1: Venice

Arrive in Venice's Marco Polo Airport (there are direct flights from the United States), hop on the bus into the main bus station in Venice, then check into your hotel, get out, and get lost in the back canals for a couple of hours before dinner. If you enjoy fish, you should indulge yourself at a traditional Venetian restaurant. There's no better place for sweet, delicate Adriatic seafood.

Logistics: At the airport, avoid the Alilaguna boat into Venice on arrival. It's expensive, slow, and singularly unromantic. The bus is quick and cheap—save the romance for later. When you get to the main station, transfer to the most delightful main-street "bus" in the world: the *vaporetto* ferry. Enjoy your first ride up the Grand Canal, and make sure you're paying attention to the *fermata* (or stop) you need to get off at. As for water taxis from the airport to the city, they're very expensive, although they'll take you directly to your hotel.

Day 2: Venice

Begin by skipping the coffee at your hotel and have a real Italian coffee at a real Italian coffee shop. Spend the day at Venice's top sights, including the Basilica di San Marco, Palazzo Ducale, and Galleria dell'Accademia; don't forget Piazza San Marco, which is probably the most intense concentration of major artistic and cultural monuments in the world. The intense anticipation as you near the giant square through a maze of tiny shop-lined alleys and streets

climaxes in the stunning vista of the Piazza (return at 7 am the next morning to see it *"senza popolo"* (without people) and it'll look like a Canaletto painting come alive. Stop for lunch, perhaps sampling Venice's traditional specialty, *sarde in saor* (grilled sardines in a mouthwatering sweet-and-sour preparation that includes onions and raisins), and be sure to check out the fish market at the foot of the Rialto Bridge, and sunset at the Zattere before dinner. Later, stop at one of the pubs around the Campo San Luca or Campo Santa Margarita, where you can toast to freedom from automobiles.

Logistics: Venice is best seen by wandering. The day's activities can be done on foot, with the occasional vaporetto ride if you feel the urge to be on the water.

Day 3: Ferrara/Bologna

Get an early start and leave Venice on a Bologna-bound train. The ride to Ferrara—your first stop in Emilia-Romagna—is about an hour and a half. Visit the Castello Estense and Duomo before lunch; a panino and a beer at one of Ferrara's cafés should fit the bill. Wander Ferrara's cobblestone streets before hopping on the train to Bologna (a ride of less than an hour). In Bologna, check into your hotel and walk around Piazza Maggiore before dinner. Later you can check out some of northern Italy's best nightlife.

Logistics: In Ferrara, the train station lies a bit outside the city center, so you may want to take a taxi into town (though the distance is easily walkable, too). Here and elsewhere in Italy, you may leave your bags at the station for a small fee. Going out, there's a taxi stand near the back of the castle, toward Corso Ercole I d'Este. In Bologna the walk into town from the station is more manageable, particularly if you're staying along Via dell'Indipendenza.

Day 4: Bologna/Florence

After breakfast, check out some of Bologna's churches and piazzas, including a climb up the leaning Torre degli Asinelli for a red rooftop–studded panorama. After lunch, head back to the train station and take the short ride to Florence. You'll arrive in time for an afternoon siesta and an evening passeggiata.

Logistics: Florence's Santa Maria Novella train station is within easy access to some hotels, and farther from others. Florence's traffic is legendary, but taxis at the station are plentiful; make sure you get into a licensed, clearly marked car; the taxi stand is just outside the station.

Day 5: Florence

This is your day to see the sights of Florence. Start with the Uffizi Gallery (reserve your tickets in advance), where you'll see Botticelli's *Primavera* and *Birth of Venus*. Next, walk to the Piazza del Duomo, the site of Brunelleschi's spectacular dome, which you can climb for an equally spectacular view. By the time you get down, you'll be more than ready for a simple lunch at a laid-back trattoria. Depending on your preferences, either devote the afternoon to art or hike up to Piazzale Michelangelo, overlooking the city. Either way, finish the evening in style with a traditional *bistecca alla fiorentina* (grilled T-bone steak with olive oil).

Day 6: Lucca/Pisa

After breakfast, board a train for Lucca. It's an easy 1½-hour trip on the way to Pisa to see this walled medieval city. Don't miss the Romanesque Duomo, or a walk in the park that lines the city's ramparts. Have lunch at a local trattoria before continuing on to Pisa, where you'll spend an afternoon seeing—what else—the Leaning Tower, along with the equally impressive

TIPS

■ The itinerary can also be completed by car on the modern *autostrade* (four-lane highway system), although you'll run into dicey traffic in Florence and Rome. For obvious reasons, you're best off waiting to pick up your car on Day 3, when you leave Venice.

■ When it comes to trains, aim for the reservations-only Eurostar Italia or relative newcomer-to-the-scene Italo—it's more comfortable and faster.

■ The sights along this route are highly touristed; you'll have a better time if you make the trip outside the busy months of June, July, and August.

Duomo and Battistero. Walk down to the banks of the Arno River, contemplate the majestic views at sunset, and have dinner at one of the many inexpensive local restaurants in the real city center—a bit away from the most touristy spots.

Logistics: Lucca's train station lies just outside the walled city, so hardier travelers may want to leave the station on foot; otherwise, take a taxi. Pisa's train station isn't far from the city center, although it's on the other side of town from the Campo dei Miracoli (site of the Leaning Tower). Since Lucca and Pisa are only 15 minutes apart by train, you may want to return from Pisa to spend the night in more-charming Lucca.

Day 7: Orvieto/Rome

Three hours south of Pisa is Orvieto, one of the prettiest and most characteristic towns of the Umbria region, conveniently situated right on the Florence-Rome train line. Check out the memorable cathedral before a light lunch accompanied by one

of Orvieto's famous white wines. Get back on a train bound for Rome, and in a little more than an hour you'll arrive in the Eternal City in time to make your way to your hotel and relax for a bit before you head out for the evening. When you do, check out Piazza Navona, Campo de' Fiori, and the Trevi Fountain—it's best in the evening—and take a stand-up *aperitivo* (Campari and soda is a classic) at an unpretentious local bar before dinner. It's finally pizza time; you can't go wrong at any of Rome's popular local pizzerias.

Logistics: To get from Pisa to Orvieto, you'll first catch a train to Florence and then get on a Rome-bound train from here. Be careful at Rome's Termini train station, which is a breeding ground for scam artists. Keep your possessions close, and only get into a licensed taxi.

Day 8: Rome

Rome took millennia to build, but on this whirlwind trip you'll only have a day and a half to see it. In the morning, head to the Vatican Museums to see Michelangelo's glorious *Creation of Adam* at the Sistine Chapel. See St. Peter's Basilica and Square before heading back into Rome proper for lunch around the Pantheon, followed by a coffee from one of Rome's famous coffee shops. Next, visit ancient

Rome—first see the magnificent Pantheon, and then head across to the Colosseum, stopping along the way along Via dei Fori Imperiali to check out the Roman Forum from above. From the Colosseum, walk or take a taxi to Piazza di Spagna, a good place to see the sunset and shop at stylish boutiques. Taxi to Piazza Trilussa at the entrance of Trastevere, a beautiful old working-class neighborhood where you'll have a relaxing dinner.

Day 9: Rome/Departure

Head by taxi to Termini station and catch the train ride to the Fiumicino airport.

Logistics: The train from Termini station to the airport is fast, not inexpensive, and easy—for most people, it's preferable to an exorbitantly priced taxi ride that, in bad traffic, can take twice as long and cost much, much more.

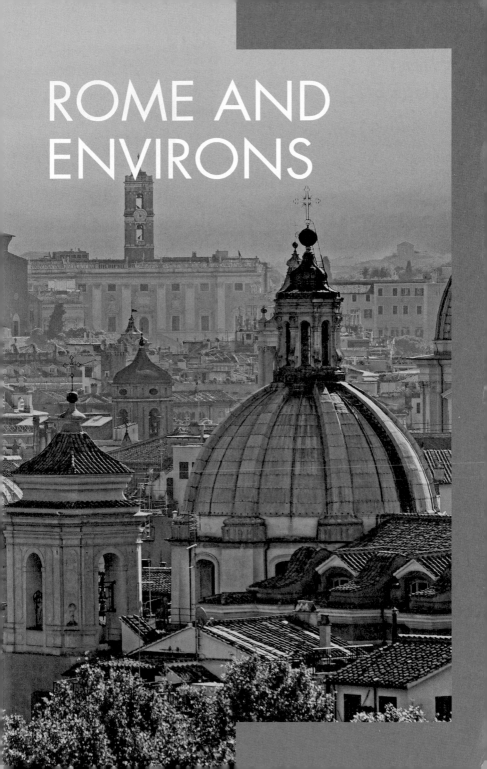

ROME AND ENVIRONS

WHAT'S WHERE

1 Ancient Rome. Backstopped by the most stupendous monument of ancient Rome—the Colosseum—the Roman Forum and Palatine Hill were once the hub of western civilization.

2 The Vatican. The Vatican draws millions of pilgrims and art lovers to St. Peter's Basilica, the Vatican Museums, and the Sistine Chapel.

3 Navona and Campo. The *cuore*—heart—of the *centro storico* (historic quarter), this district revolves around the ancient Pantheon, bustling Campo de' Fiori, and spectacular Piazza Navona.

4 Corso. Rome's "Broadway" begins at Piazza Venezia and neatly divides the city center in two—an area graced by historic landmarks like the 17th-century Palazzo Doria-Pamphilj (famed for its Old Master collection) and the Column of Marcus Aurelius.

5 Spagna. Travel back to the days of the Grand Tour in this glamorous area. After some people-watching on Piazza di Spagna, shop like a true VIP along Via dei Condotti, then be sure to throw a coin in the Trevi Fountain.

6 Repubblica and Quirinale. A largely 19th-century district, Repubblica lets art lovers go for Baroque with a bevy of Bernini works, including his *Ecstasy of St. Theresa* at Santa Maria della Vittoria. To the south looms the Palazzo Quirinale, Italy's presidential palace.

7 Villa Borghese and Piazza del Popolo. Rome's most famous park is home to playful fountains, sculptured gardens, and the treasure-packed Galleria Borghese. Piazza del Popolo—a beautiful place to watch the world go by—lies south.

8 Trastevere. Rome's left bank has kept its authentic roots thanks to mom-and-pop trattorias, medieval alleyways, and Santa Maria in Trastevere, stunningly spotlighted at night.

9 The Ghetto and Isola Tiberina. Once a Jewish quarter, the gentrified Ghetto still preserves the flavor of Old Rome. Alongside is moored Tiber Island, so picturesque it will click your camera for you.

10 The Catacombs and Appian Way. Follow in the footsteps of St. Peter to this district, home to the spirit-warm catacombs and the Tomb of Cecilia Metella.

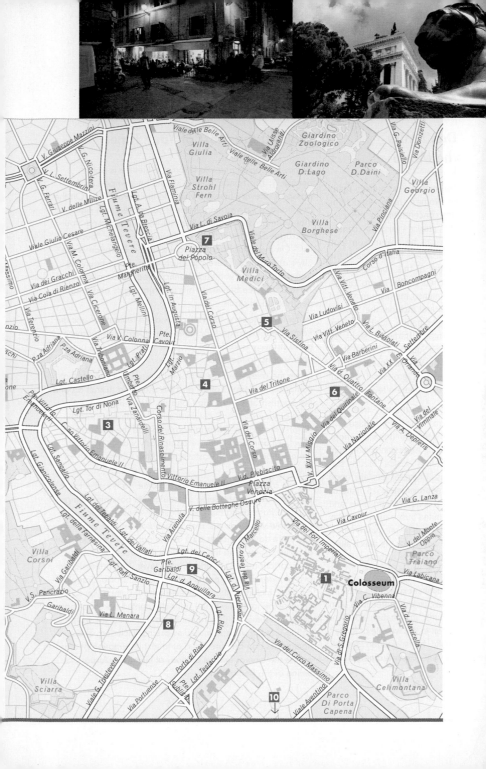

ROME AND ENVIRONS PLANNER

Don't Miss the Metro

Fortunately for tourists, many of Rome's main attractions are concentrated in the *centro storico* (historic center) and can be covered on foot. Some sights that lie nearer the border of this quarter can be reached via the Metro Line A, nicknamed the *linea rossa* (red line) and include: the Spanish Steps (Spagna stop), the Trevi Fountain (Barberini stop), St. Peter's Square (Ottaviano stop), and the Vatican Museums (Ottaviano or Cipro-Musei Vaticani stop), to name a few.

Tickets for the bus, tram, and Metro can be purchased at any *tabacchi* (tobacco shop), at some newsstands, and from machines inside Metro stations. These tickets are good for approximately 75 minutes for a single Metro ride and unlimited buses and trams. Day passes can be purchased for €4, and weekly passes, which allow unlimited use of buses, trams, and the Metro, for €16.

For a fuller explanation of Metro routes, pick up a free map from a tourist information booth or log on to the website of Rome's public transportation system, the ATAC (⊕ *www.atac.roma.it*).

Making the Most of Your Time

Roma, non basta una vita ("Rome, a lifetime is not enough"). This famous saying should be stamped on the passport of every first-time visitor to the Eternal City. On the one hand, it's a warning: Rome is so packed with sights that it's impossible to take them all in; it's easy to run yourself ragged trying to check off the items on your "bucket list." On the other hand, the saying is a celebration of the city's abundance. There's so much here, you're bound to make discoveries you hadn't anticipated. To conquer Rome, strike a balance between visits to major sights and leisurely neighborhood strolls.

In the first category, the Vatican and the remains of ancient Rome loom the largest. Both require at least half a day; a good strategy is to devote your first morning to one and your second to the other.

Leave the afternoons for exploring the neighborhoods that comprise "Baroque Rome" and the shopping district around the Spanish Steps and Via Condotti. If you have more days at your disposal, continue with the same approach. Among the sights, Galleria Borghese and the multilayered church of San Clemente are particularly worthwhile, and the neighborhoods of Trastevere and the Ghetto make for great roaming.

There's a lot of ground to cover in Rome, so it's wise to plan your busy sightseeing schedule with possible savings in mind. Purchasing the Roma Pass (⊕ *www.romapass.it*) can allow you to do just that, depending on your plans. The three-day pass costs €30 and is good for unlimited use of buses, trams, and the metro (like the three-day public transportation pass). It adds in, however, free admission to two of more than 40 participating museums or archaeological sites, including the Colosseum (and it bumps you to the head of the long line there), plus discounted tickets to many other museums. As they're not Rome museums, it's worth noting that the Vatican museums are not included. The Roma Pass can be purchased at tourist information booths across the city, at Termini Station, at Fiumicino Airport, or online at the Roma Pass website.

When to Go

Not surprisingly, spring and fall are the best times to visit, with mild temperatures and many sunny days; the famous Roman sunsets are also at their best. Summers are often sweltering. In July and August, learn to do as the Romans do—get up and out early, seek refuge from the afternoon heat, resume activities in early evening, and stay up late to enjoy the nighttime breeze. Come August, many shops and restaurants close as locals head out for vacation. Remember that air-conditioning, though increasingly available, is still not ubiquitous in this city. Roman winters are relatively mild, with persistent rainy spells.

Hop-On, Hop-Off

Rome has its own "hop-on, hop-off" sightseeing buses. The Trambus 110 Open leaves every 15 minutes from Viale Einaudi (near Termini), with a two-hour loop including the Colosseum, Circus Maximus, St. Peter's, and the Trevi Fountain. Day-long tickets, valid for 24 hours, cost €15; two-day tickets cost €20. The Archeobus departs every 30 minutes from Viale Einaudi and heads to the Via Appia Antica, with stops at the Colosseum, Baths of Caracalla, and the catacombs. Tickets, valid for 48 hours, cost €12. A cumulative ticket covering both buses costs €25 and is valid for 72 hours. The website for both is ⊕ *www.trambusopen.com*.

Roman Hours

Much of the city shuts down on Sunday, although museums and many restaurants are closed Monday. Most stores in the *centro storico* area, the part of town that caters to tourists, remain open. Shop hours generally run from 10 am to 1 pm, then reopen around 3 pm until 7 or 7:30 pm. Unless advertised as having *orario continuato* (open all day), most businesses close from 1 to 3. On Monday, shops usually don't open until around 3 or 4 pm. Pharmacies tend to have the same hours of operation as stores unless they advertise *orario notturno* (night hours); two can be found on Corso Rinascimento and Piazza dei Cinquecento (near Termini Station). As for churches, most open at 8 or 9 in the morning, close from 12:30 to 3 or 4, then reopen until 6:30 or 7. St. Peter's, however, is open 7 am to 7 pm (6:30 pm October to March).

Information, Please

Rome's main Tourist Information Office is at Via Leopardi 24 (☎ *06/0608* ⊕ *www. romaturismo.it*), near Piazza Vittorio.

Green information kiosks with multilingual personnel are located near the most important sights and squares, as well as at Termini Station and Leonardo da Vinci Airport. These kiosks, called Tourist Information Sites (Punti Informativi Turistici, or PIT) can be found at:

PIT Castel S. Angelo, Piazza Pia; open 9:30–7

PIT Navona, Piazza delle Cinque Lune (north end of Piazza Navona); open 9:30–7

PIT Fiumicino, Aeroporto Leonardo da Vinci, Arrivi Internazionali Terminal C; open 9–7:30

PIT Ciampino, Aeroporto Ciampino, Arrivi Internazionali Baggage Claim; open 9–6:30

PIT Minghetti, Via Marco Minghetti (corner of Via del Corso); open 9:30–7

PIT Nazionale, Via Nazionale (Palazzo delle Esposizioni); open 9:30–7

PIT Santa Maria Maggiore, at Via dell'Olmata; open 9:30–7

PIT Termini, Stazione Termini, at Via Giovanni Giolitti 34; open 8–8

PIT Trastevere, on Piazza Sidney Sonnino; open 9:30–7

ROME
TOP ATTRACTIONS

The Pantheon

Reputedly constructed to honor all pagan gods, this best-preserved building of ancient Rome was rebuilt in the 2nd century AD by Emperor Hadrian. The vast dome of perfect dimensions—142 feet high by 142 feet wide—was the largest freestanding dome until the 20th century.

The Vatican

Though its population numbers are just shy of a thousand, the Vatican—home base for the Catholic Church and the pope—has millions of visitors each year. Savor Michelangelo's Sistine Ceiling, attend Papal Mass, and marvel at St. Peter's Basilica, embraced by the colonnades of St. Peter's Square.

The Colosseum

(A) Legend has it that as long as the Colosseum stands, Rome will stand; and when Rome falls, so will the world. One of the "new" seven wonders of the world, the mammoth amphitheater was begun by Emperor Vespasian and inaugurated by the next emperor, his son Titus, in year AD 80. For "the grandeur that was Rome," this yardstick of eternity can't be topped.

Piazza Navona

(B) You couldn't concoct a more Roman street scene: cafés and crowded tables at street level, coral- and rust-color houses above, most lined with wrought-iron balconies, and, at the center of this urban "living room" Bernini's spectacular Fountain of the Four Rivers and Borromini's supertheatrical Sant'Agnese.

Roman Forum

(C) Set between the Capitoline and Palatine hills, this fabled labyrinth of ruins variously served as a political playground, a commerce mart, and a place where justice was dispensed during the days of the Republic and Empire (509 BC to AD 476). Once adorned with stately buildings, triumphal arches, and impressive temples, the Forum today is a silent

ruin—*sic transit gloria mundi* ("so passes away the glory of the world").

The Campidoglio

(D) Catch an emperor's-eye view of the Roman Forum from beside Michelangelo's Palazzo Senatorio, situated atop one of the highest spots in Rome, the Capitoline Hill. Next door you'll find the Vittoriano, the Capitoline Museums, and beloved Santa Maria in Aracoeli.

Trevi Fountain

(E) One of the few fountains in Rome that's actually more absorbing than the people crowding around it, the Fontana di Trevi was designed by Nicola Salvi in 1732. Immortalized in *Three Coins in a Fountain* and *La Dolce Vita,* this fountain may be your ticket back to Rome—that is, if you throw a coin into it.

The Spanish Steps

(F) Byron, Shelley, and Keats all drew inspiration from this magnificent "Scalinata," constructed in 1723. Connecting the shops at the bottom with the hotels at the top, this is the place for prime people-watching. The steps face beautiful sunsets.

Galleria Borghese

(G) Only the best could satisfy the aesthetic taste of Cardinal Scipione Borghese, and that means famed Bernini sculptures, great paintings by Titian and Raphael, and the most spectacular 17th-century palace in Rome.

Trastevere

Just across the Tiber River, this charming neighborhood is a maze of jumbled alleyways, cobblestone streets, and medieval houses. The area also boasts one of the oldest churches of Rome—Santa Maria in Trastevere.

TOP ROME EXPERIENCES

Say "Cheese," Spartacus

Taking a photo with one of those ersatz gladiators in front of Rome's ancient sights will win some smiles—but maybe some frowns, too. Many of them (who are actually costumed as centurions, not gladiators, at all) pounce on tourists who simply aim a camera at them and then proceed to shake them down for a "photo fee." Others have a craftier approach: before you know it, one may envelop your eight-year-old in his red cape and say "Formaggio." Indeed, this may turn out to be the greatest souvenir back home in fourth-grade class, so if interested, step right up, shake hands, and exchange some euros. But pick your Spartacus very carefully: some sloppy guys wear a helmet and cloak but have sweatsuits or sneakers on. Rome has cracked down on these "gladiators," but with limited success—expect to see them near the Forum, Colosseum, and along Via dei Fori Imperiali.

A Whole World Underground

From opulent villas to Mithraic temples, an entire ancient world lies beneath ground-level Rome. No, it's not because ancient Romans had a penchant for the subterranean. It's because, two millennia ago, the ground level stood 30 to 40 feet lower than it does today.

As a result, every time someone goes to dig a hole in Rome, they get a surprise. That's been a source of both pride and frustration, as most recently seen with the ongoing project for Linea C. Rome's third metro line is supposed to go through the heart of the *centro storico*—but several subway stops have had to be scrapped when workers hit (surprise!) ancient ruins. Most famously, a desired stop at Piazza Venezia had to come to a halt when workers discovered ruins of an ancient auditorium built by Emperor Hadrian in the 2nd century AD.

For a great glimpse of how modern Rome sits atop the ancient, book a tour at Palazzo Valentini, just around the corner from that doomed Piazza Venezia stop. In 2007, excavations beneath the 16th-century Palazzo Valentini—today the seat of the Province of Rome—turned up ruins of two 2nd- and 3rd-century villas. On an automated tour experience beneath the Renaissance palazzo, visitors are brought through the opulent rooms and, with light shows, shown how they once would have looked . . . all without ever emerging aboveground (⊕ *provincia.roma.it*).

Through a Keyhole

Head to the Aventine hill, just across the Circus Maximus from the Palatine, for a quirky surprise. The Order of the Knights of Malta, the only private entity to also be a sovereign state, has their headquarters here. Although their building is closed to the public unless you're on a prebooked tour, its most charming facet is open to anyone: the keyhole. Peek through for a perfectly framed view of the dome of St. Peter's Basilica—and the chance to see three countries (Vatican City, Italy, and the Order of the Knights of Malta) in one glance.

Lights, Camera, Action!

The Festival Internazionale del Film di Roma (Rome International Film Festival; ⊕ *www.romacinemafest.it*), entering its sixth year, has hosted the likes of Martin Scorsese, Robert De Niro, and Meryl Streep. Though Rome is far from reclaiming its film prominence, lost decades ago, the festival draws important players in the world of film and sees its share of world premieres. The festival is held at

the Auditorium Parco della Musica during a full week in the fall.

Three Coins in the Fountain

Rome has always been in love with *amore*. But romance is certainly nowhere more contagious than around its famous fountains. If a besotted couple can spare the time, a trip up to Tivoli's Villa D'Este (an hour outside Rome via bus) is nirvana. Its seductive garden and endless array of fountains (about 500 of them) is the perfect setting to put anyone in the mood for love.

That's your cue to return to Rome and make a beeline for the luminous Trevi Fountain, even more enchanting at night than in the daytime. Make sure you and that special someone throw your coins into the fountain for good luck. Legend has it that those who do so are guaranteed a return trip back to Rome.

L'Aperitivo

Borrowed from *i Milanesi,* the trend of *l'aperitivo* has become *moda* in Rome. Not to be confused with happy hour, l'aperitivo is not about discounts or heavy drinking, but rather a time to meet up with friends and colleagues after work or on weekends—definitely an event in which to see and be seen. Aperitivo hours are usually from 7 to 9 pm.

Depending on where you go, the price of a drink often includes an all-you-can-eat appetizer buffet of finger foods, sandwiches, and pasta salads. Some aperitivo hot spots on the *trendissimo* list are Enoteca Palatium (Via Frattina) near the Piazza di Spagna; L'Angolo Divino (Via del Balestrari) near the Campo de' Fiori; Freni e Frizioni (Via del Politeama) in Trastevere; and the 5th Floor Terrace at Il Palazzetto, set on a magical balcony right over the Spanish Steps.

Rome's Coolest Artisans

Despite the encroachment of chain stores and big brands, many of Rome's finest artisans are still hanging on—barely. But locals hope they'll be able to withstand globalization's assault, because they still produce some of the finest (and best-value!) handmade clothes, shoes, leather goods, and more in the city. Top-notch artisans can be found in neighborhoods like Trastevere and Campo dei Fiori, as well as scattered in areas like the Spanish Steps. For a glimpse of how tradition and trend can combine, wander through Monti, a neighborhood chock-a-block with young jewelers, fashion designers, and artists, many of whom use traditional artisanal techniques (and often handcraft their products right in the store)—but with an eye toward contemporary style.

Walk like a Roman

Rome was made for wandering, with relentlessly picturesque streets and alleyways, leading you past monuments, down narrow *vicoli,* through ancient Roman arches, and into hidden piazzas. A stroll is the best way to become attuned to the city's rhythm and, no matter how aimlessly you wander, chances are you'll end up somewhere magical.

The best walking tours in Rome are given by Context (⊕ *www.contexttravel. com*). Also getting raves from the public and media are the truly wonderful walking tours offered by Through Eternity (⊕ *www.througheternity.com*).

GETTING HERE AND AROUND

Getting Here by Car

The main access routes from the north are the A1 (Autostrada del Sole) from Milan and Florence. The principal route to or from points south, including Naples, is the A1, as well. All highways connect with the Grande Raccordo Anulare (GRA) Ring Road, which channels traffic into the city center. For driving directions, check out ⊕ *www.autostrade.it* and ⊕ *www.tuttocitta.it.* Note: Parking in Rome can be a nightmare—private cars are not allowed access to the entire historic center during the day (weekdays 6:30 am–8 pm; Saturday 2 pm–6 pm), except for residents.

Getting Here by Bus

Bus lines cover all of Rome's surrounding Lazio region and are operated by the Consorzio Trasporti Lazio, or COTRAL (☎ *800/174471*   ⊕ *www.cotralspa.it*). These bus routes terminate either near Tiburtina Station or at outlying Metro stops, such as Laurentina and Ponte Mammolo (Line B) and Anagnina (Line A). COTRAL buses are good options for taking short day trips from Rome, such as those that leave daily from Rome's Ponte Mammolo (Line B) Metro station for the town of Tivoli, where Hadrian's Villa and Villa D'Este await.

Getting Here by Air

Rome's principal airport is Leonardo da Vinci Airport (☎ *06/65951* ⊕ *www.adr.it*), commonly known by the name of its location, Fiumicino (FCO). It's 30 km (19 miles) southwest of the city but has a direct train link with downtown Rome. Rome's other airport, with no direct train link, is Ciampino (☎ *06/65951* ⊕ *www.adr.it*) or CIA, 15 km (9 miles) south of downtown and used mostly by low-cost airlines.

Two trains link downtown Rome with Fiumicino. Inquire at the PIT tourist information counter in the International Arrivals hall (Terminal 2) or train information counter near the tracks to determine which takes you closest to your destination in Rome. The 30-minute nonstop Airport–Termini express (called the Leonardo Express) goes direct to Termini Station, Rome's main train station; tickets cost €11. The FM1 train stops in Trastevere and Ostiense. Always stamp your tickets in the little machines near the track before you board. As for Ciampino, COTRAL buses connect to trains that go to the city and Terravision (☎ *06/97610632* ⊕ *www.terravision.eu*) buses link the airport to Termini Station for €6 each way. Taxi transport to and from Fiumicino carries a flat fee of €48; to and from Ciampino is €30. The price includes all luggage.

Getting Here by Train

State-owned Trenitalia (☎ *892021 in Italy, 06/68475475 abroad* ⊕ *www. trenitalia.it*) trains also serve some destinations on side trips outside Rome. The main Trenitalia stations in Rome are Termini, Tiburtina, Ostiense, and Trastevere. On long-distance routes (to Florence and Naples, for instance), you can either travel on the cheap, but slow *regionali* trains, or the fast but more expensive Intercity, Eurostar Alta Velocità. The state railways' website is user-friendly. The privately run Italo high-speed train (⊕ *www.italotreno. it*) has two lines serving Rome. The Turin-Salerno line stops in Bologna, Florence, Rome, Naples, and Salerno, and the Venice–Napoli line serves Padova, Bologna, Florence, and Rome.

Getting Around by Public Transportation

Rome's integrated transportation system is ATAC (☎ 06/57003 ⊕ www.atac.roma.it), which includes the Metropolitana subway, city buses, and municipal trams. A ticket (BIT) valid for 100 minutes on any combination of buses and trams and one entrance to the Metro costs €1.50. Day *giornaliero* passes are €6, three-day passes are €16.50, and weekly passes are €24.

Tickets (singly or in quantity—it's a good idea to have a few tickets handy so you don't have to hunt for a vendor when you need one) are sold at tobacconists, newsstands, some coffee bars, automatic ticket machines in Metro stations, some bus stops, and ATAC ticket booths. A handful of buses also have ticket machines onboard.

Time-stamp tickets at Metro turnstiles and in little yellow machines on buses and trams when boarding the first vehicle. The expiration date and time will be printed on the reverse side of the ticket.

Getting Around by Bus and Tram

ATAC city buses and trams are orange, gray-and-red, or blue-and-orange. Remember to board at the front or rear and to exit at the middle; in most cases, you must buy your ticket before boarding, and always stamp it in a machine as soon as you enter. The ticket is good for a single Metro ride and unlimited buses and trams within the next 75 minutes.

ATAC has a website (⊕ www.atac.roma.it) that will help you calculate the number of stops and bus routes needed.

Getting Around by Metropolitana

The Metropolitana (or Metro) is the easiest and fastest way to get around Rome. Street entrances are marked with red and white "M" signs.

The Metro A Line, known as the *linea rossa*, will take you to a chunk of the main attractions in Rome: Piazza di Spagna (Spagna stop), Piazza del Popolo (Flaminio), St. Peter's Square (Ottaviano–San Pietro), the Vatican Museums (both Ottaviano and Cipro–Musei Vaticani), and the Trevi Fountain (Barberini).

The B Line (*linea blu*) will take you to the Colosseum (Colosseo stop), Circus Maximus (Circo Massimo stop), the Pyramid (Piramide stop for Testaccio, Ostiense Station, and trains for Ostia Antica), and Basilica di San Paolo Fuori le Mura (San Paolo stop). The two lines intersect at Rome's main station, Termini.

Getting Around by Taxi

Taxis in Rome do not cruise, but if free they'll stop if you flag them down. They wait at stands, but can also be called by phone (☎ 06/5551, 06/6645, 06/3570, or 06/0609).

Always ask for a receipt (*ricevuta*) to make sure the driver charges you the correct amount, and always ensure the driver is running the meter (unless you're coming from the airport, when it's the flat fare). Use only licensed cabs with a plaque next to the license plate reading *"Servizio Pubblico."*

Getting Around by Scooter

As bikes are to Beijing, so scooters are to Rome; that means they're everywhere. Riders are required to wear helmets. You can rent a scooter at Bici & Baci (✉ Via del Viminale 5 ☎ 06/48986162 ⊕ www.bicibaci.com) from €19 per day.

ROME TODAY

...is breaking new ground

With a big push to modernize parts of Rome particularly lacking in the luster department, visitors will notice some new and novel aspects to the city skyline. First, that former eyesore, the Tiburtina train station, was completely overhauled, to the tune of some €330 million, to become the new avant-garde Tiburtina Stazione, the first rail hub in Italy to handle super-high-speed (Alstom AGVs) trains.

Even more buzz has been generated by Rome's first-ever skyscraper, the EuroSky Tower. Located in the distant EUR suburb, the 28-floor building (to be completed in 2013) will be the first to launch Romans into orbit for high-rise luxury apartment living (it's eco-sustainable, replete with solar panels, biofuel power, and channels to deliver rainwater to plants and flowers). Feathers were ruffled when Vatican officials worried that the skyscraper would clash with St. Peter's Basilica, Rome's tallest building.

Located by the Tiber River, the grandiose new "Ponte della Musica" bridge has now "bridged the gap" between the worlds of sports and music and arts: it connects the Foro Italico area (home to Rome's stunning Stadio Olimpico and Stadio dei Marmi) with the Flaminio district (Parco della Musica and the MAXXI museum). Designed by British star-engineer Buro Happold, the eco-friendly *ponte* can be used by pedestrians, cyclists, and electric buses.

Last but not least, the new convention center of Rome—EUR Congressi Roma—is expected to dazzle when completed by the end of 2013.

The renowned Italian architect Massimiliano Fuksas whipped up a vast design centered on the "Cloud," an airy futuristic structure that floats in a showcase of steel and glass. City officials have high hopes.

...is in political limbo

After playing a prominent role in politics for nearly two decades, controversial tycoon Silvio Berlusconi stepped down as prime minister at the end of 2011. To put a new government into place and turn the country's severe economic crisis around, Mario Monti—a multitasker whose background runs the gamut from professor to economist to president of the prestigious Bocconi University—was appointed not only as the new prime minister but also, due to his formidable expertise, as minister of economy and finance.

...IS CREATING NEW "IT" NEIGHBORHOODS

The leader among Rome's "It" neighborhoods is Pigneto, the working-class area once immortalized as the backdrop for Roberto Rossellini's magnificent Academy Award–nominated *Rome Open City* (*Roma Città Aperta*).

Set in the northwestern part of the city on the other side of the Porta Maggiore walls, Pigneto has come a long way since the black-and-white days of the 1950s. This hot new *quartiere* has undergone a major transformation into a colorful hub for hipsters who

tuck into the many wine bars and bookshops along main drags like Fanfulla da Lodi and Via del Pigneto.

To channel the days when legends Pier Paolo Pasolini and Luchino Visconti spent time filming here, enjoy an aperitivo at the historic Bar Necci (Via

Wasting no time, he raised taxes, cracked down on tax evaders—and made a number of enemies, especially among Italians who weren't so fond of how austerity hit their pocketbooks.

Complicating matters further, Berlusconi couldn't stay out of the ring for long. A general election at the end of February 2013 included both Monti and Berlusconi as candidates. (Conveniently, a judge ruled that Berlusconi's need to campaign for the new election impeded his ability to show up in court, thus postponing his trial for charges of paying for sex with a minor until after the election.) In the surreal world of Italian politics, the elections also include Beppe Grillo, a well-known Italian comedian. The result of the election was inconclusive, with no candidate gaining a clear majority, thus providing no real measure of where Italy stands today on austerity . . . or on the willingness of Italians to forgive and forget Berlusconi's many past transgressions.

. . . has a new Pope

Pope Benedict XVI shocked the world in February when, without prior announcement, he declared that he planned to step down at the end of the month. The last time a pope resigned, the year was 1415—and the purpose was to end the Western Schism, where there were three people all claiming to be pope simultaneously. A conclave was held in March to choose the new pope: Pope Francis, who hails from Argentina, making him the first pope from the Americas.

. . . is more commuter-connected

When it comes to train travel in Italy, the competition is growing fierce.

Thanks to the introduction of "Italo," Italy's first private railroad (owned by NTV and operated by the president of Fiat), rail travelers now have a new alternative to the state-run TrenItalia.

NTV is the first operator in the world to use the new Alstom AGV train, which currently holds the highest speed record for trains and will service various big cities around Italy, including Rome, Florence, Venice, Bologna, Naples, and Salerno.

In Rome, the high-speed trains will use Rome's new Tiburtina station rather than Termini.

Fanfulla da Lodi 68), where Pasolini once filmed scenes for his 1961 *Accatone* (an award-winning look at how a pimp living in the slums of Rome attempts to go straight).

Another young neighborhood, San Lorenzo, is set just a stone's throw away from the Termini train station. Just beyond the city walls near Via Tiburtina, Rome's new "Left Bank" district is filled with students and a young bohemian crowd, thanks to its proximity to La Sapienza University. The area has an *alternativa* feel to it, with its plethora of starving artists, tattoo studios, and hippie musicians. In fact, if you don't know what you're looking for, you could easily get lost in this maze of dark narrow streets, many now lined with underground cafés, bars, hip restaurants, and pubs with live-music venues.

EATING AND DRINKING WELL IN ROME

In Rome traditional cuisine reigns supreme. Most chefs follow the mantra of freshness over fuss, and simplicity of flavor and preparation over complex cooking methods.

So when Romans continue ordering the standbys, it's easy to understand why. And we're talking about *very* old standbys: some restaurants re-create dishes that come from ancient recipes of Apicius, probably the first celebrity chef (to Emperor Tiberius) and cookbook author of the Western world. Today Rome's cooks excel at what has taken hundreds, or thousands, of years to perfect.

Still, if you're hunting for newer-than-now developments, things are slowly changing. Talented young chefs are exploring new culinary frontiers, with results that tingle the taste buds: fresh pasta filled with carbonara sauce, cod "tiramisu," and mozzarella gelato with basil sorbet and semisweet tomatoes are just a few recent examples. Of course, there's grumbling about the number of chefs who, in a clumsy effort to be *nuovo*, end up with collision rather than fusion. That noted, Rome *is* the capital city, and the influx of residents from other regions of the country allows for many variations on the Italian theme.

FOODIE FINDS

Via Cola di Rienzo is home to two of Rome's best specialty shops: Franchi (⊠ *Via Cola di Rienzo 200, Prati* ☎ *06/6874651*), pictured above, is a gastroshop that sells high-quality cured meats, Italian cheeses, wines, pastas, and fresh truffles. Next door, Castroni (⊠ *Via Cola di Rienzo 196/198, Prati* ☎ *06/6874383*) is well known among expats for its imported foreign foods from the United States, Great Britain, Japan, India, and Mexico, as well as its impressive selection of candies, preserves, olive oils, and balsamic vinegars. Castroni is a great place to stop in for *caffè* (coffee) and a *cornetto* (an Italian croissant).

ARTICHOKES

If there's one vegetable Rome is known for, it's the artichoke, or *carciofo*. The classic Roman preparation, *carciofo alla romana*, is a large, globe-shape artichoke stripped of its outer leaves, stuffed with wild mint and garlic, then braised. It's available at restaurants throughout the city from February to May, when local artichokes are in season. For the excellent Roman-Jewish version, *carciofo alla giudia*— artichoke deep-fried until crisp and brown—head to any restaurant in the Ghetto.

BUCATINI ALL'AMATRICIANA

What may appear to the naked eye as spaghetti with red sauce is actually *bucatini all'amatriciana*—a spicy, rich, and complex dish that owes its flavor to an important ingredient: *guanciale*, or cured pork jowl. Once you taste a meaty, guanciale-flavor dish, you'll understand why Romans swear by it. Along with guanciale, the simple sauce features crushed tomatoes and red pepper flakes. It's served over *bucatini*, a hollow, spaghetti-like pasta, and topped with grated pecorino Romano cheese.

CODA ALLA VACCINARA

Rome's largest slaughterhouse in the 1800s was housed in the Testaccio neighborhood. That's where you'll find dishes like *coda alla vaccinara*, or "oxtail in the style of the cattle butcher." This dish is made from ox or veal tails stewed

with tomatoes, carrots, celery, and wine, and seasoned with cinnamon, pancetta, and myriad other flavorings. The stew cooks for hours then is finished with the sweet-and-sour element—often raisins and pine nuts or bittersweet chocolate.

GELATO

For many travelers, the first taste of gelato is one of the most memorable moments of their Italian trip. With a consistency that's a cross between regular American ice cream and soft-serve, gelato's texture is dense but softer than hard ice cream because it's kept at a higher temperature. The best gelato is extremely flavorful, and made daily. In Rome a few common flavors are caffè, *pistacchio* (pistachio), *nocciola* (hazelnut), *fragola* (strawberry), and *cioccolato fondant* (dark chocolate).

PIZZA

Roman pizza comes in two types: *pizza al taglio* (by the slice) and *pizza tonda* (round pizza). The former has a thicker focaccia-like crust and is cut into squares. These slices are sold by weight and available all day. In Rome, the typical pizza tonda has a very thin crust. It's cooked in wood-burning ovens that reach extremely high temperatures. Since they're so hot, the ovens are usually fired up in the evening, which is why Roman pizzerias are only open for dinner.

A GREAT ITINERARY

Rome wasn't built in a day, and even locals themselves will tell you that it takes a lifetime to discover all the treasures the Eternal City has to offer. Jam-packed with monuments, museums, fountains, galleries, and picturesque neighborhoods, Mamma Roma makes it hard for visitors to decide which to tackle first during their adventurous Roman holiday. As Romans like to say, this one-day itinerary *basta e avanza* ("is more than enough") to get you started!

Rome 101

So you want to taste Rome, gaze at its beauty, and inhale its special flair, all in one breathtaking (literally) day? Think Rome 101, and get ready for a spectacular sunrise-to-sunset span. Begin at 9 by exploring Rome's most beautiful neighborhood—"Vecchia Roma" (the area around Piazza Navona, Campo de' Fiori, and the Pantheon)—starting out on the Corso (the big avenue that runs into Piazza Venezia, the traffic hub of the historic center).

A block away from each other are two opulently over-the-top monuments that show off Rome at its Baroque best: the church of Sant'Ignazio and the princely Palazzo Doria-Pamphilj, aglitter with great Old Master paintings. By 10:30, head west a few blocks to find the granddaddy of monuments, the fabled Pantheon, still looking like Emperor Hadrian might arrive at any minute. A few blocks northwest is San Luigi dei Francesi, home to the greatest Caravaggio paintings in Rome. At 11:30 saunter a block or so westward into beyond-beautiful Piazza Navona, studded with Bernini fountains. Then take Via Cucagna (at the piazza's south end) and continue several blocks toward Campo de' Fiori's open-air food market for some lunch-on-the-run fixings. Two more blocks toward the Tiber brings you to fashionable Via Giulia, laid out by Pope Julius II in the early 16th century.

Walk past 10 blocks of Renaissance palaces and antiques shops to take a bus (from the stop near the Tiber) over to the Vatican. Arrive around 1 to gape at St. Peter's Basilica, then hit the treasure-filled Vatican Museums (Sistine Chapel) around 1:30—during lunch, the crowds diminish considerably. After two hours, head for the Ottaviano stop near the museum and Metro your way to the Colosseo stop.

Around 4 (earlier in winter, when last entrance to the archaeological zone is at 3:30), climb up into the Colosseum and picture it full of screaming toga-clad citizens enjoying the spectacle of gladiators in mortal combat. Striding past the massive Arch of Constantine, enter the Palatine Hill entrance at around 4:45, following signs for the Roman Forum. Photograph yourself giving a "Friends, Romans, Countrymen" oration (complete with upraised hand) among the marble fragments.

March down the Forum's Via Sacra toward the looming Vittorio Emanuele Monument (Il Vittoriano) and exit onto the Campidoglio.

Here, on the Capitoline Hill, tour the great ancient Roman art treasures of the Musei Capitolini (which are open most nights until 8, last entrance at 7), and snap the view from the terrace over the spotlighted Forum. After dinner, hail a cab—or take a long *passeggiata* (stroll) down *dolce vita* memory lane—to the Trevi Fountain, a gorgeously lit sight at night. Needless to say, toss that coin in to ensure your return trip back to the Mother of Us All.

ROME

Updated
by Amanda
Ruggeri

Coming off the Autostrada at Roma Nord or Roma Sud, you know by the convergence of heavily trafficked routes that you're entering a grand nexus: All roads lead to Rome.

And then the interminable suburbs, the railroad crossings, the intersections—no wonder they call it the Eternal City. As you forge on, features that match your expectations begin to appear: a bridge with heroic statues along its parapets; a towering slab of marble decorated with allegorical figures in extravagant poses; a piazza and an obelisk under an umbrella of pine trees. Then you spot what looks like a mul-tistory parking lot. With a gasp, you realize it's the Colosseum.

You've arrived. You're in the city's heart. You step down from your excursion bus onto the broad girdle of tarmac that encircles the great stone arena of the Roman emperors, and scurry out of the way of the passing Fiats—the motorists behind the wheels seem to display the panache of so many Ben-Hurs. The excitement of arriving here jolts the senses and sharpens expectations.

The timeless city to which all roads lead, Mamma Roma, enthralls visitors today as she has since time immemorial. More than Florence, more than Venice, this is Italy's treasure storehouse. Here the ancient Romans made us heirs-in-law to what we call Western Civilization; where centuries later Michelangelo painted the Sistine Chapel; where Gian Lorenzo Bernini's Baroque nymphs and naiads still dance in their marble fountains; and where, at Cinecittà Studios, Fellini filmed *La Dolce Vita* and *8½*. Today the city remains a veritable Grand Canyon of culture. Ancient Rome rubs shoulders with the medieval, the modern runs into the Renaissance, and the result is like nothing so much as an open-air museum.

But always remember: *Quando a Roma vai, fai come vedrai* ("When in Rome, do as the Romans do"). Don't feel intimidated by the press of art and culture. Instead, contemplate the grandeur from a table at a sun-drenched café on Piazza della Rotonda; let Rome's colorful life flow around you without feeling guilty because you haven't seen everything. It can't be done, anyway. There's just so much here that you'll have to come back again, so be sure to throw a coin in the Trevi Fountain.

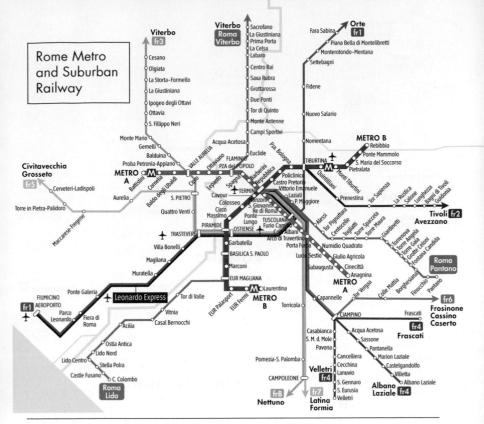

Rome Metro and Suburban Railway

EXPLORING ROME

Updated by Amanda Ruggeri

Most everyone begins by discovering the grandeur that was Rome: the Colosseum, the Forum, and the Pantheon. Then many move on to the Vatican, the closest thing to heaven on Earth for some.

The historical pageant continues with the 1,001 splendors of the Baroque era: glittering palaces, jewel-studded churches, and Caravaggio masterpieces. Arrive refreshed—with the help of a shot of espresso—at the foot of the Spanish Steps, where the picturesque world of the classic Grand Tour (peopled by such spirits as John Keats and Tosca) awaits you.

Thankfully, Rome provides delightful ways to catch your historic breath along the way: a walk through the cobblestone valleys of Trastevere or an hour stolen alongside a splashing Bernini fountain. Keep in mind that an uncharted ramble through the heart of the old city can be just as satisfying as the contemplation of a chapel or a trek through marbled museum corridors. No matter which aspect of Rome you end up enjoying the most, a visit to the Eternal City will live up to its name in memory.

Continued on page 60

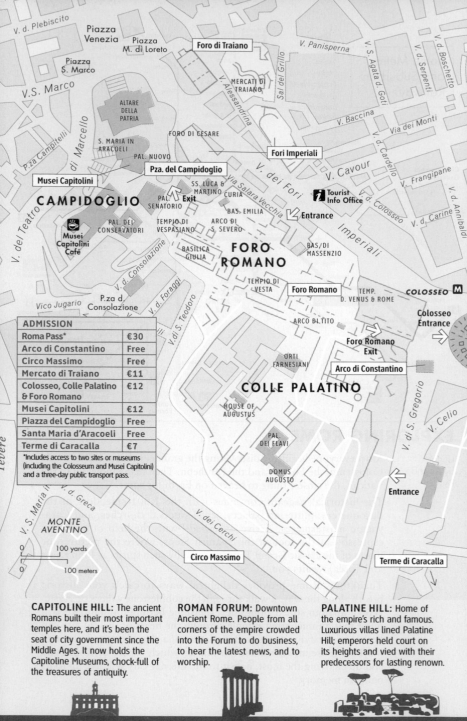

ADMISSION	
Roma Pass*	€30
Arco di Constantino	Free
Circo Massimo	Free
Mercato di Traiano	€11
Colosseo, Colle Palatino & Foro Romano	€12
Musei Capitolini	€12
Piazza del Campidoglio	Free
Santa Maria d'Aracoeli	Free
Terme di Caracalla	€7

*Includes access to two sites or museums (including the Colosseum and Musei Capitolini) and a three-day public transport pass.

MONTE AVENTINO

0 — 100 yards
0 — 100 meters

CAPITOLINE HILL: The ancient Romans built their most important temples here, and it's been the seat of city government since the Middle Ages. It now holds the Capitoline Museums, chock-full of the treasures of antiquity.

ROMAN FORUM: Downtown Ancient Rome. People from all corners of the empire crowded into the Forum to do business, to hear the latest news, and to worship.

PALATINE HILL: Home of the empire's rich and famous. Luxurious villas lined Palatine Hill; emperors held court on its heights and vied with their predecessors for lasting renown.

CAMPIDOGLIO   FORO ROMANO   COLLE PALATINO

ANCIENT ROME
GLORIES OF THE CAESARS

Time has reduced ancient Rome to fields of silent ruins, but the powerful impact of what happened here, of the genius and power that made Rome the center of the Western world, echoes across the millennia.

In this one compact area of the city, you can step back into the Rome of Cicero, Julius Caesar, and Virgil. Walk along the streets they knew, cool off in the shade of the Colosseum that loomed over the city, and see the sculptures poised above their piazzas. At the end of a day of exploring, climb one of the famous hills and watch the sun set over what was once the heart of the civilized world.

Today, this part of Rome, more than any other, is a perfect example of that layering of historic eras, the overlapping of ages, of religions, of a past that is very much a part of the present. Christian churches rise from the foundations of ancient pagan temples. An immense marble monument to a 19th-century king shares a square with a Renaissance palace built by a pope. Still, the history and memory of ancient Rome dominate the area. It's fitting that in the aftermath of centuries of such pageantry Percy Bysshe Shelley and Edward Gibbon reflected here on the meaning of *sic transit gloria mundi* (so passes away the glory of the world).

COLOSSEUM: Gladiators fought for the chance to live another day on the floor of the Colosseum, iconic symbol of ancient Rome.

KEY

☕ *Cafe / Restaurant*

CAMPIDOGLIO

The Capitoline Museums are closed on Monday. Late evening is an option for this area. Though the Santa Maria d'Aracoeli church is closed, the museums are open until 8 pm, and the views of the city lights and the illuminated Altare della Patria (aka the Victor Emmanuel II monument) and the Foro Romano are striking.

CLIMB MICHELANGELO'S DRAMATIC RAMP TO THE SUMMIT of one of Rome's famous hills, the Campidoglio (also known as Capitoline Hill), for views across the rooftops of modern Rome in one direction and across the ruins of ancient Rome in the other. Check out the stellar Musei Capitolini, crammed with a collection of masterpieces rivaled only by the Vatican museums.

★ **Piazza del Campidoglio.** In Michelangelo's piazza at the top of the Campidoglio stands a bronze equestrian statue of Marcus Aurelius (AD 121–180). A legend foretells that some day the statue's original gold surface will return, heralding the end of the world. Pending the arrival of that day, the original 2nd century statue was moved inside the Musei Capitolini; a copy sits on the piazza. Stand with your back to it to survey central Rome.

The Campidoglio, the site of the Roman Republic's first and holiest temples, had fallen into ruin by the Middle Ages and was called *Monte Caprino* (Goat Hill). In 1536 Pope Paul III (1468–1549) decided to restore its grandeur for the triumphal entry into the city of Charles V (1500–1558), the Holy Roman Emperor. He called upon Michelangelo to create the staircase ramp, the buildings and facades on the square, the pavement decoration, and the pedestal for the bronze statue.

The two buildings that make up the **Musei Capitolini** are on the piazza, flanking the **Palazzo Senatorio**. The Campidoglio has long been the seat of Rome's government; its Latin name is the root for the word capitol. Today, Rome's city hall occupies the Palazzo Senatorio. Head to the vantage points in the belvederes on the sides of the palazzo for great views of the ruins of ancient Rome.

★ **Musei Capitolini** (Capitoline Museums). Housed in the twin Palazzo dei Conservatori and Palazzo Nuovo buildings, this is a greatest hits collection of Roman art through the ages, from the ancients to the baroque.

Lining the courtyard of the **Palazzo dei Conservatori** are the colossal fragments

AN EMPEROR CHEAT SHEET

OCTAVIAN/AUGUSTUS (27 BC–AD 14)

After the death of Julius Caesar, Octavian gained control of Rome following a decade-long civil war that ended with the defeat of Antony and Cleopatra at Actium. Later known as Caesar Augustus, he was Rome's first emperor. His rule began a 200-year period of peace known as the Pax Romana.

Colle Palatino

CALIGULA (AD 37–41)

Caligula was tremendously popular when he came to power at the age of 25, but he very soon became infamous for his excessive cruelty, immorality, and erratic behavior. His contemporaries universally considered him to be insane. He was murdered by his own guard within four years.

of a head, leg, foot, and hand—all that remains of the famous statue of the emperor Constantine. These immense effigies were much in vogue throughout the Roman Empire. The renowned symbol of Rome, the *Capitoline Wolf*, a medieval bronze (long thought to be Etruscan), holds a place of honor in the museum; the suckling twins were added during the Renaissance to adapt the statue to the legend of Romulus and Remus.

The Palazzo also contains some of baroque painting's great masterpieces, including Caravaggio's *La Buona Ventura* (1595) and *San Giovanni Battista* (1602), Peter Paul Rubens's *Romulus and Remus* (1615), and Pietro da Cortona's sumptuous portrait of Pope Urban VIII (1627). When museum fatigue sets in, enjoy the view and refreshments on a large open terrace in the Palazzo dei Conservatoria.

The **Palazzo Nuovo** contains hundreds of Roman busts of philosophers and emperors—a fascinating Who's Who of the ancient world. A dozen Roman emperors are represented. Unlike the Greeks, whose portraits are idealized, the Romans preferred a more realistic representation.

Other notable sculptures include the poignant *Dying Gaul* and the regal *Capitoline Venus*. In the Capitolino courtyard is a gigantic, reclining sculpture of Oceanus, found in the Roman Forum and later dubbed *Marforio*. This was one of Rome's "talking statues" to which citizens from the 1500s to the 1900s affixed anonymous satirical verses and notes of political protest. ☎ *06/0608* ⊕ *www.museicapitolini.org* ⊙ *Tues.–Sun. 9–8.*

Santa Maria in Aracoeli. Seemingly endless, steep stairs climb from Piazza Venezia to the church of Santa Maria. There are 15th-century frescoes by Pinturicchio (1454–1513) in the first chapel on the right. ✉ *Scala dell'Arce Capitolina 14* ⊙ *May–Sept., daily, 9–12:30 and 3–6:30; Oct.–Apr., daily 7–12:30 and 3–6:30.*

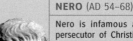

AN EMPEROR CHEAT SHEET

NERO (AD 54–68)

Nero is infamous as a violent persecutor of Christians. He also murdered his wife, his mother, and countless others. Although it's certain he didn't actually fiddle as Rome burned in AD 64, he was well known as a singer and a composer of music.

Domus Aurea

DOMITIAN (AD 81–96)

The first emperor to declare himself "Dominus et Deus" (Lord and God), he stripped away power from the Senate. After his death, the Senate retaliated by declaring him "Damnatio Memoriae" (his name and image were erased from all public records).

Colle Palatino

FORO ROMANO

It takes about an hour to explore the Roman Forum. There are entrances on the Via dei Fori Imperiali and from the Palatine Hill. A 30-minute walk will cover the Imperial Fora. You can reserve tickets online or by phone—operators speak English. If you are buying tickets in person, remember there are shorter lines here than at the Colosseum and the ticket is good for both sights.

EXPERIENCE THE ENDURING ROMANCE OF THE FORUM. Wander among its lonely columns and great, broken fragments of sculpted marble and stone— once temples, law courts, and shops crowded with people from all corners of the known world. This was the heart of ancient Rome and a symbol of the values that inspired Rome's conquest of an empire.

★ **Foro Romano** (Roman Forum). Built in a marshy valley between the Capitoline and Palatine hills, the Forum was the civic core of Republican Rome, the austere era that preceded the hedonism of the emperors. The Forum was the political, commercial, and religious center of Roman life. Hundreds of years of plunder and the tendency of later Romans to carry off what was left of the better building materials reduced it to the series of ruins you see today. Archaeological digs continue to uncover more about the sight; bear in mind that what you see are the ruins not of one period but of almost 900 years, from about 500 BC to AD 400.

The **Basilica Giulia**, which owes its name to Julius Caesar who had it built, was where the Centumviri, the hundred-or-so judges forming the civil court, met to hear cases. The open space before it was the core of the forum proper and prototype of Italy's famous piazzas. Let your imagination dwell on Mark Antony (circa 83 BC–30 BC), who delivered the funeral address in Julius Caesar's honor from the rostrum left of the **Arco di Settimio Severo**. This arch, one of the grandest of all antiquity, was built several hundred years later in AD 203 to celebrate the victory of the emperor Severus (AD 145–211) over the Parthians, and was topped by a bronze equestrian statuary group with four horses. You can explore the reconstruction of the large brick senate hall, the **Curia**; three Corinthian columns (a favorite of 19th-century poets) are all that remains of the **Tempio di Vespasiano el Tito**. In the **Tempio di Vesta**, six highly privileged vestal virgins kept the sacred fire, a tradition that dated back to the very earliest days of Rome. Their luxuious villa beside the temple was opened to the public in 2011. The cleaned and restored **Arco di Tito**, which stands in a slightly

AN EMPEROR CHEAT SHEET

	TRAJAN (AD 98–117)
	Trajan, from Southern Spain, was the first Roman emperor not born in Italy. He enlarged the empire's boundaries to include modern-day Romania, Armenia, and Upper Mesopotamia.
	Colonna di Traiano, Foro di Traiano, Mercati di Traiano

	HADRIAN (AD 117–138)
	He expanded the empire in Asia and the Middle East. He's best known for rebuilding the Pantheon, constructing a majestic villa at Tivoli, and initiating myriad other constructions across the empire, including the famed wall across Britain.

elevated position on a spur of the Palatine Hill, was erected in AD 81 to honor the recently dead Emperor Titus. It depicts the sacking of Jerusalem 10 years earlier, after the great Jewish revolt. A famous relief shows the captured contents of Herod's Temple—including its huge seven-branched menorah—being carried in triumph down Rome's Via Sacra. The temple of Venus and Roma sits between the arch and the Colosseum. Making sense of the ruins isn't always easy; consider renting an audio guide (€4) or buying a booklet that superimposes an image of the Forum in its heyday over a picture of it today. ☎ 06/39967700 ⊕ www.pierreci.it ☉ Daily, Jan.–Feb. 15 and last Sun. in Oct.–Dec., 8:30–4:30; Feb. 16–Mar. 15, 8:30–5; Mar. 16–last Sat. in Mar., 8:30–5:30; last Sun. in Mar.–Aug., 8:30–7:15; Sept., 8:30–7; Oct.1–last Sat. in Oct., 8:30–6:30.

THE OTHER FORA

Fori Imperiali (Imperial Fora). These five grandly conceived squares flanked with columnades and temples were built by Caesar, Augustus, Vespasian, Nerva, and Trajan. The original Roman Forum, built up over 500 years of Republican Rome, had grown crowded, and Julius Caesar was the first to attempt to rival it. He built the **Foro di Cesare** (Forum of Caesar), including a temple dedicated to the goddess Venus. Four emperors followed his lead, creating their own fora. The grandest was the **Foro di Traiano** (Forum of Trajan) a veritable city unto itself built by Trajan (AD 53–117). Here you find the 100-ft Colonna di Traiano (Trajan's Column, AD 110), carved with 2,600 figures in relief. In the 20th century, Benito Mussolini built the Via dei Fori Imperiali directly through the Imperial Fora area. Marble and limestone maps on the wall along the avenue portray the extent of the Roman Republic and Empire, and many of the remains of the Imperial Fora lay buried beneath its surface.

Mercati di Traiano (Trajan's Markets). This huge multilevel brick complex of 120 offices was one of the marvels of the ancient world. It provides a glimpse into Roman daily life and offers a stellar view from the belvedere at its top. ☎ 06/0608 ⊕ www.mercatiditraiano.it ☉ Tues.–Sun., 9–7.

(AD 161–180)

Remembered as a humanitarian emperor, Marcus Aurelius was a Stoic philosopher and his *Meditations* are still read today. Nonetheless, he was an aggressive leader devoted to expanding the empire.

Piazza del Campidoglio

CONSTANTINE I (AD 306–337)

Constantine changed the course of history by legalizing Christianity. He legitimized the once-banned religion and paved the way for the papacy in Rome. Constantine also established Constantinople as an Imperial capital in the East.

Arco di Constantino

COLLE PALATINO

A stroll on the Palatino, with a visit to the Museo Palatino, takes about two hours. The hill was once home to several major imperial palaces. Domitian's 1st-century AD palace is the best preserved. The Colle Palatino entrances are from the Roman Forum and at Via S. Gregorio 30.

IT ALL BEGAN HERE. ACCORDING TO LEGEND, ROMULUS, THE FOUNDER OF ROME, lived on the Colle Palatino (Palatine Hill). It was an exclusive address in ancient Rome, where emperors built palaces upon the slopes. Tour the Palatine's hidden corners and shady lanes, take a welcome break from the heat in its peaceful gardens, and enjoy a view of the Circo Massimo fit for an emperor.

★ **Colle Palatino** (Palatine Hill). A lane known as the Clivus Palatinus, paved with worn stones that were once trod by emperors and their slaves, climbs from the Forum area to a site that historians identify as one of Rome's earliest settlements. The legend goes that the infant twins Romulus and Remus were nursed by a she-wolf on the banks of the Tiber and adopted by a shepherd. Encouraged by the gods to build a city, Romulus chose this site in 753 BC. Remus preferred the Aventine. The argument that ensued left Remus dead and Romulus Rome's first king.

During the Republican era the hill was an important religious center, housing the Temple of Cybele and the Temple of Victory, as well as an exclusive residential area. Cicero, Catiline, Crassus, and Agrippa all had homes here. Augustus was born on the hill, and as he rose in power, he built

libraries, halls, and temples here; the **House of Augustus,** opened in 2008, preserves exquisite 1st-century BC frescoes. Emperor Tiberius was the next to build a palace here; others followed. The structures most visible today date back to the late 1st century AD, when the Palatine experienced an extensive remodeling under Emperor Domitian. During the Renaissance, the powerful Farnese family built gardens in the area overlooking the ruins of the Forum. Known as the **Orti Farnesiani,** they were Europe's first botanical gardens. The **Museo Palatino** charts the history of the hill. Splendid sculptures, frescoes, and mosaic intarsia from various imperial buildings are on display. ☎ *06/39967700* ⊕ *www.pierreci.it* ⊙ *Daily, Jan.–Feb. 15 and last Sun. in Oct.– Dec., 8:30–4:30; Feb. 16–Mar. 15, 8:30–5; Mar. 16–last Sat. in Mar., 8:30–5:30; last Sun. in Mar.–Aug., 8:30–7:15; Sept., 8:30– 7; Oct.1–last Sat. in Oct., 8:30–6:30.*

THE RISE AND FALL OF ANCIENT ROME

218 BC

ca. 800 BC	Rise of Etruscan city-states.
509–510	Foundation of the Roman republic; expulsion of Etruscans from Roman territory.
343	Roman conquest of Greek colonies in Campania.
264–241	First Punic War (with Carthage): increased naval power helps Rome gain control of southern Italy and then Sicily.
212–202	Second Punic War: Hannibal's attempted conquest of Italy, using elephants, is eventually crushed.

NEAR THE COLLE PALATINO

Circo Massimo (Circus Maximus). Ancient Rome's oldest and largest racetrack lies in the natural hollow between the Palatine and Aventine hills. From the imperial box in the palace on Palatine Hill, emperors could look out over the oval course. Stretching about 660 yards from end to end, the Circus Maximus could hold more than 200,000 spectators. On certain occasions there were as many as 100 chariot races a day, and competitions could last for 15 days. The central ridge was framed by two Egyptian obelisks. Check out the panoramic views of the Circus Maximus from the Palatine Hill's Belvedere. You can also see the green slopes of the Aventine and Celian hills, as well as the bell tower of Santa Maria in Cosmedin.

Terme di Caracalla (Baths of Caracalla). For the Romans, public baths were much more than places to wash. The baths also had recital halls, art galleries, libraries, massage rooms, sports grounds, and gardens. Even the smallest public baths had at least some of these amenities, and in the capital of the Roman Empire, they were provided on a lavish scale. Ancient Rome's most beautiful and luxurious public baths were opened by the emperor Caracalla in AD 217 and were used until the 6th century.

Taking a bath was a long process, and a social activity first and foremost. You began by sweating in the *sudatoria*, small rooms resembling saunas. From these you moved on to the *calidarium* for the actual business of washing, using an olive-oil-and-sand exfoliant, then removing it with a *strigil* (scraper). Next was the *tepidarium*, where you gradually cooled down. Finally, you splashed around in the *frigidarium*, in essence a cold–water swimming pool. There was a nominal admission fee, often waived by officials and emperors wishing to curry favor with the plebeians. The baths' functioning depended on the slaves who cared for the clients and stoked the fires that heated the water. ☎ 06/39967700 ⊕ *www.pierreci.it* ⊗ *Tues.–Sun., Jan.–Feb. 15 and last Sun. in Oct.–Dec., 9–4:30; Feb. 16–Mar. 15, 9–5; Mar. 16–last Sat. in Mar., 9–5:30; last Sun. in Mar.–Aug., 9–7:15; Sept., 9–7; Oct. 1–last Sat. in Oct., 9–6:30. For all Mondays, 9–2.*

150 BC	Roman Forum begins to take shape as the principal civic center in Italy.
149–146	Third Punic War: Rome razes city of Carthage and emerges as the dominant Mediterranean force.
133	Rome rules entire Mediterranean Basin except Egypt.
58–52	Julius Caesar conquers Gaul.
44	Julius Caesar is assassinated.
27	Rome's Imperial Age begins; Octavian (now named Augustus) becomes the first emperor and is later deified. The Augustan Age is celebrated in the works of Virgil (70–19 BC), Ovid (43 BC–AD 17), Livy (59 BC–AD 17), and Horace (65–8 BC).

44 BC

COLOSSEO

You can give the Colosseum a cursory look in about 30 minutes, but it deserves at least an hour. Make reservations by phone (there are English-speaking operators) or online at least a day in advance to avoid long lines. Or buy your ticket at the Roman Forum or Palatine Hill, where the lines are usually shorter.

LEGEND HAS IT THAT AS LONG AS THE COLOSSEUM STANDS, ROME WILL STAND; and when Rome falls, so will the world. No visit to Rome is complete without a trip to the obstinate oval that has been the iconic symbol of the city for centuries.

★ **Colosseo.** A program of games and shows lasting 100 days celebrated the opening of the massive and majestic Colosseum in AD 80. On the opening day Romans claimed that 5,000 wild beasts perished. More than 50,000 spectators could sit within the arena's 596-yard circumference, which had limestone facing, hundreds of statues for decoration, and a *velarium*—an ingenious system of sail-like awnings rigged on ropes manned by imperial sailors—to protect the audience from the sun and rain. Before the imperial box, gladiators would salute the emperor and cry, "*Ave, imperator, morituri te salutant*" ("Hail, emperor, men soon to die salute you"); it is said that when one day they heard the emperor Claudius respond, "Or maybe not," they were so offended that they called a strike.

Originally known as the Flavian Amphitheater, it took the name Colosseum after a truly colossal gilt bronze statue of Nero that stood nearby. Gladiator combat ended by the 5th century and staged animal hunts

by the 6th. The arena later served as a quarry from which materials were looted to build Renaissance churches and palaces, including St. Peter's Basilica. Finally, it was declared sacred by the Vatican in memory of the many Christians believed martyred here. (Scholars now maintain that Christians met their death elsewhere.) During the 19th century, romantic poets lauded the glories of the ruins when viewed by moonlight. Now its arches glow at night with mellow golden spotlights.

Expect long lines at the entrance and actors dressed as gladiators who charge a hefty fee to pose for pictures. (Agree on a price in advance if you want a photo.) Once inside you can walk around about half of the outer ring of the structure and look down into the exposed passages under what was once the arena floor, now represented by a small stage at one end. Climb the steep stairs for panoramic views in the Colosseum and out to the Palatine and Arch of Constantine. A museum

THE RISE AND FALL OF ANCIENT ROME

AD 116

58 AD	Rome invades Britain.
50	Rome is the largest city in the world, with a population of possibly as much as a million.
64–68	Emperor Nero begins the persecution of Christians in the Empire; Saints Peter and Paul are executed.
72–80	Vespasian begins the Colosseum; Titus completes it.
98–117	Trajan's military successes are celebrated with his Baths (98), Forum (110), and Column (113); the Roman Empire reaches its apogee.

space on the second floor holds temporary archaeological exhibits. ☎ 06/39967700 ⊕ *www.pierreci.it* ⊗ *Daily, Jan.–Feb. 15 and last Sun. in Oct.–Dec., 8:30–4:30; Feb. 16–Mar. 15, 8:30–5; Mar. 16–last Sat. in Mar., 8:30–5:30; last Sun. in Mar.–Aug., 8:30–7:15; Sept., 8:30–7; Oct.1–last Sat. in Oct., 8:30–6:30.*

Arco di Costantino. The largest (69 feet high, 85 feet long, 23 feet wide) and the best preserved of Rome's triumphal arches was erected in AD 315 to celebrate the victory of the emperor Constantine (280–337) over co-emperor Maxentius (died 312). According to legend, it was just before this battle that Constantine, the emperor who legalized Christianity, had a vision of a cross in the heavens and heard the words "In this sign, thou shalt conquer."

NEAR THE COLOSSEO

Domus Aurea. At this writing, Nero's "Golden House" was closed, with the prospect of reopening uncertain. The site gives a good sense of the excesses of Imperial Rome. After fire destroyed much of the city in AD 64, Nero took advantage of the resulting open space to construct a lavish palace so large that it spread over a third of the city. It had a facade of marble, seawater piped into the baths, gilded vaults, decorations of mother-of-pearl, and vast gardens. Not much of this ornamentation has survived; a good portion of the building and grounds was buried under the public works with which subsequent emperors sought to make reparation to the Roman people for Nero's phenomenal greed. As a result, the site of the Domus Aurea itself remained unknown for many centuries. A few of Nero's original halls were discovered underground at the end of the 15th century. Raphael (1483–1520) was one of the artists who had themselves lowered into the rubble-filled rooms, which resembled grottoes. The artists copied the original painted Roman decorations, barely visible by torchlight, and scratched their names on the ceilings. Raphael later used these models—known as *grotesques* because they were found in the so-called grottoes—in his decorative motifs for the Loggia of Julius II in the Vatican. The palace remains impressive in scale, even if a lot of imagination is required to envision the original. ✉ *Via della Domus Aurea* ☎ 06/39967700 ⊕ *www.pierreci.it.*

AD 450

238 AD	The first wave of Germanic invasions penetrates Italy.
293	Diocletian reorganizes the Empire into West and East.
330	Constantine founds a new Imperial capital (Constantinople) in the East.
410	Rome is sacked by Visigoths.
476	The last Roman emperor, Romulus Augustus, is deposed. The western Roman Empire falls.

NAVONA AND CAMPO: BAROQUE ROME

Called the "Campo Marzio" (Field of Mars), this time-burnished district is the city's most beautiful neighborhood. Set between Via del Corso and the Tiber bend, it's filled with narrow streets bearing curious names, airy piazzas, and half-hidden courtyards. Some of Rome's most coveted residential addresses are nestled here. So, too, are the ancient Pantheon and the Renaissance square of Campo de' Fiori, but the spectacular, over-the-top Baroque monuments of the 16th and 17th centuries predominate.

The hub of the district is the queen of squares, Piazza Navona— a cityscape adorned with the most jaw-dropping fountain by Gian Lorenzo Bernini, father of the Baroque. Streets running off the square lead to many historic must-sees, including noble churches by Borromini and Caravaggio's greatest paintings at San Luigi dei Francesi. This district has been an integral part of the city since ancient times, and its position between the Vatican and Lateran palaces, both seats of papal rule, put it in the mainstream of Rome's development from the Middle Ages onward. Craftsmen, shopkeepers, and famed artists toiled in the shadow of the huge palaces built to consolidate the power of leading figures in the papal court. Artisans and artists still live here, but their numbers are diminishing as the district becomes increasingly posh and—so critics say—"Disneyfied." But three of the liveliest piazzas in Rome—Piazza Navona, Piazza della Rotonda (home to the Pantheon), and Campo de' Fiori—are lodestars in a constellation of some of Rome's most authentic cafés, stores, and wine bars.

GETTING HERE AND AROUND

To bus it from Termini train station or the Vatican, take the No. 40 Express or the No. 64 and get off at Corso Vittorio Emanuele II, a two-minute stroll from either Campo de' Fiori or Piazza Navona, or take little electric No. 116 from Via Veneto to Campo de' Fiori. Buses Nos. 87 and 571 link the area to the Forum and Colosseum. Tram No. 8 runs from Largo Argentina to Trastevere.

TOP ATTRACTIONS

Campo de' Fiori. A bustling marketplace in the morning (Mon.–Sat. 8–1) and a trendy meeting place the rest of the day (and night), this piazza has plenty of earthy charm. By sunset, all the fish, fruit, and flower vendors disappear and this so-called *piazza trasformista* takes on another identity, becoming a circus of bars particularly favored by study-abroads, tourists, and young expats (for the full scoop, see our special photo feature, "Life is a Piazza"). Brooding over the piazza is a hooded statue of the philosopher Giordano Bruno, who was burned at the stake here in 1600 for heresy. His was the first of the executions that drew Roman crowds to Campo de' Fiori in the 17th century. ⌂ *Intersection of Via dei Baullari, Via Giubbonari, Via del Pellegrino, and Piazza della Cancelleria, Campo.*

Fodor's Choice   **Palazzo Altemps.** Containing some of the finest ancient Roman statues
★   in the world, the collection here formerly made up the core of the Museo Nazionale Romano. As of 1995, it was moved to these new, suitably grander digs. The palace's sober exterior belies a magnificence that appears as soon as you walk into the majestic courtyard, studded

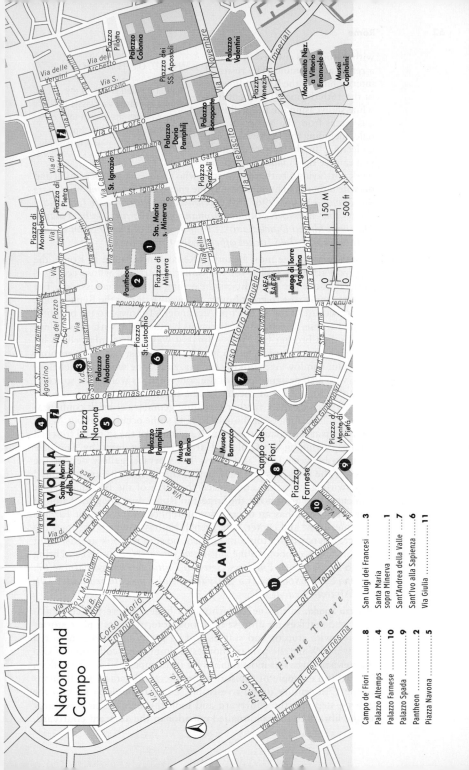

Navona and Campo

with statues and covered in part by a retractable awning. The restored interior hints at the Roman lifestyle of the 16th through 18th centuries while showcasing the most illustrious pieces from the Museo Nazionale, including the Ludovisi family collection. In the frescoed salons you can see the *Galata,* a poignant

work portraying a barbarian warrior who chooses death for himself and his wife rather than humiliation by the enemy. ⊠ *Piazza Sant'Apollinare 46, Navona* ☎ *06/39967700* ⊕ *www.coopculture.it* ▱ *€7, includes three other Museo Nazionale Romano sites (Crypta Balbi, Palazzo Massimo, Museo Diocleziano); €10 if any one of them has an exhibit* ☉ *Tues.–Sun. 9–7:45 (ticket office closes 1 hr before).*

Fodor's Choice
★

Palazzo Farnese. The most beautiful Renaissance palace in Rome, the Palazzo Farnese is fabled for the Galleria Carracci, whose ceiling is to the Baroque age what the Sistine ceiling is to the Renaissance. The Farnese family rose to great power and wealth during the Renaissance, in part because of the favor Pope Alexander VI showed to the beautiful Giulia Farnese. The massive palace was begun when, with Alexander's aid, Giulia's brother became cardinal; it was further enlarged on his election as Pope Paul III in 1534. The uppermost frieze decorations and main window overlooking the piazza are the work of Michelangelo, who also designed part of the courtyard, as well as the graceful arch over Via Giulia at the back. The facade on Piazza Farnese has recently been cleaned, further revealing geometrical brick configurations that have long been thought to hold some occult meaning. When looking up at the palace, try to catch a glimpse of the splendid frescoed ceilings, including the **Galleria Carracci** vault painted by Annibale Carracci between 1597 and 1604. The Carracci gallery depicts the loves of the gods, a supremely pagan theme that the artist painted in a swirling style that announced the birth of the Baroque. Other opulent salons are among the largest in Rome, including the Salon of Hercules, which has an overpowering replica of the ancient *Farnese Hercules* front and center. The French Embassy, which occupies the palace, offers weekly tours in English; be sure to book at least eight days in advance (book online at ⊕ *www.inventerrome.com*) and bring photo ID. ⊠ *French Embassy, Servizio Culturale, Piazza Farnese 67, Campo* ☎ *06/686011* ▱ *€5* ☉ *By tours only (no children under 10); English tour Wed. at 5.*

Palazzo Spada. In this neighborhood of huge, austere palaces, Palazzo Spada strikes an almost frivolous note, with its upper stories covered with stuccos and statues and its pretty ornament-encrusted courtyard. While the palazzo houses an impressive collection of Old Master paintings, it is most famous for its trompe l'oeil garden gallery, a delightful example of the sort of architectural games rich Romans of the 17th century found irresistible. Even if you don't go into the gallery, step into the courtyard and look through the glass window of the library to the colonnaded corridor in the adjacent courtyard.

Going Baroque

1

Flagrantly emotional, heavily expressive, and visually sensuous, the 17th-century artistic movement known as Baroque was born in Rome. It was the creation of three geniuses: the sculptor and architect Gian Lorenzo Bernini (1598–1680), the painter and architect Pietro da Cortona (1596–1669), and the architect and sculptor Francesco Borromini (1599–1667). From the drama found in the artists' works to the jewel-laden, gold-on-gold detail of 17th-century Roman palaces, the Baroque style was intended both to shock and delight by upsetting the placid, "correct" rules of proportion and scale of the Renaissance. If a building looks theatrical—like a stage or a theater, especially with curtains being drawn back—it's usually Baroque. Look for over-the-top, curvaceous marble work, trompe l'oeil, allusions to other art, and high drama to identify the style. Baroque's appeal to the emotions made it a powerful weapon in the hands of the Counter-Reformation.

See—or seem to see—Borromini's 8-meter-long gallery quadrupled in depth, a sort of optical telescope taking the Renaissance's art of perspective to another level, as it stretches out for a great distance with a large statue at the end. In fact the distance is an illusion: the corridor grows progressively narrower and the columns progressively smaller as they near the statue, which is just 2 feet tall. ⊠ *Piazza Capo di Ferro 13, Campo* ☎ *06/6861158* ⊕ *www.galleriaborghese.it* ☒ *€5* ☉ *Tues.–Sun. 8:30–7:30.*

Fodor's Choice **Pantheon.** One of the wonders of the ancient world, this onetime pagan
★   temple, a marvel of architectural harmony and proportion, is the best-preserved ancient building in Rome. It was entirely rebuilt by the emperor Hadrian around AD 120 on the site of an earlier pantheon (from the Greek *pan*, all, and *theon*, gods) erected in 27 BC by Augustus's general Agrippa.

The most striking thing about the Pantheon is not its size, immense though it is (until 1960 the dome was the largest ever built), nor even the phenomenal technical difficulties posed by so vast a construction; rather, it's the remarkable unity of the building. You don't have to look far to find the reason for this harmony: the diameter described by the dome is exactly equal to its height. It's the use of such simple mathematical balance that gives classical architecture its characteristic sense of proportion and its nobility and why some call it the world's only architecturally perfect building. The great opening at the apex of the dome, the oculus, is nearly 30 feet in diameter and was the temple's only source of light. It was intended to symbolize the "all-seeing eye of heaven."

The Pantheon is by far the best preserved of the major monuments of imperial Rome. Turned into a church in the 7th century, it holds the remains of many luminaries. Its most famous tomb is that of Raphael (between the second and third chapels on the left as you enter). One-hour tours (€10) are run regularly in English; check at the information desk on your right as you enter. ⊠ *Piazza della Rotonda, Navona*

☎ 06/68300230 ⊕ *pantheonroma.com* ▦ *Free; audio guides* €5 ⊘ *Mon.–Sat. 9–7:30, Sun. 9–6, public holidays that fall on a weekday 9–1* Ⓜ *Closest bus hub: Argentina (Bus Nos. 40, 85, 53, 46, 64, 87, 571, Tram No. 8).*

Piazza Navona. Here, everything that makes Rome unique is compressed into one beautiful Baroque piazza. Always camera-ready, Piazza Navona has Bernini sculptures, three gorgeous fountains, a magnificently Baroque church (Sant'Agnese in Agone), and, best of all, the excitement of so many people strolling, admiring the fountains, and enjoying the view.

At center stage is the Fontana dei Quattro Fiumi, created for Innocent X by Bernini in 1651. Bernini's powerful figures of the four rivers represent the four corners of the world: the Nile; the Ganges; the Danube; and the Plata, with its hand raised.

Piazza Navona is lined with cafés, though, so you can pick and choose. Just be aware that the restaurants here are geared toward tourists, so while it's a beautiful place for a coffee, you can find cheaper, more authentic, and much better meals elsewhere.

Fodor'sChoice
★
San Luigi dei Francesi. A pilgrimage spot for art lovers everywhere, San Luigi's Contarelli Chapel is adorned with three stunningly dramatic works by Caravaggio (1571–1610), the Baroque master of the heightened approach to light and dark. At the altar end of the left nave, they were commissioned for San Luigi, the official church of Rome's French colony (San Luigi is St. Louis, patron of France). The inevitable coin machine will light up his *Calling of St. Matthew, Matthew and the Angel,* and *Matthew's Martyrdom,* seen from left to right, and Caravaggio's mastery of light takes it from there. When painted, they caused considerable consternation to the clergy of San Luigi, who thought the artist's dramatically realistic approach was scandalously disrespectful. A first version of the altarpiece was rejected; the priests were not particularly happy with the other two, either. Time has fully vindicated Caravaggio's patron, Cardinal Francesco del Monte, who secured the commission for these works and stoutly defended them. They're now recognized to be among the world's greatest paintings. ✉ *Piazza San Luigi dei Francesi, Navona* ☎ 06/688271 ⊘ *Fri.–Wed. 10–12:30 and 3–7; Thurs. 10–12:30.*

Santa Maria sopra Minerva. The name of the church reveals that it was built *sopra* (over) the ruins of a temple of Minerva, ancient goddess of wisdom. Erected in 1280 by the Dominicans on severe Italian Gothic lines, it has undergone a number of more or less happy restorations to the interior. Certainly, as the city's major Gothic church, it provides a refreshing contrast to Baroque flamboyance. Have a €1 coin handy to illuminate the **Cappella Carafa** in the right transept, where Filippino Lippi's (1457–1504) glowing frescoes are well worth the small investment, opening up the deepest azure expanse of sky where musical angels hover around the Virgin. Under the main altar is the tomb of St. Catherine of Siena, one of Italy's patron saints. Left of the altar you'll find Michelangelo's *Risen Christ* and the tomb of the gentle artist Fra Angelico. Bernini's unusual and little-known monument to the Blessed

Maria Raggi is on the fifth pier from the door on the left as you leave the church. In front of the church, the little obelisk-bearing elephant (under restoration at the time of this printing) carved by Bernini is perhaps the city's most charming sculpture. An inscription on the base of **Bernini's Elephant Obelisk** references the church's ancient patroness, reading something to the effect that it takes a strong mind to sustain solid wisdom. ✉ *Piazza della Minerva, Navona* ☎ *06/6793926* ⊙ *Weekdays 8–7, weekends 8–12:30 and 3:30–7.*

Fodor's Choice **Via Giulia.** Still a Renaissance-era diorama and one of Rome's most
★ exclusive addresses, Via Giulia was the first street in Rome since ancient times to be laid out in a straight line. A stroll will reveal elegant palaces and old churches (one, **San Eligio,** at No. 18, reputedly designed by Raphael himself). The area around Via Giulia is a wonderful section to wander through and get the feel of daily life as carried on in a centuries-old setting. Remnant of a master plan by Michelangelo, the arch over the street was meant to link massive Palazzo Farnese, on the east side of Via Giulia, with the building across the street and a bridge to the Villa Farnesina, directly across the river. Finally, on the right and rather green with age, dribbles that star of many a postcard, the Fontana del Mascherone. ✉ *Between Piazza dell'Oro and Piazza San Vincenzo Palloti, Campo.*

WORTH NOTING

Sant'Andrea della Valle. Topped by the highest dome in Rome (designed by Maderno) after St. Peter's, this huge and imposing 17th-century church is remarkably balanced in design. Fortunately, its facade, which had been turned a sooty gray from pollution, has been cleaned to a near-sparkling white. Use the handy mirror that's provided to examine the early-17th-century frescoes by Domenichino in the choir vault and those by Lanfranco in the dome. One of the earliest ceilings done in full Baroque style, its upward vortex was influenced by Correggio's dome in Parma, of which Lanfranco was also a citizen. (Bring a few coins to light the paintings, which can be very dim.) The three massive paintings of Saint Andrew's martyrdom are by Maria Preti (1650–51). Richly marbled and decorated chapels flank the nave, and in such a space, Puccini set the first act of *Tosca.* ✉ *Piazza Vidoni 6, Corso Vittorio Emanuele II, Campo* ☎ *06/6861339* ⊙ *Daily 7:30–12:30 and 4–7:45.*

Sant'Ivo alla Sapienza. The main facade of this eccentric Baroque church, probably Borromini's best, is on the stately courtyard of an austere building that once housed Rome's university. Sant'Ivo has what must surely be one of the most delightful domes in all of Rome—a golden spiral said to have been inspired by a bee's stinger. ✉ *Corso Rinascimento 40, Navona* ☎ *06/6864987* ⊙ *Sept.–June. Sun. 9–noon* Ⓜ *Bus Nos. 130, 116, 186, 492, 30, 70, 81, or 87.*

CORSO AND SPAGNA: PIAZZA VENEZIA TO THE SPANISH STEPS

In spirit, and in fact, this section of the city is its most grandiose. The overblown Vittoriano monument, the labyrinthine treasure-chest palaces of Rome's surviving aristocracy, even the diamond-draped denizens of Via Condotti's shops—all embody the exuberant ego of a city at the center of its own universe. Here's where you'll see ladies in furs gobbling pastries at café tables, and walk through a thousand snapshots as you climb the famous Spanish Steps, admired by generations from Byron to Versace. Cultural treasures abound around here: gilded 17th-century churches, glittering palaces, and the greatest example of portraiture in Rome, Velázquez's incomparable *Innocent X* at the Galleria Doria Pamphilj. Have your camera ready—along with a coin or two—for that most beloved of Rome's landmarks, the Trevi Fountain.

GETTING HERE AND AROUND

One of Rome's handiest subway stations, the Spagna Metro station is tucked just to the left of the Spanish Steps. Buses No. 117 (from St. John Lateran and the Colosseum) and No. 119 (from Largo Argentina) hum through the neighborhood.

TOP ATTRACTIONS

Monumento a Vittorio Emanuele II, or Altare della Patria (*Victor Emmanuel Monument, or Altar of the Nation*). The huge white mass of the "Vittoriano" is an inescapable landmark—Romans say you can avoid its image only if you're actually standing on it. Built to honor the unification of Italy and the nation's first king, Victor Emmanuel II, it also shelters the eternal flame at the tomb of Italy's Unknown Soldier killed during World War I. You can't avoid the Monumento, so enjoy neo-imperial grandiosity at its most bombastic. The views from the top are some of Rome's most panoramic. ⊠ *Entrance at Piazza Ara Coeli, next to Piazza Venezia, around Via del Corso* 🕾 *06/0608* ⊕ *060608.it* 🖃 *Free, elevator €7* ⊙ *Elevator Mon.–Thurs. 9:30–5:45; Fri. and weekends 9:30–6:45; stairs open winter 9:30–4:30, summer 9:30–5:30.*

Fodor'sChoice ★ **Palazzetto Zuccaro.** The most amusing house in all of Italy, this folly was designed in 1591 by noted painter Federico Zuccaro to form a monster's face. Typical of the outré Mannerist style of the period, the eyes are the house's windows; the entrance portal is through the monster's mouth. Zuccaro (1540–1609)—whose frescoes adorn many Roman churches, including Trinità del Monti just up the block—sank all of his money into his new home, dying in debt before his curious memorial, as it turned out to be, was completed. Today, it is the property of the Biblioteca Hertziana, Rome's prestigious fine-arts library; at press time, it has been sheathed for a long-term renovation project. Leading up to the quaint Piazza Trinità del Monti, Via Gregoriana is a real charmer and has long been one of Rome's most elegant addresses, home to such residents as French 19th-century painter Ingres and famed couturier Valentino's first couture salon. ⊠ *Via Gregoriana 30, Spagna* 🕾 *06/69993242 Biblioteca Hertziana* Ⓜ *Spagna.*

FodorśChoice ★ **Palazzo Colonna.** Rome's grandest family built itself Rome's grandest palazzo in the 18th century—it's so immense, it faces Piazza Santi Apostoli on one side and the Quirinal Hill on the other (a little bridge over Via della Pilotta links the palace with the gardens on the hill). While still home to some Colonna patricians, the palace also holds the family picture gallery, open to the public one day a week. The galleria is itself a setting of aristocratic grandeur. At one end looms the

WORD OF MOUTH

"The Pantheon and Trevi Fountain were very busy, but the Galleria Doria Pamphilj was, as ever, virtually deserted. Why this wonderful collection of paintings, including by Brueghel and Caravaggio, isn't better known and more popular, I have no idea; it certainly deserves to be both."

—annhig

ancient red marble column (*colonna* in Italian), which is the family's emblem; above the vast room is the spectacular ceiling fresco of the Battle of Lepanto painted by Giovanni Coli and Filippo Gherardi. At 11:45, there's a guided tour in English (included in your entrance fee). In 2013 the gallery opened a new wing, including its tapestry room, to the public. ✉ *Via della Pilotta 17, around Via del Corso* ☎ *06/6784350* ⊕ *www.galleriacolonna.it* 💰 *€12* ☉ *Sat. 9–1:15 (tour in English 11:45); private tours available daily on request.*

FodorśChoice ★ **Palazzo Doria Pamphilj.** Along with the Palazzo Colonna and the Galleria Borghese, this spectacular family palace provides the best glimpse of aristocratic Rome. Here, the main attractions are the legendary Old Master paintings, including treasures by Velázquez and Caravaggio, the splendor of the main galleries, and a unique suite of private family apartments.

Housed in four wings that line the palace's courtyard, the picture gallery contains 550 paintings, including three by Caravaggio—a young *St. John the Baptist, Mary Magdalene,* and the breathtaking *Rest on the Flight to Egypt.* Off the eyepopping **Galleria degli Specchi** (Gallery of Mirrors)—a smaller version of the one at Versailles—are the famous Velázquez *Pope Innocent X,* considered by some historians to be the greatest portrait ever painted, and the Bernini bust of the same Pamphilj pope. The audio guide by Prince Jonathan Doria Pamphilj, the current heir (born in England, he was adopted by the late Principessa Orietta), provides an intimate family history well worth listening to. ✉ *Via del Corso 305, around Via del Corso* ☎ *06/6797323* ⊕ *www.doriapamphilj.it* 💰 *€11* ☉ *Daily 9–7.*

FodorśChoice ★ **Sant'Ignazio.** Rome's largest Jesuit church, this 17th-century landmark harbors some of the most city's magnificent trompe-l'oeil. To get the full effect of the marvelous illusionistic ceiling by priest-artist Andrea Pozzo, stand on the small disk set into the floor of the nave. The heavenly vision above you, seemingly extending upward almost indefinitely, represents the *Allegory of the Missionary Work of the Jesuits* and is part of Pozzo's cycle of works in this church exalting the early history of the Jesuit Order, whose founder was the reformer Ignatius of Loyola. Scattered around the nave are several awe-inspiring altars; their soaring columns, gold-on-gold decoration, and gilded statues make these the last word in splendor. The church is often host to concerts of sacred

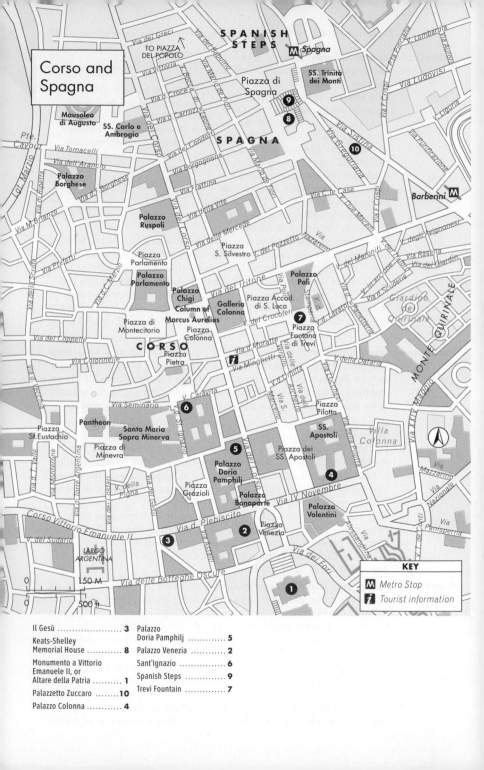

Corso and Spagna

SPANISH STEPS

TO PIAZZA DEL POPOLO

Piazza di Spagna

SS. Trinita dei Monti

Ⓜ *Spagna*

⑨

⑧

Mausoleo di Augusto

SS. Carlo e Ambrogio

SPAGNA

Pte. Cavour

Via Tomacelli

Via dell'Arancio

⑩

Palazzo Borghese

Barberini Ⓜ

Palazzo Ruspoli

Palazzo Parlamento

Piazza Parlamento

Palazzo Poli

Piazza S. Silvestro

Piazza S. Silvestro

Piazza di Montecitorio

Palazzo Chigi

Column of Marcus Aurelius

Galleria Colonna

Piazza Accad. di S. Luca

⑦

Piazza Fontana di Trevi

Giardino le Quirinale

Piazza Colonna

C O R S O

Piazza Pietra

ℹ

Piazza Pilotta

MONTE QUIRINALE

Piazza St.Eustachio

Pantheon

Santa Maria Sopra Minerva

⑥

SS. Apostoli

Villa Colonna

Piazza di Minevra

Piazza Grazioli

⑤

Piazza dei SS. Apostoli

④

Palazzo Doria Pamphilj

Palazzo Bonaparte

Via IV Novembre

Palazzo Valentini

Corso Vittorio Emanuele II

③

②

Piazza Venezia

LARGO ARGENTINA

150 M

500 ft

①

KEY

Ⓜ	*Metro Stop*
ℹ	*Tourist information*

music performed by choirs from all over the world. Look for post-ers at the church doors for more information. ⊠ *Piazza Sant'Ignazio, around Via del Corso* ☎ *06/6794406* ⊙ *Mon.–Sat 7:30–7, Sun. and religious holidays 9–7.*

FAMILY **The Spanish Steps.** That icon of postcard Rome, the Spanish Steps (often
Fodor's Choice called simply *la scalinata*—"the staircase"—by Italians) and the Piazza
★ di Spagna from which they ascend both get their names from the Spanish Embassy to the Vatican on the piazza. In an allusion to the church, the staircase is divided by three landings (beautifully banked with azaleas from mid-April to mid-May). For centuries, the scalinata and its neighborhood have welcomed tourists, dukes, and writers in search of inspiration—among them Stendhal, Honoré de Balzac, William Makepeace Thackeray, and Byron, along with today's enthusi-astic hordes. ⊠ *Intersection of vias Condotti, del Babuino, and Due Macelli, Spagna* Ⓜ *Spagna.*

Fodor's Choice **Trevi Fountain.** Alive with rushing waters commanded by an imperious
★ Oceanus, the Fontana di Trevi (Trevi Fountain) earned full-fledged iconic status in 1954 when it starred in 20th-Century Fox's *Three Coins in the Fountain*. From the very start, however, the Trevi has been all about theatrical effects. An aquatic marvel in a city filled with them, the fountain's unique drama is largely due to the site: its vast basin is squeezed into the tight meeting of three little streets (the "tre vie," which may give the fountain its name) with cascades emerging as if from the wall of Palazzo Poli. ■**TIP→** Everyone knows the famous legend that if you throw a coin into the Trevi Fountain you will ensure a return trip to the Eternal City. But not everyone knows how to do it the right way: You must toss a coin with your right hand over your left shoulder, with your back to the fountain. One coin means you'll return to Rome; two, you'll return and fall in love; three, you'll return, find love, and marry. ⊠ *Piazza di Trevi, Trevi* Ⓜ *Barberini–Fontana di Trevi.*

WORTH NOTING

Il Gesù. The mother church of the Jesuits in Rome is the prototype of all Counter-Reformation churches. Considered the first fully Baroque church, it has spectacular interior that tells a lot about an era of reli-gious triumph and turmoil. Its architecture (the overall design was by Vignola, the facade by della Porta) influenced ecclesiastical building in Rome for more than a century and was exported by the Jesuits through-out the rest of Europe.

Though consecrated as early as 1584, the interior of the church wasn't decorated for another 100 years. The most striking element is the ceil-ing, which is covered with frescoes that swirl down from on high to merge with painted stucco figures at the base. The founder of the Jesuit order himself is buried in the Chapel of St. Ignatius, in the left-hand transept. This is surely the most sumptuous Baroque altar in Rome; as is typical, the enormous globe of lapis lazuli that crowns it is really only a shell of lapis over a stucco base. The heavy bronze altar rail by architect Carlo Fontana is in keeping with the surrounding opulence. ⊠ *Piazza del Ges, off Via del Plebiscito, Campo* ☎ *06/697001* ⊕ *www.chiesadelgesu.org* ⊙ *Daily 7–12:30 and 4–7:45.*

Keats-Shelley Memorial House. Sent to Rome in a last-ditch attempt to treat his consumption, English Romantic poet John Keats lived—and died—here, in the "Casina Rossa" (the name refers to the blush-pink facade) at the foot of the Spanish Steps. At that point, this was the heart of the colorful bohemian quarter of Rome that was especially favored by the English. Keats had become celebrated through such poems as "Ode to a Nightingale" and "She Walks in Beauty," but his trip to Rome was fruitless. He breathed his last here on February 23, 1821, aged only 25, forevermore the epitome of the doomed poet. In this "Casina di Keats," you can visit his rooms, although all his furnishings were burned after his death as a sanitary measure by the local authorities. You'll also find a rather quaint collection of memorabilia of English literary figures of the period—Lord Byron, Percy Bysshe Shelley, Joseph Severn, and Leigh Hunt as well as Keats—and an exhaustive library of works on the Romantics. ✉ *Piazza di Spagna 26, Spagna* ☎ *06/6784235* ⊕ *www.keats-shelley-house.org* 💰 *€4.50* ⊗ *Weekdays 10–1 and 2–6, Sat. 11–2 and 3–6* Ⓜ *Spagna.*

Palazzo Venezia. Centerpiece of the eponymous piazza, this palace was originally built for Venetian cardinal Pietro Barbo, who became Pope Paul II. It was also the backdrop used by Mussolini to harangue crowds with dreams of empire from the balcony over the main portal. Lights were left on through the night during his reign to suggest that the Fascist leader worked without pause. The palace shows a mixture of Renaissance grace and heavy medieval lines; salons include frescoes by Giorgio Vasari and a Bernini sculpture of Pope Clement X. The café on the loggia has a pleasant view over the garden courtyard. ✉ *Via del Plebiscito 118, around Via del Corso* ☎ *06/69994388* ⊕ *museopalazzovenezia.beniculturali.it/* 💰 *€5* ⊗ *Tues.–Sun. 8:30–7:30.*

PIAZZA DELLA REPUBBLICA AND THE QUIRINALE

This sector of Rome stretches down from the 19th-century district built up around the Piazza della Repubblica—originally laid out to serve as a monumental foyer between the Termini train station and the rest of the city—and over the rest of the Quirinale. The highest of ancient Rome's famed seven hills, it's crowned by the massive Palazzo Quirinale, home to the popes until 1870 and now Italy's presidential palace. Along the way, you can see ancient Roman sculptures, Early Christian churches, and highlights from the 16th and 17th centuries, when Rome was conquered by the Baroque—and by Bernini.

Although Bernini's work feels omnipresent in much of the city center, the Renaissance-man range of his work is particularly notable here. The artist as architect considered the church of Sant'Andrea al Quirinale one of his best; Bernini the urban designer and water worker is responsible for the muscle-bound sea god who blows his conch so provocatively in the fountain at the center of whirling Piazza Barberini. And Bernini the master gives religious passion a joltingly corporeal treatment in what is perhaps his greatest work, the *Ecstasy of St. Teresa,* in the church of Santa Maria della Vittoria.

GETTING HERE AND AROUND

Bus No. 40 will get you from Termini station to Via Nazionale, an artery of the Quirinale, in one stop; from the Vatican, take Bus No. 64 or Line A to the very busy and convenient Repubblica Metro stop on the piazza of the same name. Bus No. 62 and the Metro also run from the Vatican to Piazza Barberini.

TOP ATTRACTIONS

Fodor'sChoice **Capuchin Crypt.** Not for the easily spooked, the crypt under the Church
★ of Santa Maria della Concezione holds the bones of some 4,000 dead Capuchin monks. Arranged in odd decorative designs around the shriveled and decayed skeletons of their kinsmen, a macabre reminder of the impermanence of earthly life, the crypt is strangely touching and beautiful. As one sign proclaims, "What you are, we once were. What we are, you someday will be." Upstairs in the church, the first chapel on the right contains Guido Reni's mid-17th-century *St. Michael Trampling the Devil*. The painting caused great scandal after an astute contemporary observer remarked that the face of the devil bore a surprising resemblance to the Pamphili Pope Innocent X, arch-enemy of Reni's Barberini patrons. Compare the devil with the bust of the pope that you saw in the Palazzo Doria Pamphilj and judge for yourself. ⊠ *Via Veneto 27, Quirinale* ☎ *06/4871185* ⊕ *www.cappucciniviaveneto.it* ✉ *Donation of at least €1 for crypt* ☉ *Fri.–Wed. 9–noon and 3–6* Ⓜ *Barberini.*

Palazzo Barberini. One of Rome's most splendid 17th-century palaces, the recently renovated Palazzo Barberini is a landmark of the Roman Baroque style. Pope Urban VIII had acquired the property and given it to a nephew, who was determined to build an edifice worthy of his generous uncle and the ever-more-powerful Barberini clan. The result was, architecturally, a precedent-shattering affair: a "villa suburbana" set right in the heart of the urban city and designed to be strikingly open to the outdoors. Note how Carlo Maderno's grand facade seems almost entirely composed of window tiers rising up in proto-20th-century fashion. Ascend Bernini's staircase to the Galleria Nazionale d'Arte Antica, hung with famed paintings including Raphael's *La Fornarina*. But the showstopper here is the palace's Gran Salone, a vast ballroom with a ceiling painted in 1630 by the third (and too-often neglected) master of the Roman Baroque, Pietro da Cortona. ⊠ *Via Barberini 18, Quirinale* ☎ *06/32810* ⊕ *www.galleriaborghese.it* ✉ *€7* ☉ *Tues.–Sun. 8:30–7 (ticket office closes at 6)* Ⓜ *Barberini; Bus Nos. 52, 56, 60, 95, 116, 175, 492.*

Fodor'sChoice **Palazzo Massimo alle Terme.** Come here to get a real feel for ancient
★ Roman art—the collection rivals even the Vatican's. The Roman National Museum, with a collection ranging from striking classical Roman paintings to marble bric-a-brac, has been organized in four locations: here, Palazzo Altemps, Crypta Balbi, and the Museo delle Terme di Diocleziano. The vast structure of the Palazzo Massimo holds the great ancient treasures of the archaeological collection and also the coin collection. Highlights include the *Niobid*, the famous bronze *Boxer*, and the *Discobolus Lancelloti*. Pride of place goes, however, to the great ancient frescoes on view, stunningly set up to "re-create" the look of the homes they once decorated. These include stuccos and wall paintings found in the area of the Villa della Farnesina (in Trastevere)

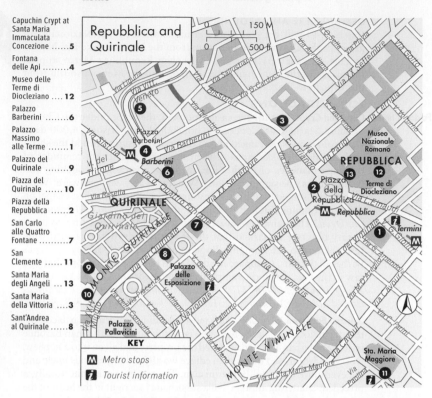

and the legendary frescoes from Empress Livia's villa at Prima Porta, delightful depictions of a garden in bloom and an orchard alive with birds. Their colors are remarkably well preserved. These delicate decorations covered the walls of cool, sunken rooms in Livia's summer house outside the city. ■TIP→ **Admission includes entrance to all four national museums, good for three days.** ✉ *Largo Villa Peretti 1, Repubblica* ☎ *06/39967700* ⊕ *www.coopculture.it* 🎟 *€7, includes three other Museo Nazional Romano sites (Crypta Balbi, Museo Diocleziano, Palazzo Altemps); €10 if any one of them has a temporary exhibit* ☉ *Tues.– Sun. 9–7:45* Ⓜ *Repubblica*.

Piazza del Quirinale. This strategic location atop the Quirinal Hill has long been of great importance. It served as home of the Sabines in the 7th century BC, then deadly enemies of the Romans, who lived on the Capitoline and Palatine Hills (all of 1 km [½ mile] away). Today it's the foreground for the presidential residence, Palazzo del Quirinale, and home to the **Palazzo della Consulta,** where Italy's Constitutional Court sits. The open side of the piazza has an impressive vista of the rooftops and domes of central Rome and St. Peter's. The **Fontana di Montecavallo,** or Fontana dei Dioscuri, is composed of a huge Roman statuary group and an obelisk from the tomb of the emperor Augustus. The group of the Dioscuri trying to tame two massive marble steeds was found in the Baths of Constantine, which occupied part of the summit of the Quirinal Hill. Unlike just about every other ancient statue in Rome, this group survived the Dark Ages intact and accordingly became one of the city's great sights, especially during the Middle Ages. Next to the figures, the ancient obelisk from the Mausoleo di Augusto (Tomb of Augustus) was put here by Pope Pius VI at the end of the 18th century. ⊠ *Quirinale* Ⓜ *Barberini.*

Fodor's Choice
★
San Clemente. One of the most impressive archaeological sites in Rome, San Clemente is a historical triple-decker. A 12th-century church was built on top of a 4th-century church, which in turn was built over a 2nd-century pagan temple to the god Mithras and 1st-century Roman apartments. The layers were rediscovered in 1857, when a curious prior, Friar Joseph Mullooly, started excavations beneath the present basilica. Today, you can descend to explore all three.

The upper church (at street level) is a gem even on its own. In the apse, a glittering 12th-century mosaic shows Jesus on a cross that turns into a living tree. In the left nave, the Castiglioni chapel holds frescoes painted around 1400 by the Florentine artist Masolino da Panicale (1383–1440), a key figure in the introduction of realism and one-point perspective into Renaissance painting.

To the right of the sacristy (and bookshop), descend the stairs to the 4th-century church, used until 1084, when it was damaged beyond repair during a siege of the area by the Norman prince Robert Guiscard. Still intact are some vibrant 11th-century frescoes depicting stories from the life of St. Clement. Descend an additional set of stairs to the mithraeum, a shrine dedicated to the god Mithras. Most such pagan shrines in Rome were destroyed by Christians, who often built churches over their remains, as happened here. ⊠ *Via San Giovanni in Laterano 108, Monti and Esquilino* ☎ *06/7740021* ⊕ *www.basilicasanclemente. com* 🖾 *Archaeological area €5* 🕘 *Mon.–Sat. 9–12:30 and 3–6; Sun. noon–6* Ⓜ *Colosseo.*

Fodor's Choice
★
Santa Maria della Vittoria. Like the church of Santa Susanna across Piazza San Bernardo, this church was designed by Carlo Maderno, but this one is best known for Bernini's sumptuous Baroque decoration of the **Cappella Cornaro** (Cornaro Chapel), on the left as you face the altar, where you'll find his interpretation of heavenly ecstasy in his statue of the *Ecstasy of St. Theresa.* Your eye is drawn effortlessly from the frescoes on the ceiling down to the marble figures of the angel and the swooning saint, to the earthly figures of the Cornaro family (who commissioned the chapel), to the two inlays of marble skeletons in the pavement, representing the hope and despair of souls in purgatory. ⊠ *Via XX Settembre 17, Largo Santa Susanna, Repubblica* ☎ *06/42740571* ⊕ *www. chiesasmariavittoria.191.it* 🕘 *Daily 7–noon and 3:30–7* Ⓜ *Repubblica.*

WORTH NOTING

Fontana delle Api (*Fountain of the Bees*). Decorated with the famous heraldic bees of the Barberini family, the upper shell and the inscription are from a fountain that Bernini designed for Pope Urban VIII. ⊠ *Via Veneto at Piazza Barberini, Quirinale* Ⓜ *Barberini.*

Museo delle Terme di Diocleziano (*Baths of Diocletian*). Though part of the ancient structure is now the church of Santa Maria degli Angeli, and other parts were transformed into a Carthusian monastery or razed to make room for later urban development, a visit gives you an idea of the scale and grandeur of this ancient bathing establishment. Upon entering the church you see the major structures of the baths, partly covered by 16th- and 17th-century overlay, some of which is by Michelangelo. The monastery cloister is filled with the lapidary collection of the Museo Nazionale Romano while other rooms have archaeological works, along with a virtual representation of Livia's villa, which you can tour with the help of a joystick. ⊠ *Viale E. De Nicola 79, Repubblica* ☎ *06/39967700* 🖅 *€7, includes three other Museo Nazional Romano sites (Crypta Balbi, Palazzo Massimo, Palazzo Altemps); €10 if any one of them has a temporary exhibit* ⊘ *Tues.–Sun. 9–7:45 (ticket office closes at 6:45)* Ⓜ *Repubblica.*

Piazza della Repubblica. Often the first view that spells "Rome" to weary travelers walking from the Stazione Termini, this broad square was laid out in the late 1800s and includes the exuberant **Fontana delle Naiadi** (Fountain of the Naiads). This pièce de résistance is draped with voluptuous bronze ladies wrestling happily with marine monsters. ⊠ *Repubblica* Ⓜ *Repubblica.*

Santa Maria degli Angeli e dei Martiri. The curving brick facade on the northeast side of Piazza della Repubblica is one small remaining part of the colossal Terme di Diocleziano, the largest and most impressive of the baths of ancient Rome. In 1561 Michelangelo was commissioned to convert the vast *tepidarium*, the central hall of the baths, into a church. His work was altered by Vanvitelli in the 18th century, but the huge transept, which formed the nave in Michelangelo's plan, has remained as he adapted it. The eight enormous monolithic columns of red granite that support the great beams are the original columns of the tepidarium, 45 feet high and more than 5 feet in diameter. The great hall is 92 feet high. ⊠ *Via Cernaia 9, Repubblica* ☎ *06/4880812* ⊕ *www. santamariadegliangeliroma.it* ⊘ *Mon.–Sat. 7–6:30, Sun. and religious holidays 7 am–7:30 pm* Ⓜ *Repubblica.*

Fodor's Choice **San Carlo alle Quattro Fontane.** Sometimes identified by the diminutive
★   San Carlino because of its tiny size, this is one of Borromini's masterpieces. In a space no larger than the base of one of the piers of St. Peter's Basilica, he created a church that is an intricate exercise in geometric perfection, with a coffered dome that seems to float above the curves of the walls. Borromini's work is often bizarre, definitely intellectual, and intensely concerned with pure form. In San Carlo, he invented an original treatment of space that creates an effect of rippling movement, especially evident in the double-S curves of the facade. Characteristically, the interior decoration is subdued, in white stucco with no more than a few touches of gilding, so as not to distract from the form. Don't miss the **cloister,** a tiny, understated baroque jewel, with a graceful portico and loggia above, echoing the lines of the church. ⇨ *For more on Borromini and this church, see our special photo feature, "Baroque and Desperate: The Tragic Rivalry of Bernini and Borromini" in this chapter.* ⊠ *Via del Quirinale 23, Quirinale* ☎ *06/4883109* ⊕ *www.sancarlino-borromini.it* ⊘ *Mon.–Sat. 10:15–1 and 3:30–6, Sun. 10:15–1* Ⓜ *Barberini.*

Sant'Andrea al Quirinale. Designed by Bernini, this is an architectural gem of the Baroque. His son wrote that Bernini considered it one of his best works and that he used to come here occasionally just to sit and enjoy it. Bernini's simple oval plan, a classic of Baroque architecture, is given drama and movement by the church's decoration, which carries the story of St. Andrew's martyrdom and ascension into heaven, starting with the painting over the high altar, up past the figure of the saint over the chancel door, to the angels at the base of the lantern and the dove of the Holy Spirit that awaits on high. ⊠ *Via del Quirinale 29, Quirinale* ☎ *06/4740807* ⊘ *Mon.–Sat. 8:30–noon and 2:30–6, Sun. 8:30–noon and 3–7* Ⓜ *Barberini.*

VILLA BORGHESE AND PIAZZA DEL POPOLO

Touring Rome's artistic masterpieces while staying clear of its hustle and bustle can be, quite literally, a walk in the park. Some of the city's finest sights are tucked away in or next to green lawns and pedestrian piazzas, offering a breath of fresh air for weary sightseers, especially in the Villa Borghese park. One of Rome's largest, this park can alleviate gallery gout by offering an oasis in which to cool off under the ilex, oak, and umbrella pine trees. If you feel like a picnic, have an *alimentari* (food shop) make you some panini before you go; food carts within the park are overpriced.

GETTING HERE AND AROUND

Electric bus No. 119 does a loop that connects Largo Argentina, Piazza Venezia, Piazza di Spagna, and Piazza del Popolo. The No. 117 connects Piazza del Popolo to Piazza Venezia and the Colosseum. The No. 116 motors through the Villa Borghese to the museum and connects the area with Piazza Navona, Campo de' Fiori, and the Pantheon. Piazza del Popolo has a Metro stop called Flaminio.

TOP ATTRACTIONS

Fodor's Choice
★

Ara Pacis Augustae (*Altar of Augustan Peace*). This vibrant monument of the imperial age has been housed in one of Rome's newest architectural landmarks: a gleaming, rectangular glass-and-travertine structure designed by American architect Richard Meier. Overlooking the Tiber on one side and the ruins of the marble-clad **Mausoleo di Augusto** (Mausoleum of Augustus), on the other, the result is a serene, luminous oasis right in Rome's center. Opened in 2006, after a decade of bitter controversy over the monument's relocation, the altar itself dates back to 13 BC; it was commissioned to celebrate the Pax Romana, the era of peace ushered in by Augustus's military victories. It is covered with spectacular and moving relief sculptures. ⊠ *Lungotevere in Augusta, around Via del Corso* ☎ *06/0608* ⊕ *www.arapacis.it* ⊠ *€8.50* ⊘ *Tues.–Sun. 9–7 (last admission 1 hr before closing)* Ⓜ *Flaminio (Piazza del Popolo).*

Fodor's Choice
★

Galleria Borghese. It's a real toss-up as to which is more magnificent: the villa built for Cardinal Scipione Borghese in 1612, or the art that lies within. Despite its beauty, the villa never was used as a residence. Instead, the luxury-loving cardinal built it as a showcase for his fabulous collection of both antiquities and more "modern" works, including those he commissioned from the masters Caravaggio and Bernini. Today, it's a monument to Roman interior decoration at its most extravagant. With the passage of time, however, the building has become less celebrated than the collections housed within, including one of the finest collections of Baroque sculpture anywhere in the world.

One of the most famous works in the collection is Canova's Neoclassical sculpture of Pauline Borghese as Venus Victrix. Scandalously, Pauline reclines on a Roman sofa, bare-bosomed, her hips swathed in classical drapery, the very model of haughty detachment and sly come-hither. The next three rooms hold three key early Baroque sculptures: Bernini's *David, Apollo and Daphne,* and *Rape of Proserpina.* The Caravaggio Room holds works by this hotheaded genius, who died of malaria at age 37. All of his paintings, even the charming *Boy with a Basket of Fruit,* seethe with an undercurrent of darkness. Upstairs, the Pinacoteca (Picture Gallery) boasts paintings by Raphael (including his moving *Deposition*), Pinturicchio, Perugino, Bellini, and Rubens. Probably the gallery's most famous painting is Titian's allegorical *Sacred and Profane Love,* a mysterious and yet-unsolved image with two female figures, one nude, one clothed.

Admission to the Museo is by reservation only. Visitors are admitted in two-hour shifts from 9 to 5. Prime-time slots can sell out days in advance, so in high season reserve by phone or directly through the Borghese's website. You need to collect your reserved ticket at the museum ticket office a half hour before your entrance. However, when it's not busy you can purchase your ticket at the museum for the next entrance appointment. ⊠ *Piazza Scipione Borghese 5, off Via Pinciana, Villa Borghese* ☎ *06/32810* for *reservations, 06/8413979* for *information* ⊕ *www.galleriaborghese.it* ✑ *€11, including €2 reservation fee; audio guide €5, English tour €5* ☉ *Tues.–Sun. 8:30–7:30, with sessions at 9, 11, 1, 3, and 5* Ⓜ *Bus No. 910 from Piazza della Repubblica, or Tram No. 19 or Bus No. 3 from Policlinico.*

Piazza del Popolo. With its obelisk and twin churches, this immense square is a famed Rome landmark. It owes its current appearance to architect Giuseppe Valadier, who designed it about 1820, also laying out the terraced approach to the Pincio and the Pincio's gardens. It marks what was for centuries the northern entrance to the city, where all roads from the north converge and where visitors, many of them pilgrims, would get their first impression of the Eternal City. The desire to make this entrance to Rome something special had been a pet project of popes and their architects for more than three centuries. The piazza takes its name from the 15th-century church of Santa Maria del Popolo, huddled on the right side of the Porta del Popolo, or city gate. In the late 17th century, the twin churches of Santa Maria in Montesanto (on the left as you face them) and Santa Maria dei Miracoli (on the right) were added to the piazza at the point where Via del Babuino, Via del

Corso, and Via di Ripetta converge. The piazza, crowded with fashionable carriages and carnival revelers in the past, is a pedestrian zone today. At election time, it's the scene of huge political rallies, and on New Year's Eve Rome stages a mammoth alfresco party in the piazza. ⊠ *Piazza del Popolo* Ⓜ *Flaminio.*

Fodor's Choice
★
Santa Maria del Popolo. Standing inconspicuously in a corner of the vast Piazza del Popolo, this church often goes unnoticed, but the treasures inside make it a must for art lovers, as they include an entire chapel designed by Raphael and one adorned with striking Caravaggio masterpieces. Bramante enlarged the apse of the church, which had been rebuilt in the 15th century on the site of a much older place of worship. Inside, in the first chapel on the right, you'll see some frescoes by Pinturicchio from the mid-15th century; the adjacent **Cybo Chapel** is a 17th-century exercise in marble decoration. Raphael's famous **Chigi Chapel,** the second on the left, was built around 1513 and commissioned by the banker Agostino Chigi (who also had the artist decorate his home across the Tiber, the Villa Farnesina). The **Cerasi Chapel,** to the left of the high altar, holds two Caravaggios, the *Crucifixion of St. Peter* and *Conversion of St. Paul.* Exuding drama and realism, both are key early Baroque works that show how "modern" 17th-century art can appear. Compare their style with the much more restrained

and classically "pure" *Assumption of the Virgin* by Caravaggio's contemporary and rival, Annibale Carracci; it hangs over the altar of the chapel. ⊠ *Piazza del Popolo 12, near Porta Pinciana, Piazza del Popolo* ☏ *06/3610836* ⊘ *Mon.–Sat. 7–noon and 4–7, Sun. 8–1:30 and 4:30–7:30* Ⓜ *Flaminio.*

WORTH NOTING

MAXXI—Museo Nazionale delle Arti del XXI Secolo (*National Museum of 21st-Century Arts*). It took 10 years and cost some €150 million, but for lovers of contemporary art and architecture, Italy's first national museum devoted to contemporary creativity was worth it. The building alone impresses; it plays with lots of natural light, curving and angular lines, and big open spaces, all meant to question the division between "within" and "without" (think glass ceilings and steel staircases that twist through the air). The MAXXI hosts temporary exhibits on art, architecture, film, and more. From the permanent collection, rotated through the museum, more than 350 works represent artists including Andy Warhol, Francesco Clemente, and Gerhard Richter. ⊠ *Via Guido Reni 4, Flaminio* ☏ *06/39967350* ⊕ *www.fondazionemaxxi. it* 🎫 *€11* ⊘ *Tues.–Fri. and Sun. 11–7, Sat. 11–10 (ticket office closes 1 hr earlier)* Ⓜ *Flaminio, then Tram No. 2 to Apollodoro; Bus Nos. 53, 217, 280, 910.*

THE VATICAN: ROME OF THE POPES

Capital of the Catholic Church, this tiny walled city-state is a place where some people go to find a work of art—Michelangelo's frescoes, rare ancient Roman marbles, or Bernini's statues. Others go to find their souls. Whatever the reason, thanks to being the seat of world Catholicism and also address to the most overwhelming architectural achievement of the 16th and 17th centuries—St. Peter's Basilica—the Vatican attracts millions of travelers every year. In addition, the Vatican Museums are famed for magnificent rooms decorated by Raphael, sculptures such as the *Apollo Belvedere* and the *Laocoön,* paintings by Giotto, frescoes by Raphael, and the celebrated ceiling of the Sistine Chapel. The Church power that emerged as the Rome of the emperors declined gave impetus to a profusion of artistic expression and shaped the destiny of the city for a thousand years. Allow yourself an hour to see St. Peter's Basilica, at least two hours for the museums, an hour for Castel Sant'Angelo, and an hour to climb to the top of the dome. Note that ushers at the entrance of St. Peter's Basilica and the Vatican Museums bar entry to people with "inappropriate" clothing—which means no bare knees or shoulders.

GETTING HERE AND AROUND

From Termini station, hop on the No. 40 Express or the No. 64 to be delivered to Piazza San Pietro. Metro stops Cipro or Ottaviano will get you within about a 10-minute walk of the entrance to the Vatican Museums. Use Ottaviano for St. Peter's.

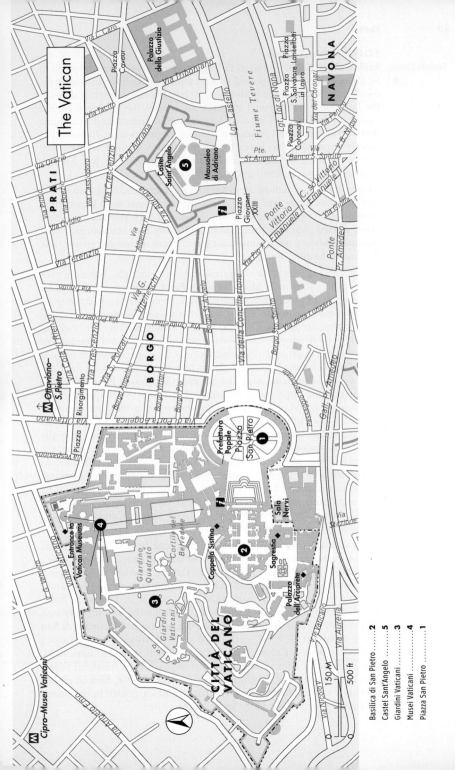

The Vatican

PRATI

Via Caio
Via Caro
Palazzo della Giustizia
Piazza Cavour
Via Tacito
Via Orazio
Via Pompeo Magno
Via Cola di Rienzo
Via Vittoria Colonna
Via Tibullo
Via Ovidio
Via Cassiodoro
Via Crescenzio
Pza Adriana
Castel Sant'Angelo
Mausoleo di Adriano
Via Terenzio
Via Ennio Q. Visconti
Via Alberico II
Via Attilio Regolo
Via Properzio
Via G. Interlenghi
Via P. Caetani
Lgt. Castello
Pte. St. Angelo
Fiume Tevere
Ponte Vittorio Emanuele
Lgt. Tor. di Nona
Lgt. Sangallo
Piazza della Giustizia
Via Triboniano
Piazza S. Salvatore Lonellotti in Lauro
Piazza Coronari
Via dei Coronari
Via del Banco S. Spirito
Piazza San Salvatore
NAVONA
C. V. Emanuele
Ponte Pr. Amedeo
Via Giulia
Via della Lungara
Piazza Giovanni XXIII
Ponte Vittorio Emanuele

5 Castel Sant'Angelo
7 Piazza Giovanni XXIII

BORGO

M Ottaviano-S.Pietro
Via Ottaviano
Via G. Cesare
Via Vespasiano
Via Cola di Rienzo
Via S. Porcari
Via Crescenzio
Via Risorgimento
Piazza Vespasiano
Borgo Pio
Borgo Vittorio
Borgo Angelico
Via di Porta Angelica
Via della Conciliazione
Borgo Sto. Spirito
Borgo S. Angelo
Borgo Vittorio
Via degli Ombrellari

Via Aurelia
Viale Vaticano
Entrance to Vatican Museums
4 Musei Vaticani
Cortile del Belvedere
Giardini Quadrato
Cortile della Pigna
3 Giardini Vaticani
Giardini Vaticani
V.le Vaticano
CITTÀ DEL VATICANO
Prefettura Papale
1 Piazza San Pietro
Basilica di San Pietro **2**
7
Cappella Sistina
Sala Nervi
Sagrestia
Sagrestia
Palazzo dell'Arciprete
Via Aurelia
Via della Stazione
Via Nicolò V

150 M
500 ft

M Cipro-Musei Vaticani
Via Andrea Doria

TOP ATTRACTIONS

Fodor's Choice ★ **Basilica di San Pietro.** The world's largest church, built over the tomb of St. Peter, is the most imposing and breathtaking architectural achievement of the Renaissance (although much of the lavish interior dates to the Baroque). The physical statistics are impressive: it covers 18,000 square yards, runs 212 yards in length, and is surmounted by a dome that rises 435 feet and measures 138 feet across its base. Its history is equally impressive. No fewer than five of Italy's greatest artists—Bramante, Raphael, Peruzzi, Antonio Sangallo the Younger, and Michelangelo—died while striving to erect this new St. Peter's.

As you climb the shallow steps up to the great church, flanked by the statues of Sts. Peter and Paul, you'll see the **Loggia delle Benedizioni** (Benediction Loggia) over the central portal. This is the balcony where newly elected popes are proclaimed, and where they stand to give their apostolic blessing on solemn feast days. Pause a moment to appraise the size of the great building.

As you enter the great nave, immediately to your right, behind a protective glass partition, is **Michelangelo's** *Pietà,* sculpted when the artist was only 25. The work was of such genius, some rivals spread rumors it was by someone else, prompting the artist to inscribe his name, unusually for him, across Mary's sash. Farther down, with its heavyweight crown barely denting its marble cushion, is Carlo Fontana's monument to Catholic convert and abdicated Queen Christina of Sweden (who is buried in the Grotte Vaticane below). Just across the way, in the **Cappella di San Sebastiano,** now lies the **tomb of Blessed Pope John Paul II.** The beloved pope's remains were moved into the chapel after his beatification on May 1, 2011. Exquisite bronze grilles and doors by Borromini open into the third chapel in the right aisle, the **Cappella del Santissimo Sacramento** (Chapel of the Most Holy Sacrament, generally open to visitors only from 7 am–8:30 am), with a Baroque fresco of the Trinity by Pietro da Cortona. The lovely carved angels are by Bernini. At the last pillar on the right (the pier with Bernini's statue of St. Longinus) is a bronze statue of St. Peter, whose right foot is ritually touched by lines of pilgrims. In the right transept, over the door to the **Cappella di San Michele** (Chapel of St. Michael), usually closed, Canova created a brooding Neoclassical monument to Pope Clement XIII.

In the central crossing, Bernini's great bronze *baldacchino*—a huge, spiral-columned canopy—rises high over the *altare papale* (papal altar). At 100,000 pounds, it's said to be the largest, heaviest bronze object in the world. Circling the baldacchino are four larger-than-life statues of saints whose relics the Vatican has; the one of St. Longinus, holding the spear that pierced Christ's side, is another Bernini masterpiece. Meanwhile, Bernini designed the splendid gilt-bronze **Cattedra di San Pietro** (throne of St. Peter) in the apse above the main altar to contain a wooden and ivory chair that St. Peter himself is said to have used, though in fact it doesn't date from farther back than medieval times. (You can see a copy of the chair in the treasury.) Above, Bernini placed a window of thin alabaster sheets that diffuses a golden light around the dove, symbol of the Holy Spirit, in the center.

Two of the major papal funeral monuments in St. Peter's Basilica are on either side of the apse and unfortunately are usually only dimly lighted. To the right is the **tomb of Pope Urban VIII**; to the left is the **tomb of Pope Paul III.** Paul's tomb is of an earlier date, designed between 1551 and 1575 by Giacomo della Porta, the architect who completed the dome of St. Peter's Basilica after Michelangelo's death. Many believed the nude figure of Justice to be a portrait of the pope's beautiful sister, Giulia. The charms of this alluring figure were such that in the 19th century, it was thought that she should no longer be allowed to distract worshippers from their prayers, and she was thenceforth clad in marble drapery. It was in emulation of this splendid late-Renaissance work that Urban VIII ordered Bernini to design his tomb. The real star here, however, is *la Bella Morte* ("Beautiful Death") who, all bone and elbows, dispatches the deceased pope above to a register of blue-black marble. The **tomb of Pope Alexander VII,** also designed by Bernini, stands to the left of the altar as you look up the nave, behind the farthest pier of the crossing. This may be the most haunting memorial in the basilica, thanks to another frightening skeletonized figure of Death, holding an hourglass in its upraised hand to tell the pope his time is up. Pope Alexander, however, was well prepared, having kept a coffin (also designed by Bernini) in his bedroom and made a habit of dining off plates embossed with skulls.

With advance notice you can take a 1¼-hour guided tour in English of the **Vatican Necropolis** (☎ *06/69885318* ✉ *€12* ⊘ *Ufficio Scavi weekdays 9–6 and Sat. 9–5, visits 9–3:30*) under the basilica, which gives a rare glimpse of Early Christian Roman burial customs and a closer look at the tomb of St. Peter. Apply by fax or email (*scavi@fsp.va*) at least 2–3 weeks in advance, specifying the number of people in the group (all must be age 15 or older), preferred language, preferred time, available dates, and your contact information in Rome.

Under the Pope Pius V monument, the entrance to the sacristy also leads to the **Museo Storico-Artistico e Tesoro** (*Historical-Artistic Museum and Treasury;* ☎ *06/69881840* ✉ *€10 includes audio guide* ⊘ *Apr.–Sept., daily 8–7; Oct.–Mar., daily 8–6:20*), a small collection of Vatican treasures. They range from the massive and beautifully sculptured 15th-century tomb of Pope Sixtus IV by Pollaiuolo, which you can view from above, to a jeweled cross dating from the 6th century and a marble tabernacle by Donatello. Continue on down the left nave past Algardi's **tomb of St. Leo.** The handsome bronze grilles in the **Cappella del Coro** (Chapel of the Choir) were designed by Borromini to complement those opposite in the Cappella del Santissimo Sacramento.

Above, the vast sweep of the basilica's dome is the cynosure of all eyes. Proceed to the right side of the Basilica's vestibule; from here, you can either take the elevator or climb the long flight of shallow stairs to the roof (☎ *06/69883462* ✉ *elevator €7, stairs €5* ⊘ *Apr.–Sept., daily 8–6; Oct.–Mar., daily 8–4; on a Papal Audience Wed., opens after the audience finishes, about noon; closed during ceremonies in piazza*). From here, you'll see a surreal landscape of vast, sloping terraces, punctuated by domes.

CLOSE UP

A Morning with the Pope

The pope holds audiences in St. Peter's Square (or a large, modern hall in inclement weather) on Wednesday morning at 10:30. Although attendance is free, you must procure tickets; either call 06/69883114 or fax 06/69885863, indicating the full names of attendants, the date you prefer, your language, and your hotel's contact information. Pick up tickets through the Portone di Bronzo, the bronze door at the end of the colonnade on the right side of the piazza, from 9 to 1 on Monday or 9 to 6 on Tuesday.

You can also arrange to pick up free tickets on Tuesday from 5 to 6:45 at the **Santa Susanna American Church** (⊠ *Via XX Settembre 15, near Piazza della Repubblica* ☎ *06/42014554* ⊕ *www.santasusanna.org*); call first. For a fee, travel agencies make arrangements that include transportation. Arrive early, as security is tight and the best places fill up fast.

Only if you're of stout heart and strong lungs should you then make the taxing climb from the drum of the dome up to the *lanterna* (lantern) at the dome's very apex. A narrow, seemingly interminable staircase follows the curve of the dome between inner and outer shells, finally releasing you into the cramped space of the lantern balcony for an absolutely gorgeous panorama of Rome and the countryside on a clear day. There's also a nearly complete view of the palaces, courtyards, and gardens of the Vatican. Be aware, however, that it's a tiring, slightly claustrophobic climb. There's one stairway for going up and a different one for coming down, so you can't change your mind halfway and turn back.

The entrance to the **Grotte Vaticane** (*Vatican Grottoes;* ⊠ *free* ☉ *Mon.– Sat. 9–4, Sun. 1:30–3:30; closed while the papal audience takes place in St. Peter's Square, until about noon on Wed.*) is to the right of the Basilica's main entrance. The crypt, lined with marble-faced chapels and tombs occupying the area of Constantine's basilica, stands over what is believed to be the tomb of St. Peter himself, flanked by two angels and visible through glass. Among the most beautiful tombs leading up to it are that of Borgia pope Calixtus III with its carving of the Risen Christ, and the tomb of Paul II featuring angels carved by Renaissance great Mino da Fiesole. ⊠ *Piazza di San Pietro, Vatican* ☉ *Apr.–Sept., daily 7–7; Oct.– Mar., daily 7–6; closed during the papal audience in St. Peter's Square on Wed. mornings until about noon* Ⓜ *Ottaviano–San Pietro.*

FAMILY **Castel Sant'Angelo.** Standing between the Tiber and the Vatican, this circular and medieval "castle" has long been one of Rome's most distinctive landmarks. Opera-lovers know it well as the setting for the final scene of Puccini's *Tosca*; at the opera's end, the tempestuous diva throws herself from the rampart on the upper terrace. In fact, the structure began life many centuries before as a mausoleum for the emperor Hadrian. Out on to the upper terrace, at the feet of the bronze angel, take in a magnificent view of the city below. ⊠ *Lungotevere Castello 50, Vatican* ☎ *06/6819111, 06/6896003 for tickets* ⊕ *www.castelsantangelo.com* ⊠ *€8.50* ☉ *Tues.–Sun. 9–7:30 (ticket office closes 6:30)* Ⓜ *Lepanto.*

Fodor's Choice
★

Musei Vaticani (*Vatican Museums*). Other than the pope and his papal court, the occupants of the Vatican are some of the most famous artworks in the world. The museums that contain them are part of the **Vatican Palace,** residence of the popes since 1377. The palace consists of an estimated 1,400 rooms, chapels, and galleries. The pope and his household occupy only a small part of the palace; most of the rest is given over to the Vatican Library and Museums. Beyond the glories of the Sistine Chapel, the collection is so extraordinarily rich you may just wish to skim the surface, but few will want to miss out on the great antique sculptures, Raphael Rooms, and the Old Master paintings, such as Leonardo da Vinci's *St. Jerome.*

Among the collections on the way to the chapel, the **Egyptian Museum** (in which Room II reproduces an underground chamber tomb of the Valley of Kings) is well worth a stop. The **Chiaramonti Museum** was organized by the Neoclassical sculptor Canova and contains almost 1,000 copies of classical sculpture. The gems of the Vatican's sculpture collection are in the **Pio-Clementino Museum,** however. Just off the hall in Room X, you can find the *Apoxyomenos* (Scraper), a beautiful 1st-century AD copy of the famous bronze statue of an athlete. There are other even more famous pieces in the **Octagonal Courtyard,** where Pope Julius II installed the pick of his private collection. On the left stands the celebrated *Apollo Belvedere.* In the far corner, on the same side of the courtyard, is the *Laocoön* group. Found on Rome's Esquiline Hill in 1506, this antique sculpture group influenced Renaissance artists perhaps more than any other.

In 1508 Pope Julius II commissioned Michelangelo to paint single-handedly the more-than-10,000-square-foot ceiling of the **Cappella Sistina** (Sistine Chapel). ⇨ *For an in-depth look at Michelangelo's masterpiece, see the Sistine Chapel feature in this chapter.*

Rivaling the Sistine Chapel for artistic interest—and for the number of visitors—are the recently restored **Stanze di Raffaello** (Raphael Rooms). Pope Julius II moved into this suite in 1507, four years after his election. Reluctant to continue living in the Borgia apartments downstairs, with their memories of his ill-famed predecessor Alexander VI, he called in Raphael to decorate his new quarters. When people talk about the Italian High Renaissance—thought to be the very pinnacle of Western art—it's probably Raphael's frescoes they're thinking about.

The rooms aren't arranged chronologically. Today, for crowd-management purposes, you head down an outdoor gallery to loop back through them; as you go, look across the way to see, very far away, the Pinecone Courtyard near where you entered the museums.

The tiny **Chapel of Nicholas V** is rarely open. But if you can access it, do: One of the Renaissance's greatest gems, it's aglow with Fra Angelico (1395–1455) frescoes of episodes from the life of St. Stephen (above) and St. Lawrence (below). If it weren't under the same roof as Raphael's and Michelangelo's works, it would undoubtedly draw greater attention.

Downstairs, enter the recently restored **Borgia apartments,** where some of the Vatican's most fascinating historical figures are depicted on elaborately painted ceilings. Pinturicchio designed the frescoes at the end of the 15th century, though the paintings were greatly retouched in later centuries.

Continued on page 92

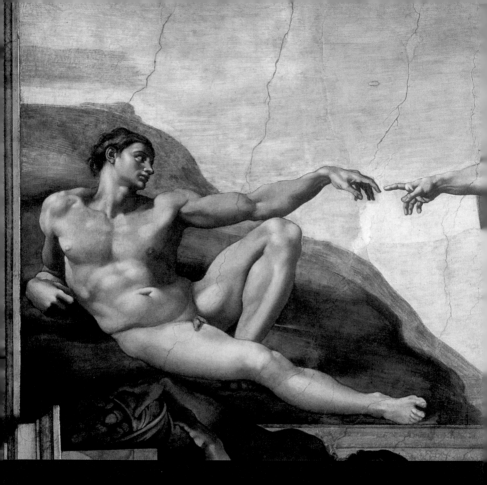

HEAVEN'S ABOVE:
THE SISTINE CEILING

Forming lines that are probably longer than those
waiting to pass through the Pearly Gates, hordes of
visitors arrive at the Sistine Chapel daily to view what
may be the world's most sublime example of artistry:

Michelangelo: *The Creation of Adam*, Sistine Chapel, The Vatican, circa 1511.

Michelangelo's Sistine Ceiling. To paint this 12,000-square-foot barrel vault, it took four years, 343 frescoed figures, and a titanic battle of wits between the artist and Pope Julius II. While in its typical fashion, Hollywood focused on the element of agony, not ecstasy, involved in the saga of creation, a recently completed restoration of the ceiling has revolutionized our appreciation of the masterpiece of masterpieces.

By Martin Wilmot Bennett

View of the Cappella Sistina

MICHELANGELO'S
MISSION IMPOSSIBLE

Designed to match the proportions of Solomon's Temple described in the Old Testament, the Sistine Chapel is named after Pope Sixtus VI, who commissioned it as a place of worship for himself and as the venue where new popes could be elected. Before Michelangelo, the barrel-vaulted ceiling was an expanse of azure fretted with golden stars. Then, in 1504, an ugly crack appeared. Bramante, the architect, managed do some patchwork using iron rods, but when signs of a fissure remained, the new Pope Julius II summoned Michelangelo to cover it with a fresco 135 feet long and 44 feet wide.

Taking in the entire span of the ceiling, the theme connecting the various participants in this painted universe could be said to be mankind's anguished waiting. The majestic panel depicting the Creation of Adam leads, through the stages of the Fall and the expulsion from Eden, to the tragedy of Noah found naked and mocked by his own sons; throughout all runs the underlying need for man's redemption. Witnessing all from the side and end walls, a chorus of ancient Prophets and Sibyls peer anxiously forward, awaiting the Redeemer who will come to save both the Jews and the Gentiles.

APOCALYPSE NOW

The sweetness and pathos of his Pietà, carved by Michelangelo only ten years earlier, have been left behind. The new work foretells an apocalypse, its congregation of doomed sinners facing the wrath of heaven through hanging, beheading, crucifixion, flood, and plague. Michelangelo, by nature a misanthrope, was already filled with visions of doom thanks to the fiery orations of Savonarola, whose thunderous preachments he had heard before leaving his hometown of Florence. Vasari, the 16th-century art historian, coined the word "terribilità" to describe Michelangelo's tension-ridden style, a rare case of a single word being worth a thousand pictures.

Michelangelo wound up using a *Reader's Digest* condensed version of the stories from Genesis, with the dramatis personae overseen by a punitive and terrifying God. In real life, poor Michelangelo answered to a flesh-and-blood taskmaster who was almost as vengeful: Pope Julius II. Less vicar of Christ than latter-day Caesar, he was intent on uniting Italy under the power of the Vatican, and was eager to do so by any means, including riding into pitched battle. Yet this "warrior pope" considered his most formidable adversary to be Michelangelo. Applying a form of blackmail, Julius threatened to wage war on Michelangelo's Florence, to which the artist had fled after Julius canceled a commission for a grand papal tomb unless Michelangelo agreed to return to Rome and take up the task of painting the Sistine Chapel ceiling.

MICHELANGELO, SCULPTOR

A sculptor first and foremost, however, Michelangelo considered painting an inferior genre—"for rascals and sissies" as he put it. Second, there was the sheer scope of the task, leading Michelangelo to suspect he'd been set up by a rival, Bramante, chief architect of the new St. Peter's Basilica. As Michelangelo was also a master architect, he regarded this fresco commission as a Renaissance mission-impossible. Pope Julius's powerful will prevailed—and six years later the work of the Sistine Ceiling was complete. Irving Stone's famous novel *The Agony and the Ecstasy*—and the granitic 1965 film that followed—chart this epic battle between artist and pope.

THINGS ARE LOOKING UP

To enhance your viewing of the ceiling, bring along opera-glasses, binoculars, or just a mirror (to prevent your neck from becoming bent like Michelangelo's). Note that no photos are permitted. Insiders know the only time to get the chapel to yourself is during the papal blessings and public audiences held in St. Peter's Square. Failing that, get there during lunch hour. Admission and entry to the Sistine Chapel is only through the Musei Vaticani (Vatican Museums).

SCHEMATIC OF THE SISTINE CEILING

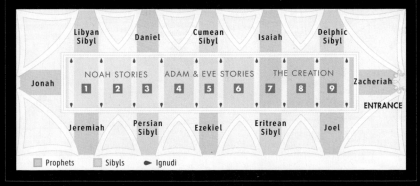

PAINTING THE BIBLE

The ceiling's biblical symbols were ideated by three Vatican theologians, Cardinal Alidosi, Egidio da Viterbo, and Giovanni Rafanelli, along with Michelangelo.

As for the ceiling's painted "framework," this *quadratura* alludes to Roman triumphal arches because Pope Julius II was fond of mounting "triumphal entries" into his conquered cities (in imitation of Christ's procession into Jerusalem on Palm Sunday).

THE CENTER PANELS

Prophet turned art-critic or, perhaps doubling as ourselves, the ideal viewer, Jonah the prophet (painted at the altar end) gazes up at the

Creation, or Michelangelo's version of it.

1 The first of three scenes taken from the Book of Genesis: God separates Light from Darkness.

2 God creates the sun and a craterless pre-Galilean moon

while the panel's other half offers an unprecedented rear view of the Almighty creating the vegetable world.

3 In the panel showing God separating the Waters from the Heavens, the Creator

tumbles towards us as in a self-made whirlwind.

4 Pausing for breath, next admire probably Western Art's most famous image—God giving life to Adam.

5 The Creation of Eve from Adam's rib leads to the sixth panel.

6 In a sort of diptych divided by the trunk of the Tree of Knowledge of Good and Evil, Michelangelo retells the Temptation and the Fall.

7 Illustrating Man's fallen nature, the last three panels narrate, in un-chronological order, the Flood. In the first Noah offers a pre-Flood sacrifice of thanks.

8 Damaged by an explosion in 1794, next comes Michelangelo's version of Flood itself.

9 Finally, above the monumental Jonah, you can just make out the small, wretched figure of Noah, lying drunk— in pose, the shrunken anti-type of the majestic Adam five panels down the wall.

THE CREATION OF ADAM

Michelangelo's Adam was partly inspired by the Creation scenes Michelangelo had studied in the sculpted doors of Jacopo della Quercia in Bologna and Lorenzo Ghiberti's Doors of Paradise in Florence. Yet in Michelangelo's version Adam's hand hangs limp, waiting God's touch to impart the spark of life. Facing his Creation, the Creator—looking a bit like the pagan god Jupiter—is for the first time ever depicted as horizontal, mirroring the Biblical "in his own likeness." Decades after its completion, a crack began to appear, amputating Adam's fingertips. Believe it or not, the most famous fingers in Western art are the handiwork, at least in part, of one Domenico Carnevale.

In the frescoed exhibition halls, the **Vatican Library** displays precious illuminated manuscripts and documents from its vast collections. The **Aldobrandini Marriage Room** contains beautiful ancient frescoes of a Roman nuptial rite, named for their subsequent owner, Cardinal Aldobrandini. The **Braccio Nuovo** (New Wing) holds an additional collection of ancient Greek and Roman statues, the most famous of which is the *Augustus of Prima Porta,* in the fourth niche from the end on the left.

> **WORD OF MOUTH**
>
> "Free Sundays are usually packed at the Vatican Museums, be aware of that."
>
> —daveesl

Equally celebrated are the works on view in the **Pinacoteca** (Picture Gallery). These often world-famous paintings, almost exclusively of religious subjects, are arranged in chronological order, beginning with works of the 12th and 13th centuries. A fitting finale to your Vatican visit can be found in the **Museo Pio Cristiano** (Museum of Christian Antiquities), where the most famous piece is the 3rd-century AD statue called the *Good Shepherd,* much reproduced as a devotional image.

To avoid the line into the museums, which can be three hours long in the high season, consider booking your ticket in advance online (⊕ *biglietteriamusei.vatican.va*); there is a €4 surcharge. For those interested in guided visits to the Vatican Museums, tours are €31 to €36, including entrance tickets, and can also be booked online. Other offerings include a regular two-hour guided tour of the Vatican gardens and the semi-regular Friday night openings, allowing visitors to the museums until 11 pm; call to confirm. For more information, call ☎ *06/69884676* or go to ⊕ *mv.vatican.va.* For information on tours, call ☎ *06/69883145* or *06/69884676*; visually impaired visitors can arrange tactile tours by calling ☎ *06/69884947.*

Note: Ushers at the entrance of St. Peter's and sometimes the Vatican Museums will bar entry to people with bare knees or bare shoulders. ✉ *Viale Vaticano, near intersection with Via Leone IV, Vatican* ⊕ *www. mv.vatican.va* 🖼 *€1; free last Sun. of month* ☉ *Mon.–Sat. 9–6 (last entrance at 4), last Sun. of month 9–12:30* ☉ *Closed Jan. 1 and 6, Feb. 11, Mar. 19, Easter and Easter Monday, May 1, June 29, Aug. 14 and 15, Nov. 1, and Dec. 8, 25, and 26* Ⓜ *Cipro–Musei Vaticani or Ottaviano–San Pietro. Bus Nos. 64, 40.*

Piazza di San Pietro. Mostly enclosed within high walls that recall the papacy's stormy history, the Vatican opens the spectacular arms of Bernini's colonnade to embrace the world only at St. Peter's Square, scene of the pope's public appearances. One of Bernini's most spectacular masterpieces, the elliptical Piazza di San Pietro was completed in 1667 after only 11 years' work and holds 400,000 people.

Surrounded by a pair of quadruple colonnades, it is gloriously studded with 140 statues of saints and martyrs. Look for the two disks set into the piazza's pavement on either side of the central obelisk. If you stand on either disk, a trick of perspective makes the colonnades look like a single row of columns. At the piazza center, the 85-foot-high Egyptian obelisk was brought to Rome by Caligula in AD 37 and moved here in 1586 by Pope Sixtus V. The emblem at the top of the obelisk is the Chigi star, in honor of Pope Alexander VII, a member of the powerful Chigi family, who commissioned the piazza. ⊠ *West end of Via della Conciliazione, Vatican* ☎ *06/69881662* ✐ *upt@scv.va* ☉ *Daily 6:30 am–11 pm (midnight during Christmas)* Ⓜ *Cipro–Musei Vaticani or Ottaviano–San Pietro.*

WORTH NOTING

Giardini Vaticani (*Vatican Gardens*). Neatly trimmed lawns and flower beds extend over the hills behind St. Peter's Basilica, an area dotted with some interesting constructions and other, duller ones that serve as office buildings. The Vatican Gardens occupy almost 40 acres of land on the Vatican hill. The gardens include a formal Italian garden, a flowering French garden, a romantic English landscape, and a small forest. You have two options for visiting the Vatican Gardens. You can take a two-hour walking tour with an official Vatican guide (make sure to wear good walking shoes). Or you can take a one-hour minibus tour of the gardens, done with an audio guide; this new offering is run by the company RomaCristiana. For either tour, a reservation is necessary. ⊠ *For official Vatican tour, Centro Servizi, south side of Piazza San Pietro; for RomaCristiana tour, ORP St. Peter's Office at Piazza Pio XII 9, Vatican* ☎ *06/69883145 Vatican tour, 06/88816186 minibus tour* ⊕ *www.mv.vatican.va* ⊠ *€32 for 2-hour tour with Vatican guide (includes €16 entrance ticket to Vatican museums) or €15 for 1-hour bus ride with RomaCristiana* ☉ *Tours with Vatican guide daily except Wed. and Sun.* Ⓜ *Ottaviano–San Pietro.*

THE GHETTO, TIBER ISLAND, AND TRASTEVERE

Staunchly resisting the tides of change, these three areas are hard to beat for the authentic atmosphere of Old Rome. You begin in the old Ghetto, once a warren of twisting, narrow streets where Rome's Jewish community was at one time confined, now a combination of medieval, Renaissance, and modern structures. Ancient bridges, the Ponte Fabricio and Ponte Cestio, link the Ghetto to Tiber Island, the diminutive sandbar that's one of Rome's most picturesque sights. On the opposite side of the Tiber lies Trastevere—literally "across the Tiber"—long cherished as Rome's Greenwich Village and now subject to rampant gentrification. In spite of this, Trastevere remains about the most tightly knit community in the city, the Trasteverini proudly (and erroneously!) proclaiming their descent from the ancient Romans. This area is Rome's enchanting, medieval heart.

GETTING HERE AND AROUND

From Termini station, nab the No. 40 Express or the No. 64 bus to Largo Torre Argentina, where you can get off to visit the Ghetto area. Switch to Tram No. 8 to get to Trastevere. The No. 75 bus departs from Termini, passes the Colosseum, runs through Trastevere, and later ascends the Janiculum Hill.

TOP ATTRACTIONS

Fontana delle Tartarughe. Designed by Giacomo della Porta in 1581 and sculpted by Taddeo Landini, this 16th-century fountain, set in venerable Piazza Mattei, is Rome's most charming. The focus of the fountain is four bronze boys, each grasping a dolphin spouting water into a marble shell. Bronze turtles held in the boys' hands drink from the upper basin. The turtles are thought to have been added in the 17th century by Bernini. ⊠ *Piazza Mattei, Ghetto.*

Isola Tiberina. It's easy to overlook this tiny island in the Tiber. Don't. In terms of history and sheer loveliness, the charming Isola Tiberina—shaped like a boat about to set sail—gets high marks.

Cross onto the island via Ponte Fabricio, constructed in 62 BC, Rome's oldest remaining bridge; on the north side of the island crumbles the romantic ruin of the Ponte Rotto (Broken Bridge), which dates back to 179 BC. Descend the steps to the lovely river embankment to see the island's claim to fame: a Roman relief of the intertwined-snakes symbol of Aesculapius, the great god of healing. In imperial times, Romans sheathed the entire island with marble to make it look like Aesculapius's ship, replete with a towering obelisk as a mast. Amazingly, the ancient sculpted ship's prow still exists. You can marvel at it on the downstream end of the embankment.

Sometimes called the world's most beautiful movie theater, the open-air Cinema d'Isola di Tiberina operates from mid-June to early September as part of Rome's big summer festival, Estate Romana (⊕ *www. estateromana.comune.roma.it*). ⊠ *Trastevere.*

Jewish Ghetto. Rome has had a Jewish community since the 2nd century BC, and from that time until the present its living conditions have varied widely according to its relations with the city's rulers. In 1555 Pope Paul IV Carafa established Rome's Ghetto Ebraico in the neighborhood marked off by the Portico d'Ottavia, the Tiber, and the Piazza dei Cenci. It measured only 200 yards by 250 yards. Jews were obligated to live there by law and the area quickly became Rome's most densely populated and least healthy. The laws were rescinded when Italy was unified in 1870 and the pope lost his political authority, but German troops tragically occupied Rome during World War II and in 1943 wrought havoc here. Today there are a few Judaica shops and kosher groceries, bakeries, and restaurants (especially on Via di Portico d'Ottavia), but the neighborhood mansions are now being renovated and much coveted by rich and stylish expats. The Museo Ebraico arranges tours of the Ghetto. The museum has exhibits detailing the millennial history of Rome's Jewish community.

Portico d'Ottavia. Looming over the Ghetto district, this huge porticoed enclosure, with a few surviving columns, comprises one of its most picturesque set pieces, with the time-stained church of Sant'Angelo in Pescheria built right into its ruins. Named by Augustus in honor of his sister Octavia, it was originally 390 feet wide and 433 feet long, encompassed two temples, a meeting hall, and a library, and served as a kind of grandiose entrance foyer for the adjacent Teatro di Marcello. The ruins of the portico became Rome's *pescheria* (fish market) during the Middle

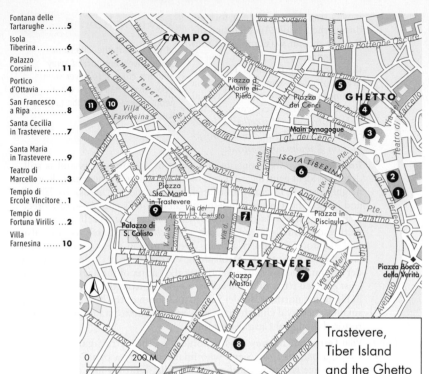

Trastevere,
Tiber Island
and the Ghetto

Ages. After restoration, the lovely medieval church of Sant'Angelo in Pescheria has reopened to the public *(Wed., Sat., and first Mon. of the month, 2–5; 06/68801819).* ⊠ *Via Tribuna di Campitelli 6, Ghetto.*

Fodor'sChoice
★   **Santa Maria in Trastevere.** Originally built sometime before the 4th century, this is certainly one of Rome's oldest, and grandest, churches. With a nave framed by a processional of two rows of gigantic columns (22 in total) taken from ancient Roman temples and an altar studded with gilded mosaics, the interior conjures up the splendor of ancient Rome better than any other in the city. Larger Roman naves exist, but none seem as majestic as this one, bathed in a sublime glow from the 12th- and 13th-century mosaics and Domenichino's gilded ceiling (1617). The 19th-century portico draws attention to the facade's 800-year-old mosaics, which represent the parable of the Wise and Foolish Virgins. They enhance the whole piazza, especially at night, when the church front and bell tower are illuminated. Back inside, the church's most important mosaics, Pietro Cavallini's six panels of the *Life of the Virgin,* cover the semicircular apse. ⊠ *Piazza Santa Maria in Trastevere, Trastevere* ☎ *06/5814802* ☉ *Daily 7:30 am–9 pm.*

Teatro di Marcello. Begun by Julius Caesar and completed by the emperor Augustus in AD 13, this was Rome's first permanent building dedicated to drama; it held 20,000 spectators. Like other Roman monuments, it was transformed into a fortress during the Middle Ages. During the Renaissance, it was converted into a residence by the Savelli, one of the city's noble families. The small archaeological zone is used as a summer venue for open-air classical music and lyrical concerts. ⊠ *Via del Teatro di Marcello, Ghetto* ☎ *06/87131590 for concert information* ⊕ *www.tempietto.it.*

Trastevere. This area consists of a maze of narrow streets and is still, despite evident gentrification, one of the city's most authentically Roman neighborhoods. Literally translated, its name means "across the Tiber," and indeed the Trasteverini—the neighborhood's natives—are a breed apart. The area is hardly undiscovered, but among its self-consciously picturesque trattorias and trendy *enoteche* (wine bars) you can also find old stores and dusty artisans' workshops in alleys festooned with laundry hung out to dry. Stroll along Via dell'Arco dei Tolomei and Via dei Salumi, shadowy streets showing the patina of the ages. One of the least affected parts of Trastevere is a block in from the Tiber: on Piazza in Piscinula, north of Via dei Salumi and south of the Ponte Cestio. The smallest medieval church in the city, San Benedetto, stands opposite the restored medieval Casa dei Mattei.

Fodor's Choice
★

Villa Farnesina. Money was no object to the extravagant Agostino Chigi, a banker from Siena who financed many a papal project. His munificence is evident in this elegant villa, built for him about 1511. He was especially proud of the delicate fresco decorations in the airy loggias, now glassed in to protect their artistic treasures. When Raphael could steal a little time from his work on the Vatican Stanze, he came over to execute some of the frescoes himself, notably a luminous *Galatea*. In the magnificent **Loggia of Psyche** on the ground floor, Giulio Romano and others worked from Raphael's designs. On the floor above you can see the trompe l'oeil effects in the aptly named **Hall of Perspectives** by Peruzzi. The palace also houses the **Gabinetto Nazionale delle Stampe,** a treasure-house of old prints and drawings. ⊠ *Via della Lungara 230, Trastevere* ☎ *06/68027268 for information, 06/68027397 for tour reservations* ⊕ *www.villafarnesina.it* ⊠ *€5* ☺ *Mon.–Sat. 9–2.*

WORTH NOTING

Palazzo Corsini. A brooding example of Baroque style, the palace houses part of the 16th- and 17th-century sections of the collection of the Galleria Nazionale d'Arte Antica and is across the road from the Villa Farnesina. Among the most famous paintings in this large, dark collection are Guido Reni's *Beatrice Cenci* and Caravaggio's *St. John the Baptist*. Stop in, if only to climb the 17th-century stone staircase, itself a drama of architectural shadows and sculptural voids. Behind, but separate from, the palazzo is the **Orto Botanico** (☺ *Mon.–Sat. 9:30–6:30 in summer, 4:30 in winter* ⊠ *€6*), Rome's only botanical park, containing 3,500 species of plants. There are various greenhouses around a recently restored stairway/fountain with 11 jets. Or, if you prefer, it's just a peaceful park where kids can run and play. ⊠ *Via della Lungara 10, Trastevere* ☎ *06/68802323 Galleria Corsini, 06/32810 Galleria Corsini tickets, 06/49912436 Orto Botanico* ⊕ *www.galleriaborghese.it* ✉ *€5* ⊙ *Tues.–Sun. 8:30–7:30.*

San Francesco a Ripa. Near Trastevere's southern end, this Baroque church attached to a 13th-century Franciscan monastery holds one of Bernini's last works, a statue of the Blessed Ludovica Albertoni. This is perhaps Bernini's most hallucinatory sculpture, a dramatically lighted figure ecstatic at the prospect of entering heaven as she expires on her deathbed. Gracing the altar is Baciccia's *Madonna and St. Anne.* St. Francis is supposed to have stayed at this monastery when visiting the city; to see his cell, ask the Sacristan. The side chapels of the church, including Bernini's, have been restored and are open to the public. ⊠ *Piazza San Francesco d'Assisi 88, Trastevere* ☎ *06/5819020* ⊙ *Daily 7–1 and 2–7.*

Santa Cecilia in Trastevere. The basilica commemorates the aristocratic St. Cecilia, patron saint of music. One of ancient Rome's most celebrated Early Christian martyrs, she was put to a supernaturally long death by the emperor Diocletian around the year AD 300. After an abortive attempt to suffocate her in the baths of her own house (a favorite means of quietly disposing of aristocrats in Roman days), she was brought before the executioner. But not even three blows of the executioner's sword could dispatch the young girl. She lingered for several days, converting others to the Christian cause, before finally dying. In 1595, her body was exhumed. It was said to look as fresh as if she still breathed— and the heart-wrenching sculpture by eyewitness Stefano Maderno that lies below the main altar was, the sculptor insisted, exactly how she looked. Time your visit to enter the cloistered convent to see what remains of Pietro Cavallini's *Last Judgment,* dating from 1293. It's the only major fresco in existence known to have been painted by Cavallini, a forerunner of Giotto. ⊠ *Piazza Santa Cecilia in Trastevere 22, Trastevere* ☎ *06/5899289* ✉ *Church free; frescoes €2.50; underground €2.50* ⊙ *Basilica and underground, Mon.–Sat. 9:30–12:30 and 4–6:30, Sun. 4–6:30; frescoes, Mon.–Sat. 10–12:30.*

Tempio della Fortuna Virilis. A picture-perfect (if dollhouse-size) Roman temple, this rectangular edifice from the 2nd century BC is built in the Greek style, as was the norm in Rome's early years. It owes its fine state of preservation to the fact that it was consecrated and used as a Christian church. ⊠ *Piazza Bocca della Verit, Aventino* Ⓜ *Circo Massimo. Bus Nos. 3, 60, 75, 81, 118, 160, 175, 271.*

Tempio di Ercole Vincitore. All but one of the 20 original Corinthian columns in Rome's most evocative small ruin remain intact. It was built in the 2nd century BC. Long considered a shrine to Vesta, it's now believed that the temple was devoted to Hercules by a successful olive merchant. ⊠ *Piazza Bocca della Verità, Ghetto.*

THE CATACOMBS AND VIA APPIA ANTICA

The Early Christian sites on the ancient Appian Way are some of the religion's oldest. Catacombs, where ancient pagans, Jews, and early Christians buried their dead, lie below the very road where tradition says Christ appeared to Saint Peter. The Via Appia Antica, built 400 years before, is a quiet, green place to walk and ponder the ancient world. There's a helpful office around the first milestone (at No. 58/60) that provides informative pamphlets and bicycle rentals.

GETTING HERE AND AROUND

You can take bus No. 118 from Circo Massimo, No. 218 from Piazza San Giovanni in Laterano, or No. 660 from the Colli Albani Metro station (Line A). There's also an Archeobus OpenTram bus from Termini (⊕ *www.trambusopen.com*).

TOP ATTRACTIONS

Catacombe di San Sebastiano (*Catacombs of St. Sebastian*). This 4th-century church was named after the saint who was buried in the catacomb, which burrows underground on four different levels. This was the only Early Christian cemetery to remain accessible during the Middle Ages, and it was from here that the term "catacomb" is derived—it's in a spot where the road dips into a hollow, known to the Romans as *catacumbas* (Greek for "near the hollow"). The Romans used the name to refer to the cemetery that had existed here since the 2nd century BC, and it came to be applied to all the underground cemeteries discovered in Rome in later centuries. ⊠ *Via Appia Antica 136, Via Appia Antica* ☏ 06/7850350 ⊕ *www.catacombe.org* ⬙ €8 ۞ *Dec. 26–late Nov. Mon.–Sat. 10–4:30* Ⓜ *Bus Nos. 118, 218, 660.*

Fodor'sChoice **Tomba di Cecilia Metella.** For centuries, sightseers have flocked to this
★ famous landmark, one of the most complete surviving tombs of ancient Rome. One of the many round mausoleums that once lined the Appian Way, this tomb is a smaller version of the Mausoleum of Augustus, but impressive nonetheless. It was the burial place of a Roman noblewoman, wife of the son of Crassus, one of Julius Caesar's rivals and known as the richest man in the Roman Empire (infamously entering the English language as "crass"). An adjacent chamber houses a small museum of the area's geological phases. ⊠ *Via Appia Antica 162, Via Appia Antica* ☏ 06/39967700 ⊕ *archeoroma.beniculturali.it* ⬙ €7, *includes Terme di Caracalla and Villa dei Quintili* ۞ *Tues.–Sun. 9–4:30; ticket office closes 1 hr earlier.*

Via Appia Antica. This Queen of Roads, "Regina Viarium," was the most important of the extensive network of roads that traversed the Roman Empire, a masterful feat of engineering that made possible Roman control of a vast area by allowing for the efficient transportation of armies and commercial goods. Begun in 312 BC by Appius Claudius, the road was ancient Europe's first major highway. The first part reached as far as Capua near Naples, ultimately being extended in 191 BC to Brindisi 584 km (365 miles) southeast of Rome on the Adriatic Coast. The ancient roadway begins at Porta San Sebastiano, southeast of the Circus Maximus, passing through grassy fields and shady groves and by the villas of movie stars (Marcello Mastroianni

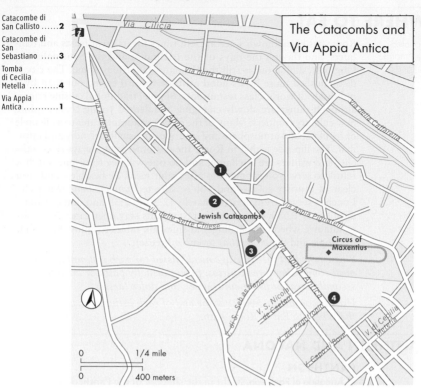

The Catacombs and Via Appia Antica

1

and Gina Lollobrigida had homes here). The area of primary interest lies between the second and third milestones and is still paved with the ancient *basoli* (basalt stones) over which the Romans drove their carriages—look for the wheel ruts. Pick a sunny day for your visit, wear comfortable shoes, and bring a bottle of water. The Appia Antica is best reached with public transportation (there are no sidewalks along the road); ⇨ *See Getting Here.* For more information, or bike rentals for exploring the Via Appia, visit the Information Point (*Via Appia Antica 58/60 P06/5135316 Open in winter from 9:30–4:30 daily, summer 9:30–5 weekdays and 9:30–6 weekends, August 9:30–5 daily, www. parcoappiaantica.it).* ⊕ *parcoappiaantica.it.*

WORTH NOTING

Catacombe di San Callisto (*Catacombs of St. Calixtus*). Burial place of many popes of the 3rd century, this is the oldest and best-preserved underground cemetery. One of the (English-speaking) friars who act as custodians of the catacomb will guide you through its crypts and galleries, some adorned with Early Christian frescoes. Watch out for wrong turns: this is a five-story-high catacomb! ⊠ *Via Appia Antica 110/126, Via Appia Antica* ☎ *06/5310151* ⊕ *www.catacombe.roma.it* ⟀ *€8* ⊙ *Thurs.–Tues. 9–noon and 2–5. Closed 3 to 4 wks late Jan. and Feb.* Ⓜ *Bus Nos. 118, 218.*

WHERE TO EAT

Updated by Amanda Ruggeri

Rome has been known since ancient times for its great feasts and banquets, and though the days of the triclinium and the Saturnalia are long past, dining out is still the Romans' favorite pastime. The city is distinguished more by its good attitude toward eating out than by a multitude of world-class restaurants. Simple, traditional cuisine reigns, although things are slowly changing as talented young chefs explore new culinary frontiers. Many of the city's restaurants cater to a clientele of regulars, and atmosphere and attitude are usually friendly and informal. The flip side is that in Rome the customer isn't always right—the chef and waiters are in charge, and no one will beg forgiveness if they refuse to serve you cappuccino after your meal. Be flexible—and steer clear of touristy spots—and you're sure to *mangiar bene* (eat well). Lunch is served from approximately 12:30 to 2:30 and dinner from 8 until about 10:30, though some restaurants stay open later, especially in summer, when patrons linger at sidewalk tables to enjoy the parade of people and the *ponentino* (evening breeze).

Please note that the "average meal" listed for each restaurant means a meal comprising three courses: primo (usually pasta or an appetizer), secondo (meat or fish main course), and dolce (dessert).

Use the coordinate (⊕ B2) at the end of each listing to locate a site on the Where to Eat in Rome map.

PANTHEON AND NAVONA

PANTHEON

$$ ROMAN 🍴 **Armando al Pantheon.** Right in the shadow of the Pantheon, this wonderful trattoria, open since 1961, delights the tourists who mostly tend to come for lunch, but there's always a buzz here and an air of authenticity, witnessed by Roman antique shop owners who have been regulars here for 25 years—you can tell these older gentlemen who come here to enjoy a four-course meal . . . and scold the waitress, by name, when she brings coffee before the profiteroles. This is just the place to try Roman artichokes or *vignarola* (a fava bean, asparagus, pea, and guanciale stew) in the spring, or the wild boar *bruschetta* in winter. Pastas are filling and great, and *secondi* deliver all the Roman staples: oxtail, baby lamb chops, tripe, meatballs, and other hearty fare. Those with a sweet tooth shouldn't miss the famous *torta "Antica Roma."* [$] *Average meal: €35* ✉ *Salita dei Crescenzi 31, Pantheon* ☎ *06/68803034* 🌐 *www.armandoalpantheon.it* 🕓 *Closed Sun. No dinner Sat.* ⊕ *1:E4.*

$ CAFÉ 🍴 **Caffè Sant'Eustachio.** Traditionally frequented by Rome's literati, this has what is generally considered Rome's best cup of coffee. Servers are hidden behind a huge espresso machine, vigorously mixing the sugar and coffee to protect their "secret method" for the perfectly prepared cup. (If you want your *caffè* without sugar here, ask for it *amaro*). [$] *Average meal: €2* ✉ *Piazza Sant'Eustachio 82, Pantheon* ☎ *06/68802048* ⊕ *1:E4.*

$$$$ MODERN ITALIAN 🍴 **Hostaria dell'Orso.** Back in the Hollywood-on-the-Tiber 1950s, this was *the* place to be. Everyone from Sophia Loren to Aristotle Onassis reveled in the historic setting: a 15th century palazzo straight out of a

Renaissance painting. Today, after several fallow decades, a face-lift has brightened the salons, and even more up-to-the-second is the menu: The *alta cucina* deftly utilizes simple ingredients like top quality baby pig or black cod, and just a handful of ingredients—some very Italian, others more esoteric—to tease out maximum flavor. One artfully presented dinner included a kidney risotto with Provolone cheese fondue and liquorice dust, a pigeon wth peanut sauce and Java black pepper, and a crème brûlée with coffee parfait, chocolate ice-cream, and cotton candy. There's a piano bar and disco on other floors. Elegant dress is recommended. $ *Average meal: €70* ✉ *Via dei Soldati 25c, Piazza Navona* ☎ *06/68301192* ⊕ *www.hdo.it* ⌦ *Reservations essential* ☾ *Closed Sun. No lunch Mon.* ✛ *1:D3.*

$$
MODERN ITALIAN

✗ **Il Bacaro.** With a handful of choice tables set outside against an ivy-draped wall, this tiny candlelit spot not far from the Pantheon makes for an ideal evening, equally suited for a romantic twosome or close friends and convivial conversation. Pastas—like *orecchiette* (little ear-shaped pasta) with prosciutto *crudo* and radicchio, a dish that lip-smacks of Puglia—are star players. As a bonus, the kitchen keeps its clients from picking at each other's plates by offering side dishes of all the pastas ordered among those at the table. The choice main courses are mostly meat—the Argentine beef with balsamic vinegar or London broil–style marinated in olive oil and rosemary are winners. $ *Average meal: €45* ✉ *Via degli Spagnoli 27, Pantheon* ☎ *06/6872554* ⊕ *www.ilbacaro.com* ⌦ *Reservations essential* ✛ *1:E3.*

$
CAFÉ

✗ **Tazza d'Oro.** Many admirers contend this is the city's best cup of coffee. The hot chocolate in winter, all thick and gooey goodness, is a treat. And in warm weather, the coffee granita is the perfect cooling alternative to a regular espresso. $ *Average meal: €4* ✉ *Via degli Orfani, Pantheon* ☎ *06/6789792* ⊕ *www.tazzadorocoffeeshop.com* ✛ *1:E4.*

NAVONA

$
CAFÉ

✗ **Caffè della Pace.** With its sidewalk tables taking in Santa Maria della Pace's adorable piazza, Caffè della Pace has long been the haunt of Rome's *beau monde.* Set on a quiet street near Piazza Navona, it also has two rooms filled with old-world personality and paparazzi-worthy patrons. The neighborhood is currently hipper than ever, creating clogged *vicoli,* so snagging a table here is now an especially prized commodity. Dinner is more of a light meal than a dining "experience," but it's worth coming for the vibe. $ *Average meal: €15* ✉ *Via della Pace 3, Navona* ☎ *06/6861216* ⊕ *www.caffedellapace.it* ✛ *1:D4.*

$$
WINE BAR
Fodor's Choice
★

✗ **Cul de Sac.** This popular wine bar near Piazza Navona is among the city's oldest enoteche and offers a book-length selection of wines from Italy, France, the Americas, and elsewhere. Food is eclectic, ranging from a huge assortment of Italian meats and cheeses (try the delicious *lonza,* cured pork loin, or *speck,* a northern Italian smoked prosciutto) to various Mediterranean dishes, including delicious baba ghanoush, a tasty Greek salad, and a spectacular wild boar pâté. Outside tables get crowded fast, so arrive early, or come late—they serve until about 12:30am. $ *Average meal: €35* ✉ *Piazza Pasquino 73, Piazza Navona* ☎ *06/68801094* ⊕ *www.enotecaculdesac.com* ⌦ *Reservations not accepted* ✛ *1:D4.*

$ PIZZA 🍴 **Da Baffetto.** Down a cobblestone street not far from Piazza Navona, this is one of Rome's most popular pizzerias and a summer favorite for street-side dining. The debate is constant whether or not this spot is massively overrated, but as with all the "great" pizzerias in Rome, it's hard to argue with the line that forms outside here on weekends (the wait can be up to an hour). Happily, outdoor tables—enclosed and heated in winter—provide much-needed additional seating. Turnover is fast and lingering not encouraged. (Baffetto 2, at Piazza del Teatro di Pompeo 18, also offer pasta and secondi, and doesn't suffer from the same overcrowding, plus you can reserve a table, an option not available at the original location.) [$] *Average meal: €22* ✉ *Via del Governo Vecchio 114, Navona* ☎ *06/6861617* 💳 *No credit cards* 🕒 *Closed Tues. and Aug. No lunch Mon.–Fri.* ✥ *1:D4.*

$$$ MEDITERRANEAN Fodor's Choice ★ 🍴 **Etablì.** On a narrow vicolo off beloved Piazza del Fico, this multidimensional locale serves as a lounge-bar, and becomes a hot spot by aperitivo hour. Beautifully finished with vaulted wood beam ceilings, wrought-iron touches, plush leather sofas, and chandeliers, it's all modern Italian farmhouse chic. In the restaurant section (the place is sprawling), it's minimalist Provençal hip (*etabli* is French for the regionally typical tables within). The food is clean and Mediterranean, with touches of Asia in the raw fish appetizers. Pastas are more traditional Italian, and the secondi run the gamut from land to sea. The place fills up by *dopo cena* ("after dinner") when it becomes a popular spot for sipping and posing. [$] *Average meal: €55* ✉ *Vicolo delle Vacche 9/a, Navona* ☎ *06/6871499* 🌐 *www.etabli.it* 🕒 *Closed Sun. No lunch* ✥ *1:D3.*

$$$$ MODERN ITALIAN Fodor's Choice ★ 🍴 **Il Convivio.** In a tiny, nondescript vicolo north of Piazza Navona, the three Troiani brothers—Angelo in the kitchen, and brothers Giuseppe and Massimo presiding over the dining room and wine cellar—have quietly been redefining the experience of Italian eclectic *alta cucina* (haute cuisine) for many years. Antipasti include a selection of ultra-fresh raw seafood preparations in the mixed crudi, while a "carbomare" pasta is a riff on tradition, substituting pancetta with fresh fish roe and house-cured *bottarga* (salted fish roe). Or opt for one of the famed signature dishes, including a fabulous version of a cold-weather pigeon main course prepared four different ways. Service is attentive without being overbearing, and the wine list is exceptional. It is definitely a splurge spot. [$] *Average meal: €110* ✉ *Vicolo dei Soldati 31, Navona* ☎ *06/6869432* ✍ *Reservations essential* 🕒 *Closed Sun. and 2 wks in Aug. No lunch* ✥ *1:D3.*

CAMPO DE' FIORI AND GHETTO

CAMPO DE' FIORI

$$ ITALIAN 🍴 **Ditirambo.** Don't let the country-kitchen ambience fool you. At this little spot off Campo de' Fiori, the constantly changing selection of offbeat takes on Italian classics is a step beyond ordinary Roman fare. The place is usually packed with diners who appreciate the adventuresome kitchen, though you may overhear complaints about the brusque service. Antipasti can be delicious and unexpected, like Gorgonzola-pear soufflé drizzled with aged balsamic vinegar, or a mille-feuille of

1

BEST BETS FOR ROME DINING

With hundreds of restaurants to choose from, how will you decide where to eat? Fodor's writers and editors have selected their favorite restaurants by price, cuisine, and experience in the Best Bets lists below. In the first column, Fodor's Choice properties represent the "best of the best" in every price category.

Fodor'sChoice★

Agata e Romeo, $$$$, p. 109

Cul de Sac, $$, p. 101

Etablì, $$$, p. 102

Filetti di Baccalà, $, p. 106

Il Convivio, $$$$, p. 102

Il Sanlorenzo, $$$$, p. 106

La Pergola, $$$$, p. 111

La Veranda dell' Hotel Columbus, $$$, p. 110

Nino, $$$, p. 108

Taverna Angelica, $$$, p. 110

Trattoria Monti, $$, p. 109

BEST BY PRICE

$

Panattoni (Ai Marmi), p. 111

$$

Cul de Sac, p. 101

Enoteca Palatium, p. 128

L'Angolo Divino, p. 106

Trattoria Monti, p. 109

$$$

Roscioli, p. 107

$$$$

Agata e Romeo, p. 109

Checchino dal 1887, p. 112

Glass Hostaria, p. 111

La Pergola, p. 111

BEST BY CUISINE

MODERN ITALIAN

Agata e Romeo, $$$$, p. 109

Glass Hostaria, $$$$, p. 111

Il Convivio, $$$$, p.102

La Pergola, $$$$, p. 111

PIZZA

Panattoni (Ai Marmi), $, p. 111

ROMAN

Checchino dal 1887, $$$$, p. 112

Perilli, $$, p. 112

WINE BAR

Cul de Sac, $$, p. 101

L'Angolo Divino $$, p. 106

Roscioli, $$$, p. 107

BEST BY EXPERIENCE

OUTDOOR DINING

La Veranda dell'Hotel Columbus, $$$, p. 110

Osteria La Quercia, $$, p. 106

GORGEOUS SETTING

Il Convivio, $$$$, p. 102

La Pergola, $$$$, p. 111

La Veranda dell'Hotel Columbus, $$$, p. 110

LOTS OF LOCALS

Perilli, $$ p. 112

Trattoria Monti, $$ p. 109

ROMANTIC

Glass Hostaria, $$$$, p. 111

Il Convivio, $$$$, p. 102

Il Sanlorenzo, $$$$, p. 106

La Pergola, $$$$, p. 111

GREAT WINE LIST

Enoteca Palatium, $$, p. 128

Glass Hostaria, $$$$, p. 111

Il Convivio, $$$$, p. 102

GOOD FOR LUNCH

Cul de Sac, $$, p. 101

L'Angolo Divino $$, p. 106

Osteria La Quercia, $$, p. 106

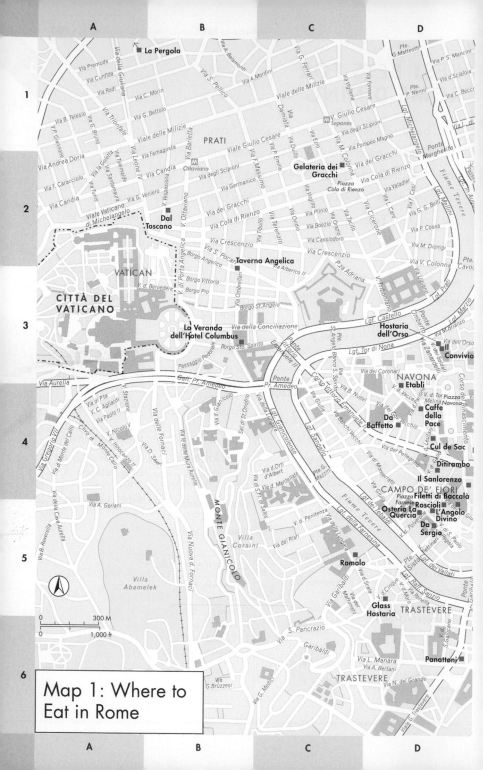

Map 1: Where to Eat in Rome

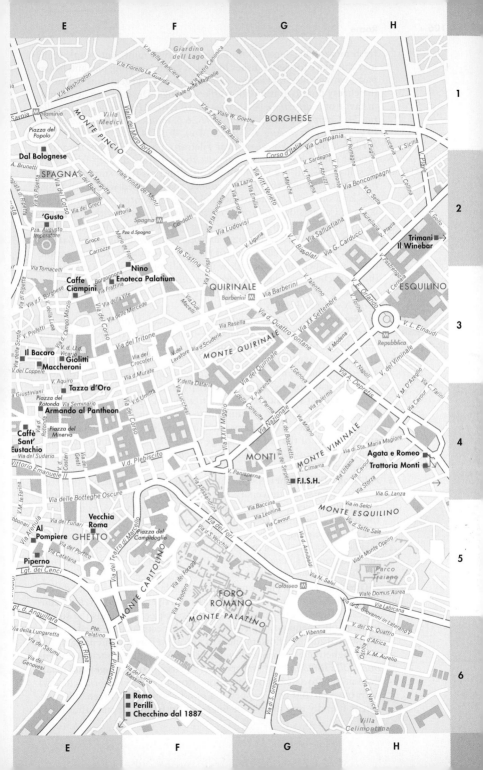

fresh mozzarella, sundried tomatoes and fresh mint. But people really love this place for rustic dishes like roast lamb, suckling pig, and hearty pasta with guinea fowl and porcini mushrooms. Vegetarians will adore the cheesy potato gratin with truffle shavings. Desserts can be skipped in favor of a *digestivo*. $ *Average meal: €40* ⊠ *Piazza della Cancelleria 74, Campo de' Fiori* ☎ *06/6871626* ⊕ *www.ristoranteditirambo.it* ⊙ *Closed 2 wks in Aug. No lunch Mon.* ✛ *1:D4.*

$ ITALIAN   Fodor'sChoice ★ ✕ **Filetti di Baccalà.** For years, Dar Filettaro a Santa Barbara (to use its official name) has been serving just that—battered, deep-fried fillets of salt cod—and not much else. You'll find no-frills starters such as *bruschette al pomodoro* (garlic-rubbed toast topped with fresh tomatoes and olive oil), sautéed zucchini, and, in winter months, the cod is served alongside *puntarelle*, chicory stems tossed with a delicious anchovy-garlic-lemon vinaigrette. The location, down the street from Campo de' Fiori in a little piazza in front of the beautiful Santa Barbara church, begs you to eat at one of the outdoor tables, weather permitting. Long operating hours allow those still on U.S. time to eat as early (how gauche!) as 5 pm. $ *Average meal: €18* ⊠ *Largo dei Librari 88, Campo de' Fiori* ☎ *06/6864018* ▭ *No credit cards* ⊙ *Closed Sun. and Aug. No lunch* ✛ *1:D5.*

$$$$ SEAFOOD   Fodor'sChoice ★ ✕ **Il Sanlorenzo.** This revamped, gorgeous space—think chandeliers and soaring original brickwork ceilings—houses one of the better seafood spots in the Eternal City. Tempting tasting menus are on offer, as well as à la carte items like a wonderful series of small plates in their crudo appetizer, which can include a perfectly seasoned fish tartare trio, sweet *scampi* (local langoustines), and a wispy-thin carpaccio of red shrimp. The restaurant's version of spaghetti with sea urchin is exquisite and delicate; follow up with a main course of a freshly caught seasonal fish prepared to order. Menu items often change based on the chef's whim and the catch of the day. $ *Average meal: €85* ⊠ *Via dei Chiavari 4/5, Campo de' Fiori* ☎ *06/6865097* ⊕ *www.ilsanlorenzo.it* ⊙ *No lunch Sat.–Mon.* ✛ *1:D4.*

$$ WINE BAR ✕ **L'Angolo Divino.** There's something about this cozy wine bar that feels as if it's in a small university town instead of a bustling metropolis. Serene blue-green walls lined with wood shelves of wines from around the Italian peninsula add to the warm atmosphere. Along with several hot plates including fresh pasta, smoked fish, cured meats, cheeses, and salads make a nice lunch or light dinner, and the kitchen stays open until the wee hours. $ *Average meal: €30* ⊠ *Via dei Balestrari 12, Campo de' Fiori* ☎ *06/6864413* ⊙ *Closed 1 wk in Aug.* ✛ *1:D5.*

$$ ROMAN ✕ **Osteria La Quercia.** The beautiful Piazza della Quercia was once devoid of any restaurants, until this casual trattoria opened its doors. Now diners can sit under the gorgeous looming oak tree that lends the square its name. Its menu is simple—the usual suspects include fried starters like stuffed zucchini flowers and baccalà, as well as Roman pasta dishes like spaghetti carbonara and *amatriciana*. Main dishes include *saltimbocca alla romana* (veal wrapped with prosciutto and sage) and meatballs in tomato sauce. The ubiquitous Roman sautéed *cicoria* (chicory) with olive oil and chili pepper is a good choice for a green side. Service is friendly and allows for lingering on balmy Roman afternoons

and evenings—so close, and yet so seemingly far from the chaos of nearby Campo de'Fiori. $ *Average meal: €30* ⊠ *Piazza della Quercia 23, Campo de' Fiori* ☎ *06/68300932* ✛ *1:D5.*

$$$ ✕ **Roscioli.** More like a Caravaggio painting than a place of business,
WINE BAR this food shop and wine bar is dark and decadent. The shop in front beckons with top-quality comestibles: wild Alaskan smoked salmon, hand-sliced prosciutto from Italy and Spain, more than 300 cheeses, and a dizzying array of wines. Venture farther inside to a cavelike room where you'll be served artisanal cheeses and *salumi*, as well as an extensive selection of unusual dishes and interesting takes on classics. Try the *mortadella* of Bologna with 3-year-aged *parmigiano, burrata* with Norwegian herring caviar, or go for pasta with sardines or Sicilian linguini with red prawns and cumin. The menu features meats, seafood (including a nice selection of tartars and other raw fish preparations), and vegetarian-friendly items. ■TIP➜ Reserve a table in the cozy wine cellar beneath the dining room. And afterward head around the corner to their bakery for rightfully famous breads and sweets. $ *Average meal: €65* ⊠ *Via dei Giubbonari 21/22, Campo de' Fiori* ☎ *06/6875287* ⊕ *www.anticofornoroscioli.com* ⋧ *Reservations essential* ☾ *Closed Sun.* ✛ *1:D5.*

GHETTO

$$$ ✕ **Al Pompiere.** The entrance on a narrow side street leads upstairs to the
ROMAN main dining room of this neighborhood favorite, all white tablecloths and high arched ceilings. Its Roman Jewish dishes, such as fried zucchini flowers, battered salt cod, and gnocchi, are all consistently good and there are also some nice, historic touches, like a beef-and-citron stew from an ancient Roman recipe of Apicius. If the traditional Roman *porchetta* (roasted suckling pig) is on the menu, order it before it runs out—it is truly divine. In 2004, there was a terrible fire in a shop below the restaurant, but the kitchen was soon back in business, though the irony here is as thick as the chef's tomato sauce: *Al Pompiere* means "the fireman." $ *Average meal: €55* ⊠ *Via Santa Maria dei Calderari 38, Ghetto* ☎ *06/6868377* ⊕ *www.alpompiereroma.com* ☾ *Closed Sun. and Aug.* ✛ *1:E5.*

$$$ ✕ **Piperno.** *The* place to go for Rome's extraordinary *carciofi alla giudia*
ROMAN (fried whole artichokes), Piperno has been in business for more than a century. The location, up a tiny hill in a piazza tucked away behind the *palazzi* of the Ghetto, lends the restaurant a rarefied air. It's a popular location for Sunday brunch. Try the exquisite prosciutto and buffalo mozzarella plate, the *fiori di zucca ripieni e fritti* (fried stuffed zucchini flowers), and *filetti di baccalà* (fillet of cod) to start. The display of fresh local fish is enticing enough to lure diners to try offerings from sea instead of land. Service is in the old school style of dignified formality. $ *Average meal: €55* ⊠ *Monte dei Cenci 9, Ghetto* ☎ *06/68806629* ⊕ *www.ristorantepiperno.it* ☾ *Closed Mon. and Aug. No dinner Sun.* ✛ *1:E5.*

$$$ ✕ **Vecchia Roma.** Though the frescoed dining rooms are lovely, the choice
SEAFOOD place to dine is outside on the piazza, under the big white umbrellas. After several decades, this is still considered one of the most solid spots on the Roman culinary scene, just the place to get acquainted

with Roman cooking, upper-middle-class style. For appetizers, the seafood selection may include an assortment of fresh anchovies in vinegary goodness, seafood salad, or baby shrimp. Chef Raffaella generally doles out large portions, so select one of her wonderful pasta dishes or skip straight to the secondi. Though meat and vegetable dishes are on offer, seafood is the specialty, and simple southern Italian preparations, such as fresh white flaky fish in a potato crust with cherry tomatoes, are excellent no-fail choices. House-made fruit desserts provide a light(ish) finish to the meal, hopefully accompanied by a dramatic sunset over the 17th-century facade of Santa Maria in Campitelli. $ *Average meal: €65* ✉ *Piazza Campitelli 18, Ghetto* ☎ *06/6864604* ⊕ *www.ristorantevecchiaroma.com* ⚠ *Reservations essential* ⊙ *Closed Wed.* ✛ *1:E5.*

SPAGNA

$$$$ ✕ **Dal Bolognese.** The darling of the media, film, and fashion communities, this classic restaurant on Piazza del Popolo is not only an "in-crowd" dinner destination but makes a convenient shopping-spree lunch spot. As the name promises, the cooking adheres to the hearty tradition of Bologna. Start with a plate of sweet *prosciutto di Parma* with melon, then move on to the traditional egg pastas of Emilia-Romagna. Second plates include the famous Bolognese *bollito misto,* a steaming tray of an assortment of boiled meats (some recognizable, some indecipherable) served with its classic accompaniment, a tangy, herby *salsa verde* (green sauce). During dessert, take in the passing parade of your fellow diners—they love to meet and greet with excessive air kisses. $ *Average meal: €75* ✉ *Piazza del Popolo 1, Spagna* ☎ *06/3611426* ⚠ *Reservations essential* ⊙ *Closed Mon. and 3 wks in Aug.* Ⓜ *Flaminio* ✛ *1:E1.*

EMILIAN (label for Dal Bolognese)

$$ ✕ **'Gusto.** There's an urban-loft feel to this trendy two-story space, a bit like a Pottery Barn exploded in Piazza Agusto Imperatore. The ground floor contains a buzzing pizzeria-trattoria, while upstairs is the more upscale restaurant. We prefer the casual-but-hopping vibe of the ground-floor wine bar in the back, where a rotating selection of wines by the glass and bottle are served up alongside a vast array of cheeses, salumi, and bread products. Lunchtime features a great value salad bar. And for the kitchen enthusiast, the 'Gusto "complex" includes a store, selling everything from cookware to cookwear. $ *Average meal: €45* ✉ *Piazza Augusto Imperatore 9, Spagna* ☎ *06/3226273* ⊕ *www. gusto.it* ✛ *1:E2.*

WINE BAR (label for 'Gusto)

$$$ ✕ **Nino.** A favorite among international journalists and the rich and famous for decades (Tom Cruise and Katie Holmes had their celeb-studded rehearsal dinner here), Nino is Rome's best-loved dressed-up trattoria. The interior is country rustic *alla Tuscana,* and, along with the classic appearance of its interior (and its waiters!), Nino sticks to the classics when it comes to its food—basically Roman and Tuscan staples. Start with a selection from the fine antipasto spread, or go for the cured meats or warm *crostini* (toasts) spread with liver pâté. Move on to pappardelle *al lepre* (a rich hare sauce) or hearty Tuscan ribollita soup, and go for the gold with a piece of juicy grilled

ITALIAN
Fodor's Choice
★
(labels for Nino)

beef. ⚠ **If you're not Italian, or a regular, or a celebrity, the chance of brusque service multiplies—insist on good service and you'll win the waiters' respect.** [$] *Average meal: €55* ✉ *Via Borgognona 11, Spagna* ☎ *06/6786752, 06/6795676* 🌐 *www.ristorantenino.it* 🕓 *Closed Sun. and Aug.* [M] *Spagna* ⊕ *1:F2.*

MONTI, ESQUILINO, AND SAN LORENZO

MONTI

$$$ SEAFOOD

🍴 **F.I.S.H.** The name stands for Fine International Seafood House, which sums up the kitchen's approach. This is fresh, *fresh* fish cooked by capable and creative hands—from Italian fish-based pastas to a Thai mollusk soup with lemongrass and coconut milk that awakens the senses. The menu is divided into sections: appetizers, tapas, Oriental, and Mediterranean. Seating is divided into the front aqua lounge, a bar for tapas and aperitivo, and the back dining room, but it is limited, so book ahead. [$] *Average meal: €50* ✉ *Via dei Serpenti 16, Monti* ☎ *06/47824962* 🌐 *www.f-i-s-h.it* ✍ *Reservations essential* 🕓 *Closed Mon., the last wk of July, and several days in mid-Aug. No lunch* [M] *Cavour* ⊕ *1:G4.*

ESQUILINO

$$$$ MODERN ITALIAN Fodor's Choice ★

🍴 **Agata e Romeo.** For the perfect marriage of fine dining, creative cuisine, and rustic Roman tradition, the husband-and-wife team of Agata Parisella and Romeo Caraccio is the top. Romeo presides over the dining room and delights in the selection of wine-food pairings. And Chef Agata was perhaps the first in the capital to put a gourmet spin on Roman ingredients and preparations, elevating dishes of the common folk to new levels. Staples like *cacio e pepe* (a traditional Roman dish: pasta tossed in pecorino romano cheese and fresh black pepper) are transformed with the addition of even richer Sicilian aged cheese and saffron; "baccala' 5 ways" showcases salt cod of the highest quality; and many dishes are the best versions of classics you can get. Prices are steep, but for those who appreciate extremely high-quality ingredients, an incredible wine cellar, and warm service, dining here is a real treat. [$] *Average meal: €100* ✉ *Via Carlo Alberto 45, Termini* ☎ *06/4466115* 🌐 *www.agataeromeo.it* ✍ *Reservations essential* 🕓 *Closed Sun. and 2 wks in Aug. No lunch Sat. and Mon.* [M] *Vittorio Emanuele* ⊕ *1:H4.*

$$ ITALIAN Fodor's Choice ★

🍴 **Trattoria Monti.** Not far from Santa Maria Maggiore, Trattoria Monti is one of the most dependable, moderately priced trattorias in the city, featuring the cuisine of Le Marche, an area to the northeast of Rome. There are surprisingly few places specializing in this humble fare considering there are more people hailing from Le Marche in Rome than currently living in that whole region. Served up by the Camerucci family, it's hearty and simple, represented by various roasted meats and game, and a selection of generally vegetarian timbales and soufflés that change seasonally. The region's rabbit dishes are much loved, and here the *timballo di coniglio con patate* (rabbit casserole with potatoes) is no exception. [$] *Average meal: €45* ✉ *Via di San Vito 13a, Monti* ☎ *06/4466573* ✍ *Reservations essential* 🕓 *Closed Aug., 1 wk at Easter, and 10 days at Christmas* [M] *Vittorio Emanuele* ⊕ *1:H4.*

REPUBBLICA

$$ | ✕ **Trimani Il Winebar.** Operating nonstop from 11 am to 12:30 am, this
WINE BAR | wine bar serves hot food at lunch and dinner. The interior is in minimalist style, and the second floor provides a subdued, candlelit space to sip wine. There's always a choice of a soup and pasta plates, as well as second courses and *torte salate* (savory tarts). Around the corner is a wineshop, one of the oldest in Rome, of the same name. Call about wine tastings and classes (in Italian). $ *Average meal: €30* ✉ *Via Cernaia 37/b, Repubblica* ☎ *06/4469630* ⊕ *www.trimani.com* ۩ *Closed Sun. and 2 wks in Aug.* Ⓜ *Castro Pretorio* ✛ *1:H2.*

VATICAN, BORGO, PRATI, AND NORTHWEST ROME

BORGO

$$$ | ✕ **La Veranda dell'Hotel Columbus.** Deciding where to sit at La Veranda is
ROMAN | not easy, since both the shady courtyard, torch-lit at night, and the fres-
Fodor's Choice | coed dining room are among Rome's most spectacular settings. While
★ | La Veranda has classic Roman cuisine on tap, the kitchen imparts nice, refreshing twists on the familiar with an innovative use of flavor combinations. The menu changes seasonally, but can include such offerings as an eggplant *caponata* with *burrata* cheese and *bottarga* (salted fish roe) from Sardinia, Piedmontese oxtail soup, or a risotto with Barolo wine, blue cheese, and quail carpacco with mustard seeds. Call ahead, especially on Saturday, because the hotel often hosts weddings, which close the restaurant, and you don't want to miss passing a few hours of your Roman Holiday in these environs. $ *Average meal: €65* ✉ *Borgo Santo Spirito 73, Borgo, near the Vatican* ☎ *06/6872973* ⊕ *www.laveranda. net* ⚸ *Reservations essential* ✛ *1:B3.*

$$$ | ✕ **Taverna Angelica.** The area surrounding St. Peter's Basilica isn't known
MODERN ITALIAN | for culinary excellence, but this is an exception. Its tiny size allows the
Fodor's Choice | chef to concentrate on each individual dish, and the menu is creative
★ | without being pretentious. Dishes such as warm scampi with artichokes and tomatoes are more about taste than presentation. The breast of duck with honey and rye bread brings hunter's cuisine to a new level, and spaghetti with crunchy pancetta and leeks is what the Brits call "more-ish" (meaning you want *more* of it). Fresh sliced tuna in a pistachio crust with orange sauce is light and delicious. It may be difficult to find, on a section of the street that's set back and almost subterranean, but Taverna Angelica is worth seeking out. $ *Average meal: €55* ✉ *Piazza A. Capponi 6, Borgo* ☎ *06/6874514* ⊕ *www.tavernaangelica. it* ⚸ *Reservations essential* ۩ *No lunch Mon.–Sat.* Ⓜ *Ottaviano* ✛ *1:B2.*

PRATI

$$$ | ✕ **Dal Toscano.** An open wood-fired grill and classic dishes such as *ribol-
TUSCAN | lita* (a thick bread and vegetable soup) and *pici* (fresh, thick pasta with wild hare sauce) are the draw at this great family-run Tuscan trattoria near the Vatican. The cuts of beef visible at the entrance tell you right away that the house special is the prized *bistecca alla fiorentina*—a thick grilled steak seared on the outside and rare in the middle, with its rub of gutsy Tuscan olive oil and sea salt forming a delicious crust to keep in the natural juices. Seating outside on the sidewalk in warm

weather is a nice touch. $\boxed{S}$ *Average meal: €55* ⊠ *Via Germanico 58/60, Prati* ☏ *06/39725717* ⊕ *www.ristorantedaltoscano.it* ☉ *Closed Mon. and 3 wks in Aug.* Ⓜ *Ottaviano–San Pietro–Musei Vaticani* ✛ *1:B2.*

NORTHWEST ROME

$$$$
MODERN ITALIAN
Fodor's Choice
★

✕ **La Pergola.** La Pergola's rooftop location offers a commanding view of the city, and as you're seated in your plush chair, you know you're in for a three–Michelin star experience, and the only one in Rome. First, your waiter will present you with menus: food, wine, and water (you read correctly). Then you must choose between the German Wunder-chef Heinz Beck's *alta cucina* specialties, though most everything will prove to be the best version of the dish you've ever tasted. Lobster is oh-so-lightly poached, and fish is cooked perfectly, including the delicious black cod with a celery sauce and curry crust. Each course comes with a flourish of sauces or extra touches that makes it an event in its own right, while the cheese cart is well explained by knowledgeable servers. The dessert course is extravagant, including tiny petits fours and treats tucked away in small drawers that make up the serving "cabinet." The wine list is as thrilling as one might expect with the financial backing of the Waldorf-Astoria and their investment in one of the top wine cellars in Italy. $\boxed{S}$ *Average meal: €150* ⊠ *Rome Cavalieri, Via Cadlolo 101, Monte Mario, Northwest Rome* ☏ *06/35092152* ⊕ *www.romecavalieri. com/lapergola.php* ⚞ *Reservations essential* 🎩 *Jacket and tie* ☉ *Closed Sun. and Mon., 2 wks in Aug., and most of Jan. No lunch* ✛ *1:A1.*

TRASTEVERE

$$$$
MODERN ITALIAN

✕ **Glass Hostaria.** After 14 years in Austin, Texas, Glass chef Cristina Bowerman returned to Rome to reconnect with her Italian roots. Her cooking is as innovative as the building she works in—which has received numerous recognitions for its architecture and design since opening in 2004—but Bowerman still abides by some cardinal Italian kitchen rules, such as the use of fresh, local, and seasonal ingredients. The menu changes frequently, but with an impassioned sense for detail, taste, and presentation, Bowerman comes up with dishes like tagliatelle pasta with eggplant, prunes and ricotta affumicata; scallops with pistachio cream and seasonal mushrooms; and for dessert, a passion fruit *crema cotta* (frozen custard) with lychees, cornbread and popcorn granita. Need help pairing your wine? Glass offers more than 600 labels for interested oenophiles. $\boxed{S}$ *Average meal: €85* ⊠ *Vicolo del Cinque 58, Trastevere* ☏ *06/58335903* ⊕ *www.glass-hostaria.com* ☉ *Closed Mon. No lunch* ✛ *1:D5.*

$
PIZZA
FAMILY

✕ **Panattoni.** Nicknamed *"ai marmi"* ("the mortuary") for its marble-slab tables, Panattoni is actually about as lively as you can get. Packed every night, it serves crisp pizzas that come out of the wood-burning ovens at top speed. The fried starters here, like a nice *baccalà* (cod), are light and tasty. Panattoni stays open well past midnight, convenient for a late meal after the theater or a movie nearby. $\boxed{S}$ *Average meal: €20* ⊠ *Viale Trastevere 53–57, Trastevere* ☏ *06/5800919* ⚞ *Reservations not accepted* ▭ *No credit cards* ☉ *Closed Wed. and 3 wks in Aug. No lunch* ✛ *1:D6.*

$$$ ROMAN 🍴 **Romolo.** Nowhere else do the lingering rays of the setting Roman sun seem more inviting than within the famed tavern garden of this charming Trastevere haunt—right by the arch of Porta Settimiana, this was reputedly the onetime home of Raphael's lady love, La Fornarina. And though belly-warming winter meals can be enjoyed in the ancient palazzo, it's the outdoor garden seating that makes this a truly coveted dining spot in the summer months. Who can resist classic spaghetti alla carbonara or pasta all'amatriciana in these surroundings? House specialties include the *mozzarella alla fornarina* (deep-fried mozzarella with ham and anchovies) and anything with the chef's legendary artichoke sauce. Service is equally warm and the wine list as local as the staff. [$] *Average meal: €50* ✉ *Via di Porta Settimiana 8, Trastevere* ☎ *06/5818284* 🌐 *www.ristoranteromolo.it* ✍ *Reservations essential* 🕒 *Closed Mon.* ✢ *1:C5.*

TESTACCIO

$$$$ ROMAN 🍴 **Checchino dal 1887.** Literally carved out of a hill of ancient shards of amphorae, Checchino remains an example of a classic, family-run Roman restaurant, with one of the best wine cellars in the region. Though the slaughterhouses of Testaccio are long gone, an echo of their past existence lives on in the restaurant's soul food—mostly offal and other less–appealing cuts like *trippa* (tripe), *pajata* (intestine with the mother's milk still inside), and *coratella* (sweetbreads and heart of beef) are all still on the menu for die-hard Roman purists. For the less adventuresome, house specialties include braised milk-fed lamb with seasonal vegetables. Head here for a taste of old Rome, but note that Checchino is really beginning to show its age. [$] *Average meal: €70* ✉ *Via di Monte Testaccio 30, Testaccio* ☎ *06/5746318* 🌐 *www.checchino-dal-1887.com* 🕒 *Closed Sun., Mon., Aug, and 1 wk at Christmas* ✢ *1:F6.*

$$ ROMAN 🍴 **Perilli.** In this restaurant dating from 1911, the old Testaccio remains, as proven by the interior style. A seasonal antipasto table starts things off, offering Roman specialties like stewed Roman artichokes and *puntarelle* (curled chicory stems in a garlicky vinaigrette with lots of lemon and anchovy). The waiters wear crooked bow ties and are just a little bit too hurried—until, that is, you order classics like pasta all'amatriciana and carbonara, which they relish tossing in a big bowl tableside. This is also the place to try rigatoni *con pajata* (with calves' intestines)—if you're into that sort of thing. Secondi plates are for meat-eaters only, and the house wine is a golden enamel-remover from the Castelli Romani. [$] *Average meal: €40* ✉ *Via Marmorata 39, Testaccio* ☎ *06/5742415* 🕒 *Closed Wed.* [M] *Piramide* ✢ *1:F6.*

$ PIZZA 🍴 **Remo.** Expect a wait at this perennial favorite in Testaccio frequented by students and locals. You won't find tablecloths or other nonessentials, just classic Roman pizza and boisterous conversation. [$] *Average meal: €18* ✉ *Piazza Santa Maria Liberatrice 44, Testaccio* ☎ *06/5746270* 💳 *No credit cards* 🕒 *Closed Sun., Aug., and Christmas wk. No lunch* ✢ *1:F6.*

WHERE TO STAY

1

Updated
by Amanda
Ruggeri

Lodging options in Rome are abundant. Over the past decade or so there's been an upswing in the number of bed-and-breakfasts, stylish boutique hotels, and lodgings with over-the-top opulence. At the same time, there continue to be many modest, budget hotels and *pensioni* (small family-run accommodations).

If swanky is what you're after, the best place to look is in the Spanish Steps and Via Veneto areas. On the flip side, many of the city's lower-cost accommodations are scattered near the Stazione Termini. But for the most convenient Roman experience, stay in or near the *centro storico* (the historic center), where you'll be able to cover most of the main attractions on foot.

Exact prices listed are for a standard double room in high season.

Hotel reviews have been condensed for this book. Please go to Fodors. com for expanded reviews of each property.

Use the coordinate (⊕ B2) at the end of each listing to locate a site on the Where to Stay in Rome map.

PANTHEON, NAVONA, AND TREVI

PANTHEON

$$$
HOTEL
Fodor'sChoice
★

Albergo Santa Chiara. If you're looking for a good location (right behind the Pantheon) and top-notch service—not to mention comfortable beds and a quiet stay—look no further. **Pros:** great location in the historical center; staff is polite and helpful; lovely terrace/sitting area in front, overlooking the piazza. **Cons:** the rooms are small and could use some restyling; some rooms don't have a window. $ *Rooms from: €250* ⊠ *Via Santa Chiara 21, Pantheon* ☎ *06/6872979* ⊕ *www. albergosantachiara.com* ➷ *96 rooms, 3 suites, 3 apartments* ⍟ *Breakfast* ⊕ *2:E4.*

$$$$
HOTEL

Pantheon. A superb little hotel right next to the monument itself, the Pantheon has a typically Roman lobby—warm and cozy yet opulent—and equally welcoming staff that exemplifies true Italian hospitality. **Pros:** proximity to the Pantheon; big, clean bathrooms; friendly staff. **Cons:** rooms are in need of some upgrading; the lighting is low and the rooms can feel a bit stuffy. $ *Rooms from: €320* ⊠ *Via dei Pastini 131, Pantheon* ☎ *06/6787746* ⊕ *www.hotelpantheon.com* ➷ *12 rooms, 1 suite* ⍟ *Breakfast* ⊕ *2:E4.*

NAVONA

$$
HOTEL

Genio. Just outside one of Rome's most beautiful piazzas—Piazza Navona—this pleasant hotel with good-size rooms has a lovely rooftop terrace where you can relax with a cup of coffee or glass of wine and enjoy the view. **Pros:** great view from the rooftop terrace; rooms are a decent size for a Roman hotel; the bathrooms are elegantly designed. **Cons:** On a busy street so there is often traffic noise; walls are paper-thin; both the decoration and the carpet have seen better days. $ *Rooms from: €180* ⊠ *Via Giuseppe Zanardelli 28, Navona* ☎ *06/6832191* ⊕ *www.hotelgenioroma.it* ➷ *60 rooms* ⍟ *Breakfast* ⊕ *2:D3.*

$$$ HOTEL

[🏨] Relais Palazzo Taverna. This little hidden gem, on a side street behind the lovely Via dei Coronari, is a pleasant surprise for travelers who happen to stumble upon it. **Pros:** centrally located; boutique-style at moderate prices. **Cons:** breakfast is served in your room; staff is on duty only until 11 pm (although in the case of an emergency, they can be contacted after hours). [$] *Rooms from: €210* ✉ *Via dei Gabrielli 92, Navona* ☎ *06/20398064* 🌐 *www.relaispalazzotaverna.com* 🛏 *11 rooms* 🍴 *Breakfast* ✣ *2:D6.*

TREVI

$$$ HOTEL

[🏨] Trevi. Location, location, location—this delightful place is tucked away down one of Old Rome's quaintest alleys near the Trevi Fountain. **Pros:** pass the Trevi Fountain each day as you come and go; comfortable rooms; roof-garden restaurant. **Cons:** breakfast room is cramped; this area can be very noisy due to foot traffic around the Trevi Fountain. [$] *Rooms from: €240* ✉ *Vicolo del Babbuccio 20/21, Trevi* ☎ *06/6789563* 🌐 *www.hoteltrevirome.com* 🛏 *29 rooms* 🍴 *Breakfast* ✣ *2:F3.*

CAMPO DE' FIORI AND GHETTO

CAMPO DE' FIORI

$$ B&B/INN Fodor's Choice ★

[🏨] Casa di Santa Brigida. The friendly sisters of Santa Brigida oversee simple, straightforward, and centrally located accommodations—right next to Campo de' Fiori—in one of Rome's loveliest convents, with a rooftop terrace overlooking Palazzo Farnese. **Pros:** no curfew in this historic convent; insider papal tickets; location in the Piazza Farnese. **Cons:** weak a/c; no TVs in the rooms (though there is a common TV room); mediocre breakfast. [$] *Rooms from: €160* ✉ *Piazza Farnese 96, entrance around the corner at Via Monserrato 54, Campo de' Fiori* ☎ *06/68892596* 🌐 *www.brigidine.org* 🛏 *2 rooms* 🍴 *Breakfast* ✣ *2:D4.*

$$$ HOTEL

[🏨] Hotel Campo de' Fiori. Each room in this ivy-draped hotel, perhaps one of Rome's most handsome, is entirely unique in its colors, furnishings, and refined feel, and the views of Roman rooftops from the terrace certainly don't disappoint. **Pros:** modern amenities such as flat-screen LCD TV with satellite, individual air-conditioning, and free Wi-Fi; rooftop terrace; a 5% discount if you pay in cash. **Cons:** some of the rooms are very small; the staff isn't as hospitable as most Italians. [$] *Rooms from: €300* ✉ *Via del Biscione 6, Campo de' Fiori* ☎ *06/68806865* 🌐 *www.hotelcampodefiori.it* 🛏 *23 rooms* 🍴 *Breakfast* ✣ *2:D4.*

$$$ HOTEL Fodor's Choice ★

[🏨] Hotel Ponte Sisto. With one of the prettiest patio-courtyards in Rome (Europe?), this hotel—a gorgeously renovated palazzo—offers its own blissful definition of *Pax Romana*: peace, indeed, will be yours, just two steps from Trastevere and Campo de' Fiori. **Pros:** staff is friendly; rooms with views (and some with balconies and terraces); luxury bathrooms; beautiful courtyard garden. **Cons:** street-side rooms can be a bit noisy; some rooms are on the small side; meals at the restaurant can only be planned for groups. [$] *Rooms from: €300* ✉ *Via dei Pettinari 64, Campo de' Fiori* ☎ *06/686310* 🌐 *www.hotelpontesisto.it* 🛏 *103 rooms, 4 suites* 🍴 *Breakfast* ✣ *2:D5.*

GHETTO

$$
HOTEL

Arenula. A hefty bargain by Rome standards, with an almost unbeatable location (in the Ghetto just across the river from Trastevere), the Arenula has an imposingly elegant stone exterior, and simple but comfortable rooms. **Pros:** a real bargain; conveniently located, close to Campo de' Fiori and Trastevere; spotless. **Cons:** totally no-frills accommodations; no elevator; can still be a bit noisy despite the double-glazed windows. $ *Rooms from: €133* ⊠ *Via Santa Maria dei Calderari 47, off Via Arenula, Ghetto* ☎ *06/6879454* ⊕ *www.hotelarenula.com* ⤴ *50 rooms* ⦿ *Breakfast* ✛ *2:E5.*

VENETO AND SPAGNA

VENETO

$$$
HOTEL
Fodor'sChoice
★

Aleph. If you're wondering where the beautiful people are, look no further than the Aleph, the most unfalteringly fashionable of Rome's design hotels, über-designed by Adam Tihany with a just-this-side-of-kitsch theme of Dante's Divine Comedy. **Pros:** free access to the spa for hotel guests; award-winning design; free Wi-Fi. **Cons:** rooms are too petite for the price; cocktails are expensive. $ *Rooms from: €280* ⊠ *Via San Basilio 15, Veneto* ☎ *06/422901* ⊕ *aleph-roma.boscolohotels.com* ⤴ *90 rooms, 6 suites* ⦿ *No meals* Ⓜ *Barberini–Fontana di Trevi* ✛ *2:G2.*

$$$
B&B/INN
Fodor'sChoice
★

Daphne Veneto. Inspired by Baroque artist Gianlorenzo Bernini's exquisite *Apollo and Daphne* sculpture at the Borghese Gallery, this is an "urban B&B" run by people who love Rome and will do their best to make sure you love it, too. **Pros:** the opportunity to see Rome "like an insider"; beds have Simmons mattresses and fluffy comforters. **Cons:** no TVs; some bathrooms are shared; only accepts Visa or MasterCard to hold bookings (though you can actually pay with an AmEx). $ *Rooms from: €230* ⊠ *Via di San Basilio 55, Veneto* ☎ *06/87450087* ⊕ *www.daphne-rome.com* ⤴ *7 rooms, 2 suites* ⦿ *Breakfast* Ⓜ *Barberini/Fontana di Trevi* ✛ *2:G3.*

$$$$
HOTEL
Fodor'sChoice
★

Eden. One of Rome's top luxury lodgings, once a favorite haunt of Hemingway, Ingrid Bergman, and Fellini, this superlative hotel combines dashing elegance, exquisitely lush interiors, and stunning vistas with true Italian hospitality. **Pros:** gorgeous mirrored roof terrace restaurant; you could be rubbing elbows with the stars; 24-hour room service. **Cons:** expensive; Wi-Fi costs €15 per day; some say the staff can be hit-or-miss. $ *Rooms from: €440* ⊠ *Via Ludovisi 49, Veneto* ☎ *06/478121* ⊕ *www.lemeridien.com/eden* ⤴ *121 rooms, 13 suites* ⦿ *No meals* Ⓜ *Spagna* ✛ *2:G2.*

SPAGNA

$$$$
HOTEL

D'Inghilterra. From monarchs and movie moguls to some of the greatest writers of all time, this hotel has welcomed Rome's most discerning tourists since it opened in 1845. **Pros:** distinct character and opulence; turndown service (with chocolates!); genuinely friendly and attentive staff. **Cons:** the elevator is small and slow; bathrooms are surprisingly petite; despite soundproofing, it's still noisy. $ *Rooms from: €520* ⊠ *Via Bocca di Leone 14, Spagna* ☎ *06/699811* ⊕ *www.hoteldinghilterraroma.it* ⤴ *81 rooms, 7 suites* ⦿ *No meals* Ⓜ *Spagna* ✛ *2:E3.*

BEST BETS FOR ROME LODGING

Fodor's offers a selective listing of quality lodgings at every price range, from the city's best budget motel to its most sophisticated luxury hotel. Here, we've compiled our top picks by price and experience. The best properties—those that provide a particularly remarkable experience in their price range—are designated in the listings with the Fodor's Choice logo.

Fodor's Choice ★

Albergo Santa Chiara, $$$, p. 113
Aleph, $$$, p. 115
The Beehive, $, p. 120
Casa di Santa Brigida, $$, p. 114
Casa di Santa Francesca Romana, $$, p. 121
Daphne Veneto, $$$, p. 115
Eden, $$$$, p. 115
Exedra, $$$$, p. 120
Hassler, $$$$, p. 117
Hotel Ponte Sisto, $$$, p. 114
Hotel Santa Maria, $$$, p. 122
Il Palazzetto, $$$$, p. 117
Relais Le Clarisse, $$$, p. 122
Residenza Paolo VI, $$$, p. 121
Scalinata di Spagna, $$$, p. 117
Yes Hotel, $, p. 121

By Price

$

The Beehive, p. 120
Hotel Trastevere, p. 122
Panda, p. 117
Yes Hotel, p. 121

$$

Casa di Santa Brigida, p. 114
Italia, p. 120

$$$

Albergo Santa Chiara, p. 113
Aleph, p. 115
Daphne Veneto, p. 115
Hotel Campo de' Fiori, p. 114
Hotel Ponte Sisto, p. 114
Hotel Santa Maria, p. 122
Relais Le Clarisse, p. 122
Scalinata di Spagna, p. 117

$$$$

Eden, p. 115
Hassler, p. 117
Hotel de Russie, p. 117
Pantheon, p. 113

Best by Experience

B&BS

Daphne Veneto, $$$, p. 115
Relais Le Clarisse, $$$, p. 122

BUSINESS TRAVEL

Exedra, $$$$, p. 120

CONCIERGE

The Beehive, $, p. 120
Daphne Veneto, $$$, p. 115
Scalinata di Spagna, $$$, p. 117

DESIGN

Exedra, $$$$, p. 120

CHILD-FRIENDLY

Hassler, $$$$, p. 117
Hotel Ponte Sisto, $$$, p. 114
Hotel de Russie, $$$$, p. 117

GREAT VIEWS

Eden, $$$$, p. 115
Genio, $$, p. 113
Hassler, $$$$, p. 117
Hotel Campo de' Fiori, $$$, p. 114

HIDDEN OASES

Domus Aventina, $$$, p. 122
Hotel Santa Maria, $$$$, p. 122

MOST ROMANTIC

Daphne Veneto, $$$, p. 115
Relais Le Clarisse, $$$$, p. 122

$$$$ HOTEL Fodor's Choice ★ **Hassler.** When it comes to million-dollar views, this exclusive hotel atop the Spanish Steps has the best seats in the house, which is why the rich and famous—Tom Cruise and Jennifer Lopez included—are willing to pay top dollar to stay here. **Pros:** charming old-world feel; prime location and panoramic views; near some of the best shopping in the world. **Cons:** VIP prices; many think the staff is too standoffish; spa facilities are far from 5-star material. [$] *Rooms from: €780* ✉ *Piazza Trinità dei Monti 6, Spagna* ☎ *06/69934755, 800/223–6800 toll-free from the U.S.* 🌐 *www.hotelhasslerroma.com* 🛏 *82 rooms, 14 suites* 🍴 *No meals* [M] *Spagna* ✥ *2:F2.*

$$$$ HOTEL FAMILY **Hotel de Russie.** A ritzy retreat for government bigwigs and Hollywood high rollers, the de Russie is just steps away from the famed Piazza del Popolo and occupies a 19th-century hotel that once hosted royalty, Picasso, and Cocteau. **Pros:** big potential for celebrity sightings; activities for children; extensive gardens (including a butterfly reserve); first-rate luxury spa. **Cons:** hotel is a bit worn around the edges; interior is generic-luxe; breakfast is not included; avoid street-side rooms. [$] *Rooms from: €750* ✉ *Via del Babuino 9, Popolo* ☎ *06/328881* 🌐 *www.rfhotels.com* 🛏 *89 rooms, 33 suites* 🍴 *No meals* [M] *Flaminio* ✥ *2:E1.*

$$ HOTEL **Hotel Suisse.** In the same family for more than three generations, this lovely little hotel is on a picturesque and fabled street minutes from the Spanish Steps and its famous boutiques. **Pros:** good value for reasonable price; the rooms are obviously cared for; great location. **Cons:** breakfast is taken in your room. [$] *Rooms from: €170* ✉ *Via Gregoriana 54, Veneto* ☎ *06/6783649* 🌐 *www.hotelsuisserome.com* 🛏 *12 rooms* 🍴 *Breakfast* [M] *Barberini–Fontana di Trevi, Spagna* ✥ *2:F3.*

$$$$ B&B/INN Fodor's Choice ★ **Il Palazzetto.** If you have ever fantasized about staying in one of those houses that perch over the Spanish Steps, you can make that dream your very special reality here, and recline on the gorgeous terrace to watch the neverending street theater that is the Scalinatella. **Pros:** that address, that view; gourmet restaurant. **Cons:** restaurant here is often rented out for crowded special events; bedrooms do not access the communal terraces. [$] *Rooms from: €350* ✉ *Vicolo del Bottino 8, Spagna* ☎ *06/6993-41000* 🌐 *www.ilpalazzettoroma.com/* 🛏 *4* 🍴 *No meals* [M] *Spagna* ✥ *2:F2.*

$ HOTEL **Panda.** You couldn't possibly find a better deal in Rome than here at the Panda—especially given its key location just behind the Spanish Steps on one of the poshest shopping streets in the centro. **Pros:** discount if you pay cash; free Wi-Fi; on a quiet street, but still close to the Spanish Steps. **Cons:** Wi-Fi signal can be a bit weak; not all rooms have private bathrooms; no elevator directly to floor; no TVs in the rooms. [$] *Rooms from: €100* ✉ *Via della Croce 35, Spagna* ☎ *06/6780179* 🌐 *www.hotelpanda.it* 🛏 *28 rooms, 20 with bath* 🍴 *No meals* [M] *Spagna* ✥ *2:E2.*

$$$ B&B/INN Fodor's Choice ★ **Scalinata di Spagna.** This tiny hotel's prime location at the top of the Spanish Steps and its quiet, sunny charm all add to the character that guests fall in love with over and over again—which explains why it's often booked up for months, even years ahead. **Pros:** friendly and helpful concierge; fresh fruit in the rooms; free Wi-Fi throughout. **Cons:** it's a hike up the hill to the hotel; no porter and no elevator; service can be hit-or-miss. [$] *Rooms from: €250* ✉ *Piazza Trinità dei Monti 17, Spagna* ☎ *06/6793006* 🌐 *www.hotelscalinata.com* 🛏 *16 rooms* 🍴 *Breakfast* [M] *Spagna* ✥ *2:F2.*

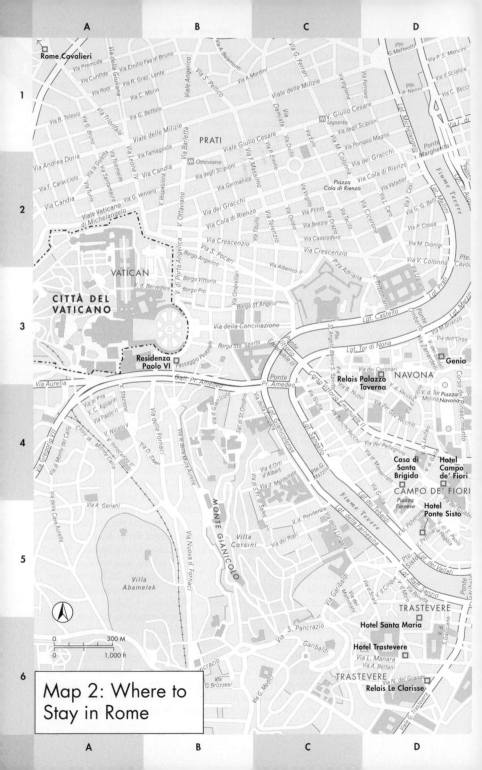

Map 2: Where to Stay in Rome

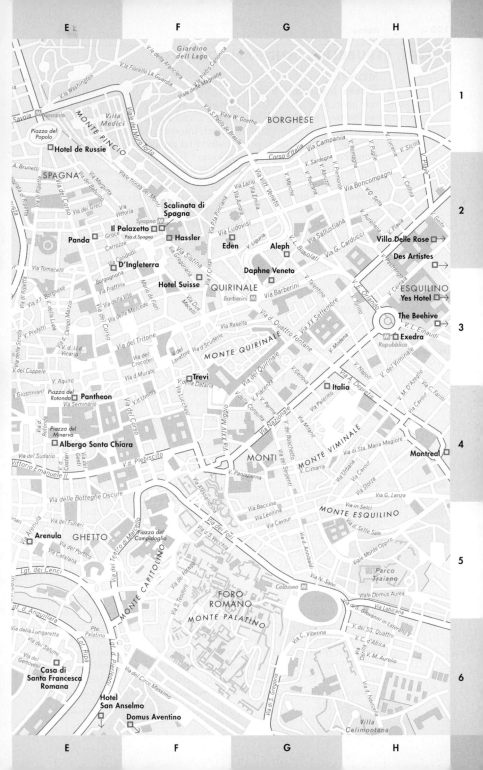

MONTI, REPUBBLICA, AND SAN LORENZO

MONTI

$$
HOTEL
▦ **Italia.** Just a block from bustling Via Nazionale, this friendly, family-run hotel feels like a classic pensione: low budget with a lot of heart, inexpensive rooms with big windows, and a generous buffet breakfast. **Pros:** free Wi-Fi throughout the hotel; Internet point for guests traveling without a laptop; great price; individual attention and personal care. **Cons:** can be a bit noisy; a/c is an extra €10. Ⓢ *Rooms from: €135* ✉ *Via Venezia 18, Monti* ☎ *06/4828355* ⊕ *www.hotelitaliaroma.com* ⮠ *35 rooms, 1 apartment* ⦿ *Breakfast* Ⓜ *Repubblica* ✚ *2:G4.*

$$
B&B/INN
▦ **Montreal.** A good choice for budget travelers, this modest hotel with bright, cozy rooms is on a central avenue across the square from Santa Maria Maggiore, and three blocks from Stazione Termini. **Pros:** informative and helpful staff provides maps and good recommendations; bathrooms are spacious. **Cons:** can be noisy at night; need to take a bus or a metro to get to most of the sights. Ⓢ *Rooms from: €125* ✉ *Via Carlo Alberto 4, Esquilino* ☎ *06/4457797* ⊕ *www.hotelmontrealroma. com* ⮠ *27 rooms* ⦿ *Breakfast* Ⓜ *Vittorio Emanuele* ✚ *2:G4.*

REPUBBLICA

$
B&B/INN
Fodor'sChoice
★
▦ **The Beehive.** Living the American dream in Italy is exactly what one Los Angeles couple did in 1999, when they opened the Beehive, a hip, alternative budget hotel near Termini station where you can go organic in the on-site caffè, or lounge the afternoon away in the lovely garden or reading lounge. **Pros:** massage and other therapies offered on-site; organic weekend brunches and dinners on Wednesday and weekends. **Cons:** some rooms share bathrooms; in classic rooms, no TV or a/c; breakfast is not included in the room rate. Ⓢ *Rooms from: €80* ✉ *Via Marghera 8, San Lorenzo* ☎ *06/44704553* ⊕ *www.the-beehive.com* ⮠ *8 rooms, 1 dormitory, 3 apartments* ⦿ *No meals* ✚ *2:H3.*

$$$$
HOTEL
Fodor'sChoice
★
▦ **Exedra.** If Rome's semi-stodgy hotel scene has an It-Girl, it's this place, where high rollers love to host splashy parties by the rooftop swimming pool and magazines love to rave about them. **Pros:** spacious and attractive rooms; great spa and pool; terrace with cocktail service; close to Termini station. **Cons:** food and beverages are expensive; beyond the immediate vicinity, parts of the neighborhood can be sketchy. Ⓢ *Rooms from: €345* ✉ *Piazza della Repubblica 47, Repubblica* ☎ *06/489381* ⊕ *www.boscolohotels.com* ⮠ *220 rooms, 18 suites* ⦿ *Breakfast* ✚ *2:H3.*

SAN LORENZO

$$
HOTEL
▦ **Des Artistes.** The three Riccioni brothers have put their hearts and souls into making this delightful hotel the crème de la crème of this neighborhood, but still offer a "hostel" floor for travelers on a budget. **Pros:** good value; decent-size rooms; relaxing roof garden. **Cons:** breakfast room is small; reception is on the fifth floor; you have to pay for Wi-Fi in your room (although it's free in common areas). Ⓢ *Rooms from: €159* ✉ *Via Villafranca 20, Castro Pretorio* ☎ *06/4454365* ⊕ *www.hoteldesartistes.com* ⮠ *48 rooms* ⦿ *Breakfast* Ⓜ *Castro Pretorio* ✚ *2:H2.*

$$ **Villa delle Rose.** When the Eternal City becomes too chaotic for
HOTEL you, head to this relaxing retreat in a charming 19th-century palazzo, minutes away from Termini Station, with its beautiful rose garden where guests can sip afternoon tea. **Pros:** delightful garden with blooming roses and jasmine; free parking; free Wi-Fi. **Cons:** some of the rooms are small (ask for a larger one); the elevator is also small; no breakfast. $ *Rooms from: €130* ⊠ *Via Vicenza 5, Repubblica* ☎ *06/4451795* ⊕ *www.villadellerose.it* ☞ *36 rooms* ᵢ◯ᵢ *No meals* Ⓜ *Termini* ✛ *2:H2.*

$ **Yes Hotel.** This chic hotel may fool you into thinking these digs are
HOTEL expensive, but the contemporary coolness comes at a budget price,
Fodor'sChoice and its location near Termini Station makes it a great base for sight-
★ seeing. **Pros:** flat-screen TVs with satellite TV; around the corner from Termini Station; doesn't have the feel of a budget hotel; discount if you pay cash; great value. **Cons:** rooms are small; charge for Wi-Fi. $ *Rooms from: €100* ⊠ *Via Magenta 15, Termini* ☎ *06/44363836* ⊕ *www.yeshotelrome.com* ☞ *38 rooms, 2 suites* ᵢ◯ᵢ *Breakfast* Ⓜ *Termini, Castro Pretorio* ✛ *2:H3.*

VATICAN AND NORTHWEST ROME

VATICAN

$$$ **Residenza Paolo VI.** In a former monastery that's still an extraterri-
HOTEL torial part of the Vatican, this hotel (pronounced Paolo Sesto) enjoys
Fodor'sChoice one of the most spectacular perches in Rome—magnificently abutting
★ Bernini's colonnade of St. Peter's Square. **Pros:** unparalleled views of St. Peter's from the roof terrace; quiet rooms; huge breakfast spread. **Cons:** the small rooms are really small; bathrooms are small; the atmosphere at night is a little too quiet. $ *Rooms from: €295* ⊠ *Via Paolo VI 29, Vatican* ☎ *06/684870* ⊕ *www.residenzapaolovi.com* ☞ *35 rooms* ᵢ◯ᵢ *Breakfast* Ⓜ *Ottaviano* ✛ *2:B3.*

NORTHWEST ROME

$$$$ **Rome Cavalieri.** Though it's outside the city center, distance has its
RESORT advantages—in addition to the magnificent view over Rome from its hilltop site, this place feels more like a ritzy resort because of it's vast grounds and Olympic-size pool. **Pros:** beautiful bird's-eye view of Rome; complimentary shuttle to the city center; three-Michelin-star dining. **Cons:** you definitely pay for the luxury of staying here—everything is expensive; outside the city center; not all rooms have the view. $ *Rooms from: €500* ⊠ *Via Cadlolo 101, Monte Mario* ☎ *06/35091* ⊕ *www.romecavalieri.com* ☞ *345 rooms, 25 suites* ᵢ◯ᵢ *Breakfast* ✛ *2:A1.*

TRASTEVERE

$$ **Casa di Santa Francesca Romana.** In the heart of Trastevere, but tucked
HOTEL away from the hustle and bustle of the medieval quarter, this simply
Fodor'sChoice delightful hotel in a former monastery has fabulous location and is
★ a spectacular buy for the money. **Pros:** the price can't be beat; excellent restaurants nearby; delicious breakfast; away from rowdy side of Trastevere. **Cons:** thin walls; interior is a bit bland; few amenities, other

than a TV room and reading room. [$] *Rooms from: €130* ✉ *Via dei Vasceillari 61, Trastevere* ☎ *06/5812125* 🌐 *www.sfromana.it* 🛏 *37 rooms* 🍴 *Breakfast* ✣ *2:E6.*

$$$ HOTEL Fodor's Choice ★ 🏨 **Hotel Santa Maria.** A Trastevere treasure with a pedigree going back four centuries, this ivy-covered, mansard-roofed, rosy-brick-red, erstwhile Renaissance-era convent is just steps away from the glorious Santa Maria in Trastevere church and a few blocks from the Tiber. **Pros:** a quaint and pretty oasis in a central location; relaxing courtyard; stocked wine bar. **Cons:** it might be tricky to find; some of the showers drain slowly; finding a cab is not always easy in Trastevere. [$] *Rooms from: €230* ✉ *Vicolo del Piede 2, Trastevere* ☎ *06/5894626* 🌐 *www.htlsantamaria.com* 🛏 *20 rooms* 🍴 *Breakfast* ✣ *2:D6.*

$ HOTEL 🏨 **Hotel Trastevere.** This tiny hotel captures the village-like charm of the Trastevere district with its exposed medieval brickwork, a scattering of antiques, and a lively food market on the piazza outside. **Pros:** cheap with a good location; convenient to transportation; free Wi-Fi; friendly staff. **Cons:** no frills; few amenities. [$] *Rooms from: €105* ✉ *Via Luciano Manara 24–25, Trastevere* ☎ *06/5814713* 🌐 *www.hoteltrastevere.net* 🛏 *18 rooms* 🍴 *Breakfast* ✣ *2:D6.*

$$$ B&B/INN Fodor's Choice ★ 🏨 **Relais Le Clarisse.** Within the former cloister grounds of the Santa Chiara order, with gardens so beautiful you'd think yourself in Sorrento or Capri, this charming oasis is exceptionally welcoming thanks to the comfortable size of the accommodations and the warm personal service. **Pros:** spacious rooms with comfy beds; high-tech showers/tubs with good water pressure; staff is multilingual, friendly, and at your service. **Cons:** this part of Trastevere can be noisy at night; the rooms here fill up quickly. [$] *Rooms from: €220* ✉ *Via Cardinale Merry del Val 20, Trastevere* ☎ *06/58334437* 🌐 *www.leclarisse.com* 🛏 *5 rooms, 3 suites* 🍴 *Breakfast* ✣ *2:D6.*

AVENTINO

$$$ HOTEL 🏨 **Domus Aventina.** The best part of this quaint, friendly hotel is that it's between two of Rome's loveliest gardens—a municipal rose garden and Rome's famous Orange Garden—in the heart of the historic Aventine district. **Pros:** quiet location; walking distance to tourist attractions; complimentary Wi-Fi throughout. **Cons:** no elevator; small showers; no tubs. [$] *Rooms from: €205* ✉ *Via di Santa Prisca 11/b, Aventino* ☎ *06/5746135* 🌐 *www.hoteldomusaventina.com* 🛏 *26 rooms* 🍴 *Breakfast* [M] *Circo Massimo* ✣ *2:F6.*

$$$ HOTEL 🏨 **Hotel San Anselmo.** With a sleek metropolitan feel, this romantic 19th-century villa atop the Aventine Hill blends bits of Baroque antique-flair (such as period chandeliers) with contemporary pieces (such as the sharp stainless steel fireplace in the public spaces), all within a charming garden. **Pros:** free Wi-Fi; historic building with artful interior; great showers with jets; a garden where you can enjoy your breakfast. **Cons:** some consider it a bit of a hike to sights; limited public transportation. [$] *Rooms from: €210* ✉ *Piazza San Anselmo 2, Aventino* ☎ *06/570057* 🌐 *www.aventinohotels.com* 🛏 *38 rooms* 🍴 *Breakfast* ✣ *2:E6.*

NIGHTLIFE AND THE ARTS

THE ARTS

Updated by Amanda Ruggeri

Rome has a good range of publications with timely information regarding events and happenings in the city. Begin with the city's official website (⊕ *www.comune.roma.it*). Likewise, events listings can be found in the *Cronaca* and *Cultura* sections of Italian newspapers, as well as in *Metro* (the free newspaper). Flip to the back for the brief yet detailed English-language section. Check out the events site ⊕ *inromenow.com* and ⊕ *www.romeing.it*, in English, as well as the monthly updated *Time Out Rome* (⊕ *www.timeout.com/travel/rome*) and *The American* (⊕ *www.theamericanmag.com*). In addition, consult the monthly English-language periodical (with accompanying website) *Wanted in Rome* (⊕ *www.wantedinrome.com*), available at many newsstands.

TICKETS

Hello Ticket. One of Italy's largest ticket vendors (both online and at ticket offices), Hello Ticket covers major musical performances and cultural events in Rome and throughout Italy. ⊠ *Viale Alessandro Manzoni 53, San Giovanni* ☎ *06/48078202* ⊕ *www.helloticket.it.*

Orbis. An in-person ticket vendor, Orbis stocks a wide array of tickets for music, cultural, and performance events. ⊠ *Piazza dell'Esquilino 37, Repubblica* ☎ *06/4827403.*

TicketOne. For blockbuster cultural performances, rock concerts, and sporting events, TicketOne is the major online ticket vendor. ⊕ *www. ticketone.it.*

MAIN VENUES

Fodor's Choice
★

Auditorium Parco della Musica. Designed by famous architect Renzo Piano, this is *the* place to perform in Rome. The amazing space features three halls with nearly perfect acoustics, and a large courtyard for outdoor classical, jazz, and pop concerts. In addition, it hosts dance troupes and cultural festivals. The venue is a 10-minute tram ride north of Piazza del Popolo. ⇨ *See the Spotlight on the Parco.* ⊠ *Viale Pietro de Coubertin 30, Flaminio* ☎ *06/802411, 06/0608 tickets* ⊕ *www.auditorium.com.*

Fodor's Choice
★

Teatro Argentina. The opulence of Rome's beautiful turn-of-the-century theater—burgundy velvet upholstery and large crystal chandeliers—evokes Belle Epoque glamour. Most productions are in Italian, but it occasionally showcases some dance performances, which don't require subtitles. ⊠ *Largo di Torre Argentina 52, Campo de' Fiori* ☎ *06/684000311* ⊕ *www.teatrodiroma.net.*

Teatro Olimpico. This is the venue for contemporary dance companies, visiting international ballet companies, and touring Broadway shows like *Stomp.* ⊠ *Piazza Gentile da Fabriano 17, Flaminio* ☎ *06/3265991* ⊕ *www.teatroolimpico.it.*

CAMPO DE' FIORI
CLASSICAL MUSIC

Oratorio del Gonfalone. A small concert hall with an internationally recognized music series of Baroque classics, the Oratorio del Gonfalone has
highly decorated walls of beautiful mannerist frescoes respresenting the
very best of the mid-16th century. ⊠ *Via del Gonfalone 32/a, Campo
de' Fiori* ☎ *06/6875952* ⊕ *www.oratoriogonfalone.com.*

GHETTO
CLASSICAL MUSIC

Il Tempietto. Music festivals and concerts are organized throughout the
year in otherwise inaccessible sites, such as the Teatro di Marcello.
Music ranges from classical to contemporary. ⊠ *Piazza Campitelli 9,
Ghetto* ☎ *06/87131590* ⊕ *www.tempietto.it.*

FLAMINIO
CLASSICAL MUSIC

Accademia di Santa Cecilia. Part of Rome's amazing and well-versed musical circuit, this venue has a program of performances ranging from
classical to contemporary and a lineup of world-renowned artists. The
futurist Auditorium Parco della Musica hosts Santa Cecilia's concerts.
⇨ *Auditorium Parco della Musica.* ⊠ *Via Pietro de Coubertin 34, Flaminio* ☎ *06/8082058* ⊕ *www.santacecilia.it.*

Accademia Filarmonica Romana. Nearly two centuries old, this is one of
Rome's historic concert venues featuring classical music. The garden
hosts occasional outdoor performances. ⊠ *Via Flaminia 118, Flaminia*
☎ *06/3201752* ⊕ *www.filarmonicaromana.org.*

NAVONA
CLASSICAL MUSIC

Chiostro del Bramante. A charming former cloister and art venue/cul-
tural center, the Chiostro has a cocktail room reminiscent of *Mad Men*
with equally inspired 1960s cocktails. The Bramante-designed bar hosts
smaller shows of modern and contemporary artists like Warhol, Balla,
and Basquiat as well as classical works. ⊠ *Via della Pace 5, Navona*
☎ *06/68809036* ⊕ *www.chiostrodelbramante.it.*

PANTHEON
CLASSICAL MUSIC

Hallowed Sounds. Throughout the year, churches like Sant'Ivo alla
Sapienza, San Francesco a Ripa, and San Paolo entro le Mura usually have afternoon and evening performances. Look for posters outside churches announcing free concerts, particularly at Sant'Ignazio
(⊠ *Piazza Sant'Ignazio, Pantheon* ☎ *06/6794560*), which often hosts
concerts in a spectacularly frescoed setting. You could also sit in
the shadow of the Theatre of Marcello (⊠ *Via del Teatro Marcello,
Ghetto* ☎ *06/87131590*) for its summertime concert series. ⊠ *Piazza
Sant'Ignazio, Pantheon* ☎ *06/6794560* ⊕ *www.amicimusicasacra.com/
chiesa_di_s_ignazio.htm.*

Entertainment Alfresco

Roman nightlife moves outdoors in summertime, and that goes not only for pubs and discos but for higher culture as well. Open-air opera in particular is a venerable Italian tradition; competing companies commandeer church courtyards, ancient villas, and soccer stadiums for performances that range from student-run mom-and-poperas to full-scale extravaganzas. The same goes for dance and for concerts covering the spectrum of pop, classical, and jazz. Look for performances at the Baths of Caracalla, site of the famous televised "Three Tenors" concert; regardless of the production quality, it's a breathtaking setting. In general, though, you can count on performances being quite good, even if small productions often resort to school-play scenery and folding chairs to cut costs. An outdoor theater is also set up in Villa Borghese; Shakespeare productions are popular. Tickets run about €15–€50. The more sophisticated productions may be listed in newspapers and magazines such as *roma c'è*, but your best sources for information are old-fashioned posters plastered all over the city, advertising classics such as *Tosca* and *La Traviata*.

REPUBBLICA

FILM

The Space Cinema Moderno. Perhaps the most "American" of all Rome's theaters (hint: great concessions, stadium seating, and comfortable, couchlike chairs), the cinema has five screens. Easy to find, the Moderno is located in the porticoes of Piazza Repubblica, next to the classic Exedra Hotel. ⊠ *Piazza della Repubblica 45–46, Repubblica* ☎ *892111* ⊕ *www.thespacecinema.it* Ⓜ *Repubblica–Teatro dell'Opera.*

OPERA

Fodor's Choice ★ **Teatro dell'Opera.** Recently Rome has come into the spotlight for opera aficionados thanks to Maestro Riccardo Muti's 2011 *Nabucco* performance and his recent support of Rome's Teatro dell'Opera. Though considered a far younger sibling of Milan's La Scala and Venice's La Fenice, the company does command an audience during its mid-November to May season. Tickets are on sale in advance of the season. In the hot summer months, the company moves to the Baths of Caracalla for its outdoor opera series. As can be expected, the oft-preferred performance is *Aida* for its spectacle, which has been known to include real elephants. The company has taken a new direction, using projections atop the ancient ruins to create cutting-edge sets. The season for the **Opera Theater of Rome** runs from November or December to May. Main performances are staged at the Teatro dell'Opera, on Piazza Beniamino Gigli, in cooler weather, and at outdoor locations, such as Piazza del Popolo and the spectacular Terme di Caracalla (Baths of Caracalla), in summer. ⊠ *Piazza Beniamino Gigli 8, Repubblica* ☎ *06/481601, 06/48160255 for tickets* ⊕ *www.operaroma.it* Ⓜ *Repubblica–Teatro dell'Opera.*

TERMINI
DANCE
Corps de Ballet, Teatro dell'Opera. Performing throughout the year at the Belle Époque opera house, the ballet company stages many of the classics, often with leading international guest stars. During the summer season, they perform ballets alfresco at the Baths of Caracalla, mixing contemporary set design with the classic structure. ⊠ *Teatro dell'Opera, Piazza Beniamino Gigli 7, Termini* ☎ *06/48160255* ⊕ *www.operaroma.it.*

TRASTEVERE
CLASSICAL MUSIC
Orto Botanico. The historic botanical garden spans more than 30 acres at the base of the Janiculum Hill in Trastevere. In this redolent and verdant setting, the spring and summer seasons promote art and summer concert series. ⊠ *Largo Cristina di Svezia 23/a, Trastevere* ☎ *06/49917107* ⊕ *sweb01.dbv.uniroma1.it.*

VILLA BORGHESE
FILM
Casa del Cinema. Dedicated to the art of the silver screen, Casa del Cinema is Rome's most modern projection house and film library. This oasis for film buffs has multiple screening rooms, a café, and a resource center with DVD library and laptops for private viewings. They shows many new and retro films, and often showcases the original language films from the fall's Venice Film Festival and Roma Cinema Fest (⊕ *www.romacinemafest.it*). Like its indoor counterpart, the outdoor projection screen shows both new and vintage movies, sometimes in original languages, though only in the warm months. ⊠ *Largo Marcello Mastroianni 1, Villa Borghese* ☎ *06/423601* ⊕ *www.casadelcinema.it.*

NIGHTLIFE

Rome's nightlife is decidedly more happening for locals and insiders who know whose palms to grease and when to go where. The "flavor of the month" factor is at work here, and many places fade into oblivion after their 15 minutes of fame. Smoking has been banned in all public areas in Italy (that's right, it actually happened), and Roman aversion to clean air has meant a decrease in crowds at bars and clubs. The best sources for an up-to-date list of nightspots are the *roma c'è, Romeing,* and *Time Out Rome* magazines. Trastevere and the area around Piazza Navona are both filled with bars, restaurants, and, after dark, people. In summer, discos and many bars close to beat the heat (although some simply relocate to the beach, where many Romans spend their summer nights). The city-sponsored Estate Romana (Rome Summer) festival takes over, lighting up hot city nights with open-air concerts, bars, and discos. Pick up the event guide at newsstands.

Most dance clubs open about 10:30 pm and charge an entrance fee of about €20, which may include the first drink (subsequent drinks cost about €10). Clubs are usually closed Monday, and all those listed here close in summer, when the city's nightlife scene goes seaside to the beaches of Ostia and Fregene. The liveliest areas for clubs with a younger clientele are the grittier working-class districts of Testaccio,

Ostiense, and San Lorenzo. Any of the clubs lining Via Galvani, leading up to Monte Testaccio, are fair game for a trendy, crowded dance-floor experience—names and ownership of clubs change frequently, but the overall scene has shown exciting staying power, growing into a DJ "Disneyland."

CAMPO DE' FIORI

CAFÉS AND WINE BARS

L'Angolo Divino. Hidden on a back alley, this quiet enoteca with wood-panelled walls offers an extensive selection of wines—some 1,000 labels—delicious homemade pastas, and local antipasti. It's a welcome respite from the chaotic, adjacent Campo de' Fiori. ⊠ *Via dei Balestrari 12, Campo de' Fiori* ☎ *06/6864413.*

Vineria Reggio. The quintessential Roman wine bar, where the first focus is whetting one's whistle and the last is style. The crowd ranges from grandfathers to glitterati. ⊠ *Campo de' Fiori 15, Campo de' Fiori* ☎ *06/68803268* ⊕ *www.vineriareggio.com.*

ROOFTOP TERRACES AND UPSCALE BARS

Rooftop Lounge Bar at the St. George Hotel. The latest front-runner in Rome's ever-growing list of rooftop sweet spots has a delicious oyster selection headlining its seafood-based menu and a dizzying drink selection that includes cocktails, beer, and many rosés—from pink champagnes to Italian *rosati.* The St. George's Wine Bar and Cigar Room make an excellent substitute in the non-summer months when the rooftop is closed. ⊠ *Via Giulia 62, Campo de' Fiori* ☎ *06/686611* ⊕ *www.stgeorgehotel.it.*

MONTI

CAFÉS AND WINE BARS

Ai Tre Scalini. This rustic hangout—think wooden walls and counters—in Monti, Rome's boho 'hood, serves delicious antipasti and light entrees and has an enticing wine list. ⊠ *Via Panisperna 251, Monti* ☎ *06/48907495* ⊕ *www.aitrescalini.org* Ⓜ *Cavour.*

NAVONA

CAFÉS AND WINE BARS

Fodor's Choice
★ **Antico Caffè della Pace.** It doesn't get any more Rome than this: a cappuccino or cocktail al fresco at a turn-of-the-20th-century-style café nestled in the picturesque side streets behind Piazza Navona. Celebrities and literati hang out at the coveted outdoor tables of Antico Caffè della Pace, also known as Bar della Pace, where the atmosphere ranges from peaceful to percolating. La Pace's location is equally enchanting, in the *piazzatina* (tiny piazza) of Santa Maria della Pace, by Baroque architect Pietro da Cortona. The only drawbacks: overpriced table service and distracted waiters. ⊠ *Via della Pace 3/7, Navona* ☎ *06/6861216* ⊕ *www.caffedellapace.it.*

Fluid. With excellent cocktails and slick design, Fluid lures in passersby with its looking-glass front window where the aperitivi crowd likes to be seen. ⊠ *Via del Governo Vecchio 46/47, Navona* ☎ *06/6832361* ⊕ *www.fluideventi.com.*

ROOFTOP TERRACES AND UPSCALE BARS

Terrace Bar of the Hotel Raphael. Noted for its bird's-eye view of the campaniles and palazzos of the Piazza Navona and seemingly floating in the moonlit sky, the Terrace Bar ranks high on Rome's list of romantic views. ⊠ *Largo Febo 2, Navona* ☎ *06/682831* ⊕ *www.raphaelhotel. com* ☾ *Summer only.*

NIGHTCLUBS AND DISCOS

Fodor'sChoice ★ **La Cabala.** Atop the medieval palazzo, La Cabala looks over the Eternal City. Rome's version of a supper club, La Cabala is part of the Hostaria dell'Orso trio of restaurant, disco, and piano bar. Dress code is stylish. ⊠ *Hostaria dell'Orso, Via dei Soldati 23, Navona* ☎ *06/68301192* ⊕ *www.hdo.it.*

Fodor'sChoice ★ **La Maison.** At Rome's best after-dinner club the large dance floor plays second fiddle to the VIP room, where wanna-be models lounge in their very best DVF dresses and manicured boys vie for their attention. Depending on the evening, vibe can be chic, hipster, or clubby. Rule of thumb: head straight to the back room and grab a couch. ⊠ *Vicolo dei Granari 4, Navona* ☎ *06/6833312.*

PIAZZA DI SPAGNA

CAFÉS AND WINE BARS

Enoteca Antica. The area between Piazza del Popolo and the Spanish Steps has plenty of eateries, but be warned: Many are touristy and overpriced. Although their service can be slow, Enoteca Antica, just off Piazza di Spagna, has a good wine list and reasonable food in a charming, old-fashioned atmosphere. ⊠ *Via della Croce 76, Spagna* ☎ *06/6790896.*

Fodor'sChoice ★ **Enoteca Palatium.** Just down the street from the Piazza di Spagna hub is this quiet gem run by Lazio's Regional Food Authority as a chic showcase for the best of Lazio's pantry and wine cellar: from its fine vintages to olive oils, cheese, and meats to a full seasonal menu of Lazio cuisine. Located where famed aesthete and poet Gabriele d'Annunzio once lived, this is not your garden-variety corner wine bar. ■TIP→ Stop by during aperitivo hour, from 6:30 pm onward (reservations recommended) to enjoy this burst of local flavor. ⊠ *Via Frattina 94, Spagna.*

ROOFTOP TERRACES AND UPSCALE BARS

Wine Bar at the Palazzetto. The prize for perfect aperitivo spot goes to the Palazzetto, with excellent drinks and appetizers and a breathtaking view of Rome's domes and rooftops, all from its 5th-floor rooftop overlooking Piazza di Spagna. ⊠ *Palazzetto, Piazza Trinità di Monti, Spagna* ☎ *06/699341000* Ⓜ *Spagna.*

NIGHTCLUBS AND DISCOS

Gilda. Every year, Gilda reinvents herself to continue the never-ending party near the Spanish Steps. Recent incarnations have added a piano bar and restaurant just off the dance floors. ⊠ *Via Mario de' Fiori 97, Spagna* ☎ *06/6784838* ⊕ *www.gildabar.it* Ⓜ *Spagna.*

PIAZZA VITTORIO
NIGHTCLUBS AND DISCOS
Casa Clementina. "There's no place like home" seems to be the motto of Rome's latest concept lounge. Casa Clementina has a truly homey vibe—an ersatz home with kitchen, living room, dining room, and bedroom at your disposal, whether to enjoy live performances or cocktails and the very abundant aperitivo hour. ⊠ *Via Clementina 9, Piazza Vittorio* ☎ *39/3347096385.*

POPOLO
ROOFTOP TERRACES AND UPSCALE BARS
Stravinskij Bar at the Hotel de Russie. Rome's dolce vita is best found in the restaurant Le Jardin de Russie, in particular the terraced garden of the Stravinskij Bar, where celebrities, blue bloods, and VIPs hang out. Mixed drinks are well above par, as are the prices. ⊠ *Hotel de Russie, Via del Babuino 9, Popolo* ☎ *06/328881* ⊕ *www.hotelderussie. it* Ⓜ *Flaminio.*

REPUBBLICA
ROOFTOP TERRACES AND UPSCALE BARS
Fodor'sChoice ★ **Champagnerie Tazio.** A chic champagne bar named after the original Italian *paparazzo*, Tazio has a red, black, and white lacquered interior with crystal chandeliers and a distinct '80s feel (think Robert Palmer, "Addicted to Love"). The favorite pastime here is sipping champagne while watching the people parade through the colonnade of the lobby. In summer, the hotel's rooftop Posh bar is the place to be, with its infinity pool and terrace view overlooking downtown. ⊠ *Hotel Exedra, Piazza della Repubblica 47, Repubblica* ☎ *06/489381* ⊕ *www. boscolohotels.com* Ⓜ *Repubblica–Teatro dell'Opera.*

TESTACCIO
NIGHTCLUBS AND DISCOS
Hulala. Still considered a designer discoteca and magnet for fashionistas, Hulala is evolving as the crowd diversifies into a younger generation. The mod interior includes lots of red-and-black styling and strobe lights. ⊠ *Via dei Conciatori 7, Testaccio* Ⓜ *Piramide.*

Ketum Bar. Excellent for people-watchers, and even better if you want to mix a bit of culture with your clubbing. The glass-covered walls show off shards of 1st-century amphorae to remind you that Ketum Bar was carved out of a mountain of pottery. ⊠ *Via Galvani 24, Testaccio* ☎ *06/57305338* ⊕ *www.ketumbar.it.*

TRASTEVERE
CAFÉS AND WINE BARS
Fodor'sChoice ★ **Freni e Frizioni.** This hipster hangout has a cute artist vibe, great for coffee, tea, aperitifs, and late-night socializing. In warmer weather, the crowd overflows the large *terrazzo* overlooking the Tiber and the side streets of Trastevere. ⊠ *Via del Politeama 4, Trastevere* ☎ *06/45497499* ⊕ *www.freniefrizioni.com.*

VENETO

NIGHTCLUBS AND DISCOS

Jackie O'. A dip into Rome's dolce vita is not complete without a visit to the historic Jackie O', a retro-hip disco and restaurant off Via Veneto. The small lounge area is where you want to be, and don't arrive before 11 pm. ⊠ *Via Boncompagni 11, Veneto* ☎ *06/42885457* ⊕ *www. jackieoroma.com.*

SHOPPING

They say when in Rome to do as the Romans do—and the Romans love to shop. After all, this is the city that gave us the Gucci "moccasin" loafer, the Fendi bag, and the Valentino dress that Jackie O wore when she became Mrs. Onassis. Stores are generally open from 10 to 1 and from 3:30 or 4 to 7 or 7:30 (with the exception of Monday, when most are closed in the morning). There's a tendency for shops in central districts to stay open all day, and hours are becoming more flexible throughout the city. Many places close all day Sunday, though this is changing, too, especially in the city center. Some stores also close Saturday afternoon from mid-June through August.

You can stretch your euros by taking advantage of the Tax-Free for Tourists V.A.T. (value-added tax) refunds, available at most large stores for purchases over €155. Or hit Rome in January and early February or in late July and August, when stores clean house with the justly famous biannual sales, or *saldi*. There are so many hole-in-the-wall boutiques selling top-quality merchandise in Rome's center that even just wandering you're sure to find something that catches your eye.

SHOPPING DISTRICTS

The city's most famous shopping district, **Piazza di Spagna,** is conveniently compact, fanning out at the foot of the Spanish Steps in a galaxy of boutiques selling gorgeous wares with glamorous labels. Here you can prance back and forth from Gucci to Prada to Valentino to Versace with less effort than it takes to pull out your credit card. If your budget is designed for lower altitudes, you also can find great clothes and accessories at less extravagant prices. But here buying is not necessarily the point—window displays can be works of art, and dreaming may be satisfaction enough. Via dei Condotti is the neighborhood's central axis, but there are shops on every street in the area bordered by Piazza di Spagna on the east, Via del Corso on the west, between Piazza San Silvestro and Via della Croce, and extending along Via del Babuino to Piazza del Popolo. **Via Margutta,** a few blocks north of the Spanish Steps, is a haven for contemporary art galleries.

Shops along **Via Campo Marzio,** and adjoining Piazza San Lorenzo in Lucina, stock eclectic, high-quality clothes and accessories—by both big names (Bottega Veneta, Louis Vuitton) and smaller European designers—at slightly lower prices. Running from Piazza Venezia to Piazza del Popolo lies **Via del Corso,** a main avenue that has more than a mile of shops. Unfortunately, these days most of it is taken up by the same chain stores you find worldwide (including Gap, H&M, and even an Athlete's Foot), rendering it little more interesting than a trip to one's local shopping mall. Running west from Piazza Navona, **Via del Governo Vecchio** has numerous women's boutiques and secondhand-clothing stores.

Via Cola di Rienzo, across the Tiber from Piazza del Popolo and extending to the Vatican, is block after block of boutiques, shoe stores, department stores, and mid-level chain shops, as well as street stalls and upscale food shops. **Via dei Coronari,** across the Tiber from Castel Sant'Angelo, has quirky antiques and home furnishings. **Via Giulia** and other surrounding streets are good bets for decorative arts. Should your gift list include religious souvenirs, look for everything from rosaries to Vatican golf balls at the shops between Piazza San Pietro and **Borgo Pio.** Liturgical vestments and statues of saints make for good window-shopping on **Via dei Cestari,** near the Pantheon.

Via Nazionale is a good bet for affordable stores along the lines of Benetton, and for shoes, bags, and gloves. The **Termini** train station has become a good one-stop place for many shopping needs, although again, most stores are the same you see worldwide. Its 60-plus shops are open until 10 pm and include a Nike store, the Body Shop, Sephora, Mango (women's clothes), a UPIM department store, a grocery store, and a three-story bookstore with selections in English. For local designers and independent boutiques, don't miss the trendy shopping districts of **Monti** near the Forum and **Trastevere** across the Tiber from the historic center.

LISTINGS BY NEIGHBORHOOD

BARBERINI
LANDMARK STORES
Antica Farmacia Pesci dal 1552. Likely Rome's oldest pharmacy, the Antica Farmacia is run by a family of pharmacists. The shop's 18th-century furnishings, herbs, and vases evoke Harry Potter's Diagon Alley; and while they don't carry Polyjuice Potion, the pharmacists can whip up a just-for-you batch of composite powders, syrups, capsules, gels, and creams to soothe what ails you. ⊠ *Piazza Trevi 89, Trevi* ☎ *06/6792210* Ⓜ *Barberini–Fontana di Trevi.*

MEN'S CLOTHING
Fodor's Choice **Brioni.** Founded in 1945 and hailed for its impeccable craftsmanship
★ and flawless execution, the Brioni label is known for attracting and keeping the best men's tailors in Italy. The exacting standards require that custom-made suits are designed from scratch and measured to the millimeter. For this personalized line, the menswear icon has 5,000 spectacular fabrics to select from. As thoughtful as they are expensive, one bespoke suit made from wool will take a minimum of 32 hours to create. Their prêt-à-porter line is also praised for peerless cutting and stitching. Past and present clients include Clark Gable, Donald Trump, Barack Obama and, of course, James Bond. And they say clothing doesn't make the man? ⊠ *Via Barberini 79, Quirinale* ☎ *06/484517* ⊕ *www.brioni.it* Ⓜ *Barberini–Fontana di Trevi* ⊠ *Via Condotti 21/A, Spagna* ☎ *06/485855* Ⓜ *Spagna.*

CORSO

BOOKSTORES

Ex Libris. Founded in 1931 and one of the oldest antiquarian bookshops in Rome, Ex Libris has a distinctive selection of scholarly and collectible books from the 16th to 21th centuries that will make bookworms drool. The selection includes rare editions on art and architecture, music and theater, and literature and humanities, as well as maps and prints. ✉ *Via dell' Umiltà 77/a* ☎ *06/6791540* ⊕ *www.exlibrisroma.it* Ⓜ *Barberini–Fontana di Trevi.*

GELATO

Caffè Ciampini. Just off the Corso in the jewel of a piazza, San Lorenzo in Lucina, sits this turn-of-the-century tearoom-gelateria-café. Stand at the elegant bar for a quick espresso, or pay a bit more to sit outdoors under a big umbrella, lingering over an aperitivo and a plateful of yummy hors d'oeuvres that come with it. ✉ *Piazza San Lorenzo in Lucina 29, Corso* ☎ *06/6876606* ⊕ *www.ciampini.net.*

MEN'S CLOTHING

Fratelli Viganò. If you are a *Mad Men* wannabe, hipster, or just maintain a particular fondness for classically styled Italian millinery, this store will have you drooling. Fratelli Viganò was founded in 1873 and has been producing handsome handmade hats ever since. Even if you aren't planning a tribute to Don Draper, the shop is sure to impress with its artisans' painstaking attention to detail. With hundreds of hats arranged in perfect order, you will surely find one to strike your fancy. Roman poet Trilussa and even Mussolini preferred their top hats, but their signature pieces are the sporty fedoras and debonair brown derbies. ✉ *Via Marco Minghetti 7, Spagna* ☎ *06/6795147* Ⓜ *Barberini–Fontana di Trevi.*

MUSIC STORES

Remix. An underground favorite for famous producers and distributors of legendary Roman vinyl labels like Sounds Never Seen, ACV, and many others, Remix specializes in techno. The shop also has a great back catalogue—all at prices that will make new collectors smile. ✉ *Via del Fiume 8/9* ☎ *06/3216514* ⊕ *www.re-mix.it* Ⓜ *Flaminio.*

STATIONERY

Fodor's Choice **Cartoleria Pantheon dal 1910.** An absolute Aladdin's cave for scribblers
★ and those inspired by the blank page, the simply sumptuous Cartoleria Pantheon dal 1910 has unique leather journals and fine handmade paper to write a special letter. Writers and artists can choose from simple, stock paper to artisanal sheets of handcrafted Amalfi paper and from among hand-bound leather journals in an extraordinary array of colors and sizes. ✉ *Via della Rotonda 15* ☎ *06/6875313* ⊕ *www. pantheon-roma.it.*

MONTI

FASHION

Hydra. An avant-garde clothing shop for older teens and twentysomethings who believe clothing should make a statement, Hydra has styles that range from voluptuous Betty Boop retro dresses to indie underground to in-your-face T-shirts that would make your grandmother blush. ✉ *Via Urbana 139* ☎ *06/48907773* Ⓜ *Cavour.*

VINTAGE CLOTHING

Fodor'sChoice
★

Le Gallinelle. This is a tiny boutique where owner Wilma Silvestri transforms vintage, ethnic, and contemporary fabrics into retro-inspired clothing with a modern edge—without smelling like mothballs from your great aunt Suzie's closet. ✉ *Via Panisperna 61* ⊕ *www.legallinelle.it.*

PANTHEON

Giolitti. For years Giolitti was considered the best gelateria in Rome, and it's still worth a stop if you're near the Pantheon. It's best known for its variety of fresh seasonal fruit flavors, which taste like the essence of the fruits themselves. ✉ *Via degli Uffici del Vicario 40, Pantheon* ☎ *06/6991243* ⊕ *www.giolitti.it.*

NAVONA

ACCESSORIES

Spazio IF. In a tiny piazza alongside Rome's historic Via dei Coronari, designers Irene and Carla Ferrara have created a tantalizing hybrid between fashion paradise and art gallery. Working with unconventional designers and artists who emphasize Sicilian design, the shop has more to say about the style of Sicily and the creativity of the island's inhabitants than flat caps, puppets, and rich pastries. Perennial favorites include handbags cut by hand in a *putia* (shop) in Palermo, swimsuits, designer textiles, jewelry, and sportswear. ✉ *Via dei Coronari 44a* ☎ *06/64760639* ⊕ *www.spazioif.it.*

ANTIQUES

Nardecchia. In the heart of Piazza Navona, in front of Bernini's Fountain of the Four Rivers, Nardecchia knows there are three major considerations when it comes to antique prints and etchings: value, aesthetics, and rarity. The shop showcases some of its beautiful 19th-century prints, old photographs, and watercolors, giving browsers a hint at what Rome looked like in centuries past. Can't afford an 18th-century etching? They have refined postcards too. ✉ *Piazza Navona 25* ☎ *06/6865318* ⊕ *www.nardecchia.it.*

Quattrocolo. This historic shop dating to 1938 showcases exquisite antique micro-mosaic jewelry painstakingly crafted in the style perfected by the masters at the Vatican mosaic studio. You'll also find 18th- and 19th-century cameos and beautiful engraved stones. Their small works are beloved by cosmopolitan clientele of the Grand Tour age and offer modern-day shoppers a taste of yesteryear's grandeur. If you are a fan of archaeology, don't miss their Etruscan-style jewelry. ✉ *Via della Scrofa 48* ☎ *06/68801367* ⊕ *www.quattrocolo.com.*

CASUAL CHIC

Vestiti Usati Cinzia. There's a fun, unique, and diverse inventory of 1960s- and '70s-style apparel and googly sunglasses at Vestiti Usati Cinzia, beloved by private clients, costume designers, and fashion designers and stylists alike. You'll find lots of flower power, embroidered tops, and psychedelic clothing here, along with trippy boots and dishy bubblegum pink shoes that Twiggy would have loved. ✉ *Via del Governo Vecchio 45* ☎ *06/6832945.*

CERAMICS AND GLASSWEAR

Fodor's Choice
★ IN.OR. dal 1952. For more than 50 years, Romans have registered their bridal china and gifts under the frescoed ceilings of this grand silver and china store occupying the piano nobile of an 18th-century palazzo in the characteristic Campo Marzo area, in hopes of receiving something elegant. With seven rooms for browsing, the shop specializes in work handcrafted by the silversmiths of Pampaloni in Florence and Bellotto of Padua. ⊠ *Via della Stelletta 23* ☎ *06/6878579* ⊕ *www.inor.it.*

FASHION

Le Tartarughe. Designer Susanna Liso, a Rome native, adds suggestive elements of playful experimentation to her haute couture and ready-to-wear lines, which are much loved by Rome's aristocracy and intelligentsia. With intense and enveloping designs, she mixes raw silks or cashmere and fine merino wool together to form captivating garments that are a mix of seduction and linear form. Le Tartarughe can be found at two locations close to the Pantheon. ⊠ *Via Piè di Marmo 17* ☎ *06/6792240* ⊕ *www.letartarughe.eu.*

FOOD AND CANDY

Moriondo e Gariglio. The Willy Wonka of Roman chocolate factories opened its doors in 1850. The shop uses the finest cocoa beans and adheres strictly to family recipes passed down from generation to generation. Known for rich, gourmet chocolates, they soon were the favored chocolatier to the House of Savoy. In 2009, the shop partnered with Bvlgari and placed 300 pieces of jewelry in their Easter eggs to benefit cancer research. While you may not find diamonds in your bonbons, marrons glacés, or dark-chocolate truffles, you'll still delight in choosing from more than 80 delicacies. ⊠ *Via Piè di Marmo 21* ☎ *06/6990856.*

JEWELRY

Delfina Delettrez. When your great grandmother is Adele Fendi, it's not surprising that creativity runs in your genes. In her early 20s, Delfina Delettrez creates edgy, conceptual collections. Using human body–inspired pieces blending skulls, wild animals, and botanical elements, she daringly merges gold, silver, bone and glass, crystals and diamonds to create gothic, edgy styles worthy of Fritz Lang's *Metropolis* or *Blade Runner*. Don't be put off by her signature goth-glam designs in the window: this dazzling emporium, with its innumerable drawers filled with baubles, has something saucy and refined for everyone's sensibilities. ⊠ *Via Governo Vecchio 67* ☎ *06/68136362* ⊕ *www.delfinadelettrez.com.*

MEN'S CLOTHING

Davide Cenci. For the discerning shopper, Davide Cenci is a Roman classic for high-quality clothing and accessories for every occasion. For most visitors on a short holiday, purchasing custom-fitted clothing is not an option. Cenci's clothiers will adjust and tailor most anything to fit your body like a glove and have it delivered to your hotel within three days. The label is famous for its sinful cashmere, sailing sportswear, and trench coats, and you will appreciate their customer service and attention to detail. ⊠ *Via Campo Marzio 1–7* ☎ *06/6990681* ⊕ *www. davidecenci.com.*

SBU. In a city famous for classically sharp suits, it can be a challenge to find hip menswear in Rome, but SBU (Strategic Business Unit) suavely fills the void. In a 19th-century former draper's workshop, it's the place where Rome's VIPs buy their soft and supple vintage low-cut Japanese denims. Behind the old wooden counters, stacked drawer chests, and iron columns, SBU offers a sophisticated range of casual clothing, sportswear, shoes, and upscale accessories. The small hidden garden around back offers a relaxing moment between shopping sprees. ⊠ *Via di San Pantaleo 68–69* ☏ *06/68802547* ⊕ *www.sbu.it.*

PERFUME AND COSMETICS

Fodor'sChoice **Ai Monasteri.** Among dark-wood paneling, choir-like alcoves, and painted
★ angels, at Ai Monasteri you'll find traditional products made by Italy's diligent friars and monks. Following century-old recipes, the herbal decoctions, liqueurs, beauty aids, and toiletries offer a look into the time-honored tradition of monastic trade. The Elixir dell'Amore (love potion) is perfect for any well-deserving valentine, or, if it isn't true love, you can opt for a bottle of the popular Elixir of Happiness. There are myriad products, ranging from colognes for children to quince-apple and Cistercian jams, made exclusively with organic produce, and Royal Jelly honey. ⊠ *Corso del Rinascimento 72* ☏ *06/68802783* ⊕ *www.monasteri.it.*

Antica Erboristeria Romana. Complete with hand-labeled wooden drawers holding its more than 200 varieties of herbs, flowers, and tinctures including aper, licorice, and hellbane, Antica Erboristeria Romana has maintained its old-world apothecary feel. The shop stocks an impressive array of herbal teas and infusions, more than 700 essential oils, bud derivatives, and powdered extracts. ⊠ *Via Torre Argentina 15* ☏ *06/6879493* ⊕ *www.anticaerboristeriaromana.it.*

STATIONERY

Il Papiro. One of Rome's preferred shops for those who appreciate exquisite writing materials and papermaking techniques that are almost extinct, Il Papiro sells hand-decorated marbleized papers made using the 17th-century marbleized technique called *a la cuve*. Their stationery and card stock are printed with great care using exacting standards. Whether you are searching for unique lithography, engraving, or delicate watermarked paper, you'll find some indulgence here. They also carry a fine selection of wax seals, presses for paper embossing, Venetian glass pens, and ink stamps. ⊠ *Via del Pantheon 50* ☏ *06/6795597* ⊕ *www.ilpapirofirenze.it.*

TOYS

Al Sogno. If you're looking for quality toys that encourage imaginative play and learning, look no further. With an emphasis on the artistic as well as the multisensory, the shop has a selection of toys that are both discerning and individual, making them perfect for children of all ages. Carrying an exquisite collection of fanciful puppets, collectible dolls, masks, stuffed animals, and illustrated books, this Navona jewel is crammed top to bottom with beautiful and well-crafted playthings. If you believe that children's toys don't have to be high-tech, you will adore reliving some of your best childhood memories here. ⊠ *Piazza Navona 53, corner of Via Agonale* ☏ *06/6864198* ⊕ *www.alsogno.com.*

Fodor's Choice ★ **Bartolucci.** Shoppers are enticed with a life-size Pinocchio pedaling furiously on a wooden bike. Inside is a shop that would have warmed Gepetto's heart. For more than 60 years and three generations, this family has been making whimsical, handmade curiosities out of pine, including clocks, bookends, bedside lamps, and wall hangings. You can even buy a child-size vintage car entirely made of wood, including the wheels. ✉ *Via dei Pastini 98* ☎ *06/69190894* ⊕ *www.bartolucci.com.*

REPUBBLICA

BOOKSTORES

Libreria IBS. If you like discounts on remainder stock and secondhand books, come to Libreria IBS (formerly Mel Bookstore). Browse through the large basement and find a treasure trove of marked-down merchandise as well as a modest selection of English-language paperbacks. Upstairs, shop for books in Italian on a variety of subjects or pick up a DVD of *Roman Holiday*. Afterward, relax with your purchases while you treat yourself to a coffee and dessert in the spacious art deco–style caffè. ✉ *Via Nazionale 254–255, Repubblica* ☎ *06/4885405* ⊕ *www. ibs.it* Ⓜ *Repubblica–Teatro dell'Opera.*

CERAMICS AND DECORATIVE ARTS

Il Giardino di Domenico Persiani. Nestled in a cool courtyard garden under the shade of an expansive oak tree is refreshing open-air terra-cotta shop Il Giardino di Domenico Persiani. Whether you're looking for a chubby cherub, a replica of Bacchus, or your very own Bocca della Verità, this is your chance to bring a little piece of Rome home to your garden. With a large selection of handmade Roman masks, busts, flower pots, and vases, there is something here for anyone with a green thumb. ✉ *Via Torino 92, Repubblica* ☎ *06/4883886* Ⓜ *Repubblica– Teatro dell'Opera.*

SHOPPING MALLS

Il Forum Termini. Rome's handiest central shopping mall is a cluster of shops that stay open until 10 pm (even on Sunday), conveniently located directly inside Rome's biggest train station, Stazione Termini. In a city not known for its convenient shopping hours, this "shop before you hop/ buy before you fly" hub is a good spot for last-minute goodies or a book for your train or airplane ride. There are more than 50 shops, including United Colors of Benetton, L'Occitane, Sephora, and Optimissimo, which has more than 3,000 super-stylish glasses and sunglasses by top Italian designers. There is even a supermarket for your picnic lunch on the train. ✉ *Stazione Temini, Repubblica* ⊕ *www.romatermini.com* Ⓜ *Termini.*

SAN LORENZO

CASUAL CHIC

Fodor's Choice ★ **L'Anatra all'Arancia.** Repetto ballerinas, roomy handbags, and funky dresses make L'Anatra all'Arancia one of the best local secrets of boho San Lorenzo. Its window display showcases innovative designer clothes from Coast, Hoss, and Donatella Baroni (the store's owner and buyer). Leaning towards the alternative with an eclectic selection of handpicked Italian and French labels, Donatella carries sinful perfumes from L'Artisan Parfumeur and beautiful jewelry from the line of Serge Thoraval. ✉ *Via Tiburtina 105* ☎ *06/4456293* Ⓜ *Termini, Castro Pretorio.*

1

SPAGNA
ACCESSORIES

Fodor's Choice ★ **Braccialini.** Founded in 1954 by Florentine stylist Carla Braccialini and her husband, and currently managed by their sons, this company makes bags that are authentic works of art in delightful shapes, such as little gold taxis or Santa Fe stagecoaches. The delightfully quirky beach bags have picture postcard scenes of Italian resorts made of brightly colored appliquéd leather: Be sure to check out their eccentric *Temi* (Theme) creature bags; the opossum-shaped handbag made out of crocodile skin makes a richly whimsical fashion statement. ⊠ *Via Mario De' Fiori 73* ☎ *06/6785750* ⊕ *braccialini.it* Ⓜ *Spagna.*

Furla. There are 15 franchises in Rome alone, and its flagship store, to the left of the Spanish Steps, sells bags like hot cakes. Be prepared to fight your way through crowds of passionate handbag lovers, all anxious to possess one of the delectable bags, wallets, or watch straps in ice-cream colors. ⊠ *Piazza di Spagna 22, Spagna* ☎ *06/69200363* ⊕ *www.furla.com* Ⓜ *Spagna.*

La Perla. This is the go-to for beautifully crafted lingerie and glamorous underwear for that special night, a bridal trousseau, or just to spoil yourself on your Roman holiday. In partnership with Jean Paul Gaultier, the brand has just launched a swimwear line alongside his second lingerie collection. If you like decadent finery that is both stylish and romantic, you will find something here to make you feel like a goddess. ⊠ *Via Bocca di Leone 28* ☎ *06/69941934* ⊕ *www.laperla.com* Ⓜ *Spagna.*

Fodor's Choice ★ **Tod's.** With just 30 years under its belt, Tod's has grown from a small family brand into a global powerhouse so wealthy that it has donated €25 million to renovate the Colosseum. Tod's has gathered a cult following among style mavens worldwide, due in large part to owner Diego Della Valle's equally famous other possession: Florence's soccer team. The shoe baron's trademark is its simple, understated designs. Sure to please are their light and flexible slip-on Gommini driving shoes with rubber-bottomed soles for extra driving-pedal grip. Now you just need a Ferrari. ⊠ *Via Fontanella di Borghese 56a–57* ☎ *06/68210066* ⊕ *www.tods.com.*

ANTIQUES

Fratelli Alinari. The gallery store of the world's oldest photography firm, Fratelli Alinari was founded by brothers Leopoldo, Giuseppe, and Romualdo Alinari in 1852. Patrons can browse through a vast archive of prints, books, rare collotypes, and finely detailed reproductions of historical images, drawings, and paintings. Several of the more interesting subjects re-created using this technique are Dante's *The Divine Comedy* and both the *Plan de Paris* and *The Origin of New York,* detailed reproductions of the first recorded maps of these two cities. ⊠ *Via Alibert 16/a* ☎ *06/6792923* ⊕ *www.alinari.it* Ⓜ *Spagna.*

Galleria Benucci. With carved and gilded late Baroque and Empire period furniture and paintings culled from the noble houses of Italy's past, Galleria Benucci is a treasure trove. An establishment favored by professionals from Europe and abroad, this elegant gallery has a astonishing selection of objects in a hushed atmosphere where connoisseurs will find the proprietors only too happy to discuss their latest finds. ⊠ *Via del Babuino 150/C* ☎ *06/36002190* ⊕ *www.galleriabenucci.it* Ⓜ *Spagna.*

BOOKSTORES

Anglo-American Book Co. Large and friendly, this English-language bookstore has more than 45,000 books, and has been a mecca for English-language reading material in Rome for more than 25 years. Whether you are a study-abroad student in need of an art history or archaeology textbook, or a visitor searching for a light read for the train, there is something for everyone here. Among shelves stuffed from floor to ceiling and sometimes several rows deep, book lovers can find British and American editions and easily spend hours just looking. The bilingual staff pamper browsers and do not rush or hover. ⊠ *Via della Vite 102, Spagna* ☎ *06/6795222* ⊕ *www.aab.it* Ⓜ *Spagna.*

La Feltrinelli. As Rome's biggest bookseller, La Feltrinelli's main attraction is the Piazza Colonna flagship store. Ensconced in the elegant 19th-century Galleria Alberto Sordi, this megabookstore fills three floors with books, music, postcards, holiday items, and small gifts. A great place to explore Italian-style book shopping, there are 12 branches peppered throughout the city. The Torre Argentina shop also has a ticketing office for music and cultural events and a caffè tucked upstairs with refreshing snacks and good coffee. The Repubblica branch carries a large section of titles in many languages in addition to a well-stocked foreign film selection. ⊠ *Piazza Colonna 31/35, Corso* ☎ *06/69755001* ⊕ *www.lafeltrinelli.it* Ⓜ *Barberini–Fontana di Trevi.*

Lion Bookshop. For half a century or so, Italy's oldest English-language bookstore, with its children's reading corner and small caffè with American snacks and cookies, has been a welcoming haven for moms in search of that special children's book. In addition to books for kids, they also have a broad assortment of contemporary and classic fiction and nonfiction titles, as well as books on Rome and Italy in general, plus art, architecture, and cooking. ⊠ *Via dei Greci 33/36* ☎ *06/32654007* Ⓜ *Spagna.*

CLOTHING

Schostal. At the end of the 19th century when ladies needed petticoats, corsets, bonnets, or white or colored stockings made of cotton thread, wool, or silk, it was inevitable for them to stop at Schostal. A Piazza di Spagna fixture since 1870, the shop still preserves that genteel ambience. Fine-quality shirts come with spare collars and cuffs. Ultraclassic underwear, handkerchiefs, and pure wool and cashmere are available at affordable prices. ⊠ *Via Fontanella Borghese 29, Spagna* ☎ *06/6791240* ⊕ *www.schostalroma.com* Ⓜ *Spagna.*

DEPARTMENT STORES

La Rinascente. Italy's best-known department store, La Rinascente is where Italian fashion mogul Giorgio Armani got his start as a window dresser. Inside the Galleria Alberto Sordi, the store has a phalanx of ready-to-wear designer sportswear and blockbuster handbags and accessories. The upscale clothing and accessories are a hit with the young and well dressed, while retail turf is geared toward people on lunch breaks and the ubiquitous tourist. The Piazza Fiume location has more floor space and a wider range of goods, including a housewares department. ⊠ *Galleria Alberto Sordi, Piazza Colonna* ☎ *06/6797691* ⊕ *www.rinascente.it* Ⓜ *Spagna.*

FASHION

Dolce & Gabbana. Dolce and Gabbana met in 1980 when both were assistants at a Milan atelier, and they opened their first store in 1982. With a modern aesthetic that screams sex appeal, the brand has always thrived on its excesses. The Rome store can be more than a little overwhelming with its glossy glamazons, but at least there is plenty of eye candy, masculine and feminine, with a spring line heavy on stars and sequins as well as enthusiastic fruits, flowers, and veggies. ⊠ *Piazza di Spagna 94–95* ☎ *06/6782990* ⊕ *www.dolcegabbana.com* Ⓜ *Spagna.*

Fodor'sChoice ★ **Fendi.** A fixture of the Roman fashion landscape since "Mamma" Fendi first opened shop with her husband in 1925. With an eye for crazy genius, she hired Karl Lagerfeld, who began working with the group at the start of his career. His furs and runway antics have made him one of the world's most influential designers of the 20th century and brought international acclaim to Fendi along the way. Recent Lagerfeld triumphs include new collections marrying innovative textures, fabrics (cashmere, felt, and duchesse satin) with exotic skins like crocodile. Keeping up with technology, they even have an iPad case that will surely win a fashionista's seal of approval. The atelier, now owned by the Louis Vuitton group, continues to symbolize Italian glamour at its finest, though the difference in owners is noticeable. ⊠ *Largo Carlo Goldoni 419–421* ☎ *06/3344501* ⊕ *www.fendi.com* Ⓜ *Spagna.*

Giorgio Armani. One of the most influential designers of Italian haute couture, Giorgio Armani creates fluid silhouettes and dazzling evening gowns with décolletés so deep they'd make a grown man blush, his signature cuts made with the clever-handedness and flawless technique that you only achieve working with tracing paper and Italy's finest fabrics over the course of a lifetime. His menswear collection uses traditional textiles like wide-ribbed corduroy and stretch jersey in nontraditional ways while staying true to a clean, masculine aesthetic. It's true that exotic runway ideas and glamorous celebrities give Armani saleability, but his staying power is casual Italian elegance with just the right touch of whimsy and sexiness. Want to live *la bella vita* for longer than your Roman holiday? Armani is also selling luxury apartments in Rome at Cavour 220, complete with his personalized interiors. ⊠ *Via Condotti 77* ☎ *06/6991460* ⊕ *www.giorgioarmani.com* Ⓜ *Spagna.*

Fodor'sChoice ★ **Gucci.** As the glamorous fashion label approaches its centenary (in 2021), the success of the double-G trademark brand is unquestionable. Survival in luxury fashion depends on defining market share, and creative director Frida Giannini has proven she knows the soul of the House of Gucci. Tom Ford may have made Gucci the sexiest brand in the world, but it's today's reinterpreted horsebit styles and Jackie Kennedy scarves that keep the design house on top. And while Gucci remains a fashion must for virtually every A-list celebrity, their designs have moved from heart-stopping sexy rock star to something classically subdued and retrospectively feminine. ⊠ *Via Condotti 8* ☎ *06/6790405* ⊕ *www.gucci.com* Ⓜ *Spagna.*

Fodor's Choice
★

Laura Biagiotti. For more than 40 years a worldwide ambassador of Italian fashion, Laura Biagiotti is considered the Queen of Cashmere. Her soft-as-velvet pullovers have been worn by Sophia Loren and her snow-white cardigans were said to be a favorite of the late Pope John Paul II. Princess Diana even sported one of Biagiotti's cashmere maternity dresses. Be sure to indulge in her line of his-and-her perfumes. ⊠ *Via Mario de' Fiori 26* ☎ *06/6791205* ⊕ *www.laurabiagiotti. it* Ⓜ *Spagna.*

Marisa Padovan. The place to go for exclusive, made-to-order lingerie and bathing suits, Marisa Padovan has been sewing for Hollywood starlets like Audrey Hepburn and the well-heeled women of Rome for more than 40 years. Whether you want to purchase a ready-made style trimmed with Swarovski crystals and polished turquoise stones or design your own bespoke bikini or one-piece, their made-to-measure precision will have you looking like Rita Hayworth. ⊠ *Via delle Carrozze 81–82* ☎ *06/6793946* ⊕ *www.marisapadovan.it* Ⓜ *Spagna.*

Fodor's Choice
★

Prada. Not just the devil, but also serious shoppers wear Prada season after season, especially those willing to sell their souls for one of their ubiquitous handbags. If you are looking for that blend of old-world luxury with a touch of fashion-forward finesse, you'll hit pay dirt here. Recent handbag designs have a bit of a 1960s Jackie Kennedy feel, and whether you like them will hinge largely on whether you find Prada's signature retro-modernism enchanting. You'll find the Rome store more service-focused than the New York City branches—a roomy elevator delivers you to a series of thickly carpeted rooms where a flock of discreet assistants will help you pick out dresses, shoes, lingerie, and fashion accessories. The men's Prada is located at Via Condotti 88/90, while women's is at Via Condotti 92/95. ⊠ *Via Condotti 92/95* ☎ *06/6790897* ⊕ *www.prada.com* Ⓜ *Spagna.*

Salvatore Ferragamo. One of the top-10 most-wanted men's footwear brands, Salvatore Ferragamo has been providing Hollywood glitterati and discerning clients with unique handmade designs for years. Ferragamo fans will think they have died and followed the white light when they enter this store. The Florentine design house also specializes in handbags, small leather goods, men's and women's ready-to-wear, and scarves and ties. Men's styles are found at Via Condotti 65, women's at 73/74. Want to sleep in Ferragamo style? Their splendid luxury Portrait Suites Hotel is on the upper floors. ⊠ *Via Condotti 65* ☎ *06/6781130* ⊕ *www.ferragamo.com* Ⓜ *Spagna* ⊠ *Via Condotti 73/74* ☎ *06/6791565* Ⓜ *Spagna.*

Save the Queen!. A hot Florentine design house with exotic and creative pieces for women and girls with artistic and eccentric frills, cut-outs, and textures, Save the Queen! has one of the most beautiful shops in the city, with window displays that are works of art unto themselves. The store is chock-full of baroque-inspired dresses, shirts, and skirts that are ultrafeminine, not the least bit discreet, and 100 percent made in Italy.

Pieces radiate charming excess, presenting a portrait of youthful chic. ⊠ *Via del Babuino 49, Spagna* ☎ *06/36003039* ⊕ *www.savethequeen. com* Ⓜ *Spagna.*

Fodor's Choice
★
Valentino. Since taking the reins a few years ago, creative directors Maria Grazia Chiuri and Pierpaolo Piccioli have faced numerous challenges, the most basic being keeping Valentino true to Valentino after the designer's retirement in 2008. Both served as accessories designers under Valentino for more than a decade and understand exactly how to make the next generation of Hollywood stars swoon. Spagna's sprawling boutiques showcase designs with a romantic edginess: think kitten heels and or a show-stopping prêt-à-porter evening gown worthy of the Oscars. ⊠ *Via Condotti 15, Spagna* ☎ *06/6739420* ⊕ *www.valentino.com* Ⓜ *Spagna* ⊠ *Via del Babuino 61, Spagna* ☎ *06/36001906* Ⓜ *Spagna.*

Versace. Occupying the ground floor of a noble palazzo with wrought-iron gratings on the windows and mosaic pavement, Versace is as imaginitive as the store is ostentatious. Here shoppers will find apparel, jewelry, watches, fragrances, cosmetics, and home furnishings. The designs are as flamboyant as Donatella and Allegra (Gianni's niece), drawing heavily on the sexy rocker gothic underground vibe. Be sure to check out the Via Veneto location for pret-à-porter and jewelry. ⊠ *Via Bocca di Leone 23, 26–27, Spagna* ☎ *06/6780521* ⊕ *www. versace.com* Ⓜ *Spagna.*

JEWELRY

Bulgari. Every capital city has its famous jeweler, and Bulgari is to Rome what Tiffany's is to New York and Cartier is to Paris. The jewelry giant has developed a reputation for meticulous craftsmanship melded with noble metals and precious gems. In the middle of the 19th century, the great-grandfather of the current Bulgari brothers began working as a silver jeweler in his native Greece and is said to have moved to Rome with less than 1,000 lire in his pocket. Today the megabrand emphasizes colorful and playful jewelry as the principal cornerstone of its aesthetic. Popular collections include Parentesi, Bulgari-Bulgari and B.zero1. ⊠ *Via Condotti 10* ☎ *06/696261* ⊕ *www.bulgari.com* Ⓜ *Spagna.*

MEN'S CLOTHING

Ermenegildo Zegna. A century-old powerhouse of men's clothing. Believing that construction and fabric are the key, Zegna is the master of both. Most of the luxury brand's suits cost in the €1,500–€2,500 range, with the top of the line, known as "Couture," costing considerably more. But don't despair if your pockets aren't that deep: their ready-to-wear dress shirts are suit-defining. ⊠ *Via Condotti 58* ☎ *06/69940678* ⊕ *www. zegna.com* Ⓜ *Spagna.*

MUSIC STORES

Messaggerie Musicali. Central Rome's largest selection of music, DVDs, and concert tickets is at Messaggerie Musicali. Owned by Mondadori, the store also has a limited book section. ⊠ *Via del Corso 472* ☎ *06/684401* ⊕ *www.mondadorishop.it* Ⓜ *Spagna.*

SHOES

A. Testoni. Born in 1905 in Bologna, the heart of Italy's shoemaking territory, Amadeo Testoni opened his first shop in 1929 and began producing shoes as artistic as the cubist and art deco artwork of the period. His shoes have adorned the art-in-motion feet of Fred Astaire and proved that lightweight shoes could be comfortable and luxurious and still make heads turn. Today the Testoni brand includes an extraordinary women's collection and a sports line that is relaxed without losing its artistic heritage. The soft, calfskin sneakers are a dream, as are the matching messenger bags. ⊠ *Via Condotti 80, Spagna* ☎ *06/6788944* ⊕ *www.testoni.com* Ⓜ *Spagna.*

Fausto Santini. Fausto Santini gives a hint of extravagance in minimally decorated shoes that fashion mavens love. For more than 30 years, Santini has successfully attracted an avant-garde clientele of both men and women who flock to his preppy-hipster/nerdy-chic shoes, which are bright and colorful and sport deconstructed forms in plush, supple leathers that scream to be tried on. ■ **TIP→** A second shop at Via Cavour 106 sells last season's shoes at a deep discount. ⊠ *Via Frattina 120* ☎ *06/6784114* ⊕ *www.faustosantini.it* Ⓜ *Spagna.*

STATIONERY

★

Pineider. They've been making exclusive stationery in Italy since 1774; this is where Rome's aristocratic families have their wedding invitations engraved and their stationery personalized. For stationery and desk accessories, hand-tooled in the best Florentine leather, it has no equal. ⊠ *Via di Fontanella Borghese 22* ☎ *06/6878369* ⊕ *www. pineider.com.*

TRASTEVERE

BOOKSTORES

Almost Corner Bookshop. This Trastevere bookstore is a well-loved meeting point for English-speaking residents and visitors to this lively neighborhood. Owner Dermot O'Connell, from Kilkenny, Ireland, stocks an inviting selection ranging from translated Italian classics to the latest bestsellers. With a reputation for being able to find anything a customer requests, the small shop is a good place to special order books, and it has a wonderful selection of obscura if you've got the time to poke around. In December 2012, Mr. O'Connell opened a second store near Campo de' Fiori (at Via di Monserrato 49) serving English book-seekers on both sides of the Tiber. ⊠ *Via del Moro 45* ☎ *06/5836942.*

FLEA MARKETS

Porta Portese. Rome's biggest flea market is at Porta Portese, which welcomes 100,000 visitors every Sunday from 7 until 2. Larger than the St. Ouen in Paris, this mecca of flea markets is easily accessible via Tram No. 8. Like one vast yard sale, the market disgorges mountains of new and secondhand clothing, furniture, pictures, old records, used books, vintage clothing, and antiques—all at rock-bottom prices (especially if you're adept at haggling). There is a jovial atmosphere, with an aroma of foods wafting in the air and people crowding around the stalls, hoping to pick up a 1960s Beatles album or a rare art deco figurine. Just make sure you bring cash, as stallholders don't accept credit cards and

1

the nearest available ATM is a hike. And watch your purse—this is a popular area with pickpockets. ⊠ *Via Portuense and adjacent streets between Porta Portese and Via Ettore Rolli.*

SHOES

Fodor's Choice
★

Joseph DeBach. The best kept shoe secret in Rome and open only in the evenings, when Trastevere diners begin to strut their stuff, Joseph DeBach has weird and wonderful creations that are more art than footwear. Entirely handmade from wood, metal, and leather in his small and chaotic studio, his abacus wedge is worthy of a museum. Styles are outrageous "wow" and sometimes finished with hand-painted strings, odd bits of comic books, newspapers, or other unexpected baubles. Individually signed and dated, his shoes are distributed, in very small numbers, in London, Paris, Tokyo, and New York. ⊠ *Vicolo del Cinque 19* ☎ *06/5562756.*

VATICAN

DEPARTMENT STORES

Coin. A perfect place for upscale merchandise in a proper department store atmosphere, Coin has convenient locations in the center of Rome. Customers can select from trendy merchandise, including clothing separates, lingerie, and sportswear for men, women, and children. Searching for a pressure-driven espresso machine, a simpler stove-top Bialetti model, or a mezzaluna? You can find these and other high-quality, stylish cookware items that are difficult to find back home. If you are hopping a train from Termini station be sure to check out the smaller version of this store, which has a fabulous emphasis on hip fashions. ⊠ *Via Cola di Rienzo 173* ☎ *06/36004298* ⊕ *www.coin.it* Ⓜ *Lepanto, Ottaviano–San Pietro–Musei Vaticani.*

FOOD, WINE, AND DELICACIES

Castroni. The legend over the door reads Castroni Droghe Coloniali, but for years this international food emporium has been known by the single moniker Castroni. Opening its flagship shop near the Vatican in 1932, this gastronomic paradise has long been Rome's port of call for decadent delicacies from around the globe. Jonesing expatriates and study-abroad students pop in for their Fauchon products from Paris, their Twinings teas, or tins of their special smoked Spanish paprika. Travelers will want to stock up on exquisite Italian goodies like Sardinian bottarga, aromatic Alba white truffles, or their in-house roasted espresso. Just be sure to bring an extra suitcase: you will want to buy everything. Need a pick-me-up? Make a stop at the bar here, where the coffee is some of the best in Rome. ⊠ *Via Cola di Rienzo 196* ☎ *06/6874383* ⊕ *www.castroni.it* Ⓜ *Lepanto, Ottaviano–San Pietro– Musei Vaticani.*

GELATO

Gelateria dei Gracchi. Thanks to its all-natural ingredients and luscious flavors (the pistacchio in particular gets rave reviews), Gelateria dei Gracchi serves up the best gelato in the Vatican area—and is a serious contender for all of Rome. A favorite with locals, the no-frills shop often bustles. Don't worry: The line moves quickly, and the gelato is more than worth the wait (and the 10-minute walk from St. Peter's Basilica or Castel Sant'Angelo). ⊠ *Via dei Gracchi 272, Vatican* ☎ *06/3216668* ⊕ *gelateriadeigracchi.com* Ⓜ *Lepanto.*

RELIGIOUS MEMENTOS

Arte Italiana. Religious souvenir shops line the avenue leading to St. Peter's Basilica and at this one, whether you're looking for a unique First Holy Communion gift, rosary bracelets, or Byzantine icons, you will find something meaningful to bestow on your parish back home. The multilingual staff will help you find what you are looking for and mean to be helpful, even if they can seem pushy. The store stocks a wide variety of detailed crèche statuettes, alabaster sculptures, tapestries, saint medals, and crucifixes handmade in Italy. The pieces aren't cheap, but they are of the highest quality and make great mementos to personalize your Vatican experience. ⊠ *Via della Conciliazione 4f* ☎ *06/68806373.*

SIDE TRIPS
FROM ROME

WELCOME TO SIDE TRIPS FROM ROME

TOP REASONS TO GO

★ **Ostia Antica:** Perhaps even more than Pompeii, the excavated port city of ancient Rome conveys a picture of everyday life in the days of the Empire.

★ **Tivoli's Villa d'Este:** Hundreds of fountains cascading and shooting skyward (one even plays music on organ pipes) will delight you at this spectacular garden.

★ **Castelli Romani:** Be a Roman for a day and enjoy an escape to the ancient hilltop wine towns on the city's doorstep.

★ **Get "Middle-Aged" in Viterbo:** This town may be modern, but it has a Gothic papal palace, a Romanesque cathedral, and the magical medieval quarter of San Pellegrino.

★ **Gardens bizarre and beautiful:** Just a few miles from each other, the 16th-century proto-Disneyland Parco dei Mostri (Monster Park) is famed for its fantastic sculptures, while the Villa Lante remains the stateliest Renaissance garden of them all.

1 Tuscia. The San Pellegrino district of **Viterbo** is a 13th-century time capsule; at the gardens and palaces of nearby **Bagnaia**, **Caprarola**, and **Bomarzo** you can time-travel back to the Renaissance.

2 Ostia Antica. This ancient Roman port is now a parklike archaeological site.

3 East of Rome. Rising above the heat of Rome is cool, green **Tivoli**, a fitting setting for the regal Villa Adriana and the unforgettable Villa d'Este, a park filled with the most gorgeous fountains in the world.

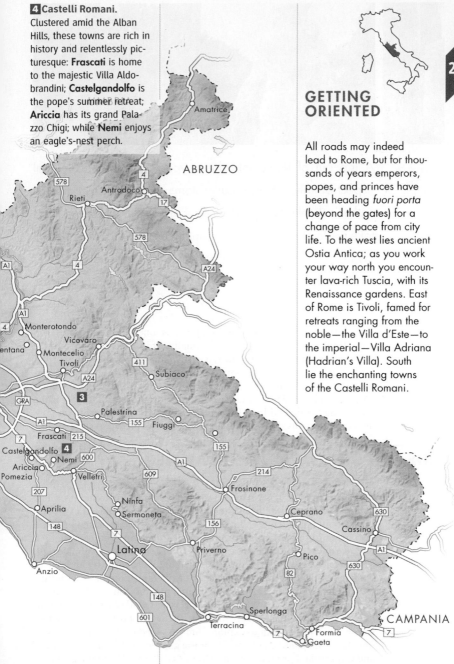

4 Castelli Romani.
Clustered amid the Alban Hills, these towns are rich in history and relentlessly picturesque: **Frascati** is home to the majestic Villa Aldobrandini; **Castelgandolfo** is the pope's summer retreat; **Ariccia** has its grand Palazzo Chigi; while **Nemi** enjoys an eagle's-nest perch.

2

GETTING ORIENTED

All roads may indeed lead to Rome, but for thousands of years emperors, popes, and princes have been heading *fuori porta* (beyond the gates) for a change of pace from city life. To the west lies ancient Ostia Antica; as you work your way north you encounter lava-rich Tuscia, with its Renaissance gardens. East of Rome is Tivoli, famed for retreats ranging from the noble—the Villa d'Este—to the imperial—Villa Adriana (Hadrian's Villa). South lie the enchanting towns of the Castelli Romani.

Updated by
Margaret
Stenhouse

A trip out of Rome introduces you to a more traditional aspect of Italy, where local customs and feast days are still enthusiastically observed, and local gastronomic specialties take pride of place on restaurant menus. Despite these small towns' proximity to the capital and the increased commuter traffic congestion of today, they still each manage to preserve their individual character.

Ostia Antica, ancient Rome's seaport, is one of the region's top attractions—it rivals Pompeii in the quality of its preservation, and for evocativeness and natural beauty, it easily outshines the Roman Forum. Emperors, cardinals, even popes have long escaped to green and verdant retreats in nearby Tivoli, Viterbo, and the Alban Hills, and their amazing villas, palaces, and gardens add to nature's allure. So if the screeching traffic and long lines at the Colosseo start to wear on you, do as the Romans do—get out of town. There's plenty to see and do.

SIDE TRIPS FROM ROME PLANNER

MAKING THE MOST OF YOUR TIME

Ostia Antica is in many ways an ideal day trip from Rome: it's a fascinating sight, not far from the city, reachable by public transit, and takes about half a day to "do." Villa d'Este and Villa Adriana in Tivoli also make for a manageable, though fuller, day trip. You can use up a flash card just on these two sights alone, but leave room to photograph Tivoli's picturesque gorge, which is strikingly crowned by an ancient Roman temple to Vesta (now it's part of the famed Sibilla restaurant). Other destinations in Lazio can be visited in a day, but you'll get more out of them if you stay the night. A classic five-day itinerary would have you first visiting Ostia Antica, the excavated port town of ancient Rome. Then head north to explore Viterbo's medieval streets on Day 2. On Day 3, take in the hot springs or the gardens of Bomarzo, Bagnaia, and Caprarola. For Day 4, head to Tivoli's delights. Then on Day 5 take a relaxing trip to the Castelli Romani, where Frascati wine is produced.

Side Trips
from Rome

Admire the monumental gardens of the aristocrats of yore and explore the narrow streets of these small hill towns. Grand villas, ancient ruins, pretty villages—what more could any vacationer want?

GETTING HERE AND AROUND

There's reliable public transit from Rome to Ostia Antica, Tivoli, and Viterbo. For other destinations in the region, a car is a big advantage—going by train or bus can add hours to your trip, and routes and schedules are often puzzling.

COTRAL. This is the regional bus company. ☎ *800/174471* ⊕ *www. cotralspa.it.*

Trenitalia. For train information, check with the national rail service. ☎ *892021* ⊕ *www.trenitalia.com.*

VISITOR INFORMATION

Tourist information kiosks in Rome can give you information about the Castelli Romani, Ostia Antica, and Tivoli.

RESTAURANTS

Please note that the "average cost" listed for each restaurant means a meal consisting of first course (primo), second course (secondo), and dessert (dolce).

HOTELS

With relatively few exceptions, accommodations in Lazio cater more to business travelers than to tourists, but there are many delightful exceptions, tucked away in historic quarters and even palaces. *Prices are for a double in high season.*

Hotel reviews have been condensed for this book. Please go to Fodors. com for full reviews of each property.

OSTIA ANTICA

30 km (19 miles) southwest of Rome.

Founded around the 4th century BC, Ostia served as Rome's port city for several centuries until the Tiber changed course, leaving the town high and dry. What has been excavated here is a remarkably intact Roman town. To get the most out of a visit, fair weather and good walking shoes are essential. To avoid the worst extremes of hot days, be here when the gates open or go late in the afternoon. A visit to the excavations takes two to three hours, including 20 minutes for the museum. Inside the site, there's a snack bar and a bookshop.

GETTING HERE AND AROUND

The best way to get to Ostia Antica is by train. The Ostia Lido train leaves every half hour from the station adjacent to Rome's Piramide Metro B subway station, stopping off at Ostia Antica en route. The trip takes 35 minutes. By car, take the Via del Mare that leads off from Rome's EUR district. Be prepared for heavy traffic, especially at peak hours, on weekends, and in summer.

2

EXPLORING

Castello della Rovere. Before exploring Ostia Antica's ruins, it's worth taking a tour through the medieval *borgo* (town). The distinctive Castello della Rovere, easily spotted as you come off the footbridge from the train station, was built by Pope Julius II when he was the cardinal bishop of Ostia in 1483. Its triangular form is unusual for military architecture. Inside are (badly faded) frescoes by Baldassare Peruzzi and a small museum of ancient Roman and medieval pottery that was found on the site. ✉ *Piazza della Rocca* ☎ *06/56358013* 🌐 *www.ostiaantica.net* 🎫 *Free* 🕒 *By tour only: Thurs. 10 and noon, Sun. 11 and noon.*

Fodor's Choice ★ **Scavi di Ostia Antica** (*Ostia Antica excavations*). Tidal mud and wind-blown sand covered the ancient port town, which lay buried until the beginning of the 20th century when it was extensively excavated. A cosmopolitan population of rich businessmen, wily merchants, sailors, slaves, and their respective families once populated the city. The great warehouses were built in the 2nd century AD to handle huge shipments of grain from Africa; the *insulae* (forerunners of the modern apartment building) provided housing for the city's growing population. Under the combined assaults of the barbarians and the malaria-carrying mosquito, and after the Tiber changed course, the port was eventually abandoned. The Ostiense Museum inside the ruined city displays sculptures, mosaics, and objects of daily use found on the site. ✉ *Viale dei Romagnoli 717* ☎ *06/56350215* 🌐 *www.ostiaantica. net* 🎫 *€6.50 includes Museo Ostiense* 🕒 *Tues.–Sun. 8:30–1 hr before sunset.*

WHERE TO EAT

$ ITALIAN 🍴 **Cipriani.** Tucked away in the little medieval town under the shadow of the castle, this cozy trattoria is decorated with reproductions of fresco fragments from a Roman palace. The kitchen offers a varied menu of Roman specialties and seasonal fare. Owner Fabrizio Cipriani speaks English and will be happy to guide you in your choice of dishes and wine from his comprehensive list. [$] *Average meal: €30* ✉ *Via del Forno 11* ☎ *06/56352956* 🌐 *www.ristorantecipriani.com* 🕒 *Closed Wed. No lunch Sun.*

TUSCIA

Tuscia (the modern name for the Etruscan domain of Etruria) is a region of dramatic beauty punctuated by deep, rocky gorges and thickly forested hills, with dappled light falling on wooded paths. This has long been a preferred locale for the retreats of wealthy Romans, a place where they could build grand villas and indulge their sometimes eccentric gardening tastes. The provincial capital, Viterbo, which overshadowed Rome as a center of papal power for a time during the Middle Ages, lies in the heart of Tuscia. The farmland east of Viterbo conceals small quarries of the dark, volcanic *peperino* stone, which shows up in the walls of many buildings here. Lake Bolsena is an extinct volcano, and the sulfur springs still bubbling up in the spas were used by the ancient Romans. Bagnaia and Caprarola are home

A GOOD WALK: OSTIA ANTICA

The **Porta Romana,** one of the city's three gates, is where you enter the Ostia Antica excavations. It opens onto the Decumanus Maximus, the main thoroughfare crossing the city from end to end. To your right, a staircase leads to a platform—the remains of the upper floor of the **Terme di Nettuno** (Baths of Neptune)—from which you get a good view of the mosaic pavements showing a marine scene with Neptune and the sea goddess Amphitrite. Behind the baths are the barracks of the fire department. On the north side of the Decumanus Maximus is the beautiful **Teatro** (Theater), built by Agrippa, remodeled by Septimius Severus in the 2nd century AD, and restored by the Rome City Council in the 20th century. In the vast Piazzale delle Corporazioni, where trade organizations had their offices, is the **Tempio di Cerere** (Temple of Ceres)—highly appropriate for a town dealing in grain imports, Ceres being the goddess of agriculture. From there you can visit the **Domus di Apuleio** (House of Apuleius), built in Pompeian style, lower to the ground and with fewer windows than was characteristic of Ostia. Next door, the **Mithraeum** has balconies and a hall decorated with symbols of the cult of Mithras, whose beliefs and symbols may have been imported from Persia.

On Via Semita dei Cippi, just off Via dei Molini, the **Domus della Fortuna Annonaria** (House of Fortuna Annonaria) is the richly decorated residence of a wealthy Ostian; one of the rooms opens onto a secluded garden. On Via dei Molini you can see a **molino** (mill), where grain was ground with stones that are still here. Along Via di Diana you come upon a **thermopolium** (bar) with a marble counter and a fresco depicting the foods sold here.

At the end of Via dei Dipinti is the **Museo Ostiense** (Ostia Museum), which displays sarcophagi, massive marble columns, and large statuary. (The last entry to the museum is a half hour before the Scavi closes.) The **Forum,** on the south side of Decumanus Maximus, holds the monumental remains of the city's most important temple, dedicated to Jupiter, Juno, and Minerva. It's also the site of other ruins of baths, a basilica (which in Roman times was a hall of justice), and smaller temples.

Via Epagathiana leads toward the Tiber, where there are large **horrea** (warehouses) erected during the 2nd century AD for the enormous amounts of grain imported into Rome during the height of the Empire. West of Via Epagathiana, the **Domus di Amore e Psiche** (House of Cupid and Psyche), a residence, was named for a statue found here (now on display in the museum); the house's enclosed garden is decorated with marble and mosaic motifs and has the remains of a large pool. The **Casa di Serapide** (House of Serapis) on Via della Foce is a 2nd-century multilevel dwelling; another apartment building stands a street over on Via degli Aurighi. Nearby, the **Termi dei Sette Sapienti** (Baths of the Seven Wise Men) are named for a group of bawdy frescoes. The **Porta Marina** leads to what used to be the seashore and the **sinagoga,** dating from the 4th century AD.

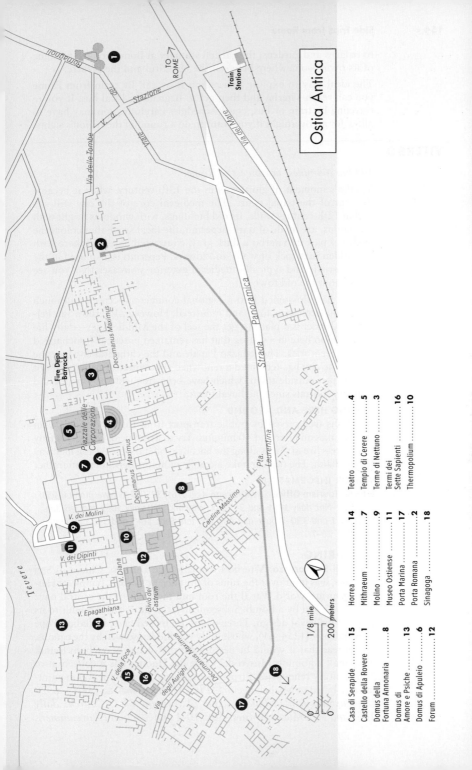

Ostia Antica

TO ROME

Train Station

Romagnoli

V.d. Stazione

Viale del Mare

Via del Mare

Via delle Tombe

Decumanus Maximus

Fire Dept. Barracks

Piazzale delle Corporazioni

Decumanus Maximus

Cardine Massimo

V. dei Molini

V. dei Dipinti

V. Diana

Bivio del Castrum

V. Epagathiana

Tevere

Strada Panoramica

Pta. Leuentina

Cardine Massimo

V. della Foce

V. degli Aurighi

Decumanus Maximus

1/8 mile
200 meters

to palaces and gardens; the garden statuary at Bomarzo is in a league of its own—somewhere between the beautiful and the bizarre.

The ideal way to explore this region is by car. By train from Rome you can reach Viterbo and then get to Bagnaia by local bus. If you're traveling by train or bus, check schedules carefully; you may have to allow for an overnight if you want to do a round of the region's sights.

VITERBO

104 km (64 miles) northwest of Rome.

Viterbo's moment of glory was in the 13th century, when it became the seat of the papal court. The medieval core of the city still sits within 12th-century walls. Its old buildings, with windows bright with geraniums, are made of dark peperino, the local stone that colors the medieval part of Viterbo a dark gray, contrasted here and there with the golden tufa rock of walls and towers. Peperino is also used in the characteristic and typically medieval exterior staircases that you see throughout the old town.

Viterbo has blossomed into a regional commercial center, and much of the modern city is loud and industrial. However, Viterbo's San Pellegrino district is a place to get the feel of the Middle Ages—daily life is carried on here in a setting that has remained practically unchanged over the centuries. The Palazzo Papale and the cathedral enhance the effect. The city has remained a renowned spa center for its natural hot springs just outside town, which have been frequented by popes and ordinary mortals since medieval times.

GETTING HERE AND AROUND

Viterbo is well served by public transport from Rome. A direct train service takes an hour and 40 minutes. Try to avoid peak hours, as many commuters live in towns along the line. By road, take the A1 toll highway to Attigliano. The trip can take a couple of hours, depending on traffic.

VISITOR INFORMATION

Viterbo Tourism Office ⊠ *Via Ascenzi 4* ☎ *0761/325992* ⊕ *www.promotuscia. it* ⊗ *Nov.–Mar. daily 10–1 and 3–5, Apr.–May and Oct. daily 10–1 and 3–6, Jun. daily 10–1 and 3:30–7, July–mid-Aug. and late Sept. 10–1 and 3–7, mid-Aug– late Sept. 10–7.*

EXPLORING

Chiesa di San Lorenzo. Viterbo's Romanesque Duomo, Chiesa di San Lorenzo, was built over the ruins of the ancient Roman Temple of Hercules. During World War II the roof and the vault of the central nave were destroyed by a bomb. Subsequently, the church was rebuilt to its original medieval design. Three popes are buried here, including Pope Alexander IV (1254–61), whose body was hidden so well by the canons, out of fear that it would be desecrated, that it has never been found. The small adjoining **Museo del Colle del Duomo** has a collection of 18th-century reliquaries, Etruscan sarcophagi, and a crucifixion painting attributed to Michelangelo. ⊠ *Piazza San Lorenzo* ☎ *338/1336529* ⊕ *www.museocolledelduomo.com* ☑ *Museum €3* ⊗ *Church: daily 10–1 and 3–6. Museum: Tues.–Sun. 10–1 and 3–6 (until 7 in summer).*

Palazzo Papale (*Papal Palace*). A Gothic palace was built in the 13th century as a residence for popes looking to get away from the city. At that time Rome was a notoriously unhealthful place, ridden with malaria and plague and rampaging factions of rival barons. In 1271 the palace was the scene of a novel type of rebellion. A conclave held here to elect a new pope had dragged on for months. The people of Viterbo were exasperated by the delay, especially as custom decreed that they had to provide for the cardinals' board and lodging for the duration of the conclave. So they tore the roof off the great hall where the cardinals were meeting, and gave them nothing but bread and water. Sure enough, a new pope—Gregory X—was elected in short order. ✉ *Piazza San Lorenzo* ☎ *338/1336529* 🌐 *www.museocolledelduomo.com* 🎫 *€7, includes Museo del Colle del Duomo* ⏲ *June–Sept., Tues.–Sun. 10-1 and 3–7; Oct.–May, Tues.–Sun. 10–1 and 3–6.*

San Pellegrino. One of the best preserved medieval districts in Italy has charming vistas of arches, vaults, towers, exterior staircases, worn wooden doors on great iron hinges, and tiny hanging gardens. You pass many antiques shops and craft workshops as you explore the little squares and byways. The **Fontana Grande** in the piazza of the same name is the largest and most extravagant of Viterbo's Gothic fountains. ✉ *Via San Pellegrino.*

Terme dei Papi. Viterbo has been a spa town for centuries, and this excellent spa continues the tradition, providing the usual health and beauty treatments an Etruscan twist: try a facial with local volcanic mud, or a steam bath in an ancient cave, where scalding hot mineral water direct from the spring splashes down a waterfall to a pool beneath your feet. The Terme dei Papi's main draw, however, is the *terme* (baths) themselves: a 21,000-square-foot outdoor limestone pool, into the shallow end of which Viterbo's famous hot water pours at 59°C (138°F)—and gives a jolt with its sulfurous odor. Floats and deck chairs are for rent, but bring your own bathrobe and towel unless you're staying at the hotel. ✉ *Strada Bagni 12, 5 km (3 miles) west of town center* ☎ *0761/3501* 🌐 *www.termedeipapi.it* 🎫 *Pool: weekdays €12, weekends €18* ⏲ *Pool: Wed.–Mon. 9–7 (until 1 am Sat. in Aug.). Spa: daily 9–7.*

WHERE TO EAT

$$$$ ITALIAN

🍴 **Enoteca La Torre.** One of the best wine cellars in Italy, with more than 1000 labels, takes center stage at the elegant Enoteca La Torre. It's also a temple to good eating: in addition to an ever-changing menu there are lists for cheeses, mineral waters, oils, and vinegars. *Baccalà* (salted cod) or ravioli with ricotta cheese and cream of chicken livers are recommended, but whatever you choose will be local, traditional, and of the highest quality. [$] *Average meal: €70* ✉ *Via della Torre 5* ☎ *0761/226467* 🌐 *www.enotecalatorrevt.com* ⏲ *Closed Tues. and Wed. No dinner Sun.*

$ ITALIAN

🍴 **Osteria Palazzo dei Mercanti.** Enjoy impeccably executed classics at extremely good prices at this casual eatery in the heart of town: it shares a kitchen with the more upscale Enoteca La Torre. Try whatever is listed as the daily rotating special, such as *pappardelle* (fresh, wide-cut pasta) or bean and pasta soup. You can select a glass or bottle from the Enoteca's epic wine list, which includes a complex matrix of ratings from Italy's foremost wine reviewers. $ *Average meal: €25* ✉ *Via della Torre 1* ☎ *0761/226467* ⊕ *www.enotecalatorrevt.com.*

$$
ITALIAN
✗ **Tre Re.** Viterbo's oldest restaurant—and one of the most ancient in Italy—has been operating in the *centro storico* (historic center) since 1622. The kitchen focuses on traditional local dishes, such as *zuppa ceci e castagne* (chickpea and chestnut soup). The wine list offers the best of Italian wines. The small, wood-paneled dining room, chummily packed with tables, was a favorite haunt of movie director Federico Fellini and, before that, of British and American soldiers during World War II. Local diners make a point of touching the old inn sign of the "Three Kings," hanging on the wall inside, as this is supposed to bring good luck. $ *Average meal: €30* ✉ *Via Macel Gattesco 3* ☎ *0761/304619* ⊕ *www.ristorantetrere.com* ☉ *Closed Thurs.*

WHERE TO STAY

For expanded hotel reviews, visit Fodors.com.

$$$
HOTEL
🏨 **Hotel Niccolò V.** An air of relaxed, country-house elegance and comfortable rooms provide a sharp contrast to the brisk and clinical atmosphere of the spa complex at Terme dei Papi, to which it is attached, bustles with doctors, bathers in bathrobes, and uniformed staff. **Pros:** friendly staff; comfortable rooms; relaxing atmosphere. **Cons:** guests lounge in the lobby in bathrobes; several miles out of town. $ *Rooms from: €280* ✉ *Strada Bagni 12, 5 km (3 miles) west of center* ☎ *0761/350555* ⊕ *www.termedeipapi.it* ⟿ *20 rooms, 3 suites* ⏍ *Some meals.*

$
B&B/INN
🏨 **La Terrazza Medioevale.** The historic Palazzo Perotti in the heart of old Viterbo's San Pellegrino district is the setting for these three stylish, elegantly furnished rooms. **Pros:** elegant surroundings at bargain price. **Cons:** no credit cards accepted; accessible only by flight of stairs. $ *Rooms from: €80* ✉ *Via S. Pellegrino 1* ☎ *0761/307034* ⊕ *www. laterrazzamedioevale.it* ⟿ *3 rooms* ⊟ *No credit cards* ⏍ *Breakfast.*

BAGNAIA

5 km (3 miles) east of Viterbo.

GETTING HERE AND AROUND

Local buses from Viterbo are one way to get here. By local train, it's 10 minutes beyond the Viterbo stop—few local trains actually do, though, so be sure to check.

EXPLORING

Villa Lante. The village of Bagnaia is the site of the 16th-century cardinal Alessandro Montalto's summer retreat; it's quite an extravaganza. The hillside garden and park that surround the two small, identical residences are the real draw—they were designed by virtuoso architect Giacomo Barozzi (circa 1507–73), known as Vignola, who later worked with Michelangelo on St. Peter's. On the lowest terrace a delightful Italian garden has a centerpiece fountain fed by water channeled down the hillside. On another terrace, a stream of water runs through a groove carved in a long stone table where the cardinal entertained his friends alfresco, chilling wine in the running water. That's only one of the most evident of the whimsical water games that were devised for the cardinal. The symmetry of the formal gardens contrasts with the wild, untamed park adjacent to it, reflecting the paradoxes of nature and artifice that are the theme of this pleasure garden. ⊠ *Via G. Baroni 71* ☎ *0761/288008* ⊕ *www.villalante.it* ⊠ *€5* ⊙ *Tues.–Sun. 8:30–1 hr before sunset.*

CAPRAROLA

21 km (16 miles) southeast of Bagnaia, 19 km (12 miles) southeast of Viterbo.

The wealthy and powerful Farnese family took over this sleepy village in the 1500s and had the architect Vignola design a huge palace and gardens to rival the great residences of Rome. He also rearranged the little town of Caprarola to enhance the palazzo's setting.

GETTING HERE AND AROUND
Caprarola is served by COTRAL bus, leaving from Rome's Saxa Rubra station on the Roma Nord suburban railway line.

EXPLORING
Palazzo Farnese. Built on an unusual pentagonal plan, this huge and splendid 400-year-old palazzo has an ingenious system of ramps and terraces that leads right up to the main portal. This nicety allowed carriages and mounts to arrive directly in front of the door. Though the salons are unfurnished, the palace's grandeur is still evident. An artificial grotto decorates one wall, the ceilings are covered with frescoes glorifying the Farnese family, and an entire room is frescoed with maps of the world as it was known to 16th-century cartographers. The palace is surrounded by a magnificent formal garden, which is open only for guided tours. ⊠ *Piazza Farnese 1* ☎ *0761/646052* ⊠ *€5* ⊙ *Palazzo: Tues.–Sun. 8:30–1 hr before sunset. Garden tour: Tues.–Sat. 10, 11, noon, and 3.*

BOMARZO

15 km (9 miles) northeast of Viterbo.

GETTING HERE AND AROUND
Bomarzo is 6 km (4 miles) from the A1 Autostrada Attigliano exit, so if you're coming to Viterbo by car, it's easy to stop off on the way. Alternatively, you can get a public bus from Viterbo.

EXPLORING
FAMILY **Parco dei Mostri** (*Monster Park*). The eerie fantasy originally known as the Village of Marvels, or the Sacred Wood, was created in 1552 by Prince Vicino Orsini. It's a kind of Disneyland forerunner, populated with weird and fantastic sculptures of mythical creatures, intended to astonish illustrious guests. The sculptures, carved in outcroppings of mossy stone in shady groves and woodland, include giant tortoises and griffins and an ogre's head with an enormous gaping mouth. Children love it, and there are photo ops galore. The park has a self-service café (closed in winter) and a souvenir shop. ⊠ *1½ km (1 mile) west of Bomarzo* ☎ *0761/924029* ⊕ *www.parcodeimostri.com* ⊠ *€10* ⊙ *Daily 8:30–sunset.*

TIVOLI AND PALESTRINA

Tivoli is a five-star draw, its attractions being its two villas—an ancient one in which Hadrian reproduced the most beautiful monuments in the then-known world, and a Renaissance one, in which cardinal Ippolito d'Este put a river to work for his delight. Unfortunately, the road from Rome to Tivoli passes through miles of uninspiring industrial areas with chaotic traffic. Grit your teeth and persevere. It'll be worth it. In the heart of this gritty shell lie two pearls that are rightly world famous. You'll know you're close to Tivoli when you see vast quarries of travertine marble and smell the sulfurous vapors of the little spa, Bagni di Tivoli. Both sites in Tivoli are outdoors and entail walking. With a car, you can continue your loop through the mountains east of Rome, taking in the ancient pagan sanctuary at Palestrina, spectacularly set on the slopes of Mount Ginestro.

TIVOLI

36 km (22 miles) northeast of Rome.

In ancient times just about anybody who was anybody had a villa in Tivoli, including Crassius, Trajan, Hadrian, Horace, and Catullus. Tivoli fell into obscurity in the medieval era until the Renaissance, when popes and cardinals came back to the town and built villas showy enough to rival those of their extravagant predecessors.

Nowadays Tivoli is small but vibrant, with winding streets and views over the surrounding countryside. The deep Aniene River gorge runs right through the center of town, and comes replete with a romantically sited bridge, cascading waterfalls, and two jewels of ancient Roman architecture that crown its cliffs—the round Temple of Vesta (or the Sybil, the prophetess credited with predicting the birth of Christ) and the ruins of the rectangular Temple of the hero-god Tibur, the mythical founder of the city. These can be picturesquely viewed across the gorge from the Villa Gregoriana park, named for Pope Gregory XVI, who saved Tivoli from chronic river damage by diverting the river through a tunnel, weakening its flow. An unexpected (but not unappreciated) side effect was the creation of the Grande Cascata (Grand Cascade), which shoots a huge jet of water into the valley below. You may also want to set your sights on the Antico Ristorante Sibilla, set right by the Temple of Vesta. From its dining terrace you can take in one of the most memorably romantic landscape views in Italy.

GETTING HERE AND AROUND

Unless you have nerves of steel, it's best not to drive to Tivoli. Hundreds of industries line the Via Tiburtina from Rome and bottleneck traffic is nearly constant. You can avoid some, but not all, of the congestion by taking the Roma–L'Aquila toll road. Luckily, there's abundant public transport. Buses leave every 15 minutes from the Ponte Mammolo stop on the Metro A line. The ride takes an hour. Regional Trenitalia trains connect from both Termini and Tiburtina stations and will have you in Tivoli in under an hour. Villa d'Este is in the town center, and a frequent bus service from Tivoli's main square goes to Hadrian's Villa.

VISITOR INFORMATION

PIT (Punto Informativo Turistico) *(Tivoli tourist office).* ✉ *Piazzale Nazioni Unite* ☎ *0774/313536* ⊕ *www.comune.tivoli.rm.it/pit* ⊙ *Tues.–Sun. 9:30–5:30.*

EXPLORING

Villa Adriana *(Hadrian's Villa).* An astonishingly grand 2nd-century villa was an emperor's theme park: an exclusive retreat below the ancient settlement of Tibur where the marvels of the classical world were reproduced for a ruler's pleasure. Hadrian, who succeeded Trajan as emperor in AD 117, was a man of genius and intellectual curiosity, fascinated by the accomplishments of the Hellenistic world. From AD 125 to 134, architects, laborers, and artists worked on the villa, periodically spurred on by the emperor himself when he returned from another voyage full of ideas for even more daring constructions (he also gets credit for Rome's Pantheon). After his death in AD 138 the fortunes of his villa declined as it was sacked by barbarians and Romans alike. Many of his statues and decorations ended up in the Vatican Museums, but the expansive ruins are nonetheless compelling. It's not the single elements but the delightful effect of the whole that makes Hadrian's Villa so great. Oleanders, pines, and cypresses growing among the ruins heighten the visual impact. To help you get your bearings, maps are issued free with the audio guides (€5). A visit here takes about two hours, more if you like to savor antiquity slowly. In summer visit early to take advantage of cool mornings. ✉ *Bivio di Villa Adriana off Via Tiburtina, 6 km (4 mile) southwest of Tivoli* ☎ *0774/382733 for reservations* 🎫 *€8* ⊙ *Daily 9–1 hr before sunset.*

Villa d'Este. Created by Cardinal Ippolito d'Este in the 16th century, this villa in the center of Tivoli was the most amazing pleasure garden of its day: it still stuns visitors with its beauty. Este (1509–72), a devotee of the Renaissance celebration of human ingenuity over nature, was inspired by the excavation of Villa Adriana. He paid architect Pirro Ligorio an astronomical sum to create a mythical garden with water as its artistic centerpiece. To console himself for his seesawing fortunes in the political intrigues of his time (he happened to be cousin to Pope Alexander VI), he had his builders tear down part of a Franciscan monastery to clear the site, then divert the Aniene River to water the garden and feed the fountains. And what fountains: big, small, noisy, quiet, rushing, running, and combining to create a late-Renaissance, proto–Busby Berkeley masterpiece in which sunlight, shade, water, gardens, and carved stone create an unforgettable experience. To this day, several hundred fountains cascade, shoot skyward, imitate birdsongs, and simulate rain. The musical **Fontana dell'Organo** has been restored to working order: the organ plays a watery tune every two hours from 10:30 to 6:30 (until 2:30 in winter). Romantics will love the night tour of the gardens and floodlit fountains, available on Friday and Saturday from July until September. Allow at least an hour for the visit, and bear in mind that there are a lot of stairs to climb. There's also a café on the upper terrace leading from the palace entrance, where you can sit and admire the view. ✉ *Piazza Trento 1* ☎ *0774/312070* ⊕ *www.villadestetivoli.info* 🎫 *€8* ⊙ *Tues.–Sun. 8:30–1 hr before sunset.*

WHERE TO EAT AND STAY

For expanded hotel reviews, visit Fodors.com.

$$$ ITALIAN Fodor's Choice ★ 🍴 **Antico Ristorante Sibilla.** This famed restaurant should be included among the most beautiful sights of Tivoli. Built in 1730 beside the circular Roman Temple of Vesta and the Sanctuary of the Sybil, the terrace garden has a spectacular view over the deep gorge of the Aniene River, with the thundering waters of the waterfall in the background. Marble plaques on the walls list the royals who have come here to dine over 2½ centuries. The food, wine, and service standards are all high, and in recent years there's been more and more emphasis placed on seasonal produce and local dishes. Be sure to sample the speciality of the house—a lavish choice of antipasti served on individual triple-tiered trays that resemble old-fashioned cake stands. Dishes for the first course may include pappardelle made with spelt and dressed with garlic, olive oil and tiny "datterini" tomatoes. For the second course, local lamb; suckling pig; and a salad with ricotta, herbs, honey, and prunes may all make an appearance. The desserts are equally strong contenders for your attention. [$] *Average meal: €50* ✉ *Via della Sibilla 50* ☎ *0774/335281* 🌐 *www.ristorantesibilla.com* 🕒 *Closed Mon. Oct.–Feb.*

$ B&B/INN 🏨 **Adriano.** Guest rooms in a converted 19th-century mansion tend to be small, with an overabundance of chintz drapes, but the position right next to the ruins of the Emperor Hadrian's palatial residence is ample compensation. **Pros:** wonderful location; peaceful garden; attentive service. **Cons:** busloads of tourists disembark under the windows; restaurant can be crowded. [$] *Rooms from: €80* ✉ *Largo Yourcenar 2, Via di Villa Adriana 194* ☎ *0774/382235* 🌐 *www.hoteladriano.it* 🛏 *10 rooms* 🍽 *Breakfast.*

$$ HOTEL 🏨 **Hotel Torre Sant'Angelo.** A former monastery and residence of the Massimo princes now offers comfortable guest rooms well equipped with modern amenities and, best of all, overlooking the old town, the Aniene Falls, and the Temple of the Sybil. **Pros:** 21st-century comfort in a historic mansion house; pool; competitive rates. **Cons:** isolated location a mile out of town. [$] *Rooms from: €150* ✉ *Via Quintilio Varo* ☎ *0774/332533* 🌐 *www.hoteltorresangelo.it* 🛏 *25 rooms, 10 suites* 🍽 *Breakfast.*

PALESTRINA

27 km (17 miles) southeast of Tivoli, 37 km (23 miles) east of Rome.

Except to students of ancient history and music lovers, Palestrina is surprisingly little known outside Italy. Its most famous native son, Giovanni Pierluigi da Palestrina, born here in 1525, is considered the master of counterpoint and polyphony. He composed 105 masses, as well as madrigals, Magnificats, and motets. But the town was celebrated long before the composer's lifetime.

Ancient Praeneste (modern Palestrina) flourished much earlier than Rome. It was the site of the Temple of Fortuna Primigenia, which dates from the 2nd century BC. This was one of the largest, richest, most frequented temple complexes in all antiquity—people came from far and wide to consult its famous oracle. In modern times no one had any idea of the extent of the complex until World War II bombings exposed ancient foundations occupying huge artificial terraces stretching from the upper part of the town as far downhill as its central Duomo.

GETTING HERE AND AROUND

COTRAL buses leave from the Anagnina terminal on Rome's Metro A line and from the Tiburtina railway station. Alternatively, you can take a train to Zagarolo, where a COTRAL bus takes you on to Palestrina. The total trip takes 40 minutes. By car, take the A1 Autostrada del Sole to the San Cesareo exit and follow the signs to Palestrina. Expect it to take about an hour.

VISITOR INFORMATION

Palestrina Tourism Office ✉ *Piazzale Caduti Senza Croce* ☎ *06/95302318* 🕒 *Daily 8–1:45 and 4–8.*

EXPLORING

Palazzo Barberini. Large arches and terraces scale the hillside up to this imposing palazzo that crowns a flight of steep, stone stairs. The palace was built in the 17th century along the semicircular lines of the original temple. It now contains the **Museo Nazionale Archeologico di Palestrina,** with material found on the site that dates from throughout the classical period. A well-labeled collection of Etruscan bronzes, pottery, and terra-cotta statuary as well as Roman artifacts must take second place to the main event, a first-century BC mosaic showing ancient Egyptian pleasure craft and African animals. This delightful, highly colorful and detailed work is worth the trip to Palestrina by itself. But there's more: a model of the temple as it was in ancient times helps you appreciate the immensity of the original construction. ✉ *Piazza della Cortina 1* ☎ *06/9538100* 🎟 *€5* 🕒 *Museum: daily 9–8. Archaeological zone: daily 9–1 hr before sunset.*

WHERE TO EAT

$$$ ITALIAN 🍴 **Il Piscarello.** Tucked away at the bottom of a steep side road, this elegant dining room comes as a bit of a surprise. The yellow damask table linen and the deep gold curtains lend a warm and sunny look, and a trim patio overlooking the garden is the setting for alfresco meals in good weather. Specialties on the menu include seafood and succulent fish or meat carpaccio. [$] *Average meal: €50* ✉ *Via del Piscarello 2* ☎ *06/9574326* 🌐 *www.ristoranteilpiscarello.it* 🕒 *Closed Mon.*

THE CASTELLI ROMANI

The "castelli" aren't really castles, as their name would seem to imply. They're little towns that are scattered on the slopes of the Alban Hills near Rome. And the Alban Hills aren't really hills, but extinct volcanoes. There were castles here in the Middle Ages, however, when each of these towns, fiefs of rival Roman lords, had its own fortress to defend it. Some centuries later, the area became given over to villas and retreats, notably the pope's summer residence at Castelgandolfo, and the 17th- and 18th-century villas that transformed Frascati into the Beverly Hills of Rome. Arrayed around the rim of an extinct volcano that encloses two crater lakes, the string of picturesque towns of the

Castelli Romani are today surrounded by vineyards, olive groves, and chestnut woods—no wonder overheated Romans have always loved to escape here.

Ever since Roman times the Castelli towns have been renowned for their wine. In the narrow, medieval alleyways of the oldest parts you can still find old-fashioned hostelries where the locals sit on wooden benches, quaffing the golden nectar straight from the barrel. Following the mapped-out **Castelli Wine Route** (⊕ *www.stradadeivinideicastelliromani. it*) around the numerous vineyards and wine cellars is a more sophisticated alternative. Exclusive local gastronomic specialties include the bread of Genzano, baked in traditional wood-fire ovens, the *porchetta* (roast suckling pig) of Ariccia, and the *pupi* biscuits of Frascati, shaped like women or mermaids with three or more breasts (an allusion to ancient fertility goddesses). Each town has its own feasts and saints' days, celebrated with costumed processions and colorful events. Some are quite spectacular, like Marino's annual Wine Festival in October, where the town's fountains flow with wine; or the Flower Festival of Genzano in June, when an entire street is carpeted with millions of flower petals, arranged in elaborate patterns.

FRASCATI

20 km (12 miles) south of Rome.

It's worth taking a stroll through Frascati's lively old center. Via Battisti, leading from the Belvedere, takes you into Piazza San Pietro with its imposing gray-and-white cathedral. Inside is the cenotaph of Prince Charles Edward, last of the Scottish Stuart dynasty, who tried unsuccessfully to regain the British Crown, and died an exile in Rome in 1788. A little arcade beside the monumental fountain at the back of the piazza leads into Market Square, where the smell of fresh baking will entice you into the Purificato family bakery to see the traditional pupi biscuits, modeled on old pagan fertility symbols.

Take your pick from the cafés and trattorias fronting the central Piazzale Marconi, or do as the locals do—buy fruit from the market gallery at Piazza del Mercato, then get a huge slice of porchetta from one of the stalls, a hunk of *casareccio* bread, and a few *ciambelline frascatane* (ring-shape cookies made with wine), and take your picnic to any one of the nearby *cantine* (homey wine bars), and settle in for some sips of tasty, inexpensive vino.

GETTING HERE AND AROUND

An hourly train service along a single-track line through vineyards and olive groves takes you to Frascati from Termini station. The trip takes 45 minutes. By car, take the Via Tuscolano, which branches off the Appia Nuova road just after St. John Lateran in Rome, and drive straight up.

VISITOR INFORMATION

Frascati Point (tourism office) ⊠ *Piazza G. Marconi 5* ☎ *06/94015378* ⊗ *Weekdays 8–8, weekends 10–8.*

2

EXPLORING
Abbey of San Nilo. In Grottaferrata, a busy village a couple of miles from Frascati, the main attraction is a walled citadel founded by the 90-year-old St. Nilo, who brought his group of Basilian monks here in 1004. The order is unique in that it's Roman Catholic but observes Greek Orthodox rites.

The fortified abbey, considered a masterpiece of martial architecture, was restructured in the 15th century by Antonio da Sangallo for the future Pope Julius II. The abbey church, inside the second courtyard, is a jewel of oriental opulence, with glittering Byzantine mosaics and a revered icon set into a marble tabernacle designed by Bernini. The Farnese chapel, leading from the right nave, contains a series of frescoes by Domenichino.

If you make arrangements in advance you can visit the library, which is one of the oldest in Italy. The abbey also has a famous laboratory for the restoration of antique books and manuscripts, where Leonardo's *Atlantic Code* was restored in 1962 and more than a thousand precious volumes were saved after the disastrous Florence flood in 1966. ⊠ *Corso del Popolo 128, Grottaferrata* ☎ *06/9459309* ⊕ *www.abbaziagreca.it* ⊠ *Free* ⊙ *Daily 7:30–12:30 and 3:30–6:30.*

Villa Aldobrandini. Frascati was a retreat of prelates and princes, who built magnificent villas on the sun-drenched slopes overlooking the Roman plain. The most spectacular of these is still owned by the Princes Aldobrandini and dominates Frascati's main square from the top of its steeply sloped park.

Built in the late 16th century and adorned with frescoes by the Zuccari brothers and the Cavalier d'Arpino, the hulking villa takes second place to the park, which is open to the public and is a marvel of Baroque fountains and majestic box-shaded avenues. There you can see the magnificent "water theater" that Cardinal Pietro Aldobrandini, Pope Clement VIII's favorite nephew, built to impress his guests, thinking nothing of diverting the water supply that served the entire area in order to make his fountains play. The gigantic central figure of Atlas holding up the world is believed to represent the pope. You can also see another water theater in the grounds of nearby Villa Torlonia, which is now a public park. ⊠ *Via Cardinale Massaia* ☎ *06/9421434* ⊠ *Free* ⊙ *Garden weekdays 9–5.*

WHERE TO EAT AND STAY
For expanded hotel reviews, visit Fodors.com.

$$ ✕ **Al Fico Vecchio.** This historic coaching inn, dating to the 16th century,
ITALIAN   is on an old Roman road a couple of miles outside Frascati. It has a charming garden shaded by the old fig tree that gave the place its name. The dining room has been tastefully renovated, preserving many of the characteristic antique features. The menu offers a wide choice of local dishes, such as gnocchi with cheese and truffles. $ *Average meal: €50* ⊠ *Via Anagnini 257* ☎ *06/9459261* ⊕ *www.alfico.it.*

$$$ ⊡ **Park Hotel Villa Grazioli.** One of the region's most famous residences,
HOTEL   this elegant patrician villa halfway between Frascati and Grottaferrata
Fodor's Choice   is now a first-class hotel, though the standard-issue guest rooms are a
★   bit of a letdown amid the frescoed salons. **Pros:** wonderful views of the countryside; elegant atmosphere; professional staff. **Cons:** difficult to

find; some rooms could do with a bit of renovation. [$] *Rooms from: €180* ✉ *Via Umberto Pavoni 19, Grottaferrata* ☎ *06/9454001* 🌐 *www.villagrazioli.com* 🛏 *60 rooms, 2 suites.*

CASTELGANDOLFO

8 km (5 miles) southwest of Frascati, 25 km (15 miles) south of Rome. This little town is well known as the pope's summer retreat. It was the Barberini Pope Urban VIII who first headed here, eager to escape the malarial miasmas that afflicted summertime Rome; before long, the city's princely families also set up country estates around here.

The 17th-century **Villa Pontificia** has a superb position overlooking Lake Albano and is set in one of the most gorgeous gardens in Italy; unfortunately, neither the house nor the park is open to the public (although crowds are admitted into the inner courtyard for papal audiences). On the little square in front of the palace there's a fountain by Bernini, who also designed the nearby Church of San Tommaso da Villanova, which has works by Pietro da Cortona.

The village has a number of interesting craft workshops and food purveyors, in addition to the souvenir shops on the square. On the horizon, the silver astronomical dome belonging to the Specola Vaticana observatory—one of the first in Europe—where the scientific Pope Gregory XIII indulged his interest in stargazing, is visible for miles around.

GETTING HERE AND AROUND

There's an hourly train service for Castelgandolfo from Termini station (Rome–Albano line). Otherwise, buses leave frequently from the Anagnina terminal of the Metro A subway. The trip takes about 30 minutes. By car, take the Appian Way from San Giovanni in Rome and follow it straight to Albano, where you branch off for Castelgandolfo (about an hour, depending on traffic).

EXPLORING

FAMILY **Lakeside Lido.** Lined with restaurants, ice-cream parlors, and cafés, this is favorite spot for Roman families to relax. No motorized craft are allowed on the lake, but you can rent paddleboats and kayaks. The waters are full of seafowl, such as swans and herons, and there is a nature trail along the wooded end of the shore for those who want to get away from the throng. There are bathing establishments where you can rent deck chairs; you might also want to stop to eat a plate of freshly prepared pasta or a gigantic Roman sandwich at one of the little snack bars under the oak and alder trees. There's also a small, permanent fairground for children.

WHERE TO EAT

$$$ ITALIAN 🍴 **Antico Ristorante Pagnanelli.** One of most refined restaurants in the Castelli Romani has been in the same family since 1882. The present generation—Aurelio Mariani, his Australian wife, Jane, and their four sons—have lovingly restored this old railway inn perched high above Lake Albano. The dining-room windows open onto a breathtaking view across the lake to the conical peak of Monte Cavo. In winter a log fire blazes in a corner; in summer you can dine on the flower-filled terrace.

Many of the dishes are prepared with produce from the family's own farm. The wine cellar, carved out of the local tufa rock, boasts more than 3,000 labels. [$] *Average meal: €70* ✉ *Via Gramsci 4* ☎ *06/9361740* 🌐 *www.pagnanelli.it.*

ARICCIA

8 km (5 miles) southwest of Castelgandolfo, 26 km (17 miles) south of Rome.

Ariccia is a gem of Baroque town planning. When millionaire banker Agostino Chigi became Pope Alexander VII, he commissioned Gian Lorenzo Bernini to redesign his country estate to make it worthy of his new station. Bernini consequently restructured not only the existing 16th-century palace, but also the town gates, the main square with its loggias and graceful twin fountains, and the round church of Santa Maria dell'Assunzione (the dome is said to be modeled on the Pantheon). The rest of the village coiled around the apse of the church down into the valley below.

Strangely, Ariccia's splendid heritage has been largely forgotten in the 20th century, and yet it was once one of the highlights of every artist's and writer's Grand Tour. Corot, Ibsen, Turner, Longfellow, and Hans Christian Andersen all came to stay here.

GETTING HERE AND AROUND

For Ariccia, take the COTRAL bus from the Anagnina terminal of the Metro A underground line. Buses on the Albano–Genzano–Velletri line stop under the monumental bridge that spans the Ariccia Valley, where an elevator whisks you up to the main town square. If you take a train to Albano, you can proceed by bus to Ariccia or go on foot (it's just under 3 km [2 miles]). If you're driving, follow the Appian road to Albano and carry on to Ariccia.

EXPLORING

Palazzo Chigi. This is a true rarity—a Baroque residence whose original furniture, paintings, drapes, and decorations are still mostly intact. Italian film director Lucchino Visconti used the villa for most of the interior scenes in his 1963 film *The Leopard*. The rooms contain intricately carved pieces of 17th-century furniture, as well as textiles and costumes from the 16th to the 20th centuries. The Room of Beauties is lined with paintings of the loveliest ladies of the day, and the Nuns' Room with portraits of 10 Chigi sisters, all of whom took the veil. The park stretching behind the palace is a wild wood, the last remnant of the ancient Latium forest, where herds of deer still graze under the trees. Book ahead for tours in English. ✉ *Piazza di Corte 14* ☎ *06/9330053* 🌐 *www.palazzochigiariccia.it* 🎫 *€7* 🕒 *Tours: Apr.–Sept., Tues.–Fri. at 11, 4, and 5:30; weekends at 10:30, 11:30, 12:30, 3, 4, 5, 6, and 7; Oct.–Mar., Tues.–Fri. at 11, 4, and 5:30; weekends at 10:30, 11:30, 12:30, 3, 4, 5, and 6.*

WHERE TO EAT

A visit to Ariccia isn't complete without tasting the local gastronomic specialty: porchetta, a delicious roast whole pig stuffed with herbs. The shops on the Piazza di Corte will make up a sandwich for you, or you can do what the Romans do: take a seat at one of the *fraschette* wine cellars that serve cheese, cold cuts, pickles, olives, and sometimes a plate of pasta. Conditions are rather rough and ready—you sit on a wooden bench at a trestle table covered with simple white paper—but there's no better place to make friends and maybe join in a sing-along.

$ ✕ **L'Aricciarola.** This is a great place for people-watching while you
ITALIAN   enjoy the local porchetta (whole roast pig stuffed with herbs), washed down with a carafe of local Castelli wine. It's tucked in a corner under the Galloro bridge. Ⓢ *Average meal: €25 ✉ Via Borgo S. Rocco 9* ☎ *06/9334103* ⊕ *www.osterialaricciarola.it* ⊘ *Closed Mon.*

NEMI

8 km (5 miles) west of Ariccia, 34 km (21 miles) south of Rome.

Nemi is the smallest and prettiest village of the Castelli Romani. Perched on a spur of rock 600 feet above the small crater lake of the same name, it has an eagle's-nest view over the rolling Roman countryside as far as the coast some 18 km (11 miles) away. The one main street, Corso Vittorio Emanuele, takes you to the (now privately owned) baronial Castello Ruspoli, with its 11th-century watchtower, and the quaint little Piazza Umberto 1, lined with outdoor cafés serving the tiny wood-strawberries harvested from the crater bowl.

If you continue on through the arch that joins the castle to the former stables, you come to the entrance of the dramatically landscaped public gardens, which curve steeply down to the panoramic **Belvedere terrace.** If you enjoy walking, you can follow the road past the garden entrance and go all the way down to the bottom of the crater.

GETTING HERE AND AROUND

Nemi is a bit difficult to get to unless you come by car. Buses from the Anagnina Metro A station go to the town of Genzano, where a local bus travels to Nemi every two hours. If the times aren't convenient, you can take a taxi or walk the 5 km (3 miles) around Lake Nemi. By car, take the panoramic route known as the Via dei Laghi (Road of the Lakes). Follow the Appia Nuova from St. John Lateran and branch off on the well-signposted route after Ciampino airport. Follow the Via dei Laghi toward Velletri until you see signs for Nemi.

EXPLORING

Museo delle Navi Romani (*Roman Ship Museum*). Nemi may be small, but it has a long and fascinating history. In Roman times it was an important sanctuary dedicated to the goddess Diana: it drew thousands of pilgrims from all over the Roman Empire. In the 1930s the Italian government drained the lake in order to recover two magnificent ceremonial ships, loaded with sculptures, bronzes, and art treasures, that were submerged for 2,000 years.

The Museo delle Navi Romani, on the lakeshore, was built to house them, but they were burned during World War II. Inside are scale models and a collection of finds from the sanctuary and the area nearby. A unique new addition is a colossal statue of the infamous Roman Emperor Caligula, who had the ships built. Italian police snatched it just in time from tomb robbers as they were about to smuggle it out of the country. ⊠ *Via del Tempio di Diana 9* ☎ *06/9398040* ▭ *€3* ⊘ *Daily 9–6:30.*

WHERE TO EAT

$ ✕ **L'Osteria del Gusto.** This quiet and refined alternative to the noisy and MODERN ITALIAN crowded fraschette will surprise you with young chef-owner Amedeo Paoloni's creative and innovative bill of fare. This includes potato dumplings with Parmesan sauce, walnuts and red chicory, hot sheep's cheese flan with pear coulis, aubergine rolls stuffed with ham and smoked cheese, and grilled Italian beef sliced fine and served with colonnata lard. Desserts are equally tempting. The small but select wine list offers the best from local Castelli cellars. $ *Average meal: €30* ⊠ *Via, Rosa 4, Ariccia* ☎ *06/9332848* ⚘ *Reservations essential* ▭ *No credit cards* ⊘ *Closed Mon. and Tues.*

$$ ✕ **Specchio di Diana.** Halfway down the main street is the town's most ITALIAN historic inn—Byron reputedly stayed here when visiting the area. A wine bar and café are on street level, while the restaurant proper on the second floor offers marvelous views, especially at sunset. Megapizzas (they stretch over two plates) are a speciality of the house, but don't neglect Nemi's regional specialties: *fettucine al sugo di lepre* (fettucine with hare sauce), roasted porcini mushrooms, and the little wood-strawberries with whipped cream. $ *Average meal: €40* ⊠ *Corso Vittorio Emanuele 13* ☎ *06/9368805* ⊕ *www.specchiodidiana.it.*

NORTHERN ITALY

WHAT'S WHERE

1 Venice. One of the world's most unusual—and beautiful—cities, Venice has canals where the streets should be and an atmosphere of faded splendor. It's also a major international cultural center.

2 The Veneto and Friuli-Venezia Giulia. The green plains stretching west of Venice hold three of northern Italy's most artistically significant midsize cities: Padua, Vicenza, and Verona. Farther north and east, Alpine foothills are dotted with welcoming villages and some of Italy's finest vineyards.

3 The Dolomites. Along Italy's northeast border, the Dolomites are the country's finest mountain playground, with gorgeous cliffs, curiously shaped peaks, lush meadows, and crystal-clear lakes. The skiing is good, and the scenery is different from what you find in the Austrian, Swiss, or French Alps.

4 Milan, Lombardy, and the Lakes. The deep-blue lakes of the Lombardy region—Como, Garda, and Maggiore—have been attracting vacationers since the days of ancient Rome. At the center of Lombardy is Milan, Italy's second-largest city and its business capital. It holds Italy's most renowned opera house, and as the epicenter of

AUSTRIA

TRENTINO-
ALTO ADIGE

3

Cortina
d'Ampezzo

FRIULI-VENEZIA
GIULIA

Bolzano

Belluno

Udine

Trento

Lake
Garda

VENETO

Treviso

Trieste

Brescia

Verona

Vicenza

2

Padua

Venice

1

Gulf of
Venice

Mantua

Adige

Po

Ferrara

EMILIA-ROMAGNA

7

Modena

Bologna

Ravenna

Adriatic Sea

Rimini

SAN MARINO

Pistoia

SAN MARINO

ca

Florence

Arno

Ancona

TUSCANY

Arezzo

THE
MARCHES

Siena

Macerata

Perugia

Assisi

UMBRIA

Grosseto

Orvieto

Italian fashion and design, it's a shopper's paradise.

5 **Piedmont and Valle d'Aosta.** A step off the usual tourist circuit, these regions in Italy's northwest corner have attractions that are well worth a visit. You'll find here great Alpine peaks along the French and Swiss borders, one of the most highly esteemed food-and-wine cultures in Italy (think of the famed white truffles of Alba!), and an elegant regional capital in Turin.

6 **The Italian Riviera.** Northern Italy's most attractive coastline runs along the Italian Riviera in the region of Liguria. The best beaches are west of Genoa, but the main appeal lies to the east, where fishing villages are interspersed along beautiful seaside cliffs and coves.

7 **Emilia-Romagna.** Many of Italy's signature foods come from here—including Parmigiano-Reggiano cheese, prosciutto di Parma, and balsamic vinegar—and the egg pasta is considered Italy's finest. But there's more than food to draw you here. Bologna has important museums, elegant piazzas, and arcaded streets; the mosaics of Ravenna are glittering late antique and Byzantine treasures; and Ferrara, Parma, and Modena all have artistic jewels.

NORTHERN ITALY PLANNER

Speaking the Language

People who interact regularly with tourists—such as hotel, restaurant, museum, and transportation personnel—generally speak some English. However, even in the cosmopolitan north, although knowledge of foreign languages is increasing, often highly educated Italians speak only Italian. Many are slightly offended if a foreigner assumes they speak English without first asking politely, "*Parla Lei inglese?*" If you do ask, most Italians, even those with no English, will try to be helpful. Perhaps because of their own linguistic limitations, Italians are tolerant of foreigners who try to speak their language and do wonders in understanding fractured Italian.

Even if you speak Italian, don't be surprised if you can't understand conversations going on around you, which may be in local dialect. Because of television and mass education, now almost everyone speaks standard Italian, and in cities such as Milan dialect has almost died out, but it still thrives in the Veneto and in areas that have not had a large influx of residents from other parts of Italy. Among friends, at home, and in moments of high emotion, standard Italian gives way to the local language.

Getting Here

Aeroporto Malpensa, 50 km (31 miles) northwest of Milan, is the major northern Italian hub for intercontinental flights and also sees substantial European and domestic traffic. Venice's **Aeroporto Marco Polo** also serves international destinations.

There are regional airports in Turin, Genoa, Bologna, Verona, Trieste, Treviso, Bolzano, and Parma, and Milan has a secondary airport, Linate. You can reach all of these on connecting flights from within Italy and from other European cities. If you fly into Malpensa, but Milan isn't your final destination, you can also get where you're going by train, using the Italian national rail system, **Ferrovie dello Stato** (☎ 199–30–30–60 *toll-free within Italy* ⊕ *www.trenitalia.com*). Shuttle buses run three times an hour (less often after 10 pm) between Malpensa and Milan's main train station, Stazione Centrale; the trip takes about 75 minutes, depending on traffic. The Malpensa Express Train, which leaves twice an hour, takes 40 minutes and delivers you to Cadorna station in central Milan.

TYPICAL TRAVEL TIMES

	Hours by Car	Hours by Train
Milan–Venice	3:30	2:35
Milan–Turin	2:00	2:00
Milan–Genoa	2:00	1:45
Milan–Bologna	2:30	1:00
Venice–Bologna	2:15	1:25
Venice–Turin	5:00	4:20
Venice–Genoa	4:45	4:30
Bologna–Genoa	3:15	3:00
Bologna–Turin	3:30	2:00
Genoa–Turin	2:00	2:00

When to Go

Spring: Late April, May, and early June are ideal times to tour northern Italy: the weather is mild, and the volume of tourists isn't as large as in summer.

Although there's some rain, springtime is generally drier in northern Italy than it is in northern Europe or the east coast of North America. By May the coastal towns of Liguria are beginning to come to life. Meanwhile, in the mountains hiking trails can remain icy well into June.

Summer: Anywhere away from the mountains, summers are warm and humid. Bring sunscreen, because it seldom rains, and when it does, it's mainly in the late afternoon and at night. Summer is prime hiking season in the Alps, and the lakes and the Riviera are in full swing (meaning lodging reservations are a must).

Note that a large portion, maybe even the majority, of tourists in northern Italy are not foreigners; they're Italians seeing their own country, and they come in summer, when the kids are out of school and families can travel together.

Fall: Much like spring, autumn, with its mild weather, is an ideal time for touring most of the region. Much of Northern Italy enjoys pleasant, sunny weather through September and well into October.

Most years it doesn't really begin to get cold until mid-November, though in the mountains temperatures drop sharply in September. Many of the mountain tourist facilities close down entirely until the ski season kicks in.

Winter: In the Dolomites most ski resorts are open from mid-December through April, but snowfall in early winter is unreliable, and the best conditions often aren't seen until late February.

Likewise, in Piedmont and Valle d'Aosta snow conditions vary drastically year to year—some years there's good snow beginning in November, while others don't see much more than a flake or two until February.

In Venice winters are relatively mild, with fewer tourists, but there are frequent rainy spells, and at the beginning and end of the season there's the threat of *acqua alta*, when tides roll in and flood low-lying parts of the city. (The floods last at most three hours.)

The larger cities are active year-round, but the resort towns of the Lake District and the Riviera are all but shut down.

On the Calendar

Taking part in seasonal events can give your trip an added dose of local culture. Here are a few of the north's best:

From December through June, the **opera season** is in full swing, most notably in Milan, Venice, Turin, Parma, and Genoa. In Milan the **Festa di Sant'Ambrogio** in early December officially launches the season at La Scala; it's celebrated by a huge street fair around the Castello Sforzesco.

Venice's **Carnevale,** during the 10 days preceding Lent (usually falling in February), includes concerts, plays, masked balls, fireworks, and indoor and outdoor happenings of every sort. It's probably Italy's most famous festival, attracting hundreds of thousands.

The **Festa del Redentore** (Feast of the Redeemer) in Venice on the third Sunday in July commemorates the end of the plague of 1575. Venetians eat a traditional dinner in boats on San Marco Basin or along the water and then watch the spectacular fireworks.

Venice's **Mostra del Cinema,** the oldest of the international film festivals, takes place in late August and early September.

L'Arena di Verona Stagione Lirica (Arena of Verona Outdoor Opera Season), from early July to late August, is known for its grand productions, performed in Verona's 22,000-seat Roman amphitheater.

NORTHERN ITALY TOP ATTRACTIONS

Venice's Piazza San Marco

(A) Perhaps nowhere else in the world gathers together so many of man's noblest artistic creations. The centerpiece of the piazza is the Basilica di San Marco, arguably the most beautiful Byzantine church in the West, with not only its shimmering Byzantine Romanesque facade, but also its jewel-like mosaic-encrusted interior. Right next door is the Venetian Gothic Palazzo Ducale, which was so beloved by the Venetians that when it burned down in the 16th century they rejected projects by the greatest architects of the Renaissance and had their palace rebuilt *come era, dove era*—exactly how and where it was. (⇨ *Chapter 3.*)

Venice's Grand Canal

(B) No one ever forgets a first trip down the Grand Canal. The sight of its magnificent palaces, with the light reflected from the canal's waters shimmering across their facades, is one of Italy's great experiences. (⇨ *Chapter 3.*)

Ravenna's Mosaics

(C) This small, out-of-the-way city houses perhaps the world's greatest treasure trove of early Christian art. After the decline of Rome, Ravenna was the capital of the Western Roman Empire and, a bit later, the seat of the Byzantine Empire in the West. The exquisite and surprisingly moving 5th- and 6th-century mosaics decorating several churches and other religious buildings still retain their startling brilliance. (⇨ *Chapter 9.*)

Palladio's Villas and Palazzi

(D) The great 16th-century architect Palladio created harmoniously beautiful buildings that were influential in spreading the Neoclassical style to northern Europe, England, and, later, America. He did most of his work in and around his native city of Vicenza. If a visit to Vicenza simply whets your appetite for Palladio, you can see another wonderful Palladian villa outside Venice (La

Malcontenta) and his famous collaboration with Veronese outside Treviso (Villa Barbaro). (⇨ *Chapter 4.*)

Lake Como
(E) Just a short drive or train ride north of Milan, Lake Como combines spectacular mountain scenery with the elegance of Baroque and Neoclassical villas and gardens and the charm of picturesque villages. It's great any time of year, but best in the spring, when the azaleas are in bloom in the gardens of Villa Carlotta. (⇨ *Chapter 6.*)

Giotto's Frescoes in the Scrovegni Chapel, Padua
(F) Dante's contemporary Giotto decorated this chapel with an eloquent and beautiful fresco cycle. Its convincing human dimension helped to change the course of Western art. (⇨ *Chapter 4.*)

Mantua
(G) This charming town, slightly off the beaten track in Lombardy, contains a high point of 15th-century painting: Mantegna's frescoes in the wedding chamber of the Palazzo Ducale, a masterpiece of spatial illusion. On the outskirts of town, Giulio Romano's Palazzo Te is an elegant pleasure palace, frescoed with illusionistic painting carrying the tradition established by Mantegna several steps further. (⇨ *Chapter 6.*)

Leonardo's *Last Supper*
(H) On the refectory wall of Santa Maria della Grazie in Milan one of the world's most famous paintings still evokes wonder, not at all trivialized by millions of reproductions or dulled by its poor state of conservation. (⇨ *Chapter 6.*)

TOP EXPERIENCES

Discovering the Cinque Terre

Along the Italian Riviera east of Genoa are five remote fishing villages known collectively as the Cinque Terre. The beauty of the landscape—with steep, vine-covered hills pushing smack-dab against an azure sea—and the charm of the villages have turned the area into one of Italy's top destinations. That is, until October 25, 2011, when two of the Cinque Terre's most picturesque towns—Vernazza and Monterossa—were devastated by a freak storm. More than 20 inches of rain lead to torrential flooding, which, in less than three hours, transformed these picture-perfect beauties into disaster areas. Happily, much of the damage was completely repaired within the year. Today the number-one activity is hiking the trails that run between the villages—the views are once-in-a-lifetime gorgeous—but if hiking isn't your thing, you can still have fun lounging about in cafés, admiring the water, and wandering through the medieval streets of the villages.

Taking Part in Venice's Festivals

Few people love a good party as much as the Venetians. The biggest is, of course, **Carnevale,** culminating on Fat Tuesday, but with revelry beginning about 10 days earlier. Visitors from the world over join the Venetians in a period of institutionalized fantasy, dressing in exquisitely elaborate costumes. The program changes each year and includes public, mostly free cultural events in all districts of the city.

The **Redentore,** on the third weekend in July, is a festival essentially for Venetians, but guests are always welcome. The Venetians pack a picnic dinner and eat in boats decorated with paper lanterns in the Bacino di San Marco. Just before midnight, there's a magnificent fireworks display. The next day (Sunday), everyone crosses a temporary bridge spanning the Canale della Giudecca to Palladio's Redentore church to light a candle.

Venice Biennale is a cutting-edge international art exposition held in odd numbered years from June to November in exhibition halls in the Venice Public Gardens (Giardini) and in the 14th-century industrial complex (Le Corderie) in the Arsenale. It's the most important exhibition of contemporary art in Italy and one of the three most important in Europe.

Feasting in Bologna

Italians recognize Emilia as the star of its culinary culture and Bologna as its epicenter. Many dishes native to Bologna, such as the slow-cooked meat-and-tomato sauce *sugo alla Bolognese*, have become so famous that they're widely available in all regions of Italy and abroad. But you owe it to yourself to try them in the city where they were born and are a subject of local pride. Take note, however: in Bologna a sugo is never served with spaghetti, but rather with an egg pasta in the form of tagliatelle, lasagne, or tortellini.

Fashion and Style in Milan

Italian clothing and furniture design are world famous, and the center of the Italian design industry is Milan. The best way to see what's happening in the world of fashion is to browse the designer showrooms and boutiques of the fabled *quadrilatero della moda,* along and around Via Montenapoleone. The central event in the world of furniture design is Milan's annual Salone Internazionale del Mobile, held at the Milan fairgrounds for a week in April. Admission is generally restricted to the trade, but the Salone is open to the general public for one day, generally on a Sunday, during the week of the show.

NORTHERN ITALY TODAY

...feels the influence of immigration

The population of northern Italy, especially the western regions, has undergone a substantial transformation due to immigration. Beginning during the economic boom of the 1960s and continuing to the 1980s, Italians from the south moved to the great industrial centers of Turin and Milan, changing the face of those cities. The southerners, or at least their children, adopted most northern customs—few now go home for a nap at midday—but their presence has had a clear influence on the culture of the north. Especially in the cities, local dialects died out, and at the dinner table the traditional polenta and risotto now share the scene with spaghetti and other pastas, and southern dishes often appear on menus.

Prosperity, and immigration, came later to the northeast. Venetians still enjoy the 18th-century dialect comedies of Goldoni, and it's not uncommon to hear dialect spoken by elegant operagoers at La Fenice.

Northern Italy, like the rest of the country, has recently experienced an influx of foreign immigrants, although their numbers are smaller relative to the local population than in many other European countries. Their welcome has varied widely: proudly cosmopolitan Venice is fairly open to the newcomers, while in cities where the government is controlled by the overtly xenophobic Northern League, integration has been contentious. In recent years some politicians have exploited the issue for their own gain, drawing criticism from various internationally respected human rights organizations, but the need for unskilled and semiskilled labor in northern factories may eventually provide the antidote.

...struggles with the global economy

Parts of northern Italy are among Europe's most prosperous areas, but recently even these economic powerhouses have run into trouble. The industrial base consists mainly of small and midsize businesses, many of which have had to close or outsource to Eastern Europe or Asia. Restrictive labor laws that impede hiring staff while remaining competitive are the crux of the problem. It remains to be seen whether Italians will accept economic and social reforms that will allow Italy to regain its competitive status.

...is feeling the effects of global warming

Venice has long suffered from a natural phenomenon called *acqua alta*—flooding that occurs when especially high tides coincide with a strong *scirocco,* a wind that blows north from Africa, forcing more sea water into the lagoon. Confined to the period between mid-October and December, the floods are temporary, lasting only for three or four hours around high tide. However, in recent years it has become clear that climate change is affecting the frequency and intensity of the flooding. While the city is geared up to cope with flooding, more buildings are being affected, and there is much concern over the long-term damage to a city already under threat.

Making matters worse, the deep channel dug in the lagoon to allow cruise ships to enter quickens the incoming tide, while waves and vibrations from the giant vessels are even more damaging. An alternative cruise port is under consideration, and movable dykes at lagoon entrances expect to be completed in 2016—but may bring their own ecological impact.

A GREAT ITINERARY

Day 1: Bellagio

If you're flying to northern Italy from overseas, there's no better way to rest up after a long flight than a day on Lake Como, combining some of Italy's most beautiful scenery with elegant historic villas and gardens.

At the center of it all is Bellagio, a pretty village with world-class restaurants and hotels, as well as more economical options. From Bellagio you can ferry to other points along the lake, take walking tours, go hiking, or just sit on a terrace watching the light play on the sapphire water and the snow-capped mountains in the distance.

Logistics: There are inexpensive bus-train combinations from Milan's Malpensa airport. A limousine service, Fly to Lake (☎ *0341/286887* ⊕ *www.flytolake.com*), leaves Malpensa four times per day (€35–€70 per person depending on the number of travelers; no service Sunday, late fall, or winter). The trip takes a little over two hours. In Bellagio you won't need a car, since most of your touring will be on foot, by ferry, or by bus.

Day 2: Milan

After a leisurely breakfast in Bellagio, take the ferry to Varenna (15 minutes) and then the train (1¼ hours) to Milan's Central Station. Milan is a leading center of fashion and design, and many visitors keep to the area of elegant shops around Via Montenapoleone.

But the city also houses some of Europe's great art treasures in the Brera Gallery and has two churches by Bramante, perhaps the most refined of the Italian High Renaissance architects. And then, of course, there's Leonardo's *Last Supper*. You may want to spend your evening taking in an opera at Italy's most illustrious opera house, La Scala.

Logistics: Central Milan is compact, with excellent public transportation. Milan does have its share of crime; keep an eye on your possessions around the train station and avoid hotels in that area.

Days 3 to 5: Verona/Mantua/Vicenza

Take an early express train to Verona (1½ hours from Milan) and settle into your hotel, where you'll stay for three nights; you'll be using this stately medieval city as your base to see three of the most important art cities in northern Italy.

Verona, with its ancient Roman arena, theater, and city gates, its brooding medieval palaces and castle, and its graceful bridge spanning the Adige, is probably the most immediately impressive of the three, and you'll want to spend the first day exploring its attractions. But the real artistic treasures are in the two smaller cities you'll see on day trips out of Verona.

The next day, take a short train trip to Mantua (30–45 minutes). Be sure to arrive in time for lunch, because Mantua has one of the most interesting local cuisines in northern Italy. The great specialty is *tortelli di zucca* (pumpkin-, cheese-, and almond-paste-filled ravioli), served with sage butter and Parmesan cheese.

The top artistic attractions are the Mantegna frescoes in the Palazzo Ducale, and you should also pay a visit to Giulio Romano's Palazzo Te, a 16th-century pleasure palace, on the outskirts of town. Take the train back to Verona in time for dinner, and perhaps catch an opera performance in Verona's Roman amphitheater.

The day after, take a short train trip to Vicenza (30 minutes) to see the palaces, villas, and public buildings of the lion of late 16th-century architecture,

Andrea Palladio. Don't miss his Teatro Olimpico and his most famous villa, La Rotonda, slightly out of town. For lunch, try the *baccalà alla vicentina*, the local version of dried salt cod, which is surprisingly good.

Also be sure to see the frescoes by Gianbattista and Giandomenico Tiepolo in the Villa dei Nani, near the Rotonda. In spring and summer there are musical performances in the Teatro Olimpico; if you want to attend, you'll have to book a hotel in Vicenza for the night, since you'll miss the last train back to Verona.

Day 6: Padua

Most people visit this important art and university center on a day trip out of Venice, but then they miss one of Padua's main attractions, the nightlife that goes on in the city's wine bars and cafés from evening until quite late.

Most cities in northern Italy, even Venice and Milan, have surprisingly little to offer after dinner or the theater, but in Padua going out for a nightcap or coffee with friends is a tradition, not only for students but also for older folks, too.

Arrive early enough to see at least the Giotto frescoes in the Cappella degli Scrovegni and the Basilica di San Antonio before lunch, then spend a relaxing

afternoon at the Villa Pisani, enjoying its gardens and important Tiepolo fresco.

Logistics: Trains are frequent to Padua from Verona (1 hour) and Vicenza (30 minutes); you don't really need to schedule ahead.

Day 7: Venice

Three days are hardly enough to see one of the world's most beautiful cities and one of the cradles of modern Western civilization. But running from museum to museum, church to church would be a mistake, since Venice is a wonderful place to stroll or "hang out," taking in some of the atmosphere that inspired such great art.

The first things you'll probably want to do in Venice are to take a vaporetto ride down the Grand Canal and see the Piazza San Marco.

These are best done in the morning: before 8:30 you'll avoid rush hour on the vaporetto, and although there's likely to be a line at San Marco when it opens, it'll be shorter than later in the day. After that, move on to the adjacent Palazzo Ducale and Sansovino's Biblioteca Marciana, facing it in the Piazzetta.

For lunch, take vaporetto #1 to the Ca' Rezzonico stop and have a sandwich and a *spritz* in the Campo Santa

Margherita, where you can mingle with the university students in one of Venice's most lively squares.

From there, make your way to the Galleria dell'Accademia and spend a few hours taking in its wonderful collection of Venetian paintings.

In the evening, take a walk up the Zattere and have a drink at one of the cafés overlooking the Canale della Giudecca.

Logistics: Be careful selecting your early train from Padua to Venice; some can be very slow. The 7:50 am (weekdays) is one of the fastest (27 minutes), and will get you into Venice in time to beat rush hour on the Grand Canal vaporetto. To get an early start, unless your hotel is very near San Marco, deposit your luggage at the station, and pick it up later, after you've seen the Piazza. Seeing the Grand Canal and Piazza San Marco in relative tranquillity will be your reward for getting up at the crack of dawn and doing a little extra planning.

Day 8: Venice

If the Accademia has just whetted your appetite for Venetian painting, start the day by visiting churches and institutions where you can see more of it.

For Titian, go to Santa Maria Gloriosa dei Frari church and Santa Maria della Salute; for Tintoretto, Scuola Grande di San Rocco; for Bellini, the Frari and San Giovanni e Paolo; for Tiepolo, Ca' Rezzonico, Scuola Grande dei Carmini, and the Gesuati; for Carpaccio, Scuola di San Giorgio; and for Veronese, San Sebastiano.

If your taste runs to more modern art, there are the Guggenheim Collection and, down the street, the Pinault Collection in the refashioned Punta della Dogana.

In the afternoon, head for the Fondamenta Nuova station to catch a vaporetto to one or more of the outer islands: Murano, where you can shop for Venetian glass and visit a glass museum and workshops; Burano, known for lacemaking and colorful houses; and Torcello, Venice's first inhabited island and home to a beautiful cathedral.

Day 9: Venice

Venice is more than a museum—it's a lively city. The best way to see that aspect of La Serenissima is to pay a visit to the Rialto Market, where the Venetians buy their fruits and vegetables and, most important, their fish, at one of Europe's largest and most varied fish markets.

Have lunch in one of the excellent restaurants in the market area.

On your last afternoon in Venice, allow time to sit and enjoy a coffee or spritz in one of the city's lively squares or in a café along the Fondamenta della Misericordia in Cannaregio, simply watching the Venetians go about their daily lives.

There's certainly a good deal more art and architecture to see in the city, and if you can't resist squeezing in another few churches, you may want to see Palladio's masterpiece of ecclesiastical architecture, the Redentore church on the Giudecca, or Tullio Lombardo's lyrical Miracoli, a short walk from the San Marco end of the Rialto Bridge.

Day 10: Venice/Departure

Take one last vaporetto trip up the Grand Canal to Piazzale Roma and, after saying good-bye to Venice, catch city bus #5 to the airport.

VENICE

WELCOME TO VENICE

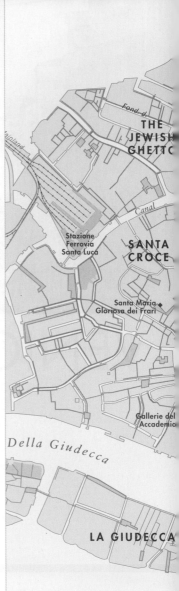

TOP REASONS TO GO

★ **Cruising the Grand Canal:** The beauty of its palaces, enhanced by light playing on the water, make a trip down Venice's "main street" unforgettable.

★ **Basilica di San Marco:** Don't miss the gorgeous mosaics inside—they're worth standing in line for.

★ **Santa Maria Gloriosa dei Frari:** Its austere, cavernous interior houses Titian's Assunta—the most beautiful altarpiece in the world.

★ **Gallerie dell'Accademia:** Legendary masterpieces of Venetian painting will overwhelm you in this fabled museum.

★ **Sipping wine and snacking at a *bacaro*:** For a sample of tasty local cuisine and excellent wines in a uniquely Venetian setting, head for one of the city's many wine bars.

1 The Grand Canal. Venice's major thoroughfare is lined with grand palazzi that once housed the city's most prosperous and powerful families.

2 San Marco. The neighborhood at the center of Venice is filled with fashion boutiques, art galleries, and grand hotels. Its Piazza San Marco—which Napoleon is said to have called "the drawing room of Europe"—is one of the world most beautiful and elegant urban spaces.

3 Dorsoduro. This graceful residential area is home to the Santa Maria della Salute, the Gallerie dell'Accademia, the Peggy Guggenheim Collection, and François Pinault Collection at the Punta della Dogana. The Zattere promenade is one of the best spots to stroll with a gelato or linger at an outdoor café.

4 Santa Croce and San Polo. These bustling *sestieri* (districts) are both residential and commercial, with all sorts of shops and artisan studios, several major churches and museums, and the Rialto fish and produce markets.

5 Cannaregio. Brimming with residential Venetian life, this sestiere provides some of the sunniest open-air canalside walks in town. The Fondamenta della Misericordia is a strand of restaurants and cafés, and the Jewish Ghetto has a fascinating history and tradition.

6 Castello. Along with Cannaregio, this area is home to most of the residents. With its gardens, park, and narrow, winding walkways, it's the sestiere least influenced by Venice's tourist culture.

GETTING ORIENTED

3

Venice proper is divided into six *sestieri,* or districts (the word *sestiere* means, appropriately, "sixth"): Cannaregio, Santa Croce, San Polo, Dorsoduro, San Marco, and Castello. More sedate outer islands float around them—San Giorgio Maggiore and the Giudecca just to the south; beyond them to the east, the Lido, the barrier island; and to the north, Murano, Burano, and Torcello.

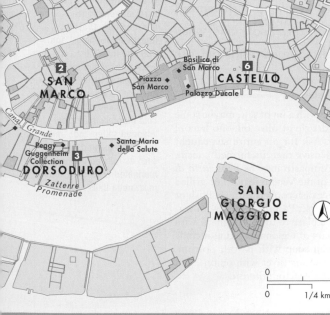

Misericordia

5
CANNAREGIO

Grande

1

Canal Grande

Ca' d'Oro

4

SAN POLO

2
SAN MARCO

Canal Grande

Piazza San Marco

Basilica di San Marco

6
CASTELLO

Palazzo Ducale

Peggy Guggenheim Collection

Santa Maria della Salute

3

DORSODURO

Zattere Promenade

SAN GIORGIO MAGGIORE

0 _____ 1/4 mi

0 _____ 1/4 km

EATING AND DRINKING WELL IN VENICE

The catchword in Venetian restaurants is fish. How do you learn about the catch of the day? A visit to the Rialto's *pescheria* (fish market) is more instructive than any book, and when you're dining at a well-regarded restaurant, ask for a recommendation.

Traditionally, fish is served with a bit of salt, maybe some chopped parsley, and a drizzle of olive oil—no lemon; lemon masks the flavor. Ask for an entire sea-caught fish; it's much more expensive than its farmed cousin, but certainly worth it. Antipasto may be *prosciutto di San Daniele* (cured ham of the Veneto region) or grilled vegetables. Risotto—a rice dish cooked with shellfish or veggies—is a great first course. Pasta? Enjoy it with seafood sauce: this is *not* the place to order spaghetti with tomato sauce. Other pillars of regional cooking include *pasta e fagioli* (thick bean soup with pasta), polenta, often with *fegato alla veneziana* (liver with onion), and that dessert invented in the Veneto: *tiramisù*.

GOING BACARO

You can sample regional wines and scrumptious *cicheti* (bite-size snacks) in *bacari* (traditional wine bars), a great Venetian tradition. *Crostini* (toast with toppings) and *polpette* (meat, fish, or vegetable croquettes) are popular cicheti, as are small sandwiches, seafood salads, *baccalà mantecato* (creamy whipped salted cod), and toothpick-speared items such as roasted peppers, marinated artichokes, and mozzarella balls.

SEAFOOD

Granseola (crab), *moeche* (soft-shell crab), sweet *canoce* (mantis shrimp), *capelunghe* (razor clams), calamari, and *seppie* or *seppioline* (cuttlefish) are all prominently featured, as well as *rombo* (turbot), *branzino* (sea bass), *San Pietro* (John Dory), *sogliola* (sole), *orate* (gilthead), and *triglia* (mullet). Trademark dishes include *sarde in saor* (panfried sardines marinated in olive oil, vinegar, onions, pine nuts, and raisins), *la frittura mista* (tempura-like fried fish and vegetables), and baccalà mantecato.

RISOTTO, PASTA, POLENTA

Although legend has it Venetian traveler Marco Polo brought pasta back from China, it isn't a traditional staple of the local cuisine. As a first course, Venetians favor the creamy rice dish risotto *all onda* ("undulating," as opposed to firm), prepared with vegetables or shellfish. When pasta is served, it's generally accompanied by seafood sauces, too: *pasticcio di pesce* is lasagna-type pasta baked with fish, and *bigoli* is a strictly local whole- or buckwheat pasta shaped like thick spaghetti, usually served *in salsa* (an anchovy-onion sauce with a dash of cinnamon), or with *nero di seppia* (squid-ink sauce). A classic first course is pasta e fagioli. *Polenta* (corn-meal gruel) is another staple that's served creamy or fried in wedges.

VEGETABLES

The larger islands of the lagoon are legendary for fine vegetables, such as the Sant'Erasmo *castraure*, sinfully expensive but heavenly tiny white artichokes that appear for a few days in spring. Spring treats are fat white asparagus from neighboring Bassano or Verona, and artichoke bottoms (*fondi*), usually sautéed with olive oil, parsley, and garlic. From December to March the prized *radicchio di Treviso*, a local red endive, is grilled and served with a bit of melted *taleggio* cheese from Lombardy. Fall brings small wild mushrooms called *chiodini*, and *zucca di Mantova*, a yellow squash with a gray-green rind used in soups, puddings, and to stuff ravioli.

SWEETS

Tiramisu lovers will have ample opportunity to sample this creamy concoction made from ladyfingers soaked in espresso and covered with sweetened mascarpone cheese—a dessert invented in the Veneto. Gelatos, sorbets, and *semifreddi* (ice cream and cake desserts) are other sweets frequently seen on Venetian menu, as are almond cakes, strudels, and dry cookies served with dessert wine. The glory of the Venetian pastry kitchen is the *focaccia veneziana*, a raised cake made in the late fall and winter. And no Carnevale celebration is complete without *fritelle*, deep fried sweet buns filled with cream, zabaglione, or raisins and pine nuts.

Updated
by Bruce
Leimsidor

It's called La Serenissima, "the most serene," a reference to the majesty, wisdom, and power of this city that was for centuries a leader in trade between Europe and the Orient, and a major center of European culture. Built on water by a people who saw the sea as a defense and ally, and who constantly invested in her splendor with magnificent architectural projects, Venice is a city unlike any other.

No matter how often you've seen it in photos and films, the real thing is more dreamlike than you could ever imagine. Its most-noted landmarks, the Basilica di San Marco and the Palazzo Ducale, are exotic mixes of Byzantine, Romanesque, Gothic, and Renaissance styles, reflecting Venice's ties with Constantinople in the east and the rest of Italy. Shimmering sunlight and silvery mist soften every perspective here; it's easy to understand how the city became renowned in the Renaissance for its artists' use of color. It's full of secrets, inexpressibly romantic, and frequently given over to pure, sensuous enjoyment.

You'll see Venetians going about their daily affairs in *vaporetti* (water buses), aboard the *traghetti* (gondola ferries) that carry them across the Grand Canal, in the *campi* (squares), and along the *calli* (narrow streets). They're quite skilled—and remarkably tolerant—in dealing with the veritable armies of tourists who fill the city's streets.

VENICE PLANNER

MAKING THE MOST OF YOUR TIME
The hoards of tourists visiting Venice are legendary, especially in spring and fall, but during other seasons, too—there's really no "off-season" in Venice. Unfortunately, tales of impassable, tourist-packed streets and endless queues to get into the Basilica di San Marco are not exaggerated. A little bit of planning, however, will help you avoid the worst of the crowds.

The majority of tourists do little more than take the *vaporetto* down the Grand Canal to Piazza San Marco, see the piazza and the basilica, and walk up to the Rialto and back to the station. You'll want to visit these areas, too, but do so in the early morning, before most tourists have finished their breakfast cappuccinos. Since many of the tourists are other Italians who come for a weekend outing, you can further decrease your competition for Venice's pleasures by choosing weekdays to visit the city.

Away from San Marco and the Rialto, the streets and quays of Venice's beautiful medieval and Renaissance residential districts receive only a moderate amount of traffic. Besides the Grand Canal and the Piazza San Marco, and perhaps Torcello, the other historically and artistically important sites are seldom overcrowded. Even on weekends you probably won't have to queue up to get into the Accademia museum.

Venice proper is quite compact, and you should be able to walk across it in a couple of hours, counting even a few minutes for getting lost. The water buses will save wear and tear on tired feet, but won't always save you much time.

PASSES AND DISCOUNTS

Avoid lines and save money by booking services and venue entry online with **Venice Connected** (⊕ *veniceconnected.com*). The service was introduced in 2009 and continues to evolve. Currently, you must book at least seven days in advance to get the lowest rates, which are also dependent on your arrival date. Venice Connected guarantees the lowest prices on parking, toilet service, museum passes, Wi-Fi access, and airport transfers. Venice Connected supplements the **VENICEcard** (☎ *041/2424* ⊕ *www.hellovenezia.com*), a pass that provides more comprehensive discounted access to sights, tours, shows, and certain shops.

Sixteen of Venice's most significant churches are part of the **Chorus Foundation** (☎ *041/2750462* ⊕ *www.chorusvenezia.org*) umbrella group, which coordinates their administration, hours, and admission fees. Churches in the group are open to visitors all day except Sunday morning. Single church entry costs €3; you have a year to visit all 16 with the €10 Chorus Pass. Family and student discounts are also available. Get a pass at any participating church or online.

The **Museum Pass** (€24.50) from **Musei Civici** (☎ *041/2715911* ⊕ *www. museicivicivenezian.it*) includes one-time entry to 12 Venice museums; it's valid for six months. The **Museums of San Marco Pass Plus** (€14) is good for the museums on the piazza All these passes are offered at ⊕ *veniceconnected.com* or at the individual museum sites. The Gallerie dell'Accademia and Ca' d'Oro are state, not city, museums, so are not covered in the Museum Pass from Musei Civici. Most comprehensive is the new MUVE pass (€45), which offers unlimited multiple access for one year to all the city museums.

GETTING HERE AND AROUND

AIR TRAVEL

Aeroporto Marco Polo. Venice's Aeroporto Marco Polo is on the mainland, 10 km (6 miles) north of the city. It's served by domestic and international flights, including connections from 21 European cities, plus direct flights from New York's JFK and other U.S. cities. Despite recent expansion, the airport is still too small for the amount of traffic it has to handle. To avoid substantial queues at check-in, it's highly advisable to use online check-in services if provided by your airline. ☎ 041/2609260 ⊕ www.veniceairport.it.

WATER TRANSFERS   From Marco Polo terminal it's a mostly covered seven-minute walk to the dock where boats depart for Venice's historic center.

Alilaguna. This company has regular ferry service from predawn until nearly midnight. The charge is €15 (€13 if bought online), including bags, and it takes about 1½ hours to reach the landing near Piazza San Marco; some ferries also stop at Fondamente Nove, Murano, Lido, the Cannaregio Canal, and the Rialto. For €25 you can take the one-hour Oro line direct to San Marco. A *motoscafo* (water taxi) carries up to four people and four bags to the city center in a powerboat—with a base cost of €95 for the 25-minute trip. Each additional person over 5 people costs €10 extra; buy a ticket on line at ⊕ www.motoscafivenezia. it or agree on a fare before boarding.

Note that the boat trip from the airport to Venice is singularly unromantic. You'll be entering Venice through its back door, with no particularly interesting views. The Alilaguna ferries have you sit in a closed area; so, you won't be able to see much, anyway. At the airport, the Alilaguna dock is a seven-minute walk from the arrivals hall, while the bus to Piazzale Roma leaves from right outside the door. Alilaguna is recommended if your hotel is close to one of its stops in Venice. Otherwise, the bus will get you there faster and cheaper. ☎ 041/2401701 ⊕ www.alilaguna.it.

LAND TRANSFERS   **ATVO.** Buses run by ATVO make a quick (20 minutes) and cheap (€7) direct trip from the airport to Piazzale Roma, from where you can get a vaporetto to the stop nearest your hotel. Tickets are sold from machines and at the airport ground transportation booth (open daily 9–7:30), and on the bus when tickets are otherwise unavailable. The public ACTV Bus No. 5 also runs to the Piazzale Roma in about the same time. Tickets (€5) are available at the airport ground transportation booth. A taxi to Piazzale Roma costs about €35. ☎ 0421/383672 ⊕ www.atvo.it.

CAR TRAVEL
Venice is at the end of SR11, just off the east–west A4 Autostrada. There are no cars in Venice; if possible, return your rental when you arrive.

A warning: Don't be waylaid by illegal touts, often wearing fake uniforms, who try to flag you down and offer to arrange parking and hotels. Use one of the established garages and consider reserving a space in advance. The **Autorimessa Comunale** (☎ 041/2727211 ⊕ www.asmvenezia. it) costs €24–€27 for 24 hours, less if you book with Venice Connected (⊕ www.veniceconnected.com). The **Garage San Marco** (☎ 041/5232213 ⊕ www.garagesanmarco.it) costs €24 for up to 12 hours and €30 for 12 to 24 hours with online reservations. On its own island, **Tronchetto** (☎ 041/5207555) charges €21 for 6 to 24 hours. Watch for signs coming over the bridge—you turn right just before Piazzale Roma. Many hotels and the casino have guest discounts with San Marco or Tronchetto garages. A cheaper alternative is to park in Mestre, on the mainland, and take a train (10 minutes, €1) or bus into Venice. The garage across from the station and the Bus No. 2 stop costs €8–€10 for 24 hours.

PUBLIC TRANSPORTATION

TRAGHETTI Many tourists are unaware of these two-man gondola ferries that cross the Grand Canal at or near many gondola stations. At €0.50, they're the cheapest and shortest gondola ride in Venice—and can also save a lot of walking. Look for "Traghetto" signs and hand your fare to the gondolier when you board; they're marked on many maps. Stand up in these gondolas, straddling the width to keep your balance, unless the gondolier tells you otherwise. Most traghetti operate only in the morning.

WATER BUSES **ACTV.** Venice's primary public transportation is the *vaporetto* (water bus). The ACTV operates vaporetti on routes throughout the city. Beginning at about 11:30 pm there's limited, but fairly frequent, night service. Although most landings are well marked, the system takes some getting used to; check before boarding to make sure the boat is going in your desired direction. Line 1 is the Grand Canal local, making all stops and continuing via San Marco to the Lido. The trip from Ferrovia to San Marco takes about 35 minutes.

Individual tickets are €7. Considerable savings are possible if you buy a one-, three-, or seven-day pass, which can, with a small surcharge, also include your bus fare to and from the airport. Tickets are available at the airport, from tobacco shops, and from machines or booths at some, but not all, vaporetto stops. Tickets are checked frequently and fines for using the bus or vaporetto without a ticket are substantial. ☎ *041/2424* ⊕ *www.hellovenezia.com.*

WATER TAXIS A *motoscafo* isn't cheap: you'll spend about €50 for a short trip in town, €70 to the Lido, and €90 per hour to visit the outer islands. It is strongly suggested to book through the Consorzio Motoscafi Venezia (☎ *041 522 2303* ⊕ *www.motoscafivenezia.it*) to avoid having to argue with the driver over prices. A water taxi can carry up to 10 passengers, with an additional charge of €10/person over 5 people, so if you're traveling in a group, it may not be that much more expensive than a vaporetto.

TRAIN TRAVEL

Venice has rail connections with many major cities in Italy and Europe. Note that Venice's train station is **Venezia Santa Lucia,** not to be confused with Venezia Mestre, which is the mainland stop prior to arriving in the historic center. Some trains don't continue beyond the Mestre station; in such cases you can catch the next Venice-bound train. Get a €1 ticket from the newsstand on the platform and validate it (in the yellow time-stamp machine) to avoid a fine.

TOURS

If you want some expert guidance around Venice, you may opt for private, semiprivate, or large group tours. Any may include a boat tour as a portion of a longer walking tour. For private tours, make sure to choose an authorized guide.

PRIVATE TOURS

A Guide in Venice. This popular company offers a wide variety of innovative, entertaining, and informative themed tours for groups of up to 10 people. Tours cost €70 per hour for the entire group, and generally last two to three hours. ☎ *3477876846 Sabrina Scaglianti* ⊕ *www. aguideinvenice.com.*

Walks Inside Venice. For a host of particularly creative group and private tours, from historic to artistic to gastronomic, opt for one run by Walks Inside Venice. Their tours cost €75 for groups up to six people; their guides include people with advanced university degrees and published authors. ☎ *041/5241706 Roberta, 041/5202434 Cristina ⊕ www. walksinsidevenice.com.*

LARGE-GROUP TOURS

Venice Tourism Office. Visit any Venice tourism office to book walking tours of the San Marco area (€21) (no Sunday tour in winter). There's also an afternoon walking tour that ends with a gondola ride (€40), and a daily serenaded gondola ride (€40). Check the main branch of the city's tourist office or their website for additional scheduled offerings, meeting places, and times. ⊠ *San Marco 2637* ☎ *041/5298711 ⊕ www.turismovenezia.it.*

VISITOR INFORMATION

The multilingual staff of the **Venice tourism office** (☎ *041/5298711 ⊕ www.turismovenezia.it*) can provide directions and up-to-the-minute information. Its free, quarterly *Show and Events Calendar* lists current happenings and venue hours. Tourist office branches are at Marco Polo Airport; the Venezia Santa Lucia train station; Garage Comunale, on Piazzale Roma; at Piazza San Marco near Museo Correr at the southwest corner; the Venice Pavilion (including a Venice-centered bookstore), on the *riva* (canal-front street) between the San Marco vaporetto stop and the Royal Gardens; and on the Lido at the main vaporetto stop. The train-station branch is open daily 8–6:30; other branches generally open at 9:30.

EXPLORING VENICE

PIAZZA SAN MARCO

One of the world's most beautiful squares, Piazza San Marco (Saint Mark's Square), a vast open space bordered by an orderly procession of arcades marching toward the fairytale cupolas and marble lacework of the Basilica di San Marco, is the spiritual and artistic heart of Venice. From mid-morning on it's generally packed with tourists. (If Venetians have business in the piazza, they try to conduct it in the early morning, before the crowds swell.) At night it can be magical, especially in winter, when mists swirl around the lampposts and the campanile. And if you can catch it at 6 am, *"senza popolo"* (without people), it looks like a 3D Canaletto painting from the 18th century.

Piazzetta San Marco is the "little square" leading from Piazza San Marco to the waters of Bacino San Marco (Saint Mark's Basin); its *molo* (landing) once served as the grand entrance to the Republic. Two imposing columns tower above the waterfront. One is topped by a winged lion, an emblem of Saint Mark that became the symbol of Venice itself; the other supports Saint Theodore, the city's first patron, along with his dragon. Though the columns are a glorious vision today, the Republic traditionally executed convicts between them. Even today, some superstitious Venetians avoid walking between the two columns.

Continued on page 198

CRUISING THE GRAND CANAL

THE BEST INTRODUCTION TO VENICE IS A TRIP DOWN MAIN STREET

Venice's Grand Canal is one of the world's great thoroughfares. It winds its way from Piazzale Roma to Piazza San Marco, passing 200 palazzi built from the 13th to the 18th centuries by Venice's richest and most powerful families. There's a theatrical quality to a boat ride on the canal: it's as if each pink- or gold-tinted façade is trying to steal your attention from its rival across the way.

In medieval and Renaissance cities, wars and sieges required defense to be an element of design; but in rich, impregnable Venice, you could safely show off what you had. But more than being simply an item of conspicuous consumption, a Venetian's palazzo was an embodiment of his person—not only his wealth, but also his erudition and taste.

The easiest, and cheapest way to see the Grand Canal is to take the Line 1 vaporetto (water bus) from Piazalle Roma to San Marco. The ride costs €6.50 and takes about 35 minutes. Invest in a day ticket (€16 buys 24 hours of unlimited passage) and you can spend the better part of a day hopping on and off at the vaporetto's many stops, visiting the sights along the banks. Keep your eyes open for the highlights listed here; some have fuller descriptions later in this chapter.

FROM PIAZZALE ROMA TO RIALTO

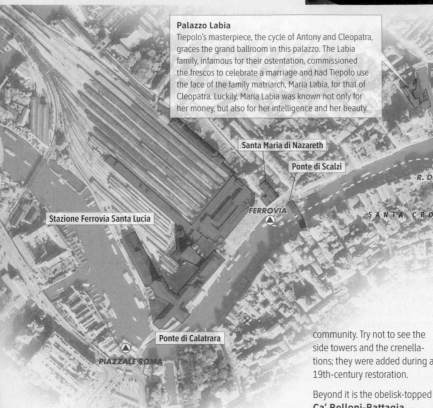

Palazzo Labia
Tiepolo's masterpiece, the cycle of Antony and Cleopatra, graces the grand ballroom in this palazzo. The Labia family, infamous for their ostentation, commissioned the frescos to celebrate a marriage and had Tiepolo use the face of the family matriarch, Maria Labia, for that of Cleopatra. Luckily, Maria Labia was known not only for her money, but also for her intelligence and her beauty.

Santa Maria di Nazareth

Ponte di Scalzi

R. DI BIASIO

Stazione Ferrovia Santa Lucia

FERROVIA

SANTA CROCE

Ponte di Calatrara

PIAZZALE ROMA

After you pass the Ferrovia, the baroque church immediately to your left is the baroque **Santa Maria di Nazareth**, called the Chiesa degli Scalzi (Church of the Barefoot).

After passing beneath the Ponte di Scalzi, ahead to the left, where the Canale di Cannaregio meets the Grand Canal, you'll spy **Palazzo Labia**, an elaborate 18th-century palace built for the social-climbing Labia family. Known for their ostentation even in this city where modesty was seldom a virtue, the Labias chose a location that required three façades instead of the usual one.

A bit farther down, across the canal, is the 13th-century **Fondaco dei Turchi**, an elegant residence that served as a combination commercial center and ghetto for the Turkish community. Try not to see the side towers and the crenellations; they were added during a 19th-century restoration.

Beyond it is the obelisk-topped **Ca' Belloni-Battagia**, designed for the Belloni family by star architect Longhena. Look for the family crest he added prominently on the façade.

On the opposite bank is architect Mauro Codussi's magnificent **Palazzo Vendramin-Calergi**, designed just before 1500. Codussi ingeniously married the fortress-like Renaissance style of the Florentine Alberti's Palazzo Rucellai to the lacy delicacy of the Venetian Gothic, creating the prototype of

Palazzo Vendramin-Calergi
Venice's first Renaissance palazzo. Immediately recognized as a masterpiece, it was so highly regarded that later, when its subsequent owners, the Calergi, were convicted of murder and their palace was to be torn down as punishment, the main building was spared.

Ca' d'Oro
Inspired by stories of Nero's Domus Aurea (Golden House) in Rome, the first owner had parts of the façade gilded with 20,000 sheets of gold leaf. The gold has long worn away, but the Ca' D'Oro is still Venice's most beautiful Gothic palazzo.

Ca' da Mosto
Venice's oldest surviving palazzo gives you an idea of Marco Polo's Venice. More than any other Byzantine palazzo in town, it maintains its original 13th-century appearance.

GHETTO

S. MARCUOLA

Ca' Belloni-Battagia

S. STAE

Ca' Pesaro

Fondaco dei Turchi

San Stae Church

CA' D'ORO

SAN POLO

Pescheria
Stop by in the morning to see the incredible variety of fish for sale. Produce stalls fill the adjacent fondamenta. Butchers and cheesemongers occupy the surrounding shops.

Rialto Mercato

Fondaco dei Tedeschi

RIALTO

SAN MARCO

the Venetian Renaissance palazzo. The palazzo is now Venice's casino.

The whimsically baroque church of **San Stae** on the right bank is distinguished by a host of marble saints on its façade.

Farther along the bank is one of Longhena's Baroque masterpieces, **Ca' Pesaro**. It is now the Museum of Modern Art.

Next up on the left is **Ca' d'Oro** (1421-1438), the canal's most spendid example of Venetian Gothic domestic design. Across from this palazzo is the loggia of the neo-Gothic **pescheria**, Venice's fish market.

Slightly farther down, on the bank opposite from the vegetable market, is the early 13th-century **Ca' da Mosto**, the oldest building on the Grand Canal. The upper two floors are later additions, but the ground floor and piano nobile give you a good idea of a rich merchant's house during the time of Marco Polo.

As you approach the Rialto Bridge, to the left, just before

the bridge, is the **Fondaco dei Tedeschi**. German merchants kept warehouses, offices, and residences here; its façade was originally frescoed by Titian and Giorgione.

FROM RIALTO TO THE PONTE DELL' ACCADEMIA

Ca' Foscari
The canal's most imposing Gothic masterpiece, Ca' Foscari was built to blot out the memory of a traitor to the Republic.

SAN POLO

Ponte di Rialto

▲ RIALTO

Palazzo Dolfin Man

S. SILVESTRO ▲

Ca' Loredan

Ca' Farsetti

Palazzo Pisani Moretta

Ca' Grimani

Ca'Corner-Spinelli

S. ANGELO ▲

TOMA ▲

Ca' Balbi

Palazzo Grassi

Ca' Rezzonico

REZZONICO ▲

SAN MARCO

ACCADEMIA ▲

Gallerie dell'Accademia

DORSODURO

The shop-lined **Ponte di Rialto** was built in stone after former wooden bridges had burned or collapsed. As you pass under the bridge, on your left stands star architect Sansovino's Palazzo Dolfin Manin. The white stone–clad Renaissance palace was built at huge expense and over the objections of its conservative neighbors.

A bit farther down stand **Ca' Loredan** and **Ca' Farsetti**, 13th-century Byzantine palaces that today make up Venice's city hall.

Along the same side is the **Ca' Grimani**, by the Veronese architect Sanmichele. Legend has it that the palazzo's oversized windows were demanded by the young Grimani's fiancée, who insisted that he build her a palazzo on the Canale Grande with windows larger than the portal of her own house.

At the Sant'Angelo landing, the vaporetto passes close to Codussi's **Ca' Corner-Spinelli**. Back on the right bank, in a lovely salmon color, is the graceful **Palazzo Pisani Moretta**, built in the mid-15th century and typical of the Venetian Gothic palazzo of the generation after the Ca' D'Oro.

A bit farther down the right bank, crowned by obelisks, is **Ca' Balbi**. Niccolò Balbi built this elegant palazzo in order to upstage his former landlord, who had insulted him in public.

Farther down the right bank, where the Canale makes a sharp turn, is the imposing **Ca' Foscari**. Doge Francesco Foscari tore down an earlier palazzo on this spot and built this splendid palazzo to erase memory of the traitorous former owner. It is now the seat of the University of Venice.

Continuing down the right bank you'll find Longhena's **Ca' Rezzonico**, a magnificent baroque palace. Opposite stands the Grand Canal's youngest palace, Giorgio Massari's **Palazzo Grassi**, commissioned in 1749. It houses part of the François Pinot contemporary art collection.

Near the canal's fourth bridge, is the former church and monastery complex that houses the world-renowned **Gallerie dell'Accademia**, the world's largest and most distinguished collection of Venetian art.

ARCHITECTURAL STYLES ALONG THE GRAND CANAL

BYZANTINE: 13th century
Distinguishing characteristics: high, rounded arches, relief panels, multicolored marble.

Examples: Fondaco dei Turchi, Ca' Loredan, Ca' Farsetti, Ca' da Mosto

GOTHIC: 14th and 15th centuries
Distinguishing characteristics: pointed arches, high ceilings, and many windows.

Examples: Ca' d'Oro, Ca' Foscari, Palazzo Pisani Moretta, Ca' Barbaro (and, off the canal, Palazzo Ducale)

RENAISSANCE: 16th century
Distinguishing characteristics: classically influenced emphasis on harmony and motifs taken from classical antiquity.

Examples: Palazzo Vendramin-Calergi, Ca' Grimani, Ca' Corner-Spinelli, Ca' dei Camerlenghi, Ca' Balbi, Palazzo Corner della Ca' Granda, Palazzo Dolfin Manin, and, off the canal, Libreria, Sansoviniana on Piazza San Marco

BAROQUE: 17th century
Distinguishing characteristics: Renaissance order wedded with a more dynamic style, achieved through curving lines and complex decoration.

Examples: churches of Santa Maria di Nazareth, San Stae, and Santa Maris della Salute; Ca' Belloni Battaglia, Ca' Pesaro, Ca' Rezzonico

FROM THE PONTE DELL'ACCADEMIA TO SAN ZACCARIA

Ca' Barbaro
John Singer Sargent, Henry James, and Cole Porter are among the guests who have stayed at Ca' Barbaro. It was a center for elegant British and American society during the turn of the 20th century.

Santa Maria Della Salute
Baldessare Longhena was only 26 when he designed this church, which was to become one of Venice's major landmarks. Its rotunda form and dynamic Baroque decoration predate iconic Baroque churches in other Italian cities.

SAN MARCO

Ca' Franchetti

Ponte dell' Accademia

Palazzo Corner della Ca' Grande

ACCADEMIA

S. M. DEL GIGLIO

DORSODURO

SALUTE

Palazzo Venier dei Leoni
Eccentric art dealer Peggy Guggenheim's personal collection of modern art is here. At the Grand Canal entrance to the palazzo stands Marino Marini's sexually explicit equestrian sculpture, the Angel of the Citadel. Numerous entertaining stories have been spun around the statue and Ms. Guggenheim's overtly libertine ways.

S. Maria della Salute

Ca' Dario
Graceful and elegant Ca' Dario is reputed to carry a curse. Almost all its owners since the 15th century have met violent deaths or committed suicide. It was, nevertheless, a center for elegant French society at the turn of the 20th century.

Down from the Accademia bridge, on the left bank next door to the fake Gothic Ca' Franchetti, is the beautiful **Ca' Barbaro**, designed by Giovanni Bon, who was also at work about that time on the Ca' D'Oro.

Farther along on the left bank Sansovino's first work in Venice, the **Palazzo Corner della Ca' Granda**, begun in 1533, still shows the influence of his Roman Renaissance contemporaries, Bramante and Giulio Romano. It faces the uncompleted **Palazzo Venier dei Leoni**, which holds the Peggy Guggenheim Collection, a good cross-section of the visual arts from 1940 to 1960.

Ca' Dario a bit farther down, was originally a Gothic palazzo, but in 1487 it was given an early Renaissance multicolored marble façade.

At this point on the canal the cupola of **Santa Maria della Salute** dominates the scene. The commission for the design of the church to celebrate the Virgin's rescuing Venice from the disastrous plague of 1630, was given to the 26-year-old

Longhena. The young architect stressed the new and inventive aspects of his design, likening the rotunda shape to a crown for the Virgin.

Across from the Salute, enjoying the magnificent view across the canal, are a string of luxury hotels whose historic

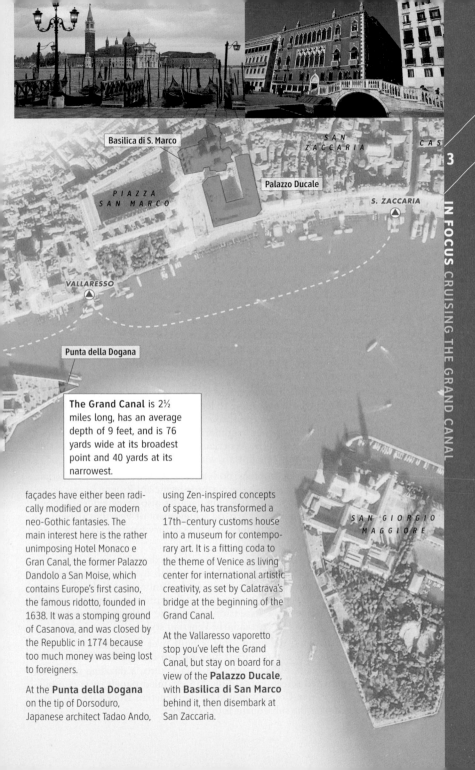

Basilica di S. Marco

SAN ZACCARIA

CAS

Palazzo Ducale

S. ZACCARIA

PIAZZA SAN MARCO

VALLARESSO

Punta della Dogana

The Grand Canal is 2½ miles long, has an average depth of 9 feet, and is 76 yards wide at its broadest point and 40 yards at its narrowest.

SAN GIORGIO MAGGIORE

façades have either been radically modified or are modern neo-Gothic fantasies. The main interest here is the rather unimposing Hotel Monaco e Gran Canal, the former Palazzo Dandolo a San Moise, which contains Europe's first casino, the famous ridotto, founded in 1638. It was a stomping ground of Casanova, and was closed by the Republic in 1774 because too much money was being lost to foreigners.

At the **Punta della Dogana** on the tip of Dorsoduro, Japanese architect Tadao Ando,

using Zen-inspired concepts of space, has transformed a 17th-century customs house into a museum for contemporary art. It is a fitting coda to the theme of Venice as living center for international artistic creativity, as set by Calatrava's bridge at the beginning of the Grand Canal.

At the Vallaresso vaporetto stop you've left the Grand Canal, but stay on board for a view of the **Palazzo Ducale**, with **Basilica di San Marco** behind it, then disembark at San Zaccaria.

TIMING

You can easily spend several days seeing the historical and artistic monuments in and around the Piazza San Marco, but at a bare minimum plan on at least an hour in the Basilica, for its wonderful mosaics. Add on another half hour if you want to see its Pala d'Oro, Galleria, and Museo di San Marco. Don't let the guards rush you through. If you politely insist, they will leave you alone. You'll want at least an hour to appreciate the Palazzo Ducale. Leave another hour for the Museo Correr, through which you also enter the archaeological museum and the Libreria Sansoviniana. If you choose to take in the piazza itself from a café table with an orchestra, keep in mind there will be an additional charge for the music.

TOP ATTRACTIONS

Fodor's Choice
★
Basilica di San Marco. The crowning glory of the Piazza San Marco, the Basilica di San Marco is not only the religious center of a great city; it is also an expression of the political, intellectual, and economic aspiration and accomplishments of a city that, for centuries, held a pivotal place in the formation of European culture. It was the *doge*'s (duke's) personal chapel, linking its religious function to the political life of the city. Over the years this Basilica stood as a symbol of Venetian wealth and power, and it was endowed with all the riches the Republic's admirals and merchants could carry off from the Byzantine Empire, earning it the nickname Chiesa D'Oro, or Golden Church. This Basilica was a monument not just to the glory of God, but also to the glory of Venice.

The original church, consecrated in 832, was built to house the body of St. Mark, which, according to legend, had been stolen by two Venetians in 828. The whole enterprise, however, was intended to establish Venice's prominence over neighboring Aquileia, a city with a glorious ancient Roman past. (The Venetians have never quite gotten over that their city is the only one in Italy without an ancient Roman past.)

The facades contain trophies, both ancient Roman and Early Christian, taken during raids, such as the gilt-bronze ancient Roman horses seized from Constantinople in 1204. The facades also show evidence, however, of the high quality of artistic achievement of Venetian artisans, as can be seen in the beautiful early 13th-century bas-reliefs on the inner arches of the main portal.

The glory of the Basilica is, of course, its medieval mosaics. The earliest mosaics, bearing the graceful lines of high Byzantine art, are in the first dome of the interior, the Dome of the Penticost, and date from the 12th century. It is probably the work of Byzantine artisans. The central dome, the Dome of the Ascension, is from the 13th century, and shows the development of a particularly Venetian style.

In the Sanctuary, the main altar is built over the tomb of St.Mark, its green marble canopy lifted high on 6th century carved alabaster columns—again, pillaged art. The Pala D'Oro, a dazzling gilt-silver, gem-encrusted screen containing 255 enamled panels, was commissioned in 976 in Constantinople by the Venetian Doge Orseolo I and enlarged over the subsequent four centuries.

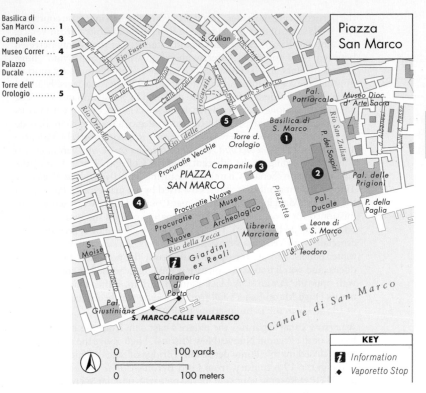

■TIP➔ To skip the line at the Basilica entrance, reserve your arrival—at no extra cost—on the Basilica website. Or check a bag at the nearby checkroom: just show your check stub to the guard at the entrance, and he will wave you in. Remember that this is a sacred place: guards will deny admission to people in shorts, sleeveless dresses, and tank tops. ⊠ *Piazza San Marco, San Marco 328, San Marco* ☎ *041/2413817 for tour info, weekdays 10–noon* ⊕ *www.basilicasanmarco.it* ⊠ *Basilica free, Treasury €3, Sanctuary and Pala D'Oro €2, Museum €5* ☉ *May–Sept., Mon.–Sat. 9:45–5, Sun. 2–5; Oct.–Apr., Mon.–Sat. 9:45–5, Sun. 2–4. Last entry 1 hr before closing; interior illuminated Mon.–Sat. 11:30–12:30, Sun. 2–5* Ⓜ *Vaporetto: Vallaresso, San Zaccaria.*

Fodor'sChoice **Palazzo Ducale** (*Doge's Palace*). Rising majestically above the Piazzetta
★ San Marco, this Gothic fantasia of pink-and-white marble is a majestic expression of Venetian prosperity and power. Although the site was the doge's residence from the 10th century, the building began to take its present form around 1340; what you seen now is essentially a product of the first half of the 15th century. It served not only as the doge's residence, but also as the central administrative center of the Venetian Republic.

Near the basilica you'll see Giovanni and Bartolomeo Bon's Gothic **Porta della Carta** (Gate of the Paper), built between 1438 and 1442, where official decrees were traditionally posted, but you enter the palazzo under the portico facing the water. You'll find yourself in an immense courtyard that holds some of the first evidence of Renaissance architecture in Venice, like Antonio Rizzo's **Scala dei Giganti** (Stairway of the Giants), erected between 1483 and 1491, directly ahead, guarded by Sansovino's huge statues of Mars and Neptune, added in 1567. Though ordinary mortals must use the central interior staircase, its upper flight is the lavishly gilded **Scala d'Oro** (Golden Staircase), also designed by Sansovino in 1555. The palace's sumptuous chambers have walls and ceilings covered with works by Venice's greatest artists. Visit the **Anticollegio,** a waiting room outside the Collegio's chamber, where you can see the *Rape of Europa* by Veronese and Tintoretto's *Bacchus and Ariadne Crowned by Venus*. Veronese also painted the ceiling of the adjacent **Sala del Collegio.** The ceiling of the **Sala del Senato** (Senate Chamber), featuring *The Triumph of Venice* by Tintoretto, is magnificent, but it's dwarfed by his masterpiece *Paradise* in the **Sala del Maggiore Consiglio** (Great Council Hall). A vast work commissioned for a vast hall, this dark, dynamic piece is the world's largest oil painting (23 by 75 feet). The room's carved gilt ceiling is breathtaking, especially with Veronese's majestic *Apotheosis of Venice* filling one of the center panels. Around the upper walls, study the portraits of the first 76 doges, and you'll notice one picture is missing near the left corner of the wall opposite *Paradise*. A black painted curtain, rather than a portrait, marks Doge Marin Falier's fall from grace; he was beheaded for treason in 1355, which the Latin inscription bluntly explains.

A narrow canal separates the palace's east side from the cramped cell blocks of the **Prigioni Nuove** (New Prisons). High above the water arches the enclosed marble **Ponte dei Sospiri** (Bridge of Sighs), which earned its name in the 19th century, from Lord Byron's *Childe Harold's Pilgrimage*. ■TIP→ Reserve your spot for the palazzo's popular Secret Itineraries tour well in advance. You'll visit the doge's private apartments, through hidden passageways to the interrogation (torture) chambers, and into the rooftop *piombi* (lead) prison, named for its lead roofing. Venetian-born writer and libertine Giacomo Casanova (1725–98), along with an accomplice, managed to escape from the piombi in 1756; they were the only men ever to do so. ⊠ *Piazzetta San Marco* ☎ *041/2715911, 041/5209070 Secret Itineraries tour* ⊕ *www.museicivivenziani.it* 🎫 *Museums of San Marco Pass €16, includes single entry also to the Museo Correr, the Archeological Museum, and the monumental rooms of the Biblioteca Marciana. Free with MUVE pass. "Secret Itineraries" tour €20* ☉ *Apr.–Oct., daily 8:30–7; Nov.–Mar., daily 8:30–5:30. Last entry 1 hr before closing. "Secret Itineraries" tour in English 9:55, 10:45, 11:35* Ⓜ *Vaporetto: San Zaccaria, Vallaresso.*

WORTH NOTING

Campanile. Construction of Venice's famous brick bell tower (325 feet tall, plus the angel) began in the 9th century, and took on its present form in 1514. During the 15th century, the tower was used as a place of punishment: immoral clerics were suspended in wooden cages from the tower, some forced to subsist on bread and water for as long as a year; others were left to starve. In 1902, the tower unexpectedly collapsed, taking with it Jacopo Sansovino's 16th-century marble loggia at its base. The largest original bell, called the *marangona*, survived. The crushed

VENICE THROUGH THE AGES

BEGINNINGS

Venice was founded in the 5th century when the Veneti, inhabitants of the mainland region roughly corresponding to today's lower Veneto, fled their homes to escape invading Germanic tribes. The unlikely city, built on islands in the lagoon and later atop wooden posts driven into the marshes, would evolve into a maritime republic lasting over a thousand years.

After liberating the Adriatic from marauding pirates, its early fortunes grew as a result of its active role in the Crusades, beginning in 1095 and culminating in the Venetian-led sacking of Constantinople in 1204. The defeat of rival Genoa in the Battle of Chioggia (1380) established Venice as the dominant sea power in Europe.

EARLY GOVERNMENT

As early as the 7th century, Venice was governed by a ruler, the doge, elected by the nobility to a lifetime term; however, since the common people had little political input or power, the city wasn't a democracy by modern definition. Beginning in the 12th century, the doge's power was increasingly subsumed by a growing number of councils, commissions, and magistrates. In 1268 a complicated procedure for the doge's election was established to prevent nepotism, but by that point power rested foremost with the Great Council, which at times numbered as many as 2,000 members.

A LONG DECLINE

Venice reached the height of its wealth and territorial expansion in the early 15th century, during which time its domain included all of the Veneto region and part of Lombardy, but the seeds of its decline were soon to be sown, with the fall of Constantinople to the Turks in 1453.

By the beginning of the 16th century, the pope, threatened by Venice's mainland expansion, organized the League of Cambrai, defeated Venice in 1505, and effectively put a stop to the Republic's mainland territorial designs. The Ottoman Empire blocked Venice's Mediterranean trade routes, and newly emerging sea powers such as Britain, Spain, Portugal, and the Netherlands ended Venice's monopoly by opening oceanic trading routes.

When Napoleon arrived in 1797, after having offered Venice first an alliance and then, having been betrayed by the Venetians' violation of a pledge of neutrality, he took the city without a fight. He gave it briefly to the Austrians, and then got it back in 1805. With his defeat Venice was ceded again to the Austrians at the Council of Vienna in 1815, and they ruled (save for a brief Venetian revolt in 1848) until the formation of the Italian Republic in 1866. During their occupation, the Austrians, as the French had before them, helped themselves to many of the city's artistic treasures. Very few of them have been returned.

3

loggia was promptly reconstructed, and the new tower, rebuilt to the old plan, reopened in 1912. Today, on a clear day the stunning view includes the Lido, the lagoon, and the mainland as far as the Alps, but, strangely enough, none of the myriad canals that snake through the city. Currently, the Campanile is undergoing foundation restoration due to deterioration caused by flooding (*acqua alta*); however, this hasn't affected the visiting hours. ⊠ *Piazza San Marco* ☎ *041/5224064* 🖃 *€8* ◷ *Easter–June, Oct., and Nov., daily 9–7; July–Sept., daily 9–9; Nov.–Easter, daily 9–3:45. Last entry 1 hr before closing* Ⓜ *Vaporetto: Vallaresso, San Zaccaria.*

Fodor's Choice   **Museo Correr.** This world-famous museum of Venetian art and history
★   contains an important sculpture collection by Antonio Canova and important paintings by Giovanni Bellini, Vittore Carpaccio (Carpaccio's famous painting of the Venetian courtesans is here), and other major local painters. It's the main repository of Venetian drawings and prints, which, unfortunately, can be seen only by special arrangement. It also houses curiosities such as the absurdly high-sole shoes worn by 16th-century Venetian ladies (who walked with the aid of a servant). The city's proud naval history is evoked in several rooms through highly descriptive paintings and numerous maritime objects, including ships' cannons and some surprisingly large iron mast-top navigation lights. The museum also has a room devoted entirely to antique games. The Correr exhibition rooms lead directly into the **Museo Archeologico**, which houses the Grimani collection—an important 16th- and 17th-century collection of Greek and Roman art—and the **Stanza del Sansovino**, the only part of the **Biblioteca Nazionale Marciana** open to visitors. ⊠ *Piazza San Marco, Ala Napoleonica (opposite the basilica)* ☎ *041/2405211* ⊕ *www. museicivicieneziani.it* 🖃 *Museums of San Marco Pass €16, includes single entry also to the Doge's Palace, the Archeological Museum, and the monumental rooms of the Biblioteca Marciana. Free with MUVE Pass.* ◷ *Apr.–Oct., daily 10–7; Nov.–Mar., daily 10–5. Last entry 1 hr before closing* Ⓜ *Vaporetto: Vallaresso, San Zaccaria.*

Torre dell'Orologio. This enameled clock, completed in 1499, was most likely designed by Venetian Renaissance architect Mauro Codussi. Twin giant figures (now called Moors because of their tarnished bronze bodies) would strike the hour, and three wise men with an angel would walk out and bow to the Virgin Mary on Epiphany (January 6) and during Ascension Week (40 days after Easter). An inscription on the tower reads "*Horas non numero nisi serenas*" ("I only count happy hours"). Originally, the clock tower had a much lighter, more graceful appearance, and was free standing. The four lateral bays were added in the early 16th century, while the upper stories and balustrades were completed in 1755. The clock itself was neglected until the 19th century, but now, after years of painstaking labor, the clockwork has been reassembled and is fully operational. Visits in English are offered daily and must be booked in advance at the Museo Correr or online. ⊠ *Piazza San Marco (north side of the piazza at the Merceria)* ☎ *0412405211* ⊕ *www.museicivicieneziani.it* 🖃 *€12* ◷ *Tours in English Mon.–Wed. at 10 and 11, Thurs.–Sun. at 2 and 3. Visits must be booked in advance through the Museo Correr.* Ⓜ *Vaporetto: Vallaresso, San Zaccaria.*

SAN MARCO AND DORSODURO

The sestiere Dorsoduro (named for its "hard back" solid clay foundation) is across the Grand Canal to the south of San Marco. It's a place of monumental churches, meandering canals, modern art galleries, the city's finest art museums, and a promenade called the Zattere, built in the early 16th century as a loading dock for timber shipped down from the Alpine regions. Now, on the Zattere, on sunny days you'll swear half the city is out for a *passeggiata*, or stroll. The eastern tip of the peninsula, the Punta della Dogana, was once the city's customs point; it became accessible to the public in 2009 when the old customs house was reopened as a contemporary art museum showcasing the François Pinault Collection. At the western end of the sestiere is the Stazione Marittima, where mammoth cruise ships line the dock all year-around.

Dorsoduro is also home to the Gallerie dell'Accademia, which has an unparalleled collection of Venetian painting, and the gloriously restored Ca' Rezzonico, which houses the Museo del Settecento Veneziano (Museum of 18th-Century Venice). Another of its landmark sites, the Peggy Guggenheim Collection, has a fine selection of 20th-century art.

TIMING

The Gallerie dell'Accademia demands a few hours, but if time is short an audio guide can help you cover the highlights in about an hour. Ca' Rezzonico deserves at least an hour.

TOP ATTRACTIONS

Fodor's Choice
★ **Ca' Rezzonico.** Designed by Baldassare Longhena in the 17th century, this gigantic palace was completed nearly 100 years later by Giorgio Massari and became the last home of English poet Robert Browning (1812–89). Stand on the bridge by the Grand Canal entrance to spot the plaque with Browning's poetic excerpt, *"Open my heart and you will see graved inside of it, Italy ..."* on the left side of the palace. The spectacular centerpiece is the eye-popping Grand Ballroom, which has hosted some of the grandest parties in the city's history, from its 18th-century heyday to the 1969 Bal Fantastica (a Save Venice charity event that attracted every notable of the day, from Elizabeth Taylor to Aristotle Onassis) to its balls recreated for Heath Ledger's 2005 *Casanova* film. Today the upper floors of the Ca' Rezzonico are home to the especially delightful **Museo del Settecento** (Museum of 18th-Century Venice). Its main floor successfully retains the appearance of a magnificent Venetian palazzo, decorated with period furniture and tapestries in gilded salons, as well as Tiepolo ceiling frescoes and oil paintings. Upper floors contain a fine collection of paintings by 18th-century Venetian artists, including the famous genre and Pucinella frescoes by Giambattista Tiepolo's son, Giandomenico, moved here from the Villa di Zianigo. There's even a restored apothecary, complete with powders and potions. ✉ *Fondamenta Rezzonico, Dorsoduro 3136* ☎ *041/2410100* ⊕ *www.museicivicivenezianai.it* 🏷 *€8. Free with MUVE pass* ☉ *Wed.–Mon. 10–6.* Ⓜ *Vaporetto: Ca' Rezzonico.*

Fodor's Choice   **Gallerie dell'Accademia.** The greatest museum of Venetian paintings in the
★   world, these galleries were founded by Napoleon back in 1807 on the
site of a religious complex he had suppressed. They were carefully and
subtly restructured between 1945 and 1959 by the renowned architect
Carlo Scarpa. In them you'll find room after room of the most treasured
Venetian masterpieces.

Jacopo Bellini is considered the father of the Venetian Renaissance, and
in Room 2 you can compare his *Madonna and Child with Saints* with
such later works as *Madonna of the Orange Tree* by Cima da Conegliano (circa 1459–1517) and *Ten Thousand Martyrs of Mt. Ararat* by
Vittore Carpaccio (circa 1455–1525). Jacopo's more-accomplished son
Giovanni (circa 1430–1516) attracts your eye not only with his subject
matter, but also with his rich color. Rooms 4 and 5 have a good selection
of his Madonnas. Room 5 contains *Tempest* by Giorgione (1477–1510),
a revolutionary work that has intrigued viewers and critics for centuries. It is unified not only by physical design elements, as was usual, but
more importantly by a mysterious, somewhat threatening atmosphere.
In Room 10, *Feast in the House of Levi*, commissioned as a Last Supper,
got Veronese summoned to the Inquisition over its depiction of dogs, jest-
ers, and other extraneous figures. The artist responded with the famous
retort, *"Noi pittori ci prendiamo le stesse libertà dei poeti e dei pazzi"*
("We painters permit ourselves the same liberties that poets and madmen
do"). He resolved the problem by simply changing the title, so that the
painting represented a different, less solemn biblical feast.

Room 10 also houses several of Tintoretto's finest works, including
three paintings from the life of St. Mark. Titian's *Presentation of the
Virgin* (Room 24) is the collection's only work originally created for
the building in which it hangs. Don't miss rooms 20 and 21, with
views of 15th- and 16th-century Venice by Carpaccio and Gentile Bellini
(1429–1507), Giovanni's brother—you'll see how little the city has
changed. (Note: The arrangement of the paintings described above may
be changed during special exhibitions.)

■**TIP→** Booking tickets in advance isn't essential, but helps during busy
seasons and costs only an additional €1.50. Booking is necessary to
see the Quadreria, where additional works cover every inch of a wide
hallway. A free map notes art and artists, and the bookshop sells a more
informative English-language booklet. In the main galleries a €4 audio
guide saves reading, but adds little to each room's excellent annotation.
✉ *Dorsoduro 1050, Campo della Carità just off the Accademia Bridge*
☎ *041/5200345 reservations 041/5222247 Quadreria reservations*
⊕ *www.gallerieaccademia.org* ✒ *€14 (includes admission to Palazzo Grimani and special exhibitions)* ☉ *Galleria: Tues.–Sun. 8:15–7:15, Mon.
8:15–2. Quadreria: Fri. 11–1, Sat. 11–noon* Ⓜ *Vaporetto: Accademia.*

■ QUICK
BITES

Fondamenta delle Zattere. There's no sunnier spot in Venice than Fondamenta delle Zattere, along the southern edge of Dorsoduro. It actually has
a micro-climate that is a few degrees warmer than the rest of the city. It is
here—on the city's gigantic public terrace, with bustling bars and gelato
shops—that people come to stroll, read in the open air, and play hooky
from sightseeing.

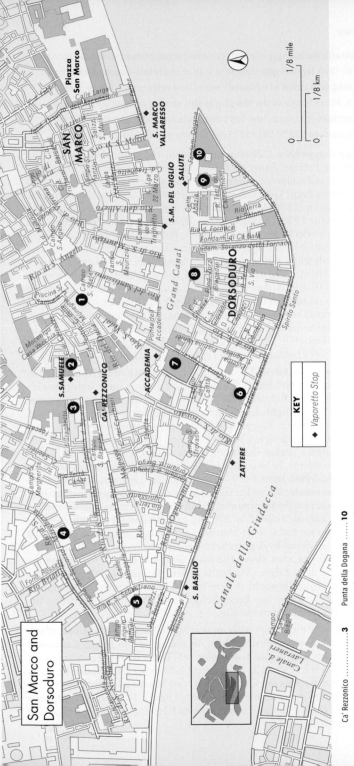

San Marco and Dorsoduro

KEY

0   1/8 km

0   1/8 mile

Gelateria Nico. Enjoy the Zattere's most scrumptious treat at Gelateria Nico—their famous *gianduiotto*, a slab of chocolate-hazelnut ice cream floating on a cloud of whipped cream—and relax on the big, welcoming deck. Nico's is one of the few places still serving authentic homemade (*artiginale*) ice cream, and has been seducing Venetians since 1935. ✉ *Dorsoduro 922* ☎ *041/5225293* ⊕ *www.gelaterianico.com.*

FAMILY **Peggy Guggenheim Collection.** Housed in the surprisingly small and charming Palazzo Venier dei Leoni, this choice selection of 20th-century painting and sculpture represents the taste and extraordinary style of the late heiress Peggy Guggenheim. Through wealth and social connections, Guggenheim (1898–1979) became an important art dealer and collector from the 1930s through the 1950s, and her personal collection here includes works by Picasso, Kandinsky, Pollock, Motherwell, and Ernst (at one time her husband). The museum serves beverages, snacks, and light meals in its refreshingly shady, artistically sophisticated garden. On Sunday at 3 the museum offers a free tour and art workshop for children 10 and under; conducted in Italian, anglophone interns are generally on hand to help those who don't *parla italiano.* Nearby is the headline-making contemporary art museum, the Punta della Dogana, now home to part of the Pinault collection. ✉ *Fondamenta Venier dei Leoni, Dorsoduro 701* ☎ *041/2405411* ⊕ *www.guggenheim-venice.it* 🎫 *€14* ◷ *Wed.–Mon. 10–6* Ⓜ *Vaporetto: Accademia.*

Fodor'sChoice **Santa Maria della Salute.** The most iconic landmark of the Grand Canal,
★ La Salute (as this church is commonly called) is most unforgettably viewed from the Riva degli Schiavoni at sunset, or from the Accademia Bridge by moonlight. En route to becoming Venice's most important Baroque architect, 32-year-old Baldassare Longhena won a competition in 1631 to design a shrine honoring the Virgin Mary for saving Venice from a plague that in the space of two years (1629–30) killed 47,000 residents, or one-third of the city's population. It was not completed, however, until 1687—five years after Longhena's death. Outside, this ornate, white Istrian stone octagon is topped by a colossal cupola with snail-like ornamental buttresses—in truth, piers encircled by finely carved "ropes," an allusion to the sail-making industry of the city (or so say today's art historians). Inside, a white-and-gray color scheme is echoed by a polychrome marble floor and the six chapels. The Byzantine icon above the main altar has been venerated as the Madonna della Salute (Madonna of Health) since 1670, when Francesco Morosini brought it here from Crete. Above it is a sculpture showing Venice on her knees before the Madonna as she drives the wretched plague from the city.

Do not leave the church without visiting the **Sacrestia Maggiore,** which contains a dozen works by Titian, including his *San Marco Enthroned with Saints* altarpiece. You'll also see Tintoretto's *The Wedding at Cana.* For the Festa della Salute, held November 21, a votive bridge is constructed across the Grand Canal, and Venetians pilgrimage here to light candles in prayer for another year's health. ✉ *Punta della Dogana* ☎ *041/2411018* 🎫 *Church free, sacristy €2* ◷ *Daily 9–noon and 3–5:30* Ⓜ *Vaporetto: Salute.*

Campo Santa Margherita. Lined with cafés and restaurants generally filled with university students, Campo Santa Margherita also has produce vendors and benches where you can sit and take in the bustling local life of the campo. Close to the Ca' Rezzonico and the Scuola dei Carmini, and only a 10-minute walk from the Gallerie dell'Accademia, it's a neat place to have a light, economical lunch of a *tramezzino* (sandwich) or panino and a spritz.

Il Caffè. For more than a portable munch, bask in the sunshine at the popular Il Caffè, commonly called Bar Rosso for its bright red exterior. It dishes up the best tramezzini in the campo, is open until midnight, and serves drinks and other light refreshments every day except Sunday. ⊠ *Dorsoduro 2963* ☎ *041/5287998.*

WORTH NOTING

Campo Santo Stefano. In Venice's most prestigious residential neighborhood, you'll find one of the city's busiest crossroads just over the Accademia Bridge; it's hard to believe this square once hosted bullfights, with bulls or oxen tied to a stake and baited by dogs. For centuries the *campo* was all grass except for a stone avenue called the *liston*. It was so popular for strolling that in Venetian dialect *"andare al liston"* still means "to go for a walk." A sunny meeting spot popular with Venetians and visitors alike, the campo also hosts outdoor fairs during Christmas and Carnevale seasons. Check out the 14th-century **Chiesa di Santo Stefano.** The pride of the church is its very fine Gothic portal, created in 1442 by Bartomomeo Bon. Inside, you'll see works by Tintoretto. ⊠ *Campo Santo Stefano, San Marco* ☎ *041/2750462 Chorus Foundation* ⊕ *www.chorusvenezia. org* ▣ *Church of Santo Stefano €3, Chorus Pass €10* ۞ *Church of Santo Stefano: Mon.–Sat. 10–5* Ⓜ *Vaporetto: Accademia.*

Gesuati. When the Dominicans took over the church of Santa Maria della Visitazione from the suppressed order of Gesuati laymen in 1668, Giorgio Massari was commissioned to build this structure. It has an important Tiepolo illusionistic ceiling and several other works by Giambattista Tiepolo (1696–1770), Giambattista Piazzetta (1683–1754), and Sebastiano Ricci (1659–1734). ⊠ *Zattere, Dorsoduro* ☎ *041/2750462* ⊕ *www.chorusvenezia.org* ▣ *€3, Chorus Pass €10* ۞ *Mon.–Sat. 10–5* Ⓜ *Vaporetto: Zattere.*

Palazzo Grassi. Built between 1748 and 1772 by Giorgio Massari for a Bolognese family, this palace is one of the last of the great noble residences on the Grand Canal. Once owned by auto magnate Giovanni Agnelli, it was bought by French businessman François Pinaut in 2005 to showcase his highly important collection of modern and contemporary art (which has now grown so large that Pinaut rented the Punta della Dogana, at the entryway to the Grand Canal, for his newest acquisitions). Pinaut brought in Japanese architect Tadao Ando to remodel the Grassi's interior. Check online for a schedule of temporary art exhibitions. ⊠ *Campo San Samuele, San Marco* ☎ *041/5231680* ⊕ *www. palazzograssi.it* ▣ *€15, €20 with Punta della Dogana* ۞ *Daily 10–7, closed Tues.* Ⓜ *Vaporetto: San Samuele.*

Fodor's Choice **Punta della Dogana.** Funded by the billionaire who owns Christie's Auc-
★ tion House, the François Pinault Foundation had Japanese architect
Tadao Ando redesign this fabled customs house—sitting at the *punta*,
"point" or head, of the Grand Canal—and now home to many eye-
popping works from Pinault's collection of contemporary art. The
streaming light, polished surfaces, and clean lines of Ando's design
contrast beautifully with the brick, massive columns, and sturdy
beams of the original Dogana. Even if you don't visit the museum, be
sure to walk down to the punta for a magnificent view of the Venetian
basin. Check online for a schedule of temporary exhibitions. ⊠ *Punta
della Dogana, Dorsoduro* 🕾 *041/5231680* ⊕ *www.palazzograssi.it*
🎫 *€15, €20 with Palazzo Grassi* ☉ *Wed.–Mon. 10–7. Last entry 1 hr
before closing.* Ⓜ *Vaporetto: Salute.*

Fodor's Choice **San Sebastiano.** Paolo Veronese (1528–88), although still in his twenties,
★ was already the official painter of the Republic when he began the oil
panels and frescoes at San Sebastiano, his parish church, in 1555. For
decades he continued to embellish the church with very beautiful illusionistic scenes. The cycles of panels in San Sebastiano are considered
to be his supreme accomplishment. Veronese is buried beneath his bust
near the organ. The church itself, remodeled by Antonio Scarpagnino
and finished in 1548, offers a rare opportunity to see a monument in
Venice where both the architecture and the pictorial decoration all date
from the same period. Be sure to check out the portal of the ex-convent,
now part of the University of Venice, to the left of the church; it was
designed in 1976–78 by Carlo Scarpa, one of the most important Italian architects of the 20th century. ⊠ *Campo San Sebastiano, Dorsoduro* 🕾 *041/2750462* ⊕ *www.chorusvenezia.org* 🎫 *€3, Chorus Pass
€10* ☉ *Mon.–Sat. 10–5, closed Sun.* Ⓜ *Vaporetto: San Basilio.*

Scuola Grande dei Carmini. When the order of Santa Maria del Carmelo
commissioned Baldassare Longhena to finish the work on the Scuola
Grande dei Carmini in the 1670s, their brotherhood of 75,000 members
was the largest in Venice and one of the wealthiest. Little expense was
spared in the decorating of stuccoed ceilings and carved ebony paneling,
and the artwork was choice, even before 1739, when Tiepolo began
painting the **Sala Capitolare.** In what many consider his best work,
Tiepolo's nine great canvases vividly transform some rather conventional religious themes into dynamic displays of color and movement.
⊠ *Campo dei Carmini, Dorsoduro 2617* 🕾 *041/5289420* 🎫 *€5* ☉ *Daily
11–4* Ⓜ *Vaporetto: Ca' Rezzonico.*

SAN POLO AND SANTA CROCE

The two smallest of Venice's six *sestieri (districts)*, San Polo and Santa
Croce, were named after their main churches, though the Chiesa di
Santa Croce was demolished in 1810. The city's most famous bridge, the
Ponte di Rialto, unites sestiere San Marco (east) with San Polo (west).
The Rialto takes its name from Rivoaltus, the high ground on which
it was built. Shops abound in the area surrounding the Rialto Bridge.
On the San Marco side you'll find fashions, on the San Polo side, food.

CLOSE UP

Speaking Venetian

Venice is one of the few Italian cities where the local dialect is still alive and well. Much of the language you'll hear in Venice is not Italian, but rather Venetian, or Italian heavily laced with Venetian. Venetian has its own rich and widely respected literature. The Venetian-dialect comedies of Goldoni, the great 18th-century playwright, are regularly performed in the city.

Even when speaking Italian, Venetians will use dialect terms to refer to certain common objects. Sometimes the term means something totally different in standard Italian.

Here are a few frequently used words:

sestiere: One of six neighborhoods in central Venice.

rio: A canal. Only the Grand Canal and a few other major waterways are called "canali." Everything else is a "rio."

fondamenta: A quay, a street running along a canal or a "rio."

calle: A street, what is elsewhere in Italy called a "via." "Via" is used in Venice, but it means "boulevard."

campo: A square—what is elsewhere in Italy called a piazza. (The only piazza in Venice is Piazza San Marco.)

bacaro: A traditional wine bar.

cicheto (pronounced chee-*kay*-toh): An hors d'oeuvre—roughly the Venetian equivalent of tapas. Generally served at a bacaro and in many cafés.

ombra: A small glass of wine.

focaccia: A traditional Venetian raised sweet cake, similar to a panettone, but much lighter and without candied fruit or raisins. (Very different from the better-known Genovese focaccia, a dense, slightly raised bread sometimes flavored with herbs or cheese.)

Venetians tend to use the informal second person form, "tu," much more readily than people do in other parts of Italy. Venetians also frequently address each other with the term *amore* (love), as is done sometimes in England. But in Venice it's used even between members of the same sex, without any romantic connotation.

3

TIMING

To do the area justice requires at least half a day. If you want to take part in the food shopping, come early to beat the crowds. Campo San Giacomo dell'Orio, west of the main thoroughfare that takes you from the Ponte di Rialto to Santa Maria Gloriosa dei Frari, is a peaceful place for a drink and a rest. The museums of Ca' Pesaro are a time commitment—you'll want at least two hours to see them both.

TOP ATTRACTIONS

Fodor'sChoice ★ **Ponte di Rialto** (*Rialto Bridge*). The competition to design a stone bridge across the Grand Canal attracted the best architects of the late 16th century, including Michelangelo, Palladio, and Sansovino, but the job went to the less-famous (but appropriately named) Antonio da Ponte (1512–95). His pragmatic design, completed in 1591, featured shop space and was high enough for galleys to pass beneath. Unlike the classical plans proposed by his more famous contemporaries, Da Ponte's bridge essentially followed the design of its wooden predecessor; it kept

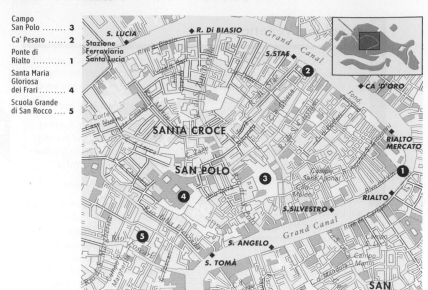

San Polo and
Santa Croce

KEY

◆ *Vaporetto Stop*

decoration and cost to a minimum at a time when the Republic's coffers were low due to continual wars against the Turks and the competition brought about by the Spanish and Portuguese opening of oceanic trade routes. Along the railing you'll enjoy one of the city's most famous views: the Grand Canal vibrant with boat traffic. Ⓜ *Vaporetto: Rialto.*

Fodor'sChoice
★

Santa Maria Gloriosa dei Frari. Completed in 1442, this immense Gothic church of russet-color brick—known locally as *I Frari*—is famous worldwide for its array of spectacular Venetian paintings. Visit the sacristy first, to see Giovanni Bellini's 1488 triptych *Madonna and Child with Saints* in all its mellow luminosity, painted for precisely this spot. The Corner Chapel on the other side of the chancel is graced by Bartolomeo Vivarini's (1415–84) 1474 altarpiece *St. Mark Enthroned and Saints John the Baptist, Jerome, Peter, and Nicholas,* which is much more conservative, displaying attention to detail generally associated with late medieval painting. In the first south chapel of the chorus, there is a fine sculpture of Saint John the Baptist by Donatello, dated 1438 (perhaps created before the artist came to Venice), which displays a psychological intensity rare for early Renaissance sculpture. You can see the rapid development of Venetian Renaissance painting by contrasting Bellini with the heroic energy of Titian's *Assumption,* over the main altar, painted only 30 years later. Unveiled in 1518, it was the artist's first public commission and, after causing a bit of controversy, did much to establish his reputation. Upon viewing this painting at the far end of the nave you'll first think it has been specially spotlit: upclose, however, you'll discover this impression is due to the painter's unrivaled use of light and color.

Titian's beautiful *Madonna di Ca' Pesaro* is in the left aisle. The painting took seven years to complete (finished in 1526), and in it Titian disregarded the conventions of his time by moving the Virgin out of center and making the saints active participants. The composition, built on diagonals, anticipates structural principals of baroque painting in the following century. The Frari also holds a Sansovino sculpture of St. John the Baptist, and Longhena's impressive baroque tomb designed for Doge Giovanni Pesaro. ⊠ *Campo dei Frari, San Polo* ☎ *041/2728618, 041/2750462 Chorus Foundation* ⊕ *www.chorusvenezia.org* ⌖ *€3, Chorus Pass €10* ⊙ *Mon.–Sat. 9–6, Sun. 1–6* Ⓜ *Vaporetto: San Tomà.*

Fodor's Choice
★ **Scuola Grande di San Rocco.** Saint Rocco's popularity stemmed from his miraculous recovery from the plague and his care for fellow sufferers. Throughout the plague-filled Middle Ages, followers and donations abounded, and this elegant example of Venetian Renaissance architecture, built between 1517 and 1560 and including the work of at least four architects, built for the essentially secular charitable confraternity bearing the saint's name, was the result. Although it is bold and dramatic outside, its contents are even more stunning—a series of more than 60 paintings by Tintoretto. In 1564 Tintoretto edged out competition for a commission to decorate a ceiling by submitting not a sketch, but a finished work, which he moreover offered free of charge. *Moses Striking Water from the Rock, The Brazen Serpent,* and *The Fall of Manna* represent three afflictions—thirst, disease, and hunger—that San Rocco and later his brotherhood sought to relieve. ⊠ *Campo San Rocco, San Polo 3052* ☎ *041/5234864* ⊕ *www.scuolagrandesanrocco.it* ⌖ *€8 (includes audio guide)* ⊙ *Daily 9:30–5:30. Last entry ½ hr before closing* Ⓜ *Vaporetto: San Tomà.*

QUICK BITES

Caffè dei Frari. Just over the bridge in front of the Frari church is Caffè dei Frari, where you'll find a delightful assortment of sandwiches and snacks. Established in 1870, it's one of the last Venetian tearooms with its original decor. It's frequented more by residents and students than by tourists. Prices are a bit higher (€3.50 for a spritz) than in caffès in nearby Campo Santa Margherita, but the decor and the friendly "retro" atmosphere seem to make the added cost worthwhile. ⊠ *Fondamenta dei Frari, San Polo 2564, San Polo* ☎ *No phone* ⊙ *Closed weekends.*

Pasticceria Tonolo. Pasticceria Tonolo, in operation since 1886, is widely considered among Venice's premier confectionaries. During Carnevale it's still one of the best places in town for *fritelle,* fried doughnuts (traditional raisin or cream-filled), and before Christmas and Easter, Venetians order their *focaccia,* the traditional raised cake eaten especially at holidays, from here well in advance. Closed Monday, and there's no seating any time. ⊠ *Calle Crosera, Dorsoduro 3764* ☎ *041/5237209.*

WORTH NOTING

Ca' Pesaro. Baldassare Longhena's grand Baroque palace is the beautifully restored home of two impressive collections. The **Galleria Internazionale d'Arte Moderna** has works by 19th- and 20th-century artists such as Klimt, Kandinsky, Matisse, and Miró. It also has a collection of representative works from Venice's Biennale art show that amounts to a panorama of 20th-century art. The pride of the **Museo Orientale** is its collection of Japanese art, and especially armor and weapons, of the Edo period (1603–1868). It also has a small but striking collection of Chinese and Indonesian porcelains and musical instruments. ⊠ *San Stae, Santa Croce 2076* ☎ *041/721127 Galleria, 041/5241173 Museo Orientale* ⊕ *www.museicivicivenezian.it* ☞ *€8.50 includes both museums. Free with MUVE pass* ⊘ *Apr.–Oct., daily 10–6; Nov.–Mar., daily 10–5. Closed Mon.* Ⓜ *Vaporetto: San Stae.*

Campo San Polo. Only Piazza San Marco is larger than this square, and the echo of children's voices bouncing off the surrounding palaces makes the space seem even bigger. Campo San Polo once hosted bull races, fairs, military parades, and packed markets, and now comes especially alive on summer nights, when it's home to the city's outdoor cinema. The **Chiesa di San Polo** has been restored so many times that little remains of the original 9th-century church, and sadly, 19th-century alterations were so costly that the friars sold off many great paintings to pay bills. Though Giambattista Tiepolo is represented here, his work is outdone by 16 paintings by his son Giandomenico (1727–1804), including the *Stations of the Cross* in the oratory to the left of the entrance. The younger Tiepolo also created a series of expressive and theatrical renderings of the saints. Look for altarpieces by Tintoretto and Veronese that managed to escape auction. San Polo's bell tower remained unchanged through the centuries—don't miss the two lions playing with a disembodied human head and a serpent that guard it. ⊠ *Campo San Polo* ☎ *041/2750462 Chorus Foundation* ⊕ *www.chorusvenezia.org* ☞ *€3, Chorus Pass €10* ⊘ *Church: Mon.–Sat. 10–5.* Ⓜ *Vaporetto: San Silvestro, San Tomà.*

San Giacomo dell'Orio. It was named after a laurel tree (*orio*), and today trees give character to this square. Add benches and a fountain (with a drinking bowl for dogs), and the pleasant, oddly shaped campo becomes a welcoming place for friendly conversation and neighborhood kids at play. Legend has it the **Chiesa di San Giacomo dell'Orio** was founded in the 9th century on an island still populated by wolves. The current church dates from 1225; its short unmatched Byzantine columns survived renovation during the Renaissance, and the church never lost the feel of an ancient temple sheltering beneath its 14th-century ship's-keel roof. In the sanctuary, large marble crosses are surrounded by a group of small medieval Madonnas. The altarpiece is *Madonna with Child and Saints* (1546) by Lorenzo Lotto (1480–1556), and the sacristies contain 12 works by Palma il Giovane (circa 1544–1628). ⊠ *Campo San Giacomo dell'Orio, Santa Croce* ☎ *041/2750462 Chorus Foundation* ⊕ *www.chorusvenezia.org* ☞ *€3, Chorus Pass €10* ⊘ *Mon.–Sat. 10–5* Ⓜ *Vaporetto: San Stae.*

San Giovanni Elemosinario. Storefronts make up the facade, and the altars were built by market guilds—poulterers, messengers, and fodder merchants—at this church intimately bound to the Rialto Market. The original church was completely destroyed by a fire in 1514 and rebuilt in 1531 by Antonio Abbondi, who had also worked on the Scuola di San Rocco. During a recent restoration, workers stumbled upon a frescoed cupola by Pordenone (1484–1539) that had been painted over centuries earlier. Don't miss Titian's *St. John the Almsgiver* and Pordenone's *Sts. Catherine, Sebastian, and Roch*, which in 2002 were returned after 30 years by the Gallerie dell'Accademia. ⊠ *Rialto Ruga Vecchia San Giovanni, Santa Croce* ☎ *041/2750462 Chorus Foundation* ⊕ *www.chorusvenezia.org* ✍ *€3, Chorus Pass €10* ⊙ *Mon.–Sat. 10–5.* Ⓜ *Vaporetto: San Silvestro, Rialto.*

San Stae. The church of San Stae—the Venetian name for San Eustacchio (Eustace)—was reconstructed in 1687 by Giovanni Grassi and given a new facade in 1707 by Domenico Rossi. The most renowned Venetian painters and sculptors of the early 18th century decorated this church around 1717 with the legacy left by Doge Alvise Mocenigo II, who's buried in the center aisle. San Stae affords a good opportunity to see the early works of Tiepolo, Ricci, and Piazzetta, as well as those of the previous generation of Venetian painters. ⊠ *Campo San Stae, Santa Croce* ☎ *041/2750462 Chorus Foundation* ⊕ *www.chorusvenezia.org* ✍ *€3, Chorus Pass €10* ⊙ *Mon.–Sat. 9–5* Ⓜ *Vaporetto: San Stae.*

CANNAREGIO

Seen from above, this part of town seems like a wide field plowed by several long, straight canals that are linked by intersecting straight streets—not typical of Venice, where the shape of the islands usually defines the shape of the canals. Cannaregio's main thoroughfare, the Strada Nova (literally, "New Street," as it was opened in 1871), is the longest street in Venice. It runs parallel to the Grand Canal, and was once a canal itself. Today it's lined with fruit and vegetable stalls (near Ponte delle Guglie), quiet shops, gelaterias, and bakeries, and serves as a pedestrian walkway from the train station almost to the Rialto.

TOP ATTRACTIONS

Fodor'sChoice
★
Ca' d'Oro. One of the postcard sights of Venice, this exquisite Venetian Gothic palace was once literally a "Golden House," when its marble traceries and ornaments were embellished with gold. It was created by Giovanni and Bartolomeo Bon between 1428 and 1430 for the patrician Marino Contarini, who had read about the Roman emperor Nero's golden house in Rome, and wished to imitate it as a present to his wife. Her family owned the land and the Byzantine *fondaco* (trading post) previously standing on it; you can still see the round Byzantine arches on the entry porch incorporated into the Gothic building. The last proprietor, Baron Giorgio Franchetti, left Ca' d'Oro to the city, after having had it carefully restored and furnished with antiquities, sculptures, and paintings that today make up the **Galleria Franchetti.** Besides Andrea Mantegna's *St. Sebastian* and other Venetian works, the Galleria Franchetti contains the type of fresco that once adorned the

exteriors of Venetian buildings (commissioned by those who could not afford a marble facade). One such detached fresco displayed here was made by the young Titian for the facade of the Fondaco dei Tedeschi near the Rialto. ✉ *Calle Ca' d'Oro, Cannaregio 3933* ☎ *041/5238790* ⊕ *www.cadoro.org* ✉ *€6, plus €1.50 to reserve; €8 when there is a special exhibition.* ☉ *Tues.–Sun. 8:15–7:15, Mon. 8:15–2. Closed Sun. in Jan.* Ⓜ *Vaporetto: Ca' d'Oro.*

Jewish Ghetto. The neighborhood that gave the world the word *ghetto* is today a quiet neighborhood surrounding a large campo. It is home to Jewish institutions, two kosher restaurants, a rabbinical school, and five synagogues. Present-day Venetian Jews live all over the city, and the contemporary Jewish life of the ghetto, with the exception of the Jewish museum and the synagogues, is an enterprise conducted almost exclusively by American Hassidic Jews of Eastern European descent and tradition.

In 1516 relentless local opposition forced the Senate to confine Jews to an island in Cannaregio, then on the outer reaches of the city, named for its *geto* (foundry). The term "ghetto" also may come from the Hebrew "ghet," meaning separation or divorce. Gates at the entrance were locked at night, and boats patrolled the surrounding canals. Jews were allowed only to lend money at low interest, operate pawnshops controlled by the government, trade in textiles, or practice medicine. Jewish doctors were highly respected and could leave the ghetto at any hour when on duty.

Though ostracized, Jews were nonetheless safe in Venice, and in the 16th century the community grew considerably—primarily with refugees from the Inquisition, which persecuted Jews in southern and central Italy, Spain, and Portugal. The ghetto was allowed to expand twice, but it still had the city's densest population and consequently ended up with the city's tallest buildings. Although the gates were pulled down after Napoleon's 1797 arrival, the ghetto was reinstated during the Austrian occupation. The Jews realized full freedom only in 1866 with the founding of the Italian state. Many Jews fled Italy as a result of Mussolini's 1938 racial laws, so that on the eve of World War II, there were about 1,500 Jews left in the ghetto. Jews continued to flee, and the remaining 247 were deported by the Nazis; only eight returned.

The area has Europe's highest density of Renaissance-era synagogues, and visiting them is interesting not only culturally, but also aesthetically. Though each is marked by the tastes of its individual builders, Venetian influence is evident throughout. Women's galleries resemble those of theaters from the same era, and some synagogues were decorated by artists who were simultaneously active in local churches; Longhena, the architect of Santa Maria della Salute, renovated the Spanish synagogue in 1635.

Museo Ebraico. The small but well-arranged Museo Ebraico highlights centuries of Venetian Jewish culture with splendid silver Hanukkah lamps and Torahs, and handwritten, beautifully decorated wedding contracts in Hebrew. Tours in Italian and in English (on the half hour) of the ghetto and its five synagogues leave from the museum. ✉ *Campo*

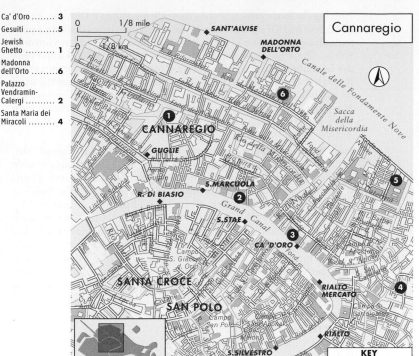

del Ghetto Nuovo, Cannaregio 2902/B ☏*041/715359* ⊕*www. museoebraico.it* ✉ *Museum €3; guided tour, museum, and synagogues €8.50* ⊘ *June–Sept., Sun.–Fri. 10–7; Oct.–May, Sun.–Fri. 10–6. Tours hourly starting at 10:30* Ⓜ *Vaporetto: San Marcuola, Guglie.*

Antico Cimitero Ebraico (*Ancient Jewish Cemetery*). You might complete your circuit of Jewish Venice with a visit to the Antico Cimitero Ebraico on the Lido, full of fascinating old tombstones half hidden by ivy and grass. The earliest grave dates from 1389; the cemetery remained in use until the late 18th century. ✉ *Via Cipro at San Nicolo, Lido* ☏ *041/715359 Jewish Museum* ✉ *€8.50* ⊘ *Tours Apr.–Oct., Sun. at 2:30, other days by appointment; call to reserve* Ⓜ *Vaporetto: Lido, San Nicolo.*

Madonna dell'Orto. Though built toward the middle of the 14th century, this church takes its character from its beautiful late-Gothic facade, added between 1460 and 1464; it's one of the most beautiful Gothic churches in Venice. Tintoretto lived nearby, and this, his parish church, contains some of his most powerful work. Lining the chancel are two huge (45 feet by 20 feet) canvases, *Adoration of the Golden Calf* and *Last Judgment*. In glowing contrast to this awesome spectacle are Tintoretto's *Presentation of the Virgin at the Temple* and the simple chapel where he and his children, Marietta and Domenico, are buried.

Paintings by Domenico, Cima da Conegliano, Palma il Giovane, Palma il Vecchio, and Titian also hang in the church. A chapel displays a photographic reproduction of a precious *Madonna with Child* by Giovanni Bellini. The original was stolen one night in 1993. ■TIP→ Don't miss the beautifully austere, late-Gothic cloister (1460), which you enter through the small door to the right of the church; it is frequently used for exhibitions, but may be open at other times as well. ⊠ *Campo della Madonna dell'Orto, Cannaregio* 🕾 *041/2750462 Chorus Foundation* ⊕ *www.chorusvenezia.org* ⊠ *€3, Chorus Pass €10* ☉ *Mon.–Sat. 10–5* Ⓜ *Vaporetto: Orto.*

Santa Maria dei Miracoli. Tiny yet harmoniously proportioned, this Renaissance gem, built between 1481 and 1489, is sheathed in marble and decorated inside with exquisite marble reliefs. Architect Pietro Lombardo (circa 1435–1515) miraculously compressed the building into its confined space, then created the illusion of greater size by varying the color of the exterior, adding extra pilasters on the building's canal side, and offsetting the arcade windows to make the arches appear deeper. The church was built to house *I Miracoli*, an image of the Virgin Mary by Niccolò di Pietro (1394-1440) that is said to have performed miracles—look for it on the high altar. ⊠ *Campo Santa Maria Nova, Cannaregio* 🕾 *041/2750462 Chorus Foundation* ⊕ *www.chorusvenezia.org* ⊠ *€3, Chorus Pass €10* ☉ *Mon.–Sat. 10–5* Ⓜ *Vaporetto: Rialto.*

WORTH NOTING

Gesuiti. The interior walls of this early-18th-century church resemble brocade drapery, and only touching them will convince skeptics that rather than embroidered cloth, the green-and-white walls are inlaid marble. This tromp l'oeil decor is typical of the late baroque's fascination with optical illusion. Towards the end of his life, Titian tended to paint scenes of suffering and sorrow in a nocturnal ambience. A dramatic example of this is on display above the first altar to the left: Titian's daring *Martyrdom of St. Lawrence* (1578), taken from an earlier church that stood on this site. ⊠ *Campo dei Gesuiti, Cannaregio* 🕾 *041/5286579* ☉ *Apr.–Oct, Thurs., Fri., Sat. 10–noon* Ⓜ *Vaporetto: Fondamente Nove.*

Palazzo Vendramin-Calergi. Hallowed as the place of Richard Wagner's death and today's Venice's most glamorous casino, this magnificent edifice found its fame centuries before: Venetian star architect Mauro Codussi (1440–1504) essentially invented Venetian Renaissance architecture with this design. Built for the Loredan family around 1500, Codussi's palace married the fortress-like design of the Florentine Alberti's Palazzo Ruccelai with the lightness and delicacy of Venetian Gothic. Note how Codussi beautifully exploits the flickering light of Venetian waterways to play across the building's facade and to pour in through the generous windows. Famously, the great German composer Richard Wagner ended his days in an apartment in the rebuilt garden wing of the palazzo. Today, the palazzo itself houses the Casino di Venezia, but even if you are not interested in gambling, you should pay a call to view some of the most sumptuous salons in Venice. ⊠ *Cannaregio 2040* 🕾 *041/5297111, 338/4164174 Sala di Wagner tours*

⊕ www.casinovenezia.it ☛ Casinò €10, Sala di Wagner tour €5 suggested donation ☹ Casinò, Sun.– Thurs. 3:30–2:30, Fri. and Sat. 3:30–3; slot machines open daily at 3. Sala di Wagner tours Tues. and Sat. at 10:30 am, Thurs. at 2:30 pm (call by noon the day before to reserve) Ⓜ *Vaporetto: San Marcuola.*

3

CASTELLO

Castello, Venice's largest sestiere (district), includes all of the land from east of Piazza San Marco to the city's easternmost tip. Its name probably comes from a fortress that once stood on one of the eastern islands.

Not every well-off Venetian family could find a spot or afford to build a palazzo on the Grand Canal. Many that couldn't instead settled in western Castello, taking advantage of its proximity to the Rialto and San Marco, and built the noble palazzos that today distinguish this area from the fishermen's enclave in the more easterly streets of the sestiere. During the days of the Republic, eastern Castello was the primary neighborhood for workers in the shipbuilding Arsenale, which is located in its midst.

TOP ATTRACTIONS

Arsenale. Visible from the street, the Arsenale's impressive Renaissance gateway, the **Porta Magna** (1460), was the first classical structure to be built in Venice. It is guarded by four lions—war booty of Francesco Morosini, who took the Peloponnese from the Turks in 1687. The 10-foot-tall lion on the left stood sentinel more than 2,000 years ago near Athens, and experts say its mysterious inscription is runic "graffiti" left by Viking mercenaries hired to suppress 11th-century revolts in Piraeus. If you look at the winged lion above the doorway, you'll notice that the Gospel at his paws is open, but lacks the customary *Pax* inscription; praying for peace perhaps seemed inappropriate above a factory that manufactured weapons. The interior is not regularly open to the public, since it belongs to the Italian Navy, but it opens for the Biennale and for Venice's festival of traditional boats, **Mare Maggio** (⊕ *www.maremaggio.it*), held every May. If you're here during those times, don't miss the chance for a look inside; you can enter from the back via a northern-side walkway leading from the Ospedale vaporetto stop.

The Arsenale is said to have been founded in 1104 on twin islands. The immense facility that evolved—it was the largest industrial complex in Europe built prior to the Industrial Revolution—was given the old Venetian dialect name *arzanà*, borrowed from the Arabic *darsina'a*, meaning "workshop." At the height of its activity, in the early 16th century, it employed as many as 16,000 *arsenalotti*, workers who were among the most respected shipbuilders in the world. The Arsenale developed a type of pre-Industrial Revolution assembly line, which allowed it to build ships with astounding speed and efficiency. (This innovation existed even in Dante's time, and he immortalized these toiling workers armed with boiling tar in his *Inferno, Canto 21.*) The Arsenale's efficiency was confirmed time and again—whether building 100 ships in 60 days to battle the Turks in Cyprus (1597) or completing one perfectly armed warship, start to finish, while King Henry III of France attended a banquet. ⊠ *Campo dell'Arsenale* Ⓜ *Vaporetto: Arsenale.*

Fodor's Choice
★
Santi Giovanni e Paolo. A venerated jewel, this gorgeous church looms over one of the most picturesque squares in Venice: the Campo Giovanni e Paolo, centered around the magnificent 15th-century equestrian statue of Bartolomeo Colleoni by the Florentine Andrea Verrocchio. Also note the beautiful facade of the Scuola Grande di San Marco (now the municipal hospital), begun by Pietro Lombardo and completed after the turn of the 16th century by Mauro Codussi. The massive Italian Gothic church itself is of the Dominican order and was consecrated in 1430. Bartolomeo Bon's portal, combining Gothic and classical elements, was added between 1458 and 1462, using columns salvaged from Torcello. The 15th-century stained-glass window near the side entrance is breathtaking for its brilliant colors and beautiful figures; it was made in Murano from drawings by Bartolomeo Vivarini and Gerolamo Mocetto (circa 1458–1531). The second official church of the Republic after San Marco, San Zanipolo is the Venetian equivalent of London's Westminster Abbey, with a great number of important people, including 25 doges, buried here. Artistic highlights include an early (1465) polyptych by Giovanni Bellini (right aisle, second altar) where the influence of Mantegna is still very evident, Alvise Vivarini's *Christ Carrying the Cross* (sacristy), and Lorenzo Lotto's *Charity of St. Antonino* (right transept). Don't miss the *Cappella del Rosario* (Rosary Chapel), off the left transept, built in the 16th century to commemorate the 1571 victory of Lepanto, in western Greece, when Venice led a combined European fleet to defeat the Turkish Navy. The chapel was devastated by a fire in 1867 and restored in the early years of the 20th century with works from other churches, among them the sumptuous Veronese ceiling paintings. However quick your visit, don't miss the Pietro Mocenigo tomb to the right of the main entrance, by Pietro Lombardo and his sons. ⊠ *Campo dei Santi Giovanni e Paolo* ☎ *041/5235913* ⊠ *€3 (Note: this is not a Chorus church, and the Chorus card is not valid here)* ⊗ *Mon.–Sat. 9:30–6, Sun. 1–6* Ⓜ *Vaporetto: Fondamente Nove, Rialto.*

QUICK BITES

Didovich Pastry Shop. To satisfy your sweet tooth, head for Campo Santa Marina and the family-owned and -operated Didovich Pastry Shop. It's a local favorite, especially for Carnevale-time *fritelle* (fried doughnuts). There is limited seating inside, but in the warmer months you can sit outside. ⊠ *Campo Santa Marina, Castello 5909, Castello* ☎ *041/5230017.*

Un Mondo di Vino. Un Mondo di Vino, below Campo Santa Maria Nova on Calle San Canciano, is a friendly place to recharge with a *cicheto* (snack) or two and some wine. ⊠ *Salizzada San Cancian, Cannaregio 5984, Cannaregio* ☎ *041/5211093* ⊗ *Closed Mon.*

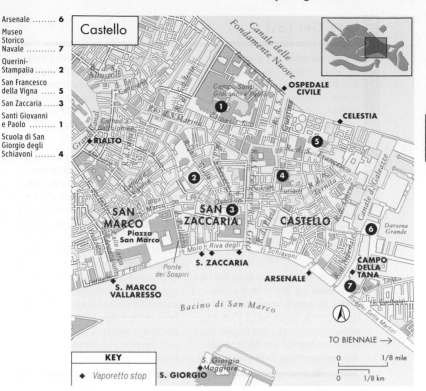

WORTH NOTING

FAMILY **Museo Storico Navale** (*Museum of Naval History*). The boat collection here includes scale models such as the doges' ceremonial *Bucintoro,* and full-size boats such as Peggy Guggenheim's private gondola complete with romantic *felze* (cabin). There's a range of old galley and military pieces, and also a large collection of seashells. ⊠ *Campo San Biagio, Castello 2148* ☎ *041/2441399* ⊕ *www.marina.difesa.it (then search Venezia Museo)* 🎫 *€1.55* ☯ *Weekdays 8:45–1:30, Sat. 8:45–1* Ⓜ *Vaporetto: Arsenale.*

Querini-Stampalia. A connoisseur's delight, this art collection at this late-16th-century palace includes Giovanni Bellini's *Presentation in the Temple* and Sebastiano Ricci's triptych *Dawn, Afternoon, and Evening.* Portraits of newlyweds Francesco Querini and Paola Priuli were left unfinished on the death of Giacomo Palma il Vecchio (1480–1528); note the groom's hand and the bride's dress. Original 18th-century furniture and stuccowork are a fitting background for Pietro Longhi's portraits. Nearly 70 works by Gabriele Bella (1730–99) capture scenes of Venetian street life; downstairs is a café. The entrance hall and the beautiful rear garden were designed by famous Venetian architect Carlo Scarpa during the 1950s. ⊠ *Campo Santa Maria Formosa, Castello 5252* ☎ *041/2711411* ⊕ *www.querinistampalia.it* 🎫 *€10* ☯ *Tues.–Sun. 10–6* Ⓜ *Vaporetto: San Zaccaria.*

CLOSE UP

Let's Get Lost

Getting around Venice presents some unusual problems: the city's layout has few straight lines; house numbering seems nonsensical, referring to the sestiere, and not to the street itself; and the six sestieri of San Marco, Cannaregio, Castello, Dorsoduro, Santa Croce, and San Polo all duplicate each other's street names. Since the sestiere carries the house number and forms part of the address, the street name itself frequently becomes irrelevant. In fact, unless a Venetian lives on a major thoroughfare, he or she may not even know the name of the street where he lives.

The numerous vaporetto lines can also be bewildering, and often the only option for getting where you want to go is to walk. Yellow signs, posted on many busy corners, point toward the major landmarks—San Marco, Rialto, Accademia, and so forth—but don't

count on finding such markers once you're deep into residential neighborhoods. Even buying a good map at a newsstand—the kind showing all street names and vaporetto routes— won't necessarily keep you from getting lost.

Fortunately, as long as you maintain your patience and sense of adventure, getting lost in Venice can be a pleasure. For one thing, being lost is a sign that you've escaped the tourist throngs. And although you might not find the Titian masterpiece you'd set out to see, instead you could wind up coming across an ageless bacaro or a quirky shop that turns out to be the highlight of your afternoon. Opportunities for such serendipity abound. Keep in mind that the city is very self-contained: sooner or later, perhaps with the help of a patient resident, you're bound to regain your bearings.

Fodor's Choice ★ **San Francesco della Vigna.** Although this church contains some interesting and beautiful paintings and sculptures, it's the architecture that makes it worth the hike through a lively, middle-class, residential neighborhood. The Franciscan church was enlarged and rebuilt by Jacopo Sansovino in 1534, giving it the first Renaissance interior in Venice; its proportions are said to reflect the mystic significance of the numbers three and seven dictated by Renaissance neo-Platonic numerology. The soaring, but harmonious facade was added in 1562 by Palladio. The church represents, therefore, a unique combination of the work of the two great stars of Veneto 16th-century architecture. As you enter, a late Giovanni Bellini *Madonna with Saints* is down some steps to the left, inside the Cappella Santa. In the Giustinian chapel to the left is Veronese's first work in Venice, an altarpiece depicting the Virgin and child with saints. In another, larger chapel, on the left, are bas-reliefs by Pietro and his son Tullio Lombardo. ⊠ *Campo di San Francesco della Vigna* ☎ *041/5206102* ☜ *Free* ☉ *Daily 8–12:30 and 3–7* Ⓜ *Vaporetto: Celestia.*

San Zaccaria. Practically more a museum than a church, San Zaccaria bears a striking Renaissance facade, with central and upper portions representing some of Mauro Codussi's best work. Most of the church was 14th-century Gothic, with its facade completed in 1515, some years after Codussi's death in 1504, and it retains the proportions of the rest of the essentially Gothic structure. Inside is one of the great treasures of Venice, Giovanni Bellini's celebrated altarpiece, *La Sacra Conversazione*, easily recognizable in the left nave. Completed in 1505, when the artist was 75, it shows Bellini's ability to incorporate the esthetics of the High Renaissance into his work. It bears a closer resemblance to the contemporary works of Leonardo (it dates from approximately the same time as the *Mona Lisa*) than it does to much of Bellini's early work. The **Cappella di San Tarasio** displays frescoes by Tuscan Renaissance artists Andrea del Castagno (1423–57) and Francesco da Faenza (circa 1400–51). Castagno's frescoes (1442) are considered the earliest examples of Renaissance painting in Venice. The three outstanding Gothic polyptychs attributed to Antonio Vivarini earned it the nickname "Golden Chapel." ✉ *Campo San Zaccaria, 4693 Castello* ☎ *041/5221257* ✆ *Church free, chapels and crypt €1* ☉ *Mon.–Sat. 10–noon, Sun. 4–6* Ⓜ *Vaporetto: San Zaccaria.*

Scuola di San Giorgio degli Schiavoni. Founded in 1451 by the Dalmatian community, this small scuola was, and still is, a social and cultural center for migrants from what is now Croatia. It contains one of Italy's most beautiful rooms, harmoniously decorated between 1502 and 1507 by Vittore Carpaccio. Carpaccio generally painted legendary and religious figures against backgrounds of contemporary Venetian architecture, but here, there is also perhaps one of the first instances of "Orientalism" in western painting. Note the turbans and exotic dress of those being baptized and converted, and even the imagined, arid Middle Eastern or North African landscape in the background of several of the paintings. Here, in a scuola for immigrants, Carpaccio focuses on "foreign" saints especially venerated in Dalmatia: Saints George, Tryphone, and Jerome. He combined keen empirical observation with fantasy, a sense of warm color, and late medieval realism. (Look for the priests fleeing Saint Jerome's lion, or the body parts in the dragon's lair.) ■**TIP→** The opening hours are quite flexible. Since this is a "must see" site, check to confirm opening hours so that you won't be disappointed. ✉ *Calle dei Furlani, Castello 3259/A* ☎ *041/5228828* ✆*€5* ☉ *Tues.–Sun. 9–12, 3–6* Ⓜ *Vaporetto: Arsenale, San Zaccaria.*

SAN GIORGIO MAGGIORE AND THE GIUDECCA

Beckoning travelers across Saint Mark's Basin, sparkling white through the mist, is the island of San Giorgio Maggiore, separated by a small channel from the Giudecca. A tall brick campanile on that distant bank nicely complements the Campanile of San Marco. Beneath it looms the stately dome of one of Venice's greatest churches, San Giorgio Maggiore, the creation of Andrea Palladio. To the west, on the Giudecca, is Palladio's other masterpiece, the Church of the Santissimo Redentore.

You can reach San Giorgio Maggiore via vaporetto Line 2 from San Zaccaria. The next three stops on the line take you to the Giudecca. The island's past may be shrouded in mystery, but despite recent gentrification by artists and well-to-do bohemians, it's still down to earth and one of the city's few remaining primarily working-class neighborhoods. Interestingly, you find that most Venetians don't even consider the Giudecchini Venetians at all.

TIMING
A half day should be plenty of time to visit the area. Allow about a half hour to see each of the churches and an hour or two to look around the Giudecca.

TOP ATTRACTIONS

Fodor'sChoice   **San Giorgio Maggiore.** There's been a church on this island since the
★   8th century, with a Benedictine monastery added in the 10th century. Today's refreshingly airy and simply decorated church of brick and white marble was begun in 1566 by Palladio and displays his architectural hallmarks of mathematical harmony and classical influence. *The Last Supper* and the *Gathering of Manna,* two of Tintoretto's later works, line the chancel. To the right of the entrance hangs *The Adoration of the Shepherds* by Jacopo Bassano (1517–92); his affection for his home in the foothills, Bassano del Grappa, is evident in the bucolic subjects and terra-firma colors he chooses. The monks are happy to show Carpaccio's *St. George and the Dragon,* hanging in a private room, if they have time. The campanile dates from 1791, the previous structures having collapsed twice.

Adjacent to the church is the complex now housing the **Cini Foundation,** containing a very beautiful cloister designed by Palladio in 1560, his refectory, and a library designed by Longhena. Guided tours are given on weekends (10–4), reservations not required. ✉ *Isola di San Giorgio Maggiore* ☎ *041/5227827* ✆ *Church free, campanile €3* ⊙ *Daily 9:30–12:30 and 2–6; Sunday 2–6 (hrs tend to be flexible)* Ⓜ *Vaporetto: San Giorgio.*

Santissimo Redentore. After a plague in 1576 claimed some 50,000 people—nearly one-third of the city's population (including Titian)— Andrea Palladio was asked to design a commemorative church. Giudecca's Capuchin friars offered land and their services, provided the building was in keeping with the simplicity of their hermitage. Consecrated in 1592, after Palladio's death, the Redentore (considered Palladio's supreme achievement in ecclesiastical design) is dominated by a dome and a pair of slim, almost minaret-like bell towers. Its deceptively simple, stately facade leads to a bright, airy interior. There aren't any paintings or sculptures of note, but the harmony and elegance of the interior makes a visit worthwhile.

For hundreds of years, on the third weekend in July the doge would make a pilgrimage here to give thanks to the Redeemer for ending the 16th-century plague. The event has become the Festa del Redentore, a favorite Venetian festival featuring boats, fireworks, and outdoor feasting. It's the one time of year you can walk to Giudecca—across a temporary pontoon bridge connecting Redentore with the Zattere. ✉ *Fondamenta San Giacomo* ☎ *041/5231415, 041/2750462 Chorus Foundation* ✆ *€3, Chorus Pass €10* ⊙ *Mon.–Sat. 10–5, closed Sun.* Ⓜ *Vaporetto: Redentore.*

WORTH NOTING
Giudecca. The island's name is something of a mystery. It may come from a possible 14th-century Jewish settlement, or because 9th-century nobles condemned to *giudicato* (exile) were sent here. It became a

pleasure garden for wealthy Venetians during the Republic's long and luxurious decline, but today it's populated by a combination of working class Venetians and generally expatriate gentrifiers. The Giudecca provides spectacular views of Venice. Thanks to several bridges, you can walk the entire length of its promenade, relaxing at one of several restaurants or just taking in the atmosphere. Accommodations run the gamut from youth hostels to the city's most exclusive hotels: the Cipriani (no longer associated with the Cipriani family), the Bauer Palladio, and the Hilton Molino Stucky, whose rooftop bar offers perhaps the most spectacular (and free) view of Venice. ⊠ *Fondamenta San Giacomo, Giudecca* Ⓜ *Vaporetto: Redentore, Palanca.*

ISLANDS OF THE LAGOON

The perfect vacation from your Venetian vacation is an escape to Murano, Burano, and sleepy Torcello, the islands of the northern lagoon. Torcello is legendary for its beauty and offers ancient mosaics, greenery, breathing space, and picnic opportunities (remember to pack lunch). Burano is an island of fishing traditions and houses painted in a riot of colors—blue, yellow, pink, ocher, and dark red. Visitors still love to shop here for "Venetian" lace, even though the vast majority of it is machine-made in Asia; visit the island's Museo del Merletto (Lace Museum) to discover the undeniable difference between the two.

Murano is renowned for its glass, plenty of which you can find in Venice itself. It's also notorious for high-pressure sales on factory tours, even those organized by top hotels. Vaporetto connections to Murano aren't difficult, and for the price of a boat ticket (included in any vaporetto pass), you'll buy your freedom and more time to explore. The Murano "guides" herding new arrivals follow a rotation so that factories take turns giving tours, but you can avoid the hustle by just walking away. ■TIP➜ Don't take a "free" taxi to Murano: it only means that should you choose to buy (and you'll be strongly encouraged), your taxi fare and commission will be included in the price you pay.

TIMING

Hitting all the sights on all the islands takes a busy, full day. If you limit yourself to Murano and San Michele, you can easily explore for an ample half day; the same goes for Burano and Torcello. In summer the express vaporetto Line 7 will take you to Murano from San Zaccaria (the Jolanda landing) in 25 minutes; Line 3 will take you from Piazzale Roma to Murano via the Canale di Cannaregio in 21 minutes; otherwise, local Line 4.1 makes a 45-minute trip from San Zaccaria every 20 minutes, circling the east end of Venice, stopping at Fondamenta Nove and San Michele island cemetery on the way. To see glassblowing, get off at Colonna; the Museo stop will put you near the Museo del Vetro.

Line 12 goes from Fondamente Nove direct to Murano and Burano every 30 minutes (Torcello is a 5-minute ferry ride—Line 9—from there); the full trip takes 45 minutes each way. To get to Burano and Torcello from Murano, pick up Line 12 at the Faro stop (Murano's lighthouse).

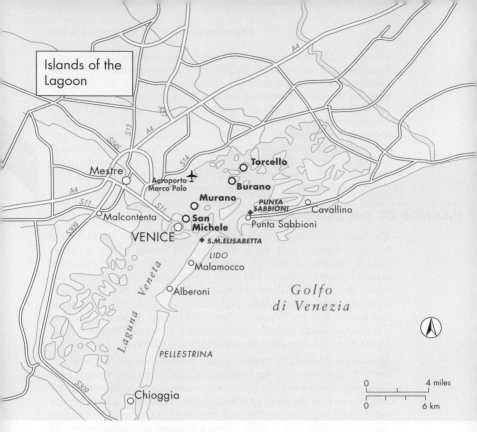

TOP ATTRACTIONS

Fodor's Choice
★

Burano. Cheerfully painted houses line the canals of this quiet village where lace making rescued a faltering fishing-based economy centuries ago. As you walk the 100 yards from the dock to Piazza Galuppi, the main square, you pass stall after stall of lace vendors. These good-natured ladies won't press you with a hard sell, but don't expect precise product information or great bargains—authentic, handmade Burano lace costs $1,000 to $2,000 for a 10-inch doily.

Museo del Merletto. The "Lace Museum" lets you marvel at the intricacies of Burano's lace making. The museum will likely continue to host a "sewing circle" of sorts, where on most weekdays you can watch local women carrying on the lace-making tradition. They may have authentic pieces for sale privately. ⊠ *Piazza Galuppi 187* ☎ *041/730034* 🎫 *€5, free with MUVE pass* ⏱ *Apr.–Oct., daily 10–6; Nov.–Mar., daily 10–5* Ⓜ *Vaporetto: Burano.*

Fodor's Choice
★

Murano. As in Venice, bridges here link a number of small islands, which are dotted with houses that once were workmen's cottages. In the 13th century the Republic, concerned about fire hazard and anxious to maintain control of its artisans' expertise, moved its glassworks to Murano, and today you can visit the factories and watch glass being made. Many of them line the Fondamenta dei Vetrai, the canalside walkway leading from the Colonna vaporetto landing. ■ **TIP→ To avoid being pressured to buy glass, take the regular vaporetto from Piazzale Roma or the Fondamente Nuove to Murano instead of succumbing to the hawkers offering you a "free" trip to Murano. They will take you to inferior glassmakers and will abandon you if you don't buy. If you do buy, rest assured that your taxi driver's commission will be added into the price you pay.** Ⓜ *Murano Colonna.*

Chiesa di San Pietro Martire. Before you reach Murano's Grand Canal (a little more than 800 feet from the landing), you'll pass Chiesa di San Pietro Martire. Reconstructed in 1511, it houses Giovanni Bellini's very beautiful and spectacular Madonna and Child with Dodge Augostino Barbarigo and Veronese's St. Jerome. ⊠ *Fondamenta dei Vetrai* ☎ *041/739704* ☾ *Weekdays 9–12 and 3–6, Sun. 3–6* Ⓜ *Vaporetto: Colonna, Faro.*

Museo del Vetro (*Glass Museum*). Although the collection at the Museo del Vetro leaves out some important periods, glassmakers, and styles, it is still the best way to get an overview of Venetian glassmaking through the ages. You can see an exhibition on the history of glass, along with a chance to review authentic Venetian styles, patterns, and works by some famous glassmakers. Don't miss the famous Barovier wedding cup (1470–80). ⊠ *Fondamenta Giustinian 8* ☎ *041/739586* ⊕ *www.museicivicivenezani.it* ▤ *€8, free with MUVE pass; admission with guided tour €13* ☾ *Apr.–Oct., daily 10–6; Nov.–Mar., daily. 10–5. Last entry 1 hr before closing. Guided tours available in English daily at 2:30* Ⓜ *Vaporetto: Museo.*

Basilica dei Santi Maria e Donato. The Basilica dei Santi Maria e Donato, just past the glass museum, is among the first churches founded by the lagoon's original inhabitants. The elaborate mosaic pavement includes the date 1140; its ship's-keel roof and Veneto-Byzantine columns add to the semblance of an ancient temple. ⊠ *Fondamenta Giustinian* ☎ *041/739056* ☾ *Mon.–Sat. 8–6, Sun. 2–6* Ⓜ *Vaporetto: Museo.*

Fodor'sChoice
★

Torcello. Some people call this tiny island the most magical place in Venice. Nearly deserted today (except for the very posh Locanda Cipriani (who loved this restaurant and inn for its solitude), the island still casts a spell, perhaps because, in the 10th century, this *was* Venice. In their flight from barbarians 1,500 years ago, the first Venetians landed here, prospering even after many left to found the city of Venice. By the 10th century, Torcello had a population of 10,000 and was more powerful than Venice. From the 12th century on, the lagoon around the island began silting up, and a malarial swamp developed. As malaria took its toll, Torcello was gradually abandoned and its palaces and houses were dismantled, their stones used for building materials in Venice. All that's left now is the hauntingly beautiful cathedral (1008), containing exquisite, although poorly restored, Byzantine mosaics. *The Virgin and the Apostles* in the apse, as well as the spectacular *Last Judgement*, date from the 12th century, predating most of the mosaics in the Basilica di San Marco. There's also the graceful 11th- and 12th-century church of Santa Fosca. And, of course, the Locanda Cipriani. ▤ *€5 for the cathedral* ☾ *Apr.–Oct. 10:30–5:30; Nov.–Mar. 10–5* Ⓜ *Torcello.*

Santa Maria Assunta. The hallowed centerpiece of Torcello, Santa Maria Assunta was built in the 11th century, and the island's wealth at the time is evident in the church's high-quality mosaics. The mosaics show the gradually increasing cultural independence of Venice from Byzantium. The magnificent late-12th-century mosaic of the Last Judgment shows the transition from the stiffer Byzantine style on the left to the more-fluid Venetian style on the right. The virgin in the main apse dates possibly from about 1185, and is of a distinctly Byzantine type, with her right hand pointing to the Christ child held with her left arm. The 12 apostles below her are possibly the oldest mosaics in the church and date from the early 12th century. The adjacent Santa Fosca church, built when the body of the saint arrived in 1011, is still used for religious services. The bell tower is undergoing renovation (completion date is unknown at this writing). It is not accessible to visitors. ⊠ *Torcello, Isola di Torcello* ☎ *041/730119* ✉ *Santa Maria Assunta €5, audio guide €1* ⊙ *Basilica: Mar.–Oct., daily 10:30–6; Nov.–Feb., daily 10–5. Campanile: currently closed for restorations.* Ⓜ *Vaporetto: Torcello.*

WORTH NOTING

San Michele. Tiny, cypress-lined San Michele is home to the gracefully elegant church of **San Michele in Isola** (1469)—and to some of Venice's most illustrious deceased. The church was designed by Mauro Codussi and is the first example of renaissance architecture in Venice; its dedication to Saint Michael is singularly appropriate, since traditionally, he holds the scales of the Last Judgement. The graves include those of poet Ezra Pound (1885–1972), impresario and art critic Sergey Diaghilev (1872–1929), and composer Igor Stravinsky (1882–1971). ⊠ *Isola di San Michele* ☎ *041/7292811* ⊙ *Church daily 7:30–12:15 and 3–4; island daily 7:30–4, 7:30–6 in summer* Ⓜ *Vaporetto: Cimitero.*

WHERE TO EAT

Dining options in Venice range from the ultrahigh end, where jackets are required and shorts are a no-go, to the very casual. Once staunchly traditional, many restaurants have revamped their menus along with their dining rooms, creating dishes that blend classic Venetian elements with ingredients and methods less common to the lagoon environs.

Mid- and upper-range restaurants are often more willing to make the break, offering innovative options while keeping dishes like sarde in saor and fegato alla veneziana available as mainstays. Restaurants are often quite small with limited seating, so make sure to reserve ahead. It's not uncommon for restaurants to have two sittings per night, one at 7 and one at 9. A traditional Italian meal includes several courses and should be a leisurely affair; so if you don't want to be rushed, opt for the later sitting.

There's no getting around the fact that Venice has more than its share of overpriced, mediocre eateries that prey on tourists. Avoid places with cajoling waiters standing outside, and beware of restaurants that don't display their prices. At the other end of the spectrum, showy *menu turistico* (tourist menu) boards make offerings clear in a dozen languages, but for the same €15–€20 you'd spend at such places, you could do better at a bacaro making a meal of cicheti (savory snacks).

Note: *The average meal listed in each restaurant review is for a three-course meal, comprising a primo (appetizer), a secondo (fish or meat), and a dolce (dessert).*

Use the coordinate (✚ B2) at the end of each listing to locate a site on the Where to Eat and Stay in Venice map.

3

SAN MARCO

$ ✕ **Caffè Florian.** Because of the prices and the tourist mobs, Venetians tend to avoid caffè in the Piazza San Marco. But when they want to indulge and regain control of their city, they go to Florian. Founded in 1720, it's not only the city's oldest caffè, but with its glittering neo-baroque decor and attractive 19th-century wall panels (depicting Venetian heroes), it's undisputedly the most beautiful. Florian is steeped in local history: favored by Venetians during the long Austrian occupation, it was the only caffè to serve women during the 18th century (hence why it secured Casanova's patronage), and it was the caffè of choice for artistic notables such as Wagner, Göthe, Goldoni, Lord Byron, Marcel Proust, and Charles Dickens. It was also the birthplace of the international art exhibition, which later blossomed into the Venice Biennale. The coffee, drinks, and snacks are quite good, but you really come here for the atmosphere and to be part of Venetian history. As with other cafés in the Piazza, there's a surcharge for music. Savvy Venetians know the prices are much lower if you have your drinks at the comfortable bar in the back. $ *Average meal: €30* ✉ *Piazza San Marco* ☎ *041/5205641* ☽ *Daily 9:30 am–11:00 pm* ✚ *E4.*

CAFÉ
Fodor'sChoice
★

$ ✕ **Enoteca al Volto.** A short walk from the Rialto Bridge, this bar has been around since 1936; the fine cicheti and primi have a lot to do with its staying power. Two small, dark rooms with a ceiling plastered with wine labels provide a classic backdrop for simple fare. The place prides itself on its considerable wine list of both Italian and foreign vintages. If you stick to a panino or some cicheti at the bar, you'll eat well for relatively little. If you take a table and opt for one of the day's exceptional primi (like the delicious risotto options), the price category goes up a notch; however, this is still one of the best restaurant bargains in Venice. There are, of course, traditional secondi, such as a very good seppie in nero. The house wine, as is to be expected in an enoteca, is quite drinkable. $ *Average meal: €30* ✉ *Calle Cavalli, San Marco 4081, San Marco* ☎ *041/5228945* ⊕ *www.alvoltoenoteca.it* ▭ *No credit cards* ☽ *Closed Thurs.* Ⓜ *Vaporetto: Rialto* ✚ *E3.*

VENETIAN

$$$$ ✕ **Harry's Bar.** For those who can afford it, and despite its recently having become the watering place of Russian oligarchs and their female spike-heeled retinues, lunch or dinner at Harry's Bar is as indispensable to a visit to Venice as a walk across the Piazza San Marco or a vaporetto ride down the Grand Canal. Harry's is not just a fine restaurant; it's a cultural institution. When founder Giuseppe Cipriani opened the doors in 1931, the place became a favorite of almost every famous name

VENETIAN
Fodor'sChoice
★

BEST BETS FOR VENICE DINING

Fodor's Choice★	By Price	$$$
Alle Testiere, $$$, p. 237	**$**	Alle Testiere, p. 237
Al Paradiso, $$$, p. 230	Al Prosecco, p. 234	Al Paradiso, p. 230
Antiche Carampane, $$$, p. 231	Botteghe di Promessi Sposi, p. 235	Antiche Carampane, p. 231
Bentigodi, $$, p. 235	Caffè Florian, p. 227	**$$$$**
Caffè Florian, $, p. 227	Cantina Do Mori, p. 231	
Harry's Bar, $$$$, p. 227	Cantinone già Schiavi, p. 229	Harry's Bar, p. 227
Il Ridotto, $$$$, p. 238	Casin dei Nobili, p. 229	Il Ridotto, p. 238
La Zucca, $, p. 234	Enoteca Do Colonne, p. 236	Osteria Da Fiore, p. 231
Osteria alla Bifora, $, p. 230	La Zucca, p. 234	**Best by**
Osteria Da Fiore, $$$$, p. 231	Osteria alla Bifora, p. 230	**Experience**
Ristorante Quadri, $$$$, p. 228	**$$**	ROMANTIC
	Anice Stellato, p. 235	Al Paradiso, $$$, p. 230
	Bentigodi, p. 235	Anice Stellato, $$, p. 235
	La Bitta, p. 230	Osteria Da Fiore, $$$$, p. 231
	Vini da Gigio, p. 236	

to visit Venice (including Charlie Chaplin, Orson Welles, and Ernest Hemingway) and still attracts much of Venetian high society as regulars. Try the delicate baked sea bass with artichokes, and don't miss the Harry's signature crêpes flambées or his famous Cipriani chocolate cake for dessert. Since a meal at Harry's is just as much about being seen, book one of the cramped tables on the ground floor—the upper floor of the restaurant, despite its spectacular view, is the Venetian equivalent of "Siberia." And be sure to order a Bellini cocktail—a refreshing mix of white peach purée and sparking prosecco—this is its birthplace, after all. On the other hand, true to its "retro" atmosphere, Harry's makes one of the best martini cocktails in town. $ *Average meal: €100* ✉ *Calle Vallaresso, San Marco 1323, Piazza San Marco* ☎ *041/5285777* 🌐 *www.harrysbarvenezia.com* ⚜ *Reservations essential* Ⓜ *Vaporetto: San Marco (Calle Vallaresso)* ✛ *E4.*

$$$$
VENETIAN
Fodor's Choice
★
✗ **Ristorante Quadri.** Located above the famed café of the same name sits one of the most legendary restaurants in Italy: Quadri, a name steeped in history (as a café, it was the first to introduce Turkish Coffee to an already over-caffinated city in the 1700s), beauty—the period dark-wood furnishings, lush burgundy damask walls, and sparkling chandeliers epitomize Venetian *ambiente* like few other places—and mise-en-scène, thanks to its extraordinary perch on, and over, the Piazza San Marco. The Alajmo family (of the celebrated Le Calandre

restaurant near Padua) has recently taken over the restaurant and put their accomplished sous-chef from Padua in charge of the kitchen. The menu, while still bearing the creative mark of the Alajmos, offers more traditional dishes than in previous years. For tasting menus that range from €180 to €220 (exclusive of wine), you can savor such delights of creative cuisine as dill-flavored tagliolini with spider crab in a sauce of sea urchins and Venetian clams, but you can also be more conservative and enjoy burrata ravioli with a seafood-tomato sauce spiked with oregano. Downstairs, the simpler abcQuadri (located next to the café)—decorated with neo-Rococo wall paintings—serves more traditional Venetian fare; however, a three-course dinner will still set you back €100, without the added pleasure of wine. As for Quadri itself: the prices, cuisine, and decor are all *alta,* so beware: some food critics find the chef in charge not up to these high prices. [$] *Average meal: €125* ✉ *Piazza San Marco 121* ☎ *041/5222105* 🌐 *www.caffequadri.it* ✍ *Reservations essential* ⏲ *Closed Mon.* ✥ *E4*

3

DORSODURO

$ VENETIAN

🍴 **Cantinone già Schiavi.** This beautiful 19th-century bacaro opposite the *squero* (gondola repair shop) of San Trovaso has original furnishings and one of the best wine cellars in town—the walls are covered floor to ceiling by bottles for purchase. Cicheti here are some of the most inventive in Venice—try the crostini-style layers of bread, smoked swordfish, and slivers of raw zucchini, or pungent slices of parmigiano-reggiano, fig, and toast. They also have a creamy version of baccalà mantecato spiced with herbs, and there are nearly a dozen open bottles of wine for experimenting at the bar. [$] *Average meal: €7* ✉ *Fondamenta Nani, Dorsoduro 992* ☎ *041/5230034* ▭ *No credit cards* ⏲ *Closed most Sun. after 2 pm and 2 wks in Aug.* [M] *Vaporetto: Zattere, Accademia* ✥ *C5.*

$ PIZZA FAMILY

🍴 **Casin dei Nobili.** When a Venetian living on the Dorsoduro side of the Grand Canal says, "*Mangiamo una pizza insieme*" ("Let's go out for pizza"), there's a good chance what he or she means is, "Lets go to the Casin dei Nobili"—a modestly priced, pleasant pizzeria just off the popular Campo San Barnaba. Pizza is not a Venetian specialty, and matters are made worse by the citywide prohibition of open, wood-fire ovens—the only way to bake a pizza, according to the Neapolitans, who invented the dish. But you can enjoy a pretty good facsimile of a Neapolitan pizza here, along with very good pasta and (moderately priced) fish dishes. The relaxed, informal atmosphere makes this a good bet for families. This is a very popular place, both among Venetians and visitors, so reservations are strongly recommended. [$] *Average meal: €25* ✉ *Off of Campo San Barnaba, Dorsoduro 2756* ☎ *041/2411841* ✍ *Reservations essential* ⏲ *Closed Mon.* ✥ *B4*

$ VENETIAN Fodor's Choice ★

🍴 **Impronta Cafe.** This sleek café is a favorite lunchtime haunt for professors from the nearby university and local businesspeople. Unlike in more traditional places, it's quite acceptable to order only pasta or a secondo, without an antipasto or dessert. Although the restaurant is also open for dinner—and you can dine well and economically in the evening—the real bargain is lunch, where you can easily have a beautifully prepared primo or secondo, plus a glass of wine, for around €12–€18. There's also a good selection of sandwiches and salads. The attentive staff speaks English, although you may be the only non-Venetian in the place. Unlike most local eateries, this spot is open from breakfast through late dinner. $ *Average meal: €20* ⊠ *Dorsoduro 3815–3817* ☎ *041/2750386* ⊕ *www.improntacafevenice.com* ⊘ *Closed Sun.* ✛ *B3.*

$$
NORTHERN
ITALIAN
✕ **La Bitta.** The decor is more discreet, the dining hours longer, and the service friendlier and more efficient here than in many small restaurants in Venice—and the non-fish menu (inspired by the cuisine of the Venetian terra firma) is a temptation at every course. Market availability keeps the menu changing almost every day, although typically you can start with a savory barley soup or gnocchi with winter squash and aged ricotta cheese. Then choose a secondo such as lamb chops with thyme, *anatra in pevarada* (duck in a pepper sauce), or guinea hen in cream. The homemade desserts are all luscious, and it's been said that La Bitta serves the best *panna cotta* (flavored custard) in town. Trust owner Deborah Civiero's selection from her excellent wine and grappa lists. $ *Average meal: €40* ⊠ *Calle Lunga San Barnaba, Dorsoduro 2753/A* ☎ *041/5230531* ⚒ *Reservations essential* ▭ *No credit cards* ⊘ *Dinner only. Closed Sun. and July.* Ⓜ *Vaporetto: Ca' Rezzonico* ✛ *B5.*

$
VENETIAN
Fodor's Choice
★
✕ **Osteria alla Bifora.** A beautiful and atmospheric bacaro, alla Bifora has such ample and satisfying food selections that most Venetians consider it a full-fledged restaurant. Most of the offerings consist of overflowing trays of cold sliced meats and cheeses, various preparations of baccalà, or Venetian classics such as *polpetti* (meatballs), sarde in saor, or marinated anchovies. La Bifora also serves up a couple of excellent hot dishes, too; the *seppie in nero* (squid in its ink) is among the best in the city. Owner and barman Franco Bernardi and his sister Mirella are warm and friendly—after a few visits, you'll be greeted like a member of the family. Always open for dinner, you may find this place open for lunch … if you're lucky. $ *Average meal: €25* ⊠ *Campo Santa Margherita, Dorsoduro 2930* ☎ *041/5236119* ⚒ *Reservations essential* ▭ *No credit cards* ✛ *B4.*

SAN POLO

$$$
MODERN ITALIAN
Fodor's Choice
★
✕ **Al Paradiso.** In a small dining room made warm and cozy by its pleasing and unpretentious decor, proprietor Giordano makes all diners feel like honored guests. Pappardelle "al Paradiso" takes pasta with seafood sauce to new heights, while risotto with shrimp, champagne, and grapefruit puts a delectable twist on a traditional dish. The inspired and original array of entrées includes meat and fish selections such as a salmon with honey and balsamic vinegar in a stunning presentation. Unlike many elegant restaurants, Al Paradiso serves generous portions and many of the delicious antipasti and primi are quite satisfying; you may want to follow the traditional Italian way of ordering and wait until you've finished your antipasto or your primo before you order your secondo. $ *Average meal: €60* ⊠ *Calle del Paradiso, San Polo 767* ☎ *041/5234910* ⚒ *Reservations essential* ⊘ *Closed Mon. and 3 wks in Jan. and Feb.* Ⓜ *Vaporetto: San Silvestro* ✛ *D3.*

$$$
VENETIAN
Fodor's Choice
★
✕**Antiche Carampane.** Judging from its rather modest and unremarkable appearance, you wouldn't guess that Piera Bortoluzzi Librai's trattoria is among the finest fish restaurants in the city both because of the quality of the ingredients and because of the chef's creative magic. Like other upscale seafood restaurants in Venice, this trattoria offers

3

a selection of modern dishes such as turbot in citrus sauce. However, Antiche Carampane's kitchen goes a step further: it explores the more complex and interesting, but lesser known, dishes from the traditional Venetian repertoire. Embark on a culinary journey with St. Peter's fish with radicchio di Treviso; mullet in red wine; or an unusual spaghetti with spicy shellfish sauce from the town of Chioggia, the major fishing port on the Venetian lagoon. If you prefer simpler fare, the perfectly grilled fish is always sea caught and fresh, and in spring, try the local, fried soft-shell crabs. $ *Average meal: €60* ✉ *Rio Terà della Carampane, San Polo 1911* ☎ *041/5240165* ⊕ *www.antichecarampane.com* ⟳ *Reservations essential* ⊗ *Closed Sun. and Mon., 10 days in Jan., and 3 wks in July and Aug.* Ⓜ *Vaporetto: San Silvestro* ✛ *D3.*

$
WINE BAR
✕**Cantina Do Mori.** This bacaro par excellence—cramped but warm and cozy under hanging antique copper pots—has been catering to the workers of the Rialto Market for generations. In addition to young, local whites and reds, the well-stocked cellar offers about 600 more-refined labels, many available by the glass. Between sips you can munch on crunchy *grissini* (breadsticks) draped with prosciutto or a few well-stuffed, tiny tramezzini, appropriately called *francobolli* (postage stamps). Don't leave without tasting the delicious baccalà mantecato. You can make a light lunch out of the cicheti here, but you'll have to do it standing at the bar; there are no tables. $ *Average meal: €10* ✉ *Calle dei Do Mori, San Polo 429* ☎ *041/5225401* ▭ *No credit cards* ⊗ *Closed Sun., 3 wks in Aug., and 1 wk in Jan.* Ⓜ *Vaporetto: Rialto Mercato* ✛ *D3.*

$$$$
VENETIAN
Fodor's Choice
★
✕**Osteria Da Fiore.** The understated atmosphere, simple decor, and quiet elegance featured alongside Da Fiore's modern take on traditional Venetian cuisine certainly merit its international reputation. With such beautifully prepared cuisine, you would expect the kitchen to be manned by a chef with a household name; however the kitchen is headed by none other than owner Maurizio Montin's wife, Mara, who learned to cook from her grandmother. The other surprise is that while this restaurant is in an upper price category, it is hardly among the priciest in Venice. It offers several moderately priced (€50), three-course, prixfixe luncheon menus, and the prix-fixe dinner menu is €80, which brings it very much into line with most of the more elegant choices in town. The menu is constantly changing, but generally *fritto misto* (deep-fried seafood) or Da Fiore's tender, aromatic version of *seppie in nero*, cuttlefish in black sauce, is almost always available. Reservations, perhaps made a few days in advance in high season, are essential for

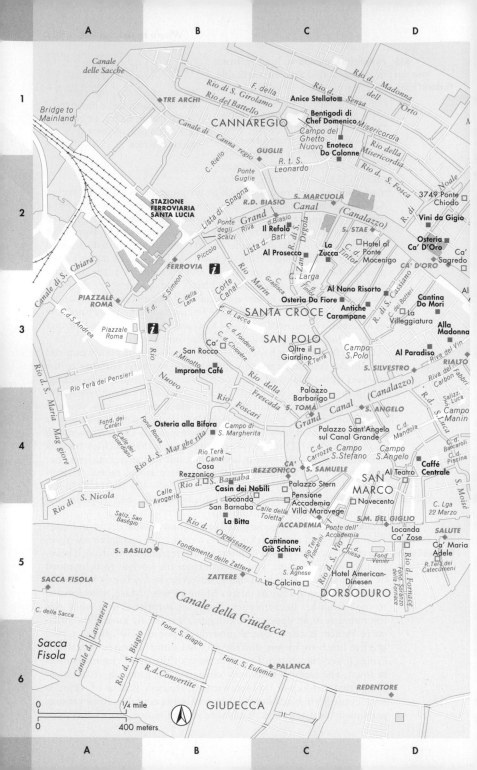

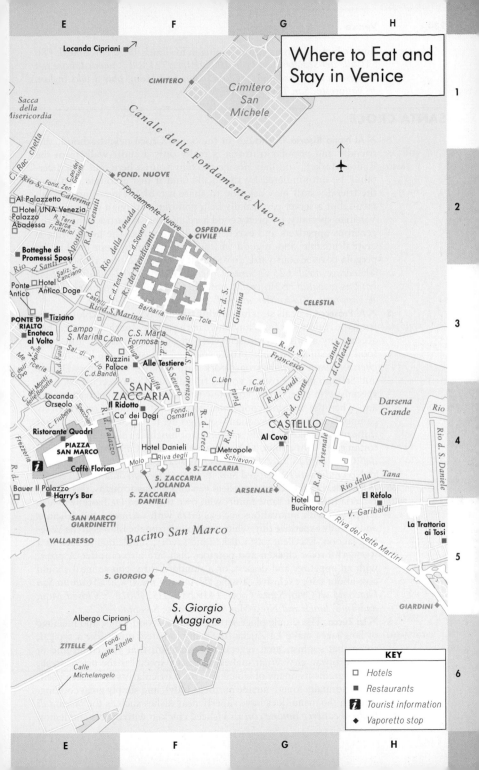

Where to Eat and Stay in Venice

dinner, but you can try just dropping in for lunch. $\boxed{S}$ *Average meal: €80* ✉ *Calle del Scaleter, San Polo 2002* ☎ *041/721308* ⊕ *www.dafiore.net* 🍴 *Reservations essential* 🕐 *Closed Sun. and Mon., plus 3 wks in Jan.* Ⓜ *Vaporetto: San Tomà* ✛ *C3.*

SANTA CROCE

$
VENETIAN
FAMILY

✕ **Al Nono Risorto.** Although in the Santa Croce neighborhood, this friendly and popular trattoria is really only a short walk from the Rialto Market. You may not be the only tourist here, but you'll certainly be outnumbered by the locals (and if just a couple or a trio, the friendly staff may ask you to share a table). There's no English menu, but a server can usually help you out. Although pizza is not a Venetian specialty, it's pretty good here, but the star attractions are the generous appetizers and excellent shellfish pastas. The house wine is quite drinkable, and in good weather, you can enjoy your meal in the pergola-covered courtyard (do reserve if you want to snag a table there). $\boxed{S}$ *Average meal: €25* ✉ *Santa Croce 2337* ☎ *041/5241169* 🍴 *Reservations essential* ☐ *No credit cards* 🕐 *Closed Wed. No lunch Thurs.* Ⓜ *Vaporetto: Rialto Mercato* ✛ *D3.*

$
WINE BAR

✕ **Al Prosecco.** Locals stream into this friendly bacaro to explore wines from the region—or from anywhere in the county for that matter. They accompany a carefully chosen selection of meats, cheeses, and other food from small, artisanal producers, used in tasty panini like the *porchetta romane verdure* (roast pork with greens). Proprietors Davide and Stefano preside over a young, friendly staff who reel off the day's specials with ease. There are a few tables in the intimate back room, and when the weather cooperates you can sit outdoors on the lively campo, watching the Venetian world go by. It's open 9 to 9, and later if the mood strikes. Mostly a favorite for lunch, it's also a special place for an early light dinner. $\boxed{S}$ *Average meal: €20* ✉ *Campo San Giacomo dell'Orio, Santa Croce 1503* ☎ *041/5240222* ⊕ *www.alprosecco.com* ☐ *No credit cards* 🕐 *Closed Sun.* Ⓜ *Vaporetto: San Stae* ✛ *C2.*

$$
PIZZA

✕ **Il Refolo.** Besides serving excellent versions of classic pizzas, this elegant pizzeria (run by the same family who own the noted Da Fiore) will also tempt you with innovations such as pizza with *castraore,* the delicious and sinfully expensive tiny, white artichokes from the islands in the Venetian lagoon. Excellent pasta dishes and savory, simple mains, such as a wonderful roast chicken and potatoes dish, are also on offer. A pizza, with an appetizer and dessert, or a standard three-course meal should cost about €30, exclusive of wine. $\boxed{S}$ *Average meal: €30* ✉ *Campo San Giacomo all'Orio, Santa Croce 1459* ☎ *041/5240016* 🕐 *Closed Mon. and Tues. lunch and Nov.–Mar.* Ⓜ *Vaporetto: San Stae* ✛ *C2.*

$
VEGETARIAN

✕ **La Zucca.** The simple place settings, lattice-wood walls, and mélange of languages make La Zucca (the pumpkin) feel much like a typical, somewhat sophisticated vegetarian restaurant that you could find in any European city. What makes La Zucca special is the use of fresh, local ingredients (many of which, like the particularly sweet zucca itself, aren't normally found outside northern Italy), and simply great cooking. Though the menu does have superb meat dishes such as the *piccata di pollo ai caperi e limone con riso* (sliced chicken with capers and lemon served with rice), more attention is paid to dishes from the garden: try the radicchio *di Treviso con funghi e scaglie di Montasio* (with mushrooms and shavings of Montasio cheese), the *finocchi piccanti con olive* (fennel in a spicy tomato-olive sauce), or the house's signature dish—the *flan di zucca,* a luscious, naturally sweet, pumpkin pudding topped with slivered, aged ricotta cheese. [$] *Average meal: €30 ✉ Calle del Tintor at Ponte de Megio, Santa Croce 1762 ☎ 041/5241570 🌐 www.lazucca.it ✍ Reservations essential ⏲ Closed Sun. and 1 wk in Dec. [M] Vaporetto: San Stae ✣ C2.*

CANNAREGIO

$$ VENETIAN

🍴 **Anice Stellato.** Off the main concourse, on one of the most romantic fondamente of Cannaregio, this family-run bacaro-trattoria is the place to stop for fairly priced, satisfying fare, though service can feel indifferent and occasionally, but not often, the kitchen is a bit inconsistent. The space has plenty of character: narrow columns rise from the colorful tile floor, dividing the room into cozy sections. There are also a few outdoor canal side tables. Venetian classics like seppie in nero are enriched with such offerings as *sarde in beccafico* (sardines rolled and stuffed with breadcrumbs, herbs and cheese) and tagliatelle with king prawns and zucchini flowers. They also serve several meat dishes, including a tender beef fillet stewed in Barolo wine with potatoes and lamb from the nearby Veneto hills. [$] *Average meal: €35 ✉ Fondamenta de la Sensa, Cannaregio 3272 ☎ 041/720744 ⏲ Closed Mon. and Tues., 1 wk in Feb., and 3 wks in Aug. [M] Vaporetto: San Alvise or San Marcuola ✣ C1.*

$$ VENETIAN Fodor's Choice ★

🍴 **Bentigodi.** Many Venetians claim that owner Domenico Iacuzio is one of the best chefs in town, even though he hails from Italy's deep south. In 2012 he moved his entire operation from La Colombina to this location just a three-minute walk away. The traditional Venetian food here comes with slight southern accents: a natural combination, as it turns out, since both cuisines share ties with the eastern Mediterranean (due to their inclusion in the Byzantine Empire). For starters, his sarde in saor perfectly balances sweet and savory, and his diced raw tuna *cipolata* is enlivened by sautéed onions and oranges. His seafood risottos are always made to order and his preparations of freshly caught—never farmed—fish are magical. For the Venetian traditionalist, Domenico prepares a first-class fritto misto dish. If you've missed his southern accent up to now, you'll find it at dessert with homemade southern specialties such as cannoli or *cassata* (candied Sicilian cake). Portions are ample, the atmosphere is informal, and the service is helpful. [$] *Average meal: €40 ✉ Cannargio 1423 ☎ 041/8223714 🌐 www.bentigodi.com [M] Vaporetto: San Marcuola or Guglie ✣ C1.*

$ VENETIAN Fodor's Choice ★

🍴 **Botteghe di Promessi Sposi.** The former Promessi Sposi eatery was rejuvenated when three *fioi* (guys) with considerable restaurant experience joined forces. Claudio mans the kitchen, while Nicola and Cristiano will serve you either an *ombra* (small glass of wine) and cicheto at the *banco* (counter), or a delightful meal in the dining room or the intimate courtyard. A season-centered menu includes local standards like calves' liver or grilled *canestrelli* (tiny Venetian scallops), along with creative variations on classic Venetian fare, like homemade ravioli stuffed with *radicchio di Treviso* (red chicory leaves) or *orechiette* (little ears—small cup-shaped pasta) with a scrumptious sauce of minced duck. The service is efficient, friendly, and helpful. This is a very popular place among Venetians, so if you don't want to have to battle crowds, be sure to make a reservation. $\boxed{\$}$ *Average meal: €30* ⊠ *Calle de l'Oca (just off Campo Santi Apostoli), Cannaregio 4367* 🕾 *041/2412747* ⚐ *Reservations essential* ⊟ *No credit cards* ⊘ *Closed Mon. No lunch Wed.* Ⓜ *Vaporetto: Ca' d'Oro* ✛ *E2.*

$ ✕ **Enoteca Do Colonne.** Venetians from this working-class neighborhood
VENETIAN frequent this friendly bacaro, not just for a glass of very drinkable wine, but also because of its excellent selection of traditional Venetian cicheti for lunch. There's not only a large selection of sandwiches and panini, but also luscious tidbits like grilled vegetables, breaded and fried sardines and shrimp, and a superb version of baccalà mantecato. For the more adventurous, there are Venetian working-class specialties such as *musetto* (a sausage made from pigs' snouts served warm with polenta) and *nervetti* (veal tendons with lemon and parsley). These dishes are worth trying at least once when in Venice, and Do Colonne offers the best musetto in town. $\boxed{\$}$ *Average meal: €12* ⊠ *Cannaregio 1814* 🕾 *041/5240453* ⊟ *No credit cards* Ⓜ *Vaporetto: San Marcuola* ✛ *C2.*

$ ✕ **Osteria Ca' D'Oro (Alla Vedova).** This traditional (and tiny) bacaro
VENETIAN doubles as an excellent mid-range restaurant—and a great bargain to boot—serving superb versions of local specialties. La Vedova is justly famous for its meatballs, which you can have either at the counter with a glass of wine, or at a table, as a starter. Follow them up with a delicious helping of *bigoli con salsa* (thick spaghetti with anchovies, onions, and a dash of cinnamon), and then a well-made fritto misto or seppie in nero. Nothing fancy nor inventive; just good food like your Venetian mamma used to make. ■ **TIP→ Forget the deserts—they were never part of a traditional Venetian meal anyway—and satisfy your sweet tooth with ice cream at Gelateria GROM, on the nearby Strada Nuova.** $\boxed{\$}$ *Average meal: €25* ⊠ *Cannaregio 3912* 🕾 *041/5285324* ⚐ *Reservations essential* ⊟ *No credit cards* ⊘ *Closed Thurs. and late July–late Aug.* Ⓜ *Vaporetto: Ca' d'Oro* ✛ *D2.*

$ ✕ **Tiziano.** A fine variety of excellent tramezzini lines the display cases
ITALIAN at this *tavola calda* (roughly the Italian equivalent of a cafeteria) on the main thoroughfare from the Rialto to Santi Apostoli; inexpensive salad plates and daily pasta specials, are also served. This is a great place for a light meal or snack before a performance at the nearby Teatro Malebran. Whether you choose to sit or stand, it's a handy—and popular—spot for a quick meal or a snack at very modest prices. Service is efficient, if somewhat grumpy. $\boxed{\$}$ *Average meal: €12* ⊠ *Salizzada San Giovanni Crisostomo, Cannaregio 5747* 🕾 *041/5235544* ⊟ *No credit cards* Ⓜ *Vaporetto: Rialto* ✛ *E3.*

$$ ✕ **Vini da Gigio.** Paolo and Laura, a brother-sister team, run this refined
VENETIAN trattoria as if they've invited you to dinner in their home, while keeping
Fodor'sChoice the service professional. Deservedly popular with Venetians and visi-
★ tors alike, it's one of the best values in the city. Indulge in pastas such as rigatoni with duck sauce and arugula-stuffed ravioli. Fish is well represented—try the sesame-encrusted tuna—but the meat dishes steal

the show. The steak with red-pepper sauce and the *tagliata di agnello* (sautéed lamb fillet with a light, crusty coating) are both superb, and you'll never enjoy a better *fegato alla veneziana* (Venetian-style liver with onions). This is a place for wine connoisseurs, as the cellar is one of the best in the city. Come at lunch or for the second sitting in the evening, to avoid being rushed. [$] *Average meal: €40* ✉ *Fondamenta San Felice, Cannaregio 3628/A* ☎ *041/5285140* 🌐 *www.vinidagigio.com* ✍ *Reservations essential* ⏲ *Closed Mon. and Tues., 2 wks in Jan., and 3 wks in Aug.* [M] *Vaporetto: Ca' d'Oro* ✥ *D2.*

CASTELLO

$$$ VENETIAN 🍴 **Al Covo.** For years, Diane and Cesare Binelli's Al Covo has set the standard of excellence for traditional, refined Venetian cuisine. The Binellis are dedicated to providing their guests with the freshest, highest quality fish from the Adriatic, and vegetables, when at all possible, from the islands of the Venetian lagoon and the fields of the adjacent Veneto region. Although their cuisine could be correctly termed "classic Venetian," it always offers surprises like the juicy crispness of their legendary fritto misto—reliant upon a secret, nonconventional ingredient in the batter—or the heady aroma of their fresh anchovies marinated in wild fennel, a herb somewhat foreign to Veneto. The main exception to Al Covo's distinct local flavor is Diane's wonderful Texas-inspired desserts, especially her dynamite chocolate cake. [$] *Average meal: €58* ✉ *Castello 3968* ☎ *041/5223812* ✍ *Reservations essential* ⏲ *Closed Wed. and Thurs.* [M] *Vaporetto: Arsenale* ✥ *G4.*

$$$ VENETIAN Fodor's Choice ★ 🍴 **Alle Testiere.** "Testiere" means "headboards," a reference to the old headboards that adorn the walls of this tiny informal restaurant, where the food (and not the decor) is undoubtedly the focus. Local foodies consider this one of the most refined in the city thanks to Chef Bruno Cavagni's gently creative take on classic Venetian fish dishes. The chef's artistry seldom draws attention to itself, but simply reveals new dimensions to familiar fare, creating dishes that stand out for their lightness and balance. A classic black risotto of cuttlefish, for example, is surrounded by a brilliant coulis of mild yellow peppers; tiny potato gnocchi are paired with tender newborn squid; and fish dishes are often accentuated with berries and fruit. The menu changes regularly to capitalize on the freshest produce of the moment, and the wine cellar is top notch. To enjoy a leisurely meal, be sure to book the second dinner sitting. [$] *Average meal: €60* ✉ *Castello 5801* ☎ *041/5227220* ✍ *Reservations essential* ⏲ *Closed Sun. and Mon., 3 wks Jan.–Feb.; 4 wks July–Aug.* ✥ *F3.*

$ WINE BAR 🍴 **El Rèfolo.** This hip hangout is named after a play by turn-of-the-20th-century emancipated lady Amalia Rosselli—look for the framed title page inside. El Rèfolo ("The Breeze," in Venetian) is a contemporary cantina in a very Venetian neighborhood, and is more for *un aperitivo* (an aperitif) and a snack than for a meal. Owner Massimiliano pairs great wines with select meat, savory cheese, and seasonal vegetable combos. In temperate weather, this niche-size *enoteca*'s exuberance effervesces out onto the city's broadest street. It's open every day but Sunday from 9:30 am to 12:30 am. [$] *Average meal: €22* ✉ *Via Garibaldi 1580* ⏲ *Closed Sun., hrs limited in winter* [M] *Vaporetto: Arsenale* ✥ *H5.*

$$$$ MODERN ITALIAN Fodor's Choice ★ 🍴 **Il Ridotto.** Longtime restaurateur Gianni Bonaccorsi has established a restaurant where he can pamper a limited number of lucky patrons with his imaginative cuisine. Ridotto, "reduced" in Italian, refers to the size of this tiny, gracious restaurant. The innovative, yet traditional menu is revised daily, with the offerings tending toward lighter, but wonderfully tasty versions of classic dishes. The €60 tasting menus—one meat, one fish—where Gianni "surprises" you with a selection of his own creations, never fail to satisfy. Choose a wine from the excellent cantina. [$] *Average meal: €80* ✉ *Campo SS Filippo e Giacomo, Castello 4509* ☎ *041/5208280* 🌐 *www.ilridotto.com* ✍ *Reservations essential* 🕓 *Closed Wed. No lunch Thurs.* [M] *Vaporetto: San Zaccaria* ✥ *F4.*

$ ITALIAN 🍴 **La Trattoria ai Tosi.** Getting off the beaten track to find good, basic local cuisine isn't easy in Venice, but La Trattoria ai Tosi (aka Ai Tosi Piccoli) fills the bill with its (not too) remote, tranquil location, homey atmosphere, and variety of fine traditional fare at prices that make it worth the walk from anywhere in the city. The baccalà mantecato "sanwicini" are excellent, as are the classic frittura mista and the traditional Venetian *bigoli in salsa* (thick, home made spaghetti with an anchovy-onion sauce). The fixed-price lunch menu, created for local workers with limited time, is another good deal, and there's even decent pizza. (Note: make sure you end up at this smaller, locally owned Tosi, rather than the Tosi Grande across the way that's no longer family owned.) [$] *Average meal: €21* ✉ *Seco Marina 738* ☎ *041/5237102* 🕓 *Closed Mon.* [M] *Vaporetto: Giardini* ✥ *H5.*

ISLANDS OF THE LAGOON

$$$$ ITALIAN 🍴 **Locanda Cipriani.** A nearly legendary restaurant and owned by a nephew of Arrigo Cipriani (the founder of Harry's Bar), this inn profits from its idyllic location on the island of Torcello. Hemingway, who loved the silence of the lagoon, came here often to eat, drink, and brood under the green veranda. The food is not exceptional, especially considering the high-end prices, but dining here is more about getting lost in Venetian magic. The menu features pastas, *vitello tonnato* (chilled poached veal in a tuna and caper sauce), baked *orata* (gilthead) with potatoes, and lots of other seafood. A vaporetto service runs until 11:30 pm, and then upon request; service is sporadic. [$] *Average meal: €75* ✉ *Piazza Santa Fosca 29, Torcello* ☎ *041/730150* ✍ *Reservations essential* 🕓 *Closed Tues. and early Jan.–early Feb.* [M] *Vaporetto: Torcello* ✥ *F1.*

WHERE TO STAY

Many of Venice's hotels are in renovated palaces, but space is at a premium—and comes at a high price—and rooms may feel cramped by American standards. The most exclusive hotels are indeed palatial, although they may well have some small, dowdy rooms (the main culprits are usually classified as "standard"), so it's best to verify ahead of time that yours isn't one of them. Smaller hotels may not have lounge areas, and because of preservation laws, some are not permitted to install elevators, so if these features are essential, ask ahead of time.

Although the city has no cars, it does have boats plying the canals and pedestrians chattering in the streets sometimes late into the night (most likely along principal thoroughfares, in San Marco and near the Rialto), so ask for a quiet room if you're concerned about noise.

Many travelers assume that a hotel near Piazza San Marco will give them the most convenient location, but keep in mind that Venice is scaled to humans (on foot) rather than automobiles; it's difficult to find a location that's *not* convenient to most of the city. Areas away from San Marco may also offer the benefit of being less overrun by day-trippers.

3

It's essential to have detailed directions to your hotel when you arrive. Arm yourself with not only a clear map and postal address (e.g., Dorsoduro 825), but the actual street name (e.g., Fondamenta San Trovaso) and the nearest campo. Also be aware that location apps on smart phones can be highly inaccurate for Venice.

You can compare Venice hotels from A to Z at **Venezia.net** (🌐 *www.venezia.net*); it furnishes links to hotels' official websites. The website of **Venezia Sì** (☎ *199/173309 in Italy, 39/0415222264 abroad* 🕒 *Mon.–Sat. 9 am–11 pm* 🌐 *www.veneziasi.it*) lists most hotels in town (with some photographs), and they offer a free reservation service over the phone. It's the public relations arm of AVA (Venetian Hoteliers Association) and has booths where you can make same-day reservations at Piazzale Roma (☎ *041/5231397* 🕒 *Daily 9 am–10 pm*), Santa Lucia train station (☎ *041/715288 or 041/715016* 🕒 *Daily 8 am–9 pm*), and Marco Polo Airport (☎ *041/5415133* 🕒 *Daily 9 am–10 pm*). Be aware that if you arrive in the afternoon without a reservation, pickings will be slim, and you may be unable to find a room at all.

Hotel reviews have been condensed for this book. Please go to Fodors.com for full reviews of each property.

Use the coordinate (✥ B2) at the end of each listing to locate a site on the Where to Eat and Stay in Venice map.

PRICES

Hotel rates are about 20% higher than in Rome and Milan but can be reduced by as much as half off-season, from November to March (excluding Christmas, New Year's, and Carnevale), and likely in August as well.

SAN MARCO

$ B&B/INN 🏨 **Al Teatro.** Behind the Fenice Theater, just off the Maria Callas Bridge, this small B&B is the renovated home of owners Fabio and Eleonora (in fact, it's where Eleanora was born) that offers three spacious, comfortable, and conscientiously appointed rooms with private baths, each overlooking a gondola-filled canal; the largest room has a broad balcony. **Pros:** airy rooms; convenient San Marco location; good for families. **Cons:** the intimacy of a family B&B is not for everyone; canal noise, especially from singing gondoliers; intense gondola traffic. [$] *Rooms from: €160* ✉ *Fondamenta della Fenice, San Marco 2554* ☎ *041/5204271* 🌐 *www.bedandbreakfastalteatro.com* 🛏 *3 rooms* 🍴 *Breakfast* [M] *Vaporetto: Santa Maria del Giglio* ✥ *D4.*

BEST BETS FOR VENICE LODGING

Fodor'sChoice★	Novecento, p. 241	CLASSIC VENETIAN DESIGN
Al Ponte Antico, $$$, p. 244	Palazzo Abadessa, p. 245	
	Palazzo Barbarigo, p. 243	Al Ponte Antico, $$$, p. 244
Hotel Danieli, $$$$, p. 246	$$$$	Ca' Sagredo Hotel, $$$$, p. 245
$–$$	Ca' Sagredo Hotel, p. 245	
Al Palazzetto, p. 244	Palazzo Stern, p. 242	Palazzo Abadessa, $$$, p. 245
La Calcina, p. 242	**Best by**	
La Villeggiatura, p. 243	**Experience**	ROMANTIC
Locanda San Barnaba, p. 242		Ca' dei Dogi, $, p. 240
	CANAL VIEWS	La Calcina, $$, p. 242
$$$	3749 Ponte Chiodo, $$, p. 244	Oltre il Giardino–Casaifrari, $$$, p. 243
Hotel Antico Doge, p. 244		
Hotel UNA Venezia, p. 245	Hotel Danieli, $$$$, p. 246	Palazzo Barbarigo, $$$, p. 243
Metropole, p. 246	La Calcina, $$, p. 242	Ruzzini Palace Hotel, $$$, p. 246

$$$$ HOTEL Fodor'sChoice ★ **Bauer Il Palazzo.** A palazzo with an ornate, 1930s neo-Gothic facade facing the Grand Canal, the Bauer Il Palazzo has lavishly decorated guest rooms (large by Venetian standards) featuring high ceilings, tufted walls of Bevilacqua and Rubelli fabrics, Murano glass, marble bathrooms, damask drapes, and imitation antique furniture—and the hotel also boasts Venice's highest rooftop terrace, appropriately named *Il Settimo Cielo* (Seventh Heaven), which offers a heavenly breakfast, and nearby is the hotel's outdoor hot tub which offers breathaking views of La Serenissima. Pros: pampering service; high-end luxury. Cons: in one of the busiest areas of the city; you will pay handsomely for a room with a canal view, and yet Wi-Fi is still an additional charge. *Rooms from: €700 ⊠ Campo San Moisè, San Marco 1413/D ☎ 041/5207022 ⊕ www.ilpalazzovenezia.com ➳ 44 rooms, 38 suites ⋈ Breakfast Ⓜ Vaporetto: Vallaresso ⊹ E4.*

$ HOTEL **Ca' dei Dogi.** Amid the crush of mediocre hotels around Piazza San Marco, this inexpensive boutique hotel, in a quiet courtyard secluded from the melee, offers an island of calm: six individually decorated guest rooms (some with private terraces) that feature contemporary furnishings and accessories. Pros: offers respite from the San Marco crowds; some rooms have terraces with views of the Doge's Palace. Cons: rooms are on the small side; furnishings are spartan and look a bit cheap; located in the middle of the most touristy part of Venice (fine dining is limited). *Rooms from: €150 ⊠ Corte Santa Scolastica, Castello 4242 ☎ 041/2413751 ⊕ www.cadeidogi.it ➳ 6 rooms ⊙ Closed Dec. ⋈ Breakfast Ⓜ Vaporetto: San Zaccaria ⊹ F4.*

$$ **HOTEL** 🏨 **Locanda Orseolo.** A relaxed atmosphere pervades at this hotel's divine hot breakfast, where it is common to become engrossed in conversation with other guests as gondolas glide lazily by the water-level windows: this lovely state-of-mind is created by this cozy, elegant hotel's attentive staff and its comfortable, well-appointed rooms (but which can be ruined by a plague of singing gondoliers!). **Pros:** intimate and romantic; friendly staff; Wi-Fi is free. **Cons:** no elevator; canalside rooms can be noisy (think singing gondoliers); rooms without a canal view can be small and dark. [$] *Rooms from: €180* ✉ *Corte Zorzi off Campo San Gallo, San Marco 1083* ☎ *041/5204827* 🌐 *www.locandaorseolo.com* 🛏 *12 rooms* 🕒 *Closed Jan.* 🍴 *Breakfast* [M] *Vaporetto: Rialto or Vallaresso* ✥ *E4.*

$$$ **HOTEL** 🏨 **Novecento.** This small, family-run hotel is on a quiet street midway between the Piazza San Marco and the Accademia museum; inside, intimate rooms are attractively furnished largely with standard but attractive late-19th- and early-20th-century furniture with some Asian decor thrown in. **Pros:** intimate, romantic atmosphere; free Wi-Fi. **Cons:** Some rooms are small indeed, and some are noisy. [$] *Rooms from: €280* ✉ *Calle del Dose, Campo San Maurizio, San Marco 2683/84* ☎ *041/2413765* 🌐 *www.novecento.biz* 🛏 *9 rooms* 🍴 *Breakfast* [M] *Vaporetto: Santa Maria del Giglio* ✥ *C4.*

$$$$ **HOTEL** 🏨 **Palazzo Sant'Angelo sul Canal Grande.** There's a distinguished yet comfortable feel to this elegant palazzo, which is large enough to deliver expected facilities and services but small enough to pamper its guests; guest rooms have tapestry-adorned walls and Carrara and Alpine marble in the bath, and those facing the Grand Canal have balconies, which practically bring the canal to you. **Pros:** convenient to vaporetto stop. **Cons:** modest breakfast; fee for Wi-Fi, and Internet available only in common areas, not in rooms. [$] *Rooms from: €420* ✉ *Campo Sant'Angelo, San Marco 3488* ☎ *041/2411452* 🌐 *www.palazzosantangelo.com* 🛏 *14 rooms* 🍴 *Breakfast* [M] *Vaporetto: Sant'Angelo* ✥ *D4.*

DORSODURO

$$$$ **HOTEL** **Fodor's Choice** ★ 🏨 **Ca' Maria Adele.** Boasting a tranquil yet convenient spot near the showpiece church of Venice—spectacular Santa Maria della Salute—this is one of Venice's most elegant small hotels. **Pros:** quiet and romantic; imaginative contemporary decor; free Wi-Fi. **Cons:** small rooms, even for Venice; few good restaurants nearby. [$] *Rooms from: €420* ✉ *Campo Santa Maria della Salute, Dorsoduro 111* ☎ *041/5203078* 🌐 *www.camariaadele.it* 🛏 *12 rooms, 4 suites* 🍴 *Breakfast* [M] *Vaporetto: Salute* ✥ *D5.*

$ **B&B/INN** 🏨 **Casa Rezzonico.** Gently priced (even canal views come at a reasonable rate), this hotel is fronted by a sunny fondamenta and canal, offers pleasant—if generic—guest rooms, and hides a private garden out back that beckons you to enjoy the inner courtyard at breakfast. **Pros:** spacious garden for relaxing; canal views at a reasonable rate; two lively squares nearby; great for families. **Cons:** must reserve well in advance; some rooms are quite small; ground-floor rooms are dark; air-conditioning and heating not totally reliable. [$] *Rooms from: €160* ✉ *Fondamenta Gherardini, Dorsoduro 2813* ☎ *041/2770653* 🌐 *www.casarezzonico.it* 🛏 *6 rooms* 🍴 *Breakfast* [M] *Vaporetto: Ca' Rezzonico* ✥ *B4.*

3

$$ HOTEL
🏨 **La Calcina.** The time-burnished and elegant Calcina sits in an enviable position along the sunny Zattere, with front rooms offering vistas across the wide Giudecca Canal; it has been host to an array of notables, including art critic John Ruskin, who may have always, as today, been attracted to the hotel's gentler prices. **Pros:** panoramic views from some rooms; elegant, historic atmosphere. **Cons:** not for travelers who prefer ultramodern surroundings; no elevator; rooms with a view are appreciably more expensive. [$] *Rooms from: €180* ✉ *Dorsoduro 780* ☎ *041/5206466* 🌐 *www.lacalcina.com* 🛏 *27 rooms, 26 with bath; 5 suites* 🍴 *Breakfast* [M] *Vaporetto: Zattere* ✥ *C5.*

$ HOTEL
🏨 **Locanda Ca' Zose.** The idea that the Campanati sisters named the 15 rooms in their 17th-century locanda after the stars and constellations of the highest magnitude in the northern hemisphere says something about how personally this place is run. That's a real plus, as it the location on one of the brightest, most tranquil canals in the Dorsoduro area, but two minutes from the Salute (both the church and the vaporetto stop) and the Guggenheim Museum, and also handy to the Zattere promenade, the Accademia, and San Marco. **Pros:** quiet but convenient location; efficient, personal service. **Cons:** no outdoor garden or terrace; no Wi-Fi in rooms; unimpressive breakfast. [$] *Rooms from: €165* ✉ *Calle del Bastion, Dorsoduro 193/B* ☎ *041/5226635* 🌐 *www.hotelcazose.com* 🛏 *10 rooms, 1 junior suite, 1 suite* 🍴 *Breakfast* [M] *Vaporetto: Salute* ✥ *D5.*

$ HOTEL
🏨 **Locanda San Barnaba.** Handily located just off the Ca' Rezzonico vaporetto stop, this family-run, value-for-money establishment is housed in a 16th-century palazzo and, if you're lucky, you'll bag one of the superior rooms or the double that have original 18th-century frescoes (one junior suite has two small balconies and is exceptionally luminous). **Pros:** garden and terrace; close to vaporetto stop. **Cons:** no elevator, minibar, or Internet access. [$] *Rooms from: €175* ✉ *Calle del Traghetto, Dorsoduro 2785–2786* ☎ *041/2411233* 🌐 *www.locanda-sanbarnaba.com* 🛏 *11 rooms, 2 junior suites* 🍴 *Breakfast* [M] *Vaporetto: Ca' Rezzonico* ✥ *C4.*

$$$$ HOTEL
🏨 **Palazzo Stern.** An opulent refurbishment of this neo-Gothic palazzo, carried out by the Stern family in the early 20th century, incorporated marble-columned arches, terrazzo floors, frescoed ceilings, mosaics, and a majestic carved staircase (copied from the Ca' d'Oro), but the gracious terrace that overlooks the Grand Canal is almost reason alone to stay here. **Pros:** excellent service; lovely views from many rooms; modern renovation retains historic ambience; steps from vaporetto stop. **Cons:** multiple renovations may turn off some Venetian architectural purists; rooms with a Grand Canal view are much more expensive; terrace bar and service are sub-standard. [$] *Rooms from: €340* ✉ *Calle del Traghetto, Dorsoduro 2792* ☎ *041/2770869* 🌐 *www.palazzostern.com* 🛏 *18 rooms, 5 junior suites, 1 suite* 🍴 *Breakfast* [M] *Vaporetto: Ca' Rezzonico* ✥ *C4.*

$$$ HOTEL Fodor's Choice ★
🏨 **Pensione Accademia Villa Maravege.** One of the most enchanting hotels in Venice, this hotel appears like a mirage: in one of the most densely packed parts of the city (actually a promontory where two side canals converge with the Grand Canal), an iron gate parts and you find yourself in a large and elegant garden set with flower beds and stone cupids, all

offering an emerald-green backdrop for the Gothic-style "villa" charmingly decorated with a connoisseur's eye, like a 3D Tiepolo painting. **Pros:** a unique "villa" in the heart of Venice. **Cons:** standard rooms are smaller than is usual in Venice, and seem to be more sparsely decorated than the more expensive options. [$] *Rooms from: €280* ✉ *Fondamenta Bollani, Dorsoduro 1058* ☎ *041/5210188* 🌐 *www.pensioneaccademia.it* 🛏 *27 rooms, 2 suites* 🍴 *Breakfast* [M] *Vaporetto: Accademia* ✥ *C4.*

3

SAN POLO

$ B&B/INN 🏨 **Ca' San Rocco.** Through an iron gate on a calle, just off the main thoroughfare from Piazzale Roma to the San Tomà vaporetto stop, you'll spy the small, inviting garden terrace of the Ca' San Rocco—a former doctor's residence that has been transformed into a green, exceptionally quiet oasis by the Cuogo sisters. **Pros:** lots of greenery and outdoor areas; extraordinarily quiet. **Cons:** No elevator or porter (so you have to carry your own bags upstairs to your room); definitely not for people with mobility problems; 3 bridges with steps to the bus or train station; Wi-Fi is extra. [$] *Rooms from: €150* ✉ *Ramo Cimesin, San Polo 3078* ☎ *041/716744* 🌐 *www.casanrocco.it* 🛏 *6 rooms* 🍴 *Breakfast* [M] *Vaporetto: Piazzale Roma or San Tomà* ✥ *B3.*

$$ HOTEL 🏨 **La Villeggiatura.** If eclectic Venetian charm is what you seek, don't be dismayed by La Villeggiatura's unprepossessing entrance or the number of stairs (36) you'll climb to reach this lofty attic lodging: your reward is a luminous residence and six individually decorated rooms, each with its own original, theatrically themed fresco by a local artist. **Pros:** relaxed atmosphere; meticulously maintained; well-located. **Cons:** positioned high over a popular and busy thoroughfare; no elevator; modest breakfast; no view to speak of, despite the climb. [$] *Rooms from: €195* ✉ *Calle dei Botteri, San Polo 1569* ☎ *041/5244673* 🌐 *www.lavilleggiatura.it* 🛏 *6 rooms* 🍴 *Breakfast* [M] *Vaporetto: Rialto Mercato* ✥ *D3.*

$$$ HOTEL 🏨 **Oltre il Giardino–Casaifrari.** It's easy to overlook—and it can be a challenge to find—this secluded palazzo, sheltered as it is behind a brick wall just over the bridge from the Frari church, but the search is well worth it: this six-room hotel, set with airy, individually decorated guest rooms and a large garden, is an oasis of peace (especially in high season). **Pros:** a peaceful, gracious, and convenient setting; walled garden. **Cons:** a beautiful, but not particularly Venetian, ambience. [$] *Rooms from: €250* ✉ *San Polo 2542* ☎ *041/2750015* 🌐 *www.oltreilgiardino-venezia.com* 🛏 *6* 🍴 *Breakfast* [M] *Vaporetto: San Tomà* ✥ *C3.*

$$$ HOTEL 🏨 **Palazzo Barbarigo.** It is not unusual to find an opulent hotel along the Grand Canal; it is unusual to discover black marble, matte lacquer, indirect lighting, and 1940s design ensconced in a 16th-century Venetian palace. **Pros:** small; lavish; an uncommon ambience. **Cons:** standard rooms have pleasant side canal, but not Grand Canal, views; at times, unpleasant odors waft from the side canal. [$] *Rooms from: €300* ✉ *San Polo 3765* ☎ *041/74072* 🌐 *www.palazzobarbarigo.it* 🛏 *8 rooms, 6 junior suites* 🍴 *Breakfast* [M] *Vaporetto: San Tomà* ✥ *C4.*

SANTA CROCE

$ HOTEL Fodor's Choice ★ **Hotel al Ponte Mocenigo.** A columned courtyard welcomes you to this elegant, charming palazzo, former home of the Santa Croce branch of the Mocenigo family (which has a few doges in its past); not surprisingly, the meticulously renovated interior has an updated 18th-century Venetian feel, incorporating a number of distinctive architectural elements such as open-beam ceilings, fireplaces transformed into writing nooks, and Murano chandeliers. **Pros:** enchanting courtyard; water access; friendly staff; free Wi-Fi. **Cons:** beds are on the hard side; standard rooms are small; rooms in the annex can be noisy. [$] *Rooms from: €145* ✉ *Fondamento de Rimpeto a Ca' Mocenigo, Santa Croce 2063* ☎ *041/5244797* 🌐 *www.alpontemocenigo.com* 🛏 *10 rooms, 1 junior suite* 🍴 *Breakfast* [M] *Vaporetto: San Stae* ✣ *C2.*

CANNAREGIO

$$ B&B/INN Fodor's Choice ★ **3749 Ponte Chiodo.** Handy to the central Ca' d'Oro vaporetto stop, this family-owned, cheery, and homey bed-and-breakfast takes its name from the bridge leading to its entrance (one of only two left in the lagoon area without hand railings) and offers attentively appointed guest rooms with geranium-filled window boxes that overlook either the bridge and canals below or the spacious enclosed garden. **Pros:** highly attentive service; warm, relaxed atmosphere; private garden; canal or garden views. **Cons:** no elevator could be a problem for some. [$] *Rooms from: €180* ✉ *Calle Racchetta, Cannaregio 3749, Cannaregio* ☎ *041/2413935* 🌐 *www.pontechiodo.it* 🛏 *6 rooms* 🍴 *Breakfast* [M] *Vaporetto: Ca' d'Oro* ✣ *D2.*

$ B&B/INN **Al Palazzetto.** Understated yet gracious Venetian decor, original open-beam ceilings and terrazzo flooring, spotless marble baths, and friendly, attentive service are hallmarks of this intimate, family-owned *locanda* (inn). **Pros:** standout service; owner on-site; quiet; free Wi-Fi. **Cons:** not for amenity-seekers or lovers of ultramodern decor. [$] *Rooms from: €100* ✉ *Calle delle Vele, Cannaregio 4057, Cannaregio* ☎ *041/2750897* 🌐 *www.guesthouse.it* 🛏 *6 rooms, 1 suite* 🍴 *Breakfast* [M] *Vaporetto: Ca' d'Oro* ✣ *E2.*

$$$ HOTEL Fodor's Choice ★ **Al Ponte Antico.** The Peruch family, proprietors of this 16th-century palace inn, has lined its Gothic windows with tiny white lights, creating an inviting glow that's emblematic of the hospitality and sumptuous surroundings that await you inside: rich brocade-tufted walls, period-style furniture, and hand-decorated beamed ceilings all contribute to a luxurious, distinctly Venetian warmth in both guest rooms and common areas. **Pros:** upper-level terrace overlooks Grand Canal; family run; superior service; Internet is free. **Cons:** in one of the busiest areas of the city. [$] *Rooms from: €315* ✉ *Cannaregio 5768, Cannaregio* ☎ *041/2411944* 🌐 *www.alponteantico.com* 🛏 *12 rooms, 1 junior suite* 🍴 *Breakfast* [M] *Vaporetto: Rialto* ✣ *E3.*

$$$ HOTEL **Hotel Antico Doge.** Once the home of Doge Marino Falier, this palazzo has been attentively modernized in elegant Venetian style: some guest rooms have *baldacchini* (canopied beds) and courtyard views, the suite and two superior rooms have canal views; all are adorned with brocades, damask tufted walls, gilt mirrors, and parquet floors and even

the breakfast room comes fitted out with a stuccoed ceiling and Murano chandelier. **Pros:** romantic, atmospheric decor; convenient to the Rialto and beyond. **Cons:** on a busy thoroughfare; no outdoor garden or terrace; no elevator. $ *Rooms from: €240* ✉ *Campo Santi Apostoli, Cannaregio 5643, Cannaregio* ☎ *041/2411570* ⊕ *www.anticodoge.com* ↝ *19 rooms, 1 suite* ⦿ *Breakfast* Ⓜ *Vaporetto: Ca' d'Oro or Rialto* ✛ *E3.*

$$$$ 📷 **Ca' Sagredo Hotel.** A study in Venetian opulence, this expansive palace
HOTEL has been the Sagredo family residence since the mid-1600s and has the
Fodor'sChoice decor to prove it: the massive staircase has Longhi frescoes soaring above
★ it and the large common areas are adorned with original art by Tiepolo, Longhi, and Ricci, among others. **Pros:** excellent location; authentic yet comfortable renovation of Venice's patrician past. **Cons:** more opulent than intimate. $ *Rooms from: €400* ✉ *Campo San Sofia, Cannaregio 4198/99* ☎ *041/2413111* ⊕ *www.casagredohotel.com* ↝ *42 rooms, 2 junior suites, 3 suites* ⦿ *Breakfast* Ⓜ *Vaporetto: Ca' d'Oro* ✛ *D2.*

$$$ 📷 **Hotel UNA Venezia.** Up a narrow calle and across the bridge from the
HOTEL bustling Strada Nova, this 15th-century palazzo lingers silently over a tranquil canal and an evocative corner campo named for its two cisterns, or *pozzi*; inside you'll find the results of a 2008 renovation that maintains a traditional Venetian decor of creams, burgundies, and elegant sages. **Pros:** an intimate, boutique hideaway still handy for exploring the city; substantial rate reduction for stays of three days or longer. **Cons:** classic rooms are quite small; extra charge for Internet. $ *Rooms from: €200* ✉ *Ruga Do Pozzi, Cannaregio 4173, Cannaregio* ☎ *041/2442711* ⊕ *www.unahotels.com* ↝ *28 rooms, 3 junior suites, 3 suites* ⦿ *Breakfast* Ⓜ *Vaporetto: Ca' d'Oro* ✛ *E2.*

$$$ 📷 **Palazzo Abadessa.** At this late-16th-century palazzo, you can experi-
HOTEL ence gracious hospitality and a luxurious atmosphere in keeping with
Fodor'sChoice Venice's heritage of opulence and splendor—unusually spacious guest
★ rooms are well appointed with antique-style furniture, frescoed or stuccoed ceilings, and silk fabrics, while the enormous garden is a rare and delightful treat in crowded Venezia. **Pros:** spacious rooms and garden; superb guest service. **Cons:** some bathrooms are small. $ *Rooms from: €295* ✉ *Calle Priuli off Strada Nova, Cannaregio 4011, Cannaregio* ☎ *041/2413784* ⊕ *www.abadessa.com* ↝ *10 rooms, 5 suites* ⦿ *Breakfast* Ⓜ *Vaporetto: Ca' d'Oro* ✛ *E2.*

CASTELLO

$$$ 📷 **Hotel Bucintoro.** "All rooms with a view" touts this pensione-turned-
HOTEL four-star-hotel—and the views are indeed expansive: from the hotel's waterfront location near lively Via Garibaldi, your windows swing open to a panorama that sweeps from the Lido across the basin to San Giorgio and San Marco; upper-floor vistas are particularly inspiring. **Pros:** recent, tasteful renovation; lagoon views from all rooms; waterfront without the San Marco crowds; reduced rates for stays of more than one night. **Cons:** yachts and huge cruise ships sometimes dock outside, blocking lagoon views, and without those views, the hotel is really overpriced. $ *Rooms from: €400* ✉ *Riva degli Schiavoni, Castello 2135/A* ☎ *041/5209909* ⊕ *www.hotelbucintoro.com* ↝ *20 rooms, 6 junior suites* ⦿ *Breakfast* Ⓜ *Vaporetto: Arsenale* ✛ *G4.*

> **WORD OF MOUTH**
>
> "I don't think you can select a 'wrong place' to stay in Venice. Each district or sestiere is unique. All are safe and delightful to be in."
>
> –Mormor

$$$$ HOTEL Fodor's Choice ★ **Hotel Danieli.** Welcoming guests with one of the most sumptuous, quintessentially Venetian locations (part of the late-14th-century Palazzo Dandolo, built by the family of the doge who conquered Constantinople), this fabled and meticulously maintained monument of Venetian history sets the standard for premium luxury hotels in Venice: marble columns here, carved archways there, and plush furniture everywhere. **Pros:** beautiful, well-maintained rooms; a sense of history; spectacular views; lower rates available for rooms without views. **Cons:** the restaurant, though acceptable, isn't of the standard of the rest of the hotel; breakfast is not included, and expensive at €52. [$] *Rooms from: €820* ✉ *Riva degli Schiavoni, Castello 4196* ☎ *041/5226480* 🌐 *www.danielihotelvenice.com* 🛏 *225* 🍴 *No meals* [M] *Vaporetto: San Zacaria* ✣ *F4.*

$$$ HOTEL **Metropole.** This atmospheric five-star hotel is a labyrinth of intimate, opulent spaces featuring classic Venetian decor combined with exotic Eastern influences: the owner—a lifelong collector of unusual objects—fills common areas and the sumptuously appointed guest rooms with an assortment of antiques and curiosities. **Pros:** owner's collection adds its own interest; hotel harkens back to a gracious Venice of times past; fine hotel bar. **Cons:** one of the most densely touristed locations in the city; rooms with views are considerably more expensive; air-conditioning not completely reliable; restaurant is very expensive (and the chef is new and untested). [$] *Rooms from: €272* ✉ *Riva degli Schiavoni, Castello 4149* ☎ *041/5205044* 🌐 *www.hotelmetropole.com* 🛏 *67 rooms, 13 junior suites, 9 suites* 🍴 *Breakfast* [M] *Vaporetto: San Zaccaria* ✣ *F4.*

$$$ HOTEL **Ruzzini Palace Hotel.** After a painstaking renovation, the historic Ruzzini Palace (which graces the northern end of the lively Campo Santa Maria Formosa) offers renaissance- and baroque-style salons, with soaring spaces, Venetian terrazzo flooring, frescoed and open-beamed ceilings, and Murano chandeliers—but some of that fabulous time-burnished patina was diminished in the process. **Pros:** excellent service; a luminous, aristocratic ambience. **Cons:** the walk from San Zaccaria or Rialto includes two bridges and can be cumbersome for those with mobility issues or significant amounts of luggage; relatively far from a vaporetto stop; no restaurant. [$] *Rooms from: €380* ✉ *Campo Santa Maria Formosa, Castello 5866* ☎ *041/2410447* 🌐 *www.ruzzinipalace.com* 🛏 *19 rooms, 6 junior suites, 3 suites* 🍴 *Breakfast* [M] *Vaporetto: San Zaccaria or Rialto* ✣ *E3.*

NIGHTLIFE AND THE ARTS

THE ARTS

Visit ⊕ *www.aguestinvenice.com* for a preview of musical, artistic, and sporting events. *Venezia News* (VENews), available at newsstands, has similar information but also includes in-depth articles about noteworthy events. The tourist office publishes a handy, free quarterly *Calendar* in Italian and English, listing daily events and current museum and venue hours. *Venezia da Vivere* is a seasonal guide listing nightspots and live music. Several Venice websites allow you to scan the cultural horizon before you arrive; try ⊕ *www.turismovenezia.it, www.veneziasi.it, www.veniceonline.it,* and *www.venicebanana.com.* And don't ignore the posters you'll see plastered on the walls as you walk—they're often the most up-to-date information you can find.

CARNEVALE

Although Carnevale has traditionally been associated with the time leading up to the Roman Catholic period of Lent, it originally started out as a principally secular annual period of partying and feasting to celebrate Venice's victory over the patriarch of Ulrich Aquileia in 1162. To commemorate the annual tribute of a bull and twelve pigs Ulrich was forced to pay, a bull and pigs were slaughtered each year on the day before Lent in Piazza San Marco. The use of masks for Carnevale was first mentioned in 1268, and its direct association with Lent was not made until the end of the 13th century. Since then, for centuries the city marked the days preceding *quaresima* (Lent) with abundant feasting and wild celebrations. The word *carnevale* is derived from the words for meat (*carne*) and to remove (*levare*), as eating meat was restricted during Lent. Venice earned its international reputation as the "city of Carnevale" in the 18th century, when partying would begin several months before Lent and the city seemed to be one continuous masquerade. During this time, income from tourists became a major source of funds in the Serenissima's coffers. With the Republic's fall in 1797, Carnevale was prohibited by the French and the Austrians. From Italian reunification in 1866 until the fall of fascism in the 1940s, the event was alternately resumed and banned depending on the government's stance.

It was revived for good in the 1970s when residents began taking to the calli and campi in their own impromptu celebrations. It didn't take long for the tourist industry to embrace the revival as a means to stimulate business during low season. The efforts were successful. Each year over the 10- to 12-day Carnevale period (ending on the Tuesday before Ash Wednesday), more than a half million people attend concerts, theater and street performances, masquerade balls, historical processions, fashion shows, and contests. Since 2008 Carnevale has been organized by **Venezia Marketing & Eventi** (⊕ *www.carnevale.venezia.it*). *A Guest in Venice* is also a complete guide to public and private Carnevale festivities. Stop by the **tourist office** (☎ *041/5298711* ⊕ *www.turismovenezia.it*) or Venice Pavilion for information, but be aware they can be mobbed. If you're not planning on joining in the revelry, you'd be wise to choose another time to visit Venice. Crowds clog the streets (which become one-way, with police directing foot traffic), bridges are designated "no-stopping" zones to avoid gridlock, and prices skyrocket.

FESTIVALS

The **Biennale** (⊕ *www.labiennale.org*) cultural institution organizes events year-round, including the Venice Film Festival, which begins the last week of August. La Biennale di Venezia, an international exhibition of contemporary art, is held in odd-numbered years, usually from mid-June to early November, at the Giardini della Biennale, and in the impressive Arsenale.

Fodor's Choice
★

Festa del Redentore. On the third Sunday in July, crowds cross the Canale della Giudecca by means of a pontoon bridge, built every year to commemorate the doge's annual visit to Palladio's Chiesa del Redentore, to offer thanks for the end of a 16th-century plague. The day before, Venetians set up tables and chairs along the canals. As evening falls, practically the whole city takes to the streets and tables, and thousands more take to the water. Boats decorated with colored lanterns, well provisioned with traditional Redentore meals, jockey for position to watch the grand event. Half an hour before midnight, Venice kicks off a fireworks display over the Bacino, with the fireworks reflecting in its waters. Anywhere along the Riva degli Schiavoni you'll find good viewing; or try Zattere, as close to Punta Dogana as you can get, or on the Zitelle end of the Giudecca. After the fireworks you can join the young folks in staying out all night and greeting sunrise on the Lido beach, or rest up and make the procession to Mass on Sunday morning. If you're on a boat, allow for a couple of hours to dislodge yourself from the nautical traffic jam when the festivities break up.

MUSIC

The majority of the music you'll hear is classical, with Venice's famed composer, Vivaldi, frequently featured. In addition to Venice's opera house, Teatro La Fenice, churches, palazzi, and scuole *grandi* host a broad variety of concerts and operas, as do the Ca' Rezzonico and Querini-Stampalia museums.

During the 17th and 18th centuries Venice was a major center of European music; Vivaldi was only one of many prominent composers—such as Handel, Monteverdi, Cavalli, and the Gabrielis—who worked and drew inspiration from the city. In recognition of Venice's contribution to European music, the **Venetian Center for Baroque Music** (⊕ *www.vcbm. it*), formed in 2011, sponsors an annual festival of (what else?) Venetian Baroque music, which draws internationally recognized artists to the city.

To find out everything that's going on, stop by the tourist pavilion, or look in the tourist office's *Shows and Events Calendar* and in *A Guest in Venice* (⊕ *www.aguestinvenice.com*). You can book at the tourist office, any travel agency, the venue itself, or online with Music in Venice (⊕ *musicinvenice.com*).

HelloVenezia. HelloVenezia, which handles public transit ticket sales, also sells tickets for events at the Fenice and Malibran theaters. Purchase tickets by phone, on their Web site, at the Fenice, or at sales kiosks at Piazzale Roma and the train station. ✉ *Isola nova del Tronchetto 21* ☎ *041/2424* ⊕ *www.hellovenezia.it* ✉ *Piazzale Roma.*

Scan the posters and notices on the streets to spot free or inexpensive concerts offered by local choral groups and music schools.

OPERA

Teatro La Fenice. The Teatro La Fenice, located between Piazza San Marco and Campo San Stefano, is one of Italy's oldest opera houses. It has witnessed many memorable operatic premieres, including, in 1853, the dismal first-night flop of Verdi's *La Traviata*. It has also witnessed its share of disasters, the most recent being a horrific fire that burned most of the interior; it was deliberately set in January 1996, and was followed by endless delays in a complicated reconstruction. In keeping with its name (which translates as The Phoenix, coined when it was built over the ashes of its predecessor in 1792), La Fenice rose again. It was restored and reopened to great fanfare in 2004, and once again hosts seasons of symphony, opera, and dance. The acoustics of the reconstructed theatre have received mainly positive reviews, but attitudes expressed toward the decoration (replicated based on the style of the early 19th century, but using cheaper, less exacting techniques) have been mixed. According to music critics, in recent years less well known and accomplished artists have been booked, the production quality has deteriorated somewhat, and some operas (because of budget cuts) are presented in *concertante* (just sung, without staging) form, without much prior notice. Daily audio-guided tours through the theatre are available in several languages, from 9:30–6. Some discerning music critics now proclaim that the legendary La Fenice has deteriorated to the point of being a musical tourist trap. ⊠ *Campo San Fantin, San Marco 1965, San Marco* ⊕ *www.teatrolafenice.it* ☎ *€8 for audio tour* Ⓜ *Vaporetto: Sant'Angelo, Giglio.*

Teatro Malibran. La Fenice's more intimate sister venue is the Teatro Malibran. When built by the powerful Grimani family in 1677, as the Teatro Grimani a San Gristostomo, it was one of Europe's most famous theaters. It was, at first, a playhouse, featuring theatrical productions, including many works by Metastasio and, later, Goldoni. It became an opera house in the early 19th century. It was renamed Malibran in 1835, after Maria Garcia Malibran, the great soprano of her day. It was converted into a movie theater in 1927 and then reopened for live performances in 2001 after a lengthy restoration. ⊠ *Campiello del Teatro Malibran, Cannaregio 5870* ☎ *041/786511 La Fenice* Ⓜ *Vaporetto: Rialto.*

NIGHTLIFE

Venice's offerings for nightlife are, even by rather sedate standards, fairly tame. Most bars must close by midnight, especially those that offer outdoor seating. Piazza San Marco is a popular meeting place in nice weather, when the cafés stay open relatively late and all seem to compete to offer the best live music. The younger crowd, Venetians and visitors alike, tends to gravitate toward the area around Rialto Bridge, with Campi San Bartolomeo and San Luca on one side and Campo Rialto Nuovo on the other. Especially popular with university students are the bars around Campo Santa Margherita. Pick up a booklet of *2Night* or visit ⊕ *venezia.2night.it* for nightlife listings and reviews.

SAN MARCO AND DORSODURO

Al Chioschetto. Al Chioschetto is among Venice's "nonbars," consisting only of a kiosk set up to serve some outdoor tables. Located on the Zattere, and hence charging somewhat inflated prices, it's popular among tourists in nice weather for late-night panini or a sunny breakfast. ⊠ *Near Ponte Lungo, Dorsoduro 1406/A* ☎ *338/1174077* Ⓜ *Vaporetto: Zattere.*

Fodor's Choice
★ **Il Caffè.** Commonly called "Bar Rosso" for its bright-red exterior, Il Caffè has far more tables outside than in. A favorite with students and faculty from the nearby university, it's a good place to enjoy a *spritz*—the preferred Venetian aperitif of white wine, Campari or Aperol, soda water, an olive, and a slice of orange. It has excellent tramezzini (among the best in town) and panini, and a hip, helpful staff. New rules force it to close at midnight. ⊠ *Campo Santa Margherita, Dorsoduro 2963* ☎ *041/5287998* ⊙ *Closed Sun.*

Imagina. This refined bar, off the Campo Santa Margherita toward the Porte dei Pugni, draws a more mature and sophisticated Venetian clientele than the student-oriented places in the campo itself. The friendly fellows running the place make an excellent (and generous) spritz, serve decent wine, and some American regulars have taught them to make a rather palatable martini cocktail. Sandwiches and snacks are limited, but what's offered is fresh and tasty. There are tables outside, but in inclement weather a backroom with upholstered chairs and couches offers one of the few pleasant indoor environments to enjoy a drink in the area. The bar hosts regular art exhibitions by local, yet-to-be-established artists. ⊠ *Dorsoduro 3126, Dorsoduro* ⊙ *Closed Sun.* Ⓜ *Vaporetto: Ca'Rezzonico.*

Orange. Modern, hip, and complemented by a nice internal garden, Orange anchors the south end of Campo Santa Margherita, the liveliest campo in Venice. You can have *piadine* sandwiches, salads, and drinks while watching soccer games on a massive screen inside, or sit at the tables in the campo. Despite being close to the university, Orange is frequented primarily by young working people from the mainland and tourists. ⊠ *Campo Santa Margherita, Dorsoduro 3054/A* ☎ *041/5234740.*

Venice Jazz Club. This spot hosts the only live jazz concerts in town; €20 gets you a concert, a table, and your first drink. They also serve cold cuts and sandwiches from when the doors open at 7 until the music begins at 9. It's best to reserve a table (you can book through the website). ⊠ *Near Ponte dei Pugni, Dorsoduro 3102* ☎ *041/5232056, 340/1504985* ⊕ *www.venicejazzclub.com* ⊙ *Closed Dec., Jan., and Aug., and occasionally on Thurs. and Sun.* Ⓜ *Vaporetto: Ca' Rezzonico.*

CASTELLO

El Refolo Wine Bar. Tiny dimensions notwithstanding, the El Refolo wine bar is inviting to anyone on their way up or down Via Garibaldi, owing to its savory snacks, wine selection, and live music on some Friday nights when the weather's fine. There's no set closing hour—they'll tell you when it's time to leave. ⊠ *Via Garibaldi, Castello 1580* Ⓜ *Vaporetto: Arsenale.*

Zanzibar. A kiosk bar that's very popular on warm summer evenings, Zanzibar offers food but that is mostly limited to sandwiches and ice cream. The most delicious thing about the place is its location along the canal near Chiesa di Santa Maria Formosa, which makes it a truly pleasant place for a drink. ⊠ *Campo Santa Maria Formosa, Castello 5840* ☎ *041/962640* Ⓜ *Vaporetto: San Zaccaria.*

SHOPPING

Alluring shops abound in Venice. You'll find countless vendors of trademark Venetian wares such as glass and lace. The authenticity of some goods can be suspect, but they're often pleasing to the eye regardless of their place of origin. For more sophisticated tastes (and deeper pockets), there are jewelers, antiques dealers, and high-fashion boutiques on a par with those in Italy's larger cities but often maintaining a uniquely Venetian flair. There are also some interesting craft and art studios, where you can find high-quality one-of-a-kind articles, from handmade shoes to decorative lamps and mirrors.

Regular store hours are usually 9 to 12:30 and 3:30 or 4 to 7:30; some stores close Saturday afternoon or Monday morning. Food shops are open 8 to 1 and 5 to 7:30, and may close Wednesday afternoon and all day Sunday. Many tourist-oriented shops are open all day, every day. Some shops close for both a summer and a winter vacation.

The **San Marco** area is full of shops and couture boutiques such as Armani, Missoni, Valentino, Fendi, and Versace. **Le Mercerie**, the Frezzeria, Calle dei Fabbri, and Calle Larga XXII Marzo, all leading from Piazza San Marco, are some of Venice's busiest shopping streets. Other good shopping areas surround Calle del Teatro and Campi San Salvador, Manin, San Fantin, and San Bartolomeo. You can find somewhat less expensive, more varied and imaginative shops between the Rialto Bridge and San Polo and in Santa Croce, and art galleries in Dorsoduro from the Salute to the Accademia.

FOOD MARKETS

Smaller fresh markets dot the city, but the morning open-air fruit-and-vegetable market at **Rialto** offers animated local color and commerce. On Tuesday through Saturday morning the **fish market** (adjacent to the Rialto produce market) will amaze you with an impressive lesson in ichthyology; it's fun to count the number of species you've never seen before. You can also find a lively food market weekday mornings on **Via Garibaldi** in the Castello district, in the San Leonardo area in Cannaregio, and in Campo San Margherita in Dorsoduro.

CLOSE UP

Venetian Art Glass

The glass of Murano is Venice's number-one product, and you'll be confronted by mind-boggling displays of traditional and contemporary glassware—much of it kitsch and not made in Venice. Traditional Venetian glass is hot, blown glass, not lead crystal; it comes in myriad forms including the classic ornate goblets and chandeliers, to beads, vases, sculpture, and more. Beware of paying "Venetian" prices for glass made elsewhere. A piece claiming to be made in Murano may guarantee its origin, but not its value or quality; the prestigious Venetian glassmakers—like Venini, Seguso, Salviati, and others—sign their pieces, but never use the "made in Murano"

label. To make a smart purchase, take your time and be selective. You can learn a great deal without sales pressure at the Museo del Vetro on Murano; unfortunately you'll likely find the least-attractive glass where public demonstrations are offered. Although prices in Venice and on Murano are comparable, shops in Venice with wares from various glassworks may charge slightly less. ■TIP➜ A "free" taxi to Murano always comes with sales pressure. Take the vaporetto that's included in your transit pass, and, if you prefer, a private guide who specializes in the subject but has no affinity to any specific furnace.

SPECIALTY STORES

SAN MARCO AND DORSODURO

Angolo del Passato. In her tempting store, Giordana Naccari collects excellent quality early and middle 20th-century Venetian glassware and produces her own intriguing cups, plates, and pitchers at prices that are quite accessible. ⊠ *Campiello dei Squelini, Dorsoduro 3276* ☎ *041/5287896.*

Fodor's Choice ★ **Bevilacqua.** Keeping the weaving tradition alive in Venice since 1875, Bevilacqua uses 18th-century handlooms for its most precious creations. Its repertoire of 3,500 different patterns and designs yields a ready-to-sell selection of hundreds of brocades, Gobelins, damasks, velvets, taffetas, and satins. You'll also find tapestry, cushions, and braiding. Fabrics made by this prestigious firm have been used to decorate the Vatican, the Royal Palace of Stockholm, and the White House.■TIP➜ This listing is for the retail outlet of the Bevilacqua establishment. If you're interested in seeing the actual 18th century looms in action making the most precious fabrics, ask for an appointment at the production center in Santa Croce. ⊠ *Campo di Santa Maria del Giglio, San Marco 2520* ☎ *041/2410662 retail outlet, 041/721566 Santa Croce production center* Ⓜ *Vaporetto: Giglio* ⊠ *Fondamenta della Canonica, San Marco 337/B* ☎ *041/5287581* ⊕ *www.luigi-bevilacqua.com* Ⓜ *Vaporetto: San Marco* ⊠ *Factory: Campiello della Comare, Santa Croce 1320* ☎ *041/721576* ☉ *Visits by appointment only* Ⓜ *Vaporetto: Riva di Biasio.*

Fodor's Choice **Jesurum.** A great deal of so-called "Burano-Venetian" lace is now made
★ in China; so, unless you're an expert—and experts really can tell the
difference—you're best off going a trusted place. Jesurum has been the
major producer of handmade Venetian lace since 1870. Its lace is, of
course, all modern production, but if you want an antique piece, the
people at Jesurum can point you in the right direction. ⊠ *Calle Larga
XII Marzo, San Marco 2401, San Marco* ☎ *041/5238969.*

Ma.Re. A visit to this shop will give you a good overview of premium
Venetian production. Ma.Re sells Salviati glass, as well as glass from
other famous Murano glassmakers like Venini, Seguso, and Moretti,
but some collectors head here for the one-of-a-kind objects created
by leading glass artists. If you've broken a piece out of a set of out
of production Venetian glasses, the friendly staff will try to help you
replace it, either by finding a substitute, or having one made for you.
⊠ *Via XXII Marzo, San Marco 2088* ☎ *041/5231191* 🖷 *041/5285745*
⊕ *www.mareglass.com* Ⓜ *Vaporetto: San Marco.*

Marina and Susanna Sent. The beautiful and elegant glass jewelry of
Marina and Susanna Sent has been featured in *Vogue.* Look also for
vases and other exceptional design pieces. ⊠ *Campo San Vio, Dorsoduro 669* ☎ *041/5208136* Ⓜ *Vaporetto: Accademia.*

Fodor's Choice **Pauly & C.** Established in 1866, Pauly & C features a truly impressive
★ selection of authentic Murano art glass (both traditional and contemporary styles) by the most accomplished masters—and at better prices than
on the island. The showroom at No. 73 houses the more traditional
collection; at No. 77 you can find works by artists and designers. ⊠ *Piazza San Marco 73 and 77, San Marco* ☎ *041/5235484, 041/2770279*
⊕ *www.pauly.it.*

3

THE VENETO AND FRIULI–VENEZIA GIULIA

WELCOME TO THE VENETO AND FRIULI–VENEZIA GIULIA

TOP REASONS TO GO

★ **Giotto's frescoes in the Cappella degli Scrovegni:** In this Padua chapel, Giotto's expressive and innovative frescoes foreshadowed the painting techniques of the Renaissance.

★ **Villa Barbaro in Maser:** Master architect Palladio's graceful creation meets Veronese's splendid frescoes in a one-time-only collaboration.

★ **Opera in Verona's ancient arena:** The performances may not be top-notch, but even serious opera fans can't resist the spectacle of these shows.

★ **Roman and early Christian ruins at Aquileia:** Aquileia's ruins offer an image of the transition from pagan to Christian Rome, and are almost entirely free of tourists.

★ **The wine roads north of Treviso:** A series of routes takes you through beautiful hillsides to some of Italy's finest wines.

1 Padua. A city of both high-rises and history, Padua is most noted for Giotto's frescoes in the Cappella degli Scrovegni, where Dante's contemporary painted with a human focus that foreshadowed the Renaissance.

2 Verona. Shakespeare placed Romeo, Juliet, and a couple of gentlemen in Verona, one of the oldest, best-preserved, and most beautiful cities in Italy. Try to catch *Aïda* at the gigantic Roman arena.

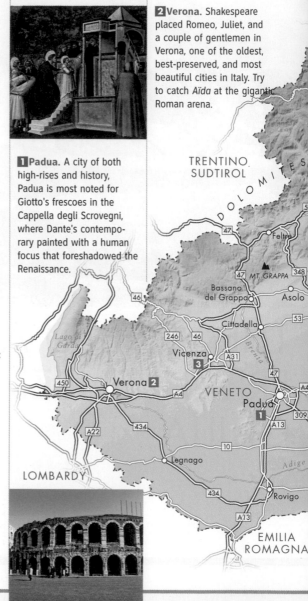

3 Vicenza. This elegant art city, on the green plain reaching inland from Venice's lagoon, bears the signature of the great 16th-century architect Andrea Palladio, including several palazzi and other important buildings.

4 Treviso and the Hillside Towns. Treviso is a busy town with a touch of Venetian style. Asolo (the City of a Hundred Horizons) is the most popular destination in a series of charming towns that dot the wine-producing hills north of Treviso.

GETTING ORIENTED

The Venetian Arc is the sweep of land curving north and east from the River Adige to the Slovenian border. It's made up of two Italian regions—the Veneto and Friuli–Venezia Giulia—that were once controlled by Venice, and the culture is a mix of Venetian, Alpine, and central European sensibilities.

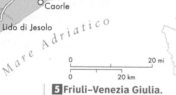

5 Friuli–Venezia Giulia. Set between the Adriatic Sea and Slovenia in the eastern corner of Italy, this is a region where menus run from gnocchi to goulash. The port city of Trieste has a mixed Venetian-Austrian heritage and an important literary history. It contains several Belle Epoque cafés and palaces built for Habsburg nobility.

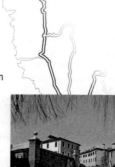

EATING AND DRINKING WELL IN THE VENETO AND FRIULI–VENEZIA GIULIA

With the decisive seasonal changes of the Venetian Arc, it's little wonder that many restaurants shun printed menus. Elements from field and forest define much of the region's cuisine, including white asparagus, herbs, chestnuts, radicchio, and wild mushrooms.

Restaurants of the Venetian Arc tend to cling to tradition, not only in the food they serve, but in how they serve it. This means that from 3 in the afternoon until about 7:30 in the evening most places are closed tight (though you can pick up a snack at a bar during these hours), and on Sunday afternoon restaurants are packed with Italian families and friends indulging in a weekly ritual of lunching out.

Meals are still sacred for most Italians, so don't be surprised if you get disapproving looks when you gobble down a sandwich or a slice of pizza while seated on the church steps or a park bench. In many places it's actually illegal to do so. If you want to fit in with the locals, eat while standing at the bar, and they may not even notice that you're a tourist.

THE BEST IN BEANS

Pasta e fagioli, a thick bean soup with pasta, served slightly warm or at room temperature, is made all over Italy. Folks in Veneto, though, take a special pride in their version. It features particularly fine beans that are grown around the village of Lamon, near Belluno.

Even when they're bought in the Veneto, the beans from Lamon cost more than double the next most expensive variety, but their rich and delicate taste is considered to be well worth the added expense. You never knew that bean soup could taste so good.

PASTA, RISOTTO, POLENTA

For *primi* (first courses), the Veneto dines on *bigoli* (thick whole-wheat pasta) generally served with an anchovy-onion sauce delicately flavored with cinnamon, and risotto—saturated with red wine in Verona and made with prosecco in Conegliano. *Polenta* (corn meal gruel) is everywhere, whether it's a stiff porridge topped with Gorgonzola or stew, or a patty grilled alongside meat or fish, *as in the photo below.*

FISH

The catch of the day is always a good bet, whether sweet and succulent Adriatic shellfish, sea bream, bass, or John Dory, or freshwater fish from Lake Garda near Verona. A staple in the Veneto is *baccalà,* dried salt cod, soaked in water or milk, and then prepared in a different way in each city. In Vicenza, baccalà *alla vicentina, pictured at left,* is cooked with onions, milk, and cheese, and is generally served with polenta.

MEAT

Because grazing land is scarce in the Veneto, beef is a rarity, but pork and veal are standards, while goose, duck, and guinea fowl are common poultry options. Lamb is best in spring, when it's young and delicate. In Friuli–Venezia Giulia, menus show the influences of Austria-Hungary: you may find deer and hare on the menu, as well as Eastern European–style goulash. Throughout

the Veneto an unusual treat is *nervetti*—cubes of gelatin from a cow's knee prepared with onions, parsley, olive oil, and lemon.

RADICCHIO DI TREVISO

In fall and winter be sure to try the radicchio di Treviso, *pictured above,* a red endive grown near that town but popular all over the region. Cultivation is very labor-intensive, so it can be a bit expensive. It's best in a stew with chicken or veal, in a risotto, or just grilled or baked with a drizzle of olive oil and perhaps a little taleggio cheese from neighboring Lombardy.

WINE

Wine is excellent here: the Veneto produces more D.O.C. (Denominazione di Origine Controllata) wines than any other region in Italy. Amarone, the region's crowning achievement, is a robust and powerful red with an alcohol content as high as 16%. Valpolicella and Bardolino are other notable appellations.

The best of the whites are Soave, sparkling prosecco, and *pinot bianco* (pinot blanc). In Friuli–Venezia Giulia the local wines par excellence are *tocai friulano*, a dry, lively white made from the sauvignon vert grape, which has attained international stature, and piccolit, perhaps Italy's most highly prized dessert wine.

Updated
by Bruce
Leimsidor

The arc around Venice—stretching from Verona to Trieste, encompassing the Veneto and Friuli–Venezia Giulia regions—has, in recent centuries, fallen under the cultural influence of its namesake city. Whether coastal or inland, the emblem of Venice, Saint Mark's winged lion, is emblazoned on palazzi or poised on pedestals. Since the 16th century, the art, architecture, and way of life have all reflected Venetian splendor.

But in the Middle Ages Padua and Verona were independent cities that developed substantial cultural traditions of their own, leaving behind many artistic treasures. And 16th-century Vicenza, even while under Venetian political domination, contributed more to the cultural heritage of La Serenissima than it took from her.

The area is primarily flat green farmland. As you move inland, though, you encounter low hills, which swell and rise in a succession of plateaus and high meadows, culminating in the snowcapped Dolomite Alps. Much of the pleasure of exploring here comes from discovering the variations on the Venetian theme that give a unique character to each of the towns. Some, such as Verona, Treviso, and Udine, have a solid medieval look. Asolo, dubbed "the town of a hundred horizons," has an idyllic setting; Padua, with its narrow arcaded streets, is romantic; Vicenza, ennobled by the architecture of Palladio, is elegant. In Friuli–Venezia Giulia, Udine is a genteel, intricately sculpted city that's home to the first important frescoes by Giambattista Tiepolo. In Trieste there's a reminder of its past as a port of the Austro-Hungarian Empire in its Viennese-inspired coffeehouses.

THE VENETO AND FRIULI–VENEZIA

PLANNING AHEAD

Reservations are required to see the Giotto frescoes in Padua's Cappella degli Scrovegni—though if there's space, you can "reserve" on the spot.

On the outskirts of Vicenza, Villa della Rotonda, one of star-architect Palladio's masterpieces, is open to the public only from mid-March through mid-November, and only on Wednesday and Saturday. (Hours for visiting the grounds are less restrictive.)

Another important Palladian villa, Villa Barbaro near Maser, is open weekends and several days during the week from March to October. From November to February, it's open only on weekends. *For details about Cappella degli Scrovegni, look in this chapter under "Top Attractions" in Padua. For the villas, see "Top Attractions" in Vicenza and Palladio Country.*

MAKING THE MOST OF YOUR TIME

Lined up in a row west of Venice are Padua, Vicenza, and Verona—three prosperous small cities that are each worth at least a day on a northern Italy itinerary. Verona has the greatest charm, and it's probably the best choice for a base in the area, even though it also draws the biggest crowds of tourists. The hills north of Venice make for good drives, with appealing villages set amid a visitor-friendly wine country.

East of the Veneto, the region of Friuli–Venezia Giulia is off the main tourist circuit. You probably won't go here on a first trip to Italy, but by your second or third visit you may be drawn by its caves and castles, its battle-worn hills, and its mix of Italian and central European culture. The port city of Trieste, famous for its elegant cafés, has quiet character that some people find dull and others find alluring.

GETTING HERE AND AROUND

BUS TRAVEL

There are interurban and interregional connections throughout the Veneto and Friuli, handled by nearly a dozen private bus lines. To figure out which line will get you where, the best strategy is to get assistance from local tourist offices.

CAR TRAVEL

Padua, Vicenza, and Verona are on the highway and train line between Venice and Milan. Seeing them without a car isn't a problem; in fact, having a car can complicate matters. The cities sometimes limit access, permitting only cars with plates ending in an even number on even days, odd on odd, or prohibiting cars altogether on weekends. There's no central source for information about these sporadic traffic restrictions; the best strategy is to check with your hotel before arrival for an update. You'll need a car to get the most out of the hill country that makes up much of the Venetian Arc, and it will be particularly useful for visiting Asolo and Aquileia, since public transportation to those quite interesting sites is very limited.

The two main access roads to the Venetian Arc from southern Italy are both linked to the A1 (Autostrada del Sole), which connects Bologna, Florence, and Rome. They are the A13, which culminates in Padua, and the A22, which passes through Verona running north–south. Linking the region from east to west is the A4, the primary route from Milan to Trieste, skirting Verona, Padua, and Venice along the way. The distance from Verona to Trieste via A4 is 263 km (163 miles, 2½ hours), with one break in the autostrada near Venice/Mestre. Branches link the A4 with Treviso (A27), Pordenone (A28), and Udine (A23).

TRAIN TRAVEL

Trains on the main routes from the south stop almost hourly in Verona, Padua, and Venice. From northern Italy and the rest of Europe, trains usually enter via Milan or through Porta Nuova station in Verona. Treviso and Udine both lie on the main line from Venice to Tarvisio. Unfortunately, there are no daytime express trains between Venice and Tarvisio, only the slower interregional and regional service.

To the west of Venice, the main line running across the north of Italy stops at Padua (30 minutes from Venice), Vicenza (1 hour), and Verona (1½ hours); to the east is Trieste (2 hours). Local trains link Vicenza to Treviso (1 hour) and Udine to Trieste (1 hour).

Be sure to take express trains whenever possible—a local "milk run" that stops in every village along the way can take considerably longer. The fastest trains are the Eurostars, but reservations are obligatory and fares are much higher than on regular express trains.

FS. You can check schedules on the Italian national railway's website. ☏ 892021 ⊕ *www.trenitalia.com.*

RESTAURANTS

Please note that restaurant prices listed as "average meal" include a meal consisting of first course *(primo)*, second course *(secondo)*, and dessert *(dolce)*.

HOTELS

There's a full range of accommodations throughout the region. Hotels often renovate and raise their prices, but good low-cost options can still be found. Ask about weekend discounts, often available at hotels catering to business clients. Rates tend to be higher in Padua and Verona; in Verona especially, seasonal rates vary widely and soar during trade fairs and the opera season. There are fewer good lodging choices in Vicenza, perhaps because more overnighters are drawn to the better restaurant scene in Verona and Padua. *Agriturismo* (farm stay) information is available at tourist offices and sometimes on their websites.

PADUA

A romantic warren of arcaded streets, Padua has long been one of the major cultural centers of northern Italy. Its university, founded in 1222 and Italy's second oldest, attracted such cultural icons as Dante (1265–1321), Petrarch (1304–74), and Galileo Galilei (1564–1642), thus earning the city the sobriquet *La Dotta* (The Learned). Padua's Basilica di Sant'Antonio, begun around 1238, attracts droves of pilgrims, especially on his feast day, June 13. Three great artists—Giotto (1266–1337), Donatello (circa 1386–1466), and Mantegna (1431–1506)—left significant works in Padua, with Giotto's Scrovegni Chapel being one of the best-known, and most meticulously preserved, works of art in the country. Today, a cycle-happy student body—some 50,000 strong—flavors every aspect of local culture. Don't be surprised if you spot a *laurea* (graduation) ceremony marked by laurel leaves, mocking lullabies, and X-rated caricatures.

GETTING HERE AND AROUND

Many people visit Padua from Venice: the train trip between the cities is short, and regular bus service originates from Venice's Piazzale Roma. By car from Milan or Venice, Padua is on the Autostrada Torino–Trieste A4/E70. Take the San Carlo exit and follow Via Guido Reni to Via Tiziano Aspetti into town. From the south, take the Autostrada Bologna Padova A13 to its Padua terminus at Via Ballaglia. Regular bus service connects Venice's Marco Polo airport with downtown Padua.

Padua is a walker's city. If you arrive by car, leave your vehicle in one of the parking lots on the outskirts, or at your hotel. Unlimited bus service is included with the Padova Card (€16 or €21, valid for 48 or 72 hours), which allows entry to all the city's principal sights (€1 extra for a Scrovegni Chapel reservation). It's available at tourist information offices and at some museums and hotels.

VISITOR INFORMATION

Padua Tourism Office ⊠ *Padova Railway Station* ☎ *049/8752077* ⊕ *www.turismopadova.it* ✉ *Galleria Pedrocchi* ☎ *049/8767927.*

EXPLORING PADUA

TOP ATTRACTIONS

Basilica di Sant'Antonio (*Basilica del Santo*). Thousands of faithful make the pilgrimage here each year to pray at the tomb of Saint Anthony. The huge church, which combines elements of Byzantine, Romanesque, and Gothic styles, was probably begun around 1238, seven years after the death of the Portuguese-born saint. It was completed in 1310, with structural modifications added from the end of the 14th century into the mid-15th century. The imposing interior contains works by the 15th-century Florentine master Donatello. He sculpted the very beautiful series of bronze reliefs illustrating the miracles of Saint Anthony, as well as the bronze statues of the Madonna and saints, on the high altar. Because of the site's popularity with pilgrims, masses are held in the basilica almost constantly, which makes it difficult to see these works. More accessible is the restored **Cappella del Santo** (housing the tomb of the saint), which dates from the 16th century. Its walls are covered with impressive reliefs by various important Renaissance sculptors, including Jacopo Sansovino (1486–1570), the architect of the library in Venice's Piazza San Marco, and Tullio Lombardo (1455–1532), the greatest in a family of sculptors who decorated many churches in the area, among them Venice's Santa Maria dei Miracoli. In front of the church is an undisputed masterpiece of Italian Renaissance sculpture, Donatello's equestrian statue (1453) of the *condottiere* (mercenary general) Erasmo da Narni, known as Gattamelata. Inspired by the ancient statue of Marcus Aurelius in Rome's Campidoglio, it is the first in a series of

4

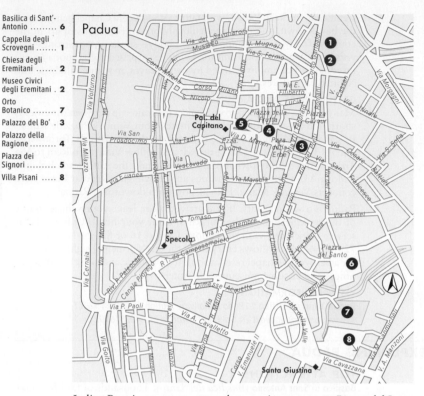

Italian Renaissance monumental equestrian statues. ⊠ *Piazza del Santo*
☎ *049/8225652* ⊕ *www.santantonio.it* ⊙ *Oct.–Apr., daily 6:20 am–7
pm; May–Sept., daily 6:20 am–7:45 pm.*

Fodor'sChoice **Cappella degli Scrovegni** (*The Arena Chapel*). This world-famous cha-
★   pel and its frescoes were commissioned by Enrico Scrovegno to atone
for the sins of his deceased father, Reginaldo, the usurer encountered
by Dante in the Seventh Circle of the Inferno in his *Divine Comedy*.
Giotto and his assistants decorated the interior from 1303 to 1305
with a universally acclaimed fresco cycle illustrating the lives of Mary
and Jesus. The 38 panels are arranged in tiers and are to be read from
left to right. The spatial depth, emotional intensity, and naturalism of
these frescoes—note the use of blue sky instead of the conventional,
depth-destroying gold background of medieval painting—broke new
ground in Western art. Opposite the altar is a *Last Judgment,* most
likely designed and painted by Giotto's assistants, where Enrico offers
his chapel to the Virgin, celebrating her role in human salvation—particularly appropriate, given the penitential purpose of the chapel.

Mandatory reservations are for a specific time and are nonrefund-
able. They can be made well in advance at the ticket office, online, or
by phone. Payments online or by phone by credit card must be made
one day in advance; payments by bank transfer (possible by phone

only) should be made four days in advance. Reservations are necessary even if you have a Padova Card. In order to preserve the artwork, doors are opened only every 15 minutes. A maximum of 25 visitors at a time must spend 15 minutes in an acclimatization room before making a 15-minute (20-minute in winter, late June, and July) chapel visit. Punctuality is essential; tickets should be picked up at least one hour before your reservation time. If you don't have a reservation, it's

sometimes possible to buy your chapel admission on the spot—but you might have to wait a while until there's a group with an opening. You can see fresco details as part of a virtual tour at Musei Civici degli Eremitani. A good place to get some background before visiting the chapel is the multimedia room, which offers films and interactive computer presentations. ⊠ *Piazza Eremitani 8* ☎ *049/2010020 for reservations* ⊕ *www.cappelladegliscrovegni.it* ⊠ *€13 includes Musei Civici, or €1 with Padova Card* ⊙ *Early Nov.–early Mar. and mid-June–early Aug., daily 9–7; early Mar.–mid-June and early Aug.–early Nov., Mon. 9–7, Tues.–Sun. 9 am–10 pm; entry by reservation only.*

Palazzo della Ragione. Also known as Il Salone, this spectacular arcaded reception hall, which divides the Piazza delle Frutta from the Piazza delle Erbe, was built between 1172 and 1219, with 14th- and 15th-century additions. Giotto painted the original frescoes, which were destroyed in a fire in 1420. The existing ones are primarily by Niccolò Miretto and Stefano di Ferrara, working from 1425 to 1440 and following the original plan of Giotto's frescoes. In the Middle Ages, as its name implies, the building housed Padua's law courts; today, its street-level arcades shelter shops and cafés. Art shows are often held upstairs in the frescoed **Salone,** which, at 85 feet high, is one of the largest halls in Italy. In this stunning space there's an enormous wooden horse, crafted for a 15th-century public tournament, with a head and tail later remodeled to replicate the steed from Donatello's *Gattamelata.* In the piazza surrounding the building are Padua's colorful open-air fruit and vegetable markets. ⊠ *Piazza della Ragione* ☎ *049/8205006* ⊠ *Salone €4, free with Padova Card* ⊙ *Feb.–Oct., Tues.–Sun. 9–7; Nov.–Jan., Tues.–Sun. 9–6.*

Piazza dei Signori. Some fine examples of 15th- and 16th-century buildings line this square. On the west side, the **Palazzo del Capitanio** (facade constructed 1598–1605) has an impressive **Torre dell'Orologio,** with an astronomical clock dating from 1344 and a portal made by Falconetto in 1532 in the form of a Roman triumphal arch. The 12th-century **Battistero del Duomo** (Cathedral Baptistry), with frescoes by Giusto de Menabuoi (1374–78), is a few steps away. ⊠ *Piazza del Duomo* ☎ *049/656914* ⊠ *Battistero: €2.80, free with Padova Card* ⊙ *Daily 10–6.*

THE VENETIAN ARC, PAST AND PRESENT

Long before Venetians made their presence felt on the mainland in the 15th century, Ezzelino III da Romano (1194–1259), whose soul, because of its cruel and violent nature, Dante consigned to Hell, laid claim to Verona, Padua, and the surrounding lands and towns. He was the first of a series of brutal and aggressive rulers who dominated the cities of the region until the rise of Venetian rule.

After Ezzelino was ousted, powerful families such as Padua's Carrara and Verona's della Scala (Scaligeri) vied throughout the 14th century to dominate these territories. With the rise of Venetian rule came a time of relative peace, when noble families from the lagoon and the mainland commissioned Palladio and other accomplished architects to design their palazzi and villas. This rich classical legacy, superimposed upon medieval castles and fortifications, is central to the identities of present-day Padua, Vicenza, and Verona.

The region remained under Venetian control until the Napoleonic invasion and the fall of the Venetian Republic in 1797. The Council of Vienna ceded it, along with Lombardy, to Austria in 1815. The region revolted against Austrian rule and joined the Italian Republic in 1866.

Friuli–Venezia Giulia's complicated history is reflected in its architecture, language, and cuisine. It's been marched through, fought over, hymned by patriots, and romanticized by writers that include James Joyce, Rainer Maria Rilke, Pier Paolo Passolini, and Jan Morris. The region has seen Fascists and Communists, Romans, Habsburgs, and Huns. It survived by forging sheltering alliances—Udine beneath the wings of San Marco (1420), Trieste choosing Duke Leopold of Austria (1382) over Venetian domination.

Some of World War I's fiercest fighting took place in Friuli–Venezia Giulia, where memorials and cemeteries commemorate hundreds of thousands who died before the arrival of Italian troops in 1918 finally liberated Trieste from Austrian rule. Trieste, along with the whole of Venezia Giulia, was annexed to Italy in 1920. During World War II the Germans occupied the area and placed Trieste in an administrative zone along with parts of Slovenia. The only Nazi extermination camp on Italian soil, the Risiera di San Sabba, was near Trieste. After the war, during a period of Cold War dispute, Trieste was governed by an allied military administration; it was officially re-annexed to Italy in 1954, when Italy ceded the Istrian peninsula to the south to Yugoslavia. These arrangements were not finally ratified by Italy and Yugoslavia until 1975.

FAMILY **Villa Pisani.** Extensive grounds with rare trees, ornamental fountains, and garden follies surround this extraordinary palace in Stra, 13 km (8 miles) southeast of Padua. Built in 1721 for the Venetian doge Alvise Pisani, it recalls Versailles more than a Veneto villa. This was one of the last and grandest of many stately residences constructed along the Brenta River from the 16th to 18th century by wealthy Venetians for their *villeggiatura*—vacation and escape from the midsummer humidity. Giambattista Tiepolo's (1696–1770) spectacular frescoes on the ballroom ceiling alone are worth the visit. For a relaxing afternoon, explore the gorgeous park and maze. To get here from Venice, take Bus No. 53 from Piazzale Roma. The villa is a five-minute walk from the bus stop in Stra.■**TIP→** This is the place where Mussolini invited Hitler for their first meeting, but they only stayed one night because of the mosquitos. The dictators are, thankfully, no longer there, but the mosquitoes remain: If you're visiting the park in the late afternoon in the summer, be sure to bring some mosquito repellant. ⊠ *Via Doge Pisani 7, Stra* ☎ *049/502074* ⊕ *www.villapisani.beniculturali.it* ⊠ *€7.50; park only, €4.50* ⊙ *Villa and park: Apr.–Sept., Tues.–Sun. 9–7; Oct., Tues.–Sun. 9–5; Nov.–Mar., Tues.–Sun. 9–4. Maze closed Nov.–Feb.*

WORTH NOTING

Chiesa degli Eremitani. This 13th-century church houses substantial fragments of Andrea Mantegna's frescoes (1448–50), damaged by Allied bombing in World War II. Despite their fragmentary condition, Mantegna's still beautiful and historically important frescoes, which depict the martyrdom of Saint James and Saint Christopher, show the young artist's mastery of extremely complex problems of perspective. ⊠ *Piazza degli Eremitani* ☎ *049/8756410* ⊙ *Mon.–Sat. 8–6, Sun. 10–1 and 4–7.*

Musei Civici degli Eremitani (*Civic Museum*). A former monastery now houses works of Venetian masters, as well as fine collections of archaeological finds and ancient coins. Notable are the Giotto Crucifix, which once hung in the Scrovegni Chapel, and the *Portrait of a Young Senator* by Giovanni Bellini (1430–1516). ⊠ *Piazza Eremitani 8* ☎ *049/82045450* ⊠ *€10, €13 with Scrovegni Chapel, free with Padova Card* ⊙ *Tues.–Sun. 9–7.*

Orto Botanico (*Botanical Garden*). The Venetian Republic ordered the creation of Padua's botanical garden in 1545 to supply the university with medicinal plants, and it still maintains its original layout. You can stroll the arboretum—still part of the university—and wander through hothouses and beds of plants that were first introduced to Italy in this late-Renaissance garden. A St. Peter's palm, planted in 1585, inspired Goethe to write his 1790 essay called "The Metamorphosis of Plants." ⊠ *Via Orto Botanico 15* ☎ *049/8272119* ⊕ *www.ortobotanico.unipd. it* ⊠ *€4, free with Padova Card* ⊙ *Apr.–Oct., daily 9–1 and 3–7; Nov.–Mar., Mon.–Sat. 9–1.*

Palazzo del Bo'. The University of Padua, founded in 1222, centers around this predominently16th-century palazzo with an 18th-century facade. It's named after the Osteria del Bo' (*bo'* means "ox"), an inn that once stood on the site. It's worth a visit to see the exquisite and perfectly proportioned anatomy theater (1594), the beautiful "Old Courtyard," and a hall with a lectern used by Galileo. You can enter only as part of a guided tour. Most guides speak English, but it is worth checking ahead by phone. ⊠ *Via VIII Febbraio* ☎ *049/8275111 University switchboard* ⊕ *www.unipd.it* ⊠ *€5* ⊙ *Nov.–Feb., Mon., Wed., and Fri. at 3:15 and 4:15, Tues., Thurs., and Sat. at 10:15 and 11:15; Mar.–Oct., Mon., Wed., and Fri. at 3:15, 4:15, and 5:15; Tues., Thurs., and Sat. at 9:15, 10:15, and 11:15.*

WHERE TO EAT

$ NORTHERN ITALIAN

🍴 **Enoteca dei Tadi.** In this cozy and atmospheric cross between a wine bar and a restaurant you can put together an inexpensive dinner from the various classic dishes on offer. Portions are small, but so are the prices—just follow the local custom and order a selection. Dishes are made with first-rate ingredients and are coupled with a fine selection of wines. Start with fresh *burrata* (mozzarella's creamier, richer cousin) with tomatoes, or choose from a selection of *prosciutto crudo* or salamis. Don't pass up the house specialty, lasagna, with several kinds are on the menu. Main courses are limited, but include a savory Veneto stew with polenta. [$] *Average meal: €25* ✉ *Via dei Tadi 16, Padua* ☎ *049/8364099, 388/4083434 cell phone* 🌐 *www.enotecadeitadi.it* ✍ *Reservations essential* 🕒 *Closed Mon. No lunch.*

$$$ MODERN ITALIAN

🍴 **La Finestra.** One of the trendier restaurants in Padua, La Finestra is cozy yet elegant. The carefully prepared and creatively presented dishes may not always stick to tradition, but no one can claim that owners Carlo Vidali and Hélène Dao don't know what they're doing in the kitchen. Try their wonderful black bean soup with ginger, prawns and sour cream—not grandma's bean soup, but it's heavenly—followed by seared tuna with saffron and onions, or a more traditional beef tagliata with rosmary. The service is attentive and helpful. [$] *Average meal: €55* ✉ *Via dei Tadi 15* ☎ *049/650313* 🌐 *www.ristorantefinestra.it* ✍ *Reservations essential* 🕒 *Closed Mon., first week in Feb. and 3 wks in Aug. No lunch Tues.–Thurs. No dinner Sun.*

$ WINE BAR

🍴 **L'Anfora.** This mix between a traditional *bacaro* (wine bar) and an *osteria* (tavernlike restaurant) is a local institution. Stand at the bar shoulder-to-shoulder with a cross-section of Padovano society, from construction workers to professors, and let the friendly and knowledgeable proprietors help you choose a wine. The reasonably priced menu offers simple *casalinga* (home-cooked dishes), plus salads and a selection of cheeses. Portions are ample, and no one will look askance if you don't order the full meal. The place is packed with loyal regulars at lunchtime, so come early or expect a wait. [$] *Average meal: €27* ✉ *Via Soncin 13* ☎ *049/656629* 🕒 *Closed Sun. (except in Dec.), 1 wk in Jan., and 1 wk in Aug.*

$$$$ MODERN ITALIAN

🍴 **Le Calandre.** If you are willing to shell out around €500 for a dinner for two and are gastronomically adventurous, include quietly elegant Le Calandre on your itinerary: major critics consistently judge it to be one of Italy's top three restaurants. Traditional Veneto recipes are given a highly sophisticated and creative treatment—traditional squid in its ink comes as a "cappuccino," in a glass with a crust of potato foam—while dishes such as sole with a grapefruit and curry sauce leave the Veneto far behind. Owner-chef Massimiliano Alajmo's creative impulses, together with seasonal changes, augment the signature dishes, but Alajmo considers food to be an art form rather than nourishment, so be prepared for minuscule portions. Reserve well in advance. [$] *Average meal: €220* ✉ *Via Liguria 1, 7 km (4 miles) west of Padua, Sarmeola di Rubano* ☎ *049/630303* 🌐 *www.calandre.com* ✍ *Reservations essential* 🕒 *Closed Sun. and Mon., Jan. 1–17, and Aug. 14–31.*

$$ ✕**Osteria Dal Capo.** A friendly trat-
VENETIAN toria in the heart of what used to
be Padua's Jewish ghetto, Osteria
Dal Capo serves almost exclu-
sively traditional Veneto dishes
and does so with refinement and
care. The liver and onions is
extraordinarily tender. Even the
accompanying polenta is grilled to
perfection—slightly crisp on the
outside and moist on the inside.
And the desserts are nothing to
scoff at, either. Word is out among
locals about this place, and the
tiny place fills up quickly, so res-
ervations are necessary. $ *Aver-
age meal: €35 ⊠ Via degli Oblizzi
2 ☎049/663105 ☝ Reservations
essential ☾ Closed Sun., 2 wks in
early Jan., and 3 wks in Aug. No
lunch Mon.*

> ### COCKTAIL HOUR ON PADUA'S PIAZZAS
>
> One of Padua's greatest traditions is the outdoor en-masse consumption of aperitifs: *spritz* (a mix of Aperol or Campari, soda water, and wine), prosecco (sparkling wine), or wine. It all happens in the Piazza delle Erbe and Piazza delle Frutta. Several bars there provide drinks in plastic cups, so you can take them outside and mingle among the crowds. The ritual, practiced primarily by students, begins at 6 or so, at which hour you can also pick up a snack from one of the outdoor vendors. On weekends, the open-air revelry continues into the wee hours.

WHERE TO STAY

For expanded hotel reviews, visit Fodors.com.

$ 🛏**Al Fagiano.** This delightfully funky budget hotel sits near Basilica
HOTEL di Sant'Antonio, and some rooms have views of the church's spires
and cupolas. **Pros:** large rooms; relaxed atmosphere; convenient loca-
tion. **Cons:** no room service or help with baggage; some find the eccen-
tric decoration a bit much. $ *Rooms from: €75 ⊠ Via Locatelli 45
☎049/8750073 ⊕ www.alfagiano.com ➽40 rooms ⦿No meals.*

$$ 🛏**Albergo Verdi.** Close to the Piazza dei Signori, this is one of the best-
HOTEL situated hotels in the city. **Pros:** excellent location; attentive staff; pleas-
ant and warm atmosphere; quiet. **Cons:** rooms, while ample, are not
large; few views; charge for WiFi access; hefty parking fee. $ *Rooms
from: €150 ⊠ Via Dondi dell'Orlogio 7 ☎049/8364163 ⊕www.
albergoverdipadova.it ➽14 rooms ⦿Breakfast.*

$ 🛏**Methis.** Strikingly modern, this hotel takes its name from the Greek
HOTEL word for style and spirit. **Pros:** attractive rooms; helpful and attentive
staff; pleasant little extras like umbrellas. **Cons:** a 15-minute walk from
major sights and restaurants; public spaces are cold and uninviting.
$ *Rooms from: €120 ⊠ Riviera Paleocapa 70 ☎049/8725555 ⊕ www.
methishotel.com ➽52 rooms, 7 suites ⦿Breakfast.*

NIGHTLIFE AND THE ARTS

CAFES AND WINE BARS

Fodor'sChoice **Caffè Pedrocchi.** No visit to Padua is complete without a trip to Caffè
★ Pedrocchi. You can still sit here, as the French writer Stendahl did
shortly after the café was established in 1831, and observe a good slice

of Veneto life, especially, as he noted, the elegant ladies sipping their coffee. Built in a style reflecting the fashion set by Napoléon's expeditions in Egypt, the massive café has long been central to the city's social life. Its restaurant also serves lunch (12:30 to 2:30), and is proud of its innovative menu. ⊠ *Piazzetta Pedrocchi* ☎ *049/8781231* ⊕ *www. caffepedrocchi.it.*

Hostaria Ai Do Archi. The most popular local *bacari*, the Ai Do Archi is famous for its impressive platters of sliced meats, its selections of wine, and as a meeting place for Padova's reggae fans. The music can be overwhelming, there are very few tables so you may have to stand all evening, and the service a bit casual, but if reggae is your passion or you want a good taste of Padua student nightlife, this is the place. ⊠ *Via Nazario Sauro 23* ☎ *049/652335.*

Prato della Valle. Surrounded by a canal and 78 statues, parklike Prato della Valle hosts a Saturday market where you can buy everything from clothes to kitchenware; there's an antiques market here on the third Sunday of every month.

VICENZA

Vicenza bears the distinctive signature of the 16th-century architect Andrea Palladio, whose name has been given to the "Palladian" style of architecture. He emphasized the principles of order and harmony using the classical style of architecture established by Renaissance architects such as Brunelleschi, Alberti, and Sansovino. He used these principles and classical motifs not only for public buildings but also for private dwellings. His elegant villas and palaces were influential in propagating classical architecture in Europe, especially Britain, and later in America—most notably at Thomas Jefferson's Monticello.

In the mid-16th century Palladio was commissioned to rebuild much of Vicenza, which had been greatly damaged during wars waged against Venice by the League of Cambrai (1505), an alliance of the papacy, France, the Holy Roman Empire, and several neighboring city-states. He made his name with the renovation of the Basilica, begun in 1549 in the heart of Vicenza, and then embarked on a series of lordly buildings, all of which adhere to the same classicism and principles of harmony.

GETTING HERE AND AROUND
Vicenza is midway between Padua and Verona, and several trains leave from both cities every hour. By car, take the Autostrada Brescia–Padova/Torino–Trieste A4/E70 to SP247 North directly into Vicenza.

VISITOR INFORMATION
Vicenza Tourism Office ⊠ *Piazza Giacomo Matteotti 12* ☎ *0444/320854* ⊕ *www.vicenzae.org.*

EXPLORING VICENZA

TOP ATTRACTIONS

Fodor's Choice
★

Teatro Olimpico. Palladio's last, and perhaps most spectacular work, was begun in 1580 and completed in 1585, after his death, by Vincenzo Scamozzi (1552–1616). Based closely on the model of ancient Roman theaters, it represents an important development in theater and stage design and is noteworthy for its acoustics and the cunning use of perspective in Scamozzi's permanent backdrop. The anterooms are frescoed with images of important figures in Venetian history. As the oldest surviving covered theater, it's still used for concerts and other performances. ⊠ *Piazza Matteotti* ☎ *0444/222800* ⊕ *www.teatrolimpico.it* ✍ *€8.50, includes admission to Palazzo Chiericati* ☉ *Tues.–Sun. 9–5.*

Fodor's Choice
★

Villa della Rotonda (Villa Almerico Capra). This beautiful Palladian villa, commissioned in 1556 as a suburban residence for Paolo Almerico, is undoubtedly the purest expression of Palladio's architectural theory and aesthetic. It's more a villa-temple than a residence, and in this respect it contradicts the rational utilitarianism of Renaissance architecture. Rather, it can be called a prime example of mannerist architecture, demonstrating the priority Palladio gave to architectural symbolism of celestial harmony over practical considerations. Although a visit to view the interior may be difficult to schedule—it's still privately owned—it is well worth the effort in order to get an idea of how the people who commissioned the villa actually lived. Even without a peek inside, viewing the exterior and the grounds is a must for any visit to Vicenza. The villa is a 20-minute walk from town or a short ride on bus 8 from Vicenza's Piazza Roma. ⊠ *Via della Rotonda* ☎ *0444/321793* ⊕ *www.villalarotonda.it* ✍ *€10; grounds only €5* ☉ *Villa interior: Mar. 13–early Nov., Wed. 10–noon and 3–6. Grounds: Mar. 13–early Nov., Tues.–Sun. 10–noon and 3–6; early Nov.–Mar. 12, Tues.–Sun. 10–noon and 2:30–5. Hours may be modified during inclement weather.*

Fodor's Choice
★

Villa Valmarana ai Nani. Inside this 17th- to 18th-century country house, named for the statues of dwarfs adorning the garden, is a series of frescoes executed in 1757 by Giambattista Tiepolo depicting scenes from classical mythology, *The Illiad*, Tasso's *Gerusalemme Liberata*, and Ariosto's *Orlando Furioso*. They include his *Sacrifice of Iphigenia*, a major masterpiece of 18th-century painting. The neighboring *foresteria* (guest house) is also part of the museum; it contains frescoes showing 18th-century life at its most charming, and scenes of chinoiserie popular in the 18th century, by Tiepolo's son Giandomenico (1727–1804). The garden dwarves are probably taken from designs by Giandomenico. You can reach the villa on foot by following the same path that leads to Palladio's Villa della Rotonda. ⊠ *Via dei Nani 2/8* ☎ *0444/321803* ✉ *valmarana@villavalmarana. com* ⊕ *www.villavalmarana.com* ✍ *€9* ☉ *Early Mar.–early Nov., Tues.–Sun. 10–12:30 and 3–6. Visits at other times are possible at an additional price; to arrange, contact by phone or email.*

WORTH NOTING

Palazzo Chiericati. This imposing Palladian palazzo (1550) would be worthy of a visit even if it didn't house Vicenza's **Museo Civico.** Because of the ample space surrounding the building, Palladio combined elements of an urban palazzo with those he used in his country villas. The museum's important Venetian collection includes significant paintings by Cima, Tiepolo, Piazetta, and Tintoretto, but its main attraction is an extensive collection of highly interesting and rarely found painters from the Vicenza area, such as Jacopo Bassano (1515–92) and the eccentric and innovative Francesco Maffei (1605–60), whose work foreshadowed important currents of Venetian painting of subsequent generations. ✉ *Piazza Matteotti* ☎ *0444/325071* 🎟 *€8.50 includes admission to Teatro Olimpico* ⏲ *Tues.–Sun. 9–5.*

Piazza dei Signori. At the heart of Vicenza, this square contains the **Palazzo della Ragione** (1549), commonly known as Palladio's basilica, a courthouse, and public meeting hall (the original Roman meaning of the term "basilica"). With this project Palladio made his name by successfully modernizing the medieval building, grafting a graceful two-story exterior loggia onto the existing Gothic structure. The palazzo is open only when it houses exhibits, but the building's main point of interest is the loggia, which is visible from the piazza. Take a look also at the **Loggia del Capitaniato,** opposite, which Palladio designed but never completed.

WHERE TO EAT

$$ NORTHERN ITALIAN 🍴 **Antico Ristorante agli Schioppi.** When they want to eat well, Vicentini generally head to the countryside, so it is telling that this is one of the few restaurants in the city frequented by local families and the business community. In Veneto country style, with enormous murals, it offers simple, well-prepared regional cuisine with some modern touches. The risotto, delicately flavored with wild mushrooms and zucchini flowers, is creamy and beautifully textured—or try the Vicenza specialty baccalà. The "Menu Palladiana" presents 16th-century dishes featuring spices common during that period, such as cinnamon and cloves, and omitting items like tomatoes and potatoes, which were new to Europe at that time. [$] *Average meal: €35* ✉ *Contrà Piazza del Castello 26* ☎ *0444/543701* 🌐 *www.ristoranteaglischioppi.com* ⏲ *Closed Sun. No lunch Mon.*

$ PIZZA 🍴 **Da Vittorio.** It has little in the way of atmosphere or style, but Vicentini flock to this small, casual place for what may be the best pizza north of Naples. There's an incredible array of toppings, from the traditional to the exotic (mangoes), but the pizzas are all so authentic that they will make you think you are sitting by the Bay of Naples. The service is friendly and efficient. This is a great place to stop for lunch if you're walking to Palladio's Rotonda or the Villa Valmarana. [$] *Average meal: €14* ✉ *Borgo Berga 52* ☎ *0444/525059* 💳 *No credit cards* ⏲ *Closed Tues. and 2 wks in July.*

$$ NORTHERN ITALIAN 🍴 **Ponte delle Bele.** Vicenza lies at the foot of the Alps, and many wealthier residents spend at least a part of summer in the mountains to escape the heat. The Alpine cuisine that's been incorporated into the local

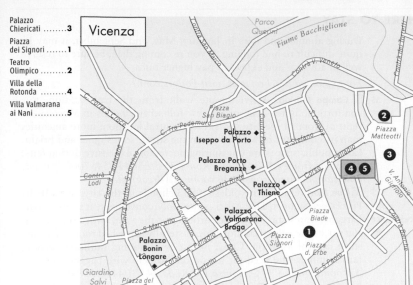

culture can be enjoyed at this popular and friendly Veneto trattoria. The house specialty, *stinco di maiale al forno* (roast port shank), is wonderfully fragrant, with herbs and aromatic vegetables. Game dishes include venison with blueberries and guinea fowl roasted with white grapes. They're also justly proud of their baccalà alla vicentina, served with polenta. The rather kitschy interior in no way detracts from the good, hearty food. $ *Average meal: €35* ⊠ *Contrà Ponte delle Bele 5* ☎ *0444/320647* ⊕ *www.pontedellebele.it* ☉ *Closed Sun. and 2 wks in mid-Aug.*

$ ✕ **Righetti.** For a city of its size, Vicenza has few outstanding restaurants.

ITALIAN That's why many people gravitate to this popular cafeteria, which serves excellently prepared classic dishes without putting a dent in your wallet. There's frequently a hearty soup such as *orzo e fagioli* (barley and bean) on the menu. The classic baccalà alla vicentina is a great reason to stop by on Tuesday or Friday. Righetti tends to be a bit crowded at lunch, so be patient. It's also open until 10 or so for dinner. $ *Average meal: €14* ⊠ *Piazza Duomo 3* ☎ *0444/543135* ▭ *No credit cards* ☉ *Closed weekends, 1st wk in Jan., and Aug.*

WHERE TO STAY

During annual gold fairs in January, May, and September, it may be quite difficult to find lodging. If you're coming then, be sure to reserve well in advance and expect to pay higher rates.

For expanded hotel reviews, visit Fodors.com.

$$ HOTEL **Campo Marzio.** A five-minute walk from the train station, this comfortable hotel—one of the few full-service hotels in Vicenza—is right in front of the city walls. **Pros:** central location; more amenities than its competitors; set back from the street, so it's quiet and bright. **Cons:** public spaces are uninspiring; incredibly expensive during fairs. [$] *Rooms from: €140* ✉ *Viale Roma 21* ☎ *0444/5457000* 🌐 *www.hotelcampomarzio.com* *36 rooms* 🍴 *Breakfast.*

$ HOTEL Fodor's Choice ★ **Due Mori.** One of the oldest (1883) hotels in the city, just off the Piazza dei Signori, Due Mori is not only convenient, it's also a true bargain—rates stay the same throughout the year, with no high-season price hikes. **Pros:** comfortable, tastefully furnished rooms; friendly staff; central location. **Cons:** no air-conditioning (although ceiling fans minimize the need for it); no one to help with baggage; no TV. [$] *Rooms from: €90* ✉ *Contrà Do Rode 24* ☎ *0444/321886* 🌐 *www.hotelduemori.com* *53 rooms* 🕒 *Closed 1st 2 wks of Aug. and 2 wks in late Dec.* 🍴 *No meals.*

VERONA

On the banks of the fast-flowing River Adige, enchanting Verona, 60 km (37 miles) west of Vicenza, has timeless monuments, a picturesque town center, and a romantic reputation as the setting of Shakespeare's *Romeo and Juliet.* With its lively Venetian air and proximity to Lake Garda, it attracts hordes of tourists, especially Germans and Austrians. Tourism peaks during summer's renowned season of open-air opera in the arena and during spring's **Vinitaly** (✉ *Fiera di Verona, Viale del Lavoro 8* ☎ *045/829817* 🌐 *www.vinitaly.com*), one of the world's most important wine expos. For five days you can sample the wines of more than 3,000 wineries from dozens of countries.

Verona grew to power and prosperity within the Roman Empire as a result of its key commercial and military position in northern Italy. With its Roman arena, theater, and city gates, it has the most significant monuments of Roman antiquity north of Rome. After the fall of the empire, the city continued to flourish under the guidance of barbarian kings such as Theodoric, Alboin, Pepin, and Berenger I, reaching its cultural and artistic peak in the 13th and 14th centuries under the della Scala (Scaligero) dynasty. (Look for the *scala*, or ladder, emblem all over town.) In 1404 Verona traded its independence for security and placed itself under the control of Venice. (The other recurring architectural motif is the lion of Saint Mark, a symbol of Venetian rule.)

If you're going to visit more than one or two sights, it's worth purchasing a VeronaCard, available at museums, churches, and tobacconists for €15 (two days) or €20 (five days). It buys a single admission to most of the city's significant museums and churches, plus you can ride

Continued on page 280

PALLADIO COUNTRY

Wealthy 16th-century patrons commissioned Andrea Palladio to design villas that would reflect their sense of cultivation and status. Using a classical vocabulary of columns, arches, and domes, he gave them a series of masterpieces in the towns and hills of the Veneto that exemplify the neo-Platonic ideals of harmony and proportion. Palladio's creations are the perfect expression of how a learned 16th century man saw himself and his world, and as you stroll through them today, their serene beauty is as powerful as ever. Listen closely and you might even hear that celestial harmony, the music of the spheres, that so moved Palladio and his patrons.

TOWN & COUNTRY

Although the villa, or "country residence," was still a relatively new phenomenon in the 16th century, it quickly became all the rage once the great lords of Venice turned their eyes from the sea toward the fertile plains of the Veneto. They were forced to do this once their trade routes had faltered when Ottoman Turks conquered Constantinople in 1456 and Columbus opened a path to the riches of America in 1492. In no time, canals were built, farms were laid out, and the fashion for *villeggiatura*—the attraction of idyllic country retreats for the nobility—became a favored lifestyle. As a means of escaping an overheated Rome,

villas had been the original brainchild of the ancient emperors and it was no accident that the Venetian lords wished to emulate this palatial style of country residence. Palladio's method of evaluating the standards, and standbys, of ancient Roman life through the eye of the Italian Renaissance, combined with Palladio's innate sense of proportion and symmetry, became the lasting foundation of his art. In turn, Palladio threw out the jambalaya of styles prevalent in Venetian architecture—Oriental, Gothic, and Renaissance—for the pure, noble lines found in the buildings of the Caesars.

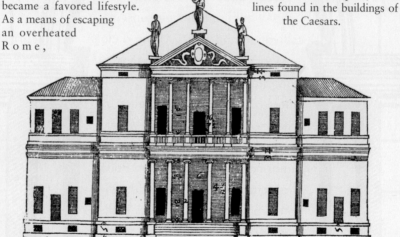

PALLADIO, STAR ARCHITECT

Andrea Palladio (1508–1580)

"Face dark, eyes fiery. Dress rich. His appearance that of a genius." So was Palladio described by his wealthy mentor, Count Trissino. Trissino encouraged the young student to trade in his birth name, Andrea di Pietro della Gondola, for the elegant Palladio. He did, and it proved a wise move indeed. Born in Padua in 1508, Andrea moved to nearby Vicenza in 1524 and was quickly taken up by the city's power elite. He experienced a profound revela-

THE OLD BECOMES NEW

La Malcontenta

Studying ancient Rome with the eyes of an explorer, Palladio employed a style that linked old with new—but often did so in unexpected ways. Just take a look at Villa Foscari, nicknamed **"La Malcontenta"** (Mira, 041/5470012, www.lamalcontenta.com €10. Open May–Oct., Tues. and Sat. 9–noon; from Venice, take an ACTV bus from Piazzale Roma to Mira or opt for a boat ride up on the Burchiello). Shaded by weeping willows and mirrored by the Brenta Canal, "The Sad Lady" was built for Nicolò and Alvise Foscari and is the quintessence of Palladian poetry. Inspired by the grandeur of Roman public buildings, Palladio applied the ancient motif of a temple facade to a domestic dwelling, topped off by a pediment, a construct most associated with religious structures. Inside, he used the technique of vaulting seen in ancient Roman baths, with giant windows and immense white walls ready-made for the colorful frescoes painted by Zelotti. No one knows for certain the origin of the villa's nickname—some say it came from a Venetian owner's wife who was exiled there due to her scandalous behavior. Regardless of the name, it's hard today to associate such a beautiful, graceful villa with anything but harmony and contentment.

tion on his first trip, in 1541, to Rome, where he sensed the harmony of the ancient ruins and saw the elements of classicism that were working their way into contemporary architecture. This experience led to his spectacular conversion of the Vicenza's Palazzo della Ragione (1545) into a basilica recalling the great meeting halls of antiquity. In years to come, after relocating to Venice, he created some memorable churches, such as S. Giorgio Maggiore (1564). Despite these varied projects, Palladio's unassailable position as one of the world's greatest architects is tied to the countryside villas, which he spread across the Veneto plains like a firmament of stars. Nothing else in the Veneto illuminates more clearly the idyllic beauty of the region than these elegant residences, their stonework now nicely mellowed and suntanned after five centuries.

VICENZA, CITY OF PALLADIO

Palazzo della Ragione

La Rotonda

To see Palladio's pageant of palaces, head for Vicenza. His **Palazzo della Ragione**, or "Basilica," marks the city's heart, the Piazza dei Signori. This building rocketed young Palladio from an unknown to an architectural star. Across the way is his redbrick **Loggia dei Capitaniato**.

One block past the Loggia is Vicenza's main street, appropriately named Corso Andrea Palladio. Just off this street is the Contrà Porti, where you'll find the **Palazzo Barbaran da Porto** (1570) at No. 11, with its fabulously rich facade erupting with Ionic and Corinthian pillars. Today, this is the Centro Internazionale di Studi di Architettura Andrea Palladio (0444/323014, www.cisapalladio.org), a study center which mounts impressive temporary exhibitions. A few steps away, on the Contrà San Gaetano Thiene, is the Palazzo Thiene (1542-58), designed by Giulio Romano and completed by Palladio.

Doubling back to Contrà Porti 21, you find the **Palazzo Iseppo da Porto** (1544), the first palazzo where you can see the neoclassical effects of young Palladio's trip to Rome. Following the Contrà Reale, you come to Corso Fogazzaro 16 and the **Palazzo Valmarana Braga** (1565). Its gigantic pilasters were a first for domestic architecture.

Returning to the Corso Palladio, head left to the opposite end of the Corso, about five blocks, to the Piazza Mattoti and **Palazzo Chiericati** (1550). This was practically a suburban area in the 16th century, and for the palazzo Palladio combined elements of urban and rural design. The pedestal raising the building and the steps leading to the entrance—unknown in urban palaces—were to protect from floods and to keep cows from wandering in the front door. (For opening times and details, see the main text).

Across the Corso Palladio is Palladio's last and one of his most spectacular works, the **Teatro Olimpico** (1580). By careful study of ancient ruins and architectural texts, he reconstructed a Roman theater with archaeological precision. Palladio died before it was completed, but he left clear plans for the project. (For opening times and details, see the main text.)

Although it's on the outskirts of town, the **Villa Almerico Capra**, better known as **La Rotonda** (1566), is an indispensable part of any visit to Vicenza. It's the iconic Palladian building, the purest expression of his aesthetic. (For opening times, details, and a discussion of the villa, see the main text.)

A MAGNIFICENT COLLABORATION

Villa Barbaro

At the **Villa Barbaro** (1554) near the town of Maser in the province of Treviso, 48 km (30 miles) northeast of Vicenza, you can see the results of a one-time collaboration between two of the greatest artists of their age.

Palladio was the architect, and Paolo Veronese decorated the interior with an amazing cycle of trompe l'oeil frescoes—walls dissolve into landscapes, and illusions of courtiers and servants enter rooms and smile down from balustrades.

Legend has it a feud developed between Palladio and Veronese, with Palladio feeling the illusionistic frescoes detracted from his architecture; but there is practically nothing to support the idea of such a rift.

It's also noteworthy that Palladio for the first time connected the two lateral granaries to the main villa. This was a working farm, and Palladio thus created an architectural unity by connecting with graceful arcades the working parts of the estate to the living quarters, bringing together the Renaissance dichotomy of the active and the contemplative life. *Via Cornuda 7, Maser, 0432/923004 www.villadimaser. it , €6, Open Nov.–Feb., weekends 11–5; Apr.–June, and Sept.–Oct., Tues.–Sat. 10–6, Sun. 11–6; Mar., July–Aug., Tues., Thurs, Sat. 10:30–6, Sun. 11–6.*

ALONG THE BRENTA CANAL

During the 16th century the Brenta was transformed into a landlocked version of Venice's Grand Canal with the building of nearly 50 waterside villas.

Back then, boating parties viewed them in *"burchielli"*—beautiful boats. Today, the Burchiello excursion boat (Via Orlandini 3, Padua, 049/8206910, www.ilburchiello. it) makes full- and half-day tours along the Brenta, from March to November, departing from Padua and Venice Tues.–Sun., running in both directions; tickets are €55–€95 and can also be bought at travel agencies. You visit three houses, including the Villas Pisani and Foscari, with a lunchtime break in Oriago (€30 extra). Note that most houses are on the left side coming from Venice, or the right from Padua.

free on city buses. If you're mostly interested in churches, a €6 Chiese Vive Card is sold at Verona's major houses of worship and gains you entry to the Duomo, San Fermo Maggiore, San Zeno Maggiore, and Sant'Anastasia. Note that Verona's churches strictly enforce their dress code: no sleeveless shirts, shorts, or short skirts.

GETTING HERE AND AROUND

Verona is midway between Venice and Milan. It's served by a small airport, Aeroporto Valerio Catullo, which accommodates domestic and European flights; however, many travelers still prefer to fly into Venice or Milan and drive or take the train to Verona. Several trains per hour depart from any point on the Milan–Venice line. By car, from the east or west, take the Autostrada Trieste–Torino A4/E70 to the SS12 and follow it north into town. From the north or south, take the Autostrada del Brennero A22/E45 to the SR11 East (initially, called the Strada Bresciana) directly into town.

VISITOR INFORMATION

Verona Tourism Office ⊠ Piazza Brà, Via Degli Alpini 9 ☎ 045/8068680 ⊕ www.tourism.verona.it.

EXPLORING VERONA

TOP ATTRACTIONS

Fodor'sChoice
★
Ancient City Gates/Triumphal Arch. In addition to ancient Verona's famous arena and Roman theater, two of its city gates and a beautiful triumphal arch have survived. These graceful and elegant portals give us an idea of the high aesthetic standards of the time. The oldest, the Porta dei Leoni (on Via Leoni, just a few steps from Piazza delle Erbe), dates from the 1st century BC, but its original earth-and-brick structure was sheathed in local marble during early Imperial times. The Porta dei Borsari was, as its elegant decoration suggests, the main entrance to ancient Verona, and, in its present state, dates from the 1st century AD. It's at the beginning of Corso Porta Borsari, just a few steps from the opposite side of Piazza della Erbe. Continuing down Corso Cavour, which starts on the other (front) side of Porta dei Borsari, you can find the beautiful Arco dei Gavi, which is simpler and less imposing, but also more graceful, than the triumphal arches in Rome. It was built in the 1st century AD by the architect Lucius Vitruvius Cerdo to celebrate the accomplishments of the patrician Gavia family. It was highly esteemed by several Renaissance architects, including Palladio.

FAMILY
Fodor'sChoice
★
Arena di Verona. Only Rome's Colosseum and Capua's arena would dwarf this amphitheater. Though four arches are all that remain of the arena's outer arcade, the main structure is complete. It dates from the early Imperial age, and was used for gymnastic competitions, choreographed sacrificial rites, and games involving hunts, fights, battles, and wild animals. Unlike at Rome's Colosseum, there is no evidence that Christians were ever put to death here. Today you can visit the arena year-round; in summer, you can join up to 16,000 people packing the stands for one of Verona's spectacular opera productions. Even those who aren't crazy about opera can sit in the stands and enjoy Italians enjoying themselves—including, at times, singing along with

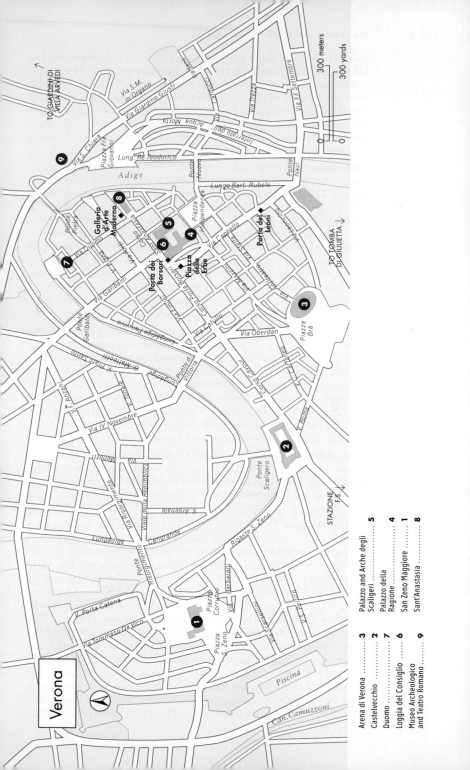

Verona

Arena di Verona	3	
Castelvecchio	2	
Duomo	7	
Loggia del Consiglio	6	
Museo Archeologico and Teatro Romano	9	
Palazzo and Arche degli Scaligeri	5	
Palazzo della Ragione	4	
San Zeno Maggiore	1	
Sant'Anastasia	8	

300 meters
300 yards

their favorite hits. Note that the open hours are sometimes reduced in the late fall and winter. ■ **TIP→** The main interest is to see an opera in the arena; when there is no opera performance, for €6 you can still enter the interior, but be aware that the Arena di Verona is much less impressive inside than the Colosseum or other Roman amphitheaters. ⊠ *Piazza Brà 5* ☎ *045/596517* ⊕ *www.arena.it* ✍ *€6, free with Chiese Vive and VeronaCard* ⊙ *8:30–7:30 (closes at 5 on days when operas are performed).*

Fodor's Choice ★ **Castelvecchio.** This crenellated, russet brick building with massive walls, towers, turrets, and a vast courtyard was built for Cangrande II della Scala in 1354. It presides over a street lined with attractive old buildings and palaces of the nobility. Only by going inside the **Museo di Castelvecchio** can you really appreciate this massive castle complex with its vaulted halls. You also get a look at a significant collection of Venetian art, medieval weapons, and jewelry. The interior of the castle was restored and redesigned as a museum between 1958 and 1975 by the notable architect Carlo Scarpa. Behind the castle is the Ponte Scaligero (1355), which spans the River Adige. ⊠ *Corso Castelvecchio 2* ☎ *045/8062611* ✍ *€6, free with Chiese Vive and VeronaCard* ⊙ *Mon. 1:30–7:30, Tues.–Sun. 8:30–7:30; last entry 6:45.*

Duomo. The present church was begun in the 12th century in the Romanesque style; its later additions are mostly Gothic. On pilasters guarding the main entrance are 12th-century carvings thought to represent Oliver and Roland, two of Charlemagne's knights and heroes of several medieval epic poems. Inside, Titian's *Assumption* (1532) graces the first chapel on the left. ⊠ *Via Duomo* ☎ *045/592813* ⊕ *www.chieseverona.it* ✍ *€3, free with Chiese Vive and VeronaCard* ⊙ *Mar.–Oct., Mon.–Sat. 10–5:30, Sun. and holidays 1:30–5:30; Nov.–Feb., Mon.–Sat. 10–4, Sun. and holidays 1:30–4. Open at other times for religious purposes.*

Piazza delle Erbe. Frescoed buildings surround this beautiful medieval square, where a busy Roman forum once stood. During the week it's still bustling, as vendors hawk produce and trinkets, much as they have been doing for generations. Relax at one of the cafés and take in the lively scene.

Fodor's Choice ★ **San Zeno Maggiore.** One of Italy's finest Romanesque churches, San Zeno Maggiore has a rose window by the 13th-century sculptor Brioloto. It represents a wheel of fortune, with six of the spokes formed by statues depicting the rising and falling fortunes of mankind. The 12th-century porch is the work of Maestro Niccolò. Eighteen 12th-century marble reliefs flanking the porch by Niccolò and Maestro Guglielmo depict scenes from the Old and New Testaments and scenes from the legend of Theodoric. The bronze doors are from the 11th and 12th centuries; some were probably imported from Saxony and some are from Veronese workshops. They combine allegorical representations with scenes from the lives of saints. Inside, look for the 12th-century statue of San Zeno to the left of the main altar. In modern times it has been dubbed the "Laughing San Zeno" because of a misinterpretation of its conventional Romanesque grin. A justly famous *Madonna and Saints* triptych by Andrea Mantegna (1431–1506) hangs over the main altar, and a peaceful cloister (1120–38) lies to the left of the nave. The detached bell tower was begun in 1045, before the construction of much of the present church, and finished in 1173. ⊠ *Piazza San Zeno* ☎ *045/592813* ⊕ *www.chieseverona.it* ✉ *€3, free with Chiese Vive and VeronaCard* ☻ *Nov.–Feb., Mon.–Sat. 10–1 and 1:30–5, Sun. 12:30–5; Mar.–Oct., Mon.–Sat. 8:30–6, Sun. 12:30–6.*

Sant'Anastasia. Verona's largest church, begun in 1290 but only consecrated in 1471, is a fine example of Gothic brickwork and has a grand doorway with elaborately carved biblical scenes. The main reason for visiting this church, however, is *St. George and the Princess* (dated 1434, but perhaps earlier) by Pisanello (1377–1455) above the Pellegrini Chapel off the main altar. As you come in, look also for the *gobbi* (hunchbacks) supporting holy-water stoups. ⊠ *Vicolo Sotto Riva 4* ☎ *045/592813* ✉ *€2.50, free with Chiese Vive and VeronaCard* ☻ *Nov.–Feb., Mon.–Sat. 10–1 and 1:30–5, Sun. 12:30–5; Mar.–Oct., Mon.–Sat. 9–6, Sun. 1–6.*

WORTH NOTING

Arche Scaligere. On a little square off the Piazza dei Signori are the fantastically sculpted Gothic tombs of the della Scalas, who ruled Verona during the late Middle Ages. The 19th-century English traveler and critic John Ruskin described the tombs as graceful places where people who have fallen asleep live. The tomb of Cangrande I (1291–1329) hangs over the portal of the adjacent church and is the work of the Maestro di Sant'Anastasia. The tomb of Mastino II, begun in 1345, has an elaborate baldachin, originally painted and gilded, and is surrounded by an iron grillwork fence and topped by an equestrian statue. The latest and most elaborate tomb is that of Cansignorio (1375), the work principally of Bonino di Campione. The major tombs are all visible from the street. ⊠ *Via Arche Scaligere.*

Loggia del Consiglio. This graceful structure on the north flank of the Piazza dei Signori was finished in 1492 and built to house city council meetings. Although the city was already under Venetian rule, Verona still had a certain degree of autonomy, which was expressed by the splendor of the loggia. Very strangely for a Renaissance building of this quality, its architect remains unknown, but it is undoubtedly the finest surviving example of late-15th-century architecture in Verona. The building is not open to the public, but the exterior is worth a visit. ⊠ *Piazza dei Signori.*

Museo Archeologico and Teatro Romano. Housed in a 15th-century former monastery, the museum's archeological collections were amassed largely out of the donated collections of Veronese citizens proud of their city's classical past. Though there are few blockbusters here, there are some very noteworthy pieces (especially among the bronzes), and it is interesting to see what was collected by cultured Veronese during the 17th to 19th centuries. The museum sits high above the Teatro Romano, ancient Verona's theater, dating from the 1st century AD, which is open to visitors. ⊠ *Rigaste del Redentore 2* ☎ *045/8000360* ✉ *€4.50, free with VeronaCard* ☻ *Mon. 1:30–7:30, Tues.–Sun. 8:30–7:30; last entry 6:45.*

Palazzo degli Scaligeri (Palazzo di Cangrande). The della Scalas ruled Verona from this stronghold, built at the end of the 13th century by Cangrande I. At that time Verona controlled the mainland Veneto from Treviso and Lombardy to Mantua and Brescia. The portal facing the Piazza dei Signori was added in 1533 by the accomplished Renaissance architect Michele Sanmicheli. You have to admire the palazzo from the outside, as it's not open to the public. ⊠ *Piazza dei Signori.*

Palazzo della Ragione. An elegant 15th-century pink marble staircase leads up from the *mercato vecchio* (old market) courtyard to the magistrates' chambers in this 12th-century palace, built at the intersection of the main streets of the ancient Roman city. The renovated interior is now used for occasional exhibitions of art from the Galleria dell'Arte Moderna, which was recently moved to this location. You can get the highest view in town from atop the attached 270-foot-high, romanesque Torre dei Lamberti. About 50 years after a lightning strike in 1403 knocked its top off, it was rebuilt and extended to its current height. ⊠ *Piazza dei Signori* ☎ *045/8032726* 🖂 *Free; tower €6 or free with VeronaCard* ☯ *Tower: daily 8:30–7:30 (until 8:30 in summer). Palazzo open only for exhibitions.*

WHERE TO EAT

$
NORTHERN
ITALIAN
✕ **Antica Osteria al Duomo.** This friendly side-street eatery, lined with old wood paneling and decked out with musical instruments, serves Veronese food to a Veronese crowd; they come for the local wine (€1 to €3 per glass) and to savor excellent versions of local dishes like *bigoli con sugo di asino* (thick whole-wheat spaghetti with sauce made from donkey meat) and *pastissada con polenta* (horse-meat stew with polenta). Don't be deterred by the unconventional meats—they're tender and delicious, and this is probably the best place in town to sample them. First-rate Veronese home cooking is reasonably priced and served by helpful, efficient staff. It's popular, so arrive early. Reservations are not possible on weekends. ⓢ *Average meal: €25* ⊠ *Via Duomo 7/A* ☎ *045/8007333* ☯ *Closed Sun. (except in Dec. and during wine fair).*

$$$$
NORTHERN
ITALIAN
✕ **Dodici Apostoli.** In a city where many high-end restaurants tend toward nouvelle cuisine, this highly esteemed restaurant is an exceptional place to enjoy classic dishes made with elegant variations on traditional recipes. Near Piazza delle Erbe, it stands on the foundations of a Roman temple. Specialties include gnocchi *di zucca e ricotta* (with squash and ricotta cheese) and *vitello alla Lessinia* (veal with mushrooms, cheese, and truffles) and a signature pasta e fagioli. ⓢ *Average meal: €70* ⊠ *Vicolo Corticella San Marco 3* ☎ *045/596999* ⊕ *www.12apostoli.it* ✍ *Reservations essential* ☯ *Closed Mon., 2 wks in Jan. and 2 wks in June. No dinner Sun.*

$$$$ MODERN ITALIAN 🍴 **Il Desco.** *Cucina dell'anima*—food of the soul—is how Chef Elia Rizzo describes his cuisine. True to Italian culinary traditions, he preserves natural flavors through quick cooking and selective ingredients, but tradition gives way to invention, even daring, in the combination of ingredients in dishes such as duck breast with grappa, grapes, and eggplant puree, or beef cheeks with goose liver and caramelized pears. Some find his creative combinations, such as adding truffles to a fish filet, difficult to understand. For a spendy gastronomic adventure, there's a multicourse tasting menu (€135, exclusive of wine). The interior is elegant, if overdone, with tapestries, paintings, and an impressive 16th-century lacunar ceiling. Service, while efficient, is not exactly friendly. [$] *Average meal: €120* ✉ *Via Dietro San Sebastiano 7* ☎ *045/595358* ✍ *Reservations essential* 🕒 *Closed Sun. and Mon. (open for dinner Mon. in July, Aug., and Dec.), 2 wks in June and Christmas wk.*

$$$ MODERN ITALIAN 🍴 **Ostaria La Fontanina.** Veronese go to La Fontanina to enjoy a sumptuous meal under vine-covered balconies on a quiet street in one of the oldest sections of town. The Tapparini family takes great pride in the kitchen's modern versions of traditional dishes. There are such standards as risotto *al Amarone* made with Verona's treasured red wine, and an excellent version of baccalà, or for the more adventurous, a luscious wild boar confit with a savory fruit sauce laced with *ricioto,* Verona's famous sweet wine. There are several reasonably priced set menus. [$] *Average meal: €60* ✉ *Portichiette fontanelle S. Stefano 3* ☎ *045/913305* 🌐 *www.ristorantelafontanina.com* ✍ *Reservations essential* 🕒 *Closed Sun., 1 wk in Jan., and 2 wks in Aug. No lunch Mon.*

WHERE TO STAY

Book hotels months in advance for spring's Vinitaly, usually the second week in April, and for opera season. Verona hotels are also very busy during the January, May, and September gold fairs in neighboring Vicenza. Hotels jack up prices considerably at all these times.

For expanded hotel reviews, visit Fodors.com.

$$$ HOTEL 🏨 **Hotel Accademia.** The columns and arches of this hotel's stately facade are a good indication of what you can discover inside: an elegant, full-service, historic hotel in the center of old Verona. **Pros:** central location; old-world charm; up-to-date services. **Cons:** expensive parking; few standard rooms; prices go way up during the summer opera season and trade fairs. [$] *Rooms from: €225* ✉ *Via Scala 12* ☎ *045/596222* 🌐 *www.accademiavr.it* 🛏 *93 rooms* 🍽 *Breakfast.*

$$$$ HOTEL 🏨 **Hotel Victoria.** Busy business executives and tourists seeking a bit of pampering frequent this full-service hotel near the Piazza delle Erbe. **Pros:** quiet and tasteful rooms; central location; good business center. **Cons:** no views; expensive parking (and rates); staff not particularly helpful. [$] *Rooms from: €306* ✉ *Via Adua 8* ☎ *045/5905664* 🌐 *www.palazzovictoria.com* 🛏 *58 rooms, 13 suites* 🍽 *No meals.*

$ B&B/INN 🏨 **Torcolo.** In addition to a central location close to Piazza Brà, you can also count on this budget hotel for a warm welcome from the owners and courteous, helpful service. **Pros:** nice rooms; staff gives reliable advice. **Cons:** some street noise; no help with baggage; pricey parking.

[$] *Rooms from: €95* ✉ *Vicolo Listone 3* ☎ *045/8007512* 🌐 *www.hoteltorcolo.it* 🛏 *19 rooms* 🕒 *Closed Christmas and 2 wks in Jan. and Feb.* 🍴 *Breakfast.*

NIGHTLIFE AND THE ARTS

Fodor's Choice ★ **Arena di Verona.** Milan's La Scala or Parma's Teatro Regio offer performances more likely to satisfy serious opera fans, but none offers a greater spectacle than the Arena di Verona. Many Italian opera lovers claim their enthusiasm was initiated when they were taken as children to a production at the arena. During its summer season (July–September) audiences of as many as 16,000 sit on the original stone terraces or in modern cushioned stalls. Most of the operas presented are the big, splashy ones, like *Aïda* or *Turandot,* which demand huge choruses, lots of color and movement, and, if possible, camels, horses, or elephants. Order tickets by phone or online through the Arena website: if you book a spot on the cheaper terraces, be sure to take or rent a cushion—four hours on a 2,000-year-old stone bench can be an ordeal. ✉ *Box office, Via Dietro Anfiteatro 6/b* ☎ *045/8005151* 🌐 *www.arena.it* 🎫 *Tickets for most performances start at €21* 🕒 *Box office Sept.–June 20, weekdays 9–noon and 3:15–5:45, Sat. 9–noon; June –Aug (during the opera festival), performance days 10–9, non–performance days 10–5:45.*

FOOD AND WINE

Istituto Enologico Italiano. Verona is the epicenter of wine culture in northern Italy, and the shop run by the Istituto Enologico is undoubtedly the best place to sample and buy choice wines, not only from the Veneto, but from all over northern Italy. The atmospheric, historic wine cellar pairs a suberb shopping opportunity with a pleasant and informative cultural experience. ✉ *Via Sottoriva 7, Verona* ☎ *045/590366* 🌐 *www.istitutoenologico.it.*

TREVISO AND THE HILLSIDE TOWNS

North of Venice, the Dolomites spawn rivers and streams that flow through market towns dotting the foothills. Villa Barbaro, one of Palladio's most graceful country villas *(see the "Palladio Country" feature)*, is nearby, as are the arcaded streets and romantic canals of undiscovered Treviso and the graceful Venetian Gothic structures of smaller hill towns.

ASOLO

16 km (10 miles) east of Bassano del Grappa, 33 km (20½ miles) northwest of Treviso.

Fodor's Choice ★ Considered the most romantic and charming of Veneto towns, the visually striking hillside hamlet of Asolo is a top place to use as a base for touring the surrounding countryside—at the very least plan to stop here for lunch after a visit to the Palladian villa at Maser.

Through the centuries, Veneto aristocrats built elegant villas on the hillside, and in the 19th century Asolo became the idyllic haunt of musicians, poets, and painters. And it's no wonder why—this is one of

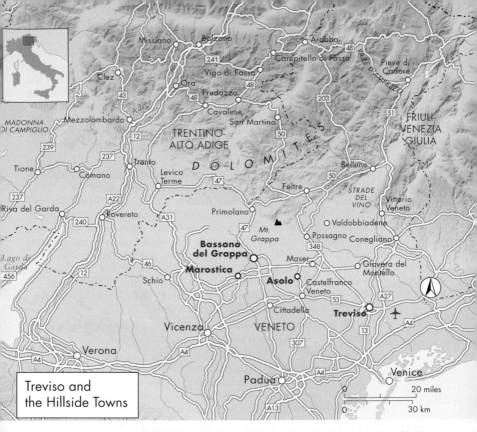

Treviso and
the Hillside Towns

Italy's most perfectly situated villages, with views across miles of hilly countryside. Be warned that the town's charm vaporizes on weekends and holidays when the crowds pour in. Even on weekdays, the village, given over to tourism and vacation houses, has almost no local population. Asolo hosts a modest antiques market on the second Sunday of every month except July and August.

GETTING HERE AND AROUND

There's no train station in Asolo; the closest one is in Montebelluna, 12 km (7½ miles) away. Bus connections are infrequent, and buses are not coordinated with trains, making it about a 2½-hour trip from Venice via public transportation. The best option is to drive.

By car from Treviso take Via Feltrina and continue onto Via Padre Agostino Gemelli (SR348). Follow SR348 about 16 km (10 miles), then turn left on SP667, which you follow for almost 4 km (2½ miles). At the roundabout, take the first exit, Via Monte Grappa (SP284) and follow it for 6½ km (4 miles) to Via Loredan, where you turn right and then left onto Via Bordo Vecchio. Asolo is less than 7 km (4½ miles) away from the Palladian Villa Barbaro at Maser.

VISITOR INFORMATION

Asolo Tourism Office ⊠ *Piazza Garibaldi* ☎ *0423/529046* ⊕ *www.asolo.it.*

EXPLORING

Brion Family Tomb. One of the major monuments of contemporary Italian architecture, the Brion family tomb was designed and built by the architect Carlo Scarpa (1906–78) between 1970 and 1972. Combining Western rationalism with Eastern spirituality, Scarpa avoids the gloom and bombast of conventional commemorative monuments, creating, in his words, a secluded Eden. ✉ *SP6, Via Castellan, about 7 km (4½ miles) south of Asolo, near village of San Vito* 🎟 *Free* ⏲ *Apr.–Sept., daily 8–7; Oct.–Mar., daily 9–3:30.*

Fodor's Choice ★ **Museo Canova (Gypsoteca).** The most significant cultural monument in the area is the Museo Canova (Gypsoteca), dedicated to the work of the Italian neoclassical sculptor Antonio Canova (1757–1822), whose sculptures are featured in many major European and North American museums. Set up shortly after the sculptor's death in his hometown, the village of Possagno, a short ride from Asolo, the gypsoteca houses most of the original plaster casts, models, and drawings made by the artist in preparation for his marble sculptures. In 1957 the museum was extended by the Italian architect Carlo Scarpa. ✉ *Via Canova 74, 13.5 km (8¼ miles) from Asolo, Possagno* ☎ *0423/544323* 🌐 *www.museocanova.it* 🎟 *€8* ⏲ *Tues.–Sun. 9:30–6.*

Piazza Maggiore. Renaissance palaces and long-established cafés grace this piazza, Asolo's town center.

Museo Civico. In the piazza, the frescoed 15th-century Loggia del Capitano contains the Museo Civico, which displays memorabilia—Eleonora Duse's correspondence, Robert Browning's spinet, and portraits of Caterina Cornaro. ✉ *Piazza Maggiore* ☎ *0423/952313* 🎟 *€5* ⏲ *Weekends 10–noon and 3–7, and by reservation*

QUICK BITES

Caffè Centrale. While away some idle moments at Caffè Centrale, which has overlooked the fountain in Piazza Maggiore and the Duomo since about 1700. Now half-café and half-tourist shop, it's open until 1 am. ✉ ***Via Roma 72*** ☎ ***0423/952141*** 🌐 ***www.caffecentrale.com*** ⏲ ***Closed Tues.***

Tempio Canoviano. This church, designed by Canova in 1819 and finished in 1830, combines motifs from the rotunda of the Roman Pantheon and the *pronaos* (inner portico) of the Parthenon. It contains several works by Canova, including his tomb, along with paintings by Luca Giordano, Palma il Giovane, and il Pordenone. One of the most impressive and historically significant neo-classical buildings in Italy, theTempio is in the village of Possagno, a short drive north of Asolo. ✉ *Piazza Canova, Possagno* ☎ *0423544323* ⏲ *Winter, daily 9–noon and 2–5; summer, daily 9–noon and 3–6.*

WHERE TO EAT

$ NORTHERN ITALIAN 🍴 **Al Bacaro.** This family-style restaurant offers affordable home-style food. Take the leap and try a dish with stewed game, tripe, or snails. Less adventurous diners can go for goulash, polenta with cheese and mushrooms, or one of Bacaro's open-face sandwiches, generously topped with fresh salami, speck, or other cold cuts. [$] *Average meal: €25* ✉ *Via Browning 165* ☎ *0423/55150* ⏲ *Closed Wed.*

$$$
NORTHERN
ITALIAN
Fodor's Choice
★

✕**Locanda Baggio.** Even if you are put off by the swarms of tourists and commercialization in Asolo, a lunch or dinner in this family-run restaurant makes a trip to the once-elegant hillside village worthwhile. This is the best restaurant in Asolo, and the prix-fixe menu is one of the best values in the region. Chef Nino Baggio specializes in elegant versions of traditional cuisine—the rabbit stuffed with sausage, for example, is deboned and served with a crust of grana cheese—and takes pride in his homemade pasta, bread, and desserts. If you are there in November be sure to try one of Nino's heavenly dishes with the precious white truffles from Alba. $ *Average meal: €50* ⊠ *Via Bassane 1* ☎ *0423/529648* ⊕ *www.caderton.com* ☾ *Closed Mon. and 2 wks in Aug. No lunch Tues.*

WHERE TO STAY
For expanded hotel reviews, visit Fodors.com.

$$$
B&B/INN

Al Sole. This elegant pink-washed hotel in a 16th-century building overlooks the main square and enjoys wider views over picturesque Asolo or its leafy hinterland. **Pros:** central location; beautiful views; attentive service. **Cons:** restaurant open only in summer; rates increase greatly in the high season. $ *Rooms from: €245* ⊠ *Via Collegio 33* ☎ *0423/951332* ⊕ *www.albergoalsole.com* ⤴ *22 rooms, 1 suite* ⑩ *Breakfast.*

$
B&B/INN

Duse. A spiral staircase winds its way up this narrow, centrally located building to rooms with a view of the main square. **Pros:** simple but tasteful rooms; central location. **Cons:** some street noise; not as much of a bargain when you add the cost of breakfast and parking. $ *Rooms from: €120* ⊠ *Via Browning 190* ☎ *0423/55241* ⊕ *www.hotelduse.com* ⤴ *14 rooms* ☾ *Closed 3 wks in Jan. and Feb.* ⑩ *No meals.*

$$$
HOTEL

Villa Cipriani. A romantic garden surrounded by gracious country homes is the setting for this luxurious 16th-century villa, which once belonged to the Venice restaurateur and hotelier Harry Cipriani. **Pros:** incomparable views; truly elegant grounds; good spa services. **Cons:** small bathrooms; furnishings are old but not always tasteful; restaurant is pricey, rooms in the annex are very small. $ *Rooms from: €240* ⊠ *Via Canova 298* ☎ *0423/523411* ⊕ *www.villaciprianiasolo.com* ⤴ *31 rooms* ⑩ *Breakfast.*

TREVISO

35 km (22 miles) southeast of Maser, 30 km (19 miles) north of Venice.

Treviso has been dubbed "Little Venice" because of its meandering, moss-banked canals. They can't really compare with Venice's spectacular waterways, but on the whole, Treviso's historic center, with its medieval arcaded streets, has a great deal of charm. It's a fine place to stop for a few hours on the way from Venice to the wine country to the north or to the Palladian villas in the hinterland.

Treviso is one of the wealthiest small cities in the country, with fashionable shops and boutiques at every turn in the busy city center. Though a World War II Allied bombing on Good Friday 1944 destroyed half the city—it was tragically bombed by mistake after a

CLOSE UP

Traveling the Wine Roads

You'd be hard-pressed to find a more stimulating and varied wine region than northeastern Italy. From the Valpolicella, Bardolino, and Soave produced near Verona to the superlative whites of the Collio region, wines from the Veneto and Friuli–Venezia Giulia earn more Denominazione di Origine Controllata seals for uniqueness and quality than those of any other area of Italy.

You can travel on foot, by car, or by bicycle over hillsides covered with vineyards, each field nurturing subtly different grape varieties. On a casual trip through the countryside you're likely to come across wineries that will welcome you for a visit; for a more organized tour, check local tourist information offices, which have maps of roads, wineries, and vendors. Be advised that Italy has become more stringent about its driving regulations; designated drivers can save fines, embarrassment, or worse.

One of the most hospitable areas in the Veneto for wine enthusiasts is the stretch of country north of Treviso, where you can follow designated wine roads—tours that blend a beautiful rural setting with the delights of the grape. Authorized wineshops where you can stop and sample are marked with a sign showing a triangular arrangement of red and yellow grapes. There are three routes to choose from, and they're manageable enough that you can do them all comfortably over the course of a day or two.

MONTELLO AND ASOLO HILLS

This route provides a good balance of vineyards and nonwine sights. It winds from Nervesa della Battaglia, 18 km (10 miles) north of Treviso, past two prime destinations in the area, the lovely village of Asolo and the Villa Barbaro at Maser. Asolo produces good prosecco, whereas Montello, a hill near Nervesa, favors merlot and cabernet. Both areas also yield pinot and chardonnay.

PIAVE RIVER

The circular route follows the Piave River and runs through orchards, woods, and hills. Among the area's gems are the desert wines Torchiato di Fregona and Refrontolo Passito, both made according to traditional methods.

Raboso del Piave, renowned since Roman times, ages well and complements local dishes such as beans and pasta or goose stuffed with chestnuts. Other reds are cabernet, merlot, and cabernet sauvignon. As an accompaniment to fish, try a Verduzzo del Piave or, for an aperitif, the warm-yellow Pinot Grigio del Piave.

PROSECCO

This route runs for 47 km (29 miles) between Valdobbiadene and Conegliano, home of Italy's first wine institute, winding between knobby hills covered in grapevines. These hang in festoons on row after row of pergolas to create a thick mantle of green.

Turn off the main route to explore the narrower country lanes, most of which eventually join up. They meander through tiny hamlets and past numerous family wineries where you can taste and purchase the wines. Spring is an excellent time to visit, with no fewer than 15 local wine festivals held between March and early June.

report that Hitler would be in Tarvisio, on the Austrian border, was misread—Treviso meticulously preserved what remained of its old town's narrow streets while introducing modernity far more gently than in many other parts of Italy.

GETTING HERE AND AROUND

Treviso is 30 minutes by train from Venice; there are frequent daily departures. By car from Venice, pick up the SS13 in Mestre (Via Terraglio) and follow it all the way to Treviso; the trip takes about 45 minutes.

VISITOR INFORMATION

Treviso Tourism Office ⊠ *Palazzo Scotti, Via S. Andrea 3* ☎ *0422/547632* ⊕ *turismo.provincia.treviso.it* ☉ *Tues.–Fri. 9–1 and 2–6; Mon. and Sat. 9–1.*

EXPLORING

Duomo. Inside Treviso's Duomo, which was modified during the 19th century, is the Malchiostro Chapel. There you'll find an *Annunciation* by Titian (1520) and frescoes by Pordenone (1484–1539), including an *Adoration of the Magi.* The crypt has 12th-century columns. Bring a handful of coins for the coin-operated lights that illuminate the artwork. To the left of the Duomo is the Romanesque Battistero di San Giovanni (11th to 12th century), which is probably quite similar in style to the medieval Duomo. It's open only for special exhibitions. ⊠ *Piazza del Duomo* ☎ *0422/545720* ☉ *Mon.–Sat. 7:30–noon and 3:30–7, Sun. 7:30–1 and 3:30–8.*

Piazza dei Signori. The center of medieval Treviso, this piazza remains the town's social hub, with outdoor cafés and some impressive public buildings. The most important of these, the Palazzo dei Trecento (1185–1268), was the seat of the city government, composed of the Council of 300, during the Middle Ages. Behind it is a small alley that leads to the *pescheria* (fish market), on an island in one of the small canals that flow through town.

Quartiere Latino. While strolling the city, take in this restored district between Riviera Garibaldi and Piazza Santa Maria Battuti. It's the site of university buildings, upscale apartments, and a number of bustling restaurants and shops. If you walk along the northern part of the historic city wall, you'll look down on the island home of a number of ducks, geese, and goats. Their little farm occupies some of the city's prettiest real estate.

San Nicolò. The most important church in Treviso, this is a huge Venetian Gothic structure of the early 14th century, with an ornate vaulted ceiling and frescoes (circa 1350) of saints by Tommaso da Modena (circa 1325–79) on the columns; the depiction of *St. Agnes* on the north side is particularly interesting. Also worth examining are Tommaso's realistic portraits of 40 Dominican friars, found in the Sala del Capitolo of the seminary next door. They include the earliest-known painting of a subject wearing eyeglasses, an Italian invention (circa 1280–1300). ⊠ *Seminario Vescovile, Via San Nicolò* ☎ *0422/548626* ☉ *Church daily, 8–12:30 and 3:30–7; Seminary daily 8-6.*

Conegliano. This attractive town, with Venetian-style villas and arcaded streets, is 23 km (14 miles) north of Treviso in wine-producing country, and is known for its prosecco. Its other claim to fame is its connection with Gianbattista Cima—called Cima di Conegliano. Alongside Giovanni Bellini, Cima is one of the greatest painters of the early Venetian Renaissance, and the town's elegant 14th-century Duomo houses an altarpiece that he painted in 1492. The front of the Duomo is formed by the frescoed late medieval facade and Gothic arcade of the Scuola dei Battuti. If you stop in town, be sure to taste the prosecco, sold in local wine bars and shops. ⊠ *Conegliano.*

WHERE TO EAT

$$$
NORTHERN
ITALIAN

✕ Beccherie. The name means butcher shop, and this area behind Treviso's Palazzo Trecento is where people bought and sold meat for centuries. It is only fitting that Beccherie should specialize in *bollito,* a celebrated dish of assorted boiled meats and sauces, which originated in Piedmont but is now so much a part of Veneto cooking that most Veneti regard it as their own. The varied menu, based on the local cuisine, changes according to the season, offering hearty fare in winter and lighter choices in summer. The owner's mother, Depillo Alba Campeol, invented the famous dessert tiramisù in the 1960s, and the Beccharie still makes it to the original, feather-light recipe. Locals have been keeping this family-owned restaurant busy since 1939. Reservations are recommended for dinner. Ⓢ *Average meal: €47* ⊠ *Piazza Ancilotto 10* ☎ *0422/540871* ⊕ *www.anticoristorantebeccherie.it* ☉ *Closed Mon. and last 2 wks in July. No dinner Sun.*

$$$
VENETIAN

✕ Il Basilisco. Gastronomically adventurous diners who visit this simple restaurant will find Veneto cuisine in the *cucina povera* (poor people's food) tradition and discover that, with talent and imagination, wonderful dishes can be created from the most humble and unusual ingredients. Start with a savory dish of pasta with rabbit tripe, or *nervetti,* gelatinous veal tendons in a sauce of celery root. Main courses are somewhat more conventional, such as a timbale of local anchovies with a sauce of chicory and sundried tomatoes. If all this sounds a little too unusual, there are dishes such as veal liver in a pepper sauce, or a couscous of calamari and vegetables. Ⓢ *Average meal: €50* ⊠ *Via Bison 34, Treviso* ☎ *0422/541822* ⊕ *www.ristorantebasilisco.com* ⌧ *Reservations essential* ☉ *Closed Sun. No lunch Mon. and Sat.*

$$
VENETIAN
Fodor's Choice
★

✕ Toni del Spin. Wood paneled and with a 1930s-style interior, this friendly, bustling place oozes old-fashioned character. The reasonably priced, wholesome menu, chalked on a hanging wooden board, is based on local Veneto cooking. The "Spin" in the restaurant's name is the spine of the baccalà, one of the restaurant's famous specialties (served, of course, minus the actual spine). In autumn and winter, don't miss trying Treviso's hallmark product, radicchio, in risotto or pasta. The chef-owner, Alfredo Sturlese, is also justly proud of his *sopa coada* (pigeon-and-bread soup). Reservations are essential, even for lunch, since the word is out that this is the best value for money in town. Ⓢ *Average meal: €30* ⊠ *Via Inferiore 7* ☎ *0422/543829* ⊕ *www. ristorantetonidelspin.com* ⌧ *Reservations essential* ☉ *Closed 3 wks in July and Aug. No lunch Mon.*

WHERE TO STAY

For expanded hotel reviews, visit Fodors.com.

$$ ⚏ **Carlton Hotel.** Pass the river flowing outside, walk through the lobby,
HOTEL and seek out the huge terrace right on top of the old city wall—and
even the parking lot of this comfortable hotel has a view. **Pros:** central
location; one of very few hotels in the city center. **Cons:** interior is not
always that appealing; some of the rooms need refurbishing. $ *Rooms
from: €140* ✉ *Largo di Porta Altinia 15* ☎ *0422/411661* ⊕ *www.
hotelcarlton.it* ⤏ *93 rooms* ❍ *Breakfast.*

FRIULI–VENEZIA GIULIA

4

The peripheral location of the Friuli–Venezia Giulia region in Italy's
northeastern corner makes it easy to overlook, but with its mix of
Italian, Slavic, and central European cultures, along with a legend-
ary wine tradition, it's a fascinating area to explore. Venetian culture
spread northward until it merged with northern European style evi-
dent in places like the medieval city of Udine. Cividale del Friuli and
the Collio wine regions are a short hop away from Udine, and the old
Austrian port of Trieste was, in the late 19th and early 20th centuries,
an important center of Italian literature.

UDINE

*94 km (58 miles) northeast of Treviso, 127 km (79 miles) northeast
of Venice.*

Udine, the largest city on the Friuli side of the region, has a provincial,
genteel atmosphere and lots of charm. The city sometimes seems com-
pletely unaffected by tourism, and things are still done the way they
were decades ago. In the medieval and Renaissance historical center
of town, you'll find unevenly spaced streets with appealing wine bars
and open-air cafés. Friulani are proud of their culture, with many res-
taurants featuring local cuisine, and street signs and announcements
written in both Italian and Friulano (Furlan), which, although it is
classified as a dialect, is really a separate language from Italian. But the
main reason for devoting some time to Udine is to see works by the
last of the great Italian painters, Giambattista Tiepolo (1696–1770).
Distributed in several palaces and churches around town, this is the
greatest assembly of his art outside Venice. Udine calls itself, in fact,
la città di Tiepolo.

Commanding a view from the Alpine foothills to the Adriatic Sea, Udine
stands on a mound that, according to legend, was erected so Attila the
Hun could watch the burning of Aquileia, an important Roman center to
the south. Although the legend is unlikely (Attila burned Aquileia about
500 years before the first historical mention of Udine), the view from
Udine's castle across the alluvial plane down to the sea is impressive. In
the Middle Ages Udine flourished, thanks to its favorable trade location
and the right granted by the local patriarch to hold regular markets.

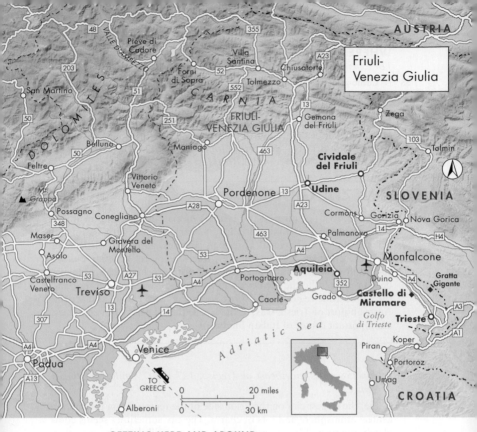

GETTING HERE AND AROUND

There's frequent train service from both Venice and Trieste; the trip takes about two hours from Venice, and a little over an hour from Trieste. By car from Venice, take the SR11 to the E55 and head east. Take the E55 (it eventually becomes the Autostrada Alpe Adria) to SS13 (Viale Venezia) east into Udine. Driving from Trieste, take the SS202 to the E70, which becomes the A4. Turn onto the E55 north, which is the same road you would take coming from Venice. Driving times are 1½ hours from Venice and 1 hour from Trieste.

VISITOR INFORMATION

Udine Tourism Office ⊠ *Piazza I Maggio 7* ☎ *0432/295972* ⊕ *www.turismo.fvg. it* ⊙ *Mon.–Sat. 9–7 (until 6 Oct.–Apr.), Sun. and holidays 9–1.*

EXPLORING

Castello. From its hilltop site, the castle (construction began 1517) has panoramic views extending to Monte Nero (7,360 feet) in neighboring Slovenia. Here Udine's civic museums of art and archaeology are centralized under one roof. Particularly worth seeing is the national and regional art collection in the **Galleria d'Arte Antica,** which has canvases by Venetians Vittore Carpaccio (circa 1460–1525) and Giambattista Tiepolo, an excellent Caravaggio, and a carefully selected collection of works by lesser known but still interesting Veneto and Friuli artists.

The museum also has a small but wonderful collection of drawings, containing several by Tiepolo; some find his drawings even more moving than his paintings. ⊠ *Via Lionello 1* ☎ *0432/271591* 💰 *€3, or free with Card Udine Museale (€6), which allows admission to most museums in Udine and the Chiesa della Purità* ⊙ *Tues.–Sat. 9:30–12:30 and 3–6, Sun. 9:30–noon.*

Duomo. A few steps from the Piazza della Libertà is Udine's 1335 Duomo. Its Cappella del Santissimo has important early frescoes by Tiepolo, and the Cappella della Trinità sports a Tiepolo altarpiece. There is also a beautiful late Tiepolo *Resurrection* (1751) in an altar by the sculptor Giuseppi Toretti. Ask the Duomo's attendant to let you into the adjacent **Chiesa della Purita** to see more important late paintings by Tiepolo. ⊠ *Piazza del Duomo 1* ☎ *0432/506830* 💰 *Free* ⊙ *Daily 7–noon and 4–7.*

Fodor's Choice
★ **Palazzo Arcivescovile.** The Palazzo Arcivescovile (aka Palazzo Patriarcale) contains several rooms of frescoes by the young Giambattista Tiepolo, painted from 1726 to 1732. They comprise the most important collection of early works by Italy's most brilliant 18th-century painter. The Galleria del Tiepolo (1727) contains superlative Tiepolo frescoes depicting the stories of Abraham, Isaac, and Jacob. The *Judgment of Solomon* (1729) graces the Pink Room. There are also beautiful and important Tiepolo frescoes in the staircase, throne room, and palatine chapel of this palazzo. Even in these early works we can see the Venetian master's skill in creating an illusion of depth, not only through linear perspective, but also through subtle gradations in the intensity of the colors, with the stronger colors coming forward and the paler ones receding into space. Tiepolo was one of the first artists to use this method of representing space and depth, which reflected the scientific discoveries of perception and optics in the 17th century. In the same building, the **Museo Diocesano** features a collection of sculptures from Friuli churches from the 13th through the 18th century. ⊠ *Piazza Patriarcato 1* ☎ *0432/25003* ⊕ *www.musdioc-tiepolo.it* 💰 *€5, includes Museo Diocesano* ⊙ *Wed.–Sun. 10–1 and 3–6.*

Piazza della Libertà. Udine was conquered by the Venetians in 1420, so there is a distinctly Venetian stamp on the architecture of the historic center, most noticeably here, in the large main square. The Loggia del Leonello, begun in 1428, dominates the square and houses the municipal government. Its similarity to the facade of Venice's Palazzo Ducale (finished in 1424) is clear, but there is no evidence that it is an imitation of that palace. It's more likely a product of the same architectural fashion. Opposite stands the Renaissance Porticato di San Giovanni (1533–35) and the Torre dell'Orologio, a 1527 clock tower with naked *mori* (Moors, who strike the hours) on the top.

WHERE TO EAT

$$
FRIULIAN
Fodor's Choice
★ ╳ **Hostaria alla Tavernetta.** One of Udine's most trusted food addresses since 1954, this restaurant is steps from the Piazza Duomo. It has rustic fireside dining downstairs and smaller, more elegantly decorated rooms upstairs, where there's also a small terrace. On the menu are regional specialties such as *orzotto* (barley prepared like risotto), delicious *cjalzòns* (ravioli stuffed with ricotta, apples, raisins, and spices and topped

with smoked ricotta, butter, and cinnamon), and perhaps the most tender suckling pig you have ever eaten. The restaurant offers a reasonably priced (€25) prix-fixe menu. The service is pleasant and attentive, and there's a fine selection of Friuli's celebrated wines and grappas. [$] *Average meal: €35* ✉ *Via di Prampero 2* ☎ *0432/501066* ⏲ *Closed Sun. and Mon., 2nd wk in Jan., 1 wk in June, 2 wks in mid-Aug.*

$ FRIULIAN 🍴 **Osteria Al Vecchio Stallo.** This former stable bursts with character, its beautiful courtyard shaded by grape arbors. The menu includes a wide choice of traditional Friuli home cooking prepared simply, without much elaboration. As an appetizer, try the prized prosciutto from the neighboring village of San Daniele, which some regard even more highly than the famous Parma version. Start with cjalzòns, or the *mignàculis con luagne* (pasta with local sausage), followed by Friuli classics such as *frico con patate* (hash-brown potatoes with Montasio cheese) or goulash with polenta. On Friday there are also fish dishes. There's a great selection of wines by the glass. [$] *Average meal: €25* ✉ *Via Viola 7* ☎ *0432/21296* 💳 *No credit cards* ⏲ *Closed Wed. Sept.–June, Sun. in July and Aug., 3 wks in Aug., and Dec. 25–Jan. 7.*

WHERE TO STAY

For expanded hotel reviews, visit Fodors.com.

$$ HOTEL 🏨 **Hostaria Hotel Allegria.** In a residential area, but within easy walking distance to the center and most sights, this 15th-century building has grown from a humble osteria into a modern, comfortable family-run hotel. **Pros:** well-appointed rooms; great staff; discounted weekend rates. **Cons:** rooms may be too minimalist for some; restaurant is closed Sunday and for Monday lunch; fee for parking. [$] *Rooms from: €140* ✉ *Via Grazzano 18* ☎ *0432/201116* 🌐 *www.hotelallegria.it* 🛏 *21 rooms* 🍽 *Breakfast.*

$ HOTEL 🏨 **Hotel Clocchiatti.** You have two choices here: stay in the restored 19th-century villa or opt for the ultramodern (and slightly more expensive) "Next" wing. **Pros:** individually decorated rooms; quiet surroundings; swimming pool; excellent breakfast. **Cons:** 10-minute drive from town center; small bathrooms; no restaurant. [$] *Rooms from: €90* ✉ *Via Cividale 29* ☎📠 *0432/505047* 🌐 *www.hotelclocchiatti.it* 🛏 *27 rooms* 🍽 *Breakfast.*

CIVIDALE DEL FRIULI

17 km (11 miles) east of Udine, 144 km (89 miles) northeast of Venice.

Cividale is the best place to see the art of the Lombards, a Germanic people who entered Italy in 568 and ruled until the late 8th century. The city was founded in AD 53 by Julius Caesar, then commander of Roman legions in the area. Here you can also find Celtic, Roman, and medieval Jewish ruins alongside Venetian Gothic buildings, including the Palazzo Comunale. Strolling through the part of the city that now occupies the former Gastaldia, the Lombard ducal palace, gives you spectacular views of the medieval city and the river.

GETTING HERE AND AROUND

There's hourly train service from Udine. Since the Udine–Cividale train line isn't part of the Italian national rail system, you have to buy the tickets from the tobacconist or other retailers within the Udine station. You can't buy a ticket through to Cividale from another city.

By car from Udine, take Via Cividale, which turns into SS54; follow SS54 into Cividale.

EXPLORING

Duomo. Cividale's Renaissance Duomo is largely the work of Pietro Lombardo, principal architect of Venice's Santa Maria dei Miracoli. It contains a magnificent 12th-century silver gilt altarpiece. ✉ *Piazza Duomo* ☎ *0432/731144* ⏲ *Daily 7:30–7:30.*

Museo Cristiano e Tesoro del Duomo. Entered via a courtyard off to the right of the Duomo, this museum contains two interesting and important monuments of Lombard art: the Altar of Duke Ratchis (737–744) and the Baptistry of Patriarch Callisto (731–776). Both were found under the floor of the present Duomo in the early 20th century. The museum also has two fine paintings by Veronese, one by Pordenone, and a small but fine collection of medieval and Renaissance vestments. ✉ *Via Candotti 1* ☎ *0432/730403* 🎟 *€4; €6 combined ticket with Tempietto Longobardo* ⏲ *Summer, Wed.–Sun. 10–1 and 3–6; winter, weekends 10–1 and 3–6.*

Fodor's Choice ★ **Tempietto Longobardo** (*Lombard Church*). Seeing the beautiful and historically important Tempietto Longobardo from the 8th century is more than enough reason to visit Cividale. Now within the Monastery of Santa Maria in Valle (16th century), the Tempietto was originally the chapel of the ducal palace, known as the Gastaldia. The west wall is the best-preserved example of the art and architecture of the Lombards, a Germanic people who entered Italy in 568. It has an archway with an exquisitely rendered vine motif, guarded by an 8th-century procession of female figures, showing the Lombard interpretation of classical forms that resembles the style of the much earlier Byzantine mosaics in Ravenna, which had passed briefly to Lombard rule in 737. This procession of female figures had originally extended to the side walls of the Tempietto, but was destroyed by an earthquake in 1222. The post-Lombard frescoes decorating the vaults and the east wall date from the 13th and 14th centuries, and the fine carved wooden stalls also date from the 14th century. ✉ *Via Monastero Maggiore* ☎ *0432/700867* 🎟 *€4; €6 combined ticket with Museo del Duomo* ⏲ *Oct.–Mar., Mon.–Sat. 10–1 and 3–5, Sun. 10–5; Apr.–Sept., Mon.–Sat. 10–1 and 3–6:30, Sun. 10–7.*

WHERE TO STAY

For expanded hotel reviews, visit Fodors.com.

$ B&B/INN 🏨 **La Cjase dai Toscans.** In a central location, this 15th-century palazzo, once home to the Dukes of Tuscany, is now a charming and romantic bed-and-breakfast, with large rooms furnished in antique style. **Pros:** large, well-appointed rooms; high-speed Wi-Fi; good breakfast; nearby parking is free or at moderate cost, depending on the distance. **Cons:** some noise from the street and the cathedral bells. [$] *Rooms from: €75* ✉ *Corso Mazzini 15/1, Cividale del Friuli* ☎ *3490765288 cell phone* 🌐 *www.lacjasedaitoscans.it* 🛏 *3* 🍴 *No meals.*

$$ HOTEL **Locanda Al Castello.** On a peaceful hillside a few minutes' drive out of town, this crenellated and creeper-covered hotel was once a monastery. **Pros:** quiet area; discounts possible, depending on availability; excellent restaurant. **Cons:** need a car to get around; the spa is small and sometimes closes early; spa services overpriced at €50 for a massage. [$] *Rooms from: €150* ✉ *Via del Castello 12* ☎ *0432/733242* 🌐 *www.alcastello.net* 🛏 *25 rooms, 2 suites* 🍴 *Breakfast.*

Aquileia Tourism Office ✉ *Bus Terminal, Via Iulia Augusta, Aquileia* ☎ *0431/919491.*

Archaeological Site. Beyond the basilica and across the road, the archaeological site among the cypresses reveals Roman remains of the forum, houses, cemetery, and port. The little stream was once an important waterway extending to Grado. The area is well signposted. Unfortunately, many of the excavations of Roman Aquileia could not be left exposed because of the extremely high water table under the site and had to be reburied after archaeological studies had been conducted; nevertheless, what remains aboveground, along with the monuments in the archaeological museum, gives an idea of the grandeur of this ancient city. ✉ *Aquileia* 🌐 *www.museoarcheo-aquileia.it* 🎟 *Free* 🕐 *Daily 8:15–7.*

Fodor's Choice ★ **Basilica.** Aquileia's Basilica was founded by Theodore, its first patriarch, who built two parallel basilicas, now the north and the south halls, on the site of a 3rd-century Gnostic chapel. These were joined by a third hall, forming a U, with the baptismal font in the middle. The complex was rebuilt between 1021 and 1031, and later accumulated the Romanesque portico and the Gothic bell tower, producing the church you see today. The highlight of this monument is the spectacular 3rd- to 4th-century mosaic covering the entire floor of the basilica and the adjacent crypt, comprising one of the most beautiful and important of early Christian monuments. The mosaic floor of the present-day basilica is essentially the remains of the floor of Theodore's south hall, while those of the Cripta degli Scavi are those of his north hall, along with the remains of the mosaic floor of a pre-Christian Roman house and warehouse.

The mosaics of the basilica are important not only because of their beauty, but also because they provide a window into Gnostic symbolism and the conflict between Gnosticism and the early Christian church. In his north hall, Theodore retained much of the floor of the earlier Gnostic chapel, whose mosaics, done largely in the 3rd century, represent the ascent of the soul, through the realm of the planets and constellations, to God, who is represented as a ram. (The ram, at the head of the zodiac, is the Gnostic generative force.) Libra is not the scales, but rather a battle between good (the rooster) and evil (the tortoise); the constellation Cancer is represented as a shrimp on a tree. The basis for the representation in Aquileia is the Pistis Sophia, a 2nd-century Gnostic tract written in Alexandria.

The 4th-century mosaics of the south hall (the present-day nave of the basilica) are somewhat more doctrinally conventional, and represent the story of Jonah as prefiguring the salvation offered by the Church.

Down a flight of steps, the **Cripta degli Affreschi** contains beautiful 12th-century frescoes, among them Saint Peter sending Saint Mark to Aquileia and the beheading of Saints Hermagoras and Fortunatus, to whom the basilica is dedicated. ✉ *Aquileia* ☎ *0431/91067* ⊕ *www. aquileia.net* ✉ *Basilica free, both crypts €3, campanile €1.20* ☉ *Basilica: Apr.–Sept, daily 9–7; Mar. and Oct. daily 9–6; Nov.–Mar., weekdays 9–4:30, weekends 9–5. Campanile: Apr.–Sept., 9:30–1:30 and 3:30–6:30; Oct., weekends 10–5; closed Nov.–Mar. Note: The Basilica sometimes has shorter hours or is even closed for a day. Phone ahead or check the website.*

TRIESTE

71 km (44 miles) southeast of Cividale del Friuli, 163 km (101 miles) east of Venice.

Trieste is built along a fringe of coastline where a rugged *karst* plateau tumbles abruptly into the beautiful Adriatic. It was the only port of the Austro-Hungarian Empire and, therefore, a major industrial and financial center. In the early years of the 20th century, Trieste and its surroundings also became famous by their association with some of the most important names of Italian literature, such as Italo Svevo, and Irish and German writers. James Joyce drew inspiration from the city's multiethnic population, and Rainer Maria Rilke was inspired by the seacoast west of the city.

The city has lost its importance as a port and a center of finance, but perhaps because of its multicultural nature, at the juncture of Latin, Slavic, and Germanic Europe, it's never fully lost its role as an intellectual center. In recent years the city has become a center for science and technology. The streets hold a mix of monumental, neoclassical, and art nouveau architecture built by the Austrians during Trieste's days of glory, granting an air of melancholy stateliness to a city that lives as much in the past as the present.

Italian revolutionaries of the 1800s rallied their battle cry around Trieste, because of what they believed was foreign occupation of their motherland. After World War II the sliver of land including Trieste and a small part of Istria became an independent, neutral state that was officially recognized in a 1947 peace treaty. Although it was actually occupied by British and American troops for its nine years of existence, the Free Territory of Trieste issued its own currency and stamps. In 1954 a Memorandum of Understanding was signed in London, giving civil administration of Trieste to Italy.

GETTING HERE AND AROUND

Trains to Trieste depart regularly from Venice, Udine, and other major Italian cities. By car, it's the eastern terminus of the Autostrada Torino–Trieste (E70). Trieste is served by Ronchi dei Ligioneri Airport, which receives flights from major Italian airports and some European cities. The airport is 33 km (20½ miles) from the city; transportation into Trieste is by taxi or Bus No. 51.

VISITOR INFORMATION

Trieste Tourism Office ✉ *Via dell'Orlogio 1, corner of Piazza dell'Unità d'Italia* ☎ *040/3478312* ⊕ *www.triesteturismo.com* ☉ *Mon.–Sat. 9–6, Sun. 9–1.*

EXPLORING

Castello di San Giusto. This hilltop castle, built between 1470 and 1630, was constructed on the ruins of the Roman town of Tergeste. Given the excellent view, it's no surprise that 15th-century Venetians turned the castle into a shipping observation point; the structure was further enlarged by Trieste's subsequent rulers, the Habsburgs. The castle also contains the Civic Museum, which has a small collection of furnishings, tapestries, and weaponry. ⊠ *Piazza della Cattedrale 3* ☎ *040/309362* ⊠ *€4* ☉ *Daily 9–5.*

Cattedrale di San Giusto. Dating from the 14th century and occupying the site of an ancient Roman forum, the cathedral contains remnants of at least three previous buildings, the earliest a hall dating from the 5th century. A section of the original floor mosaic still remains, incorporated into the floor of the present church. In the 9th and 11th centuries two adjacent churches were built—the Church of the Assumption and the Church of San Giusto. The beautiful apse mosaics of these churches, done in the 12th and 13th centuries by a Venetian artist, still remain in the apses of the side aisles of the present church. The mosaics in the main apse date from 1932. In the 14th century the two churches were joined and a Romanesque-Gothic facade was attached, ornamented with fragments of Roman monuments taken from the forum. The jambs of the main doorway are the most conspicuous Roman element. ⊠ *Piazza della Cattedrale 3* ☎ *040/309666* ☉ *Daily 8:30–noon and 4–7.*

Civico Museo di Storia ed Arte. On the hill near the Castello, this is an eclectic history and art museum with statues from the Roman theater and artifacts from Egypt, Greece, and Rome. There's also an assortment of glass and manuscripts. The **Orto Lapidario** (Lapidary Garden) has classical statuary, pottery, and a small Corinthian temple. ⊠ *Via Cattedrale 1* ☎ *040/310500* ⊠ *€4* ☉ *Tues.–Sun. 10–5.*

Piazza della Borsa. A statue of Habsburg emperor Leopold I looks out over this square, which contains Trieste's original stock exchange, the **Borsa Vecchia** (1805), an attractive neoclassical building now serving as the chamber of commerce. It sits at the end of the Canal Grande, dug in the 18th century by the Austrian empress Maria Theresa as a first step in the expansion of what was then a small fishing village of 7,000 into the port of her empire.

Piazza dell'Unità d'Italia. The sidewalk cafés on this vast seaside piazza are popular meeting places in the summer months. The imposing square, ringed by grandiose facades, was set out as a plaza open to the sea, like Venice's Piazza San Marco, in the late Middle Ages. It underwent countless changes through the centuries and its present size and architecture are essentially products of late-19th- and early-20th-century Austria. Named and renamed, according to the political fortunes of the city, it was given its current name in 1955, when Trieste was finally given to Italy. On the inland side of the piazza note the facade of the **Palazzo Comunale** (Town Hall), designed by the Triestino architect Giuseppi Bruni in 1875. It was from this building's balcony in 1938 that Mussolini proclaimed the infamous racial laws, depriving Italian Jews of most of their rights.

Risiera di San Sabba. In September 1943 the Nazi occupation established Italy's only concentration camp in this rice-processing factory outside of Trieste. In April 1944 a crematorium was put into operation. The Nazis destroyed much of the evidence of their atrocities before their retreat, but a good deal of the horror of the place is still perceivable in the reconstructed museum (1975). It has been an Italian national monument since 1965, and now receives more than 100,000 visitors per year. It can be reached easily by Bus No. 8 or 10; by car it is off the Autostrada A4, exit Valmaura/Stadio/Cimitero. ⊠ *Via Giovanni Palatucci 5* ☎ *040/826202* ☜ *Free, €3 guided tour* ☉ *Daily 9–7.*

San Silvestro. This beautiful, small Romanesque church, dating from the 9th to 12th centuries, is the oldest church in Trieste that's still in use and in approximately its original form. Its interior walls still have some fragmentary remains of Romanesque frescoes. The church was deconsecrated under the secularizing reforms of the Austrian emperor Josef II in 1785 and was later sold to the Swiss Evangelical community. It then became, and is still, the Reformed Evangelical and Waldesian Church of Trieste. ⊠ *Piazza San Silvestro 1* ☎ *040/363952* ☉ *Thurs. and Sat. 10–noon; services Sun. morning.*

Teatro Romano. The ruins of this 1st century AD amphitheater, near the Via Giuseppi Mazzini opposite the city's *questura* (police station), were discovered during 1938 demolition work. Its statues are now displayed at the Museo Civico, and the space is used for summer plays and concerts. ⊠ *Via del Teatro Romano.*

OFF THE
BEATEN
PATH

Castello Di Duino. This 14th-century castle, where in 1912 Rainer Maria Rilke wrote his masterpiece, the *Duino Elegies*, is just 12 km (7½ miles) from Trieste. Take Bus No. 44 or 51 from the Trieste train station. The easy path along the seacoast from the castle toward Trieste has gorgeous views that rival the Amalfi Coast and the Cinque Terre. The castle itself, still the property of the Princes of Thurn and Taxis, contains a fine collection of antique furnishings and an amazing Palladian circular staircase, but the main attractions are the surrounding gardens and the spectacular views. ⊠ *Frazione Duino 32, Duino-Ausina* ☎ *040/208120* ⊕ *www.castellodiduino.it* ☜ *€7* ☉ *Apr.–Oct., Wed.–Mon. 9:30–5:30; Nov.–Mar., weekends 9:30–4; open sporadically at other times.*

WHERE TO EAT

$$$

SEAFOOD

✕ **Al Bagatto.** At this warm little seafood restaurant near the Piazza Unità, chef-owner Roberto Marussi personally shepherds your meal from start to finish. The menu includes both traditional dishes, such as *baccalà mantecato* (creamed cod with olive oil), and more inventive creations, such as a tartare of sea bass with fresh ricotta. Robert'ʾ dishes often integrate nouvelle ingredients without overshadowing freshness of whatever local fish he bought in the market that 'erva- Ⓢ *Average meal: €60* ⊠ *Via L. Cadorna 7* ☎ *040/30177* tions essential ☉ *Closed Sun.*

$

SEAFOOD

✕ **Antipastoteca di Mare.** Hidden halfway up the hill San Giusto, in what the Triestini call the old city taurant specializes in traditional preparation literally the "cooking of the poor," tho movement in which creative flair transforms the humblest ingredients. The inexpensive fish—bluefish, sardines, mackerel, mussels, and squid—are accompanied by salad, potatoes, polenta, and house wine. The consistently tasty and fresh dishes, especially the fish soup and the *sardoni in savor* (large sardines with raisins, pine nuts, and caramelized onions—"savor" is the Triestino-dialect equivalent of the Venetian "saor"), show what a talented chef can do on a limited budget. [$] *Average meal: €20* ✉ *Via della Fornace 1* ☎ *040/309606* ✍ *Reservations essential* 💳 *No credit cards* ⏲ *Closed Mon. No dinner Sun.*

$ NORTHERN ITALIAN FAMILY 🍴 **Buffet da Siora Rosa.** Serving delicious and generous portions of traditional Triestino buffet fare—think boiled pork and sausages, with savory sauerkraut—Siora Rosa is a bit more comfortable than many buffets. In addition to ample seating in its simple but cozy dining room, it has tables outside for when the weather is good. It is frequented mainly by Triestini, including students and faculty from the nearby university, and you may be the only tourist in the place, but the helpful waitresses generally speak English. [$] *Average meal: €20* ✉ *Piazza Hortis 3* ☎ *040/301460* 💳 *No credit cards* ⏲ *Closed weekends and holidays.*

$ NORTHERN ITALIAN 🍴 **Da Pepi.** A Triestino institution, this is the oldest and most esteemed of the many "buffet" restaurants—small steam-table restaurants serving pork and sausages—around town. It and similar holes-in-the-wall (few tables, simple interior) are as much a part of the Triestino scene as the cafés. It specializes in *bollito di maiale,* a dish of boiled pork and pork sausages accompanied by delicately flavored sauerkraut, mustard, and grated horseradish. Unlike other Italian restaurants, buffets don't close between lunch and dinner, and tap beer is the drink of choice. [$] *Average meal: €12* ✉ *Via Cassa di Risparmio 3* ☎ *040/366858* ⏲ *Closed Sun. and last 2 wks in July.*

$$$ NORTHERN ITALIAN 🍴 **Suban.** An easy trip just outside town, this landmark trattoria operated by the hospitable Suban family has been in business since 1865. Sit by the dining room fire or relax on a huge terrace and watch the sunset. This is Triestino food with a Slovene, Hungarian, and Austrian accent. Start with *jota carsolina* (a rich soup of cabbage, potatoes, and beans), and then you might order a roast joint of veal fragrant with rosmary and thyme, or a tender pork filet with red and yellow peppers, sausage, and sweet paprika. ■ **TIP→ Although the kitchen has central European roots, portions tend to be small, so if you're hungry, be sure to order both a first and second course, and maybe an antipasto, too. To get here you can take Bus No. 35 from Piazza Oberdan.** [$] *Average meal: €60* ✉ *Via Comici 2* ☎ *040/54368* ✍ *Reservations essential* ⏲ *Closed Tues., 2 wks in early Jan. and 1st 3 wks in Aug. No lunch.*

WHERE TO STAY

For expanded hotel reviews, visit Fodors.com.

$$ Fodo TEL 🏨 **Duchi d'Aosta.** On the spacious Piazza Unità d'Italia, this hotel, beautifully furnished in Venetian Renaissance style, has come a long way since its original incarnation as a 19th-century dockers' café. **Pros:** lots f charm paired with modern convenience; great location; attentive ff; sumptuous breakfast; upgrades sometimes available at no addi- cost. **Cons:** rooms overlooking the piazza can be very expen- nding on the season; restaurant overpriced; late check-in (3

pm), although rooms are frequently ready sooner; expensive parking. [$] *Rooms from: €189* ✉ *Piazza Unità d'Italia 2/1* ☎ *040/7600011* 🌐 *www.grandhotelduchidaosta.com* 🛏 *55* 🍴 *Breakfast.*

$$ HOTEL 🏨 **Filoxenia.** The reasonable prices and waterfront location make this small hotel a good budget choice. **Pros:** central; friendly staff; great price given the location. **Cons:** some very small, spartan rooms; some street noise; showers are cramped. [$] *Rooms from: €150* ✉ *Via Mazzini 3* ☎ *040/3481644* 🌐 *www.filoxenia.it* 🛏 *20 rooms* 🍴 *Breakfast.*

$$ B&B/INN 🏨 **L'Albero Nascosto Hotel Residence.** On a busy, narrow street in the historic center, this hotel residence, with interesting artwork and historic features, is one of the best values in Trieste. **Pros:** very central; spacious and simple but tasteful rooms. **Cons:** no elevator; no staff onsite after 8 pm (though late arrivals can be arranged); street noise can be a problem—if you are noise-sensitive, ask for a room in the back. [$] *Rooms from: €165* ✉ *Via Felice Venezian 18* ☎ *040/300188* 🌐 *www.alberonascosto.it* 🛏 *10 rooms* 🍴 *Breakfast.*

NIGHTLIFE AND THE ARTS

Teatro Verdi. This is Trieste's main opera house, built under Austrian rule in 1801. It is of interest not only for music lovers, but also for its architecture—the interior was designed by the architect of Venice's La Fenice, Gian Antonio Selva, and the facade was designed by the architect of Milan's La Scala, Matteo Pertsch. You'll have to go to a performance to see the interior, since guided tours are not given to individuals.

The opera season here runs from October through May, with a brief operetta festival in July and August. ✉ *Piazza Verdi 1* ☎ *040/9869883* 🌐 *www.teatroverdi-trieste.com.*

CAFES

Trieste is justly famous for its coffee. The elegant civility of Trieste plays out beautifully in a caffè culture combining the refinement of Vienna with the passion of Italy. In Trieste, as elsewhere in Italy, ask for a caffè and you'll get a thimbleful of high-octane espresso. Your cappuccino here will come in the Viennese fashion, with a dollop of whipped cream. Many cafés are part of a *torrefazione* (roasting shop), so you can sample a cup and then buy beans to take with you.

Antico Caffè San Marco. Few cafés in Italy can rival Antico Caffè San Marco for its bohemian atmosphere. First founded in 1914, it was largely destroyed in World War I. It was rebuilt in the 1920s, and then restored several more times, but some of the original art nouveau interior remains. It became a meeting place for local intellectuals and was the haunt of the Triestino writers Italo Svevo and Umberto Saba. ✉ *Via Battisti 18, Trieste* ☎ *040/363538* 🕒 *Tues.–Sun. 8 am–midnight.*

Caffè Degli Specchi. For a great view of the great piazza, you couldn't do better than Caffè Degli Specchi, where the many mirrors heighten the opportunities for people-watching. Originally opened in 1839, it was taken over by the British Navy after World War II, and Triestini were not allowed in unless accompanied by an Englishman. Because of its location, it is the café most frequented by tourists, and it's open from 8 am to 9 pm. ✉ *Piazza dell'Unità d'Italia 7, Trieste* ☎ *040/3*

Caffè Tommaseo. Founded in 1830, classic Caffè Tommaseo is a comfortable place to linger, especially on weekend evenings and Sunday lunchtime (11–1:30), when there's live music. While you can still have just a coffee, Tommaseo has evolved into a pastry shop and restaurant, with an extensive menu. It's open daily from 8 am until 12:30 am. ⊠ *Piazza Tommaseo 4/C, Trieste* ☎ *040/362666.*

I Paesi del Caffè. The atmosphere here is more modern than Old World, and they brew coffee and sell beans of most of the top varieties, including Jamaica Blue Mountain. ⊠ *Via Einaudi 1, Trieste* ☎ *040/633897* ⊗ *Mon.–Sat. 7 am–8:30 pm.*

CASTELLO DI MIRAMARE

7 km (4½ miles) northwest of Trieste.

GETTING HERE AND AROUND

Bus No. 36 from Piazza Oberdan in Trieste runs here every half hour.

EXPLORING

FAMILY **Miramar.** Maximilian of Habsburg, brother of Emperor Franz Josef and retired commander of the Austrian Navy, built this seafront extravaganza from 1856 to 1860, complete with a throne room under a ship's-keel wooden ceiling. In keeping with late 19th-century taste, the rooms are generally furnished with very elaborate, somewhat ponderous versions of medieval, Renaissance, and French period furniture, and the walls are covered in red damask. Maximilian's retirement was interrupted in 1864, when he became emperor of Mexico at the initiative of Napoléon III. He was executed three years later by a Mexican firing squad. His wife, Charlotte of Belgium, went mad and returned to Miramar, and later to her native country. During the last years of the Habsburg reign, Miramar became one of the favorite residences of Franz Josef's wife, the Empress Elizabeth (Sissi). The castle was later owned by Duke Amadeo of Aosta, who renovated some rooms in the rationalist style and installed modern plumbing in his art deco bathroom. Tours in English are available by reservation. Surrounding the castle is a 54-acre park, partly wooded and partly sculpted into attractive gardens. ⊠ *Viale Miramare, off SS14* ☎ *040/224143* ⊕ *www. castello-miramare.it* ⊠ *Castle €6, park free* ⊗ *Castle: daily 9–7 (last entry ½ hr before closing); park: Apr.–Sept., daily 8–7; Nov.–Feb., daily 8–5; Mar. and Oct., daily 8–6.*

5

THE DOLOMITES

Trentino–Alto Adige

WELCOME TO THE DOLOMITES

TOP REASONS TO GO

★ **Driving in the Dolomites:** Your rental Fiat will think it's a Ferrari on a gorgeous drive through the heart of the Dolomites.

★ **Hiking:** No matter your fitness level, there's an unforgettable walk in store for you here.

★ **Museo Archeologico dell'Alto Adige, Bolzano:** The impossibly well-preserved body of the iceman Ötzi, the star attraction here, provokes countless questions about what life was like 5,000 years ago.

★ **Trento:** A graceful fusion of Austrian and Italian styles, this breezy, frescoed town is famed for its imposing castle.

1 Trentino. This butterfly-shape province is Italy with a German accent. Its principal city, history-rich Trento, is at the center. To the northwest are Madonna di Campiglio, one of Italy's most fashionable ski resorts, and Bormio, another notable skiing destination, which doubles as a gateway to the Parco Nazionale dello Stelvio.

2 Bolzano. Alto Adige's capital is the Dolomites' liveliest city. Look for high-gabled houses, wrought-iron signs, and centuries-old wine cellars.

3 Alto Adige. This region was a part of Austria until the end of World War I, and Austrian sensibilities still predominate over Italian. At the spa town of Merano you can soak in hot springs, take the "grape cure," and stroll along lovely walkways. To the southwest, Caldaro has an appealing wine-growing region.

4 Heart of the Dolomites. The spectacular Sella mountain range and the surrounding Val di Fassa and Val Gardena make up this region. It's distinguished by great views and great mountain sports, both summer and winter. At the town of Canazei, the cable car 3,000 feet up to the Col Rodella lookout packages the vast panorama perfectly.

AUSTRIA

SWITZERLAND

Glorenza
Spondigna

40
41
38
38

Parco Nazionale
dello Stelvio

Bormio

ORTLES ORTLERGRUPPE

38
PIEMONTE

VAL DI SOLE

Madonna di
Campiglio

42

Pinzolo

TRENTINO

239

Tione

237

Arco

240

Brenner Pass

A L P S

AUSTRIA

A22

49 Brunico

Bressanone

Dobbiaco

51

3

ALTO ADIGE

49

Merano

38

2 Bolzano

VAL GARDENA

SELLA MT. RANGE

48

5 Cortina d'Ampezzo

51

12

4

Grande Strada delle Dolomiti

Col Rodella

Canazei

42

Cles

A22

VAL DI FASSA

43

Mezzelombardo

48 Predazzo

Trento

Lago di
Caldonazzo

47 Strigno

12

A22

Rovereto

46

0   10 mi
0   10 km

S

5

GETTING ORIENTED

Shadowed by the Dolomite
Mountains, the north-
east Italian provinces
of Trentino and Alto
Adige are centered on
the valleys of the Adige
and Isarco rivers, which
course from the Brenner
Pass south to Bolzano.

5 **Cortina d'Ampezzo.**
Once a trendy hangout, Cortina has aged gracefully into
the grande dame of Italian
ski resorts. But it's arguably
at its best in summer, when
there are countless options
for hiking and mountain
activities.

EATING AND DRINKING WELL IN THE DOLOMITES

Everything in Alto Adige (and, to a lesser extent, Trentino) has more than a tinge of the Teutonic—and the food is no exception. The rich and creamy cuisine here, including fondues, polentas, and barley soups, reflects the Alpine climate and Austrian and Swiss influences.

The quintessential restaurant here is the wood-panel Tirolean *Stube* (pub) serving hearty meat-and-dumpling fare, and there's also a profusion of pastry shops and lively beer halls.

Although the early dining schedule you'll find in Germany or Austria is somewhat tempered here, your options for late-night meals are more limited than they are in places farther south, where *la dolce vita* has a firmer grip.

Thankfully, the coffee is every bit as good as in parts south—just expect to hear "*danke, grazie*" when paying for your cappuccino.

BEST OF THE WURST

Not to be missed are the outdoor wurst carts, even (or perhaps especially) in colder weather. After placing your order you'll get a sheet of wax paper, followed by a dollop of mustard, a Kaiser roll, and your chosen sausage.

You can sometimes make your selection by pointing to whatever picture is most appealing; if not, pass on the familiar-sounding *Frankfurter* and try the local *Meraner*. Carts can reliably be found in Bolzano (try Piazza delle Erbe, or in front of the archaeological museum) and Merano (Piazza del Grano, or along the river).

POLENTA AND DUMPLINGS

Polenta is a staple in the region, in both its creamy and firm varieties, often topped with cheese or mushrooms (or both). Dumplings also appear on many menus; the most distinctive to the region are *canederli* (also known as *Knoedel*), *pictured at right,* made from seasoned bread in many variations, and served either in broth or with a sauce.

Other dumplings to look for are the dense *strangolapreti* (literally "priest-chokers") and *gnocchi di ricotta alla zucca* (ricotta and pumpkin dumplings).

CHEESE

Every isolated mountain valley in the Trentino–Alto Adige seems to make its own variety of cheese, and the local specialty is often simply called *nostrano* (ours).

The best known of the cheeses are the mild Asiago and *fontal* and the more pungent *puzzone di Moena* (literally, "stinkpot"). Try the *schiz*: fresh cheese that's sliced and fried in butter, sometimes with cream added.

PASTRIES AND BAKED GOODS

Bakeries turn out a wide selection of crusty dark rolls and caraway-studded rye breads—maybe not typical Italian bread, but full of flavor. Pastries are reminiscent of what you'd expect to find in Vienna. Apple strudel, *pictured below,* is everywhere, and for good reason: the best apples in Italy are grown here.

There are other exceptional fruits as well, including pears, plums, and grapes that make their way into baked goods.

ALIMENTARI

If you're planning a picnic or getting provisions for a hike, you'll be well served by the fine *alimentari* (food shops) of Trentino and Alto Adige. They stock a bounty of regional specialties, including cheeses, pickles, salami, and smoked meats. These are good places to pick up a sample of *speck tirolese*, the salt-cured, cold-smoked, deboned ham hock usually cut in paper-thin slices, like prosciutto (though proud speck producers often bristle at the comparison). Don't discard the fat—it's considered the best part.

WINE

Though Trentino and Alto Adige aren't as esteemed for their wines as many other Italian regions, they produce a wide variety of crisp, dry, and aromatic whites—Kerner, Müller Thurgau, and Traminer, to name a few—not surprisingly, more like what you'd expect from German vineyards than Italian. Among the reds, look for Lagrein and the native Teroldego, a fruity, spicy variety produced only in the tiny valley north of Trento. The Trento D.O.C. appellation yields a marvelous sparkling wine in a class with Champagne.

5

Updated by
Lorna Holland

The Dolomites, the inimitable craggy peaks Le Corbusier called "the most beautiful work of architecture ever seen," are never so arresting as at dusk, when the last rays of sun create a pink hue that languishes into purple—locals call this magnificent transformation the *enrosadira*. You can certainly enjoy this glow from a distance, but the Dolomites are such an appealing year-round destination precisely because of the many ways to get into the mountains themselves. In short order, your perspective—like the peaks around you—will only become more rose colored.

The Dolomites are strange, rocky pinnacles that jut straight up like chimneys: the otherworldly pinnacles that Leonardo depicted in the background of his *Mona Lisa*. In spite of this incredible beauty, the vast, mountainous domain of northeastern Italy has remained relatively undeveloped. Below the peaks, rivers meander through valleys dotted with peaceful villages, while pristine lakes are protected by picture-book castles. In the most secluded Dolomite vales, unique cultures have flourished: the Ladin language, an offshoot of Latin still spoken in the Val Gardena and Val di Fassa, owes its unlikely survival to centuries of topographic isolation.

The more accessible parts of Trentino–Alto Adige, on the other hand, have a history of near-constant intermingling of cultures. The region's Adige and Isarco valleys make up the main access route between Italy and central Europe, and as a result, the language, cuisine, and architecture are a blend of north and south. The province of Trentino is largely Italian-speaking, but Alto Adige is predominantly Germanic: until World War I the area was Austria's south Tirol. As you move north toward the famed Brenner Pass—through the prosperous valley towns of Rovereto, Trento, and Bolzano—the Teutonic influence is increasingly dominant; by the time you reach Bressanone, it's hard to believe you're in Italy at all.

THE DOLOMITES PLANNER

MAKING THE MOST OF YOUR TIME

For a brief stay, your best choice for a base is vibrant Bolzano, where you can get a sense of the region's contrasts—Italian and German, medieval and modern. After a day or two in town, venture an hour south to history-laden Trento, north to the lovely spa town of Merano, or southwest to Caldaro and its Strada di Vino; all are viable day trips from Bolzano, and Trento and Merano make good places to spend the night as well.

If you have more time, you'll want to get up into the mountains, which are the region's main attraction. The trip on the Grande Strada delle Dolomiti (Great Dolomites Road) through the Heart of the Dolomites from Bolzano to Cortina d'Ampezzo is one of Italy's most spectacular drives. Summer or winter, this is a great destination for mountain sports, with scores of trails for world-class hiking and skiing.

GETTING HERE AND AROUND

BUS TRAVEL

Regular bus service connects larger cities to the south (Verona, Venice, and Milan) with valley towns in Trentino–Alto Adige (Rovereto, Trento, Bolzano, and Merano). You'll need to change to less frequent local buses to reach resorts and smaller villages in the mountains beyond.

If you're equipped with current schedules and don't mind adapting your schedules to theirs, it's possible to visit even the remotest villages by bus.

ATVO. A handy way to reach Cortina from Venice is via ATVO, which provides year-round service to Cortina from Venice's Piazzale Roma bus park. ☎ *0421/594672* ⊕ *www.atvo.it.*

CortinaExpress. Winter service via fast bus connects the resort with Venice airport and the nearby Mestre train station. ☎ *0436/867350* ⊕ *www. cortinaexpress.it.*

DolomitiBus. Local service covers the eastern Dolomites, including a number of small towns. ☎ *0437/217111* ⊕ *www.dolomitibus.it.*

SIT (*Servizio Integrato di Trasporto*). ✉ *Alto Adige* ☎ *0471/415480* ⊕ *www.sii.bz.it.*

Trentino Trasporti ☎ *0461/821000* ⊕ *www.ttesercizio.it.*

CAR TRAVEL

Driving is easily the most convenient way to travel in the Dolomites; it can be difficult to reach the ski areas (or any town outside of Rovereto, Trento, Bolzano, and Merano) without a car. Driving is also the most exhilarating way to get around, as you rise from broad valleys into mountains with narrow, winding roads straight out of a sports-car ad. The most important route in the region is the A22, the main north–south highway linking Italy with central Europe by way of the Brenner Pass. It connects Innsbruck with Bressanone, Bolzano, Trento, and Rovereto, and near Verona joins Autostrada A4 (which runs east–west across northern Italy, from Trieste to Turin). By car, Trento is 3 hours from Milan and 2½ hours from Venice. Bolzano is another hour's drive to the north, with Munich four hours farther on.

If you're planning a driving tour of the Dolomites, consider flying into Munich. Car rentals are less expensive in Germany, and it's easier to get automatic transmission if that's what you need to drive. Manual is better, however, for challenging mountain roads.

Caution is essential (tap your horn in advance of hairpin turns), as are chains in winter, when roads are often covered in snow. Sudden closures are common, especially on high mountain passes, and can occur as early as November and as late as May. Even under the best conditions, expect to negotiate mountain roads at speeds no greater than 50 kph (30 mph).

TRAIN TRAVEL

The rail line following the course of the Isarco and Adige valleys—from Munich and Innsbruck, through the Brenner Pass, and southward past Bressanone, Bolzano, Trento, and Rovereto en route to Verona—is well trafficked, making trains a viable option for travel between these towns. Eurocity trains on the Dortmund–Venice and Munich–Innsbruck–Rome routes stop at these stations, and you can connect with other Italian lines at Verona. Although branch lines from Trento and Bolzano do extend into some of the smaller valleys (including hourly service between Bolzano and Merano), most of the mountain attractions are beyond the reach of trains.

Trenitalia ☎ *892021 within Italy* ⊕ *www.trenitalia.com.*

RESTAURANTS

Please note that restaurant prices listed as "average meal" include a meal consisting of first course *(primo)*, second course *(secondo)*, and dessert *(dolce)*.

HOTELS

Classic Dolomite lodging options include restored castles, chalets, and stately 19th-century hotels. The small villages that pepper the Dolomites often have scores of flower-bedecked inns, many of them inexpensive. Hotel information offices at train stations and tourist offices can help if you've arrived without reservations. The Bolzano train station has a 24-hour hotel service, and tourist offices will give you a list of all the hotels in the area, arranged by location, stars, and price. Hotels at ski resorts cater to longer stays at full or half board. Many Italians come to the Dolomites every winter for their *Settimana Bianca* (White Week), and if you care to join them you should book ski vacations as packages well in advance. Most rural accommodations close from early November to mid- or late December, as well as for a month or two after Easter.

TRENTINO

Until the end of World War I, Trentino was Italy's frontier with the Austro-Hungarian Empire, and although this province remains unmistakably Italian, Germanic influences are tangible in all aspects of life here, including architecture, cuisine, culture, and language. Visitors are drawn by historical sights reflecting a strategic position at the intersection of southern and central Europe: Trento was the headquarters of the Catholic Counter-Reformation. Numerous year-round mountain resorts, including fashionable Madonna di Campiglio, are in the wings of the butterfly-shape region.

TRENTO

51 km (32 miles) south of Bolzano, 24 km (15 miles) north of Rovereto.

Trento is a prosperous, cosmopolitan university town that retains an architectural charm befitting its historical importance. It was here, from 1545 to 1563, that the structure of the Catholic Church was redefined at the Council of Trent. This was the starting point of the Counter-Reformation, which brought half of Europe back to Catholicism. The word *consiglio* (council) appears everywhere in Trento—in hotel, restaurant, and street names, and even on wine labels.

Today the Piazza del Duomo remains splendid, and its enormous medieval palazzo dominates the city landscape in virtually its original form. The 24-hour Trento Card (€10), which grants admission to all major town sights, can be bought at the tourist office or any museum. A 48-hour card (€15) is also available, and includes entrance to the modern art museum in nearby Rovereto. Both cards provide a number of other perks, including tours, free public transportation, wine tastings, and the cable car ride to Belvedere di Sardagna.

VISITOR INFORMATION

Trento Tourism Office ✉ *Via Manci 2* ☎ *0461/216000* ⊕ *www.apt.trento.it.*

EXPLORING

Belvedere di Sardagna. You can take the Funivia Trento–Sardagna cable car up to the Belvedere di Sardagna, a lookout point 1,200 feet above medieval Trento. ✉ *Ponte San Lorenzo* ☎ *0461/232154* 🎫 *€5 round trip* ⊘ *Daily 7 am–10:30 pm.*

Castello del Buonconsiglio (*Castle of Good Counsel*). The position and size of this stronghold of the prince-bishops made it easier to defend than the Palazzo Pretorio. Look for the evolution of architectural styles: the medieval fortifications of the Castelvecchio section (on the far left) were built in the 13th century; the fancier Renaissance Magno Palazzo section (on the far right) wasn't completed until 300 years later. Part of the Castello now houses the **Museo Provinciale d'Arte,** where permanent and visiting exhibits of art and archaeology hang in frescoed medieval halls or under Renaissance coffered ceilings. The 13th-century **Torre dell'Aquila** (Eagle's Tower) is home to the castle's artistic highlight, a 15th-century *ciclo dei mesi* (cycle of the months). The four-wall fresco is full of charming and detailed scenes of medieval life in both court and countryside. Reservations are required to visit the tower; check the schedule at the ticket office. ✉ *Via Bernardo Clesio 5* ☎ *0461/233770* ⊕ *www.buonconsiglio.it* 🎫 *€8, Torre dell'Aquila €1 extra* ⊘ *Mid-May–mid-Nov., Tues.–Sun 10–6; mid-Nov.–late Apr., Tues.–Sun. 9:30–5.*

Duomo. This massive Romanesque church, also known as the Cathedral of San Vigilio, forms the southern edge of the Piazza del Duomo. Locals refer to this square as the city's *salotto* (sitting room), as in fine weather it's always filled with students and residents drinking coffee, sipping an

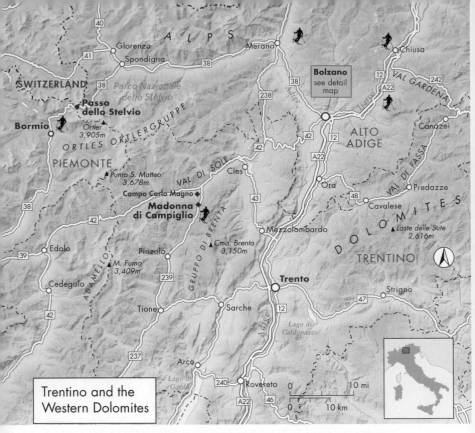

Trentino and the
Western Dolomites

aperitif, or reading the newspaper. The baroque **Fontana del Nettuno** presides over it all. When skies are clear, pause here to savor the view of the mountaintops enveloping the city.

Within the Duomo, unusual arcaded stone stairways border the austere nave. Ahead is the *baldacchino* (altar canopy), a copy of Bernini's masterpiece in St. Peter's in Rome. To the left of the altar is a mournful 16th-century crucifixion, flanked by the Virgin Mary and John the Apostle. This crucifix, by German artist Sisto Frey, was a focal point of the Council of Trent: each decree agreed upon during the two decades of deliberations was solemnly read out in front of it. Stairs on the left side of the altar lead down to the 4th-century Paleo-Christian burial vault. Outside, walk around to the back of the cathedral to see an exquisite display of 14th-century stonemason's art, from the small porch to the intriguing knotted columns on the graceful apse. ⊠ *Piazza del Duomo* ☎ *0461/980132* ⏱ *Daily 6:30–noon and 2–7.*

Guided Tours of Trento. Guided tours of Trento depart Saturdays from the Trento tourism office. You can meet at 10 am for a visit to the Castello del Buonconsiglio (€14, including admission to the castle), or at 3 pm for a tour of the city center (€6). Reservations are not required; these tours and others are included in the Trento Card. Tours are not always offered in English; to guarantee an English-speaking guide, call for reservations. ⊠ *Via Manci 2* ☎ *0461/216000* ⊕ *www.apt.trento.it.*

Museo d'Arte Moderna e Contemporanea di Trento e Rovereto. The Palazzo delle Albere, a Renaissance villa on the Adige River, houses works from the 19th and 20th centuries, but the real focus here is the rotating exhibitions of contemporary artists. ⊠ *Via Roberto da Sanseverino 45* ☎ *800/397760* ⊕ *www.mart.trento.it* ⊠ *€11* ☉ *Tues.–Sun. 10–6.*

Palazzo Pretorio. The fortified residence of the prince-bishops, who enjoyed considerable power and autonomy within the medieval hierarchy, was built in the 13th century and situated so as to seem like a wing of the Duomo. The remarkable palazzo has lost none of its original splendor. The crenellations are not merely decorative: the square pattern represents ancient allegiance to the Guelphs (the triangular crenellations seen elsewhere in town represent Ghibelline loyalty). The palazzo now houses the **Museo Diocesano Tridentino,** where you can see paintings showing the seating plan of the prelates during the Council of Trent; early-16th-century tapestries by Pieter van Aelst (1502–56), the Belgian artist who carried out Raphael's 15th-century designs for the Vatican tapestries; carved wood altars and statues; and an 11th-century sacramentary, or book of services. These and other precious objects all come from the cathedral's treasury. Accessible through the museum, a subterranean archaeological area reveals the 1st-century Roman Porta Veronensis, which marked the road to Verona. ⊠ *Piazza del Duomo 18* ☎ *0461/234419* ⊕ *www.museodiocesanotridentino.it* ⊠ *€5* ☉ *June–Sept., Wed.–Mon. 9:30–12:30 and 2:30–6; Oct.–May, Wed.–Mon. 9:30–12:30 and 2–5:30.*

Santa Maria Maggiore. Many sessions of the Council of Trent met in this Renaissance church. Limited light enters through the simple rose window over the main door, so you have to strain to see the magnificent ceiling, an intricate combination of stucco and frescoes. The church is off the northwest side of the Piazza del Duomo, about 200 yards down Via Cavour. ⊠ *Vicolo Orsoline 1* ☎ *0461/980132* ☉ *Daily 8–noon and 2–6.*

Tridentum. The ancient Roman city of Tridentum lies beneath much of Trento's city center. Centuries of Adige River flooding buried ruins that only recently have been unearthed on public and private land. Beneath this piazza lies the largest of the archaeological sites, revealing some marvels of Roman technology, such as under-floor home heating and under-street sewers complete with manhole covers. The Romans also used lead pipes for four centuries before recognizing it was hazardous to health. Other excavations you can visit lie beneath the Palazzo Pretoria and the Scrigno del Duomo restaurant. ⊠ *Piazza Cesare Battisti* ☎ *0461/230171* ⊠ *€2.50* ☉ *June–Sept., Tues.–Sun. 9:30–1 and 2–6; Oct.–May, Tues.–Sun. 9–1 and 2–5:30.*

QUICK
BITES

Scrigno del Duomo. More than 30 wines by the glass, accompanied by an excellent selection of local cheeses, are served in an upstairs room with some of the oldest frescoes in town. Salads and regional specialties are also available; the *canederli* (seasoned bread dumplings) are especially flavorful here. ⊠ *Piazza del Duomo 29* ☎ *0461/220030* ⊕ *www.scrignodelduomo.com.*

Via Belenzani. Locals refer to this street as Trento's outdoor gallery because of the frescoed facades of the hallmark Renaissance palazzi. It's an easy 50-yard walk up the lane behind the church of Santa Maria Maggiore.

WHERE TO EAT

$ ✕ **Al Vò.** Trento's oldest trattoria (it's the descendant of a 14th-century
NORTHERN tavern) remains one of its most popular lunch spots. Locals crowd into
ITALIAN a simple, modern dining room to enjoy regional specialites like *crema di zucca e castagne* (squash and chestnut soup) and grilled meats, such as the reliable *filetto di maialino* (pork fillet), served in copper skillets. An impressive (and inexpensive) selection of local wines is available; try the food-friendly red Teroldego, made in the valley north of Trento. $ *Average meal: €25* ⊠ *Vicolo del Vò 11* ☎ *0461/985374* ⊕ *www. ristorantealvo.it* ⊘ *Closed Sun. No dinner Mon.–Wed. and Sat.*

$ ✕ **Antica Birreria Pedavena.** Come here for the beer—a half dozen variet-
NORTHERN ies are brewed in-house (as evidence by the big vats looming in front of
ITALIAN you) and served in a cavernous beer hall. Meals include wursts, meat and cheese platters, pizzas, and huge salads. It's open continuously from 9 am to midnight (until 1 am on Friday and Saturday). Smaller wood-paneled dining rooms and a summer terrace allow for more peaceful dining. $ *Average meal: €19* ⊠ *Piazza Fiera 13* ☎ *0461/986255* ⊕ *www.birreriapedavena.com* ⊘ *Closed Tues.*

$$ ✕ **Le Due Spade.** An intimate dining room that started out as a Tiro-
NORTHERN lean tavern around the time of the Council of Trent is known for
ITALIAN superb cuisine, both traditional and more innovative, adeptly served amid the coziness of wood paneling and an antique stove. You can sample *maialino* (suckling pig) wrapped in a crust of speck, or be more adventurous with *agnello in manto alle fave di cacao* (lamb coated with cocoa beans) served with foie-gras sauce. Given the restaurant's deserved popularity with locals and the limited seating, reservations are a must. $ *Average meal: €45* ⊠ *Via Rizzi 11* ☎ *0461/234343* ⊕ *www.leduespade.com* ⊜ *Reservations essential* ⊘ *Closed Sun. No lunch Mon.*

$ ✕ **Pizzeria Laste.** Owner Guido Rizzi is a national pizza-making cham-
PIZZA pion; he invented pizza Calabrese, a white pizza with garlic, mozza-rella, and red-pepper flakes. Each of his 35 pies—especially the *sedano* (mozzarella, celery root, aged Parmesan cheese, oregano)—is delectable. Save room for desserts like the pizza *dolce* (sweet), which is made with bananas, strawberries, kiwi, and caramel. In a pleasant hilltop villa above the city center, the pizzeria is a bit hard to reach, but worth it. $ *Average meal: €18* ⊠ *Via alle Laste 37* ☎ *0461/231570* ⊕ *www. pizzerialaste.it* ⊘ *Closed Tues.*

$$ ✕ **Trattoria Orso Grigio.** The family-run "gray bear," just off the main
NORTHERN piazza, serves tasty fare in a congenial atmosphere. Choose from typi-
ITALIAN cal regional dishes—look for *rufioi* (homemade ravioli stuffed with savoy cabbage)—served in a bright garden courtyard when the weather is fine. The wine list is mostly regional and pairs well with the menu. $ *Average meal: €32* ⊠ *Via degli Orti 19* ☎ *0461/984400* ⊕ *www. orsogrigiotrento.com* ⊘ *Closed Sun.*

WHERE TO STAY

For expanded hotel reviews, visit Fodors.com.

$$ HOTEL 🏨 **Accademia.** Stylishly contemporary bedrooms with comfortable beds and handsome lithographs occupy an ancient, character-filled house close to Piazza del Duomo. **Pros:** central location; charming outdoor restaurant. **Cons:** some rooms are small; stark decor; basic breakfast. [$] *Rooms from: €165 ✉ Vicolo Colico 4 ☎ 0461/233600 🌐 www.accademiahotel.it 🛏 35 rooms, 5 suites ⏲ Closed late Dec.–early Jan. 🍴 Breakfast.*

$$ B&B/INN 🏨 **Castel Pergine.** Tucked into a 13th-century castle's labyrinth of stone and brick chambers, prisons, and chapels are sparse, rustic rooms with carved-wood trim, lace curtains, and heavy wooden beds, some canopied. **Pros:** romantic setting; great restaurant. **Cons:** simple accommodations; need a car to get around. [$] *Rooms from: €145 ✉ Via al Castello 10, Pergine Val Sugana ✥ 12 km (7½ miles) east of Trento ☎ 0461/531158 🌐 www.castelpergine.it 🛏 21 rooms, 14 with bath ⏲ Closed Nov.–Mar. No lunch Mon. 🍴 Multiple meal plans.*

$$ HOTEL 🏨 **Hotel Garni Aquila d'Oro.** Each room has its own contemporary design, some have saunas and terraces with hot tubs and stunning views, and all enjoy a prime location near Piazza del Duomo. **Pros:** excellent location; friendly service. **Cons:** common areas rather cramped. [$] *Rooms from: €160 ✉ Via Belenzani 76 ☎ 0461/986282 🌐 www.aquiladoro.it 🛏 16 rooms 🍴 Breakfast.*

$ B&B/INN 🏨 **Hotel Garni Venezia.** For reasonably priced accommodations, it's hard to beat this *garni* (bed-and-breakfast) right on Piazza Duomo, where six of the simple rooms have wonderful views. **Pros:** great location; friendly environs. **Cons:** piazza can be noisy; not all rooms have private baths or TVs. [$] *Rooms from: €80 ✉ Piazza Duomo 45 ☎ 0461/234559 🌐 www.hotelveneziatn.it 🛏 43 rooms 🍴 Breakfast.*

$$$ HOTEL 🏨 **Imperial Grand Hotel Terme.** If you're in the mood for some pampering, choose a grand room with a frescoed ceiling in the graciously restored, golden yellow palace in the nearby spa town of Levico Terme. **Pros:** beautiful park setting; pleasant indoor pool. **Cons:** standard rooms are small; use of thermal baths costs extra. [$] *Rooms from: €220 ✉ Via Silva Domini 1, Levico Terme ✥ 20 km (12 miles) east of Trento ☎ 0461/706104 🌐 www.imperialhotel.it 🛏 69 rooms, 12 suites ⏲ Closed Nov.–Mar. 🍴 Some meals.*

NIGHTLIFE AND THE ARTS

I Suoni delle Dolomiti (*The Sounds of the Dolomites*). This annual series of free concerts is held high in the hills of Trentino in July and August, offering the wonderful experience of enjoying chamber music played in grassy meadows. ☎ *0461/219500* 🌐 *www.isuonidelledolomiti.it.*

SHOPPING

Enoteca di Corso. This atmospheric shop, a bit outside the town center, is laden with local products, including wine and sweets. ✉ *Corso 3 Novembre 64* ☎ *0461/916424.*

La Salumeria Mattei. A picnic can be handily assembled from a huge assortment of local salamis and cheeses. ✉ *Via Mazzini 46* ☎ *0461/238053* 🌐 *www.salumeriamattei.it.*

5

Panificio Pulin. Whole grain breads and delicate pastries are on offer in this fragrant bakery. ⊠ *Via Cavour 23* ☏ *0461/234544.*

Piazza Alessandro Vittoria. You can pick up meats, cheeses, produce, local truffles, and porcini mushrooms at the small morning market in the square.

EN ROUTE Traveling west and then north from Trento to Madonna di Campiglio, you zigzag through lovely mountain valleys, past small farming communities such as Tione.

San Vigilio. Outside the small mountain village of Pinzolo (on the SS239), stop at the church of San Vigilio to see the remarkable 16th-century fresco on the exterior south wall. Painted in 1539 by the artist Simone Baschenis, the painting describes the Dance of Death: a macabre parade of 40 sinners from all walks of life (in roughly descending order of worldly importance), each guided to his end by a ghoulish escort. The church's interior is closed to the public. ⊠ *Via San Vigilio, Pinzolo, Italy.*

MADONNA DI CAMPIGLIO

80 km (50 miles) northwest of Trento, 100 km (62 miles) southwest of Bolzano.

The winter resort of Madonna di Campiglio vies with Cortina d'Ampezzo as the most fashionable place for Italians to ski and be seen in the Dolomites. Madonna's popularity is well deserved, with 39 lifts connecting more than 120 km (75 miles) of well-groomed ski runs and equally good lodging and trekking facilities. The resort itself is a modest 5,000 feet above sea level, but the downhill runs, summer hiking paths, and mountain-biking trails venture high up into the surrounding peaks (including Pietra Grande at 9,700 feet).

VISITOR INFORMATION
Madonna di Campiglio Tourism Office ⊠ *Via Pradalago 4* ☏ *0465/447501* ⊕ *www.campigliodolomiti.it.*

EXPLORING
Campo Carlo Magno. The stunning pass at Campo Carlo Magno (5,500 feet) is 3 km (2 miles) north of Madonna di Campiglio. This is where Charlemagne is said to have stopped in AD 800 on his way to Rome to be crowned emperor. Stop here to glance over the whole of northern Italy. If you continue north, take the descent with caution—in the space of a mile or so, hairpin turns and switchbacks deliver you down more than 2,000 feet.

WHERE TO EAT
$$
NORTHERN
ITALIAN
✕ **Cascina Zeledria.** Although the majority of meals in Madonna are taken in resort hotels, Italians consider an on-mountain dinner like one in this remote, rustic refuge to be an indispensable part of a proper ski week. In winter, you'll be collected on a Sno-Cat and ferried up the slopes (you'll hike up in warmer months). After the 10-minute ride, sit down to grill your own meats and vegetables over stone griddles; the kitchen-prepared mushrooms and polenta are house specialties. Call

in advance to reserve a table and arrange for transportation. $ *Average meal: €35* ✉ *Località Zeledria* ☎ *0465/440303* ⊕ *www.zeledria.it* ⚲ *Reservations essential* ⊘ *Closed May, June, Oct., and Nov.*

$$
WINE BAR
✕**Ferrari Spazio Bollicine Nabucco.** This intimate venue has the feel of a rustic-yet-stylish chalet and is done in a black-and-white color scheme. Guests settle into these pleasant surroundings for an après-ski aperitif or a light meal, based on local ingredients and paired with sparkling wines from Ferrari, a well-known Trentino vintner. $ *Average meal: €30* ✉ *Piazza Righi, B3, Madonna di Campiglio* ☎ *0465/440756.*

WHERE TO STAY
For expanded hotel reviews, visit Fodors.com.

$$$
HOTEL
🛏**Golf Hotel.** You need to make your way north to the Campo Carlo Magno Pass to reach this grand hotel, the former summer residence of Habsburg emperor Franz Josef, replete with verandas, Persian rugs, and bay windows. **Pros:** attractive indoor pool; elegant rooms. **Cons:** long walk into town; popular with business groups. $ *Rooms from: €190* ✉ *Via Cima Tosa 3* ☎ *0465/441003* ⊕ *www.atahotels.it/golf-campiglio* 🛏 *109 rooms, 13 suites* ⊘ *Closed late Mar.–June and Sept.–late Nov.* ⦿ *Breakfast.*

$$$
HOTEL
🛏**Grifone.** At this comfortable lodge with a distinctive wood facade, flower-bedecked balconies catch the sun and contemporary guest rooms and suites have views of the forested slopes. **Pros:** convenient location; charming decor. **Cons:** half board is mandatory; lacks air-conditioning; a bit out of town (but the Spinale cable car is nearby). $ *Rooms from: €180* ✉ *Via Vallesinella 7* ☎ *0465/442002* ⊕ *www.hotelgrifone.it* 🛏 *38 rooms, 2 suites* ⊘ *Closed mid-Apr.–June and Sept.–Nov.* ⦿ *Some meals.*

$$$$
HOTEL
🛏**Savoia Palace.** At Madonna's most traditional lodging, guest rooms and lounges are full of carved-wood and mountain-style furnishings and two fireplaces blaze away in the bar, where you can relax as you recall the day's exploits on the ski slopes. **Pros:** central location in town; warm atmosphere; nice spa. **Cons:** half board is mandatory; some rooms need refurbishing; faces a busy street. $ *Rooms from: €310* ✉ *Viale Dolomiti di Brenta 18* ☎ *0465/441004* ⊕ *www.savoiapalace.com* 🛏 *55 rooms* ⊘ *Closed mid-Apr.–June and Sept.–Dec.* ⦿ *Some meals.*

SPORTS AND THE OUTDOORS
HIKING AND CLIMBING
The Madonna di Campiglio tourism office has maps of a dozen trails leading to waterfalls, lakes, and stupefying views.

Punta Spinale (*Spinale Peak*). The cable car to 6,900-foot-high Punta Spinale offers skiers magnificent views of the Brenta Dolomites in winter. It also runs during peak summer season. ✉ *Off Via Monte Spinale* ☎ *0465/447744* 💶 *€9 round trip.*

SKIING
Funivie Madonna di Campiglio. Miles of interconnecting ski runs—some of the best in the Dolomites—are linked by the cable cars and lifts of Funivie Madonna di Campiglio. Advanced skiers will like the extremely difficult terrain found on certain mountain faces, but there are also many intermediate and beginner runs, all accessible from town. There

are also plenty of off-piste opportunities. Passes can be purchased at the main *funivia* (cable car) in town. ☒ *Via Presanella 12* ☎ *0465/447744* ⊕ *www.funiviecampiglio.it* ☒ *Passes €39–€44 per day.*

EN ROUTE The route between Madonna di Campiglio and Bormio (2½ hours) takes you through a series of high mountain passes. After Campo Carlo Magno, turn left at Dimaro and continue 37 km (23 miles) west through Passo del Tonale (6,200 feet). At Ponte di Legno, turn north on SS300. You pass the Lago Nero (Black Lake) on your left just before the summit. Continue on to Bormio through the Passo di Gavia (8,600 feet).

THE WESTERN DOLOMITES

The Parco Nazionale dello Stelvio extends through western Trentino and the Altoatesino area of Alto Adige, and even into eastern Lombardia. It's named for the famed Stelvio, Europe's highest road pass and the site of the highest battle fought during World War I. The well-preserved town of Bormio merits a visit for its history and character, even if you don't want to ski its trails or indulge in one of its equally renowned spa treatments.

BORMIO

97 km (60 miles) northwest of Madonna di Campiglio, 100 km (62 miles) southwest of Merano.

At the foot of Stelvio Pass, Bormio is the most famous ski resort on the western side of the Dolomites, with 38 km (24 miles) of long pistes and a 5,000-plus-foot vertical drop. In summer its cool temperatures and clean air entice Italians away from cities in the humid Lombard plain. This dual-season, winter/summer popularity supports the plentiful shops, restaurants, and hotels in town. Bormio has been known for the therapeutic qualities of its waters since the Roman era, and there are numerous spas.

VISITOR INFORMATION
Bormio Tourism Office ☒ *Via Roma 131/B* ☎ *0342/903300* 🖷 *0342/904696* ⊕ *www.aptbormio.it.*

EXPLORING
Bagni Vecchi (*Old Baths*). Ancient Roman baths predate the thermal springs, caves, and waterfalls now known as the Bagni Vecchi; Leonardo da Vinci soaked here in 1493. ☒ *Via Bagni Vecchi* ☎ *0342/910131* ⊕ *www.bagnidibormio.it* ☒ *€48* ⊙ *Daily 10–8.*

Bormio Terme. Modern facilities and comprehensive spa treatments are available at these municipal baths. ☒ *Via Stelvio 14* ☎ *0342/901325* ⊕ *www.bormioterme.it* ☒ *€16* ⊙ *Sat.–Tues. and Thurs. 10–8, Wed. and Fri. 10–10.*

Parco Nazionale dello Stelvio. The Alps' biggest national park is spread over 1,350 square km (520 square miles) and four provinces. Opened in 1935 to preserve flora and protect fauna, today it has more than 1,200 types of plants, 600 different mushrooms, and more than 160 species of animals, including the chamois, ibex, and roe deer. There are many entrances to the park, and a dozen visitor centers. Bormio makes a good base for exploring—the closest entrance to town is the year-round gateway at Torre Alberti. ✉ *Via de Simone 42* ☎ *0342/900811* 🌐 *www.parks.it/parco.nazionale.stelvio* 🎟 *Free.*

WHERE TO EAT

$$ NORTHERN ITALIAN 🍴 **Caffe Kuerc.** This building was for centuries where justice was publicly served to accused witches, among others. These days, things at the restaurant are less momentous: enjoy local specialties like *bresaola* (salted, air-dried beef) with lemon and olive oil, or *pizzoccheri* (buckwheat pasta) with garlic and winter vegetables. [$] *Average meal: €28* ✉ *Piazza Cavour 8* ☎ *0342/910787* ⏲ *Closed Tues.*

WHERE TO STAY

For expanded hotel reviews, visit Fodors.com.

$ HOTEL 🏨 **La Genzianella.** Alpine chic without high expense or pretense includes contemporary decor with warm pine, ceramics, rich textiles, and beamed ceilings; all but three rooms have balconies and "charme" suites include hydromassage tubs. **Pros:** great for bikers; handy to slopes and town. **Cons:** no pool. [$] *Rooms from: €125* ✉ *Via Zandilla 6* ☎ *0342/904485* 🌐 *www.genzianella.com* 🛏 *40 rooms* ⏲ *Closed May and mid-Sept.–Dec.* 🍽 *Breakfast.*

$$$ B&B/INN 🏨 **Nazionale.** Behind the Alpine exterior of this inn on the edge of Stelvio National Park are small but nicely furnished rooms with balconies in all but those on the top floor. **Pros:** great location; winter and summer activities; family-friendly environment. **Cons:** may require a 20% supplement for stays of fewer than three nights. [$] *Rooms from: €160* ✉ *Via al Forte 28* ☎ *0342/903361* 🌐 *www.nazionalebormio.it* 🛏 *48 rooms* 🍽 *Breakfast.*

SPORTS AND THE OUTDOORS

SKIING

Funivia. You can buy a ski pass (€34–€38 per day) and pick up a trail map at the base in the center of town to connect to the Bormio 2000 station (6,600 feet) on Vallecetta, the main resort mountain. From there, you can ski down intermediate trails (which comprise the majority of Bormio's runs), use the extensive lift network to explore secondary ski areas, or get another funivia up to the Bormio 3000 station at Cima Bianca (9,800 feet) for more challenging terrain. The cable car also runs July to mid-September, when it is used by mountain bikers to reach long trails through breathtaking Alpine terrain; less-ambitious visitors can wander around and then ride the cable car back down. ✉ *Via Battaglion Morbegno 25* ☎ *0342/902770* 🌐 *www.skipassaltavaltellina.it.*

PASSO DELLO STELVIO

20 km (12 miles) north of Bormio, 80 km (48 miles) west of Merano.

Passo dello Stelvio. At more than 9,000 feet, the Passo dello Stelvio is the second-highest pass in Europe, connecting the Valtellina in Lombardy with the Val Venosta in Alto Adige. The view from the top is well worth the drive; looking north you can see Switzerland. The pass is open from

5

May or June to October, depending on weather conditions. Stelvio itself is a year-round skiing center, with many of its runs open in summer.

EN
ROUTE
Between the Stelvio Pass and the town of Spondigna, 30 km (19 miles) of road wind down 48 hair-raising hairpin turns. The views are spectacular, but this descent is not for the faint of heart. In Spondigna keep to the right for the road to Naturno.

BOLZANO (BOZEN)

32 km (19 miles) south of Merano, 50 km (31 miles) north of Trento.

Bolzano (Bozen), capital of the autonomous province of Alto Adige, is tucked among craggy peaks in a Dolomite valley 77 km (48 miles) from the Brenner Pass and Austria. Tirolean culture dominates Bolzano's language, food, architecture, and people. It may be hard to remember that you're in Italy when walking the city's colorful cobblestone streets and visiting its lantern-lighted cafés, where you may enjoy sauerkraut and a beer among a lively crowd of blue-eyed German speakers. However, the fine Italian espresso and the boutiques will help remind you where you are. The long, narrow arcades of its Via dei Portici house shops that specialize in Tirolean crafts and clothing, as well as many Italian designers. With castles and steeples topping the landscape, this quiet city at the confluence of the Isarco (Eisack) and Talvera rivers has retained its provincial appeal. Proximity to fabulous skiing and mountain climbing—not to mention the world's oldest preserved body—make it a worthwhile tourist destination. And its streets are immaculate: its residents have the highest per capita earnings of any city in Italy.

VISITOR INFORMATION
Bolzano Tourism Office ⊠ *Piazza Walther 8* ☎ *0471/307000*
⊕ *www.bolzano-bozen.it* ⊙ *Weekdays 9–7, Sat. 9:30–6.*

EXPLORING BOLZANO

TOP ATTRACTIONS

Chiesa dei Domenicani. The 13th-century Dominican Church is renowned as Bolzano's main repository for paintings, especially frescoes. In the adjoining **Cappella di San Giovanni** you can see works from the Giotto school that show the birth of a pre-Renaissance sense of depth and individuality; come prepared with 50-cent coins for the lights. ⊠ *Piazza Domenicani* ☎ *0471/973133* ⊙ *Mon.–Sat. 9:30–5, Sun. noon–6.*

Duomo. A lacy spire looks down on the mosaic-like roof tiles of the city's Gothic cathedral, built between the 12th and 14th century. Inside are 14th- and 15th-century frescoes and an intricately carved stone pulpit dating from 1514. Outside, don't miss the **Porta del Vino** (Wine Gate) on the northeast side; decorative carvings of grapes and harvest workers attest to the long-standing importance of wine to this region. ⊠ *Piazza della Parrocchia 27* ☎ *0471/978676* ⊙ *Mon.–Sat. 10–noon and 2–5.*

Fodor's Choice
★   **Museo Archeologico dell'Alto Adige.** This museum has gained international fame for Ötzi, its 5,300-year-old iceman, discovered in 1991 and the world's oldest naturally preserved body. In 1998 Italy acquired it from

Austria after it was determined that the body lay 100 yards inside Italian territory. The iceman's leathery remains are displayed in a freezer vault, preserved along with his longbow, ax, and clothing. The rest of the museum relies on models and artifacts from nearby archaeological sites, and exhibits are changed out regularly. An eloquent English audio guide leads you not only through Ötzi's Copper Age, but also into the preceding Mesolithic and Neolithic eras, and the Bronze and Iron ages that followed. In July and August, the museum's supervised play area keeps young children entertained while adults experience the museum. ⊠ *Via Museo 43* 🖃 *0471/320100, 0471/320123* ⊕ *www.iceman.it* 🖃 *€9* ⊗ *July, Aug., and Dec., daily 10–6; Jan.–June and Sept.–Nov., Tues.– Sun. 10–6; last entry 5:30.*

Piazza delle Erbe. A bronze statue of Neptune, which dates to 1745, presides over a bountiful fruit-and-vegetable market in this square. The stalls spill over with colorful displays of local produce; bakeries and grocery stores showcase hot breads, pastries, cheeses, and delicatessen meats—a complete picnic. Try the speck tirolese and the apple strudel.

Piazza Walther. This pedestrians-only square is Bolzano's heart; in warmer weather it serves as an open-air living room where locals and tourists can be found at all hours sipping a drink (such as a glass of chilled Riesling). In the center stands Heinrich Natter's white-marble, neo-Romanesque **Monument to Walther,** built in 1889. The piazza's namesake was the 12th-century German wandering minstrel Walther von der Vogelweide, whose songs lampooned the papacy and praised the Holy Roman Emperor.

WORTH NOTING

Castel Roncolo (*Schloss Runkelstein*). Green hills and farmhouses north of town surround this meticulously kept castle with a red roof. It was built in 1237, destroyed half a century later, and then rebuilt soon thereafter. There's a beautifully preserved cycle of medieval frescoes inside. A tavern in the courtyard serves excellent local food and wines. To get here from Piazza Walther, take the free shuttle (Tuesday–Sunday every half hour 10–5), or the No. 12 bus. It's a 20-minute walk from Piazza delle Erbe: head north along Via Francescani, continue through Piazza Madonna, connecting to Via Castel Roncolo. ✉ *Via San Antonio 15* ☎ *0471/329808 castle, 0471/324073 tavern* 🌐 *www.roncolo.info* 🎫 *€8* 🕒 *Tues.–Sun. 10–6; last entry 5:30.*

Messner Mountain Museum Firmian. Perched on a peak overlooking Bolzano, 10th-century Castle Sigmundskron is home to one of five Dolomite museums established by Reinhold Messner—the first climber to conquer Everest solo and the first to reach its summit without oxygen. The Tibetan tradition of *kora,* a circular pilgrimage around a sacred site, is an inspiration for the museum, where visitors contemplate the relationship between man and mountain, guided by images and objects Messner collected during his adventures. Guided tours begin every half hour. The museum is 3 km (2 miles) southwest of Bolzano, just off the Appiano exit on the highway to Merano. ✉ *Via Castel Firmiano 53* ☎ *0471/631264* 🌐 *www.messner-mountain-museum.it* 🎫 *€8* 🕒 *Mar.–late Nov., Fri.–Wed. 10–6; last entry 5.*

Museo Civico. Bolzano's municipal museum has a rich collection of traditional costumes, wood carvings, and archaeological exhibits. ✉ *Via Cassa di Risparmio 14* ☎ *0471/997960* 🌐 *www.bolzano.net/museocivico.htm* 🎫 *Varies with exhibitions* 🕒 *Tues.–Sun. 10–6.*

Passeggiata del Guncina. An 8-km (5-mile) botanical promenade dating from 1892 ends with a panoramic view of Bolzano. ✉ *Entrance near Vecchia Parrocchiale, in Gries, across river and up Corso Libertà.*

Vecchia Parrocchiale (*Old Parish Church*). Visit this church, said to have been built in 1141, to see its two medieval treasures: an 11th-century Romanesque crucifix and an elaborately carved 15th-century wooden altar by Michael Pacher—a masterpiece of the Gothic style. ✉ *Via Martin Knoller, in Gries, across river and up Corso Libertà* ☎ *0471/283089* 🕒 *Apr.–Oct., weekdays 10:30–noon and 2:30–4.*

WHERE TO EAT

$ NORTHERN ITALIAN

🍴 **Alexander.** Typical Tirolean dishes are served at this convivial spot. The venison ham and the lamb cutlets *al timo con salsa all'aglio* (with thyme and garlic sauce) are particularly good, but make sure to leave room for the rich chocolate cake. [$] *Average meal: €30* ✉ *Via Aosta 37* ☎ *0471/918608* 🕒 *Closed Sat.*

CLOSE UP

Enrosadira and the Dwarf King

The French nobleman and geologist Déodat Guy Silvain Tancrède Gratet de Dolomieu (1750–1801) got his name applied to the Dolomite range after demonstrating that the peaks have a particular composition of stratified calcium magnesium carbonate that generates a rosy evening glow, a spectacle known as "enrosadira." For those unconvinced that such a phenomenon can be explained by geology alone, Ladin legend offers a compelling alternative.

Laurin, King of the Dwarfs, became infatuated with the daughter of a neighboring (human) king, and captured her with the aid of a magic hood that made him invisible. As he spirited her back to the mountains, the dwarf king was pursued by many knights, who were able to track the kidnapper after spotting his beloved rose garden. Laurin was captured and imprisoned, and when he finally managed to escape and return home, he cast a spell turning the betraying roses into rocks—so they could be seen neither by day nor by night. But Laurin forgot to include dusk in his spell, which is why the Dolomites take on a rosy glow just before nightfall. (This story is the subject of frescoes in the bar of Bolzano's Parkhotel Laurin.)

5

$ WINE BAR 🍴 **Batzenhausl.** Locals hold animated conversations over glasses of regional wine in a modern take a traditional Stube. Tasty south Tirolean specialties include speck tirolese and *mezzelune casarecce ripiene* (house-made stuffed half-moons of pasta). If you're seeking a quiet meal, ask for a table on the second floor, near the handsome stained-glass windows. This is a good place for a late bite, as food is served until midnight. [$] *Average meal: €30* ✉ *Via Andreas Hofer 30* ☎ *0471/050950* 🌐 *www.batzen.it.*

$ NORTHERN ITALIAN 🍴 **Cavallino Bianco.** A spacious, comfortable dining room near Via dei Portici is a dependable favorite with residents as well as visitors. A wide selection of Italian and German dishes are served to large tables of families enjoying their meals together. [$] *Average meal: €21* ✉ *Via Bottai 6* ☎ *0471/973267* 🌐 *www.weissesroessl.org* 🕓 *Closed Sun. No dinner Sat.*

$ NORTHERN ITALIAN 🍴 **Hopfen & Co.** Fried white *Würstel* (sausage), sauerkraut, and grilled ribs complement the excellent home-brewed Austrian-style pilsner and wheat beer at this bustling pub-restaurant. There's live music on Thursday night, attracting Bolzano's students and young professionals. [$] *Average meal: €25* ✉ *Piazza delle Erbe, Obstplatz 17* ☎ *0471/300788* 🌐 *www.boznerbier.it.*

$$ NORTHERN ITALIAN 🍴 **Wirthaus Vögele.** Ask residents of Bolzano where they like to dine out, and odds are good they'll tell you Vögele, one of the area's oldest inns. The classic wood-panel dining room on the ground level is often packed, but don't despair, as the restaurant has two additional floors. The menu features Sud Tyrol standards, including canederli with speck and venison. [$] *Average meal: €35* ✉ *Goethestr 3* ☎ *0471/973938* 🌐 *www.voegele.it* 🕓 *Closed Sun.*

WHERE TO STAY

For expanded hotel reviews, visit Fodors.com.

$$$
HOTEL
Fodor'sChoice
★

⊞ **Hotel Greif.** A revamp has filled individually designed guest rooms in a centuries-old Bolzano landmark with clean-line modern furnishings and contemporary art paired with 19th-century paintings and sketches. **Pros:** elegant decor; helpful staff; central location. **Cons:** rooms vary in size; sometimes filled with tour groups. $ *Rooms from: €220* ⊠ *Piazza Walther 1* ☎ *0471/318000* ⊕ *www.greif.it* ⤳ *27 rooms, 6 suites* ⦿ *Breakfast.*

$$
HOTEL

⊞ **Luna-Mondschein.** Comfortable, wood-paneled rooms, some with balconies, overlook a garden or the mountains, and all are swathed in the charming ambience of this inn from 1798. **Pros:** central location; great buffet breakfast. **Cons:** rooms vary in size; rooms facing garage can be noisy. $ *Rooms from: €141* ⊠ *Via Piave 15* ☎ *0471/975642* ⊕ *www.hotel-luna.it* ⤳ *80 rooms* ⦿ *Breakfast.*

$$
HOTEL

⊞ **Parkhotel Laurin.** An exercise in art nouveau opulence, presiding over a large park in the middle of town, is one of the best hotels in all of Alto Adige, with art-filled modern guest rooms and handsome public spaces. **Pros:** convenient location; excellent restaurant. **Cons:** rooms facing park can be noisy; can be packed with business groups. $ *Rooms from: €174* ⊠ *Via Laurin 4* ☎ *0471/311000* ⊕ *www.laurin.it* ⤳ *93 rooms, 7 suites* ⦿ *Breakfast.*

$$$
B&B/INN

⊞ **Schloss Korb.** This romantic 13th-century castle with crenellations and a massive tower is perched in a park amid vine-covered hills, viewed through some of the cozy rooms through Romanesque arched windows. **Pros:** romantic setting; charming traditional furnishings. **Cons:** not all rooms are in the castle; need a car to get around. $ *Rooms from: €230* ⊠ *Via Castel d'Appiano 5, Missiano/Appiano* ☎ *0471/636000* ⊕ *www.schlosskorb.com* ⤳ *35 rooms, 10 suites* ⊘ *Closed Nov.–Mar.* ⦿ *Breakfast.*

ALTO ADIGE

Prosperous valley towns (such as the famed spa center of Merano) and mountain resorts entice those seeking both relaxation and adventure. Alto Adige (Südtirol) was for centuries part of the Austro-Hungarian Empire, only ceded to Italy at the end of World War I. Ethnic differences led to inevitable tensions in the 1960s and again in the '80s, though a large measure of provincial autonomy has, for the most part, kept the lid on nationalist ambitions. Today Germanic and Italian balance harmoniously, as do medieval and modern influences, with ancient castles regularly playing host to contemporary art exhibitions.

MERANO (MERAN)

24 km (15 miles) north of Bolzano, 16 km (10 miles) east of Naturno.

The second-largest town in Alto Adige, Merano (Meran) was once the capital of the Austrian region of Tirol. When the town and surrounding area were ceded to Italy as part of the 1919 Treaty of Versailles, Innsbruck became Tirol's capital. Merano continued to be known as a

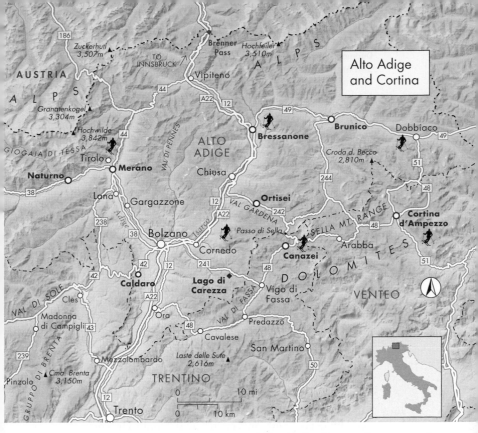

spa town, attracting European nobility for its therapeutic waters and its grape cure, which consists simply of eating the grapes grown on the surrounding hillsides. Sheltered by mountains, Merano has an unusually mild climate, with summer temperatures rarely exceeding 80°F (27°C) and winters that usually stay above freezing, despite the skiing that's within easy reach. Along the narrow streets of Merano's old town, houses have little towers and huge wooden doors, and the pointed arches of the Gothic cathedral sit next to neoclassical and art nouveau buildings. Merano serves as a good respite from mountain adventures, or from the bustle of nearby Trento and Bolzano.

VISITOR INFORMATION
Merano Tourism Office ⊠ *Corso Libertà 45* ☏ *0473/272000* ⊕ *www.meran.eu.*

EXPLORING
Castel Trauttmansdorff. This Gothic castle was restored in the 19th century and now serves as a museum, celebrating 200 years of tourism in south Tirol. Outside, a sprawling garden has an extensive display of exotic flora organized by country of origin. An English-language audio guide is available for €2.50. The castle is about 2 km (1 mile) southeast of town. ⊠ *Via Valentino 51a* ☏ *0473/235730* ⊕ *www.trauttmansdorff. it* ⎙*€11* ⏱ *Apr.–Oct., daily 9–7; Jun.–Aug., Fri. 9 am–11 pm; early Nov., daily 9–5.*

Duomo. The 14th-century Gothic cathedral, with a crenellated facade and an ornate campanile, sits in the heart of the old town. The Capella di Santa Barbara, just behind the Duomo, is an octagonal church containing a 15th-century pietà. Mass is only held in German. ⊠ *Piazza del Duomo* ☎ *0473/230174* ☉ *Daily 8–6.*

Museo Agricolo di Brunnenburg. Overlooking the town atop Mt. Tappeinerweg is Castel Fontana, which was the home of poet Ezra Pound from 1958 to 1964. Still in the Pound family, the castle now houses the Museo Agricolo di Brunnenburg, devoted to Tirolean country life. Among its exhibits are a blacksmith's shop and a room with Pound memorabilia. To get here, take Bus No. 3, which departs every hour on the hour, from Merano to Dorf Tirol (20 minutes). ⊠ *Via Castello 17, Brunnenburg* ☎ *0473/923533* ⊠ *€3* ☉ *Easter–Oct., Sun.–Thurs. 10–5.*

Fodor's Choice
★

Promenades. A stroll along one of Merano's well-marked, impossibly pleasant promenades may yield even better relaxation than time in its famous spa. **Passeggiata Tappeiner** (Tappeiner's Promenade) is a 3-km (2-mile) path with panoramic views from the hills north of the Duomo and diverse botanical pleasures along the way. **Passeggiata d'Estate** (Summer Promenade) runs along the shaded south bank of the Passirio River, and the **Passeggiata d'Inverno** (Winter Promenade), on the exposed north bank, provides more warmth and the Wandelhalle—a sunny area decorated with idyllic paintings of surrounding villages. The popular Austrian empress Sissi (Elisabeth of Wittelsbach, 1837–98) put Merano on the map as a spa destination; a trail named in her honor, the **Sentiero di Sissi** (Sissi's Walk), follows a path from Castel Trauttmansdorff to the heart of Merano.

FAMILY

Terme di Merano. This sprawling spa complex has 25 pools (including a brine pool with underwater music) and eight saunas (with an indoor "snow room" available for cooling down). Along with the family-friendly options for bathing, personalized services for grown-ups include traditional cures using local products, such as grape-based applications and whey baths. An admission charge of about €12.50 gets you two hours in thermal baths; €24.50 is for a full day's use of all baths and saunas. ⊠ *Piazza Terme 9* ☎ *0473/252000* ⊕ *www.termemerano. it* ☉ *Daily 9 am–10 pm.*

QUICK
BITES

Cafe Glif. You can enjoy a rich hot chocolate or a cold beer above a gurgling waterfall at the northeast edge of the Passeggiata d'Inverno. ⊠ *Passeggiata Glif 51* ☎ *0473/690321* ☉ *Fri.–Wed. 10–8.*

Cafe Saxifraga. An extensive selection of teas and other beverages can be enjoyed on the patio; the cafe has an enviable position overlooking Merano and the peaks enveloping the town. ⊠ *Passeggiata Tappeiner* ☎ *0473/239249* ⊕ *www.saxifraga.it.*

WHERE TO EAT

$
NORTHERN
ITALIAN

✗ **Haisrainer.** Among the rustic wine taverns lining Via dei Portici, this one is most popular with locals and tourists alike; a menu in English is available. Warm wooden walls provide a comfortable setting for Tirolean and Italian standards: try the *zuppa al vino bianco* (stew with white wine) or the seasonal risottos (with asparagus in spring, or Barolo wine in chillier months). $ Average meal: €25 ⊠ Via dei Portici 100 ☎ 0473/237944 ⊘ Closed Sun.

$$
ITALIAN
✗ **Sieben.** Young Meraners crowd the bar on the ground floor of this modern bistro, in the town's central arcade. Upstairs, an older crowd enjoys the contemporary cooking and attentive service in the jazz-themed dining room. Sieben occasionally hosts jazz concerts in summer. $ Average meal: €30 ⊠ Via dei Portici 232 ☎ 0473/210636 ⊕ www. bistrosieben.it ⊘ Closed Tues. Nov.–Apr.

$$$
NORTHERN
ITALIAN
✗ **Sissi.** In relaxed, light-filled surroundings just off Via dei Portici, rustic regional dishes are prepared with precision. Menu choices may include gnocchi di formaggio con salsa all' erba cipollina (with cheese and chives) and vitello alle castagne e tartufo nero (veal with chestnuts and black truffles). $ Average meal: €50 ⊠ Via Galilei 44 ☎ 0473/231062 ⊕ www.andreafenoglio.com ⌲ Reservations essential ⊘ Closed Mon. and 3 wks Feb.–Mar. No lunch Tues.

$
NORTHERN
ITALIAN
✗ **Vinoteca-Pizzeria Relax.** If you have difficulty choosing from the long list of tasty pizzas here, ask the friendly English-speaking staff for help with the menu. You're unlikely to find a better selection of wine, or a more pleasant environment for sampling. You can also buy bottles of the locally produced vintage to take home. $ Average meal: €25 ⊠ Via Cavour 31, opposite Palace Hotel ☎ 0473/236735 ⊕ www.weine-relax. it ⊘ Closed Sun. and 2 wks Feb.–Mar.

WHERE TO STAY
For expanded hotel reviews, visit Fodors.com.

$$$
HOTEL
Fodor'sChoice
★
⌂ **Castello Labers.** Behind the red-tile gables, towers, and turrets of a Tirolean-style castle is a realm of distinctive luxury, where ceiling beams and frescoes are complimented with sumptuous art nouveau furnishings. **Pros:** romantic setting on a hilltop; spectacular views; pool and sauna. **Cons:** long walk into town; some bathrooms are small. $ Rooms from: €280 ⊠ Via Labers 25 ☎ 0473/234484 ⊕ www. labers.it ⌂ 32 rooms, 1 suite ⊘ Closed early Nov.–late Apr. ⦿ Multiple meal plans.

$
HOTEL
⌂ **Conte di Merano.** Steps away from Via dei Portici and open year-round, these simple, comfortable rooms done in pleasing traditional style are an efficient base for exploring the town. **Pros:** central; reasonable rates. **Cons:** basic decor. $ Rooms from: €90 ⊠ Via delle Corse 78 ☎ 0473/490260 ⊕ www.grafvonmeran.com ⌂ 20 rooms ⦿ Breakfast.

NATURNO (NATURNS)

44 km (27 miles) northwest of Bolzano, 61 km (38 miles) east of Passo dello Stelvio.

Colorful houses covered with murals line the streets of Naturno (Naturns).

VISITOR INFORMATION
Naturno Tourism Office ⊠ Piazza Municipio 1 ☎ 0473/666077 ⊕ www.naturns.it.

5

EXPLORING

Castel Juval. Since 1983 this 13th-century castle in the hills above the hamlet of Stava has been the home of the south Tirolese climber and polar adventurer Reinhold Messner—the first climber to conquer Everest solo. Part of the castle has been turned into one of five in Messner's chain of Dolomite museums, giving guided tours of his collection of Tibetan art and masks from around the world. It's a five-minute shuttle ride from Naturno (there's no parking at the castle), or an hour hike on many local trails. ✉ *Viale Europa 2* ☎ *0473/631264, 0473/668058 shuttle* 🌐 *www.messner-mountain-museum.it* 🎟 *€9* 🕓 *Mar.–Nov., Fri.–Wed. 10–6.*

San Procolo (*Prokolus*). Frescoes here are some of the oldest in the German-speaking world, dating from the 8th century. A small, modern museum offers multimedia installations (in Italian or German only) presenting four epochs in the region's history: ancient, medieval, Gothic, and the era of the Great Plague of 1636 (which claimed a quarter of Naturno's population, some of whom are buried in the church's cemetery). There are leaflets and other information in English upon request. ✉ *Via San Procolo* ☎ *0473/667312* 🌐 *www.procolo.org* 🎟 *€2 (suggested donation)* 🕓 *2 wks before Easter–mid-Oct., Tues.–Sun. 9:30–noon and 2:30–5:30; mid-Oct.–Nov., Tues.–Sun. 2–5.*

WHERE TO EAT

$ NORTHERN ITALIAN 🍴 **Schlosswirt Juval.** Reinhold Messner's restored farmhouse, which is below Castel Juval, holds an old-style restaurant serving Mediterranean standards and traditional local dishes. Not to be missed are the smoked hams and flavorful cheeses provisioned from the farm outside; they are well paired with the estate's Castel Juval wine. Dinner is often accompanied by live jazz. [$] *Average meal: €30* ✉ *Juval 2* ☎ *0473/668056* 🌐 *www.schlosswirtjuval.it* 💳 *No credit cards* 🕓 *Closed Wed. and mid-Dec.–Mar.*

CALDARO (KALTERN)

15 km (9 miles) south of Bolzano.

A vineyard village with clear views of castles high up on the surrounding mountains represents the centuries of division that forged the unique character of the area. Caldaro architecture is famous for the way it blends Italian Renaissance elements of balance and harmony with the soaring windows and peaked arches of the Germanic Gothic tradition. The church of Santa Caterina, on the main square, is a good example.

VISITOR INFORMATION

Caldaro Tourism Office ✉ *Piazza Mercato 8* ☎ *0471/963169* 🌐 *www.kaltern.com.*

EXPLORING

South Tyrolean Wine Museum. Head here for exhibits on how local wine has historically been made, stored, served, and worshipped. You can board the bus in front of the tourist office at 10 each Thursday for a museum tour and wine tasting in the cellar, or call ahead to reserve. ✉ *Via dell'Oro 1, near main square* ☎ *0471/963168* 🌐 *www.weinmuseum.it* 🎟 *€4, wine tasting €5* 🕓 *Easter–Oct., Tues.–Sat. 10–5, Sun. 10–noon.*

BRESSANONE (BRIXEN)

40 km (25 miles) northeast of Bolzano.

Bressanone (Brixen) is an important artistic center and was the seat of prince-bishops for centuries. Like their counterparts in Trento, these medieval administrators had the delicate task of serving two masters—the pope (the ultimate spiritual authority) and the Holy Roman Emperor (the civil and military power), who were virtually at war throughout the Middle Ages. Bressanone's prince-bishops became experts at tact and diplomacy.

VISITOR INFORMATION
Bressanone Tourism Office ✉ *Via Stazione 9* ☎ *0472/836401* ⊕ *www.brixen.org.*

EXPLORING
Abbazia di Novacella. This Augustinian abbey founded in 1142 has been producing wine for at least nine centuries and is most famous for the delicate stone-fruit character of its dry white Sylvaner. You can wander the delightful grounds; note the progression of Romanesque, Gothic, and Baroque building styles. Guided tours of the abbey (in Italian and German) depart daily at 10, 11, 2, 3, and 4, as well as at noon and 1 in summer; from January through March, tours are by reservation only. ✉ *Località Novacella 1, Varna* ✛ *3 km (2 miles) north of Bressanone* ☎ *0472/836189* ⊕ *www.kloster-neustift.it* 🖙 *Grounds and tasting room free, guided tours €6* ⊙ *Grounds and tasting room: Mon.–Sat. 10–7.*

Duomo. The imposing town cathedral was built in the 13th century but acquired a Baroque facade 500 years later; its 14th-century cloister is decorated with medieval frescoes. ✉ *Piazza Duomo* ⊙ *Easter–Oct., daily 7–6; Nov.–Sat. before Easter, daily 7–noon and 3–6.*

Museo Diocesano (*Diocesan Museum*). The Bishop's Palace houses an abundance of local medieval art, particularly Gothic wood carvings. The wooden statues and liturgical objects were all collected from the cathedral treasury. During the Christmas season, curators arrange the museum's large collection of antique Nativity scenes; look for the shepherds wearing Tirolean hats. ✉ *Palazzo Vescovile 2* ☎ *0472/830505* ⊕ *www.dioezesanmuseum. bz.it* 🖙 *€7* ⊙ *Mid-Mar.–Oct. and Dec.–Jan. 6, Tues.–Sun. 10–5.*

WHERE TO EAT AND STAY
For expanded hotel reviews, visit Fodors.com.

$$
NORTHERN
ITALIAN
✕ **Fink.** This rustic, wood-paneled, upstairs dining room is under the arcades of the pedestrians-only town center. Among the house specialties are *carré di maiale gratinato* (pork chops roasted with cheese and served with cabbage and potatoes) and *castrato alla paesana*, a substantial lamb stew. In addition to hearty Tirolean specialties, there's an affordable daily set menu, as well as homemade pastries. ⓢ *Average meal: €35* ✉ *Via Portici Minori 4* ☎ *0472/834883* ⊕ *www.restaurant-fink.it* ⊙ *Closed Wed. No dinner Tues.*

$$$
HOTEL
🏨 **Elephant.** At this cozy inn, 550 years old and still one of the region's best, each room is unique and many are filled with antiques and paintings. **Pros:** lovely ambience; good restaurant; lavish breakfast. **Cons:** rooms vary in size; often filled with groups. ⓢ *Rooms from: €236* ✉ *Via Rio Bianco 4* ☎ *0472/832750* ⊕ *www.hotelelephant.com* 🛏 *44 rooms* 🍽 *Breakfast.*

Hiking the Dolomites

For many overseas visitors, the Dolomites conjure images of downhill skiing at Cortina d'Ampezzo and Madonna di Campiglio. But summer, not winter, is high season here; Italians, German-speaking Europeans, and in-the-know travelers from farther afield come here for clear mountain air and world-class hiking. In 2009 UNESCO (the United Nations Educational, Scientific, and Cultural Organization) added the Dolomites to its list of natural heritage sites.

The dramatic terrain, inspiring vistas, and impossibly pleasant climate are complemented by excellent facilities for enjoying the mountains.

PICKING A TRAIL
The Dolomites have a well-maintained network of trails for hiking and rock climbing. As long as you're in reasonably good shape, the number of appealing hiking options can be overwhelming.

Trails are well marked and designated by grades of difficulty: T for tourist path, H for hiking path, EE for expert hikers, and EEA for equipped expert hikers. On any of these paths you're likely to see carpets of mountain flowers between clutches of dense evergreens, with chamois and roe deer mulling about.

If you're just out for a day in the mountains, you can leave the details of your walk open until you're actually on the spot; local tourist offices (especially those in Cortina and Madonna) can help you choose the right route based on trail conditions, weather, and desired exertion level.

TRAVELING THE VIE FERRATE
If you're looking for an adventure somewhere between hiking and

climbing, consider a guided trip along the *Vie Ferrate* (Iron Paths).

These routes offer fixed climbing aids (steps, ladders, bridges, safety cables) left by Alpine divisions of the Italian and Austro-Hungarian armies and later converted for recreational use.

Previous experience is generally not required, but vertigo-inducing heights do demand a strong stomach.

Detailed information about Vie Ferrate in the eastern Dolomites can be found at ⊕ *www.dolomiti.org*. Capable tour organizers include **Scuola di Alpinismo** (Mountaineering School) in Madonna di Campiglio (☎ *0465/442634* ⊕ *www. guidealpinecampiglio.it*) and Cortina d'Ampezzo (☎ *0436/868505* ⊕ *www.guidecortina.com*).

EATING WELL
Food is as much a draw at *rifugi* (refuges) as location. The rustic dishes, such as salami, dumplings, hearty stews, are all excellent—an impressive feat, made all the more remarkable when you consider that supplies often have to arrive by helicopter.

Your dinner may cost as much as your bed for the night—about €20 per person—and it's difficult to determine which is the better bargain.

Snacks and packed lunches are available for purchase, but many opt to sit down for the midday meal.

Serving as both holiday hiking destination and base camp for difficult ascents, the rifugi welcome walkers and climbers of all stripes from intersecting trails and nearby faces. Multilingual stories are swapped, food and wine shared, and new adventures launched.

BEDDING DOWN

One of the pleasures of an overnight adventure in the Dolomites is staying at a *rifugio*, one of the refuges that dot the mountainsides, often in remote locations.

There are hundreds of them, and they range in comfort from spartan to posh. Most fall somewhere in between—they're cozy mountain lodges with dormitory-style accommodations. Pillows and blankets are provided (there's no need to carry a sleeping bag), but you have to supply your own sheet.

Bathrooms are usually shared, as is the experience of a cold shower in the morning.

The majority of rifugi are operated by the **Club Alpino Italiano** (⊕ *www. cai.it*). Contact information for both CAI-run and private rifugi is available from local tourist offices; most useful are those in Madonna di Campiglio (⊕ *www.campiglio.to*), Cortina d'Ampezzo (⊕ *www.dolomiti.org*), Val di Fassa (⊕ *www.fassa.com*), and Val Gardena (⊕ *www.val-gardena.net*).

Reservations are a must, especially in August, although Italian law requires rifugi to accept travelers for the night if there's insufficient time to reach other accommodations before dark.

STUMBLING ON ÖTZI

It was at the Similaun rifugio in September 1991 that a German couple arrived talking of a dead body they'd discovered near a "curious pickax."

This was to be the world's introduction to Ötzi, the oldest mummy ever found.

The couple, underestimating the age of the corpse by about 5,300 years, thought it was a matter for the police.

World-famous mountaineers Reinhold Messner and Hans Kammerlander happened to be passing through the same rifugio during a climbing tour, and a few days later they were on the scene, freeing the iceman from the ice.

Ötzi's remarkable story was under way. You can see him on display, along with his longbow, ax, and clothes, at Bolzano's Museo Archeologico dell'Alto Adige, where he continues to be preserved at freezing temperatures.

5

BRUNICO (BRUNECK)

★ *33 km (20 miles) east of Bressanone, 65 km (40 miles) northwest of Cortina d'Ampezzo.*

Brunico's medieval quarter nestles below a 13th-century bishop's castle. In the heart of the Val Pusteria, this quiet and quaint town is divided by the Rienza River, with the old quarter on one side and the modern town on the other.

VISITOR INFORMATION
Brunico Tourism Office ⌧ *Piazza Municipio 7* ☎ *0474/555722* ⊕ *www.bruneck.com.*

EXPLORING
Museo Etnografico dell'Alto Adige (*Alto Adige Ethnographic Museum*). A recreation of a Middle Ages farming village is built around a 300-year-old mansion. The wood-carving displays are especially interesting. ⌧ *Herzog-Diet-Straße 24* ☎ *0474/552087* ⊕ *www.volkskundemuseum. it* ⌧ *€6* ⊙ *Sept.–July, Tues.–Sat. 10–5, Sun. 2–6; Aug., Tues.–Sat. 10–6, Sun. 2–6.*

SPORTS AND THE OUTDOORS
SKIING
Alta Badia. The Alta Badia ski area, which includes 52 ski lifts and 130 km (80 miles) of slopes, can be reached by heading 30 km (19 miles) south on SS244 from Brunico. It's cheaper and more Austrian in character than the more famous ski destinations in this region. Groomed trails for cross-country skiing (usually loops marked off by the kilometer) accommodate differing degrees of ability. Inquire at the local tourist office. ☎ *0471/836366 Corvara* ⊕ *www.altabadia.org.*

THE HEART OF THE DOLOMITES

The area between Bolzano and the mountain resort Cortina d'Ampezzo is dominated by two major valleys, Val di Fassa and Val Gardena. Both share the spectacular panorama of the Sella mountain range, known as the Heart of the Dolomites. Val di Fassa cradles the beginning of the Grande Strada delle Dolomiti (Great Dolomites Road—SS48 and SS241), which runs from Bolzano as far as Cortina. This route, opened in 1909, comprises 110 km (68 miles) of relatively easy grades and smooth driving between the two towns—a slower, more scenic alternative to traveling by way of Brunico and Dobbiaco along SS49. Scenic it is—the road passes into a stark, high-altitude landscape punctuated with the needle-like mountain peaks, climbing to 7,346 feet.

In both Val di Fassa and Val Gardena, recreational options are less expensive, though less comprehensive, than in better-known resorts like Cortina. The culture here is firmly Germanic. Val Gardena is freckled with well-equipped, photo-friendly towns with great views overlooked by the oblong Sasso Lungo (Long Rock), which is more than 10,000 feet above sea level. It's also home to the Ladins, descendants of soldiers sent by the Roman emperor Tiberius to conquer the Celtic population of the area in the 1st century AD. Forgotten in the narrow cul-de-sacs of isolated mountain valleys, the Ladins have developed their own folk traditions and speak an ancient dialect that is derived from Latin and similar to the Romansch spoken in some high valleys in Switzerland.

CANAZEI

60 km (37 miles) west of Cortina d'Ampezzo, 52 km (32 miles) east of Bolzano.

Of the year-round resort towns in the Val di Fassa, Canazei is the most popular. The mountains around this small town are threaded with hiking trails and ski slopes, surrounded by large clutches of conifers.

VISITOR INFORMATION
Canazei Tourism Office ⊠ *Stréda de Pareda 67* ☏ *0462/608811* ⊕ *www.canazei.org.*

EXPLORING
Col Rodella. An excursion from Campitello di Fassa, about 4 km (2½ miles) west of Canazei, to the vantage point at Col Rodella is a must. A cable car rises some 3,000 feet to a full-circle vista of the Heart of the Dolomites, including the Sasso Lungo and the rest of the Sella range. ⊠ *Localita' Ischia 1* 🚡 *Cable car €15 round trip* ☉ *Open early Dec.– Easter and mid-June–mid-Oct.*

WHERE TO STAY
For expanded hotel reviews, visit Fodors.com.

$$ 🍴 **Alla Rosa.** The view of the imposing Dolomites is the real attraction in
HOTEL rooms that pleasantly blend rustic and contemporary furnishings, so ask for a balcony. **Pros:** in the center of town; great views. **Cons:** half board mandatory in winter high season; busy neighborhood. Ⓢ *Rooms from: €180* ⊠ *Strèda del Faure 18* ☏ *0462/601107* ⊕ *www.hotelallarosa.com* 🛏 *49 rooms* ⦁⊙⦁ *Breakfast.*

LAGO DI CAREZZA

22 km (14 miles) west of Canazei, 29 km (18 miles) east of Bolzano.

EXPLORING
Lago di Carezza. When this glacial lake is not covered by snow, the crystal, almost florescent azure blue of the waters can at times change to magical greens and purples, reflections of the dense surrounding forest and rosy peaks of the Dolomites. You can hike down from the nearby village of the same name.

EN ROUTE **Passo di Sella** (*Sella Pass*). The Passo di Sella can be approached from the SS48, affording some of the most spectacular mountain vistas in Europe before it descends into the Val Gardena. The road continues to Ortisei, passing the smaller resorts of Selva Gardena and Santa Cristina.

ORTISEI (ST. ULRICH)

28 km (17 miles) north of Canazei, 35 km (22 miles) northeast of Bolzano.

Ortisei (St. Ulrich), the jewel in the crown of Val Gardena's resorts, is a hub of activity in both summer and winter; there are hundreds of miles of hiking trails and accessible ski slopes.

For centuries Ortisei has also been famous for the expertise of its wood-carvers, and there are still numerous workshops. Apart from making religious sculptures—particularly the wayside calvaries you come upon everywhere in the Dolomites—Ortisei's carvers were long known for producing wooden dolls, horses, and other toys. As itinerant peddlers they traveled every spring on foot with their loaded packs as far as Paris, London, and St. Petersburg. Shops in town still sell woodcrafts.

VISITOR INFORMATION
Ortisei Tourist Office ⊠ *Via Rezia 1* ☎ *0471/777600* ⊕ *www.valgardena.it.*

EXPLORING
Museo della Val Gardena. Fine historic and contemporary examples of local woodworking are on display here. ⊠ *Via Rezia 83* ☎ *0471/797554* ⊕ *www.museumgherdeina.it* 💰 *€7* ⊙ *Mid-Jan.–Mar., Tues.–Fri. 10–noon and 2–5; May 15–June and Sept.–Oct., weekdays 10–noon and 2–6; July–Aug., Mon.–Sat. 10–noon and 2–6, Sun. 3–6; early Dec. and late Dec.–early Jan., daily 10–noon and 2–5.*

SPORTS AND THE OUTDOORS
SKIING
With almost 600 km (370 miles) of accessible downhill slopes and more than 90 km (56 miles) of cross-country skiing trails, Ortisei is one of the most popular ski resorts in the Dolomites. Prices are good, and facilities are among the most modern in the region. In warmer weather, the slopes surrounding Ortisei are a popular hiking destination, as well as a playground for vehicular mountain adventures: biking, rafting, and paragliding.

Sella Ronda. An immensely popular ski route, the Sella Ronda relies on well-placed chairlifts to connect 26 km (16 miles) of downhill skiing around the colossal Sella massif, passing through several towns along the way. You can ski the loop, which requires intermediate ability and a full day's effort, either clockwise or counterclockwise. Going with a guide is recommended. ⊕ *www.sella-ronda.info.*

Val Gardena Tourism Office. The Val Gardena tourism office can provide detailed information about sport-equipment rental outfits and guided-tour operators. ⊠ *Via Dursan 81, Santa Cristina* ☎ *0471/777777* ⊕ *www.valgardena.it.*

CORTINA D'AMPEZZO

The archetypal Dolomite resort, Cortina d'Ampezzo entices those seeking both relaxation and adventure. The town is the western gateway to the Strade Grande delle Dolomiti, and actually crowns the northern Veneto region and an area known as Cadore in the northernmost part of the province of Belluno. Like Alto Adige to the west, Cadore (birthplace to the Venetian Renaissance painter Titian) was on the Alpine front during the World War I, and the scene of many battles commemorated in refuges and museums. Although its appeal to younger Italians has been eclipsed by steeper, sleeker Madonna di Campiglio, Cortina remains, for many, Italy's most idyllic incarnation of an Alpine ski town.

WORD OF MOUTH

"The drive from Cortina to Bolzano is spectacular—its only about 76 km but will take a full day. We also like the hiking and lakes around Cortina. The funicular takes you up the mountain, where you can either hike or just enjoy the views."

—cmeyer54

Surrounded by mountains and dense forests, the "Queen of the Dolomites" is in a lush meadow 4,000 feet above sea level. The town hugs the slopes beside a fast-moving stream, and a public park extends along one bank. Higher in the valley, luxury hotels and the villas of the rich are identifiable by their attempts to hide behind stands of firs and spruces. The bustling center of Cortina d'Ampezzo has little nostalgia, despite its Alpine appearance. The tone is set by shops and cafés as chic as their well-dressed patrons, whose corduroy knickerbockers may well have been tailored by Armani. Unlike neighboring resorts that have a strong Germanic flavor, Cortina d'Ampezzo is unapologetically Italian and distinctly fashionable.

VISITOR INFORMATION
Cortina d'Ampezzo Tourism Office ✉ *Piazzetta San Francesco 8* ☎ *0436/3231* ⊕ *www.infodolomiti.it.*

WHERE TO EAT

$$$
NORTHERN
ITALIAN

✗ **Ristorante Lago Pianozes.** This small, family-run establishment is just outside of Cortina beside the picturesque Lago Pianozes. Fabrizio, the owner, is friendly and knowledgeable, not only about his food and wine, but also about the surrounding region. The menu varies according to the seasons, always incorporating local foods and recipies. Reservations are recommended, as seating is limited. $ *Average meal: €75* ✉ *1, Campo di Sotto Pianozes* ☎ *0436/5601* ⚓ *Reservations essential.*

$$
NORTHERN
ITALIAN

✗ **Tavernetta.** These Tirolean-style wood-paneled dining rooms near the Olympic ice-skating rink are a Cortona institution. Join the local clientele in sampling local specialties such as pasta with a *ragù bianco tartuffato* (white truffle sauce), and wild game. $ *Average meal: €36* ✉ *Via Castello 53* ☎ *0436/868102* ☉ *Closed Tues. and mid-June–mid-July.*

WHERE TO STAY
For expanded hotel reviews, visit Fodors.com.

$$
HOTEL

🏨 **Corona.** Noted ski instructor Luciano Rimoldi, who has coached such luminaries as Alberto Tomba, runs a cozy Alpine lodge where modern art adorns small but comfortable pine-paneled rooms. **Pros:** cozy atmosphere; friendly staff; quiet location; ski shuttle stops out front. **Cons:** small rooms; outside the town center. $ *Rooms from: €240* ✉ *Via Val di Sotto 12* ☎ *0436/3251* ⊕ *www.hotelcoronacortina.it* 🛏 *44 rooms* ☉ *Closed Apr., May, and mid-Sept.–Nov.* ❑ *Multiple meal plans.*

$$$$ **☷ De la Poste.** Loyal skiers return year after year to this old-school
HOTEL   mountain retreat, where each unique room has antiques in characteristic
Dolomite style (almost all have wooden balconies) and the main terrace
bar is one of Cortina's social centers. **Pros:** professional service; romantic. **Cons:** a bit stuffy; expensive; in a busy neighborhood. $ *Rooms
from: €449* ✉ *Piazza Roma 14* ☎ *0436/4271* ⊕ *www.delaposte.it* ⟿ *83
rooms* ⊙ *Closed Apr.–mid-June and Oct.–mid-Dec.* ⧉ *Breakfast.*

$$$$ **☷ Miramonti Majestic.** A touch of luxurious formality rather than rustic
RESORT   charm comes through in the imperial Austrian design of this century-old
landmark tucked into a magnificent mountain valley. **Pros:** magnificent
location; loads of old-world charm in lounges and guest rooms alike;
splendid views; great pool and spa. **Cons:** about 1 km (½ mile) outside
town center; minimum stay three nights; sky-high rates. $ *Rooms from:
€880* ✉ *Località Peziè 103* ☎ *0438/493500* ⊕ *www.miramontimajestic.
it* ⟿ *122 rooms* ⊙ *Closed Apr.–June and Sept.–mid-Dec.* ⧉ *Breakfast.*

SPORTS AND THE OUTDOORS
HIKING AND CLIMBING
Hiking information is available from the excellent local tourism office.

Gruppo Guide Alpine Cortina Scuola di Alpinismo (*Mountaineering School*).
This group organizes climbing trips and trekking adventures. ✉ *Corso
Italia 69/a* ☎ *0436/868505* ⊕ *www.guidecortina.com.*

SKIING
Cortina's long and picturesque ski runs will delight intermediates, but
advanced skiers might lust for steeper terrain, which can be found only
off-piste. Efficient ski bus service connects the town with the high-speed
chairlifts and gondolas that ascend in all directions from the valley.

Dolomiti Superski pass. The Dolomiti Superski pass provides access to the
surrounding Dolomites (€40–€45 per day), with 450 lifts and gondolas
serving 1,200 km (750 miles) of trails. Buy one at the ticket office next
to the bus station and at other outlets in the Dolomites. ✉ *Via Marconi
15* ☎ *0471/795397* ⊕ *www.dolomitisuperski.com.*

Faloria gondola. The Faloria gondola runs from the center of town. From
its top you can get up to most of the central mountains. ✉ *Via Ria de
Zeta 10* ☎ *0436/2517* 🎫 *€16 round trip.*

Monte Cristallo. Some of the most impressive views (and steepest slopes)
are on Monte Cristallo, based at Misurina, 15 km (9 miles) northeast
of Cortina by car or bus.

Passo Falzarego. The topography of the Passo Falzarego ski area, 16 km
(10 miles) east of town, is dramatic. The cable car takes you to one of
the highest points in the Dolomites. From here, it's easy to see why this
was such a deadly area for soldiers in World War I.

6

MILAN, LOMBARDY, AND THE LAKES

WELCOME TO MILAN, LOMBARDY, AND THE LAKES

TOP REASONS TO GO

★ **Lake Como—the most beautiful lake in the world?:** Ferries crisscross the waters, taking you from picture-book villages to stately villas to edenic gardens, all backdropped in the distance by the snow-capped Alps.

★ **Decoding Da Vinci:** Leonardo da Vinci's *Last Supper* used to be known only as one of the world's most famous works of art until *The Da Vinci Code* made everyone wonder if the apostle John was in fact Mary Magdalene

★ **The sky's no limit:** A funicular ride in Bergamo whisks you up to the magnificent medieval city.

★ **Milan alla Moda:** As you window-shop the afternoon away in Milan's Quadrilatero shopping district, catch a glimpse of fashion's latest trends.

★ **A night at La Scala:** What the Louvre is to art, Milan's La Scala is to the world of opera.

1 Milan. The country's center of finance and commerce is constantly looking to the future. Home of the Italian stock exchange, it's also one of the world's fashion capitals and has cultural and artistic treasures that rival those of Florence and Rome.

2 Pavia, Cremona, and Mantua. South of Milan are the walled cities where Renaissance dukes built towering palaces and ornate churches. They sit on the Po Plain, one of Italy's wealthiest regions.

3 Lake Garda. Italy's largest lake measures 16 km (10 miles) across at its widest point and 50 km (31 miles) from end to end. With a more laid-back feel than the other lakes, the waters and shores are a haven for outdoor enthusiasts.

4 Lake Como. This relatively narrow lake is probably the country's best-known and most charmingly populated body of water. You can almost always see across to the other side, which lends a great sense of intimacy. Lake Lecco, to the southeast, is actually a branch of Lake Como.

5 Lake Maggiore. It may be smaller than Lake Garda and less famous than Lake Como, but Lake Maggiore is impressively picturesque with the Alps as a backdrop. One of the greatest pleasures here is exploring the lake's islands.

GETTING ORIENTED

In Lombardy jagged mountains and deep glacial lakes stretch from the Swiss border down to Milan's outskirts, where they meet the flat, fertile plain that extends from the banks of the River Po. Lake Como is north of Milan, while Lake Maggiore is to the northwest and Lake Garda is to the east. Scattered across the plains to the south are the Renaissance city-states of Pavia, Cremona, and Mantua.

6

SWITZERLAND

A L P S

Chiavenna

36

4

Sondrio

Edolo

38

Morbegno

Cong...

llagio

42

Darfo-Boario

TRENTINO-
ALTO ADIGE

Lecco

LOMBARDY

42

Lago
d'Iseo

Bergamo

342

Gargnano

R. Adda

A4

A4

510

Gardone Riviera

11

Brescia

3

Lago
Garda

11

235

Sirmione

415

Oglio

A21

236

VENETO

Melegnano

Crema

A1

Lodi

River

9

2

River

10

Mantua

me Po

Cremona

River

0   20 mi

0   20 km

EMILIA-
ROMAGNA

EATING WELL IN MILAN, LOMBARDY, AND THE LAKES

Lombardy may well offer Italy's most varied, rich and refined cuisine. Local cooking is influenced by the neighboring regions of the north; foreign conquerors have left their mark; and today well-traveled Milanese, business visitors, and industrious immigrants are likely to find more authentic ethnic cuisine in Milan than any other Italian city.

Milan runs counter to many of the established Italian dining customs. A "real" traditional Milanese meal is a rarity; instead, Milan offers something for every taste, budget, and time of day, from expense-account elegance in fancy restaurants to abundant *aperitivo*-time nibbles. The city's cosmopolitan nature means trends arrive here first, and things move fast. Meals are not the drawn-out pastime they tend to be elsewhere in Italy. But food is still consistently good—competition among restaurants is fierce and the local clientele is demanding, which means you can be reasonably certain that if a place looks promising, it won't disappoint.

THE COTOLETTA QUESTION

Everyone has an opinion on *cotoletta (photo upper right)*, the breaded veal cutlet known across Italy as *una Milanese*.

It's clearly related to Austria's Wiener schnitzel, but did the Austrians introduce it when they dominated Milan or take it home when they left? Should it be with bone or without? Some think it's best with fresh tomato and arugula on top; others find this sacrilege.

Two things unite all camps: the meat must be well beaten until it's thin, and it must never leave a grease spot after it's fried.

REGIONAL SPECIALTIES

Ask an Italian what Lombards eat, and you're likely to hear *cotoletta, càsoeûla,* and *risotto giallo*—all dishes that reinforce Lombardy's status as the crossroads of Italy. *Cotoletta alla Milanese* may very well have Austrian roots. *Càsoeûla* is a cabbage-and-pork stew that resembles French cassoulet, though some say it has Spanish origins. *Risotto giallo* (also known as *Milanese*), *pictured at left*, is colorful and perfumed with exotic saffron. With no tomatoes, olive oil, or pasta, these dishes hardly sound Italian.

BUTTER AND CHEESE

Agricultural traditions and geography mean that animal products are more common here than in southern Italy— and that means butter and cream take olive oil's place. A rare point of agreement about cotoletta is that it's cooked in butter. The first and last steps of risotto making—toasting the rice and letting it "repose" before serving— use ample amounts of butter. And the second-most-famous name in Italian cheese (after Parmesan) is likely Gorgonzola, named for a town near Milan. The best now comes from Novara.

RISOTTO

Rice is Lombardy's answer to pasta, and the region is the center of Italian (and European) rice production. From Milan's risotto giallo with its costly saffron tint to Mantua's risotto with pumpkin or sausage, there's no end to the variety of rice dishes. Canonical risotto should be *all'onda*, or flow off the spoon like a wave. Keeping with the Italian tradition of nothing wasted, yesterday's risotto is flattened in a pan and fried in butter to produce *riso al salto*, which at its best has a crispy crust and a tender middle.

PANETTONE

Panettone, a tall, fluffy sweet yeast bread, is flavored with sweet candied fruit, *pictured below left*. Invented in Milan, it graces nearly every table during the Christmas holiday. It's now so ubiquitous that its price is used as an economic indicator: is it up or down, compared to last year? Consumption begins on December 7, Milan's patron saint's day, and goes until supplies run out at January's end.

WINE

Lombardy isn't one of Italy's most heralded wine regions, but its reputation is growing. The Valtellina area to the northeast of Milan produces two notable reds from the nebbiolo grape: Valtellina Superiore and the intense dessert wine Sforzato di Valtellina. The Franciacorta region around Brescia makes highly regarded sparkling wines. Lake breezes bring crisp, smooth whites from the shores around Lake Garda.

6

Updated by
Sofia Celeste

Lombardy is one of Italy's most dynamic regions—offering everything from world-class ski slopes to luxurious summer lake resorts. Milan is the pulse of the nation—commercial, fashionable, and forward-looking. The great Renaissance cities of the Po Plain—Pavia, Cremona, and Mantua—offer the romantic Italian characteristics tourists dream about, embracing their past by preserving national treasures while ever keeping an eye on the present. Topping any list of the region's attractions are the glacial lakes. Above them stand the Alps, which have been praised as the closest thing to paradise by writers throughout the ages, from Virgil to Hemingway.

Millions of travelers have concurred: for sheer beauty, the lakes of northern Italy—Como, Maggiore, Garda, and Orta—have few equals. Along their shores are 18th- and 19th-century villas, exotic formal gardens, sleepy villages, and dozens of Belle Epoque–era resorts that were once Europe's most fashionable, and still retain a powerful allure.

Milan can be disappointingly modern and congested—a little too much like the place you've come to Italy to escape—but its historic buildings and art collections in many ways rival those of Florence and Rome. And if you love to shop, Milan is one of the world's great fashion centers, and offers experiences and goods for every taste, from Corso Buenos Aires, which has a higher ratio of stores per square foot than anywhere else in Europe, to the edgy street style of Corso di Porta Ticinese and upscale Via Montenapoleone, where there's no limit on what you can spend. Milan is home to global fashion giants such as Armani, Prada, Versace, Salvatore Ferragamo, and Ermenegildo Zegna; behind them stands a host of less-famous designers who help fill all those fabulous shops.

MILAN, LOMBARDY, AND THE LAKES PLANNER

MAKING THE MOST OF YOUR TIME

Italy's commercial hub isn't usually at the top of the list for visiting tourists, but Milan is the nation's most modern city with its own sophisticated appeal: its fashionable shops rival those of New York and Paris, its soccer teams are Italy's answer to the Yankees and the Mets, its opera performances set the standard for the world, and its art treasures are well worth the visit.

The biggest draw in the region, though, is the Lake District. Throughout history, the magnificently beautiful lakes of Como, Garda, Maggiore, and Orta have attracted their fair share of well-known faces—from Winston Churchill and Russian royalty to American heartthrob George Clooney and singer-songwriting powerhouse Madonna. Each lake town has its own history and distinct character. If you have limited time, visit the lake you think best suits your style, but if you have time to spare, make the rounds to two or three to get a sense of their contrasts.

GETTING HERE AND AROUND

AIR TRAVEL

The region's international gateway airport is Aeroporto Mapleusa (☎ *02/74852200* ⊕ *www.sea-aeroportimilano.it*), 48 km (28 miles) north of Milan.

BOAT TRAVEL

Frequent daily ferry and hydrofoil services link the lakeside towns and villages. Residents take them to get to work and school, while visitors use them for exploring the area. There are also special round-trip excursions, some with (optional) dining service on board.

Navigazione Laghi. Schedules and ticket price are available on the website and are posted at the landing docks. ✉ *Via Ariosto 21, Milan* ☎ *02/4676101, 03/9149511 Lake Garda* ⊕ *www.navigazionelaghi.it.*

To get around the lakes by car, you have to follow secondary roads—often of great beauty. S572 follows the southern and western shores of Lake Garda, SS45b edges the northernmost section of the western shore, and S249 runs along the eastern shore. Around Lake Como, follow S340 along the western shore, S36 on the eastern shore, and S583 on the lower arms. S33 and S34 trace the western shore of Lake Maggiore. Although the roads around the lake can be beautiful, they're full of harrowing twists and turns, making for a slow, challenging drive—often with an Italian speedracer on your tail.

There's regular bus service between the small towns on the lakes. It's less convenient than going by boat or by car, and it's used primarily by locals (particularly schoolchildren), but sightseers can use it as well. The bus service around Lake Garda serves mostly towns on the western shore.

SIA. Call the bus operator SIA for information. ☎ *030/44061* ⊕ *www. sia-autoservizi.it.*

6

BUS TRAVEL

Bus service isn't the best way to travel between cities here, because the region's extensive train network provides service that is faster, cheaper, and more convenient. However, a bus is an option for reaching Bellagio and many other lake towns (a boat is another).

Autostradale. For those determined to travel by bus, Autostradale goes to Turin and airports Linate, Malpensa and Bergamo's Orio al Serio from its hub at Lampugnano (red line metro) northwest of Milan's city center or Milan's central train station. There are also bus services from Milan to resort towns like St. Moritz and Cortina. Reservations are required. ☎ 02/33910794 ⊕ www.autostradale.it.

CAR TRAVEL

Getting almost anywhere by car is a snap, as several major highways intersect at Milan, all connected by the *tangenziale,* the road that rings the city. The A4 runs west to Turin and east to Venice; A1 leads south to Bologna, Florence, and Rome; A7 angles southwest down to Genoa. A8 goes northwest toward Lake Maggiore, and A9 north runs past Lake Como and into Switzerland's southernmost tip.

ACI. Your car-rental company should be your first resource if you have a problem while driving in Italy, but it's also good to know that the ACI, the Italian auto club, offers 24-hour roadside assistance (free for members, for a fee for nonmembers). ☎ 803/116 ⊕ www.aci.it.

Regularly spaced roadside service phones are available on the autostrade.

TRAIN TRAVEL

Milan's majestic Central Station (Milano Centrale), 3 km (2 miles) northwest of the Duomo, is Italy's version of Grand Central Station, with frequent service within the region to Como, Bergamo, Brescia, Sirmione, Pavia, Cremona, and Mantua. Soaring domed glass ceilings and plenty of signage have significantly improved the renovated station's navigability, but its sheer size requires considerable walking and patience, so allow for some extra time here.

For general information on trains and schedules, as well as online ticket purchases, visit the website of the Italian national railway, **FS** (⊕ www. trenitalia.com).

Tickets bought without a reservation need to be validated by stamping them in yellow machines on the train platforms. Tickets with reservations don't require validation. When in doubt, validate: it can't hurt.

RESTAURANTS

Please note that restaurant prices listed as "average meal" include a meal consisting of first course *(primo)*, second course *(secondo)*, and dessert *(dolce)*.

HOTELS

The hotels in Italy's wealthiest region generally cater to a clientele willing to pay for extra comfort. Outside Milan, many are converted villas with well-landscaped grounds. Most of the famous lake resorts are expensive; many smaller lakeside hotels are quite reasonably priced. Local tourism offices throughout the region are an excellent source of information about affordable lodging.

Please note that hotel prices are for a double in high season, though when "high season" is can vary—in the lakes it's at the height of summer, not surprisingly, but in Milan it depends on what fairs and exhibitions are being staged. Prices in almost all hotels can go up dramatically during the Furniture Fair in early April. Fashion, travel, and tech fairs also draw big crowds throughout the year, raising prices. In contrast to other cities in Italy, however, you can often find discounts on weekends. The three lake districts—Maggiore, Garda, and Como—have little to offer except quiet from November to March, when most gardens, hotels, and restaurants are closed.

MILAN

Milan is Italy's business hub and crucible of chic. Between the Po's rich farms and the industrious mountain valleys, it's long been the country's capital of commerce, finance, fashion, and media. Rome may be bigger and have the political power, but Milan and the affluent north are what really make the country go. It's also Italy's transport hub, with the biggest international airport, the most rail connections, and the best subway system. Leonardo da Vinci's *The Last Supper* and other great works of art are here, as well as a spectacular Gothic Duomo, the finest of its kind. Milan even reigns supreme where it really counts (in the minds of many Italians), routinely trouncing the rest of the nation with its two premier soccer teams.

And yet, Milan hasn't won the battle for hearts and minds. Most tourists prefer Tuscany's hills and Venice's canals to Milan's hectic efficiency and wealthy indifference, and it's no surprise that in a country of medieval hilltop villages and skilled artisans a city of grand boulevards and global corporations leaves visitors asking the real Italy to please stand up. They're right, of course. Milan is more European than Italian, a new buckle on an old boot, and although its old city can stand cobblestone for cobblestone against the best of them, seekers of Roman ruins and fairy-tale towns may pass. But Milan's secrets reveal themselves slowly to those who look. A side street conceals a garden complete with flamingos (Via dei Cappuccini, just off Corso Venezia), and a renowned 20th-century art collection hides modestly behind an unspectacular facade a block from Corso Buenos Aires (the Casa Museo Boschi-di Stefano). Visitors lured by the world-class shopping will appreciate Milan's European sophistication while discovering unexpected facets of a country they may have only thought they knew.

Virtually every invader in European history—Gaul, Roman, Goth, Lombard, and Frank—as well as a long series of rulers from France, Spain, and Austria, took a turn at ruling the city. After being completely sacked by the Goths in AD 539 and by the Holy Roman Empire under Frederick Barbarossa in 1157, Milan became one of the first independent city-states of the Renaissance. Its heyday of self-rule proved comparatively brief. From 1277 until 1500 it was ruled by the Visconti and subsequently the Sforza dynasties. These families were known, justly or not, for a peculiarly aristocratic mixture of refinement, classical learning, and cruelty, and much of the surviving grandeur of Gothic and Renaissance art and architecture is their doing. Be on the lookout in your wanderings for the Visconti family emblem—a viper, its jaws straining wide, devouring a child.

GETTING HERE AND AROUND

The city center is compact and walkable; trolleys and trams make it even more accessible, and the efficient Metropolitana (subway) and buses provide access to locations farther afield. Driving in Milan is difficult and parking miserable, so a car is a liability. In addition, drivers within the second ring of streets (the *bastioni*) must hold an Ecopass. (Ask your hotel about getting a pass.)

BICYCLE TRAVEL

BikeMI. The innovative BikeMI makes hop-on, drop-off bicycles available at designated spots around the city. There are more than 200 stations. Weekly and daily rates for tourists are available. Buy your subscription online; the site has a map showing stations and availability. Keep in mind, though, that traffic makes biking in the city dangerous for inexperienced cyclists, and be careful not to get your tires caught on the tram tracks. ⊕ *www.bikemi.com.*

PUBLIC TRANSIT TRAVEL

A standard public transit ticket costs €1.50 and is valid for a 90-minute trip on a subway, bus, or tram. An all-inclusive subway, bus, and tram pass costs €4.50 for 24 hours or €8.25 for 48 hours. Individual tickets and passes can be purchased from news vendors and tobacconists, and at ticket counters and ticket machines at larger stops. Another option is a carnet (€13.80), good for 10 tram or subway rides. Once you have your ticket or pass, either stamp it or insert it into the slots in station turnstiles or on poles inside trolleys and buses. (The electronic tickets won't function if bent or demagnetized. If you have a problem, contact a station manager, who can usually issue a new ticket.) Trains run from 6 am to 12:30 am.

ATM (*Azienda Trasporti Milanesi*). For more information, check the ATM website or visit information offices at the Duomo, Stazione Cadorna, Stazione Centrale, Garibaldi, and Loreto stops. ⊕ *www. atm-mi.it/en.*

Radiobus. From 8 pm to 2 am, Radiobus will pick you up and drop you off anywhere in Milan for a €2 supplement to a transit pass. Advance booking is required. ☎ *02/48034803* ⊕ *www.atm-mi.it/en.*

TAXI TRAVEL

Taxi fares in Milan are higher than in American cities. A short ride will run about €15. Taxis wait at stands marked by an orange "Taxi" sign, or you can call one of the city's taxi companies.

Amicotaxi ☎ *02/4000.*

Autoradiotaxi ☎ *02/8585.*

Radiotaxi–Yellow Taxi ☎ *02/6969.*

Taxiblu ☎ *02/4040.*

Dispatchers may speak some English; they'll ask for the phone number you're calling from, and they'll tell you the number of your taxi and how long it'll take to arrive. If you're in a restaurant or bar, ask the staff to call a cab for you.

Autonoleggio Pini. For car service, contact Autonoleggio Pini. Most drivers and reservation staff speak english. ☎ *02/29400555* ⊕ *www. limousinepini.eu.*

TOURS

City Sightseeing Milano. Open-top double-decker buses provide hop-on/ hop-off tours on two routes departing from Piazza Castello. An all-inclusive day pass costs €20. ⊕ *www.milano.city-sightseeing.it.*

VISITOR INFORMATION

Milan Tourism Office. The tourism office in Piazza Castello is the per-fect place to begin your visit. There are excellent maps, booklets with museum descriptions, itineraries on a variety of themes, and a selection of brochures about smaller museums and cultural initiatives. Pick up a copy of the English-language *Hello Milano* (ask, if it is not on display, or see ⊕ *www.hellomilano.it*), a monthly publication with a day-to-day schedule of events of interest to visitors and a comprehensive map. The Autostradale bus operator, sightseeing companies, and a few theaters have desks in the tourism office where you can buy tickets.

There is also a location at the central railway station in front of tracks 13 and 14. ✉ *Piazza Castello 1, Castello Sforzesco* ☎ *02/77404343* ⊕ *www.visitamilano.it* ⊙ *Weekdays 9–6, Sat. 9–1:30 and 2–6, Sun. 9–1:30 and 2–5.*

EXPLORING MILAN

THE DUOMO AND POINTS NORTH

Milan's main streets radiate out from the massive Duomo, a late-Gothic cathedral that was started in 1386. Heading north is the handsome Gal-leria Vittorio Emanuele, an enclosed shopping arcade that opens at one end to the world-famous opera house known as La Scala. Beyond are the winding streets of the elegant Brera neighborhood, once the city's bohemian quarter. Heading northeast from La Scala is Via Manzoni, which leads to the *Quadrilatero della moda,* or fashion district.

Heading northeast from the Duomo is the pedestrians-only street Corso Vittorio Emanuele. Northwest of the Duomo is Via Dante, at the top of which is the imposing outline of the Castello Sforzesco.

TOP ATTRACTIONS

Castello Sforzesco. For the serious student of Renaissance military engi-neering, the Castello must be something of a travesty, so often has it been remodeled or rebuilt since it was begun in 1450 by the *condottiere* (hired mercenary) who founded the city's second dynastic family, Fran-cesco Sforza, fourth duke of Milan. Though today "mercenary" has a pejorative ring, during the Renaissance all Italy's great soldier-heroes were professionals hired by the cities and principalities that they served. Of them—and there were thousands—Francesco Sforza (1401–66) is considered one of the greatest, most honest, and most organized. It is said he could remember the names not only of all his men but of their horses as well. His rule signaled the enlightened age of the Renaissance but preceded the next foreign rule by a scant 50 years.

Milan

TO STAZIONE CENTRALE

TO AEROPORTO MALPENSA

Parco Sempione

Stazione Cadorna

Pza. S. Maria delle Grazie

San Ambrogio

Sant'Agostino

Pza. Genova

Pta. Ticinese

Moscova Ⓜ

Lanza Ⓜ

Cadorna Ⓜ

Cairoli Ⓜ

Duomo

Pza. della Scala

Pza. del Duomo

Missori Ⓜ

San Babila Ⓜ

Monte Napoleon

Turati

Republica Ⓜ

Pza. di Republica

Giardini Pubblici

Palestro Ⓜ

San Ambrogio Ⓜ

TO AEROPORTO MILANO LINATE

Pta. S. Babila

1/4 mile

400 meters

KEY

Ⓜ Metro stops

ℹ Tourist information

Basilica di
Sant'Ambrogio 15

Battistero
Paleocristiano 2

Castello Sforzesco 8

Duomo 1

Galleria Vittorio
Emanuele 3

GAM 6

Museo Civico
Archeologico 13

Museo Nazionale della
Scienza e Tecnica 16

Museo Poldi-Pezzoli 5

Navigli district 18

Parco Sempione 9

Pinacoteca
Ambrosiana 12

Pinacoteca di Brera 7

San Lorenzo
Maggiore alle Colonne 17

San Satiro 11

Santa Maria
delle Grazie 14

Teatro alla Scala 4

Triennale Design
Museum 10

The castle's crypts and battlements, including a tunnel that emerges well into the Parco Sempione behind, can be visited with privately reserved guides from **Ad Artem** (☎ 02/6596937 ⊕ www.adartem.it) or **Opera d'Arte** (☎ 02/45487400 ⊕ www.operadartemilano.it). Since the turn of the 20th century, the Castello has been the depository of several city-owned collections of Egyptian and other antiquities, musical instruments, arms and armor, decorative arts and textiles, prints and photographs (on consultation), paintings, and sculpture. Highlights include the **Sala delle Asse,** a frescoed room still sometimes attributed to Leonardo da Vinci (1452–1519), which, at the time of writing, is closed for restoration (scheduled to reopen sometime before 2015). Michelangelo's unfinished *Rondanini Pietà* is believed to be his last work—an astounding achievement for a man nearly 90, and a moving coda to his life. The *pinacoteca* (picture gallery) features paintings from medieval times to the 18th century, including 230 works by Antonello da Messina, Canaletto, Andrea Mantegna, and Bernardo Bellotto. The **Museo dei Mobili** (furniture museum), which illustrates the development of Italian furniture from the Middle Ages to current design, includes a delightful collection of Renaissance treasure chests of exotic woods with tiny drawers and miniature architectural details. A single ticket purchased in the office in an inner courtyard admits visitors to these separate installations, which are dispersed around the castle's two immense courtyards. ✉ *Piazza Castello, Brera* ☎ 02/88463700 ⊕ *www.milanocastello.it* 🎟 *Castle: free. Museums: €3, free Fri. 2–5:30, Thurs,. and weekends 4:30–5:30* ⏱ *Castle: Apr.–Oct, daily 7–7; Nov.–Mar., daily 7–6. Museums: Tues.–Sun. 9–5:30; last entry at 5* Ⓜ *Cadorna, Lanza, or Cairoli; Tram No. 1, 2, 4, 12, 14, or 19.*

Fodor'sChoice
★
Duomo. This intricate Gothic structure has been fascinating and exasperating visitors and conquerors alike since it was begun by Galeazzo Visconti III (1351–1402), first duke of Milan, in 1386. Consecrated in the 15th or 16th century, it was not completed until just before the coronation of Napoleon as king of Italy in 1809. Whether you concur with travel writer H. V. Morton's 1964 assessment that the cathedral is "one of the mightiest Gothic buildings ever created," there is no denying that for sheer size and complexity it is unrivaled. It is the second-largest church in the world—the largest being St. Peter's in Rome. The capacity is estimated to be 40,000. Usually it is empty, a sanctuary from the frenetic pace of life outside and the perfect place for solitary contemplation.

The building is adorned with 135 marble spires and 2,245 marble statues. The oldest part is the apse. Its three colossal bays of curving and counter-curved tracery, especially the bay adorning the exterior of the stained-glass windows, should not be missed. At the end of the southern transept down the right aisle lies the **tomb of Gian Giacomo Medici.** The tomb owes some of its design to Michelangelo but was executed by Leone Leoni (1509–90) and is generally considered to be his masterpiece; it dates from the 1560s. Directly ahead is the Duomo's most famous sculpture, the gruesome but anatomically instructive figure of San Bartolomeo (St. Bartholomew), whose glorious martyrdom consisted of being flayed alive. It is usually said the saint stands "holding" his skin, but this is not quite accurate. It would appear more that he is luxuriating in it, much as a 1950s matron might have shown off a new fur stole.

Don't miss the view from the Duomo's roof; walk out the left (north) transept to the stairs and elevator. Sadly, air pollution drastically reduces the view on all but the rarest days. As you stand among the forest of marble pinnacles, remember that virtually every inch of this gargantuan edifice, including the roof itself, is decorated with precious white marble dragged from quarries near Lake Maggiore by Duke Visconti's team along road laid fresh for the purpose and through the newly dredged canals. Audio guides can be rented inside the Duomo from March to December and at Duomo Point in Piazza Duomo (just behind the cathedral) all year long. Exhibits at the **Museo del Duomo** shed light on the cathedral's history and include some of the treasures removed from the exterior for preservation purposes. At this writing, the museum is closed for restoration with no estimated date for completion. ✉ *Piazza del Duomo* ☎ *02/72023375* ⊕ *www.duomomilano.it* ✉ *Stairs to roof €10, elevator €12* ☉ *Cathedral: Mon.–Sat. 8:30–6, Sun. 1:30–5. Roof: Nov.–Mar., daily 9–6; Apr.–Oct., daily 9–9.* Ⓜ *Duomo.*

Galleria Vittorio Emanuele. This spectacular, late-19th-century glass-topped, Belle Époque, barrel-vaulted tunnel is essentially one of the planet's earliest and most select shopping malls. Like its suburban American cousins, the Galleria Vittorio Emanuele fulfills numerous social functions. This is the city's heart, midway between the Duomo and La Scala. It teems with life, inviting people-watching from the tables that spill from the bars and restaurants, where you can enjoy an overpriced coffee. Books, records, clothing, food, pens, pipes, hats, and jewelry are all for sale. Known as Milan's "parlor," the Galleria is often viewed as a barometer of the city's well-being. By the 1990s, the quality of the stores (with the exception of the Prada flagship) and restaurants was uninspired. The city government, which owns the Galleria, and merchants' groups evicted some longtime tenants who had enjoyed anomalously low rents, in favor of Gucci, Tod's, and Louis Vuitton. The historic, if somewhat overpriced and inconsistent, Savini restaurant hosts the beautiful and powerful of the city, just across from McDonald's. Like the cathedral, the Galleria is cruciform in shape. Even in poor weather the great glass dome above the octagonal center is a splendid sight. Look up! The paintings at the base of the dome represent Europe, Asia, Africa, and America. Those at the entrance arch are devoted to science, industry, art, and agriculture. And the floor mosaics are a vastly underrated source of pleasure, even if they are not to be taken too seriously. Be sure to follow tradition and spin your heels once or twice on the more "delicate" parts of the bull beneath your feet in the northern apse; the Milanese believe it brings good luck. ✉ *Piazza del Duomo* Ⓜ *Duomo.*

QUICK BITES

Caffè Zucca. One thing has remained constant in the Galleria: the Caffè Zucca, known by the Milanese as Camparino. Its inlaid counter, mosaics, and wrought-iron fixtures have been welcoming tired shoppers since 1867. Enjoy a Campari or Zucca *aperitivo* (aperitif) as well as the entire range of Italian coffees, served either in the Galleria or in an elegant upstairs room where lunch is also available. ✉ *Galleria Vittorio Emanuele* ⊕ *www.caffemiani.it.*

Museo Poldi-Pezzoli. This exceptional museum, opened in 1881, was once a private residence and collection, and contains not only pedigreed paintings but also porcelain, textiles, and a cabinet with scenes from Dante's life. The gem is undoubtedly the *Portrait of a Lady* by Antonio Pollaiuolo (1431–98), one of the city's most prized

treasures and the source of the museum's logo. The collection also includes masterpieces by Botticelli (1445–1510), Andrea Mantegna (1431–1506), Giovanni Bellini (1430–1516), and Fra Filippo Lippi (1406–69). Private guided tours are available by reservation. ⊠ *Via Manzoni 12, Quadrilatero* ☎ *02/794889* ⊕ *www.museopoldipezzoli. it* ⌑ *€9* ☉ *Wed.–Mon. 10–6* Ⓜ *Montenapoleone.*

Parco Sempione. Originally the gardens and parade grounds of the Castello Sforzesco, this open space was reorganized during the Napoleonic era, when the arena on its northeast side was constructed, and then turned into a park during the building boom at the end of the 19th century. It is still the lungs of the city's fashionable western neighborhoods, and the **Aquarium** still attracts Milan's schoolchildren (⊠ *Viale Gadio 2* ☎ *02/884957* ⊕ *www.acquariocivicomilano.eu.* ⌑ *Free.* ☉ *Tues.–Sun. 9–1 and 2–5:30*) The park became a bit of a design showcase in 1933 with the construction of the Triennale.

Fiat Café offers outdoor dining in summer along with a view of De Chirico's sculpture-filled fountain *Bagni Misteriosi* (Mysterious Baths). ⊠ *Parco Sempione: Piazza Castello, Sempione-Castello* ☉ *Oct.–Apr., daily 6:30–9; May, daily 6:30–10; June–Sept., daily 6:30–11:30* Ⓜ *Cairoli, Lanza, or Cadorna; Tram No. 1, 2, 4, 12, 14, 19, or 27; Bus No. 43, 57, 61, 70, or 94.*

  Torre Branca. It is worth visiting Parco Sempione just to see the Torre Branca. Designed by architect Gio Ponti, who was behind so many of the projects that made Milan the design capital that it is, this steel tower rises 330 feet over the Triennale. Take the elevator to get a nice view of the city, then have a drink at the glitzy Just Cavalli Café (☉ *Mon.–Sat. 8 pm–2 am*) at its base. ⊠ *Parco Sempione* ☎ *02/3314120* ⊕ *www.branca. it/torre/dati.asp* ⌑ *€3* ☉ *Irregular, seasonal hrs.*

Pinacoteca di Brera (*Brera Gallery*). The collection here is star-studded even by Italian standards. The entrance hall (Room I) displays 20th-century sculpture and painting, including Carlo Carrà's (1881–1966) confident, stylish response to the schools of cubism and surrealism. The museum has nearly 40 other rooms, arranged in chronological order—so pace yourself.

The somber, moving *Cristo Morto* (Dead Christ) by Mantegna dominates Room VI, with its sparse palette of umber and its foreshortened perspective. Mantegna's shocking, almost surgical precision—in the rendering of Christ's wounds, the face propped up on a pillow, the day's growth of beard—tells of an all-too-human agony. It's one of

Renaissance painting's most quietly wondrous achievements, finding an unsuspected middle ground between the excesses of conventional gore and beauty in representing the Passion's saddest moment.

Room XXIV offers two additional highlights of the gallery. Raphael's (1483–1520) *Sposalizio della Vergine* (Marriage of the Virgin) with its mathematical composition and precise, alternating colors, portrays the betrothal of Mary and Joseph (who, though older than the other men gathered, wins her hand when the rod he is holding miraculously blossoms). *La Vergine con il Bambino e Santi* (Madonna with Child and Saints), by Piero della Francesca (1420–92), is an altarpiece commissioned by Federico da Montefeltro (shown kneeling, in full armor, before the Virgin); it was intended for a church to house the duke's tomb. The ostrich egg hanging from the apse, depending on whom you ask, either commemorates the miracle of his fertility—Federico's wife died months after giving birth to a long-awaited male heir—or alludes to his appeal for posthumous mercy, the egg symbolizing the saving power of grace. Room XXXVIII houses one of the most romantic paintings in Italian history. *Il Bacio* by Francesco Hayez (1791–1882) depicts a couple from the Middle Ages engaged in a passionate kiss. The painting was meant to portray the patriotic spirit of Italy's Unification and freedom from the Austro-Hungarian empire. ✉ *Via Brera 28, Brera* ☎ *02/72263264* ⊕ *www.brera.beniculturali.it* 💶 *€10 general admisison, €12 during special exhibitions* ☉ *Tues.–Sun. 8:30–7:15; last admission 35 mins before closing* Ⓜ *Montenapoleone or Lanza.*

Teatro alla Scala. You need know nothing of opera to sense that, like Carnegie Hall, La Scala is closer to a cathedral than an auditorium. Here, Verdi established his reputation and Maria Callas sang her way into opera lore. It looms as a symbol—both for the performer who dreams of singing here and for the opera buff who knows every note of *Rigoletto* by heart. Audiences are notoriously demanding and are apt to jeer performers who do not measure up. The opera house was closed after destruction by Allied bombs in 1943, and reopened with a performance led by famed conductor Arturo Toscanini in 1946.

If you are lucky enough to be here during the opera season, which runs from December to June, do whatever is necessary to attend. Tickets go on sale two months before the first performance and are usually sold out the same day. Hearing opera sung in the magical setting of La Scala is an unparalleled experience.

At **Museo Teatrale alla Scala** you can admire an extensive collection of librettos, paintings of the famous names of Italian opera, posters, costumes, antique instruments, and design sketches for the theater. It is also possible to take a look at the theater, which was completely restored in 2004. Special exhibitions reflect current productions. ✉ *Piazza della Scala; museum, Largo Ghiringhelli 1, Duomo* ☎ *02/72003744 theater, 02/88797473 museum* ⊕ *www.teatroallascala. org* 💶 *Museum €5* ☉ *Museum daily 9–12:30 and 1:30–5:30; last entry ½ hr prior to closing* Ⓜ *Duomo.*

Triennale Design Museum. After decades of false starts and controversy, Milan's Triennale is a museum that honors Italy's design talent, as well as offering a regular series of exhibitions on design from around the world. A spectacular bridge entrance leads to a permanent collection, an exhibition space, and a stylish café (whose seating is an encyclopedia of design icons). The Triennale also manages the museum-studio of designer Achille Castiglioni in nearby Piazza Castello. ⊠ *Via Alemagna 6, Parco Sempione* ☎ *02/724341* ⊕ *www.triennaledesignmuseum.it* ☞ *€8* ⊙ *Tues.–Sun. 10:30–8:30; Thurs. 10:30 am–11 pm; last entrance 1 hr before closing* Ⓜ *Cadorna.*

WORTH NOTING

Battistero Paleocristiano. Beneath the Duomo's piazza lies this baptistery ruin dating from the 4th century. Although opinion remains divided, it is widely believed to be where Ambrose, Milan's first bishop and patron saint, baptized Augustine. Tickets are available at the kiosk inside the cathedral. ⊠ *Piazza del Duomo, enter through Duomo* ☎ *02/72022656* ☞ *€4* ⊙ *Daily 9:30–5:30* Ⓜ *Duomo.*

Casa-Museo Boschi di Stefano (*Boschi di Stefano House and Museum*). To most of people, Italian art means Renaissance art. But the 20th century in Italy was also productive, if less well known as a time of artistic achievement. An apartment on the second floor of a stunning art deco building designed by Milan architect Portaluppi houses this collection, which was donated to the city of Milan in 2003 and is a tribute to the enlightened private collectors who replaced popes and nobles as Italian patrons. The walls are lined with the works of postwar greats, such as Fontana, De Chirico, and Morandi. Along with the art, the museum holds distinctive postwar furniture and stunning Murano glass chandeliers. ⊠ *Via Jan 15, Corso Buenos Aires* ☎ *02/20240568* ⊕ *www.fondazioneboschidistefano.it* ☞ *Free* ⊙ *Tues.–Sun. 10–6; last entry at 5:30* Ⓜ *Lima; Tram No. 33; Bus No. 60.*

GAM: Galleria d'Arte Moderna/Villa Reale. One of the city's most beautiful buildings is an outstanding example of neoclassical architecture, built between 1790 and 1796 as a residence for a member of the Belgioioso family. It later became known as the Villa Reale (royal) when it was donated to Napoleon, who lived here briefly with Empress Josephine. Its origins as a residence are reflected in the elegance of its proportions and its private garden behind. The museum provides a unique glimpse of the splendors hiding behind Milan's discreet and often stern facades.

The collection derives from private donations from Milan's hereditary and commercial aristocracies and includes the collection left by prominent painter and sculptor Marino Marini. The immense *Quarto Stato* (*Fourth Estate*) is at the top of the grand staircase. Completed in 1901 by Pellizza da Volpedo, this painting of striking workers is an icon of 20th-century Italian art and labor history, and as such it has been satirized almost as much as the *Mona Lisa.* ⊠ *Via Palestro 16* ☎ *02/88445947* ⊕ *www.gam-milano.com* ☞ *Free* ⊙ *Tues.–Sun. 9–1 and 2–5:30; last entry 15 mins before closing* Ⓜ *Palestro or Turati.*

FAMILY **Giardini Pubblici** (*Public Gardens*). Giuseppe Piermarini, architect of La Scala, laid out these gardens across Via Palestro from the Villa Realein in 1770. Designed as public pleasure gardens, today they still are popular with families who live in the city center. Generations of Milanese have taken pony rides and gone on the miniature train and merry-go-round. The park also contains a small planetarium and the **Museo Civico di Storia Naturale** (Municipal Natural History Museum). ⊠ *Corso Venezia 55* ☎ *02/88463337* ⊕ *www.assodidatticamuseale.it* ⊠ *€3; free on Fri. 2–5:30* ⊙ *Tues.–Sun. 9–5:30 (last entry at 5)* Ⓜ *Palestro.*

SOUTH AND WEST OF THE DUOMO

If the part of the city to the north of the Duomo is dominated by its shops, the section to the south is famous for its works of art. The most famous is *Il Cenacolo*—known in English as *The Last Supper*. If you have time for nothing else, make sure you see this masterpiece, which has now been definitively restored, after many, many years of work. You will need reservations to see this fresco, housed in the refectory of Santa Maria delle Grazie. Make these at least three weeks before you depart for Italy, so you can plan the rest of your time in Milan.

TOP ATTRACTIONS

Basilica di Sant'Ambrogio (*Basilica of Saint Ambrose*). Milan's bishop, Saint Ambrose (one of the original Doctors of the Catholic Church), consecrated this church in AD 387. Saint Ambroeus, as he is known in Milanese dialect, is the city's patron saint, and his remains—dressed in elegant religious robes, a miter, and gloves—can be viewed inside a glass case in the crypt below the altar. Until the construction of the more imposing Duomo, this was Milan's most important church. Much restored and reworked over the centuries (the gold-and-gem-encrusted altar dates from the 9th century), Sant'Ambrogio still preserves its Romanesque characteristics (5th-century mosaics may be seen for €2). The church is often closed for weddings on Saturday. ⊠ *Piazza Sant'Ambrogio 15* ☎ *02/86450895* ⊕ *www.basilicasantambrogio.it* ⊙ *Mon.–Sat. 7:30–12:30 and 2:30–7; Sun. 7:30–1 and 3–8* Ⓜ *Sant'Ambrogio.*

QUICK
BITES

Bar Magenta. Open since 1907, Bar Magenta maintains its old-school charm with its vintage Campari and Moretti beer posters and its quintessential Milanese clientele. The bar overflows at night, when teenagers virtually block the sidewalk and traffic. Beyond coffee at all hours, lunch, and beer, the real attraction is its mix of old and new, working-class, trendy and aristocratic. ⊠ *Via Carducci 13, at Corso Magenta, Sant'Ambrogio* ☎ *02/8053808* ⊕ *www.barmagenta.it* Ⓜ *Sant'Ambrogio or Cadorna.*

Pinacoteca Ambrosiana. Cardinal Federico Borromeo, one of Milan's native saints, founded this picture gallery in 1618 with the addition of his personal art collection to a bequest of books to Italy's first public library. More recent renovations have reunited the core works of the collection, including such treasures as Caravaggio's *Basket of Fruit*; Raphael's monumental preparatory drawing (known as a "cartoon") for *The School of Athens*, which hangs in the Vatican; and the *Codice Atlantico*, the largest collection of designs by Leonardo da Vinci (on display through 2015). In addition to works by Lombard artists are paintings by Botticelli, Luini,

Titian, and Jan Brueghel. A wealth of charmingly idiosyncratic items on display include 18th-century scientific instruments and gloves worn by Napoleon at Waterloo. Access to the library, the Biblioteca Ambrosiana, is limited to researchers who apply for entrance tickets. ⊠ *Piazza Pio XI 2, near Duomo* ☎ *02/806921* ⊕ *www.ambrosiana.it* 🎫 *€15* ⊙ *Tues.– Sun. 8:30–7, Mon. 9:30–1 and 2–6* Ⓜ *Duomo.*

San Lorenzo Maggiore alle Colonne. Sixteen ancient Roman columns line the front of this sanctuary; 4th-century paleo-Christian mosaics survive in the Cappella di Sant'Aquilino (Chapel of Saint Aquilinus). ⊠ *Corso di Porta Ticinese 39* ☎ *02/89404129* ⊕ *www.sanlorenzomaggiore. com* 🎫 *Mosaics €2* ⊙ *Mon., Fri., and Sat. 7:30–6:30; Tues., Wed., and Thurs. 7:30–12:30 and 2:30–6:30; Sun. 9–7.*

San Satiro. Just a few steps from the Duomo, this architectural gem was first built in 876 and later perfected by Bramante (1444–1514), demonstrating his command of proportion and perspective, keynotes of Renaissance architecture. Bramante tricks the eye with a famous optical illusion that makes a small interior seem extraordinarily spacious and airy, while accommodating a beloved 13th-century fresco. ⊠ *Via Speronari 3, near Duomo* ☎ *02/874683* ⊙ *Weekdays 7:30–12 and 3–6:30, Sat. 3:30–7, Sun. 8:30–12:30 and 3:30–7* Ⓜ *Duomo; Tram No. 2, 3 , 4, 12, 14, 19, 20, 24, or 27.*

Fodor's Choice **Santa Maria delle Grazie.** Leonardo da Vinci's *The Last Supper,* housed
★ in this church and former Dominican monastery, has had an almost unbelievable history of bad luck and neglect—its near destruction in an American bombing raid in August 1943 was only the latest chapter in a series of misadventures, including, if one 19th-century source is to be believed, being whitewashed over by monks. Well-meant but disastrous attempts at restoration have done little to rectify the problem of the work's placement: it was executed on a wall unusually vulnerable to climatic dampness. Yet Leonardo chose to work slowly and patiently in oil pigments—which demand dry plaster—instead of proceeding hastily on wet plaster according to the conventional fresco technique. After years of restorers patiently shifting from one square centimeter to another, Leonardo's masterpiece is free of the shroud of scaffolding—and centuries of retouching, grime, and dust. Astonishing clarity and luminosity have been regained.

Reservations are required to view the work. Viewings are in 15-minute, timed slots, and visitors must arrive 15 minutes before their assigned time in order not to lose their place. Reservations can be made by phone or through the website; it is worthwhile to call, as tickets are set aside for phone reservations. Call at least three weeks ahead if you want a Saturday slot, two weeks ahead for a weekday slot. The telephone reservation office is open 9 to 6 weekdays and 9 to 2 on Saturday. Operators do speak English, though not fluently, and to reach one you must wait for the Italian introduction to finish and then press "2." However, you can sometimes get tickets from one day to the next. Some city bus tours include a visit in their regular circuit, which may be a good option. Guided tours in English are available for €3.50 and also require a reservation.

6

The painting was executed in what was the order's refectory, which is now referred to as the **Cenacolo Vinciano**. Take a moment to visit Santa Maria delle Grazie itself. It's a handsome, completely restored church, with a fine dome, which Bramante added along with a cloister about the time that Leonardo was commissioned to paint *The Last Supper*. If you're wondering how two such giants came to be employed decorating and remodeling the refectory and church of a comparatively modest religious order, and not, say, the Duomo, the answer lies in the ambitious but largely unrealized plan to turn Santa Maria delle Grazie into a magnificent Sforza family mausoleum. Though Ludovico il Moro Sforza (1452–1508), seventh duke of Milan, was but one generation away from the founding of the Sforza dynasty, he was its last ruler. Two years after Leonardo finished *The Last Supper*, Ludovico was defeated by Louis XII and spent the remaining eight years of his life in a French dungeon. ⊠ *Piazza Santa Maria delle Grazie 2, off Corso Magenta, Sant'Ambrogio* ☎ *02/4987588 Last Supper, 02/92800360 reservations, 02/4676111 church* ⊕ *www.cenacolovinciano.net* ⊠ *Last Supper €6.50 plus €1.50 reservation fee; church free* ☉ *Last Supper: Tues.–Sun. 8–7:30. Church: weekdays 7–noon and 3–7, Sun. 7:30–12:15 and 3:30–9* Ⓜ *Cadorna; Tram No. 16.*

WORTH NOTING

Museo Civico Archeologico (*Municipal Archaeological Museum*). Appropriately situated in the heart of Roman Milan, this museum housed in a former monastery displays everyday utensils, jewelry, silver plate, and several fine examples of mosaic pavement from Mediolanum, the ancient Roman name for Milan. The museum opens into a garden that is flanked by the square tower of the roman circus and the polygonal Ansperto tower, adorned with frescoes dating to the end of the 13th and 14th centuries, portraying St. Francis and other saints receiving the stigmata. ⊠ *Corso Magenta 15, Sant'Ambrogio* ☎ *02/88445208* ⊕ *www.poliarcheo.it* ⊠ *€2* ☉ *Tues.–Sun. 9–5:30; last entry at 5* Ⓜ *Cadorna; Tram No. 16 or 27.*

FAMILY **Museo Nazionale della Scienza e Tecnica** (*National Museum of Science and Technology*). This converted cloister is best known for the collection of models based on Leonardo da Vinci's sketches (although these are not captioned in English, the labeling in many other exhibits is bilingual). On the ground level—in the hallway between the courtyards—is a room featuring interactive, moving models of the famous *vita aerea* (aerial screw) and *ala battente* (beating wing), thought to be forerunners of the modern helicopter and airplane, respectively. The museum also houses a varied collection of industrial artifacts including trains, a celebrated Italian-built submarine, and several reconstructed workshops including a watchmaker's, a lutemaker's, and an antique pharmacy. Displays also illustrate papermaking and metal founding, which were fundamental to Milan's—and the world's—economic growth. There's a bookshop and a bar. ⊠ *Via San Vittore 21, Sant'Ambrogio* ☎ *02/485551* ⊕ *www. museoscienza.org* ⊠ *€10* ☉ *Tues.–Fri. 9:30–5, weekends 9:30–6:30* Ⓜ *Sant'Ambrogio; Bus No. 50, 58, or 94.*

Navigli District. In medieval times, a network of *navigli,* or canals, crisscrossed the city. Almost all have been covered over, but two—Naviglio

Grande and Naviglio Pavese—are still navigable. Once a down-at-the-heels neighborhood, the Navigli district has undergone some gentrification over the past 20 years. Humble workshops have been replaced by boutiques, art galleries, cafés, bars, and restaurants, and at night the Navigli serves up a scene about as close as you will get to southern-style Italian street life in Milan. On weekend nights, it is difficult to walk (and impossible to park, although an underground parking area has been under construction for years) among the youthful crowds thronging the narrow streets along the canals. Check out the antiques fair on the last Sunday of the month. ⊠ *South of Corso Porta Ticinese, Porta Genova* Ⓜ *Porta Genova; Tram No. 2, 3, 9, 14, 15, 29, or 30.*

Villa Necchi Campiglio. In 1932, architect Piero Portaluppi designed this sprawling estate in an art deco style, with inspiration coming from the decadent cruise ships of the 1920s. Once owned by the Necchi Campiglio industrial family, the tasteful and elegant home—which sits on one of Milan's most exclusive streets, Via Mozart—is a reminder of the refined, modern culture of the nouveau riche who accrued financial power in Milan during that era. *I Am Love*, directed by Luca Guadagnino, was mostly set in Villa Necchi, where actors Tilda Swinton and Marisa Berenson were allowed to sit on the plush velvet furniture and mill about freely among the impressive artwork and sculptures. The villa was reopened to the public in 2008 after an extensive restoration. Tickets can be purchased at the ticket counter on the estate grounds. There is also a restaurant-café on the grounds that is open for lunch. ⊠ *Via Mozart 14, Palestro* ☎ *02/76340121* ⊕ *www.casemuseo.it* 🎟 *€8* ☉ *Wed.–Sun. 10–6* Ⓜ *Montenapoleone.*

WHERE TO EAT

BRERA

$$
MODERN ITALIAN

✕ **Fioraio Bianchi Caffè.** This French-style bistro in the heart of Milan was opened more than 40 years ago by Raimondo Bianchi, a great lover of flowers. In fact, eating at this restaurant is like eating in the middle of a boutique Parisian flower shop. It's a popular haunt for local glitterati, and despite the French atmosphere, many dishes like julienne of squid with red pesto and Livornese sea bass with basmati rice and cinnamon ensure a classy, inventive Italian meal. Reservations recommended. Ⓢ *Average meal: €40* ⊠ *Via Montebello 7* ☎ *02/29014390* ⊕ *www.fioraiobianchicaffe.it* ☉ *Closed Sun.* Ⓜ *Turati.*

$
VEGETARIAN

✕ **La Vecchia Latteria.** With only two small dining rooms, this family-owned lunch spot—run by Giorgio Notari, his wife Teresa, and their daughter Francesca—dishes out an impressive amount of vegetarian cuisine. Opened in 1951 by Giorgio's parents, La Vecchia Latteria (The Old Dairy) began life as a breakfast place, but transformed into a vegetarian restaurant when Giorgio's wife Teresa started introducing her Sicilian influence into the kitchen in the 1980s. Nestled on a small street just steps away from the Duomo, it offers an array of freshly prepared, in-season delights ranging from *parmigiana di melanzane* (eggplant parmesan) to lasagna with taleggio cheese, and *scamorza dolce* (sweet cheese made from Italian cows' milk). The menu changes daily; try the mixed plate, which offers a taste of eight different small dishes. To beat the lunch rush, arrive before 1 pm. Between the months of February and July, on Tuesday and Thursday nights, the restaurant hosts an aperitivo called "Eppi Auar" (Happy Hour) from 7 to 10 with live music and an all-you-can-eat buffet for €9. [$] *Average meal: €20* ✉ *Via dell'Unione, 6, Duomo* ☎ *02/874401* 🕒 *Closed Sun.* [M] *Duomo or Missori.*

CINQUE GIORNATE

$$$ ITALIAN 🍴 **Da Giacomo.** The fashion and publishing crowd, as well as international bankers and businessmen, favor this Tuscan/Ligurian restaurant. The emphasis is on fish; even the warm slice of pizza served while you study the menu has seafood on it. The specialty, gnocchi *Da Giacomo,* has a savory seafood-and-tomato sauce. Service is friendly and efficient; the wine list broad; and the most celebrated dish on the dessert cart is the *bomba Da Giacomo,* a savory mountain of chantilly cream, mascarpone, and strawberries. With its tile floor and bank of fresh seafood, the place has a refined neighborhood-bistro style. [$] *Average meal: €60* ✉ *Via P. Sottocorno 6, entrance in Via Cellini, Cinque Giornate* ☎ *02/76023313* 🌐 *www.giacomomilano.com* ✍ *Reservations essential* [M] *Tram No. 9, 12, 27, 29, or 30; Bus No. 54 or 60.*

DUOMO

$$$$ MODERN ITALIAN 🍴 **Cracco.** In an elegant dining room favoring cool earth tones and clean lines, tasting menus are a good way to savor many of chef Carlo Cracco's delicate inventions, though an à la carte menu is available. Specialties include Milanese classics revisited—Cracco's take on saffron risotto and *cotoletta* (breaded veal cutlet) should not be missed. Delightful appetizers and desserts vary seasonally, but may include scampi cream with freshwater shrimp, the disk of "caramelized Russian salad," and mango cream with mint gelatin. [$] *Average meal: €80* ✉ *Via Victor Hugo 4, Duomo* ☎ *02/876774* 🌐 *www.ristorantecracco.it* ✍ *Reservations essential* 🕒 *Closed 3 wks in Aug. and last wk in Dec. Sept.–July: no lunch Sat. or Mon., closed Sun.* [M] *Duomo.*

$$$ MODERN ITALIAN 🍴 **Don Carlos.** One of the few restaurants open after La Scala lets out, Don Carlos, in the Grand Hotel et de Milan, is nothing like its indecisive operatic namesake (whose betrothed was stolen by his father). Flavors are bold, presentation is precise and full of flair, and service is attentive. The walls are blanketed with sketches of the theater, and the low-key opera recordings are every bit as well chosen as the wine list, setting the perfect stage for discreet business negotiation or, better yet, refined romance. [$] *Average meal: €65* ✉ *Grand Hotel et de Milan, Via Manzoni 29, Duomo* ☎ *02/7234640* 🌐 *www.ristorantedoncarlos.it* ✍ *Reservations essential* 🕒 *No lunch* [M] *Montenapoleone; Tram 1 or 2.*

$$ ECLECTIC 🍴 **Rinascente Food & Restaurants.** The seventh floor of this famous Italian department store is a gourmet food market surrounded by several small restaurants that can be a good option for lunch, an aperitivo, or dinner if you've been shopping or touring the Duomo. There are several places to eat, including the popular mozzarella bar Obika, My Sushi, De Santis for "slow food" sandwiches, and the sophisticated Maio restaurant. A terrace overlooking the Duomo is shared by three locations.

It's best to get here early—it's popular, and there are often lines at meal-times. $ *Average meal: €30* ⊠ *Piazza Duomo* ☎ *02/8852471* ⊕ *www. rinascente.it* Ⓜ *Duomo.*

GARIBALDI

$

NORTHERN
ITALIAN

✕ **Osteria Vecchi Sapori.** Simple but savory fare and a menu that varies weekly characterize one osteria with two locations run by two brothers, Paolo and Roberto. Specialties include their truffle tagliolini, and primi of stuffed pasta like Gorgonzola-filled fiocchetti, or pear and Parmesan-filled ravioli with a saffron butter sauce. Their extensive, meat-rich second-course dishes are paired with creamy *polenta taragna* (made with cornmeal and buckwheat flour) or their hand-cut fried potatoes. The dessert menu changes daily with in-house cakes, tiramisu, and *crostate* (fruit tarts) reflecting traditional tastes and seasonal availability. $ *Average meal: €25* ⊠ *Via Carmagnola 3, Garbaldi* ☎ *02/6686148* ⊕ *www.vecchisapori.it* ⚐ *Reservations essential* ۞ *Closed Sun. No lunch Sat.* Ⓜ *Garibaldi or Zara; Tram No. 3, 4, 7, or 31; Bus No. 82, 86, 90, or 91.*

$$

PIZZA

✕ **Pizzeria La Fabbrica.** This lively pizzeria has two wood-burning ovens going full-steam every day of the week. Skip the appetizers and go straight to the pizzas, which vary from traditional (*quattro stagioni*) to vegetable-based (with leeks and Gorgonzola) to in-house specialties like the *tartufona* (with truffles). The menu also offers pasta like *pici* with Tuscan sausage and main secondi dishes. Save room for a worthy dessert like the *torta caprese al cioccolato* or tiramisu—though after pizza, you might want to share. The Fabbrica is spacious enough to handle groups; seek out a seat in the spacious garden area when the weather's nice. $ *Average meal: €30* ⊠ *Viale Pasubio 2, Garbaldi* ☎ *02/6552771* ⊕ *www.lafabbricapizzeria.it* Ⓜ *Garibaldi.*

LORETO

$$

MILANESE

✕ **Da Abele.** If you love risotto, then make a beeline for this neighborhood trattoria. The superb risotto dishes change with the season, and there may be just two or three on the menu at any time. It is tempting to try them all. The setting is relaxed, the service informal, the prices strikingly reasonable. Outside the touristy center of town but quite convenient by subway, this trattoria is invariably packed with locals. $ *Average meal: €30* ⊠ *Via Temperanza 5, Loreto* ☎ *02/2613855* ۞ *8 pm-midnight* ۞ *Closed Mon., Aug., and Dec. 24–Jan. 3. No lunch* Ⓜ *Pasteur.*

PORTA ROMANA

$$

NORTHERN
ITALIAN

✕ **U Barba.** Simple, fresh, authentic Ligurian specialties (in Ligurian dialect the name means "the uncle") will take you back to lazy summer days on the Italian Riviera—even during Milan's wet winter weather. Such classic coastal specialties as *trofie al pesto* (an egg-free pasta served with pesto) and *muscoli ripieni* (stuffed mussels), coupled with a complimentary basket of warm focaccia, reign supreme in this favorite of Milan's fashion crowd. $ *Average meal: €35* ⊠ *33 Via Pier Candido Decembrio, Porta Romana* ☎ *02/45487032* ⊕ *www.ubarba.it* ⚐ *Reservations essential* ۞ *Closed Mon.*

6

PORTA VENEZIA

$$$$ VEGETARIAN

🍴 **Joia.** At this haute-cuisine vegetarian haven near Piazza della Repubblica, delicious dishes are artistically prepared by Chef Pietro Leemann. Vegetarians, who often get short shrift in Italy, will marvel at the variety of culinary traditions—Asian and European—and artistry offered here. The ever-changing menu offers dishes in unusual formats: tiny glasses of creamed vegetables or ravioli in the shape of a human hand. Fish also makes an appearance. Joia's restful dining room has been refurbished, another room added, and its kitchen enlarged. [$] *Average meal: €100* ✉ *Via Panfilo Castaldi 18, Porta Venezia* ☎ *02/29522124* 🌐 *www.joia.it* ✍ *Reservations essential* 🕒 *Closed Sun., 3 wks in Aug., and Dec. 24–Jan. 7. No lunch Sat.* [M] *Repubblica; Tram No. 1, 5, 11, 29, or 30.*

$ PIZZA

🍴 **Pizza OK.** Pizza is almost the only item on the menu at this family-run pizzeria with three locations, the oldest near Corso Buenos Aires in the Porta Venezia area. The pizza is extra thin and large, and possibilities for toppings seem endless. A good choice for families, this dining experience will be easy on your pocketbook. Other locations are on Via San Siro 9 in Corso Vercelli, and Piazza Sempione 8. [$] *Average meal: €11* ✉ *Via Lambro 15, Porta Venezia* ☎ *02/29401272* 🌐 *www.pizzaokgroup.it* 🕒 *Closed Aug. 7–20 and Dec. 24– 26* [M] *Porta Venezia.*

QUADRILATERO

$ MODERN ITALIAN

🍴 **Chic & Go Milano.** Step into these chic and trendy surroundings for a quick sandwich as exquisite as the fashion found in the nearby shops. With ingredients like angus tartare, lobster, and wild salmon, you may not mind paying prices that match those on the designer labels that abound in the neighborhood. [$] *Average meal: €15* ✉ *25 Via Montenapoleone, Quadrilatero* ☎ *39/02782648.*

$$ ITALIAN

🍴 **Paper Moon.** This cross between a neighborhood restaurant and a celebrity hangout is hidden behind Via Montenapoleone and thus handy to the restaurant-scarce Quadrilatero. Clients include families from this well-heeled area, professionals, football players, and television stars. What the menu lacks in originality it makes up for in reliable consistency—pizza and cotoletta, to name just two. Like any Italian restaurant, it's not child-friendly in an American sense—no high chairs or children's menu—but children will find food they like. It's open until 12:30 am. [$] *Average meal: €35* ✉ *Via Bagutta 1, Quadrilatero* ☎ *02/76022297* 🕒 *Closed Sun. and 2 wks in Aug.* [M] *San Babila.*

BEYOND CITY CENTER

$$$$ ITALIAN

Fodor's Choice ★

🍴 **Antica Osteria del Ponte.** Rich, imaginative seasonal cuisine composed according to the inspired whims of Chef Fabio Barbaglini is reason enough to make your way 25 km (12 miles) southwest of Milan to one of Italy's finest restaurants. The setting is a traditional country inn, where a wood fire warms the rustic interior in winter. The menu changes regularly; in fall, wild porcini mushrooms are among the favored ingredients. Various fixed-price menus offer broad samplings of antipasti, primi, and meat or fish; some include appropriate wine selections, too. [$] *Average meal: €70* ✉ *Piazza G. Negri 9, Beyond City Center, Cassinetta di Lugagnano* ☎ *02/9420034* 🌐 *www.anticaosteriadelponte.it* ✍ *Reservations essential* 🕒 *Closed Sun. and Mon., Aug., and Dec. 24–Jan. 10.*

$$$
MILANESE
✕ **ATMosfera.** Take a ride on Milan's 1930s-era trams, enjoy a tour of the city, and have a romantic dinner at the same time. With many cable cars out of service these days, ATMosfera shows that in Milan, old traditions die hard. The menu is limited, but patrons can choose between the meat, fish, and vegetarian set menu, which varies throughout the year. Dinner lasts about two hours and visitors are asked to arrive at least 15 minutes prior to departure, which is at 8 from Piazza Castello, at the corner of Via Beltrami. Due to limited space, reservations are mandatory. $ *Average meal: €65* ✉ *Piazza Castello* ☎ *800/808181* ⊕ *www. atm-mi.it* ⚲ *Reservations essential* ☉ *Closed Jan. 1–16 and Aug.*

WHERE TO STAY

For expanded hotel reviews, visit Fodors.com.

DUOMO

$$
HOTEL
⌕ **Ariston.** The soothing, minimally decorated rooms offer a soothing respite in a city-center location, close to the lively Porta Ticinese shops and restaurants and the young people's fashion mecca, Via Torino. **Pros:** central; parking available. **Cons:** plain rooms; a longish walk from the metro (but well served by tram). $ *Rooms from: €150* ✉ *Largo Carrobbio 2, Duomo* ☎ *02/72000556* ⊕ *www.aristonhotel.com* ⤴ *52 rooms* ⦿ *Breakfast* Ⓜ *Duomo; Tram No. 2 or 14.*

$$
HOTEL
⌕ **Hotel Gran Duca di York.** Spare but classically elegant and efficient rooms are arranged around a courtyard—four have private terraces—and are an exceptional value. **Pros:** central; airy; updated and well-decorated rooms. **Cons:** rooms are simple. $ *Rooms from: €180* ✉ *Via Moneta 1/a, Duomo* ☎ *02/874863* ⊕ *www.ducadiyork.com* ⤴ *33 rooms* ☉ *Closed Aug.* ⦿ *Breakfast* Ⓜ *Cordusio; Duomo.*

$$$
HOTEL
⌕ **Hotel Spadari al Duomo.** That this chic city center inn is owned by an architect's family shows in the details, including custom-designed furniture and paintings by young Milanese artists on rotating display in the stylish guest rooms. **Pros:** good breakfast; central location; attentive staff, environmentally friendly toiletries. **Cons:** pricey option; some rooms on the small side. $ *Rooms from: €290* ✉ *Via Spadari 11, Duomo* ☎ *02/72002371* ⊕ *www.spadarihotel.com* ⤴ *40 rooms, 3 suites* ⦿ *Breakfast* Ⓜ *Duomo.*

$$$$
HOTEL
Fodor's Choice
★
⌕ **Park Hyatt Milan.** Extensive use of warm travertine stone and modern art creates a sophisticated, yet inviting and tranquil backdrop in the spacious and opulent guest rooms, a worthy splurge. **Pros:** central; contemporary; refined. **Cons:** not particularly intimate. $ *Rooms from: €520* ✉ *Via Tommaso Grossi 1, Duomo* ☎ *02/88211234* ⊕ *milan.park. hyatt.com* ⤴ *106 rooms, 25 junior suites* Ⓜ *Duomo.*

$$$
HOTEL
⌕ **The Yard.** Ralph Lauren–style polo culture (mixed with contemporary flair) inspires the dark leather couches, polished silver plates, and other decor in this extremely stylish outpost at the foot of the lively Corso di Porta Ticinese. **Pros:** extremely attractive and comfortable; well-priced for expensive Milan. **Cons:** too design-oriented for some guests; lacking some of the amenities of large hotels. $ *Rooms from: €230* ✉ *Piazza XXIV Maggio 8, Porta Ticinese* ☎ *0289415901* ⊕ *www.theyardmilano. com* ⤴ *15 rooms* ⦿ *Breakfast.*

6

$$$
HOTEL

⊞ **UNA Maison Milano.** Inside a faithfully restored palazzo dates from the early 1900s spaciousness is accentuated with soft white interiors, muted fabrics and marbles, and clean, contemporary lines. **Pros:** the warmth of a residence and luxury of a design hotel; lovely bathrooms and other modern amenities. **Cons:** breakfast not included. $ *Rooms from:* €300 ⊠ *Via Mazzini 4, Duomo* ☎ *02/85605* ⊕ *www.unamaison milano.it* 🖘 *27 rooms, 6 junior suites, 3 suites* ⏀ *No meals* Ⓜ *Duomo.*

> **'LET'S GO TO THE COLUMNS'**
>
> *Andiamo al Le Colonne* in Milanese youthspeak means to meet up at the sober Roman columns in front of the Basilica San Lorenzo Maggiore. Attracted by the bars and shops along Corso di Porta Ticinese, Milan's alternative, hipsters spill out on the street to chat and drink. Neighbors may complain about the noise and confusion, but students and nighthawks find it indispensable for socializing at all hours. It's a street—no closing time.

PIAZZA REPUBBLICA

$
HOTEL

⊞ **Hotel Casa Mia Milan.** These simple, clean rooms are easy to reach from the central train station (a few blocks away) and easy on the budget. **Pros:** clean; good value; free Wi-Fi for guests. **Cons:** not the nicest neighborhood in Milan; up a flight of stairs. $ *Rooms from:* €100 ⊠ *Viale Vittorio Veneto 30, Piazza Repubblica* ☎ *02/6575249* ⊕ *www. hotelcasamiamilano.it* 🖘 *15 rooms* ⏀ *Breakfast* Ⓜ *Repubblica.*

$$
HOTEL

⊞ **Hotel Star.** The decor may seem out of date (the animal murals may be a bit off-putting), but the price is extremely reasonable, the staff is helpful and cheerful, and the rooms are well equipped and comfortable. **Pros:** central; reasonably priced; breakfast is included. **Cons:** outdated decor. $ *Rooms from:* €160 ⊠ *Via dei Bossi 5, La Scala* ☎ *02/801501* ⊕ *www.hotelstar.it* 🖘 *30 rooms* ⏀ *Breakfast.*

$$$$
HOTEL

⊞ **Hotel Principe di Savoia Milano.** Milan's grande dame has all the trappings of an exquisite traditional luxury hotel: lavish mirrors, drapes, and carpets, limousine services, and the city's largest guest rooms, outfitted with eclectic fin de siècle furnishings. **Pros:** substantial spa–health club (considered chic by Milanese); close to Central Station. **Cons:** overblown luxury in a not-very-central or attractive neighborhood. $ *Rooms from:* €400 ⊠ *Piazza della Repubblica 17, Piazza Repubblica* ☎ *02/62301* ⊕ *www.hotelprincipedisavoia.com* 🖘 *335 guest rooms, 66 suites* ⏀ *No meals* Ⓜ *Repubblica.*

QUADRILATERO

$$$$
HOTEL

⊞ **Four Seasons.** Built in the 15th century as a convent and surrounding a colonnaded cloister, this luxurious retreat that is often cited as Milan's best hotel exudes a feeling that is anything but urban. **Pros:** beautiful setting that feels like Tuscany rather than central Milan. **Cons:** luxury does not come cheap. $ *Rooms from:* €610 ⊠ *Via Gesù 6–8, Quadrilatero* ☎ *02/7708167* ⊕ *www.fourseasons.com/milan* 🖘 *67 rooms, 51 suites* ⏀ *No meals* Ⓜ *Montenapoleone.*

SANT'AMBROGIO

$$ HOTEL **Antica Locanda Leonardo.** Half the rooms in this 19th-century building face a courtyard and the others a back garden; many have balconies and one ground-floor room has a private garden with table and chairs. **Pros:** very quiet and homey; breakfast is ample. **Cons:** more like a bed-and-breakfast than a hotel. [$] *Rooms from: €170* ✉ *Corso Magenta 78, Sant'Ambrogio* ☎ *02/463317* 🌐 *www.anticalocandaleonardo.com* 🛏 *16 rooms* 🕒 *Closed 1st wk in Jan. and 3 wks in Aug.* 🍴 *Breakfast* [M] *Sant'Ambrogio.*

SCALA

$$$$ HOTEL **Grand Hotel et de Milan.** Only blocks from La Scala you'll find everything you hope for in a traditional European hotel; dignified but not stuffy, elegant but not ostentatious, with moss-green and persimmon velvet enlivening the 19th-century look without sacrificing dignity and luxury. **Pros:** traditional and elegant; great location. **Cons:** gilt decor may not suit those who like more modern design. [$] *Rooms from: €700* ✉ *Via Manzoni 29, Scala* ☎ *02/723141* 🌐 *www.grandhoteletdemilan.it* 🛏 *72 rooms, 23 suites* 🍴 *No meals* [M] *Montenapoleone.*

VIA SANTA SOFIA

$$ HOTEL **Hotel Canada.** Nice wood flooring, thorough soundproofing, and contemporary furnishings that maximize space and bring in light all provide a stylish bargain in pricey Milan. **Pros:** good value; central location; allows small pets. **Cons:** although trams and buses are handy, it's a short walk to the nearest metro stop. [$] *Rooms from: €150* ✉ *Via San Sofia 16, Via San Sofia* ☎ *02/58304844* 🌐 *www.canadahotel.it* 🛏 *37 rooms* 🍴 *Breakfast* [M] *Repubblica.*

NIGHTLIFE AND THE ARTS

THE ARTS

For events likely to be of interest to non–Italian speakers, see *Hello Milano* (🌐 *www.hellomilano.it*), a monthly magazine available online and in print at the tourist office in Piazza Duomo; *Easy Milano* (🌐 *www.easymilano.it*); or *The American* (🌐 *www.theamericanmag.com*), which is available online and at international bookstores and newsstands, and which has a thorough cultural calendar. The tourist office publishes the monthly *Milano Mese,* which also includes some listings in English.

MUSIC

Auditorium di Milano. This modern hall, known for its excellent acoustics, is home to the **Orchestra Verdi,** founded by Milan-born conductor Richard Chailly. The season, which runs from September to June, includes many top international performers and rotating guest conductors. ✉ *Largo Gustav Mahler, Corso San Gottardo, 39 at Via Torricelli, Conchetta, Navigli* ☎ *02/83389401* 🌐 *www.laverdi.org.*

Conservatorio. The two halls belonging to the Conservatorio host some of the leading names in classical music. Series are organized by several organizations, including the venerable chamber music society, the **Società del Quartetto** (☎ *02/76005500* 🌐 *www.quartettomilano.it*). ✉ *Via del Conservatorio 12, Duomo* ☎ *02/762110* 🌐 *www.consmilano.it* [M] *San Babila.*

6

Teatro Dal Verme. Frequent classical music concerts are staged here from October to May. ⊠ *Via San Giovanni sul Muro 2, Castello* ☎ *02/87905* ⊕ *www.dalverme.org* Ⓜ *Cairoli.*

OPERA

Teatro alla Scala. The season runs from December 7, the feast day of Milan patron Saint Ambrose, through June. Plan well in advance, as tickets sell out quickly. For tickets, visit the **Biglietteria Centrale** (*Galleria del Sagrato, Piazza Del Duomo* <img src=”assets/images/C.png”/>*Daily noon–6 Duomo*), which is in the Duomo subway station. Tickets are also available via La Scala's automated booking system (*02/860775*). To pick up tickets for performances—from two hours prior until 15 minutes after the start of a performance—go to the box office at the theater, which is around the corner at Via Filodrammatici 2. Although you might not get seats for the more popular operas with big-name stars, it is worth trying; ballets are easier. The theater is closed from the end of July through August and on national and local holidays. ⊠ *Piazza della Scala* ☎ *02/72003744* ⊕ *www.teatroallascala.org* ⊗ *Daily 9–noon* Ⓜ *Duomo.*

NIGHTLIFE

The *aperitivo,* or prelunch or predinner drink, is available everywhere Italy, but in Milan it is a big part of life and a must-try. Milan bar owners have enriched the usual nibbles of olives, nuts, and chips with full finger (and often fork) buffets serving cubes of pizza and cheese, fried vegetables, rice salad, sushi, and even pasta, and they baptized it 'Appy Hour—with the first "h" dropped and the second one pronounced. For the price of a drink (around €8), you can make a meal of hors d'oeuvres (though don't be a glutton; remember Italians value the quality of the food, not the quantity).

BARS

Armani/Lounge. The Lounge at the Armani Hotel Milano has kept Milan abuzz since its opening. A modern architectural marvel boasts high ceilings, louvered windows, and expansive views of the city's rooftops. It's a great place for a relaxing after-work tea with friends or a predinner aperitivo. ⊠ *Via Manzoni 31* ☎ *02/8883-8888.*

Bar STRAF. An architecturally stimulating, yet dimly lit, atmosphere has such artistic features as recycled fiberglass panels and vintage 1970s furnishings. The music is an eclectic mix of mellow tunes during the daytime with more lively and vibrant tracks pepping it up at night. Located on a quiet side street near the Duomo, STRAF draws an attractive international crowd. ⊠ *Via San Raffaele 3, Duomo* ☎ *02/80508715* ⊕ *www.straf.it/en/bar.html.*

Blue Note. The first European branch of the famous New York nightclub features regular performances by some of the most famous names in jazz, as well as blues and rock concerts. Dinner is available, and there's a popular jazz brunch on Sunday. It's closed Monday. ⊠ *Via Borsieri 37, Garibaldi* ☎ *02/69016888* ⊕ *www.bluenotemilano.com.*

Brellin Café. This popular spot in the arty Navigli district has live music and serves late-night snacks. ⊠ *Vicolo Lavandai at Alzaia Naviglio Grande* ☎ *02/58101351* ⊕ *www.brellin.it.*

Bulgari Hotel Bar. Having drinks or a light lunch at the Bulgari Hotel Bar allows patrons to step off the asphalt and into one of the city's most impressive, private urban gardens—even indoors you seem to be outside, separated from the elements by a spectacular wall of glass. This is a great place to run into international hotel guests and jet-setting Milanese, and the bar staff mixes up a wide range of traditional and invented drinks—including the exclusive Bulgari Cocktail. ⊠ *Via Privata Fratelli Gabba 7/b, Brera* ☎ *02/8058051* ⊕ *www.bulgarihotels.com.*

Café Trussardi. Open throughout the day, this is a great place for coffee and bumping into Milan's elite, who are entertained by video art on an enormous plasma screen. ⊠ *Piazza della Scala 5, Duomo* ☎ *02/80688295* ⊕ *www.trussardi.it.*

Capo Verde. A bar housed in a greenhouse/nursery is especially popular for after-dinner drinks. ⊠ *Via Leoncavallo 16* ☎ *02/26820430.*

Giamaica. A traditional hangout for students from the nearby Brera art school pulses with life on summer nights, when street vendors and fortune-tellers jostle for space alongside the outdoor tables. ⊠ *Via Brera 32* ☎ *02/876723* ⊕ *www.jamaicabar.it.*

Le Scimmie. Head to this perennial favorite for an evening of live music—predominantly rock to jazz. The club features international stars, some of whom jet in just to play here, while others, including Ronnie Jones, are longtime residents in Milan. Dinner is an option. ⊠ *Via Ascanio Sforza 49, Navigli* ☎ *02/89402874* ⊕ *www.scimmie.it* ⊘ *Closed Tues.*

'N Ombra de Vin. This highly rated enoteca in the Brera neighborhood serves wine by the glass and, in addition to the plates of sausage and cheese nibbles, has light food and not-so-light desserts. It's a great place for people-watching on Via San Marco, while indoors offers a more dimly lit, romantic setting. Check out the impressive vaulted basement where bottled wine and spirits are sold. ⊠ *Via S. Marco 2, Brera* ☎ *02/6599650* ⊕ *www.nombradevin.it.*

Peck. The Milan gastronomical shrine near the Duomo also has a bar and restaurant that serves up traditional—and excellent—pastas, pizza slices, olives, and toasted nuts in a refined setting. ⊠ *Via Cesare Cantù 3* ☎ *02/8023161* ⊕ *www.peck.it.*

Sheraton Diana Majestic. This hotel bar, which has a splendid garden, is a prime meeting place for young professionals and the fashion people from the showrooms of the Porta Venezia neighborhood. ⊠ *Viale Piave 42* ☎ *02/20581.*

SHU. For a break from the traditional, check out this ultratrendy gleaming interior that looks like a cross between something from *Star Trek* and Cocteau's *Beauty and the Beast.* ⊠ *Via Molino delle Armi, Ticinese* ☎ *02/58315720* ⊕ *www.shucafe.it.*

NIGHTCLUBS

Note that the cover charges at clubs can change depending on the day of the week.

Milan's Furniture Fair

During the Salone del Mobile, Milan's furniture fair, in early April, the city is abuzz—there are showroom openings, cocktail parties, and product launches, and design types dressed in black and wearing funny glasses fill the sidewalks and bars.

Except for a few free days, the Salone del Mobile is for professionals only, but you can still participate. Newspapers such as *Corriere della Sera* usually run an English supplement, and special design-week freebies list public events around Milan called "Fuorisalone" (⊕ *www. fuorisalone.it*). Major players such as bathroom and kitchen specialist Boffi (✉ *Via Solferino 11*) and Capellini (✉ *Via Santa Cecilia 4*) launch new products in their stores. Warning: Don't visit if you haven't planned ahead. Hotel rooms and restaurant seating are impossible to find. See ⊕ *www.fieramilano.it* for dates.

Magazzini Generali. What was once an abandoned warehouse is now a fun, futuristic venue for dancing and concerts. The cover charge includes a drink, and entrance is free on Wednesday. It's usually standing room only for concerts. ✉ *Via Pietrasanta 14, Porta Vigentina* ☎ *02/5393948* ⊕ *www.magazzinigenerali.it.*

Plastic. Its venerable age notwithstanding, this is still Milan's most transgressive, avant-garde, and fun club, complete with drag-queen shows. The action starts late, even by Italian standards—don't bother going before midnight. ✉ *Viale Umbria 120* ☎ *02/733996* ⊕ *www. thisisplastic.com* ⊗ *Closed Mon.–Wed.*

Tocqueville. Regular discotheque fare is embellished with two nights per week of live music, featuring young and emerging talent. ✉ *Via Alexis de Tocqueville, Corso Como* ☎ *3939463842 3428102013* ⊕ *www. tokvill.com* ⊗ *Closed Mon.*

SHOPPING

Milan is the birthplace of many of the world's most celebrated brands and high-ticket retail establishments: Prada, Versace, and Armani all call Milan home. The city has produced some of the industry's biggest talents and reigns as one of the most important fashion capitals in the world, and "fashion tourists" come from cities like Shanghai, Moscow, and Tokyo to shop here.

QUADRILATERO

The heart of Milan's shopping reputation is the **Quadrilatero della moda** district north of the Duomo. Here the world's leading designers compete for shoppers' attention, showing off their ultrastylish clothes in stores that are works of high style themselves. It's difficult to find any bargains, but regardless of whether you're making a purchase, the area is a great place for window-shopping and people-watching.

Armani Megastore. This monumental megastore on Via Manzoni houses the eponymous Giorgio Armani label, as well as the Armani Collezioni,

Armani Casa, Armani Junior, Emporio Armani, Armani Jeans, EA7, and Giorgio Armani beauty brands all under one roof. ⊠ *Via Manzoni 31, Quadrilatero* ☏ 02/72318600 ⊕ *www.armani.com.*

Borsalino. The kingpin of milliners, Borsalino has managed to stay trendy since it opened in 1857. ⊠ *Galleria Vittorio Emanuele II 92, Quadrilatero* ☏ 02/89015436 ⊕ *www.borsalino.com.*

DMagazine Outlet. This store boasts some of the best prices in the Quadrilatero district for luxury items such as Prada, Gucci, Lanvin, and Cavalli. ⊠ *Via Montenapoleone 26, Quadrilatero* ☏ 02/76006027 ⊕ *www.dmagazine.it.*

Fodor'sChoice
★
Dolce & Gabbana. Still as hot and chic as ever, put on the global map by Madonna, this fabulous duo has created an empire based on hot, sultry designs for men and women. ⊠ *Via della Spiga 2, Quadrilatero* ☏ 02/795747 ⊕ *www.dolcegabbana.it.*

Fay. Part of the Tod's empire, Fay carries women's and men's clothes and accessories at its flagship store designed by Philip Johnson. ⊠ *Via della Spiga 15, Quadrilatero* ☏ 02/76017597 ⊕ *www.fay.it.*

Gallo Boutique. Known for their signature colorful striped socks, Gallo also carries casual wear and accessories for men, women, and kids. ⊠ *Via Manzoni 16B, Quadrilatero* ☏ 02783602 ⊕ *www.gallospa.it.*

Gio Moretti. A true luxury destination, Gio Moretti carries everything from designer gowns to books on design and architecture. ⊠ *Via della Spiga 4, Quadrilatero* ☏ 02/76003186 ⊕ *www.giomoretti.com.*

Giorgio Armani. One of the Italian fashion industry's most successful labels, Giorgio Armani is a 360-degree brand that produces everything from evening gowns to fine chocolates. ⊠ *Via Alessandro Manzoni 31, Quadrilatero* ☏ 02/72318600 ⊕ *www.armani.com.*

Gucci. This Florence-born brand is now part of French conglomerate PPR's vast galaxy of companies, but it hasn't lost its charm with fashion-forward tourists in hot pursuit of its monogrammed bags, shoes, and accessories. ⊠ *Galleria Vittorio Emanuele II, Quadrilatero* ☏ 02/8597991 ⊕ *www.gucci.com.*

Malo. One of the finest Italian names in knitwear, Malo carries luxurious casual looks for men, women, and the home. ⊠ *Via della Spiga 7, Quadrilatero* ☏ 02/76016109 ⊕ *www.malo.it.*

Missoni. Famous for their kaleidoscope-patterned prints, this family-run brand offers whimsical designs for men and women. ⊠ *Via Montenapoleone 8, Quadrilatero* ☏ 02/76003555 ⊕ *www.missoni.it.*

Miu Miu. Prada's more upbeat, youthful brand has a wide offering of bold-printed women's fashions and accessories. ⊠ *Via Sant' Andrea 12, Quadrilatero* ☏ 02/76001799 ⊕ *www.miumiu.com.*

Moschino. Known for its bold prints, colors, and appliqués, Moschino is a brand for daring fashionistas. ⊠ *Via Sant'Andrea 12, Quadrilatero* ☏ 02/76009404 ⊕ *www.moschino.com.*

Prada. Founded in Milan, Prada has several locations throughout the city. Its Via della Spiga location carries upscale accessories and bags coveted by women worldwide. ⊠ *Via della Spiga 18, Quadrilatero* ☎ *02/76394336* ⊕ *www.prada.com.*

Roberto Cavalli. Famous for his wild animal prints, Roberto Cavalli serves up sexy designs for men and women. ⊠ *Via della Spiga 30, Quadrilatero* ☎ *02/76020900* ⊕ *www.robertocavalli.com.*

Salvatore Ferragamo Donna. This Florence-based brand is a leader in leather goods and accessories, and carries designs for women in this store. ⊠ *Via Montenapoleone 20/3, Quadrilatero* ☎ *02/76000054* ⊕ *www.ferragamo.com.*

Salvatore Ferragamo Uomo. Ferragamo's men's accessories, leather goods, and ties are a staple for Milan's male fashion set. ⊠ *Via Montenapoleone 20/4, Quadrilatero* ☎ *02/76006660* ⊕ *www.ferragamo.com.*

Tod's. A leader in the leather goods market, the della Valle family's products range from luxury handbags to casual loafers for men and women. ⊠ *Via della Spiga 22, Quadrilatero* ☎ *02/783511* ⊕ *www.tods.com.*

Trussardi. This family-run label offers sleek, fashion-forward accessories, leather goods, and clothes at its flagship store. ⊠ *Piazza della Scala 5, Quadrilatero* ☎ *02/76020380* ⊕ *www.trussardi.com.*

Valentino. Even after the departure of its founding father Valentino Garavani, this Roman-based fashion brand still flourishes. ⊠ *Via Montenapoleone 20, Quadrilatero* ☎ *02/76006182* ⊕ *www.valentino.com.*

BRERA

With its narrow streets and outdoor cafés, Brera is one Milan's most charming neighborhoods. Wander through it to find smaller shops with some appealing offerings from lesser-known names that cater to the well-schooled taste of this upscale area. The densest concentration is along Via Brera, Via Solferino, and Corso Garibaldi.

VIA TORINO

For inexpensive and trendy clothes—for the under-25 set—stroll Via Torino, which begins in Piazza Duomo. Stay away on Saturday afternoon if you don't like crowds.

Milan has several shopping streets that serve nearby residential concentrations. **Corso Buenos Aires** is in the Porta Venezia area, and runs northeast from the Giardini Pubblici. The wide and busy street is lined with affordable shops. It has the highest concentration of clothing stores in Europe, so be prepared to give up halfway. Avoid Saturday after 3, when it seems the entire city is here looking for bargains.

Near the Corso Magenta area, walk a few blocks beyond *The Last Supper* to **Corso Vercelli,** where you'll find everything from a branch of the Coin department store to the quintessentially Milanese **Gemelli** (⊠ *Corso Vercelli 16* ☎ *02/48004689* ⊕ *www.gemelli.it*).

CORSO COMO

10 Corso Como. A shrine to Milan's creative fashion sense, 10 Corso Como was founded by former fashion editor and publisher Carla Sozzani. The clothing and design establishment also includes a garden cafe, workshop, and gallery. ⊠ *Corso Como 10, Corso Como* ☎ *02/29013581* ⊕ *www.10corsocomo.com.*

Pasticceria Biffi. This Milan institution opened its doors in 1847, before Italy's Unification, and is the official pastry shop of this traditionally wealthy neighborhood. Have a coffee or a rich hot chocolate in its paneled rooms before facing the crowds in Corso Vercelli. ⊠ *Corso Magenta 87* ☎ *02/48006702* ⊕ *www.biffipasticceria.it.*

MARKETS

Weekly open markets selling fruits and vegetables—and a great deal more—are still a regular sight in Milan. Many also sell clothing and shoes.

Mercato di Via S. Marco. Monday- and Thursday-morning markets here cater to the wealthy residents of this central neighborhood. In addition to food stands where you can get cheese, roast chicken, and dried beans and fruits, there are several clothing and shoe stalls that are important stops for some of Milan's most elegant women. Check out the knitwear at Valentino, about midway down on the street side. Muscle in on the students from the prestigious high school nearby who rush here for the french fries and potato croquettes at the chicken stand at the Via Montebello end. ⊠ *Brera.*

Mercato Papiniano. Bargains in designer apparel can be found at this huge market all day on Saturday and from about 8:30 to 1 on Tuesday. The stalls to look for are at the Piazza Sant'Agostino end of the market. It's very crowded and demanding—watch out for pickpockets. ⊠ *Sant' Agostino.*

BERGAMO, PAVIA, CREMONA, AND MANTUA

Once proud medieval towns rivaling Milan in power, these centers of industry and commerce still play a key role in Italy's wealthiest, most populous region. Pavia is celebrated for its extraordinarily detailed Carthusian monastery, and Cremona for its incomparable violin-making tradition. Mantua—the most picturesque of the towns—was the home of the fantastically wealthy Gonzaga dynasty for almost 300 years. While Pavia, Cremona, and Mantua are on the low-lying Po Plain, Bergamo is nestled against the foothills of the Alps.

BERGAMO

52 km (32 miles) northeast of Milan.

If you're driving from Milan to Lake Garda, the perfect deviation from your autostrada journey is the lovely medieval town of Bergamo. Easily one of Italy's most elegant, well-kept, picturesque cities, Bergamo is also a wonderful side trip by train from Milan. With direct train service from Milan, you'll be whisked from the restless pace of city life to the medieval grandeur of Bergamo Alta in less than an hour.

From behind a set of battered Venetian walls high on an Alpine hilltop, Bergamo majestically surveys the countryside. Behind are the snow-capped Bergamese Alps, and two funiculars connect the modern **Bergamo Bassa** (Lower Bergamo) to the ancient **Bergamo Alta** (Upper

Bergamo). Bergamo Bassa's long arteries and ornate piazze speak to its centuries of prosperity, but it's nonetheless overshadowed by Bergamo Alta's, whose magnificent architecture has a fairy-tale allure.

GETTING HERE AND AROUND

Bergamo is along the A4 Autostrada. By car from Milan, take A51 out of the city to pick up A4; the drive is 52 km (32 miles) and takes about 45 minutes. By train, Bergamo is about one hour from Milan and 1½ hours from Sirmione.

VISITOR INFORMATION

Bergamo Tourism Office ✉ *Torre del Gombito, Via Gombito 13, Bergamo Alta* ☎ *035/242226* ⊕ *www.turismo.bergamo.it* ⊙ *Daily 9–12:30 and 2–5:30* ✉ *Viale Papa Giovanni XXIII 57* ☎ *035/210204* ⊙ *Closed holidays and weekends in winter.*

EXPLORING

Accademia Carrara. Bergamo is home to an art collection that's surprisingly rewarding given its size and remote location. Many of the Venetian masters are represented—Mantegna, Bellini, Carpaccio (circa 1460–1525/26), Tiepolo (1727–1804), Francesco Guardi (1712–93), Canaletto (1697–1768)—as well as Botticelli (1445–1510). The museum is undergoing remodeling, but a selection of works can be seen at Palazzo della Regione in Piazza Vecchia, Bergamo Alta. ✉ *Bergamo Bassa, Piazza Carrara 82* ☎ *035/270413* 🎟 *€5* ⊙ *Palazzo della Regione: June–Sept., Sun. and Tues.–Fri. 10–9, Sat. 10 am–11 pm; Oct.–May, Sun. and Tues.–Fri. 9:30–5:30, Sat. 10–6.*

■ NEED A BREAK?
Pasticceria Nessi. Save room for dessert while dining in Bergamo, because Pasticceria Nessi serves up the most delightful local treat. *Polenta e Osei* is a hand-decorated, fluffy golden mound made with an ever-so-soft sponge cake and filled with maraschino cherries, hazelnut cream, almond paste, and chocolate. ✉ *Via Gombito 34* ☎ *39/035 247073.*

Cappella Colleoni. Bergamo's **Duomo** and **Battistero** are the most substantial buildings in Piazza Duomo. But the most impressive structure is the Cappella Colleoni, which boasts a kaleidoscope of marble decoration and golden accents. ✉ *Piazza Duomo* ☎ *035/210223 Duomo, 035/210061 cappella* ⊙ *Duomo: daily 7:30–11:45 and 3–5:30. Cappella: Mar.–Oct., daily 9–12:30 and 2:30–6, Nov.–Feb., Tues.–Sun. 9–12:30 and 2–4:30.*

Torre Civica. The massive 13th-century Torre Civica offers a great view of the two cities. Take an elevator to the top of the tower, where the bells ring every half hour. ✉ *Piazza Vecchia* ☎ *035/210104* 🎟 *€5* ⊙ *Mar.–Oct., Tues.–Fri. 9:30–7, weekends 9:30–9:30; Nov.–Feb., Tues.–Fri. by appointment, weekends 9:30–1 and 2–5:30.*

WHERE TO EAT

$$
NORTHERN
ITALIAN
✕ **Agnello d'Oro.** A 17th-century tavern on Upper Bergamo's main promenade is furnished with wooden booths and a plethora of copper cookware. It has a cozy northern Italian vibe, local clientele, and and a wide variety of bold local wines. Specialties include Bergamo-style risotto and varieties of polenta served with game and mushrooms. Upstairs

are several floors of small, simple, but extremely cozy and well-priced guest rooms. $ *Average meal: €40* ✉ *Via Gombito 22, Bergamo Alta* ☏ *035/249883* ⊕ *www.agnellodoro.it* ☯ *Closed Mon. and Jan. 7–Feb. 5. No dinner Sun.*

$$
NORTHERN
ITALIAN
Fodor's Choice
★

✕ **Al Donizetti.** Find a table in the back of this central, cheerful restaurant before choosing local cured meats and cheeses to accompany your wine (more than 800 bottles are available, many by the glass). Heartier meals are also available, such as polenta with asiago cheese and smoked ham, but save room for the desserts, which are well paired with dessert wines. $ *Average meal: €40* ✉ *Via Gombito 17/a, Bergamo Alta* ☏ *035/242661* ⊕ *www.donizetti.it.*

$$
NORTHERN
ITALIAN

✕ **Da Ornella.** The vaulted ceilings of this popular trattoria on the main street in the upper town are marked with ancient graffiti, created by (patiently) holding candles to the stone overhead. Ornella herself is in the kitchen, turning out casoncelli in butter, *pancetta* (smoked bacon) and sage, and platters of assorted roast meats. Ask her to suggest the perfect wine pairing for your meal. $ *Average meal: €30* ✉ *Via Gombito 15, Bergamo Alta* ☏ *035/232736* ☯ *Closed Thurs.*

$$$
INTERNATIONAL

✕ **Taverna Colleoni dell'Angelo.** Pierangelo Cornaro is the name behind the Taverna Colleoni, on the Piazza Vecchia right behind the Duomo. He serves imaginative fish, mushrooms, and meat dishes, both regional and international, all expertly prepared. $ *Average meal: €60* ✉ *Piazza Vecchia 7, Bergamo Alta* ☏ *035/232596* ⊕ *www.colleonidellangelo. com* ☯ *Closed Mon.*

WHERE TO STAY

For expanded hotel reviews, visit Fodors.com.

$$$
HOTEL

🏨 **Excelsior San Marco.** The most comfortable hotel in Lower Bergamo is a short walk from the walls of the upper town, and some of the comfortable-if-generic rooms have expansive views of the city. **Pros:** modern, upscale businesslike surroundings; lots of rooms, so a good chance of availability. **Cons:** not in Bergamo Alta or near the tourist attractions. $ *Rooms from: €280* ✉ *Piazza della Repubblica 6* ☏ *035/366111* ⊕ *www.hotelsanmarco.com* ⇆ *155 rooms* ⦿ *Breakfast.*

PAVIA

41 km (25 miles) south of Milan.

Pavia was once Milan's chief regional rival. The city dates from at least the Roman era and was the capital of the Lombard kings for two centuries (572–774). It was at one time known as "the city of a hundred towers," but only a few have survived the passing of time. Its prestigious university was founded in 1361 on the site of a 10th-century law school, but it has roots that can be traced to antiquity.

GETTING HERE AND AROUND

By car from Milan, start out on the A7 Autostrada and exit onto A53 as you near Pavia; the drive is 40 km (25 miles) and takes about 45 minutes. Pavia is 30 to 40 minutes by train from Milan and 1½ hours (by slower regional service) from Cremona. The Certosa is 30 minutes by train from several Milan stations.

VISITOR INFORMATION

Pavia Tourism Office ⊠ *Palazzo del Broletto, Piazza della Vittoria 14, Pavia* ☏ *0382/079943* ⊕ *www.comune.pv.it.*

EXPLORING

Castello Visconteo. The town's 14th-century fortress/castle now houses the local **Museo Civico** (Municipal Museum), with a Romanesque and Renaissance sculpture gallery, an archaeological collection, and a large picture gallery featuring works by Correggio, Bellini, Tiepolo, Hayez, Pelizza da Volpedo, and La Foppa, among others. ⊠ *Viale XI Febbraio 35, near Piazza Castello, Pavia* ☏ *0382/33853* ⊕ *www.museicivici. pavia.it* ▣ *€6* ⊘ *July, Aug., Dec,. and Jan., Tues.–Sun. 9–1:30; rest of the year, Tues.–Sun. 10–5:30. Last entry 45 mins before closing.*

Certosa (*Carthusian monastery*). The main draw in Pavia is the Certosa, 9 km (5½ miles) north of the city center. Its elaborate facade shows the same relish for ornamentation as the Duomo in Milan. The Certosa's extravagant grandeur was due in part to the plan to have it house the tombs of the family of the first duke of Milan, Galeazzo Visconti III (who died during a plague, at age 49, in 1402). Though the floor plan may be Gothic—a cross shape divided into a series of squares—the gorgeous fabric that rises above it is triumphantly Renaissance. On the facade, in the lower frieze, are medallions of Roman emperors and Eastern monarchs; above them are low reliefs of scenes from the life of Christ and from the career of Galeazzo Visconti III.

The first duke was the only Visconti to be interred here, and not until some 75 years after his death, in a tomb designed by Gian Cristoforo Romano. Look for it in the right transept. In the left transept is a more appealing tomb—that of a rather stern middle-aged man and a beautiful young woman. The man is Ludovico il Moro Sforza, seventh duke of Milan, who commissioned Leonardo to paint *The Last Supper*. The woman is Ludovico's wife, Beatrice d'Este (1475–97), one of the most celebrated women of her day, the embodiment of brains, culture, birth, and beauty. Married when he was 40 and she was 16, they had enjoyed six years together when she died while delivering a stillborn child. Ludovico commissioned the sculptor Cristoforo Solari to design a joint tomb for the high altar of Santa Maria delle Grazie in Milan. Originally much larger, the tomb for some years occupied the honored place as planned. Then, for reasons that are still mysterious, the Dominican monks sold the tomb to their Carthusian brothers in Pavia and part of it and its remains were lost. ⊠ *Certosa, Località Monumento 4, 9 km (5½ miles) north of Pavia, Pavia* ☏ *0382/925613* ⊕ *www.comune.pv.it/certosadipavia* ▣ *Donations accepted* ⊘ *May–Aug., Tues.–Sun. 9–11:30 and 2:30–6; Apr. and Sept., Tues.–Sun. 9–11:30 and 2:30–5:30; Mar. and Oct., Tues.–Sun. 9–11:30 and 2:30–5; Nov.–Feb., Tues.–Sun. 9–11 and 2:30–4:30.*

San Pietro in Ciel d'Oro. This Romanesque masterpiece houses the tomb of Christianity's most celebrated convert, Saint Augustine, who rests in an intricately carved, Gothic, white marble ark on the high altar. ⊠ *San Pietro in Ciel d'Oro 2, Pavia* ☏ *0382/303036* ⊕ *santagostinopavia.wordpress.com* ⊘ *Daily 7–noon and 3–7. Mass: Mon.–Sat. 9 and 6:30; Sun. 9, 11, and 6:30.*

WHERE TO EAT

$$ NORTHERN ITALIAN

🍴 **Locanda Vecchia Pavia al Mulino.** In sophisticated art nouveau surroundings 150 yards from the Certosa you can find creative versions of traditional regional cuisine, including risotto *alla certosina* (with sturgeon eggs, frogs' legs, and river shrimp). All seafood dishes are done with similar style, as are *casoncelli* (stuffed pasta), *petto d'anatra* (duck breast), and veal cutlet alla Milanese. A veranda that's open in summer has a view of the Certosa. [$] *Average meal: €50* ✉ *Via al Monumento 5, Certosa* ☎ *0382/925894* 🌐 *www.vecchiapaviaalmulino.it* ✍ *Reservations essential* 🕒 *Apr.–Oct., closed Mon., no lunch Tues.; Nov.–Mar., closed Sun., no lunch Mon..*

CREMONA

104 km (65 miles) east of Pavia, 106 km (66 miles) southeast of Milan.

Cremona is a classical music–lover's dream. With violin shops on every block along its crooked old streets, it is where the world's best violins are crafted. Andrea Amati (1510–80) invented the modern instrument here in the 16th century. Though cognoscenti continue to revere the Amati name, it was an apprentice of Amati's nephew for whom the fates had reserved wide and lasting fame. In a career that spanned an incredible 68 years, Antonio Stradivari (1644–1737) made more than 1,200 instruments—including violas, cellos, harps, guitars, and mandolins, in addition to his fabled violins. Labeled simply with a small printed slip reading "Antonius stradivarius cremonensis. Faciebat anno," followed by the date inserted in a neat italic hand, they remain the most coveted, most expensive stringed instruments in the world.

Strolling about this quiet, medium-size city, you can't help noting that violin making continues to flourish. There are, in fact, more than 50 *liutai* (violin makers), many of them graduates of the Scuola Internazionale di Liuteria (International School of Violin Making). You're usually welcome in these ateliers, where traditional craftsmanship reigns supreme, especially if you're contemplating the acquisition of your own instrument; the tourist office can provide addresses.

Cremona's other claim to fame is *torrone* (nougat), which is said to have been created here in honor of the marriage of Bianca Maria Visconti and Francesco Sforza, which took place in October 1441. The new confection, originally prepared by heating almonds, egg whites, and honey over low heat, and shaped and named after the city's tower, was created in symbolic celebration. The annual Festa del Torrone is held in the main piazza on the third Sunday in October.

GETTING HERE AND AROUND

By car from Milan, start out on the A1 Autostrada and switch to A21 at Piacenza; the drive is 100 km (62 miles) and lasts about 1½ hours. From Pavia, take SS617 to A21; the trip is 70 km (44 miles) and lasts about 1¼ hours. By train, Cremona is about an hour from Milan and 1½ hours from Desenzano, near Sirmione on Lake Garda.

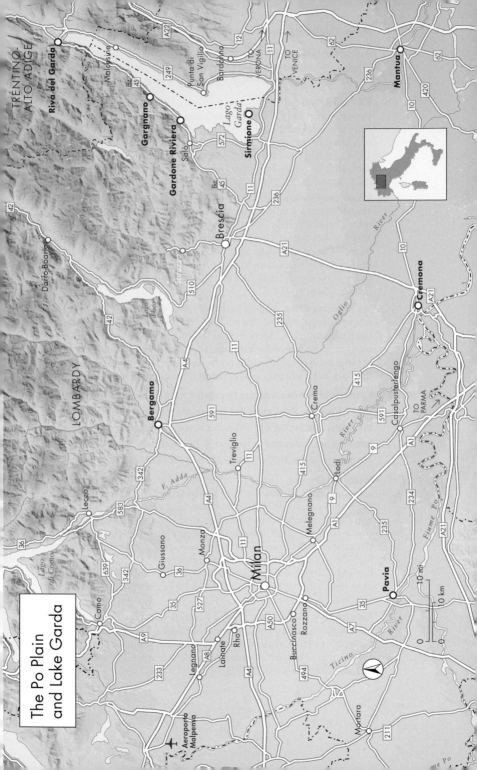

VISITOR INFORMATION
Cremona Tourism Office ⊠ *Piazza del Comune 5* ☎ *0372/406391*
⊕ *www.turismocremona.it* ⊙ *Sept.–June, daily 9:30–1 and 2–5.*

EXPLORING

Duomo. Cremona's Romanesque cathedral was consecrated in 1190.
Here you can find the beautiful *Story of the Virgin Mary and the Passion
of Christ*, the central fresco of an extraordinary cycle commissioned in
1514 and featuring the work of local artists, including Boccaccio Boc-
canccino, Giovanni Francesco Bembo, and Altobello Melone. ⊠ *piazza
del Comune* ☎ *0372/495011* ⊙ *weekdays 7:30–noon and 3:30–7.*

Museo Stradivariano (*Stradivarius Museum/Museo Civico*). This collection in Palazzo Affaitati includes antique and modern instruments and
informative exhibits of Stradivari's paper patterns, wooden models,
and various tools. The Stradivariano Museum sits inside the larger
Museo Civico, which is also home to Michelangelo Merisi da Caravaggio San Francesco in Meditation, a somber work of art that is said
to be autobiographical. ⊠ *Via Ugolani Dati 4* ☎ *0372/803622* ☞ *€7*
⊙ *Tues.–Sun. 10–5.*

No. 1 Piazza Roma. Legendary violin maker Antonio Stradivari lived,
worked, and died near the verdant square at No. 1 Piazza Roma (not
open to the public). According to local lore, Stradivari kept each instru-
ment in his bedroom for a month before varnishing it, imparting part of
his soul before sealing and sending it out into the world. In the center of
the park is **Stradivari's grave,** marked by a simple tombstone.

**QUICK
BITES**

Pasticceria Dondeo. Prepare to visit the sites of Cremona or wait for the
next train at the Pasticceria Dondeo, visible from and just to the right of
the station. Dating back to 1912, this is one of Cremona's oldest and most
beautiful artn cafés and pastry shops. The fresh zabaglione and beignets
are heaven. ⊠ *Via Alghieri Dante 38* ☎ *0372/21224.*

Piazza del Comune. The Duomo, tower, baptistery, and Palazzo Communale (city hall) surround this distinctive and harmonious square:
the combination of old brick, rose- and cream-color marble, terra
cotta, and old copper roofs brings Romanesque, Gothic, and Renaissance together with unusual success. Palazzo Communale houses
Cremona's collection of stringed treasures: a viola and five violins,
including the golden-orange "Il Cremonese 1715" of Stradivarius and
one made by Andrea Amati for Charles IX of France in 1566. ⊠ *Piazza del Comune 8* ☎ *0372/803618* ☞ *violin collection €6* ⊙ *tues.–
Sat. 9–6, Sun. 10–6.*

Torrazzo (*Big Tower*). Dominating Piazza del Comune is perhaps the tallest campanile in Italy, visible for a considerable distance across the Po
Plain. It's open to visitors, but in winter, hours fluctuate depending on
the weather. The tower's astronomical clock is the 1583 original. ⊠ *piazza del Comune* ☎ *0372/495029* ☞ *€5* ⊙ *tues.–Sun. 10–1 and 2:30–6.*

WHERE TO EAT AND STAY

For expanded hotel reviews, visit Fodors.com.

$$
NORTHERN
ITALIAN
✕**Centrale.** Close to the cathedral, this old-style trattoria is a favorite among locals for traditional regional fare, such as succulent *cotechino* (pork sausage) and *tortelli di zucca* (a small pasta with pumpkin filling), at moderate prices. Centrale prides itself on its *bolliti,* boiled meats like veal tongue and cheek, which are served with *salsa verde* (a sauce of parsely and capers), as well as Cremona's most famous condiment, *mostarda,* a spicy, candied fruit. $ *Average meal: €35* ✉ *Via Pertusio 4* ☎ *0372/28701* ⊕ *www.ristorantecentralecremona.com* ⊘ *closed Thurs. and July.*

$$
NORTHERN
ITALIAN
✕**La Sosta.** This traditional *osteria* prides itself as being part of the international Slow Food movement and looks to the 16th century for culinary inspiration, following a time-tested recipe for a favored first course, gnocchi *Vecchia Cremona,* which are filled with Lombard cheese. The homemade salami is also excellent. To finish off the evening, try the *semifreddo al torroncino* (chilled almond cake) and a dessert wine. $ *Average meal: €40* ✉ *Via Sicardo 9* ☎ *0372/456656* ⊕ *www. osterialasosta.it* ⊘ *Closed 3 wks in Aug. No dinner Sun.*

$$
HOTEL
▥ **Delle Arti Design Hotel.** The name suits the elegant modern interiors and eclectic designer furniture, all geared to solid comfort. **Pros:** ultramodern, industrial design; friendly staff; lots of amenities; garage nearby. **Cons:** probably too contemporary for those seeking traditional Italy. $ *Rooms from: €169* ✉ *Via Bonomelli 8* ☎ *0372/23131* ⊕ *www. dellearti.com* ⊅ *33 rooms, 3 suites* ⊘ *Closed Aug. 5–29 and late Dec.* ⦿*Breakfast.*

$
HOTEL
▥ **Hotel Impero.** This comfortable, modern hotel is well equipped to satisfy both leisure and business travelers, offering both pleasant, functional rooms, the best of which overlook the piazza. **Pros:** highly professional staff; quiet rooms. **Cons:** rooms may seem bland and a little out of style for some. $ *Rooms from: €120* ✉ *Piazza della Pace 21* ☎ *0372/413013* ⊕ *www.hotelimpero.cr.it* ⊅ *53 rooms* ⦿*Breakfast.*

SHOPPING

Sperlari. Head to this famed shop for a taste of Cremona's specialty nougat. Cremona's best *mostarda* (a condiment made from preserved fruit served with meat and cheese) has also been sold from this handsome shop since 1836; Sperlari and parent company Fieschi have grown into a confectionary empire. Look for the historical product display in the back. The store also sells teas, marmalades and other Italian delights. ✉ *Via Solferino 25* ☎ *0372/232346* ⊕ *www.fieschi1867.com.*

MANTUA

192 km (119 miles) southeast of Milan.

Mantua (Mantova in Italian) stands tallest among the ancient walled cities of the Po Plain. Its fortifications are circled on three sides by the passing Mincio River, which long provided Mantua with protection, fish, and a steady stream of river tolls as it meandered from Lake Garda to join the Po. Mantua may not be flashy or dramatic, but its beauty is subtle and deep, hiding a rich trove of artistic, architectural, and cultural gems beneath its slightly somber facade.

Although Mantua first came to prominence in Roman times as the home of Virgil, its grand monuments date from the glory years of the Gonzaga dynasty. From 1328 until the Austrian Habsburgs sacked the city in 1708, the dukes and marquesses of the Gonzaga clan reigned over a wealthy independent commune, and the arts thrived in the relative peace of that period. Raphael's star pupil Andrea Mantegna, who served as court painter for 50 years, was the best known of a succession of artists and architects who served Mantua through the years, and some of his finest work, including his only surviving fresco cycle, can be seen here. Giulio Romano (circa 1499–1546), Mantegna's apprentice, built his masterpiece, Palazzo Te, on an island in the river. Leon Battista Alberti (1404–72), who designed two impressive churches in Mantua, was widely emulated later in the Renaissance.

> **WORD OF MOUTH**
>
> "Mantua! A small city, midway between Venice and Milan, surrounded on three sides by lagoons which are covered by flowering lotus in the summer, a funny sort of place where they eat donkey ragù and pumpkin ravioli and drink fizzy wine. Italians go there for the art and the lakes, but tourists from other countries haven't discovered it yet. Oh, and the art! Astonishing, amazing Renaissance art!"
>
> —Julia1

GETTING HERE AND AROUND

Mantua is 5 km (3 miles) west of the A22 Autostrada. The drive from Milan, following A4 to A22, takes a little more than two hours. The drive from Cremona, along SS10, is 1¼ hours. Most trains arrive in just under two hours from Milan, depending on the type of service, and about 1½ hours from Desenzano, near Sirmione on Lake Garda, via Verona.

VISITOR INFORMATION

Mantua Tourism Office. Ask about the museum pass, which entitles you to reduced entrance fees at participating museums (not including the Palazzo Ducale or the Palazzo Te). ⊠ *Piazza A. Mantegna 6* ☎ *0376/432432* ⊕ *www.turismo.mantova.it* ☉ *May–Sept., weekdays 9–1:30 and 2:30–6, weekends 10–6; Oct. and Nov., weekdays 9–1:30 and 2:30–5, weekends 10–5.*

EXPLORING

Casa di Andrea Mantegna. Serious Mantegna aficionados will want to visit the house the artist designed and built around an intriguing circular courtyard, which is usually open to view. The exterior is interesting for its unusual design, and the interior, with its hidden frescoes, can be seen by appointment or during occasional art exhibitions. Prices vary depending on the exhibition. ⊠ *Via Acerbi 47* ☎ *0376432432* ⊕ *www. casadelmantegna.it* ☉ *Tues.–Sat. 10–12:30 and 3–7.*

Palazzo Ducale. The 500-room palace that dominates the Mantua skyline was built for the Gonzaga family, though much of the art within the castle was sold or stolen as the dynasty waned in power and prestige. A glmpse of past grandeur is still in evidence in the Camera Degli Sposi—literally, the "Chamber of the Wedded Couple"—where Duke

Ludovico and his wife held court. Mantegna painted the hall over a nine-year period at the height of his power, finishing at age 44. He made a startling advance in painting by organizing the picture plane in a way that systematically mimics the experience of human vision. Even now, more than five centuries later, you can sense the excitement of a mature artist, fully aware of the great importance of his painting, expressing his vision with a masterly, joyous confidence. The circular trompe l'oeil around the vaulted ceiling is famous for the many details that attest to Mantegna's greatness: the three-dimensional quality of the seven Caesars (the Gonzagas saw themselves as successors to the Roman emperors and paid homage to classical culture throughout the palazzo); the self-portrait of Mantegna (in purple, on the right side of the western fresco); and the dwarf peering out from behind the dress of Ludovico's wife (on the northern fresco). Only 20 people at a time are allowed in the Camera Degli Sposi, and only for 10 minutes at a time. Read about the room before you enter so that you can spend your time looking up. Reservations are mandatory for Camera Degli Sposi, though visitors may take a fast-paced guided tour of the rest of the castle conducted in Italian; signs in each room provide explanations in English. Parts of the castle are not open as restoration work continues after the earthquake of 2012. ⊠ *Piazza Sordello 40* ☎ *041/2411897* ⊕ *www.mantovaducale. beniculturali.it* ⊠ *€6.50, additional €1 for reservation to see Camera Degli Sposi* ⊙ *Tues.–Sun. 8:15–7:15; last entry at 6:20.*

Palazzo Te. One of the greatest of all Renaissance palaces, built between 1525 and 1535 by Federigo II Gonzaga, is the mannerist masterpiece of artist-architect Giulio Romano, who created a pavilion where the strict rules of courtly behavior could be relaxed for libertine pastimes. Romano's purposeful breaks with classical tradition are lighthearted and unprecedented. For example, note the "slipping" triglyphs along the upper edge of the inside courtyard. Two highlights are the *Camera di Amore e Psiche* (Room of Cupid and Psyche) that depicts a wedding set among lounging nymphs, frolicking satyrs, and even a camel and an elephant; and the gasp-producing *Camera dei Giganti* (Room of the Giants) that shows Jupiter expelling the Titans from Mount Olympus. The scale of the work is overwhelming; the floor-to-ceiling work completely envelops the viewer. The room's rounded corners, and the river rock covering the original floor, were meant to give it a cavelike feeling. It is a "whisper chamber" in which words softly uttered in one corner can be heard in the opposite one. Note the graffiti from as far back as the 17th century. ⊠ *Viale Te 13* ☎ *0376/323266* ⊕ *www. centropalazzote.it* ⊠ *€8* ⊙ *Mon.–Fri. 9–6.*

Sant'Andrea. Mantegna's tomb is in the first chapel to the left in the basilica of Sant'Andrea, most of which was built in 1472. The current structure, a masterwork by the architect Alberti, is the third built on this spot to house the relic of the Precious Blood: the crypt holds two reliquaries containing earth believed to be soaked in the blood of Christ, brought to Mantua by Longinus, the soldier who pierced his side. They are displayed only on Good Friday. ⊠ *Piazza di Mantegna* ☎ *0376/328504* ⊠ *Church free, crypt €1* ⊙ *Mon.–Sun. 8–noon and 3 –7.*

WHERE TO EAT

$$$$ ✕**Ambasciata.** Heralded by food critics the world over as one of Italy's
NORTHERN   finest restaurants, Ambasciata (Italian for "embassy") takes elegance and
ITALIAN   service to new levels. Chef Romano Tamani, who is co-owner with his
brother Francesco, makes frequent appearances abroad but is at home
in tiny Quistello, 20 km (12 miles) southeast of Mantua. He offers those
willing to make the trek (and pay the bill) an ever-changing array of
superlative creations such as *timballo di lasagne verdi con petto di piccione sauté alla crème de Cassis* (green lasagna with breast of pigeon and
red currant). $ *Average meal: €80* ✉ *Via Martiri di Belfiore 33, Quistello*
📞 *0376/619169* ⊕ *www.ristoranteambasciata.com* ⚜ *Reservations
essential* ⏱ *Closed Mon., Jan. 1–15, and 2 wks in Aug. No dinner Sun.*

$ ✕**Pasticceria Duomo.** This portal to the past opened in 1883 and still
CAFÉ   serves up such handmade local delights as *pan torrone* (a loaf cake made
with chunks of nougat) and *torta cremona* (a cake made with almond
flour and filled with amarena cherries). A relaxing stop between visiting museums, it's the perfect place to have a cappuccino and relax by
the fireplace. $ *Average meal: €10* ✉ *Via Boccaccino 6* 📞 *037222273.*

$ ✕**Ristorante Pavesi.** Locals have been coming to this central restaurant for
ITALIAN   delicious food at reasonable prices since 1918. The menu changes every
other month; homemade pasta is always a good bet. In warmer months
you can dine on Mantua's handsome main square. $ *Average meal: €15*
✉ *Piazza delle Erbe 13* 📞 *0376/323627* ⊕ *www.ristorantepavesi.com*
⏱ *Closed Tues. and Jan. 6–14.*

WHERE TO STAY

For expanded hotel reviews, visit Fodors.com.

$ ⌂ **Casa Poli.** Refreshing, minimalist influences, creative touches (like
HOTEL   the room number projected onto the hall floor), and attention to detail
create a welcoming ambience with contemporary flair. **Pros:** attentive
staff; tasteful and modern; families welcome. **Cons:** although convenient, not in the absolute center of the city. $ *Rooms from: €150*
✉ *Corso Garibaldi 32* 📞 *0376/288170* ⊕ *www.hotelcasapoli.it* 🛏 *27
rooms* ❙◯❙ *Breakfast.*

$$ ⌂ **Hotel Rechigi.** Unpretentious and comfortable rooms are done in
HOTEL   contemporary style, with crisp blue-and-white color schemes, offer-
ing a quiet refuge from the busy streets of Mantua. **Pros:** quiet and
central with friendly service. **Cons:** modern, cold design might leave
guests wanting for a more characteristic lodging. $ *Rooms from: €160*
✉ *Via Pier Fortunato Calvi 30* 📞 *059/283600* ⊕ *www.rechigi.com* 🛏 *72
rooms, 3 suites* ❙◯❙ *No meals.*

LAKE GARDA

Lake Garda has had a perennial attraction for travelers and writ-
ers alike; even essayist Michel de Montaigne (1533–92), whose 15
months of travel journals contain not a single other reference to nature,
paused to admire the view down the lake from Torbole, which he
called "boundless."

Lake Garda is 50 km (31 miles) long, ranges roughly 1 km to 16 km (½ mile to 10 miles) wide, and is as much as 1,135 feet deep. The terrain is flat at the lake's southern base and mountainous at its northern tip. As a consequence, its character varies from stormy inland sea to crystalline Nordic-style fjord. It's the biggest lake in the region and by most accounts the cleanest. Drivers should take care on the hazardous hairpin turns on the lake road.

> ### WORD OF MOUTH
>
> "You definitely need a car at Lake Garda. The landscape is so fantastic. Nowhere else on earth you will see such a dramatic meeting of mountain and lake as in the northern section. And the only way to see it is driving by car."
>
> —traveller1959

GETTING HERE AND AROUND

The town of Sirmione, at the south end of the lake, is 10 km (6 miles) from Desenzano, which has regular train service; it's about an hour and 20 minutes by train from Milan and 25 minutes from Verona. The A4 Autostrada passes to the south of the lake, and A22 runs north–south about 10 km (6 miles) from the eastern shore.

SIRMIONE

138 km (86 miles) east of Milan.

Dramatically rising out of Lake Garda is the enchanting town of Sirmione. *"Paene insularum, Sirmio, insularumque ocelle,"* sang Catullus in a homecoming poem: "It is the jewel of peninsulas and islands, both." The forbidding Castello Scaligero stands guard behind the small bridge connecting Sirmione to the mainland; beyond, cobbled streets wind their way through medieval arches past lush gardens, stunning lake views, and gawking crowds. Originally a Roman resort town, Sirmione served under the dukes of Verona and later Venice as Garda's main point of defense. It's now reclaimed its original function, bustling with visitors in summer. Cars aren't allowed into town; parking is available by the tourist office at the entrance.

VISITOR INFORMATION

Sirmione Tourism Office ✉ *Viale Marconi 2* ☎ *030/916114* ⊕ *www.sirmionebs.it.*

EXPLORING

Castello Scaligero. As hereditary rulers of Verona for more than a century before control of the city was seized by the Visconti in 1402, the Della Scala counted Garda among their possessions and they built this lakeside redoubt, along with almost all the other castles on the lake. You can go inside to take in the nice view of the lake from the tower, or you can swim at the nearby beach. ✉ *Piazza Castello* ☎ *030/916468* 🎟 *€4* ⏱ *Tues.–Sun. 8:30–7:30.*

Grotte di Catullo (*Grottoes of Catullus*). Locals will almost certainly tell you that these romantic lakeside ruins were once the site of the villa of Catullus (87–54 BC), one of the greatest pleasure-seeking poets of all time. Present archaeological wisdom, however, does not concur, and there is some consensus that this was the site of two villas of slightly different periods, dating from about the 1st century AD. But never mind—the view through the cypresses and olive trees is lovely, and even if Catullus didn't have a villa here, he is closely associated with the area and undoubtedly did have a villa nearby. The ruins are at the top of the isthmus and are poorly signposted: walk through the historic center and past the various villas to the top of the spit; the entrance is on the right. A small **museum** offers a brief overview of the ruins (on the far wall). ✉ *Piazzale Orti Manara* ☎ *030/916157* 🎟 *€4* 🕒 *Apr.–Oct., Tues.–Sat. 8:30–7:30, Sun. 8:30–6:30; Nov.–Feb., Tues.–Sat. 8:30–7:30, Sun. 8:30–1:30; Mar., Tues.–Sat. 8:30–7, Sun. 8:30–2.*

WHERE TO EAT

$$$$ ITALIAN 🍴 **La Rucola.** Next to Sirmione's castle, this elegant, intimate restaurant tucked into three charming rooms has a creative menu, with seafood and meat dishes accompanied by a good choice of wines. Fixed-price menus are available. [$] *Average meal: €90* ✉ *Via Strentelle 3* ☎ *030 916326* 🌐 *www.ristorantelarucola.it* 🕒 *Closed Thurs. and Jan.–mid-Feb. No lunch Fri.*

$ SEAFOOD 🍴 **Ristorante Al Pescatore.** Lake fish is the specialty at this simple, popular restaurant in Sirmione's historical center. For a reasonably priced meal, try grilled trout with a bottle of local white wine and settle your meal with a walk in the nearby park. [$] *Average meal: €23* ✉ *Via Piana 20* ☎ *030/916216* 🌐 *ristorantealpescatore.com* 🕒 *Closed Wed. and Dec. 10–25.*

WHERE TO STAY

For expanded hotel reviews, visit Fodors.com.

$$$$ HOTEL 🏨 **Hotel Sirmione.** Scandinavian slat beds, matching floral draperies and wall coverings, and built-in white furniture impart a homey feel that, along with the attentiveness of the staff, keeps many guests returning year after year. **Pros:** next to the lake; beautiful grounds. **Cons:** the price of all this beauty is high. [$] *Rooms from: €388* ✉ *Piazza Castello 19* ☎ *030/916331* 🌐 *www.termedisirmione.com* 🛏 *101 rooms* 🍽 *Breakfast.*

$$$$ HOTEL 🏨 **Villa Cortine.** This former private villa in a secluded park risks being just plain ostentatious, but it's saved by the sheer luxury of the lakeside setting, the charming decor of the older rooms, and the extraordinary professionalism of its staff. **Pros:** an opulent experience. **Cons:** in summer a three-night minimum stay and half board are required. [$] *Rooms from: €420* ✉ *Via Grotte 6* ☎ *030/9905890* 🌐 *www.palacehotelvillacortine.com* 🛏 *54 rooms, 2 suites* 🕒 *Closed mid-Oct.–Mar.* 🍽 *Breakfast.*

TOWNS ALONG LAKE GARDA'S EASTERN SHORE

VISITOR INFORMATION

Malcesine Tourism Office ✉ *Via Capitanato 6, Malcesine* ☎ *0457/400044* ⊕ *www.malcesinepiu.it.*

EXPLORING

Bardolino. The town famous for its eponymous red wine hosts the Cura dell'Uva (Grape Cure Festival) in late September–early October. It's a great excuse to indulge in the local vino, which is light, dry, and often slightly sparkling. (Bring aspirin, just in case the *cura* turns out to be worse than the disease.) Bardolino is one of the most popular summer resorts on the lake, on the eastern shore at the wider end. Here there are two handsome Romanesque churches: **San Severo,** from the 11th century, and **San Zeno,** from the 9th. Both are in the center of the small town. ⊕ *www.bardolinoweb.it.*

Malcesine, about 30 km (20 miles) north of Punta San Vigilio, is one of the loveliest areas along the upper eastern shore of Lake Garda. It's principally known as a summer resort, with sailing and windsurfing schools. It tends to be crowded in season, but there are nice walks from the town toward the mountains. Six lifts and more than 11 km (7 miles) of runs of varying degrees of difficulty serve skiers.

Castello Scaligero. Dominating the town is another 12th-century castle built by Verona's dynastic Della Scala family. ☎ *045/6570333* ⊠ *€4* ⊙ *Tues.–Sun. 8:30–7:30.*

Monte Baldo. The futuristic *funivia* (cable car), zipping visitors to the top of Monte Baldo (5,791 feet), is unique because it rotates. After a 10-minute ride, you're high in the Veneto where you can take a stroll and enjoy spectacular views of the lake. You can ride the cable car down or bring along a mountain bike (or hang glider) for the descent. ✉ *Via Navene Vecchia 12, Malcesine* ☎ *045/7400206* ⊕ *www.funiviedelbaldo.it* ⊠ *€19 round trip* ⊙ *Dec. 22–Mar. 10, daily 8–5; Mar. 24–Oct., daily 8–7.*

RIVA DEL GARDA

18 km (11 miles) north of Malcesine, 180 km (112 miles) east of Milan.

Riva del Garda is set on the northern tip of Lake Garda against a dramatic backdrop of jagged cliffs and miles of beaches. The old city, surrounding a pretty harbor, was built up during the 15th century, when it was a strategic outpost of the Venetian Republic.

VISITOR INFORMATION

Riva del Garda Tourism Office ✉ *Largo Medaglie d'Oro al Valor Militare 5* ☎ *0464/554444* ⊕ *www.gardatrentino.it.*

EXPLORING

Piazza 3 Novembre. This lakeside plaza, the heart of Riva del Garda, is surrounded by medieval palazzi. Standing in the piazza and looking out onto the lake you can understand why Riva del Garda has become a windsurfing mecca: air currents ensure good breezes on even the most sultry midsummer days.

Torre Apponale. Predating the Venetian period by three centuries, this sturdy tower looms above the medieval residences of the main square; its crenellations recall its defensive purpose. Visitors can climb the 165 steps to see the view from the top. ☎ *0464/573869* 🌐 *www.gardatrentino.it* 🎫 *€1* 🕓 *Late Mar.–May and Oct.–early Nov., Tues.–Sun. 10–12:30 and 1:30–6; June–Sept., Tues.–Sun. 10–12:30 and 1:30–6.*

EN ROUTE After passing the town of Limone—where it's said the first lemon trees in Europe were planted—take the fork to the right about 5 km (3 miles) north of Gargnano and head to Tignale. The view from the Madonna di Monte Castello church, some 2,000 feet above the lake, is spectacular. Adventurous travelers will want to follow this pretty inland mountain road to Tremosine. Be warned that the road winds its way up the mountain through hairpin turns and blind corners that can test even the most experienced drivers.

WHERE TO EAT AND STAY

For expanded hotel reviews, visit Fodors.com.

$$ NORTHERN ITALIAN 🍴 **Ristorante Castel Toblino.** A lovely stop for a lakeside drink or a romantic dinner, this castle is right on a lake in Sarche, about 20 km (12 miles) north of Riva toward Trento. The compound is said to have been a prehistoric, then Roman, village, and was later associated with the Church of Trento. Bernardo Clesio had it rebuilt in the 16th century in the Renaissance style. It's now a sanctuary of fine food, serving such local specialties as lake fish and guinea fowl. [$] *Average meal: €40* ✉ *Via Caffaro 1, Sarche* ☎ *0461/864036* 🌐 *www.casteltoblino.com* 🕓 *Closed Tues. and Jan. and Feb.*

$$$ RESORT 🏨 **Hotel du Lac et du Parc.** Riva's most splendid hotel has elegance befitting its cosmopolitan name, with comfortable, well-appointed rooms and personalized service rarely found on Lake Garda since its aristocratic heyday. **Pros:** expansive and lush surroundings offering myriad lodging options; a pampering and indulgent staff. **Cons:** not a cozy atmosphere. [$] *Rooms from: €250* ✉ *Viale Rovereto 44* ☎ *0464/566600* 🌐 *www.dulacetduparc.com* 🛏 *159 rooms, 67 suites* 🕓 *Closed Nov.–Mar.* 🍽 *Breakfast.*

$ HOTEL 🏨 **Hotel Sole.** Comfortable, affordable rooms occupy a lakeside 15th-century palazzo in the center of town, and those in front have terraces that open to breathtaking views of the lake. **Pros:** a classic lake resort with modern hotel conveniences. **Cons:** not for those looking for ultra-contemporary design. [$] *Rooms from: €100* ✉ *Piazza 3 Novembre 35* ☎ *0464/552686* 🌐 *www.hotelsole.net* 🛏 *52 rooms* 🕓 *Closed Nov.–Dec. 19 and mid-Jan.–mid-Mar.* 🍽 *Breakfast.*

GARGNANO

30 km (19 miles) south of Riva del Garda, 144 km (89 miles) east of Milan.

This small port town was an important Franciscan center in the 13th century, and now comes alive in the summer months when German tourists, many of whom have villas here, crowd the small pebble beach. An Austrian flotilla bombarded the town in 1866, and some of the houses still bear marks of cannon fire. Mussolini owned two houses in Gargnano: one is now a language school and the other, Villa Feltrinelli, has been restored and reopened as a luxury hotel.

VISITOR INFORMATION
Gargnano Tourism Office ✉ *Piazza Boldini 2* ☎ *0365/791243* ⊕ *www.gargnanosulgarda.it.*

WHERE TO EAT AND STAY
For expanded hotel reviews, visit Fodors.com.

$$$

NORTHERN ITALIAN

✕ **La Tortuga.** This rustic trattoria is more sophisticated than it first appears, with an extensive wine cellar and nouvelle-style twists on local dishes. Specialties include *agnello con rosmarino e timo* (lamb with rosemary and thyme), *persico con rosmarino* (perch with rosemary), and *carpaccio d'anatra all'aceto balsamico* (duck carpaccio with balsamic vinegar). The *assaggio di pesce di lago* (assortment of lake fish) is a worthy introduction to regional delights. $ *Average meal: €80* ✉ *Via XXIV Maggio at small harbor* ☎ *0365/71251* ☉ *Closed Tues. and Nov.–Mar. No dinner Sun.*

$

HOTEL

🏠 **Garni Bartabel.** At this cozy inn on the main street of town, rooms are small but attractive, with Venetian-style furnishings and pastel decor, and reasonable prices. **Pros:** very attractive; a bargain for this area. **Cons:** simple with few luxuries. $ *Rooms from: €85* ✉ *Via Roma 35* ☎ *0365/71300* ⊕ *www.hotelbartabel.it* ⇱ *12 rooms* ☉ *Closed Nov.–mid-Mar.* ⊖*No meals.*

GARDONE RIVIERA

12 km (7 miles) south of Gargnano, 139 km (86 miles) east of Milan.

EXPLORING

Giardino Botanico Hruska. More than 2,000 Alpine, subtropical, and Mediterranean species thrive at the Giardino Botanico Hruska. ✉ *Via Roma* ☎ *0366/410877* ⊕ *www.hellergarden.com* ☑ *€9* ☉ *Mar.–Oct., daily 9–7.*

Il Vittoriale. Gardone Riviera, a once-fashionable 19th-century resort now pleasantly faded, is the former home of the flamboyant Gabriele d'Annunzio (1863–1938), one of Italy's greatest modern poets. D'Annunzio's estate, Il Vittoriale, perched on the hills above the town, is an elaborate memorial to himself, filled with the trappings of conquests in art, love, and war (of which the largest is a ship's prow in the garden), and complete with an imposing mausoleum. ✉ *Via Vittoriale 12* ☎ *0365/296511* ⊕ *www.vittoriale.it* ☑ *€12 for house or museum, €16 for both* ☉ *Grounds: Apr.–Sept., daily 8:30–8; Oct.–Mar., daily 9–5. House and museum: Apr.–Sept., Tues.–Sun. 9:30–7; Oct.–Mar., Tues.–Sun. 9–1 and 2–5.*

OFF THE BEATEN PATH

Salò Market. Four kilometers (2½ miles) south of Gardone Riviera is the enchanting lakeside town of Salò, which history buffs may recognize as the capital of the ill-fated Social Republic set up in 1943 by the Germans after they liberated Mussolini from the Gran Sasso. Every Saturday morning an enormous market is held in the Piazza dei Martiri della Libertà, with great bargains on everything from household goods to clothing to foodstuffs. In August or September a lone vendor often sells locally unearthed *tartufi neri* (black truffles) at affordable prices.

WHERE TO STAY

For expanded hotel reviews, visit Fodors.com.

$$$ HOTEL **Grand Hotel Gardone.** At this majestic 1800s palace surrounded by an attractive landscaped gardens, nearly all the rooms look out over the water, and all bathrooms have been renovated in marble. **Pros:** well-appointed; expansive gardens; lakeside pool; lauded service. **Cons:** with meeting rooms, banquet, and wedding facilities, this may not make for a quiet, cozy getaway. [$] *Rooms from: €250* ✉ *Via Zanardelli 84* ☎ *0365/20261* 🌐 *www.grangardone.it* 🛏 *143 rooms, 25 suites* 🕒 *Closed mid-Oct.–late Mar.* 🍴 *Breakfast.*

$$ HOTEL **Grand Hotel Fasano.** A former 19th-century hunting lodge between Gardone and Maderno, the Fasano has matured into a seasonal hotel of a high standard, with opulent, old-fashioned-style rooms and salons and many amenities. **Pros:** exquisitely stylish rooms; relaxing surroundings. **Cons:** not all rooms have Wi-Fi or lake views; no credit cards accepted. [$] *Rooms from: €240* ✉ *Corso Zanardelli 190* ☎ *0365/290220* 🌐 *www.ghf.it* 🛏 *75 rooms* 💳 *No credit cards* 🕒 *Closed mid-Oct.–Mar.* 🍴 *Breakfast.*

$$$$ HOTEL **Villa Fiordaliso.** This pink-and-white lakeside villa—once home to Claretta Petacci, given to her by Benito Mussolini—is a high-quality restaurant, but it also has seven tastefully furnished rooms, some overlooking the lake. **Pros:** has the charm of an intimate B&B. **Cons:** short on amenities given the price category. [$] *Rooms from: €350* ✉ *Corso Zanardelli 150* ☎ *0365/20158* 🌐 *www.villafiordaliso.it* 🛏 *6 rooms, 1 suite* 🕒 *Closed Nov.–mid-Mar.* 🍴 *Breakfast.*

$ HOTEL **Villa Maria Elisabetta.** An economical option with the comforts and amenities of a three-star hotel, complete with lake views, is run by a group of hospitable nuns. **Pros:** a great bargain for a laid-back stay; Internet access. **Cons:** extremely simple decor; no a/c; some rooms have no TV. [$] *Rooms from: €80* ✉ *Corso Zanardelli 180* ☎ *0365/20206* 🌐 *www.monasterystays.com* 🛏 *51 rooms* 🕒 *Closed Oct. 15–Dec. 20* 🍴 *Breakfast.*

LAKE COMO

If your idea of nirvana is palatial villas, rose-laden belvederes, hanging wisteria and bougainvillea, lanterns casting a glow over lakeshore restaurants, and majestic Alpine vistas, then proceed immediately to Lake Como. Though summer crowds threaten to diminish the lake's dreamy mystery and slightly faded old-money gentility, the allure of this spectacular place endures. Como remains a consummate pairing of natural and man-made beauty. The villa gardens, like so many in Italy, are a union of two landscape traditions: that of Renaissance Italy, which values order, and that of Victorian England, which strives to create the illusion of natural wildness. Such gardens are often framed by vast areas of picturesque farmland—fruit trees, olive groves, and vineyards.

Lake Como is some 47 km (30 miles) long north to south and is Europe's deepest lake (almost 1,350 feet). Car ferries and *vaporetti* (water buses) traverse the lake in season, making it easy to get to the other main

towns, Cernobbio, Tremezzo, and Varenna. Many travelers hasten to boats waiting to take them to Bellagio and the *centro di lago,* the center region of the lake's three branches, and its most beautiful section. You should not pass by the 2,000-year-old walled city of Como, a leading textile center famous for its silks, however—even if you only linger long enough to see the medieval town center and pretty lakefront. Remember that Como is extremely seasonal: if you go to Bellagio, for example, from November through February, you'll find nothing open—not a bar, restaurant, or shop.

GETTING HERE AND AROUND

Trains run regularly from Milan to the town of Como; the trip takes half an hour from the Central Station and an hour from the Cardorna Station. There's also service to the tiny town of Varenna, just across the lake from Bellagio; the trip from Milan takes 1¼ hours. Como is off the A9 Autostrada. To get to the town from Milan, take A8 to A9; the drive takes about an hour. Ferries (mainly pedestrian) run regularly from Como and Varenna to different spots around the lake. Schedules can be consulted online at ⊕ *www.navigazionelaghi.it.*

BELLAGIO

Fodor's Choice
★

30 km (19 miles) northeast of Como, 56 km (35 miles) northwest of Bergamo.

Sometimes called the prettiest town in Europe, Bellagio always seems perfectly adorned with geraniums ablaze in every window and bougainvillea veiling the staircases, or *montées*, which thread through the town. At dusk Bellagio's nightspots—including the wharf, where an orchestra serenades dancers under the stars—beckon you to come and make merry. It's an impossibly enchanting location, one that inspired French composer Gabriel Fauré to call Bellagio "a diamond contrasting brilliantly with the sapphires of the three lakes in which it is set."

Boats ply the lake to Tremezzo, where Napoleon's worst Italian enemy, Count Sommariva, resided at Villa Carlotta; and a bit farther south of Tremezzo, to Villa Balbianello. Check with the tourist office for the hours of the launch to Tremezzo.

VISITOR INFORMATION
Bellagio Tourism Office ✉ *Piazza Mazzini (Pontile Imbarcadero)* ☎ *031/950204* ⊕ *www.bellagiolakecomo.com.*

EXPLORING

Villa Melzi. The famous gardens of the Villa Melzi were once a favorite picnic spot for Franz Lizst, who advised author Louis de Ronchaud in 1837: "When you write the story of two happy lovers, place them on the shores of Lake Como. I do not know of any land so conspicuously blessed by heaven." The gardens are open to the public, and though you can't get into the 19th-century villa, don't miss the lavish Empire-style family chapel. The Melzi were Napóleon's greatest allies in Italy (the family has passed down the name "Josephine" to the present day). Guided tours available upon request. ✉ *Via Melzi d'Eril 8* ☎ *3394573838* ⊕ *www.giardinidivillamelzi.it* ✍ *€6.50* ۞ *Late Mar.–early Nov., daily 9:30–6:30.*

Villa Monastero. By ferry from Bellagio it's a quick trip across the lake to Varenna. The principal sight here is the spellbinding garden of the Villa Monastero, which, as its name suggests, was originally a monastery. Now it's an international science and convention center. Guided tours can be booked. ✉ *Viale Polvani 2, Varenna* ☎ *0341/295450* ⊕ *www. villamonastero.eu* ✍ *Garden €5, house and garden €8* ۞ *Garden: Mar. and Apr., Mon.–Sun. 9–6; May–Sept., Mon.–Thurs. 9–7, Fri. 9–2, weekends 9–7; Oct. and Nov., Mon.–Sun. 9–6. House museum: Mar. and Apr., weekends 9–6; May–Sept., Fri. 2–7, weekends 9–7; Oct., weekends 9–6.*

Villa Serbelloni. This property of the Rockefeller Foundation has celebrated gardens on the site of Pliny the Elder's villa overlooking Bellagio. There are only two 1½-hour-long guided visits per day, restricted to 30 people each, and in May these tend to be commandeered by group bookings. It's wise to arrive early to sign up. ✉ *Near Palazza della Chiesa* ☎ *031/951555* ⊕ *www.bellagiolakecomo.com* ✍ *€9* ۞ *Apr.–early Nov., Tues.–Sun. at 11 and 3:30; tours gather 15 mins before start.*

WHERE TO EAT

$ NORTHERN ITALIAN 🍴 **La Pergola.** Try to reserve a table on the terrace at this popular lakeside restaurant a short walk (with many steps) from central Bellagio on the east side of the peninsula. The food is average, with the best option being the freshly caught fish; the view and the tranquility of the terrace are the main draws. You can also stay in one of the inn's 11 rooms, all of which have baths. [$] *Average meal: €25* ✉ *Piazza del Porto 4, Pescallo* ☎ *031/950263* 🌐 *www.lapergolabellagio.it* 🕒 *Closed Nov.–Mar.*

WORD OF MOUTH

"Because you're most likely to get around among the main towns on Lake Como by steamer or ferry, you'll be best off scheduling dinners in your own town and doing lunches in others, since transport is quite frequent during the day and less so, even ending early, in the evening."

—JulieVikmanis

$ NORTHERN ITALIAN 🍴 **Silvio.** At the edge of town, this family-owned trattoria with a lakeshore terrace specializes in fresh fish. Served cooked or marinated, with risotto or as a ravioli stuffing, the lake's bounty is caught by Silvio's family—it's local cooking at its best. There are also 21 modestly priced ($) guest rooms with balconies and lake views. [$] *Average meal: €25* ✉ *Lòppia di Bellagio, Via Carcano 12* ☎ *031/950322* 🌐 *www.bellagiosilvio.com* 🕒 *Closed Jan. and Feb.*

WHERE TO STAY

For expanded hotel reviews, visit Fodors.com.

$$ HOTEL 🏨 **Du Lac.** Most rooms at this comfortable old hotel owned by an Anglo-Italian family have views of the lake and mountains, while the rooftop terrace garden is a perfect spot for drinks or dozing. **Pros:** pleasant in-house restaurant; comfortable ambience; friendly service. **Cons:** some decor a little worn around the edges. [$] *Rooms from: €225* ✉ *Piazza Mazzini 32* ☎ *031/950320* 🌐 *www.bellagiohoteldulac.com* 🛏 *42 rooms* 🕒 *Closed Nov.–Mar.* 🍽 *Breakfast.*

$$$$ HOTEL 🏨 **Grand Hotel Villa Serbelloni.** The sense of 19th-century luxury has not so much faded as mellowed at this grand lakeside hotel set in lovely gardens: the rooms are immaculate and plush; public areas are gilt and marble with thick, colorful carpets; and breakfast is served in a ballroom, Salone Reale. **Pros:** historic lake hotel; great pool and health club; good low-season deals. **Cons:** limited deluxe amenities. [$] *Rooms from: €404* ✉ *Via Roma 1* ☎ *031/950216* 🌐 *www.villaserbelloni.com* 🛏 *95 rooms* 🕒 *Closed early Nov.–early Apr.* 🍽 *Breakfast.*

$$$ HOTEL 🏨 **Hotel Belvedere.** In Italian, belvedere means "beautiful view," and it's an apt name for this enchanting spot where antique furniture and eye-catching rugs complement the modern rooms, many of which have balconies and views of the lake. **Pros:** attention to detail; great views; pool. **Cons:** breakfast is only so-so; a climb from the waterfront. [$] *Rooms from: €295* ✉ *Via Valassina 31* ☎ *031/950410* 🌐 *www.belvederebellagio.com* 🛏 *59 rooms, 5 suites* 🕒 *Closed Nov.–mid-Apr.* 🍽 *Breakfast.*

$$ HOTEL 🏨 **Hotel Florence.** Most large and comfortable rooms in this villa dating from the 1880s are furnished with interesting antiques and have splendid views of the lake. **Pros:** central location; appealing public spaces.

6

Cons: location may feel too central if you're looking to get away from it all. $ *Rooms from: €200* ✉ *Piazza Mazzini 46* ☎ *031/950342* 🌐 *www.hotelflorencebellagio.it* 🛏 *30 rooms* 🕒 *Closed Nov.–Mar.* 🍴 *Multiple meal plans.*

TREMEZZO

34 km (21 miles) north of Cernobbio, 78 km (48 miles) north of Milan.

VISITOR INFORMATION

Tremezzo Tourism Office ✉ *Via Regina 3* ☎ *0344/40493* 🌐 *www.tremezzo.it* 🕒 *Daily 9–6:30.*

EXPLORING

Villa Balbianello. Villa Balbianello may be the most magical house in all of Italy. It sits on its own little promontory, Il Dosso d'Avedo—separating the bays of Venus and Diana—around the bend from the tiny fishing village of Ossuccio. Relentlessly picturesque, the villa is composed of loggias, terraces, and *palazzini* (tiny palaces), all spilling down verdant slopes to the lakeshore, where you'll find an old Franciscan church, a magnificent stone staircase, and a statue of San Carlo Borromeo blessing the waters. The villa is most frequently reached by launch from Como and Bellagio and leaves you at Lenno. Marked signs lead you to the villa and is accessible by foot (20-minute walk) on Tuesday and weekends, while the villa provides private boat service for visitors to the villa on Thursday and Friday. Visits are usually restricted to the gardens, but guided tours (€60, must be arranged in advance) include the villa. ✉ *Il Dosso d'Avedo; ferry stop Lenno* ☎ *0344/56110* 🌐 *www.fondoambiente.it* 🎫 *Gardens €13* 🕒 *Mid-Mar.–mid-Nov., Tues. and Thurs.–Sun. 10–6; last entry to gardens 5:30.*

Villa Carlotta. If you're lucky enough to visit the small lakeside town of Tremezzo in late spring or early summer, you will find the magnificent Villa Carlotta a riot of color, with more than 14 acres of azaleas and dozens of varieties of rhododendrons in full bloom. The height of the blossoms is late April to early May. The villa was built between 1690 and 1743 for the luxury-loving marquis Giorgio Clerici. The garden's collection is remarkable, particularly considering the difficulties of transporting delicate plants before the age of aircraft. Palms, banana trees, cacti, eucalyptus, a sequoia, orchids, and camellias are counted among the more than 500 species.

According to local lore, one reason for the Villa Carlotta's magnificence was a competition between the marquis's son-in-law, who inherited the estate, and the son-in-law's archrival, who built *his* summer palace directly across the lake (Villa Melzi, in Bellagio). Whenever either added to his villa and garden, it was tantamount to taunting the other in public. Eventually the son-in-law's insatiable taste for self-aggrandizement prevailed. The villa's last (and final) owners were Prussian royalty (including the "Carlotta" of the villa's name); the property was confiscated during World War I.

The villa's interior is worth a visit, particularly if you have a taste for the romantic sculptures of Antonio Canova (1757–1822). The best known is his *Cupid and Psyche,* which depicts the lovers locked in an odd but graceful embrace, with the young god above and behind, his wings extended, while Psyche awaits a kiss that will never come. The villa can be reached by boats from Bellagio and Como. ✉ *Via Regina 2* ☎ *0344/40405* 🌐 *www.villacarlotta.it* 🎟 *€9* 🕒 *mid-Mar.–mid-Nov., daily 10–5.*

WHERE TO STAY

For expanded hotel reviews, visit Fodors.com.

$$$$ HOTEL 🏨 **Grand Hotel Tremezzo.** Creature comforts in this turn-of-the-20th-century building include a private park, three heated swimming pools (one of them actually floats on pontoons on the lake), and sumptuous guest rooms where old-world style is accented with modern amenities. **Pros:** lakeside location; beautiful views. **Cons:** not well situated if you're looking for shopping or nightlife. [$] *Rooms from: €500* ✉ *Via Regina 8* ☎ *0344/42491* 🌐 *www.grandhoteltremezzo.com* 🛏 *88 rooms, 10 suites* 🕒 *Closed mid-Nov.–Feb.* 🍴 *Breakfast.*

$ B&B/INN 🏨 **Hotel Rusall.** On the hillside above Tremezzo in the midst of a large garden, these small, comfortably simple rooms offer quiet, privacy, and the chance to lie by the pool and enjoy a nice view. **Pros:** lovely walks into town and in the countryside; more intimate than grander lake hotels. **Cons:** takes some effort to reach the hillside location. [$] *Rooms from: €120* ✉ *Via San Martino 2* ☎ *0344/40408* 🌐 *www.rusallhotel.com* 🛏 *23 rooms* 🍴 *Breakfast.*

CERNOBBIO

5 km (3 miles) north of Como, 53 km (34 miles) north of Milan.

The legendary resort of Villa d'Este is reason enough to visit this jewel on the lake, but the town itself is worth a stroll. Despite the fact that George Clooney lunches here regularly, the place still has a neighborhood feel to it, especially on summer evenings and weekends when the piazza is full of families and couples taking their *passeggiata* (stroll).

VISITOR INFORMATION

Cernobbio Tourism Office ✉ *Via Regina 23* ☎ *031/349341* 🌐 *www.comune.cernobbio.co.it.*

EXPLORING

Villa d'Este. Built on the site of a former nunnery as Cardinal Tolomeo Gallio's summer residence, this lakeside retreat has had a colorful and somewhat checkered history since its completion in 1568, swinging wildly between extremes of grandeur and dereliction. Its tenants have included the Jesuits, two generals, a ballerina, Caroline of Brunswick—the disgraced and estranged wife of the future king of England George IV—a family of ordinary Italian nobles, and, finally, a czarina of Russia. Its life as a private summer residence ended in 1873, when it was turned into the fashionable hotel it has remained ever since.

WHERE TO EAT AND STAY

For expanded hotel reviews, visit Fodors.com.

$$ NORTHERN ITALIAN 🍴 **Il Gatto Nero.** A vantage point in the hills above Cernobbio provides a splendid view of the lake. Specialties include *filetto con aceto balsamico* (filet mignon with balsamic vinegar), *pappardelle al ragù di selvaggini* (pasta with wild game sauce), and lake fish. Save room for the warm chocolate torte with its delicious liquid chocolate center. Reservations are encouraged as this is a regular haunt of Italian soccer stars as well as the jet set. [$] *Average meal: €40* ✉ *Via Monte Santo 69, Rovenna* ☎ *031/512042* 🌐 *www.gattonerocernobbio.com* 🕓 *Closed Mon. No lunch Tues.*

$ NORTHERN ITALIAN 🍴 **Il Giardino.** "The Garden" has an expansive shaded patio that's a welcome respite from the summer sun. With an extensive menu balanced between fish, meat, pizza, and salads, there's something for everyone. You can also stay the night in one of Il Giardino's 12 basic rooms. [$] *Average meal: €30* ✉ *Via Regina 73* ☎ *031/511154* 🌐 *www.giardinocernobbio.com.*

$$$$ HOTEL 🏨 **Villa d'Este.** One of the grandest hotels in Italy has long wlecomed Europe's rich and famous, housing them in grand guest rooms still furnished in the Empire style. **Pros:** fine service; world-renowned clientele. **Cons:** may seem too formal to some. [$] *Rooms from: €750* ✉ *Via Regina 40* ☎ *031/3481* 🌐 *www.villadeste.it* 🛏 *152 rooms 7 suites, 2 private villas* 🕓 *Closed mid-Nov.–first wk of Mar.* 🍽 *Breakfast.*

COMO

5 km (3 miles) south of Cernobbio, 30 km (19 miles) southwest of Bellagio, 49 km (30 miles) north of Milan.

Como commands the south shore of the lake. It is only part elegant resort, though in the center of town cobbled pedestrian streets wind their way past parks and bustling cafés. The city has an industrial heritage, deeply rooted in the production of textiles, particularly silk and the silk trade. If you're traveling by car, leave it at the edge of the town center in the clean, well-lighted underground parking facility right on the lake.

VISITOR INFORMATION

Como Tourism Office ✉ *Piazza Cavour 17* ☎ *031/269712* ✉ *akecomo@tin.it* 🌐 *www.lakecomo.com* 🕓 *Mon.–Sat. 9–1 and 2:30–6; Sun. 9:30–1.*

EXPLORING

Duomo. The splendid 15th-century Renaissance-Gothic Duomo was begun in 1396. The facade was added in 1455, and the transepts were completed in the mid-18th century. The dome was designed by Filippo Juvara (1678–1736), chief architect of many of the sumptuous palaces of the royal house of Savoy. The facade has statues of two of Como's most famous sons, Pliny the Elder and Pliny the Younger, whose writings are among the most important documents from antiquity. Inside, the works of art include Luini's *Holy Conversation,* a fresco cycle by Morazzone, and the *Marriage of the Virgin Mary* by Ferrari. ✉ *Piazza del Duomo* ☎ *031/265244* 🕓 *Daily 7–noon and 3–7.*

Museo Didattico della Seta (*Silk Museum*). From silkworm litters to moire-finishing machinery, this small but complete collection preserves the history of a manufacturing region that continues to supply almost three-fourths of Europe's silk. The friendly staffers will give you an overview of the museum; they are also happy to provide brochures and information about local retail shops. The location isn't well marked: follow the textile school's driveway around to the low-rise concrete building on the left, and take the shallow ramp down to the entrance. ✉ *Via Castelnuovo 9* ☎ *031/303180* 🌐 *www.museosetacomo.com* 🎟 *€10* 🕒 *Tues.–Fri. 9–noon and 3–6. Guided tours Mon. and weekends (book in advance).*

San Fedele. At the heart of Como's medieval quarter, the city's first cathedral is well worth a peek. The apse walls and ceiling are completely frescoed, as are the ceilings above the altar. ✉ *Piazza San Fedele* ☎ *031/272334* 🕒 *Daily 7–noon and 3–7.*

Sant'Abbondio. If you brave Como's industrial quarter, you will come upon this beautiful church, a gem of Romanesque architecture begun by Benedictine monks in 1013 and consecrated by Pope Urban II in 1095. Inside, the five aisles converge on a presbytery with a semicircular apse decorated with a cycle of 14th-century frescoes—now restored to their original magnificence—by Lombard artists heavily influenced by the Sienese school. To see them, turn right as you enter and put €0.50 in the mechanical box for a few minutes of lighting. In the nave, the cubical capitals are the earliest example of this style in Italy. ✉ *Via Sant'Abbondio* 🕒 *Daily 8–5.*

6

WHERE TO STAY

For expanded hotel reviews, visit Fodors.com.

$$ HOTEL 🏨 **Terminus.** Commanding a panoramic view over Lake Como, this early-20th-century art nouveau landmark is the city's best hotel, with marbled public spaces and old-fashioned guest rooms done in floral patterns and furnished with large walnut wardrobes and silk-covered sofas. **Pros:** old-world charm; right on the lake; sauna and gym; good value. **Cons:** limited number of rooms with lake views; decor in some rooms seems dated with busy floral decor. [$] *Rooms from: €152* ✉ *Lungolario Trieste 14* ☎ *031/329111* 🌐 *www.albergoterminus.com* 🛏 *50 rooms* 🍴 *Breakfast.*

$$ HOTEL 🏨 **Tre Re.** Although the exterior gives away the age of this 16th-century former convent a few steps from the cathedral, the rooms are airy, comfortable, and modern. **Pros:** friendly staff; homey atmosphere. **Cons:** rooms are functional, not elegant—decor is spartan. [$] *Rooms from: €160* ✉ *Via Boldoni 20* ☎ *031/265374* 🌐 *www.hoteltrere.com* 🛏 *48 rooms* 🕒 *Closed mid-Dec.–mid-Jan.* 🍴 *Breakfast.*

SPORTS AND THE OUTDOORS

Lake Como has many opportunities for sports enthusiasts, from windsurfing at the lake's northern end, to boating, sailing, and Jet Skiing at Como and Cernobbio. The lake is also quite swimmable in summer. For hikers there are lovely paths all around the lake. For an easy trek, take the funicular up to Brunate, and walk along the mountain to the lighthouse for a stunning view of the lake.

LAKE MAGGIORE

Magnificently scenic, Lake Maggiore has a unique geographical position: its mountainous western shore is in Piedmont, its lower eastern shore is in Lombardy, and its northern tip is in Switzerland. The lake stretches nearly 50 km (30 miles) and is up to 5 km (3 miles) wide. The better-known resorts are on the western shore.

GETTING HERE AND AROUND

Trains run regularly from Milan to the town of Stresa on Lake Maggiore; the trip takes from 1 to 1½ hours, depending on the type of train. By car from Milan to Stresa, take the A8 Autostrada to A8dir, and from A8dir take A26; the drive is about 1¼ hours.

STRESA AND THE ISOLE BORROMEE

80 km (50 miles) northwest of Milan.

One of the better-known resorts on the western shore, Stresa is a tourist town that provided one of the settings for Hemingway's *A Farewell to Arms*. It's capitalized on its central lakeside position, though the luxurious elegance that distinguished its heyday has faded; the grand hotels are still grand, but traffic now encroaches on their parks and gardens. The best way to escape to yesteryear is to head for the Isole Borromee (Borromean Islands) in Lake Maggiore.

VISITOR INFORMATION

Stresa Tourism Office ⊠ *Piazza Marconi 16* ☎ *0323/30150* ⊕ *www.comune.stresa.vb.it.*

EXPLORING

Funivia. For amazing views, take the funivia—a cable car that takes you to heights from which you can see seven lakes: Maggiore, Orta, Mergozzo, Varese, Camabbio, Monate, and Biandronno. Situated between Lakes Maggiore and Orta, it offers tourists 360-degree views of the Po Valley right across to the distant Alpine peaks. At the top, nature- and adventure-lovers can rent mountain bikes and ride on properly marked paths, while others can just relax at a local restaurant. ⊠ *Piazzale Lido 8* ☎ *0323/30295* ⊕ *www.stresa-mottarone.it* ⊠ *€17.50 round trip* ☉ *Mar. 26–Oct. 31, daily 9:30–6; Nov.–mid-Mar., daily 8:10–5:40.*

Isole Borromee. Boats to the three islands depart every 15 to 30 minutes from the dock at Stresa's Piazza Marconi, as well as from Piazzale Lido at the northern end of the promenade. There's also a boat from Verbania; check locally for the seasonal schedule. Although you can hire a private boatman, it's cheaper and just as convenient to use the regular service. Make sure you buy a ticket allowing you to visit all the islands—Bella, Dei Pescatori, and Madre. The islands take their name from the Borromeo family, which has owned them since the 12th century. ⊕ *www.borromeoturismo.it.*

   Isola Bella (*Beautiful Island*). The most famous of the three islands, and the first that you'll visit, is named after Isabella, whose husband, Carlo III Borromeo (1538–84), built the palace and terraced gardens for her as a wedding present. Before Count Carlo began his project, the island was rocky and almost devoid of vegetation; the soil for the garden had to be transported from the mainland. Wander up the 10 terraces of the gardens, where peacocks roam among the scented shrubs, statues, and fountains, for a splendid view of the lake. Visit the palazzo to see the rooms where famous guests—including Napoleon and Mussolini—stayed in 18th-century splendor. Those three interlocked rings on walls and even streets represent the powerful Borromeo, Visconti, and Sforza families. ☎ *0323/30556* 🌐 *www.borromeoturismo.it* 🎟 *Garden and palazzo €13* 🕒 *Late Mar.–late Oct., daily 9–5:30. Painting gallery: daily 9–1 and 1:30–5.*

Isola dei Pescatori (*Island of the Fishermen, aka Isola Superiore*). Stop for a while at the smallest island, less than 100 yards wide and only about ½ km (¼ mile) long. It's the perfect place for a seafood lunch before, after, or in between your visit to the other two islands. Of the 10 or so restaurants on this tiny island, the three worth visiting are **Ristorante Unione** (☎ *0323/933798*), **Ristorante Verbano** (☎ *0323/30408*), and **Ristorante Belvedere** (☎ *0323/32292*). The island's little lanes strung with fishing nets and dotted with shrines to the Madonna are the definition of picturesque; little wonder that in high season the village is crowded with postcard stands.

6

Isola Madre (*Mother Island*). The entire island is a botanical garden, whose season stretches from late March to late October due to the climatic protection of the mighty Alps and the tepid waters of Lago Maggiore. The vision of cacti and palm trees on Isola Madre, its position so far north and so near the border of Switzerland, is a beautiful and unexpected surprise. Take time to see the profusion of exotic trees and shrubs running down to the shore in every direction. Two special times to visit are April (for the camellias) and May (for azaleas and rhododendrons). Also on the island is a 16th-century palazzo, where the Borromeo family still resides at different times throughout the year and where an antique puppet theater is on display, complete with string puppets, prompt books, and elaborate scenery designed by Alessandro Sanquirico, who was a scenographer at La Scala in Milan. ☎ *0323/31261* 🎟 *€11* 🕒 *Late Mar.–Oct., daily 9–5:30*

Villa Pallavicino. As you wander around the palms and semitropical shrubs, don't be surprised if you're followed by a peacock or even an ostrich: they're part of the zoological garden and are allowed to roam almost at will. From the top of the hill on which the villa stands you can see the gentle hills of the Lombardy shore of Lake Maggiore and, nearer and to the left, the jewel-like Borromean Islands. In addition to a bar and restaurant, the grounds also have picnic spots. ✉ *Via Sempione 8* ☎ *0323/31533* 🌐 *www.parcozoopallavicino.it* 🎟 *€9.50* 🕒 *mid-Mar.–Oct., daily 9–6.*

WHERE TO EAT AND STAY

For expanded hotel reviews, visit Fodors.com.

$ PIEDMONTESE 🍴 **Da Cesare.** Off Piazza Cadorna and close to the embarcadero, this popular spot serves tasty risotto *con filetti di persico* (with perch fillets) and typical Piedmontese meat dishes, such as beef braised in Barolo wine. Da Cesare also has hotel rooms. [$] *Average meal: €30* ✉ *Via Mazzini 14* ☎ *0323/31386* 🌐 *www.dacesare.com.*

$$$$ HOTEL **Grand Hotel des Iles Borromees.** This palatial, Liberty-style establishment has catered to a demanding European clientele since 1863, and spacious salons and guest rooms still have lavish furnishings of the turn of the 20th century. **Pros:** the grace and style of a bygone era, with modern amenities. **Cons:** some might consider it isolated on the outskirts of town. [$] *Rooms from: €400* ✉ *Corso Umberto I 67* ☎ *0323/938938* 🌐 *www.borromees.it* 🛏 *179 rooms, 11 suites* 🕓 *Closed mid-Oct.–Mar.* 🍴 *Breakfast.*

$ HOTEL **Primavera.** These compact, simply furnished rooms in a 1950s building hung with flower boxes are a few blocks up from the lake. **Pros:** good value; convenient location. **Cons:** no lake views; small, plainly furnished rooms. [$] *Rooms from: €100* ✉ *Via Cavour 39* ☎ *0323/31286* 🌐 *www.hotelprimaverastresa.com* 🛏 *37 rooms* 🕓 *Closed mid-Nov.–mid-Mar.* 🍴 *Breakfast.*

VERBANIA

16 km (10 miles) north of Stresa, 95 km (59 miles) northwest of Milan.

EXPLORING

Villa Taranto. Quaint Verbania is across the Gulf of Pallanza from its touristy neighbor Stresa. It is known for the Villa Taranto, which has magnificent botanical gardens. The villa was acquired in 1931 by Scottish captain Neil McEachern, who expanded the gardens considerably, adding terraces, waterfalls, more than 3,000 plant species from all over the world, and broad meadows sloping gently to the lake. In 1938 McEachern donated the entire complex to the Italian people. ✉ *Via Vittorio Veneto 111* ☎ *0323/404555* 🌐 *www.villataranto.it* 🎫 *€10* 🕓 *Late Mar.–early Nov., daily 8:30–6:30; last entry 1 hr before closing.*

WHERE TO STAY

For expanded hotel reviews, visit Fodors.com.

$ HOTEL **Il Chiostro.** A 17th-century monastery has expanded into the adjoining 19th-century textile factory, offering clean, functional rooms, some overlooking a lovely garden. **Pros:** friendly and efficient staff. **Cons:** rooms are fairly plain. [$] *Rooms from: €120* ✉ *Via Fratelli Cervi 14* ☎ *0323/404077* 🌐 *www.chiostrovb.it* 🛏 *100 rooms* 🍴 *Breakfast.*

$$$ HOTEL Fodor's Choice ★ **Il Sole di Ranco.** For more than 150 years the same family has run this elegant lakeside inn, where guest rooms and suites are in two late-19th-century villas surrounded by a garden perched high on the banks of the lake opposite Stresa. **Pros:** classic lake setting; tranquil grounds, meticulously maintained. **Cons:** a bit distant from lake's tourist center (although hotel offers excursions with private driver). [$] *Rooms from: €250* ✉ *Piazza Venezia 5, near Angera, Ranco* ☎ *0331/976507* 🌐 *www.ilsolediranco.it* 🛏 *2 rooms, 10 suites* 🕓 *Closed Nov. 15–Jan. 21. Restaurant closed Tues. No lunch Mon.* 🍴 *Breakfast.*

PIEDMONT AND VALLE D'AOSTA

WELCOME TO PIEDMONT AND VALLE D'AOSTA

TOP REASONS TO GO

★ **Sacra di San Michele:** Explore one of the country's most spectacularly situated religious monuments

★ **Castello Fénis:** This castle transports you back in time to the Middle Ages.

★ **Monte Bianco:** A cable car ride over the snowcapped mountain will take your breath away.

★ **Turin's Museo Egizio:** A surprising treasure— one of the world's richest collections of Egyptian art outside Cairo.

★ **Regal wines:** Some of Italy's most revered reds—led by Barolo, dubbed "the king of wines"—come from the hills of southern Piedmont.

★ **Turin's Galleria Sabauda:** Witness to the regal splendor of the reigning House of Savoy, this museum is famed for its spectacular Old Master collection

1 Turin. The region's main city isn't just the car capital of Italy and home to the Holy Shroud. Neoclassical piazzas, shops filled with chocolates and chic fashions, and elegant Baroque palazzos have been restored in grand style.

2 Monferrato and the Langhe. These hills are famous among food and wine connoisseurs. Asti gave the world Asti Spumante, Alba is known for its truffles and mushrooms, and the Langhe hills produce some of Italy's finest wines.

3 Valle d'Aosta. The mountains and valleys of this region cry out to be strolled, climbed, and skied. Here, the highest Alpine peaks—including Monte Bianco (aka Mont Blanc) and the Matterhorn—shelter resorts such as Breuil-Cervinia and Courmayeur and the great nature preserve known as the Gran Paradiso.

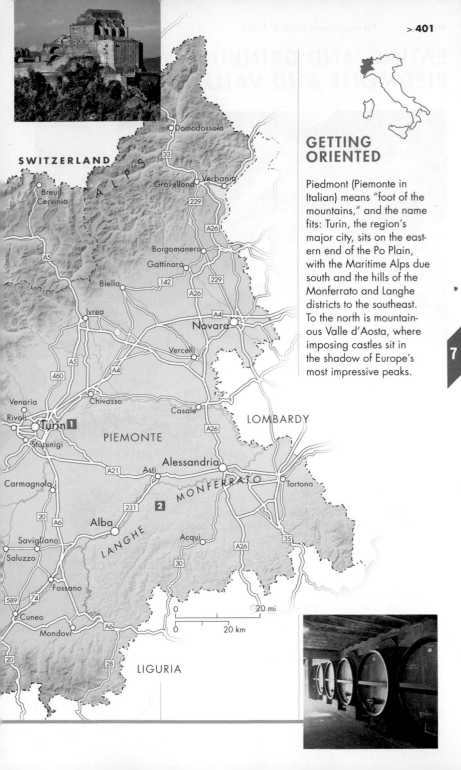

GETTING ORIENTED

Piedmont (Piemonte in Italian) means "foot of the mountains," and the name fits: Turin, the region's major city, sits on the eastern end of the Po Plain, with the Maritime Alps due south and the hills of the Monferrato and Langhe districts to the southeast. To the north is mountainous Valle d'Aosta, where imposing castles sit in the shadow of Europe's most impressive peaks.

7

SWITZERLAND

Domodossola

Breuil-Cervinia

Gravellona

Verbania

33

229

A26

Borgomanero

Gattinara

Biella

142

229

A26

Ivrea

A5

Novara

A4

Vercelli

A5

A4

460

Venaria

Chivasso

Rivoli

Casale

LOMBARDY

Turin 1

Stupinigi

A26

PIEMONTE

Carmagnola

Alessandria

A21

Asti

Tortona

MONFERRATO

20

A6

Alba

231

2

Savigliano

Acqui

35

Saluzzo

30

A26

589 74

Fossano

Cuneo

20 mi

20 km

Mondovi

A6

28

LIGURIA

EATING AND DRINKING WELL IN PIEDMONT AND VALLE D'AOSTA

In Piedmont and Valle d'Aosta you can find rustic specialties from farmhouse hearths, fine cuisine with a French accent, and everything in between. The Piedmontese take their food and wine very seriously.

There's a significant concentration of upscale restaurants in Piedmont, with refined cuisine designed to showcase the region's fine wines. Wine-oriented menus are prevalent both in cities and in the country, where even simply named trattorias may offer a *menu di degustazione* (a multicourse tasting menu) accompanied by wines paired to each dish.

In Turin the ritual of the *aperitivo* (aperitif) has been finely tuned, and most cafés from the early evening onward provide lavish buffets that are included in the price of a cocktail—a respectable substitute for dinner if you're traveling on a limited budget. As a result, restaurants in Turin tend to fill only after 9 pm.

GREAT GRISSINI

Throughout the region, though especially in Turin, you'll find that most meals are accompanied by *grissini* (bread sticks), *pictured above.*

Invented in Turin in the 17th century to ease the digestive problems of little Prince Vittorio Amedeo II (1675–1730), these, when freshly made and hand-rolled, are a far cry from the thin and dry, plastic-wrapped versions available elsewhere.

Napoléon called them *petits batons* and was, according to legend, addicted to them.

TRUFFLES

The *tartufo* (truffle) is a peculiar delicacy—a gnarly clump of fungus that grows wild in forests a few inches underground. It's hunted down using truffle-sniffing dogs and can sell for a small fortune. The payoff is a powerful, perfume flavor that makes gourmets swoon. Though truffles are more abundant farther south in Umbria, the most coveted ones are the *tartufi bianchi* (white truffles), *pictured at right*, from Alba in Piedmont. A thin shaving of truffle often tops pasta dishes; they're also used to flavor soups and other dishes.

POLENTA AND PASTA

The area's best-known dish is probably polenta, creamy cornmeal served with *carbonada* (a meat stew), melted cheese, or wild mushrooms. *Agnolotti*—crescent-shaped pasta stuffed with meat filling, *pictured below*—is another specialty, often served with the pan juices of roast veal. *Agnolotti del Plin* is a smaller version topped with melted butter and shaved truffles.

CHEESE

In keeping with their northern character, a regional specialty in both Piedmont and Valle d'Aosta is *fonduta,* a version of fondue made with melted cheese, eggs, and sometimes grated truffles. Fontina and ham also often deck out the ubiquitous French-style crepes *alla valdostana,* served casserole style.

MEAT

The locally raised beef of Piedmont is some of Italy's most highly prized; it's often braised or stewed with the region's hearty red wine. In winter, *bollito misto* (various meats, boiled and served with a rich sauce) shows up on many menus, and *fritto misto,* a combination of fried meats and vegetables, is another specialty.

DESSERTS AND SWEETS

Though desserts here are less sweet than in some other Italian regions, treats like *panna cotta* (a cooked milk custard), *torta di nocciole* (hazelnut torte), and *bonet* (a pudding made with hazelnuts, cocoa, milk, and macaroons) are delights. Turin is renowned for its delicate pastries and fine chocolates, especially for *gianduiotti,* made with hazelnuts.

WINE

Piedmont is one of Italy's most important wine regions, producing full-bodied reds, such as Barolo, Barbaresco, Freisa, Barbera, and the lighter Dolcetto. Asti Spumante, a sweet sparkling wine, comes from the region, while Valle d'Aosta is famous for schnapps-like brandies made from fruits or herbs.

7

Updated
by Peter
Blackman
Northwest Italy's Piedmont and Valle d'Aosta regions yield a big dose of mountain splendor, bourgeois refinement, culinary achievement, and scenic beauty. Two of Europe's most famous peaks—Monte Bianco (aka Mont Blanc) and Monte Cervino (the Matterhorn)—straddle Valle d'Aosta's borders with France and Switzerland, and the region is a magnet for skiers and hikers.

To the south, the mist-shrouded lowlands skirting the Po River are home to Turin, a city that may not have the artistic treasures of Rome or the cutting-edge style of Milan, but has developed a sense of urban sophistication that makes it a pleasure to visit. Farther south, vineyards carpet rolling hills and yield Piedmontese wines commonly held to be some of Italy's finest.

PIEDEMONT AND VALLE D'AOSTA PLANNER

MAKING THE MOST OF YOUR TIME

Turin, the first capital of unified Italy and the fourth largest city in the country, is a commercial center once overlooked on tourist itineraries. It's got a much higher profile now, and for good cause: the museum system is second to none, great restaurants abound, the nightlife is hopping, and there are an unusual number of attractions for children. If you also like the idea of an Italian city with touches of Parisian sophistication, Turin will strike your fancy.

In the mountains that surround Turin the hiking, climbing, and skiing are exceptional. On the Piedmont–Valle d'Aosta border, the Gran Paradiso National Park has beautiful trails. Farther north is Monte Bianco, which should be a priority; you can ascend by cable car, or, if you're an experienced climber, make a go of it with professional guides. You'll find extensive ski slopes in Sestriere in Piedmont and in Breuil-Cervinia on the Matterhorn. Food and wine lovers should head for the hills of the Langhe, just south of Turin, home to world-class wines and aromatic white truffles.

GETTING HERE AND AROUND
BUS TRAVEL
Turin's main bus station is on the corner of Corso Inghilterra and Corso Vittorio Emanuele. There's also a major bus station at Aosta, across the street from the train station.

GTT. Urban buses, trams, and the subway are all operated by this agency. ☎ *800/019152 toll-free in Italy ⊕ www.comune.torino.it/gtt.*

SADEM. This Turin-based bus line provides service throughout Piedmont and Valle d'Aosta. ☎ *800/801600 toll-free in Italy ⊕ www.sadem.it.*

SAVDA. This Aosta-based company specializes in mountain service, providing frequent links between Aosta, Turin, and Courmayeur as well as Milan. ☎ *0165/262027 ⊕ www.savda.it.*

CAR TRAVEL
Like any mountainous region, the Italian Alps can be tricky to navigate by car. Roads that look like highways on the map can be narrow and twisting, with steep slopes and cliff-side drops. Generally, roads are well maintained, but the distance covered by all of those curves tends to take longer than you might expect, so it's best to figure in extra time for getting around. This is especially true in winter, when weather conditions can cause slow traffic and close roads. Check with local tourist offices or, in a pinch, with the police, to make sure roads are passable and safe, and to find out whether you need tire chains for snowy and icy roads.

For travel across the French, Swiss, and Italian borders in Piedmont and Valle d'Aosta, only a few routes are usable year-round: the 12-km (7-mile) Mont Blanc tunnel connecting Chamonix with Courmayeur; the Colle del Gran San Bernardo/Col du Grand St. Bernard (connecting Martigny with Aosta on Swiss highway E27 and Italian highway SS27, with 6 km [4 miles] of tunnel); and the Traforo del Fréjus (between Modane and Susa, with 13 km [8 miles] of tunnel). Other passes become increasingly unreliable between November and April.

TRAIN TRAVEL
Turin is on the main Paris–Rome TGV express line and is also connected with Milan, only 90 minutes away on the fast train. The fastest (Frecciarossa) trains cover the 667-km (414-mile) trip to Rome in just over four hours; other trains take between five and seven hours.

Services to the larger cities east of Turin are part of the extensive and reliable train network of the Lombard Plain. West of the region's capital, however, the train services soon peter out in the mountains. Continuing connections by bus serve these valleys; information about train-bus mountain services can be obtained from train stations and tourist information offices, or by contacting FS–Trenitalia, the Italian national train service.

RESTAURANTS

In the region's restaurants you'll taste a mountain/city contrast: the hearty peasant cooking served in tiny stone villages and the French-accented delicacies found in the plain are both eminently satisfying. Please note that restaurant prices listed as "average meal" include a meal consisting of first course *(primo)*, second course *(secondo)*, and dessert *(dolce)*.

HOTELS

High standards and opulence are characteristic of Turin's better hotels, and the same is true, translated into the Alpine idiom, at the top mountain resorts. Hotels in Turin and other major towns are generally geared to business travelers; make sure to ask whether lower weekend rates or special deals for two- or three-night stays are available.

Summer vacationers and winter skiers keep occupancy rates and prices high at the resorts during peak seasons. Many mountain hotels accept half- or full-board guests only and require that you stay for several nights; some have off-season rates that can reduce the cost by a full price category. If you're planning to ski, ask about package deals that give you a discount on lift tickets. *Hotel prices are for two people in a standard double room in high season, including tax and service.*

TURIN

Turin—Torino, in Italian—is roughly in the center of Piedmont/Valle d'Aosta and 128 km (80 miles) west of Milan; it's on the Po River, on the edge of the Po Plain, which stretches east all the way to the Adriatic. Turin's flatness and wide, angular, tree-lined boulevards are a far cry from Italian *metropoli* to the south; the region's decidedly northern European bent is quite evident in its nerve center. Apart from its role as northwest Italy's major industrial, cultural, intellectual, and administrative hub, Turin also has a reputation as Italy's capital of black magic and the supernatural. This distinction is enhanced by the presence of Turin's most famous and controversial relic, the Sacra Sindone (Holy Shroud), still believed by many Catholics to be Christ's burial shroud. (For its part, the Vatican has not taken an official position on its authenticity.)

GETTING HERE AND AROUND

Turin is well served by the Italian *autostrade* (highway) system and can be reached easily by car from all directions: from Milan on the A4 Autostrada (2 hours); from Bologna (4 hours) and Florence (5 hours) on A1 and A21; from Genoa on the A6 Autostrada (2 hours).

Bus service to and from other major Italian cities is also plentiful, and Turin can be reached by fast train service from Paris in less than six hours. Fast train service also connects the city with Milan, Genoa, Bologna, Florence, and Rome.

Public boats, operated by Turin's public transport system (☎ *800/019152 or 011/5764733 ⊕ www.comune.torino.it/gtt*), make for a pleasant way to reach the Borgo Medioevale from the Murazzi dock at the northern end of the Parco del Valentino.

VISITOR INFORMATION

Turin's group and personally guided tours are organized by the city's tourist office. They also provide maps and details about a wide range of thematic self-guided walks through town. The Torino+Piemonte card, which provides discounts on transportation and museum entrances for two-, three-, five-, or seven-day visits can be purchased here, as well as Turin's unique Chocopass, which allows you to indulge in 10 tastings in as many chocolate shops.

Turin Tourism Office ⊠ *Piazza Castello* ☎ *011/535181* ⊕ *www.turismotorino.org.*

EXPLORING TURIN

DOWNTOWN TURIN
TOP ATTRACTIONS

Duomo di San Giovanni. The most impressive part of Turin's 15th-century cathedral is the shadowy black marble–walled **Cappella della Sacra Sindone** (Chapel of the Holy Shroud), where the famous relic was housed before a fire in 1997. The chapel was designed by the priest and architect Guarino Guarini (1604–83), a genius of the Baroque style who was official engineer and mathematician to the court of Duke Carlo Emanuele II of Savoy. The fire caused severe structural damage, and the chapel is closed indefinitely while restoration work proceeds.

The Sacra Sindone is a 4-yard-long sheet of linen, thought by millions to be the burial shroud of Christ, bearing the light imprint of his crucified body. The shroud first appeared around the middle of the 15th century, when it was presented to Ludovico of Savoy in Chambéry. In 1578 it was brought to Turin by another member of the Savoy royal family, Duke Emanuele Filiberto. It was only in the 1990s that the Catholic Church began allowing rigorous scientific study of the shroud. The results have been hazy, bolstering both sides of the argument. On one hand, three university teams—in Switzerland, Britain, and the United States—have concluded, as a result of carbon 14 dating, that the cloth is a forgery dating from between 1260 and 1390. On the other hand, they are unable to explain how medieval forgers could have created the shroud's image, which resembles a photographic negative, and how they could have had the knowledge or means to incorporate traces of Roman coins covering the eyelids and endemic Middle Eastern pollen woven into the cloth. Either way, the shroud continues to be revered as a holy relic, exhibited to the public on very rare occasions. In lieu of the real thing, a photocopy is on permanent display near the altar of the Duomo. ⊠ *Via XX Settembre 87, Centro* ☎ *011/4361540* ☉ *Mon.–Fri. 7–12:30 and 3–7; weekends 8–12:30 and 3–7.*

Galleria Sabauda. Housed in the restored *Manica Nuova* (new wing) of the **Palazzo Reale** the gallery displays some of the most important paintings from the vast collections of the house of Savoy. The collection is particularly rich in 16th- and 17th-century Dutch and Flemish paintings: note the *Stigmate di San Francesco* (*St. Francis Receiving Stigmata*) by Jan Van Eyck (1395–1441), in which the saint receives the marks of Christ's wounds while a companion cringes beside him. Other Dutch masterpieces include paintings by Anthony Van Dyck (1599–1641) and

Turin

QUADRILATERO

TO DOCKS
DORA

TO
SUPERGA

Teatro
Romano

Palazzo
di Città

Piazza
C. Augusto

Porta
Palatina

Piazza
Giulio

Pza. San
Giovanni

Pza.
Reale

Piazza
Castello

Piazza
Carlo
Alberto

Piazza
San Carlo

Corso Regina Margherita

Dora Riparia

Via Giuseppe Verdi

Piazza
Vittorio
Veneto

Piazza
Carlo
Emanuele II

MURAZZI

TO
GAM

Piazza
Carlo
Felice

Piazza
Bodoni

Piazza
C. Balbo

Piazza
Cavour

Train
Station

Corso Vittorio Emanuele II

Piazza Maria
Cristina

Ponte
Vittorio
Emanuele I

Ponte
Umberto I

Corso G. Marconi

Corso del Fiume

Parco
del
Valentino

Palazzo
Torino
Esposizioni

TO
LINGOTTO

Ponte Princ.
Isabella

Po

0   500 meters
0   500 yards

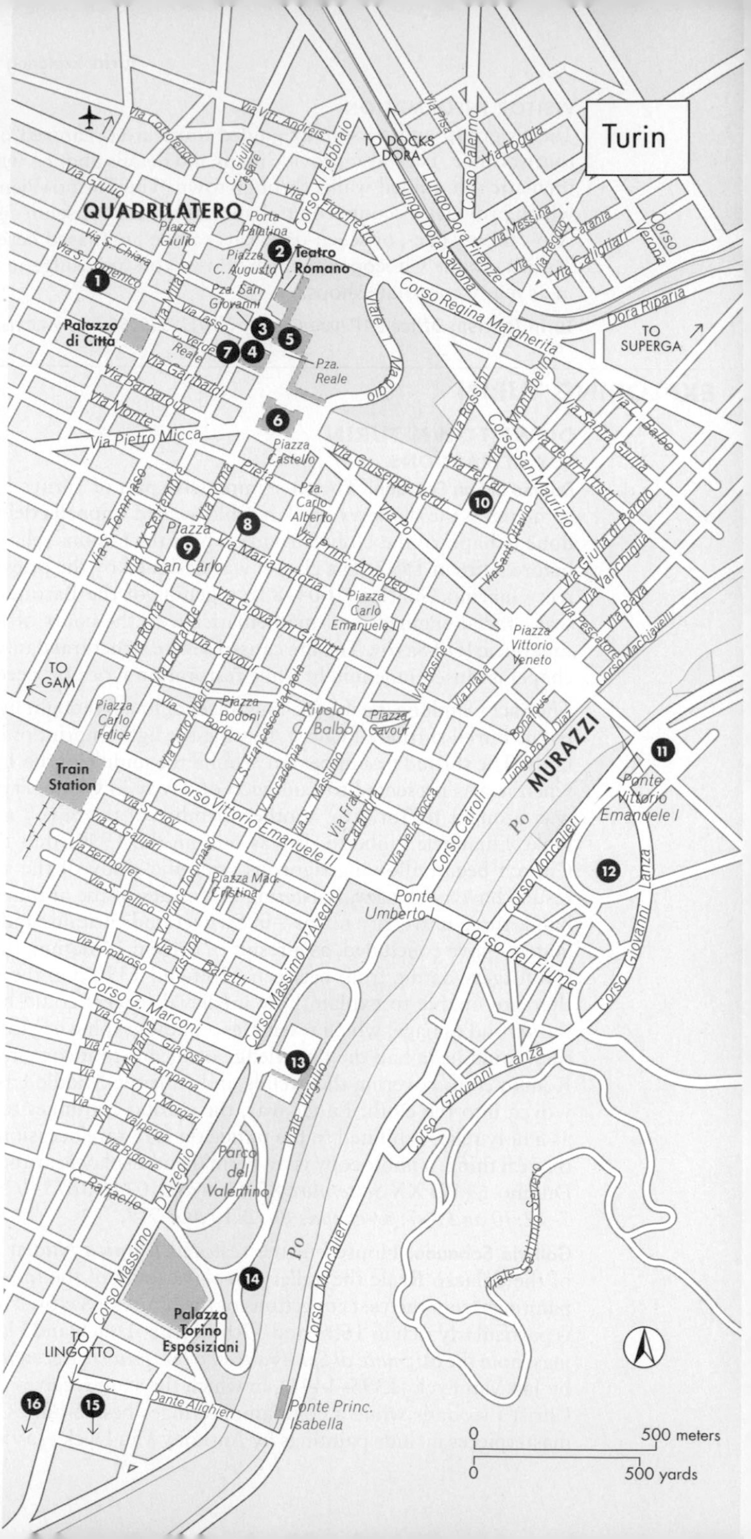

Rembrandt (1606–69). *L'arcangelo Raffaele e Tobiolo (Tobias and the Angel)* by Piero del Pollaiuolo (circa 1443–96) is showcased, and other featured Italian artists include Fra Angelico (circa 1400–55), Andrea Mantegna (1431–1506), and Paolo Veronese (1528–88). At time of writing ongoing restoration, due for completion in 2014, allows only a portion of the collection to be displayed. ⊠ *Via XX Settembre 88, Centro* ☎ *011/5641749* ⊕ *www.artito.arti.beniculturali.it* ⌨ *€10, includes the Palazzo Reale and the Armeria Reale* ⊙ *Tues.–Sun. 8:30–7:30.*

Mole Antonelliana. You can't miss the unusual square dome and thin, elaborate spire of this Turin landmark above the city's rooftops. This odd structure, built between 1863 and 1889, was originally intended to be a synagogue, but costs escalated and eventually it was bought by the city of Turin. In its time it was the tallest brick building in the world, and it is still the tallest building in Italy. You can take the crystal elevator to reach the terrace at the top of the dome for an excellent view of the city, the plain, and the Alps beyond. Also worth a visit is the Mole Antonelliana's **Museo Nazionale del Cinema** (National Cinema Museum), which covers more than 34,000 square feet and houses many items of film memorabilia as well as a film library with some 7,000 titles. ⊠ *Via Montebello 20, Centro* ☎ *011/8138560 museum* ⊕ *www.museocinema.it* ⌨ *Museum €9, elevator €6, combination ticket €12* ⊙ *Museum: Tues.–Fri. and Sun. 9–8, Sat. 9 am–11 pm. Elevator: Tues.–Fri. and Sun. 10–8, Sat. 10 am–11 pm. Ticket sales end 1 hr before closing.*

Museo d'Arte Orientale. Housed in the magnificently renovated 17th-century Palazzo Mazzonis, this collection of Southeast Asian, Chinese, Japanese, Himalayan, and Islamic art is a must-see for anyone interested in Asian sculpture, painting, and ceramics. Highlights include a towering 13th-century wooden statue of the Japanese temple guardian Kongo Rikishi and a sumptuous assortment of Islamic manuscripts. ⊠ *Via San Domenico 11, Centro* ☎ *011/4436927* ⊕ *www.maotorino.it* ⌨ *€10* ⊙ *Tues.–Sun. 10–6; ticket sales end 1 hr before closing.*

QUICK BITES

Al Bicerin. A chocolate lover's pilgrimage to Turin inevitably leads to this small coffee shop, which opened in 1763. Nietzsche, Puccini, Dumas, and the politicical reformer Cavour have all sipped here, and if you order the house specialty, the *bicerin* (a hot drink with layers of chocolate, coffee, and cream), you'll understand why. Don't be surprised if the friendly owner, Marité Costa, also tries to tempt you with one of her flavored *zabajoni* (warm eggnogs). Chocolate goodies are for sale in the café store. ⊠ *Piazza della Consolata 5, Centro* ☎ *011/4369325* ⊕ *www.bicerin.it* ⊙ *Closed Wed. and Aug.*

Caffè San Carlo. This historic coffee shop is usually filled with locals gathered at the marble-top tables under the huge crystal chandelier. Breakfast and lunch, afternoon snacks, and evening aperitifs are all served in a particularly elegant neoclassical setting. ⊠ *Piazza San Carlo 156, Centro* ☎ *011/532586* ⊕ *www.caffesancarlo.it.*

7

Fodor's Choice **Museo Egizio.** The Egyptian Museum's superb collection includes stat-
★ ues of pharaohs and mummies and entire frescoes taken from royal
tombs—all in all, it's one of the world's finest and largest museums of
its kind. The striking sculpture gallery, designed by Oscar-winner Dante
Ferretti, is a veritable "who's who" of ancient Egypt. Look for the magnificent 13th-century-BC statue of Ramses II and the fascinating Tomb
of Kha. The latter was found intact with furniture, supplies of food and
clothing, writing instruments, and a complete set of personal cosmetics and toiletries. Unfortunately, the museum's objects are not always
displayed according to modern standards. Along with carefully constructed exhibits with detailed information in English and Italian you
will also find rooms that resemble warehouses filled with objects, with
little or no information provided. The museum is housed in the **Palazzo
dell'Accademia delle Scienze,** a Baroque tour de force designed by the
priest and architect Guarino Guarini. ⊠ *Via Accademia delle Scienze 6,
Centro* ☎ *011/5617776* ⊕ *www.museoegizio.it* 🎫 *€7.50* ☉ *Tues.–Sun.
8:30–7:30; ticket sales end 1 hr before closing.*

Palazzo Madama. In the center of Piazza Castello, this castle was named
for the Savoy queen Madama Maria Cristina, who made it her home
in the 17th century. The building incorporates the remains of a Roman
gate with later-medieval and Renaissance additions. The castle's monumental Baroque facade and grand entrance staircase were designed
by Filippo Juvarra (1678–1736). The palace now houses the **Museo
Civico d'Arte Antica,** whose collections comprise more than 30,000
items dating from the Middle Ages to the Baroque era. The paintings,
sculptures, illuminated manuscripts, and various decorative objects on
display illustrate almost 10 centuries of Italian and European artistic
production. Works by Jan van Eyck, Antonella da Messina (circa 1430–
79), and Orazio Gentileschi (1563–1639) highlight the collection. ⊠ *Piazza Castello, Centro* ☎ *011/4433501* ⊕ *www.palazzomadamatorino.it*
🎫 *Grand staircase and medieval courtyard free, museum €10* ☉ *Grand
staircase and medieval courtyard: Tues.–Sun. 9–7. Museum: Tues.–Sat.
10–6, Sun. 10–7. Ticket sales end 1 hr before closing.*

Palazzo Reale. This 17th-century palace, a former Savoy royal residence,
is an imposing work of brick, stone, and marble that stands on the
site of one of Turin's ancient Roman city gates. In contrast to its sober
exterior, the two main floors of the palace's interior are swathed in luxurious, mostly rococo trappings, including tapestries, gilt ceilings, and
sumptuous 17th- to 19th-century furniture. You also can head down to
the basement and the old kitchens to see where food for the last kings
of Italy was once dished up. Currently the royal gardens behind the
palace are closed for extensive restoration. ⊠ *Piazzetta Reale 1, Centro* ☎ *011/4361455* 🎫 *€10, includes the Armeria Reale and Galleria
Sabauda* ☉ *Tues.–Sun. 8:30–7:30.*

Armeria Reale (*Royal Armory*). This wing of the Royal Palace holds
one of Europe's most extensive collections of arms and armor. It's a
must-see for connoisseurs. ⊠ *Piazza Castello 191, Centro* ☎ *011/543889*
🎫 *€10, includes the Palazzo Reale and Galleria Sabauda* ☉ *Tues.–Fri.
9–2, weekends 1–7.*

NORTHWEST ITALY, PAST AND PRESENT

Ancient history. Piedmont and Valle d'Aosta were originally inhabited by Celtic tribes, who over time were absorbed by the conquering Romans. As allies of Rome, the Celts held off Hannibal when he came down through the Alpine passes with his elephants, but they were eventually defeated, and their capital—Taurasia, the present Turin—was destroyed. The Romans rebuilt the city, giving its streets the grid pattern that survives today. (Roman ruins can be found throughout both regions and are particularly conspicuous in the town of Aosta.)

The Middle Ages and the Savoy. With the fall of the Roman Empire, the region suffered the fate of the rest of Italy and was successively occupied and ravaged by barbarians from the east and the north. In the 11th century the feudal French Savoy family ruled Turin briefly; toward the end of the 13th century it returned to the area, where it would remain, almost continuously, for 500 years. In 1798 the French republican armies invaded Italy, but when Napoléon's empire fell, the house of Savoy returned to power.

Risorgimento. Beginning in 1848, Piedmont was one of the principal centers of the Risorgimento, the movement for Italian unity. In 1861 the Chamber of Deputies of Turin declared Italy a united kingdom, with Turin as the new nation's capital. The capital moved to Florence in 1865, and then to Rome in 1870, effectively marking the end of Piedmont's prominence in national politics.

Industry and affluence. Piedmont became one of the first industrialized regions in Italy, and the automotive giant FIAT—the Fabbrica Italiana Automobili Torino—was established here in 1899. Today the region is the center of Italy's automobile, metalworking, chemical, and candy industries, having attracted thousands of workers from Italy's south. The FIAT company, led by the Agnelli family, has been arguably the most important factor in the region's rise to affluence.

Piazza San Carlo. Surrounded by shops, arcades, fashionable cafés, and elegant Baroque palaces, this is one of the most beautiful squares in Turin. In the center stands a statue of Duke Emanuele Filiberto of Savoy, victor at the battle of San Quintino in 1557. The melee heralded the peaceful resurgence of Turin under the Savoy after years of bloody dynastic fighting. The fine bronze statue erected in the 19th century is one of Turin's symbols. At the southern end of the square, framing the continuation of Via Roma, are the twin baroque churches of San Carlo and Santa Cristina. ⊠ *Centro.*

San Lorenzo. Architect Guarino Guarini was in his mid-sixties when he began this church in 1668. The masterful use of geometric forms and the theatrical control of light and shadow show him working at his mature and confident best. Stand in the center of the church and look up into the cupola for the full effect. ⊠ *Via Palazzo di Città 4, Centro* ☎ *011/4361527* ⊕ *www.sanlorenzo.torino.it* ☉ *Mon.–Sat. 7:30–noon and 4–7; Sun. 9–1 and 3–7:30.*

Baratti e Milano. In the glass-roofed Galleria Subalpina, near Via Po, stands one of Turin's charming old cafés. It's famous for its exquisite chocolates—indulge your sweet tooth or buy some *gianduiotti* (hazelnut chocolates) or candied chestnuts to take home to friends. Light lunches are served at the tables to the rear of the shop. ⊠ *Piazza Castello 27, Centro* ☎ *011/4407138* ⊕ *www.barattiemilano.it* ☉ *Closed Mon.*

Mulassano. This tiny café, decorated with marble and finely carved wood panels, is famous for its *tramezzini* (small triangular sandwiches made with white bread), invented here in the 1920s. Popular with the pre- and post-theater crowd, the café also offers a unique roulette system for clients trying to decide on who pays the bill—ask the cashier for an explanation. ⊠ *Piazza Castello 15, Centro* ☎ *011/547990* ⊕ *www.caffemulassano.com.*

WORTH NOTING

Galleria Civica d'Arte Moderna e Contemporanea (GAM). In 1863 Turin was the first Italian city to begin a public collection devoted to contemporary art. Housed in a modern building on the edge of downtown, a permanent display of more than 600 paintings, sculptures, and installation pieces provides an exceptional glimpse of how Italian contemporary art has evolved since the late 1800s. The futurist, pop, neo-Dada, and arte povera movements are particularly well represented, and the gallery has a fine video and art film collection. ⊠ *Via Magenta 31, Centro* ☎ *011/4429518* ⊕ *www.gamtorino.it* 🎟 *€10; ticket sales end 1 hr before closing* ☉ *Tues.–Sun. 10–6.*

Museo di Antichità. A small but fascinating collection of artifacts found at archaeological sites in and around Turin is on display here. A spiral ramp winds through the subterranean museum, and like in a real archaeological site, the deeper you go the older the objects displayed. A life-size silver bust of the Roman Emperor Lucio Vero (AD 161–169) is one of the masterpieces of the collection. ⊠ *Via XX Settembre 88c, Centro* ☎ *011/5212251* ⊕ *museoarcheologico.piemonte.beniculturali. it* 🎟 *€4* ☉ *Tues.–Sun. 8:30–7:30.*

Palazzo Carignano. This Baroque triumph is by Guarino Guarini, the priest and architect who designed several of Turin's most noteworthy structures. Built between 1679 and 1685, the palace played an important role in creating the modern-day nation. Vittorio Emanuele II of Savoy (1820–78), the first king of a united Italy, was born here, and Italy's first parliament met here from 1860 to 1865. The palace now houses the **Museo del Risorgimento,** a museum honoring the 19th-century movement for Italian unity. ⊠ *Via Accademia delle Scienze 5, Centro* ☎ *011/5621147* ⊕ *www.museorisorgimentotorino.it* 🎟 *€10* ☉ *Tues.–Sun. 10–6; ticket sales end 1 hr before closing.*

ALONG THE PO
TOP ATTRACTIONS

FAMILY **Borgo Medioevale.** Along the banks of the Po, this complex, built for a General Exhibition in 1884, is a faithful reproduction of a typical Piedmont village in the Middle Ages. Crafts shops, houses, a church, and stores cluster the narrow lanes, and in the center of the village is the **Rocca Medioevale,** a medieval castle that's the ersatz town's main attraction. ⊠ *Viale Virgilio 107, San Salvario* ☎ *011/4431701* ⊕ *www. borgomedioevaletorino.it* ☞ *Village free, Rocca Medioevale €6* ☉ *Village: Apr.–Oct., daily 9–8; Nov.–Mar., daily 9–7. Rocca Medioevale: Apr.–Oct., daily 9–7; Nov.–Mar., Tues.–Sun. 9–6; groups of no more than 25 enter castle every 30 mins. Ticket counter closes at 6:15.*

FAMILY **Museo dell'Automobile.** No visit to this motor city would be complete without a pilgrimage to see perfectly preserved Bugattis, Ferraris, and Isotta Fraschinis. Here you can get an idea of the importance of FIAT—and automobiles in general—to Turin's economy. There's a collection of antique cars from as early as 1896, and displays show how the city has changed over the years as a result of the auto industry. ⊠ *Corso Unità d'Italia 40, Millefonti* ☎ *011/677666* ⊕ *www.museoauto.it* ☞ *€8* ☉ *Mon. 10–2, Tues. 2–7, Wed., Thurs. and Sun. 10–7, Fri. and Sat. 10–9; last entrance 1 hr before closing.*

Parco del Valentino. This pleasant riverside park is a great place to stroll, bike, or jog. Originally the grounds of a relatively simple hunting lodge, the park owes its present arrangement to Madama Maria Cristina of France, who received the land and lodge as a wedding present after her marriage to Vittorio Amedeo I of Savoy. With memories of 16th-century French châteaux in mind, she began work in 1620 and converted the lodge into a magnificent palace, the **Castello del Valentino.** The building, now home to the University of Turin's Faculty of Architecture, is not open to the public. Next to the palace are the university's botanical gardens, established in 1729, where local and exotic flora can be seen in a hothouse, herbarium, and arboretum. ⊠ *Parco del Valentino, San Salvario* ☎ *011/6705985 botanical gardens* ☞ *Botanical gardens €3* ☉ *Botanical gardens: mid-Apr.–Sept., weekends 9–1 and 3–7.*

Fodor's Choice **Pinacoteca Giovanni e Marella Agnelli.** This gallery was opened in 2002 ★ by Gianni Agnelli (1921–2003), the head of FIAT and patriarch of one of Italy's most powerful families. The emphasis here is on quality rather than quantity: 25 works of art from the Agnelli private collection are on permanent display, along with temporary exhibitions. There are four magnificent scenes of Venice by Canaletto (1697–1768); two splendid views of Dresden by Canaletto's nephew, Bernardo Bellotto (1720–80); several works by Manet (1832–83), Renoir (1841–1919), Matisse (1869–1954), and Picasso (1881–1973); and fine examples of the work of Italian futurist painters Balla (1871–1958) and Severini (1883–1966). The gallery is on the top floor of the **Lingotto,** a former FIAT factory that was completely transformed between 1982 and 2002 by architect Renzo Piano. The multilevel complex now holds a shopping mall, several movie theaters, restaurants, two hotels, and an auditorium. ⊠ *Via Nizza 230, Lingotto* ☎ *011/0062713* ⊕ *www.pinacoteca-agnelli. it* ☞ *€4* ☉ *Tues.–Sun. 10–7; last entrance at 6:15.*

WORTH NOTING

Basilica di Superga. Visible from miles around, this thoroughly Baroque church was designed by Juvarra in the early 18th century and since 1731 has been the burial place of kings: no fewer than 58 members of the Savoy family are memorialized in the crypt. ⊠ *Strada della Basilica di Superga 75, Sassi* ☎ *011/8997456* ⊕ *www.basilicadisuperga.com* 🖃 *Basilica free, crypt €4* ⊙ *Basilica: weekdays 9–noon and 3–5, weekends 9–noon and 3–6. Crypt: Mar.–Oct., daily 9:30–7:30; Nov.–Feb., weekends 9:30–6:30; last entrance 45 mins before closing.*

Gran Madre di Dio. On the east bank of the Po, this neoclassical church is modeled after the Pantheon in Rome. It was built between 1827 and 1831 to commemorate the return of the house of Savoy to Turin after the fall of Napoléon's empire. ⊠ *Piazza Gran Madre di Dio 4, Borgo Po* ☎ *011/8193572* ⊙ *Mon.–Sat. 7:30–noon and 4:30–7, Sun. 7:30–1 and 3:30–7.*

Santa Maria del Monte. The church and convent standing on top of 150-foot Monte dei Cappuccini date from 1583. Don't be surprised if you find yourself in the middle of a wedding party, as couples often come here to be photographed. Next to the church is the tiny **Museo Nazionale della Montagna,** dedicated to mountains and mountaineers. ⊠ *Piazzale Monte dei Cappuccini, above Corso Moncalieri, Borgo Po* ☎ *011/6604414 church, 011/6604104 museum* ⊕ *www.museomontagna.org* 🖃 *Church free, museum €10* ⊙ *Church: daily 9–noon and 2:30–6. Museum: Tues.–Sun. 10–6.*

FAMILY   **Sassi–Superga Cog Train.** The 18-minute ride from Sassi up the Superga hill is an absolute treat on a clear day. The view of the Alps is magnificent at the hilltop **Parco Naturale Collina Torinese,** a tranquil retreat from the bustle of the city. If you feel like a little exercise, you can walk back down to Sassi (about two hours) on one of the well-marked wooded trails that start from the upper station. Other circular trails lead through the park and back to Superga. ⊠ *Piazza G. Modena, Sassi* ☎ *800019152 toll-free in Italy* ⊕ *www.comune.torino.it/gtt* 🖃 *Weekdays €4 one-way, weekends €6 one-way* ⊙ *Hourly service Mon. and Wed.–Fri. 9–noon and 2–5, hourly service weekends 9–8; bus service replaces train on Tues.*

Sacra di San Michele. Perhaps best known as inspiration for the setting of Umberto Eco's novel *The Name of the Rose,* Sacra di San Michele was built on Monte Pirchiriano in the 11th century so it would stand out: it occupies the most prominent location for miles around, hanging over a 3,280-foot bluff. When monks came to enlarge the abbey they had to build part of the structure on supports more than 90 feet high—an engineering feat that was famous in medieval Europe and is still impressive today. By the 12th century this important abbey controlled 176 churches in Italy, France, and Spain; one of the abbeys under its influence was Mont-Saint-Michel in France. Because of its strategic position the Abbey of Saint Michael came under frequent attacks over the next five centuries and was eventually abandoned in 1622. It was restored, somewhat heavy-handedly, in the late 19th and early 20th centuries.

From **Porta dello Zodiaco,** a splendid Romanesque doorway decorated with the signs of the zodiac, you climb 150 steps, past 12th-century sculptures, to reach the church. On the left side of the interior are 16th-century frescoes representing New Testament themes; on the right are depictions of the founding of the church. In the crypt are some of the oldest parts of the structure, three small 9th- to 12th-century chapels. Note that some sections of the abbey are open only on weekends and, when particularly crowded, visits may be limited to hour-long tours. ✉ *Via Sacra di San Michele 14, Sant'Ambrogio di Torino, Italy* ☎ *011/939130* 🌐 *www.sacradisanmichele.com* 🎫 *€5* 🕓 *Mid-Mar.–mid-Oct., Tues.–Sat. 9:30–12:30 and 2:30–6, Sun. 9:30–noon and 2:40–6:30; July–Sept., Mon.–Sat. 9:30–12:30 and 4:30–6, Sun. 9:30–noon and 2:40–6:30; mid-Oct.–mid-Mar., Tues.–Sat. 9:30–12:30 and 2:30–5, Sun. 9:30–noon and 2:40–5; Closed Mon. except Jul.–Sept., 9:30–12:30 and 2:30–6.*

WHERE TO EAT

$$$ PIEDMONTESE **Fodor's Choice** ★

🍴 **Al Garamond.** The ocher-color walls and the ancient brick vaulting in this small, bright space set the stage for traditional meat and seafood dishes served with creative flair. Try the tantalizing *rombo in crosta di patate al barbera* (turbot wrapped in sliced potatoes and baked with Barbera wine). For dessert, the mousse *di liquirizia e salsa di cioccolato bianco* (licorice mousse with white-chocolate sauce) is delightful, even if you don't usually like licorice. The level of service here is high, even by demanding Turin standards. [$] *Average meal: €60* ✉ *Via G. Pomba 14, Centro* ☎ *011/8122781* 🌐 *www.algaramond.it* 🕓 *Closed Jan. 1–6 and 3 wks in Aug. No dinner weekends.*

$$$ PIEDMONTESE

🍴 **Casa Vicina.** Hidden away in the basement of the Lingotto food emporium, this establishment is one of Turin's top restaurants. The decor is starkly modern and, without windows, might seem claustrophobic to some, but the food makes up for everything. Traditional dishes, particularly those from northern Piedmont, are served up with creative style. Among the antipasti, the *insalata russa con acciuga* (Russian salad with anchovies) is as tasty as it is unusual. The agnolotti *alla Vecchia Eporedia* are an equally delicious rendition of the commonly found pasta dish, served with the pan juices of roast veal. The wine list is an encylopedia, with many small wineries included. [$] *Average meal: €60* ✉ *Via Nizza 224, Centro* ☎ *011/19506840* 🌐 *www.casavicina.it* ✍ *Reservations essential* 🕓 *Closed Sun. and Mon.*

$$ PIEDMONTESE

🍴 **Consorzio.** Very popular at lunchtime during the week, this small and informal osteria is right in the heart of Turin's business district. The service is relaxed, the decor low-key, and the menu highlights organic meats and vegetables from the region. The *tortino di verdura* (vegetable flan) and the gnocchi *con pecorino, pancetta e fave* (with sheep's cheese, bacon, and broad beans) make for a light and satisfying meal. There's a good selection of Piedmont wines. [$] *Average meal: €35* ✉ *Via Monte di Pietà 23, Centro* ☎ *011/2767661* 🌐 *www.ristoranteconsorzio.it* ✍ *Reservations essential* 🕓 *Closed Sat. for lunch, all day Sun.*

$ TUSCAN

🍴 **Da Mauro.** This bustling spot in the center of Turin's business district teems with locals at both lunch and dinner. After Tuscan migrants moved to Turin in the sixties, Da Mauro was one of the first restaurants to cater to their tastes. The menu changes daily and is as long and as varied as one might wish, with both Tuscan-style seafood and meat courses always present. The tagliatelle *con sugo di anatra* (with duck sauce), and the *misto pesce alla livornese* (Livorno-style fish stew) are both excellent. Service is brisk and efficient—it's not the place to come for a slow-paced meal. [$] *Average meal: €18* ✉ *Via Maria Vittoria 21, Centro* ☎ *011/8170604* 💳 *No credit cards.*

$$$$ ✗ **Del Cambio.** Set in a palace dating from 1757, this is one of Europe's
PIEDMONTESE most beautiful and historic restaurants, with decorative moldings, mirrors, and hanging lamps that look just as they did when Italian national
hero Cavour dined here more than a century ago. The cuisine draws
heavily on Piedmontese tradition and is paired with fine wines of the
region. Agnolotti pasta with *sugo d'arrosto* (pan juice of roast veal) is
a recommended first course. $ *Average meal: €75* ✉ *Piazza Carignano
2, Centro* ☎ *011/546690* ⊕ *www.delcambio.it* ⚭ *Reservations essential*
☉ *Closed Sun., Jan. 1–6, and 3 wks in Aug.*

$$ ✗ **L'Agrifoglio.** This local favorite has just 10 tables. Specialties change
PIEDMONTESE with the seasons, but you might find such delicacies as risotto *al Bar-
baresco* (with Barbaresco wine) and agnolotti *farciti di brasato* (cres-
cent-shaped stuffed pasta) on the menu. L'Agrifoglio stays open late for
the post-movie and -theater crowds. $ *Average meal: €45* ✉ *Via Andrea
Provana 7, Centro* ☎ *011/8136837* ⊕ *www.lagrifoglioristorante.com*
☉ *Closed Sun. and Mon.*

$ ✗ **La Dentera.** For a break (gastronomic, and for the wallet as well) to
ITALIAN the usually elaborate slow-food style of Piedmont cuisine try one of
the 34 different pizzas served up at this lively spot near the base of the
Sassi–Superga cog train. The chef's pizza specials include the *dentera*
(with anchiovies, red bell pepper, oil and garlic) and the *cremagliera*
(with gorgonzola). It's a great spot for a quick-bite before or after vis-
iting the Superga Basilica. $ *Average meal: €10* ✉ *Corso Casale 321,
Sassi, Turin* ☎ *011/8987108.*

$ ✗ **Pastificio Defilippis.** Famous for freshly made pasta since 1872, this
PIEDMONTESE shop also serves pasta creations to a packed lunch crowd all week
long. Some of the favorites include *rigatoni all'arrabbiata* (with a spicy
tomato and meat sauce) and *agnolotti di prosciutto e zucchine al burro*
(with ham, zucchini, and melted butter). Second courses and desserts are
also available, but the pasta is the main event. Dining is on two floors
so even if you find it full when you arrive, the wait is never very long.
$ *Average meal: €15* ✉ *Via Lagrange 39, Centro, Turin* ☎ *011/542137*
⊕ *www.pastificiodeifilippis.com* ▤ *No credit cards* ☉ *No dinner.*

$$ ✗ **Porta di Po.** They're vigilant about sticking to Piedmontese special-
PIEDMONTESE ties at this elegant restaurant with minimalist decor. All the seasonal
favorites are here: the delicious *tajarin ai quaranta uova con salsiccia
di Bra* (pasta made with 40 eggs and served with sausage) is sure to
top up your cholesterol levels, and the *brasato di vitello piemontese al
Barbera* (veal braised in red wine) melts in your mouth. Desserts are
all traditional, and the limited wine list presents a reasonable collection of regional wines. $ *Average meal: €40* ✉ *Piazza Vittorio Veneto
1, Centro* ☎ *011/8127642* ⊕ *www.portadipo.it* ☉ *Closed Sun. and 2
wks in Sept. No lunch Mon.*

$ ✗ **Trattoria Anna.** If you are hankering for something different from the
SEAFOOD usual meat-based Piedmontese cuisine, give this simple, extremely popular, family-run spot a try. They serve only seafood, and they do it well.
The *tagliatelle Walter* (pasta with shellfish) and the *grigliata di pesce*
(mixed grilled fish) are both excellent. $ *Average meal: €30* ✉ *Via Belle-
zia 20, Centro* ☎ *011/4362134* ⚭ *Reservations essential* ☉ *Closed Sun.
and 2 wks in Aug. No lunch.*

$$$ NORTHERN ITALIAN 🍴 **Vintage 1997.** The first floor of an elegant town house in the center of Turin makes a fitting location for this restaurant. You might try such specialties as *vitello tonnato alla vecchia maniera* (roast veal with a light tuna sauce made without mayonnaise) or *merluzzo in crosta di erbette con patate e scalogno caramellato* (cod filet in a crust of herbs served with potatoes and caramelized scallions). For the especially hungry gourmet there's the *menu del Vintage,* a 13-course feast that covers the full range of the restaurant's cuisine. [$] *Average meal: €65* ✉ *Piazza Solferino 16/H, Centro* ☎ *011/535948* 🌐 *www.vintage1997.com* 🕒 *Closed Sun. and 3 wks in Aug. No lunch Sat.*

WHERE TO STAY

The Turin Tourist Board provides a booking service for accommodations in the city and throughout the region. You must book hotels 48 hours in advance and B&Bs seven days in advance.

For expanded hotel reviews, visit Fodors.com.

$$ HOTEL 🏨 **Genio.** Though they're just steps away from the main train station, these spacious and tastefully decorated rooms provide a quiet haven from the bustle of the city. **Pros:** close to the central train station; very friendly service. **Cons:** 15-minute walk to the center of town; area around the hotel is a little seedy. [$] *Rooms from: €175* ✉ *Corso Vittorio Emanuele II 47, Centro* ☎ *011/6505771* 🌐 *www.hotelgenio.it* 🛏 *125 rooms, 3 suites* 🍽 *Breakfast.*

$$$ HOTEL 🏨 **Grand Hotel Sitea.** One of the city's finest, in the historic center, is decorated in a classical style, and public areas and guest rooms are elegant and comfortable. **Pros:** central location; well-appointed rooms; large bathrooms. **Cons:** air-conditioning can be noisy; carpets are a little worn. [$] *Rooms from: €198* ✉ *Via Carlo Alberto 35, Centro* ☎ *011/5170171* 🌐 *www.grandhotelsitea.it* 🛏 *118 rooms, 4 suites* 🍽 *Breakfast.*

$$ HOTEL 🏨 **LingottoTech.** Designed by architect Renzo Piano, this luxury hotel is part of the former Lingotto FIAT factory. **Pros:** interesting design and location; good weekend rates sometimes available. **Cons:** outside the city center; some signs of wear and tear. [$] *Rooms from: €160* ✉ *Via Nizza 230, Lingotto* ☎ *011/6642000* 🌐 *www.nh-hotels.it* 🛏 *141 rooms, 1 suite* 🍽 *Breakfast.*

$$$ HOTEL Fodor's Choice ★ 🏨 **Victoria.** Rare style, attention to detail, and comfort are the hallmarks of in-town retreat that's furnished and managed along the lines of a refined English town house. **Pros:** tranquil location in the center of town; excellent spa facilities; wonderful breakfast. **Cons:** entrance is a little run-down; hotel parking lot is a couple of blocks away and finding a spot on the street is difficult; no views from the rooms. [$] *Rooms from: €270* ✉ *Via Nino Costa 4, Centro* ☎ *011/5611909* 🌐 *www.hotelvictoria-torino.com* 🛏 *97 rooms, 9 suites* 🍽 *Breakfast.*

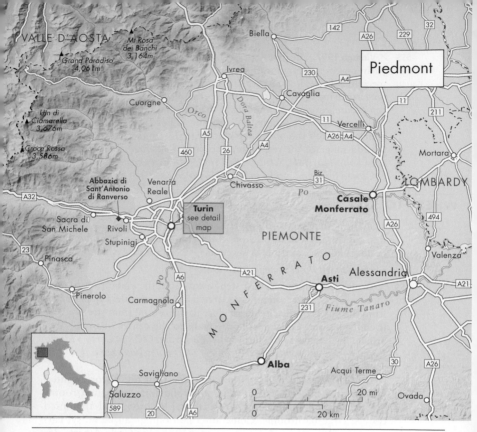

NIGHTLIFE AND THE ARTS

THE ARTS

MUSIC

Duomo. Traditional sacred music and some modern religious pieces are performed in the cathedral on Sunday evening; performances are usually advertised in the vestibule or in the local edition of Turin's nationally distributed newspaper, *La Stampa*. The Friday edition comes with a supplement on music and other entertainment. ⊠ *Via XX Settembre 87, Centro* ☏ *011/4361540.*

Giovanni Agnelli Auditorium. Classical music concerts are held at the theatre designed by Renzo Piano in the renovated Lingotto building; internationally famous conductors and orchestras are frequent guests. ⊠ *Via Nizza 280, Lingotto* ☏ *011/6677415* ⊕ *www.lingottomusica.it.*

MITO Settembre Musica Festival. Held for three weeks in September in a variety of venues, this is a popular festival of classical music. The program of performances and tickets become available in May each year. ⊠ *Via San Francesco da Paola 3* ☏ *011/4424787* ⊕ *www. mitosettembremusica.it.*

OPERA

Teatro Regio. Premieres at one of Italy's leading opera houses sell out well in advance. You can buy tickets for most performances at the box office or on the website, where discounts are offered on the day of the performance. The season runs from October through June. ⊠ *Piazza Castello 215, Centro* ☏ *011/8815557* ⊕ *www.teatroregio.torino.it.*

NIGHTLIFE

Two areas of Turin are enormously popular nightlife destinations: the Quadrilatero, to the north of the city center, and the Murazzi embankment, near the Ponte Vittorio Emanuele I. The center of town is also popular, especially earlier in the evening.

Caffè Elena. This wine bar is a trendy place for an aperitif or a pre-disco drink. It's in the piazza at the end of Via Po. ⊠ *Piazza Vittorio Veneto 5, Centro* ☏ *011/8123341.*

Jammin'. On the Murazzi, near the Ponte Vittorio Emanuele I, this is a popular disco with live music on Friday. ⊠ *Murazzi del Po 17, Centro* ☏ *011/882869* ⊙ *May–Sept., Mon.–Sat. 9 pm–4 am.*

Pastis. The Quadrilatero Romano, which roughly corresponds to the grid pattern of Roman Turin near Piazza della Reppublica, is a hopping area filled with nightclubs and ethnic restaurants. Places open and close with startling frequency here, but Pastis has shown considerable staying power—several local cultural groups hold their meetings in the bar. ⊠ *Piazza Emanuele Filiberto 9b, Centro* ☏ *011/5211085.*

SPORTS AND THE OUTDOORS

BICYCLING

Ufficio Iniziative Ambientali (*Office for Environmental Initiatives*). Turin has about 160 km (100 miles) of bike paths running through the city and its parks. From April to October, bicycles are available for daily rental at stands. The UIA website provides a detailed map of the bike paths and rental locations. ⊠ *Via Padova 29, Madonna di Campagna* ☏ *011/4020177* ⊕ *www.comune.torino.it/ambiente/bici.*

SHOPPING

CHOCOLATE

The tradition of making chocolate began in Italy in Turin during the early 17th century. Chocolate at that time was an aristocratic drink, but in the 19th century a Piedmontese invention made it possible to further refine cocoa to create solid bars and candies.

Peyrano. The most famous of all Turin chocolates is the wedge-shape *gianduiotto*, flavored with hazelnuts and first concocted in 1867. The tradition has been continued at this small, family-run shop, where more than 80 types of chocolates are made. ⊠ *Corso Moncalieri 47, Centro* ☏ *011/6602202* ⊕ *www.peyrano.it.*

Stratta. In business since 1836, this famed shop sells confectionery of all kinds—not just the chocolates in the lavish window displays but also fancy cookies, rum-laced fudges, and magnificent cakes. ⊠ *Piazza San Carlo 191, Centro* ☎ *011/547920.*

MARKETS

Balon Flea Market. Go to this famous market on Saturday morning for excellent bargains on secondhand books and clothing. There is good browsing to be had among stalls, which include local specialties such as gianduiotti. (Be aware, however, that the market is also famous for its pickpockets.) ⊠ *Piazza Repubblica, Centro.*

Gran Balon. The second Sunday of every month this antiques market sets up shop in Piazza Repubblica. ⊠ *Piazza Repubblica, Centro.*

SPECIALTY STORES

Many people know that Turin produces more than 75% of Italy's cars, but they're often unaware that it's also a hub for clothing manufacturing. Top-quality boutiques stocking local, national, and international lines are clustered along Via Roma and Via Garibaldi. Piazza San Carlo, Via Po, and Via Maria Vittoria are lined with antiques shops, some of which specialize in 18th-century furniture and domestic items.

Borgiattino. Specialty food stores and delicatessens abound in central Turin, but for a truly spectacular array of cheeses and other delicacies this should be your first stop. ⊠ *Corso Vinzaglio 29, Centro* ☎ *011/5629075.*

Eataly. Now with branches in Milan, Bologna, New York, and Tokyo, this is perhaps Turin's most famous food emporium. In addition to a food market, food-related bookstore, kitchen equipment, and a wine bar, there are several different food counters and restaurants serving hamburgers, haute cuisine, and lots more in between. ⊠ *Via Nizza 230, Lingotto* ☎ *011/19506801* ⊕ *www.eatalytorino.it.*

THE MONFERRATO AND THE LANGHE

Southeast of Turin, in the hilly wooded area around Asti known as the Monferrato, and farther south in a similar area around Alba known as the Langhe, the landscape is a patchwork of vineyards and dark woods dotted with hill towns and castles. This is wine country, producing some of Italy's most famous reds and sparkling whites. And hidden away in the woods are the secret places where hunters and their dogs unearth the precious, aromatic truffles worth their weight in gold at Alba's truffle fair.

Continued on page 424

ON THE TRAIL OF BAROLO

Picture yourself in the background of a grand medieval mural, and you won't be far off from what you experience driving through the idyllic wooded landscape south of Turin, in Piedmont's Langhe district.

The crests of the graceful hills are dotted with villages, each lorded over by an ancient castle. The gentle slopes of the valleys below are lined with row upon row of Nebbiolo grapes, the choicest of which are used to make Barolo wine. Dubbed "the king of wines and wine of kings" in the 19th century after finding favor with King Carlo Alberto, Barolo still wears the crown, despite stiff competition from all corners of Italy.

The Langhe district is smaller and surprisingly less visited by food-and-wine enthusiasts than Chianti and the surrounding areas of Tuscany, but it yields similar rewards. The best way to tour the Barolo-producing region is on day trips from the delightful truffle town of Alba—getting around is easy, the country roads are gorgeous, and the wine is fit for a king.

Above, Serralunga's castle
Right, bottles of old vintage Barolo

ALL ABOUT BAROLO

The Nebbiolo grapes that go into this famous wine come not just from Barolo proper (the area surrounding the tiny town of Barolo), but also from a small zone that encompasses the hill towns of Novello, Monforte d'Alba, Serralunga d'Alba, Castiglione Falletto, La Morra, and Verduno. All are connected by small but easy-to-navigate roads.

When wine lovers talk about Barolo, they talk about tannins—the quality that makes red wine dry out your mouth. Tannins come from the grape skins; red wine—which gets its color from the skins—has them, white wine doesn't. Tannins can be balanced out by acidity (the quality that makes your mouth water), but they also soften over time. As a good red wine matures, flavors emerge more clearly, achieving a harmonious balance of taste and texture.

A bottle of Barolo is often born so overwhelmingly tannic that many aficionados won't touch the stuff until it has aged 10 or 15 years. But a good Barolo ages beautifully, eventually spawning complex, intermingled tastes of tobacco, roses, and earth. It's not uncommon to see bottles for sale from the 1960s, 1950s, or even the 1930s.

WHERE TO DRINK IT

The word *enoteca* in Italian can mean a wine store, or a wine bar, or both. The words "wine bar," on the other hand—which are becoming increasingly trendy—mean just that. Either way, these are great places to sample and buy the wines of the Langhe.

An excellent enoteca in Alba is **Vincafé** (Via V. Emanuele, 12, Alba, 0173/364603, www.vincafe.com). It specializes in tastes of Langhe wines, accompanied by *salumi* (cured meats), cheeses, and other regional products. More than 350 wines, as well as grappas and liqueurs, grace Vincafé's distinguished list. It's open from noon to midnight, and there's food until 9 pm.

In Barolo visit the **Enoteca Regionale del Barolo** (Castello di Barolo, Piazza Falletti 1, 0173/5627, www.enotecadelbarolo.it) which represents all the wine producers of the region and offers tastings of selected wines.

HOW MUCH DOES IT COST?

The most reasonably priced, but still enjoyable Barolos will cost you €20 to €30. A very good but not top-of-the-line bottle will cost €40 to €60. For a top-of-the-line bottle you may spend anywhere from €80 to €200.

LABELS TO LOOK FOR

Barolo is a strictly controlled denomination, but that doesn't mean all Barolos are equal. Legendary producers include Prunotto, Aldo Conterno, Giacomo Conterno, Bruno Giacosa, Famiglia Anselma, Mascarello, Pio Cesare, and Michele Chiarlo.

WINE ESTATES TO VISIT

Right in the town of Barolo, an easy, if touristy, option for a visit is **Marchesi di Barolo** (Via Alba 12, Barolo, 0173/564400, www.marchesibarolo.com). In the estate's user-friendly enoteca you can taste wine, buy thousands of different bottles from vintages going way back, and look at display bottles, including an 1859 Barolo. Marchesi di Barolo's *cantine* (wine cellars, Via Roma 1, Barolo) are open daily 10:30–5:30. The staff here is used to catering to visitors, so you won't have to worry too much about endearing yourself to them.

From there you might want to graduate to **Famiglia Anselma** (Loc. Castello della Volta, Barolo, 0173/560511, www.anselma.it). Winemaker Maurizio Anselma, in his mid-20s, is something of a prodigy in the Barolo world, and he's quite open to visitors. He is known for his steadfast commitment to produce only Barolo—nothing else—and for his policy of holding his wines for several years before release.

A good, accessible example of the new school of Barolo winemaking is **Podere Rocche dei Manzoni** (3, Loc. Manzini Soprano, Monforte d'Alba, 0173/78421, www.barolobig.com). The facade of the cantina is like a Roman temple of brick, complete with imposing columns. Rocche dei Manzoni's reds include four Barolos, one Dolcetto, one Langhe Rosso, two Langhe DOCs, and two Barbera d'Albas.

WINE TOUR TIPS

Keep in mind that visiting wineries in Italy is different from what you might have experienced in the Napa Valley or in France. Wherever you go, reservations are required and you may be the only person or group on the tour.

Wine buyers and wine professionals are the expected audience for tours. While this attitude is slowly changing and many winemakers are beginning to welcome interested outsiders, it's important to come in with an open mind and respect that the winemaker probably knows more about wine than you do. It helps to speak Italian, but if you don't, the international language of effusive compliments can still go a long way.

BEYOND BAROLO

Neive, in the Barbaresco region

By no means do the fruits of the Langhe end with Barolo. The region boasts Italy's highest concentration of DOC (denominazione di origine controllata) and DOCG (denominazione di origine controllata e garantita) wines, the two most prestigious categories of appellation in Italy. The other DOCG in the Langhe is Barbaresco, which, like Barolo, is made from the Nebbiolo grape. Barbaresco is not quite as tannic as Barolo, however, and can be drunk younger. www.enotecadelbarbaresco.it

7

IN FOCUS ON THE TRAIL OF BAROLO

ASTI

60 km (37 miles) southeast of Turin.

Asti is best known outside Italy for its wines—excellent reds as well as the famous sparkling white spumante—and its strategic position on trade routes at Turin, Milan, and Genoa has given it a broad economic base. In the 12th century Asti began to develop as a republic, at a time when other Italian cities were also flexing their economic and military muscles. It flourished in the following century, when the inhabitants began erecting lofty **towers** (⊠ *West end of Corso Vittorio Alfieri*) for its defense. As in Pavia, near Milan, this gave rise to the medieval nickname "city of a hundred towers." In the center of Asti some of these remain, among them the 13th-century **Torre Comentina** and the well-preserved **Torre Troyana,** a tall, slender tower attached to the **Palazzo Troya.** The 18th-century church of **Santa Caterina** has incorporated one of Asti's medieval towers, the **Torre Romana** (itself built on an ancient Roman base), as its bell tower. Corso Vittorio Alfieri is Asti's main thoroughfare, running west–east across the city. This road, known in medieval times as Contrada Maestra, was built by the Romans.

GETTING HERE AND AROUND
Asti is less than an hour away from Turin by car on the A21. GTT bus service connects the two towns, but isn't direct. Train service to Asti, on the other hand, is frequent and fast.

WHEN TO GO
Douja d'Or National Wine Festival. For 10 days in early September Asti is host to a popular wine festival—an opportunity to see Asti and celebrate the product that made it famous. During the course of the festival a competition is held to award "Oscars" to the best wine producers, and stands for wine tastings allow visitors to judge the winners for themselves. Musical events and other activities accompany the festival. Contact the tourist office for the schedule of events. ☎ *0141/53035 tourist office* ⊕ *www.astiturismo.it.*

Palio di Asti. September is a month of fairs and celebrations in Asti, and this horse race that's run through the streets of town is the highlight. First mentioned in 1275, this annual event has been going strong ever since. After an elaborate procession in period costumes, nine horses and jockeys representing different sections of town vie for the honor of claiming the *palio,* a symbolic flag of victory.

VISITOR INFORMATION
Asti Tourism Office ⊠ *Piazza Alfieri 34* ☎ *0141/530357* ⊕ *www.astiturismo.it.*

EXPLORING
Duomo. Dedicated to the Assumption of the Virgin, the Duomo is an object lesson in the evolution of Gothic architecture. Built in the early 14th century, it is decorated so as to emphasize geometry and verticality: pointed arches and narrow vaults contrast with the earlier, Romanesque attention to balance and symmetry. The porch on the south side of the cathedral facing the square was built in 1470 and represents the Gothic style at its most florid and excessive. ⊠ *Via San Giovanni 8* ☎ *0141/592924* ☉ *Daily 8:30–noon and 3:30–5:30.*

Skiing in Piedmont and Valle d'Aosta

Skiing is the major sport in both Piedmont and Valle d'Aosta. Excellent facilities abound at resort towns such as Courmayeur and Breuil-Cervinia. The so-called Via Lattea (Milky Way)—five skiing areas near Sestriere with 400 km (almost 250 miles) of linked runs and 90 ski lifts—provides practically unlimited skiing. Lift tickets, running around €35 for a day's pass, are a good deal compared to those at major U.S. resorts.

To Italian skiers, a weeklong holiday on the slopes is known as a *settimana*

bianca (white week). Ski resort hotels in Piedmont and Valle d'Aosta encourage these getaways by offering six- and seven-day packages, and though they're designed with the domestic market in mind, you can get a bargain by taking advantage of the offers. The packages usually, though not always, include half or full board.

You should have your passport with you if you plan a day trip into Switzerland—though odds are you won't be asked to show it.

San Secondo. This Gothic church is dedicated to Asti's patron saint, reputedly decapitated by the Emperor Hadrian on this same spot. San Secondo is also the patron of the city's favorite folklore and sporting event, the annual Palio di Asti, a colorful medieval-style horse race that's similar to Siena's. It's held each year on the third Sunday of September in the vast Campo del Palio to the south of the church. ⊠ *Piazza San Secondo, south of Corso Vittorio Alfieri* ☎ *0141/530066* ⊗ *Mon.–Sat. 10:45–noon and 3:30–5:30, Sun. 3:30–5:30.*

WHERE TO EAT

$$$$
PIEDMONTESE
Fodor's Choice
★

✕ **Gener Neuv.** This family-run restaurant, one of Italy's finest, is known for its rustic elegance. The setting on the bank of the Tanaro River is splendid. The menu of regional specialties may include agnolotti *ai tre stufati* (with fillings of ground rabbit, veal, and pork), and to finish, *zabaione caldo al vino Vecchio Samperi* (warm eggnog flavored with a dessert wine). Fixed-price menus are available with or without the wine included. As you might expect, the wine list is first-rate. $ *Average meal: €75* ⊠ *Lungo Tanaro 4* ☎ *0141/557270* ⊕ *www.generneuv. it* ⌂ *Reservations essential* ⊗ *Closed Aug. and Mon. No dinner Sun.*

$$
PIEDMONTESE

✕ **L'Angolo del Beato.** Regional specialties such as *bagna cauda* (literally "hot bath," a dip for vegetables made with anchovies, garlic, butter, and olive oil) and *tagliolini al ragu di anatra* (pasta with a duck sauce) are the main attractions at this Asti institution, housed in a building that dates to the 12th century. There's also a good wine list. $ *Average meal: €45* ⊠ *Via Guttuari 12* ☎ *0141/531668* ⊕ *www.angolodelbeato. it* ⊗ *Closed Sun., last wk of Dec., 1st wk of Jan., and 3 wks in Aug.*

WHERE TO STAY

For expanded hotel reviews, visit Fodors.com.

$
B&B/INN

▦ **Reale.** Spacious rooms in a 19th-century building on Asti's main square are eclectically decorated, with a mix of contemporary and period furniture. **Pros:** spacious rooms; central location. **Cons:** lobby area is a little worn; rooms facing the main square can be noisy.

$ *Rooms from: €120* ✉ *Piazza Alfieri 6* ☎ *0141/530240* ⊕ *www.
hotelristorantereale.it* ⇌ *24 rooms* ❍❘ *Breakfast.*

$

HOTEL

🛏 **Relais Sant'Uffizio.** It's surprising to know that this now delightfully
peaceful and elegant retreat, with a luxurious spa and swimming pool,
surrounded by vineyards and rolling hills, was once home to the 16th-
century Roman Catholic inquisition. **Pros:** tranquil and beautiful location; excellent spa and exercise facilities; friendly staff; very good value.
Cons: 20 km (12 miles) north of Asti and isolated; private transportation required. $ *Rooms from: €120* ✉ *Strada Sant Uffizio 1, Cioccaro
di Penango, Asti* ☎ *0141/916292* ⊕ *www.relaissantuffizio.com* ⇌ *39
rooms, 2 suites* ☉ *Closed Feb.* ❍❘ *Breakfast.*

SHOPPING

Tuit. This shop and café on a quiet street just off Piazza Alfieri is a branch
of Turin's Eataly food emporium. It's a great place to shop for local
and regional food specialties or to enjoy a light meal. Both the *tortino
di melanzane di pomodori pachino* (eggplant flan with Sicilian cherry
tomatoes) and the risotto *mantecato alla zucca e amaretti* (with butter,
pumpkin, and macaroons) are quite delicious. ✉ *Via Carlo Grandi 3*
☎ *0141/095813* ⊕ *www.tuit.it* ☉ *Tues.–Sat. 10–10.*

ALBA

30 km (18 miles) southwest of Asti.

This small town has a gracious atmosphere and a compact core studded
with medieval towers and Gothic buildings. In addition to being a wine
center of the region, Alba is known as the "City of the White Truffle"
for the dirty little tubers that command a higher price per ounce than
diamonds. For picking out your truffle and having a few wisps shaved
on top of your food, expect to shell out an extra €16 or so—which may
be worth it, at least once.

GETTING HERE AND AROUND

By car from Turin follow the A6 south to Marene and then take the A33
east. The A33 *autostrada* connects Asti and Alba. GTT offers frequent
bus service between Alba and Turin—the journey takes approximately
1½ hours. There's no direct train service, but you can get to Alba from
Turin by making one transfer in Asti, Bra, or Cavallermaggiore; the
entire trip takes about 1½ hours.

VISITOR INFORMATION

Alba Tourism Office ✉ *Piazza Risorgimento 2* ☎ *0173/35833*
⊕ *www.langheroero.it.*

WHERE TO EAT

$$

PIEDMONTESE

✗ **La Libera.** Modern and subdued, this small spot on a quiet back street
is conducive to slow, relaxed dining. The antipasti include a splendid
piatto della tradizione (an array of typical Piedmont starters). As a
first course, the ravioli *in brodo di cappone* (pasta in a fish broth) is
excellent. A variety of tasty meat dishes make up the list of second
courses, and there's a superb selection of cheeses to follow. The des-
serts are divine and the wine list extensive, with over six pages dedi-
cated to Barolo alone. $ *Average meal: €45* ✉ *Via Elvio Pertinace 24a*

☎ 0173/293155 🌐 *www.lalibera.com* ⏲ *Closed for several wks in Feb. and July. No lunch Sun. and Mon.*

$$$ PIEDMONTESE 🍴 **Locanda del Pilone.** The elegant, formal dining room of the Locanda del Pilone hotel is one of the best restaurants in the region, serving refined variations of traditional dishes. The risotto *carnaroli cru "Campo dell'Aia," scampi e cardi Gobbi di Nizza Monferrato* (a white-wine risotto with shrimp and cardoons) is as delicious as it is unusual. [$] *Average meal: €60* ✉ *Località Madonna di Como 34* ☎ *0173/366616* 🌐 *www.locandadelpilone.com.*

$ PIEDMONTESE 🍴 **Vigin Mudest.** Delicious regional specialties are served at this bustling, family-run restaurant in the center of Alba. There's a sumptuous buffet spread of hot and cold antipasti, and their version of *carne cruda albese* (beef carpaccio in the style of Alba) is a favorite with the locals who flock here. All of the pasta (including the thin egg yolk–rich *tajarin* traditional to the region) is homemade, and the risotto *al Barolo* is particularly tasty. Outdoor seating is available in summer. [$] *Average meal: €25* ✉ *Via Vernazza 11* ☎ *0173/441701* 🌐 *www.viginmudest.it* ✍ *Reservations essential* ⏲ *Closed Mon.*

WHERE TO STAY

For expanded hotel reviews, visit Fodors.com.

$ B&B/INN 🏨 **La Meridiana.** The Belle Epoque reigns in this lovely manor house on a hill overlooking the historic center (the views are enjoyed from the many terraces and balconies) and surrounded by grapevines. **Pros:** friendly, family atmosphere; in a secluded setting convenient for exploring the Langhe. **Cons:** long walk to nearest restaurants (though some units have kitchens); no air-conditioning in some rooms. [$] *Rooms from: €95* ✉ *Località Altavilla 9* ☎📠 *0173/440112* 🌐 *www.villalameridianaalba.it* 🛏 *8 rooms, 2 suites* 💳 *No credit cards* 🍽 *Breakfast.*

$$ B&B/INN 🏨 **Locanda del Pilone.** It would be hard to imagine a more commanding position for these simply but tastefully decorated accommodations above Alba. **Pros:** spectacular location with 360-degree views; excellent restaurant. **Cons:** isolation makes own transportation a must; no air-conditioning. [$] *Rooms from: €185* ✉ *Località Madonna di Como 34* ☎ *0173/366616* 🌐 *www.locandadelpilone.it* 🛏 *7 rooms, 1 suite* 🍽 *Breakfast.*

$$ B&B/INN 🏨 **Palazzo Finati.** A carefully restored 19th-century town house with rooms decorated individually in contemporary style has charm and character that set it apart from the other more business-oriented hotels in Alba. **Pros:** quiet location in the center of town; rooms facing the courtyard have terraces; changing exhibitions of contemporary art adorn the walls. **Cons:** staff coverage is limited at night; breakfast room is a bit gloomy. [$] *Rooms from: €170* ✉ *Via Vernazza 8* ☎📠 *0173/366324* 🌐 *www.palazzofinati.it* 🛏 *4 rooms, 5 suites* ⏲ *Closed 2 wks in Aug., and Christmas–mid-Jan.* 🍽 *Breakfast.*

FESTIVALS

Fiera Internazionale del Tartufo Bianco (*International White Truffle Fair*). From the second Saturday in October to the second Sunday in November, Alba hosts an internationally famous truffle fair, held on weekends. Aficionados of this pungent, yet delicious, fungus come from all over

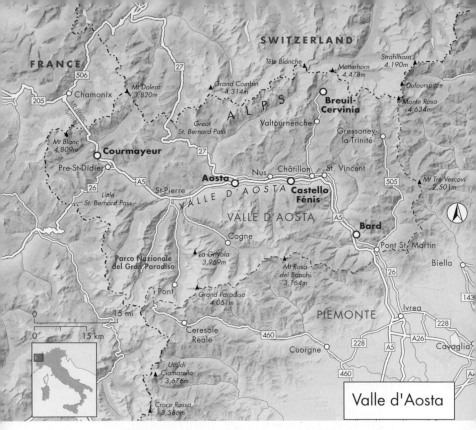

Valle d'Aosta

the world to buy and to taste white truffles at the height of their season. Though the affair is very commercialized, it still makes Alba a great place to visit in the fall. Note that hotel and restaurant reservations for October and November should be made well in advance. ☒ *Cortile della Madalena* ☎ *0173/361051* ⊕ *www.fieradeltartufo.org.*

Palio degli Asini. Alba's hilarious donkey race, a spoof of Asti's serious horse race, is held on the first Sunday of October. Tickets to watch this competition, with riders dressed in medieval garb astride their stubborn beasts, can be hard to get; they go on sale at the beginning of July each year. Contact Alba's tourist information office for details. ☎ *0173/35833 tourist office* ⊕ *www.langheroero.it.*

VALLE D'AOSTA

In Valle d'Aosta, a semiautonomous, bilingual region tucked away at the border with France and Switzerland, the unspoiled beauty of the highest peaks in the Alps, the Matterhorn and Monte Bianco, competes with the magnificent scenery of Italy's oldest national park, Gran Paradiso. Luckily, you don't have to choose—the region is small, so you can fit skiing, après-ski, and wild ibex into one memorable trip. The main Aosta Valley, largely on an east–west axis, is hemmed in by high mountains where glaciers have gouged out 14 tributary valleys, six to the north and eight to the south. A car is helpful here, but take care: though distances are relatively short as the crow flies, steep slopes and winding roads add to your mileage and travel time.

Coming up from Turin, beyond Ivrea, the road takes you through countryside that passes through steep ravines guarded by brooding, romantic castles. Pont St. Martin, about 18 km (11 miles) north of Ivrea, is the beginning of bilingual (Italian and French) territory.

BARD

65 km (40 miles) north of Turin.

GETTING HERE AND AROUND

Bard is just off the A5 Autostrada that runs north from Turin into the Valle d'Aosta—by car the trip takes about an hour. Train service from Turin is infrequent, but there's regular service to and from Aosta. Traveling to Bard by bus is not a viable option.

EXPLORING

FAMILY **Forte di Bard.** A few minutes beyond the French-speaking village of Pont St. Martin, you pass through the narrow Gorge de Bard to reach the fortress that has stood guarding the valley entrance for more than eight centuries. In 1800 Napoléon entered Italy through this valley, using the cover of darkness to get his artillery units past the castle unnoticed. Ten years later he remembered this inconvenience and had the fortress destroyed. The fort was rebuilt in the 19th century; these days it houses the lavishly multimedia **Museo degli Alpi,** dedicated to the history and culture of the Alps and the Valle d'Aosta region. ☎ *0125/833811* ⊕ *www.fortedibard.it* 🎫 *€8* ☉ *Wed.–Fri. 10–6, weekends 10–7; last entrance 1 hr before closing.*

EN ROUTE Between Bard and the town of Donnas, 5 km (3 miles) south along the S26, you can walk on a short but fascinating section of a 1st-century Roman consular road that passed here on its way to France. Still showing the deeply worn tracks left by the passage of cart and chariot wheels, this section of road includes an archway carved through solid rock (used during the Middle Ages as the city gate of Donnas) and a milestone (XXXVI, to indicate 36 Roman miles from Aosta).

BREUIL-CERVINIA/THE MATTERHORN

50 km (30 miles) north of Bard, 116 km (72 miles) north of Turin.

GETTING HERE AND AROUND

From Aosta take the A5 and then the SR46 (one hour); from Turin take the A5 and then the SR46 (90 minutes). SADEM has regular bus service from Turin; SAVDA buses travel here from Milan. Breuil-Cervinia isn't on a train line.

VISITOR INFORMATION

Breuil-Cervinia Tourism Office ✉ *Piazzale Funivie* ☎ *0166/944311* ⊕ *www.cervinia.it.*

EXPLORING

Matterhorn (*Monte Cervino in Italian; Mont Cervin in French*). The famous peak straddles the border between Italy and Switzerland, and all sightseeing and skiing facilities are operated jointly. Splendid views of the peak can be seen from **Plateau Rosa** and the **Cresta del Furggen,** both of which can be reached by cable car from the center of Breuil-Cervinia. Although many locals complain that the tourist facilities and condominiums have changed the face of their beloved village, the cable car does give access to climbing and off-trail skiing in ridges that were once inaccessible.

WHERE TO STAY

For expanded hotel reviews, visit Fodors.com.

$$ B&B/INN **Cime Bianche.** This calm, quiet mountain lodge offers commanding views of the Matterhorn and surrounding peaks from the balconies of its simply furnished, wood-paneled guest rooms. **Pros:** next to the ski slopes; great restaurant; lovely views. **Cons:** lobby is showing wear; busy during the ski season; location is far from everything but slopes; multiday stays with some meals usually required. [$] *Rooms from: €160* ✉ *Località La Vieille 44, near ski lift* ☎ *0166/949046* 🌐 *www.hotelcimebianche.com* *13 rooms* 🕓 *Closed May, June, and Oct. Restaurant closed Mon.* 🍴 *Some meals.*

$$$$ RESORT **Hermitage.** The entryway's marble relief of Saint Theodolus reminds you that this was the site of a hermitage, but asceticism has given way to comfort and elegance—a fire is always glowing in the enormous hearth, the dining room is candlelighted, the bright bedrooms have balconies, and suites have antique fireplaces and 18th-century furnishings. **Pros:** superlative staff; refined atmosphere; frequent shuttle service into town and to ski lifts. **Cons:** located 2 km (1 mile) from the town center; half board is mandatory during the winter season. [$] *Rooms from: €720* ✉ *Via Piolet 1, Località Chapellette* ☎ *0166/948998* 🌐 *www.hotelhermitage.com* *30 rooms, 6 suites* 🕓 *Closed May, June, Sept., and Nov.* 🍴 *Some meals.*

$$$ B&B/INN **Les Neiges d'Antan.** In an evergreen forest at Perrères, just outside Cervinia, this family-run inn is quiet and cozy, with three big fireplaces and a nice view of the Matterhorn. **Pros:** secluded and beautiful setting; excellent restaurant; well-designed spa facilities. **Cons:** 5 km (3 miles) outside Breuil-Cervinia (a car is essential); entrance and lobby areas are showing some wear. [$] *Rooms from: €280* ✉ *Frazione Perrères 10* ☎ *0166/948775* 🌐 *www.lesneigesdantan.it* *21 rooms, 3 suites* 🕓 *Closed May and June* 🍴 *Breakfast.*

SPORTS AND THE OUTDOORS

CLIMBING

Serious climbers can make the ascent of the Matterhorn from Breuil-Cervinia after registering with the local mountaineering officials at the tourist office. This ascent is for experienced climbers only.

Società delle Guide Alpine. The Society's guides are available to accompany you on treks and also lead skiing, canyoning, and ice-climbing excursions. ✉ *Strada Villair 2, Courmayeur* ☎ *0165/842064* 🌐 *www.guidecourmayeur.com.*

Less demanding hikes follow the lower slopes of the valley of the River Marmore, to the south of town.

SKIING

Sixty lifts and a few hundred miles of ski runs ranging from beginner to expert make Breuil-Cervinia one of the best and most popular resort areas in Italy. Because the slopes border a glacier, there's skiing year-round.

CASTELLO FÉNIS

34 km (22 miles) northwest of Bard, 104 km (65 miles) north of Turin.

GETTING HERE AND AROUND

To reach the castle by car, take the Nus exit from the main A5 Autostrada. SAVDA buses provide infrequent service between Aosta and Fénis. The closest train station, in Nus, is a 5-km (3-mile) walk from the castle.

EXPLORING

FAMILY

Fodor's Choice

★

Castello Fénis. The best-preserved medieval fortress in Valle d'Aosta, this many-turreted castle was built in the mid-14th century by Aimone di Challant, a member of a prolific family related to the Savoys. The castle, which used a double ring of walls for its defense, would make a perfect setting for a fairy tale, given its pointed towers, portcullises, and spiral staircases. The 15th-century courtyard surrounded by wooden balconies is elegantly decorated with well-preserved frescoes. Inside you can see the kitchen, with an enormous fireplace that provided central heat in winter; the armory; and the spacious, well-lighted rooms used by the lord and lady of the manor. If you have time to visit only one castle in Valle d'Aosta, this should be it. ⊠ *Frazione Chez Croiset 22* 📞 *0165/764263* 🎫 *€5* ⏱ *Mar.–Sept., daily 9–7; Oct.–Feb., daily 10–12:30 and 1:30–5. Maximum of 25 people allowed to enter every ½ hr.*

EN
ROUTE

The highway continues climbing through Valle d'Aosta to the town of Aosta itself. The road at this point is heading almost due west, with rivulets from the wilderness reserve Parco Nazionale del Gran Paradiso streaming down from the left to join the Dora Baltea River, one of the major tributaries of the Po and an increasingly popular spot for rafting. Be careful driving here in late spring, when melting snow can turn some of these streams into torrents.

AOSTA

12 km (7 miles) west of Castello Fénis, 113 km (70 miles) north of Turin.

GETTING HERE AND AROUND

Aosta can easily be reached by car or bus from Milan and Turin. The town is off the main A5 Autostrada. SAVDA buses regularly travel to and from Milan, Turin, and Chamonix in France. Direct train service (two hours) is also available from Turin, but a change of trains is required if traveling here from Milan (three hours).

WHEN TO GO

Sant'Orso Fair. On the last weekend of January, the streets of Aosta are brightened by an arts-and-crafts market that brings artisans from all over the Valle d'Aosta. All the traditional techniques are featured: wood carving and sculpture, soapstone work, wrought iron, leather, wool, lace, and household items of all kinds. Food and wine are sold at outdoor stands and wandering minstrels enliven the whole event. Contact the tourist office for details.

VISITOR INFORMATION

Aosta Tourism Office ⊠ *Piazza Porta Praetoria 3* ☎ *0165/236627* ⊕ *www.lovevda.it.*

EXPLORING

Arco di Augusto. Aosta stands at the junction of two of the important trade routes that connect France and Italy—the valleys of the Rhône and the Isère. Its significance as a trading post was recognized by the Romans, who built a garrison here in the 1st century BC. At the eastern entrance to town, in the Piazza Arco d'Augusto and commanding a fine view over Aosta and the mountains, stands the Arco di Augusto (Arch of Augustus), built in 25 BC to mark Rome's victory over the Celtic Salassi tribe. (The sloping roof was added in 1716 in an attempt to keep rain from seeping between the stones.) The present-day layout of streets in this small city tucked away in the Alps more than 644 km (400 miles) from Rome is the clearest example of Roman urban planning in Italy. Well-preserved Roman walls form a perfect rectangle around the center of Aosta, and the regular pattern of streets reflects its role as a military stronghold. Saint Anselm, born in Aosta, later became England's Archbishop of Canterbury.

Collegiata di Sant'Orso. This church has layers of history literally visible in its architecture. Originally there was a 6th-century chapel on this site founded by the Archdeacon Orso, a local saint. Most of this structure was destroyed or hidden when an 11th-century church was erected over it. This church, in turn, was encrusted with Gothic, and later Baroque, features, resulting in a jigsaw puzzle of styles, but, surprisingly, not a chaotic jumble. The 11th-century features are almost untouched in the crypt, and if you go up the stairs on the left from the main church you can see the 11th-century frescoes (ask the sacristan who let you in). These restored frescoes depict the life of Christ and the apostles. Although only the tops are visible, you can see the expressions on the faces of the disciples. Take the outside doorway to the right of the main entrance to see the church's crowning glory, its 12th-century cloister, enclosed by some 40 stone columns with masterfully carved capitals depicting scenes from the Old and New Testaments and the life of Saint Orso. The turrets and spires of Aosta peek out above. ⊠ *Via Sant'Orso 10* ☎ *0165/262026* ◷ *Apr.–Sept., daily 9–5; Oct.–Mar., daily 10–5.*

Duomo. Aosta's cathedral dates from the 10th century, but all that remains from that period are the bell towers. The decoration inside is primarily Gothic, but the main attraction predates that era by 1,000 years: among the many ornate objects housed in the treasury is a carved ivory diptych from AD 406 portraying the Roman Emperor Honorius.

✉ *Via Monsignor de Sales 3* ☎ *0165/40251* ⏲ *Duomo: Easter–Sept. 7, Mon.–Sat. 6:30 pm–8 pm, Sun. 7 am–8 pm; Sept. 8–Easter, Mon.–Sat. 6:30–noon and 3–7, Sun. 7–noon and 3–7. Treasury: Apr.–Sept., Tues.–Sun. 9–11:30 and 3–5:30; Oct.–Mar., Sun. 3–5:30.*

Roman Porta Pretoria. This huge gateway, regally guarding the city, is a remarkable relic from the Roman era. The area between the massive inner and outer walls was used as a small parade ground for the changing of the guard. ✉ *West end of Via Sant'Anselmo.*

Teatro Romano. The 72-foot-high ruin of the facade of the Teatro Romano guards the remains of the 1st-century BC amphitheater, which once held 20,000 spectators. Only a bit of the outside wall and seven of the amphitheater's original 60 arches remain. The latter, once incorporated into medieval buildings, are being brought to light by ongoing archaeological excavations. ✉ *Via Anfiteatro 4.*

WHERE TO EAT

$$ ITALIAN 🍴 **La Brasserie du Commerce.** In the heart of Aosta, near the Piazza Emile Chanoux, stands this small and busy restaurant. On a sunny summer day try to snag a table in the restaurant's courtyard garden. La Brasserie specializes in grilled meat dishes; also on the menu are typical valley dishes such as fonduta, as well as many vegetable dishes and chef's salads. Pizza is also served, but only on the ground floor. [$] *Average meal: €35* ✉ *Via de Tillier 10* ☎ *0165/35613* 🌐 *www.brasserieducommerce.com* ⏲ *Closed Sun.*

$$ NORTHERN ITALIAN 🍴 **Praetoria.** Just outside the Porta Pretoria, this simple and unpretentious restaurant serves hearty local dishes such as *crespelle alla valdostana* (crepes with cheese and ham). The pasta is made on the premises, and all of the menu offerings are prepared from traditional recipes. [$] *Average meal: €35* ✉ *Via Sant'Anselmo 9* ☎ *0165/44356* ⏲ *Closed Thurs. No dinner Wed.*

$$$ NORTHERN ITALIAN 🍴 **Vecchio Ristoro.** The elegant, intimate spaces of a converted mill are furnished with antiques, and a traditional ceramic stove provides additional warmth in cool weather. The chef-proprietor takes pride in creative versions of regional recipes, including *gnocchetti di castagnesu crema di zucca* (chestnut gnocchi with pumpkin cream) and *quaglietto disossata farcita alle castagne fatta al forno* (roast quail with chestnut stuffing). [$] *Average meal: €60* ✉ *Via Tourneuve 4* ☎ *0165/33238* 🌐 *www.ristorantevecchioristoro.it* ⏲ *Closed Sun., June, and 1 wk in Nov. No lunch Mon.*

WHERE TO STAY

For expanded hotel reviews, visit Fodors.com.

$ B&B/INN 🏨 **Casa Ospitaliera del Gran San Bernardo.** Here's your chance to sleep in a 12th-century castle without emptying your wallet. **Pros:** good base for budget-conscious skiers and hikers; secluded atmosphere. **Cons:** isolated location (no towns or restaurants nearby); extremely simple accommodations. [$] *Rooms from: €105* ✉ *Rue de Flassin 3, Saint-Oyen* ☎ *0165/78247* 🌐 *www.gsbernard.net* 🛏 *15 rooms* ⏲ *Closed May* 🍽 *Breakfast.*

$$ B&B/INN 🏨 **Le Miramonti.** Built on the banks of a branch of the Dora Baltea River, this delightful, small, family-run establishment offers all the woody Alpine interiors, traditional regional furnishings, and other homey

7

comforts needed for a relaxing evening after a day of hiking, skiing, mountain biking, or river rafting. **Pros:** friendly, efficient service; excellent location for outdoor sports. **Cons:** isolated location in a small village; some rooms are a bit noisy. $ *Rooms from: €180* ✉ *Via Piccolo San Bernardo 3, La Thuile* ☎ *0165/883084* ⊕ *www.lemiramonti.it* ⏎ *35 rooms, 5 suites* ☉ *Closed May, Oct., and Nov.* ⏐○⏐ *Breakfast.*

$$
B&B/INN
Fodor's Choice
★

⊡ **Milleluci.** At this small and inviting family-run hotel overlooking Aosta, bedrooms, some with balconies, are bright and charmingly decorated; all have splendid views of the city and mountains. **Pros:** panoramic views; great spa facilities; cozy and traditionally decorated rooms. **Cons:** 1 km (½ mile) north of town—need a car to get around; no air-conditioning. $ *Rooms from: €170* ✉ *Località Porossan Roppoz 15* ☎ *0165/235278* ⊕ *www.hotelmilleluci.com* ⏎ *31 rooms* ⏐○⏐ *Breakfast.*

COURMAYEUR/MONTE BIANCO

35 km (21 miles) northwest of Aosta, 150 km (93 miles) northwest of Turin.

GETTING HERE

Courmayeur is on the main A5 Autostrada and can easily be reached by car from both Turin and Milan via Aosta. SAVDA buses run regularly from both Turin and Milan. Train service isn't available.

VISITOR INFORMATION

Courmayeur Tourism Office ✉ *Piazzale Monte Bianco 15* ☎ *0165/842060* ⊕ *www.courmayeur.it.*

EXPLORING

Monte Bianco (*Mont Blanc*). The main attraction of Courmayeur is a knock-'em-dead view of Europe's tallest peak, Monte Bianco. The celebrities that still come here are following a tradition that dates from the late 17th century, when Courmayeur's natural springs first began to draw visitors. The spectacle of the Alps gradually surpassed the springs as the biggest draw (the Alpine letters of the English poet Percy Bysshe Shelley were almost advertisements for the region), but the biggest change came in 1965 with the opening of the Mont Blanc tunnel. Since then, ever-increasing numbers of travelers have passed through the area.

Planners have managed to keep some restrictions on wholesale development within the town, and its angled rooftops and immaculate cobblestone streets maintain a cozy (if prepackaged) feeling.

From La Palud, a small town 4 km (2½ miles) north of Courmayeur, you can catch the cable car up to the top of Monte Bianco. In summer, if you get the inclination, you can then switch cable cars and descend into Chamonix, in France. In winter you can ski parts of the route off-piste. The Funivie La Palud whisks you up first to the Pavillon du Mont Fréty—a starting point for many beautiful hikes—and then to the Rifugio di Torino, before arriving at the viewing platform at **Punta Helbronner** (more than 11,000 feet), which is also the border post with France. Monte Bianco's attraction is not so much its shape (much less distinctive than that of the Matterhorn) as its expanse and the vistas from the top.

The next stage up—only in summer—is on the **Télépherique de L'Aiguille du Midi,** as you pass into French territory. The trip is particularly impressive: you dangle over a huge glacial snowfield (more than 2,000 feet below) and make your way slowly to the viewing station above Chamonix. It's one of the most dramatic rides in Europe. From this point you're looking down into France, and if you change cable cars at the Aiguille du Midi station you can make your way down to Chamonix itself. The return trip, through the Monte Bianco tunnel, is made by bus. Schedules are unpredictable, depending on weather conditions and demand; contact the Funivie Monte Bianco for information. ⊠ *Frazione La Palud 22* ☎ *0165/89925 in Courmayeur, 0450/532275 in Chamonix* ⊕ *www.montebianco.com* ⊠ *€15 round-trip to Pavillon du Mont Fréty, €38 round-trip to Helbronner, €62 round-trip to Aiguille du Midi, €96 round-trip to Chamonix with return by bus* ⊙ *Closed mid-Oct.–mid-Dec., depending on demand and weather.*

Parco Nazionale del Gran Paradiso. Cogne, 52 km (32 miles) southeast of Courmayeur, is the gateway to this huge park, which was once the domain of King Vittorio Emanuele II (1820–78). Bequeathed to the nation after World War I, it is one of Europe's most rugged and unspoiled wilderness areas, with wildlife and many plant species protected by law. The park is one of the few places in Europe where you can see the ibex (a mountain goat with horns up to 3 feet long) and the chamois (a small antelope). The park, which is 703 square km (271 square miles), is open free of charge throughout the year; there's an information office in Cogne. Try to visit in May, when spring flowers are in bloom and most of the meadows are clear of snow. ⊠ *Villaggio Cogne 12, Cogne* ☎ *0165/749264* ⊕ *www.grand-paradis.it.*

WHERE TO EAT

$$
NORTHERN
ITALIAN
✕ **Cadran Solaire.** The Garin family made over the oldest tavern in Courmayeur to create a warm and inviting restaurant that has a 17th-century stone vault, old wooden floor, and huge stone fireplace. The menu offers seasonal specialties and innovative interpretations of regional dishes: when available, the ravioli maison (filled with ricotta cheese flavored with walnuts and bathed with butter and sage) are particularly delicious. The cozy bar is a popular place for a before-dinner drink. Ⓢ *Average meal: €40* ⊠ *Via Roma 122* ☎ *0165/844609* ⌖ *Reservations essential* ⊙ *Closed Tues., May, and Oct.*

$$
NORTHERN
ITALIAN
✕ **Maison de Filippo.** Here you'll find country-style home cooking in a mountain house with lots of atmosphere, furnished with antiques, farm tools, and bric-a-brac of all kinds. There's a set menu only, which includes an abundance of antipasti, a tempting choice of local soups and pasta dishes, and an equally impressive array of traditional second courses, including fonduta *valdostana* (cheese fondue), and an equally hearty *carbonada* (beef stew and polenta). Cheese, dessert, and fresh fruit complete the meal. Don't head here if you are looking for something light to eat, and make sure to reserve in advance—it's one of the most popular restaurants in Valle d'Aosta. Ⓢ *Average meal: €45* ⊠ *Via Passerin d'Entrèves 8* ☎ *0165/869797* ⌖ *Reservations essential* ⊙ *Closed Tues., mid-May–June, Oct., and Nov.*

WHERE TO STAY

For expanded hotel reviews, visit Fodors.com.

$$$ HOTEL **Auberge de la Maison.** Most of these cozy rooms have views of Monte Bianco, and Alpine prints on the walls, plush fabrics, and wood-burning stoves give the feeling of a country inn. **Pros:** secluded location in the center of Entrèves; nice spa; charming decor. **Cons:** isolated location (a car is essential); not all standard rooms have views of Monte Bianco. [$] *Rooms from: €210* ✉ *Via Passerin d'Entrèves 16* ☎ *0165/869811* 🌐 *www.aubergemaison.it* 🛏 *30 rooms, 3 suites* ⏲ *Closed May and 15 days in Nov.* 🍴 *Breakfast.*

$$ HOTEL **Croux.** Half the rooms at this bright, comfortable hotel near the town center have balconies, the other half have great views of the mountains. **Pros:** central location; great views. **Cons:** only half the rooms have views; on a busy road. [$] *Rooms from: €160* ✉ *Via Croux 8* ☎ *0165/846735* 🌐 *www.hotelcroux.it* 🛏 *31 rooms* ⏲ *Closed mid-Apr.–mid-June, Oct., and Nov.* 🍴 *Breakfast.*

$$$ HOTEL **Royal e Golf.** With wide terraces and wood paneling, this longtime landmark in the center of Courmayeur is the most elegant spot in town, and the cheery rooms have plenty of amenities. **Pros:** central location on Courmayeur's main pedestrian street; panoramic views; heated outdoor pool. **Cons:** standard rooms can be small; meal plan required; very expensive; town center can be busy. [$] *Rooms from: €240* ✉ *Via Roma 87* ☎ *0165/831611* 🌐 *www.hotelroyalegolf.com* 🛏 *80 rooms, 6 suites* ⏲ *Closed wk after Easter–mid-June and mid-Sept.–Nov.* 🍴 *Breakfast.*

$$$ B&B/INN Fodor's Choice ★ **Villa Novecento.** Run with the friendly charm and efficiency of Stefano Cavaliere, the Novecento is a peaceful haven with the style of a comfortable mountain lodge, complete with a log fire in winter, traditional fabrics, wooden furnishings, and early 19th-century prints. **Pros:** charming and cozy; good restaurant; close to town center but away from the hubbub. **Cons:** parking is limited; no air-conditioning. [$] *Rooms from: €270* ✉ *Viale Monte Bianco 64* ☎ *0165/843000* 🌐 *www.villanovecento.it* 🛏 *26 rooms* 🍴 *Breakfast.*

SPORTS AND THE OUTDOORS

SKIING

Funivie Courmayeur/Mont Blanc. Courmayeur pales in comparison to its French neighbor, Chamonix, in both the quality and the number of its ski runs (it has only 24). But with good natural snow cover, the trails and vistas are spectacular. A huge gondola leads from the center of Courmayeur to Plan Checrouit, where other gondolas and lifts lead to the slopes. The skiing around Monte Bianco is particularly good, and the off-piste options are among the best in Europe. The routes from Cresta d'Arp (the local peak) to Dolonne, and from La Palud area into France, should be done with a guide. Contact the Funivie Courmayeur/Mont Blanc for complete information about lift tickets, ski runs, and weather conditions. ✉ *La Palud 22* ☎ *0165/89925* 🌐 *www.montebianco.com.*

Società delle Guide Alpine (*Alpine Guide Society*). The society provides year-round Alpine guiding services. ✉ *Strada Villair 2* ☎ *0165/842064* 🌐 *www.guidecourmayeur.com.*

THE ITALIAN RIVIERA

WELCOME TO
THE ITALIAN RIVIERA

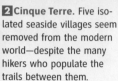

TOP REASONS
TO GO

★ **Walking the Cinque Terre:** Hike the famous Cinque Terre trails past gravity-defying vineyards, rock-perched villages, and the deep blue sea.

★ **Portofino:** See the world through rose-tinted sunglasses at this glamorous little harbor village.

★ **Genoa's historical center and port:** From the palaces of Via Garibaldi to the labyrinthine backstreets of the old city to the world-class aquarium, the city is full of surprising delights.

★ **Giardini Botanici Hanbury:** A spectacular natural setting harbors one of Italy's largest, most exotic botanical gardens.

★ **Pesto:** The basil-rich sauce was invented in Liguria, and it's never been equaled elsewhere.

1 Riviera di Levante. East of Genoa, the Riviera of the Rising Sun has tiny bays and inlets, set among dramatic cliffs, making for some of the most beautiful coastline in Italy. The pastel-hue town of Portofino has charmed generations of the rich and famous.

2 Cinque Terre. Five isolated seaside villages seem removed from the modern world—despite the many hikers who populate the trails between them.

3 Genoa. Birthplace of Christopher Columbus, this city is an urban anomaly among Liguria's charming villages. At its heart is Italy's largest historic district, filled with beautiful architecture.

4 **Riviera di Ponente.**
The Riviera of the Setting
Sun, reaching from the
French border to Genoa,
has protected bays and
sandy beaches. The seaside
resorts of Bordighera and
San Remo share some of
the glitter of their French
cousins to the west.

GETTING ORIENTED

A thin crescent of rug-
ged and verdant land
surrounded by France,
Piedmont, Tuscany,
the Alps, and the
Mediterranean Sea,
Liguria is best known as
the Italian Riviera. Genoa,
the region's largest city
and one of Italy's most
important ports, lies directly
in the middle, with the
Riviera di Ponente to the
west and the Riviera di
Levante to the east. It's here
that the Italians perfected
il dolce far niente—the
sweet art of idleness.

8

0 _____ 20 mi
0 _____ 20 km

EMILIA-ROMAGNA

Busalla
A26
35
45
Rosso
A10
3
Genoa
Nervi
A12
225
Camogli
Portofino
Rapallo
Santa
Margherita
Ligure
Chiavari
Lavagna
Golfo di
Genova

TUSCANY

1
Sestri Levante
Moneglia
Monterosso
al Mare
Vernazza
Manarola
Riomaggiore
CINQUE TERRE
2
La
Spezia
A12
1
RIVIERA DI LEVANTE

a

EATING AND DRINKING WELL IN THE ITALIAN RIVIERA

Ligurian cuisine might surprise you. As you'd expect given the long coastline, it employs all sorts of seafood, but the real claim to fame is the exemplary use of vegetables and herbs.

Basil is practically revered in Genoa (the word is derived from the Greek *basileus*, meaning "king"), and the city is considered the birthplace of pesto, the basil-rich pasta sauce. This and other herbs—laurel, fennel, and marjoram—are cultivated but also grow wild on the sun-kissed hillsides. Naturally, seafood plays a prominent role on the menu, appearing in soups, salads, and pasta dishes. Especially bountiful are anchovies, sea bass, squid, and octopus. Vegetables—particularly artichokes, eggplant, and zucchini—are abundant, usually prepared with liberal amounts of olive oil and garlic.

Like much of Italy, Liguria has a full range of eating establishments from cafeteria-like *tavole calde* to family-run trattorias to sophisticated *ristoranti*. Lunch is served between 12:30 and 2:30 and dinner between 7:30 and 11. Also popular, especially in Genoa, are *enoteche* (wine bars), which serve simply prepared light meals late into the night.

FABULOUS FOCACCIA

When you're hankering for a snack, turn to bakeries and small eateries serving focaccia *(pictured above)*. The flat bread here is more dense and flavorful than what's sold as focaccia in American restaurants; it's the region's answer to pizza, usually eaten on the go.

It comes simply salted and dribbled with olive oil; flavored with rosemary and olives; covered with cheese or anchovies; and even *ripiena* (filled), usually with cheese or vegetables and herbs. Another local delicacy is *farinata*, a chickpea pancake baked like a pizza.

ANTIPASTI
Seafood antipasti are served in abundance at most Ligurian restaurants. These usually include marinated anchovies from Monterosso, *cozze ripiene* (mussel shells stuffed with minced mussel meat, prosciutto, Parmesan, herbs, and bread crumbs), and *sopressato di polpo* (flattened octopus in olive oil and lemon sauce).

PASTA
Liguria's classic pasta sauce is pesto, made from basil, garlic, olive oil, pine nuts, and hard cheese. It's usually served with *trenette* (similar to spaghetti) or the slightly sweet *testaroli* (a flat pasta made from chestnut flour).

You can also find *pansotti* (triangular pockets of pasta filled with a cheese mixture) *(pictured below)*, and *trofie* (doughy, short pasta twists) with *salsa di noci,* a rich sauce of garlic, walnuts, and cream that, as with pesto, is ideally pounded with a mortar and pestle.

Spaghetti *allo scoglio* is an olive oil, tomato, and white wine–based sauce containing an assortment of local *frutti di mare* (seafood) including shrimp, clams, mussels, and cuttlefish.

FISH AND MEAT
Fish is the best bet for a second course: the classic preparation is a whole grilled or baked whitefish—*branzino* (sea bass) and *orata* (dorado) are good choices—served with olives, potatoes, Ligurian

spices, and a drizzle of olive oil. A popular meat dish is *cima alla Genovese,* a veal roll stuffed with a mixture of eggs and vegetables, served as a cold cut.

PANIGACCI
One of the real treats of the region is *panigacci* from the Lunigiana area, the valley extending inland along the border between Liguria and Tuscany. Balls of dough are laid in a small, terra-cotta dishes known as *testine* and stacked one on top of the other in order to flatten the dough. Then they are placed over hot coals (or in a pizza oven), and what emerges is flat, firm, almost pitalike bread. Panigacci is usually served with *stracchino* cheese (similar to cream cheese), pesto, or nut sauce and cold cuts—a delicious, hearty meal.

WINE
Local vineyards produce mostly light and refreshing whites such as Pigato, Vermentino, and Cinque Terre. Rossese di Dolceacqua, from near the French border, is the best red wine the region has to offer, but for a more robust accompaniment to meats opt for the more full-bodied reds of the neighboring Piedmont region.

Updated by Megan McCaffrey-Guerrera

Like the jewelry that bedecks its habitual visitors, the Italian Riviera is glamorous, but in an old-fashioned way. The resort towns and coastal villages that stake intermittent claim on the rocky shores of the Ligurian Sea are the long-lost cousins of newer seaside paradises found elsewhere.

Here the grandest palazzi share space with frescoed, angular, late-19th-century apartment buildings. The rustic and elegant, the provincial and chic, the small-town and cosmopolitan all collide here in a sun-drenched blend that defines the Italian side of the Riviera. There's the glamour of its chic resorts such as San Remo and Portofino, the tranquil beauty and outdoor adventures of the Cinque Terre, plus the history and architectural charm of Genoa. Mellowed by the balmy breezes blowing off the sea, travelers bask in the sun, explore the picturesque fishing villages, and pamper themselves at the resorts that dot this ruggedly beautiful landscape.

THE ITALIAN RIVIERA PLANNER

MAKING THE MOST OF YOUR TIME
Your first decision, particularly with limited time, is between the two Rivieras. The Riviera di Levante, east of Genoa, is quieter and has a more distinct personality with the rustic Cinque Terre, ritzy Portofino, and the panoramic Gulf of Poets. The Riviera di Ponente, west of Genoa, is a classic European resort experience with many white-sand beaches and more nightlife—similar to, but not as glamorous as, the French Riviera across the border.

In either case, your second choice is whether to visit Genoa. Despite its rough exterior and (diminishing) reputation as a seamy port town, Genoa's artistic and cultural treasures are significant—you won't find anything remotely comparable elsewhere in the region. Unless your goal is to avoid urban life entirely, consider a night or two in the city.

Season is everything. Shops, cafés, clubs, and restaurants stay open late in resorts during high season (at Easter and from June through August), but during the rest of the year they close early, if they're open at all.

GETTING HERE AND AROUND
BUS TRAVEL
Generally speaking, buses are a difficult way to come and go in Liguria.

Volpibus. This firm provides service from the airport in Nice as well as Milan, but there's no bus service between Genoa and other major Italian cities. ☎ *010/561661* ⊕ *www.volpibus.com.*

While there are local buses that run between villages along the Riviera Ponente, it's not an extensive network and can be a challenge to navigate.

ATP. Things run somewhat easier along the Riviera Levante where ATP has regular, regional services. ☎ *0185/373275* ⊕ *www.atp-spa.it.*

CAR TRAVEL
With the freedom of a car, you could drive from one end of the Riviera to the other on the autostrada in less than three hours. Two good roads run parallel to each other along the coast of Liguria. Closer to shore and passing through all the towns and villages is SS1, the Via Aurelia, which was laid out by the ancient Romans and has excellent views at almost every turn but gets crowded in July and August.

More direct and higher up than SS1 are the autostrade, A10 west of Genoa and A12 to the south—engineering wonders with literally hundreds of long tunnels and towering viaducts. These routes save time on weekends, in summer, and on days when festivals slow traffic in some resorts to a standstill.

TRAIN TRAVEL
Train travel is by far the most convenient mode of transportation throughout the region. It takes three hours for an express train to cover the entire Liguria coast. Local trains take upward of five hours to get from one end of the coast to the other, stopping in or near all the towns along the way.

For schedules, check the website of the national railway, **FS** (☎ *892021* ⊕ *www.trenitalia.com*).

HIKING
Walking Liguria's extensive network of trails, and taking in the gorgeous views, is a major outdoor activity. The mild climate and laid-back state of mind can lull you into underestimating just how strenuous such walks can be. Wear good shoes, use sunscreen, and carry plenty of water—you'll be glad you did. Trail maps are available from tourist information offices, or upon entry to the Cinque Terre National Park.

Other walks to consider: On Portofino promontory, the relatively easy walk to the Abbazia di San Fruttuoso is popular, and there's a more challenging hike from Ruta to the top of Monte Portofino. From Genoa, you can take the Zecca–Righi funicular up to Righi and walk along the ring of fortresses that used to defend the city, or ride the Genova–Casella railroad to one of the trailheads near the station stops.

Walking tours can introduce you to lesser-known aspects of the region.

For the Cinque Terre and the rest of the Province of La Spezia, the **Cooperativa Arte e Natura** (✉ *Viale Amendola 172, La Spezia* ☎ *0187/739410* ✍ *coop.arte@tin.it* ⊕ *www.guideartenatura.it*) is a good source for English-speaking guides. A full day costs around €210 for groups up to 25 people.

RESTAURANTS

Please note that restaurant prices listed as "average meal" include a meal consisting of first course *(primo)*, second course *(secondo)*, and dessert *(dolce)*.

HOTELS

Liguria's lodging options may be a step behind such resort areas as Positano and Taormina, so reservations for its better accommodations, and limited ones in the Cinque Terre, should be made far in advance. Lodging tends to be pricey in high season, particularly June to August. At other times of year, ask for a *sconto bassa stagione* (low-season discount).

RIVIERA DI LEVANTE

East of Genoa lies the Riviera di Levante (Riviera of the Rising Sun). It has a more raw, unpolished side to it than the Riviera di Ponente, and its stretches of rugged coastline are dotted with fishing villages. Around every turn of this area's twisting roads the hills plummet sharply to the sea, forming deep, hidden bays and coves. Beaches on this coast tend to be rocky, backed by spectacular sheer cliffs. (Yet there are some rather lovely sandy beaches in Lerici, Monterosso, Levanto, and Paraggi.) It's also home to one of Europe's well-known playgrounds for the rich and famous, the inlet of Portofino.

Still growing in popularity are the photogenic, preposterously beautiful towns of the Cinque Terre, the Cinderella of the Italian Riviera. In their rugged simplicity the five old fishing towns of Monterosso, Vernazza, Corniglia, Manarola, and Riomaggiore seem to mock the caked-on artifice of glitzy neighboring resorts. With a clear blue sea in the foreground, spectacularly multicolored buildings emerge almost seamlessly from cliff, and rocky mountains rise precipitously to gravity-defying vineyards and dusty olive groves. The geography here prevents expansion or any real technological advancement, and the small towns can't help but retain their enchanting intimacy.

LERICI

106 km (66 miles) southeast of Genoa, 65 km (40 miles) west of Lucca.

Lerici is located in the glorious Bay of La Spezia, famous for its natural beauty. Near Liguria's border with Tuscany, this picturesque village dates back to medieval times when, under the rule of Pisa, it fought cross-bay battles with Genovese Portovenere as well as with local pirates. The town is set on a magnificent coastline of gray cliffs jutting down into a crystal-clear sea and surrounded by a national park that is nearly an unframed painting of pine forests, olive trees, and tiny colorful hamlets. The waterfront piazza is filled with trompe-l'oeil frescoed buildings, and seaside cafés line a charming little harbor that holds boats of all sizes.

There are several white beaches and bathing establishments dotting the 2-km (1-mile) walk along the bay from the village center to nearby San Terenzo. From the village, you can also reach some beautiful hiking trails that head southeast to both seaside and hilltop villages like Fiascherino, Tellaro, and Montemarcello.

GETTING HERE AND AROUND

By car, Lerici is less than a 10-minute drive west from the A12 with plenty of blue signs indicating the way. There's a large pay–parking lot about a 10-minute walk along the seaside promenade from the center. By train, the closest station is either Sarzana (10-minute drive) or La Spezia Centrale (20-minute drive) on the main north–south line between Genoa and Pisa.

VISITOR INFORMATION

Lerici Tourism Office ✉ *Via Biaggini 6* ☎ *0187/967164* 🌐 *www.aptcinqueterre.sp.it.*

EXPLORING

Castello di Lerici. The promontory is dominated by this 13th-century Pisan castle that now houses a museum of paleontology. ✉ *Piazza S. Giorgio 1* ☎ *0187/969042* 🌐 *www.castellodilerici.it* 🎟 *€6* 🕒 *Hours vary but usually open Tues.–Sun. 10:30–12:30.*

WHERE TO EAT

$ ITALIAN 🍴 **Bonta Nascoste.** In the local dialect, *bonta nascoste* means "hidden goodness," a reference to the back-alleyway location and consistently delicious dishes, including fresh pasta and local fish. This charming spot also serves a handful of delicious meat choices. There are only eight tables (and a couple more outside in summer), so reserve ahead. [$] *Average meal: €30* ✉ *Via Cavour 52* ☎ *0187/965500* 🌐 *www.bontanascoste.it* ✍ *Reservations essential* 🕒 *Closed Tues. and 2 wks in Nov. and June.*

$ LIGURIAN 🍴 **Miranda.** Perched amid the clustered old houses in seaside Tellaro, 4 km (2½ miles) southeast of Lerici, this small family-run restaurant has become a gourmet's destination because of chef Angelo Cabani's imaginative Ligurian cooking. His seafood menu changes daily, but might include shrimp and lobster salad with fennel, or risotto with asparagus and shrimp. This pretty building also houses a small inn with seven charming and comfortable rooms. [$] *Average meal: €60* ✉ *Via Fiascherino 92, Tellaro* ☎ *0187/964012* 🌐 *www.miranda1959.com* 🕒 *Closed Mon. and Nov. and Jan.*

$ LIGURIAN 🍴 **Osteria di Redarca.** Within the pine forest of the Montemarcello National Park, this *osteria* (a simple, informal restaurant) serves some of the best homemade pastas in the area. It also offers a "surf-and-turf" menu, with abundant cooked-to-perfection fish platters and succulent meat dishes. The location may not be seaside, but the setting and the food are both a treat. [$] *Average meal: €45* ✉ *Rocchetta Località Redarca 6* ☎ *0187/966140* 🕒 *Closed Wed. and 2 wks in Jan.*

WHERE TO STAY

For expanded hotel reviews, visit Fodors.com.

$ HOTEL 🏨 **Doria Park.** The junior suites have large terraces and Jacuzzi tubs, but any of the sea-view rooms are a real value, and the location, between olive-tree hills and the village center, is the best in Lerici. **Pros:** sea views; comfortable beds; not far from the main piazza and harbor.

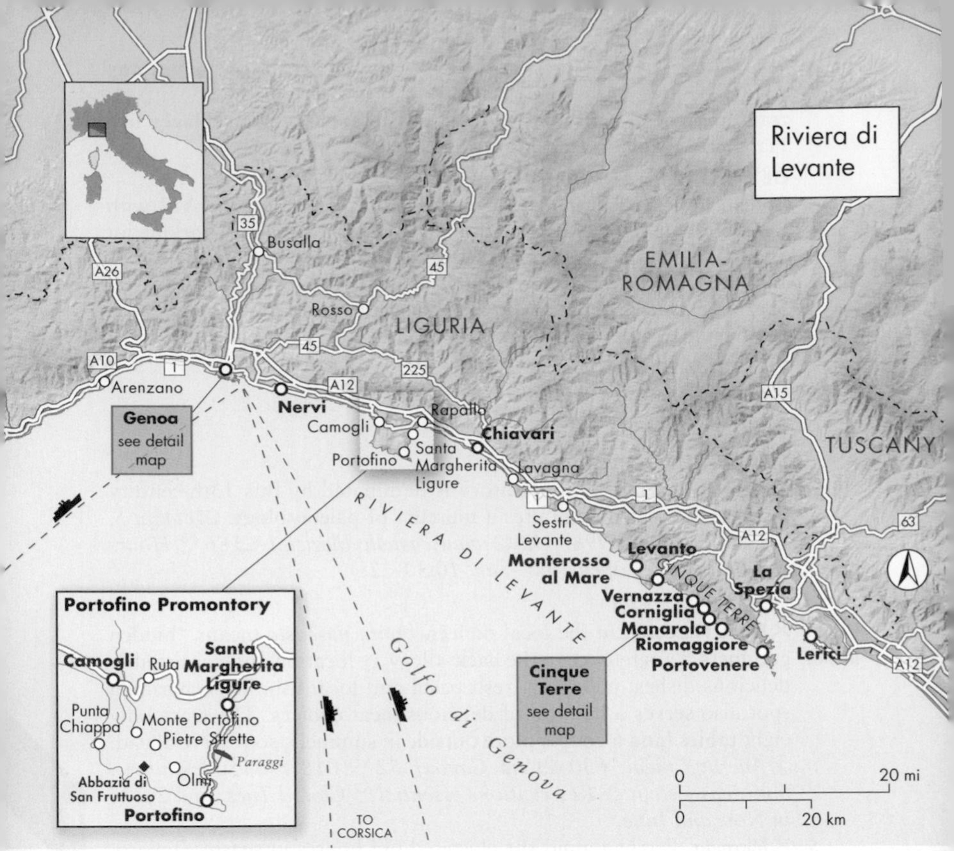

Cons: many stairs, including several sets that can be challenging for people with weak knees or heavy bags. *$ Rooms from: €125 ✉ Via Doria 2 ☎ 0187/967124 🌐 www.doriaparkhotel.it 🛏 48 rooms, 5 suites 🍴 Breakfast.*

$ HOTEL 🏨 **Florida.** Extras such as sea-view balconies make this seafront, family-run establishment well worth the euros. **Pros:** beachfront location; bay views; friendly staff. **Cons:** small rooms; beach across the street can be noisy, especially in summer. *$ Rooms from: €190 ✉ Lungomare Biaggini 35 ☎ 0187/967332 🌐 www.hotelflorida.it 🛏 40 rooms 🕒 Closed Dec.–Feb. 🍴 Breakfast.*

$ HOTEL 🏨 **Piccolo Hotel del Lido.** Each of the 12 tastefully decorated waterfront rooms has a private rooftop terrace where you can sunbathe or sip a glass of local wine while watching the sunset. **Pros:** beachfront; great views; large bathrooms. **Cons:** limited parking; adjacent beach club can get noisy by day during high season. *$ Rooms from: €230 ✉ Lungomare Biaggini 24 ☎ 0187/968159 🌐 www.locandadellido.it 🛏 12 rooms 🕒 Closed mid-Oct.–Easter 🍴 Breakfast.*

EN ROUTE

Ten minutes inland from Lerici is the medieval village of **Sarzana,** designed by the military leader Castruccio Castracani, who also designed Lucca. Here you'll find some of the most authentic and well-restored palazzos in Liguria. Its pedestrians-only cobblestone streets bustling with people, fine boutiques, and packed cafés are perfect for a *passeggiata* (evening stroll). For three weeks in August it hosts a lively antiques market with great buys and opportunities for people watching.

LA SPEZIA

11 km (7 miles) northwest of Lerici, 103 km (64 miles) southeast of Genoa.

La Spezia is sometimes thought of as nothing but a large, industrialized naval port en route to the Cinque Terre and Portovenere, but it does possess some charm, and it gives you a look at a less tourist-focused part of the Riviera. Its palm-lined promenade, fertile citrus parks, renovated Liberty-style palazzos, and colorful balcony-lined streets make parts of La Spezia surprisingly beautiful. On Monday through Saturday mornings you can stroll through the fresh fish, produce, and local-cheese stalls at the outdoor market on Piazza Cavour, and on Friday take part in the busy flea market on Via Garibaldi.

GETTING HERE AND AROUND

By car, take La Spezia exit off the A12. La Spezia Centrale train station is on the main north–south railway line between Genoa and Pisa.

VISITOR INFORMATION

La Spezia Tourism Office ✉ *Via Mazzini 45* ☎ *0187/770900* 🌐 *turismocultura.spezianet.it.*

EXPLORING

Castel San Giorgio. The remains of this massive 13th-century castle atop a small hill above the modern town now house a small museum dedicated to local archaeology. ✉ *Via XX Settembre* ☎ *0187/751142* 🎫 *€5* 🕒 *June–Aug., Wed.–Mon. 9:30–12:30 and 5–8; Apr., May, and Sept., Wed.–Mon. 9:30–12:30 and 3–8; Oct.–Mar., Wed.–Mon. 9:30–12:30 and 2–5.*

8

WHERE TO EAT

$ PIZZA 🍴 **La Pia.** Considered an institution, this *farinateria* and pizzeria dates back to 1887. During the lunch hour, you will find a line out the door while inside—and on the patio in summer—locals munch on *farinata,* a chickpea pancake that's a Ligurian delicacy, and on thick-crust pizzas served hot out of the wood-burning oven. [$] *Average meal: €15* ✉ *Via Magenta 12* ☎ *0187/739999* 🕒 *Closed Wed. and 2 wks in Aug. and Nov.*

PORTOVENERE

12 km (7 miles) south of La Spezia, 114 km (70 miles) southeast of Genoa.

The colorful facades and pedestrians-only *calata* (promenade) make Portovenere the quintessential Ligurian seaside village. As a UNESCO World Heritage Site, its harbor is lined with tall, thin "terratetto" houses that date from as far back as the 11th century and are connected in a wall-like formation to protect against attacks by the Pisans and local pirates. Its tiny, *carruggi* (alley-like passageways) lead to an array of charming shops, homes, and gardens and eventually to the village's impressive **Castle Doria** high on the olive tree covered hill. To the west standing guard over the Mediterranean is the picturesque medieval **Chiesa di San Pietro,** once the site of a temple to Venus (Venere in Italian), from which Portovenere gets its name. Nearby, in a rocky area leading to the sea, is Byron's Cave, a favorite spot that the poet loved to swim out into the sea from.

GETTING HERE AND AROUND

By car from the port city of La Spezia, follow the blue signs for Portovenere. It's about a 20-minute winding drive along the sea through small fishing villages. From La Spezia train station you can hire a taxi for about €30. By bus from Via Garibaldi in La Spezia (a 10-minute walk from the train station) it takes 20 minutes.

VISITOR INFORMATION

Portovenere doesn't have a tourist office; you get information at the Comune (Town Hall) or at the tourist office in La Spezia Centrale train station.

EXPLORING

Grotto Arpaia. Lord Byron (1788–1824) is said to have written *Childe Harold's Pilgrimage* in Portovenere. Near the entrance to the huge, strange Grotto Arpaia, at the base of the sea-swept cliff, is a plaque recounting the poet's strength and courage as he swam across the gulf to the village of San Terenzo, near Lerici, to visit his friend Shelley (1792–1822).

San Pietro. This 13th-century Gothic church is built on the site of an ancient pagan shrine, on a formidable solid mass of rock above the Grotto Arpaia. With its black-and-white-striped exterior, it is a landmark recognizable from far out at sea. There's a spectacular view of the Cinque Terre coastline from the front porch of the church. ✉ *Waterfront promenade* ⏲ *Daily 9–6.*

WHERE TO EAT

$ WINE BAR 🍴 **Bacicio.** Tucked away on Portovenere's main caruggio, this enoteca and antipasto bar is popular with locals and being discovered by tourists looking for good, local dishes. The owner whips up some wonderful finger food—including *crostini* (grilled bread) with fresh anchovies and smoked herring with spicy orange salsa—and offers a robust list of local wines. He also designed the place, right down to the tables and chairs made from anchors and pieces of old boats. [$] *Average meal: €20* ✉ *Via Cappellini 17* ☎ *0187/792054* ✍ *Reservations not accepted* 💳 *No credit cards* ⏲ *Closed Wed., Jan., and Nov.*

$ LIGURIAN 🍴 **Le Bocche.** At the end of the Portovenere promontory in the shadow of San Pietro, this is the village's most exclusive and possibly most delicious restaurant. The menu consists of only the freshest in-season fish, prepared with a creative touch, such as marinated tuna encrusted with pistachios. The setting is romantic and unique, as you feel almost immersed in the Mediterranean. The dinner menu is quite expensive (as is the lengthy wine list), but you can get a real deal at lunch with a limited but equally good menu at lower prices. [$] *Average meal: €70* ✉ *Calata Doria 102* ☎ *0187/790622* 🌐 *www.lebocche.it* ⏲ *Closed Nov.–Feb.*

$ LIGURIAN 🍴 **Locanda Lorena.** Across the small bay of Portovenere lies the rugged island of Palmaria. There is only one restaurant on the island,

and here Iseo (aka Giuseppe), an accomplished chef, does the cooking. Fresh pasta and local fish such as branzino are headliners at this fun dining spot with lovely views looking back toward Portovenere. To get here, take the restaurant's free speedboat from the Portovenere jetty. [$] *Average meal: €50* ✉ *Palmaria Island* ☎ *0187/792370* 🌐 *www.locandalorena.com* 🕘 *Closed Nov.*

WHERE TO STAY

For expanded hotel reviews, visit Fodors.com.

$$ HOTEL 🏨 **Hotel Belvedere.** True to the name, the best rooms in this sunny Liberty-style building face the bay of Portovenere, with lovely views of Palmaria Island and the Gulf of Poets. **Pros:** reasonably priced rooms with water views. **Cons:** parts of the hotel could use a makeover; limited parking. [$] *Rooms from: €165* ✉ *Via Garibaldi 26* ☎ *0187/790608* 🌐 *www.belvedereportovenere.it* 🛏 *19 rooms* 🕘 *Closed Nov.–mid-Mar.* 🍴 *Breakfast.*

RIOMAGGIORE

17 km (11 miles) northwest of La Spezia, 101 km (60 miles) from Genova.

At the eastern end of the Cinque Terre, Riomaggiore is built into a river gorge (thus the name, which means "river major") and is easily accessible from La Spezia by train or car. The landscape is terraced and steep—be prepared for many stairs!—which leads down to a small harbor protected by large slabs of alabaster and marble that serve as tanning beds for sunbathers, as well as being the site of several outdoor cafés with fine views. According to legend, the settlement of Riomaggiore dates as far back as the 8th century, when Greek religious refugees came here to escape persecution by the Byzantine emperor.

The village is divided into two parts. If you arrive by train, you will have to pass through a tunnel that flanks the train tracks in order to arrive to the historic side of town. To avoid the crowds and get a great view of the Cinque Terre coast, walk straight uphill as soon as you exit the station. This winding road takes you over the hill to the 14th-century **church of Saint John the Baptist,** toward the medieval town center and the Genovese-style tower houses that dot the village. Follow Via Roma (the Old Town's main street) downhill, pass under the train tracks, and you'll arrive in the charming fishermen's port of the village. Lined with traditional fishing boats and small trattorias, this is a lovely spot for a romantic lunch or dinner. Unfortunately, Riomaggiore doesn't have as much old-world charm as its sister villages; its easy accessibility has brought traffic and more modern construction here than elsewhere in the Cinque Terre.

Riomaggiore is also the starting point for the **"Via dell'Amore,"** the easily accessible path that leads to Manarola. The Bar dell'Amore—located halfway between the two villages—offers drinks and simple dishes with a great view.

GETTING HERE AND AROUND

New travelers to the Cinque Terre should be happy to know that the enormous parking problems presented by these cliff-dwelling villages has been mitigated somewhat by a large, covered parking structure at the La Spezia

Centrale station. It costs €1.50 per hour but is secure and clean (you cannot enter without a ticket code to open the door), and it's open 24/7. Parking is always so difficult here and nearly impossible in the five villages. This is a good back-up solution for those with cars, although others may choose to be day-trippers from Pisa or Lucca and rely on the bus and train services.

VISITOR INFORMATION

Riomaggiore ✉ *Stazione Ferroviaria* ☎ *0187/762287* 🌐 *www.aptcinqueterre.sp.it and www.parconazionale5terre.it.*

WHERE TO EAT

$ LIGURIAN 🍴 **La Lanterna.** Colorful chalkboards out in front of this small trattoria by the harbor list the day's selection of fresh fish; the set-up might sound modest, but this is arguably the finest restaurant in the Cinque Terre. During the winter, Chef Massimo serves as a teacher at the Culinary Academy in Switzerland, and he always returns with new ideas for his menu. When available, the cozze ripiene (stuffed mussels) shouldn't be missed. Other offerings may be a touch exotic, such as stingray with Ligurian herbs and white wine. [$] *Average meal: €40* ✉ *Via San Giacomo 10* ☎ *0187/920589* 🕒 *Closed Jan. and 2 wks in Nov.*

$$ LIGURIAN 🍴 **Dau Cila.** The lovely dining room overlooking the harbor is built into the rock of the gorge on which the village is settled. The menu is expansive and specializes in seafood dishes. The wine list is also quite interesting featuring many unique wines of the region not found elsewhere. A not-to-be-missed plate is the *calamari gratinati* (grilled calamari). [$] *Average meal: €35* ✉ *Via San Giacomo 65, Riomaggiore* ☎ *0187/760032* 🌐 *www.ristorantedaucila.com* 🕒 *Closed Jan. and Feb. and Mon., except in summer.*

MANAROLA

Fodor's Choice ★ *16 km (10 miles) northwest of La Spezia, 117 km (73 miles) southeast of Genova.*

The enchanting pastel houses of Manarola spill down a steep hill overlooking a spectacular turquoise swimming cove and a bustling harbor. The whole town is built on black rock. Above the town, ancient terraces still protect abundant vineyards and olive trees. This village is the center of the wine and olive-oil production of the region, and its streets are lined with shops selling local products.

Surrounded by steep terraced vineyards, Manarola's one road tumbles from the **Chiesa di San Lorenzo** (14th century) settled high above the village, down to the rocky port below. Since the Cinque Terre wine cooperative is located in **Groppo,** a hamlet overlooking the village (and reachable by foot or by the green Park bus; ask at Park offices for schedules), the vineyards are well maintained and accessible. If you'd like to snap a shot of the most famous view of the town, you can walk from the port area up to the cemetery above. Along the way you'll pass the town's play-yard, uncrowded bathrooms, and a tap with clean drinking water.

VISITOR INFORMATION

Manarola 🌐 *www.aptcinqueterre.sp.it and www.parconazionale5terre.it.*

Continued on page 457

HIKING THE CINQUE TERRE

FIVE REMOTE VILLAGES MAKE ONE MUST-SEE DESTINATION

"Charming" and "breathtaking" are adjectives that get a workout when you're traveling in Italy, but it's rare that both apply to a single location. The Cinque Terre is such a place, and this combination of characteristics goes a long way toward explaining its tremendous appeal.

The area is made up of five tiny villages (Cinque Terre literally means "Five Lands") clinging to the cliffs along a gorgeous stretch of the Ligurian coast. The terrain is so steep that for centuries footpaths were the only way to get from place to place. It just so happens that these paths provide beautiful views of the rocky coast tumbling into the sea, as well as access to secluded beaches and grottoes.

Backpackers "discovered" the Cinque Terre in the 1970s, and its popularity has been growing ever since. Despite summer crowds, much of the original appeal is intact. Each town has maintained its own distinct charm, and views from the trails in between are as breathtaking as ever.

Monterosso

Corniglia

Terracing around Corniglia

HIKING THE CINQUE TERRE

Monterosso—Vernazza Trail
The most demanding portion of the trail. Often narrow, with significant climbs and descents, particularly near Vernazza. Your labors are rewarded with the Trail No. 2's best views.

Mount Malpertuso ▲

Mount ▲ Castello

Le Stalle

Trail No 8a

Mount Gaginara ▲

Drignana

(Red Trail)

Vernazza—Corniglia Trail
Ups and downs interspersed with olive groves and terraced vineyards.

38

370

Madonna di Soviore

Trail No 1

Santuario del Reggio
1hr

1hr 30min

Trail No 89

51

Trail No 8

Santuario Bernardino
1hr

S. Bernardo
Trail No 8

Trail No 2 (Blue Trail)
3 km/2 mi—2 hrs

Trail No 7

3 km/2 mi—1 hr 30 min

Guvano Beach

Vernazza

Molinara Pt

del Frate Island

Palma Pt

Monterosso al Mare

FERRY TO LEVANTO

0   1 mi

0   1 km

Monterosso
The most resort-like of the villages, with the largest beach.

Vernazza
Pretty and visitor-friendly. The best spot for lingering in a café and watching waves crash against the shore.

THE CLASSIC HIKE

Hiking is the most popular way to experience the Cinque Terre, and Trail No. 2, the Sentiero Azzurro (Blue Trail), is the most traveled path. To cover the entire trail is a full day: it's approximately 13 km (8 miles) in length, takes you to all five villages, and requires about five hours, not including stops, to complete. The best approach is to start at the eastern-most town of Riomaggiore and warm up your legs on the easiest segment of the trail. As you work your way west, the hike gets progressively more demanding. For a less strenuous experience, you can choose to skip a leg or two and take the ferry (which provides its own beautiful views) or the inland train running between the towns instead.

Manarola

Along Trail No.2

Via dell'Amore

Corniglia– Manarola Trail
Runs through the hills near Manarola, descends to rocky beach near Corniglia.

Manarola–Riomaggiore Trail
Known as the Via dell'Amore (Lovers' Lane). A wide, paved, flat path with fine views.

KEY

····················	*Major footpaths*
- - - - - - - -	*Sanctuary footpaths*
················	*Connecting footpaths*
45min	*Hiking times*
☥	*Sanctuaries*

Mount Capri

Mount Galera

Mount Grosso

Trail No 1 (Red Trail)

Mount Cuna

Trail No 6

Trail No 02

Trail No 7a

Trail No 6d

1hr 30min

Madonna della Salute

1hr

Volastra

3 km/2 mi–1 hr
Trail No 2 (Blue Trail)

51

Trail No 3

Madonna di Montenero
45min

370

370

TO
LA SPEZIA

Spiaggione di Corniglia

Corniglia

el Luogo Pt

Manarola

Buonfiglio Pt

30min

Via dell' Amore

Riomaggiore

Ligurian Sea

Trail No 2 (Blue Trail)

Torre Guardiola

C di M Nero

8

Corniglia
Perched on a cliff 500 ft. above the sea, reached by a switchback path (or by shuttle bus).

Manarola
The most photogenic of the villages, best seen from the cemetery a few minutes up the path toward Corniglia.

Riomaggiore
Cliff-clinging buildings are almost as striking as those in Manarola. Stairs to the left of the train station entrance cross over the tracks and lead to the trailhead.

BEYOND TRAIL NO.2

Trail No. 2 is just one of a network of trails crisscrossing the hills. If you're a dedicated hiker, spend a few nights and try some of the other routes. Trail No. 1, the Sentiero Rosso (Red Trail), climbs from Portovenere (east of Riomaggiore) and returns to the sea at Levanto (west of Monterosso al Mare). To hike its length takes from 9 to 12 hours; the ridge-top trail provides spectacular views from high above the villages, each of which can be reached via a steep path. Other shorter trails go from the villages up into the hills, some leading to religious sanctuaries. Trail No. 9, for example, starts from the old section of Monterosso and ends at the Madonna di Soviore Sanctuary.

WELCOME TO HIKING HEAVEN

While often described as beautiful, relaxing, and easy, it would be fair to say that the first applies to anywhere in Le Cinque Terre, but best to leave the other two for your time after hiking between the villages. Many people do not realize just how "demanding" parts of these trails can be; it's best to come prepared. We recommend bringing: a Cinque Terre Card, see below, and cash (smaller shops, eateries, as well as the park entrances do not accept credit cards).

A hike through the entire region takes about 4–5 hours plus time for exploring each village and taking a lunch break. It's an all-day, if not two-day trek. We recommend an early start, especially in summer when midday temperatures can rise to 90 degrees. Note that only "Sentiero Azzuro" (Trail No. 2)requires the Cinque Terre Card. The other 20–plus trails in the area, including the famous "Via dell'Amore," or Lovers' Lane, are free. All trails are well marked with a red and white hiking trail sign. The trails from village to village get progressively steeper as you move from south (Riomaggiore) to the north (Monterosso). If you're a day-tripper arriving by car, use the new underground lot at the La Spezia Centrale train station (€1.50/hour in summer) and take the train to Riomaggiore (6–8 minutes) to begin your hiking adventure.

FOR MORE INFO

⊕ www.cinqueterre.com; ⊕ www.lecinqueterre.org; ⊕ www.parconazionale-5terre.it; ⊕ www.rebuildmonterosso.com; ⊕ savevernazza.com; ⊕ www.littleparadiso.com (blog); ⊕ lifeinliguria.blogspot.it (blog).

PRECAUTIONS

If you're hitting the trails, you'll want to carry water with you, wear sturdy shoes (hiking boots are best), and have a hat and sunscreen handy. ⚠ Check weather reports; especially in late fall and winter, thunderstorms can make the shelterless trails slippery and dangerous. Rain in October and November can cause landslides and close the trails. Note that the lesser-used trails aren't as well maintained as Trail No. 2. If you're undertaking the full Trail No. 1 hike, bring something to snack on as well as your water bottle.

ADMISSION

Entrance tickets for use of the trails are available at ticket booths located at the start of each section of Trail No. 2, and at information offices in the Levanto, Monterosso, Vernazza, Corniglia, Manarola, Riomaggiore, and La Spezia train stations.

A one-day pass costs €5, which includes a trail map and an information leaflet. A one-day Cinque Terre Card costs €4, €12 for the weekend. The card combines park entrance fees with unlimited daily use of the regional train between villages.

WHEN TO GO

The ideal times to visit the Cinque Terre are September and May, when the weather is mild and the summer tourist season isn't in full swing.

GETTING HERE AND AROUND

The local train on the Genoa–La Spezia line stops at each of the Cinque Terre villages, and runs approximately every 30 minutes. Tickets for each leg of the journey (€1.80–2) are available at the five train stations. In Corniglia, the only one of the Cinque Terre that isn't at sea level, a shuttle service (€1) is provided for those who don't wish to climb (or descend) 300-plus steps that link the train station with the cliff-top town.

Strolling the Via dell'Amore, also known as Lovers' Lane.

Along the Cinque Terre coast two ferry lines operate. From June to September, Golfo Paradiso runs from Genoa and Camogli to Monterosso al Mare and Vernazza. The smaller but more frequent Golfo dei Poeti stops at each village from Lerici (east of Riomaggiore) to Monterosso, with the exception of Corniglia, four times a day. A one-day ticket costs €22.

OUR FAVORITES

Each town has something that passes for a beach, but there are only two options for both sand and decent swimming. The more accessible is in Monterosso, opposite the train station; it's equipped with chairs, umbrellas, and snack bars. The other is the secluded, swimwear-optional Guvano Beach, between Corniglia and Vernazza. To reach it from the Corniglia train station, bypass the steps leading up to the village, instead following signs to an abandoned train tunnel. Ring a bell at the tunnel's entrance, and the gate will automatically open; after a dimly lit 10-minute walk, you'll emerge at the beach. Both beaches have a nominal admission fee. Other trails to consider include: Monterosso to Santuario Madonna di Soviore, a fairly strenuous but rewarding 1½ hours up to a lovely 8th–century sanctuary. There is also a restaurant and a priceless view. Riomaggiore to Montenero and Portovenere is 1 hour up to the sanctuary and another 3 on to Portovenere, passing through some gorgeous, less traveled terrain. Manarola to Volastra to Corniglia runs high above the main trail and through vineyards and lesser-known villages. Monterosso to Levanto is a good 2½-hour hike, passing over Punta Mesco with glorious views of Cinque Terre to the south, Corsica to the west, and the Alps to the north.

Monterosso al Mare

WHERE TO STAY

For expanded hotel reviews, visit Fodors.com.

$$$ HOTEL Fodor's Choice ★ **La Torretta.** The Cinque Terre's only "boutique" hotel is located in a 17th-century tower and sits high on the hill above the rainbow-hued village of Manarola with truly lovely views of the terraced vineyards, colorful village homes, and the Mediterranean sea; inside, decor is chic, sleek, and antiques-bedecked. **Pros:** well maintained; a cut above most lodging in the Cinque Terre. **Cons:** if the luggage shuttle is not running during its limited hours, it is a steep walk up (and a lot of exercise!) to the hotel. [$] *Rooms from: €300* ✉ *Vico Volto 20, Cinque Terre* ☎ *0187/920327* 🌐 *www.torrettas.com* 🛏 *5 rooms, 2 suites* 🕓 *Closed Nov. to mid-Mar.*

CINQUE TERRE ONLINE

For those making a trip to the Cinque Terre, the following websites and blogs will be of great help: 🌐 *www.lecinqueterre.org*; 🌐 *www.parconazionale5terre.it*; 🌐 *www.rebuildmonterosso.com*; 🌐 *www.littleparadiso.com*; 🌐 *lifeinliguria.blogspot.it.*

CORNIGLIA

Fodor's Choice ★ *27 km (17 miles) northwest of La Spezia, 100 km (60 miles) southeast of Genova.*

The buildings, narrow lanes, and stairways of Corniglia are strung together amid vineyards high on the cliffs. On a clear day views of the entire coastal strip are excellent, from Elba in the south to the Italian Alps in the north. The high perch and lack of harbor make this farming community the most remote and therefore less crowded of the Cinque Terre. In fact, the 365 steps that lead from the train station to the town center dissuade many tourists from making the hike to the village. You can also take the green Park bus, but they run infrequently and are usually packed with tired hikers.

Corniglia is built along one road edged with small shops, bars, gelaterias, and restaurants. Midway along Via Fieschi is the **Largo Taragio,** the main square and heart of the village. Shaded by leafy trees and umbrellas, this is a lovely spot for a mid-hike gelato break. Here you'll find the 14th-century **Chiesa di San Pietro.** Its rose window of marble imported from Carrara is impressive, particularly considering the work required to get it here!

VISITOR INFORMATION

WHERE TO STAY

For expanded hotel reviews, visit Fodors.com.

$ HOTEL **Cecio.** Many of the spotless rooms at this family-run inn at the edge of Corniglia have spectacular views of the town clinging to the cliffs above the bay. **Pros:** stunning views; good value. **Cons:** rooms are very basic; nearby bell tower may distract light sleepers. [$] *Rooms from: €60* ✉ *Via Serra 58, toward Vernazza* ☎ *0187/812043* 📠 *0187/812138* 🛏 *12 rooms* 🍴 *Breakfast.*

8

VERNAZZA

Fodor's Choice ★ *27 km (17 miles) northwest of La Spezia, 96 km (59 miles) southeast of Genova.*

With its narrow streets and small squares, Vernazza is arguably the most charming of the five Cinque Terre towns. Historically, it was the most important of them as it was the only one fortunate enough to have a natural port and, therefore, became wealthier than its neighbors—as evident by the elaborate arcades, loggias, and marble work lining Via Roma and Piazza Marconi.

The village's pink, slate-roof houses and colorful squares contrast with the remains of the medieval fort and castle, including two towers, in the Old Town. The Romans first inhabited this rocky spit of land in the 1st century.

Today, Vernazza has a fairly lively social scene. **Piazza Marconi** looks out across Vernazza's small sandy beach to the sea, towards Monterosso. The numerous restaurants and bars crowd their tables and umbrellas on the outskirts of the piazza creating a patchwork of sights and sounds that form one of the most unique and beautiful places in the world.

If mass is not going on (there will be a cord blocking the entrance if there is), take a peek into the **church of Saint Margaret of Antioch.** Little changed since its enlargement in the 1600s, this 14th-century edifice has simple interiors but truly breathtaking views toward the sea: a stark contrast to the other, elaborate churches of the Cinque Terre.

On the other side of the Piazza, stairs lead to a look-out **fortress and cylindrical watchtower,** built in the 11th century as protection against pirate attacks. For a small fee you can climb to the top of the tower for a spectacular view of the coastline.

VISITOR INFORMATION

Vernazza 🌐 *www.aptcinqueterre.sp.it and www.parconazionale5terre.it.*

WHERE TO EAT AND STAY

For expanded hotel reviews, visit Fodors.com.

$ LIGURIAN 🍴 **Gambero Rosso.** Relax on Vernazza's main square at this fine trattoria looking out at a church. Enjoy such delectable dishes as shrimp salad, vegetable torte, and squid-ink risotto. The creamy pesto, served atop spaghetti, is some of the best in the Cinque Terre. End your meal with Cinque Terre's own *sciacchetrà*, a dessert wine served with semisweet biscotti. Don't drink it out of the glass—dip the biscotti in the wine instead. [$] *Average meal: €45* ✉ *Piazza Marconi 7* ☎ *0187/812265* 🌐 *www.ristorantegamberorosso.net* 🕓 *Closed Mon., Jan., and Feb.*

$$ B&B/INN Fodor's Choice ★ 🏨 **La Malà.** A cut above other lodging options in the Cinque Terre, these small guest rooms are equipped with flat-screen TVs, air-conditioning, marble showers, comfortable bedding, and have views of the sea or the port, which can also be enjoyed at their most bewitching from the shared terrace literally suspended over the Mediterranean. **Pros:** clean, fresh-feeling rooms; attentive staff; oh, the views. **Cons:** there are some stairs involved; breakfast (extra) is served at a local bar and is not abundant. [$] *Rooms from: €160* ✉ *Giovanni Battista 29* ☎ *334/2875718* 🌐 *www.lamala.it* 🛏 *4 rooms* 🕓 *Closed Jan. 10–Mar.* 🍽 *No meals.*

MONTEROSSO AL MARE

Fodor's Choice
★ *32 km (20 miles) northwest of La Spezia, 89 km (55 miles) southeast of Genova.*

It's the combined draw of beautiful beaches, rugged cliffs, crystal-clear turquoise waters, and plentiful small hotels and restaurants that make Monterosso al Mare into the largest of the Cinque Terre villages (population 1,800) and also the busiest in midsummer.

From the train station, heading west, you pass through a tunnel and exit into the *centro storico* (historic center) of the village. Nestled into the wide valley that leads to the sea, Monterosso is built above numerous streams, which now have been covered and make up the major streets of the village. Via Buranco, the oldest street in Monterosso leads out to the most characteristic piazza of the village, Piazza Matteotti (locals pass through here daily to shop at the supermarket and butcher). This piazza also contains the oldest and most typical wine shop of the village, Enoteca da Eliseo—stop here between 6 pm and midnight to share tables with fellow tourists and locals over a bottle of Cinque Terre wine. There's also the **Chiesa di San Francesco,** built in the 12th century, and is an excellent example of the Ligurian Gothic style. Its distinctive black stripes and marble rose window make it one of the most photographed sites in the Cinque Terre.

Fegina, the "new side" of the village (and site of the train station), has "modern" homes ranging from Stil Liberty (art nouveau) to the early 1970s. At the far eastern end of town, you'll run into the private sailing club sheltered by a vast rock (carved with an impressive statue of Neptune). From here, you can reach the challenging trail to Levanto. This trail has the added bonus of a five-minute detour, which leads to the **ruins of a 14th-century monastery.** The expansive view from this vantage point allowed the monks that were housed here to easily scan the waters for enemy ships that could invade the villages, therefore alerting the residents to coming danger. Have your camera ready for this Cinerama-like vista.

Though having the most nightlife on the Cinque Terre, thanks to its numerous wine bars and pubs, Monterosso is also the most family-friendly. With its expanse of free and equipped beaches, extensive pedestrian areas, large children's play park, and summer activities, Monterosso is a top spot for kids.

The **local outdoor market** is held on Thursday and attracts crowds of tourists and villagers from along the coast to shop for everything from pots, pans, and underwear to fruits, vegetables, and fish. Often a few stands sell local art and crafts, as well as olive oil and wine.

Monterosso has the most festivals of the five villages, starting with the Lemon Feast on the Saturday preceding Ascension Sunday, followed by the Flower Festival of Corpus Christi, celebrated yearly on the second Sunday after Pentecost. During the afternoon, the streets and alleyways of the historic center are decorated with thousands of colorful flower petals set in beautiful designs that the evening procession passes over. Finally, the Salted Anchovy and Olive Oil Festival takes place each year during the second weekend of September.

8

WHERE TO EAT

$ 🍴 **Enoteca Internazionale.** Located on the main street in Centro, this wine
WINE BAR bar offers a large variety of vintages, both local and from further afield, plus delicious light fare; its umbrella-covered patio is a perfect spot to recuperate after a day of hiking. The owner, Susanna, is a certified sommelier who's always forthcoming with helpful suggestions on local wines. [$] *Average meal: €20* ✉ *Via Roma 62* ☎ *0187/817278* 🕒 *Closed Tues. and Jan.–Mar.*

$$ 🍴 **Miki.** Miki has a beautiful little garden in the back, perfect for lunch
SEAFOOD on a sunny day, where you can enjoy the seafood specialties Miki is known for, including an *insalata di mare* (seafood salad), with squid and fish, that is more than tasty. If you're not up for grilled fish or calamari, opt for a pizza. [$] *Average meal: €45* ✉ *Via Fegina 104* ☎ *0187/817608* 🕒 *Closed Nov. and Dec. and Tues., Sept.–July.*

$$ 🍴 **Ristorante Belforte.** High above the sea in one of Vernazza's remaining
LIGURIAN stone towers is this unique spot serving delicious Cinque Terre cuisine
Fodor's Choice ★ such as branzino *sotto sale* (cooked under salt), stuffed mussels, and *insalata di polpo* (octopus salad). The setting is magnificent, so try for an outdoor table. [$] *Average meal: €45* ✉ *Via Guidoni 42, Vernazza* ☎ *0187/812222* 🌐 *www.ristorantebelforte.it* ✍ *Reservations essential* 🕒 *Closed Tues., Nov.–Easter.*

WHERE TO STAY

For expanded hotel reviews, visit Fodors.com.

$$ 🏨 **Il Giardino Incantato.** With wood-beam ceilings and stone walls, the
B&B/INN stylishly restored and updated rooms in this 16th-century house in the
Fodor's Choice ★ historic center of Monterosso ooze comfort and Old World charm. **Pros:** spacious rooms; gorgeous garden; excellent hosts. **Cons:** located towards the upper end of town; no views. [$] *Rooms from: €170* ✉ *Via Mazzini 18* ☎ *0185/818315* 🌐 *www.ilgiardinoincantato.net* 🛏 *3 rooms, 1 junior suite* 🕒 *Closed Nov.–Mar.* 🍽 *Breakfast.*

$$$$ 🏨 **Porto Roca.** Far from the crowds, Cinque Terre's only "high-end"
HOTEL hotel is perched on the famous terraced cliffs right over the main beach, with large balconies to savor all the panoramic views; inside, decor is more than a bit dowdy and, replete with flowered wallpapers and faux antiques, seems to have little changed from the 1960s. **Pros:** unobstructed sea views; tranquil location; pool. **Cons:** some of the rooms could use a revamp; back-facing rooms can be a bit dark; expensive for level of comfort offered. [$] *Rooms from: €320* ✉ *Via Corone 1* ☎ *0187/817502* 📠 *0187/817692* 🌐 *www.portoroca.it* 🛏 *39 rooms, 2 junior suites, 1 apartment* 🕒 *Closed Nov.–Mar.* 🍽 *No meals.*

LEVANTO

8 km (5 miles) northwest of Monterosso al Mare, 60 km (36 miles) southeast of Genoa.

Nestled at the end of a valley of pine forests, olive groves, vineyards, and medieval villages lies this sunny seaside town: an alternative and usually less expensive base to explore the Cinque Terre and the Riviera di Levante. There's a long sandy beach and a charming, colorful old quarter with plenty of shops, bars, and restaurants. Levanto has become a haven for not only sun worshippers but also divers, surfers, and hikers (and the path between Levanto and Monterosso, about a 2.5-mile hike with free entrance, is breathtakingly beautiful in its own right). It's also an ideal starting point for day trips by train or boat to many interesting places along the Riviera such as Portovenere, Lerici, Tellaro, and Fiascherino heading toward La Spezia; and Portofino, Santa Margherita, Camogli, and Sestri Levante heading toward Genoa.

GETTING HERE AND AROUND
By car, take the Carodanno/Levanto exit off the A12 for 25 minutes to the town center. By train, Levanto is on the main north–south railway, one stop north of Monterosso.

VISITOR INFORMATION
Levanto Tourism Office ✉ *Piazza Mazzini 1* ☎ *0187/808125*
⊕ *www.aptcinqueterre.sp.it.*

WHERE TO STAY
For expanded hotel reviews, visit Fodors.com.

$$　🏨 **La Giada del Mesco.** Tastefully decorated and bright guest rooms on
HOTEL　the Punto Mesco headland have unobstructed vistas of the Mediterranean Sea and Riviera coastline. **Pros:** great position; nice pool. **Cons:** shuttle service is not always available; the 3½ km (1½ mile) into town is quite a walk, so you'll want a car. $ *Rooms from: €170* ✉ *Via Mesco 16* ☎ *0187/802674* ⊕ *www.lagiadadelmesco.com* 🛏 *12 rooms* ☽ *Closed mid-Nov.–Feb.* ⦿ *Breakfast.*

CHIAVARI

46 km (29 miles) northwest of Levanto, 38 km (23 miles) southeast of Genoa.

Chiavari is a fishing town (rather than village) of considerable character, with narrow, twisting streets and a good harbor. Chiavari's citizens were intrepid explorers, and many emigrated to South America in the 19th century. The town boomed, thanks to the wealth of the returning voyagers, but Chiavari retains many medieval traces in its buildings.

GETTING HERE AND AROUND
By car, take the Chiavari exit off the A12. The Chiavari train station is located on the main north–south train line between Genoa and Pisa.

VISITOR INFORMATION
Chiavari Tourism Office ✉ *Corso Assaroti 1* ☎ *0185/325198*
⊕ *www.turismoinliguria.it.*

EXPLORING
Museo Archeologico. A worthy collection in the town center displays objects from an 8th-century BC necropolis, or ancient cemetery, excavated nearby. ✉ *Palazzo Costaguta, Via Costaguta 4, Piazza Matteotti* ☎ *0185/320829* 🎟 *Free* ☽ *Tues.–Sat. and 2nd and 4th Sun. of month 9–1:30.*

SANTA MARGHERITA LIGURE

60 km (37 miles) northwest of Levanto, 31 km (19 miles) southeast of Genoa.

A beautiful old resort town favored by well-to-do Italians, Santa Margherita Ligure has everything a Riviera playground should have—plenty of palm trees and attractive hotels, cafés, and a marina packed with yachts. Some of the older buildings here are still decorated on the outside with the trompe-l'oeil frescoes typical of this part of the Riviera. This is a pleasant, convenient base, which for many represents a perfect balance on the Italian Riviera: more spacious than the Cinque Terre; less glitzy than San Remo; more relaxing than Genoa and environs; and ideally situated for day trips, such as an excursion to Portofino.

GETTING HERE AND AROUND

By car, take the Rapallo exit off the A12 and follow the blue signs, about a 10-minute drive. The Santa Margherita Ligure train station is on the main north–south line between Genoa and Pisa.

VISITOR INFORMATION

Santa Margherita Ligure Tourism Office ✉ *Piazza G. Mazzini 46* ☎ *0185/2055456* 🌐 *www.smlturismo.it.*

WHERE TO EAT

$$ LIGURIAN 🍴 **La Paranza.** From the piles of tiny *bianchetti* (young sardines) in oil and lemon that are part of the antipasto *di mare* (of the sea), to the simple, perfectly grilled whole sole, fresh seafood in every shape and form is the specialty here. Mussels, clams, octopus, salmon, or whatever else is fresh that day is what's on the menu. Locals say this is the town's best restaurant, but if you're looking for a stylish evening out, look elsewhere—La Paranza is about food, not fashion. It's just off Santa Margherita's port. [$] *Average meal: €45* ✉ *Via Jacopo Ruffini 46* ☎ *0185/283686* ✍ *Reservations essential* ⏰ *Closed Mon. and Nov.*

$$$ LIGURIAN Fodor's Choice ★ 🍴 **La Stalla dei Frati.** The breathtaking, hilltop views of Santa Margherita from this villa-turned-restaurant are worth the harrowing 3-km (2-mile) drive from the port. Cesare Frati, your congenial host, is likely to tempt you with his homemade fettuccine *ai frutti di mare* (with seafood) followed by the *pescato del giorno alla moda ligure* (catch of the day baked Ligurian style, with potatoes, olives, and pine nuts) and a delightfully fresh lemon sorbet to complete the feast. [$] *Average meal: €60* ✉ *Via G. Pino 27, Nozarego* ☎ *0185/289447* 🌐 *www.ristorantelastalladeifrati.it* ⏰ *Closed Mon. and Nov.*

$$$ ECLECTIC 🍴 **Oca Bianca.** The menu breaks away from the local norm—there is no seafood on offer. Meat dishes are the specialty, and choices may include mouthwatering preparations of lamb from France or New Zealand, steak from Ireland or Brazil, South African ostrich, and Italian pork. Delicious antipasti, an extensive wine list, and the attentive service add to the experience. Dinner is served until 1 am. [$] *Average meal: €65* ✉ *Via XXV Aprile 21* ☎ *0185/288411* 🌐 *www.ristoranteocabianca.net* ✍ *Reservations essential* ⏰ *Closed Mon. and Jan. Lunch by reservation only.*

$$ LIGURIAN Fodor's Choice ★ 🍴 **U' Giancu.** Owner Fausto Oneto is a man of many hats. Though original cartoons cover the walls of his restaurant and a playground is the main feature of the outdoor seating area, he is completely serious about his cooking. Lamb dishes are particularly delicious, his own garden provides the freshest possible vegetables, and the wine list (ask to visit the cantina) is excellent. For those who want to learn the secrets of Ligurian cuisine, Fausto provides lively morning cooking lessons. U' Giancu is 8 km (5 miles) northwest of Santa Margherita Ligure. [$] *Average meal: €45* ✉ *Via San Massimo 78, Località San Massimo, Rapallo* ☎ *0185/261212* 🌐 *www.ugiancu.it* ⏲ *Closed Wed. and mid-Jan.–mid-Feb.*

WORD OF MOUTH

"Portofino is a beautiful site. I wouldn't miss a hike to Castello Brown or the scenic path to the lighthouse at Punta da Capo. Both offer lovely and very photogenic views."

—waggis

WHERE TO STAY

For expanded hotel reviews, visit Fodors.com.

$$$ HOTEL 🏨 **Continental.** A stately seaside mansion surrounded by a lush garden shaded by tall palms and pine trees offers stylish accommodations done in a blend of classic furnishings, mostly inspired by the 19th century. **Pros:** lovely location; private beach. **Cons:** rooms in the annex are not as nice as those in the main building; breakfast is unimaginative. [$] *Rooms from: €230* ✉ *Via Pagana 8* ☎ *0185/286512* 🌐 *www.hotel-continental.it* 🛏 *69 rooms, 4 suites* 🍽 *Breakfast.*

$$$$ RESORT 🏨 **Grand Hotel Miramare.** Classic Riviera elegance prevails at this palatial hotel overlooking the bay, where antique furniture and crystal chandeliers fill the high-ceilinged rooms. **Pros:** top-notch service; private beach; well-maintained rooms and marble bathroons. **Cons:** traffic in summer from the road in front of the hotel. [$] *Rooms from: €450* ✉ *Via Milite Ignoto 30* ☎ *0185/287013* 🌐 *www.grandhotelmiramare.it* 🛏 *75 rooms, 9 suites* ⏲ *Closed Jan. 6–Mar. 18* 🍽 *Breakfast.*

$ HOTEL 🏨 **Hotel Jolanda.** They may not have sea views, but stylish, comfortable, and spacious rooms are tastefully decorated, and some have large balconies. **Pros:** reasonable rates in a high-price area. **Cons:** no sea view; parking is limited and expensive. [$] *Rooms from: €150* ✉ *Via Luisito Costa 6* ☎ *0185/287512* 🌐 *www.hoteljolanda.it* 🛏 *47 rooms, 3 suites* 🍽 *Breakfast.*

8

PORTOFINO

5 km (3 miles) south of Santa Margherita Ligure, 36 km (22 miles) east of Genoa.

One of the most photographed villages along the coast, with a decidedly romantic and affluent aura, Portofino has long been a popular destination for the rich and famous. Once an ancient Roman colony and taken by the Republic of Genoa in 1229, it's also been ruled by the French, English, Spanish, and Austrians, as well as by marauding bands of 16th-century pirates. Elite British tourists first flocked to the lush harbor in the mid-1800s. Some of Europe's wealthiest drop anchor in Portofino in summer, but they stay out of sight by day, appearing in the evening after buses and boats have carried off the day-trippers.

There's not actually much to *do* in Portofino other than stroll around the wee harbor, see the castle, walk to Punta del Capo, browse at the pricey boutiques, and sip a coffee while people-watching. However, weaving through picture-perfect cliffside gardens and gazing at yachts framed by the turquoise Ligurian Sea and the cliffs of Santa Margherita can make for quite a relaxing afternoon. There are also several tame, photo-friendly hikes into the hills to nearby villages.

Unless you're traveling on a deluxe budget, you may want to stay in Camogli or Santa Margherita Ligure rather than at one of Portofino's few very expensive hotels. Restaurants and cafés are good but also pricey (don't expect to have a beer here for much under €10).

GETTING HERE AND AROUND
By car, exit at Rapallo off the A12 and follow the blue signs (about a 20-minute drive mostly along the coast). The nearest train station is Santa Margherita Ligure.

Trying to reach Portofino by bus or car on the single narrow road can be a nightmare in summer and on holiday weekends. No trains go directly to Portofino: you must stop at Santa Margherita and take the No. 82 public bus from there (€1.20). An alternative is to take a boat from Santa Margherita.

Portofino can also be reached from Santa Margherita on foot: it's about a 40-minute (very pleasant) walk along the sea.

VISITOR INFORMATION
Portofino Tourism Office ⊠ *Via Roma 35* ☎ *0185/269024*
⊕ *www.commune.portofino.genova.it.*

EXPLORING
Abbazia di San Fruttuoso (*Abbey of San Fruttuoso*). A medieval stronghold built by the Benedictines of Monte Cassino protects a minuscule fishing village that can be reached only on foot or by water—a 20-minute boat ride from Portofino and also reachable from Camogli, Santa Margherita Ligure, and Rapallo. The restored abbey is now the property of a national conservation fund (FAI) and occasionally hosts temporary exhibitions and contains the tombs of some illustrious members of the Doria family. Plan on spending a few hours enjoying the abbey and grounds, and perhaps lunching at one of the modest beachfront trattorias nearby (open only in summer). Boatloads of visitors can make this place very crowded very fast; you might appreciate it most off-season. ⊠ *15-min boat ride or 2-hr walk northwest of Portofino* ☎ *0185/772703* 🎫 *€5* ☉ *June–Sept. 15, daily 10–5:45; May and Sept. 16–30, daily 10–4:45; Oct.–Mar., Tues.–Sun. 10–3:45. Last entry 1 hr before closing.*

Castello Brown. From the harbor, follow the signs for the climb to Castello Brown—the most worthwhile sight in Portofino—with its medieval relics, impeccable gardens, and sweeping views. The castle was founded in the Middle Ages but restored from the 16th through 18th centuries. In true Portofino form, it was owned by Genoa's English consul from 1870 until it opened to the public in 1961. ⊠ *Above harbor*

📷 *0185/269046* ⊕ *www.castellobrown.it* 🎫*€3* ⊙ *Apr.–Sept., Wed.–Mon. 10–6; Oct.–Mar., Wed.–Mon. 10–5.*

Paraggi. The only sand beach near Portofino is at Paraggi, a cove on the road between Santa Margherita and Portofino. The bus will stop here on request.

Punta Portofino. Pristine views can be had from the deteriorating *faro* (lighthouse) at Punta Portofino, a 15-minute walk along the point that begins at the southern end of the port. Along the seaside path you can see numerous impressive, sprawling private residences behind high iron gates.

San Giorgio. This small church, sitting on a ridge above Portofino, is said to contain the relics of its namesake, brought back from the Holy Land by the Crusaders. Portofino enthusiastically celebrates Saint George's Day every April 23. ⊠ *Above harbor* 📷 *0185/269337* ⊙ *Daily 7–6.*

WHERE TO EAT

$ ✕**Canale.** If the staggering prices of virtually all of Portofino's restaurants put you off, the long line outside this family-run bakery indicates
BAKERY that you're not alone and that something special is in store. Here all the focaccia Genovese is baked on the spot and served fresh from the oven, along with all kinds of sandwiches, pastries, and other refreshments. The only problem is there's nowhere to sit—time for a picnic! $ *Average meal: €10* ⊠ *Via Roma 30* 📷 *0185/269248* ▭ *No credit cards* ⊙ *Closed Nov.–Feb.*

$$$ ✕**Ristorante Puny.** A table at this tiny restaurant is difficult to come by
LIGURIAN in summer, as the manager caters mostly to friends and regulars. If you are lucky enough to get in, however, the food will not disappoint, nor will the cozy but elegant yellow interior. The unforgettable pappardelle *al portofino* delicately blends two of Liguria's tastes: tomato and pesto. Ligurian seafood specialties include baked fish with bay leaves, potatoes, and olives, as well as the inventive *moscardini al forno* (baked mini-octopus with lemon and rosemary in tomato sauce). $ *Average meal: €60* ⊠ *Piazza Martiri dell'Olivetta 4–5, on harbor* 📷 *0185/269037* ▲ *Reservations essential* ⊙ *Closed Thurs. and Jan.–Feb.*

WHERE TO STAY

For expanded hotel reviews, visit Fodors.com.

$$$$ 🛏**Eight Hotel Portofino.** Immaculate, comfortable, and soothingly
HOTEL designed guest rooms with canopy beds, pastel walls, and ultramodern bathrooms spread across two small 19th-century town houses on a quiet backstreet. **Pros:** luxurious accommodations in the middle of the village; secluded garden at the back. **Cons:** some of the lower-level rooms don't receive much light; no sea views. $ *Rooms from: €490* ⊠ *Via Del Fondaco 11* 📷 *0185/26991* ⊕ *www.eighthotels.it* 📭*17 rooms, 1 suite* ⊙ *Closed Dec.–Mar.* 🍽*Breakfast.*

$$$$ 🛏**Splendido.** Arriving at this 1920s luxury hotel and settling into one
HOTEL of the gorgeous rooms is like entering a Jazz Age film set. **Pros:** all rooms have garden or sea views; caring staff; lovely gardens. **Cons:** be prepared to spend upward of €100 for a simple lunch for two (it's not just the rooms that are pricey). $ *Rooms from: €1200* ⊠ *Salita Baratta 16* 📷 *0185/267801* ⊕ *www.hotelsplendido.com* 📭*69 rooms, 39 suites* ⊙ *Closed mid-Nov.–late Mar.* 🍽*Some meals.*

8

SPORTS AND THE OUTDOORS

HIKING

If you have the stamina, you can hike to the Abbazia di San Fruttuoso from Portofino. It's a steep climb at first, and the walk takes about 2½ hours one-way. If you're extremely ambitious and want to make a day of it, you can hike another 2½ hours all the way to Camogli. Much more modest hikes from Portofino include a one-hour uphill walk to Cappella delle Gave, a bit inland in the hills, from where you can continue downhill to Santa Margherita Ligure (another 1½ hours) and a gently undulating paved trail leading to the beach at Paraggi (½ hour). Finally, there's a 2½-hour hike from Portofino that heads farther inland to Ruta, through Olmi and Pietre Strette. The trails are well marked and maps are available at the tourist information offices in Rapallo, Santa Margherita, Portofino, and Camogli.

CAMOGLI

15 km (9 miles) northwest of Portofino, 20 km (12 miles) east of Genoa.

Camogli, at the edge of the large promontory and nature reserve known as the Portofino Peninsula, has always been a town of sailors. By the 19th century it was leasing its ships throughout the continent. Today multicolor houses, remarkably deceptive trompe-l'oeil frescoes, and a massive 17th-century seawall mark this appealing harbor community, which is perhaps as beautiful as Portofino but without the glamour. When exploring on foot, don't miss the boat-filled second harbor, which is reached by ducking under a narrow archway at the northern end of the first one.

GETTING HERE AND AROUND

By car, exit the A12 at Recco and follow the blue signs. There are several pay-parking lots near the village center. Camogli is on the main north–south railway line between Genoa and La Spezia.

VISITOR INFORMATION

Camogli Tourism Office ⊠ *Via XX Settembre 33/R* ☎ *0185/771066* ⊕ *www.prolococamogli.it.*

EXPLORING

Acquario (*Aquarium*). The "Castello di Dragonara," built onto a sheer rock face near the harbor, is home to the Acquarium and Maritime Museum, where tanks filled with local marine life are built into the ramparts and exhibits feature artifacts of the region's martime history. ⊠ *Via Isola* ☎ *0185/773375* ⊠ *€3* ☉ *Summer, 10–12 and 3–7; Winter, 10–11:45 and 2–5:45.*

OFF THE BEATEN PATH

Ruta. The footpaths that leave from Ruta, 4 km (2½ miles) east of Camogli, thread through rugged terrain and contain a multitude of plant species. Weary hikers are sustained by stunning views of the Riviera di Levante from various vantage points along the way.

WHERE TO EAT

$$

SEAFOOD

✕ **Vento Ariel.** This small, friendly restaurant serves some of the best seafood in town. Dine on the shaded terrace in summer and watch the bustling activity in the nearby port. Only the freshest seafood is served; try the spaghetti *alle vongole* (with clams) or the mixed grilled fish. [$] *Average meal: €45* ✉ *Calata Porto* ☎ *0185/771080* 🌐 *www.ventoariel.it* 🕓 *Closed Wed., 1st half of Dec., and Jan.*

WHERE TO STAY

For expanded hotel reviews, visit Fodors.com.

$$ HOTEL 🏨 **Cenobio dei Dogi.** Perched majestically a step above Camogli, many of the rooms in the former summer palace of Genoa's doges have expansive balconies with commanding vistas of Camogli's cozy port. **Pros:** location and setting are wonderful; lovely pool and gardens; private beach. **Cons:** crowds make it seem overbooked in summer; decor is a bit old-fashioned. [$] *Rooms from: €230* ✉ *Via Cuneo 34* ☎ *0185/7241* 🌐 *www.cenobio.it* 🛏 *102 rooms, 4 suites* 🍴 *Breakfast.*

$$$ B&B/INN 🏨 **Villa Rosmarino.** A beautiful Ligurian villa in the beautiful hills just above Camogli offers chic, contemporary, and comfortable accommodations, along with well-manicured gardens and a welcoming pool. **Pros:** large beds; well-equipped bathrooms; total sense of relaxation. **Cons:** rooms are small and may not have enough amenities for everyone's taste. [$] *Rooms from: €250* ✉ *Via Figari 38* ☎ *0185/771580* 🌐 *www.villarosmarino.com* 🛏 *6 rooms* 🍴 *Breakfast.*

NIGHTLIFE AND THE ARTS

Sagra del Pesce. The highlight of the festival of San Fortunato is held on the second Sunday of May each year. It's a crowded, colorful, and free-to-the-public feast of freshly caught fish, cooked outside at the port in a frying pan 12 feet wide.

8

GENOA

Genoa (Genova in Italian) was the birthplace of Christopher Columbus, but the city's proud history predates that explorer by hundreds of years. Genoa was already an important trading station by the 3rd century BC, when the Romans conquered Liguria. The Middle Ages and the Renaissance saw it rise to become a jumping-off place for the Crusaders, a commercial center of tremendous wealth and prestige, and a strategic bone of international contention. A network of fortresses defending the city connected by a wall second only in length to the Great Wall of China was constructed in the hills above, and Genoa's bankers, merchants, and princes adorned the city with palaces, churches, and impressive art collections.

Crammed into a thin crescent of land between sea and mountains, Genoa expanded up rather than out, taking on the form of a multilayer wedding cake, with churches, streets, and entire residential neighborhoods built on others' rooftops. Public elevators and funiculars are as common as buses and trains.

But with its impressive palaces and museums, the largest medieval city center in Europe, and an elaborate network of ancient hilltop fortresses, Genoa may be just the dose of culture you're looking for. Europe's biggest boat show, the annual Salone Nautico Internazionale, is held here. Fine restaurants are abundant, and classical dance and music are richly represented. The Teatro Carlo Felice is the local opera venue, and where the internationally renowned annual Niccolò Paganini Violin Contest takes place.

GETTING HERE AND AROUND

By car, take the Genoa Ovest exit off the A12 and take the upper bridge (*sopralevata*) to the second exit, Genova Centro–Piazza Corvetto. But be forewarned: driving in Genoa is harrowing and best avoided whenever possible. If you want to see the city on a day trip, go by train; if you're staying in the city, park in a garage or by valet and go by foot and taxi throughout your stay.

Regular train service operates from Genoa's two stations.

The best way by far to get around Genoa is on foot, with the occasional assistance of public transportation. Many of the more interesting districts are either entirely closed to traffic, have roads so narrow that no car could fit, or are, even at the best of times, blocked by gridlock. Although it might seem a daunting task, exploring the city is made simple by its geography. The historical center of Genoa occupies a relatively narrow strip of land running between the mountains and the sea. You can easily visit the most important monuments in one or two days.

Transportation Contacts

AMT. The main bus station in Genoa is at Piazza Principe. Local buses, operated by the municipal transport company AMT, serve the steep valleys that run to some of the towns along the western coast. Tickets may be bought at local bus stations or at newsstands. (You must have a ticket before you board.) AMT also operates the funicular railways and the elevators that service the steeper sections of the city. ⊠ *Piazza Acquaverde* ☎ *010/5582414* ⊕ *www.amt.genova.it.*

Stazione Brignole. Departures from Stazione Brignole go to points east and south. All the coastal resorts are on this line. ⊠ *Piazza Giuseppe Verdi, Foce* ☎ *892021.*

Stazione Principe. Departures from Stazione Principe travel to points west. ⊠ *Piazza del Principe, San Teodoro.*

VISITOR INFORMATION

Genoa Tourism Offices ⊠ *Via Garibaldi 12r, Maddalena* ☎ *010/5572903* ⊕ *www.genova-turismo.it* ⏱ *Daily 9–1 and 2:30–6:30.* ⊠ *Largo Pertini 13* ☎ *010/8606122* ⊠ *Terminale Crociere, Ponte dei Mille.*

EXPLORING GENOA

THE MEDIEVAL CORE AND POINTS ABOVE

TOP ATTRACTIONS

Cimitero Monumentale di Staglieno. One of the most famous of Genovese landmarks is this bizarrely beautiful cemetery; its fanciful marble and bronze sculptures sprawl haphazardly across a hillside on the outskirts of town. A pantheon holds indoor tombs and some remarkable works like an 1878 *Eve* by Villa. Don't miss Rovelli's 1896 **Tomba Raggio,** which shoots Gothic spires out of the hillside forest. The cemetery began operation in 1851 and has been lauded by such visitors as Mark Twain and Evelyn Waugh. It covers a good deal of ground (allow at least half a day to explore). Take Bus No. 12, 13, or 14 from the Stazione Genova Brignole, Bus No. 34 or 48 from Stazione Principe, or a taxi. ⊠ *Piazzale Resasco, Piazza Manin* ☎ *010/870184* ▦ *Free* ⊙ *Daily 7:30–5; last entry at 4:30.*

Galleria Nazionale. Housed in the richly adorned **Palazzo Spinola** north of Piazza Soziglia, this beautiful museum contains masterpieces by Luca Giordano and Guido Reni. The *Ecce Homo,* by Antonello da

WORD OF MOUTH

"Be sure to wander around the maze of narrow lanes in the ancient part of [Genoa] by the port—all scrubbed up recently—this warren of tiny lanes is the epitome of old-world charm—once a dicey area now all gussied up for tourists."

—PalenQ

Messina, is a hauntingly beautiful painting, of historical interest because it was the Sicilian da Messina who first brought Flemish oil paints and techniques to Italy from his sojourns in the Low Countries. ⊠ *Piazza Pelliceria 1, Maddalena* ☎ *010/2705300* ⊕ *www.palazzospinola.it* ▦ *€4, €6.50 with Palazzo Reale* ⊙ *Tues.–Sat. 8:30–7:30, Sun. 1:30–7:30.*

Palazzo Bianco. It's difficult to miss the splendid white facade of this town palace as you walk down Via Garibaldi, once one of Genoa's most important streets. The building houses a fine collection of 17th-century art, with the Spanish and Flemish schools well represented. ⊠ *Via Garibaldi 11, Maddalena* ☎ *010/2759185* ⊕ *www.museidigenova.it* ▦ *€9, includes Palazzo Rosso and Palazzo Doria Tursi* ⊙ *Tues.–Fri. 9–7, weekends 10–7.*

Fodor'sChoice **Palazzo Reale.** Lavish rococo rooms provide sumptuous display space
★ for paintings, sculptures, tapestries, and Asian ceramics. The 17th-century palace—also known as Palazzo Balbi Durazzo—was built by the Balbi family, enormously wealthy Genovese merchants. Its regal pretensions were not lost on the Savoy, who bought the palace and turned it into a royal residence in the early 19th century. The gallery of mirrors and the ballroom on the upper floor are particularly decadent. Look for works by Sir Anthony Van Dyck, who lived in Genoa for six years, beginning in 1621, and painted many portraits of the Genovese nobility. The formal gardens, which you can visit for €1, provide a welcome respite from the bustle of the city beyond the palace walls, as well as great views of the harbor. ⊠ *Via Balbi 10, Pré* ☎ *010/2710236* ⊕ *www.palazzorealegenova.it* ▦ *€4, €6.50 with Galleria Nazionale* ⊙ *Tues. and Wed. 9–1:30, Thurs.–Sun. 9–7.*

Palazzo Rosso. This 17th-century Baroque palace was named for the red stone used in its construction. It now contains, apart from a number of lavishly frescoed suites, works by Titian, Veronese, Reni, and Van Dyck. ⊠ *Via Garibaldi 18, Maddalena* ☎ *010/2759185* ⊕ *www. museidigenova.it* ▦ *€9, includes Palazzo Bianco and Palazzo Doria Tursi* ⊙ *Tues.–Fri. 9–7, weekends 10–7.*

Zecca-Righi funicular. A seven-stop commuter funicular begins at Piazza della Nunziata and ends at a high lookout on the fortified gates in the 17th-century city walls. Ringed around the circumference of the city are a number of huge fortresses; this gate was part of the city's system

8

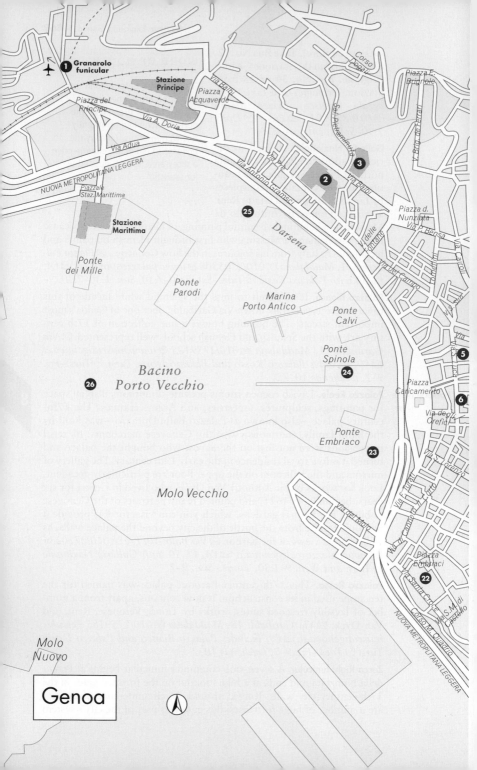

Genoa

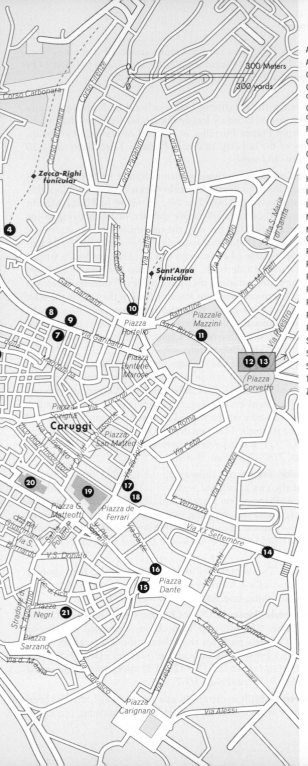

of defenses. From Righi you can undertake scenic all-day hikes from one fortress to the next. ⊠ *Piazza della Nunziata, Pré* ☎ *010/5582414* ⊕ *www.amt.genova.it* 🖭 *€2* ☾ *Daily 6 am–11:45 pm.*

WORTH NOTING

Castelletto. To reach this charming neighborhood high above the city center, you take one of Genoa's handy municipal elevators that whisk you skyward from Piazza Portello, at the end of Galleria Garibaldi, for a good view of the old city. ⊠ *Piazza Portello, Castelletto* 🖭 *€1.20* ☾ *Daily 6:40 am–midnight.*

FAMILY **Ferrovia Genova–Casella.** In continuous operation since 1929, the Genova–Casella Railroad runs from Piazza Manin in Genoa (follow Via Montaldo from the center of town, or take Bus No. 33 or 34 to Piazza Manin) through the beautiful countryside above the city, finally arriving in the rural hill town of Casella. On the way, the tiny train traverses a series of precarious switchbacks that afford sweeping views of the forested Ligurian hills. In Casella Paese (the last stop) you can hike, eat lunch, or just check out the view and ride back. There are two restaurants and two pizzerias near the Casella station; try local cuisine at Trattoria Teresin in Località Avosso. **Canova** (two stops from the end of the line) is the start of two possible hikes through the hills: one a two-hour, one-way trek to a small sanctuary, **Santuario della Vittoria,** and the other a more grueling four-hour hike to the hill town of **Creto.** Another worthwhile stop along the rail line is **Sant'Olcese Tullo,** where you can take a half-hour (one-way) walk along a river and through the **Sentiero Botanico di Ciaé,** a botanical garden and forest refuge with labeled specimens of Ligurian flora and a tiny medieval castle. For Canova and Sant'Olcese, inform your conductor that you want him to stop. The Genova–Casella Railroad is a good way to get a sense of the rugged landscape around Genoa, and you may have it to yourself. The train departs about every hour. ⊠ *Piazza Manin* ☎ *010/837321* ⊕ *www.ferroviagenovacasella.it* 🖭 *€3.40 round trip* ☾ *Mon.–Sat. 7:30–7:30, Sun. 9–8:15.*

FAMILY **Granarolo Funicular.** Take a cog railway up the steeply rising terrain to another part of the city's fortified walls. It takes 15 minutes to hoist you from Stazione Principe, on Piazza Acquaverde, to **Porta Granarolo,** 1,000 feet above, where the sweeping view gives you a sense of Genoa's size. The funicular departs about every half hour. ⊠ *Piazza del Principe, San Teodoro* ☎ *010/5582414* ⊕ *www.amt.genova.it* 🖭 *€2* ☾ *Daily 6 am–11:45 pm.*

Loggia dei Mercanti. This merchants' row dating from the 16th century is lined with shops selling local foods and gifts, as well as raincoats, rubber boots, and fishing line. ⊠ *Piazza Banchi, Maddalena.*

Museo d'Arte Orientale Chiossone. One of Europe's most noteworthy collections of Japanese, Chinese, and Thai objects is housed in galleries in the Villetta di Negro park on the hillside above Piazza Portello. There's also a fine view of the city from the museum's terrace. ⊠ *Piazzale Mazzini 4, Maddalena* ☎ *010/542285* ⊕ *www.museidigenova.it* 🖭 *€5* ☾ *Tues.–Fri. 9–7, weekends 10–7.*

Palazzo dell'Università. Built in the 1630s as a Jesuit college, this has been Genoa's university since 1803. The exterior is unassuming, but climb the stairway flanked by lions to visit the handsome courtyard, with its portico of double Doric columns. ✉ *Via Balbi 5, Pré* ☎ *01020991* ⊕ *www.unige.it.*

Palazzo Doria Tursi. In the 16th century, wealthy resident Nicolò Grimaldi had a palace built of pink stone quarried in the region. It's been reincarnated as Genoa's Palazzo Municipale (Municipal Building), and so most of the goings-on inside are the stuff of local politics and quickie weddings. You can visit the richly decorated **Sala Paganini**, where the famous Guarnerius violin that belonged to Niccolò Paganini (1782–1840) is displayed, along with the gardens that connect the palace with the neighboring Palazzo Bianco. ✉ *Via Garibaldi 9, Maddalena* ☎ *010/2759185* ⊕ *www.museidigenova.it* ✎ *€9, includes Palazzo Bianco and Palazzo Rosso* ☾ *Tues.–Fri. 9–7, weekends 10–7.*

San Siro. Genoa's oldest church was the city's cathedral from the 4th to the 9th century. Rebuilt in the 16th and 17th centuries, it now feels a bit like a haunted house—imposing frescoes line dank hallways, and chandeliers hold crooked candles flickering in the darkness. ✉ *Via San Luca, Maddalena* ☎ *010/22461468* ☾ *Daily 8–noon and 3–7.*

Santissima Annunziata del Vastato. Exuberantly frescoed vaults decorate the 16th- to 17th-century church, which is an excellent example of Genovese baroque architecture. There's a 40-minute guided tour each Sunday at 11:30 (minimum of five people). ✉ *Piazza della Nunziata, Pré* ☎ *010/2465525* ☾ *Mon.–Fri. 7:30 am–8:00 pm, Sat. 7:30–1 and 3–8:30, Sun. 8–1 and 3–8.*

SOUTHERN DISTRICTS AND THE AQUARIUM
TOP ATTRACTIONS

FAMILY **Acquario di Genova.** Europe's biggest aquarium, second in the world only to Osaka's in Japan, is the third-most-visited museum in Italy and a must for children. Fifty tanks of marine species, including sea turtles, dolphins, seals, eels, penguins, and sharks, share space with educational displays and re-creations of marine ecosystems, including a tank of coral from the Red Sea. An entire "Aquarium Village" has been created, which also includes a biosphere, hummingbird forest, and interactive submarine exhibit. If arriving by car, take the Genova Ovest exit from the autostrada. ✉ *Ponte Spinola, Porto Vecchio* ☎ *0101/2345678* ⊕ *www. acquario.ge.it* ✎ *€19 for adults, €13 for kids ages 4–12, free for children 3 and under. Aquarium Village tickets (for entrance to all attractions): €39 for adults, €27 for children 4–12, free for children 3 and under.* ☾ *Mar.–June, weekdays 9–7:30, weekends 8:45–8:30; July and Aug., daily 8:30 am–10 pm; Nov.–Feb., weekdays 9:30–7:30, weekends 9:30–8:30. Entry permitted every ½ hr; last entry 1½ hrs before closing.*

Galata Museo del Mare. Devoted entirely to the city's seafaring history, this museum is probably the best way, at least on dry land, to get an idea of the changing shape of Genoa's busy port. Highlighting the displays is a full-size replica of a 17th-century Genovese galleon. ✉ *Calata de Mari 1, Ponte dei Mille* ☎ *010/2345655* ⊕ *www.galatamuseodelmare.it* ✎ *€17 for aults, €7 for kids 4–12, free for children 3 and under* ☾ *Mar.–Oct., daily 10–7:30; Nov.–Feb., Tues.–Fri. 10–6, weekends 10–7:30. Last entry 1 hr. before closing.*

8

The Harbor. A boat tour gives you a good perspective on the layout of the harbor, which dates to Roman times. The Genoa inlet, the largest along the Italian Riviera, was also used by the Phoenicians and Greeks as a harbor and a staging area from which they could penetrate inland to form settlements and to trade.

The port is guarded by the Diga Foranea, a striking wall 5 km (3 miles) long built into the ocean. The **Lanterna,** a lighthouse more than 360 feet tall, was built in 1544; it's one of Italy's oldest lighthouses and a traditional emblem of Genoa.

Consorzio Liguria Viamare. Boat tours of the harbor, operated by the Consorzio Liguria Viamare, launch from the aquarium pier and last about an hour. The tours include a visit to the breakwater outside the harbor, the Bacino delle Grazie, and the Molo Vecchio (Old Port). There are also daily excursions down the coast as far as the Cinque Terre and Portovenere. ⊠ *Via Sottoripa 7/8, Porto Vecchio* ☎ *010/265712* ⊕ *www.liguriaviamare.it* ⊠ *€6 for port tour, €33 and up for tours to Cinque Terre* ☉ *Daily; departure times vary.*

Palazzo Ducale. This palace was built in the 16th century over a medieval hall, and its facade was rebuilt in the late 18th century and later restored. It now houses temporary exhibitions and a restaurant-bar serving fusion cuisine. Reservations are necessary to visit the dungeons and tower. Guided tours (€5) of the palace, its prison tower, and its exhibitions are available. ⊠ *Piazza Matteotti 9, Portoria* ☎ *010/5574004* ⊕ *www.palazzoducale.genova.it* ⊠ *€4* ☉ *Daily 9–7.*

San Lorenzo. Contrasting black slate and white marble, so common in Liguria, embellishes the cathedral at the heart of medieval Genoa, inside and out. Consecrated in 1118, the church honors Saint Lawrence, who passed through the city on his way to Rome in the 3rd century. For hundreds of years the building was used for religious and state purposes such as civic elections. Note the 13th-century Gothic portal, the fascinating twisted barbershop columns, and the 15th- to 17th-century frescoes inside. The last campanile dates from the early 16th century. The **Museo del Tesoro di San Lorenzo** (San Lorenzo Treasury Museum) housed inside has some stunning pieces from medieval goldsmiths and silversmiths, for which medieval Genoa was renowned. ⊠ *Piazza San Lorenzo, Molo* ☎ *010/2471831* ⊠ *Cathedral free, museum €4.50* ☉ *Cathedral: Daily 8–12 and 3–7. Museum: Mon.–Sat. 9–12 and 3–6, and 1st Sunday of the month 3–6.*

Sant'Agostino. This 13th-century Gothic church was damaged during World War II, but still has a fine campanile and two well-preserved cloisters that house an excellent museum displaying pieces of medieval architecture and fresco paintings. Highlights of the collection are the enigmatic fragments of a tomb sculpture by Giovanni Pisano (circa 1250–1315). ⊠ *Piazza Sarzano 35/R, Molo* ☎ *010/2511263* ⊕ *www. museidigenova.it* ⊠ *€4* ☉ *Tues.–Fri. 9–7, weekends 10–7.*

CLOSE UP

The Art of the Pesto Pestle

You may have known Genoa primarily for its salami or its brash explorer, but the city's most direct effect on your life away from Italy may be through its cultivation of one of the world's best pasta sauces. The sublime blend of basil, extra-virgin olive oil, garlic, pine nuts, and grated pecorino and Parmigiano-Reggiano cheeses that forms *pesto alla Genovese* is one of Italy's crowning culinary achievements, a concoction that Italian food guru Marcella Hazan has called "the most seductive of all sauces for pasta." Ligurian pesto is served only over spaghetti, gnocchi, lasagna, or—most authentically— *trenette* (a flat, spaghetti-like pasta)

or *trofie* (short, doughy pasta twists), and then typically mixed with boiled potatoes and green beans. Pesto is also occasionally used to flavor minestrone. The small-leaf basil grown in the region's sunny seaside hills is considered by many to be the best in the world, and pesto sauce was invented primarily as a showcase for that singular flavor. The simplicity and rawness of pesto is one of its virtues, as cooking (or even heating) basil ruins its delicate flavor. In fact, pesto aficionados refuse even to subject the basil leaves to an electric blender; Genovese (and other) foodies insist that true pesto can be made only with mortar and pestle.

Santa Maria di Castello. One of Genoa's most significant religious buildings, an early Christian church, was rebuilt in the 12th century and finally completed in 1513. You can visit the adjacent cloisters and see the fine artwork contained in the museum. Hours vary during religious services. ⊠ *Salita di Santa Maria di Castello 15, Molo* 🕾 *010/25495-225* ⊕ *www.santamariadicastello.it* 🖭 *Free* ☼ *Daily 9–noon and 3:30–6:30.*

8

WORTH NOTING

Accademia delle Belle Arti. Founded in 1751, the city's famous art school houses a collection of paintings from the 16th to the 19th century. Genovese artists of the Baroque period are particularly well represented. ⊠ *Largo Pertini 4, Portoria* 🕾 *010/581957* ⊕ *www.accademialigustica. it* 🖭 *Free* ☼ *Mon.–Sat. 9–1.*

Childhood home of Christopher Columbus. The ivy-covered remains of this fabled medieval house stand in the gardens below the Porta Soprana. A small and rather disappointing collection of objects and reproductions relating to the life and travels of Columbus are on display inside. ⊠ *Piazza Dante, Molo* 🕾 *010/2465346* 🖭 *€4* ☼ *Tues.–Sun. 9–5.*

FAMILY **Il Bigo.** This spiderlike white structure, designed by world-renowned architect Renzo Piano, was erected in 1992 to celebrate the Columbus quincentenary. You can take its **Ascensore Panoramico Bigo** (Bigo Panoramic Elevator) up 650 feet for a 360-degree view of the harbor, city, and sea. In winter there's an ice-skating rink next to the elevator, in an area covered by sail-like awnings. ⊠ *Ponte Spinola, Porto Vecchio* 🕾 *010/2345278 skating rink* 🖭 *Elevator €4; skating rink €8* ☼ *Elevator: Jan. 7–Feb. and Nov.–Dec. 25, weekends 10–5; Mar.–May, Sept., and Oct., Mon. 2–6, Tues.–Sun. 10–6; June–Aug., Mon. 4–11 pm, Tues.–Sun. 10 am–11 pm; Dec. 26–Jan. 6, daily 10–5. Skating rink: Nov. or Dec.– Mar., weekdays 8 am–9:30 pm, Sat. 10 am–2 am, Sun. 10 am–midnight.*

Mercato Orientale. In the old cloister of a church along Via XX Settembre, this bustling produce, fish, and meat market is a wonderful sensory overload. Get a glimpse of colorful everyday Genovese life watching the merchants and buyers banter over prices. ⊠ *Via XX Settembre, Portoria* ⊕ *www.mercatoorientale.org* ⊙ *Mon.–Sat. 7–1 and 3:30–7:30.*

Porta Soprana. A striking 12th-century twin-tower structure, this medieval gateway stands on the spot where a road from ancient Rome entered the city. It is just steps uphill from Columbus's boyhood home, and legend has it that the explorer's father was employed here as a gatekeeper. ⊠ *Piazza Dante, Molo.*

San Donato. Although somewhat marred by 19th- and 20th-century restorations, the 12th-century San Donato—with its original portal and octagonal campanile—is a fine example of Genovese Romanesque architecture. Inside, an altarpiece by the Flemish artist Joos Van Cleve (circa 1485–1540) depicts the Adoration of the Magi. ⊠ *Piazza San Donato, Portoria* ☏ *010/2468869* ⊙ *Mon.–Sat. 8–noon and 3–7, Sun. 9–12:30 and 3–7.*

San Matteo. This typically Genovese black-and-white-striped church dates from the 12th century; its crypt contains the tomb of Andrea Doria (1466–1560), the Genovese admiral who maintained the independence of his native city. The well-preserved Piazza San Matteo was, for 500 years, the seat of the Doria family, which ruled Genoa and much of Liguria from the 16th to the 18th century. The square is bounded by 13th- to 15th-century houses decorated with portals and loggias. ⊠ *Piazza San Matteo, Maddalena* ☏ *010/2474361* ⊙ *Mon.–Sat. 8–noon and 4–7, Sun. 9:30–10:30 and 4–5.*

Teatro Carlo Felice. The World War II–ravaged opera house in Genoa's modern center, Piazza de Ferrari, was rebuilt and reopened in 1991 to host the fine Genovese opera company; its massive tower has been the subject of much criticism. Lavish productions of old favorites and occasional world premieres are staged from October to May. ⊠ *Passo Eugenio Montale 4, Piazza de Ferrari, Portoria* ☏ *010/53811* ⊕ *www.carlofelice.it.*

WHERE TO EAT

$$$$
LIGURIAN

✕ **Antica Osteria del Bai.** Look out from a large dark wood-paneled room over the Ligurian Sea from this romantic spot perched high on a cliff in a nice suburb of the city. A seaside theme pervades the art and menu, which might include black gnocchi with lobster sauce or ravioli ai frutti di mare. The restaurant's traditional elegance is reflected in its white tablecloths, dress code, and prices. $ *Average meal: €65* ⊠ *Via Quarto 16, Quarto* ☏ *010/387478* ⊕ *www.osteriadelbai.it* ⚲ *Jacket and tie* ⊙ *Closed Mon., Jan. 10–20, and Aug. 1–20.*

$
LIGURIAN

✕ **Bakari.** Hip styling and ambient lighting hint at this eatery's creative, even daring, takes on Ligurian classics. Sure bets are the spinach-and-cheese gnocchi, any of several carpaccios, and the delicate beef dishes. Reserve ahead, request a table on the more imaginative ground floor, or just stop by for an aperitivo and people-watching. $ *Average meal: €30* ⊠ *Vico del Fieno 16/R, northwest of Piazza San Matteo, Maddalena* ☏ *010/291936* ⊕ *www.bakari.it* ⊙ *closed Sun. No lunch Sat.*

$$$ WINE BAR 🍴 **Enoteca Sola.** Menus are chosen specifically to complement wines at Pino Sola's airy, casually elegant enoteca in the heart of the modern town. The short menu emphasizes seafood and varies daily but might include stuffed artichokes or baked stockfish. The real draw, though, is the wine list, which includes some of the winners of the prestigious Italian *Tre Bicchieri* (Three Glasses) Award, denoting only the very best. [$] *Average meal: €45* ✉ *Via C. Barabino 120/R, Foce* ☎ *010/594513* ⏲ *Closed Sun. and 2 wks in Aug.*

$ LIGURIAN 🍴 **Exultate.** When the weather permits, umbrella-shaded tables spread out from this tiny eatery into the nearby square. The inexpensive daily menu is presented on a chalkboard for all to see; excellent pizza, meal-size salads, and delicious homemade desserts highlight the list. [$] *Average meal: €20* ✉ *Piazza Lavagna 15/R, Maddalena* ☎ *010/2468724* ⏲ *Closed Sun.*

$$$ LIGURIAN 🍴 **Le Rune.** The intimate setting, creative Ligurian dishes, and fine service make this a favorite with local businessmen and the after-opera crowd from nearby Teatro Carlo Felice. Standouts from the menu include the *tagliata di tonno* (sliced tuna) served with fresh fennel and a grapefruit sauce, and for an antipasto, the wonderful *timballo di robiola*, which is similar to a cheese soufflé served with a pear and cinnamon sauce. It's so good you could almost have it again for dessert. [$] *Average meal: €45* ✉ *Vico Domoculta 14/R, just off Via XXV Aprile, Portoria* ☎ *010/594951* ⏲ *No lunch Sun.*

$$ ITALIAN 🍴 **Maxela.** Beef is king in these lovely surroundings where meals were first served in 1790. The owners have retained most of its original design, including wood benches and slabs of marble for tables. Daily specials are listed on chalkboards, or you can just walk up to the butcher counter and pick your cut of choice. They also have a very reasonable prix-fixe lunch menu (under €20 per person) with abundant choices. [$] *Average meal: €40* ✉ *Vico Inferiore del Ferro 9/R, Maddalena* ☎ *010/2474209* 🌐 *www.maxela.it* ⏲ *Closed Sun.*

8

WHERE TO STAY

For expanded hotel reviews, visit Fodors.com.

$ HOTEL 🏨 **Agnello d'Oro.** A few of the simple, modern rooms have balconies, and a few others have vaulted ceilings. **Pros:** 100 yards from Stazione Principe; near the Palazzo Reale. **Cons:** few amenities. [$] *Rooms from: €75* ✉ *Vico delle Monachette 6, Pré* ☎ *010/2462084* 🌐 *www.hotelagnellodoro.it* 🛏 *25 rooms* 🍽 *Breakfast.*

$$ HOTEL 🏨 **Melia Bentley Genova.** Bright and sleekly decorated guest rooms and the in-house "Genovese-gourmet" restaurant frequented by celebrities and soccer players bring a lot of glamour to the city. **Pros:** for top-of-the-line style and amenities at a good price. **Cons:** it's a bit of a walk to the port and centro. [$] *Rooms from: €175* ✉ *Via Corsica 4, Carignano* ☎ *010/5315111* 🌐 *www.melia-hotels.com* 🛏 *85 rooms, 14 suites* 🍽 *Breakfast.*

$$ HOTEL 🏨 **Best Western City.** A bland apartment-building exterior gives way to a polished lobby and light, modern rooms, many with spectacular city views. **Pros:** location can't be beat; great views from upper floors. **Cons:**

regular rooms are small. $ Rooms from: €170 ⊠ Via San Sebastiano 6, Portoria ☎ 010/584707 🖷 010/586301 ⊕ www.bwcityhotel-ge.it ⇘ 63 rooms, 3 suites ᝢ Breakfast.

$$
HOTEL
☲ **Best Western Metropoli.** Rooms and bathrooms are bright and spacious at this welcoming inn on the border of the historic district and Via Garibaldi. **Pros:** guest rooms and bathrooms are large. **Cons:** parking lot is a bit of a hike; can be confusing to find if you are driving. $ *Rooms from: €130* ⊠ *Piazza Fontane Marose, Portoria* ☎ *010/2468888* ⊕ *www.bestwestern.it* ⇘ *48 rooms* ᝢ *Breakfast.*

$$$$
HOTEL
☲ **Bristol Palace.** One of Europe's gracious 19th-century grand hotels carefully guards its reputation for courtesy, service, and elegance, with spacious, high-ceilinged, handsomely furnished guest rooms and lovely public spaces. **Pros:** in the heart of the shopping district. **Cons:** busy street outside can sometimes be noisy. $ *Rooms from: €295* ⊠ *Via XX Settembre 35, Portoria* ☎ *010/592541* ⊕ *www.hotelbristolpalace.com* ⇘ *128 rooms, 5 suites* ᝢ *Breakfast.*

NERVI: A SIDE TRIP FROM GENOA

11 km (7 miles) east of Genoa.

The identity of this stately late-19th-century resort, famous for its 1½-km-long (1-mile-long) seaside promenade—the **Passeggiata Anita Garibaldi**—its palm-lined roads, and its 300 acres of parks rich in orange trees, is given away only by the sign on the sleepy train station. Although Nervi is technically part of the city, its peace and quiet are as different from Genoa's hustle and bustle as its clear blue water is from Genoa's crowded port. From the centrally located train station, walk east along the seaside promenade to reach the beaches, a cliff-hanging restaurant, and the 2,000 varieties of roses in the public **Parco Villa Grimaldi,** all the while enjoying one of the most breathtaking views on the Riviera. Nervi, and the road between it and Genoa, is known for its nightlife in summer.

GETTING HERE

By car, exit the A12 at Genova Nervi and follow the "Centro" signs. The Nervi train station is located on the main north–south line, and you can also take the local commuter trains from Genova Principe and Brignole. It can also be reached on Bus No. 15 from Genoa's Piazza Cavour.

WHERE TO EAT AND STAY

For expanded hotel reviews, visit Fodors.com.

$$
LIGURIAN
✕ **Marinella.** Here you can have a casual but sophisticated dining experience while overlooking the Ligurian Sea. Try the *zuppa di pesce* (fish soup) and freshly baked focaccia; main dishes change according to the day's catch. The restaurant perches on seaside shoals: be sure to ask for one of the tables on the terrace, where you are suspended above the sea. There's an inexpensive hotel on-site as well. $ *Average meal: €40* ⊠ *Passeggiata Anita Garibaldi 18/R* ☎ *010/3728343* ⊙ *Closed Mon., Tues., and Nov. 1–Dec. 20.*

$$ 📟 **Romantik Hotel Villa Pagoda.** A 19th-century merchant's mansion mod-
HOTEL   eled after a Chinese temple has a private park, access to the famed cliff-
Fodor's Choice   top walk, and magnificent ocean views; request a tower room for the
★   best vantage point. **Pros:** lovely guest and common rooms; everything
has a touch of class. **Cons:** nearby train can be softly heard. $ *Rooms*
from: €110 ⊠ *Via Capolungo 15* 📞 *010/3726161* ⊕ *www.villapagoda.*
it 🛏 *13 rooms, 4 suites* ⊘ *Closed Nov.–Mar.* 🍽 *Breakfast.*

RIVIERA DI PONENTE

The Riviera di Ponente (Riviera of the Setting Sun) covers the nar-
row strip of northwest Liguria from Genoa to the French border. The
sapphire-color Mediterranean Sea to one side and the verdant foot-
hills of the Alps on the other allow for temperate weather and a long
growing season—"Riviera dei Fiori" (Riviera of the Flowers). Once
filled with charming seaside villages, elegant structures, and "sophisti-
cated" visitors, this area now struggles to maintain a balance between
its natural beauty and development. Highly populated resort areas and
some overly industrialized areas are jammed into the thin stretch of
white-sand and pebble beaches. Yet, while its sister Riviera (Levante)
may retain more of its natural beauty, the Ponente remains a popular
and well-organized retreat for visitors looking for sunshine, nightlife,
and relaxation.

ALBISOLA MARINA

43 km (27 miles) west of Genoa.

GETTING HERE AND AROUND

By car, take the Albisola exit off the A10 and follow the signs for the
Albisola marina center. Albisola is on the main railway line between
Genoa and France.

EXPLORING

Lungomare degli Artisti. Albisola Marina has a centuries-old tradition
of ceramics making. Numerous shops here sell the distinctive wares,
and a whole sidewalk, Lungomare degli Artisti, which runs along the
beachfront, has been transformed by the colorful ceramic works of
well-known artists.

Villa Faraggiana. The gorgeous 18th-century Villa Faraggiana, near the
parish church, has exhibits on the history of pottery and hosts an array
of events from concerts to weddings. ⊠ *Via dell'Oratorio* 📞 *019/480622*
⊕ *www.villafaraggiana.it* 🎫 *€8* ⊘ *Mid-Mar.–Sept., Tues.–Sun. 3–7.*

SHOPPING

Ceramiche San Giorgio. Ceramiche San Giorgio has been producing
ceramics since the 17th century, and is known for both classic and
modern designs. ⊠ *Corso Matteotti 5* 📞 *019/482747.*

8

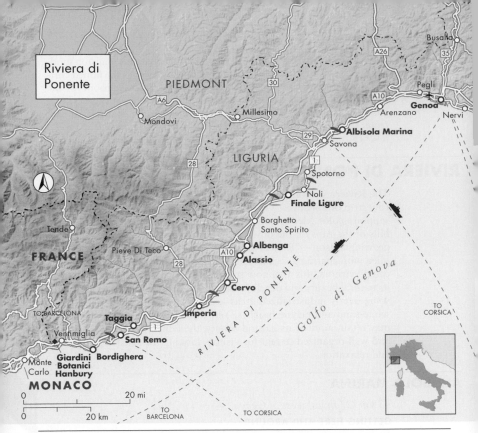

FINALE LIGURE

*30 km (19 miles) southwest of Albisola Marina, 72 km (44 miles)
southwest of Genoa.*

Finale Ligure is actually made up of three small villages: Finalmarina,
Finalpia, and Finalborgo. The former two have fine sandy beaches and
modern resort amenities. The most attractive of the villages is Finalborgo, less than 1 km (½ mile) inland. It's a hauntingly preserved
medieval settlement, planned to a rigid blueprint, with 15th-century
walls. The surrounding countryside is pierced by deep, narrow valleys and caves; the limestone outcroppings provide the warm pinkish
stone found in many buildings in Genoa. Rare reptiles lurk among the
exotic flora.

GETTING HERE AND AROUND

By car, take the Finale Ligure exit off the A10 and follow the "Centro"
signs. Finale Ligure is on the main train line between Genoa and France.

VISITOR INFORMATION

Finale Ligure Tourism Office ✉ *Piazza Porta Testa, Finalborgo* ☎ *019/680954*
⊕ *www.visitfinaleligure.it.*

EXPLORING

OFF THE
BEATEN
PATH

Noli. Just 9 km (5½ miles) northeast of Finale Ligure, the ruins of a castle loom benevolently over the tiny medieval gem of Noli. It's hard to imagine that this charming seaside village was—like Genoa, Venice, Pisa, and Amalfi—a prosperous maritime republic in the Middle Ages. Let yourself get lost among its labyrinth cobblestone streets filled with shops and cafés or enjoy a day in the sun on its lovely stretch of beach. If you don't have a car, get a bus for Noli at Spotorno, where local trains stop.

WHERE TO EAT AND STAY

For expanded hotel reviews, visit Fodors.com.

$$$$
LIGURIAN

✕ **Ai Torchi.** You could easily become a homemade-pesto snob at this Finalborgo eatery. The high prices are justified by excellent inventive seafood and meat dishes and by the setting—a restored 5th-century olive-oil refinery. $ *Average meal: €60* ✉ *Via dell'Annunziata 12, Finalborgo* ☎ *019/690531* ⊘ *Closed Jan. 7–Feb. 7 and Tues. during Sept.–July.*

$$
B&B/INN

⌂ **Ca de' Tobia.** Five rooms and a suite on the seafront promenade of Noli are stylishly done with wood floors, splashes of bright colors, and modern decor. **Pros:** ultrachic; full of modern amenities. **Cons:** right on the main road through town, so you can hear some street noise. $ *Rooms from: €150* ✉ *Via Aurelia 35, Noli* ☎ *0197/485845* ⊕ *www.cadetobia.it* ⇨ *5 rooms, 1 suite* ⫶⊙⫶ *Breakfast.*

$$$
HOTEL

⌂ **Punta Est.** An old villa with a newer wing is perched on a fragrant hillside just above the white-sand beaches, making this a wonderful retreat from the crowds down at the water's edge. **Pros:** nice pool and charming garden areas. **Cons:** some rooms are a bit outdated. $ *Rooms from: €225* ✉ *Via Aurelia 1* ☎ *39/019600611* ⊕ *www.puntaest.com* ⇨ *40 rooms* ⊘ *Closed Nov.–Apr.* ⫶⊙⫶ *Breakfast.*

8

ALBENGA

20 km (12 miles) southwest of Finale Ligure, 90 km (55 miles) southwest of Genoa.

Albenga has a medieval core, with narrow streets laid out by the ancient Romans. A network of alleys is punctuated by centuries-old towers surrounding the 18th-century Romanesque cathedral, with a late-14th-century campanile and a baptistery dating to the 5th century. It's a nice place to take an afternoon stroll and explore its many quaint shops and cafés.

GETTING HERE AND AROUND

By car, take the Albenga exit off the A10 and follow the "Centro" signs. Albenga is on the main train line between Genoa and France.

VISITOR INFORMATION

Albenga Tourism Office ✉ *Piazza Martiri della Libèrta* ☎ *0182/5685223* ⊕ *www.inforiviera.it.*

EXPLORING

OFF THE
BEATEN
PATH

Bardineto. For a look at some of the Riviera's mountain scenery, make an excursion by car to this attractive village in the middle of an area rich in mushrooms, chestnuts, and raspberries, as well as local cheeses. A ruined castle stands above the village. From Borghetto Santo Spirito (between Albenga and Finale Ligure), drive inland 25 km (15 miles).

ALASSIO

100 km (62 miles) southwest of Genoa.

Although Alassio is no longer a sleepy fishing village, the centro still possesses some old-world charm, colorful buildings, a great beachfront promenade, and white-sand beaches. Spend the day soaking up some sun, grab a seafood lunch or pizza along the boardwalk, and then finish off with a passeggiata and shopping on its caruggi.

GETTING HERE AND AROUND

By car, take the Albenga exit off the A10 and follow the blue signs for Alassio. Alassio is on the main train line between Genoa and France.

VISITOR INFORMATION

Alassio Tourism Office ⊠ *Piazza Paccini, 28* ☎ *0182/602253* ⊕ *www.comune.alassio.sv.it.*

CERVO

23 km (14 miles) southwest of Albenga, 106 km (65 miles) southwest of Genoa.

Cervo is the quintessential sleepy Ligurian coastal village, nicely polished for the tourists who come to explore its narrow byways and street staircases. It's a remarkably well-preserved medieval town, crowned with a big Baroque church. In July and August the square in front of the church is the site of chamber music concerts.

GETTING HERE AND AROUND

By car, take the Diano Marina exit off the A10 and follow the signs for Cervo located just east of Diano Marina. Diano Marina is on the main train line between Genoa and France.

IMPERIA

12 km (7 miles) west of Cervo, 116 km (71 miles) southwest of Genoa.

Imperia actually consists of two towns: Porto Maurizio, a medieval town built on a promontory, and Oneglia, now an industrial center for oil refining and pharmaceuticals. Porto Maurizio has a virtually intact medieval center, an intricate spiral of narrow streets and stone portals, and some imposing 17th- and 18th-century palaces. There's little of interest in modern Oneglia, except for a visit to the olive-oil museum.

GETTING HERE AND AROUND

By car, take the Imperia Est exit off the A10 and follow the signs for "Centro" or "Porto Maurizio." Both Imperia and Porto Maurizio are on the main rail line between Genoa and France.

VISITOR INFORMATION

Imperia Tourism Office ⊠ *Piazza Dante 4, Oneglia* ☎ *0183/2744982* ⊕ *www.visitrivieradeifiori.it or www.rivieradeifiori.org.*

EXPLORING

Museo dell'Olivo. Imperia is king when it comes to olive oil, and the story of the olive is the theme of this small museum. Displays of the history of the olive tree, farm implements, presses, and utensils show how olive oil has been made in many countries throughout history. A multilanguage audio guide is available for €4. ✉ *Via Garessio 11/13* ☎ *0183/295762* ⊕ *www.museodellolivo.com* 🖾 *€5* ⊗ *Mon.–Sat. 9–12:30 and 3–6:30.*

WHERE TO STAY

For expanded hotel reviews, visit Fodors.com.

$$
B&B/INN
$$

🖾 **Relais San Damian.** All the rooms are suites at this charming bed-and-breakfast, set among the olive trees high above Porto Maurizio. **Pros:** large suites and plenty of outdoor space; gorgeous pool area. **Cons:** limited amenities (no TVs or phones). $ *Rooms from: €150* ✉ *Strada Vasia 47* ☎ *0183/280309* ⊕ *www.san-damian.com* ↬ *9 suites* ⊗ *Closed Nov.–Feb.* ⦿ *Breakfast.*

SAN REMO

50 km (31 miles) southwest of Cervo, 146 km (90 miles) southwest of Genoa.

Once the crown jewel of the Riviera di Ponente, San Remo is still the area's largest resort, lined with polished hotels, exotic gardens, and seaside promenades. Renowned for its VIPs, glittering casino, and romantic setting, San Remo maintains remnants of its glamorous past from the late 19th century to World War II, but it also suffers from the same epidemic of overbuilding that has changed so much of the western Riviera for the worse. Still, it continues to be a lively town, even in the off-season.

The Mercato dei Fiori, Italy's most important wholesale flower market, is held here in a market hall between Piazza Colombo and Corso Garibaldi, though it's open to dealers only. More than 20,000 tons of carnations, roses, mimosa flowers, and innumerable other cut flowers are dispatched from here each year. As the center of northern Italy's flower-growing industry, the town is surrounded by hills where verdant terraces are now blanketed with plastic to form immense greenhouses.

GETTING HERE AND AROUND

By car, take the San Remo exit off the A10 and follow the "Centro" signs. San Remo is on the main train line between Genoa and France.

VISITOR INFORMATION

San Remo Tourism Office ✉ *Palazzo Riviera, Largo Nuvoloni 1* ☎ *0184/59059* ⊗ *Mon.–Sat. 8–7 and Sun. 9–1.*

EXPLORING

Cristo Salvatore, Santa Caterina d'Alessandria, e San Serafino di Sarov. This onion-dome Russian Orthodox church testifies to a long Russian presence on the Italian Riviera. Russian empress Maria Alexandrovna, wife of Czar Alexander I, built a summer house here, and in winter San Remo was a popular destination for other royal Romanovs. The church was consecrated in 1913. ✉ *Via Nuvoloni 2* ☎ *0184/531807* 🖾 *€1 donation* ⊗ *Daily 9:30–12:30 and 3–6:30.*

8

La Pigna (*The Pinecone*). San Remo's "old city" climbs upward to Piazza Castello, which offers a splendid view of the town and sea below. Some lovely old palazzi and squares have been restored, and the neighborhood gives you a sense of what it is was like to live in San Remo in centuries gone by.

San Remo Casinò. In addition to gaming, this lovely art nouveau landmark offers a restaurant, a nightclub, and a theater that hosts concerts and the annual San Remo Music Festival. If you want to try your luck at the gaming tables, there's a €7.50 cover charge on weekends. Dress is elegant, with jacket and tie requested at the French gaming tables. ⊠ *Corso Inglesi 18* ☎ *0184/5951* ⊙ *Slot machines: Sun.–Fri. 10 am–2:30 am, Sat. 10 am–3:30 am. Tables: Sun.–Fri. 2:30 pm–2:30 am, Sat. 2:30 pm–3:30 am.*

OFF THE BEATEN PATH

Bussana Vecchia. In the hills where flowers are cultivated for export, this self-consciously picturesque former ghost town is a flourishing artists' colony. The town was largely destroyed by an earthquake in 1877, when the inhabitants packed up and left en masse. For almost a century the houses, church, and crumbling bell tower were empty shells, overgrown by weeds and wildflowers. Since the 1960s painters, sculptors, artisans, and bric-a-brac dealers have restored the dwellings as houses and studios. ⊠ *8 km (5 miles) east of San Remo.*

WHERE TO EAT AND STAY

For expanded hotel reviews, visit Fodors.com.

$

LIGURIAN

✕ **Nuovo Piccolo Mondo.** Old wooden chairs dating from the 1920s, when the place opened, evoke the homey charm of this small, family-run trattoria. A faithful clientele keeps the kitchen busy, so get here early to grab a table and order Ligurian specialties such as *sciancui* (a roughly cut flat pasta with a mixture of beans, tomatoes, zucchini, and pesto) and *polpo e patate* (stewed octopus with potatoes). Ⓢ *Average meal: €30* ⊠ *Via Piave 7* ☎ *0184/509012* ⊙ *Closed Sun.*

$$

HOTEL

☷ **Paradiso.** Bright, well-equipped rooms face a quiet palm-fringed garden and pool or the sea; some enjoy sea views from nice-size balconies. **Pros:** friendly service; nice pool; free loungers and umbrellas at nearby beach. **Cons:** a steep walk up some stairs and a hill from town. Ⓢ *Rooms from: €200* ⊠ *Via Roccasterone 12* ☎ *0184/571211* ⊕ *www.paradisohotel.it* ⇝ *41 rooms* ⏐⊙⏐ *Breakfast.*

$$$

HOTEL

☷ **Royal.** This is arguably Liguria's second-most-luxurious resort after the Splendido in Portofino: each room is beautifully decorated differently, all have modern amenities, and most have views of the sea. **Pros:** the glamour of yesteryear with all the expected high-end amenities; reasonable prices given the surroundings. **Cons:** on-site meals and beverages are expensive. Ⓢ *Rooms from: €285* ⊠ *Corso Imperatrice 80* ☎ *0184/5391* ⊕ *www.royalhotelsanremo.com* ⇝ *114 rooms, 13 suites* ⊙ *Closed Nov.–mid-Feb.* ⏐⊙⏐ *Breakfast.*

BORDIGHERA

12 km (7 miles) west of San Remo, 155 km (96 miles) southwest of Genoa.

On a lush promontory, Bordighera sits as a charming seaside resort with panoramas from Genoa (on a clear day) to Monte Carlo. A large English colony, attracted by the mild climate, settled here in the second half of the 19th century and is still very much in evidence today; you regularly find people taking afternoon tea in the cafés, and streets are named after Queen Victoria and Shakespeare. This garden spot was the first town in Europe to grow date palms, and its citizens still have the exclusive right to provide the Vatican with palm fronds for Easter celebrations.

Thanks partly to its many year-round English residents, Bordighera doesn't close down entirely in the off-season like some Riviera resorts but rather serves as a quiet winter haven for all ages. With plenty of hotels and restaurants, Bordighera makes a good base for exploring the region and is quieter and less commercial than San Remo.

GETTING HERE AND AROUND

By car, take the Bordighera exit off the A10 and follow the signs for "Centro," about a 10-minute drive. Bordighera is on the main railway line between Genoa and France.

VISITOR INFORMATION

Bordighera Tourism Office ⊠ *Via Roberto 1* ☎ *0184/262322* ⊕ *www.bordighera.it.*

EXPLORING

Lungomare Argentina. Running parallel to the ocean, Lungomare Argentina is a pleasant promenade, 1½ km (1 mile) long, which begins at the western end of the town and provides good views westward to the French Côte d'Azur.

WHERE TO EAT AND STAY

For expanded hotel reviews, visit Fodors.com.

$ | LIGURIAN
✗ **Bagni Sant'Ampeglio.** This combination beach club (more than 200 lounge chairs during the season!) and seafront restaurant has wonderful choices for both lunch and dinner. Try the house-specialty branzino *in carciofi* (with artichokes) and its homemade desserts. [$] *Average meal: €25* ⊠ *Lungomare Argentina 3* ⊕ *www.santampeglio.it* ⊘ *Closed Wed. during these times: Sept.–Nov., 2nd half of Jan., and Feb.–May.*

$ | WINE BAR
✗ **Il Tempo Ritrovato.** A small wine bar and restaurant combine forces here on Bordighera's seaside promenade. Simple pasta dishes and a spectacular wine list make this a great choice. They also have live music and specially priced menus weekly. [$] *Average meal: €30* ⊠ *Lungomare Argentina 1* ☎ *0184/261207* ⊘ *Closed Sun. and Mon.*

$$ | LIGURIAN | Fodor'sChoice ★
✗ **Magiargè.** A mix of great charm and great food make this small osteria in the historic center an absolute dining delight. Dishes are Ligurian with a creative twist, such as the *stoccafisso sopra panizza* (salt cod served over a chickpea polenta) and *fritteline di bianchetti* (small frittatas made with tiny white fish). The selection of local wines is excellent. [$] *Average meal: €40* ⊠ *Via della Loggia 6* ☎ *0184/262946* ⊕ *www.magiarge.it* ⊘ *Closed 2 wks in Feb. and Oct. No lunch June–Aug.*

8

$ HOTEL **Hotel Piccolo Lido.** Sea-view rooms at this quaint little spot along the promenade have nice little balconies, and there's a terrace perfect for enjoying the sunset and vistas of France. **Pros:** a good value; nice views. **Cons:** few amenities. [$] *Rooms from: €138* ✉ *Lungomare Argentina 2* ☎ *0184/261297* 🌐 *www.hotelpiccololido.it* 🛏 *33 rooms* 🍴 *Breakfast.*

$ HOTEL **Hotel Villa Elisa.** On a street filled with beautiful old villas, this Victorian-era former residence has a relaxed and friendly atmosphere, beautiful gardens, and well-equipped rooms at reasonable prices. **Pros:** helpful staff; a good value; pool and garden make this a good choice for children. **Cons:** only partial views in sea-view rooms; limited parking; covered parking costs extra. [$] *Rooms from: €130* ✉ *Via Romana 70* ☎ *0184/261313* 🌐 *www.villaelisa.com* 🛏 *33 rooms, 2 suites, 1 apt for up to 6 people* 🍴 *Breakfast.*

EN ROUTE From Ventimiglia, a provincial road swings 10 km (6 miles) up the Nervi River valley to a lovely sounding medieval town, **Dolceacqua** (its name translates as Sweetwater), with a ruined castle. Liguria's best-known red wine is the local Rossese di Dolceacqua. A further 6 km (4 miles) along the road sits Pigna, a fascinating medieval village built in concentric circles on its hilltop.

GIARDINI BOTANICI HANBURY

6 km (4 miles) west of Ventimiglia, 10 km (6 miles) west of Bordighera.

GETTING HERE AND AROUND

Take the SS1 along the coast west from Bordighera, through the town of Ventimiglia, and toward the French border. The gardens are about 1 km (½ mile) beyond the tunnel.

EXPLORING

Fodor's Choice ★ **Giardini Botanici Hanbury.** Mortola Inferiore, only 2 km (1 mile) from the French border, is the site of the world-famous Giardini Botanici Hanbury (Hanbury Botanical Gardens), one of the largest and most beautiful in Italy. Planned and planted in 1867 by a wealthy English merchant, Sir Thomas Hanbury, and his botanist brother, Daniel, the terraced gardens contain species from five continents, including many palms and succulents. There are panoramic views of the sea from the gardens. ✉ *Corso Montecarlo 43, Località Mortola Inferiore* ☎ *0184/229507* 🌐 *www.giardinihanbury.com* 🎟 *€7.50 July 1–Mar. 19, €9 Mar. 20–June 30* 🕒 *Mar. 1–mid-June, daily 9:30–6; mid-June–mid-Sept., daily 9:30–7; mid-Sept.–mid-Oct., daily 9:30–6; mid-Oct.–Feb. 28, Tues.–Sun. 9:30–6. Last entry 1 hr before closing.*

EMILIA–ROMAGNA

WELCOME TO EMILIA-ROMAGNA

TOP REASONS TO GO

★ **The signature food of Emilia:** This region's food—prosciutto *crudo,* Parmigiano-Reggiano, balsamic vinegar, and above all, pasta—makes the trip to Italy worthwhile.

★ **Mosaics that take your breath away:** The intricate tiles in Ravenna's Mausoleo di Galla Placidia, in brilliantly well-preserved colors, depict vivid portraits and pastoral scenes.

★ **Arguably Europe's oldest wine bar:** Nicholas Copernicus tippled here while studying at Ferrara's university in the early 1500s; Osteria al Brindisi, in the *centro storico* (historic center), has been pouring wine since 1435.

★ **The nightlife of Bologna:** This red-roofed city has had a lively student culture since the university—Europe's oldest—was founded in the late 11th century.

★ **The medieval castles of San Marino:** Its three castles dramatically perch on a rock more than 3,000 feet above the flat landscape of Romagna.

1 Emilia. A landscape of medieval castles and crumbling farmhouses begins just east of Milan, in the western half of Emilia-Romagna. You'll find here the delicious delights of **Parma**, with its buttery prosciutto, famous cheese, and dazzling palaces. Next along the road, continuing east, comes **Reggio Emilia**, of Parmigiano-Reggiano cheese fame, then **Modena**, the city of balsamic vinegar.

2 Bologna. Emilia's principal cultural and intellectual center is famed for its arcaded sidewalks, grandiose medieval towers, and sublime restaurants.

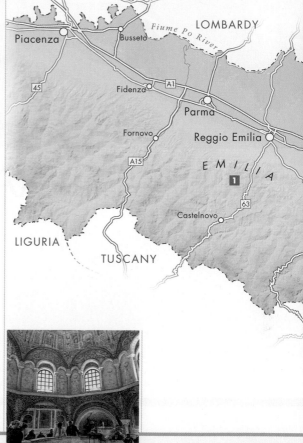

3 **Ferrara.** This prosperous, tidy city to the north of Bologna has a rich medieval past and its own distinctive cuisine.

4 **Romagna.** The eastern half of Emilia-Romagna begins east of Bologna—where spa towns span to the north and south of the Via Emilia and the A1 Autostrada—and extends to the Adriatic. **San Marino**, south of Rimini, is an anomaly in every way. As its own tiny republic, it hangs implausibly on a cliff above the Romagna plain.

5 **Ravenna.** The main attractions of this well-preserved Romagna city are its memorable mosaics, glittering treasures left from Byzantine rule.

GETTING ORIENTED

Emilia-Romagna owes its beginnings to the Romans, who built the Via Emilia in 187 BC. Today the road bisects the flat, foggy region, paralleling the Autostrada del Sole (A1), making it easy to drive straight through. Bologna is in the middle of everything, with Piacenza, Parma, and Modena to the northwest, and the Adriatic to the southeast. Ferrara and Ravenna are the only detours—they're north of Via Emilia.

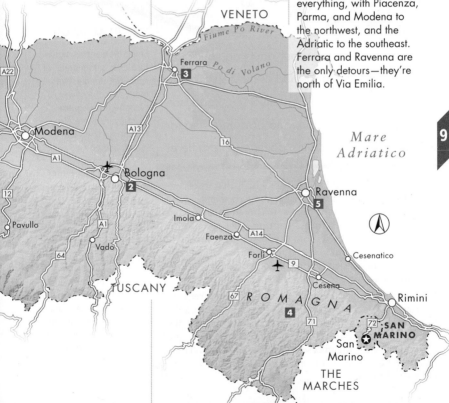

9

VENETO

Fiume Po River

A22

Ferrara *Po di Volano*
3

Modena A13

16

A1

Bologna
2

12

A1

Imola

Pavullo

Vado

Faenza A14

64

Forlì 9

Cesena

TUSCANY

67 R O M A G N A
4

71

San Marino

THE MARCHES

Mare Adriatico

Ravenna
5

Cesenatico

Rimini

72 SAN MARINO

EATING AND DRINKING WELL IN EMILIA-ROMAGNA

Italians rarely agree about anything, but most would say that the best food in the country is in Emilia-Romagna. Tortellini, fettuccine, Parmesan cheese, prosciutto *crudo*, and balsamic vinegar are just a few of the Italian delicacies born here.

One of the beauties of Emilia-Romagna is that its exceptional food can be had without breaking the bank. Many trattorias serve up classic dishes, mastered over the centuries, at reasonable prices. Cutting-edge restaurants and wine bars are often more expensive; their inventive menus are full of *fantasia*—reinterpretations of the classics. For the budget-conscious, Bologna (being a university town) has great places for cheap eats.

Between meals, you can sustain yourself with the region's famous sandwich, the *piadina*. It's made with pitalike thin bread, usually filled with prosciutto or mortadella, cheese, and vegetables; then put under the grill and served hot, with the cheese oozing at the sides. These addictive sandwiches can be savored at sit-down places or ordered to go.

THE REAL RAGÙ

Emilia-Romagna's signature dish is *tagliatelle al ragù* (flat noodles with meat sauce), known as "spaghetti Bolognese" most everywhere else. This primo is on every menu, and no two versions are the same. The sauce starts in a sauté pan with finely diced carrots, onions, and celery. Purists add nothing but minced beef, but some use *guanciale* (pork cheek), sausage, veal, or chicken. Regular ministrations of broth are added, and sometimes wine, milk, or cream. After a couple of hours of cooking, the ragù is ready to be joined with pasta and Parmesan and brought to the table.

PORK PRODUCTS

It's not just mortadella and cured pork products like prosciutto and *culatello* that Emilia-Romagnans go crazy for—they're wild about the whole hog.

You'll frequently find *cotechino* and *zampone,* both *secondi* (second courses), on menus. Cotechino, *photo below,* is a savory, thick, fresh sausage served with lentils on New Year's Day (the combination is said to augur well for the new year) and with mashed potatoes year-round. Zampone, a stuffed pig's foot, is redolent of garlic and deliciously fatty.

BOLLITO MISTO

The name means "mixed boil," and they do it exceptionally well in this part of Italy. According to Emilia-Romagnans, it was invented here (its true origins are up for grabs, as other northern Italians, especially from Milan and the Piedmont, would argue this point). Chicken, beef, tongue, and zampone are tossed into a stockpot and boiled; they're then removed from the broth and served with a fragrant *salsa verde* (green sauce), made green by parsley and spiced with anchovies, garlic, and capers. This simple yet rich dish is usually served with mashed potatoes on the side, and savvy diners will mix some of the piquant salsa verde into the potatoes as well.

STUFFED PASTA

Among the many Emilian variations on stuffed pasta, tortellini (*pictured at left*),

are the smallest. *Tortelli* (*photo upper right*), and *cappellacci* are larger pasta "pillows," about the size of a Brussels sprout, but with the same basic form as tortellini. They're often filled with pumpkin or spinach and cheese.

Tortelloni are, in theory, even bigger, although their sizes vary. Stuffed pastas are generally served simply, with melted butter, sage, and (what else?) Parmigiano-Reggiano cheese, or (in the case of tortellini) *in brodo* (in beef, chicken, or capon broth—or a combination of any of them), which brings out the subtle richness of the filling.

WINES

Emilia-Romagna's wines accompany the region's fine food rather than vying with it for accolades. The best known is lambrusco, a sparkling red produced on the Po Plain that has some admirers and many detractors. It's praised for its tartness and condemned for the same quality. The region's best wines include Sangiovese di Romagna (somewhat similar to Chianti), from the Romagnan hills, and barbera, from the Colli Piacetini and Apennine foothills. Castelluccio, Bonzara, Zerbina, Leone Conti, and Tre Monti are among the region's top producers—keep an eye out for their bottles.

9

Updated by Patricia Rucidlo

Gourmets the world over claim that Emilia-Romagna's greatest contribution to humankind has been gastronomic. Birthplace of fettuccine, tortellini, lasagna, prosciutto, and Parmesan cheese, the region has a spectacular culinary tradition. But there are many reasons to come here aside from the desire to be well fed: Parma's Correggio paintings, Giuseppe Verdi's villa at Sant'Agata, the medieval splendor of Bologna's palaces and Ferrara's alleyways, the rolling hills of the Romagna countryside, and, perhaps foremost, the Byzantine beauty of mosaic-rich Ravenna—glittering as brightly today as it did 1,500 years ago.

As you travel through Emilia, the western half of the region, you'll encounter the sprawling plants of Italy's industrial food giants, like Barilla and Fini, standing side by side with the fading villas and farmhouses that have long punctuated the flat, fertile land of the Po Plain. Bologna, the principal city of Emilia, is a busy cultural and, increasingly, business center, less visited but in many ways just as engaging as the country's more famous tourist destinations—particularly given its acknowledged position as the leading city of Italian cuisine. The rest of the region follows suit: eating is an essential part of any Emilian experience.

The area's history is laden with culinary legends, such as how the original *tortellino* (singular of tortellini) was modeled on the shape of Venus's navel and the original *tagliolini* (long, thin egg pasta) was served at the wedding banquet of Annibale Bentivoglio and Lucrezia d'Este—a marriage uniting two of the noblest families in the region. You'll need to stay focused just to make sure you try all the basics: Parma's famed prosciutto and Parmigiano-Reggiano cheese; Modena's balsamic vinegar; the ragù—slow-simmered meat sauce—whose poor imitations are known elsewhere in the world as "Bolognese"; and, of course, the best pasta in the world.

The historic border between Emilia to the west and Romagna to the east lies near the fortified town of Dozza. Emilia is flat; but just east of the Romagnan border the landscape gets hillier and more sparsely settled, in places covered with evergreen forests and steaming natural springs. Finally, it flattens again into the low-lying marshland of the Po Delta, which meets the Adriatic Sea. Each fall, in both Romagna and Emilia, the trademark fog rolls in off the Adriatic to hang over the flatlands in winter, coloring the region with a spooky, gray glow.

EMILIA-ROMAGNA PLANNER

MAKING THE MOST OF YOUR TIME

Plan on spending at least two days or nights in Bologna, the region's cultural and historical capital. You shouldn't miss Parma, with its stunning food and graceful public spaces. Also plan on visiting Ferrara, a misty, mysterious medieval city. If you have time, go to Ravenna for its memorable Byzantine mosaics and Modena for its harmonious architecture and famous balsamic vinegar.

If you have only a few days in the region, it's virtually impossible to do all five of those cities justice. If you're a dedicated gourmand (or *buona forchetta,* as Italians say), move from Bologna west along the Via Emilia (SS9) to Modena and Parma. If you're more interested in architecture, art, and history, choose the eastern route, heading north on the A13 to Ferrara and then southeast on the SS16 to Ravenna.

If you have more time, you won't have to make such tough choices. You can start in Milan, go east, and finish on the Adriatic—or vice versa.

GETTING HERE AND AROUND

CAR TRAVEL

Driving is the best way to get around Emilia-Romagna. Roads are wide, flat, and well marked; distances are short; and beautiful farmhouses and small villages offer undemanding detours. A car is particularly useful for visiting the spa towns of Romagna, which aren't well connected by train. Historic centers are off-limits to cars, but they're also quite walkable, so you may just want to park your car and get around on foot once you arrive.

Entering Emilia-Romagna by car is as easy as it gets. Coming in from the west on the Autostrada del Sole (A1), Piacenza will be the first city you'll hit. It's a mere 45 minutes southeast of Milan. On the other side of the region, Venice is about an hour from Ferrara by car on the A13.

Bologna is on the autostrada, so driving between cities is a breeze, though do take special care if you're coming from Florence, as the road is winding and drivers speed. The Via Emilia (SS9), one of the oldest roads in the world, runs through the heart of the region. Straight, low-lying, and now thoroughly modern, its length can be traveled in a few hours. Although less scenic, the A1 toll highway, which runs parallel to the Via Emilia from Bologna, can get you where you're going about twice as fast. From Bologna, the A13 runs north to Ferrara, and the A14 takes you east to Ravenna. Note that much of the historic center of Bologna is closed off to cars daily from 7 am to 8 pm.

TRAIN TRAVEL

When it comes to public transportation in the region, trains are better than buses—they're fairly efficient, quite frequent, and most stations aren't too far from the center of town. The railroad track follows the Via Emilia (SS9). In Emilia it's generally 30 to 45 minutes from one major city to the next. To reach Ferrara or Ravenna, you typically have to change to a local train at the Bologna station. Trains run often, and connections are easy. Ferrara is a half hour north of Bologna on the train, and Ravenna is just over an hour.

Bologna is an important rail hub for northern Italy and has frequent, fast service to Milan, Florence, Rome, and Venice. The routes from Bologna to the south usually go through Florence, which is an hour away. The high-speed train service Alta Velocità cuts the time from Milan to Bologna to only one hour. On the northeastern edge of the region, Venice is 1½ hours east of Ferrara by train. Check the website of the state railway, the **Ferrovie dello Stato** (⊕ *www.trenitalia.com*), for information, or stop in a travel agency, as many sell train tickets (without a markup) and agents often speak English. The Italo (⊕ *www. italotreno.it*), another (privately owned) high-speed train line, now offers competition for the state-sponsored service. The Turin-Salerno line makes stops in Bologna, Florence, Rome, Naples, and Salerno; the Venice-Napoli line stops in Padova, Bologna, Florence, and Rome. Some of these also stop in secondary stations.

RESTAURANTS

Please note that restaurant prices listed as "average meal" include a meal consisting of first course *(primo)*, second course *(secondo)*, and dessert *(dolce)*.

HOTELS

Emilia-Romagna has a reputation for demonstrating a level of efficiency uncommon in most of Italy. Even the smallest hotels are usually well run, with high standards of quality and service. Bologna is very much a businessperson's city, and many hotels here cater to the business traveler, but there are smaller, more intimate hotels as well. It's smart to book in advance—the region hosts many fairs and conventions that can fill up hotels even during low season.

Though prices are sometimes high, you can expect an experience delightfully free of the condescending attitude that sometimes mars Italy's tourist meccas.

Hotel reviews have been condensed for this book. Please go to Fodors. com for full reviews of each property.

EMILIA

The Via Emilia runs through Emilia's heart in a straight shot from medieval Piacenza, 67 km (42 miles) southeast of Milan, through Bologna, and ultimately to Romagna and the Adriatic Coast. On the way you encounter many of Italy's cultural riches—from the culinary and artistic treasures of Parma to the birthplace and home of Giuseppe Verdi. Take time to veer into the countryside, with its ramshackle

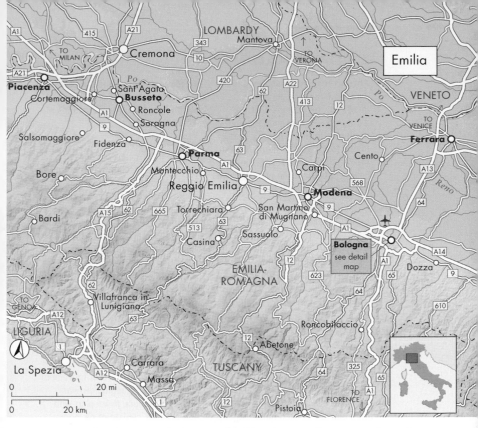

farmhouses and 800-year-old abbeys; to stop for a taste of prosciutto; and to detour north to the mist-shrouded tangle of streets that make up Ferrara's old Jewish ghetto.

PIACENZA

67 km (42 miles) southeast of Milan, 150 km (93 miles) northwest of Bologna.

Piacenza has always been associated with industry and commerce. Its position on the Po River has made it an important inland port since the earliest times; the Etruscans, and then the Romans, had thriving settlements here. As you approach the city today you could be forgiven for thinking that it holds little of interest. Piacenza is surrounded by ugly industrial suburbs (with particularly unlovely concrete factories and a power station), but if you forge ahead you'll discover a delightfully preserved medieval center and an unusually clean city. Its prosperity is evident in the great shopping to be had along Corso Vittorio Emanuele II.

GETTING HERE AND AROUND
Regional trains run often from Milan to Piacenza and take a little more than an hour; Eurostar service cuts the travel time in half, and Alta Velocità trains make it from Milan to Bologna in an hour. The Intercity

EMILIA-ROMAGNA THROUGH THE AGES

Ancient History. Emilia-Romagna owes its beginnings to a road. In 187 BC the Romans built the Via Aemilia—a long road running northwest from the Adriatic port of Rimini to the central garrison town of Piacenza—and it was along this central spine that the primary towns of the region developed.

Despite the unifying factor of what came to be known as the Via Emilia, this section of Italy has had a fragmented history. Its eastern part, roughly the area from Faenza to the coast (known as Romagna), first looked to the Byzantine east and then to Rome for art, political power, and, some say, national character. The western part, from Bologna to Piacenza (Emilia), looked more to the north with its practice of self-government and dissent.

Bologna was founded by the Etruscans and eventually came under the influence of the Roman Empire. The Romans established a garrison here, renaming the old Etruscan settlement Bononia. It was after the fall of Rome that the region began its fragmentation. Romagna, centered in Ravenna, was ruled from Constantinople. Ravenna eventually became the capital of the empire in the west in the 5th century, passing to papal control in the 8th century. Even today, the city is still filled with reminders of two centuries of Byzantine rule.

Family Ties. The other cities of the region, from the Middle Ages on, became the fiefdoms of important noble families—the Este in Ferrara and Modena, the Pallavicini in Piacenza, and the Bentivoglio in Bologna. Today all these cities bear the marks of their noble patrons. When in the 16th century the papacy managed to exert its power over the entire area, some of these cities were divided among the papal families—hence the stamp of the Farnese family on Parma and Piacenza.

A Leftward Tilt. Bologna and Emilia-Romagna have established a robust tradition of rebellion and dissent. The Italian socialist movement was born in the region, as was Benito Mussolini. In keeping with the political climate of his home state, he was a firebrand socialist during the early part of his career. Despite having Mussolini as a native son, Emilia-Romagna didn't take to fascism: it was here that the antifascist resistance was born, and during World War II the region suffered terribly at the hands of the fascists and the Nazis.

from Bologna to Piacenza takes about 1½ hours and closer to two hours on regional trains. Both have frequent service. Piacenza is easily accessible by car via the A1, either from Milan or from Bologna. If you're coming from Milan, take the Piacenza Nord exit; from Bologna, the Piacenza Est exit.

VISITOR INFORMATION
Piacenza Tourism Office ✉ Piazza Cavalli 7 ☎ 0523/329324 ⊕ www.comune.piacenza.it.

EXPLORING

Duomo. Attached like a sinister balcony to the bell tower of Piacenza's 12th-century cathedral is a *gabbia* (iron cage), where miscreants were incarcerated naked and subjected to the scorn of the crowd in the marketplace below. Inside the cathedral, less evocative but equally impressive medieval stonework decorates the pillars and the crypt, and there are extravagant frescoes in the dome of the cupola begun by Morazzone (1573–1626). Guercino (1591–1666) completed them upon Morazzone's death. The Duomo can be reached by following Via XX Settembre from Piazza dei Cavalli. ✉ *Piazza Duomo* ☎ *0523/335154* 🕒 *Daily 7:30–noon and 4–7.*

Musei di Palazzo Farnese. The city-owned museum of Piacenzan art and antiquities is housed in the vast **Palazzo Farnese.** The ruling family had commissioned a monumental palace, but construction, begun in 1558, was never completed as planned. The highlight of the museum's rather eclectic collection is the tiny 2nd-century BC Etruscan *Fegato di Piacenza,* a bronze tablet shaped like a *fegato* (liver), marked with the symbols of the gods of good and ill fortune. By comparing this master "liver" with one taken from the body of a freshly-slaughtered sacrifice, priests predicted the future. The collection also contains Botticelli's recently restored *Madonna and Child with St. John the Baptist.* Because it's under glass, you have the rare opportunity of getting very close to the piece to admire the artist's brushwork. Reserve ahead for free 1½-hour guided tours. ✉ *Piazza Cittadella 29* ☎ *0523/492661* 🌐 *www.palazzofarnese.piacenza.it* 🎟 *€6* 🕒 *Tues.–Thurs. 9–1, Fri. and Sat. 9–1 and 3–6, Sun. 9:30–1 and 3–6.*

Piazza dei Cavalli (*Square of the Horses*). The hub of the city is the Piazza dei Cavalli. The flamboyant equestrian statues from which the piazza takes its name are depictions of Ranuccio Farnese (1569–1622) and, on the left, his father, Alessandro (1545–92). The latter was a beloved ruler, enlightened and fair; Ranuccio, his successor, less so. Both statues are the work of Francesco Mochi, a master baroque sculptor. Dominating the square is the massive 13th-century **Palazzo Pubblico,** also known as il Gotico. This two-tone, marble-and-brick, turreted and crenellated building was the seat of town government before Piacenza fell under the iron fists of the ruling Pallavicini and Farnese families.

WHERE TO EAT

$$$$ MODERN ITALIAN Fodor's Choice ★

🍴 **Antica Osteria del Teatro.** A simple 15th-century palazzo on a lovely little square in the center of town gives no hint to what awaits inside. Warm yellow walls adorned with contemporary prints provide the backdrop for some serious food. Chef Filippo Chiappini Dattilo has combined his love of Italian dishes with French influences, creating a marvelous menu. The local specialty, *culatello,* is served with exquisite *porcini sott'olio* (mushrooms in olive oil). Another traditional dish, *pisarei e faso* (Piacentinian for pasta *fagioli*), is livened up with shrimp and squid. The colorful risotto *mantecato con granchio reale* (risotto with crab) arrives redolent of mandarin, with which it has been generously seasoned. Excellent service and an equally excellent wine list make dining here a true pleasure. [$] *Average meal: €70* ✉ *Via Verdi 16* ☎ *0523/323777* 🌐 *www.anticaosteriadelteatro.it* ✍ *Reservations essential* 🕒 *Closed Sun. and Mon. year-round. Closed Jan. 1–10, and Aug. 1–25.*

BUSSETO

30 km (19 miles) southeast of Piacenza, 25 km (16 miles) southeast of Cremona in Lombardy.

GETTING HERE AND AROUND

If you're coming by car from Parma, drive along the A1/E35 and follow signs for the A15 in the direction of Milan/La Spezia. Choose the exit in the direction of Fidenza/Salsomaggiore Terme, following signs to the SP12, which connects to the SS9W. At Fidenza, take the SS588 heading north, which will take you into Busseto. If you're without a car, you'll have to take a bus from Parma, as there's no train service.

VISITOR INFORMATION

Busseto Tourism Office ⊠ *Piazza G. Verdi 10* 🕾 *0524/92487* ⊕ *www.bussetolive.com.*

EXPLORING

Teatro Verdi. In the center of Busseto is the lovely Teatro Verdi, dedicated, as you might expect, to the works of the hamlet's famous son. Guided tours of the well-preserved, ornate 19th-century-style theater are offered every half hour. Check with the Busseto tourist office for the performance schedule. ⊠ *Piazza G. Verdi 10* 🕾 *0524/92487* 🎫 *Tours €4* ⊙ *Tours: Nov.–Feb., daily 9:30–1 and 2:30–5:30; Mar.–Oct., Tues.– Sun., daily 9:30–1 and 3–6.*

Villa Pallavicino. Busseto's main claim to fame is its native son, master composer Giuseppe Verdi (1813–1901), whose bicentennial was celebrated last year. The 15th-century Villa Pallavicino is where Verdi worked and lived with his mistress (and later wife) Giuseppina Strepponi. Recently renovated, it displays the maestro's piano, scores, composition books, and walking sticks. ⊠ *Via Provesi 35* 🕾 *0524/931002* ⊕ *www.museogiuseppeverdi. it* 🎫 *€9* ⊙ *Mar.–Oct., Tues.–Sun. 10–6:30; Nov., Tues.–Sun. 10–5:30; Dec.–Feb., weekends. 10–5:30, Tues.–Fri. by reservation only.*

Villa Sant'Agata. For Verdi lovers, Villa Sant'Agata (also known as Villa Verdi) is a veritable shrine. It's the grand country home Verdi built for himself in 1849—and the place where some of his greatest works were composed. Visits are by tour only, and you have to reserve a few days in advance by phone or online. ⊠ *Via Verdi 22, Sant'Agata Villanova sull'Arda ✛ 4 km (2½ miles) north of Busseto on SS588, toward Cremona* 🕾 *0523/830000* ⊕ *www.villaverdi.org* 🎫 *Tours €9* ⊙ *Tours: mid-Jan.– Feb. Sat. and holidays 8:30–11:45 and 2:30–5:30; Mar.–Oct., Tues.–Sun. 9:30–11:45 and 2:30–6:15 (no midday closure mid-Apr.– mid-June and Sept.–Oct.).*

PARMA

40 km (25 miles) southeast of Busseto, 97 km (60 miles) northwest of Bologna.

Parma stands on the banks of a tributary of the Po River. Despite damage during World War II, much of the stately historic center seems untouched by modern times. This is a prosperous city, and it shows in its well-dressed residents, clean streets, and immaculate piazzas.

Bursting with gustatory delights, Parma draws crowds for its sublime cured pork product, prosciutto *crudo di Parma* (known locally simply as "prosciutto crudo"). The pale-yellow Parmigiano-Reggiano cheese produced here and in nearby Reggio Emilia is the original—and best—of a class known around the world as Parmesan.

Almost every major European power has had a hand in ruling Parma at one time or another. The Romans founded the city—then little more than a garrison on the Via Emilia—after which a succession of feudal lords held sway. In the 16th century came the ever-conniving Farnese family, which died out in 1731 on the death of Antonio Farnese. It then went to the Spanish, and fell into French hands in 1796. In 1805 Marie-Louise (better known to the parmigiani as Maria Luigia), the wife of Napoleon, took command of the city. She was a much-beloved figure in her adopted town until her death in 1847.

GETTING HERE AND AROUND
Train service, via Eurostar, Intercity, and Regionale trains, runs frequently from Milan and Bologna. It takes a little over an hour from Milan and slightly less than an hour from Bologna. By car, Parma is just off the A1 Autostrada, halfway between Bologna and Piacenza.

VISITOR INFORMATION
Parma Tourism Office ✉ *Via Melloni 1/a* ☎ *0521/218889* ⊕ *www.turismo.comune.parma.it.*

EXPLORING
Battistero (*Baptistery*). Baptisms still happen (one Saturday and one Sunday each month) in this baptistery, which has a simple pink-stone Romanesque exterior and an uplifting Gothic interior. The doors are richly decorated with figures, animals, and flowers, and inside, the building is adorned with stucco figures (probably carved by Antelami) showing the months and seasons. Early 14th-century frescoes depicting scenes from the life of Christ grace the walls. ✉ *Piazza del Duomo* 💶 *€6* 🕐 *Daily 9–12:30 and 3–6:30.*

Fodor's Choice ★ **Camera di San Paolo.** This was the reception room for the erudite abbess Giovanna da Piacenza. In 1519 she hired Correggio to provide its decoration. Mythological scenes depict glorious frescoes of the *Triumphs of the Goddess Diana,* the *Three Graces,* and the *Three Fates.* ✉ *Via Melloni 15, off Strada Garibaldi, near Piazza Pilotta* ☎ *0521/233309* 💶 *€2* 🕐 *Tues.–Sun. 8:30–2.*

Duomo. The magnificent 12th-century cathedral has two vigilant stone lions standing guard beside the main door. The arch of the entrance is decorated with a delicate frieze of figures representing the months of the year, a motif repeated inside the baptistery. Some of the church's original artwork still survives, notably the simple yet evocative *Descent from the Cross*: a carving in the right transept by sculptor and architect Benedetto Antelami (active 1178–1230), whose masterwork is this cathedral's baptistery. It's an odd juxtaposition to turn from his austere work to the exuberant fresco in the dome, the *Assumption of the Virgin* by Antonio Allegri, better known to us as Correggio (1494–1534). The fresco was not well received when it was unveiled in 1530. "A mess of frogs' legs," the bishop of Parma is said to have called it. Today

9

Correggio is acclaimed as one of the leading masters of Mannerist painting. It's best viewed when the sun's strong, as this building is not particularly well lit. ⊠ *Piazza del Duomo* ☎ *0521/235886* ⊘ *Daily 7:30–12:30 and 3–7.*

Musei del Cibo (*Food Museums*). Four museums outside Parma showcase the city and the region's most famous foods. The Musei del Cibo, as they're collectively known, offer tastings, a bit of history, and a tour through the process of making these specialties. None is more than a 20-minute drive or taxi ride from the city. It's a good idea to call before making the trek, though, as opening hours are limited. ⊕ *www. museidelcibo.it.*

Museo del Parmigiano Reggiano. The trademark crumbly cheese is the focus of this museum. ⊠ *c/o Corte Castellazzi, Via Volta 5, 32 km (20 miles) northwest of Parma, Soragna* ☎ *0524/596129* ⊕ *www. museidelcibo.it* 🖭 *€5* ⊘ *Mar.–early Dec., weekends 10–1 and 3–6, weekdays by reservation only. Dec.–Feb. by reservation only.*

Museo del Pomodoro. It's hard to imagine what Italian cuisine would be like without the New World tomato. This museum explains all the mysteries. ⊠ *Strada Giarola 11, Corte di Giarola, Collecchio* ☎ *0521/228152* ⊕ *www.museidelcibo.it* 🖭 *€4* ⊘ *Mar. 1–Dec. 8, weekends 10–6, weekdays by reservation only.*

Museo del Prosciutto di Parma. Visit this museum for an in-depth look at Italy's most famous cured pork product. ⊠ *Via Bocchialini, Langhirano* ☎ *0521/864324* ⊕ *www.museidelcibo.it* 🖭 *€4, plus €3 for tasting* ⊘ *Mar.–Dec. weekends 10–6 by reservation only.*

Museo del Salame. This museum is all about cured meats. ⊠ *Castello di Felino, 23 km (14 miles) southwest of Parma* ☎ *0521/431809* ⊕ *www. museidelcibo.it* 🖭 *€4* ⊘ *Mar.–Dec. weekends 10–1 and 3–6 by reservation only.*

Piazza del Duomo. This spacious cobblestone piazza contains the cathedral and the Battistero, plus the Palazzo del Vescovado (Bishop's Palace). Behind the duomo is the baroque church of San Giovanni.

Piazza Garibaldi. This is the heart of Parma, where people gather to pass the time of day, start their *passeggiata* (evening stroll), or simply hang out. Strada Cavour, leading off the piazza, is Parma's prime shopping street: it's also crammed with wine bars teeming with locals. This square and nearby Piazza del Duomo make up one of the loveliest historic centers in Italy. So it's a perfect place to stop for a snack or light lunch.

San Giovanni Evangelista. Beyond the elaborate Baroque facade of San Giovanni Evangelista, the Renaissance interior reveals several works by Correggio: *St. John the Evangelist* (in the lunette above the door in the left transept) is considered among his finest. Also in this church (in the second and fourth chapels on the left) are works by Parmigianino, a contemporary of Correggio's. Once seen, Parmigianino's long-necked Madonnas are never forgotten. ⊠ *Piazzale San Giovanni 1, Piazza del Duomo* ☎ *0521/235311* ⊘ *Daily 8–noon and 3–5:45.*

Santa Maria della Steccata. Dating from the 16th century, this delightful church has one of Parma's most recognizable domes. In the dome's large arch there's a wonderful decorative fresco by Francesco Mazzola, better known as Parmigianino (1503–40). He took so long to complete it that his patrons briefly imprisoned him for breach of contract. ✉ *Piazza Steccata 9, off Via Dante near Piazza Garibaldi* ☎ *0521/234937* ⊕ *www.santuari.it/steccata* ☉ *Daily 9–noon and 3–6.*

Teatro Farnese/Galleria Nazionale. To enter the gallery, you pass through the magnificent baroque Teatro Farnese, built in 1617–18. Made entirely of wood, it was largely destroyed in a 1944 Allied bombing; fortunately, it's been flawlessly restored. Inside the gallery masterpieces by Correggio, Parmigianino, Leonardo da Vinci (1452–1519), El Greco (1541–1614), and Bronzino (1503–72) hang at the little-visited Galleria Nazionale. The museum is housed on the piano nobile of the massive and somewhat forbidding **Palazzo della Pilotta**, which was constructed on the riverbank in 1618. The palazzo takes its name from the game *pilotta*, a sort of handball played within the palace precincts in the 17th century. The building also suffered much damage in a May 1944 Allied bombing, and has been greatly restored. ✉ *Piazza della Pilotta* ⊕ *www.gallerianazionaleparma.it* 🎫 *€6* ☉ *Tues.–Sat. 8:30–6:30, Sun. 8:30–1:30.*

WHERE TO EAT

$
WINE BAR

✗ **Enoteca Antica Osteria Fontana.** Gregarious locals flock to this old-school *enoteca* (wine bar). The interior may be minimal, with yellow walls and wooden tables, but the wine list and sandwich menu are substantial. You can feast on a selection of *tartine* (little bread squares with creative toppings) or chow down on a grilled panini—the seemingly endless options for the latter include such standards as *coppa* (a cured pork product), pancetta, and Gorgonzola. Low prices make this a real draw for Parma's twentysomethings . . . and everyone else . . . so it's crammed with people, who spill out into the streets, wine glasses in hand. There's an enormous selection of wine bottles to go, so you can avoid the madding crowd with takeout. Ⓢ *Average meal: €5* ✉ *Strada Farini 24/a, near Piazza Garibaldi* ☎ *0521/286037* 🕭 *Reservations not accepted* ☉ *Closed Sun. and Mon.*

$$
EMILIAN

✗ **La Filoma.** If you want to try Parmesan specialties without breaking the bank, this is the place to go. The dining room evokes the turn of two centuries ago with its high ceilings and damask drapes, though an element of kitsch prevails. The food shines, from the classic *anolini in brodo di manzo e cappone* (a local variation on tortellini in broth) to the exquisite guinea fowl stuffed with prosciutto and Parmesan. Vegetarian options include a fragrant and tasty *tortina di zucca con porcini fritti* (pumpkin flan with fried porcini mushrooms). Friendly staff and a terrific wine list add to the enjoyment. $ *Average meal: €35* ⊠ *Borgo XX Marzo 15* ☏ *0521/2061811* ⊕ *www.lafiloma.it* ⚏ *Reservations essential* ⊘ *Closed Tues. No lunch Wed. Closed weekends July and Aug.*

$$ ✕ **La Greppia.** Just down the street from Palazzo Pilotta, this terrific
EMILIAN spot offers up some of the best Parmesan cooking in the historic center. Chef Paola Cavazzini's all-female crew turns out innovative treats like *anelli con cavolo nero e mostarda della Paola* (small ring-shaped pasta with Tuscan kale and caramelized fruits) and *faraona al tartufo nero di Fragno* (guinea hen with black truffle and chestnut puree). Though the dessert tray delivers some stunners, you might want to simply ask for Parmesan cheese, carved from a big wheel, to conclude your meal. Service is personal and friendly, in part because the place is tiny; and the unpretentious surroundings keep the focus on the food. $ *Average meal: €42* ⊠ *Via Garibaldi 39/a* ☏ *0521/233686* ⚏ *Reservations essential* ⊘ *Closed Mon. and Tues., July, and Dec. 23–Jan. 5.*

$$$$ ✕ **Parizzi Ristorante.** Chef-owner Marco Parizzi is the third-generation
EMILIAN cook in this elegant restaurant, which evolved from his grandfather's
Fodor's Choice *salumeria* (delicatessen) into a restaurant serving Parmesan classics and
★ contemporary cuisine. The *Piatti Tipici* (list of typical dishes) offers an *anolini in brodo di gallina e manzo* (stuffed pasta in meat broth), redolent of nutmeg, that shouldn't be missed. Contemporary creations are tasty flights of fancy: *petto di anatra caramellato,* for one, beautifully pairs the decidedly non-Italian Jerusalem artichoke with caramelized duck breast served with a very Italian type of chicory. There are two tasting menus—"Terra" (earth) and "Mare" (sea)—and a well-priced wine list, culled by Marco's wife Cristina, with contemporary wines and a section of "*Rarità*" collected by the two elder Parizzi. $ *Average meal: €55* ⊠ *Strada Repubblica 71* ☏ *0521/285952* ⊕ *www.ristoranteparizzi. it* ⚏ *Reservations essential* ⊘ *Closed Mon., Aug., and Jan. 8–15.*

$$ ✕ **Trattoria Santa Chiara.** In a little cul-de-sac, a stone's throw from bus-
EMILIAN tling Piazza Garibaldi, this trattoria offers some terrifically tasty Parmesan treats, drawing in locals and visitors alike. Genial host Daniele Ghidini tends his restaurant, and his diners, with great care, beginning with the plate laden with chunks of Parmesan cheese freshly shaved off the wheel. Start with the *misto di salumi* (thinly sliced culatello, Parma ham, and salame), and then consider either the classic *anolini in brodo* (pasta rings stuffed with meat in chicken broth) or *tortelli al erbette* (herb-cheese pasta sauced with butter and Parmesan). A real winner is the *guancialini di maiale alla Parma* (sliced roast pork with a Marsala reduction sauce, polenta on the side). The s*emifreddo al croccante* (an eggy semi-frozen ice cream with caramel and toasted nuts) is divine. $ *Average meal: €35* ⊠ *Piazzale Cervi 5, Parma* ☏ *0521/286098* ⊕ *www.trattoriasantachiara.it* ⊘ *Closed Sun. and 3 wks in Aug.*

WHERE TO STAY

For expanded hotel reviews, visit Fodors.com.

$$$ ⊞ **Palazzo dalla Rosa Prati.** Vittorio dalla Rosa Prati has converted part
HOTEL of his family's 15th-century palace on Piazza del Duomo into luxuri-
Fodor's Choice ous, self-catering accommodations, and those with connecting rooms
★ are ideal for families. **Pros:** the hotel has an opera box at Teatro Regio

that guests may reserve; Penhaligon's bath products; room service of continental breakfast included in the price. **Cons:** staff leaves at 10 pm; parking can sometimes be a problem. [$] *Rooms from: €230* ✉ *Strada al Duomo 7* ☎ *0521/386429* 🌐 *www.palazzodallarosaprati.it* 🛏 *7 rooms, 11 apartments* 🍴 *Breakfast.*

$$ B&B/INN 🏨 **Parizzi Suites and Studio.** A 17th-century palace has been refurbished with 21st-century amenities to provide a lovely place to rest one's head. **Pros:** central location; great staff; breakfast served in rooms. **Cons:** staff not always at desk. [$] *Rooms from: €135* ✉ *Strada della Republica 71, Parma* ☎ *0521/207032* 🌐 *www.parizzisuite.it* 🛏 *13 suites* 🍴 *Breakfast.*

MODENA

56 km (35 miles) southeast of Parma, 38 km (24 miles) northwest of Bologna.

Modena is famous for local products: Maserati, Ferrari, and opera star Luciano Pavarotti, who was born near here and buried in his family plot in Montale Rangone in 2007. However, it's Modena's heavenly scented balsamic vinegar, aged up to 40 years, that's probably its greatest achievement. The town has become another Emilian food mecca, with terrific restaurants and *salumerie* (delicatessens) at every turn. Though extensive modern industrial sprawl surrounds the city, the small historic center is filled with narrow medieval streets, pleasant piazzas, and typical Emilian architecture.

GETTING HERE AND AROUND

Modena is easily accessible by train, as it's on the Bologna-Milan line. Trains run frequently, and it's an easy walk from the station to the *centro storico* (historic center). There's an Intercity connection from Florence that takes about an hour and a half. By car, Modena is just off the A1 Autostrada, between Bologna and Parma.

VISITOR INFORMATION

Modena Tourism Office ✉ *Piazza Grande, Via Scudari 8* ☎ *059/2032660* 🌐 *www.comune.modena.it.*

EXPLORING

Consorzio Produttori Aceto Balsamico Tradizionale di Modena. Connoisseurs of balsamic vinegar can do a tasting with this organization. They'll arrange for you to visit one of their local producers: to set things up, it's best to contact the Consorzio through their website. ✉ *Strada Vaciglio Sud 1085/1* ☎ *059/395633* 🌐 *www.balsamico.it* 🎟 *Free* 🕒 *By appointment.*

Duomo. The 12th-century Romanesque cathedral was begun by the architect Lanfredo in 1099 and consecrated in 1184. Medieval sculptures depicting scenes from Genesis adorn the facade, but walk around to the Piazza Grande side as well to see the building's marvelous arcading. It's a rare example of a cathedral having more than one principal view. The interior, completely clad in brick, imparts a sober and beautiful feel. An elaborate gallery has scenes of the Passion of Christ carved by Anselmo da Campione and his assistants circa 1160–80. The tomb of San Geminiano is in the crypt. The white-marble bell tower is known as **La Torre Ghirlandina** (the Little Garland Tower) because of its distinctive weather vane. ✉ *Piazza Grande* ☎ *059/216078* 🌐 *www.duomodimodena.it* ⏲ *Daily 6:30–12:30 and 3:30–7.*

Galleria Ferrari. This museum has become a pilgrimage site for auto enthusiasts. It takes you through the illustrious history of Ferrari, from early 1951 models to the present—the legendary F50 and cars driven by Michael Schumacher in Formula One victories being highlights. You can also take a look at the glamorous life of founder Enzo Ferrari (a re-creation of his office is onsite), and a glance into the production process. ✉ *Via Dino Ferrari, Maranello, 17 km (11 miles) south of Modena* ☎ *0536/943204* 🌐 *www.galleria.ferrari.com* 🎫 *€13* ⏲ *Oct.–Apr., daily 9:30–6; May–Nov., daily 9:30–7.*

WHERE TO EAT

$ EMILIAN 🍴 **Aldina.** On the second floor of a building across from the covered market, steps from the Piazza Grande, this simple, typical trattoria is in the very nerve center of the city. Here you'll find exemplary preparations of the region's crown jewels: tortellini in brodo, tagliatelle al ragù, and roast meats. Wash it down with lambrusco, as locals have for ages, and save room for the *zuppa inglese* (layered sponge cake with custard), which is terrific. The kitchen also turns out dishes with *fantasia,* putting a contemporary twist on classics. [$] *Average meal: €18* ✉ *Via Albinelli 40* ☎ *059/236106* 💳 *No credit cards* ⏲ *Closed Sun., and July and Aug. No dinner Mon.–Thurs.*

$ EMILIAN 🍴 **Da Enzo.** The Nora-Tassi family has been operating this cheerful and crowded no-frills trattoria since 1950. Enzo and son Giovanni run the front, and Argia, Enzo's wife, makes all the tasty desserts. It's packed with Modenesi eager to eat terrific food at relatively inexpensive prices. The tortellini in brodo makes an excellent starter, as does *maccheroncini di Enzo* (macaroni in a minced veal-prosciutto ragù). The bollito misto comes with the usual salsa verde and mostarda (a fruit condiment) made in house. Many meats are served *al balsamico*—and since you're in the town that gave the world this precious commodity, why not indulge? Wash it down with the local wine, which happens to be a frizzy lambrusco served slightly chilled. Note that the trattoria is up two flights of stairs. [$] *Average meal: €24* ✉ *Via Coltellini 17* ☎ *059/225177* ⏲ *Closed Mon. and Aug. No dinner Sun.*

$ EMILIAN 🍴 **Ermes.** Ebullient host Ermes greets you as you walk in and seats you wherever he happens to have room—no matter that you might be put with people you don't know. It's part of the fun, as this quasi-communal style of lunching encourages conviviality. In the kitchen, Bruna, Ermes's wife, turns out splendid versions of *cucina casalinga modenesi* (home cooking, Modena-style). Ermes recites the short list of *primi* and *secondi*, which change daily and arrive promptly. The accompanying wine is local, simple, and cheap. So it's no wonder this place is favored by everyone from suits to construction workers to students. [$] *Average meal: €15* ✉ *Via Ganaceto 89–91* ☎ *059/238065* 💳 *No credit cards* ⏲ *Closed Sun. No dinner.*

Continued on page 510

EMILIA
ONE TASTE AT A TIME

4 towns, dozens of foods, and a mouthful of flavors you'll never forget

Imagine biting into the silkiest prosciutto in the world or the most delectable homemade tortellini you've ever tasted. In Emilia, Italy's most famous food region, you'll discover simple tastes that exceed all expectations. Beginning in Parma and moving eastward to Bologna, you'll find the epicenters of such world-renowned culinary treats as *prosciutto crudo*, Parmigiano-Reggiano, *aceto balsamico*, and tortellini. The secret to this region is not the discovery of new and exotic delicacies, but rather the rediscovery of foods you thought you already knew—in much better versions than you've ever tasted before.

TASTE 1 | PROSCIUTTO CRUDO

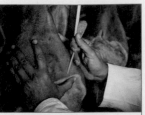

Quality testing

From Piacenza to the Adriatic, ham is the king of meats in Emilia-Romagna, but nowhere is this truer than in **Parma**.

Parma is the world's capital of *prosciutto crudo*, raw cured ham (*crudo* for short). Ask for *crudo di Parma* to signal its local provenance; many other regions also make their own crudo.

Greasing the ham

CRUDO LANGUAGE

It's easy to get confused with the terminology. Crudo is the product that Americans simply call "prosciutto" or the Brits might call "Parma ham." *Prosciutto* in Italian, however, is a more general term that means any kind of ham, including *prosciutto cotto*, or simply *cotto*, which means "cooked ham." Cotto is an excellent product and frequent pizza topping that's closer to (but much better than) what Americans would put in a deli sandwich.

Crudo is traditionally eaten in one of three ways: in a dry sandwich (*panino*); by itself as an appetizer, often with shaved butter on top; or as part of an appetizer or snack platter of assorted *salumi* (cured meats).

Fire branding

WHAT TO LOOK FOR

For the best crudo di Parma, look for slices, always cut to order, that are razor thin and have a light, rosy red color (not dark red). Don't be shy about going into a simple *salumeria* (a purveyor of cured meats) and ordering crudo by the pound. You can enjoy it straight out of the package on a park bench—and why not?

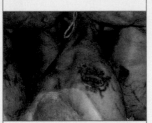

Quality trademark

BEST SPOT FOR A SAMPLE

You can't go wrong with any of Parma's famed salumerie, but **Salumeria Garibaldi** (Via Garibaldi 42) is one of the town's oldest and most reliable. You'll find not only spectacular prosciutto crudo, but also delectable cheeses, wines, porcini mushrooms, and more.

LEARN MORE

For more information on crudo di Parma, contact the **Consorzio del Prosciutto di Parma** (Largo Calamandrei 1/a, 0521/246211, www.prosciuttodiparma.com/eng).

TASTE 2 | PARMIGIANO-REGGIANO

From Parma, it's only a half-hour trip east to **Reggio Emilia**, the birthplace of the crumbly and renowned Parmigiano-Reggiano cheese. Reggio (not to be confused with Reggio di Calabria in the south) is a charming little Emilian town that has been the center of production for this legendary cheese for more than 70 years.

Warming milk in copper cauldrons

SAY CHEESE
Grana is the generic Italian term for hard, aged, full-flavored cheese that can be grated. Certain varieties of Pecorino Romano, for example, or Grana Padano, also fall under this term, but Parmigiano-Reggiano, aged for as long as four years, is the foremost example.

Breaking up the curds

NOT JUST FOR GRATING
In Italy, Parmigiano-Reggiano is not only grated onto pasta, but also often served by itself in chunks, either as an appetizer—perhaps accompanied by local salumi (cured meats)—or even for dessert, when it might be drizzled with honey or Modena's balsamic vinegar.

Placing cheese in molds

MEET THE MAKERS
If you're a cheese enthusiast, you shouldn't miss the chance to take a free two-hour guided tour of a Parmigiano-Reggiano–producing farm. You'll witness the entire process and get to meet the cheesemakers. Tours can be arranged by contacting the **Consorzio del Formaggio Parmigiano-Reggiano** in Reggio Emilia (sezionepr@parmareggiano.it) at least 20 days in advance. (Ask specifically for an English-language tour if that's what you want.)

Aging cheese wheels

BEST SPOT FOR A SAMPLE
The production of Parmigiano-Reggiano is heavily controlled by the Consorzio del Formaggio, so you can buy the cheese at any store or supermarket in the region and be virtually guaranteed equal quality and price. For a more distinctive shopping experience, however, try buying Parmigiano-Reggiano at the street market on Reggio's central square. The market takes place on Tuesday and Friday from 8 AM to 1 PM year-round.

Parmigiano-Reggiano

TASTE 3 | ACETO BALSAMICO DI MODENA

Tasting tradizionale vinegar

Modena is home to *Aceto Balsamico Tradizionale di Modena*, a kind of balsamic vinegar unparalleled anywhere else on Earth. The balsamic vinegar you've probably tried—even the pricier versions sold at specialty stores—may be good on salads, but it bears only a fleeting resemblance to the real thing.

HOW IS IT MADE?
The *tradizionale* vinegar that passes strict government standards is made with Trebbiano grape must, which is cooked over an open fire, reduced, and fermented from 12 to 25 or more years in a series of specially made wooden casks. As the vinegar becomes more concentrated, so much liquid evaporates that it takes more than 6 gallons of must to produce one quart of vinegar 12 years later. The result is an intense and syrupy concoction best enjoyed sparingly on grilled meats, strawberries, or Parmigiano-Reggiano cheese. The vinegar has such a complexity of flavor that some even drink it as an after-dinner liqueur.

Wooden casks for fermenting

BEST SPOT FOR A SAMPLE
The **Consorzio Produttori Aceto Balsamico Tradizionale di Modena** (Strada Vaciglia Sud 1085/1, 059/395633, www.balsamico.it) offers tours and tastings by reservation only. The main objective of the consortium is to monitor the quality of the authentic balsamic vinegar, made by only a few licensed restaurants and small producers.

The consortium also limits production, keeping prices sky high. Expect to pay €60 for a 100-ml (3.4 oz) bottle of tradizionale, which is generally aged 12 to 15 years, or €90 and up for the older tradizionale extra vecchio variety, which is aged 25 years.

WHERE TO EAT
In Modena, it's hard to find a bad meal. Local trattorie do great versions of tortellini and other stuffed pasta. If you can find *zampone* (a sausage made from stuffed pig's trotter), don't miss it—it's an adventurous Modena specialty. **Hosteria Giusti** (Vicolo Squallore 46, 059/10712, www.giusti1605.com) is a particularly good place to try local specialties; the adjacent **Salumeria Giusti** is reputedly the world's oldest deli, founded in 1605.

OTHER TASTES OF EMILIA
❑ **Cotechino**: a sausage made from pork and lard, a specialty of Modena

❑ **Culatello de Zibello**: raw cured ham produced along the banks of the Po River, and cured and aged for more than 11 months

❑ **Mortadella**: soft, smoked sausage made with beef, pork, cubes of pork fat, and seasonings, a specialty of Bologna

❑ **Ragù**: a sauce made from minced pork and beef, simmered in milk, onions, carrots, and tomatoes

❑ **Salama da sugo**: salty, oily sausage aged and then cooked, a specialty of Ferrara

❑ **Tortelli and cappellacci**: pasta pillows with the same basic form as tortellini, but stuffed with cheese and vegetables

TASTE 4 | TORTELLINI

The venerable city of **Bologna** is called "the Fat" for a reason: this is the birthplace of tortellini, not to mention other specialties such as mortadella and ragù. Despite the city's new reputation for chic nightclubs and flashy boutiques, much of the food remains as it ever was.

You'll find the many Emilian variations on stuffed pasta all over the region, but they're perhaps at their best in Bologna, especially the native tortellini.

INSPIRED BY THE GODS
According to one legend, tortellini was inspired by the navel of Venus, goddess of love. As the story goes, Venus and some other gods stopped at a local inn for the night. A nosy chef went to their room to catch a glimpse of Venus. Peering through the keyhole, he saw her lying only partially covered on the bed. He was so inspired after seeing her perfect navel that he created a stuffed pasta, tortellini, in its image.

ON THE MENU
Tortellini is usually filled with beef (sometimes cheese), and is served two ways: *asciutta* is "dry," meaning it is served with a sauce such as ragù, or perhaps just with butter and Parmigiano. *Tortellini in brodo* is immersed in a lovely, savory beef broth.

BEST SPOT TO BUY
Don't miss **Tamburini** (Via Drapperie 1, 051/234726), Bologna's best specialty food shop, where smells of Emilia-Romagna's famous specialties waft out through the room and into the streets.

WHERE TO EAT

The classic art deco restaurant **Rosteria Luciano** (Via Nazario Sauro 19, 051/231249, www.rosterialuciano.it) is a great place to try tortellini in brodo, one of the best choices on their fixed menu. A changing list of daily specials augments the menu. For a meat course it's usually best to order whatever special the kitchen has that day. The selection of local cheeses is also good. Please note that the restaurant is closed on Wednesday, the whole month of August, and Sunday from June through September.

Stretching the dough

Adding the filling

Shaping each piece

Tortellini di Bologna

$$ EMILIAN Fodor's Choice ★ 🍴 **Hosteria Giusti.** In the back room of the Salumeria Giusti, established in 1605 and reportedly the world's oldest deli, you'll find four tables in a room tastefully done with antique furnishings. You'll also find some of the best food in Emilia Romagna—perfectly executed takes on traditional dishes. The *gnocco fritto* (fried dough) with *salumi* (cured meats) arrives as little clouds of lightly fried dough, topped with pancetta, or prosciutto, among other things. The *anolini* (tiny cheese-stuffed pasta) in brodo might feature the most fragrant broth in the world—inhale the aroma before tucking in. If you're tempted by too many things, half-portions may be available. Just leave room for dessert, especially *La Tassina*: served in a little espresso cup, it bursts with chocolate, anise, and egg. The wine list is divine, as is the staff. Reserve well ahead. [$] *Average meal: €45* ✉ *Vicolo Squallore 46* ☎ *059/222533* 🌐 *www.hosteriagiusti.it* ✍ *Reservations essential* ⏲ *Closed Sun. and Mon. and Dec.–Jan. 10. No dinner.*

$$$$ EMILIAN Fodor's Choice ★ 🍴 **Osteria Francescana.** Chef/proprietor Massimo Bottura says he learned about food from under his grandmother's table. He's done stints with Adria and Ducasse, takes inspiration from music and literature, and pours all these influences into creating some of the most memorable food in all of Italy while remaining true to his Modenese roots. The restaurant contains only 11 tables; colors are muted, and service superior. Though it's possible to order à la carte, most everyone opts for one of the three tasting menus—*Tradizioni, Classici,* and *Sensazioni* (Traditional, Classic, and Sensational). One of his signature dishes is *5 stagionature di Parmigiano Reggiano* (five versions of Parmesan in various stages, served in five different textures and temperatures). His tortellini alla crema is light, delicate, and perhaps the definitive version of this dish. [$] *Average meal: €110* ✉ *Via Stella 22, Modena* ☎ *059/210118* 🌐 *www.osteriafrancescana.it* ✍ *Reservations essential* ⏲ *Closed Sun. No lunch Sat.*

WHERE TO STAY

For expanded hotel reviews, visit Fodors.com.

$$ HOTEL 🏨 **Hotel Canalgrande.** Once a ducal palace, the Canalgrande today has a lobby so gilded it's over the top, and rooms are large and airy, with ornate dark-wood and upholstered pieces. **Pros:** significant discounts for solo travelers; cheaper rates if booking online. **Cons:** caters to business travelers; feels somewhat impersonal. [$] *Rooms from: €147* ✉ *Corso Canalgrande 6* ☎ *059/217160* 🌐 *www.canalgrandehotel.it* 🛏 *62 rooms, 2 suites* 🍽 *Breakfast.*

BOLOGNA

Bologna, a city rich with cultural jewels, has long been one of the best-kept secrets in northern Italy. Tourists in the know can bask in the shadow of its leaning medieval towers and devour the city's wonderful food.

The charm of the centro storico, with its red-arcaded passageways and sidewalks, can be attributed to wise city counselors who, at the beginning of the 13th century, decreed that roads couldn't be built without *portici* (porticoes). Were these counselors to return to town eight centuries later, they'd marvel at how little has changed.

Bologna, with a population of about 373,000, has a university-town vibe—and it feels young and lively in a way that many other Italian cities don't. It also feels full of Italians in a way that many other towns, thronged with tourists, don't. Bolognesi come out at aperitivo time, and you might be struck by the fact that it's not just youngsters who are out doing the *passeggiata* (evening stroll), or having a glass of wine with *affettati misti* (mixed cured meats). The pleasure is shared by all Bolognesi.

Known as "Bologna the Fat" from as early as the Middle Ages, the town's agricultural prosperity led to a well-fed population, one that survives into the 21st century. Bolognese food is, arguably, the best in Italy. With its sublime food, lively spirit, and largely undiscovered art, Bologna is a memorable destination.

GETTING HERE AND AROUND
Frequent train service from Florence to Bologna makes getting here easy. The Italo and *Frecciarossa* (high-speed trains) run several times an hour and take just under 40 minutes; *frecciabianca* (slightly less-high-speed trains) run regularly as well and take a little over an hour. Otherwise, you're left with the *regionali* (regional) trains, which putter along and get you to Bologna in just over two hours. The historic center is an interesting and relatively effortless walk from the station. If you're driving from Florence, take the A1, exiting onto the A14, and then get on the RA1 to Uscita 7–Bologna Centrale. The trip takes about an hour. From Milan, take the A1, exiting to the A14 as you near the city; from there, take the A13 and exit at Bologna; then follow the RA1 to Uscita 7–Bologna Centrale. The trip takes just under three hours.

VISITOR INFORMATION
Bologna Tourism Offices ✉ *Aeroporto di Bologna* ☎ *051/239660* ⊕ *www.bolognawelcome.it* ✉ *Piazza Maggiore 1* ☎ *051/239660.*

EXPLORING BOLOGNA

Piazza Maggiore and the adjacent Piazza del Nettuno are the historic centers of the city. Arranged around these two squares are the imposing Basilica di San Petronio, the massive Palazzo Comunale, the Palazzo del Podestà, the Palazzo Re Enzo, and the Fontana del Nettuno—one of the most visually harmonious groupings of public buildings in the country. From here, sights that aren't on one of the piazzas are but a short walk away, along delightful narrow cobblestone streets or under the ubiquitous arcades that double as municipal umbrellas. Take at least a full day to explore Bologna; it's compact and lends itself to easy exploration, but there's plenty to see.

TOP ATTRACTIONS
Basilica di San Petronio. Construction on this vast cathedral began in 1390; and the work, as you can see, still isn't finished more than 600 years later. The wings of the transept are missing and the facade is only partially decorated, lacking most of the marble that was intended to adorn it. The main doorway was carved in 1425 by the great Sienese master Jacopo della Quercia. Above the center of the door is a Madonna and Child flanked by saints Ambrose and Petronius,

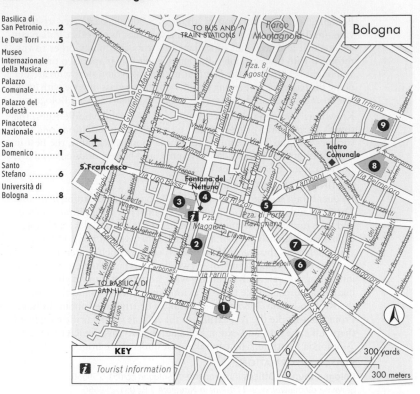

KEY

i *Tourist information*

0   300 yards

0   300 meters

the city's patrons. Michelangelo, Giulio Romano, and Andrea Palladio (among others), submitted designs for the facade, which were all eventually rejected.

The interior of the basilica is huge. The Bolognesi had planned an even bigger church—you can see the columns erected to support the larger version outside the east end—but had to tone down construction when the university seat was established next door in 1561. The **Museo di San Petronio** contains models showing how it was originally supposed to look. The most important art in the church is in the fourth chapel on the left: these frescoes by Giovanni di Modena date from 1410–15. ⊠ *Piazza Maggiore* ☎ *051/22544* ✎ *Free* ☉ *Church: daily 7:45–1 and 3–6. Museum: weekdays 9:30–12:30 and 3–5:30, Sat. 9:30–12:30 and 3–4:30, Sun. 3–5:30.*

Fontana del Nettuno. Sculptor Giambologna's elaborate 1563–66 Baroque fountain and monument to Neptune occupying Piazza Nettuno has been aptly nicknamed *Il Gigante* ("The Giant"). Its exuberantly sensual mermaids and undraped God of the sea drew fire when it was constructed, but not enough, apparently, to dissuade the populace from using the fountain as a public washing stall for centuries. ⊠ *Piazza Nettuno, next to Palazzo Re Enzo, Piazza Maggiore area.*

Le Due Torri. Two landmark towers, mentioned by Dante in *The Inferno,* stand side by side in the compact Piazza di Porta Ravegnana. Once every family of importance had a tower as a symbol of prestige and power—and as a potential fortress. Now only 60 remain out of more than 200 that once presided over the city. **Torre Garisenda** (from the late 11th century), which tilts 10 feet off perpendicular, was shortened to 165 feet in the 1300s and is now closed to visitors. **Torre degli Asinelli** (circa 1109) is 320-feet tall and leans 7½ feet. If you're up to a serious physical challenge—and not claustrophobic—you may want to climb its 500 narrow, wooden steps to get the view over Bologna. ⊠ *Piazza di Porta Ravegnana, east of Piazza Maggiore* 🔊 *€3* ⊙ *Torre degli Asinelli: daily 9–5.*

FAMILY
Fodor'sChoice
★

Santo Stefano. This splendid and unusual basilica actually contains between four and seven connected churches (authorities differ). A 4th-century temple dedicated to Isis was originally on this site, though much of what you see dates from the 10th through the 12th centuries. The oldest existing building is **Santi Vitale e Agricola,** parts of which date from the 5th century. The exquisite beehive-shape San Sepolcro contains a Nativity scene much loved by Bologna's children, who come at Christmastime to pay their respects to the Christ Child. Just outside the church, which probably dates from the 5th century with later alterations, is the **Cortile di Pilato** (Pilate's Courtyard), named for the basin in the center. It's said that Pontius Pilate washed his hands in this basin after condemning Christ—despite the fact that it was probably crafted around the 8th century. Also in the building is a museum displaying various medieval religious works with a shop selling honey, shampoos, and jams made by the monks. ⊠ *Via Santo Stefano 24, Piazza Santo Stefano, University area* ☎ *051/223256* ⊙ *Daily 9–noon and 3:30–6.*

Università di Bologna. Take a stroll through the streets of the university area: a jumble of buildings, some dating as far back as the 15th century and most to the 17th and 18th. The neighborhood, as befits a college town, is full of bookshops, coffee bars, and inexpensive restaurants. None of them are particularly distinguished, but they're all characteristic of student life in the city. Try eating at the *mensa universitaria* (cafeteria) if you want to strike up a conversation with local students (most speak English). Political slogans and sentiments are scrawled on walls all around the university and tend to be ferociously leftist, sometimes juvenile, and often entertaining. Among the university museums, the most interesting is the **Museo di Palazzo Poggi,** which displays scientific instruments plus paleontological, botanical, and university-related artifacts. ⊠ *Via Zamboni 33, University area* ☎ *051/2099610* ⊕ *www.museopalazzopoggi.unibo.it* 🔊 *€3* ⊙ *Tues.–Fri. 10–1 and 2–4, weekends 10:30–1:30 and 2:30–5:30.*

9

WORTH NOTING

MAMbo. The name of this museum stands for Museo d'Arte Moderna di Bologna, or Bologna's Museum of Modern Art. It houses a permanent collection of modern art (defined as post-World War II up until five minutes ago) and stages a revolving series of temporary exhibitions by cutting-edge artists. All of this is set within a remarkable space: you might have a hard time telling that the sleek minimalist structure was built in

1915 as the Forno del Pane, a large bakery that made bread for many of the city's residents. A bookshop and a restaurant complete the complex, the latter offering Sunday brunch and delicious *aperitivi* (aperitifs). ⊠ *Via Don Minzoni 14* 🏛 *051/6496611* ⊕ *www.mambo-bologna.org* 🎫 *€6* ⊙ *Tues., Wed., and Fri. noon–6, Thurs. and weekends noon–8.*

Museo Internazionale della Musica. The music museum in the spectacular Palazzo Aldini Sanguinetti, with its 17th- and 18th-century frescoes, offers among its exhibits a 1606 harpsichord and a collection of beautiful music manuscripts dating from the 1500s. ⊠ *Strada Maggiore 34, University area* 🏛 *051/2757711* ⊕ *www.museomusicabologna.it* 🎫 *Free* ⊙ *Oct.–July, Tues.–Fri. 9:30–4, weekends 10–6:30.*

Palazzo Comunale. A mélange of building styles and constant modifications characterize this huge palace dating from the 13th to 15th centuries. When Bologna was an independent city-state, this was the seat of government—a function it still serves today. Over the door is a statue of Bologna-born Pope Gregory XIII (reigned 1572–85), most famous for reorganizing the calendar. There are good views from the upper stories of the palace. The first-floor **Sala Rossa** (Red Room) is open on advance request and during some exhibitions; while the **Sala del Consiglio Comunale** (City Council Hall) is open to the public for a few hours in the late morning. The old stock exchange, part of the Palazzo Comunale which you enter from Piazza Nettuno, has been turned into a library: dubbed the **Sala Borsa** (⊕ *www.bibliotecasalaborsa.it*), it has an impressive interior courtyard. Within the palazzo there are also two museums. The **Collezioni Comunali d'Arte** exhibits paintings from the Middle Ages as well as some Renaissance works by Luca Signorelli (circa 1445–1523) and Tintoretto (1518–94). The **Museo Giorgio Morandi** (⊕ *www.museomorandi.it*) is dedicated to the 20th-century still-life artist Giorgio Morandi. In addition to his paintings, there's a re-creation of his studio and living space. Underground caves and the foundations of the old cathedral can be visited by appointment made through the tourist office. ⊠ *Piazza Maggiore 6* 🏛 *051/2194400 Palazzo/Sala Borsa, 051/6496611 Museo* 🎫 *€6, except during special art exhibitions* ⊙ *Sala del Consiglio Comunale: Tues.–Sat. 10–1. Sala Borsa: Tues.–Fri. 10–8, Sat. 10–7. Collezioni and Museo: Tues.–Wed. and Fri. noon–6, Thurs. and weekends noon–8.*

Palazzo del Podestà. This classic Renaissance palace facing the Basilica di San Petronio was erected in 1484, and attached to it is the soaring **Torre dell'Arengo.** The bells in the tower have rung whenever the city has celebrated, mourned, or called its citizens to arms. ⊠ *Piazza Nettuno, Piazza Maggiore area* 🏛 *051/224500* ⊙ *During exhibitions only.*

Palazzo Re Enzo. Built in 1244, this palace became home to King Enzo of Sardinia, who was imprisoned here in 1249 after he was captured during the fierce battle of Fossalta. He died here 23 years later. The palace has other macabre associations as well: common criminals received last rites in the tiny courtyard chapel before being executed in Piazza Maggiore. The courtyard is worth peeking into, but the palace merely houses government offices. ⊠ *Piazza Re Enzo, Piazza Maggiore area* 🏛 *051/224500* ⊙ *During exhibitions only.*

Pinacoteca Nazionale. Bologna's principal art gallery contains many works by the immortals of Italian painting spanning the 13th to the 19th centuries. Its prize possession is the famous *Ecstasy of St. Cecilia* by Raphael (1483–1520). There's also a beautiful polyptych by Giotto (1267–1337), as well as *Madonna and Child with Saints Margaret, Jerome, and Petronio* by Parmigianino: note the rapt eye contact between St. Margaret and the Christ Child. ✉ *Via delle Belle Arti 56, University area* ☎ *051/4209411* 🌐 *www.pinacotecabologna.beniculturali.it* 🎟 *€4* 🕘 *Tues.–Sun. 9–7.*

San Domenico. The tomb of St. Dominic, who died here in 1221, is called the **Arca di San Domenico,** and is found in this church in the sixth chapel on the right. Many artists participated in its decoration, notably Niccolò di Bari, who was so proud of his contribution that he changed his name to Niccolò dell'Arca to recall this famous work. The young Michelangelo (1475–1564) carved the angel on the right. In the right transept of the church is a tablet marking the last resting place of hapless King Enzo, the Sardinian ruler imprisoned in the Palazzo Re Enzo. The attached museum contains religious relics. ✉ *Piazza San Domenico 13, off Via Garibaldi, south of Piazza Maggiore* ☎ *051/6400411* 🌐 *www.domenicani.bo.it* 🕘 *Church: daily 8–12:30 and 3:30–6:30. Museum: weekdays 10–noon and 3:30–6, Sat. 9:30–noon and 3:30–5:30, Sun. 3:30–5:30.*

WHERE TO EAT

$$ EMILIAN Fodor's Choice ★

🍴 **Da Cesari.** Just off Piazza Maggiore, this lovely one-room restaurant has white tablecloths, dark-wood paneling, and wine bottle–lined walls. Genial host Paolino Cesari has been presiding over his eatery since 1955, and both he and his staff go out of the way to make you feel at home. The food's terrific—if you love pork products, try anything on the menu with *mora romagnola.* Paolino has direct contact with the people who raise this once nearly-extinct breed (he calls it "my pig"). The meat is deep, highly flavorful, and makes divine salame, among other things. All the usual Bolognesi classics are here, as well as—in fall and winter—an inspired *scaloppa all Petroniano* (veal cutlet with prosciutto and fontina) that comes smothered in white truffles. [$] *Average meal: €31* ✉ *Via de' Carbonesi 8, south of Piazza Maggiore* ☎ *051/237710* 🌐 *www.da-cesari.it* ✍ *Reservations essential* 🕘 *Closed Sun., Aug., and 1 wk in Jan.*

$$ EMILIAN

🍴 **Da Gianni a la Vecia Bulagna.** Locals simply call it "da Gianni," and they fill these two unadorned rooms at lunch and at dinner. Though the interor is plain and unremarkable, it doesn't much matter—this place is all about food. The usual starters such as a tasty tortellini in brodo are on hand, as are daily specials such as gnocchi made with pumpkin, then sauced with melted cheese. *Bollito misto* (mixed meats boiled in a rich broth) is a fine option here, and the *cotechino con purè di patate* (a deliciously oily sausage with mashed potatoes) is elevated to sublimity by the accompanying salsa verde. [$] *Average meal: €30* ✉ *Via Clavature 18, Piazza Maggiore area* ☎ *051/229434* ✍ *Reservations essential.*

$ ITALIAN 🍴 **Divinis.** Bottles lining the walls on both floors of this spot are a testimony to its commitment to serving fine wines, whether by the glass or by the bottle. The wine list runs to 102 pages—and terrific food accompanies the oenophilic splendor. Cheese and cured meat plates are on offer, as are superlative soups, salads, and secondi on a frequently changing menu. Special events, such as wine tastings and tango dancing, happen throughout the week. Divinis's continuous opening hours, a rarity in Italy, are an added plus. You could have a coffee at 11 am or a glass of wine well after midnight. [$] *Average meal: €15* ✉ *Via Battibecco 4/c, Piazza Maggiore* ☎ *051/2961502* 🌐 *www.divinis.it* ✍ *Reservations essential* 🕒 *Closed Sun.*

$$$ MODERN EUROPEAN 🍴 **Marco Fadiga Bistrot.** If you're looking for terrific food and something out of the ordinary—an Italian restaurant that also serves non-Italian food—dine at this French-styled bistrot: a warren of brilliantly colored rooms lit by chandelier. Chef Marco Fadiga has spent much time in England and France, and their culinary influences show. What's on offer each night is written on a blackboard, which is brought to the table. You can have marvelous raw oysters, as well as the *plateau* (a very un-Italian assortment of raw things from the sea). Traditionalists will thrill to his tortellini in brodo, and adventurous sorts might like the *tartare di orata* (sea bream tartare) served with fresh and candied fruit. [$] *Average meal: €50* ✉ *Via Rialto 23/c, Piazza Maggiore area* ☎ *051/220118* 🌐 *www.marcofadigabistrot.it* ✍ *Reservations essential* 🕒 *Closed Sun. and Mon. No lunch.*

$ WINE BAR 🍴 **Tamburini.** Two small rooms inside plus kegs and bar stools outside make up this lively, packed little spot. At lunchtime, office workers swarm to the "bistrot self service" for remarkably tasty primi and secondi. After lunch, it becomes a wine bar with a vast array of selections by the glass and the bottle. The overwhelming plate of *affettati misti* is crammed with top-quality local ham products and succulent cheeses (including, sometimes, a goat Brie). An adjacent salumeria offers many wonderful things to take away. [$] *Average meal: €10* ✉ *Via Drapperie 1, Piazza Maggiore area* ☎ *051/234726* 🕒 *No dinner.*

$$$ EMILIAN Fodor's Choice ★ 🍴 **Trattoria Battibecco.** This sleek eatery has been in the hands of the Costa family since 1978. Starting out as a humble trattoria, it has evolved into something entirely different, with terra-cotta floors and sponged walls the color of saffron providing the backdrop for truly exceptional fare. Bolognesi swarm here, and with good reason. The menu offers Emilian classics such as tortellini in brodo and other meat-based secondi, all executed with a deft turn. But it seems that most diners go the fish route. Start with the *spiedino di gamberi* (shrimp kebabs), rolled in toasted hazelnuts and mustard, and served over a bed of delicately shaved raw artichokes before choosing between the *tagliata di rana pescatrice in crosta di pane e bacon* (thinly sliced monkfish wrapped in bacon and lightly breaded) or the lobster. An impeccable wine list completes the picture. [$] *Average meal: €55* ✉ *Via Battibecco 4, south of Piazza Maggiore, Bologna* ☎ *051/223298* 🌐 *www.battibecco.com* ✍ *Reservations essential* 🕒 *Closed Sun. No lunch Sat.*

$ EMILIAN 🍴 **Trattoria del Rosso.** Although its interior—glaring yellow walls and the oddly placed ceramic plate—is nothing to write home, this trattoria teems with locals. A mostly young crowd chows down on delicious, basic regional fare at rock-bottom prices. Nimble staff bearing multiple plates sashay neatly between the closely-spaced tables delivering such standards as *crescentine con salumi e squacquerone* (deep-fried flour puffs with cured meats and soft cheese) and tortellini in brodo. It is the kind of place where there's always a line of hungry people outside waiting to get in, but where they don't glare at you if you only order a plate of pasta: another reason, perhaps, why it's a favorite of university students. $ *Average meal: €22* ⊠ *Via Augusto Righi 30, University area* ☎ *051/236730* ⊕ *www.trattoriadelrosso.com* ☉ *Closed Thurs.*

WHERE TO STAY

For expanded hotel reviews, visit Fodors.com.

$$
HOTEL

Albergo Centrale. A stone's throw from Piazza Maggiore, this place started out as a pensione in 1875, but has been brought firmly into the 21st century and offers the winning combination of comfort, affordability, and some family-size rooms. **Pros:** very good value; excellent location. **Cons:** might be too plain for some tastes; street-facing rooms can get some noise. $ *Rooms from: €145* ⊠ *Via della Zecca 2, Piazza Maggiore* ☎ *051/225114* ⊕ *www.albergocentralebologna.it* ☞ *31 rooms, 26 rooms with bath* ⦿ *Breakfast.*

$$$
HOTEL
Fodor'sChoice
★

Art Hotel Novecento. This swank place, inspired by the 1930s Viennese Secession movement, is in a remarkably serene cul-de-sac just minutes from Piazza Maggiore. **Pros:** spacious single rooms ideal for solo travelers; friendly, capable concierge service, sumptuous buffet breakfast. **Cons:** some standard doubles are small; might be too trendy for some. $ *Rooms from: €250* ⊠ *Piazza Galileo 4/3, Piazza Maggiore area* ☎ *051/7457311* ⊕ *www.bolognarthotels.it/novecento* ☞ *24 rooms, 1 suite* ⦿ *Breakfast.*

$$$
HOTEL
Fodor'sChoice
★

Art Hotel Orologio. The location of this stylish and welcoming hotel can't be beat: it's right around the corner from Piazza Maggiore, tucked in a quiet little side street. **Pros:** central location; family-friendly rooms; welcomes all animals. **Cons:** some steps to elevator; pet-friendly environment may not appeal to allergy sufferers. $ *Rooms from: €220* ⊠ *Via IV Novembre 10, Piazza Maggiore area* ☎ *051/7457411* ⊕ *www.bolognarthotels.it/orologio* ☞ *26 rooms, 6 suites, 1 apartment* ⦿ *Breakfast.*

NIGHTLIFE AND THE ARTS

THE ARTS
MUSIC AND OPERA

Teatro Comunale. This 18th-century theater presents concerts by Italian and international orchestras throughout the year, but is dominated by the highly acclaimed opera performances November–May, so reserve seats well in advance. The ticket office is open Tuesday–Saturday 10–2. ⊠ *Largo Respighi 1, University area* ☎ *051/529958* ⊕ *www.tcbo.it.*

NIGHTLIFE

As a university town, Bologna has long been known for its busy night-life. As early as 1300 it was said to have 150 taverns. Most of the city's current 200-plus pubs and bars are frequented by Italian students, young adults, and international students, with the university district forming the hub. In addition to the university area, the pedestrians-only zone on Via del Pratello, lined with plenty of bars, also has a hopping night scene; as does Via delle Moline, which promises cutting-edge cafés and bars. A more upscale, low-key evening experience can be had at one of Bologna's many wine bars, where the food is often substantial enough to constitute dinner.

BARS

Bar Calice. A year-round indoor-outdoor operation (with heat lamps), this bar is extremely popular with thirtysomethings, sometimes pushing baby carriages. Its large menu includes raw oysters. ⊠ *Via Clavature 13/a, at Via Marchesana, Piazza Maggiore area* ☎ *051/6569296.*

Nu Bar Lounge. This lively, high-energy place draws a cocktail-loving crowd, who enjoy bartenders mixing up fun drinks like "I'm Too Sexy for This Place"—in this case, a combination of vodka, triple sec, apple juice, and lemon. ⊠ *Via de' Musei 6, off Buca San Petronio, Piazza Maggiore area* ☎ *051/222532* ⊕ *www.nu-lounge.com.*

Osteria del Sole. Though "osteria" suggests that food will be served in an establishment, such is not the case here. This place is all about drinking wine; the entrance door has warnings such as "He who doesn't drink will please stay outside" and "Dogs who don't drink are forbidden to come in." It's been around since 1465, and locals pack in—bringing with them, of course, food from outside to accompany the wine. ⊠ *Vicolo Ranocchi 1/d, Piazza Maggiore area* ☎ *347/9680171* ⊕ *www.osteriadelsole.it.*

CAFÉS

Zanarini. Chic Bolognesi congregate at this bar, which serves coffee in the morning and swank aperitivi in the evening. Tasty sandwiches and pastries are also available. ⊠ *Piazza Galvani 1* ☎ *051/2750041.*

MUSIC VENUES

Cantina Bentivoglio. With live music staged every evening, Cantina Bentivoglio is one of Bologna's most appealing nightspots. You can enjoy light and more substantial meals here as well. ⊠ *Via Mascarella 4/b, University area* ☎ *051/265416* ⊕ *www.cantinabentivoglio.it.*

Osteria Buca delle Campane. In a 13th-century building, this underground tavern has good, inexpensive food and a lively after-dinner scene that's popular with locals, including students, who come to listen to live music. ⊠ *Via Benedetto XIV 4/a, University area* ☎ *051/220918* ⊕ *www.bucadellecampane.it.*

SHOPPING

CLOTHING

Castel Guelfo Outlet City. If you don't feel like paying Galleria Cavour prices, this mall is about 20 minutes outside Bologna on the autostrada A14 toward Imola (take the Castel San Pietro Terme exit; 980 feet after the tollbooth, turn right onto Via San Carlo). It includes about 50 discounted stores, some from top designers such as Ferré. It's closed Monday morning. ⊠ *Via del Commercio 20/a, Loc. Poggio Piccolo, Castel Guelfo* ☎ *0542/670765* ⊕ *www.thestyleoutlets.it.*

Galleria Cavour. One of the most upscale malls in Italy, the Galleria Cavour houses many of the fashion giants, including Gucci, Versace, and jeweler-watchmaker Bulgari. ⊠ *Via Luigi Carlo Farini, south of Piazza Maggiore* ⊕ *www.galleriacavour.net.*

WINE AND FOOD

Bologna is a good place to buy wine. Several shops have a bewilderingly large selection—to go straight to the top, ask the managers which wines have won the prestigious Tre Bicchieri (Three Glasses) award from Gambero Rosso's wine bible, *Vini d'Italia.*

Eataly. You can grab a bite to eat or a glass of wine while stocking up on the best quality olive oil, vinegar, cured meats, and artisanal pasta at this lively shop while browsing in the attached bookstore. You can also have a full-fledged trattoria meal on the top floor. ⊠ *Via degli Orafici 19, Piazza Maggiore area* ☎ *051/0952820* ⊕ *www.eataly.it.*

Enoteca Italiana. Consistently recognized as one of the best wine stores in the country, Enoteca Italiana lives up to its reputation with shelves lined with excellent selections from all over Italy at reasonable prices. Their delicious sandwiches with wines by the glass also make a great light lunch. ⊠ *Via Marsala 2/b, north of Piazza Maggiore* ☎ *051/235989* ⊕ *www.enotecaitaliana.it.*

La Baita. Fresh tagliolini, tortellini, and other Bolognese pasta delicacies are sold here, as well as sublime food to take away. Their cheese counter is laden with local cheeses of superlative quality. ⊠ *Via Pescherie Vecchia 3/a, Piazza Maggiore area* ☎ *051/223940.*

Le Dolcezze. If you favor sweets, head to Le Dolcezze, a top local *pasticceria* (pastry shop). Its cakes are excellent and the *panettone* (a sweet bread produced only around Christmas) is considered by some to be the best in town. ⊠ *Via Murri 121, Piazza Maggiore area* ☎ *051/444582* ⊕ *www.ledolcezze.eu.*

Majani. They've been making chocolate at this classy little establishment sice 1796. Its staying power may be attributed to high-quality candies, which are as nice to look at as they are to eat. ⊠ *Via de'Carbonesi 5, Piazza Maggiore area* ☎ *051/969157* ⊕ *www.majani.com.*

Mercato delle Erbe. This bustling food market is open Monday through Wednesday and Friday 7–1:15 and 5–7:30 (4:30–7:30 October–March), and Thursday and Saturday 7–1:15. ⊠ *Via Ugo Bassi 25, Piazza Maggiore area* ☎ *051/230186* ⊕ *www.mercatodelleerbe.it.*

Mercato di Mezzo. Specialty foods, fruits, and vegetables provide an intense barrage of sights and smells at this market. It's open Monday through Saturday 7–1 and 4:15–7:30, with the exception of Thursday afternoon, when it's closed. ⊠ *Via Peschiere Vecchie, Piazza Maggiore area.*

Paolo Atti & Figli. This place has been producing some of Bologna's finest pastas, cakes, and other delicacies for more than 130 years. ⊠ *Via Caprarie 7, Piazza Maggiore area* ☎ *051/220425* ⊕ *www.paoloatti.com.*

9

Roccati. Sculptural works of chocolate, as well as basic bonbons and simpler sweets, have been crafted here since 1909. ⊠ *Via Clavature 17/a, Piazza Maggiore area* ☎ *051/261964* ⊕ *www.roccaticioccolato.com.*

Scaramagli. Friendly owners run this midsize, down-to-earth wine store. ⊠ *Strada Maggiore 31/d, University area* ☎ *051/227132* ⊕ *www. scaramagli.it.*

Via Oberdan. For fresh produce, meats, and other foods, head to this street, just off Via dell'Indipendenza downtown. ⊠ *Piazza Maggiore area.*

FERRARA

47 km (29 miles) northeast of Bologna, 74 km (46 miles) northwest of Ravenna.

When the legendary Ferrarese filmmaker Michelangelo Antonioni called his beloved hometown "a city that you can see only partly, while the rest disappears to be imagined," perhaps he was referring to the low-lying mist that rolls in off the Adriatic each winter and shrouds Ferrara's winding knot of medieval alleyways, turreted palaces, and ancient wine bars—once inhabited by the likes of Copernicus—in a ghostly fog. But perhaps Antonioni was also suggesting that Ferrara's striking beauty often conceals a dark and tortured past.

Today you're likely to be charmed by Ferrara's prosperous air and meticulous cleanliness, its excellent restaurants and coffeehouses, and its lively wine bar scene. You'll find aficionados gathering outside any of the wine bars near the Duomo even on the foggiest of weeknights. Though Ferrara is a UNESCO World Heritage site, the city still draws amazingly few tourists—which only adds to its appeal.

If you plan to explore the city fully, consider buying a Card Musei ("museum card," €17, valid for one year) at the Palazzo dei Diamanti or at any of the museums around town; it grants admission to every museum, palace, and castle in Ferrara. The first Monday of the month is free at many museums.

GETTING HERE AND AROUND

Train service is frequent from Bologna (usually three trains per hour) and takes either a half hour or 45 minutes, depending on which train type you take. It's 37 minutes from Bologna to Florence, and then about a half hour from Bologna to Ferrara. Trains run frequently. The walk from the station is easy but not particularly interesting. If you're driving from Bologna, take the RA1 out of town; then the A13 in the direction of Padova, exiting at Ferrara Nord. Follow the SP19 directly into the center of town. The trip should take about 45 minutes.

VISITOR INFORMATION

Ferrara Tourism Office ⊠ *Castello Estense, Piazza Repubblica* ☎ *0532/299303* ⊕ *www.ferrarainfo.com* ⊠ *Piazza Municipale 11* .

EXPLORING FERRARA

TOP ATTRACTIONS

Fodor's Choice ★ **Castello Estense.** The former seat of Este power, this massive castle dominates the center of town. The building was a suitable symbol for the ruling family: cold and menacing on the outside, lavishly decorated within. The public rooms are grand, but deep in the bowels of the castle are chilling dungeons where enemies of the state were held in wretched conditions—a function these quarters served as recently as 1943, when antifascist prisoners were detained there. In particular, the **Prisons of Don Giulio, Ugo, and Parisina** have some fascinating features, like 15th-century graffiti protesting the imprisonment of lovers Ugo and Parisina, who were beheaded in 1425 because Ugo's father, Niccolò III, didn't like the fact that his son was cavorting with Niccolò's wife.

The castle was established as a fortress in 1385, but work on its luxurious ducal quarters continued into the 16th century. Representative of Este grandeur are the **Sala dei Giochi,** extravagantly painted with athletic scenes, and the **Sala dell'Aurora,** decorated to show the times of the day. The terraces of the castle, and the hanging garden—once reserved for the private use of the duchesses—have fine views of the town and the surrounding countryside. You can cross the castle's moat, traverse its drawbridge, and wander through many of its arcaded passages at any time. ⊠ *Piazza Castello* ☎ *0532/299233* ⊕ *www.castelloestense.it* 🎫 *€8 (€12 during special exhibitions)* ⊗ *Tues.–Sun. 9:30–5:30; ticket office closes at 4:45.*

QUICK BITES

Caffetteria Castello. Spectacularly sited amid centuries of history, the second floor provides a great place to break for coffee while touring the castle or to mingle with locals enjoying the lunchtime buffet. Right next door is a small book-and-gift shop. ⊠ *Largo Castello* ☎ *0532/299337* ⊗ *Tues.–Sun. 9:30–5:30.*

Duomo. The magnificent Gothic cathedral, a few steps from the Castello Estense, has a three-tier facade of slender arches and beautiful sculptures over the central door. Work began in 1135 and took more than 100 years to complete. The interior was completely remodeled in the 17th century. ⊠ *Piazza Cattedrale* ☎ *0532/207449* ⊗ *Mon.–Sat. 7:30–noon and 3–6:30, Sun. 7:30–12:30 and 3:30–7:30.*

Museo Ebraico (*Jewish Museum*). The collection of ornate religious objects here bears witness to the long history of the city's Jewish community. This history had its high points—1492, for example, when Ercole I invited the Jews to come over from Spain—and its lows, notably 1627, when Jews were enclosed within the **ghetto,** where they were forced to live until the advent of a united Italy in 1860. The triangular warren of narrow cobbled streets that made up the ghetto originally extended as far as Corso Giovecca (originally Corso Giudecca, or Ghetto Street). When it was enclosed, the neighborhood was restricted to the area between Via Scienze, Via Contrari, and Via di San Romano. The museum, in the center of the ghetto, was once Ferrara's synagogue.

All visits are led by a museum guide. ⊠ *Via Mazzini 95* ☎ *0532/210228* 🖃 *€4* ☉ *Tours: Sun.–Thurs. at 10, 11, and noon.*

Palazzo dei Diamanti (*Palace of Diamonds*). Named for the 12,600 small, pink-and-white marble pyramids (or "diamonds") that stud its facade, this building was designed to be viewed in perspective—both faces at once—from diagonally across the street. Work began in the 1490s and finished around 1504. Today the palazzo contains the **Pinacoteca Nazionale,** an extensive art gallery that also has rotating exhibits. ⊠ *Corso Ercole I d'Este 19–21* ☎ *0532/244949* ⊕ *www.palazzodiamanti.it* 🖃 *€10* ☉ *Daily 9–7.*

Palazzo Schifanoia. The oldest, most characteristic area of Ferrara is south of the Duomo, stretching between the Corso Giovecca and the city's ramparts. Here various members of the Este family built pleasure palaces, the best known of which is the Palazzo Schifanoia (*schifanoia* means "carefree" or, literally, "fleeing boredom"). Begun in the late 14th century, the palace was remodeled between 1464 and 1469. The lavish interior is well worth visiting—particularly the **Salone dei Mesi,** which contains an extravagant series of frescoes showing the months of the year and their mythological attributes. ⊠ *Via Scandiana 23* ☎ *0532/244949* ⊕ *www.artecultura.fe.it* 🖃 *€6* ☉ *Tues.–Sun. 9–6, call ahead to confirm.*

Via delle Volte. One of the best-preserved medieval streets in Europe, the Via delle Volte clearly evokes Ferrara's past. The series of ancient *volte* (arches) along the narrow cobblestone alley once joined the merchants' houses on the south side of the street to their warehouses on the north side. The street ran parallel to the banks of the Po River, which was home to Ferrara's busy port.

WORTH NOTING

Casa Romei. This ranks among Ferrara's loveliest Renaissance palaces. Built by the wealthy banker Giovanni Romei (1402–83), it's a vast structure with a graceful courtyard. Mid-15th-century frescoes decorate rooms on the ground floor; the *piano nobile* (main floor) contains detached frescoes from local churches as well as lesser-known Renaissance sculptures. The Sala delle Sibelle has a very large 15th-century fireplace and beautiful wood-coffered ceilings. ⊠ *Via Savonarola 30* ☎ *0532/234130 tickets, 0532/234100 information* ⊕ *www. soprintendenzaravenna.beniculturali.it* 🖃 *€3* ☉ *Mon. 8:30–2, Tues.– Fri. 8:30–7:30, Sat. 2–7:30, Sun. 8:30–2.*

Museo della Cattedrale. Some of the original decorations of the town's main church, the former church and cloister of San Romano, reside in the Museo della Cattedrale, which is across the piazza from the Duomo. Inside you'll find 22 codices commissioned between 1477–1535; moving early-13th-century sculpture by the Maestro dei Mesi; a mammoth oil on canvas by Cosmé Tura from 1469; and an exquisite Jacopo della Quercia, the *Madonna della Melograno*. Though this last work dates from 1403–1408, the playful expression on the Christ child seems very 21st century. ⊠ *Via San Romano 1* ☎ *0532/244949* ⊕ *www.artecultura. fe.it* 🖃 *€6* ☉ *Tues.–Sun. 9:30–1 and 3–6.*

Palazzina di Marfisa d'Este. On the busy Corso Giovecca, this grandiose 16th-century palace belonged to a great patron of the arts. It has painted ceilings, fine 16th-century furniture, and a garden containing a grotto and an outdoor theater. ✉ *Corso Giovecca 170* ☎ *0532/207450* 🌐 *www.artecultura.fe.it* 🎫 *€4* 🕘 *Tues.–Sun. 9–1 and 3–6.*

WHERE TO EAT

$$$$ MODERN ITALIAN

🍴 **Il Don Giovanni.** Just down the street from Castello Estense, this warm and inviting restaurant offers a handful of tables inside a lovely 17th-century palace. Chef Pier Luigi Di Diego and partner Marco Merighi pay strict attention to what's seasonal, and the menu reflects this. Here tortellini are stuffed with guinea fowl and sauced with *zabaione* (custard), Parmesan, and prosciutto *crocante* (fried prosciutto). Equally inventive is the delicate *tegame di pernice rossa ai frutti di bosco* (partridge in a fruit sauce), which delights the palate. Next door, the same proprietors run the less expensive, but more crowded, **La Borsa**. This trendy wine bar has excellent cured meats, cheeses, lovely primi and secondi, plus a fantastic wine-by-the-glass list. (Note the wine bar is open for lunch; the restaurant isn't.) [$] *Average meal: €65* ✉ *Corso Ercole I d'Este 1* ☎ *0532/243363* 🌐 *www.ildongiovanni.com* ✍ *Reservations essential* 🕘 *Closed Mon. No lunch.*

$$ EMILIAN Fodor's Choice ★

🍴 **L'Oca Giuliva.** Food, service, and ambience unite in blissful harmony at this casual yet elegant restaurant minutes from Piazza Repubblica. Enter through a tiny wine bar, where you could pause for glass of wine before proceeding into the restaurant. Two well-appointed rooms in a 12th-century building provide the backdrop for exquisitely prepared local foods—the chef has a deft hand with area specialties, either in *tradizionale* (traditional) or *rivisitata* (updated) style. The *cappellacci di zucca al ragù* (pumpkin-stuffed pasta) might be the best version in town. Meat-and-potatoes folk can opt for the *salama da sugo* (a salty, garlicky boiled sausage on mashed potatoes); fish-lovers might try the *trancio di anguilla* (roasted eel) with polenta. For a break from Italian food, the "Bistrot" section of the menu includes tuna burger, on house-made naturally leavened bread. The amazing wine list is complemented by a terrific cheese plate. [$] *Average meal: €31* ✉ *Via Boccanale di Santo Stefano 38* ☎ *0532/207628* 🌐 *www.ristorantelocagiuliva.it* 🕘 *Closed Mon. No lunch Tues.*

$ WINE BAR

🍴 **Osteria al Brindisi.** Ferrara is a city of wine bars, beginning with this one—allegedly Europe's oldest—which opened in 1435. Copernicus drank here while a student in the late 1400s, and the place still has a somewhat undergraduate aura. Most of the staff and clientele are twentysomethings. Perfectly dusty wine bottles line the walls, and there are wooden booths in another small room for those who want to eat while they drink. A young staff pours terrific wines by the glass, and offers three different sauces (butter-and-sage, tomato, or ragù) with its *cappellacci di zucca*. Those in search of lighter fare might enjoy any of the salads or the grilled vegetable plate with melted pecorino. [$] *Average meal: €10* ✉ *Via degli Adelardi 11* ☎ *0532/209142* 🌐 *www.albrindisi.net.*

9

$$ ✕ **Quel Fantastico Giovedì.** Locals and other cognoscenti flock to this
EMILIAN sleek eatery just minutes away from Piazza del Duomo. Two small
rooms (one white, the other with red accents) have linen tablecloths
and jazz playing softly in the background. Chef Gabriele Romagnoli
uses primo local ingredients to create gustatory taste sensations: his
sformatino di patate more closely resembles a French gratin, but he
sauces it with *salamina e Parmigiano* (that deliciously unctuous pork
product made into a smooth sauce with the help of Parmesan cheese),
thus rendering it deliciously Ferraresi. Fish also figures prominently on
the menu, including a well-priced tasting menu. The wine list is divine,
and the service, led by hands-on gregarious proprietor Mara Farinelli, is
top-notch. $ *Average meal: €33* ⊠ *Via Castelnuovo 9* ☎ *0532/760570*
⊕ *www.quelfantasticogiovedi.com* ⌕ *Reservations essential* ⊘ *Closed
Wed. No lunch Tues.*

$$ ✕ **Zafferano.** Veneto-born Chef Renzo Geminiano has worked outside
EMILIAN Italy, and it shows in his inventive cuisine. He clearly knows the clas-
sics—and how to make them dazzle. Chef Renzo runs this small, intimate restaurant—a favorite of many locals who like to eat well—with
his wife, sommelier Stefania Angelini (a native of Ferrara), whose wine
list is carefully culled and well priced. The menu's divided into fish and
meat, and choosing is agonizing. In winter, much game is on offer and
the *carpaccio di cervo e finocchi* (venison carpaccio with slivers of fennel
atop a wild berry coulis) is a perfect way to begin; followed, perhaps,
by deboned quail and artichokes. Fish is equally well prepared: the
antipasto of raw shrimp with grapefruit and avocado is heavenly. $ *Av-
erage meal: €34* ⊠ *Via Fondo Banchetto 2/a* ☎ *0532/763492* ⊕ *www.
zafferanoristorante.it.*

WHERE TO STAY

For expanded hotel reviews, visit Fodors.com.

$$ ⊡ **Hotel Ripagrande.** The courtyards, vaulted brick lobby, and break-
HOTEL fast room of this 15th-century noble's palazzo retain much of their
lordly Renaissance flair. **Pros:** beyond-helpful staff; good choice for
families. **Cons:** staff goes home at midnight; parking can be a problem.
$ *Rooms from: €150* ⊠ *Via Ripagrande 21* ☎ *0532/765250* ⊕ *www.
ripagrandehotel.it* ⤶ *20 rooms, 20 suites* ⦿ *Breakfast.*

$ ⊡ **Locanda Borgonuovo.** In the early 18th century it began life as a con-
B&B/INN vent (later suppressed by Napoleon) but now it's a delightful city-center
bed-and-breakfast, popular with performers at the city's Teatro Comu-
nale. **Pros:** phenomenal breakfast featuring local foods and terrific cakes
made in house; bicycles can be borrowed for free. **Cons:** steep stairs to
reception area and rooms; must reserve far in advance. $ *Rooms from:
€120* ⊠ *Via Cairoli 29* ☎ *0532/211100* ⊕ *www.borgonuovo.com* ⤶ *4
rooms, 2 apartments* ⦿ *Breakfast.*

ROMAGNA

Anywhere in Emilia-Romagna, the story goes, a weary, lost traveler will be invited into a family's home and offered a drink. But the Romagnesi claim that he'll be served water in Emilia and wine in Romagna. The hilly, mostly rural, and largely undiscovered Romagna region has crumbling farmhouses dotting rolling hills, smoking chimneys, early Christian churches, and rowdy local bars dishing out rounds and rounds of *piadine* (a pitalike thin bread filled with meat, cheese, vegetables, or any combination thereof, and then quickly grilled). Ravenna, the site of shimmering Byzantine mosaics, dominates the region.

Heading southeast from Bologna, Via Emilia (SS9) and the parallel A14 Autostrada lead to the town of Faenza. From here, go north to the Adriatic Coast on the SS71 to reach Ravenna. Alternatively, the slower SS16 cuts a northwest–southeast swath through Romagna.

IMOLA

42 km (26 miles) southeast of Bologna.

Affluent Imola, with its wide and stately avenues, lies on the border between Emilia and Romagna. It was populated as early as the Bronze Age, came under Roman rule, and was eventually annexed to the Papal States in 1504. Now it's best known for its Formula One auto-racing tradition: the San Marino Grand Prix has been held here every spring since 1981. Auto-racing as a serious sport in Imola dates to 1953, when, with the support of Enzo Ferrari, the racetrack just outside the city center was inaugurated. However, unless you happen to pop into town in mid-April for the race, you'll more likely find yourself in Imola shopping for its well-known ceramics or sampling the cuisine at the town's world-famous restaurant, San Domenico.

9

GETTING HERE AND AROUND

Imola is a straightforward train ride from Bologna; local trains run often and take a little under a half hour. If you're coming from Milan, you can catch the Eurostar to Bologna, and then transfer to the local train. Travel time from Milan to Bologna is a little over an hour; it's about 25 minutes from Bologna to Imola. The walk from the station to the centro storico is easy. If you're driving from Bologna, take the RA1 to the A14 (following signs for Ancona). Take the exit for Imola.

VISITOR INFORMATION

Imola Tourism Office ⊠ *Arcade of the City Center 135* ☎ *0542/602111* ⊕ *www.comune.imola.bo.it.*

WHERE TO EAT

$$$$
MODERN ITALIAN
Fodor'sChoice
★

✕ **San Domenico.** This restaurant has defended its position as one of Italy's most refined dining destinations year after year, and heads of state, celebrities, and those with bottomless pocketbooks flock here to savor the fare. The majestic appointments complement chef Valentino Marcattili's wondrous creations, like his memorable *uovo in raviolo San Domenico,* in which a large raviolo is stuffed with a raw egg yolk—which miraculously cooks only a little, then spills out and mixes with

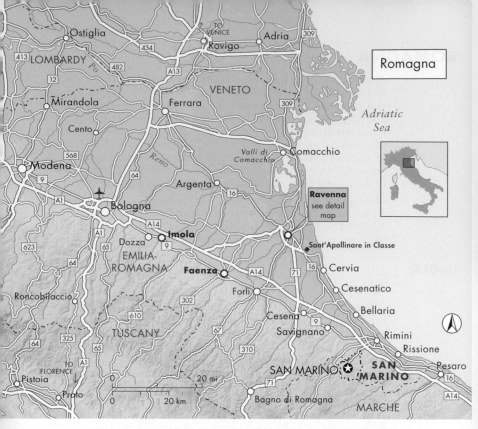

Parmesan cheese, *burro di malga* (butter from an Alpine dairy farm), and sensational white truffles. The impressive wine list has more than 3,000 choices. $ *Average meal: €110* ✉ *Via G. Sacchi 1* ☎ *0542/29000* ⊕ *www.sandomenico.it* ⚄ *Reservations essential* ⊘ *Closed Sun. and Mon., 1 wk in Jan., and 1 wk in Aug. No lunch.*

FAENZA

49 km (30 miles) southeast of Bologna.

In the Middle Ages Faenza was the crossroads between Emilia-Romagna and Tuscany, and the 15th century saw many Florentine artists working in town. In 1509, when the Papal States took control, Faenza became something of a backwater. It did, however, continue its 12th-century tradition of making top-quality ceramics. In the 16th century local artists created a color called *bianchi di Faenza* ("Faenza white"), which was wildly imitated and wildly desired all over Europe. The Frenchified *faience,* referring to the color and technique, soon entered the lexicon, where it remains to this day. In the central **Piazza del Popolo**, dozens of shops sell the native ceramic wares.

GETTING HERE AND AROUND

Trains run frequently from Bologna to Faenza, making the trip in about a half hour. There's also sporadic service from Florence, a beautiful two-hour ride. The walk to the centro storico, though easy, isn't especially interesting. By car it takes about an hour from Bologna. Follow the SP253 to the RA1, at which point pick up on the A14/E45 heading in the direction of Ancona. Exit and take the SP8 into Faenza.

VISITOR INFORMATION

Faenza Tourism Office ⊠ *Voltore Molinella 21* ☎ *0546/25231* ⊕ *www.prolocofaenza.it.*

EXPLORING

Museo Internazionale delle Ceramiche. One of the largest ceramics museums in the world has a well-labeled, well-lit collection, with objects from the Renaissance among its highlights. Though the emphasis is clearly on local work, the rest of Italy is also represented. Don't miss the 20th- and 21st-century galleries, which prove that decorative arts often surpass their utile limitations and become genuinely sculptural. ⊠ *Viale Baccarini 19* ☎ *0546/697311* ⊕ *www.micfaenza.org* ⊴ *€8* ⊙ *Apr.–Sept., Tues.–Sun. 10–7; Oct.–Mar., Tues.–Thurs. 10–1:30, Fri.–Sun. 9:30–5:30.*

WHERE TO EAT

$

EMILIAN

✗ **Marianaza.** A large open-hearth fireplace dominates this simple trattoria, and wonderful aromas of grilled meats and garlic greet you as you walk in. Marianaza, like the town of Faenza itself, successfully blends the best of Emilian-Romagnan and Tuscan cuisine: the extraordinary primi are mostly tortellini-based, and the secondi rely heavily on the grill. Grilled garlic toasts topped with prosciutto crudo delightfully whet the appetite; and the *tortellini in brodo* is tasty. The mixed grill is perfect for sharing. (Note that the person responsible for the grilling is a woman: a true rarity in Italy.) $ *Average meal: €25* ⊠ *Via Torricelli 21* ☎ *0546/681461.*

SAN MARINO

90 km (56 miles) southeast of Faenza, 139 km (86 miles) southeast of Bologna.

The world's smallest and oldest republic, as San Marino dubs itself, is surrounded entirely by Italy. It consists of three ancient castles perched on sheer cliffs rising implausibly out of the flatlands of Romagna, and a tangled knot of cobblestone streets below that are lined with tourist boutiques, cheesy hotels and restaurants, and gun shops. The 1½-hour drive from Faenza is justified, however, by the sweeping views from the castle of the countryside. The 3,300-foot-plus precipices will make jaws drop and acrophobes quiver.

Visiting San Marino in winter—off-season—increases the appeal of the experience, as tourist establishments shut down and you more or less have the castles to yourself. In August every inch of walkway on the rock is mobbed with sightseers. Don't worry about changing money, showing passports, and the like (although the tourist office at Contrada del Collegio will stamp your passport for €2.50). San Marino is, for all practical purposes, Italy—except, that is, for its majestic perch, its gun laws, and its reported 99% national voter turnout rate.

GETTING HERE AND AROUND

To get to San Marino by car, take highway SS72 west from Rimini. From Borgo Maggiore, at the base of the rock, a cable car will whisk you up to the town. Alternatively, you can drive up the winding road; public parking is available in the town. There is a regular bus service to and from Rimini, with service sometime every hour throughout the year (less frequent service on Sunday); one-way ticket from Rimini to San Marino is 4.50 and the trip takes about 45 minutes.

VISITOR INFORMATION

State Board of Tourism ✉ *Contrada Omagnano, 20, San Marino* ☎ *0549/882914* ⊕ *www.visitsanmarino.com.*

EXPLORING SAN MARINO

Tre Castelli. San Marino's headline attractions are its Tre Castelli—medieval architectural wonders that appear on every coat of arms in the city. Starting in the center of town, walk a few hundred yards past the trinket shops, along a paved cliff-top ridge, from the 10th-century **Rocca della Guaita** to the 13th-centuury **Rocca della Cesta** (containing a museum of ancient weapons that's worthwhile mostly for the views from its terraces and turrets), and finally to the 14th-century **Rocca Montale** (closed to the public), the most remote of the castles.

Every step of the way affords spectacular views of Romagna and the Adriatic—it's said that on a clear day you can see Croatia. The walk makes for a good day's exercise, but is by no means arduous. Even if you arrive after visiting hours, it's supremely rewarding. ✉ *San Marino* ☎ *0549/882670* ⊕ *www.museidistato.sm* ✉ *Il Torre Guaita and il Torre Cesta €4.50* ⊗ *Mid-Sept.–mid-June, daily 9–5; mid-June–mid-Sept., daily 8–8.*

Piazza della Libertà. A must-see is the Piazza della Libertà, where the Palazzo Pubblico is guarded by soldiers in green uniforms. As you'll notice by peering into the shops along the old town's winding streets, the republic is famous for crossbows and other items (think fireworks or firearms) that are illegal almost everywhere else. ✉ *San Marino.*

RAVENNA

76 km (47 miles) east of Bologna, 93 km (58 miles) southeast of Ferrara.

A small, quiet, well-heeled city, Ravenna has brick palaces, cobblestone streets, magnificent monuments, and spectacular Byzantine mosaics. The high point in civic history occurred in the 5th century, when Pope Honorious moved his court here from Rome. Gothic kings Odoacer and Theodoric ruled the city until it was conquered by the Byzantines in AD 540. Ravenna later fell under the sway of Venice, and then, inevitably, the Papal States.

Because Ravenna spent much of its past looking to the East, its greatest art treasures show that influence. Churches and tombs with the most unassuming exteriors contain within them walls covered with sumptuous mosaics. These beautifully preserved Byzantine mosaics put great emphasis on nature, which you can see in the delicate rendering of sky, earth, and animals. Outside Ravenna, the town of Classe hides even more mosaic gems.

GETTING HERE AND AROUND
By car from Bologna, take the SP253 to the RA1, and then follow signs for the A14/E45 in the direction of Ancona. From here, follow signs for Ravenna, taking the A14dir Ancona–Milano–Ravenna exit. Follow signs for the SS16/E55 to the center of Ravenna. From Ferrara the drive is more convoluted, but also more interesting. Take the SS16 to the RA8 in the direction of Porto Garibaldi taking the Roma/Ravenna exit. Follow the SS309/E55 to the SS309dir/E55, taking the SS253 Bologna/Ancona exit. Follow the SS16/E55 into the center of Ravenna.

VISITOR INFORMATION
Ravenna Tourism Office ⊠ *Via Salara 8* 🖀 *0544/35404* ⊕ *www.turismo.ravenna.it.*

EXPLORING RAVENNA

A combination ticket (available at ticket offices of all included sights) admits you to four of Ravenna's important monuments: the Mausoleo di Galla Placidia, the Basilica di San Vitale, the Battistero Neoniano, and Sant'Apollinare Nuovo. Start out early in the morning to avoid lines (reservations are necessary for the Mausoleo and Basilica in May and June). A half day should suffice to walk the town; allow a half hour for the Mausoleo and the Basilica.

TOP ATTRACTIONS
Basilica di San Vitale. The octagonal church of San Vitale was built in AD 547, after the Byzantines conquered the city, and its interior shows a strong Byzantine influence. In the area behind the altar are the most famous works in the church, depicting Emperor Justinian and his retinue on one wall, and his wife, Empress Theodora, with her retinue, on the opposite wall. Notice how the mosaics seamlessly wrap around the columns and curved arches on the upper sides of the altar area. Reservations are recommended from March through mid-June. ⊠ *Via San Vitale, off Via Salara* 🖀 *0544/541688 reservations* ⊕ *www.ravennamosaici.it* ⊠ *€9.50 combination ticket (includes all diocesan monuments)* ⊙ *Nov.–Feb., daily 9:30–4:45; Mar. and Oct., daily 9–5:15; Apr.–Sept., daily 9–6:45 (last entry 15 min before closing).*

Battistero Neoniano. Next door to Ravenna's 18th-century cathedral, the baptistery has one of the town's most important mosaics. It dates from the beginning of the 5th century AD, with work continuing through the century. In keeping with the building's role, the great mosaic in the dome shows the baptism of Christ, and beneath are the Apostles. The lowest register of mosaics contains Christian symbols, the Throne of God, and the Cross. Note the naked figure kneeling next to Christ—he is the

9

Ravenna

KEY

Tourist information

personification of the River Jordan. ✉ *Via Battistero* ☎ *0544/541688 reservations, 800/303999 toll-free information* ⊕ *www.ravennamosaici. it* ✉ *€9.50 combination ticket (includes all diocesan monuments)* ⊘ *Nov.–Feb., daily 10–4:45; Mar. and Oct., daily 9:30–5:15; Apr.– Sept., daily 9–6:45 (last entry 15 min before closing).*

Fodor'sChoice   **Mausoleo di Galla Placidia.** The little tomb and the great church stand
★   side by side, but the tomb predates the Basilica di San Vitale by at
least a hundred years. These two adjacent sights are decorated with
the best-known, most elaborate mosaics in Ravenna. Galla Placidia
was the sister of the Roman emperor Honorius, who moved the imperial capital to Ravenna in AD 402. She is said to have been beautiful
and strong-willed, and to have taken an active part in the governing
of the crumbling empire. This mausoleum, constructed in the mid-5th
century, is her memorial.

Viewed from the outside, it's a small, unassuming red-brick building: the
exterior's seeming poverty of charm only serves to enhance by contrast
the richness of the interior mosaics, in deep midnight blue and glittering gold. The tiny central dome is decorated with symbols of Christ,
the evangelists, and striking gold stars. Over the door is a depiction of
the Good Shepherd. Eight of the Apostles are represented in groups of
two on the four inner walls of the dome; the other four appear singly

on the walls of the two transepts. Notice the small doves at their feet, drinking from the water of faith. Also in the tiny transepts are some delightful pairs of deer (representing souls), drinking from the fountain of resurrection. There are three sarcophagi in the tomb, none of which are believed to contain the remains of Galla Placidia. She died in Rome in AD 450, and there's no record of her body's having been transported back to the place where she wished to lie. Reservations are required for the Mausoleo from March through mid-June. ⊠ *Via San Vitale, off Via Salara* ☎ *0544/541688 reservations* ⊕ *www.ravennamosaici.it* ▭ *€9.50 combination ticket (includes all Diocesan monuments), plus €2, Mar. 1–June 15* ⊙ *Nov.–Feb., daily 9:30–4:45; Mar. and Oct., daily 9–5:15; Apr.–Sept., daily 9–6:45 (last entry 15 min before closing).*

Sant'Apollinare Nuovo. The mosaics displayed in this church date from the early 6th century, making them slightly older than those in San Vitale. Since the left side of the church was reserved for women, it's only fitting that the mosaics on that wall depict 22 virgins offering crowns to the Virgin Mary. On the right wall are 26 men carrying the crowns of martyrdom. They approach Christ, surrounded by angels. ⊠ *Via Roma, at Via Guaccimanni* ☎ *0544/219518, 0544/541688 reservations* ⊕ *www.ravennamosaici.it* ▭ *€9.50 combination ticket (includes all diocesan monuments)* ⊙ *Nov.–Feb., daily 10–4:45; Mar. and Oct., daily 9:30–5:15; Apr.–Sept., daily 9–6:45 (last entry 15 min before closing).*

WORTH NOTING

Domus dei Tappeti di Pietra (*Ancient Home of the Stone Carpets*). This archaeological site was uncovered in 1993 during digging for an underground parking garage near the 18th-century church of Santa Eufemia. Below ground level (10 feet down) lie the remains of a Byzantine palace dating from the 5th and 6th centuries AD. Its beautiful and well-preserved network of floor mosaics displays elaborately-designed patterns, creating the effect of luxurious carpets. ⊠ *Via Barbiani, enter through Sant'Eufemia* ☎ *0544/32512* ⊕ *www.domusdeitappetidipietra.it* ▭ *€4* ⊙ *July and Aug., daily 10–6 and 8:30–10:30; Mar.–June and Sept.–Oct., daily 10–6:30; Nov.–Feb., Tues.–Fri. 10–5, weekends 10–6.*

Museo Nazionale (*National Museum of Ravenna*). Next to the Church of San Vitale and housed in a former Benedictine monastery, the museum contains artifacts from ancient Rome, Byzantine fabrics and carvings, and pieces of early Christian art. The collection is well displayed and artfully lighted. In the delightful first cloister are marvelous Roman tomb slabs from excavations nearby; upstairs, you can see a reconstructed 18th-century pharmacy. ⊠ *Via Fiandrini* ☎ *0544/543711* ▭ *€5* ⊙ *Tues.–Sun. 8:30–7:30.*

Sant'Apollinare in Classe. This church, about 5 km (3 miles) southeast of Ravenna, is landlocked now, but when it was built it stood in the center of the busy shipping port known to the ancient Romans as Classis. The arch above and the area around the high altar are rich with mosaics. Those on the arch, older than the ones behind it, are considered superior. They show Christ in Judgment and the 12 lambs of Christianity leaving the cities of Jerusalem and Bethlehem. In the apse is the figure of Sant'Apollinare himself, a bishop of Ravenna, and above him is a magnificent Transfiguration against blazing green grass, animals in odd perspective, and flowers. ✉ *Via Romea Sud, Classe* ☎ *0544/473569* 🎟 *€5* 🕒 *Daily 8:30–7.*

Tomba di Dante. The tomb of Dante is in a small neoclassical building next door to the large church of St. Francis. Exiled from his native Florence, the author of *The Divine Comedy* died here in 1321. The Florentines have been trying to reclaim their famous son for hundreds of years, but the Ravennans refuse to give him up, arguing that since Florence did not welcome Dante in life, it does not deserve him in death. ✉ *Via Dante Alighieri 4 and 9* 🎟 *Free* 🕒 *Daily 9–noon and 2–5.*

WHERE TO EAT

$ EMILIAN 🍴 **Bella Venezia.** Pale yellow walls, crisp white tablecloths, and warm light provide the backdrop for some seriously good regional food. The menu offers local specialties, but also gives a major nod to Venice—Ravenna's conqueror of long ago. The flavorful and delicate cappelleti *romagnoli* (stuffed pasta in broth) is a lovely starter. Follow up with *cotoletta alla Bisanzio* (a fried veal cutlet topped with cherry tomatoes and arugula), a house specialty. Desserts are made daily on the premises; save room for their killer tiramisù. [$] *Average meal: €27* ✉ *Via IV Novembre 16* ☎ *0544/212746* 🌐 *www.bellavenezia.it* 🕒 *Closed Sun. and 3 wks in Dec. and Jan.*

$ EMILIAN 🍴 **I Battibecchi.** Simple, honest food doesn't get any tastier than that served at this tiny venue (there are about 20 seats) with its even tinier kitchen. The short menu provides the usual local specialties, like cappelletti in broth or al ragù, supplemented by an ever-changing list of daily specials. The *polpettini al lesso* (little meatballs) in a lively tomato sauce with peas and pancetta, is one of many winning dishes that may be on offer. [$] *Average meal: €26* ✉ *Via della Tesoreria Vecchia 16* ☎ *0544/219536* 🌐 *www.osteriadeibattibecchi.it.*

$ EMILIAN 🍴 **Locanda del Melarancio.** In a late-16th-century palazzo in the heart of the centro storico, this contemporary inn has an osteria on the ground floor and a more formal restaurant on the second. Downstairs, the interior is minimalist without being stark. At a long counter, which extends practically through the entire length of the narrow room, lunching locals enjoy ample plates of *affettati misti* (mixed cured pork products, often served with caramelized figs) and daily specials, like the *pollo impannato alla griglia* (lightly breaded chicken breast, cooked on the grill). The menu changes frequently: goulash, a rarity in these parts, lights it up in winter. [$] *Average meal: €20* ✉ *Via Mentana 33* ☎ *0544/215258* 🌐 *www.locandadelmelarancio.it.*

$$ EMILIAN 🍴 **Osteria del Tempo Perso.** A couple of jazz-, rock-, and food-loving friends joined forces to open this smart little restaurant in the center. Inside, warm, terra-cotta-sponged walls give off an orange glow; wine bottles line the walls, interspersed with photographs of musical greats. They cook the classics well here, and offer the local specialty *capelletti* ("little hats"), in three different ways—sauced with butter, with a meat ragù, or in broth. But *fantasia* also emanates from the kitchen. The *gamberi croccanti con riso venere e vellutata di zucca*—shrimp

so lightly fried you'd hardly know it was served with wild rice and a pumpkin purèe—is an absolute winner, as is everything else on the menu. The carefully-culled wine list includes lots of local wines, and service is stellar. [$] *Average meal: €37* ✉ *Via Gamba 12, Ravenna* ☎ *0544/215393* 🌐 *www.osteriadeltempoperso.it* ⏲ *No lunch weekdays and July and Aug.*

WHERE TO STAY

For expanded hotel reviews, visit Fodors.com.

$ HOTEL 🏨 **Albergo Cappello.** In operation since the late 19th century and marvelously restored a century later, this charming place reflects a Venetian influence, with many Murano chandeliers hanging in the high-ceiling, wood-coffered public rooms. **Pros:** good location; accommodating staff; good restaurant. **Cons:** only seven rooms. [$] *Rooms from: €80* ✉ *Via IV Novembre 41* ☎ *0544/219876* 🌐 *www.albergocappello.it* 🛏 *2 rooms, 5 suites* 🍴 *No meals.*

$ B&B/INN 🏨 **Sant'Andrea.** For a lovely little B&B on a residential street a stone's throw from the Basilica of San Vitale, look no further—it even has a delightful garden. **Pros:** children under 12 stay free; discounts for stays of three nights or more; cheery and helpful staff. **Cons:** can get a little noisy; staff goes home in the early evening. [$] *Rooms from: €80* ✉ *Via Carlo Cattaneo 33* ☎📠 *0544/215564* 🌐 *www.santandreahotel.com* 🛏 *11 rooms, 1 suite* 🍴 *Breakfast.*

NIGHTLIFE AND THE ARTS

Mosaics by Night. On Friday night from June to August the Byzantine mosaic masterpieces in town are illuminated. The event is also held on certain Tuesdays. To check, call the tourist office, which offers guided tours.

Ravenna Festival. This music festival runs annually in June and July, when orchestras from all over the world come to perform in city churches and theaters. 🌐 *www.ravennafestival.org.*

Teatro di Tradizione Dante Alighieri. Operas and dance productions are staged here, usually on weekends, from November to March. If your Italian is up to it, you could also attend any of the theatrical productions—the season starts in late November and extends to late April. ✉ *Via Mariani 2* ☎ *0544/249211* 🌐 *www.teatroalighieri.org.*

CENTRAL ITALY

WHAT'S WHERE

1 Florence. It's hard to think of a place that's more closely linked to one specific historical period than Florence. In the 15th century the city was at the center of an artistic revolution, later labeled the Renaissance, which changed the way people see the world. Five hundred years later the Renaissance remains the reason people see Florence—the abundance of treasures is mind-boggling. Present-day Florentines have a somewhat uneasy relationship with their city's past; the never-ending stream of tourists is something they seem to tolerate more often than embrace. Still, they pride themselves on living well, and that means you'll find exceptional restaurants and first-rate shopping to go with all that amazing art.

2 Tuscany. Nature outdid herself in Tuscany, the central Italian region that has Florence as its principal city. Descriptions and photographs can't do the landscape justice—the hills, draped with woods, vineyards, and olive groves, may not have the drama of mountain peaks or waves crashing on the shore, yet there's an undeniable magic about them. Aside from Florence, Tuscany has several midsize cities that are well worth visiting, but the greatest

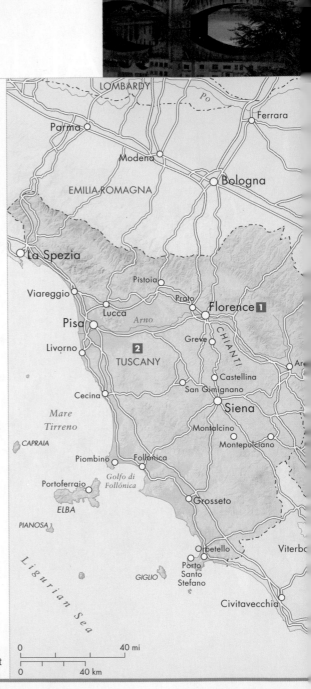

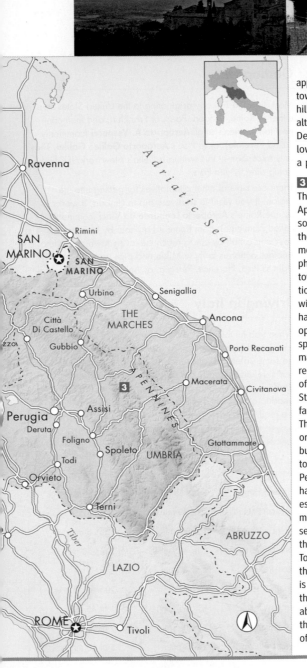

appeal lies in the smaller towns, often perched on hilltops and not significantly altered since the Middle Ages. Despite its popularity with fellow travelers, Tuscany remains a place you can escape to.

3 Umbria and the Marches. This region is closer to the Appenines than Tuscany is, so the landscape is wilder, the valleys deeper, and the mountains higher. The greater physical isolation of Umbria's towns and, until the unification of Italy, their association with the Papal States, may have encouraged the development of a keen sense of spirituality. Several of Italy's major saints are from the region, including St. Benedict of Norcia, St. Rita of Cascia, St. Chiara of Assisi, and most famously St. Francis of Assisi. There's no city with the size or significance of Florence, but a number of the smaller towns, particularly Assisi, Perugia, Spoleto, and Orvieto, have lots to hold your interest. Umbria's Roman past is much in evidence—expect to see Roman villas, aqueducts, theaters, walls, and temples. To the east, in the region of the Marches, the main draw is the town of Urbino, where the Ducal Palace reveals more about the artistic energy of the Renaissance than a shelf of history books.

CENTRAL ITALY PLANNER

Biking and Hiking

In spring, summer, and fall, bicyclists pedaling up and down Tuscany's hills are as much a part of the landscape as the cypress trees. Many are on weeklong organized tours, but it's also possible to rent bikes for jaunts in the countryside or to join afternoon or daylong rides.

Hiking is a simpler matter: all you need is a pair of sturdy shoes. The tourist information offices in most towns can direct you on walks ranging from an hour to a full day in duration. You can also sign on for more elaborate guided tours.

Italy by Design (⊠ *Via delle Lame 52, Florence* 🖀 *055/6532381* ⊕ *www.italybydesign. com*) provides city walks in Florence with expert guides, and made-to-measure hiking and driving vacations throughout Italy. The Salerno-based **Genius Loci** (⊠ *Via Rotondo 5, Salerno* 🖀 *089/791896* ⊕ *www.genius-loci. it*) offers guided and self-guided biking and walking tours for the budget-conscious throughout Italy. **Italian Connection** (⊠ *11825-11B Ave. Edmonton, AB* 🖀 *800/4627911 or 780/438/5712* ⊕ *www. italian-connection.com*) conducts high-end walking and culinary trips throughout Italy.

Getting Here

Most flights to Tuscany originating in the United States stop either in Rome, London, Paris, or Frankfurt, and then connect to Florence's small **Aeroporto A. Vespucci** (commonly called **Peretola**), or to Pisa's **Aeroporto Galileo Galilei**. The only exception at this writing is Delta's New York/JFK flight going directly into Pisa.

There are several other alternatives for getting into the region. If you want to start your trip in Umbria, it works to fly into Rome's **Aeroporto Leonardo da Vinci** (commonly called Fiumicino); from Rome it's an hour by train or an hour and a half by car to reach the lovely town of Orvieto. Another option is to fly to Milan and pick up a connecting flight to Pisa, Florence, Perugia, or Ancona in the Marches.

Driving in Italy

When you hit the road, don't be surprised to encounter tailgating and high-risk passing. Your best response is to take the same safety-first approach you use at home. On the plus side, Italy's roads are usually well maintained (though *strade regionali*—local roads—often are not). Note that wearing a seat belt and having your lights on at all times are required by law.

TYPICAL TRAVEL TIMES

	Hours by Car	Hours by Train
Florence–Rome	3 hrs	1 hr 35 min
Florence–Venice	3 hrs 30 min	2 hrs 5 min
Florence–Bologna	1 hr 30 min	40 min
Florence–Pisa	1 hr 30 min	1 hrs 5 min
Florence–Perugia	1 hr 45 min	2 hrs 10 min
Siena–Perugia	1 hr 30 min	3 hrs
Perugia–Assisi	30 min	20 min
Perugia–Orvieto	1 hr 15 min	1 hr 45 min
Assisi–Rome	2 hrs 15 min	2 hrs 10 min
Orvieto–Rome	1 hr 30 min	1 hr 10 min

On the Calendar: Events and Festivals

Several major events mark the calendar in Tuscany and Umbria, drawing attendees from around the world.

For the two weeks leading up to Lent, the town of Viareggio along the coast of northwest Tuscany is given over to the sometimes-bawdy revels of **Carnevale.** The festivities are second only to Venice's in size and lavishness.

Twice a year, on July 2 and August 16, Siena goes medieval with the **Palio,** a bareback horse race around its main square. It's more than a race—it's a celebration of tradition and culture dating back 1,000 years.

For two weeks in late June and early July, stars from the worlds of classical music and the performing arts make their way to the Umbria hill town of Spoleto to take part in the **Festival dei Due Mondi.** Opera fans crowd the outdoor **Puccini Festival** held in July and August at Torre del Lago, while Florence's **Maggio Musicale,** which extends through most of the year, attracts an international audience for performances of opera, classical music, and ballet.

While the big events are impressive, the calendar also overflows with smaller traditional *sagre* (festivals or fairs). You'll find them in towns of every size, January through December, with names like Sagra del Cinghiale (Wild Boar Festival), Sagra della Castagna (Chestnut Festival), and Festa del Fungo (Mushroom Festival). There's the Befanate (celebrating Italy's witchlike Santa equivalent) in Grosshetto during Epiphany, the Teatro Povero (a folk theater production) in Monticchiello in July, and, throughout southern Tuscany on the night of April 30, the Canta il Maggio (Songs for Spring) are performed.

Sagre are fun, and there's often delicious traditionally prepared food to be had. You can check with the local or regional tourist information offices for the dates and times of any sagre that happen to coincide with your visit.

When to Go

Throughout Tuscany and Umbria the best times to visit are spring and fall. Days are warm, nights are cool, and though there are still tourists, the crowds are smaller. In the countryside the scenery is gorgeous, with abundant greenery and flowers in spring, and burnished leaves in autumn.

July and August are the most popular times to visit. Note, though, that the heat is often oppressive and mosquitoes are prevalent. Try to start your days early and visit major sights first to beat the crowds and the midday sun. For relief from the heat, head to the mountains of the Garfagnana, where hiking is spectacular, or hit the beach at resort towns such as Forte dei Marmi and Viareggio, along the Maremma coast, or on the island of Elba.

November through March you might wonder who invented the term "sunny Italy." The panoramas are still beautiful, even with overcast skies, frequent rain, and occasional snow. In winter Florence benefits from shorter museum lines and less competition for restaurant tables. Outside the cities, though, many hotels and restaurants close for the season.

CENTRAL ITALY
TOP ATTRACTIONS

Galleria degli Uffizi, Florence

(A) Florence has many museums, but the Uffizi is king. Walking its halls is like stepping into an art history textbook, except here you're looking at the genuine article—masterpieces by Leonardo, Michelangelo, Raphael, Botticelli, Caravaggio, and dozens of other luminaries. When planning your visit, make a point to reserve a ticket in advance. (⇨ *Chapter 10.*)

Duomo, Florence

(B) The Cathedral of Santa Maria del Fiore, commonly known as the Duomo, is Florence's most distinctive landmark, sitting at the very heart of the city and towering over the neighboring rooftops. Its massive dome is one of the world's great engineering masterpieces. For an up-close look, you can climb the 463 steps to the top—then gaze out at the city beneath you. (⇨ *Chapter 10.*)

Leaning Tower, Pisa

(C) This tower may be too famous for its own good (it's one of Italy's most popular tourist attractions), but there's something undeniably appealing about its perilous tilt, and climbing to the top is a kick. The square on which it sits, known as the Campo dei Miracoli, has a majestic beauty that no quantity of tourists can diminish. (⇨ *Chapter 11.*)

Piazza del Campo, Siena

(D) The sloping, fan-shape square in the heart of Siena is one of the best places in Italy to engage in the distinctly Italian activity of hanging out and people-watching. The flanking Palazzo Pubblico and Torre del Mangia are first-rate sights. (⇨ *Chapter 11.*)

San Gimignano, Central Tuscany

(E) This classic Tuscan hill town has been dubbed a "medieval Manhattan" because of its numerous towers, built by noble families of the time, each striving to outdo

its neighbors. The streets fill with tour groups during the day, but if you stick around until sunset the crowds diminish and you see the town at its most beautiful. (⇨ *Chapter 11.*)

Abbazia di Sant'Antimo, Southern Tuscany

In a peaceful valley, surrounded by gently rolling hills, olive trees, and thick oak woods, Sant'Antimo is one of Italy's most beautifully situated abbeys—and a great "off the beaten path" destination. Stick around for mass and you'll hear the halls resound with Gregorian chant. (⇨ *Chapter 11.*)

Palazzo Ducale, Urbino, the Marches

(F) East of Umbria in the Marches region, Urbino is a college town in the Italian style—meaning its small but prestigious university dates to the 15th century. The highlight here is the Palazzo Ducale, a palace that exemplifies the Renaissance ideals of grace and harmony. (⇨ *Chapter 12.*)

Basilica di San Francesco, Assisi

(G) The basilica, built to honor Saint Francis, consists of two great churches: one Romanesque, fittingly solemn with its low ceilings and guttering candles; the other Gothic, with soaring arches and stained-glass windows (the first in Italy). They're both filled with some of Europe's finest frescoes. (⇨ *Chapter 12.*)

Duomo, Orvieto

(H) The facade of Orvieto's monumental Duomo contains a bas-relief masterpiece depicting the stories of the Creation and the Last Judgment (with the horrors of hell shown in striking detail). Inside, there's more glorious gore in the right transept, frescoed with Lucca Signorelli's *Stories of the Antichrist and the Last Judgment.* (⇨ *Chapter 12.*)

TOP EXPERIENCES

The View from Florence's Piazzale Michelangelo

One of the best ways to introduce yourself to Florence is by walking up to this square on the hill south of the Arno. From here you can take in the whole city, and much of the surrounding countryside, in one spectacular vista. To extend the experience, linger at one of the outdoor cafés, and for the finest view of all, time your visit to correspond with sunset.

Strolling the Ramparts of Lucca

Lucca, 80 km (50 miles) west of Florence, isn't situated on a hilltop in the way commonly associated with Tuscan towns, and it doesn't have quite the abundance of art treasures that you find in Siena or Pisa (to say nothing of Florence). Yet for many visitors Lucca is a favorite Tuscan destination, and the source of its appeal has everything to do with its ramparts.

These hulking barricades have surrounded the city center since the 17th century; built as a source of security, they now are part of an elevated, oval park, complete with walkways, picnic areas, grass, and trees. The citizens of Lucca spend much of their spare time here, strolling, biking, and lounging, oblivious to the novelty of their situation but clearly happy with it.

Taking the Waters at a Tuscan Spa

Tuscany is dotted throughout with small *terme* (thermal baths), where hot water flows from natural springs deep beneath the earth's surface. It's been believed for millennia that these waters have the power to cure whatever ails you.

Although their medicinal power may be questionable, that doesn't mean a dip isn't an extremely pleasant way to spend an afternoon.

In northwest Tuscany you can take the waters at Montecatini Terme (made famous as a setting for Fellini's 8½ and seemingly little has changed since then) or Bagni di Lucca (which had its heyday in the era of the 19th-century Romantic poets). To the south, Saturnia is the biggest draw, along with the more humble Chianciano Terme and Bagno Vignoni.

Wine Tasting in Chianti

The gorgeous hills of the Chianti region, between Florence and Siena, produce exceptional wines, and they never taste better than when sampled on their home turf. Many Chianti vineyards are visitor-friendly, but the logistics of a visit are different from what you may have experienced in other wine regions.

If you just drop in, you're likely to get a tasting, but for a tour you usually need to make an appointment several days ahead of time. The upside is that your tour may end up being a half day of full immersion—including extended conversation with the winemakers and even a meal.

Hiking in the Footsteps of Saint Francis

Umbria, which bills itself as "Italy's Green Heart," is fantastic hiking country. Among the many options are two with a Franciscan twist. From the town of Cannara, 16 km (10 miles) south of Assisi, an easy half-hour walk leads to the fields of Pian d'Arca, where Saint Francis delivered his sermon to the birds.

For a slightly more demanding walk, you can follow the saint's path from Assisi to the Eremo delle Carceri (Hermitage of Prisons), where Francis and his followers went to "imprison" themselves in prayer, and from here continue along the trails that crisscross Monte Subasio.

CENTRAL ITALY TODAY

. . . invests in culture

Money has been found to complete Florence's new opera house. Though officially inaugurated in November 2012, with Zubin Metha conducting Puccini's *Turandot,* almost 100 million euro has been required to finish the state-of-the-art structure. The first stage of the work should be finished by 2014, but it remains to be seen when the entire project will be finalized.

The church is spending money as well, on the expansion of Florence's Museo dell'Opera del Duomo. In order to meet the completion deadline of October 2015, the museum will be closed as of spring 2013. But, if you have gone to Florence hoping to see Lorenzo Ghiberti's "Doors of Paradise" or Michelangelo's "Pietà," you won't be disappointed. Plans are to leave these masterpieces open to the public. In addition, the north doors of the Battistero (Baptistery), also by Ghiberti, will go into restoration in March 2013, and they will almost certainly soon be displayed in the new gallery, too. In 2013, during early work on the foundations of the new building, excavations unearthed a brick model of the dome of Florence's Duomo—it's quite possibly an early prototype used by architect Filippo Brunelleschi to test his new building technique. It, too, will most likely be on display.

Restoration, expansion, and new displays mark the future of the Uffizi Gallery as well, making second and third visits a must over the next several years—even if you think you've seen it all before.

. . . lives with its past

The Etruscans are still with us. A study published in 2013, using bone samples from burial sites has proved that their DNA is identical to that of some contemporary inhabitants of Volterra and the Casentino, a mountain region in eastern Tuscany. So don't be suprised if you spot a face that resembles someone who lived 2,500 years ago!

. . . moves slowly into the future

Controversy swirls around a new high-speed train line in and beneath Florence, with a proposed tunnel being the main bone of contention. Work starts and stops, and the completion date slips inexorably away. The project also involves the ultramodern redesign of Florence's second train station, Campo di Marte, by British architect Sir Norman Foster.

. . . deals with scandal

It used to be said that there are three types of Sienese: those who work for the Monte dei Paschi bank, those who used to work for the bank, and those who are waiting for a job at the bank. Founded in 1475, it's the oldest operating bank in the world and the third largest in Italy, but came perilously close to closing after derivatives scandals were revealed in early 2013. The news has shaken Siena badly and the effects of the scandal and the subsequent investigation will be felt for years to come. Once a major supporter of the town, providing funding for everything from road works to art exhibitons, the bank will undoubtedly embrace a new reign of austerity that may limit such largesse.

A GREAT ITINERARY

Day 1: Florence

If you're coming in on an international flight, you'll probably settle in Florence in time for an afternoon stroll or siesta (depending on your jet-lag strategy) before dinner.

Logistics: On your flight in, read through the restaurant listings in this guide and begin anticipating the first dinner of your trip. Look for a place near your hotel, and when you arrive, reserve a table (or have your concierge do it for you).

Making a meal the focus of your first day is a great way to ease into Italian life. Note that Sunday and Monday are favorite closing days for many Florence restaurants, and Monday sees most important museums closed.

Day 2: Florence

Begin your morning at the **Uffizi Gallery** (reserve your ticket in advance). The extensive collection will occupy much of your morning. Next, take in the neighboring **Piazza della Signoria,** one of Florence's impressive squares, then head a few blocks north to the **Duomo.** There, check out Ghiberti's famous bronze doors on the **Battistero** (they're high-quality copies; the originals are in the Museo dell'Opera del Duomo), and work up an appetite by climbing the 463 steps to the cupola of Brunelleschi's splendid cathedral dome, atop which you'll experience a memorable view.

Spend the afternoon relaxing, shopping, and wandering Florence's medieval streets; or, if you're up for a more involved journey, head out to **Fiesole** to experience the ancient amphitheater and beautiful views of the Tuscan countryside.

Day 3: Florence

Keep the energy level up for your second full day in Florence, sticking with art and architecture for the morning, trying to see most of the following: Michelangelo's *David* at the **Galleria dell'Accademia,** the **Medici Chapels,** the **Palazzo Pitti** and **Boboli Gardens,** and the churches of **Santa Maria Novella** and **Santa Croce.**

If it's a clear day, spend the afternoon on a trip to **Piazzale Michelangelo,** high on a hill, for sweeping views of idyllic Florentine countryside. Given all the walking you've been doing, this would be a good night to recharge by trying the famed *bistecca alla fiorentina* (a grilled T-bone steak with olive oil).

Logistics: You can get up to the Piazzale Michelangelo by taxi or by taking Bus No. 12 or 13 from the Lungarno. Otherwise, do your best to get around on foot; Florence is a brilliant city for walking.

Day 4: San Gimignano

Now that you've been appropriately introduced to the bewildering splendor of Renaissance Italy, it's time for a change of pace—and time for a rental car, which will enable you to see the back roads of Tuscany and Umbria. After breakfast, head on out. On a beautiful day the lazy drive from Florence to **San Gimignano,** past vineyards and typical Tuscan landscapes, is truly spectacular.

The first thing that will hit you when you arrive at the hill town of San Gimignano will be its multiple towers. The medieval skyscrapers of Italy once occupied the role now played by Ferraris or Hummers: they were public displays of wealth and family power. After finding your way to a hotel in the old town, set out on foot and check out the city's turrets and alleyways, doing your best to get away from the trinket

shops, and later enjoying a leisurely dinner with the light but delicious local white wine, Vernaccia di San Gimignano.

Logistics: Some hotels might be able to coordinate with some rental-car agencies so that your car can be brought to your hotel for you. The historic center of Florence is closed to nonresidents' cars (including rentals). You can drive out of the center, but must give your license plate number to your hotel if you drive in—there's a heavy fine otherwise.

Once you navigate your way out of Florence (no easy task), San Gimignano is only 57 km (35 miles) to the southwest, so it's an easy drive; you could even take a detour on the SR222 (Strada Chiantigiana), stop at one of the Chianti wine towns, and visit a winery along the way.

Day 5: Siena

In the morning, set out for nearby **Siena,** which is known worldwide for its Palio, a festival that culminates in an elaborate horse-race competition among the 17 *contrade* (medieval neighborhoods) of the city. Because of the enormous influx of tourists, especially in summer, Siena isn't everyone's cup of tea, but it's still one of Tuscany's most impressive sights.

However many tourists you have to bump elbows with, it's hard not to be blown away by the city's precious medieval streets and memorable fan-shape **Piazza del Campo.**

Not to be missed while in town are the spectacular **Duomo,** the **Battistero,** and the **Spedale di Santa Maria della Scala,** an old hospital and hostel that now contains an underground archaeological museum.

Logistics: It's a short and pretty drive from San Gimignano to Siena, but once there, parking can be a challenge. Look for the *stadio* (soccer stadium), where there's a parking lot that often has space. Try to avoid arriving in Siena on Wednesday morning—the town's weekly market is in full swing, and the traffic and parking can be nightmarish.

Day 6: Arezzo/Cortona

Get an early start, because there's a lot to see today. From Siena you'll first head to **Arezzo,** home to the **Basilica di San Francesco,** which contains important frescoes by Piero della Francesca. Check out the **Piazza Grande** along with its beautiful Romanesque church of **Pieve di Santa Maria.**

Try to do all of this before lunch, after which you'll head straight to **Cortona.** If Arezzo didn't capture your imagination, Cortona, whose origins date to the 5th century BC, will. Olive trees and vineyards give way to a medieval hill town

with views over ridiculously idyllic Tuscan countryside and Lake Trasimeno. Cortona is a town for walking and relaxing, not sightseeing, so enjoy yourself, wandering through the **Piazza della Repubblica** and **Piazza Signorelli,** and perhaps doing a bit of shopping.

Logistics: Siena to Arezzo is 63 km (39 miles) on the E78. From Arezzo to Cortona, it's 30 km (18 miles)—take S71.

Day 7: Assisi

Today you'll cross over into Umbria, a region just as beautiful as Tuscany but still less trodden. Yet another impossibly beautiful hill town, **Assisi,** is the home of Saint Francis and host to the many religious pilgrims that come to celebrate his legacy. Visiting here is the most treasured memory of many a traveler's visit to Italy.

Upon arriving and checking into your lodging, head straight for the **Basilica di San Francesco,** which displays the tomb of Saint Francis and unbelievable frescoes. From here take Via San Francesco to **Piazza del Commune** and see the **Tempio di Minerva** before a break for lunch. After lunch, see **San Rufino,** the town cathedral, and then go back through the piazza to Corso Mazzini and see **Santa Chiara.** If you're a true Franciscan, you could instead devote the afternoon to heading out 16 km (10 miles) to **Cannara,** where Saint Francis delivered his sermon to the birds.

Logistics: From Cortona, take the S71 to the A1 autostrada toward Perugia. After about 40 km (24 miles), take the Assisi exit (E45), and it's another 14 km (8 miles) to Assisi.

Day 8: Spoleto

This morning will take you from a small Umbrian hill town to a slightly bigger one: **Spoleto,** a walled city that's home to a world-renowned arts festival each summer. But Spoleto needs no festival to be celebrated. Its **Duomo** is wonderful. Its fortress, **La Rocca,** is impressive. And the **Ponte delle Torri,** a 14th-century bridge that separates Spoleto from Monteluco, is a marvelous sight, traversing a gorge 260 feet below and built on the foundations of a Roman aqueduct.

See all these during the day, stopping for a light lunch of a panino (sandwich) or salad, saving your appetite for a serious last dinner in Italy: Umbrian cuisine is excellent everywhere, but Spoleto is a memorable culinary destination. Do your best to sample black truffles, a proud product of the region; they're delicious on pasta or meat.

Logistics: One school of thought would be to time your visit to Spoleto's worldrenowned arts festival that runs from mid-June through mid-July. Another would be to do anything you can to avoid it. It all depends on your taste for big festivals and big crowds.

The trip from Assisi to Spoleto is a pretty 47-km (29-mile) drive (S75 to the S3) that should take you less than an hour, a little longer if you plan a stop in the charming town of Spello on the way.

Day 9: Spoleto/Departure

It's a fair distance from Spoleto to the Florence airport, your point of departure. Depending on your comfort level with Italian driving, allow at least 2½ hours to get there.

FLORENCE

WELCOME TO FLORENCE

TOP REASONS TO GO

★ **Galleria degli Uffizi:** Italian Renaissance art doesn't get much better than this vast collection bequeathed to the city by the last Medici, Anna Maria Luisa.

★ **The dome of the Duomo:** Brunelleschi's work of engineering genius is the city's undisputed centerpiece.

★ **Michelangelo's *David*:** See it in person and you'll know why this is the one of the world's most famous sculptures.

★ **The view from Piazzale Michelangelo:** From this perch the city is laid out before you. The colors at sunset heighten the experience.

★ **Piazza Santa Croce:** After you've had your fill of Renaissance masterpieces, hang out here and watch the world go by.

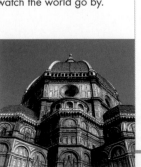

1 **The Duomo to the Ponte Vecchio.** Among the numerous landmarks here are the city's greatest museum (the Uffizi) and its most impressive square (Piazza della Signoria).

2 **San Lorenzo to the Accademia.** The blocks from the basilica of San Lorenzo to the Accademia museum bear the imprints of the Medici and of Michelangelo, culminating in the masterful *David*. To the north, the former convent of San Marco is filled with ethereal paintings by Fra Angelico.

3 **Santa Maria Novella to the Arno.** This part of town includes the train station, 16th-century palaces, and the city's chicest shopping street, Via Tornabuoni.

4 **Santa Croce.** The district centers on its namesake basilica, which is filled with the tombs of Renaissance luminaries. The area is also known for its leather shops, some of which have been open for centuries.

5 **The Oltrarno.** Across the Arno you find the massive Palazzo Pitti and the narrow streets of the Santo Spirito district, which is filled with artisans' workshops and antiques stores. A climb to Piazzale Michelangelo gives you a spectacular view of the city.

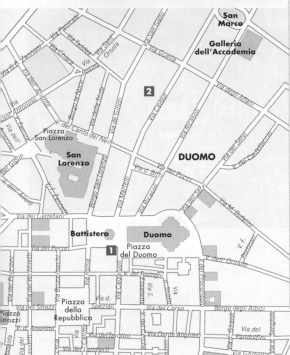

GETTING ORIENTED

The historic center of Florence is flat and compact—you could walk from one end to the other in half an hour. In the middle of everything is the Duomo, with its huge dome towering over the city's terracotta rooftops. Radiating out from the Duomo are Renaissance-era neighborhoods identified by their central churches and piazzas. Though the majority of sights are north of the Arno River, the area to the south, known as the Oltrarno, has its charms as well.

10

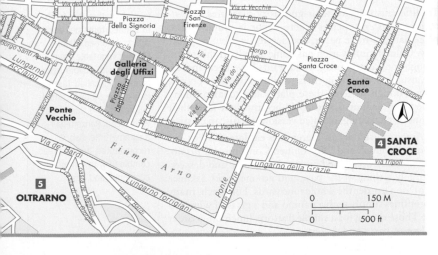

EATING AND DRINKING WELL IN FLORENCE

In Florence simply prepared meats, grilled or roasted, are the culinary stars, usually paired with seasonal vegetables like artichokes, porcini, and cannellini beans. *Bistecca*'s big, but there's plenty more that tastes great on the grill.

Traditionalists go for their gustatory pleasures in *trattorie* and *osterie*, places where decor is unimportant, placemats are mere paper, and service is often perfunctory. Culinary innovation has come slowly to this town, though some cutting-edge restaurants have been appearing, usually with young chefs who have worked outside Italy. Though some of these places lack charm (many have an international, you-could-be-anywhere feel), their menus offer exciting, updated versions of Tuscan classics.

By American standards, Florentines eat late: 1:30 or 2 is typical for lunch and 9 for dinner. Consuming a *primo*, *secondo*, and *dolce* (first and second course and dessert) is largely a thing of the past, and no one looks askance if you don't order the whole nine yards. For lunch, many Florentines simply grab a panino and a glass of wine at a bar. Those opting for a simple trattoria lunch often order a plate of pasta and dessert.

STALE AND STELLAR

Florence lacks signature pasta and rice dishes, perhaps because it has raised frugality with bread to culinary craft. Stale bread is the basis for three classic Florentine primi: *pappa al pomodoro, ribollita,* and *panzanella.* "Pappa" is made with either fresh or canned tomatoes and that stale bread. Ribollita is a vegetable soup fortified with *cavolo nero* (sometimes called Tuscan kale in the States), cannellini beans, and thickened with bread. Panzanella, a summertime dish, is reconstituted Tuscan bread combined with tomatoes, cucumber, and basil.

A CLASSIC ANTIPASTO: *CROSTINI DI FEGATINI*

This beloved dish consists of a chicken-liver spread, served warm or at room temperature, on toasted, garlic-rubbed bread. It can be served smooth, like a pâté, or in a rougher spread. It's made by sautéing chicken livers with finely diced carrot and onion, enlivened with the addition of wine, broth, or Marsala reductions, and mashed anchovies and capers.

A CLASSIC SECONDO: *BISTECCA FIORENTINA*

The town's culinary pride and joy is a thick slab of beef, resembling a T-bone steak, from large white oxen called *chianina*. The meat's slapped on the grill and served extremely rare, sometimes with a pinch of salt.

It's always seared on both sides, and just barely cooked inside (experts say five minutes per side, and then 15 minutes with the bone sitting perpendicularly on the grill). To ask for it more well done is to incur disdain; most restaurants simply won't serve it any other way but rare.

A CLASSIC CONTORNO: CANNELLINI BEANS

Simply boiled, they provide the perfect accompaniment to bistecca. The small white beans are best when they go straight from the garden into the pot. They should be anointed with a

generous outpouring of Tuscan olive oil; the combination is oddly felicitous, and it goes a long way toward explaining why Tuscans are referred to as *mangiafagioli* (bean eaters) by other Italians.

A CLASSIC DOLCE: *BISCOTTI DI PRATO*

These are sometimes the only dessert on offer, and are more or less an afterthought to the glories that have preceded them. *Biscotti* means twice-cooked (or, in this case, twice baked). They're hard almond cookies that soften considerably when dipped languidly into *vin santo* ("holy wine"), a sweet dessert wine, or into a simple caffè.

A CLASSIC WINE: CHIANTI CLASSICO

This blend from the region just south of Florence relies mainly on the local, hardy Sangiovese grape; it's aged for at least one year before hitting the market. (*Riserve*—reserves—are aged at least an additional six months.)

Chianti is usually the libation of choice for Florentines, and it pairs magnificently with grilled foods and seasonal vegetables. Traditionalists opt for the younger, fruitier (and usually less expensive) versions often served in straw flasks. You can sample *Chianti classico* all over town, and buy it in local *salumerie* (delicatessens) *enoteche* (wine bars), and supermarkets.

10

Updated
by Patricia
Rucidlo

Florence, the city of the lily, gave birth to the Renaissance and changed the way we see the world. For centuries it has captured the imaginations of travelers, who have come seeking "a room with a view" and phenomenal art. Indeed, no city in Italy can match Florence's astounding artistic wealth. Important paintings and sculptures are everywhere, and art scholars have been investigating their subtleties for hundreds of years. But what makes the art of Florence a revelation to the ordinary sightseer is a simple fact that scholarship often ignores: As astonishing percentage of Florence's art is just plain beautiful. Nowhere in Italy—perhaps in all Europe—is the act of looking at art more rewarding.

As a city, Florence has a subtle beauty—its staid, unprepossessing palaces built in local stone are not showy. Their architecture retains many of the stern, fortresslike features of pre-Renaissance palazzi, whose facades were mostly meant to keep intruders out rather than to invite sightseers in. The typical Florentine exterior gives nothing away, as if obsessively guarding secret treasures within.

The treasures, of course, are very real. And far from being a secret, they are famous the world over. The city is an artistic treasure trove of unique proportions. A single historical fact explains the phenomenon: Florence gave birth to the Renaissance. In the early 15th century the study of antiquity—of the glory that was Greece and the grandeur that was Rome—became a Florentine passion, and with it came a new respect for learning and a new creativity in art and architecture. It was funded by the city's leading businessmen: the Medici were first and foremost bankers until the most famous of them, Lorenzo de'Medici gathered around him, in the late 15th century, a court of poets, artists, philosophers, architects, and musicians. Art began to make great leaps toward a new naturalism through the study of perspective and anatomy, when architects forged a new style based on the techniques used by the ancient Romans. The Renaissance man was born, a man who, like Leonardo da Vinci, could design a canal, paint a fresco, or solve a mathematical problem with equal ease.

Happily, Leonardo could still take a walk along the Arno and find little changed, which is why so many visitors enjoy the experience. Navigating Piazza Signoria, almost always packed with tourists and locals alike, still, as has been the case for almost 700 years, requires patience. There's a reason why everyone seems to be here, however. It's the heart of the city, and, today, home to the Uffizi—arguably the world's finest repository of Renaissance art.

Florence—Firenze in Italian—was "discovered" in the 1700s by upper-class northerners making the Grand Tour. It became a mecca for travelers, particularly the Romantics, particularly those English ladies of the Room-with-a-View type who flocked to the city to stay in charming pensioni and paint romantic watercolors of the surrounding countryside. They were captivated by a wistful Botticelli smile, impressed by the graceful dignity of Donatello's bronze *David,* and moved by Michelangelo's provocative *Slaves* pulling free from their marble prisons. Today millions of modern visitors follow in their Grand Tour footsteps. When the sun sets over the Arno and, as Mark Twain described it, "overwhelms Florence with tides of color that make all the sharp lines dim and faint and turn the solid city to a city of dreams," it's hard not to fall under the city's magic spell.

FLORENCE PLANNER

MAKING THE MOST OF YOUR TIME

Even for the most dedicated art enthusiast, trying to take in Florence's abundance of masterpieces can turn into a headache—there's just too much to see. In fact, the surfeit of art and wonders has given rise to a "malady" to which foreign tourists are especially susceptible: "Stendhal's syndrome," named after the 19th-century French novelist, who was the first to describe it in print. The symptoms can be severe: confusion, dizziness, disorientation, depression, and sometimes persecution anxiety and loss of identity. Some victims immediately suspect food poisoning, but the true diagnosis is far more outlandish. They are suffering from "art poisoning," brought on by overexposure to so-called Important Works of High Culture. The victims seem to view Florentine art as an exam (Art History 101, 10 hours per day, self-taught, pass/fail), and they are terrified of flunking.

Obviously, the art of Florence should not be a test. So if you are not an inveterate museumgoer or church collector, take it easy. Remember to pace yourself. Allow time to wander and follow your whims, and ignore any pangs of guilt if you'd rather relax in a café and watch the world go by than trudge on sore feet through another breathtaking palace or

10

church. Remember: Florence isn't a city that can be "done." It's a place you can return to again and again, confident there will always be more treasures to discover.

Now that you have this advice, take heart: with some planning, you can see Florence's most famous sights in a couple of days. Start off at the city's most awe-inspiring work of architecture, the **Duomo**, climbing to the top of the dome if you have the stamina. On the same piazza, check out Ghiberti's bronze doors at the **Battistero**. (They're actually high-quality copies; the Museo dell'Opera del Duomo has the originals.) Set aside the afternoon for the **Galleria degli Uffizi**, making sure to reserve tickets in advance.

On Day 2, visit Michelangelo's *David* in the **Galleria dell'Accademia**— reserve tickets here, too. Linger in **Piazza della Signoria**, Florence's central square, where a copy of *David* stands in the spot the original occupied for centuries, then head east a couple of blocks to **Santa Croce**, the city's most artistically rich church. Double back and walk across Florence's landmark bridge, the **Ponte Vecchio**.

Do all that, and you'll have seen some great art, but you've just scratched the surface. If you have more time, put the **Bargello**, the **Museo di San Marco**, and the **Cappelle Medicee** at the top of your list. When you're ready for an art break, stroll through the **Boboli Gardens** or explore Florence's lively shopping scene, from the food stalls of the **Mercato Centrale** to the chic boutiques of the **Via Tornabuoni**.

HOURS

Florence's sights keep tricky hours. Some are closed on Wednesday, some on Monday, some on every other Monday, or every other Sunday. Quite a few shut their doors each day (or on most days) by 2 in the afternoon. Things get even more confusing on weekends. Make it a general rule to check the hours closely for any place you're planning to visit; if it's someplace you have your heart set on seeing, it's worthwhile to call to confirm.

Here's a selection of major sights that might not be open when you'd expect—*consult the sight listings within this chapter for full details.* And be aware that, as always, hours can and do change.

The **Uffizi** and the **Accademia** are both closed Monday. All but a few of the galleries at Palazzo Pitti are closed Monday as well.

The **Duomo** closes at 3:30 on Thursday (as opposed to 5:30 on other weekdays, 4:45 on weekends). The dome of the Duomo is closed on Sunday.

The **Battistero** is open from 11:15 until 7, Monday through Saturday, and on Sunday from 8:30 to 2. On the first Saturday of the month, it's open from 8:30 to 2.

The **Bargello** closes at 1:50 pm, and is closed entirely on alternating Sundays and Mondays. However, it's often open much later during high season and when there's a special exhibition on.

The **Cappelle Medicee** are closed on alternating Sundays and Mondays.

Museo di San Marco closes at 1:50 on weekdays but stays open until 7 on weekends—except for alternating Sundays and Mondays, when it's closed entirely.

Palazzo Medici-Riccardi is closed Wednesday.

RESERVATIONS

At most times of day you'll see a line of people snaking around the Uffizi. They're waiting to buy tickets, and you don't want to be one of them. Instead, call ahead for a reservation (☎ *055/294883; reservationists speak English*). You'll be given a reservation number and a time of admission—the farther ahead you call, the more time slots you'll have to choose from. Go to the museum's reservation door at the appointed hour, give the clerk your number, pick up your ticket, and go inside. You'll pay €4 for this privilege, but it's money well spent. You can also book tickets online through the website ⊕ *www.polomuseale.firenze.it*; the booking process takes some patience, but it works.

Use the same reservation service to book tickets for the Galleria dell'Accademia, where lines rival those of the Uffizi. (Reservations can also be made for the Palazzo Pitti, the Bargello, and several other sights, but they usually aren't needed.) An alternative strategy is to check with your hotel—many will handle reservations.

GETTING HERE AND AROUND
AIR TRAVEL

Aeroporto A. Vespucci. Florence's small Aeroporto A. Vespucci, commonly called **Peretola**, is just outside of town, and receives flights from Milan, Rome, London, and Paris. ⊠ *10 km (6 miles) northwest of Florence* ☎ *055/30615* ⊕ *www.aeroporto.firenze.it.*

To get into the city center from the airport by car, take the autostrada A11. A SITA bus will take you directly from the airport to the center of town. Tickets can be purchased on the bus.

Aeroporto Galileo Galilei. Pisa's Aeroporto Galileo Galilei is the closest landing point with significant international service, including a few direct flights from New York each week on Delta. Sadly, the flight is seasonal and shuts down when it's cold outside. It's a straight shot down the SS67 to Florence. A train service connects Pisa's airport station with Santa Maria Novella, roughly a 1 hour trip. Sometimes are non-stop to Florence; other times, you must change at Pisa Centrale. Trains start running about 7 am from the airport, 4:30 am from Florence, and continue service every hour until about 1 am from the airport, 10 pm from Florence. ⊠ *12 km (7 miles) south of Pisa and 80 km (50 miles) west of Florence* ☎ *050/849300* ⊕ *www.pisa-airport.com.*

BUS TRAVEL

Long-distance buses provide inexpensive if somewhat claustrophobic service between Florence and other cities in Italy and Europe. Lazzi Eurolines and SITA are the major lines; they have neatly divided up their routes, so there's little overlap.

Once you're here, Florence's flat, compact city center is made for walking, but when your feet get weary you can use the efficient bus system, which includes small electric buses making the rounds in the center.

10

Buses also climb to Piazzale Michelangelo and San Miniato south of the Arno.

Maps and timetables for local bus service are available for a small fee at most newsagents, or for free at visitor information offices. Tickets must be bought in advance from tobacco shops, newsstands, automatic ticket machines near main stops, or ATAF booths. The ticket must be canceled in the small validation machine immediately upon boarding.

You have several ticket options, all valid for one or more rides on all lines. A €1.20 ticket is good for one hour from the time it's first canceled. A multiple ticket—four tickets, each valid for 70 minutes—costs €4.50. A 24-hour tourist ticket costs €5. Two-, three-, and seven-day passes are also available.

Contacts Lazzi Eurolines ⊠ *Via Mercadante 2, Santa Maria Novella* ☎ *0573/193-7900* ⊕ *www.lazzi.it.* **SITA** ⊠ *Via Santa Caterina da Siena 17/r, Santa Maria Novella* ☎ *055/47821* ⊕ *www.sita-on-line.it.*

CAR TRAVEL

Florence is connected to the north and south of Italy by the Autostrada del Sole (A1). It takes about an hour and a half of driving on scenic roads to get to Bologna (although heavy truck traffic over the Apennines often makes for slower going), about 3 hours to Rome, and 3 to 3½ hours to Milan. The Tyrrhenian Coast is an hour west on the A11.

An automobile in Florence is a major liability. If your itinerary includes parts of Italy where you'll want a car (such as Tuscany), pick the vehicle up on your way out of town.

TAXI TRAVEL

Taxis usually wait at stands throughout the city (in front of the train station and in Piazza della Repubblica, for example), or you can call for one (☎ *055/4390 or 055/4798*). The meter starts at €3.30, with extra charges at night, on Sunday, for radio dispatch, and for luggage. Women out on the town from 9 pm to 2 am seeking taxis are entitled to a 10% discount on the fare; you must, however, request it.

TRAIN TRAVEL

Florence is on the principal Italian train route between most European capitals and Rome, and within Italy it's served frequently from Milan, Venice, and Rome by Intercity (IC) and nonstop Eurostar and Frecce trains.

Stazione Centrale di Santa Maria Novella. Florence's main train station is in the center of town. ☎ *892021* ⊕ *www.trenitalia.com.*

VISITOR INFORMATION

The Florence tourist office, known as the **APT** (☎ *055/290832* ⊕ *www. firenze.turismo.toscana.it*), has branches next to the Palazzo Medici-Riccardi, across the street from Stazione di Santa Maria Novella (the main train station) and just beside the Baptistery. The offices are generally open from 9 in the morning until 7 in the evening (and are often closed on Sunday afternoon). The multilingual staff will give you directions and the latest on happenings in the city. It's particularly worth a stop if you're interested in finding out about performing-arts events. The APT website provides information in both Italian and English.

EXPLORING FLORENCE

THE DUOMO TO THE PONTE VECCHIO

The heart of Florence, stretching from the Piazza del Duomo south to the Arno, is dense with artistic treasures. The churches, medieval towers, Renaissance palaces, and world-class museums and galleries contain some of the most outstanding aesthetic achievements of Western history.

Much of the *centro storico* (historic center) is closed to automobile traffic, but you still must dodge mopeds, cyclists, and masses of fellow tourists as you walk the narrow streets, especially in the area bounded by the Duomo, Piazza della Signoria, Galleria degli Uffizi, and Ponte Vecchio.

TOP ATTRACTIONS

Bargello. This building started out as the headquarters for the Capitano del Popolo (captain of the people) during the Middle Ages, and was later used as a prison. The exterior served as a "most wanted" billboard: effigies of notorious criminals and Medici enemies were painted on its walls. Today it houses the **Museo Nazionale,** home to what is probably the finest collection of Renaissance sculpture in Italy. The concentration of masterworks by Michelangelo (1475–1564), Donatello (circa 1386–1466), and Benvenuto Cellini (1500–71) is remarkable; the works are distributed among an eclectic collection of arms, ceramics, and miniature bronzes, among other things. For Renaissance art lovers, the Bargello is to sculpture what the Uffizi is to painting.

In 1401 Filippo Brunelleschi (1377–1446) and Lorenzo Ghiberti (circa 1378–1455) competed to earn the most prestigious commission of the day: the decoration of the north doors of the Baptistery in Piazza del Duomo. For the contest, each designed a bronze bas-relief panel depicting the sacrifice of Isaac; the panels are displayed together in the room devoted to the sculpture of Donatello, on the upper floor. The judges chose Ghiberti for the commission; see if you agree with their choice. ⊠ *Via del Proconsolo 4, Bargello* ☎ *055/294883* ⊕ *www.polomuseale. firenze.it* 🎫*€4* ☉ *Daily 8:15–1:50; closed 2nd and 4th Mon. of month and 1st, 3rd, and 5th Sun. of month.*

Battistero (*Baptistery*). The octagonal Baptistery is one of the supreme monuments of the Italian Romanesque style and one of Florence's oldest structures. Local legend has it that it was once a Roman temple dedicated to Mars, and modern excavations suggest that its foundations date from the 1st century AD. The round Romanesque arches on the exterior date from the 11th century, and the interior dome mosaics from the beginning of the mid-13th century are justly renowned, but—glittering beauties though they are—they could never outshine the building's famed bronze Renaissance doors decorated with panels crafted by **Lorenzo Ghiberti.** These doors—or at least copies of them—on which Ghiberti worked most of his adult life (1403–52) are on the north and east sides of the Baptistery, and the Gothic panels on the south door were designed by Andrea Pisano (circa 1290–1348) in 1330.

10

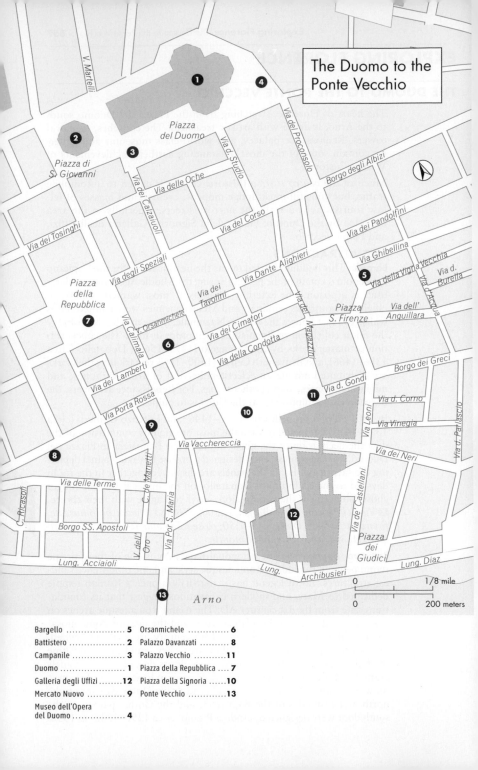

The Duomo to the
Ponte Vecchio

Piazza
del Duomo

Piazza di
S. Giovanni

Piazza
della
Repubblica

Piazza
S. Firenze

Piazza
dei
Giudici

Arno

V. Martelli

Via del Proconsolo

Via d. Studio

Via d. Calzaiuoli

Via delle Oche

Borgo degli Albizi

Via dei Tosinghi

Via del Corso

Via dei Pandolfini

Via degli Speziali

Via Ghibellina

Via Dante Alighieri

Via della Vigna Vecchia

Via d. Burella

Via dei Tavolini

Via dell' Anguillara

V. Orsanmichele

Via dei Cimatori

Via d. Acqua

Via della Condotta

Via d. Magazzini

Via dei Lamberti

Borgo dei Greci

Via d. Gondi

Via d. Corno

Via Porta Rossa

Via Leoni

Via Vinegia

Via d. Parlascio

Via Vaccherreccia

Via dei Neri

C. de Magnetti

Via de' Castellani

Via delle Terme

C. Ricasoli

V. delle Oro

Via Por S. Maria

Borgo SS. Apostoli

Lung. Acciaioli

Lung. Archibusieri

Lung. Diaz

1/8 mile

200 meters

Arno

Bargello 5
Battistero 2
Campanile 3
Duomo 1
Galleria degli Uffizi 12
Mercato Nuovo 9
Museo dell'Opera
del Duomo 4

Orsanmichele 6
Palazzo Davanzati 8
Palazzo Vecchio 11
Piazza della Repubblica ... 7
Piazza della Signoria 10
Ponte Vecchio 13

Ghiberti's original doors were removed to protect them from the effects of pollution and acid rain and have been beautifully restored; they are now on display in the Museo dell'Opera del Duomo. Ghiberti's north doors depict scenes from the life of Christ; his later east doors (dating from 1425–52), facing the Duomo facade, render scenes from the Old Testament. Both merit close examination, for they are very different in style and illustrate the artistic changes that marked the beginning of the Renaissance. Look at the far right panel of the middle row on the earlier (1403–24) north doors (*Jesus Calming the Waters*). Ghiberti here captured the chaos of a storm at sea with great skill and economy, but the artistic conventions he used are basically pre-Renaissance: Jesus is the most important figure, so he is the largest; the disciples are next in size, being next in importance; the ship on which they founder looks like a mere toy.

The exquisitely rendered panels on the east doors are larger, more expansive, more sweeping—and more convincing. The middle panel on the left-hand door tells the story of Jacob and Esau, and the various episodes of the story—the selling of the birthright, Isaac ordering Esau to go hunting, the blessing of Jacob, and so forth—have been merged into a single beautifully realized street scene. Ghiberti's use of perspective suggests depth: the background architecture looks far more credible than on the north-door panels, the figures in the foreground are grouped realistically, and the naturalism and grace of the poses (look at Esau's left leg and the dog next to him) have nothing to do with the sacred message being conveyed. Although the religious content remains, the figures and their place in the natural world are given new prominence, and are portrayed with a realism not seen in art since the fall of the Roman Empire nearly a thousand years before.

As a footnote to Ghiberti's panels, one small detail of the east doors is worth a special look. To the lower left of the Jacob and Esau panel, Ghiberti placed a tiny self-portrait bust. From either side, the portrait is extremely appealing—Ghiberti looks like everyone's favorite uncle—but the bust is carefully placed so that you can make direct eye contact with the tiny head from a single spot. When that contact is made, the impression of intelligent life—of *modern* intelligent life—is astonishing. It's no wonder that these doors received one of the most famous compliments in the history of art from an artist known to be notoriously stingy with praise: Michelangelo declared them so beautiful that they could serve as the Gates of Paradise. ⊠ *Piazza del Duomo* ☏ *055/2302885* ⊕ *www. operaduomo.firenze.it* ☏ *€5* ⊙ *Mon.–Sat. 11:15–7, Sun. 8:30–2, 1st Sat. of month 8:30–2.*

10

Fodor'sChoice
★
Galleria degli Uffizi. The venerable Uffizi Gallery occupies two floors of the U-shaped **Palazzo degli Uffizi,** designed by Giorgio Vasari (1511–74) in 1560 to hold the *uffizi* (administrative offices) of the Medici grand duke Cosimo I (1519–74). Later, the Medici installed their art collections here, creating what was Europe's first modern museum, open to the public (at first only by request) since 1591.

Among the highlights are Paolo Uccello's *Battle of San Romano*, its brutal chaos of lances one of the finest visual metaphors for warfare ever

FLORENCE THROUGH THE AGES

Guelph vs. Ghibelline. Though Florence can lay claim to a modest importance in the ancient world, it didn't come into its own until the Middle Ages. In the early 1200s the city, like most of the rest of Italy, was rent by civic unrest.

Two factions, the Guelphs and the Ghibellines, competed for power. The Guelphs supported the papacy, and the Ghibellines supported the Holy Roman Empire. Bloody battles—most notably one at Montaperti in 1260—tore Florence and other Italian cities apart. By the end of the 13th century the Guelphs ruled securely and the Ghibellines had been vanquished. This didn't end civic strife, however: the Guelphs split into the Whites and the Blacks for reasons still debated by historians. Dante, author of the *Divine Comedy,* was banished from Florence in 1301 because he was a White.

The Guilded Age. Local merchants had organized themselves into guilds by 1250. In that year they proclaimed themselves the *primo popolo* (literally, "first people"), making a landmark attempt at elective, republican rule.

Though the episode lasted only 10 years, it constituted a breakthrough in Western history. Such a daring stance by the merchant class was a by-product of Florence's emergence as an economic powerhouse. Florentines were papal bankers; they instituted the system of international letters of credit; and the gold florin became the international standard of currency. With this economic strength came a building boom. Palaces and basilicas were erected, enlarged, or restructured. Sculptors such as Donatello and Ghiberti decorated them; painters such as Giotto and Botticelli frescoed their walls.

Mighty Medici. Though ostensibly a republic, Florence was blessed (or cursed) with one very powerful family, the Medici, who came to prominence in the 1430s and were the de facto rulers of Florence for several hundred years. It was under patriarch Cosimo il Vecchio (1389–1464) that the Medici's position in Florence was securely established. Florence's golden age occurred during the reign of his grandson Lorenzo de' Medici (1449–92). Lorenzo was not only an astute politician but also a highly educated man and a great patron of the arts. Called "Il Magnifico" (the Magnificent), he gathered around him poets, artists, philosophers, architects, and musicians.

Lorenzo's son, Piero (1471–1503), proved inept at handling the city's affairs. He was run out of town in 1494, and Florence briefly enjoyed its status as a republic while dominated by the Dominican friar Girolamo Savonarola (1452–98). After a decade of internal unrest, the republic fell and the Medici were recalled to power, but Florence never regained its former prestige. By the 1530s most of the major artistic talent had left the city—Michelangelo, for one, had settled in Rome. The now-ineffectual Medici, eventually attaining the title of grand dukes, remained nominally in power until the line died out in 1737, after which time Florence passed from the Austrians to the French and back again until the unification of Italy (1865–70), when it briefly became the capital under King Vittorio Emanuele II.

captured in paint (in returned from a glorious restoration in the summer of 2012); the *Madonna and Child with Two Angels,* by Fra Filippo Lippi (1406–69), in which the impudent eye contact established by the angel would have been unthinkable prior to the Renaissance; the *Birth of Venus* and *Primavera* by Sandro Botticelli (1445–1510), the goddess of the former seeming to float on air and the fairy-tale charm of the latter exhibiting the painter's idiosyncratic

genius at its zenith; the portraits of the Renaissance duke Federico da Montefeltro and his wife Battista Sforza, by Piero della Francesca (circa 1420–92); the *Madonna of the Goldfinch* by Raphael (1483–1520), which underwent a stunning years-long restoration, completed in 2009 (check out the brilliant blues that decorate the sky, as well as the eye contact between mother and child, both clearly anticipating the painful future; Michelangelo's *Doni Tondo*; the *Venus of Urbino* by Titian (circa 1488/90–1576); and the splendid *Bacchus* by Caravaggio (circa 1571/72–1610). In the last two works, the approaches to myth and sexuality are diametrically opposed, to put it mildly. Don't forget to see the Caravaggios, which are in an easily-missable room during the exiting process. In the summer of 2012, many new rooms were opened (complementing the blue rooms housing non-Italian art which occurred the year before) which means that getting out of the museum takes even longer; don't think you've missed the Raphaels, which used to live in the room next door to Michelangelo's stunning panel painting. They are now practically the last things you'll see before leaving, so remember to save some stamina in order to truly appreciate their splendor. And don't think you've missed the Michelangelo, as in winter 2013 it was moved from Sala 25 to Sala 35. At press time, and at last count, the Uffizi numbered 79 rooms, many of which were empty awaiting more recent, non-Italian Renaissance additions. In addition, a restaurant is forecast, which should be open sometime in 2013.

10

Late in the afternoon is the least crowded time to visit. For a €4 fee, advance tickets can be reserved by phone, online, or, once in Florence, at the Uffizi reservation booth (⌧ *Consorzio ITA, Piazza Pitti 1* ☎ *055/294883)* at least one day in advance of your visit. Keep the confirmation number and take it with you to the door at the museum marked "Reservations." In the past, you wer ushered in almost immediately. But overbooking (especially in high season) has led to long lines and long waits even with a reservation. Come with cash, because credit cards are not accepted (though you can use a credit card when booking online). When there's a special exhibit on, which is often, the base ticket price goes up to €11. ⌧ *Piazzale degli Uffizi 6, Piazza della Signoria* ☎ *055/23885* ⊕ *www.uffizi.firenze.it; www.polomuseale.firenze.it reservations* ⊠ *€10, €11 during special exhibitions; €4 reservation fee* ☉ *Tues.–Sun. 8:15–6:50.*

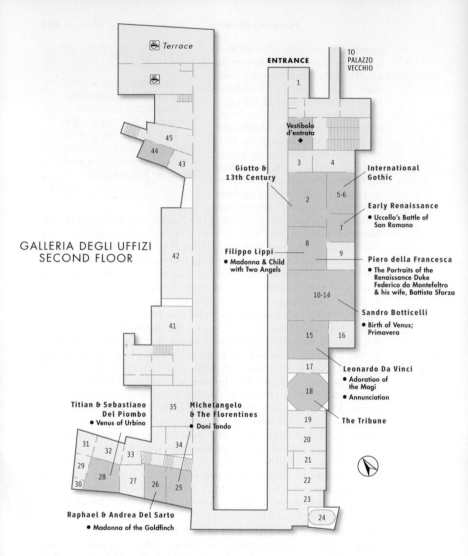

Terrace

ENTRANCE

TO PALAZZO VECCHIO

1

Vestibolo d'entrata ◆

3   4

5-6

2

7

8

9

45

44

43

42

41

GALLERIA DEGLI UFFIZI
SECOND FLOOR

Giotto &
13th Century

International
Gothic

Early Renaissance
● Uccello's Battle of
San Romano

Filippo Lippi
● Madonna & Child
with Two Angels

Piero della Francesca
● The Portraits of the
Renaissance Duke
Federico da Montefeltro
& his wife, Battista Sforza

10-14

15   16

Sandro Botticelli
● Birth of Venus;
Primavera

17

18

Leonardo Da Vinci
● Adoration of
the Magi
● Annunciation

19

The Tribune

35

Titian & Sebastiano
Del Piombo
● Venus of Urbino

Michelangelo
& The Florentines
● Doni Tondo

20

21

22

23

24

34

31   32
33
29
30   28   27   26   25

Raphael & Andrea Del Sarto
● Madonna of the Goldfinch

Piazza della Signoria. This is by far the most striking square in Florence. It was here, in 1497, that the famous "bonfire of the vanities" took place, when the fanatical friar Savonarola induced his followers to hurl their worldly goods into the flames; it was also here, a year later, that he was hanged as a heretic and, ironically, burned. A bronze plaque in the piazza pavement marks the exact spot of his execution.

The statues in the square and in the 14th-century **Loggia dei Lanzi** on the south side vary in quality. Cellini's famous bronze *Perseus* holding the severed head of Medusa is certainly the most important sculpture in the loggia. Other works here include *The Rape of the Sabine* and *Hercules and the Centaur*, both late-16th-century works by Giambologna (1529–1608), and in the back, a row of sober matrons dating from Roman times.

In the square, the Neptune Fountain, created between 1550 and 1575, takes something of a booby prize. It was created by Bartolomeo Ammannati, who himself considered it a failure. The Florentines call it il Biancone, which may be translated as "the big white man" or "the big white lump." Giambologna's equestrian statue, to the left of the fountain, portrays Grand Duke Cosimo I. Occupying the steps of the Palazzo Vecchio are a copy of Donatello's proud heraldic lion of Florence, the *Marzocco* (the original is now in the Bargello); a copy of Donatello's *Judith and Holofernes* (the original is in the Palazzo Vecchio); a copy of Michelangelo's *David* (the original is in the Galleria dell'Accademia); and Baccio Bandinelli's *Hercules* (1534). The Marzocco, the Judith, and the David were symbols of Florentine civic pride—the latter two subjects had stood up to their oppressors. They provided apt metaphors for the republic-loving Florentines, who often chafed at Medici hegemony.

Ponte Vecchio (*Old Bridge*). This charmingly simple bridge was built in 1345 to replace an earlier bridge swept away by flood. Its shops first housed butchers, then grocers, blacksmiths, and other merchants. But in 1593 the Medici grand duke Ferdinand I (1549–1609), whose private corridor linking the Medici palace (Palazzo Pitti) with the Medici offices (the Uffizi) crossed the bridge atop the shops, decided that all this plebeian commerce under his feet was unseemly. So he threw out the butchers and blacksmiths and installed 41 goldsmiths and eight jewelers. The bridge has been devoted solely to these two trades ever since.

10

The **Corridoio Vasariano** (✉ *Piazzale degli Uffizi 6, Piazza della Signoria* ☎ *055/23885 or 055/294883*), the private Medici corridor, was built by Vasari in 1565. Though the ostensible reason for its construction was one of security, it was more likely designed so that the Medici family wouldn't have to walk amid the commoners. The corridor is notoriously fickle with its operating hours; at this writing, it is temporarily open but only to groups. It can sometimes be visited by prior special arrangement. Call for the most up-to-date details. Take a moment to study the Ponte Santa Trinita, the next bridge downriver, from either the bridge or the corridor. It was designed by Bartolomeo Ammannati in 1567 (probably from sketches by Michelangelo), blown up by the retreating Germans during World War II, and painstakingly reconstructed after the war. The view from the Ponte Santa Trinita is beautiful, which might explain why so many young lovers seem to hang out there.

Continued on page 569

THE DUOMO
FLORENCE'S BIGGEST MASTERPIECE

For all its monumental art and architecture, Florence has one undisputed centerpiece: the Cathedral of Santa Maria del Fiore, better known as the Duomo. Its cupola dominates the skyline, presiding over the city's rooftops like a red hen over her brood. Little wonder that when Florentines feel homesick, they say they have *"nostalgia del cupolone."*

The Duomo's construction began in 1296, following the design of Arnolfo da Cambio, Florence's greatest architect of the time. By modern standards, construction was slow and haphazard—it continued through the 14th and into the 15th century, with some dozen architects having a hand in the project.

In 1366 Neri di Fioravante created a model for the hugely ambitious cupola: it was to be the largest dome in the world, surpassing Rome's Pantheon. But when the time finally came to build the dome in 1418, no one was sure how—or even if—it could be done. Florence was faced with a 143-ft hole in the roof of its cathedral, and one of the greatest challenges in the history of architecture.

Fortunately, local genius Filippo Brunelleschi was just the man for the job. Brunelleschi won the 1418 competition to design the dome, and for the

next 18 years he oversaw its construction. The enormity of his achievement can hardly be overstated. Working on such a large scale (the dome weighs 37,000 tons and uses 4 million bricks) required him to invent hoists and cranes that were engineering marvels. A "dome within a dome" design and a novel herringbone bricklaying pattern were just two of the innovations used to establish structural integrity. Perhaps most remarkably, he executed the construction without a supporting wooden framework, which had previously been thought indispensable.

Brunelleschi designed the lantern atop the dome, but he died soon after its first stone was laid in 1446; it wouldn't be completed until 1461. Another 400 years passed before the Duomo received its façade, a 19th-century neo-Gothic creation.

DUOMO TIMELINE

1296 Work begins, following design by Arnolfo di Cambio.

1302 Arnolfo dies; work continues, with sporadic interruptions.

1331 Management of construction taken over by the Wool Merchants guild.

1334 Giotto appointed project overseer, designs campanile.

1337 Giotto dies; Andrea Pisano takes leadership role.

1348 The Black Plague; all work ceases.

1366 Vaulting on nave completed; Neri di Fioravante makes model for dome.

1417 Drum for dome completed.

1418 Competition is held to design the dome.

1420 Brunelleschi begins work on the dome.

1436 Dome completed.

1446 Construction of lantern begins; Brunelleschi dies.

1461 Antonio Manetti, a student of Brunelleschi, completes lantern.

1469 Gilt copper ball and cross added by Verrocchio.

1587 Original façade is torn down by Medici court.

1871 Emilio de Fabris wins competition to design new façade.

1887 Façade completed.

WHAT TO LOOK FOR INSIDE THE DUOMO

The interior of the Duomo is a fine example of Florentine Gothic with a beautiful marble floor, but the space feels strangely barren—a result of its great size and the fact that some of the best art has been moved to the nearby **Museo dell'Opera del Duomo.**

Notable among the works that remain are two towering equestrian frescoes of famous mercenaries: *Niccolò da Tolentino* (1456), by Andrea del Castagno, and *Sir John Hawkwood* (1436), by Paolo Uccello. There's also fine terra-cotta work by Luca della Robbia. Ghiberti,

Brunelleschi's great rival, is responsible for much of the stained glass, as well as a reliquary urn with gorgeous reliefs. A vast fresco of the Last Judgment, painted by Vasari and Zuccari, covers the dome's interior. Brunelleschi had wanted mosaics to go there; it's a pity he didn't get his wish.

In the crypt beneath the cathedral, you can explore excavations of a Roman wall and mosaic fragments from the late sixth century; entry is near the first pier on the right. On the way down you pass Brunelleschi's modest tomb.

1. Entrance; stained glass by Ghiberti
2. Fresco of Niccolò da Tolentino by Andrea del Castagno
3. Fresco of John Hawkwood by Paolo Uccello
4. *Dante and the Divine Comedy* by Domenico di Michelino
5. Lunette: *Ascension* by Luca della Robbia
6. Above altar: two angels by Luca della Robbia. Below the altar: reliquary of St. Zenobius by Ghiberti.
7. Lunette: *Resurrection* by Luca della Robbia
8. Entrance to dome
9. Bust of Brunelleschi by Buggiano
10. Stairs to crypt
11. Campanile

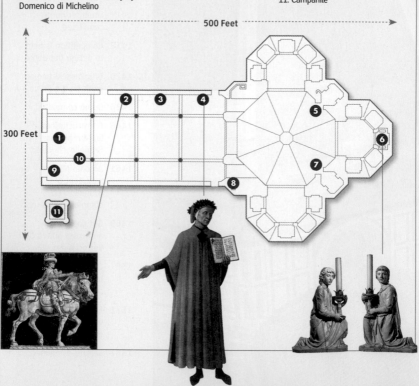

MAKING THE CLIMB

Climbing the 463 steps to the top of the dome is not for the faint of heart—or for the claustrophobic—but those who do it will be awarded a smashing view of Florence ❶. Keep in mind that the way up is also the way down, which means that while you're huffing and puffing in the ascent, people very close to you in a narrow staircase are making their way down ❷.

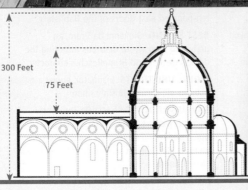

300 Feet

75 Feet

DUOMO BASICS

• Even first thing in the morning during high season (May through September), a line is likely to have formed to climb the dome. Expect an hour wait.

• For an alternative to the dome, consider climbing the less trafficked campanile, which gives you a view from on high of the dome itself.

• Dress code essentials: covered shoulders, no short shorts, and hats off upon entering.

✉ Piazza del Duomo

☎ 055/2302885

⊕ www.operaduomo.firenze.it

🎟 Free, crypt €3, cupola €8

🕐 Crypt: Mon.–Wed., Fri., Sun. 10–5; Thurs. 10–4:30; Sat. 10–5:45; first Sat. of month 10–3:30. Cupola: Weekdays 8:30–7, Sat. 8:30–5:40, 1st Sat. of month 8:30–4. Duomo: Mon.–Wed. and Fri. 10–5, Thurs. 10–4:30, Sat., 10–4:45, Sun 1:30–4:45, 1st Sat. of month 10–3:30.

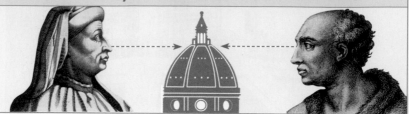

BRUNELLESCHI vs. GHIBERTI
The Rivalry of Two Renaissance Geniuses

In Renaissance Florence, painters, sculptors, and architects competed for major commissions, with the winner earning the right to undertake a project that might occupy him (and keep him paid) for a decade or more. Stakes were high, and the resulting rivalries fierce—none more so than that between Filippo Brunelleschi and Lorenzo Ghiberti.

The two first clashed in 1401, for the commission to create the bronze doors of the Baptistery. When Ghiberti won, Brunelleschi took it hard, fleeing to Rome, where he would remain for 15 years. Their rematch came in 1418, over the design of the Duomo's cupola, with Brunelleschi triumphant. For the remainder of their lives, the two would miss no opportunity to belittle each other's work.

FILIPPO BRUNELLESCHI (1377–1446)

MASTERPIECE: The dome of Santa Maria del Fiore.

BEST FRIENDS: Donatello, whom he stayed with in Rome after losing the Baptistery doors competition; the Medici family, who rescued him from bankruptcy.

SIGNATURE TRAITS: Paranoid, secretive, bad tempered, practical joker, inept businessman.

SAVVIEST POLITICAL MOVE: Feigned sickness and left for Rome after his dome plans were publicly criticized by Ghiberti, who was second-in-command. The project proved too much for Ghiberti to manage on his own, and Brunelleschi returned triumphant.

MOST EMBARRASSING MOMENT: In 1434 he was imprisoned for two weeks for failure to pay a small guild fee. The humiliation might have been orchestrated by Ghiberti.

OTHER CAREER: Shipbuilder. He built a huge vessel, *Il Badalone*, to transport marble for the dome up the Arno. It sank on its first voyage.

INSPIRED: The dome of St. Peter's in Rome.

LORENZO GHIBERTI (1378–1455)

MASTERPIECE: *The Gates of Paradise*, the ten-paneled east doors of the Baptistery.

BEST FRIEND: Giovanni da Prato, an underling who wrote diatribes attacking the dome's design and Brunelleschi's character.

SIGNATURE TRAITS: Instigator, egoist, know-it-all, shrewd businessman.

SAVVIEST POLITICAL MOVE: During the Baptistery doors competition, he had an open studio and welcomed opinions on his work, while Brunelleschi labored behind closed doors.

OTHER CAREER: Collector of classical artifacts, historian.

INSPIRED: *The Gates of Hell* by Auguste Rodin.

The Gates of Paradise detail

WORTH NOTING

Campanile. The Gothic bell tower designed by Giotto (circa 1266–1337) is a soaring structure of multicolor marble originally decorated with sculptures by Donatello and reliefs by Giotto, Andrea Pisano, and others (which are now in the Museo dell'Opera del Duomo). A climb of 414 steps rewards you with a close-up of Brunelleschi's cupola on the Duomo next door and a sweeping view of the city. ⊠ *Piazza del Duomo* ☎ *055/2302885* ⊕ *www.operaduomo.firenze.it* 🔳 *€6* ☾ *Daily 8:30–7:30.*

FAMILY **Mercato Nuovo** (*New Market*). The open-air loggia, built in 1551, teems with souvenir stands, but the real attraction is a copy of Pietro Tacca's bronze *Porcellino* (which translates as "little pig" despite the fact the animal is, in fact, a wild boar). The *Porcellino* is Florence's equivalent of the Trevi Fountain: put a coin in his mouth, and if it falls through the grate below (according to one interpretation), it means you'll return to Florence someday. What you're seeing is a copy of a copy: Tacca's original version, in the Museo Bardini, is actually a copy of an ancient Greek work. ⊠ *Corner of Via Por Santa Maria and Via Porta Rossa, Piazza della Repubblica* ☾ *Tues.–Sat. 8–7, Mon. 1–7.*

Museo dell'Opera del Duomo (*Cathedral Museum*). At press time, the museum was undergoing some serious expansion, and the results will be splendid when work is completed in October 2015. In the meantime, you can still see two of the museum's greatest treasures, Lorenzo Ghiberti's newly and brilliantly restored "Doors of Paradise" and Michelangelo's "Pietà," which are on temporary display. Michelangelo's heart-wrenching *Pietà* (not to be confused with his more famous *Pietà* in St. Peter's in Rome) was unfinished at his death; the female figure supporting the body of Christ on the left was added by Tiberio Calcagni (1532–65), and never has the difference between competence and genius been manifested so clearly. ⊠ *Piazza del Duomo 9* ☎ *055/2302885* ⊕ *www.operaduomo.firenze.it* 🔳 *€6* ☾ *Mon.–Sat. 9–7:30, Sun. 9–1:45.*

Orsanmichele. This multipurpose structure began as an 8th-century oratory and then in 1290 was turned into an open-air loggia for selling grain. Destroyed by fire in 1304, it was rebuilt as a loggia-market. Between 1367 and 1380 the arcades were closed and two stories were added above; finally, at century's end it was turned into a church. Inside is a beautifully detailed 14th-century Gothic tabernacle by Andrea Orcagna (1308–68). The exterior niches contain sculptures (all copies) dating from the early 1400s to the early 1600s by Donatello and Verrocchio (1435–88), among others, which were paid for by the guilds. Although it is a copy, Verrocchio's *Doubting Thomas* (circa 1470) is particularly

10

deserving of attention. Here you see Christ, like the building's other figures, entirely framed within the niche, and St. Thomas standing on its bottom ledge, with his right foot outside the niche frame. This one detail, the positioning of a single foot, brings the whole composition to life. It's possible to see the original sculptures at the **Museo di Orsanmichele**, which is open Mondays only. ⊠ *Via dei Calzaiuoli, Piazza della Repubblica* ☎ *055/284944* ⊙ *Museum: Mon. 10–5.*

Palazzo Davanzati. The prestigious Davanzati family owned this 14th-century palace in one of Florence's swankiest medieval neighborhoods. The place is a delight, as you can wander through the surprisingly light-filled courtyard, and climb the steep stairs to the *piano nobile* (there's also an elevator), where the family did most of its living. The beautiful *Sala dei Pappagalli* (Parrot Room) is adorned with trompe-l'oeil tapestries and gaily painted birds. ⊠ *Piazza Davanzati 13, Piazza della Repubblica* ☎ *055/2388610* ⊡ *€2* ⊙ *Daily 8:15–1:50. Closed 1st, 3rd, and 5th Sun. of month; closed 2nd and 4th Mon. of month.*

Palazzo Vecchio (*Old Palace*). Florence's forbidding, fortresslike city hall was begun in 1299, presumably designed by Arnolfo di Cambio, and its massive bulk and towering campanile dominate Piazza della Signoria. It was built as a meeting place for the guildsmen governing the city at the time; today it is still City Hall. The interior courtyard is a good deal less severe, having been remodeled by Michelozzo (1396–1472) in 1453; a copy of Verrocchio's bronze *puttino* (cherub), topping the central fountain, softens the space. (The original is upstairs.)

The main attraction is on the second floor: two adjoining rooms that supply one of the most startling contrasts in Florence. The first is the opulently vast **Sala dei Cinquecento** (Room of the Five Hundred), named for the 500-member Great Council, the people's assembly established after the death of Lorenzo the Magnificent, that met here. Giorgio Vasari and others decorated the room, around 1563–65, with gargantuan frescoes celebrating Florentine history; depictions of battles with nearby cities predominate. Continuing the martial theme, the room also contains Michelangelo's *Victory,* intended for the never-completed tomb of Pope Julius II (1443–1513), plus other sculptures of decidedly lesser quality.

In comparison, the little **Studiolo,** just off the Sala dei Cinquecento's entrance, was a private room meant for the duke and those whom he invited in. Here's where the melancholy Francesco I (1541–87), son of Cosimo I, stored his priceless treasures and conducted scientific experiments. Designed by Vasari, it was decorated by him, Giambologna, and many others. ⊠ *Piazza della Signoria* ☎ *055/2768465* ⊡ *€6* ⊙ *Mon.–Wed. and Fri.–Sun. 9–7, Thurs. 9–2.*

Piazza della Repubblica. The square marks the site of the ancient forum that was the core of the original Roman settlement. While the street plan around the piazza still reflects the carefully plotted Roman military encampment, the Mercato Vecchio (Old Market), which had been here since the Middle Ages, was demolished and the current piazza was constructed between 1885 and 1895 as a neoclassical showpiece. The piazza is lined with outdoor cafés, affording an excellent opportunity for people-watching.

SAN LORENZO AND BEYOND

A sculptor, painter, architect, and a poet, Florentine native son Michelangelo was a consummate genius, and some of his finest creations remain in his hometown. A key to understanding Michelangelo's genius can be found in the magnificent Cappelle Medicee, where both his sculptural and architectural prowess can clearly be seen. Planned frescoes were never completed—sadly so, for they would have shown in one space the artistic triple threat that he certainly was. The towering yet graceful *David,* his most famous work, resides in the Galleria dell'Accademia.

After visiting San Lorenzo, resist the temptation to explore the market that surrounds the church. You can always come back later, after the churches and museums have closed; the market is open until 7 pm. Note that the Museo di San Marco closes at 1:50 on weekdays.

TOP ATTRACTIONS

Cappelle Medicee (*Medici Chapels*). This magnificent complex includes the **Cappella dei Principi,** the Medici chapel and mausoleum that was begun in 1605 and kept marble workers busy for several hundred years, and the **Sagrestia Nuova** (New Sacristy), designed by Michelangelo and so called to distinguish it from Brunelleschi's Sagrestia Vecchia (Old Sacristy) in San Lorenzo.

Michelangelo received the commission for the New Sacristy in 1520 from Cardinal Giulio de' Medici (1478–1534), who later became Pope Clement VII. The cardinal wanted a new burial chapel for his cousins Giuliano, Duke of Nemours (1478–1534), and Lorenzo, Duke of Urbino (1492–1519), and he also wanted to honor his father, also named Giuliano, and his uncle, Lorenzo il Magnifico. The result was a tour de force of architecture and sculpture. Architecturally, Michelangelo was as original and inventive here as ever, but it is, quite properly, the powerfully sculpted tombs that dominate the room. The scheme is allegorical: on the tomb on the right are figures representing Day and Night, and on the tomb to the left are figures representing Dawn and Dusk; above them are idealized sculptures of the two men, usually interpreted to represent the active life and the contemplative life. But the allegorical meanings are secondary; what is most important is the intense presence of the sculptural figures and the force with which they hit the viewer. Ticket prices jump to €9 when special exhibitions are on—which is frequently. ⊠ *Piazza di Madonna degli Aldobrandini, San Lorenzo* ☎ *055/294883 reservations* 🖃 *€6; €9 during special exhibits* ☉ *Mar.–Nov., daily 8:15–3:50; Dec.–Feb., daily 8:15–1:50. Closed 1st, 3rd, and 5th Mon. and 2nd and 4th Sun. of month.*

10

FAMILY **Galleria dell'Accademia** (*Accademia Gallery*). The collection of Florentine paintings, dating from the 13th to the 18th centuries, is largely unremarkable, but the sculptures by Michelangelo are worth the price of admission. The unfinished *Slaves*, fighting their way out of their marble prisons, were meant for the tomb of Michelangelo's overly demanding patron Pope Julius II (1443–1513). But the focal point is the original *David*, moved here from Piazza della Signoria in 1873. *David* was commissioned in 1501 by the Opera del Duomo (Cathedral Works Committee), which gave the 26-year-old sculptor a leftover block of marble that had been ruined forty years earlier by two other sculptors. Michelangelo's success with the block was so dramatic that the city showered him with honors, and the Opera del Duomo voted to build him a house and a studio in which to live and work.

> **WORD OF MOUTH**
>
> "When you go to see *David* at the Accademia, go later in the afternoon (about 5 pm), the bus groups will have gone by then and the queue will be short. The gallery doesn't close until about 7 pm so you have plenty of time to see the very divine *David*."
>
> —cathies

Today *David* is beset not by Goliath but by tourists, and seeing the statue at all—much less really studying it—can be a trial. Save yourself a long wait in line by reserving tickets in advance. A Plexiglas barrier surrounds the sculpture, following a 1991 attack on it by a self-proclaimed hammer-wielding art anarchist who, luckily, inflicted only a few minor nicks on the toes. The statue is not quite what it seems. It is so poised and graceful and alert—so miraculously alive—that it is often considered the definitive sculptural embodiment of the High Renaissance perfection. But its true place in the history of art is a bit more complicated.

As Michelangelo well knew, the Renaissance painting and sculpture that preceded his work were deeply concerned with ideal form. Perfection of proportion was the ever-sought Holy Grail; during the Renaissance, ideal proportion was equated with ideal beauty, and ideal beauty was equated with spiritual perfection. But *David*, despite its supremely calm and dignified pose, departs from these ideals. Michelangelo didn't give the statue perfect proportions. The head is slightly too large for the body, the arms are too large for the torso, and the hands are dramatically large for the arms. The work was originally commissioned to adorn the exterior of the Duomo and was intended to be seen from a distance and on high. Michelangelo knew exactly what he was doing, calculating that the perspective of the viewer would be such that, in order for the statue to appear proportioned, the upper body, head, and arms would have to be bigger, as they are farther away from the viewer. But he also did it to express and embody, as powerfully as possible in a single figure, an entire biblical story. David's hands *are* big, but so was Goliath, and these are the hands that slew him.

Music lovers might want to check out the Museo degli Instrumenti Musicali contained within the Accademia; its Stradivarius is the main attraction. ⊠ *Via Ricasoli 60, San Marco* ☎ *055/294883 reservations, 055/2388609 gallery* ⊕ *www.gallerieaccademia.org* ✉ *€11, €4 reservation fee* ☉ *Tues.–Sun. 8:15–6:50.*

Florence's Trial by Fire

One of the most striking figures of Renaissance Florence was Girolamo Savonarola, a Dominican friar who, for a moment, captured the conscience of the city. In 1491 he became prior of the convent of San Marco, where he adopted a life of austerity and delivered sermons condemning Florence's excesses and the immorality of his fellow clergy. Following the death of Lorenzo de' Medici, Savonarola was instrumental in the formation of the Republic of Florence, ruled by a representative council with Christ enthroned as monarch. In one of his most memorable acts, he urged Florentines to toss worldly possessions—from frilly dresses to Botticelli paintings—onto a "bonfire of the vanities" in Piazza della Signoria. Savonarola's antagonism toward church hierarchy led to his undoing: he was excommunicated in 1497, and the following year was hanged and burned on charges of heresy. Today, at the Museo di San Marco, you can visit Savonarola's cell and see his arresting portrait.

Museo di San Marco. A Dominican convent adjacent to the church of San Marco now houses this museum, which contains many stunning works by Fra Angelico (circa 1400–55), the Dominican friar famous for his piety as well as for his painting. When the friars' cells were restructured between 1439 and 1444, he decorated many of them with frescoes meant to spur religious contemplation. His unostentatious and direct paintings exalt the simple beauties of the contemplative life. Fra Angelico's works are everywhere, from the friars' cells to the superb panel paintings on view in the museum. Don't miss the famous *Annunciation,* on the upper floor, and the works in the gallery off the cloister as you enter. Here you can see his beautiful *Last Judgment;* as usual, the tortures of the damned are far more inventive and interesting than the pleasures of the redeemed. ⊠ *Piazza San Marco 1* ☎ *055/2388608* ✉ *€4* ☉ *Weekdays 8:15–1:50, weekends 8:15–4:50. Closed 1st, 3rd, and 5th Sun., and 2nd and 4th Mon. of month.*

San Lorenzo. Brunelleschi designed this great basilica in the 15th century but never lived to see it finished. Note the dark marble lines on the floor, whose geometry underscores the "new" use of perspective. The Sagrestia Vecchia (Old Sacristy), at the end of the left transept, is the Renaissance at its purest; the roundels are by Donatello. ⊠ *Piazza San Lorenzo San Lorenzo* ✉ *€2.50* ☎ *No phone* ☉ *Nov.–Feb., Mon.–Sat. 10–5; Mar.–Oct., Mon.–Sat. 10–5, Sun. 1:30–5.*

WORTH NOTING

Biblioteca Medicea Laurenziana (*Laurentian Library*). Michelangelo the architect was every bit as original as Michelangelo the sculptor. Unlike Brunelleschi (the architect of the Spedale degli Innocenti), however, he wasn't obsessed with proportion and perfect geometry. He was interested in experimentation and invention and in the expression of a personal vision that was at times highly idiosyncratic.

It was never more idiosyncratic than in the Laurentian Library, begun in 1524 and finished in 1568 by Bartolomeo Ammannati. Its famous

10

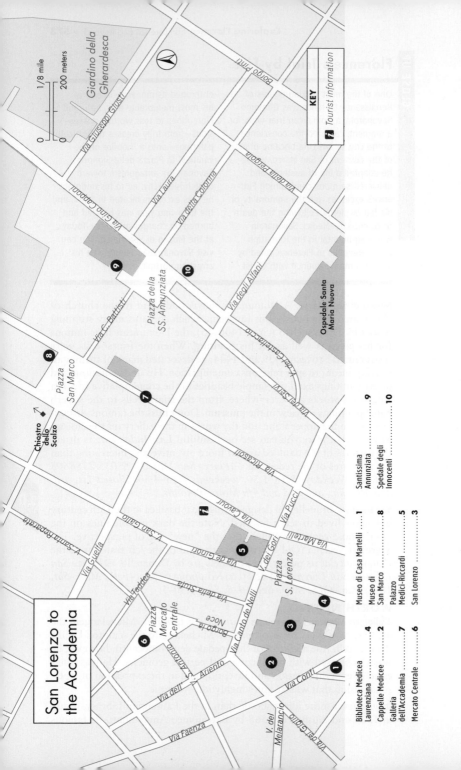

San Lorenzo to the Accademia

Giardino della Gherardesca

Piazza della SS. Annunziata

Piazza San Marco

Chiostro dello Scalzo

Ospedale Santa Maria Nuova

Piazza S. Lorenzo

Piazza Mercato Centrale

Via Giuseppe Giusti
Via Laura
Via della Colonna
Via della Pergola
Via degli Alfani
Borgo Pinti
Via Gino Capponi
Via C. Battisti
Via del Castellaccio
Via degli Servi
Via Ricasoli
Via Cavour
Via Pucci
Via Martelli
Via de' Gori
V. del Gori
Via Canto de Nelli
Via della Stufa
Via Taddea
V. San Gallo
Via Guelfa
V. Santa Reparata
Via dell' Ariento
Borgo la Noce
Via dell' Antonino
Via Conti
Via Faenza
V. del Melarancio
V. del Giglio

KEY

🛈 Tourist information

Biblioteca Medicea Laurenziana 4
Cappelle Medicee 2
Galleria dell'Accademia 7
Mercato Centrale 6
Museo di Casa Martelli 1
Museo di San Marco 8
Palazzo Medici-Riccardi 5
San Lorenzo 3
Santissima Annunziata 9
Spedale degli Innocenti 10

0   1/8 mile
0   200 meters

vestibolo, a strangely shaped ante-room, has had scholars scratching their heads for centuries. In a space more than two stories high, why did Michelangelo limit his use of columns and pilasters to the upper two-thirds of the wall? Why didn't he rest them on strong pedestals instead of on huge, decorative curli-cue scrolls, which rob them of all visual support? Why did he recess them into the wall, which makes

WORD OF MOUTH

"For a different experience, go to the Mercato Centrale (Central Market) which is full of specialty food stalls that will just amaze you! This is only a few blocks from the Accademia where the Michelangelo *David* is."

—Charnees

them look weaker still? The architectural elements here do not stand firm and strong and tall, as inside San Lorenzo, next door; instead, they seem to be pressed into the wall as if into putty, giving the room a soft, rubbery look that is one of the strangest effects ever achieved by 16th-century architecture. It's almost as if Michelangelo intentionally flouted the conventions of the High Renaissance to see what kind of bizarre, mannered effect might result. His innovations were tremendously influential, and produced a period of architectural experimentation. As his contemporary Giorgio Vasari put it, "Artisans have been infinitely and perpetually indebted to him because he broke the bonds and chains of a way of working that had become habitual by common usage."

The anteroom's staircase (best viewed straight-on), which emerges from the library with the visual force of an unstoppable lava flow, has been exempted from the criticism, however. In its highly sculptural conception and execution, it is quite simply one of the most original and fluid staircases in the world. ⊠ *Piazza San Lorenzo 9, entrance to left of San Lorenzo* ☏ *055/210760* ⊕ *www.bml.firenze.sbn.it* ⊠ *Special exhibitions €5, museum €3* ☉ *Sun.–Fri. 9–1.*

Mercato Centrale. Some of the food at this huge, two-story market hall is remarkably exotic. The ground floor contains meat and cheese stalls, as well as some very good bars that have *panini* (sandwiches), and the second floor teems with vegetable stands. At press time, the second floor was closed for renovations. ⊠ *Piazza del Mercato Centrale, San Lorenzo* ☉ *Mon.–Sat. 7–2.*

Museo di Casa Martelli. The wealthy Martelli family, long associated with the all-powerful Medici, lived, from the 16th century, in this palace on a quiet street near the basilica of San Lorenzo. The last Martelli died in 1986, and in October 2009 the *casa-museo* (house-museum) opened to the public. It's the only non-reconstructed example of such a house in all of Florence, and for that reason alone it's worth a visit. The family collected art, and while most of the stuff is B-list, a couple of gems by Beccafumi, Salvatore Rosa, and Piero di Cosimo adorn the walls. Reservations are essential, and you will be shown the glories of this place by well-informed, English-speaking guides. ⊠ *Via Zanetti 8, San Lorenzo* ☏ *055/294883* ⊕ *www.uffizi.firenze.it* ⊠ *€3* ☉ *Guided tours Thurs. 2, 3:30, and 5; Sat. 9, 10:30, and noon.*

10

Palazzo Medici-Riccardi. The main attraction of this palace, begun in 1444 by Michelozzo for Cosimo de' Medici, is the interior chapel, the so-called **Cappella dei Magi** on the *piano nobile* (second floor). Painted on its walls is Benozzo Gozzoli's famous *Procession of the Magi,* finished in 1460 and celebrating both the birth of Christ and the greatness of the Medici family. Gozzoli wasn't a revolutionary painter, and today is considered by some not quite first-rate because of his technique, which was old-fashioned even for his day. Gozzoli's gift, however, was for entrancing the eye, not challenging the mind, and on those terms his success here is beyond question. Entering the chapel is like walking into the middle of a magnificently illustrated children's storybook, and this beauty makes it one of the most enjoyable rooms in the city. Do note that officially only eight visitors are allowed in at a time for a maximum of seven minutes; sometimes, however, there are lenient guards. ✉ *Via Cavour 1, San Lorenzo* ☎ *055/2760340* 🎫 *€7* ⊘ *Thurs.–Tues. 9–7.*

Santissima Annunziata. Dating from the mid-13th century, this church was restructured in 1447 by Michelozzo, who gave it an uncommon (and lovely) entrance cloister with frescoes by Andrea del Sarto (1486–1530), Pontormo (1494–1556), and Rosso Fiorentino (1494–1540). The interior is a rarity for Florence: an overwhelming example of the Baroque. But it's not really a fair example, because it's merely 17th-century Baroque decoration applied willy-nilly to an earlier structure—exactly the sort of violent remodeling exercise that has given the Baroque a bad name. The **Cappella dell'Annunziata**, immediately inside the entrance to the left, illustrates the point. The lower half, with its stately Corinthian columns and carved frieze bearing the Medici arms, was commissioned by Piero de' Medici in 1447; the upper half, with its erupting curves and impish sculpted cherubs, was added 200 years later. Fifteenth-century-fresco enthusiasts should also note the very fine *Holy Trinity with St. Jerome* in the second chapel on the left. Done by Andrea del Castagno (circa 1421–57), it shows a wiry and emaciated St. Jerome with Paula and Eustochium, two of his closest followers. ✉ *Piazza di Santissima Annunziata* ☎ *055/266186* ⊘ *Daily 7–12:30 and 4–6:30.*

Spedale degli Innocenti. The orphanage built by Brunelleschi in 1419 to serve as an orphanage takes the historical prize as the very first Renaissance building. Brunelleschi designed its portico with his usual rigor, constructing it from the two shapes he considered mathematically (and therefore philosophically and aesthetically) perfect: the square and the circle. Below the level of the arches, the portico encloses a row of perfect cubes; above the level of the arches, the portico encloses a row of intersecting hemispheres. The entire geometric scheme is articulated with Corinthian columns, capitals, and arches borrowed directly from antiquity. At the time he designed the portico, Brunelleschi was also designing the interior of San Lorenzo, using the same basic ideas. But because the portico was finished before San Lorenzo, the Spedale degli Innocenti can claim the honor of ushering in Renaissance architecture. The 10 ceramic medallions depicting swaddled infants that decorate the portico are by Andrea della Robbia (1435–1525/28), done in about 1487.

Within the Spedale degli Innocenti is a small museum, or **Pinacoteca** (🖼€5 ☉ *Thurs.–Tues.* 9–7). Most of the objects are minor works by major artists, but well worth a look is Domenico Ghirlandaio's (1449–94) *Adorazione dei Magi* (*Adoration of the Magi*), executed in 1488. His use of color, and his eye for flora and fauna, shows that art from north of the Alps made a great impression on him. ⊠ *Piazza di Santissima Annunziata 12* ☎ *055/20371* 🖼*€4* ☉ *Mon.–Sat. 8:30–7, Sun. 8:30–2.*

SANTA MARIA NOVELLA TO THE ARNO

Piazza Santa Maria Novella, near the train station, has been restored to its former glory. The streets in and around the piazza have their share of architectural treasures, including some of Florence's most tasteful palaces. Between Santa Maria Novella and the Arno is Via Tornabuoni, Florence's finest shopping street.

TOP ATTRACTIONS

Museo Stibbert. Federico Stibbert (1838–1906), born in Florence to an Italian mother and an English father, liked to collect things. Over a lifetime of doing so, he amassed some 50,000 objects. This museum, which was also his home, displays many of them. He had a fascination with medieval armor and also collected costumes, particularly Uzbek costumes, which are exhibited in a room called the Moresque Hall. These are mingled with an extensive collection of swords, guns, and other devices whose sole function was to kill people. The paintings, most of which date from the 15th century, are largely second-rate. The house itself is an interesting amalgam of neo-Gothic, Renaissance, and English eccentric. To get here, take Bus 4 (across the street from the station at Santa Maria Novella) and get off at the stop marked "Fabbroni 4." Then follow signs to the museum. ⊠ *Via Federico Stibbert 26* ☎ *055/475520* ⊕ *www.museostibbert.it* 🖼*€5* ☉ *Mon.–Wed. 10–2, Fri.–Sun. 10–6. Tours every half hr.*

Santa Maria Novella. The facade of this church looks distinctly clumsy by later Renaissance standards, and with good reason: it is an architectural hybrid. The lower half was completed mostly in the 14th century; its pointed-arch niches and decorative marble patterns reflect the Gothic style of the day. About 100 years later (around 1456), architect Leon Battista Alberti was called in to complete the job. The marble decoration of his upper story clearly defers to the already existing work below, but the architectural motifs he added evince an entirely different style. The central doorway, the four ground-floor half-columns with Corinthian capitals, the triangular pediment atop the second story, the inscribed frieze immediately below the pediment—these are borrowings from antiquity, and they reflect the new Renaissance style in architecture, born some 35 years earlier at the Spedale degli Innocenti. Alberti's most important addition—the S-curve scrolls (called *volutes*) surmounting the decorative circles on either side of the upper story—had no precedent whatsoever in antiquity. The problem was to soften the abrupt transition between wide ground floor and narrow upper story. Alberti's solution turned out to be definitive. Once you start to look for them, you will find scrolls such as these (or sculptural variations of them) on churches all over Italy, and every one of them derives from Alberti's example here.

10

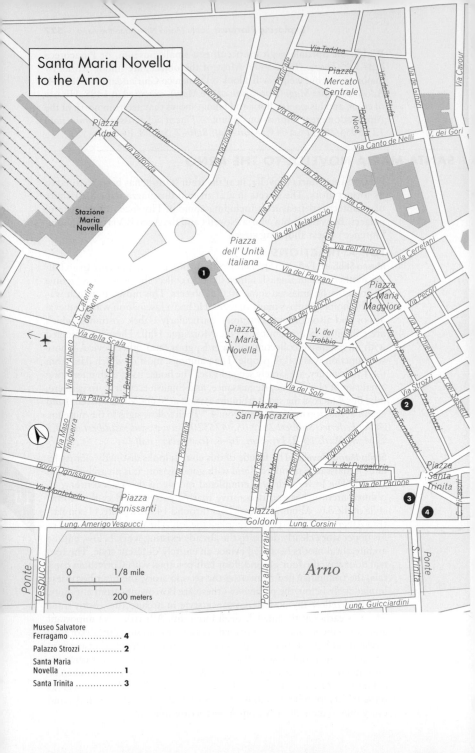

Santa Maria Novella
to the Arno

Via Taddea

Piazza
Mercato
Centrale

Via Panicale

Via Faenza

Via Nazionale

Via dell' Ariento

Via della Stufa

Noce

Via Guelfa

Via Cavour

Via del Gori

Via Canto de Nelli

V. dei Gori

Piazza
Adua

Via Fiume

Via Valfonda

Via S. Antonio

Via Faenza

Via Conti

Via del Melarancio

Via dell'Alloro

Via Cerretani

Stazione
Maria
Novella

Piazza
dell' Unità
Italiana

1

Via dei Panzani

Piazza
S. Maria
Maggiore

Via Pecori

V. S. Caterina
da Siena

Via della Scala

Via dei Banchi

Via Rondinelli

Via de' Vecchietti

Piazza
S. Maria
Novella

V. d. Belle Donne

V. del
Trebbio

Via d. Corsi

Via de' Pescioni

Via Strozzi

Via de' Tornabuoni

Via de' Sassetti

2

Via del Sole

Via Spada

Por. Rossa

Via de' Cerchi

Via dell'Albero

Via dei Conti

Via Benedetta

Via Palazzuolo

Piazza
San Pancrazio

Via Vigna Nuova

V. del Purgatorio

Piazza
Santa
Trinita

Via Maso
Finiguerra

Via d. Porcellana

Via Federighi

Via del Parione

3

4

Borgo Ognissanti

Via dei Fossi

Via del Moro

Via Montebello

Piazza
Ognissanti

Piazza
Goldoni

Lung. Amerigo Vespucci

Lung. Corsini

Ponte
Vespucci

Ponte alla Carraia

Arno

Ponte
S. Trinita

0   1/8 mile

0   200 meters

Lung. Guicciardini

The architecture of the interior is, like that of the Duomo, a dignified but somber example of Florentine Gothic. Exploration is essential, however, because the church's store of art treasures is remarkable.
Highlights include the 14th-century stained-glass rose window depicting
the *Coronation of the Virgin* (above the central entrance); the Cappella
Filippo Strozzi (to the right of the altar), containing late-15th-century
frescoes and stained glass by Filippino Lippi; the *cappella maggiore*
(the area around the high altar), displaying frescoes by Ghirlandaio;
and the Cappella Gondi (to the left of the altar), containing Filippo
Brunelleschi's famous wood crucifix, carved around 1410 and said to
have so stunned the great Donatello when he first saw it that he dropped
a basket of eggs.

Of special interest for its great historical importance and beauty is
Masaccio's *Trinity,* on the left-hand wall, almost halfway down the
nave. Painted around 1426–27 (at the same time he was working on
his frescoes in Santa Maria del Carmine), it unequivocally announced
the arrival of the Renaissance. The realism of the figure of Christ was
revolutionary in itself, but what was probably even more startling to
contemporary Florentines was the barrel vault in the background. The
mathematical rules for employing single-point perspective in painting
had just been discovered (probably by Brunelleschi), and this was one
of the first works of art to employ them with utterly convincing success.

In October 2012, the entire complex was opened to the public under a
single ticket. The resulting visit is a revelation, as the space flows, easily
and continuously, from the interior of the basilica, to the cloister outside, which leads directly to the Spanish Chapel, which in turn leads to
other, previously closed-to-the-public spaces (including the marvelous
Chiostro dei Morti).

In the first cloister is a faded and damaged fresco cycle by Paolo Uccello
depicting tales from Genesis, with a dramatic vision of the Deluge (at
press time, in restoration). Earlier and better-preserved frescoes painted
in 1348–55 by Andrea da Firenze are in the chapter house, or the
Cappellone degli Spagnoli (Spanish Chapel), off the cloister. ⊠ *Piazza
Santa Maria Novella 19* ☎ *055/210113, 055/282187 museo* ⊕ *www.
museicivicifiorentini.it* ✉ *€5* ⊘ *Mon.–Thurs. 9–5:30, Fri. 11–5:30, Sat.
9–5, Sun. 12–5 (1–5 Oct.–June).*

Santa Trinita. Started in the 11th century by Vallombrosian monks and
originally Romanesque in style, the church underwent a Gothic remodeling during the 14th century. (Remains of the Romanesque construction are visible on the interior front wall.) The major works are the
fresco cycle and altarpiece in the Cappella Sassetti, the second to the
high altar's right, painted by Ghirlandaio between 1480 and 1485.
His work here possesses such graceful decorative appeal as well as a
proud depiction of his native city (most of the cityscapes show 15th-
century Florence in all her glory). The wall frescoes illustrate scenes
from the life of St. Francis, and the altarpiece, depicting the *Adoration
of the Shepherds,* veritably glows. ⊠ *Piazza Santa Trinita* ☎ *055/216912*
⊘ *Mon.–Sat. 8–noon and 4–6.*

10

CLOSE UP

Meet the Medici

The Medici were the dominant family of Renaissance Florence, wielding political power and financing some of the world's greatest art. You'll see their names at every turn around the city. These are some of the clan's more notable members:

Cosimo il Vecchio (1389–1464), incredibly wealthy banker to the popes, was the first in the family line to act as de facto ruler of Florence. He was a great patron of the arts and architecture, and the moving force behind the family palace and the Dominican complex of San Marco.

Lorenzo il Magnifico (1449–92), grandson of Cosimo il Vecchio, presided over a Florence largely at peace with her neighbors. A collector of cameos, a writer of sonnets, and lover of ancient texts, he was the preeminent Renaissance man.

Leo X (1475–1521), also known as Giovanni de' Medici, became the first Medici pope, helping extend the family power base to include Rome and the Papal States. His reign was characterized by a host of problems, the biggest one being a former friar named Martin Luther.

Catherine de' Medici (1519–89), was married by her cousin Pope Clement VII to Henry of Valois, who later became Henry II of France. Wife of one king and mother of three, she was the first Medici to marry into European royalty. Lorenzo il Magnifico, her great-grandfather, would have been thrilled.

Cosimo I (1519–74), the first grand duke of Tuscany, should not be confused with his ancestor Cosimo il Vecchio.

WORTH NOTING

Museo Salvatore Ferragamo. If there's such a thing as a temple for footwear, this is it. The shoes in this dramatically displayed collection were designed by Salvatore Ferragamo (1898–1960) beginning in the early 20th century. Born in southern Italy, the late master jump-started his career in Hollywood by creating shoes for the likes of Mary Pickford and Rudolph Valentino. He then returned to Florence and set up shop in the 13th-century Palazzo Spini Ferroni. The collection includes about 16,000 shoes, and those on exhibition are frequently rotated. Special exhibitions are also mounted here and are well worth visiting—past shows have been devoted to Audrey Hepburn, Greta Garbo, and Marilyn Monroe. ⊠ *Via dei Tornabuoni 2* ☎ *055/3561* 🎫 *€5* ☉ *Wed.–Mon. 10–6.*

Palazzo Strozzi. The Strozzi family built this imposing palazzo in an attempt to outshine the nearby Palazzo Medici. Based on a model by Giuliano da Sangallo (circa 1452–1516) dating from around 1489 and executed between 1489 and 1504 under il Cronaca (1457–1508) and Benedetto da Maiaino (1442–97), it was inspired by Michelozzo's earlier Palazzo Medici-Riccardi. The palazzo's exterior is simple, severe, and massive: it's a testament to the wealth of a patrician, 15th-century Florentine family. The interior courtyard, entered from the rear of the palazzo, is another matter altogether. It is here that the classical vocabulary—columns, capitals, pilasters, arches, and cornices—is given uninhibited and powerful expression. The palazzo frequently hosts blockbuster art shows. ⊠ *Via Tornabuoni, Piazza della Repubblica* ☎ *055/2776461* ⊕ *www.palazzostrozzi.org* ⊒ *Free, except during exhibitions* ☉ *Daily 10–7.*

SANTA CROCE

The Santa Croce quarter, on the southeast fringe of the historic center, was built up in the Middle Ages outside the second set of medieval city walls. The centerpiece of the neighborhood was the basilica of Santa Croce, which could hold great numbers of worshippers. Since the middle of the 16th century, the vast piazza served as a playing field for no-holds-barred soccer games. A center of leather working since the Middle Ages, the neighborhood is still packed with leatherworkers and leather shops.

TOP ATTRACTIONS

Piazza Santa Croce. Originally outside the city's 12th-century walls, this piazza grew with the Franciscans, who used the large square for public preaching. During the Renaissance it was used for *giostre* (jousts), including one sponsored by Lorenzo de' Medici. "Bonfires of the vanities" occurred here, as well as soccer matches in the 16th century. Lined with many palazzi dating from the 15th century, the square remains one of Florence's loveliest piazze and is a great place to people-watch.

Fodor'sChoice
★ **Santa Croce.** Like the Duomo, this church is Gothic, but, also like the Duomo, its facade dates from the 19th century. As a burial place, the church probably contains more skeletons of Renaissance celebrities than any other in Italy. The tomb of Michelangelo is on the right at the front of the basilica; he is said to have chosen this spot so that the first thing he would see on Judgment Day, when the graves of the dead fly open, would be Brunelleschi's dome through Santa Croce's open doors. The tomb of Galileo Galilei (1564–1642) is on the left wall; he was not granted a Christian burial until 100 years after his death because of his controversial contention that Earth was not the center of the universe. The tomb of Niccolò Machiavelli (1469–1527), the political theoretician whose brutally pragmatic philosophy so influenced the Medici, is halfway down the nave on the right. The grave of Lorenzo Ghiberti, creator of the Baptistery doors, is halfway down the nave on the left. Composer Gioacchino Rossini (1792–1868) is buried at the end of the nave on the right. The monument to Dante Alighieri (1265–1321), the greatest Italian poet, is a memorial rather than a tomb (he is buried in Ravenna); it's on the right wall near the tomb of Michelangelo.

10

The collection of art within the complex is by far the most important of any church in Florence. The most famous works are probably the Giotto frescoes in the two chapels immediately to the right of the high altar. Among the church's other highlights are Donatello's *Annunciation*, 14th-century frescoes by Taddeo Gaddi, and Donatello's *Crucifix*, criticized by Brunelleschi for making Christ look like a peasant (in the chapel at the end of the left transept). Outside the church proper, in the **Museo dell'Opera di Santa Croce** off the cloister, is the 13th-century

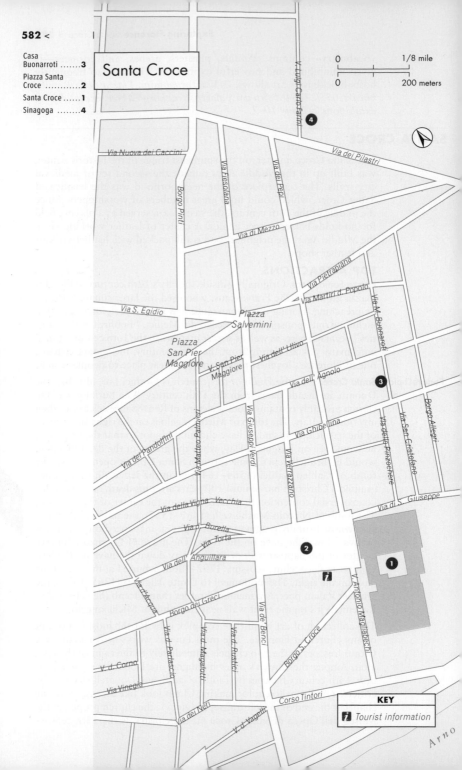

Santa Croce

0 _____ 1/8 mile

0 _____ 200 meters

V. Luigi Carlo Farini

4

Via Nuova dei Caccini

Via dei Pilastri

Borgo Pinti

Via Fiesolana

Via dei Pepi

Via di Mezzo

Via Pietrapiana

Via Martiri d. Popolo

Via M. Buonarroti

Via S. Egidio

Piazza
Salvemini

Piazza
San Pier
Maggiore

V. San Pier
Maggiore

Via dell' Ulivo

Via dell' Agnolo

3

Via Giuseppi Verdi

Via Ghibellina

Via della Pinzochere

Via San Cristofano

Borgo Allegri

Via dei Pandolfini

Via Matteo Palmieri

Via Verrazzano

Via di S. Giuseppe

Via della Vigna Vecchia

Via d. Burella

Via Torta

2

Via dell' Anguillara

V. Antonio Magliabechi

1

7

Via dell' Acqua

Borgo dei Greci

Via de' Benci

Borgo S. Croce

V. d. Parlascio

V. d. Corno

V. d. Magalotti

V. d. Rustici

Via Vinegia

Corso Tintori

Via dei Neri

V. d. Vagellai

KEY

7 Tourist information

Arno

Triumphal Cross by Cimabue (circa 1240–1302), badly damaged by the flood of 1966. A model of architectural geometry, the Cappella Pazzi, at the end of the cloister, is the work of Brunelleschi. ⊠ *Piazza Santa Croce 16* 🕿 *055/2466105* ⊕ *www.santacroceopera.it* 🎫*€6 combined admission to church and museum; €8.50 combined ticket with Casa Buonarroti* ⊗ *Mon.–Sat. 9:30–5:30, Sun. 1–5.*

Sinagoga. Jews were well settled in Florence by the end of the 14th century, but by 1570 they were required to live within the large "ghetto," at the north side of today's Piazza della Repubblica, by decree of Cosimo I, who had cut a deal with Pope Pius V (1504–72): in exchange for ghettoizing the Jews, he would receive the title Grand Duke of Tuscany.

Construction of the modern Moorish-style synagogue began in 1874 as a bequest of David Levi, who wished to endow a synagogue "worthy of the city." Falcini, Micheli, and Treves designed the building on a domed Greek cross plan with galleries in the transept and a roofline bearing three distinctive copper cupolas visible from all over Florence. The exterior has alternating bands of tan travertine and pink granite, reflecting an Islamic style repeated in Giovanni Panti's ornate interior. Of particular interest are the cast-iron gates by Pasquale Franci, the eternal light by Francesco Morini, and the Murano glass mosaics by Giacomo dal Medico. The gilded doors of the Moorish ark, which fronts the pulpit and is flanked by extravagant candelabra, are decorated with symbols of the ancient Temple of Jerusalem and bear bayonet marks from vandals. The synagogue was used as a garage by the Nazis, who failed to inflict much damage in spite of an attempt to blow up the place with dynamite. Only the columns on the left side were destroyed, and even then, the Women's Balcony above did not collapse. Note the Star of David in black and yellow marble inlay on the floor. The original capitals can be seen in the garden.

Some of the oldest and most beautiful Jewish ritual artifacts in all of Europe are displayed upstairs in the small **Museo Ebraico.** Exhibits document the Florentine Jewish community and the building of the synagogue. The donated objects all belonged to local families and date from as early as the late 16th century. Take special note of the exquisite needlework and silver pieces. A small but well-stocked gift shop is downstairs. ⊠ *Via Farini 4* 🕿 *055/2346654* 🎫 *€6.50 synagogue and museum* ⊗ *Apr.–Sept., Sun.–Thurs. 10–6, Fri. 10–2; Oct.–Mar., Sun.– Thurs. 10–3, Fri. 10–2. English guided tours: 10, 11, noon, 1, 2 (no tour at 2 on Fri.).*

WORTH NOTING

Casa Buonarroti. If you are really enjoying walking in the footsteps of the great genius, you may want to complete the picture by visiting the Buonarroti family home. Michelangelo lived here from 1516 to 1525, and later gave it to his nephew, whose son, called Michelangelo il Giovane (Michelangelo the Younger) turned it into a gallery dedicated to his great-uncle. The artist's descendants filled it with art treasures, some by Michelangelo himself. Two early marble works—the *Madonna of the Steps* and the *Battle of the Centaurs*—hint at the marvels to come. ⊠ *Via Ghibellina 70* 🕿 *055/241752* ⊕ *www.casabuonarroti.it* 🎫*€6.50* ⊗ *Fri.–Wed. 9:30–2.*

THE OLTRARNO

A walk through the Oltrarno (literally "the other side of the Arno") takes in two different aspects of Florence: the splendor of the Medici, manifest in the riches of the mammoth Palazzo Pitti and the gracious Giardino di Boboli; and the charm of the Oltrarno, a slightly gentrified but still fiercely proud working-class neighborhood with artisans' and antiques shops.

Farther east across the Arno, a series of ramps and stairs climbs to Piazzale Michelangelo, where the city lies before you in all its glory (skip this trip if it's hazy). You can avoid the long walk by taking Bus No. 12 or 13 at the west end of Ponte alle Grazie and getting off at Piazzale Michelangelo; you still have to climb the monumental stairs to and from San Miniato, but you can then take the bus from Piazzale Michelangelo back to the center of town. If you decide to take a bus, remember to buy your ticket before you board.

TOP ATTRACTIONS

Giardino di Boboli (*Boboli Gardens*). The main entrance to these land-scaped gardens is from the right side of the courtyard of **Palazzo Pitti**. The gardens began to take shape in 1549, when the Pitti family sold the palazzo to Eleanor of Toledo, wife of the Medici grand duke Cosimo I. Niccolò Tribolo (1500–50) laid out the first landscaping plans, and after his death, Ammannati, Giambologna, Bernardo Buontalenti (circa 1536–1608), and Giulio (1571–1635) and Alfonso Parigi (1606–56), among others, continued his work. Italian landscaping is less formal than French, but still full of sweeping drama. A copy of the famous *Morgante,* Cosimo I's favorite dwarf astride a particularly unhappy tortoise, is near the exit. Sculpted by Valerio Cioli (circa 1529–99), the work seems to illustrate the perils of culinary overindulgence. A visit here can be disappointing, because the gardens are somewhat underplanted and under-cared for, but it's still a great walk with some terrific views. ⊠ *Enter through Palazzo Pitti* ☎ *055/294883* ⊕ *www. polomuseale.firenze.it* 🖾 *€10, combined ticket with Museo degli Argenti, Museo delle Porcellane, Villa Bardini, and Giardino Bardini* ☉ *Jan., Feb., Nov., and Dec., daily 8:15–4:30; Mar., daily 8:15–5:30; Apr., May, Sept., and Oct., daily 8:15–6:30; June–Aug., daily 8:15–7:30. Closed 1st and last Mon. of month.*

Palazzo Pitti. This enormous palace is one of Florence's largest architectural set pieces. The original palazzo, built for the Pitti family around 1460, comprised only the main entrance and the three windows on either side. In 1549 the property was sold to the Medici, and Bartolomeo Ammannati was called in to make substantial additions. Although he apparently operated on the principle that more is better, he succeeded only in producing proof that more is just that: more.

Today the palace houses several museums: The **Museo degli Argenti** displays a vast collection of Medici treasures, including exquisite antique vases belonging to Lorenzo the Magnificent. The **Galleria del Costume** showcases fashions from the past 300 years. The **Galleria d'Arte Moderna** holds a collection of 19th- and 20th-century paintings, mostly Tuscan. Most famous of the Pitti galleries is the **Galleria**

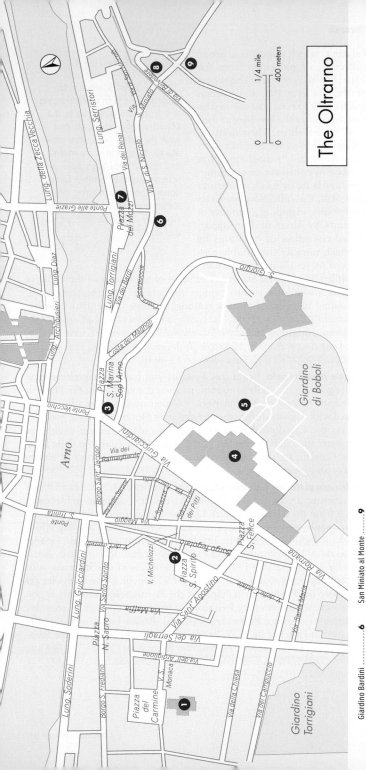

The Oltrarno

0   1/4 mile

0   400 meters

Giardino Bardini **6**
Giardino di Boboli **5**
Museo Bardini **7**
Palazzo Pitti **4**
Piazzale
Michelangelo **8**

San Miniato al Monte **9**
Santa Felicita **3**
Santa Maria del Carmine ... **1**
Santo Spirito **2**

Palatina, which contains a broad collection of paintings from the 15th to 17th centuries. The rooms of the Galleria Palatina remain much as the Lorena, the rulers who took over after the last Medici died in 1737, left them. Their floor-to-ceiling paintings are considered by some to be Italy's most egregious exercise in conspicuous consumption, aesthetic overkill, and trumpery. Still, the collection possesses high points, including a number of portraits by Titian and an unparalleled collection of paintings by Raphael, notably the double portraits of Angelo Doni and his wife, the sullen Maddalena Strozzi. The price of admission to the Galleria Palatina also allows you to explore the former **Appartamenti Reali,** containing furnishings from a remodeling done in the 19th century. ✉ *Piazza Pitti* ☎ *055/210323* ✉ *Galleria Palatina and Galleria d'Arte Moderna, combined ticket €13; Galleria del Costume, Giardino Bardini, Giardino di Boboli, Museo degli Argenti, and Museo Porcelleane, combined ticket €10* ☉ *Tues.–Sun. 8:15–6:50.*

> ## WORD OF MOUTH
>
> "My advice for Florence is to explore the city in early morning and nighttime walks. Go to the Oltrarno across the river. And walk the side streets—the crowds always tramp the same routes, and they're easy to escape—just take a couple of random turns down a pokey side street or two. It's amazing how very few tourists stray off the beaten path in this city."
>
> —Apres Londee

FAMILY **Piazzale Michelangelo.** From this lookout you have a marvelous view of Florence and the hills around it, rivaling the vista from the Forte di Belvedere. A copy of Michelangelo's *David* overlooks outdoor cafés packed with tourists during the day and with Florentines in the evening. In May the **Giardino dell'Iris** (Iris Garden) off the piazza is abloom with more than 2,500 varieties of the flower. The **Giardino delle Rose** (Rose Garden) on the terraces below the piazza is also in full bloom in May and June.

San Miniato al Monte. This church, like the Baptistery, is a fine example of Romanesque architecture and is one of the oldest churches in Florence, dating from the 11th century. A 12th-century mosaic topped by a gilt bronze eagle, emblem of San Miniato's sponsors, the Calimala (cloth merchants' guild) crowns the lovely green-and-white marble facade. Inside are a 13th-century inlaid-marble floor and apse mosaic. Artist Spinello Aretino (1350–1410) covered the walls of the **Sagrestia** with frescoes depicting scenes from the life of St. Benedict. The **Cappella del Cardinale del Portogallo** (Chapel of the Portuguese Cardinal) is one of the richest 15th-century Renaissance works in Florence. It contains the tomb of a young Portuguese cardinal, Prince James of Lusitania, who died in Florence in 1459. Its glorious ceiling is by Luca della Robbia, and the sculpted tomb by Antonio Rossellino (1427–79). ✉ *Viale Galileo Galilei, Piazzale Michelangelo, Lungarno Sud* ☎ *055/2342731* ☉ *Daily 8–12:30 and 3–5:15.*

Continued on page 593

WHO'S WHO IN RENAISSANCE ART

Michelangelo. Leonardo da Vinci. Raphael. This heady triumvirate of the Italian Renaissance is synonymous with artistic genius. Yet they are only three of the remarkable cast of characters whose work defines the Renaissance, that extraordinary flourishing of art and culture in Italy, especially in Florence, as the Middle Ages drew to a close. The artists were visionaries, who redefined painting, sculpture, architecture, and even what it means to be an artist.

THE PIONEER. In the mid-14th century, a few artists began to move away the flat, two-dimensional painting of the Middle Ages. **Giotto**, who painted seemingly three-dimensional figures who show emotion, had a major impact on the artists of the next century.

THE GROUNDBREAKERS. The generations of **Brunelleschi** and **Botticelli** took center stage in the 15th century. **Ghiberti, Masaccio, Donatello, Uccello, Fra Angelico**, and **Filippo Lippi** were other major players. Part of the Renaissance (or "re-birth") was a renewed interest in classical sources—the texts, monuments, and sculpture of Ancient Greece and Rome. Perspective and the illusion of three-dimensional space in painting was another discovery of this era, known as the Early Renaissance. Suddenly the art appearing on the walls looked real, or more realistic than it used to.

Roman ruins were not the only thing to inspire these artists. There was an incredible exchange of ideas going on. In Santa Maria del Carmine, Filippo Lippi was inspired by the work of Masaccio, who in turn was a friend of Brunelleschi. Young artists also learned from the masters via the apprentice system. Ghiberti's workshop (*bottega* in Italian) included, at one time or another, Donatello, Masaccio, and Uccello. Botticelli was apprenticed to Filippo Lippi.

THE BIG THREE. The mathematical rationality and precision of 15th-century art gave way to what is known as the High Renaissance. **Leonardo, Michelangelo**, and **Raphael** were much more concerned with portraying the body in all its glory and with achieving harmony and grandeur in their work. Oil paint, used infrequently up until this time, became more widely employed: as a result, Leonardo's colors are deeper, more sensual, more alive. For one brief period, all three were in Florence at the same time. Michelangelo and Leonardo surely knew one another, as they were simultaneously working on frescoes (never completed) inside Palazzo Vecchio.

When Michelangelo left Florence for Rome in 1508, he began the slow drain of artistic exodus from Florence, which never really recovered her previous glory.

10

A RENAISSANCE TIMELINE

IN THE WORLD

Black Death in Europe kills one third of the population, 1347-50.

Joan of Arc burned at the stake, 1431.

IN FLORENCE

Dante, a native of Florence, writes *The Divine Comedy*, 1302-21.

Founding of the Medici bank, 1397.

Medici family made official papal bankers.

1434, Cosimo il Vecchio becomes de facto ruler of Florence. The Medici family will dominate the city until 1494.

1300

1400

IN ART

EARLY RENAISSANCE

GIOTTO (ca. 1267-1337)

Masaccio and Masolino fresco Santa Maria del Carmine, 1424-28.

Giotto fresoes in Santa Croce, 1320-25.

BRUNELLESCHI (1377-1446)

LORENZO GHIBERTI (ca. 1381-1455)

DONATELLO (ca. 1386-1466)

PAOLO UCCELLO (1397-1475)

FRA ANGELICO (ca. 1400-1455)

MASACCIO (1401-1428)

FILIPPO LIPPI (ca. 1406-1469)

1334, 67-year-old Giotto is appointed chief architect of Santa Maria del Fiore, Florence's Duomo (below). He begins to work on the Campanile, which will be completed in 1359, after his death.

Donatello sculpts his bronze *David*, ca. 1440.

Fra Angelico frescoes friars' cells in San Marco, c 1438-45.

Uccello's *Sir John Hawkwood*, ca. 1436.

Ghiberti wins the competition for the Baptistery doors (above) in Florence, 1401.

Brunelleschi wins the competition for the Duomo's cupola (right), 1418.

▼ Gutenberg Bible is printed, 1455.

▼ Columbus discovers America, 1492.

▼ Martin Luther posts his 95 theses on the door at Wittenberg, kicking off the Protestant Reformation, 1517.

▼ Constantinople falls to the Turks, 1453.

▼ Machiavelli's *Prince* appears, 1513.

▼ Copernicus proves that the earth is not the center of the universe, 1530-43.

▼ Lorenzo "il Magnifico" (right), the Medici patron of the arts, rules in Florence, 1449-92.

▼ Two Medici popes Leo X (1513-21) and Clement VII (1523-34) in Rome.

▼ Catherine de' Medici becomes Queen of France, 1547.

1450   **1500**   **1550**

HIGH RENAISSANCE   MANNERISM

▼ Fra Filippo Lippi's *Madonna and Child*, ca. 1452.

▼ 1508, Raphael begins work on the chambers in the Vatican, Rome.

▼ Giorgio Vasari publishes his first edition of *Lives of the Artists*, 1550.

▼ 1504, Michelangelo's *David* is put on display in Piazza della Signoria, where it remains until 1873.

Botticelli paints the *Birth of Venus*, ca. 1482.

▼ Michelangelo begins to fresco the Sistine Chapel ceiling, 1508.

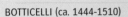
BOTTICELLI (ca. 1444-1510)

LEONARDO DA VINCI (1452-1519)

RAPHAEL (1483-1520)

MICHELANGELO (1475-1564)

Leonardo paints *The Last Supper* in Milan, 1495-98.

10

Giotto's *Nativity*   Donatello's *St. John the Baptist*   Ghiberti's *Gates of Paradise*

GIOTTO (CA. 1267-1337)
Painter/architect from a small town north of Florence.
He unequivocally set Italian painting on the course that led to the triumphs of the Renaissance masters. Unlike the rather flat, two-dimensional forms found in then prevailing Byzantine art, Giotto's figures have a fresh, life-like quality. The people in his paintings have bulk, and they show emotion, which you can see on their faces and in their gestures. This was something new in the late Middle Ages. Without Giotto, there wouldn't have been a Raphael.
In Florence: Santa Croce; Uffizi; Campanile; Santa Maria Novella
Elsewhere in Italy: Scrovegni Chapel, Padua; Vatican Museums, Rome

FILIPPO BRUNELLESCHI (1377-1446)
Architect/engineer from Florence.
If Brunelleschi had beaten Ghiberti in the Baptistery doors competition in Florence, the city's Duomo most likely would not have the striking appearance and authority that it has today. After his loss, he sulked off to Rome, where he studied the ancient Roman structures first-hand. Brunelleschi figured out how to vault the Duomo's dome, a structure unprecedented in its colossal size and great height. His Ospedale degli Innocenti employs classical elements in the creation of a stunning, new architectural statement; it is the first truly Renaissance structure.
In Florence: Duomo; Ospedale degli Innocenti; San Lorenzo; Santo Spirito; Baptistery Doors Competition Entry, Bargello; Santa Croce

LORENZO GHIBERTI (CA. 1381-1455)
Sculptor from Florence.
Ghiberti won a competition—besting his chief rival, Brunelleschi—to cast the gilded bronze North Doors of the Baptistery in Florence. These doors, and the East Doors that he subsequently executed, took up the next 50 years of his life. He created intricately worked figures that are more true-to-life than any since antiquity, and he was one of the first Renaissance sculptors to work in bronze. Ghiberti taught the next generation of artists; Donatello, Uccello, and Masaccio all passed through his studio.
In Florence: Door Copies, Baptistery; Original Doors, Museo dell'Opera del Duomo; Baptistry Door Competition Entry, Bargello; Orsanmichele

DONATELLO (CA. 1386-1466)
Sculptor from Florence.
Donatello was an innovator who, like his good friend Brunelleschi, spent most of his long life in Florence. Consumed with the science of optics, he used light and shadow to create the effects of nearness and distance. He made an essentially flat slab look like a three-dimensional scene. His bronze *David* is probably the first free-standing male nude since antiquity. Not only technically brilliant, his work is also emotionally resonant; few sculptors are as expressive.
In Florence: *David*, Bargello; *St. Mark*, Orsanmichele; Palazzo Vecchio; Museo dell'Opera del Duomo; San Lorenzo; Santa Croce
Elsewhere in Italy: Padua; Prato; Venice

Fra Angelico's *The Deposition*   Masaccio's *Trinity*   Filippo Lippi's *Madonna and Child*

PAOLO UCCELLO (1397-1475)
Painter from Florence.
Renaissance chronicler Vasari once observed that had Uccello not been so obsessed with the mathematical problems posed by perspective, he would have been a very good painter. The struggle to master single-point perspective and to render motion in two dimensions is nowhere more apparent than in his battle scenes. His first major commission in Florence was the gargantuan fresco of the English mercenary Sir John Hawkwood (the Italians called him Giovanni Acuto) in Florence's Duomo.
In Florence: *Sir John Hawkwood,* **Duomo;** *Battle of San Romano,* **Uffizi; Santa Maria Novella**
Elsewhere in Italy: Urbino, Prato

FRA ANGELICO (CA. 1400-1455)
Painter from a small town north of Florence.
A Dominican friar, who eventually made his way to the convent of San Marco, Fra Angelico and his assistants painted frescoes for aid in prayer and meditation. He was known for his piety; Vasari wrote that Fra Angelico could never paint a crucifix without a tear running down his face. Perhaps no other painter so successfully translated the mysteries of faith and the sacred into painting. And yet his figures emote, his command of perspective is superb, and his use of color startles even today.
In Florence: Museo di San Marco; Uffizi
Elsewhere in Italy: Vatican Museums, Rome; Fiesole; Cortona; Perugia; Orvieto

MASACCIO (1401-1428)
Painter from San Giovanni Valdarno, southeast of Florence.
Masaccio and Masolino, a frequent collaborator, worked most famously together at Santa Maria del Carmine. Their frescoes of the life of St. Peter use light to mold figures in the painting by imitating the way light falls on figures in real life. Masaccio also pioneered the use of single-point perspective, masterfully rendered in his *Trinity*. His friend Brunelleschi probably introduced him to the technique, yet another step forward in rendering things the way the eye sees them. Masaccio died young and under mysterious circumstances.
In Florence: Santa Maria del Carmine; *Trinity,* **Santa Maria Novella**

FILIPPO LIPPI (CA. 1406-1469)
Painter from Prato.
At a young age, Filippo Lippi entered the friary of Santa Maria del Carmine, where he was highly influenced by Masaccio and Masolino's frescoes. His religious vows appear to have made less of an impact; his affair with a young nun produced a son, Filippino (Little Philip, who later apprenticed with Botticelli), and a daughter. His religious paintings often have a playful, humorous note; some of his angels are downright impish and look directly out at the viewer. Lippi links the earlier painters of the 15th century with those who follow; Botticelli apprenticed with him.
In Florence: Uffizi; Palazzo Medici Riccardi; San Lorenzo; Palazzo Pitti
Elsewhere in Italy: Prato

Botticelli's *Primavera*

Leonardo's *Portrait of a Young Woman*

Raphael's *Madonna on the Meadow*

BOTTICELLI (CA. 1444-1510)
Painter from Florence.
Botticelli's work is characterized by stunning, elongated blondes, cherubic angels (something he undoubtedly learned from his time with Filippo Lippi), and tender Christs. Though he did many religious paintings, he also painted monumental, nonreligious panels—his *Birth of Venus* and *Primavera* being the two most famous of these. A brief sojourn took him to Rome, where he and a number of other artists frescoed the Sistine Chapel walls.
In Florence: ***Birth of Venus*, *Primavera*, Uffizi; Palazzo Pitti**
Elsewhere in Italy: **Vatican Museums, Rome**

LEONARDO DA VINCI (1452-1519)
Painter/sculptor/engineer from Anchiano, a small town outside Vinci.
Leonardo never lingered long in any place; his restless nature and his international reputation led to commissions throughout Italy, and took him to Milan, Vigevano, Pavia, Rome, and, ultimately, France. Though he is most famous for his mysterious *Mona Lisa* (at the Louvre in Paris), he painted other penetrating, psychological portraits in addition to his scientific experiments: his design for a flying machine (never built) predates Kitty Hawk by nearly 500 years. The greatest collection of Leonardo's work in Italy can be seen on one wall in the Uffizi.
In Florence: ***Adoration of the Magi*, Uffizi**
Elsewhere in Italy: ***Last Supper*, Santa Maria delle Grazie, Milan**

RAPHAEL (1483-1520)
Painter/architect from Urbino.
Raphael spent only four highly productive years of his short life in Florence, where he turned out made-to-order panel paintings of the Madonna and Child for a hungry public; he also executed a number of portraits of Florentine aristocrats. Perhaps no other artist had such a fine command of line and color, and could render it, seemingly effortlessly, in paint. His painting acquired new authority after he came up against Michelangelo toiling away on the Sistine ceiling. Raphael worked nearly next door in the Vatican, where his figures take on an epic, Michelangelesque scale.
In Florence: **Uffizi; Palazzo Pitti**
Elsewhere in Italy: **Vatican Museums, Rome**

MICHELANGELO (1475-1564)
Painter/sculptor/architect from Caprese.
Although Florentine and proud of it (he famously signed his St. Peter's *Pietà* to avoid confusion about where he was from), he spent most of his 89 years outside his native city. He painted and sculpted the male body on an epic scale and glorified it while doing so. Though he complained throughout the proceedings that he was really a sculptor, Michelangelo's Sistine Chapel ceiling is arguably the greatest fresco cycle ever painted (and the massive figures owe no small debt to Giotto).
In Florence: ***David*, Galleria dell'Accademia; Uffizi; Casa Buonarroti; Bargello**
Elsewhere in Italy: **St. Peter's Basilica, Vatican Museums, and Piazza del Campidoglio in Rome**

Santa Maria del Carmine. The **Cappella Brancacci,** at the end of the right transept of this church, houses a masterpiece of Renaissance painting: a fresco cycle that changed the course of Western art. Fire almost destroyed the church in the 18th century; miraculously, the Brancacci Chapel survived almost intact. The cycle is the work of three artists: Masaccio and Masolino (1383–circa 1447), who began it around 1424, and Filippino Lippi, who finished it some 50 years later, after a long interruption during which the sponsoring Brancacci family was exiled. It was Masaccio's work that opened a new frontier for painting, as he was among the first artists to employ single-point perspective; tragically, he died in 1428 at the age of 27, so he didn't live to experience the revolution his innovations caused.

Masaccio collaborated with Masolino on several of the frescoes, but his style predomintates in the *Tribute Money,* on the upper-left wall; *St. Peter Baptizing,* on the upper altar wall; the *Distribution of Goods,* on the lower altar wall; and the *Expulsion of Adam and Eve,* on the chapel's upper-left entrance pier. If you look closely at the last painting and compare it with some of the chapel's other works, you should see a pronounced difference. The figures of Adam and Eve possess a startling presence primarily thanks to the dramatic way in which their bodies seem to reflect light. Masaccio here shaded his figures consistently, so as to suggest a single, strong source of light within the world of the painting but outside its frame. In so doing, he succeeded in imitating with paint the real-world effect of light on mass, and he thereby imparted to his figures a sculptural reality unprecedented in his day.

These matters have to do with technique, but with the *Expulsion of Adam and Eve* his skill went beyond mere technical innovation. In the faces of Adam and Eve, you see more than finely modeled figures; you see terrible shame and suffering depicted with a humanity rarely achieved in art. Reservations to see the chapel are mandatory, but can be booked on the same day. Your time inside is limited to 15 minutes—a frustration that's only partly mitigated by a highly informative 40-minute DVD about the history of the chapel you can watch either before or after your visit. ⊠ *Piazza del Carmine, Santo Spirito* ☎ *055/2768224 reservations* ⛫*€4* ☾ *Mon. and Wed.–Sat. 10–5, Sun. 1–5.*

10

WORTH NOTING

Giardino Bardini. Garden lovers, those who crave a view, and those who enjoy a nice hike should visit this lovely villa and garden, whose history spans centuries. The villa had a walled garden as early as the 14th century; the "Grand Stairs"—a zigzag ascent well worth scaling—has been around since the 16th. The garden is filled with irises, roses, and heirloom flowers, and includes a Japanese garden and statuary. A very pretty walk (all for the same admission ticket) takes you through the Giardino di Boboli and past the Forte Belvedere to the upper entrance to the giardino. ⊠ *Via de'Bardini, San Niccolò* ☎ *005/294883* ⛫*€10 combined ticket with Galleria Costume, Giardino di Boboli, Museo Argenti, Museo Porcellane* ☾ *Jan., Feb., Nov., and Dec., daily 8:15–4:30; Mar., daily 8:15–5:30; Apr., May, Sept., and Oct., daily 8:15–6:30; June–Aug., daily 8:15–7:30. Closed 1st and last Mon. of month.*

Museo Bardini. The 19th-century collector and antiquarian Stefano Bardini turned his palace into his own private museum. Upon his death, the collection was turned over to the state and includes an interesting assortment of Etruscan pieces, sculpture, paintings, and furniture that dates mostly from the Renaissance and the Baroque. ✉ *Piazza de' Mozzi 1* ☎ *055/2342427* ⊕ *www.museifiorentini.it* ▧ *€5* ⊙ *Thurs.–Mon. 11–5.*

Santa Felicita. This late-Baroque church (its facade was remodeled between 1736 and 1739) contains the mannerist Jacopo Pontormo's *Deposition,* the centerpiece of the Cappella Capponi (executed 1525–28) and a masterpiece of 16th-century Florentine art. The remote figures, which transcend the realm of Renaissance classical form, are portrayed in tangled shapes and intense pastel colors (well preserved because of the low lights in the church), in a space and depth that defy reality. Note, too, the exquisitely frescoed *Annunciation,* also by Pontormo, at a right angle to the *Deposition.* The granite column in the piazza was erected in 1381 and marks a Christian cemetery. ✉ *Piazza Santa Felicita, Via Guicciardini, Palazzo Pitti* ⊙ *Mon.–Sat. 9–noon and 3–6, Sun. 9–1.*

Santo Spirito. The plain, unfinished facade gives nothing away, but the interior, although it appears chilly compared with later churches, is one of the most important examples of Renaissance architecture in Italy.

The interior is one of a pair designed in Florence by Filippo Brunelleschi in the early decades of the 15th century (the other is San Lorenzo). It was here that Brunelleschi supplied definitive solutions to the two major problems of interior Renaissance church design: how to build a cross-shaped interior using classical architectural elements borrowed from antiquity, and how to reflect in that interior the order and regularity that Renaissance scientists (among them Brunelleschi himself) were at the time discovering in the natural world around them.

Brunelleschi's solution to the first problem was brilliantly simple: turn a Greek temple inside out. While ancient Greek temples were walled buildings surrounded by classical colonnades, Brunelleschi's churches were classical arcades surrounded by walled buildings. This brilliant architectural idea overthrew the previous era's religious taboo against pagan architecture once and for all, triumphantly claiming that architecture for Christian use.

Brunelleschi's solution to the second problem—making the entire interior orderly and regular—was mathematically precise: he designed the ground plan of the church so that all its parts were proportionally related. The transepts and nave have exactly the same width; the side aisles are precisely half as wide as the nave; the little chapels off the side aisles are exactly half as deep as the side aisles; the chancel and transepts are exactly one-eighth the depth of the nave; and so on, with dizzying exactitude. For Brunelleschi, such a design technique was a matter of passionate conviction. Like most theoreticians of his day, he believed that mathematical regularity and aesthetic beauty were flip sides of the same coin, that one was not possible without the other.

In the refectory, adjacent to the church, you can see Andrea Orcagna's highly damaged fresco of the Crucifixion. ✉ *Piazza Santo Spirito* ☎ *055/210030* ▧ *Church free, refectory €3*

WHERE TO EAT

Florence's popularity with tourists means that, unfortunately, there's a higher percentage of mediocre restaurants here than you'll find in most Italian towns. Some restaurant owners cut corners and let standards slip, knowing that a customer today is unlikely to return tomorrow, regardless of the quality of the meal. So, if you're looking to eat well, it pays to do some research, starting with the recommendations here—we promise there's not a tourist trap in the bunch. Try to avoid places where waiters stand outside and invite you in, as well as those spots with little billboards outside showing pictures of their food. (Both practices are prevalent around San Lorenzo.)

Hours start at around 1 for lunch and 8 for dinner. Many of Florence's restaurants are small, so reservations are a must. You can sample such specialties as creamy *fegatini* (a chicken-liver spread) and *ribollita* (minestrone thickened with bread and beans and swirled with extra-virgin olive oil) in a bustling, convivial trattoria, where you share long wooden tables set with paper place mats, or in an upscale *ristorante* with linen tablecloths and napkins.

Those with a sense of culinary adventure should not miss the tripe sandwich, served from stands throughout town. This Florentine favorite comes with a fragrant *salsa verde* (green sauce) or a piquant red hot sauce—or both. Follow the Florentines' lead and take a break at an *enoteca* (wine bar) during the day and discover some excellent Chiantis and Super Tuscans from small producers who rarely export.

Please note that restaurant prices for "average meal" include first course (primo), second course (secondo), and dessert (dolce).

Use the coordinate (⊕ B2) at the end of each listing to locate a site on the Where to Eat and Stay in Florence map.

THE DUOMO TO THE PONTE VECCHIO

10

$ ITALIAN 🍴 **Caffè delle Carrozze.** The convenient Caffè delle Carrozze, around the corner from the Uffizi and practically at the foot of the Ponte Vecchio, has many terrific flavors, especially the chocolate-chip laced coffee. [$] *Average meal: €3* ✉ *Piazza del Pesce 3–5/r, Piazza della Signoria* ☎ *055/2396810* 💳 *No credit cards* ⊕ *D3.*

$ ITALIAN 🍴 **Coquinarius.** This rustically elegant space, which has served many purposes over the past 600 years, offers some of the tastiest food in town at great prices. It's the perfect place to come if you aren't sure what you're hungry for, as they offer a little bit of everything: salad-lovers will have a hard time choosing from among the lengthy list (the Scozzese, with poached chicken, avocado, and bacon, is a winner); those with a yen for pasta will face agonizing choices (the ravioli with pecorino and pears is particularly good). A revolving list of *piatti unici* (single dishes that can be ordered on their own, usually served only at lunch) can also whet the whistle, as well as terrific cheese and cured meat plates. The well-culled wine list has lots of great wines by the glass, and even more by the bottle. [$] *Average meal: €20* ✉ *Via delle Oche 15/r, Piazza della Signoria* ☎ *055/2302153* 🌐 *www.coquinarius.it* ✍ *Reservations essential* ⊕ *E3.*

BEST BETS FOR FLORENCE DINING

With hundreds of restaurants to choose from, how will you decide where to eat? Fodor's writers and editors have selected their favorite restaurants by price, cuisine, and experience in the Best Bets lists below. In the first column, Fodor's Choice properties represent the "best of the best."

Fodor'sChoice★

Cibrèo, $$$$, p. 602
Mario, $, p. 598
Ora d'Aria, $$$$, p. 597
Taverna del Bronzino, $$$, p. 598

Best by Price

$

All'Antico Vinaio, p. 599
Baldovino, p. 602
Cibrèo Trattoria, p. 602
da Nerbone, p. 597
da Rocco, p. 602
Il Santo Bevitore, p. 604
La Casalinga, p. 604
Mario, p. 598
Osteria Antica Mescita San Niccolò, p. 605

$$

Il Latini, p. 599
Osteria de'Benci, p. 603

$$$

La Giostra, p. 603
Taverna del Bronzino, p. 598

$$$$

Borgo San Jacopo, p. 604
Cibrèo, p. 602

Best Experiences

ALTA CUCINA (SOPHISTICATED CUISINE)

Enoteca Pinchiorri, $$$$, p. 602
Ora d'Aria, $$$$, p. 597
Taverna del Bronzino, $$$, p. 598

BISTECCA FIORENTINA (TUSCAN STEAK)

Buca Lapi, $$$$, p. 598
Il Latini, $$, p. 599
La Giostra, $$$, p. 603

Osteria de'Benci, $$, p. 603

CASALINGA (HOME COOKING)

La Casalinga, $, p. 604
Mario, $, p. 598

EXCEPTIONAL WINE LIST

Cantinetta Antinori, $$$, p. 598
Enoteca Pinchiorri, $$$$, p. 602
Fuori Porta, $, p. 604
Taverna del Bronzino, $$$, p. 598

GOOD FOR KIDS

Baldovino, $, p. 602
Il Latini, $$, p. 599

GOOD FOR PEOPLE-WATCHING

Cantinetta Antinori, $$$, p. 598
La Giostra, $$$, p. 603

GOOD FOR VEGETARIANS

Antico Noe, $$, p. 599
La Giostra, $$$, p. 603

Ora d'Aria, $$$$, p. 597
Osteria de'Benci, $$, p. 603

LUNCH SPOTS

Antico Noe, $$, p. 599
Cantinetta Antinori, $$$, p. 598
Mario, $, p. 598

OUTDOOR DINING

Fuori Porta, $, p. 604
Osteria de'Benci, $$, p. 603

POPULAR WITH LOCALS

La Casalinga, $, p. 604
La Giostra, $$$, p. 603
La Vecchia Bettola, $$, p. 605
Mario, $, p. 598
Osteria de'Benci, $$, p. 603

ROMANTIC

Enoteca Pinchiorri, $$$$, p. 602

WINE BARS

Casa del Vino, p. 611
Il Santino, p. 611
Le Volpi e l'Uva, p. 611

$ 🍴 **Grom.** A stone's throw from the Duomo, this is one of the best gelaterias in town. Flavors change frequently according to the season, so expect a fragrant *gelato di cannella* (cinnamon ice cream) in winter and lively fresh fruit flavors in summer. Though the original Grom hails from Turin (and there's a Grom in New York City), this is still probably the best gelato in town. [$] *Average meal: €5* ✉ *Via del Campanile, Duomo* ☎ *055/216158* 🌐 *www.grom.it* 💳 *No credit cards* ✥ *E3.*

ITALIAN
Fodor's Choice ★

$ 🍴 **'ino.** Serving arguably the best *panini* (sandwiches) in town, proprietor Alessandro sources only the very best ingredients. Located right behind the Uffizi, 'ino is a perfect place to grab a tasty sandwich and glass of wine before forging on to the next museum. [$] *Average meal: €8* ✉ *Via dei Georgofili 3/r–7/r, Piazza della Signoria, Piazza della Signoria* ☎ *055/219208* ✥ *E4.*

ITALIAN

$$$$ 🍴 **Ora d'Aria.** The name means "Hour of Air" and refers to the time of day when prisoners were let outside for fresh air—alluding to the fact that this gem was originally located across the street from what was once the old prison. In the kitchen, gifted young chef Marco Stabile turns out exquisite Tuscan classics as well as more fanciful dishes, which are as beautiful as they are delicious; intrepid diners will be vastly rewarded for ordering the tortellini *farciti con piccione* (stuffed with pigeon) if it's on the day's menu. Two tasting menus give Stabile even greater opportunity to shine, and the carefully culled wine list has something to please every palate. Do not miss his tiramisù espresso—something halfway between a dessert and a coffee. In fact, if you're a serious food lover, do not miss this place. (If the prices seem daunting, the lunch menu is significantly less expensive than dinner.) [$] *Average meal: €76* ✉ *Via Georgofili 79/r, Piazza della Signoria* ☎ *055/2001699* ✍ *Reservations essential* ⏲ *Closed Sun.* ✥ *E4.*

MODERN ITALIAN
Fodor's Choice ★

$$ 🍴 **Pegna.** Looking for some cheddar cheese to pile in your panino? Pegna has been selling both Italian and non-Italian food since 1860. It's closed Saturday afternoon in July and August, Wednesday afternoon September through June, and Sunday year-round. [$] *Average meal: €25* ✉ *Via dello Studio 8, Duomo* ☎ *055/282701* 🌐 *www.pegnafirenze.com* ✥ *F3.*

ITALIAN

SAN LORENZO AND BEYOND

$ 🍴 **Baroni.** The cheese collection at Baroni may be the most comprehensive in Florence. They also have high-quality truffle products, vinegars, and other delicacies. [$] *Average meal: €10* ✉ *Mercato Central, enter at Via Signa, San Lorenzo* ☎ *055/289576* 🌐 *www.baronialimentari.it* ✥ *E1.*

INTERNATIONAL

$ 🍴 **da Nerbone.** This *tavola calda* in the middle of the covered Mercato Centrale has been serving up food to Florentines who like their tripe since 1872. Tasty primi and secondi are available every day, but cognoscenti come for the *panino con il lampredotto* (tripe sandwich). Less adventurous sorts might want to sample the *panino con il bollito* (boiled beef sandwich). Ask that the bread be *bagnato* (briefly dipped in the tripe cooking liquid), and have both the salsa verde and *salsa piccante* (a spicy cayenne sauce) slathered on top. [$] *Average meal: €13* ✉ *Mercato Centrale San Lorenzo* ☎ *055/219949* 💳 *No credit cards* ⏲ *Closed Sun. No dinner* ✥ *D1.*

TUSCAN

$ ╳ **Gelateria Carabe.** Specializing in things Sicilian, this shop is known
ITALIAN for its tart and flavorful *granità* (granular flavored ices), made only
in the summer, which are great thirst-quenchers. [$] *Average meal: €3*
✉ *Via Ricasoli 60/r, San Marco* ☎ *055/289476* ⊕ *www.gelatocarabe.
com* ▭ *No credit cards* ✛ *F1.*

$ ╳ **Mario.** Florentines flock to this narrow family-run trattoria near San
TUSCAN Lorenzo to feast on Tuscan favorites served at simple tables under a
Fodor's Choice wooden ceiling dating from 1536. A distinct cafeteria feel and genuine
★ Florentine hospitality prevail: you'll be seated wherever there's room,
which often means with strangers. Yes, there's a bit of extra oil in most
dishes, which imparts calories as well as taste, but aren't you on vacation in Italy? Worth the splurge is *riso al ragù* (rice with ground beef
and tomatoes). [$] *Average meal: €20* ✉ *Via Rosina 2/r, corner of Piazza
del Mercato Centrale* ☎ *055/218550* ⚐ *Reservations not accepted*
⊘ *Closed Sun. and Aug. No dinner* ✛ *E1.*

$ ╳ **Perini.** Closed Sunday, Perini sells prosciutto, mixed meats, sauces
ITALIAN for pasta, and a wide assortment of antipasti. It's possible to break the
bank here, as this might be the best salumeria in Florence. [$] *Average
meal: €20* ✉ *Mercato Centrale, enter at Via dell'Aretino, San Lorenzo*
☎ *055/2398306* ✛ *E1.*

$$$ ╳ **Taverna del Bronzino.** Want to have a sophisticated meal in a 16th-
TUSCAN century Renaissance artist's studio? The former studio of Santi di Tito,
Fodor's Choice a student of Bronzino's, has a simple, formal decor, with white table-
★ cloths and place settings. The classic, elegantly presented Tuscan food
is superb, and the solid, afforable wine list rounds out the menu—espe-
cially because Stefano, the sommelier, really knows his stuff. The service
is outstanding. Reservations are advised, especially for eating at the wine
cellar's only table. [$] *Average meal: €45* ✉ *Via delle Ruote 25/r, San
Marco* ☎ *055/495220* ⊘ *Closed Sun. and 3 wks in Aug.* ✛ *G1.*

SANTA MARIA NOVELLA TO THE ARNO

$$$$ ╳ **Buca Lapi.** The Antinori family started selling wine from their palace's
TUSCAN basement in the 15th century. Six hundred years later, this *buca* (hole)
is a lively, subterranean restaurant filled with Florentine aristocrats
chowing down on what might be the best (and most expensive) bistecca
fiorentina in town. The classical Tuscan menu has the usual suspects:
crostino di cavolo nero (black cabbage on toasted garlic bread), along
with *ribollita* and *pappa al pomodoro* (two bread-based soups). You
might want to cut directly to the chase, however, and order the bistecca,
an immense slab of Chianina beef impeccably grilled on the outside,
just barely warmed on the inside. (If you're not into rare meat, order
something else from the grill.) Roast potatoes and cannellini beans make
perfect accompaniments. [$] *Average meal: €45* ✉ *Via del Trebbio 1,
Santa Maria Novella* ☎ *055/213768* ⊕ *www.bucalapi.com* ⚐ *Reserva-
tions essential* ✛ *D3.*

$$$ ╳ **Cantinetta Antinori.** After a morning of shopping on Via Tornabuoni,
TUSCAN stop for lunch in this 15th-century palazzo in the company of Florentine
ladies (and men) who come to see and be seen over lunch. The panache
of the food matches its clientele: expect treats such as *tramezzino con
pane di campagna al tartufo* (country pâté with truffles served on bread)

and the *insalata di gamberoni e gamberetti con carciofi freschi* (crayfish and prawn salad with shaved raw artichokes). [$] *Average meal: €52* ✉ *Piazza Antinori 3, Santa Maria Novella* ☎ *055/292234* ⏲ *Closed weekends, 20 days in Aug., and Dec. 25–Jan. 6* ✥ *D3.*

$$ TUSCAN 🍴 **Il Latini.** It may be the noisiest, most crowded trattoria in Florence, but it's also one of the most fun. The genial host, Torello ("little bull") Latini, presides over his four big dining rooms, and somehow it feels as if you're dining in his home. Ample portions of ribollita prepare the palate for the hearty meat dishes that follow. Both Florentines and tourists alike tuck into the *agnello fritto* (fried lamb) with aplomb. There's almost always a wait, even with a reservation. [$] *Average meal: €32* ✉ *Via dei Palchetti 6/r* ☎ *055/210916* ⏲ *Closed Mon. and 15 days at Christmas* ✥ *C3.*

$$ TUSCAN 🍴 **Trattoria Sostanza (il Troia).** Since opening its doors in 1869, this trattoria has been serving top-notch, unpretentious food to Florentines who like their bistecca fiorentina very large and very rare. A single room with white tiles on the wall and paper mats on the tables provides the setting for delicious meals. Along with fine Tuscan classics, they have two signature dishes: the *tortino di carciofi* (artichoke tart) and the *pollo al burro* (chicken with butter). The latter is an amazing surprise, a succulent chicken breast cooked very quickly and served as soon as it leaves the grill. Leave room for dessert, as their *torta alla Meringa* (a semi-frozen dessert flecked with chocolate and topped with meringue) is scrumptious. [$] *Average meal: €30* ✉ *Via della Porcellana 25* ☎ *055/212691* ✍ *Reservations essential* 💳 *No credit cards* ✥ *B3.*

SANTA CROCE

$ DELI 🍴 **All'Antico Vinaio.** Florentines liked to grab a quick bite to eat at this narrow little sandwich shop near the Uffizi and now, too, does everyone else: word is out, the lines are long (and clog the street). A handful of stools offer places to perch while devouring one of their very fine sandwiches; most folks, however, simply grab a sandwich, pour themselves a glass of inexpensive wine in a paper cup (more serious wines can be poured into glasses), and mingle on the pedestrians-only street in front. If *porchetta* (a very rich, deliciously fatty roasted pork) is on offer, don't miss it. They also offer first-rate primi, which change daily. [$] *Average meal: €8* ✉ *Via de' Neri 65, Santa Croce* 💳 *No credit cards* ✥ *F4.*

$$ TUSCAN 🍴 **Antico Noe.** If Florence had diners (it doesn't), this would be the best diner in town. The short menu at the one-room eatery relies heavily on seasonal ingredients picked up daily at the market. Though the secondi are good, it's the antipasti and primi that really shine. The menu comes alive particularly during truffle and artichoke season (don't miss the grilled artichokes if they're on the menu). Locals rave about the tagliatelle *ai porcini* (with mushrooms); the fried eggs liberally laced with truffle might be the greatest truffle bargain in town. Ask for the menu in Italian, as the English version is much more limited. The short wine list has some great bargains. [$] *Average meal: €29* ✉ *Volta di San Piero 6/r, Santa Croce* ☎ *055/2340838* ⏲ *Closed Sun. and 2 wks in Aug.* ✥ *G3.*

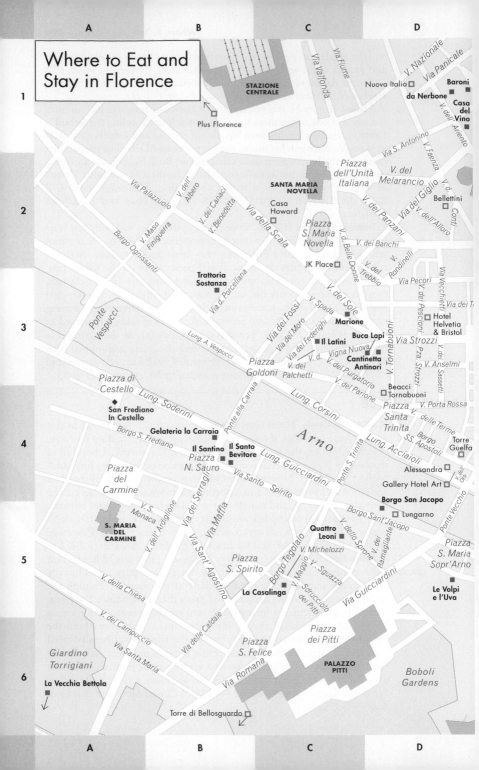

Where to Eat and Stay in Florence

A **B** **C** **D**

1

STAZIONE CENTRALE

Via Fiume

Via Vallonda

Nuova Italia □
da Nerbone
Baroni
Casa del Vino
V. Nazionale
V. Panicale

Plus Florence □

Via dell'Ariento
Via Faenza

2

Via Palazzuolo
V. dell'Albero
V. dei Canacci
v. Benedetta
Via della Scala

Borgo Ognissanti
V. Maso Finiguerra

SANTA MARIA NOVELLA

Casa Howard

Piazza S. Maria Novella

Via S. Antonino

Piazza dell'Unità Italiana

V. del Melarancio

Via dei Panzani

V. dei Banchi

V. del Giglio
v. dell'Alloro
Bellettini
Conti
V. di

Via dell'Albero

3

Ponte Vespucci

Lung. A. Vespucci

Piazza di Cestello

Lung. Soderini

Via d. Porcellana

Trattoria Sostanza

Via dei Fossi
V. Spada
V. del Sole
V. d. Belle Donne
V. del Trebbio
V. del Moro

Piazza Goldoni
Via del Moro
V. dei Palchetti
V. d.

JK Place □

Marione
Il Latini
Vigna Nuova
Buca Lapi
Cantinetta Antinori

V. del Purgatorio
V. del Parione

Beacci Tornabuoni □
Piazza Santa Trinita

Via Pecori
V. dei Pescioni
V. del Tosinghi
□ Hotel Helvetia & Bristol
Via dei T
Via Strozzi
V. dei Sassetti
V. Anselmi
Pza. Strozzi
V. Porta Rossa
Via Tornabuoni
V. Vecchietti
Via Vecchietti

4

San Frediano In Cestello ◆

Borgo S. Frediano

Gelateria la Carraia

Ponte alla Carraia

Il Santino
Piazza N. Sauro
Il Santo Bevitore

Lung. Corsini

Arno

Lung. Guicciardini

Ponte S. Trinita
Lung. Acciaioli
Borgo SS. Apostoli
V. delle Terme
V. Porta Rossa
Torre Guelfa

Alessandra □
Gallery Hotel Art □

Ponte Vecchio
V. del Oro

5

Piazza del Carmine

S. MARIA DEL CARMINE

V. S. Monaca
V. dell'Ardiglione
Via S. Agostino

Via Maffia

Via dei Serragli

Via Santo Spirito

Piazza S. Spirito

Borgo Tegolaio
V. Maggio
V. Michelozzi
V. Squazza
Scruccolo dei Pitti

La Casalinga

Quattro Leoni

V. dello Sprone
V. dei Ramaglianti

Borgo Sant'Jacopo
Borgo San Jacopo
□ **Lungarno**

Via Guicciardini

Piazza S. Maria Sopr'Arno

Le Volpi e l'Uva

6

Giardino Torrigiani

La Vecchia Bettola ■
↓

V. della Chiesa
V. del Campuccio
Via Santa Maria
Via delle Caldaie

Via Romana

Piazza S. Felice

Piazza S. Spirito

Piazza dei Pitti

PALAZZO PITTI

Torre di Bellosguardo □ ↙

Boboli Gardens

A **B** **C** **D**

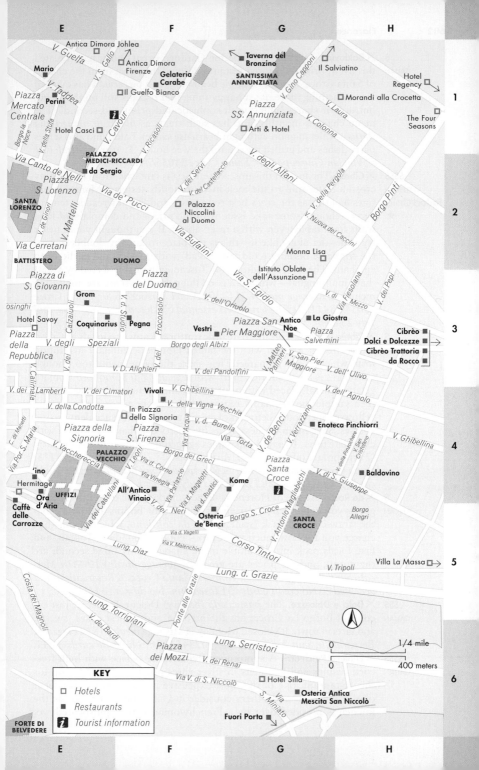

$ ITALIAN 🍴 **Baldovino.** David and Catherine Gardner, expat Scots, have created this lively, brightly colored restaurant down the street from the church of Santa Croce. From its humble beginnings as a pizzeria, it has evolved into something more. It's a happy thing that pizza is still on the menu, but now it shares billing with sophisticated primi and secondi. The menu changes monthly, and has such treats as *filetto di manzo alla Bernaise* (filet mignon with light béarnaise sauce). Baldovino also serves pasta dishes and grilled meat until the wee hours. [$] *Average meal: €31* ✉ *Via San Giuseppe 22/r, Santa Croce* ☎ *055/241773* ✥ *H4.*

$$$$ TUSCAN Fodor's Choice ★ 🍴 **Cibrèo.** The food at this upscale trattoria is fantastic, from the creamy crostini di fegatini to the melt-in-your-mouth desserts. Many Florentines hail this as the city's best restaurant, and Fodor's readers tend to agree—though some take issue with the prices and complain of long waits for a table (even with a reservation). If you thought you'd never try tripe—let alone like it—this is the place to lay any doubts to rest: the *trippa in insalata* (cold tripe salad) with parsley and garlic is an epiphany. The food is traditionally Tuscan, impeccably served by a staff that's multilingual—which is a good thing, because there are no written menus. [$] *Average meal: €71* ✉ *Via A. del Verrocchio 8/r, Santa Croce* ☎ *055/2341100* ✍ *Reservations essential* ⏲ *Closed Sun. and Mon. and July 25–Sept. 5* ✥ *H3.*

$ TUSCAN 🍴 **Cibrèo Trattoria.** This intimate little trattoria, known to locals as Cibreino, shares its kitchen with the famed Florentine culinary institution from which it gets its name. They share the same menu, too, though Cibreino's is much shorter. Start with *il gelatina di pomodoro* (tomato gelatin) liberally laced with basil, garlic, and a pinch of hot pepper, and then sample the justifiably renowned *passato in zucca gialla* (puréed yellow-pepper soup) before moving on to any of the succulent second courses. Save room for dessert, as the pastry chef has a deft hand with chocolate tarts. To avoid sometimes agonizingly long waits, come early (7 pm) or late (after 9:30). [$] *Average meal: €28* ✉ *Via dei Macci 118, Santa Croce* ☎ *055/2341100* ✍ *Reservations not accepted* 💳 *No credit cards* ⏲ *Closed Sun. and Mon. and July 25–Sept. 5* ✥ *H3.*

$ TUSCAN 🍴 **da Rocco.** At one of Florence's biggest markets you can grab lunch to go, or you could cram yourself into one of the booths and pour from the straw-cloaked flask (wine here is *da consumo,* which means they charge you for how much you drink). Food is abundant, Tuscan, and fast; locals pack in. The ample menu changes daily (nine secondi are the norm), and the prices are great. [$] *Average meal: €10* ✉ *In Mercato Sant'Ambrogio, Piazza Ghiberti, Santa Croce* ✍ *Reservations not accepted* 💳 *No credit cards* ⏲ *Closed Sun. No dinner* ✥ *H3.*

$$$ ITALIAN 🍴 **Dolci e Dolcezze.** The *pasticceria* (bakery) Dolci e Dolcezze, just off colorful Borgo La Croce, has the prettiest and tastiest cakes, sweets, and tarts in town. It's closed Monday. [$] *Average meal: €15* ✉ *Piazza C. Beccaria 8/r, Sant'Ambrogio* ☎ *055/2345458* 💳 *No credit cards* ✥ *H3.*

$$$$ ITALIAN 🍴 **Enoteca Pinchiorri.** A sumptuous Renaissance palace with high frescoed ceilings and bouquets in silver vases provides the backdrop for this restaurant, one of the most expensive in Italy. Some consider it one of the best, and others consider it a non-Italian rip-off, as the kitchen is presided over by a Frenchwoman with sophisticated, yet

internationalist, leanings. Prices are high (think $100 for a plate of spaghetti) and portions are small; the vast holdings of the wine cellar (undoubtedly the best in Florence), as well as stellar service, dull the pain, however, when the bill is presented. $ *Average meal: €240* ✉ *Via Ghibellina 87, Santa Croce* ☎ *055/242777* ⊕ *www.enotecapinchiorri. com* ⚱ *Reservations essential Jacket required* ☉ *Closed Sun., Mon., and Aug. No lunch.* ✛ *G4.*

$$
JAPANESE
✕ **Kome.** If you're looking for a break from the ubiquitous ribollita, stop in at this eatery, which may be the only Japanese restaurant in the world to be housed in a 15th-century Renaissance palazzo. High, vaulted arches frame the Kaiten sushi conveyor belt. It's Japanese food, cafeteria style: selections, priced according to the color of the plate, make their way around a bar, where diners pick whatever they find appealing. Those seeking a more substantial meal head to the second floor, where Japanese barbecue is prepared at your table. The minimalist basement provides a subtle but dramatic backdrop for a well-prepared cocktail. $ *Average meal: €20* ✉ *Via de' Benci 41/r, Santa Croce* ☎ *055/2008009* ⊕ *www.komefirenze.it* ✛ *G4.*

$$$
ITALIAN
✕ **La Giostra.** This clubby spot, whose name means "carousel" in Italian, was created by the late Prince Dimitri Kunz d'Asburgo Lorena, and is now expertly run by his handsome twin sons. In perfect English they will describe favorite dishes, such as the *taglierini con tartufo bianco,* a decadently rich pasta with white truffles. The constantly changing menu has terrific vegetarian and vegan options, and any meal that does not include truffles is significantly less expensive than those that do. For dessert, this might be the only show in town with a sublime tiramisù *and* a wonderfully gooey Sacher torte. $ *Average meal: €61* ✉ *Borgo Pinti 12/r, Santa Croce* ☎ *055/241341* ⊕ *www.ristorantelagiostra.com* ⚱ *Reservations essential* ☉ *No lunch weekends.* ✛ *G3.*

$$
ITALIAN
✕ **Osteria de'Benci.** A few minutes from Santa Croce, this charming osteria serves some of the most eclectic food in Florence. Try the spaghetti *degli eretici* (in tomato sauce with fresh herbs). The grilled meats are justifiably famous; the *carbonata* is a succulent piece of grilled beef served rare. Weekly specials complement what's happening in the market, and all of the food pairs beautifully with their wine list, which is heavy on things Tuscan. When it's warm, you can dine outside with a view of the 13th-century tower belonging to the prestigious Alberti family. $ *Average meal: €30* ✉ *Via de' Benci 11–13/r, Santa Croce* ☎ *055/2344923* ⚱ *Reservations essential* ☉ *Closed 2 wks in Aug.* ✛ *F5.*

$
ITALIAN
✕ **Vestri.** This shop is devoted to chocolate in all its guises. The small but sublime selection of chocolate-based gelati includes one with hot peppers. $ *Average meal: €3* ✉ *Borgo Albizi 11/r, Santa Croce* ☎ *055/2340374* ⊕ *www.vestri.it* ▭ *No credit cards* ✛ *F3.*

$
ITALIAN
✕ **Vivoli.** The reputation of Vivoli as the best gelateria in town is somewhat dated, but it's still worth visiting this Florentine institution. $ *Average meal: €3* ✉ *Via Isola delle Stinche 7/r, Santa Croce* ☎ *055/292334* ⊕ *www.vivoli.it* ▭ *No credit cards* ✛ *F4.*

10

THE OLTRARNO

$$$$ ITALIAN

🍴 **Borgo San Jacopo.** It makes perfect sense that any restaurant owned by the Ferragamo family would look sleek, elegant, and sophisticated. In the kitchen is Beatrice Segoni, one of the few female chefs in Florence. Her intimate, romantic restaurant has low lighting, white walls lined with prints, and a stunning view of the Arno. If you're lucky enough to book the terrace when it's warm, you will float over the river as you enjoy her remarkable offerings. The menu changes every three months or so, and fish is the emphasis. Before tucking into her delicious *grigliata* (mixed grill, including sole, sea bass, and stuffed squid), start with the innovative *sformato di carciofi con petto d'anatra ai tre pepi* (an artichoke flan topped with three-peppered duck), while remembering to leave room for her amazing desserts. [$] *Average meal: €65* ✉ *Borgo San Jacopo, 14, Lungarno Sud* ☎ *055/281661* 🌐 *www.lungarnohotels.com* ✍ *Reservations essential* 🕘 *Closed Tues. No lunch.* ✣ *D5.*

$ WINE BAR

🍴 **Fuori Porta.** One of the oldest and best wine bars in Florence, this place serves cured meats and cheeses, as well as daily specials such as the sublime spaghetti *al curry. Crostini* and *crostoni*—grilled breads topped with a mélange of cheeses and meats—are the house specialty; the *verdure sott'olio* (vegetables with oil) are divine. The lengthy wine list offers great wines by the glass, and terrific bottles from all over Italy and beyond. All this can be enjoyed at rustic wooden tables, and outdoors when weather allows. [$] *Average meal: €10* ✉ *Via Monte alle Croci 10/r, San Niccolò* ☎ *055/2342483* ✣ *G6.*

$ ITALIAN

🍴 **Gelateria la Carraia.** Though it's a bit of a haul to get here (it's at the foot of Ponte Carraia, two bridges down from the Ponte Vecchio), you'll be well-rewarded for doing so. They do standard flavors, and then creative ones such as limone con biscotti (lemon sorbet biscuits), and they do both of these very well. [$] *Average meal: €3* ✉ *Piazza Nazario Sauro 2, Santo Spirito, Florence* ☎ *055/280 695* 🌐 *www.lacarraiagroup.eu* 💳 *No credit cards* ✣ *B4.*

$ TUSCAN

🍴 **Il Santo Bevitore.** Florentines and other lovers of good food flock to "The Holy Drinker" for tasty, well-priced dishes. Unpretentious white walls, dark wood furniture, and paper placemats provide the simple decor; start with the exceptional vegetables *sott'olio* (marinated in olive oil) or the *terrina di fegatini* (terrine with a creamy chicken-liver spread) before sampling any of the divine pastas, such as the fragrant spaghetti with shrimp sauce. Count yourself lucky if the extraordinary potato gratin, served in compact triangular wedges, is on the menu. The extensive wine list is well priced, and the well-informed staff is happy to explain it. [$] *Average meal: €26* ✉ *Via Santo Spirito 64/66r, Santo Spirito* ☎ *055/211264* 🕘 *No lunch Sun.* ✣ *B4.*

$ TUSCAN

🍴 **La Casalinga.** *Casalinga* means "housewife," and this place has the nostalgic charm of a 1950s kitchen with Tuscan comfort food to match. If you eat ribollita anywhere in Florence, eat it here—it couldn't be more authentic. Mediocre paintings clutter the semipaneled walls, tables are set close together, and the place is usually jammed. The menu is long, portions are plentiful, and service is prompt and friendly. For dessert, the lemon sorbet perfectly caps off the meal. [$] *Average* *meal: €20* ✉ *Via Michelozzi 9/r, Santo Spirito* ☎ *055/218624* ⊘ *Closed Sun., 1 wk at Christmas, and 3 wks in Aug.* ✛ *C5.*

$$
TUSCAN ✕ **La Vecchia Bettola.** The name doesn't exactly mean "old dive," but it comes pretty close. This lively trattoria has been around only since 1979, but it feels as if it's been a whole lot longer. Tile floors and simple wood tables and chairs provide the interior decoration, such as it is. The recipes come from "wise grandmothers" and celebrate Tuscan food in its glorious simplicity. Here prosciutto is sliced with a knife, portions of grilled meat are tender and ample, service is friendly, and the wine list is well priced and good. This place is worth a taxi ride, even though it's just outside the centro storico. $ *Average meal: €30* ✉ *Viale Vasco Pratolini, Oltrarno* ☎ *055/224158* ▭ *No credit cards* ✛ *A6.*

$ TUSCAN ✕ **Osteria Antica Mescita San Niccolò.** It's always crowded, always good, and always inexpensive. The osteria is next to the church of San Niccolò, and if you sit in the lower part you'll find yourself in what was once a chapel dating from the 11th century. The subtle but dramatic background is a nice complement to the food, which is simple Tuscan at its best. The *pollo con limone* is tasty pieces of chicken in a lemon-scented broth. In winter, try the *spezzatino di cinghiale con aromi* (wild boar stew with herbs). Reservations are advised. $ *Average meal: €20* ✉ *Via San Niccolò 60/r, San Niccolò* ☎ *055/2342836* ⊘ *Closed Sun. and Aug.* ✛ *G6.*

WHERE TO STAY

No stranger to visitors, Florence is equipped with hotels for all budgets; you can even find both budget and luxury hotels in the centro storico and along the Arno. Florence has so many famous landmarks that it's not hard to find lodging with a panoramic view. The equivalent of the genteel pensioni of yesteryear still exist, though they're now officially classified as hotels. Generally small and intimate, they often have a quaint appeal that usually doesn't preclude modern plumbing.

Florence's importance not only as a tourist city but as a convention center and the site of the Pitti fashion collections guarantees a variety of accommodations. The high demand also means that, except in winter, reservations are a must.

If you find yourself in Florence with no reservations, go to **Consorzio ITA** (✉ *Stazione Centrale, Santa Maria Novella* ☎ *055/282893*). You must go there in person to make a booking.

Use the coordinate (✛ B2) at the end of each listing to locate a site on the Where to Eat and Stay in Florence map.

Hotel reviews have been condensed for this book. Please go to Fodors. com for full reviews of each property.

THE DUOMO TO THE PONTE VECCHIO

$$ HOTEL ⚎ **Hermitage.** All rooms here are decorated with lively wallpaper, and some have views of Palazzo Vecchio and others of the Arno. **Pros:** views; friendly, English-speaking staff; enviable position a stone's

throw from the Ponte Vecchio. **Cons:** short flight of stairs to reach elevator. $ *Rooms from: €186* ⊠ *Vicolo Marzio 1, Piazza della Signoria* ☎ *055/287216* ⊕ *www.hermitagehotel.com* ↻ *27 rooms, 1 suite* ¶ *Breakfast* ✛ *E4.*

$$$$ ⊞ **Hotel Helvetia and Bristol.** From the cozy yet sophisticated lobby with
HOTEL its stone columns to the guest rooms decorated with prints, you might feel as if you're a guest in a sophisticated manor house. **Pros:** central location; superb staff. **Cons:** rooms facing the street get some noise. $ *Rooms from: €345* ⊠ *Via dei Pescioni 2, Piazza della Repubblica* ☎ *055/26651* ⊕ *www.hbf.royaldemeure.com* ↻ *54 rooms, 13 suites* ¶ *No meals* ✛ *D3.*

$$ ⊞ **In Piazza della Signoria.** A cozy feeling permeates these charming
HOTEL rooms, all of which are uniquely decorated and lovingly furnished;
Fodor'sChoice some have damask curtains, others fanciful frescoes in the bathroom.
★ **Pros:** marvelous staff; tasty breakfast with a view of Piazza della Signoria. **Cons:** short flight of stairs to reach elevator. $ *Rooms from: €250* ⊠ *Via dei Magazzini 2, Near Piazza della Signoria* ☎ *055/2399546* ⊕ *www.inpiazzadellasignoria.com* ↻ *10 rooms, 3 apartments* ¶ *Breakfast* ✛ *F4.*

$$$ ⊞ **Palazzo Niccolini al Duomo.** The graceful Marchesa Ginevra Niccolini
HOTEL di Camugliano has taken her husband's family's palazzo (acquired by an ancestor in 1532) and turned it into a luxurious place that still manages to evoke a cozy, yet highly sophisticated, home. **Pros:** steps away from the Duomo. **Cons:** street noise sometimes a problem. $ *Rooms from: €240* ⊠ *Via dei Servi 2* ☎ *055/282412* ⊕ *www.niccolinidomepalace. com* ↻ *5 rooms, 5 suites* ✛ *F2.*

SAN LORENZO AND BEYOND

$ ⊞ **Antica Dimora Firenze.** Each simply furnished room in the intimate
B&B/INN *residenza* is painted a different pastel color—peach, rose, powderblue—while double-glazed windows ensure a peaceful night's sleep. **Pros:** ample DVD library; honor bar with Antinori wines. **Cons:** staff goes home at 8; no credit cards accepted. $ *Rooms from: €107* ⊠ *Via San Gallo 72, San Marco* ☎ *055/4627296* ⊕ *www.anticadimorafirenze. it* ↻ *6 rooms* ▬ *No credit cards* ¶ *Breakfast* ✛ *F1.*

$$ ⊞ **Antica Dimora Johlea.** Lively color runs rampant on the top floor of
B&B/INN this 19th-century palazzo, with a charming flower-filled rooftop terrace
Fodor'sChoice where you can sip a glass of wine while taking in a view of Brunelleschi's cupola. **Pros:** great staff; cheerful rooms; honor bar. **Cons:** staff
★ goes home at 7; narrow staircase to get to roof terrace. $ *Rooms from: €119* ⊠ *Via San Gallo 80, San Marco* ☎ *055/4633292* ⊕ *www.johanna. it* ↻ *6 rooms* ▬ *No credit cards* ¶ *Breakfast* ✛ *E1.*

$$ ⊞ **Hotel Casci.** In this refurbished 14th-century palace, the home of
HOTEL Giacchino Rossini in 1851–55, the friendly Lombardi family runs a hotel with spotless, functional rooms. **Pros:** helpful staff; good option for families; English-language DVD collection with good selections for kids. **Cons:** bit of a college-dorm atmosphere; small elevator $ *Rooms from: €150* ⊠ *Via Cavour 13, San Marco* ☎ *055/211686* ⊕ *www. hotelcasci.com* ↻ *25 rooms* ¶ *Breakfast* ✛ *E1.*

$$ HOTEL 🏨 **Il Guelfo Bianco.** The 15th-century building has all modern conveniences, but Renaissance charm still shines in the high-ceilinged rooms. **Pros:** stellar multilingual staff. **Cons:** rooms facing the street can be noisy. [$] *Rooms from: €250* ✉ *Via Cavour 29, San Marco* ☎ *055/288330* 🌐 *www.ilguelfobianco.it* 🛏 *40 rooms* 🍴 *Breakfast* ✥ *F1.*

SANTA MARIA NOVELLA TO THE ARNO

$$ B&B/INN 🏨 **Alessandra.** An aura of grandeur pervades this clean, ample rooms a block from the Ponte Vecchio. **Pros:** several rooms have views of the Arno; the spacious suite is a bargain. **Cons:** stairs to elevator; some rooms share bath. [$] *Rooms from: €150* ✉ *Borgo Santi Apostoli 17, Santa Maria Novella* ☎ *055/283438* 🌐 *www.hotelalessandra.com* 🛏 *26 rooms, 19 with bath; 1 suite; 1 apartment* ⏲ *Closed Dec. 10–26* 🍴 *Breakfast* ✥ *D4.*

$$$ HOTEL 🏨 **Beacci Tornabuoni.** Florentine pensioni don't get any classier than this: old-fashioned style, enough modern comfort to keep you happy, and a 14th-century palazzo. **Pros:** multilingual staff; flower-filled terrace. **Cons:** hall noise can sometimes be a problem. [$] *Rooms from: €200* ✉ *Via Tornabuoni 3, Santa Maria Novella* ☎ *055/212645* 🌐 *www.tornabuonihotels.com* 🛏 *37 rooms, 16 suites* 🍴 *Breakfast* ✥ *D4.*

$$ B&B/INN 🏨 **Casa Howard.** This unassuming little inn has no two rooms alike, and an aura of eclectic funk pervades: one room takes its inspiration from Japan; others are geared to families; others have access to a garden. **Pros:** great location near the basilica of Santa Maria Novella; good vibe. **Cons:** very limited concierge service; staff goes home in the early evening. [$] *Rooms from: €127* ✉ *Via della Scala 18, Near Santa Maria Novella* ☎ *06/699 24555* 🌐 *www.casahoward.it* ✥ *C2.*

$$$ HOTEL 🏨 **Gallery Hotel Art.** High design resides at this art showcase near the Ponte Vecchio, where sleek, uncluttered rooms are dressed mostly in neutrals and luxe touches, such as leather headboards and kimono robes, abound. **Pros:** cool atmosphere; beautiful people; miso soup on the breakfast menu; the in-house Fusion Bar, which pours delightful cocktails. **Cons:** sometimes elevator is slow; too cool for some. [$] *Rooms from: €250* ✉ *Vicolo dell'Oro 5, Santa Maria Novella* ☎ *055/27263* 🌐 *www.lungarnohotels.com* 🛏 *65 rooms, 9 suites* 🍴 *Breakfast* ✥ *D4.*

$$$$ HOTEL Fodor's Choice ★ 🏨 **JK Place.** Sumptuous appointments provide all the comforts of a luxe home away from home; soothing earth tones prevail in the guest rooms, some of which have chandeliers, others canopied beds. **Pros:** intimate feel; stellar staff; free minibar; linen sheets; organic meals on room-service menu; Wi-Fi. **Cons:** breakfast at a shared table (which can be easily gotten around with room service). [$] *Rooms from: €380* ✉ *Piazza Santa Maria Novella 7* ☎ *055/2645181* 🌐 *www.jkplace.com* 🛏 *14 doubles, 6 suites* 🍴 *Breakfast* ✥ *C2.*

$ HOTEL 🏨 **Nuova Italia.** The genial English-speaking Viti family oversees these clean and simple rooms near the train station and well within walking distance of the sights. **Pros:** reasonable rates. **Cons:** no elevator. [$] *Rooms from: €89* ✉ *Via Faenza 26, Santa Maria Novella* ☎ *055/268430* 🌐 *www.hotel-nuovaitalia.com* 🛏 *20 rooms* ⏲ *Closed Dec. 8–Dec. 26* 🍴 *Breakfast* ✥ *D1.*

$$ B&B/INN [🏨] **Torre Guelfa.** If you want a taste of medieval Florence, try one of these character-filled guest rooms—some with canopied beds, some with balconies—housed within a 13th-century tower. **Pros:** rooftop terrace with tremendous views; wonderful staff; some family-friendly triple and quadruple rooms. **Cons:** 72 steps to get to the terrace. [$] *Rooms from: €180* ✉ *Borgo Santi Apostoli 8, Santa Maria Novella* ☎ *055/2396338* 🌐 *www.hoteltorreguelfa.com* 🛏 *28 rooms, 3 suites* 🍴 *Breakfast* ✥ *D4.*

SANTA CROCE

$$$$ HOTEL [🏨] **The Four Seasons.** Seven years of restoration have turned this 15th-century palazzo in Florence's center into a luxury hotel where no two guest rooms are alike; many have original 17th-century frescoes, some face the garden, others quiet interior courtyards. **Pros:** a unique "city meets country" experience; the marvelous garden. **Cons:** for this price, breakfast really should be included; some feel it's a little too removed from the historic center. [$] *Rooms from: €590* ✉ *Borgo Pinti 99e, Santa Croce* ☎ *055/26261* 🌐 *www.fourseasons.com/florence* 🛏 *117 rooms* 🍴 *No meals* ✥ *H1.*

$$$$ HOTEL [🏨] **Hotel Regency.** Rooms dressed in richly colored fabrics and antique-style furniture remain faithful to the premises' 19th-century origins as a private mansion. **Pros:** faces one of the few green parks in the center of Florence. **Cons:** a small flight of stairs takes you to reception. [$] *Rooms from: €360* ✉ *Piazza d'Azeglio 3, Santa Croce* ☎ *055/245247* 🌐 *www.regency-hotel.com* 🛏 *30 rooms, 4 suites* 🍴 *Breakfast* ✥ *H1.*

$ B&B/INN [🏨] **Istituto Oblate dell'Assunzione.** Seven nuns run this convent, minutes from the Duomo, with spotlessly clean, simple rooms; some have views of the cupola, and others look out onto a carefully tended garden where you are welcome to relax. **Pros:** bargain price; great location; quiet rooms; garden. **Cons:** curfew; no credit cards. [$] *Rooms from: €90* ✉ *Borgo Pinti 15, Santa Croce* ☎ *055/2480582* 📠 *055/2346291* 🌐 *www.sanctuarybbfirenze.com* 🛏 *28 rooms, 22 with bath* 💳 *No credit cards* 🍴 *No meals* ✥ *G3.*

$$$$ HOTEL [🏨] **Monna Lisa.** Though some rooms are small, they are tasteful, and best of all, housed in a 15th-century palazzo that retains some of its wood-coffered ceilings from the 1500s, as well as its original staircase. **Pros:** lavish buffet breakfast; cheerful staff; garden. **Cons:** rooms in annex are less charming than those in palazzo; street noise in some rooms. [$] *Rooms from: €259* ✉ *Borgo Pinti 27, Santa Croce* ☎ *055/2479751* 🌐 *www.monnalisa.it* 🛏 *45 rooms* 🍴 *Breakfast* ✥ *G2.*

$$ B&B/INN [🏨] **Morandi alla Crocetta.** You're made to feel like privileged friends of the family at this charming and distinguished residence, furnished comfortably in the classic style of a gracious Florentine home. **Pros:** interesting, offbeat location near the sights; terrific staff; great value. **Cons:** two flights of stairs to reach reception and rooms. [$] *Rooms from: €150* ✉ *Via Laura 50, Santissima Annunziata* ☎ *055/2344747* 🌐 *www.hotelmorandi.it* 🛏 *10 rooms* ✥ *H1.*

THE OLTRARNO

$$
HOTEL
Hotel Silla. Rooms in this 15th-century palazzo, entered through a courtyard lined with potted plants and sculpture-filled niches, are simply furnished and walls are papered; some have views of the Arno. **Pros:** a Fodor's reader raves, "It's in the middle of everything except the crowds." **Cons:** some readers complain of street noise and too-small rooms. $ *Rooms from: €140 ⊠ Via de' Renai 5, San Niccolò* ☎ *055/2342888* ⊕ *www.hotelsilla.it* ↝ *35 rooms* ❖| *Breakfast* ✣ *G6.*

$$$$
HOTEL
Lungarno. Many rooms and suites here have private terraces that jut out right over the Arno, granting stunning views of the Palazzo Vecchio and the Lungarno. **Pros:** upscale without being stuffy. **Cons:** rooms without Arno views feel less special. $ *Rooms from: €351 ⊠ Borgo San Jacopo 14, Lungarno Sud* ☎ *055/27261* ⊕ *www.lungarnohotels.com* ↝ *59 rooms, 14 suites* ❖| *Breakfast* ✣ *D5.*

OUTSIDE THE CITY

$$$$
Il Salviatino. There's no reception area, but the intention is to make you feel at home—that is, if home were a restored 14th-century villa at the end of a cypress-studded winding drive. **Pros:** great views; attentive staff. **Cons:** no reception area; some hall noise. $ *Rooms from: €458* ⊠ *Via del Salviatino 21* ☎ *055/904111* ⊕ *www.salviatino.com* ↝ *23 rooms, 22 suites* ❖| *Breakfast.*

$$$
B&B/INN
Torre di Bellosguardo. *Bellosguardo* means "beautiful view"; given the view of Florence you get here, the name is fitting. **Pros:** great for escaping heat of the city in summer; a villa experience with the city just minutes away. **Cons:** a car is a necessity, breakfast is not included. $ *Rooms from: €290* ⊠ *Via Roti Michelozzi 2* ☎ *055/2298145* ⊕ *www. torrebellosguardo.com* ↝ *9 rooms, 7 suites.*

$$$$
HOTEL
Villa La Massa. In this tall and imposing villa, 15 minutes out of town, public rooms are outfitted in Renaissance style and guest rooms have high ceilings, plush carpeting, and deep bathtubs. **Pros:** pleasing mix of city and country life; sumptuous buffet breakfast; views of the Tuscan hills; phenomenal staff. **Cons:** even with shuttle, a car is a necessity; not open year-round. $ *Rooms from: €550* ⊠ *Via della Massa 24, Candeli* ☎ *055/62611* ⊕ *www.villalamassa.com* ↝ *19 rooms, 18 suites* ☾ *Closed Dec.–Mar.* ❖| *Breakfast.*

10

NIGHTLIFE AND THE ARTS

THE ARTS

MUSIC

Accademia Bartolomeo Cristofori. Also known as the Amici del Fortepiano (Friends of the Fortepiano), the Accademia Bartolomeo Cristofori sponsors fortepiano concerts throughout the year. ⊠ *Via di Camaldoli 7/r, Santo Spirito/San Frediano* ☎ *055/221646* ⊕ *www.accademiacristofori.it.*

Amici della Musica. This organization sponsors classical and contemporary concerts at the **Teatro della Pergola** (*Box office* ⊠ *Via Alamanni*

39, Lungarno North ☎ *055/210804* ⊕ *www.teatrodellapergola.com*). ⊕ *www.amicimusica.fi.it.*

Maggio Musicale Fiorentino. At press time, construction had been halted due to lack of funds on the **Parco della Musica** (Music Park) designed by Paolo Desideri and associates. Three concert halls (two indoor, one outdoor) are planned, and only one has been completed. Maggio Musicale plans to re-locate once construction is finished. In the meantime, it continues to be held at the **Teatro Comunale** (✉ *Corso Italia 16, Lungarno North* ☎ *055/287222* ⊕ *www.maggiofiorentino.com*). Within Italy you can purchase tickets from late April through July directly at the box office or by phone at ☎ *055/2779350.* You can also buy them online. Call ahead to confirm if performances are taking place in this venue or have switched over to the new space. ✉ *Via Alamanni 39* ☎ *055/210804.*

Orchestra da Camera Fiorentina. This orchestra performs various concerts of classical music throughout the year at Orsanmichele, the grain-market-turned-church. ✉ *Via Monferrato 2, Piazza della Signoria* ☎ *055/783374* ⊕ *www.orcafi.it.*

Orchestra della Toscana. The concert season of the Orchestra della Toscana runs from November to June. ✉ *Via Ghibellina 101, Santa Croce* ☎ *055/2340710* ⊕ *www.orchestradellatoscana.it.*

NIGHTLIFE

Florentines are rather proud of their nightlife options. Most bars now have some sort of happy hour, which usually lasts for many hours and often has snacks that can substitute for a light dinner. (Check, though, that the buffet is free or comes with the price of a drink.) Clubs typically don't open until very late in the evening and don't get crowded until 1 or 2 in the morning. Though the cover charges can be steep, finding free passes around town is fairly easy.

BARS

Kitsch. Choose from indoor or outdoor seating and take advantage of the great list of wines by the glass. At aperitivo time €8.50 will buy you a truly tasty cocktail and give you access to the tremendous buffet; it's so good, you won't need dinner afterward—in fact, they called it "Apericena." That means, roughly, "drink and dinner." ✉ *Via San Gallo 22/r, San Marco* ☎ *328/9039289* ⊕ *www.kitschfirenze.it.*

Rex. A trendy, artsy clientele frequents this bar at aperitivo time; around 10, the place is packed with mostly young folks sipping artfully made cocktails. ✉ *Via Fiesolana 23–25/r, Santa Croce* ☎ *055/2480331.*

Sant'Ambrogio Caffè. Come here in the summer for outdoor seating with a view of an 11th-century church (Sant'Ambrogio) directly across the street. ✉ *Piazza Sant'Ambrogio 7–8/r, Santa Croce* ☎ *055/2477277* ⊕ *www.caffesantambrogio.it.*

Zoe. Though it's called a "caffetteria," and coffee is served (as well as terrific salads and burgers at lunchtime), Zoe's fine cocktails are the real draw for elegant youngish Florentines who come here to see and be seen. Here's people-watching at its very best, done while listening to the latest CDs imported from England. ⊠ *Via de' Renai 13/r, San Niccolò* ☎ *055/243111* ⊕ *www.zoebar.it.*

WINE BARS

Casa del Vino. Come here for creative panini, such as *sgrombri e carciofini sott'olio* (mackerel and marinated baby artichokes), and an ever-changing list of significant wines by the glass. They also have a well-stocked collection of bottles to go, at more than fair prices. ⊠ *Via dell'Ariento 16/r, San Lorenzo* ☎ *055/215609.*

Il Santino. Though it has only four tables and four small stools at an equally small bar, Il Santino is blessed with a big wine list and superior cheeses, cured meats, and other delicacies to match. ⊠ *Via Santo Spirito 60/r, Santo Spirito* ☎ *055/2302820.*

Le Volpi e l'Uva. Le Volpi e l'Uva, off Piazza Santa Trinita, is an oenophile's dream: the waiters pour highly esteemed wines by the glass and serve equally impressive cheeses and little sandwiches to go with them. ⊠ *Piazza de' Rossi 1, Palazzo Pitti* ☎ *055/2398132.*

CAFÉS

Cafés in Italy serve not only coffee concoctions and pastries but also drinks; some also serve light and inexpensive lunches. They open early in the morning and usually close around 8 pm.

Caffè Giacosa. This cafe opens early in the morning for coffee, serves tasty light lunches, and makes excellent cocktails in the evening. ⊠ *Via della Spada 10/r* ☎ *055/2776328* ⊕ *www.caffegiacosa.it.*

Gran Caffè. A perfect stop for a marvelous panino or sweet while raving about the majesty of Michelangelo's David is just down the street from the Accademia. Do be aware that sitting at a table is more expensive at most cafés, and this place is particularly notorious in trying to get you to sit down. ⊠ *Piazza San Marco 11/r* ☎ *055/215833.*

Procacci. At this classy Florentine institution dating to 1885, try one of the panini tartufati and swish it down with a glass of Prosecco. It's closed Sunday. ⊠ *Via Tornabuoni 64/r, Santa Maria Novella* ☎ *055/211656.*

Rivoire. One of the best spots in Florence for people-watching offer stellar service, light snacks, and terrific aperitivi. It's been around since the 1860s, and has been famous for its hot and cold chocolate (with or without cream) for more than a century. Though the food is mostly good (it's not a bad place for a light, but expensive, lunch), it's best to stick to drinks (both alcoholic and non-) and their terrific cakes, pies, and pastries. ⊠ *Via Vacchereccia 4/r* ☎ *055/214412.*

10

SHOPPING

Window-shopping in Florence is like visiting an enormous contemporary-art gallery. Many of today's greatest Italian artists are fashion designers, and most keep shops in Florence. Discerning shoppers may find bargains in the street markets. ■TIP➔ Don't buy any knockoff goods from any of the hawkers plying their fake Prada (or any other high-end designer) on the streets. It's illegal, and fines are astronomical if the police happen to catch you. (The vendor doesn't pay the fine, you do.)

Shops are generally open 9 to 1 and 3:30 to 7:30 and are closed Sunday and Monday mornings most of the year. Summer (June to September) hours are usually 9 to 1 and 4 to 8, and some shops close Saturday afternoon instead of Monday morning. When looking for addresses, you'll see two color-coded numbering systems on each street. The red numbers are commercial addresses and are indicated, for example, as 31/r. The blue or black numbers are residential addresses. Most shops take major credit cards and ship purchases, but because of possible delays it's wise to take your purchases with you.

MARKETS

Mercato Centrale. This huge indoor food market offers a staggering selection of all things edible. ⊠ *Piazza del Mercato Centrale, San Lorenzo.*

Mercato dei Fiori (*flower market*). Every Thursday morning from September through June the covered loggia in Piazza della Repubblica hosts a Mercato dei Fiori; it's awash in a lively riot of plants, flowers, and difficult-to-find herbs. ⊠ *Piazza della Repubblica.*

Mercato del Porcellino. If you're looking for cheery, inexpensive trinkets to take home, you might want to stop and roam through the stalls under the loggia of the Mercato del Porcellino. ⊠ *Via Por Santa Maria at Via Porta Rossa, Piazza della Repubblica.*

Mercato di San Lorenzo. The clothing and leather-goods stalls of the Mercato di San Lorenzo in the streets next to the church of San Lorenzo have bargains for shoppers on a budget.

Mercato di Sant'Ambrogio. It's possible to strike gold at this lively market, where clothing stalls abut the fruit and vegetables. ⊠ *Piazza Ghiberti, off Via dei Macci, Santa Croce.*

Piazza dei Ciompi flea market. You can find bargains here Monday through Saturday and on the last Sunday of the month. ⊠ *Sant'Ambrogio, Santa Croce.*

Santo Spirito flea market. The second Sunday of every month brings the Santo Spirito flea market. On the third Sunday of the month, vendors at the Fierucola organic fest sell such delectables as honeys, jams, spice mixes, and fresh vegetables.

SHOPPING DISTRICTS

Florence's most fashionable shops are concentrated in the center of town. The fanciest designer shops are mainly on **Via Tornabuoni** and **Via della Vigna Nuova**. The city's largest concentrations of antiques shops are on **Borgo Ognissanti** and the Oltrarno's **Via Maggio**. The **Ponte Vecchio** houses reputable but very expensive jewelry shops, as it has since the 16th century. The area near **Santa Croce** is the heart of the leather merchants' district.

SPECIALTY STORES

BOOKS AND PAPER

Alberto Cozzi. You'll find an extensive line of Florentine papers and paper products here. The artisans in the shop rebind and restore books and works on paper. Their hours are tricky, so it's best to call first before stopping by. ⊠ *Via del Parione 35/r, Santa Maria Novella* ☎ *055/294968.*

Giulio Giannini e Figlio. One of Florence's oldest paper-goods stores is *the* place to buy the marbleized stock, which comes in many shapes and sizes, from flat sheets to boxes and even pencils. ⊠ *Piazza Pitti 37/r, Lungarno Sud* ☎ *055/212621* ⊕ *www.giuliogiannini.it.*

Il Torchio. Photograph albums, frames, diaries, and other objects dressed in handmade paper are high quality, and the prices lower than usual. ⊠ *Via dei Bardi 17, San Niccolò* ☎ *055/2342862* ⊕ *www. legatoriailtorchio.com.*

Libreria Salimbeni. One of Florence's best art-book shops has an outstanding selection. ⊠ *Via Matteo Palmieri 14–16/r, Santa Croce* ☎ *055/2340905* ⊕ *www.liberiasalimbeni.com.*

Pineider. Though it has shops throughout the world, Pineider started out in Florence and still does all its printing here. Stationery and business cards are the mainstay, but the stores also sell fine leather desk accessories as well as a less stuffy, more lighthearted line of products. ⊠ *via della Vigna Nuova 4–6/r, Santa Maria Novella to the Arno* ☎ *055/284655* ⊕ *www.pineider.com.*

CLOTHING

The usual fashion suspects—Prada, Gucci, Versace, to name but a few—all have shops in Florence.

Bernardo. Come here for men's trousers, cashmere sweaters, and shirts with details like mother-of-pearl buttons. ⊠ *Via Porta Rossa 87/r, Piazza della Repubblica* ☎ *055/283333.*

Cabó. Missoni knitwear is the main draw at Cabó. ⊠ *Via Porta Rossa 77–79/r, Piazza della Repubblica* ☎ *055/215774.*

Diesel. Trendy Diesel started in Vicenza; its gear is on the "must-have" list of many self-respecting Italian teens. ⊠ *Via dei Lamberti 13/r, Piazza della Signoria* ☎ *055/2399963* ⊕ *www.diesel.com.*

Emilio Pucci. The aristocratic Marchese di Barsento, Emilio Pucci, became an international name in the late 1950s when the stretch ski clothes he designed for himself caught on with the dolce vita crowd—his pseudo-psychedelic prints and "palazzo pajamas" became all the rage. ⊠ *Via Tornabuoni 20–22/r, Santa Maria Novella* ☎ *055/2658082* ⊕ *www. emiliopucci.com.*

Giorgio Vannini. You can take home a custom-made suit or dress from the designer, who has a showroom for his prêt-à-porter line. ⊠ *Borgo Santi Apostoli 43/r, Santa Maria Novella* ☎ *055/293037* ⊕ *www. giorgiovannini.it.*

The intrepid shopper might want to check out some other, lesser-known shops.

10

Maçel. Browse collections by lesser-known Italian designers, many of whom use the same factories as the A-list, at this women's clothing shop. ⊠ *Via Guicciardini 128/r, Palazzo Pitti* ☎ *055/287355.*

Patrizia Pepe. The Florentine designer has body-conscious clothes perfect for all ages, especially for women with a tiny streak of rebelliousness. Women who are not size zero—or close to it—need not apply. ⊠ *Via Strozzi 11/19r, Duomo* ☎ *055/2302518* ⊕ *www.patriziapepe.com.*

Principe. This Florentine institution sells casual clothes for men, women, and children at far-from-casual prices. It also has a great housewares department. ⊠ *Via del Sole 2, Santa Maria Novella* ☎ *055/292764* ⊕ *www.principedifirenze.com.*

Spazio A. For cutting-edge fashion, these fun and funky window displays merit a stop. The shop carries such well-known designers as Alberta Ferretti and Moschino, as well as lesser-known Italian, English, and French designers. ⊠ *Via Porta Rossa 109–115/r, Piazza della Repubblica* ☎ *055/212995* ⊕ *www.albertaferretti.com.*

FRAGRANCES

Antica Officina del Farmacista Dr. Vranjes. Dr. Vranjes elevates aromatherapy to an art form, with scents for the body and for the house. ⊠ *Via della Spada 9, Santa Maria Novella to the Arno* ☎ *055/288796* ⊕ *www. drvranjes.it.*

Lorenzo Villoresi. Proprietor Lorenzo Villoresi makes one-of-a-kind fragrances, which he develops after meeting with you. Such personalized attention does not come cheap. ⊠ *Via de'Bardi 14, Lungarno Sud* ☎ *055/2341187* ⊕ *www.lorenzovilloresi.it.*

Officina Profumo Farmaceutica di Santa Maria Novella. The essence of a Florentine holiday is captured in the sachets of this art nouveau emporium of herbal cosmetics and soaps that are made following centuries-old recipes created by friars. It celebrated its 400th birthday in 2012. ⊠ *Via della Scala 16, Santa Maria Novella* ☎ *055/216276* ⊕ *www. smnovella.it.*

JEWELRY

Angela Caputi. Angela Caputi wows Florentine cognoscenti with her highly creative, often outsized plastic jewelry. A small, but equally creative, collection of women's clothing made of fine fabrics is also on offer. ⊠ *Borgo Santi Apostoli 44/46* ☎ *055/292993.*

Carlo Piccini. Still in operation after several generations, this Florentine institution sells antique jewelry and makes pieces to order; you can also get old jewelry reset here. ⊠ *Ponte Vecchio 31/r, Piazza della Signoria* ☎ *055/292030* ⊕ *www.carlopiccini.com.*

Cassetti. This jeweler combines precious and semiprecious stones and metals in contemporary settings. ⊠ *Ponte Vecchio 54/r, Piazza della Signoria* ☎ *055/2396028* ⊕ *www.cassetti.it.*

Gatto Bianco. This contemporary jeweler has breathtakingly beautiful pieces worked in semiprecious and precious stones. ⊠ *Borgo Santi Apostoli 12/r, Santa Maria Novella* ☎ *055/282989.*

Oro Due. Gold jewelry and other beauteous objects are priced according to the level of craftsmanship and the price of gold bullion that day. ⊠ *Via Lambertesca 12/r, Piazza della Signoria* ☎ *055/292143.*

Penko. Renaissance goldsmiths provide the inspiration for this dazzling jewelry with a contemporary feel. ⊠ *Via F. Zannetti 14/16r, Duomo* ☎ *055/211661* ⊕ *www.paolopenko.com.*

Tiffany. One of Florence's oldest jewelers has supplied Italian (and other) royalty with finely crafted gems for centuries. Its selection of antique-looking classics has been updated with a selection of contemporary silver. ⊠ *Via Tornabuoni 25/r, Santa Maria Novella* ☎ *055/215506* ⊕ *www.tiffany.it.*

LINENS AND FABRICS

Loretta Caponi. Synonymous with Florentine embroidery, the luxury lace, linens, and lingerie have earned the eponymous signora worldwide renown. ⊠ *Piazza Antinori 4/r, Santa Maria Novella* ☎ *055/213668.*

Valli. Gifted seamstresses (and seamsters) should look no further than this place, which sells sumptuous silks, beaded fabrics, lace, wool, and tweeds by the meter. ⊠ *Via della Vigna Nuova 81/r, Santa Maria Novella* ☎ *055/282485* ⊕ *www.tessutialtamodavalli.it.*

OUTLETS

For bargains on Italian designer clothing, you need to leave the city.

Barberino Designer Outlet. Prada, Pollini, Missoni, and Bruno Magli, among others, are all found at Barberino Designer Outlet. To get here, take the A1 to the Barberino di Mugello exit, and follow signs to the mall. ⊠ *Via Meucci snc* ☎ *055/842161* ⊕ *www.mcarthurglen.com.*

Mall. One-stop bargain shopping awaits at this collection of stores selling goods by such names as Bottega Veneta, Giorgio Armani, Loro Piana, Sergio Rossi, and Yves St. Laurent. ⊠ *Via Europa 8* ☎ *055/8657775* ⊕ *www.themall.it.*

Prada Outlet. Cognoscenti drive 45 minutes (or take the train to Montevarchi, and then a taxi) to find a bargain here. ⊠ *Levanella Spacceo, Estrada Statale 69, Montevarchi* ☎ *055/9196528* ⊕ *www.prada.com.*

10

SHOES AND LEATHER ACCESSORIES

Casadei. The ultimate fine leathers are crafted into classic shapes, winding up as women's shoes and bags. ⊠ *Via Tornabuoni 33/r, Santa Maria Novella* ☎ *055/287240* ⊕ *www.casadei.com.*

Cellerini. In a city where it seems just about everybody wears an expensive leather jacket, Cellerini is an institution. ⊠ *Via del Sole 37/r, Santa Maria Novella* ☎ *055/282533* ⊕ *www.cellerini.it.*

Ferragamo. This classy institution, in a 13th-century palazzo, displays designer clothing and accessories, though elegant footwear still underlies the Ferragamo success. ⊠ *Via Tornabuoni 2/r, Santa Maria Novella* ☎ *055/292123* ⊕ *www.ferragamo.com.*

Furla. Internationally renowned Furla makes beautiful leather bags, shoes, and wallets in up-to-the-minute designs. ⊠ *Via Calzaiuoli 47/r, Piazza della Repubblica* ☎ *055/2382883* ⊕ *www.furla.com.*

Giotti. You'll find a full line of leather goods, including clothing, here. ✉ *Piazza Ognissanti 3–4/r, Lungarno Nord* ☎ *055/294265* ⊕ *www. giotti.com.*

Madova. Complete your winter wardrobe with a pair of high-quality leather gloves, available in a rainbow of colors and a choice of linings (silk, cashmere, and unlined), from Madova. ✉ *Via Guicciardini 1/r, Palazzo Pitti* ☎ *055/2396526* ⊕ *www.madfi@madova.com.*

Paolo Carandini. Stop in here for exquisite leather objects such as picture frames, jewelry boxes, and desk accessories. ✉ *Borgo Allegri 17/r, Santa Croce* ☎ *055/245397* ⊕ *www.paolocarandini.com.*

Scuola del Cuoio. A consortium of leatherworkers plies its trade at La Scuola del Cuoio (Leather School), in the former dormitory of the convent of Santa Croce; high-quality, fairly priced jackets, belts, and purses are sold here. ✉ *Piazza Santa Croce 16* ☎ *055/244533* ⊕ *www. scuoladelcuoio.com.*

FIESOLE: A SIDE TRIP FROM FLORENCE

A half-day excursion to Fiesole, in the hills 8 km (5 miles) above Florence, gives you a pleasant respite from museums and a wonderful view of the city. From here the view of the Duomo, with Brunelleschi's powerful cupola, gives you a new appreciation for what the Renaissance accomplished. Fiesole began life as an ancient Etruscan and later Roman village that held some power until it succumbed to barbarian invasions. Eventually it gave up its independence in exchange for Florence's protection. The medieval cathedral, ancient Roman amphitheater, and lovely old villas behind garden walls are clustered on a series of hilltops. A walk around Fiesole can take from one to three hours, depending on how far you stroll from the main piazza.

GETTING HERE AND AROUND

The simplest way to get to Fiesole from Florence is by public bus: Take the No. 7, marked "Fiesole," which you can pick up at Piazza San Marco. If you decide to drive (the bus is so much easier), go to Piazza Liberta and cross the Ponte Rosso heading in the direction of the SS65/SR65. Turn right onto Via Salviati and continue onto Via Roccettini. Make a left turn to Via Vecchia Fiesolana, which will take you directly into the center of town.

There are several possible routes for a two-hour walk from central Florence to Fiesole. One begins in a residential area of Florence called Salviatino (Via Barbacane, near Piazza Edison, on the Bus No. 7 route), and after a short time offers views over garden walls of beautiful villas, as well as the view over your shoulder at the panorama of Florence in the valley.

VISITOR INFORMATION

Fiesole tourism office ✉ *Via Portigiani 3* ☎ *055/5961323* ⊕ *www.fiesoleforyou.it.*

EXPLORING

Anfiteatro Romano (*Roman Amphitheater*). The beautifully preserved 2,000-seat Anfiteatro Romano, near the Duomo, dates from the 1st century BC and is still used for summer concerts. To the right of the amphitheater are the remains of the **Terme Romani** (Roman Baths), where you can see the gymnasium, hot and cold baths, and rectangular chamber where the water was heated. A beautifully designed **Museo Archeologico**, its facade evoking an ancient Roman temple, is built amid the ruins and contains objects dating from as early as 2000 BC. The nearby **Museo Bandini** is filled with the private collection of Canon Angelo Maria Bandini (1726–1803); he fancied 13th- to 15th-century Florentine paintings, terra-cotta pieces, and wood sculpture, which he later bequeathed to the Diocese of Fiesole. ⊠ *Via Portigiani 1* 🕾 *055/5961293* 🖃 *€12, includes access to the archaeological park and museums* ⊘ *Apr.–Sept., daily 9:30–7; Oct.–Mar., Wed.–Mon. 10–4:30.*

Badia Fiesolana. From the church of San Domenico it's a five-minute walk northwest to the Badia Fiesolana, which was Fiesole's original cathedral. Dating to the 11th century, it was first the home of the Camaldolese monks. Thanks to Cosimo il Vecchio, the complex was substantially restructured. The facade, never completed owing to Cosimo's death, contains elements of its original Romanesque decoration. The attached convent once housed Cosimo's valued manuscripts. Its mid-15th-century cloister is well worth a look. ⊠ *Via della Badia dei Roccettini 11* 🕾 *055/46851* ⊕ *www.iue.it* ⊘ *Weekdays 9–6, Sat. 9:30–12:30.*

Duomo. A stark medieval interior yields many masterpieces. In the raised presbytery, the **Cappella Salutati** was frescoed by 15th-century artist Cosimo Rosselli, but it was his contemporary, sculptor Mino da Fiesole (1430–84), who put the town on the artistic map. The Madonna on the altarpiece and the tomb of Bishop Salutati are fine examples of the artist's work. ⊠ *Piazza Mino da Fiesole* 🕾 *055/59400* ⊘ *Nov.–Mar., daily 7:30–noon and 2–5; Apr.–Oct., daily 7:30–noon and 3–6.*

San Domenico. If you really want to stretch your legs, walk 4 km (2½ miles) toward the center of Florence along Via Vecchia Fiesolana, a narrow lane in use since Etruscan times, to the church of San Domenico. Sheltered in the church is the *Madonna and Child with Saints* by Fra Angelico, who was a Dominican friar here. ⊠ *Piazza San Domenico, off Via Giuseppe Mantellini* 🕾 *055/59230* ⊘ *Mon.–Sat. 8–noon.*

San Francesco. This lovely hilltop church has a good view of Florence and the plain below from its terrace and benches. Off the little cloister is a small, eclectic museum containing, among other things, two Egyptian mummies. Halfway up the hill you'll see sloping steps to the right; they lead to a fragrant wooded park with trails that loop out and back to the church.

10

WHERE TO EAT

$$
ITALIAN
✕ **La Reggia degli Etruschi.** If you want a breath of fresh air—literally—this lovely little eatery is worth a detour. Stamina is necessary to get here, as it's on a steep hill on the way up to the church of San Francesco. The rewards upon arrival, in the form of inventive reworkings of Tuscan classics, are well worth it. The *mezzaluna di pera a pecorino* (little half moon pasta stuffed with pear and pecorino) is sauced with Roquefort and poppy seeds. Slivers of papaya—a rare commodity on restaurant menus in these parts—anoint the tasty *carpaccio di tonno affumicato* (smoked tuna carpaccio). The wine list and the attentive service help make this a terrific place to have a meal. When it's warm, you can sit on the little terrace outside. $ *Average meal: €30* ✉ *Via San Francesco* ☎ *055/59385* ⊕ *www.lareggiadeglietruschi.com.*

$$
TUSCAN
✕ **Le Cave di Maiano.** If you're looking to get out of town, hop in your car (or take a taxi) to this simple trattoria in the hills just outside Florence. Italians flock here for the *buon rapporto fra qualità e prezzo* (the good rapport between quality and price). Tuscan staples are on hand, as is a fine plate of spaghetti with truffled asparagus. They grill well here, so consider something from the grill to follow. By all means leave room for dessert. Though the food is typical, they do it exceedingly well: the *zuppa cotta* (a trifle-like derssert made with meringue and cream) should not be missed. $ *Average meal: €35* ✉ *Via Cave di Maiano 16* ☎ *055/59133.*

WHERE TO STAY

For expanded hotel reviews, visit Fodors.com.

$$
HOTEL
⌂ **Villa Aurora.** The attractive hotel on the main piazza takes advantage of its hilltop spot, with beautiful views in many of the rooms, some of which are on two levels with beamed ceilings and balconies. **Pros:** some rooms have pretty views; air quality better than in Florence. **Cons:** a little worn at the edges. $ *Rooms from: €149* ✉ *Piazza Mino da Fiesole 39* ☎ *055/59363* 🖷 *055/59587* ⊕ *www.villaurorafiesole.com* ⟿ *23 rooms, 2 suites* ⦿*Breakfast.*

$$$$
HOTEL
⌂ **Villa San Michele.** The cypress-lined driveway provides an elegant preamble to this incredibly gorgeous (and very expensive) hotel nestled in the hills of Fiesole. **Pros:** exceptional convent conversion. **Cons:** money must be no object. $ *Rooms from: €645* ✉ *Via Doccia 4* ☎ *055/5678200* 🖷 *055/5678250* ⊕ *www.villasanmichele.com* ⟿ *21 rooms, 24 suites* ⊙ *Closed Nov.–Easter.*

NIGHTLIFE AND THE ARTS

Estate Fiesolana. From June through August, Estate Fiesolana, a festival of theater, music, dance, and film, takes place in Fiesole's churches and in the Roman amphitheater—demonstrating that the ancient Romans knew a thing or two about acoustics. ✉ *Teatro Romano* ☎ *055/5961323* ⊕ *www.comune.fiesole.fi.it.*

TUSCANY

WELCOME TO TUSCANY

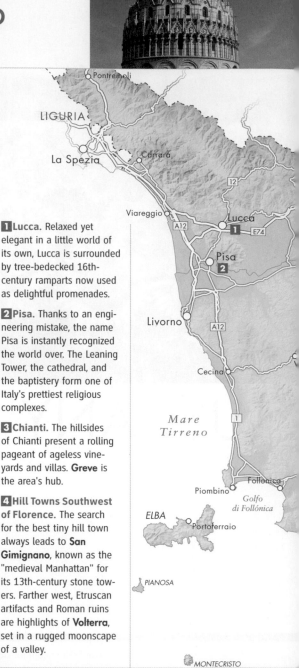

TOP REASONS TO GO

★ **Piazza del Campo, Siena:** Sip a cappuccino, lick some gelato, and take in this spectacular shell-shape piazza.

★ **Piero della Francesca's True Cross frescoes, Arezzo:** If your holy grail is great Renaissance art, seek out these 12 enigmatic scenes.

★ **San Gimignano:** Grab a spot at sunset on the steps of the Collegiata church as swallows swoop in and out of the famous medieval towers.

★ **Wine tasting in Chianti:** Sample the fruits of the region's gorgeous vineyards, at either the wineries themselves or the wine bars found in the towns.

★ **Leaning Tower of Pisa:** It may be touristy, but now that you can once again climb to the top, it's touristy fun.

1 Lucca. Relaxed yet elegant in a little world of its own, Lucca is surrounded by tree-bedecked 16th-century ramparts now used as delightful promenades.

2 Pisa. Thanks to an engineering mistake, the name Pisa is instantly recognized the world over. The Leaning Tower, the cathedral, and the baptistery form one of Italy's prettiest religious complexes.

3 Chianti. The hillsides of Chianti present a rolling pageant of ageless vineyards and villas. **Greve** is the area's hub.

4 Hill Towns Southwest of Florence. The search for the best tiny hill town always leads to **San Gimignano**, known as the "medieval Manhattan" for its 13th-century stone towers. Farther west, Etruscan artifacts and Roman ruins are highlights of **Volterra**, set in a rugged moonscape of a valley.

11

5 **Siena.** The privileged hilltop site that helped Siena flourish in the Middle Ages keeps it one of Italy's most enchanting medieval towns today. At its heart is il Campo, where the frenzied 700-year-old horse race, the Palio, is held every July 2 and August 16.

6 **Arezzo and Cortona.** These two towns south of Chianti are rewarding side trips. **Arezzo** is best known for its sublime frescoes by Piero della Francesca. **Cortona** sits high above the perfectly flat Valdichiana valley, offering great views of beautiful countryside.

7 **Southern Tuscany.** Among the highlights of Tuscany's southern reaches are the wine-producing centers of **Montalcino** and **Montepulciano**.

GETTING ORIENTED

Hillsides blanketed with vineyards, silver-green olive groves, and enchanting towns are the essence of Tuscany, one of Italy's most beautiful landscapes. Little seems changed since the Renaissance: to the west of Florence, Pisa's tower still leans; to the south, Chianti's roads wind through cypress groves, taking you to Siena, with its captivating piazza.

EATING AND DRINKING WELL IN TUSCANY

The influence of the ancient Etruscans—who favored the use of fresh herbs—is still felt in Tuscan cuisine three millennia later. Simple and earthy, Tuscan food celebrates the seasons with fresh vegetable dishes, wonderful bread-based soups, and meats perfumed with sage, rosemary, and thyme.

Throughout Tuscany there are excellent upscale restaurants that serve elaborate dishes, but to get a real taste of the flavors of the region, head for the family-run trattorias found in every town. The service and setting are often basic, but the food can be memorable.

Few places serve lighter fare at midday, so expect substantial meals at lunch and dinner, especially in out-of-the-way towns. Dining hours are fairly standard: lunch between 12:30 and 2, dinner between 7:30 and 10.

HOLD THE SALT

Tuscan bread is famous for what it's missing: it's made without salt. That's because it's intended to pick up seasoning from the food it accompanies; it's not meant to be eaten alone or dipped in a bowl of oil (which is a custom developed by American restaurants—it's not standard practice in Italian ones).

That doesn't mean Tuscans don't like to start a meal with bread, but usually it's prepared in some way. It can be grilled and drizzled with olive oil (*fettunta*), covered with chicken liver spread (*crostino nero*), or rubbed with garlic and topped with tomatoes (*bruschetta*).

AFFETTATI MISTI

The name, roughly translated, means "mixed cold cuts," pictured left, and it's something Tuscans do exceptionally well. A platter of cured meats, served as an antipasto, is sure to include *prosciutto crudo* (ham, cut paper thin) and *salame* (dry sausage, prepared in dozens of ways—some spicy, some sweet). The most distinctly Tuscan affettati are made from *cinta senese* (a once nearly extinct pig found only in the heart of the region) and *cinghiale* (wild boar, which roam all over central Italy). You can eat these delicious slices unadorned or layered on a piece of bread.

PASTA

Restaurants throughout Tuscany serve dishes similar to those in Florence, but they also have their own local specialties. Many recipes are from the *nonna* (grandmother) of the restaurant's owner, handed down through time but never written down.

Look in particular for pasta creations made with *pici* (a long, thick, hand-rolled spaghetti), *pictured below*. *Pappardelle* (a long, ribbon-like pasta noodle, pictured upper right) is frequently paired with sauces made with game, such as *lepre* (hare) or cinghiale. In the northwest, a specialty of Lucca is *tordelli di carne al ragù* (meat-stuffed pasta with a meat sauce).

MEAT

Bistecca fiorentina (a thick T-bone steak, grilled rare) is the classic meat dish of Tuscany, but there are other specialties as well. Many menus will include *tagliata di manzo* (thinly sliced, roasted beef, drizzled with olive oil), *arista di maiale* (roast pork with sage and rosemary), and *salsiccia e fagioli* (pork sausage and beans). In the southern part of the region, don't be surprised to find *piccione* (pigeon), which can be roasted, stuffed, or baked.

WINE

Grape cultivation here also dates from Etruscan times, and, particularly in Chianti, vineyards are abundant. The resulting medium-body red wine is a staple on most tables; however, you can select from a multitude of other varieties, including such reds as Brunello di Montalcino and Vino Nobile di Montepulciano and such whites as Vermentino and Vernaccia.

Super Tuscans (a fanciful name given to a group of wines by American journalists) now command attention as some of the best produced in Italy; they have great depth and complexity. The dessert wine *vin santo* is made throughout the region, and is often sipped with *biscotti* (twice-baked almond cookies), perfect for dunking.

Updated by Peter Blackman and Patricia Rucidlo

Midway down the Italian peninsula, Tuscany (Toscana in Italian) is distinguished by rolling hills, snowcapped mountains, dramatic cypress trees, and miles of coastline on the Tyrrhenian Sea—which all adds up to gorgeous views at practically every turn. The beauty of the landscape proves a perfect foil for the region's abundance of superlative art and architecture. It also produces some of Italy's finest wines and olive oils. The combination of unforgettable art, sumptuous landscapes, and eminently drinkable wines that pair beautifully with its simple food makes a trip to Tuscany something beyond special.

Many of Tuscany's cities and towns have retained the same fundamental character over the past 500 years. Civic rivalries that led to bloody battles centuries ago have given way to soccer rivalries. Renaissance pomp lives on in the celebration of local feast days and centuries-old traditions such as the Palio in Siena and the Giostra del Saracino (Joust of the Saracen) in Arezzo. Often, present-day Tuscans look as though they might have served as models for paintings produced hundreds of years ago. In many ways, the Renaissance still lives on in Tuscany.

TUSCANY PLANNER

MAKING THE MOST OF YOUR TIME
Tuscany isn't the place for a jam-packed itinerary. One of the greatest pleasures here is indulging in rustic hedonism, marked by long lunches and showstopping sunsets. Whether by car, bike, or on foot, you'll want to get out into the glorious landscape, but it's smart to keep your plans modest. Set a church or a hill town or an out-of-the-way restaurant as your destination, knowing that half the pleasure is in getting

there—admiring as you go the stately palaces, the tidy geometry of row upon row of grapevines, the fields vibrant with red poppies, sunflowers, and yellow broom. You'll need to devise a strategy for seeing the sights. Take Siena. This beautiful, art-filled town simply can't be missed; it's compact enough that you can see the major sights on a day trip, and that's exactly what most people do. Spend the night, though, and you'll get to see the town breathe a sigh and relax on the day-trippers' departure. In Pisa, the famous tower and rest of the Camposanto are not only worth seeing but a must-see, a highlight of any trip to Italy. But nearby Lucca must not be overlooked either. In fact, this walled town has greater charms than Pisa does, making it a better choice for an overnight, so you should come up with a plan that takes in both places.

GETTING HERE AND AROUND

BUS TRAVEL

Buses are a reliable but time-consuming means of getting around the region because they tend to stop in every town. Trains are a better option in virtually every respect when you're headed to Pisa, Lucca, Arezzo, and other cities with good rail service. But for most smaller towns, buses are the only option. Be aware that making arrangements for bus travel, particularly for a non-Italian speaker, can be a test of patience.

CPT. This company has infrequent buses between Volterra and Colle di Val d'Elsa, and also connects Volterra with the nearest train station in Saline. ☎ *050/505511* ⊕ *www.cpt.pisa.it.*

SENA. The trip between Siena and Rome takes three hours on the regular service provided by SENA. ☎ *0861/1991900* ⊕ *www.sena.it.*

SITA. From Florence, SITA buses serve Siena (one hour) and numerous towns in Chianti. ☎ *0577/204246, 800/373760 toll-free in Italy* ⊕ *www.sitabus.it.*

Tra-In. This bus company covers much of the territory south of Florence, and the province of Siena. ✉ *Strada Statale, 73, Levante, 23, Località Due Ponti* ☎ *892021* ⊕ *www.trainspa.it.*

CAR TRAVEL

Driving is the only way (other than hiking or biking) to get to many of Tuscany's small towns and vineyards. The cities west of Florence are easily reached by the A11, which leads to Lucca and then to the sea. The A1 takes you south from Florence to Arezzo and Chiusi (where you turn off for Montepulciano). Florence and Siena are connected by a superstrada and also the scenic Via Cassia (SR2) and even more panoramic Strada Chiantigiana (SR222), both of which thread through Chianti, skirting rolling hills and vineyards. The hill towns north and west of Siena lie along superstrade and winding local roads—all are well marked, but still you should arm yourself with a good map.

TRAIN TRAVEL

Trains on Italy's main north–south rail line stop in Florence as well as Prato, Arezzo, and Chiusi. Another major line connects Florence with Pisa, and the coastal line between Rome and Genoa passes through Pisa as well. There's regular, nearly hourly service from Florence to Lucca, and several trips a day between Florence and Siena. Siena's train station is 2 km (1 mile) north of the *centro storico* (historic center), but cabs and city buses are readily available.

For other parts of Tuscany—Chianti, Montalcino, and Montepulciano, for example—you're better off traveling by bus or by car. Train stations, when they exist, are far from the historic centers (usually in the valleys below hill towns), and service is infrequent.

Ferrovie dello Stato. You can check the website of the state railway, the Ferrovie dello Stato, for information. You can also get information and tickets at most travel agencies. ☎ *892021 toll-free within Italy* ⊕ *www.trenitalia.com.*

RESTAURANTS

Please note that restaurant prices listed as "average meal" include a meal consisting of first course *(primo)*, second course *(secondo)*, and dessert *(dolce)*.

HOTELS

A visit to Tuscany is a trip into the country. There are plenty of good hotels in the larger towns, but the classic experience is to stay in one of the rural accommodations—often converted private homes, sometimes working farms or vineyards (known as *agriturismi*).

Though it's tempting to think you can stumble upon a little out-of-the-way hotel at the end of the day, you're better off not testing your luck. Make reservations before you go. If you don't have a reservation, you may be able to get help finding a room from the local tourist office.

Hotel prices are for two people in a standard double room in high season, including tax and service. Hotel reviews have been condensed for this book. Please go to Fodors.com for full reviews of each property.

VISITOR INFORMATION

Many towns in Tuscany have tourist information offices, which can be useful resources for trip-planning advice (and sometimes maps). Such offices are typically open from 8:30 to 1 and 3:30 to 6 or 7; those in smaller towns are usually closed Saturday afternoon and Sunday, and often shut down entirely from early November through Easter.

The tourist information office in Greve is particularly noteworthy as an excellent source for general information about the Chianti wine region and its hilltop towns. In Siena the centrally located tourist office, in Piazza del Campo, has information about Siena and its province. Both offices book hotel rooms for a nominal fee. Offices in smaller towns can also be a good place to check if you need last-minute accommodations.

LUCCA

Ramparts built in the 16th and 17th centuries enclose a charming town filled with churches (99 of them), terra-cotta-roof buildings, and narrow cobblestone streets, along which locals maneuver bikes to do their daily shopping. Here Caesar, Pompey, and Crassus agreed to rule Rome as a triumvirate in 60 BC. Lucca was later the first Tuscan town to accept Christianity, and it still has a mind of its own: when most of Tuscany was voting communist as a matter of course, Lucca's citizens rarely followed suit. The famous composer Giacomo Puccini (1858–1924) was born here; his work forms the nucleus of the summer Opera Theater and Music Festival, staged in open-air venues from mid-June through mid-July. The ramparts circling the center city are the perfect place to take a stroll, ride

a bicycle, kick a ball, or just stand and look down upon Lucca.

GETTING HERE AND AROUND

You can reach Lucca easily by train from Florence; the historic center is a short walk from the station. If you're driving, take the A11/E76; Lucca is 51 km (31 miles) west of Florence.

VISITOR INFORMATION

Lucca Tourism Office ✉ *Piazza Santa Maria* ☎ *0583/91991* ⊕ *www.luccaturismo.it.*

EXPLORING LUCCA

The walled historic center of Lucca restricts motorized traffic. Walking and biking are the most efficient and most enjoyable ways to get around the mostly flat town center.

TOP ATTRACTIONS

Duomo. The blind arches on the cathedral's facade are a fine example of the rigorously ordered Pisan Romanesque style, in this case happily enlivened by an extremely varied collection of small, carved columns. Take a closer look at the decoration of the facade and that of the portico below; they make this one of the most entertaining church exteriors in Tuscany. The Gothic interior contains a moving Byzantine crucifix—called the Volto Santo, or Holy Face—brought here, according to legend, in the 8th century (though it probably dates from between the 11th and early 13th centuries). The masterpiece of the Sienese sculptor Jacopo della Quercia (circa 1371–1438) is the marble *Tomb of Ilaria del Carretto* (1407–08). ✉ *Piazza del Duomo* ☎ *0583/490530* ⊕ *www. museocattedralelucca.it* 🎟 *Church free, tomb €3* 🕐 *Duomo: Nov. 3–Mar. 14, weekdays 9:30–4:45, Sat. 9:30–6:45, Sun. 9:30–10:45 and noon–5; Mar. 15–Nov. 2, weekdays 9:30–5:45, Sat. 9–6:45, Sun. 9:30–10:45 and 11:30–6.*

Passeggiata delle Mura. Any time of day when the weather is clement, you can find the citizens of Lucca cycling, jogging, strolling, or kicking a soccer ball in this green, beautiful, and very large park—neither inside nor outside the city but rather right atop the ring of ramparts that defines Lucca. Sunlight streams through two rows of tall plane trees to dapple the *passeggiata delle mura* (walk on the walls), which is 4.2 km (2½ miles) in length. Ten bulwarks are topped with lawns, many with picnic tables and some with play equipment for children. Be aware at all times of where the edge is—there are no railings, and the drop to the ground outside the city is a precipitous 40 feet. ⊕ *www.lemuradilucca.it.*

Gelateria Veneta. Gelateria Veneta makes outstanding gelato, sorbet, and ices (some sugar-free). They prepare their confections three times a day, using the same recipes with which the Brothers Arnoldo opened the place in 1927. The pièces de résistance are frozen fruits stuffed with creamy filling: don't miss the apricot sorbet-filled apricot. Note that they close up shop in October and reopen around Easter. ⊠ *Via V. Veneto 74* ☎ *0583/467037.*

Piazza dell'Anfiteatro Romano. Here's where the ancient Roman amphitheater once stood; some of the medieval buildings built over the amphitheater retain its original oval shape and brick arches. ⊠ *Off Via Fillungo, near north side of old town.*

San Frediano. A 14th-century mosaic decorates the facade of this church just steps from the Anfiteatro. Inside are works by Jacopo della Quercia (circa 1371–1438) and Matteo Civitali (1436–1501), as well as the lace-clad mummy of Saint Zita (circa 1218–78), the patron saint of household servants. ⊠ *Piazza San Frediano* ☎ *No phone* ☉ *Mon.–Sat. 8:30–noon and 3–5, Sun. 10:30–5.*

San Michele in Foro. The facade here is even more fanciful than that of the Duomo. Its upper levels have nothing but air behind them (after the front of the church was built, there were no funds to raise the nave), and the winged Archangel Michael, who stands at the very top, seems precariously poised for flight. The facade, heavily restored in the 19th century, displays busts of such 19th-century Italian patriots as Garibaldi and Cavour. Check out the superb Filippino Lippi (circa 1457/58–1504) panel painting of Saints Jerome, Sebastian, Rocco, and Helen in the right transept. ⊠ *Piazza San Michele* ☉ *Nov.–Mar., daily 9–noon and 3–5; Apr.–Oct., daily 9–noon and 3–6.*

FAMILY **Torre Guinigi.** The tower of the medieval Palazzo Guinigi contains one of the city's most curious sights: a grove of ilex trees has grown at the top of the tower, and their roots have pushed their way into the room below. From the top you have a magnificent view of the city and the surrounding countryside. (Only the tower is open to the public, not the palazzo.) ⊠ *Palazzo Guinigi, Via Sant'Andrea* ☎ *0583/583 086* ⊕ *www. lemuradilucca.it* ☎ *€4* ☉ *Nov.–Feb., daily 9:30–4:30; Mar. and Oct, daily 9:30–5:30; Apr.–Sept., daily 9:30–7:30.*

WORTH NOTING

Museo Nazionale di Villa Guinigi. On the eastern end of the historic center, this sadly overlooked museum has an extensive collection of local Etruscan, Roman, Romanesque, and Renaissance art. The museum represents an overview of Lucca's artistic traditions from Etruscan times until the 17th century, housed in the former 15th-century villa of the Guinigi family. ⊠ *Villa Guinigi, Via della Quarquonia* ☎ *0583/496033* ☎ *€4* ☉ *Tues.–Sat. 9–7, Sun. 9–2.*

Lucca

200 yards

200 meters

Duomo **1**
Museo Nazionale
di Villa Guinigi **6**
Piazza dell'Anfiteatro
Romano **4**
San Frediano **3**
San Michele in Foro **2**
Torre Guinigi **5**

WHERE TO EAT

$$
TUSCAN
Fodor'sChoice
★

✕ **Buca di Sant'Antonio.** The staying power of Buca di Sant'Antonio—it's been around since 1782—is the result of superlative Tuscan food brought to the table by waitstaff who doesn't miss a beat. The menu includes the simple but blissful, like *tortelli lucchesi al sugo* (meat-stuffed pasta with a tomato-and-meat sauce), and more daring dishes such as roast *capretto* (kid) with herbs. A white-wall interior hung with copper pots and brass musical instruments creates a classy but comfortable dining space. $ *Average meal: €28* ✉ *Via della Cervia 3* ☎ *0583/55881* ⊙ *Closed Mon., 1 wk in Jan., and 1 wk in July. No dinner Sun.*

$$
TUSCAN

✕ **Il Giglio.** This place for all seasons, with a big fireplace for chilly weather and an outdoor terrace in summer, has quiet, late-19th-century charm and classic cuisine. If mushrooms are in season, try the *tacchonni con funghi*, a homemade pasta with mushrooms and a local herb called *nepitella*. A local favorite during winter is the *coniglio con olive* (rabbit stew with olives). $ *Average meal: €34* ✉ *Piazza del Giglio 2* ☎ *0583/494508* ⊙ *Closed Wed. and 15 days in Nov. No dinner Tues.*

$
ITALIAN

✕ **La Pecora Nera.** This lively, gaily colored little trattoria (the name means "black sheep") with a high-vaulted ceiling is staffed by *giovani disabili* (both mentally challenged and learning-disabled young people), who wait tables under the supervision of a non-disabled companion. The food's terrific, from the made-in-house *tordelli lucchesi* (meat-stuffed tortelli sauced with a fragrant meat ragù) to the tasty crostata. Great care is taken with sourcing, when possible, local organic ingredients, and such care translates into a lovely meal. $ *Average meal: €25* ✉ *Piazza San Francesco 4* ☎ *0583/469738* ⊕ *www.lapecoraneralucca.it* ⊙ *Closed Mon.–Tues. No lunch Wed.–Fri.*

$$
ITALIAN

✕ **Port Ellen Clan.** This somewhat odd name refers to a town on the Scottish island of Islay, in the Hebrides, where the proprietor and his family vacation. It calls itself a restaurant and a wine bar, and it also is a whiskey bar serving up fine single malts and blends. The interesting and short menu offers a selection of primi and secondi, as well as some tasty antipasti like the *panino di magro di lesso con salsa verde e tazzina di consommé* (a boiled beef sandwich with a herby green sauce served with a little cup of consommé). All secondi come with a side dish, which is somewhat of a novelty on Italian menus. Eclectic desserts such as the *pera cotta nel wine con gelato* (pears poached in red wine served with ice cream) provide a lovely final note. The place is small, intimate, and candle-lit: perfect for a romantic meal. $ *Average meal: €25* ✉ *Via del Fosso 120* ☎ *0583/493952* ⊕ *www.portellenclan.com* ⚑ *Reservations essential* ⊙ *Closed Mon. and Tues. No lunch Wed.–Fri.*

$
ITALIAN

✕ **Trattoria da Leo.** A few short turns away from the facade of San Michele, this noisy, informal, traditional trattoria delivers *cucina alla casalinga* (home cooking) in the best sense. Try the typical minestra di farro to start or just go straight to secondi piatti; in addition to the usual roast meats, there's excellent chicken with olives and a good cold dish of boiled meats served with a sauce of parsley and pine nuts. Save some room for a dessert, such as the rich, sweet, fig-and-walnut torte or the lemon sorbet brilliantly dotted with bits of sage, which tastes almost like mint, and is indescribably delicious. So, too, is the chestnut ice cream. $ *Average meal: €20* ⊠ *Via Tegrimi 1, at corner of Via degli Asili* ☎ *0583/492236* ▭ *No credit cards* ☉ *Closed Sun. Nov.–Mar. No lunch Sun.*

WHERE TO STAY

For expanded hotel reviews, visit Fodors.com.

$$ ⊡ **Albergo San Martino.** The brocade bedspreads are fresh and crisp, the
HOTEL proprietor friendly, the breakfast, served in a cheerful apricot room, more than ample. **Pros:** comfortable beds; great breakfast (extra). **Cons:** parking is difficult; surroundings are pleasant and stylish though not luxurious. $ *Rooms from: €110* ⊠ *Via della Dogana 9* ☎ *0583/469181* ⊕ *www.albergosanmartino.it* ⇆ *6 rooms, 2 suites* ⎮◯⎮ *No meals.*

$$ ⊡ **Hotel Ilaria.** The former stables of the Villa Bottini have been trans-
HOTEL formed into a modern hotel with stylish rooms done in a warm wood veneer with blue-and-white fittings. **Pros:** a Fodor's reader sums it up as a "nice, modern small hotel"; free bicycles. **Cons:** though in the city center, it's a little removed from main attractions. $ *Rooms from: €129* ⊠ *Via del Fosso 26* ☎ *0583/47615* ⊕ *www.hotelilaria.com* ⇆ *36 rooms, 5 suites* ⎮◯⎮ *Breakfast.*

$$ ⊡ **Palazzo Alexander.** The building, dating from the 12th century, has
HOTEL been restructured to create the ease common to Lucchesi nobility: timbered ceilings, warm yellow walls, and brocaded chairs adorn the public rooms, and guest rooms have high ceilings and that same glorious damask. **Pros:** intimate feel; gracious staff; bacon and eggs included in the buffet breakfast; a short walk from San Michele in Foro. **Cons:** some Fodor's readers complain of too-thin walls. $ *Rooms from: €160* ⊠ *Via S. Giustina 48* ☎ *0583/583571* ⊕ *www.palazzoalexander.it* ⇆ *9 rooms, 3 suites, 1 apartment* ⎮◯⎮ *Breakfast.*

$ ⊡ **Piccolo Hotel Puccini.** Steps away from the busy square and church
HOTEL of San Michele, this little hotel is quiet and calm—and a great deal. **Pros:** cheery, English-speaking staff. **Cons:** breakfast costs extra; some rooms are on the dark side. $ *Rooms from: €97* ⊠ *Via di Poggio 9* ☎ *0583/55421* ⊕ *www.hotelpuccini.com* ⇆ *14 rooms* ⎮◯⎮ *No meals.*

SPORTS AND THE OUTDOORS

A splendid bike ride may be had by circling the entire historic center along the top of the bastions—affording something of a bird's-eye view.

Poli Antonio Biciclette. This is the best option for bicycle rental on the east side of town. ⊠ *Piazza Santa Maria 42, Lucca East* ☎ *0583/493787* ⊕ *www.biciclettepoli.com.*

SHOPPING

Lucca's justly famed olive oils are available throughout the city (and exported around the world). Look for those made by Fattoria di Fubbiano and Fattoria Fabbri—two of the best.

Antica Bottega di Prospero. Stop by this shop for top-quality local products, including farro, dried porcini mushrooms, olive oil, and wine. ⊠ *Via San Lucia 13.*

Caniparoli. Chocolate lovers will be pleased with the selection of artisanal chocolates. This artisinal shop is so serious about their sweets that they do not make them from June to August, because of the heat. ⊠ *Via San Paolino 96* ☎ *0583/53456.*

My Walit. Brightly colored wallets, purses, and other lovely leather accessories are on offer here at affordable prices. ⊠ *Piazza Anfiteatro 40* ☎ *0583/051578.*

PISA

Most people think "Leaning Tower of" when they think of Pisa. Its position as one of Italy's most famous landmarks attracts hordes of day-trippers from around the world. But even if the building doesn't captivate you, Pisa has other treasures that make a visit worthwhile. Taken as a whole, the Campo dei Miracoli—the "Field of Miracles" where the Leaning Tower, the Duomo, the Camposanto, and the Baptistery are located—is one of the most dramatic and beautiful architectural complexes in Italy.

Pisa may have been inhabited as early as the Bronze Age. It was certainly populated by the Etruscans and, in turn, became part of the Roman Empire. In the early Middle Ages it flourished as an economic powerhouse—along with Amalfi, Genoa, and Venice, it was one of the maritime republics. The city's economic and political power ebbed in the early 15th century as it fell under the domination of Florence, though it enjoyed a brief resurgence under Cosimo I in the mid-16th century. Pisa endured heavy Allied bombing—miraculously, the Duomo and Leaning Tower, along with some other grand Romanesque structures, were spared, but the Camposanto sustained heavy damage.

GETTING HERE AND AROUND

About 84 km (52 miles) west of Florence, Pisa is a straight shot on the Fi-Pi-Li autostrada. By train it's an easy hour-long ride. The Pisa–Lucca train runs frequently and takes about 30 minutes.

VISITOR INFORMATION

Pisa Tourism Office ⊠ *Piazza Vittorio Emanuele II* ☎ *050/42291* ⊕ *www.pisaunicaterre.it.*

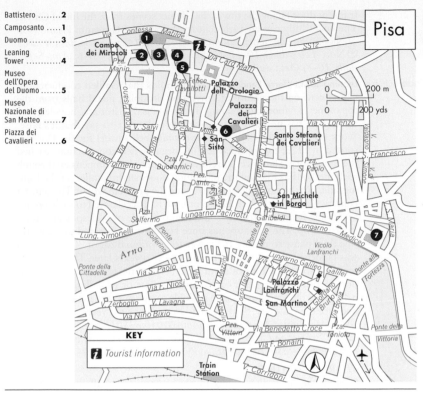

EXPLORING PISA

Pisa, like many Italian cities, is best explored on foot, and most of what you'll want to see is within walking distance. The views along the Arno River are particularly grand and shouldn't be missed—there's a feeling of spaciousness that isn't found along the Arno in Florence.

As you set out, note that there are various combination-ticket options for sights on the Piazza del Duomo.

TOP ATTRACTIONS

Battistero. This lovely Gothic baptistery, which stands across from the Duomo's facade, is best known for the pulpit carved by Nicola Pisano (circa 1220–84; father of Giovanni Pisano) in 1260. Every half hour, an employee will dramatically close the doors, then intone and chant, thereby demonstrating how remarkable the acoustics are in the place. ⊠ *Piazza del Duomo* ☎ *050/835011* ⊕ *www.opapisa.it* ⊠ *€5, discounts available if bought in combination with tickets for other monuments* ☉ *Nov.–Feb., daily 10–5; Mar., daily 9–6; Apr.–Sept., daily 8–8; Oct., daily 9–7.*

Duomo. Pisa's cathedral brilliantly utilizes the horizontal marble-stripe motif (borrowed from Moorish architecture) that became common to Tuscan cathedrals. It is famous for the Romanesque panels on the transept door facing the tower that depict scenes from the life of Christ. The beautifully carved 14th-century pulpit is by Giovanni Pisano (son of Nicola). ⊠ *Piazza del Duomo* ☎ *050835011* ⊕ *www.opapisa.it* ᴤ *€5* ⊙ *Nov.–Feb., daily 10–12:45 and 2–5; Mar., daily 10–6; Apr.–Sept., daily 10–8; Oct., daily 10–7.*

Fodor's Choice
★

Leaning Tower (Torre Pendente). Legend holds that Galileo conducted an experiment on the nature of gravity by dropping metal balls from the top of the 187-foot-high Leaning Tower of Pisa. Historians, however, say this legend has no basis in fact—which isn't quite to say that it's false. Work on this tower, built as a *campanile* (bell tower) for the Duomo, started in 1173: the lopsided settling began when construction reached the third story. The tower's architects attempted to compensate through such methods as making the remaining floors slightly taller on the leaning side, but the extra weight only made the problem worse. The settling continued, and by the late 20th century it had accelerated to such a point that many feared the tower would simply topple over, despite all efforts to prop it up. The structure has since been firmly anchored to the earth. The final phase to restore the tower to its original tilt of 300 years ago was launched in early 2000 and finished two years later. The last phase removed some 100 tons of earth from beneath the foundation. Reservations, which are essential, can be made online or by calling the Museo dell'Opera del Duomo; it's also possible to arrive at the ticket office and book for the same day. Note that children under eight years of age are not allowed to climb. ⊠ *Piazza del Duomo* ☎ *050/835011* ⊕ *www.opapisa.it* ᴤ *€18* ⊙ *Dec. and Jan., daily 10–4:30; Nov. and Feb., daily 9:30–5:30; Mar., daily 9–5:30; Apr.–Sept., daily 8:30–8; Oct., daily 9–7.*

WORTH NOTING

Camposanto. According to legend, the cemetery—a walled structure on the western side of the Campo dei Miracoli—is filled with earth that returning Crusaders brought back from the Holy Land. Contained within are numerous frescoes, notably *The Drunkenness of Noah*, by Renaissance artist Benozzo Gozzoli (1422–97), presently under restoration; and the disturbing *Triumph of Death* (14th century; artist uncertain), whose subject matter shows what was on people's minds in a century that saw the ravages of the Black Death. ⊠ *Piazza del Duomo* ☎ *050/835011* ⊕ *www.opapisa.it* ᴤ *€5, discounts available if bought in combination with tickets for other monuments* ⊙ *Nov.–Feb., daily 10–5; Mar., daily 9–6; Apr.–Sept., daily 8–8; Oct., daily 9–7.*

Museo dell'Opera del Duomo. At the southeast corner of the sprawling Campo dei Miracoli, this museum holds a wealth of medieval sculptures and the ancient Roman sarcophagi that inspired Nicola Pisano's figures. ⊠ *Piazza del Duomo* ☎ *050/835011* ⊕ *www.opapisa.it* ᴤ *€5, discounts available if bought in combination with tickets for other monuments* ⊙ *Nov.–Feb., daily 10–5; Mar., daily 9–6; Apr.–Sept., daily 8–8; Oct., daily 9–7.*

Museo Nazionale di San Matteo. On the north bank of the Arno, this museum contains some beautiful examples of local Romanesque and Gothic art. ⊠ *Lungarno Mediceo* ☎ *050/541865* ᴤ *€5* ⊙ *Tues.–Sat. 9–7, holidays 9–2.*

Piazza dei Cavalieri. The piazza, with its fine Renaissance **Palazzo dei Cavalieri, Palazzo dell'Orologio,** and Chiesa di **Santo Stefano dei Cavalieri,** was laid out by Giorgio Vasari in about 1560. The square was the seat of the Ordine dei Cavalieri di San Stefano (Order of the Knights of St. Stephen), a military and religious institution meant to defend the coast from possible invasion by the Turks. Also in this square is the prestigious **Scuola Normale Superiore,** founded by Napoléon in 1810 on the French model. Here graduate students pursue doctorates in literature, philosophy, mathematics, and science. In front of the school is a large statue of Ferdinando I de' Medici dating from 1596. On the extreme left is the tower where the hapless Ugolino della Gherardesca (died 1289) was imprisoned with his two sons and two grandsons; legend holds that he ate them. Dante immortalized him in Canto XXXIII of his *Inferno.* Duck into the **Church of Santo Stefano** (if you're lucky enough to find it open) and check out Bronzino's splendid *Nativity of Christ* (1564–65).

WHERE TO EAT

$$ ITALIAN   ✕ **Beny.** Apricot walls hung with etchings of Pisa make this small, single-room restaurant warmly romantic. Husband and wife Damiano and Sandra Lazzerini have been running the place for two decades, and it shows in their obvious enthusiasm while talking about the menu and daily specials (which often astound). Fish is a specialty here: the *ripieno di polpa di pesce a pan grattato con salsa di seppie e pomodoro* (fish-stuffed ravioli with tomato-octopus sauce) delights. Seasonal ingredients are key throughout the menu; Sandra works wonders with *tartufi estivi* (summer truffles), artichokes, and market fish of the day. Ⓢ *Average meal: €46* ⊠ *Piazza Gambacorti 22* ☎ *050/25067* ◷ *Closed Sun. and 2 wks in mid-Aug. No lunch Sat.*

$$ ITALIAN   ✕ **Osteria dei Cavalieri.** This charming white-wall restaurant, a few steps from Piazza dei Cavalieri, is reason enough to come to Pisa. They can do it all here—serve up exquisitely grilled fish dishes, please vegetarians, and prepare *tagliata* (thin slivers of rare beef) for meat lovers. Three set menus, from the sea, garden, and earth, are available, or you can order à la carte. For dinner there's an early seating (around 7:30) and a later one (around 9); opt for the later one if you want time to linger over your meal. Ⓢ *Average meal: €30* ⊠ *Via San Frediano 16* ☎ *050/580858* ⌖ *Reservations essential* ◷ *Closed Sun., 2 wks in Aug., and Dec. 29–Jan. 7. No lunch Sat.*

$ ITALIAN   ✕ **Trattoria la Faggiola.** It's only seconds away from the Leaning Tower, which probably explains the "No Pizza" sign written in big, bold letters on the blackboard outside. Inside, another blackboard lists two or three primi and secondi. The amiable Carlo Silvestrini presides over this little eatery, and he cares if you don't clean your plate. That's not a problem though, because everything's good, from the *pasta pasticciata con speck e carciofi* (oven-baked penne with cured ham and artichokes) to the finishing touch of *castagnaccio con crema di ricotta* (a chestnut flan topped with ricotta cream). Ⓢ *Average meal: €23* ⊠ *Via della Faggiola 1* ☎ *050/556179* ⌖ *Reservations essential* ▭ *No credit cards.*

WHERE TO STAY

For expanded hotel reviews, visit Fodors.com.

$$$
HOTEL
Hotel Relais dell'Orologio. What used to be a private family palace is now an intimate hideaway where 18th-century antiques fill the rooms and public spaces and some rooms have stenciled walls and wood-beam ceilings. **Pros:** location—in the center of town, but on a quiet side street. **Cons:** breakfast costs extra; a bit pricey. $ Rooms from: €250 ✉ Via della Faggiola 12/14, off Campo dei Miracoli, Santa Maria ☎ 050/830361 ⊕ www.hotelrelaisorologio.com ⇆ 16 rooms, 5 suites ⏲ No meals.

$
HOTEL
Royal Victoria. In a pleasant palazzo facing the Arno, a 10-minute walk from the Campo dei Miracoli, room styles range from the 1800s, complete with frescoes, to the 1920s; the most charming are in the old tower. **Pros:** friendly staff; lovely views of the Arno from many rooms. **Cons:** rooms vary significantly in size; all are a little worn. $ Rooms from: €70 ✉ Lungarno Pacinotti 12 ☎ 050/940111 ⊕ www.royalvictoria.it ⇆ 48 rooms, 40 with bath ⏲ Breakfast.

CHIANTI

Chianti, directly south of Florence, is one of Italy's most famous wine-producing regions; its hill towns, olive groves, and vineyards are quintessential Tuscany. Many British and northern Europeans have relocated here, drawn by the unhurried life, balmy climate, and charming villages; there are so many Britons, in fact, that the area has been nicknamed Chiantishire. Still, it remains strongly Tuscan in character, with drop-dead views of vine-quilted hills and elegantly elongated cypress trees.

The sinuous SR222 highway, known as the Strada Chiantigiana, runs from Florence through the heart of Chianti. Its most scenic section connects Strada in Chianti, 16 km (10 miles) south of Florence, and Greve in Chianti, whose triangular central piazza is surrounded by restaurants and vintners offering degustazioni (wine tastings), 11 km (7 miles) farther south.

GREVE IN CHIANTI

27 km (17 miles) south of Florence, 40 km (25 miles) northeast of Colle Val d'Elsa.

If there's a capital of Chianti, it's Greve, a friendly market town with no shortage of cafés, enoteche (wine bars), and crafts shops lining its streets.

GETTING HERE AND AROUND
Driving from Florence or Siena, Greve is easily reached via the Strada Chiantigiana (SR222). SITA buses travel frequently between Florence and Greve. Tra-In and SITA buses connect Siena with Greve, but a direct trip is virtually impossible. There's no train service to Greve.

VISITOR INFORMATION
Greve in Chianti Tourism Office ✉ Piazza Matteotti 11 ☎ 055/8546299.

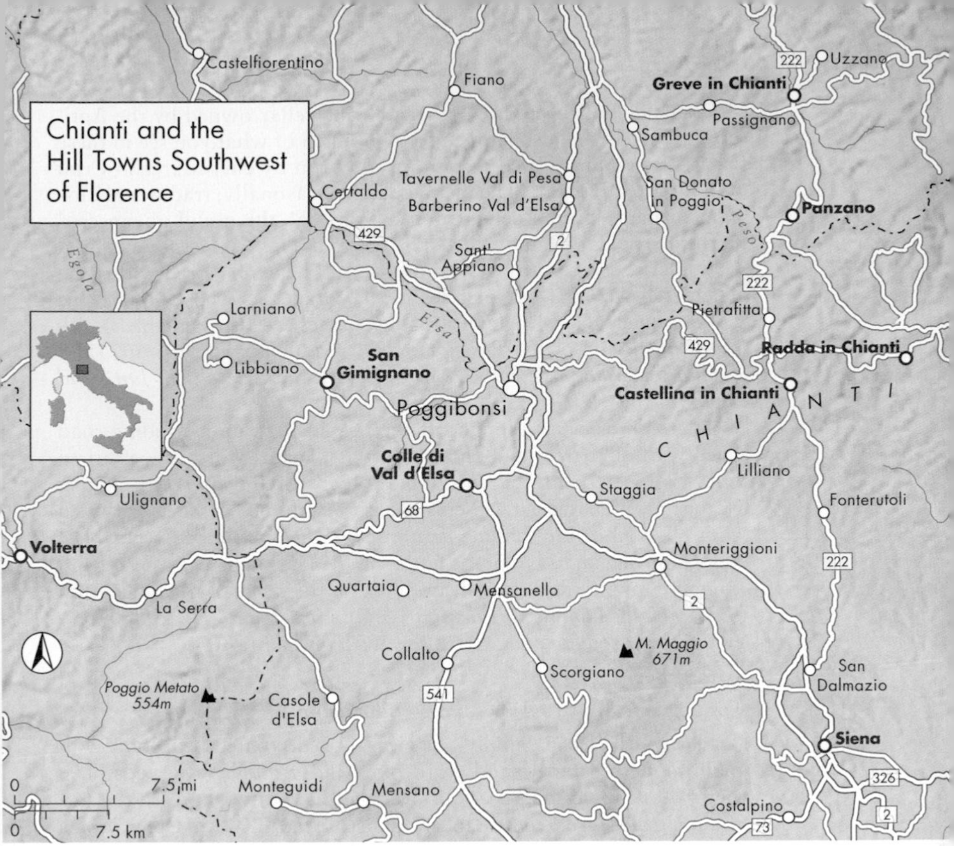
Chianti and the Hill Towns Southwest of Florence
Castelfiorentino
Fiano
Greve in Chianti
Uzzano
Passignano
Sambuca
Tavernelle Val di Pesa
Barberino Val d'Elsa
Certaldo
San Donato in Poggio
Panzano
Pesa
Egola
Sant' Appiano
Elsa
Larniano
Libbiano
San Gimignano
Poggibonsi
Pietrafitta
Radda in Chianti
Castellina in Chianti
CHIANTI
Colle di Val d'Elsa
Lilliano
Ulignano
Staggia
Fonterutoli
Volterra
Monteriggioni
Quartaia
Mensanello
La Serra
Collalto
M. Maggio 671m
Scorgiano
Poggio Metato 554m
Casole d'Elsa
San Dalmazio
Siena
Monteguidi
Mensano
Costalpino
0 7.5 mi
0 7.5 km
222
429
2
68
541
326
73

EXPLORING

Montefioralle. A tiny hilltop hamlet, about 2 km (1 mile) west of Greve in Chianti, Montefioralle is the ancestral home of Amerigo Vespucci (1454–1512), the mapmaker, navigator, and explorer who named America. (His niece Simonetta may have been the inspiration for Sandro Botticelli's *Birth of Venus*, painted sometime in the 1480s.)

Piazza Matteotti. Greve's gently sloping and asymmetrical central piazza is surrounded by an attractive arcade with shops of all kinds. In the center stands a statue of the discoverer of New York harbor, Giovanni da Verrazano (circa 1480–1527). Check out the lively market held here on Saturday morning.

WHERE TO EAT

$ TUSCAN 🍴 **Enoteca Fuoripiazza.** Detour off Greve's flower-strewn main square for food that relies heavily on local ingredients (like cheese and salami produced nearby). The lengthy wine list provides a bewildering array of choices to pair with *affettati misti* (a plate of cured meats) or one of their primi—the *pici* (a thick, short noodle) is deftly prepared here. All the dishes are made with great care. [$] *Average meal:* €26 ✉ *Via I Maggio* ☎ *055/8546313* 🕒 *Closed Mon.*

$$ ITALIAN 🍴 **Osteria di Passignano.** In an ancient wine cellar owned by the Antinori family—who also happen to own much of what you see in these parts—is a sophisticated restaurant ably run by chef Marcello Crini and his attentive staff. The menu changes seasonally; traditional Tuscan cuisine is given a delightful twist through the use of unexpected herbs. Particularly tantalizing is the *filetto di vitello alle spezie* (spiced veal fillet), served with roast tomatoes and beans flavored with sage. The extensive wine list includes local vintages as well as numerous international labels. Daylong cooking courses are also available. [$] *Average meal: €35* ✉ *Via Passignano 33, Passignano* ☎ *055/8071278* 🌐 *www.osteriadipassignano.com* ⏲ *Closed Sun., 3 wks in Jan., and 1 wk in Aug.*

$$ TUSCAN 🍴 **Ristoro di Lamole.** Although off the beaten path up a winding road lined with olive trees and vineyards, this place is worth the effort to find. The view from the outdoor terrace is divine, as is the simple, exquisitely prepared Tuscan cuisine. Start with the bruschetta drizzled with olive oil or the sublime *verdure sott'olio* (marinated vegetables) before moving on to any of the fine secondi. The kitchen has a way with *coniglio* (rabbit); don't pass it up if it's on the menu. [$] *Average meal: €35* ✉ *Via di Lamole 6, Località Lamole in Chianti* ☎ *055/8547050* 🌐 *www.ristorodilamole.it* ⏲ *Closed Wed. and Nov.–Apr.*

WHERE TO STAY

For expanded hotel reviews, visit Fodors.com.

$ B&B/INN 🏨 **Albergo del Chianti.** Simply but pleasantly decorated bedrooms with plain modern cabinets and wardrobes and wrought-iron beds have views of the town square or out over the tile rooftops toward the surrounding hills. **Pros:** central location; best value in Greve. **Cons:** rooms facing the piazza can be noisy; small bathrooms. [$] *Rooms from: €100* ✉ *Piazza Matteotti 86* ☎ *055/853763* 🌐 *www.albergodelchianti.it* 🛏 *16 rooms* ⏲ *Closed Jan.* 🍽 *Breakfast.*

$$$ B&B/INN Fodor's Choice ★ 🏨 **Villa Bordoni.** David and Catherine Gardner, Scottish expats, have transformed a ramshackle 16th-century villa into a stunning little retreat where no two rooms are alike—all have stenciled walls; some have four-poster beds, others small mezzanines. **Pros:** splendidly isolated in the hills above Greve; beautiful decor; wonderful hosts. **Cons:** on a long and bumpy dirt road; need a car to get around. [$] *Rooms from: €250* ✉ *Via San Cresci 31/32, Località Mezzuola* ☎ *055/8547453* 🌐 *www.villabordoni.com* 🛏 *8 rooms, 3 suites* ⏲ *Closed 3 wks in Jan. and Feb.* 🍽 *Breakfast.*

$$ B&B/INN Fodor's Choice ★ 🏨 **Villa Il Poggiale.** Renaissance gardens, beautiful rooms with high ceilings and elegant furnishings, a panoramic pool, and expert staff are just a few of the things that make a stay at this 16th-century villa memorable. **Pros:** beautiful gardens and panoramic setting; elegant historical building; exceptionally professional staff. **Cons:** a little isolated, making private transportation necessary; some rooms face a country road and may be noisy during the day. [$] *Rooms from: €160* ✉ *Via Empolese 69, 20 km (12 miles) northwest of Greve, San Casciano Val di Pesa* ☎ *055/828311* 🌐 *www.villailpoggiale.it* 🛏 *20 rooms, 4 suites* ⏲ *Closed Jan.–Feb.* 🍽 *Breakfast.*

Continued on page 645

GRAPE ESCAPES
THE PLEASURES OF TUSCAN WINE

The vineyards stretching across the landscape of Tuscany may look like cinematic backdrops, but in fact they're working farms, and they produce some of Italy's best wines. No matter whether you're a wine novice or a connoisseur, there's great pleasure to be had from exploring this lush terrain, visiting the vineyards, and uncorking a bottle for yourself.

GETTING TO KNOW TUSCAN WINE

Most of the wine produced in Tuscany is red (though there are some notable whites as well), and most Tuscan reds are made primarily from one type of grape, sangiovese. That doesn't mean, however, that all wines here are the same. God (in this case Bacchus) is in the details: differences in climate, soil, and methods of production result in wines with several distinct personalities.

Chianti

Chianti is the most famous name in Tuscan wine, but what exactly the name means is a little tricky. It once identified wines produced in the region extending from just south of Florence to just north of Siena. In the mid-20th century, the official Chianti zone was expanded to include a large portion of central Tuscany. That area is divided into eight subregions. **Chianti Classico** is the name given to the original zone, which makes up 17,000 of the 42,000 acres of Chianti-producing vineyards.

Classico wines, which bear the *gallo nero* (black rooster) logo on their labels, are the most highly regarded Chiantis (with **Rùfina** running second), but that doesn't mean Classicos are always superior. All Chiantis are strictly regulated (they must be a minimum 75% to 80% sangiovese, with other varieties blended in to add nuance), and they share a strong, woodsy character that's well suited to Tuscan food. It's a good strategy to drink the local product—**Colli Senesi Chianti** when in Siena, for example. The most noticeable, and costly, difference comes when a Chianti is from *riserva* (reserve) stock, meaning it's been aged for at least two years.

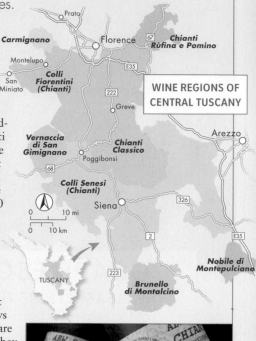

WINE REGIONS OF CENTRAL TUSCANY

DOC & DOCG The designations "DOC" and "DOCG"—Denominazione di Origine Controllata (e Garantita)—mean a wine comes from an established region and adheres to rigorous standards of production. Ironically, the esteemed Super Tuscans are labeled *vini da tavola* (table wines), the least prestigious designation, because they don't use traditional grape blends.

Brunello di Montalcino

The area surrounding the hill town of Montalcino, to the south of Siena, is drier and warmer than the Chianti regions, and it produces the most powerful of the sangiovese-based wines. Regulations stipulate that Brunello di Montalcino be made entirely from sangiovese grapes (no blending) and aged at least four years. **Rosso di Montalcino** is a younger, less complex, less expensive Brunello.

The Super Tuscans

Beginning in the 1970s, some winemakers, chafing at the regulations imposed on established Tuscan wine varieties, began blending and aging wines in innovative ways. Thus were born the so-called Super Tuscans. These pricey, French oak–aged wines are admired for their high quality, led by such star performers as **Sassicaia**, from the Maremma region, and **Tignanello**, produced at the Tenuta Marchesi Antinori near Badia a Passignano. Purists, however, lament the loss of local identity resulting from the Super Tuscans' use of nonnative grape varieties such as cabernet sauvignon and merlot.

Vino Nobile di Montepulciano

East of Montalcino is Montepulciano, the town at the heart of the third, and smallest, of Tuscany's top wine districts.

Blending regulations aren't as strict for Vino Nobile as for Chianti and Brunello, and as a result it has a wider range of characteristics. Broadly speaking, though, Vino Nobile is a cross between Chianti and Brunello—less acidic than the former and softer than the latter. It also has a less pricey sibling, **Rosso di Montepulciano**.

The Whites

Most whites from Tuscany are made from **trebbiano** grapes, which produce a wine that's light and refreshing but not particularly aromatic or flavorful—it may hit the spot on a hot afternoon, but it doesn't excite connoisseurs.

Golden-hewed **Vernaccia di San Gimignano** is a local variety with more limited production but greater personality—it's the star of Tuscan whites. Winemakers have also brought chardonnay and sauvignon grapes to the region, resulting in wines that, like some Super Tuscans, are pleasant to drink but short on local character.

TOURING & TASTING IN TUSCAN WINE COUNTRY

Strade del Vino di Toscana > Tuscany has visitor-friendly wineries, but the way you go about visiting is a bit different here from what it is in California or France. Many wineries welcome drop-ins for a tasting, but for a tour you usually need to make an appointment a few days in advance. There are several approaches you can take, depending on how much time you have and how serious you are about wine:

PLAN 1: FULL IMMERSION. Make an appointment to tour one of the top wineries (see our recommendations on the next page), and you'll get the complete experience: half a day of strolling through vineyards, talking grape varieties, and tasting wine, often accompanied by food. Groups are small; in spring and fall, it may be just you and the winemaker. The cost is usually €10 to €20 per person, but can go up to €40 if a meal is included. Remember to specify a tour in English.

PLAN 2: SEMI-ORGANIZED. If you want to spend a few hours going from vineyard to vineyard, make your first stop one of the local tourist information offices—they're great resources for maps, tasting itineraries, and personalized advice about where to visit. The offices in **Greve, Montalcino,** and **Montepulciano** are the best equipped. **Enoteche** (for more about them, turn the page) can also be good places to pick up tips about where to go for tastings.

PLAN 3: SPONTANEOUS. Along Tuscany's country roads you'll see signs for wineries offering **vendita diretta** (direct sales) and **degustazioni** (tastings). For a taste of the local product with some atmosphere thrown in, a spontaneous visit is a perfectly viable approach. You may wind up in a simple shop or an elaborate tasting room; either way, there's a fair chance you'll sample something good. Expect a small fee for a three-glass tasting.

THE PICK OF THE VINEYARDS

Within the Chianti Classico region, these wineries should be at the top of your to-visit list, whether you're dropping in for a taste or making a full tour. (Tours require reservations unless otherwise indicated.)

CHIANTI CLASSICO

Badia a Coltibuono

(✉ Gaiole in Chianti ☎ 0577/749498 ⊕ www.coltibuono. com). Along with an extensive prelunch tour and tasting, there are shorter afternoon tours, no reservation required, starting on the hour from 2 to 5. (See "Radda in Chianti" in this chapter.)

Castello di Fonterutoli

(✉ Castellina in Chianti ☎ 0577/741385 ⊕ www. fonterutoli.it). Hour-long tours include a walk through the neighboring village.

Castello di Volpaia

(✉ Radda in Chianti ☎ 0577/738066 ⊕ www. volpaia.com). The tour here includes a visit to the olive oil press and a tour of the town.

Castello di Verrazzano

(✉ Via S. Martino in Valle 12, Greve in Chianti ☎ 055/854243 ⊕ www. verrazzano.com). Tours here take you down to the cellars, through the gardens, and into the woods in search of wild boar.

Villa Vignamaggio

(✉ Via Petriolo 5, Greve in Chianti ☎ 055/854661 ⊕ www. vignamaggio.com). Along with a wine tour, you can spend the night at this villa where Mona Lisa is believed to have been born. (See "Where to Stay" under "Greve in Chianti" in this chapter.)

Rocca delle Màcie

(✉ Località Le Macìe 45, Castellina in Chianti ☎ 0577/732236 ⊕ www.rocca dellemacie.com). A full lunch or dinner can be incorporated into your tasting here.

Castello di Brolio

(✉ Gaiole in Chianti ☎ 0577/730220 ⊕ www.ricasoli.it). One of Tuscany's most impressive castles also has a centuries-old winemaking tradition. (See "Radda in Chianti" in this chapter.)

REMEMBER ⚠

Always have a designated driver when you're touring and tasting. Vineyards are usually located off narrow, curving roads. Full sobriety is a must behind the wheel.

MORE TUSCAN WINE RESOURCES

Enoteche: Wine Shops

The word *enoteca* in Italian can mean "wine store," "wine bar," or both. In any event, *enoteche* (the plural, pronounced "ay-no-*tek*-ay") are excellent places to sample and buy Tuscan wines, and they're also good sources of information about local wineries. There are scores to choose from. These are a few of the best:

Enoteca Italiana, Siena (Fortezza Medicea, Viale Maccari ☎ 0577/288497 ⊕ www. enoteca-italiana.it). The only one of its kind, this *enoteca* represents all the producers of DOC and DOCG wines in Italy and stocks over 400 labels. Wine by the glass and snacks are available.

Enoteca Osticcio, Montalcino (✉ Via Matteotti 23 ☎ 0577/848271 ⊕ www. osticcio.com). There are more than one thousand labels in stock. With one of the best views in Montalcino, it is also a very pleasant place to sit and meditate over a glass of Brunello.

Enoteca del Gallo Nero, Greve in Chianti (✉ Piazzetta S. Croce 8 ☎ 055/853297). This is one of the best stocked *enoteche* in the Chianti region.

La Dolce Vita, Montepulciano (Via di Voltaia nel Corso 80/82 ☎ 0578/757872). An elegantly restored monastery is home to the excellent enoteca in the upper part of Montepulciano, which has a wide selction of wines by the glass.

Wine on the Web

Tuscan wine country is well represented on the Internet. A good place for an overview is ⊕ www.terreditoscana.regione. toscana.it. (Click on "Le Strade del Vino"; the page that opens next will give you the option of choosing an English-language version.) This site shows 14 *strade del vino* (wine roads) that have been mapped out by consortiums representing major wine districts (unfortunately, Chianti Classico isn't included), along with recommended itineraries. You'll also find links to the consortium Web sites, where you can dig up more detailed information on touring. The Chianti Classico consortium's site is ⊕ www.chianticlassico.com. The Vino Nobile di Montepulciano site is ⊕ www.vinonobiledimontepulciano.it, and Brunello di Montalcino is ⊕ www. consorziobrunellodimontalcino.it. All have English versions.

PANZANO

7 km (4½ miles) south of Greve, 29 km (18 miles) south of Florence. The magnificent views of the valleys of the Pesa and Greve rivers easily make Panzano one of the prettiest stops in Chianti. The triangular Piazza Bucciarelli is the heart of the new town. A short stroll along Via Giovanni da Verrazzano brings you up to the old town, Panzano Alto, which is still partly surrounded by medieval walls. The town's 13th-century castle is now almost completely absorbed by later buildings (its central tower is now a private home).

GETTING HERE AND AROUND

From Florence or Siena, Panzano is easily reached by car along the Strada Chiantigiana (SR222). SITA buses travel frequently between Florence and Panzano. From Siena, though, the round-trip by bus can be difficult because SITA and Tra-In don't coordinate their schedules, leaving you stranded in Panzano longer than you want to be. There's no train service to Panzano.

EXPLORING

San Leolino. Ancient even by Chianti standards, this hilltop church probably dates from the 10th century, but was completely rebuilt in the Romanesque style sometime in the 13th century. It has a 14th-century cloister worth seeing. The 16th-century terra-cotta tabernacles are attributed to Giovanni della Robbia, and there's also a remarkable triptych (attributed to the Master of Panzano) that was executed sometime in the mid-14th century. Open days and hours are unpredictable; check with the tourist office in Greve in Chianti for the latest. ✉ *Località San Leolino, 3 km (2 miles) south of Panzano* ☎ *055/8546299.*

WHERE TO EAT

$ INTERNATIONAL 🍴 **Dario +.** Local butcher and restaurateur Dario Cecchini has extended his empire of meat to include this space located directly above his butcher's shop. Here you'll find only two items on the menu: the "Dario +," a half-pound burger in a crisp crumb crust served with roast potatoes and onions; and the "Welcome," four different dishes of beef and pork served with fresh garden vegetables. Both are a nice change from the more standard options found at restaurants throughout Chianti. Outdoor seating is available in summer, but get here early—it's enormously popular. Enter from the public parking area behind the restaurant. [$] *Average meal: €10* ✉ *Via XX Luglio 11* ☎ *055/852176* 🌐 *www.dariocecchini.com* ✍ *Reservations not accepted* 🕒 *Closed Sun.*

$ TUSCAN 🍴 **Solociccia.** "Abandon all hope, ye who enter here," announces the menu. "You're in the hands of a butcher." Indeed you are, for this restaurant is the creation of Dario Cecchini, Panzano's local merchant of meat. Served at communal tables, the set meal consists of no less than six meat courses, chosen at Dario's discretion. They are accompanied by seasonal vegetables, white beans with olive oil, and focaccia bread. Though Cecchini emphasizes that steak is never on the menu, this lively, crowded place is definitely not for vegetarians. The entrance is on Via XX Luglio. [$] *Average meal: €30* ✉ *Via Chiantigiana 5* ☎ *055/852727* 🌐 *www.solociccia.it* ✍ *Reservations essential* 🕒 *Closed Mon.–Wed. No dinner Sun.*

WHERE TO STAY

For expanded hotel reviews, visit Fodors.com.

$$$$ B&B/INN Fodor's Choice ★ **Villa Le Barone.** Once the home of the Viviani della Robbia family, this 16th-century villa in a grove of ancient cypress trees retains many aspects of a private country dwelling, complete with homey guest quarters. **Pros:** beautiful location; wonderful restaurant; great base for exploring the region. **Cons:** rooms vary in size; 20-minute walk to nearest town. [$] *Rooms from: €280* ✉ *Via San Leolino 19* ☎ *055/852621* 🌐 *www.villa-lebarone.com* *28 rooms* ⏲ *Closed Nov.–Easter* 🍴 *Breakfast.*

RADDA IN CHIANTI

26 km (15 miles) south of Panzano, 52 km (32 miles) south of Florence.

Radda in Chianti sits on a hill separating two valleys, Val di Pesa and Val d'Arbia. It's one of many tiny Chianti villages that invite you to stroll their steep streets; follow the signs pointing you toward the *camminamento,* a covered medieval passageway circling part of the city inside the walls.

GETTING HERE AND AROUND

Radda can be reached by car from either Siena or Florence along the SR222 (Strada Chiantigiana), and from the A1 highway. Three Tra-In buses a day make their way from Siena to Radda. One morning SITA bus travels from Florence to Radda. There's no train service convenient to Radda.

VISITOR INFORMATION

Radda in Chianti Tourism Office ✉ *Piazza Castello 6* ☎ *0577/738494.*

EXPLORING

Badia a Coltibuono (*Abbey of the Good Harvest*). North of Gaiole a turnoff leads to this Romanesque abbey that has been owned by Lorenza de' Medici's family for more than a century and a half (the family isn't closely related to the Renaissance-era Medici). Wine has been produced here since the abbey was founded by Vallombrosan monks in the 11th century. Today the family continues the tradition, making Chianti Classico and other wines, along with cold-pressed olive oil and various flavored vinegars and floral honeys. A small church with campanile is surrounded by 2,000 acres of oak, fir, and chestnut woods threaded with walking paths—open to all—that pass two small lakes. Though the abbey itself, built between the 11th and 18th centuries, serves as the family's home, parts are open for tours (in English, German, or Italian). Visit the jasmine-draped main courtyard, the inner cloister with its antique well, the musty old aging cellars, and the Renaissance-style garden redolent of lavender, lemons, and roses. In the shop, **L'Osteria,** you can taste wine and honey, as well as pick up other items like homemade beeswax hand lotion in little ceramic dishes. The Badia is closed on public holidays. ✉ *Località Badia a Coltibuono, 4 km (2½ miles) north of Gaiole, Gaiole in Chianti* ☎ *0577/74481 for tours, 0577/749479 for shop* 🌐 *www.coltibuono.com* 🎟 *Abbey €5* ⏲ *Tours: Easter–Oct., weekdays at 2, 3, 4, and 5. Shop: Mar.–mid-Jan., daily 9–1 and 2–7.*

Castello di Brolio. If you have time for only one castle in Tuscany, this is it. At the end of the 12th century, when Florence conquered southern Chianti, Brolio became Florence's southernmost outpost, and it was often said, "When Brolio growls, all Siena trembles." Brolio was built about AD 1000 and owned by the monks of the Badia Fiorentina; the "new" owners, the Ricasoli family, have been in possession since 1141. Bettino Ricasoli (1809–80), the so-called Iron Baron, was one of the founders of modern Italy, and is said to have invented the original formula for Chianti wine. Brolio, one of Chianti's best-known labels, is still justifiably famous. Its cellars may be toured by appointment. The grounds are worth visiting, even though the 19th-century manor house is not open to the public. A small museum, where the Ricasoli Collection is housed in a 12th-century tower, displays objects that relate the long history of the family and the origins of Chianti wine. There are two apartments here available for rent by the week. ✉ *Località Brolio, 2 km (1 mile) southeast of Gaiole, Gaiole in Chianti* ☎ *0577/730280* 🌐 *www.ricasoli.it* 🎟 *€5 gardens, €8 gardens and museum, €10 guided tours* 🕐 *Last 2 wks Mar., weekdays 10–6:30, weekends 11–6:30; Apr.–Oct., daily 10–7; last entrance 1 hr before closing time. Guided tours, Wed. and Fri.–Mon. at 10:30, daily at 3, and Mon. and Fri. at 5; must be booked in advance.*

Palazzo del Podestà. Radda's town hall (aka Palazzo Comunale), in the middle of town, was built in the second half of the 14th century and has served the same function ever since. Fifty-one coats of arms (the largest is the Medicis') are embedded in the facade, representing the past governors of the town, but unless you have official business, the building is closed to the public. ✉ *Piazza Ferrucci 1.*

WHERE TO EAT

$ TUSCAN Fodor's Choice ★

🍴 **Osteria Le Panzanelle.** Silvia Bonechi's experience in the kitchen—with the help of a few precious recipes handed down from her grandmother—is one of the reasons for the success of this small restaurant. The other is the front-room hospitality of Nada Michelassi. These two *panzanelle* (women from Panzano) serve a short menu of tasty and authentic dishes at what the locals refer to as *il prezzo giusto* (the right price). Both the *pappa al pomodoro* (tomato soup) and the *peposo* (peppery beef stew) are exceptional. Whether you are eating inside or under large umbrellas on the terrace near a tiny stream, the experience is always congenial. "The best food we had in Tuscany," writes one user of Fodors.com. Reservations are essential in July and August. [$] *Average meal: €25* ✉ *Località Lucarelli 29, 8 km (5 miles) northwest of Radda on the road to Panzano* ☎ *0577/733511* 🌐 *www.osteria.lepanzanelle.it* 🕐 *Closed Mon. and Jan. and Feb.*

WHERE TO STAY

For expanded hotel reviews, visit Fodors.com.

$ B&B/INN

🏨 **La Bottega di Giovannino.** This is a fantastic place for the budget-conscious traveler, as rooms are immaculate and most have a stunning view of the surrounding hills. **Pros:** great location in the center of town; close to restaurants and shops; super value. **Cons:** some rooms are small; some bathrooms are down the hall; basic decor. [$] *Rooms from: €80* ✉ *Via Roma 6–8* ☎📠 *0577/738056* 🌐 *www.labottegadigiovannino.it* 🛏 *9 rooms, 1 apartment* 🍽 *No meals.*

$$ ⊞ **Palazzo San Niccolò.** The wood-beamed ceilings, terra-cotta floors,
HOTEL   and some of the original frescoes of a 19th-century town palace remain,
but the marble bathrooms have all been updated, some with Jacuzzi
tubs. **Pros:** central location; friendly service. **Cons:** some rooms face
a main street; room sizes vary. $ *Rooms from: €120* ⊠ *Via Roma 16*
☎ *0577/735666* ⊕ *www.hotelsanniccolo.com* ⤳ *17 rooms, 1 suite*
⊙ *Closed Nov.–Mar.* ⦙Ⓞ⦙ *Breakfast.*

$$$ ⊞ **Relais Fattoria Vignale.** A refined and comfortable country house offers
B&B/INN   numerous sitting rooms with terra-cotta floors and attractive stonework
and wood-beamed guest rooms filled with simple wooden furnishings
and handwoven rugs. **Pros:** intimate public spaces; excellent restaurant;
helpful and friendly staff; nice grounds and pool. **Cons:** north-facing
rooms blocked by tall cypress trees; single rooms are small; annex across
a busy road. $ *Rooms from: €185* ⊠ *Via Pianigiani 9* ☎ *0577/738300*
hotel, 0577/738094 restaurant ⊕ *www.vignale.it* ⤳ *37 rooms, 5 suites*
⊙ *Closed Nov.–Mar. 15* ⦙Ⓞ⦙ *Breakfast.*

CASTELLINA IN CHIANTI

14 km (8 miles) west of Radda, 59 km (35 miles) south of Florence.

Castellina in Chianti, or simply Castellina, is on a ridge above the Val di
Pesa, Val d'Arbia, and Val d'Elsa, with beautiful panoramas in every direction. The imposing 14th-century tower in the central piazza hints at the
history of this village, which was an outpost during the continuing wars
between Florence and Siena. Don't miss a walk along Via delle Volte, a
covered passage that follows the medieval walls on one side of the town.

GETTING HERE AND AROUND

As with all the towns along the Strada Chiantigiana (SR222), Castellina
is an easy drive from either Siena or Florence. From Siena, Castellina is
well served by the local Tra-In bus company. However, only one bus a
day travels here from Florence. The closest train station is at Castellina
Scalo, some 15 km (9 miles) away.

VISITOR INFORMATION

Castellina in Chianti Tourism Office ⊠ *Via Ferruccio 40* ☎ *0577/741392.*

WHERE TO EAT

$$$ ✕ **Albergaccio.** The fact that the dining room can seat only 35 guests
TUSCAN   makes a meal here an intimate experience. The ever-changing menu
mixes traditional and creative dishes. In late September and Octo-
ber *zuppa di funghi e castagne* (mushroom and chestnut soup) is a
treat; grilled meats and seafood are on the list throughout the year.
There's also an excellent wine list. When the weather is warm, make
sure you dine on the terrace. $ *Average meal: €50* ⊠ *Via Fiorentina 25*
☎ *0577/741042* ⊕ *www.albergacciocast.com* ⥱ *Reservations essential*
⊟ *No credit cards* ⊙ *Closed Sun. No lunch Wed. and Thurs.*

$ ✕ **Ristorante Le Tre Porte.** Grilled meat dishes are the specialty at this
TUSCAN   popular restaurant, with a Florentine beefsteak (served very rare) tak-
ing pride of place. Paired with grilled fresh porcini mushrooms when in
season (in spring and fall), it's a particularly heady dish. The panoramic
terrace is a good choice for dining in summer. Inside, the upper floor

offers an umistakably Tuscan setting, while the downstairs is more modern and intimate. Reservations are essential in July and August. $ *Average meal: €25* ⊠ *Via Trento e Trieste 4* ☎ *0577/741163* ⊗ *Closed Tues.*

$

TUSCAN

✕ **Sotto Le Volte.** As the name suggests, you'll find this small restaurant under the arches of Castellina's medieval walkway. The restaurant has vaulted ceilings, which make for a particularly romantic setting. The menu is short and eminently Tuscan, with typical soups and pasta dishes. The *costolette di agnello alle erbe* (herbed lamb chops) are especially tasty. $ *Average meal: €25* ⊠ *Via delle Volte 14–16* ☎ *0577/056530* ▤ *No credit cards* ⊗ *Closed Wed.*

WHERE TO STAY

For expanded hotel reviews, visit Fodors.com.

$$

B&B/INN

Fodor's Choice

★

▦ **Palazzo Squarcialupi.** In this lovely 15th-century palace rooms are spacious, with high ceilings, tile floors, and 18th-century furnishings, and many have views of the valley below. **Pros:** great location in town center; elegant public spaces; nice spa, pool, and grounds. **Cons:** on a street with no car access; across from a busy restaurant. $ *Rooms from: €120* ⊠ *Via Ferruccio 22* ☎ *0577/741186* ⊕ *www.palazzosquarcialupi. com* ⟿ *17 rooms* ⊗ *Closed Nov.–Mar.* ⦿*Breakfast.*

HILL TOWNS SOUTHWEST OF FLORENCE

Submit to the draw of Tuscany's enchanting fortified cities that crown the hills west of Siena, many dating to the Etruscan period. San Gimignano, known as the "medieval Manhattan" because of its forest of stout medieval towers built by rival families, is the most heavily visited. This onetime Roman outpost, with its tilted cobbled streets and ancient buildings, can make the days of Guelph-Ghibelline conflicts palpable. Rising from a series of bleak gullied hills and valleys, Volterra has always been popular for its minerals and stones, particularly alabaster, which was used by the Etruscans for many implements. Examples are now displayed in the exceptional (and exceptionally large) Museo Etrusco Guarnacci.

VOLTERRA

75 km (47 miles) southwest of Florence.

Unlike other Tuscan hill towns rising above sprawling vineyards and rolling fields of green, Volterra is surrounded by desolate terrain marred with industry and mining equipment. D. H. Lawrence described it as "somber and chilly alone on her rock" in his *Etruscan Places.* Its fortress (now a maximum-security prison), walls, and gates still stand mightily over Le Balze, a distinctive series of gullied hills and valleys to the west that were formed by irregular erosion. But don't be put off by this gloomy introduction. Volterra is a lively and fascinating town that grows on you with each visit. There are spectacular views from the outer walls, winding narrow streets bustling with activity, and some amazing museums and archaeological sites. (Even the inmates of the prison have become internationally famous for their theatrical performances!) The town has also long been known for its alabaster, which has been mined since Etruscan times; today the Volterrans use it to make ornaments and souvenirs. You'll find it sold all over town, and you may have the chance to peek into an artisan's studio to see the work in progress.

GETTING HERE AND AROUND
By car, the best route from Florence follows the Florence–Siena autostrada as far as the Col di Val d'Elsa exit, where you get on the SS68 for the trip 30 km (19 miles) west to Volterr. There's a long, winding climb at the end of your trip. Getting here by train is complicated; avoid it if possible. From Florence or Siena, the journey by bus involves a change in Colle di Val d'Elsa.

VISITOR INFORMATION
Volterra Tourism Office ✉ *Piazza dei Priori 20* ☎ *0588/87257* ⊕ *www.volterratur.it.*

EXPLORING
Duomo. Behind the textbook 13th-century Pisan–Romanesque facade is proof that Volterra counted for something during the Renaissance, when many important Tuscan artists came to decorate the church. Three-dimensional stucco portraits of local saints are on the gold, red, and blue ceiling (1580) designed by Francesco Capriani, including Saint Linus, the successor to Saint Peter as pope and claimed by the Volterrans to have been born here. The highlight of the Duomo is the brightly painted 13th-century wooden life-size *Deposition* in the chapel of the same name. The unusual Cappella dell'Addolorata (Chapel of the Grieved) has two terra-cotta Nativity scenes; the depiction of the arrival of the Magi has a background fresco by Benozzo Gozzoli. The 16th-century pulpit in the middle of the nave is lined with fine 14th-century sculpted panels, attributed to a member of the Pisano family. Across from the Duomo in the center of the piazza is the **Battistero,** with stripes that match the Duomo. Evidently this baptistery got a lot of use, as the small marble baptismal font carved by Andrea Sansovino in 1502 was moved to the wall to the right of the entrance in the mid-18th century to make room for a much larger one. ✉ *Piazza San Giovanni* ☎ *0588/88524* ⊘ *Daily 7–7.*

Museo Etrusco Guarnacci. An extraordinarily large and unique collection of Etruscan relics is made all the more interesting by clear explanations in English. The bulk of the collection is comprised of roughly 700 carved funerary urns: the oldest, dating from the 7th century BC, were made from tufa (volcanic rock); a handful are made of terra-cotta; and the vast majority—from the 3rd to 1st century BC—are from alabaster. The urns are grouped by subject and taken together form a fascinating testimony about Etruscan life and death. Some illustrate domestic scenes, others the funeral procession of the deceased. Greek gods and mythology, adopted by the Etruscans, also figure prominently. The sculpted figures on many of the covers may have been made in the image of the deceased, reclining and often holding the cup of life overturned. Particularly well known is *Gli Sposi* (*Husband and Wife*), a haunting, elderly duo in terra cotta. Also on display are Attic vases, bucchero ceramics, jewelry, and household items. ✉ *Via Don Minzoni 15* ☎ *0588/86347* 🎟 *€8; €10 including the Museo Diocesano di Arte Sacra and the Pinacoteca* ⏲ *Mid-Mar.–early Nov., daily 9–6:45; early Nov.–mid-Mar., daily 9–1:15.*

Pinacoteca. One of Volterra's best-looking Renaissance buildings contains an impressive collection of Tuscan paintings arranged chronologically on two floors. Head straight for Room 12, with Luca Signorelli's (circa 1445–1523) *Madonna and Child with Saints* and Rosso Fiorentino's *Deposition.* Though painted just 30 years apart, they serve to illustrate the shift in style from the early-16th-century Renaissance ideals to full-blown mannerism: the balance of Signorelli's composition becomes purposefully skewed in Fiorentino's painting, where the colors go from vivid but realistic to emotively bright. Other important paintings in the small museum include Ghirlandaio's *Apotheosis of Christ with Saints* and a polyptych of the *Madonna and Saints* by Taddeo di Bartolo, which once hung in the Palazzo dei Priori. ✉ *Via dei Sarti 1* ☎ *0588/87580* 🎟 *€8; €10 including the Museo Etrusco Guarnacci and the Museo Diocesano di Arte Sacra* ⏲ *Mid-Mar.–early Nov., daily 9–7; early Nov.–mid-Mar., daily 8:30–1:45.*

Porta all'Arco Etrusco. Even if a good portion of the arch was rebuilt by the Romans, the three dark, weather-beaten, 3rd-century BC heads carved in basaltic rock (thought to represent Etruscan gods) still face outward, greeting those who enter. A plaque recalls the efforts of the locals who saved the arch from destruction by filling it with stones during the German withdrawal at the end of World War II.

Teatro Romano. Just outside the walls past Porta Fiorentina are the ruins of the 1st-century-BC Roman theater, one of the best-preserved in Italy, with adjacent remains of the Roman *terme* (baths). You can enjoy an excellent bird's-eye view of the theater from Via Lungo le Mura. ✉ *Viale Francesco Ferrucci* 🎟 *€3.50* ⏲ *Mar.–May and Sept.–Nov., daily 10–1 and 2–4; June–Aug., daily 10–6:45; Dec.–Feb., weekends 10–1 and 2–4.*

WHERE TO EAT

$ TUSCAN ✕ **Il Sacco Fiorentino.** Start with the *antipasti del Sacco Fiorentino*—a medley of sautéed chicken liver, porcini mushrooms, and polenta drizzled with balsamic vinegar. The meal just gets better when you move on to the *tagliatelle del Sacco Fiorentino,* a riot of curried spaghetti with chicken and roasted red peppers. The wine list is a marvel, as it's long and very well priced. White walls, tile floors, and red tablecloths create an understated tone that is unremarkable, but once the food starts arriving, it's easy to forgive the lack of decoration. [$] *Average meal: €25* ✉ *Piazza XX Settembre 18* ☎ *0588/88537* ⏲ *Closed Wed.*

WHERE TO STAY

For expanded hotel reviews, visit Fodors.com.

$ B&B/INN 🏨 **Etruria.** The rooms are modest and some of the bathrooms are out-of-date, but the central location, the ample buffet breakfast, and the modest rates make this a good choice for those on a budget. **Pros:** great central location; friendly staff; tranquil garden. **Cons:** some rooms can be noisy during the day; no a/c. [$] *Rooms from: €99* ✉ *Via Matteotti 32* ☎ *0588/87377* 🌐 *www.albergoetruria.it* 🛏 *21 rooms* 🍽 *Breakfast.*

$ HOTEL 🏨 **San Lino.** Within the town's medieval walls, this convent-turned-hotel has wood-beam ceilings, graceful archways, and terra-cotta floors, with nice contemporary furnishings and ironwork in the rooms. **Pros:** steps away from center of town; friendly and helpful staff; convenient parking. **Cons:** rooms facing the street can be noisy; breakfast is adequate, but nothing to write home about. [$] *Rooms from: €90* ✉ *Via San Lino 26* ☎ *0588/85250* 🌐 *www.hotelsanlino.com* 🛏 *43 rooms* ⏲ *Closed Nov., Jan. and Feb.* 🍴 *Breakfast.*

SAN GIMIGNANO

27 km (17 miles) east of Volterra, 57 km (35 miles) southwest of Florence.

Fodor's Choice ★ When you're on a hilltop surrounded by soaring medieval towers silhouetted against the sky, it's difficult not to fall under the spell of San Gimignano. The tall walls and narrow streets are typical of Tuscan hill towns, but it's the medieval "skyscrapers" that set the town apart from its neighbors. Today 14 towers remain, but at the height of the Guelph–Ghibelline conflict there was a forest of more than 70, and it was possible to cross the town by rooftop rather than by road. The towers were built partly for defensive purposes—they were a safe refuge and useful for pouring boiling oil on attacking enemies—and partly for bolstering the egos of their owners, who competed with deadly seriousness to build the highest tower in town.

Today San Gimignano isn't much more than a gentrified walled city, touristy but still very much worth exploring because, despite the profusion of cheesy souvenir shops lining the main drag, there's some serious Renaissance art to be seen here. Tour groups arrive early and clog the wine-tasting rooms—San Gimignano is famous for its light white Vernaccia—and art galleries for much of the day, but most sights stay open through late afternoon, when all the tour groups have long since departed.

San Gimignano is particularly beautiful in the early morning. Take time to walk up to the *rocca* (castle), at the highest point of town. Here you can enjoy 360-degree views of the surrounding countryside. Apart from when it's used for summer outdoor film festivals, it's always open.

GETTING HERE AND AROUND

From Volterra, it's an easy drive to San Gimignano on the SS68 and SP47. You can reach San Gimignano by car from the Florence–Siena Superstrada by exiting at Poggibonsi Nord and following signs for San Gimignano. Although a bus trip involves a change in Poggibonsi, the journey is a relatively straightforward affair. SITA operates the service between Siena or Florence and Poggibonsi, while Tra-In takes care of the Poggibonsi to San Gimignano route. If you're traveling with luggage, be aware that there are no storage facilities available. You cannot reach San Gimignano by train.

VISITOR INFORMATION

San Gimignano Tourism Office ✉ *Piazza Duomo 1* ☎ *0577/940008* 🌐 *www.sangimignano.com.*

EXPLORING

Collegiata. The town's main church is not officially a *duomo* (cathedral), because San Gimignano has no bishop. But behind the simple facade of the Romanesque Collegiata lies a treasure trove of fine frescoes, covering nearly every part of the interior. Bartolo di Fredi's 14th-century fresco cycle of Old Testament scenes extends along one wall. Their distinctly

medieval feel, with misshapen bodies, buckets of spurting blood, and lack of perspective, contrasts with the much more reserved scenes from the *Life of Christ* (attributed to 14th-century artist Lippo Memmi), painted on the opposite wall just 14 years later. Taddeo di Bartolo's otherworldly *Last Judgment* (late 14th century), with its distorted and suffering nudes, reveals the great influence of Dante's horrifying imagery in *The Inferno* and was surely an inspiration for later painters. Proof that the town had more than one protector, Benozzo Gozzoli's arrow-riddled *St. Sebastian* was commissioned in gratitude after the locals prayed to the saint for relief from plague. The Renaissance **Cappella di Santa Fina** is decorated with a fresco cycle by Domenico Ghirlandaio illustrating the life of Saint Fina. A small girl who suffered from a terminal disease, Fina repented for her sins—among them having accepted an orange from a boy—and in penance lived out the rest of her short life on a wooden board, tormented by rats. The scenes depict the arrival of Saint Gregory, who appeared to assure her that death was near; the flowers that miraculously grew from the wooden plank; and the miracles that accompanied her funeral, including the healing of her nurse's paralyzed hand and the restoration of a blind choirboy's vision. ✉ *Piazza Pecori 1–2* ☎ *0577/940316* 🖭 *€3.50; €5.50 including the Museo d'Arte Sacra* ☉ *Apr.–Oct., weekdays 10–7:10, Sat. 10–5:10, Sun. 12:30–4:40; Nov. 1–15, Dec. 1–Jan. 15, and Feb. 1–Mar., Mon.–Sat. 10–4:40, Sun. 12:30–4:40. Closed Nov. 16–30 and Jan. 16–31.*

Museo Civico. The impressive civic museum occupies what was the "new" Palazzo del Popolo; the Torre Grossa is adjacent. Dante visited San Gimignano for only one day as a Guelph ambassador from Florence to ask the locals to join the Florentines in supporting the pope—just long enough to get the main council chamber, which now holds a 14th-century *Maestà* by Lippo Memmi, named after him. Off the stairway is a small room containing the racy frescoes by Memmo di Filippuccio (active 1288–1324), depicting the courtship, shared bath, and wedding of a young, androgynous-looking couple. That the space could have been a private room for the commune's chief magistrate may have something to do with the work's highly charged eroticism.

Upstairs, paintings by famous Renaissance artists Pinturicchio (*Madonna Enthroned*), and Benozzo Gozzoli (*Madonna and Child*), and two large *tondi* (circular paintings) by Filippino Lippi (circa

1457–1504) attest to the importance and wealth of San Gimignano. Also worth seeing are Taddeo di Bartolo's *Life of San Gimignano,* with the saint holding a model of the town as it once appeared; Lorenzo di Niccolò's gruesome martyrdom scene in the *Life of St. Bartholomew* (1401); and scenes from the *Life of St. Fina* on a tabernacle that was designed to hold her head. Admission includes the steep climb to the top of the Torre Grossa, which on a clear day has spectacular views. ✉ *Piazza Duomo 2* ☎ *0577/990312* 🎟 *€5* 🕓 *Jan., daily 12:30–5:30; Feb.–Mar. and Oct.–Dec., daily 11–5:30; Apr.–Sept., daily 9:30–7.*

Sant'Agostino. Make a beeline for Benozzo Gozzoli's superlative 15th-century fresco cycle depicting scenes from the life of Saint Augustine. The saint's work was essential to the early development of church doctrine. As thoroughly discussed in his autobiographical *Confessions* (an acute dialogue with God), Augustine, like many saints, sinned considerably in his youth before finding God. But unlike the lives of other saints, where the story continues through a litany of deprivations, penitence, and often martyrdom, Augustine's life and work focused on philosophy and the reconciliation of faith and thought. Benozzo's 17 scenes on the choir wall depict Augustine as a man who traveled and taught extensively in the 4th and 5th centuries. The 15th-century altarpiece by Piero del Pollaiolo (1443–96) depicts *The Coronation of the Virgin* and the various protectors of the city. On your way out of Sant'Agostino, stop in at the **Cappella di San Bartolo,** with a sumptuously elaborate tomb by Benedetto da Maiano (1442–97). ✉ *Piazza Sant'Agostino 10* ☎ *0577/907012* 🎟 *Free* 🕓 *Apr.–Oct., daily 7–noon and 3–7; Nov.–Mar., daily 7–noon and 3–6.*

WHERE TO EAT

$ TUSCAN 🍴 **Enoteca Gustavo.** There's no shortage of places to try Vernaccia di San Gimignano, the justifiably famous white wine with which San Gimignano would be singularly associated—if it weren't for all those towers. At this wine bar, run by energetic Maristella Becucci, you can buy a glass of Vernaccia di San Gimignano and sit down with a cheese plate or with one of the fine crostini. [$] *Average meal: €8* ✉ *Via San Matteo 29* ☎ *0577/940057.*

$ ITALIAN 🍴 **Osteria del Carcere.** Though it calls itself an *osteria* (a tavern), this place much more resembles a wine bar, with a bill of fare that includes several different types of pâtés and a short list of seasonal soups and salads. The sampler of goat cheeses, which can be paired with local wines, should not be missed. Operatic arias play softly in the background, and service is courteous. [$] *Average meal: €25* ✉ *Via del Castello 13* ☎ *0577/941905* 💳 *No credit cards* 🕓 *Closed Wed. and early Jan.–Mar. No lunch Thurs.*

WHERE TO STAY

For expanded hotel reviews, visit Fodors.com.

$$$$ HOTEL 🏨 **La Collegiata.** After serving as a Franciscan convent and then the residence of the noble Strozzi family, the Collegiata has been converted into a fine hotel, with no expense spared in the process. **Pros:** gorgeous views from terrace; elegant rooms in main building. **Cons:** long walk into town; service can be impersonal; some rooms are dimly lit.

$ *Rooms from: €340* ⊠ *Località Strada 27, 1 km (½ mile) north of San Gimignano town center* ☏ *0577/943201* ⊕ *www.lacollegiata.it* ⤳ *20 rooms, 1 suite* ☉ *Closed Nov.–Mar.* ¶❍| *Breakfast.*

$

B&B/INN

⊡ **Pescille.** A rambling farmhouse has been transformed into a handsome hotel with understated contemporary furniture in the bedrooms and country-classic motifs such as farm implements hanging on the walls in the bar. **Pros:** splendid views; quiet atmosphere; 10-minute walk to town. **Cons:** furnishings a bit austere; there's an elevator for luggage but not for guests. $ *Rooms from: €95* ⊠ *Località Pescille, 4 km (2½ miles) south of San Gimignano* ☏ *0577/940186* ⊕ *www.pescille.it* ⤳ *38 rooms, 12 suites* ☉ *Closed Nov.–Mar.* ¶❍| *Breakfast.*

$$

B&B/INN

⊡ **Torraccia di Chiusi.** A perfect retreat for families, this tranquil hilltop *agriturismo* (farm stay) offers simple, comfortably decorated accommodations on extensive grounds 5 km (3 miles) from the hubbub of San Gimignano. **Pros:** tranquil haven close to San Gimignano; great walking possibilities; family-run hospitality; delightful countryside views. **Cons:** 30 minutes from the nearest town on a windy gravel road; need a car to get here. $ *Rooms from: €140* ⊠ *Località Montauto* ☏ *0577/941972* ⊕ *www.torracciadichiusi.com* ⤳ *8 rooms, 3 apartments* ¶❍| *Breakfast.*

COLLE DI VAL D'ELSA

15 km (9 miles) southeast of San Gimignano, 50 km (31 miles) southwest of Florence.

Most people pass through on their way to and from popular tourist destinations Volterra and San Gimignano—a shame, because Colle di Val d'Elsa has much to offer. It's another town on the Via Francigena that benefited from trade along the pilgrimage route to Rome. Colle got an extra boost in the late 16th century when it was given a bishopric, probably related to an increase in trade when nearby San Gimignano was cut off from the well-traveled road.

The town is arranged on two levels, and from the 12th century onward the flat lower portion was given over to a flourishing paper-making industry; today the area is mostly modern, and efforts have shifted toward the production of fine glass and crystal—surprisingly, 15% of the world's fine crystal is made here. Colle *alto* (the upper town) is essentially a one-street affair that runs gently uphill from a panoramic terrace overlooking Colle *basso* (the lower town), past the house where Arnolfo di Cambio (architect of the Duomo in Florence) was born, along a road lined with 16th-century town palaces, to the upper defensive ramparts built by the Florentines. If you don't like the idea of the short climb, you can take a free public elevator linking the upper and lower sections of the town.

GETTING HERE AND AROUND

You can reach Colle di Val d'Elsa by car on either the SR2 from Siena or the Florence-Siena Superstrada. From San Gimignano, it's a short trip on SS68. Bus service to and from Siena and Florence is frequent.

VISITOR INFORMATION

Colle di Val d'Elsa Tourism Office ⊠ *Via del Castello 33/b* ☏ *0577/922791.*

WHERE TO EAT

$$$$
MODERN ITALIAN
Fodor's Choice
★

✕ **Ristorante Arnolfo.** Food lovers should not miss Arnolfo, one of Tuscany's most highly regarded restaurants. Chef Gaetano Trovato sets high standards of creativity; his dishes daringly ride the line between innovation and tradition, almost always with spectacular results. The menu changes frequently but you are always sure to find fish and lots of fresh vegetables in the summer. You're in for a treat if the specials include *carrè di agnello al vino rosso e sella alle olive* (rack of lamb in a red wine sauce and lamb saddle with olives). $ *Average meal:* €125 ⊠ *Piazza XX Settembre 52* ☎ *0577/920549* ⊕ *www.arnolfo.com* ⚍ *Reservations essential* ⊗ *Closed Tues. and Wed., last wks in Jan., Feb., and Aug.*

WHERE TO STAY

For expanded hotel reviews, visit Fodors.com.

$$
B&B/INN

⊡ **Palazzo San Lorenzo.** A 17th-century palace in the historic center of Colle boasts rooms that exude warmth and comfort, with light-color wooden floors, soothingly tinted fabrics, and large windows. **Pros:** central location; spotless; extremely well maintained. **Cons:** caters to business groups; some of the public spaces feel rather sterile. $ *Rooms from: €124* ⊠ *Via Gracco del Secco 113* ☎ *0577/923675* ⊕ *www. palazzosanlorenzo.it* ⮈ *43 rooms, 6 suite, 6 apartments* ◉ *Breakfast.*

SIENA

With its narrow streets and steep alleys, a stunning Gothic cathedral, a bounty of early Renaissance art, and the glorious Palazzo Pubblico overlooking its magnificent Piazza del Campo (or just, "Campo"), Siena is often described as Italy's best-preserved medieval city. Victory over Florence in 1260 at Montaperti marked the beginning of Siena's golden age. During the following decades Siena erected its greatest buildings (including the Duomo); established a model city government presided over by the Council of Nine; and became a great art, textile, and trade center. Siena succumbed to Florentine rule in the mid-16th century, when a yearlong siege virtually eliminated the native population. Ironically, it was precisely this decline that, along with the steadfast pride of the Sienese, prevented further development, to which we owe the city's marvelous medieval condition today.

Although much looks as it did in the early 14th century, Siena is no museum. Walk through the streets and you can see that the medieval *contrade*, 17 neighborhoods into which the city has been historically divided, are a vibrant part of modern life. You may see symbols of the contrade—Tartuca (turtle), Oca (goose), Istrice (porcupine), Torre (tower)—emblazoned on banners and engraved on building walls. The Sienese still strongly identify themselves by the contrada where they were born and raised; loyalty and rivalry run deep. At no time is this more visible than during the centuries-old Palio, a twice-yearly horse race held in the Piazza del Campo. But you need not visit during the wild festival to come to know the rich culture and enchanting pleasures of Siena; those are evident at every step.

GETTING HERE AND AROUND

From Florence, the quickest way to make the 75-km (45-mile) drive to Siena is via the Florence-Siena Superstrada. Otherwise, take the Via Cassia (SR2), for a scenic route. Coming from Rome, leave the A1 at Valdichiana, and follow the Siena-Bettole Superstrada. SITA provides excellent bus service between Florence and Siena. Because buses are direct and speedy, they're preferable to the train, which sometimes involves a change in Empoli.

If you come by car, you're better off leaving it in one of the parking lots around the perimeter of town. Driving is difficult or impossible in most parts of the city center. Practically unchanged since medieval times, Siena is laid out in a "Y" over the slopes of several hills, dividing the city into *terzi* (thirds).

TIMING

It's a joy to walk in Siena—hills notwithstanding—as it's a rare opportunity to stroll through a medieval city rather than just a town. (There's quite a lot to explore, in contrast to tiny hill towns that can be crossed in minutes.) The walk can be done in as little as a day, with minimal stops at the sights. But stay longer and you'll have time to tour the church and museums, and to enjoy the streetscapes themselves. Several of the sites have reduced hours on Sunday afternoon and Monday.

VISITOR INFORMATION

Siena Tourism Office ⊠ *Piazza del Campo 56* ☎ *0577/280551* ⊕ *www.comune.siena.it.*

EXPLORING SIENA

Tra-In. City buses run frequently within and around Siena, including the centro storico. Tickets cost €1.30 and should be bought in advance at tobacconists or newsstands. Routes are marked with signposts. ☎ *0577/204111* ⊕ *www.trainspa.it.*

TOP ATTRACTIONS

Fodor's Choice ★ **Cripta.** After it had lain unseen for possibly 700 years, a crypt was rediscovered under the grand *pavimento* (floor) of the Duomo during routine excavation work and was opened to the public in 2003. An unknown master executed the breathtaking frescoes here sometime between 1270 and 1280; they retain their original colors and pack an emotional punch even with sporadic damage. The *Deposition/Lamentation* gives strong evidence that the Sienese school could paint emotion just as well as the Florentine school—and did it some 20 years before Giotto. Guided tours in English take place more or less every half hour and are limited to no more than 35 persons. ⊠ *Piazza del Duomo, entrance on the right side of the cathedral, Città* ☎ *0577/286300* ⊠ *€6; €10 combined ticket includes the Duomo, Battistero, and Museo dell'Opera Metropolitana* ⊙ *Mar.–mid-June and mid-Sept.–Oct., daily 9:30–7:30; mid-June–mid-Sept. and June–Aug., daily 9:30–8; Nov.–Feb., daily 10–5.*

Fodor's Choice ★ **Duomo.** Siena's cathedral is beyond question one of the finest Gothic churches in Italy. The multicolored marbles and painted decoration are typical of the Italian approach to Gothic architecture—lighter and

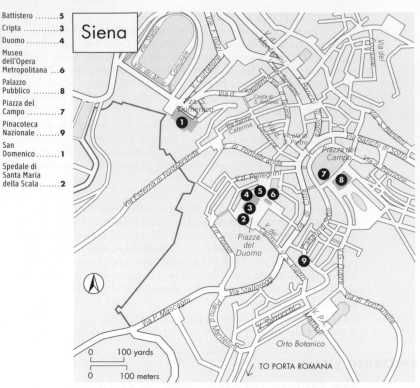

much less austere than the French. The amazingly detailed facade has few rivals in the region, although it's quite similar to the Duomo in Orvieto. It was completed in two brief phases at the end of the 13th and 14th centuries. The statues and decorative work were designed by Nicola Pisano and his son Giovanni, although most of what we see today are copies, the originals having been removed to the nearby Museo dell'Opera Metropolitana. The gold mosaics are 18th-century restorations. The Campanile (no entry) is among central Italy's finest, the number of windows increasing with each level, a beautiful and ingenious way of reducing the weight of the structure as it climbs to the heavens.

The Duomo's interior, with its black-and-white striping throughout and finely coffered and gilded dome, is simply striking. Step in and look back up at Duccio's (circa 1255–1319) panels of stained glass that fill the circular window. Finished in 1288, it's the oldest example of stained glass in Italy. The Duomo is most famous for its unique and magnificent inlaid-marble floors, which took almost 200 years to complete; more than 40 artists contributed to the work, made up of 56 separate compositions depicting biblical scenes, allegories, religious symbols, and civic emblems. The floors are covered for most of the year for conservation purposes, but are unveiled during September and October. The Duomo's carousel pulpit, also much appreciated, was carved by Nicola Pisano (circa 1220–84) around 1265; the *Life of Christ* is depicted on the rostrum frieze. In striking contrast to all the Gothic decoration in the nave are the magnificent Renaissance frescoes in the **Biblioteca Piccolomini,** off the left aisle. Painted by Pinturicchio (circa 1454–1513) and

> **WORD OF MOUTH**
>
> "The one thing I'd do in Siena—short of attending the Palio—is stay overnight. All the tourists leave and it's very dark and medieval. It feels like you've time-traveled back 500 years."
>
> —Mimar

completed in 1509, they depict events from the life of native son Aeneas Sylvius Piccolomini (1405–64), who became Pope Pius II in 1458. The frescoes are in excellent condition, and have a freshness rarely seen in work so old.

The Duomo is grand, but the medieval Sienese people had even bigger plans. They wanted to enlarge the building by using the existing church as a transept for a new church, with a new nave running toward the southeast, to make what would be the largest church in the world. But only the side wall and part of the new facade were completed when the Black Death struck in 1348, decimating Siena's population. The city fell into decline, funds dried up, and the plans were never carried out. (The dream of building the biggest church was actually doomed to failure from the start—subsequent attempts to get the project going revealed that the foundation was insufficient to bear the weight of the proposed structure.) The beginnings of the new nave, extending from the right side of the Duomo, were left unfinished, perhaps as a testament to unfulfilled dreams, and ultimately enclosed to house the adjacent **Museo dell'Opera Metropolitana.** The **Cripta** was discovered during routine preservation work on the church and has been opened to the public. ⊠ *Piazza del Duomo, Città* ☎ *0577/286300* 🖵 *€3 Nov.–Aug.; €6 Sept. and Oct.; €10 combined ticket includes the Cripta, Battistero, and Museo dell'Opera Metropolitana* ☼ *Mar.–mid-June, Mon.–Sat. 10:30–7:30, Sun. 1:30–6; mid-June–mid-Sept., Mon.–Sat. 10:30–8, Sun. 1:30–6; mid-Sept.–Oct., Mon.–Sat. 10:30–7:30, Sun. 1:30–6; Nov.–Feb., Mon.–Sat. 10:30–6:30, Sun. 1:30–5:30.*

WORTH NOTING

Battistero. The Duomo's 14th-century Gothic Baptistery was built to prop up the apse of the cathedral. There are frescoes throughout, but the highlight is a large bronze 15th-century baptismal font designed by Jacopo della Quercia (1374–1438). It's adorned with bas-reliefs by various artists, including two by Renaissance masters: the *Baptism of Christ* by Lorenzo Ghiberti (1378–1455) and the *Feast of Herod* by Donatello. ⊠ *Piazza San Giovanni* ☎ *0577/286300* 🖵 *€3; €10 combined ticket includes the Duomo, Cripta, and Museo dell'Opera del Duomo* ☼ *Mar.–mid-June, daily 9:30–7:30; mid-June–mid-Sept., daily 9:30–8; mid-Sept.–Oct., daily 9:30–7:30; Nov.–Feb., daily 10–5.*

Continued on page 664

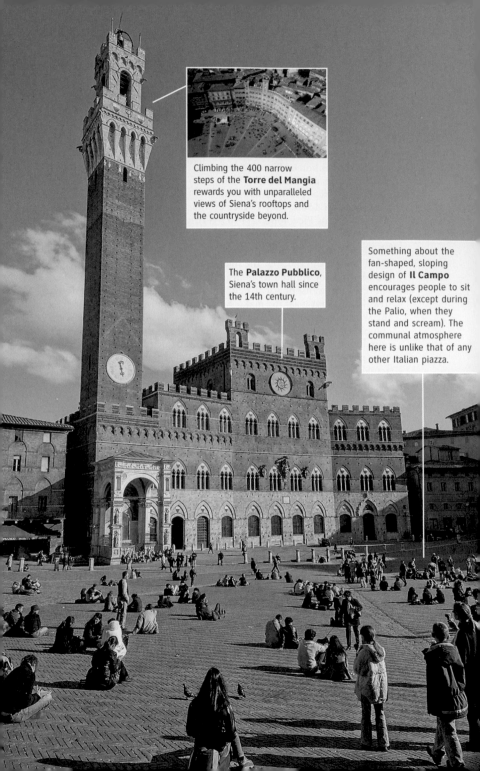

Climbing the 400 narrow steps of the **Torre del Mangia** rewards you with unparalleled views of Siena's rooftops and the countryside beyond.

The **Palazzo Pubblico**, Siena's town hall since the 14th century.

Something about the fan-shaped, sloping design of **Il Campo** encourages people to sit and relax (except during the Palio, when they stand and scream). The communal atmosphere here is unlike that of any other Italian piazza.

PIAZZA DEL CAMPO

Fodor'sChoice ★

9 The fan-shaped **Piazza del Campo,** known simply as il Campo (The Field), is one of the finest squares in Italy. Constructed toward the end of the 12th century on a market area unclaimed by any contrada, it's still the heart of town. The bricks of the Campo are patterned in nine different sections—representing each member of the medieval Government of Nine. At the top of the Campo is a copy of the **Fonte Gaia,** decorated in the early 15th century by Siena's greatest sculptor, Jacopo della Quercia, with 13 sculpted reliefs of biblical events and virtues. Those lining the rectangular fountain are 19th-century copies; the originals are in the Spedale di Santa Maria della Scala. On Palio horse race days (July 2 and August 16), the Campo and all its surrounding buildings are packed with cheering, frenzied locals and tourists craning their necks to take it all in.

[Map of Piazza del Campo area showing: Via Banchi di Sopra, Banchi di Sotto, Fonte Gaia, Palazzo Sansedoni, Palazzo Piccolomini, Via di Fontebranda, Il Campo, Torre del Mangia, Via del Porrione, Palazzo d'Elci, Sinagoga, Palazzo Pubblico, Via di Salicotto, Casato di Sotto, Via Giov. Dupré, Piazza del Mercato, Palazzo Patrizi, scale 0–50 yards, 0–50 meters]

10 The Gothic **Palazzo Pubblico,** the focal point of the Piazza del Campo, has served as Siena's town hall since the 1300s. It now also contains the **Museo Civico,** with walls covered in early Renaissance frescoes. The nine governors of Siena once met in the Sala della Pace, famous for Ambrogio Lorenzetti's frescoes called *Allegories of Good and Bad Government,* painted in the late 1330s to demonstrate the dangers of tyranny. The good government side depicts utopia, showing first the virtuous ruling council surrounded by angels and then scenes of a perfectly running city and countryside. Conversely, the bad government fresco tells a tale straight out of Dante. The evil ruler and his advisers have horns and fondle strange animals, and the town scene depicts the seven mortal sins in action. Interestingly, the bad government fresco is severely damaged, and the good government fresco is in terrific condition. The **Torre del Mangia,** the palazzo's famous bell tower, is named after one of its first bell ringers, Giovanni di Duccio (called Mangiaguadagni, or earnings eater). The climb up to the top is long and steep, but the view makes it worth every step. ⊠ *Piazza del Campo 1, Città* ☎ *0577/41169* ☒ *Museo €8, Torre €8, combined ticket €13* ⊗ *Museo Nov.–Mar. 15, daily 10–6:30; Mar. 16–Oct., daily 10–7. Torre Nov.–Mar. 15, daily 10–4; Mar. 16–Oct., daily 10–7.*

THE PALIO

The three laps around a makeshift racetrack in Piazza del Campo are over in less than two minutes, but the spirit of Siena's Palio—a horse race held every July 2 and August 16—lives all year long.

The Palio is contested between Siena's contrade, the 17 neighborhoods that have divided the city since the Middle Ages. Loyalties are fiercely felt. At any time of year you'll see on the streets contrada symbols—Tartuca (turtle), Oca (goose), Istrice (porcupine), Torre (tower)—emblazoned on banners and engraved on building walls. At Palio time, simmering rivalries come to a boil.

It's been that way since at least August 16, 1310, the date of the first recorded running of the Palio. At that time, and for centuries to follow, the race went through the streets of the city. The additional July 2 running was instituted in 1649; soon thereafter the location was moved to the Campo and the current system for selecting the race entrants established. Ten of the contrade are chosen at random to run in the July Palio. The August race is then contested between the 7 contrade left out in July, plus 3 of the 10 July participants, again chosen at random. Although the races are in theory of equal importance, Sienese will tell you that it's better to win the second and have bragging rights for the rest of the year.

The race itself has a raw and arbitrary character—it's no Kentucky Derby. There's barely room for the 10 horses on the makeshift Campo course, so falls and collisions are inevitable. Horses are chosen at random three days before the race, and jockeys (who ride bareback) are mercenaries hired from surrounding towns. Almost no tactic is considered too underhanded. Bribery, secret plots, and betrayal are commonplace—so much so that the word for "jockey," *fantino,* has come to mean "untrustworthy" in Siena. There have been incidents of drugging (the horses) and kidnapping (the jockeys); only sabotaging a horse's reins remains taboo.

Above: The tension of the starting line. Top left: The frenzy of the race. Bottom left: A solemn flag bearer follows in the footsteps of his ancestors.

AQUILA

BRUCO

CHIOCCIOLA

17 MEDIEVAL CONTRADE

Festivities kick off three days prior to the Palio, with the selection and blessing of the horses, trial runs, ceremonial banquets, betting, and late-night celebrations. Residents don their contrada's colors and march through the streets in medieval costumes. The Campo is transformed into a racetrack lined with a thick layer of sand. On race day, each horse is brought to the church of the contrada for which it will run, where it's blessed and told, "Go little horse and return a winner." The Campo fills through the afternoon, with spectators crowding into every available space until bells ring and the piazza is sealed off. Processions of flag wavers in traditional dress march to the beat of tambourines and drums and the roar of the crowds. The *palio* itself—a banner for which the race is named, dedicated to the Virgin Mary—makes an appearance, followed by the horses and their jockeys.

The race begins when one horse, chosen to ride up from behind the rest of the field, crosses the starting line. There are always false starts, adding to the frenzied mood. Once underway, the race is over in a matter of minutes. The victorious rider is carried off through the streets of the winning contrada (where in the past tradition dictated he was entitled to the local girl of his choice), while winning and losing sides use television replay to analyze the race from every possible angle. The winning contrada will celebrate into the night, at long tables piled high with food and drink. The champion horse is guest of honor.

Reserved seating in the stands is sold out months in advance of the races; contact the Siena Tourist Office (✉ Piazza del Campo 56 ☎ 0577/280551) to find out about availability, and ask your hotel if it can procure you a seat. The entire area in the center is free and unreserved, but you need to show up early in order to get a prime spot against the barriers.

CIVETTA

DRAGO

GIRAFFA

ISTRICE

LEOCORNO

LUPA

NICCHIO

OCA

ONDA

PANTERA

SELVA

TARTUCA

TORRE

VALDIMONTONE

Fodor's Choice   **Museo dell'Opera Metropolitana.** Part of the unfinished nave of what was
★   to have been a new cathedral, the museum contains the Duomo's treasury and some of the original decoration from its facade and interior.
The first room on the ground floor displays weather-beaten 13th-
century sculptures by Giovanni Pisano (circa 1245–1318) that were
brought inside for protection and replaced by copies, as was a tondo of
the *Madonna and Child* (now attributed to Donatello) that once hung
on the door to the south transept. The masterpiece is unquestionably
Duccio's *Maestà*, one side with 26 panels depicting episodes from the
Passion, the other side with a *Madonna and Child Enthroned.* Painted
between 1308 and 1311 as the altarpiece for the Duomo (where it
remained until 1505), its realistic elements, such as the lively depiction
of the Christ child and the treatment of interior space, proved an enormous influence on later painters. The second floor is divided between
the treasury, with a crucifix by Giovanni Pisano and several statues and
busts of biblical characters and classical philosophers, and La Sala della
Madonna degli Occhi Grossi (the Room of the Madonna with the Big
Eyes), named after the namesake painting it displays by the Maestro
di Tressa, who painted in the early 13th century. The work originally
decorated the Duomo's high altar, before being displaced by Duccio's
Maestà. There is a fine view from the tower inside the museum. ⊠ *Piazza del Duomo 8, Città* ☎ *0577/286300* ✆ *€6; €10 combined ticket
includes the Duomo, Cripta, and Battistero* ☉ *Mar.–mid-June, daily
9:30–7:30; mid-June–mid-Sept., daily 9:30–8; mid-Sept.–Oct., daily
9:30–7:30; Nov.–Feb., daily 10–5.*

Pinacoteca Nazionale. The superb collection of five centuries of local
painting in Siena's national picture gallery can easily convince you that
the Renaissance was by no means just a Florentine thing—Siena was
arguably just as important a center of art and innovation as its rival
to the north, especially in the mid-13th century. Accordingly, the most
interesting section of the collection, chronologically arranged, has several important "firsts." Room 1 contains a painting of the *Stories of
the True Cross* (1215) by the so-called Master of Tressa, the earliest
identified work by a painter of the Sienese school, and is followed in
Room 2 by late-13th-century artist Guido da Siena's *Stories from the
Life of Christ,* one of the first paintings ever made on canvas (earlier
painters used wood panels). Rooms 3 and 4 are dedicated to Duccio,
a student of Cimabue (circa 1240–1302) and considered to be the last
of the proto-Renaissance painters. Ambrogio Lorenzetti's landscapes
in Room 8 are the first truly secular paintings in Western art. Among
later works in the rooms on the floor above, keep an eye out for the
preparatory sketches used by Domenico Beccafumi (1486–1551) for
the 35 etched marble panels he made for the floor of the Duomo. ⊠ *Via
San Pietro 29, Città* ☎ *0577/286143* ⊕ *www.pinacotecanazionale.siena.
it* ✆ *€4* ☉ *Tues.–Sat. 8:15–7:15; Sun. and Mon. 9–1; last entrance ½
hr before closing.*

San Domenico. Although the Duomo is celebrated as a triumph of 13th-
century Gothic architecture, this church, built at about the same time,
turned out to be an oversize, hulking brick box that never merited a
finishing coat in marble, let alone a graceful facade. Named for the

founder of the Dominican order, the church is now more closely associated with Saint Catherine of Siena. Just to the right of the entrance is the chapel in which she received the stigmata. On the wall is the only known contemporary portrait of the saint, made in the late 14th century by Andrea Vanni (circa 1332–1414). Farther down is the famous **Cappella di Santa Caterina,** the church's official shrine. Catherine, or bits and pieces of her, was literally spread all over the country—a foot is in Venice, most of her body is in Rome, and only her head (kept in a reliquary on the chapel's altar) and her right thumb are here. She was revered throughout the country long before she was officially named a patron saint of Italy in 1939. On either side of the chapel are well-known frescoes by Sodoma (aka Giovanni Antonio Bazzi, 1477–1549) of *St. Catherine in Ecstasy.* Don't miss the view of the Duomo and town center from the apse-side terrace. ⊠ *Via Camporegio 2, Camollia* ☎ *0577/280893* ⊕ *www.basilicacateriniana.com* ⊘ *May–Oct., daily 7–7; Nov.–Apr., daily 9–6.*

Spedale di Santa Maria della Scala. For more than a thousand years, this complex across from the Duomo was home to Siena's hospital, but now it serves as a museum to display some terrific frescoes and other Sienese Renaissance treasures. Restored 15th-century frescoes in the Sala del Pellegrinaio (once the emergency room) tell the history of the hospital, which was created to give refuge to passing pilgrims and to those in need, and to distribute charity to the poor. Incorporated into the complex is the church of the Santissima Annunziata, with a celebrated *Risen Christ* by Vecchietta (also known as Lorenzo di Pietro, circa 1412–80). Down in the dark Cappella di Santa Caterina della Notte is where Saint Catherine went to pray at night. The subterranean archaeological museum contained within the *ospedale* (hospital) is worth seeing even if you're not particularly taken with Etruscan objects: the interior design is sheer brilliance—it's beautifully lighted, eerily quiet, and an oasis of cool on hot summer days. The displays—including the *bucchero* (dark, reddish clay) ceramics, Roman coins, and tomb furnishings—are clearly marked and can serve as a good introduction to the history of regional excavations. Don't miss della Quercia's original sculpted reliefs from the Fonte Gaia. Although the fountain has been faithfully copied for the Campo, there's something incomparably beautiful about the real thing. ⊠ *Piazza del Duomo 1, Città* ☎ *0577/534511* ⊕ *www.santamariadellascala.com* ⊠€6 ⊘ *Mid-Mar.–mid-Oct., daily 10:30–6:30; mid-Oct.–mid-Mar., daily 10:30–4:30; ticket office closes 1 hr before closing.*

WHERE TO EAT

$$$

TUSCAN

✕ **Le Logge.** Bright flowers provide a dash of color at this classic Tuscan dining room, and stenciled designs on the ceilings add some whimsy. The wooden cupboards (now filled with wine bottles) lining the walls recall its past as a turn-of-the-19th-century grocery store. The menu, with four or five primi and secondi, changes regularly, but almost always includes their classic *malfatti all'osteria* (ricotta and spinach dumplings in a cream sauce). Desserts such as *coni con mousse al cioccolato e* *gelato allo zafferano* (two diminutive ice-cream cones with chocolate mousse and saffron ice cream) provide an inventive ending to the meal. When not vying for one of the outdoor tables, make sure to ask for one in the main downstairs room. $ *Average meal: €55* ⊠ *Via del Porrione 33, San Martino* ☎ *0577/48013* ⊕ *www.osterialelogge.it* ⚍ *Reservations essential* ⊘ *Closed Sun. and 3 wks in Jan.*

$

TUSCAN

✕ **Osteria Il Grattacielo.** Wiped out from too much sightseeing? Consider a meal at this hole-in-the-wall restaurant where locals congregate for a simple lunch over a glass of wine. There's a collection of *verdure sott'olio* (marinated vegetables), a wide selection of *affettati misti* (cured meats), and various types of frittatas. All off this can be washed down with the cheap, yet eminently drinkable, house red. A couple of bench tables provide outdoor seating in summer. Don't be put off by the absence of a written menu. All the food is displayed at the counter, so you can point if you need to. $ *Average meal: €14* ⊠ *Via Pontani 8, Camollìa* ☎ *0577/289326* ⚍ *Reservations not accepted* ⊟ *No credit cards* ⊘ *Closed Sun.*

$$

TUSCAN

✕ **Trattoria Papei.** The menu hasn't changed for years, and why should it? The *pici al cardinale* (handmade spaghetti with a duck and bacon sauce) is wonderful, and all the other typically Sienese dishes are equally delicious. Grilled meats are the true speciality; the *bistecca di vitello* (grilled veal steak) is melt-in-your-mouth wonderful. Tucked away behind the Palazzo Pubblico in a square that serves as a parking lot for most of the day, the restaurant's location isn't great, but the food is. Thanks to portable heaters, there is outdoor seating all year-round. $ *Average meal: €30* ⊠ *Piazza del Mercato 6, Città* ☎ *0577/280894* ⊘ *Closed Mon.*

WHERE TO STAY

For expanded hotel reviews, visit Fodors.com.

$$

B&B/INN

🏨 **Antica Torre.** The cordial Landolfo family has carefully evoked a private home with their eight guest rooms inside a restored 16th-century tower. **Pros:** near the town center; charming atmosphere. **Cons:** narrow stairway up to the rooms; low ceilings; cramped bathrooms. $ *Rooms from: €120* ⊠ *Via Fieravecchia 7, San Martino* ☎☎ *0577/222255* ⊕ *www.anticatorresiena.it* ⤳ *8 rooms* ⦿ *Breakfast.*

$$

B&B/INN

🏨 **Hotel Santa Caterina.** Manager Lorenza Capannelli and her fine staff are welcoming, hospitable, enthusiastic, and go out of their way to ensure a fine stay in rooms where dark, straight-lined wood furniture stands next to beds with floral spreads. **Pros:** friendly staff; a short walk to center of town; breakfast in the garden. **Cons:** on a busy intersection; outside city walls. $ *Rooms from: €185* ⊠ *Via Piccolomini 7, San Martino* ☎ *0577/221105* ⊕ *www.hscsiena.it* ⤳ *22 rooms* ⦿ *Breakfast.*

$

B&B/INN

🏨 **Palazzo Fani Mignanelli.** You'll find all the trimmings of an old-style town palace in this quiet haven where rooms with a view over the rooftops of Siena are decorated with period antiques. **Pros:** peaceful retreat; excellent location for exploring town. **Cons:** on the third floor of an otherwise run-down building; some stairs; basic breakfast. $ *Rooms from: €99* ⊠ *Banchi di Sopra 15, Città* ☎ *0577/283566* ⊕ *www. residenzadepoca.it* ⤳ *11 rooms.*

$$$ HOTEL **Palazzo Ravizza.** This romantic palazzo exudes a sense of genteel shabbiness, and lovely guest rooms have high ceilings, antique furnishings, and bathrooms decorated with hand-painted tiles. **Pros:** 10-minute walk to the center of town; pleasant garden with a view beyond the city walls; professional staff. **Cons:** not all rooms have views; some rooms are a little cramped. [$] *Rooms from: €175* ✉ *Pian dei Mantellini 34, Città* ☎ *0577/280462* 🌐 *www.palazzoravizza.it* *38 rooms, 4 suites* 🍴 *Breakfast.*

ARREZZO AND CORTONA

The hill towns of Arezzo and Cortona carry on age-old local traditions—in June and September, for example, Arezzo's Romanesque and Gothic churches are enlivened by the Giostra del Saracino, a costumed medieval joust. Arezzo has been home to important artists since ancient times, when Etruscan potters produced their fiery-red vessels here. Fine examples of the work of Luca Signorelli are preserved in Cortona, his hometown.

AREZZO

63 km (39 miles) northeast of Siena, 81 km (50 miles) southeast of Florence.

The birthplace of the poet Petrarch (1304–74) and the Renaissance artist and art historian Giorgio Vasari (1511–74), Arezzo is today best known for the magnificent Piero della Francesca frescoes in the church of San Francesco. The city dates from pre-Etruscan times and thrived as an Etruscan capital from the 7th to the 4th century BC. During the Middle Ages it was fully embroiled in the conflict between the Ghibellines (pro–Holy Roman Emperor) and the Guelphs (pro-pope), losing its independence to Florence at the end of the 14th century after many decades of doing battle.

Urban sprawl testifies to the fact that Arezzo (population 90,000) is the third-largest city in Tuscany (after Florence and Pisa). But the old town, set on a low hill, is relatively small, and almost completely closed to traffic. Look for parking along the roads that circle the lower part of town and walk into town from there. You can explore the most interesting sights in a few hours, adding time to linger for some window-shopping at Arezzo's many antiques shops. Several scenes of Roberto Benigni's award-winning film *Life is Beautiful* were shot here; the tourist office provides a map that highlights the locations.

GETTING HERE AND AROUND

Arezzo is easily reached by car from the A1 (Autostrada del Sole), the main highway running between Florence and Rome. When you arrive, look for the "Pietri" parking lot, on the far side of town, and take the public escalators to the upper part of town. Direct trains connect Arezzo with Rome (2½ hours) and Florence (1 hour). Direct bus service is available from Florence, but not from Rome.

VISITOR INFORMATION

Arezzo Tourism Office ✉ *Piazza della Libertà 3* ☎ *0575/392274* 🌐 *arezzo.intoscana.it.*

EXPLORING

Fodor's Choice
★ **Basilica di San Francesco.** The famous Piero della Francesca frescoes depicting *The Legend of the True Cross* (1452–66) were executed on the three walls of the Capella Bacci, the main apse of this 14th-century church. What Sir Kenneth Clark called "the most perfect morning light in all Renaissance painting" may be seen in the lowest section of

WORD OF MOUTH

"Arezzo holds a huge antiques fair the first weekend of each month that takes over the streets in the historical center of town. You may want to check your dates, either to avoid or take advantage of it."

—shellio

the right wall, where the troops of Emperor Maxentius flee before the sign of the cross. The view of the frescoes from the nave of the church is limited, but a much closer look is available from the Capella Bacci. The ticket office for the latter is located directly in front of the main entrance, down steps in the lower church. Reservations are recommended June–September. ⊠ *Piazza San Francesco* 🕾 *0575/352727 Capella Bacci tickets and reservations* ⊕ *www.pierodellafrancesca.it* 🖾 *Church free, Capella Bacci €8* ⊙ *Weekdays 9–5:30, Sat. 9–5, Sun. 1–5.*

Duomo. Arezzo's medieval cathedral at the top of the hill contains an eye-level fresco of a tender *Magdalene* by Piero della Francesca (1420–92); look for it in the north aisle next to the large marble tomb near the organ. Construction of the Duomo began in 1278, but twice came to a halt, and the church wasn't completed until 1510. The facade, designed by Arezzo's Dante Viviani, was added later (1901–14). ⊠ *Piazza del Duomo 1* 🕾 *0575/23991* ⊙ *Daily 6:30–12:30 and 3–6:30.*

▌ NEED A
▌ BREAK?

Caffè dei Costanti. Outdoor seating on Arezzo's main pedestrian square and a tasty range of chef's salads (named after the waitresses that serve here) make this a very pleasant spot for a light lunch during a tour of town. In continuous operation since 1886, it's the oldest café in Arezzo, and the charming old-world interior served as backdrop to scenes in Roberto Benigni's 1997 film *Life is Beautiful.* If you're here in the early evening, the dei Costanti serves up an ample buffet of snacks to accompany pre-dinner aperitifs. ⊠ *Piazza San Francesco 19* 🕾 *0575/1824075.*

Piazza Grande. With its irregular shape and sloping brick pavement, framed by buildings of assorted centuries, Arezzo's central piazza echoes Siena's Piazza del Campo. Though not quite so magnificent, it's lively enough during the outdoor antiques fair the first Sunday of the month and when the **Giostra del Saracino** (Saracen Joust), featuring medieval costumes and competition, is held here on the third Saturday of June and on the first Sunday of September.

Santa Maria della Pieve (*Church of Saint Mary of the Parish*). The curving, tiered apse on Piazza Grande belongs to a fine Romanesque church that was originally Paleo-Christian, built on the remains of an old Roman temple. It was redone in Romanesque style in the 12th century. The facade dates from the early 13th century, but it includes granite columns from the Roman period. Interior frescoes by Piero della Francesca, Lorenzo Ghiberti (1378–1455), and Pietro Lorenzetti (circa

1290–1348) were sadly lost in the 16th, 17th, and 18th centuries. To the left of the altar there is a 16th-century episcopal throne by Vasari. ✉ *Corso Italia 7* ☎ *0575/22629* ⏲ *May–Sept., daily 8–1 and 3–7; Oct.–Apr., daily 8–noon and 3–6.*

WHERE TO EAT

$ SEAFOOD 🍴 **I Tre Bicchieri.** Chef Luigi Casotti hails from Amalfi and this shows through in his fine adaptations of dishes more commonly served near the Bay of Naples. The *raviolone farcito con gamberi rossi di Sicilia e tonno* (a large raviolo stufffed with Sicilian prawns and tuna served with a sauce of tomatoes, capers, and olives) and the *filetto di Branzino in panuria di erbe* (breaded filet of sea bass) are particularly delicious. [$] *Average meal: €25* ✉ *Piazzetta Sopra i Ponti 3–5* ☎ *0575/26557.*

$ ITALIAN 🍴 **La Torre di Gnicche.** Wine lovers shouldn't miss this wine bar–eatery with more than 700 labels on the list, just off Piazza Grande. Seasonal dishes of traditional fare, such as *acquacotta del casentino* (porcini mushroom soup) and *baccalà in umido* (salt-cod stew), are served in the simply decorated, vaulted dining room. You can accompany your meal with one, or more, of the almost 30 wines that are available by the glass. Limited outdoor seating is available in warm weather. [$] *Average meal: €25* ✉ *Piaggia San Martino 8* ☎ *0575/352035* 🌐 *www.latorredignicche.it* ⏲ *Closed Wed., Jan., and 2 wks in July.*

WHERE TO STAY

For expanded hotel reviews, visit Fodors.com.

$$ HOTEL 🏨 **Castello di Gargonza.** Enchantment reigns at this tiny 13th-century countryside hamlet, part of the fiefdom of the aristocratic Florentine Guicciardini and reinvented by the modern Count Roberto Guicciardini as an agriturismo. **Pros:** romantic, one-of-a-kind accommodation in a medieval castle; peaceful, isolated setting. **Cons:** standard rooms are extremely basic; a little out of the way for exploring the region; private transportation is a necessity. [$] *Rooms from: €150* ✉ *SR73 28 km (17 miles) southwest of Arezzo, Località Gargonza, Monte San Savino* ☎ *0575/847021* 🌐 *www.gargonza.it* 🛏 *37 rooms, 8 apartments* ⏲ *Closed last 3 wks in Jan., and Feb.* 🍽 *Breakfast.*

$$$$ HOTEL 🏨 **Il Borro.** The location has been described as "heaven on earth," and a stay at Salvatore Ferragamo's estate is sure to bring similar descriptions to mind. **Pros:** superlative service; great location for exploring eastern Tuscany; unique setting and atmosphere. **Cons:** off the beaten track making private transport a must; not all suites have country views; ultramodern spa facility seems out of place. [$] *Rooms from: €275* ✉ *Località Il Borro, outside the village of San Giustino Valdarno, 20 km (12 miles) northwest of Arezzo* ☎ *055/977053* 🌐 *www.ilborro.com* 🛏 *16 suites, 3 villas, 7 farmhouses, 4 apartments* 🍽 *Breakfast.*

SHOPPING

Ever since Etruscan goldsmiths set up their shops here more than 2,000 years ago, Arezzo has been famous for its jewelry. Today the town lays claim to being one of the world's capitals of jewelry design and manufacture, and you can find an impressive display of big-time baubles in the town center's shops.

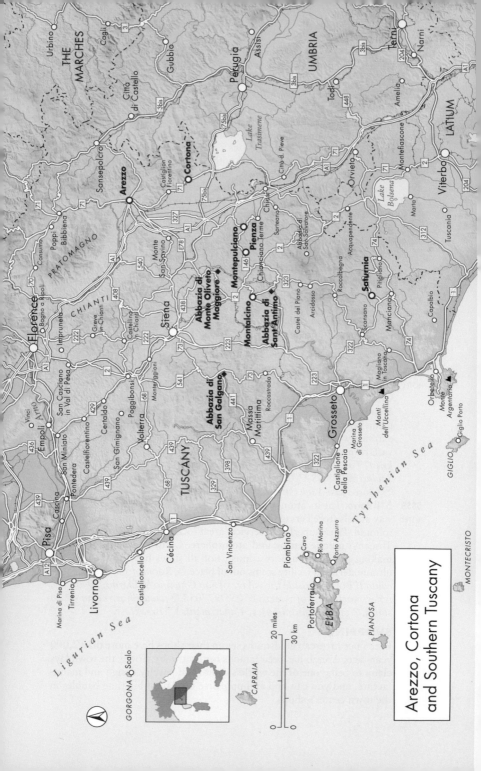

Arezzo, Cortona
and Southern Tuscany

Arezzo is also famous, at least in Italy, for its antiques dealers. The first weekend of every month, between 8:30 and 5:30, a popular and colorful flea market selling antiques and not-so-antique items takes place in the town's main square and in the streets and parks nearby.

CORTONA

29 km (18 miles) south of Arezzo, 79 km (44 miles) east of Siena, 117 km (73 miles) southeast of Florence.

With olive trees and vineyards creeping up to its walls, pretty Cortona—popularized by Frances Mayes's glowing descriptions in *Under the Tuscan Sun*—commands sweeping views over Lake Trasimeno and the plain of the Valdichiana. Its two galleries and churches are rarely visited; its delightful medieval streets are a pleasure to wander for their own sake. The heart of town is formed by Piazza della Repubblica and the adjacent Piazza Signorelli; both contain pleasant shops to browse in.

GETTING HERE AND AROUND

Cortona is easily reached by car from the A1 (Autostrada del Sole): take the Valdichiana exit toward Perugia, then follow signs for Cortona. Regular bus service, provided by Etruria Mobilità, is available between Arezzo and Cortona (1 hour). Cortona's train station is in the valley 3 km (2 miles) steeply below the town itself. From there, you can take a local bus (frequent service) or taxi to get up to Cortona.

VISITOR INFORMATION

Cortona Tourism Office ⊠ *Piazza Signorelli 9* ☎ *0575/637223* ⊕ *arezzo.intoscana.it.*

EXPLORING

Museo Diocesano. Housed in part of the original cathedral structure, this nine-room museum houses an impressive number of large, splendid paintings by native son Luca Signorelli (1445–1523), as well as a beautiful *Annunciation* by Fra Angelico (circa 1400–1455), which is a delightful surprise in this small town. The former oratory of the Compagnia del Gesù, reached by descending the 1633 staircase opposite the Duomo, is part of the museum. The church was built between 1498 and 1505 and restructured by Giorgio Vasari in 1543. Frescoes depicting sacrifices from the Old Testament by Doceno (1508–56), based on designs by Vasari, line the walls. ⊠ *Piazza Duomo 1* ☎ *0575/62830* ⊠ *€5* ⊗ *Apr.–Oct., daily 10–7; Nov.–Mar., Tues.–Sun. 10–5.*

Santa Maria al Calcinaio. Legend has it that the image of the Madonna appeared on a wall of a medieval *calcinaio* (lime pit used for curing leather), the site on which the church was then built between 1485 and 1513. The linear gray-and-white interior recalls Florence's Duomo. Sienese architect Francesco di Giorgio (1439–1502) most likely designed the sanctuary: the church is a terrific example of Renaissance architectural principles. ⊠ *Località Il Calcinaio 227, 3 km (2 miles) southeast of Cortona's center* ☎ *0575/604830* ⊗ *Mon.–Sat. 3:30–6, Sun. 10–12:30.*

WHERE TO EAT

$$
TUSCAN

✕ **Osteria del Teatro.** Photographs from theatrical productions spanning many years line the walls of this tavern off Cortona's large Piazza del Teatro. The food is simply delicious—try the *filetto al lardo di colonnata e prugne* (beef cooked with bacon and prunes); service is warm and friendly. $ *Average meal: €35* ✉ *Via Maffei 2* ☎ *0575/630556* ⊕ *www.osteria-del-teatro.it* ⊘ *Closed Wed., and 2 wks in Nov. and Feb.*

WHERE TO STAY

For expanded hotel reviews, visit Fodors.com.

$
HOTEL

🏨 **Hotel San Michele.** Cortona might tempt you to step back in time and stay there awhile, and the spacious, beamed, richly furnished rooms in a 15th-century palazzo in the center of town provide the perfect hideaway. **Pros:** lovely surroundings in perfect hilltown location; character-filled rooms; excellent service, including valet parking. **Cons:** limited views from some rooms; some street noise. $ *Rooms from: €99* ✉ *Via Guelfa 15* ☎ *0575/604348* ⊕ *www.hotelsanmichele.net* ⇨ *42 rooms* ⦿ *Breakfast.*

$$$$
B&B/INN

🏨 **Il Falconiere.** Accommodation options here include rooms in an 18th-century villa, suites in the *chiesetta* (chapel, or little church), or for more seclusion, Le Vigne del Falco suites at the far end of the property. **Pros:** attractive setting in the valley beneath Cortona; excellent service; elegant, but relaxed. **Cons:** a car is a must; some find rooms in main villa a little noisy; a bit fancy for the environs. $ *Rooms from: €290* ✉ *Località San Martino 370, 3 km (1½ miles) north of Cortona* ☎ *0575/612679* ⊕ *www.ilfalconiere.com* ⇨ *13 rooms, 7 suites* ⊘ *Hotel closed last 3 wks in Jan.–mid-Feb.* ⦿ *Breakfast.*

SOUTHERN TUSCANY

Along the roads leading south from Siena, soft green olive groves give way to a blanket of oak, cypress, and reddish-brown earth. Towns are small and as old as the hills. The scruffy mountain landscapes of Monte Amiata make up some of the wildest parts of Tuscany, and once you're across the mountains the terrain is still full of cliffs. Aside from stunning scenery, southern Tuscany has good wine (try Brunello di Montalcino or the fruity, lesser-known Morellino di Scansano for a true treat), Etruscan ruins, and medieval towns.

MONTEPULCIANO

64 km (40 miles) southeast of Siena.

Perched high on a hilltop, Montepulciano is made up of a cluster of Renaissance buildings set within a circle of cypress trees. At an altitude of almost 2,000 feet, it's cool in summer and chilled in winter by biting winds that sweep the spiraling streets. Vino Nobile di Montepulciano, a robust red wine, is justifiably the town's greatest claim to fame. You can sample it in various wineshops and bars lining the twisting roads, as well as in most restaurants.

GETTING HERE

From Rome or Florence, take the Chiusi-Chianciano exit from the A1 highway (Autostrada del Sole). The town is 13 km (8 miles) west of the Chiusi/Chianciano exit. From Siena, take the SR2 south to San Quirico and then the SP146 to Montepulciano. Tra-In offers bus service from Siena to Montepulciano several times a day. Montepulciano's train station is in Montepulciano Stazione, 10 km (6 miles) away.

VISITOR INFORMATION

Montepulciano Tourism Office ✉ *Piazza Don Minzoni 1* ☎ *0578/757341* 🌐 *www.prolocomontepulciano.it.*

EXPLORING

Duomo. On the Piazza Grande the unfinished facade of Montepulciano's cathedral doesn't measure up to the beauty of its neighboring palaces. On the inside, however, its Renaissance roots shine through. The high altar has a splendid triptych painted in 1401 by Taddeo di Bartolo (circa 1362–1422), and you can see fragments of the tomb of Bartolomeo Aragazzi, secretary to Pope Martin V, which was sculpted by Michelozzo between 1427 and 1436. ✉ *Piazza Grande* ☎ *0578/757341* 🕒 *Daily 9–12:30.*

Piazza Grande. Filled with handsome buildings, this large square on the heights of the old historic town is Montepulciano's pièce de résistance.

San Biagio. Designed by Antonio da Sangallo il Vecchio, and considered his masterpiece, this church sits on the hillside below the town walls and is a model of High Renaissance architectural perfection. Inside the church is a painting of the Madonna that according to legend, was the only thing remaining in an abandoned church that two young girls entered on April 23, 1518. The girls saw the eyes of the Madonna moving, and that same afternoon so did a farmer and a cow, who knelt down in front of the painting. In 1963 the image was proclaimed the *Madonna del Buon Viaggio* (Madonna of the Good Journey), the protector of tourists in Italy. ✉ *Via di San Biagio* ☎ *0578/757164* 🕒 *Daily 9–12:30 and 3:30–7:30.*

WHERE TO EAT

$$$ TUSCAN

🍴 **La Grotta.** You might be tempted to pass right by the innocuous entrance across the street from San Biagio, but you'd miss some fantastic food. Try the *tagliolini con carciofi e rigatino* (thin noodles with artichokes and bacon) or *tagliatelle di grano saraceno con asparagi e zucchine* (flat, buckwheat-flour noodles with asparagus and zucchini). Wash it down with the local wine, which just happens to be one of Italy's finest—Vino Nobile di Montepulciano. The desserts, such as an extravagantly rich triple-chocolate flan, are prepared with particular flair. [$] *Average meal: €55* ✉ *Via di San Biagio 15* ☎ *0578/757479* 🌐 *www.lagrottamontepulciano.it* 🕒 *Closed Wed., and Jan.–mid-Mar.*

$ TUSCAN

🍴 **Osteria del Conte.** As high in Montepulciano as you can get, just behind the Duomo, this small and intimate restaurant is expertly run by the mother and son team of Lorena and Paolo Brachi. Passionate about the food they prepare, both have a flair for the region's traditional dishes—the *pici all'aglione* (handmade spaghetti with garlic sauce) and the *filetto ai funghi porcini* (steak with porcini mushrooms) are mouthwateringly good. The wine list, though limited in range, presents a decent selection of wines from both Montepulciano and Montalcino. For a change from the usual Tuscan meat dishes, fresh fish is served on Friday. Outdoor seating is limited. [$] *Average meal: €30* ✉ *Via di San Donato 19* ☎ *0578/756062* 🌐 *www.osteriadelconte.it* 🕒 *Closed Wed.*

WHERE TO STAY

For expanded hotel reviews, visit Fodors.com.

$$$$ B&B/INN 🏨 **Podere Dionora.** At this secluded and serene country inn, earth-tone fabrics complement antiques in the individually decorated rooms, all of which have functioning fireplaces. **Pros:** secluded setting; great views; attentive service. **Cons:** long walk to the nearest town; need a car to get around. [$] *Rooms from: €330* ✉ *Via Vicinale di Poggiano 9, 3 km (2 miles) east of Montepulciano town center* ☎ *0578/717496* 🌐 *www.dionora.it* 🛏 *6 rooms* 🕒 *Closed mid-Dec.–mid-Feb.* 🍴 *Breakfast.*

$$$ B&B/INN 🏨 **Relais San Bruno.** Alberto Pavoncelli converted his family's summer home, just minutes from the town center, into a splendid inn where well-appointed rooms are filled with views. **Pros:** king-size beds in most rooms; functioning fireplaces; relaxed but attentive service. **Cons:** cottages can be chilly; need a car to get around. [$] *Rooms from: €250* ✉ *Via di Pescaia 5/7* ☎ *0578/716222* 🌐 *www.sanbrunorelais.com* 🛏 *7 rooms, 1 suite* 🍴 *Breakfast.*

$$ B&B/INN 🏨 **San Biagio.** A five-minute walk from the church of the same name, this family-run inn makes a great base for exploring Montepulciano and the surrounding countryside. **Pros:** heated indoor pool; family-friendly atmosphere. **Cons:** some rooms face a busy road; lots of tour groups. [$] *Rooms from: €125* ✉ *Via San Bartolomeo 2* ☎ *0578/717233* 🌐 *www.albergosanbiagio.it* 🛏 *27 rooms* 🍴 *Breakfast.*

PIENZA

15 km (9 miles) east of Montepulciano, 52 km (32 miles) southeast of Siena.

Pienza owes its urban design to Pope Pius II, who had grand plans to transform his home village of Corsignano—the town's former name—into a model Renaissance town. The man entrusted with the project was Bernardo Rossellino (1409–64), a protégé of the great Renaissance architectural theorist Leon Battista Alberti (1404–74). His mandate was to create a cathedral, a papal palace, and a town hall (plus miscellaneous other buildings) that adhered to the humanist pope's principles. The result was a project that expressed Renaissance ideals of art, architecture, and civilized good living in a single scheme: it stands as a fine example of the architectural canon that Alberti formulated in the 15th century and emulated in many of Italy's finest buildings and piazzas. Today the cool nobility of Pienza's center seems almost surreal in this otherwise unpretentious village, though at times it can seem overwhelmed by the tourists it attracts. Pienza's pecorino, a sheep's-milk cheese, is a superior gastronomic experience.

GETTING HERE AND AROUND

It's a short and scenic drive from Montepulciano to Pienza on the SP146. From Siena, drive south along the SR2 to San Quirico d'Orcia and then the SP146. The trip should take just over an hour. Tra-In shuttles passengers between Siena and Pienza. There's no train service to Pienza.

VISITOR INFORMATION

Pienza Tourism Office ✉ *Piazza Dante 18* ☎ *0578/749071* 🌐 *www.pienza.info.*

EXPLORING

Duomo. This 15th-century cathedral was built by the architect Rossellino under the influence of Alberti. The travertine facade is divided in three parts, with Renaissance arches under the pope's coat of arms encircled by a wreath of fruit. Inside, the cathedral is simple but richly decorated with Sienese paintings. The building's perfection didn't last long—the first cracks appeared immediately after the building was completed, and its foundations have shifted slightly ever since as rain erodes the hillside behind. You can see this effect if you look closely at the base of the first column as you enter the church and compare it with the last. ✉ *Piazza Pio II* ☎ *0578/749071* 🕓 *Tues.–Sun. 10–1 and 3–7.*

Palazzo Piccolomini. In 1459 Pius II commissioned Rossellino to design the perfect palazzo for his papal court. The architect took Florence's Palazzo Rucellai by Alberti as a model and designed this 100-room palace. Three sides of the building fit perfectly into the urban plan around it, while the fourth, looking over the valley, has a lovely loggia uniting it with the gardens in back. Guided tours departing every 30 minutes take you to visit the papal apartments, including a beautiful library, the Sala delle Armi (with an impressive weapons collection), and the music room, with its extravagant wooden ceiling forming four letter Ps, for Pope, Pius, Piccolomini, and Pienza. The last tour departs 30 minutes before closing. ✉ *Piazza Pio II* ☎ *0578/748392* 🌐 *www.palazzopiccolominipienza.it* 🎟 *€7* 🕓 *Mid-Mar.–mid-Oct., Tues.–Sun. 10–6:30; mid-Oct.–mid-Mar., Tues.–Sun. 10–4:30. Last entrance ½ hr before closing.*

WHERE TO EAT

$ TUSCAN 🍴 **La Chiocciola.** Take the few minutes to walk from the old town for typical Pienza fare, including homemade pici with hare or wild-boar sauce. The restaurant's version of *formaggio in forno* (baked cheese) with assorted accompaniments such as fresh porcini mushrooms is reason enough to venture here. [$] *Average meal: €25* ✉ *Viale Mencatelli 2* ☎ *0578/748683* 🌐 *www.trattorialachiocciola.it* 🕓 *Closed Wed., and 10 days in Feb.*

$ TUSCAN 🍴 **Osteria Sette di Vino.** Tasty dishes based on the region's cheeses are the specialty at this simple and inexpensive osteria on a quiet, pleasant square in the center of Pienza. Try versions of pici or the starter of radicchio baked quickly to brown the edges. The local pecorino cheese appears often on the menu—the pecorino *grigliata con pancetta* (grilled with cured bacon) is divine. Can't decide? Try the pecorino tasting menu. [$] *Average meal: €15* ✉ *Piazza di Spagna 1* ☎ *0578/749092* 💳 *No credit cards* 🕓 *Closed Wed., July 1–15, and Nov.*

WHERE TO STAY

For expanded hotel reviews, visit Fodors.com.

$ B&B/INN **Agriturismo Cerreto.** Built a short distance from Pienza in the 18th and 19th centuries, this grouping of farm buildings is now done in traditional Tuscan decor with terra-cotta flooring, wood beams, wrought-iron beds, and heavy oak furniture. **Pros:** peaceful country setting; great for families and small groups; good base for exploring the Val d'Orcia. **Cons:** private transportation a must; closest restaurants and town 5 km (3 miles) away. [$] *Rooms from: €110* ✉ *Strada Provinciale per Sant'Anna in Camprena, 5 km (3 miles) north of Pienza* ☎ *0578/749121* 🌐 *www.agriturismocerreto.com* ⇨ *7 rooms* 🍴 *Breakfast.*

MONTALCINO

24 km (15 miles) west of Pienza, 41 km (25 miles) south of Siena.

Another medieval hill town with a special claim to fame, Montalcino is the source for Brunello di Montalcino, one of Italy's most esteemed red wines. You can sample it in wine cellars in town or visit one of the nearby wineries for a guided tour and tasting; you must call ahead for reservations—your hotel or the local tourist office can help with arrangements.

GETTING HERE AND AROUND

By car, follow the SR2 south from Siena, then follow the SP45 to Montalcino. From Pienza, follow the SP146. Several Tra-In buses travel between Siena and Montalcino daily, making a tightly scheduled day trip possible. There's no train service available.

VISITOR INFORMATION

Montalcino Tourism Office ✉ *Costa del Municipio 1* ☎ *0577/849331* 🌐 *www.prolocomontalcino.it.*

EXPLORING

La Fortezza. Providing refuge for the last remnants of the Sienese army during the Florentine conquest of 1555, the battlements of this 14th-century fortress are still in excellent condition. Climb up the narrow, spiral steps for the 360-degree view of most of southern Tuscany. An enoteca for tasting wines is on-site. ✉ *Piazzale Fortezza* ☎ *0577/849211* 🎫 *€3* ⏲ *Nov.–Mar., Tues.–Sun. 9–6; Apr.–Oct., daily 9–8.*

Museo Civico e Diocesano d'Arte Sacra. This fine museum is housed in a building that once belonged to 13th-century Augustinian monks. The ticket booth is in the glorious refurbished cloister, and the sacred art collection, gathered from churches throughout the region, is displayed on two floors in former monastic quarters. Though the art here might be called "B-list," a fine altarpiece by Bartolo di Fredi (circa 1330–1410), the *Coronation of the Virgin,* makes dazzling use of gold. In addition, there's a striking 12th-century crucifix that originally adorned the high altar of the church of Sant'Antimo. Also on hand are many wood sculptures, a typical medium in these parts during the Renaissance. ✉ *Via Ricasoli 31* ☎ *0577/846014* 🎫 *€8* ⏲ *Jan.–Mar., Tues.–Sun. 10–1 and 2–4; Apr.–Dec., Tues.–Sun. 10–6.*

WHERE TO EAT

$ 🍴 **Enoteca Osteria Osticcio.** Tullio and Francesca Scrivano have beautifully remodeled this restaurant and wineshop. Upon entering, you descend a staircase to a tasting room filled with rustic wooden tables. Adjacent is a small dining area with a splendid view of the hills far below, and outside is a lovely little terrace perfect for sampling Brunello di Montalcino when the weather is warm. The menu is light and pairs nicely with the wines, which are the main draw. The *acciughe sotto pesto* (anchovies with pesto) is a particularly fine treat. [$] *Average meal: €25* ✉ *Via Matteotti 23* ☎ *0577/848271* 🌐 *www.osticcio.it* 🕒 *Closed Sun.*

WINE BAR

WHERE TO STAY

For expanded hotel reviews, visit Fodors.com.

$$$$ 🏨 **Castiglion del Bosco.** This estate, one of the largest still in private hands in Tuscany, was purchased by Massimo Ferragamo at the beginning of this century and meticulously converted into a second-to-none resort that incorporates a medieval *borgo* (village) and surrounding farmhouses. **Pros:** extremely secluded; exclusive and tranquil location; top-notch service; breathtaking scenery. **Cons:** well off the beaten track, the nearest town is 12 km (7.5 miles) away; private transportation required. [$] *Rooms from: €545* ✉ *Località Castiglion del Bosco* ☎ *0577/1913111* 🌐 *www.castigliondelbosco.com* 🛏 *23 suites, 9 villas* 🍴 *Breakfast.*

HOTEL

$ 🏨 **La Crociona.** A quiet and serene family-owned farm in the middle of a small vineyard with glorious views houses guests in lovely apartments that can sleep up to five people. **Pros:** peaceful location; great for families; friendly atmosphere. **Cons:** no a/c; need a car to get around. [$] *Rooms from: €120* ✉ *Località La Croce 15* ☎ *0577/848007* 🌐 *www.lacrociona.com* 🛏 *11 apartments* 🍴 *No meals.*

B&B/INN

ABBAZIA DI SANT'ANTIMO

10 km (6 miles) south of Montalcino, 51 km (32 miles) south of Siena.

GETTING HERE AND AROUND

Abbazia di Sant'Antimo is a 15-minute drive from Montalcino. Tra-In bus service is extremely limited. The abbey cannot be reached by train.

EXPLORING

Fodor's Choice ★ **Abbazia di Sant'Antimo.** It's well worth your while to go out of your way to visit this 12th-century Romanesque abbey, as it's a gem of pale stone in the silvery green of an olive grove. The exterior and interior sculpture is outstanding, particularly the nave capitals, a combination of French, Lombard, and even Spanish influences. The sacristy (seldom open) forms part of the primitive Carolingian church (founded in AD 781), its entrance flanked by 9th-century pilasters. The small vaulted crypt dates from the same period. Above the nave runs a *matroneum* (women's gallery), an unusual feature once used to separate the congregation. Equally unusual is the ambulatory, for which the three radiating chapels were almost certainly copied from a French model. Stay to hear the canonical hours celebrated in Gregorian chant.

On the road that leads up toward Castelnuovo dell'Abate is a small shop that sells souvenirs and has washrooms. A 2½-hour hiking trail (signed as #2) leads to the abbey from Montalcino. Starting near Montalcino's small cemetery, the trailheads south through woods, along a ridge road to the tiny hamlet of Villa a Tolli, and then downhill to Sant'Antimo. ✉ *Castelnuovo dell'Abate* ☎ *0577/835659* ⊕ *www. antimo.it* ⊙ *Daily 6 am–9 pm.*

UMBRIA AND THE MARCHES

WELCOME TO UMBRIA AND THE MARCHES

TOP REASONS TO GO

★ **Palazzo Ducale, Urbino:** A visit here reveals more about the ideals of the Renaissance than a shelf of history books.

★ **Assisi, shrine to Saint Francis:** Recharge your soul in this rose-color hill town with a visit to the gentle saint's majestic basilica, adorned with great frescoes.

★ **Spoleto, Umbria's musical Mecca:** Crowds may descend and prices ascend here during summer's Festival dei Due Mondi, but Spoleto's hushed charm enchants year-round.

★ **Tantalizing truffles:** Are Umbria's celebrated "black diamonds" most coveted for their pungent flavor, their rarity, or their power in the realm of romance?

★ **Orvieto's Duomo:** Arresting visions of heaven and hell on the facade and brilliant frescoes within make this Gothic cathedral a dazzler.

1 **Perugia.** Umbria's largest town is easily reached from Rome, Siena, or Florence. Home to some of Perugino's great frescoes and a hilltop *centro storico* (historic center), it's also favored by chocolate lovers, who celebrate their passion at October's Eurochocolate Festival.

2 **Assisi.** The city of Saint Francis is a major pilgrimage site, crowned by one of Italy's greatest churches. Despite the throngs of visitors, it still maintains its medieval hill-town character.

3 **Northern Umbria.** The quiet towns lying around Perugia include **Deruta**, which produces exceptional ceramics. A trip through the rugged terrain of northeast Umbria takes you to **Gubbio**, where from the Piazza della Signoria you can admire magnificent views of the countryside below.

4 **Spoleto.** Though it's known to the world for its annual performing-arts festival, Spoleto offers much more than Puccini in its Piazza del Duomo. There are Filippo Lippi frescoes in the cathedral, a massive castle towering over the town, and a bridge across the neighboring valley that's an engineering marvel.

12

5 Southern Umbria.
Of central Italy's many hill towns, none has a more impressive setting than **Orvieto**, perched on a plateau 1,000 feet above the surrounding valley. Its cathedral ranks with Assisi's as the most spectacular in Umbria. Between Spoleto and Orvieto there's a collection of quiet, laid-back hill towns, including the jewel of the area, **Todi**.

GETTING ORIENTED

Central Italy doesn't begin and end with Tuscany; the pastoral, hilly provinces of Umbria and the Marches pick up where the more famous neighbor leaves off. Divided by the Apennine range, both regions are studded with Renaissance-era villages and fortresses—a landscape hallowed by Saint Francis and immortalized in the works of native son Raphael.

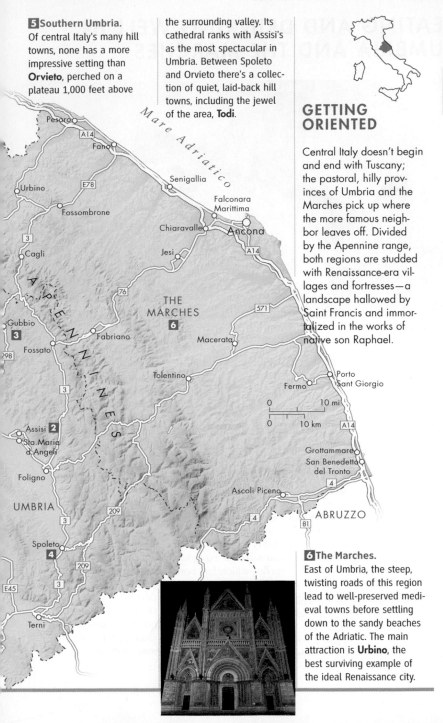

6 The Marches.
East of Umbria, the steep, twisting roads of this region lead to well-preserved medieval towns before settling down to the sandy beaches of the Adriatic. The main attraction is **Urbino**, the best surviving example of the ideal Renaissance city.

EATING AND DRINKING WELL IN UMBRIA AND THE MARCHES

Central Italy is mountainous, and its food is hearty and straightforward, with a stick-to-the-ribs quality that for centuries has seen hard-working farmers and artisans through a long day's work and helped them make the steep climb home at night.

In restaurants here, as in much of Italy, you're rewarded for seeking out the local cuisines, and you'll often find better and cheaper food if you're willing to stray a few hundred yards from the main sights. Spoleto is noted for its good food and service, probably a result of high expectations from the international arts crowd. For gourmets, however, it's hard to beat Spello, which has both excellent restaurants and first-rate wine merchants.

A rule of thumb for eating well throughout Umbria is to order what's in season; the trick is to stroll through local markets to see what's for sale. A number of restaurants in the region offer *degustazione* (tasting) menus, which give you a chance to try different local specialties without breaking the bank.

TASTY TRUFFLES

More truffles are found in Umbria than anywhere else in Italy. Spoleto and Norcia are prime territory for the *tartufo nero* (reddish-black interior and fine white veins), *pictured below right*, prized for its extravagant flavor and intense aroma.

The mild summer truffle, *scorzone estivo* (black outside and beige inside), is in season from May through December. The *scorzone autunnale* (burnt brown color and visible veins inside) is found from October through December. Truffles can be shaved into omelets or over pasta, pounded into sauces, or chopped and mixed with oil.

12

OLIVE OIL

Nearly everywhere you look in Umbria, olive trees grace the hillsides. The soil of the Apennines allows the olives to ripen slowly, guaranteeing low acidity, a cardinal virtue of fine oil. Look for restaurants that proudly display their own oil, often a sign that they care about their food.

Umbria's finest oil is found in Trevi, where the local product is intensely green and fruity. You can sample it in the town's wine bars, which often do double duty, offering olive-oil tastings.

PORK PRODUCTS

Much of traditional Umbrian cuisine revolves around pork. It can be cooked in wood-fire stoves, sometimes basted with a rich sauce made from innards and red wine. The roasted pork known as *porchetta, pictured at left*, is grilled on a spit and flavored with fennel and herbs, leaving a crisp outer sheen.

The art of pork processing has been handed down through generations in Norcia, so much so that charcuterie producers throughout Italy are often known as *norcini*. Don't miss *prosciutto di Norcia*, which is aged for two years.

LENTILS AND SOUPS

The town of Castelluccio di Norcia is particularly known for its lentils and its *farro* (an ancient grain used by the Romans, similar to wheat), and a variety of beans used in soups. Throughout

Umbria, look for *imbrecciata*, a soup of beans and grains, delicately flavored with local herbs.

Other ingredients that find their way into thick Umbrian soups are wild beet, sorrel, mushrooms, spelt, chickpeas, and the elusive, fragrant saffron, grown in nearby Cascia.

WINE

Sagrantino grapes are the star in Umbria's most notable red wines. For centuries they've been used in Sagrantino *passito,* a semisweet wine made by leaving the grapes to dry for a period after picking in order to intensify their sugar content.

In recent decades, the *secco* (dry) Sagrantino has occupied the front stage. Both passito and secco have a deep red-ruby color, with a full body and rich flavor.

In the past few years the phenomenon of the *enoteca* (wineshop and wine bar) has taken off, making it easier to arrange wine tastings.

Many also let you sample different olive oils on toasted bread, known as *bruschetta.*

Some wine information centers, such as La Strada del Sagrantino in the town of Montefalco, will help set up appointments for tastings.

Updated
by Jonathan
Willcocks

Birthplace of saints and home to some of the country's greatest artistic treasures, central Italy is a collection of misty green valleys and picture-perfect hill towns laden with centuries of history.

Umbria and the Marches are the Italian countryside as you've imagined it: verdant farmland, steep hillsides topped with medieval fortresses, and winding country roads. No single town here has the extravagant wealth of art and architecture of Florence, Rome, or Venice, but this works in your favor: small jewels of towns feel knowable, not overwhelming. And the cultural cupboard is far from bare. Orvieto's cathedral and Assisi's basilica are two of the most important sights in Italy, while Perugia, Todi, Gubbio, and Spoleto are rich in art and architecture.

East of Umbria, the Marches (Le Marche to Italians) stretch between the Apennines and the Adriatic Sea. It's a region of great turreted castles on high peaks defending passes and roads—a testament to the centuries of battles that have taken place here. Rising majestically in Urbino is a splendid palace, built by Federico da Montefeltro, where the humanistic ideals of the Renaissance came to their fullest flower, while the town of Ascoli Piceno can lay claim to one of the most beautiful squares in Italy. Virtually every small town in the region has a castle, church, or museum worth a visit—but even without them, you'd still be compelled to stop for the interesting streets, panoramic views, and natural beauty.

UMBRIA AND THE MARCHES PLANNER

MAKING THE MOST OF YOUR TIME

Umbria is a nicely compact collection of character-rich hill towns; you can settle in one, then explore the others, as well as the countryside and forest in between, on day trips.

Perugia, Umbria's largest and liveliest city, is a logical choice for your base, particularly if you're arriving from the north. If you want something a little quieter, virtually any other town in the region will suit your purposes; even Assisi, which overflows with bus tours during the day, is delightfully quiet in the evening and early morning. Spoleto and Orvieto are the most developed towns to the south, but they're still of modest proportions.

If you have the time to venture farther afield, consider trips to Gubbio, northeast of Perugia, and Urbino, in the Marches. Both are worth the time it takes to reach them, and both make for pleasant overnight stays. In southern Umbria, Valnerina and the Piano Grande are out-of-the-way spots with the region's best hiking.

12

FESTIVALS

If you want to attend one of these events, you should make arrangements in advance. And if you don't want to attend, you should plan to avoid the cities during festival time, when hotel rooms and restaurant tables are at a premium. A similar caveat applies for Assisi during religious festivals at Christmas, Easter, the feast of Saint Francis (October 4), and Calendimaggio (May 1), when pilgrims arrive en masse.

Eurochocolate Festival. If you've got a sweet tooth and are visiting in fall, book up early and head to Perugia for the Eurochocolate Festival. This is one of the biggest chocolate festivals in the world, with a million visitors, and is held the third week of October. ⊕ *www.eurochocolate.com*.

Festival dei Due Mondi. Each summer Umbria hosts one of Italy's biggest arts festivals: Spoleto's Festival dei Due Mondi, the Festival of the Two Worlds. Starting out as a classical music festival, it has now evolved into one of Italy's brightest gatherings of arts aficionados. Running from late June through early July, it features modern and classical music, theatre, dance, and opera. Increasingly there are also a number of small cinema producers and their films. ⊕ *www.festivaldispoleto.com*.

Sagra Musicale Umbra. Held from mid-August to mid-September, the Sagra Musicale Umbra celebrates sacred music. ☎ *075/5721374* ⊕ *www.perugiamusicaclassica.com*.

Umbria Jazz Festival. Perugia is hopping for 10 days in July, when more than a million people flock to see famous names in contemporary music perform at the Umbria Jazz Festival. In recent years the stars have included B. B. King, Wynton Marsalis, Sting, Eric Clapton, and Elton John. ⊕ *www.umbriajazz.com*.

GETTING HERE AND AROUND
BUS TRAVEL

Local bus services between all the major and minor towns of Umbria are good. Some of the routes in rural areas are designed to serve as many places as possible and are, therefore, quite roundabout and slow. Schedules change often, so consult with local tourist offices before setting out. In many hill towns bus stations are closer to the town center than train stations, which are usually in the valleys below.

Bucci. Connections between Rome, Spoleto, and the Marches are provided. ☎ *800/664332, 0722/376738* ⊕ *www.adriabus.eu*.

Sulga Line. Perugia is served by the Sulga Line, which has daily departures to Rome's Stazione Tiburtina and to Florence's Piazza Adua. ☎ *075/5009641* ⊕ *www.sulga.it*.

CAR TRAVEL

On the western edge of the region is the Umbrian section of the Auto-strada del Sole (A1), Italy's principal north–south highway. It links Florence and Rome with Orvieto and passes near Todi and Terni. The S3 intersects with A1 and leads on to Assisi and Urbino. The Adriat-ica superhighway (A14) runs north–south along the coast, linking the Marches to Bologna and Venice.

The steep hills and deep valleys that make Umbria and the Marches so idyllic also make for challenging driving. Fortunately, the area has an excellent, modern road network, but be prepared for tortuous mountain roads if your explorations take you off the beaten track. Central Umbria is served by a major highway, the S75bis, which passes along the shore of Lake Trasimeno and ends in Perugia. Assisi is served by the modern highway S75; the S75 connects to the S3 and S3bis, which cover the heart of the region. Major inland routes connect coastal A14 to large towns in the Marches, but inland secondary roads in mountain areas can be winding and narrow. Always carry a good map, a flashlight, and, if possible, a cell phone in case of a breakdown.

TRAIN TRAVEL

Several direct daily trains run by the Italian state railway, **Ferrovia dello Stato** (☎ 892021 toll-free in Italy ⊕ www.trenitalia.com), link Florence and Rome with Perugia and Assisi, and local service to the same area is available from Terontola (on the Rome–Florence line) and from Foligno (on the Rome–Ancona line). Intercity trains between Rome and Flor-ence make stops in Orvieto, and the main Rome–Ancona line passes through Narni, Terni, Spoleto, and Foligno.

Within Umbria, a small, privately owned railway operated by **Ferrovia Centrale Umbra** (☎ 024/73000541) runs from Città di Castello in the north to Terni in the south via Perugia. Note: train service isn't available to either Gubbio or Urbino. Also, train stations are often located in the valleys below hill towns, quite a distance from town centers.

RESTAURANTS

Please note that restaurant prices listed as "average meal" include a meal consisting of first course *(primo)*, second course *(secondo)*, and dessert *(dolce)*.

HOTELS

Virtually every older town, no matter how small, has some kind of hotel. A trend, particularly around Gubbio, Orvieto, and Todi, is to convert old villas, farms, and monasteries into first-class hotels. The natural splendor of the countryside more than compensates for the distance from town—provided you have a car. Hotels in town tend to be simpler than their country cousins, with a few notable exceptions in Spoleto, Gubbio, and Perugia.

Hotel reviews have been condensed for this book. Please go to Fodors. com for expanded reviews of each property.

VISITOR INFORMATION
Umbria's Regional Tourism Office. Umbria's regional tourism office is in Perugia. The staff is well informed about the area and can give you a wide selection of leaflets and maps to assist you during your trip. It's open Monday to Saturday 9 to 7. ✉ *Piazza Matteotti 18, Perugia* 🕿 *075/5736458* ⊕ *www.regioneumbria.eu.*

PERUGIA

Thanks to Perugia's hilltop position, the medieval city remains almost completely intact. It's the best-preserved hill town of its size, and few other places in Italy better illustrate the model of the self-contained city-state that so shaped the course of Italian history.

Strolling through the city center you could be forgiven for imagining that the Renaissance started in Perugia, with its proud white palaces and its stunning 13th-century fountain. Often considered the heart and soul of Umbria, the city attracts a student population of more than 30,000, many of whom come to learn Italian, meaning that the town is abuzz with activity throughout the year. Umbria Jazz, one of Europe's most important music festivals, attracts music lovers from around the world every July, and Eurochocolate, the international chocolate festival, is an irresistible draw for anyone with a sweet tooth each October.

GETTING HERE AND AROUND
The best approach to the city is by train. The area around the station doesn't attest to the rest of Perugia's elegance, but buses running from the station to Piazza d'Italia, the heart of the old town, are frequent. If you're in a hurry, take the minimetro, a one-line subway, to Stazione della Cupa. If you're driving to Perugia and your hotel doesn't have parking facilities, leave your car in one of the lots close to the center. Electronic displays indicate the location of lots and the number of spaces free. If you park in the Piazza Partigiani, which is also where the bus station is located, take the escalators that pass through the fascinating subterranean excavations of the Roman foundations of the city and lead to the town center.

EXPLORING PERUGIA

TOP ATTRACTIONS
Collegio del Cambio (*Bankers' Guild Hall*). These elaborate rooms, on the ground floor of the **Palazzo dei Priori,** served as the meeting hall and chapel of the guild of bankers and moneychangers. Most of the frescoes were completed by the most important Perugian painter of the Renaissance, Pietro Vannucci, better known as Perugino. He included a remarkably honest self-portrait on one of the pilasters. The iconography includes common religious themes, such as the Nativity and the Transfiguration seen on the end walls. On the left wall are female figures representing the virtues, and beneath them are the heroes and sages of antiquity. On the right wall are figures presumed to have been painted in part by Perugino's most famous pupil, Raphael. (His hand, experts say, is most apparent in the figure of Fortitude.) The *cappella* (chapel)

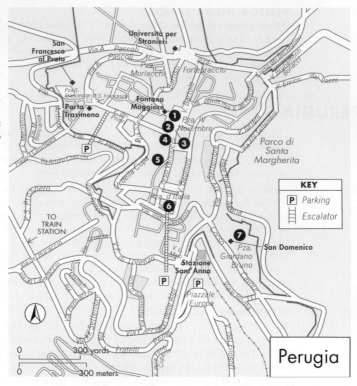

Perugia

of San Giovanni Battista has frescoes painted by Giannicola di Paolo, another student of Perugino's. ✉ *Corso Vannucci 25* ☎ *075/5728599* 🎫 *€4.50 with Collegio della Mercanzia* ☉ *Mon.–Sat. 9–12:30 and 2:30–5:30, Sun. 9–1.*

Corso Vannucci. A string of elegantly connected *palazzi* (palaces) expresses the artistic nature of this city center, the heart of which is concentrated along Corso Vannucci. Stately and broad, this pedestrians-only street runs from Piazza d'Italia to Piazza IV Novembre. Along the way, the entrances to many of Perugia's side streets might tempt you to wander off and explore. But don't stray too far as evening falls, when Corso Vannucci fills with Perugians out for their evening *passeggiata,* a pleasant pre-dinner stroll that may include a pause for an aperitif at one of the many bars that line the street.

Fodor'sChoice **Galleria Nazionale dell'Umbria.** The region's most comprehensive art gallery is housed on the fourth floor of the **Palazzo dei Priori.** Enhanced by skillfully lit displays and computers that allow you to focus on the works' details and background information, the collection includes work by native artists—most notably Pintoricchio (1454–1513) and Perugino (circa 1450–1523)—and others of the Umbrian and Tuscan schools, among them Gentile da Fabriano (1370–1427), Duccio (circa 1255–1318), Fra Angelico (circa 1400–1455), Fiorenzo di Lorenzo (1445–1525), and

Piero della Francesca (1420–92). In addition to paintings, the gallery has frescoes, sculptures, and some superb examples of crucifixes from the 13th and 14th centuries. Some rooms are dedicated to Perugia itself, showing how the medieval city evolved. ⊠ *Corso Vannucci 19, Piazza IV Novembre* ☎ *075/58668410* ⊕ *www.gallerianazionaleumbria.it* ☎ *€6.50* ⊙ *Tues.–Sun. 8:30–7:30; last admission ½ hr before closing.*

Palazzo dei Priori (*Palace of Priors*). A series of elegant connected buildings, the palazzo serves as Perugia's city hall and houses three of the city's museums. The buildings string along Corso Vannucci and wrap around the Piazza IV Novembre, where the original entrance is located. The steps here lead to the **Sala dei Notari** (Notaries' Hall). Other entrances lead to the **Galleria Nazionale dell'Umbria,** the **Collegio del Cambio,** and the **Collegio della Mercanzia.** The Sala dei Notari, which dates back to the 13th century and was the original meeting place of the town merchants, had become the seat of the notaries by the second half of the 15th century. Wood beams and an interesting array of frescoes attributed to Maestro di Farneto embellish the room. Coats of arms and crests line the back and right lateral walls; you can spot some famous figures from Aesop's *Fables* on the left wall. The palazzo facade is adorned with symbols of Perugia's pride and past power: the griffin is the city symbol, and the lion denotes Perugia's allegiance to the Guelph (or papal) cause. ⊠ *Piazza IV Novembre, 25* ☎ *Free* ⊙ *June–Sept., Tues.–Sun. 9–1 and 3–7.*

Rocca Paolina. A labyrinth of little streets, alleys, and arches, this underground city was originally part of a fortress built at the behest of Pope Paul III between 1540 and 1543 to confirm papal dominion over the city. Parts of it were destroyed after the end of papal rule, but much still remains. Begin your visit by taking the escalators that descend through the subterranean ruins from Piazza Italia down to Via Masi. In the summer this is the coolest place in the city. ⊠ *Piazza Italia* ☎ *€3.50* ⊙ *Tues.–Sun. 10–1:30 and 2:30–6.*

WORTH NOTING

Duomo. Severe yet mystical, the Cathedral of San Lorenzo is most famous for being the home of the wedding ring of the Virgin Mary, stolen by the Perugians in 1488 from the nearby town of Chiusi. The ring, kept high up in a red-curtained vault in the chapel immediately to the left of the entrance, is stored under lock—15 locks, to be precise—and key most of the year. It's shown to the public on July 30 (the day it was brought to Perugia) and the second-to-last Sunday in January (Mary's wedding anniversary). The cathedral itself dates from the Middle Ages, and has many additions from the 15th and 16th centuries. The most visually interesting element is the altar to the Madonna of Grace; an elegant fresco on a column at the right of the entrance of the altar depicts *La Madonna delle Grazie* and is surrounded by prayer benches decorated with handwritten notes to the Holy Mother. Around the column are small amulets—symbols of gratitude from those whose prayers were answered. There are also elaborately carved choir stalls, executed by Giovanni Battista Bastone in 1520. The altarpiece (1484), an early masterpiece by Luca Signorelli (circa 1441–1523), shows the Madonna with Saint John the Baptist, Saint Onophrius, and Saint Lawrence. Sections of the church may be closed to visitors during religious services.

UMBRIA THROUGH THE AGES

The earliest inhabitants of Umbria, the Umbri, were thought by the Romans to be the most ancient inhabitants of Italy. Little is known about them; with the coming of Etruscan culture the tribe fled into the mountains in the eastern portion of the region. The Etruscans, who founded some of the great cities of Umbria, were in turn supplanted by the Romans. Unlike Tuscany and other regions of central Italy, Umbria had few powerful medieval families to exert control over the cities in the Middle Ages—its proximity to Rome ensured that it would always be more or less under papal domination.

In the center of the country, Umbria has for much of its history been a battlefield where armies from north and south clashed. Hannibal destroyed a Roman army on the shores of Lake Trasimeno, and the bloody course of the interminable Guelph–Ghibelline conflict of the Middle Ages was played out here. Dante considered Umbria the most violent place in Italy. Trophies of war still decorate the Palazzo dei Priori in Perugia, and the little town of Gubbio continues a warlike rivalry begun in the Middle Ages—every year it challenges the Tuscan town of Sansepolcro to a crossbow tournament. Today the bowmen shoot at targets, but neither side has forgotten that 500 years ago they were shooting at each other. In spite of—or perhaps because of—this bloodshed, Umbria has produced more than its share of Christian saints. The most famous is Saint Francis, the decidedly pacifist saint whose life shaped the Church of his time. His great shrine at Assisi is visited by hundreds of thousands of pilgrims each year. Saint Clare, his devoted follower, was Umbria-born, as were Saint Benedict, Saint Rita of Cascia, and the patron saint of lovers, Saint Valentine.

The **Museo Capitolare** displays a large array of precious objects associated with the cathedral, including vestments, vessels, and manuscripts. Outside the Duomo is the elaborate **Fontana Maggiore,** which dates from 1278. It's adorned with zodiac figures and symbols of the seven arts. ⊠ *Piazza IV Novembre* ☏ *075/5723832* 🖼 *Museum €3.50* ⊙ *Duomo: Mon.–Sat. 7:30–12:30 and 4–6, Sun. 8–12 and 4–6:30. Museum: daily 10–1 and 2:30–5:30; last admission ½ hr before closing.*

Museo Archeologico Nazionale. An excellent collection of Etruscan artifacts from throughout the region sheds light on Perugia as a flourishing Etruscan city long before it fell under Roman domination in 310 BC. Little else remains of Perugia's mysterious ancestors, although the Arco di Augusto, in Piazza Fortebraccio, the northern entrance to the city, is of Etruscan origin. ⊠ *Piazza G. Bruno 10* ☏ *075/5727141* ⊕ *www.archeopg.arti.beniculturali.it* 🖼 *€4* ⊙ *Mon. 10–7:30, Tues.–Sun. 8:30–7:30.*

WHERE TO EAT

$ **✕ Antica Trattoria San Lorenzo.**
UMBRIAN Brick vaults are not the only distinguishing feature of this small, popular eatery next to the Duomo, as both the food and the service are outstanding. Particular attention is paid to adapting traditional Umbrian cuisine to the modern palate. There's also a nice variety of seafood dishes on the menu. The *trenette alla farina di noce con pesce di mare* (flat noodles made with walnut flour topped with fresh fish) is a real treat. $ *Average meal: €22* ✉ *Piazza Danti 19-A* ☎ *075/5721956* ⊕ *www.anticatrattoriasanlorenzo.com* ⊘ *Closed Sun.*

$ **✕ Dal Mi' Cocco.** A great favorite with Perugia's university students is fun,
UMBRIAN crowded, and inexpensive. You may find yourself seated at a long table with other diners, but some language help from your neighbors could come in handy—the menu is in pure Perugian dialect. The fixed-price meals change with the season, and each day of the week brings some new creation *dal cocco* (from the "coconut," or head) of the chef. $ *Average meal: €18* ✉ *Corso Garibaldi 12* ☎ *075/5732511* ⊿ *Reservations essential* ▭ *No credit cards* ⊘ *Closed late July–mid-Aug.*

$ **✕ Il Falchetto.** Exceptional food at reasonable prices makes this Peru-
UMBRIAN gia's best bargain. Service is smart but relaxed in the two medieval dining rooms that put the chef on view. The house specialty is *falchetti* (homemade gnocchi with spinach and ricotta cheese). $ *Average meal: €22* ✉ *Via Bartolo 20* ☎ *075/5731775* ⊘ *Closed Mon. and last 2 wks in Jan.*

$ **✕ La Rosetta.** The dining room of the hotel of the same name is a peace-
ITALIAN ful, elegant spot. In winter you dine inside under medieval vaults; in summer, in the cool courtyard. The food is simple but reliable, and flawlessly served. The restaurant caters to travelers seeking to get away from the bustle of central Perugia. $ *Average meal: €22* ✉ *Piazza d'Italia 19* ☎ *075/5720841* ⊿ *Reservations essential.*

$ **✕ La Taverna.** Medieval steps lead to a rustic two-story space where wine
UMBRIAN bottles and artful clutter decorate the walls. Good choices from the regional menu include *caramelle al gorgonzola* (pasta rolls filled with red cabbage and mozzarella and topped with a Gorgonzola sauce) and grilled meat dishes, such as the *medaglioni di vitello al tartuffo* (grilled veal with truffles). $ *Average meal: €20* ✉ *Via delle Streghe 8, off Corso Vannucci* ☎ *075/5724128* ⊘ *Closed Mon.*

12

WHERE TO STAY

For expanded hotel reviews, visit Fodors.com.

$$ HOTEL 🏨 **Castello dell'Oscano.** A splendid neo-Gothic castle, a late-19th-century villa, and a converted farmhouse hidden in the tranquil hills north of Perugia offer a wide range of accommodations. **Pros:** quiet elegance; fine gardens; Umbrian wine list. **Cons:** distant from Perugia; not easy to find. [$] *Rooms from: €180* ✉ *Strada della Forcella 32, Cenerente* ☎ *075/584371* 🌐 *www.oscano.it* 🛏 *24 rooms, 8 suites, 13 apartments* 🍴 *Breakfast.*

$$ HOTEL 🏨 **Hotel Fortuna.** The elegant decor in the large rooms, some with balconies, complements the frescoes, which date from the 1700s. **Pros:** central but quiet; cozy, friendly atmosphere; elevator. **Cons:** some small rooms; no restaurant. [$] *Rooms from: €128* ✉ *Via Bonazzi 19, Corso Vannucci* ☎ *075/5722845* 🌐 *www.hotelfortunaperugia.com* 🛏 *51 rooms* 🍴 *Breakfast.*

$ HOTEL 🏨 **Locanda della Posta.** Renovations have left the lobby and other public areas rather bland, but the rooms in this converted 18th-century palazzo are soothingly decorated in muted colors. **Pros:** some fine views; central position. **Cons:** some street noise; some small rooms; no restaurant. [$] *Rooms from: €120* ✉ *Corso Vannucci 97* ☎ *075/5728925* 🛏 *38 rooms, 1 suite* 🍴 *Breakfast.*

$$$ HOTEL 🏨 **Posta dei Donini.** Beguilingly comfortable guest rooms are set on lovely grounds, where gardeners go quietly about their business. **Pros:** plush atmosphere; a quiet and private getaway. **Cons:** outside Perugia; uninteresting village. [$] *Rooms from: €200* ✉ *Via Deruta 43, San Martino in Campo* ☎ *075/609132* 🌐 *www.postadonini.it* 🛏 *33 rooms.*

$ HOTEL 🏨 **Sangallo Palace.** This comfy business hotel with standard-issue accommodations is just outside the old city walls, but within easy reach of the escalators leading up to the city center. **Pros:** handy to bus station for travel around Umbria; comfortable if not luxurious. **Cons:** a bit removed from city center. [$] *Rooms from: €100* ✉ *Via L. Masi 9, Perugia* ☎ *075/5730202* 🌐 *www.sangallo.it.*

$$$ HOTEL 🏨 **Tre Vaselle.** Rooms spread throughout four stone buildings are spacious and graced with floors of typical red-clay Tuscan tiles. **Pros:** perfect for visiting Torgiano wine area and Deruta; friendly staff; nice pool. **Cons:** somewhat far from Perugia; in center of uninspiring village. [$] *Rooms from: €200* ✉ *Via Garibaldi 48, Torgiano* ☎ *075/9880447* 🌐 *www.3vaselle.it* 🛏 *47 rooms.*

NIGHTLIFE AND THE ARTS

With its large student population, the city has plenty to offer in the way of bars and clubs. The best ones are around the city center, off Corso Vanucci. *Viva Perugia* is a good source of information about nightlife. The monthly, sold at newsstands, has a section in English. Summer brings thousands of music lovers to town for two bug music festivals, Umbria Jazz and Sagra Musicale Umbra.

SHOPPING

Take a stroll down any of Perugia's main streets, including Corso Vannucci, Via dei Priori, Via Oberdan, and Via Sant'Ercolano, and you'll see many well-known designer boutiques and specialty shops.

The most typical thing to buy in Perugia is some Perugina chocolate, which you can find almost anywhere. The best-known chocolates made by Perugina are the chocolate-and-hazelnut-filled nibbles called Baci (literally, "kisses"). They're wrapped in silver paper that includes a sliver of paper, like the fortune in a fortune cookie, with multilingual romantic sentiments or sayings.

ASSISI

Especially in the early morning, Assisi can seem like a lost corner of the Middle Ages, a city of legends and mysteries that has remained a focus of interest for artists and writers. As Assisi wakes up the pilgrims and visitors arrive—the small town is one of the Christian world's most important pilgrimage sites and home of the Basilica di San Francesco—built to honor Saint Francis (1182–1226) and erected in swift order after his death.

Like most other towns in the region, Assisi began as an Umbri settlement in the 7th century BC and was conquered by the Romans 400 years later. The town was Christianized by Saint Rufino, its patron saint, in the 3rd century, but it's the spirit of Saint Francis, a patron saint of Italy and founder of the Franciscan monastic order, that's felt throughout its narrow medieval streets. The famous 13th-century basilica was decorated by the greatest artists of the period.

Assisi is pristinely medieval in architecture and appearance, owing in large part to relative neglect from the 16th century until 1926, when the celebration of the 700th anniversary of Saint Francis's death brought more than 2 million visitors. Since then, pilgrims have flocked here in droves, and today several million arrive each year to pay homage. But not even the constant flood of visitors to this town of just 3,000 residents can spoil the singular beauty of this significant religious center, the home of some of the Western tradition's most important works of art. The hill on which Assisi sits rises dramatically from the flat plain, and the town is dominated by a medieval castle at the very top.

Even though Assisi is sometimes besieged by busloads of sightseers who clamor to visit the famous basilica, it's difficult not to be charmed by the tranquility of the town and its medieval architecture. Once you've seen the basilica, stroll through the town's narrow winding streets to see beautiful vistas of the nearby hills and valleys peeking through openings between the buildings.

GETTING HERE AND AROUND
Assisi lies on the Terontola–Foligno rail line, with almost hourly connections to Perugia and direct trains to Rome and Florence several times a day. The Stazione Centrale is 4 km (2½ miles) from town, with a bus service about every half hour. Assisi is easily reached from

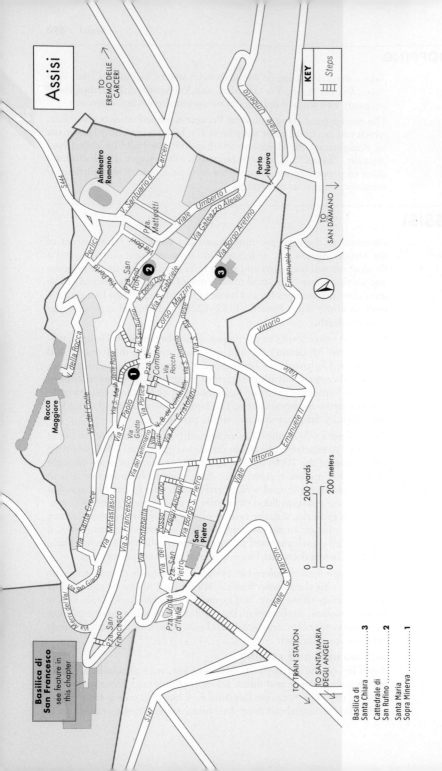

Assisi

TO EREMO DELLE CARCERI →

Anfiteatro Romano

Basilica di San Francesco
see feature in this chapter

Rocca Maggiore

Porto Nuova

TO SAN DAMIANO →

TO SANTA MARIA DEGLI ANGELI ↓

TO TRAIN STATION ↓

KEY

Steps

0 — 200 yards
0 — 200 meters

Basilica di Santa Chiara **3**

Cattedrale di San Rufino **2**

Santa Maria Sopra Minerva **1**

the A1 Motorway (Rome–Florence) and the S75b highway. The walled town is closed to traffic, so cars must be left in the parking lots at Porta San Pietro, near Porta Nuova, or beneath Piazza Matteotti. Pay your parking fee at the *cassa* (ticket booth) before you return to your car to get a ticket to insert in the machine that will allow you to exit. It's a short but sometimes steep walk into the center of town; frequent minibuses (buy tickets from a newsstand or tobacco shop near where you park your car) make the rounds for weary pilgrims.

VISITOR INFORMATION
Assisi Tourism Office ⊠ *Piazza del Commune 22* ☎ *075/8138680* ⊕ *www.regioneumbria.eu.*

EXPLORING ASSISI

TOP ATTRACTIONS

For Assisi's legendary Basilica di San Francesco, see the special photo feature in this chapter.

Basilica di Santa Chiara. The lovely, wide piazza in front of this church is reason enough to visit. The red-and-white-striped facade frames the piazza's panoramic view over the Umbrian plains. Santa Chiara is dedicated to Saint Clare, one of the earliest and most fervent of Saint Francis's followers and the founder of the order of the Poor Ladies—or Poor Clares—which was based on the Franciscan monastic order. The church contains Clare's body, and in the **Cappella del Crocifisso** (on the right) is the cross that spoke to Saint Francis. A heavily veiled nun of the Poor Clares order is usually stationed before the cross in adoration of the image. ⊠ *Piazza Santa Chiara* ☎ *075/812282* ◷ *Nov.–mid-Mar., daily 7–noon and 2–6; mid-Mar.–Oct., daily 7–noon and 2–7.*

Cattedrale di San Rufino. Saint Francis and Saint Clare were among those baptized in Assisi's Cattedrale, which was the principal church in town until the 12th century. The baptismal font has since been redecorated, but it's possible to see the crypt of Saint Rufino, the bishop who brought Christianity to Assisi and was martyred on August 11, 238 (or 236 by some accounts). Admission to the crypt includes the small **Museo Capitolare**, with its detached frescoes and artifacts. ⊠ *Piazza San Rufino* ☎ *075/5812283* ⊕ *www.sistemamuseo.it* 🎟 *Crypt and Museo Capitolare €3* ◷ *Cathedral: daily 7–noon and 2–6. Crypt and Museum: mid-Mar.–mid-Oct., daily 10–1 and 3–6; mid-Oct.–mid-Mar., daily 10–1 and 2:30–6.*

WORTH NOTING

Eremo delle Carceri. About 4 km (2½ miles) east of Assisi is a monastery set in a dense wood against Monte Subasio. The "Hermitage of Prisons" was the place where Saint Francis and his followers went to "imprison" themselves in prayer. The only site in Assisi that remains essentially unchanged since Saint Francis's time, the church and monastery are the kinds of tranquil places that Saint Francis would have appreciated. The walk out from town is very pleasant, and many trails lead from here across the wooded hillside of Monte Subasio (now a protected forest), with beautiful vistas across the Umbrian countryside. True to their Franciscan heritage, the friars here are entirely dependent on alms from visitors. ✉ *Via Santuario delle Carceri 4 km (2½ miles) east of Assisi* ☎ *075/812301* 🌐 *www.eremocarceri.it* 🎫 *Donations accepted* 🕒 *Nov.–Mar., daily 6:30–6; Apr.–Oct., daily 6:30 am–7:00 pm.*

Santa Maria Sopra Minerva. Dating from the time of the Emperor Augustus (27 BC–AD 14), this structure was originally dedicated to the Roman goddess of wisdom, in later times used as a monastery and prison before being converted into a church in the 16th century. The expectations raised by the perfect classical facade are not met by the interior, which was subjected to a thorough baroque transformation in the 17th century. ✉ *Piazza del Comune* ☎ *075/812268* 🕒 *Daily 7:15 am–8 pm.*

WHERE TO EAT

Assisi isn't a late-night town, so don't plan on any midnight snacks. What you can count on is the ubiquitous *stringozzi* (thick spaghetti), as well as the local specialty *piccione all'assisana* (roasted pigeon with olives and liver). The locals eat *torta al testo* (a dense flatbread, often stuffed with vegetables or cheese) with their meals.

$ UMBRIAN 🍴 **Buca di San Francesco.** In summer, dine in a cool green garden; in winter, under the low brick arches of the cozy cellars. The unique settings and the first-rate fare make this central restaurant Assisi's busiest. Try homemade spaghetti *alla buca,* served with a roasted mushroom sauce. [$] *Average meal: €20* ✉ *Via Eugenio Brizi 1* ☎ *075/812204* 🕒 *Closed Mon. and 10 days in late July.*

$ UMBRIAN Fodor's Choice ★ 🍴 **La Pallotta.** At this homey, family-run trattoria with a crackling fireplace and stone walls, the women do the cooking and the men serve the food. Try the stringozzi *alla pallotta* (with a pesto of olives and mushrooms). Connected to the restaurant is an inn whose eight rooms have firm beds and some views across the rooftops of town. [$] *Average meal: €21* ✉ *Vicolo della Volta Pinta 3* ☎ *075/812649* 🌐 *www.pallottaassisi.it* 🕒 *Closed Tues. and 2 wks in Jan. or Feb.*

$ UMBRIAN 🍴 **Osteria Piazzetta dell'Erba.** Hip service and sophisticated presentations attract locals, who enjoy a wide selection of appetizers, including smoked goose breast, and four or five types of pasta, plus various salads and a good selection of *torta al testo* (dense flatbread stuffed with vegetables or cheese). For dessert, try the homemade biscuits, which you dunk in sweet wine. The owners carefully select wine at local vineyards, buy it in bulk, and then bottle it themselves, resulting in high quality and reasonable prices. Outdoor seating is available. [$] *Average meal: €20* ✉ *Via San Gabriele dell'Addolorata 15b* ☎ *075/815352* 🕒 *Closed Mon. and a few wks in Jan. or Feb.*

Continued on page 701

ASSISI'S BASILICA DI SAN FRANCESCO

The legacy of St. Francis, founder of the Franciscan monastic order, pervades Assisi. Each year the town hosts several million pilgrims, but the steady flow of visitors does nothing to diminish the singular beauty of one of Italy's most important religious centers. The pilgrims' ultimate destination is the massive Basilica di San Francesco, which sits halfway up Assisi's hill, supported by graceful arches.

The basilica is not one church but two. The Romanesque **Lower Church** came first; construction began in 1228, just two years after St. Francis's death, and was completed within a few years. The low ceilings and candlelit interior make an appropriately solemn setting for St. Francis's tomb, found in the crypt below the main altar. The Gothic **Upper Church**, built only half a century later, sits on top of the lower one, and is strikingly different, with soaring arches and tall stained-glass windows (the first in Italy). Inside, both churches are covered floor to ceiling with some of Europe's finest frescoes: the Lower Church is dim and full of candlelit shadows, and the Upper Church is bright and airy.

VISITING THE BASILICA

THE LOWER CHURCH

The most evocative way to experience the basilica is to begin with the dark Lower Church. As you enter, give your eyes a moment to adjust. Keep in mind that the artists at work here were conscious of the shadowy environment—they knew this was how their frescoes would be seen.

In the first chapel to the left, a superb fresco cycle by Simone Martini depicts scenes from the life of St. Martin. As you approach the main altar, the vaulting above you is decorated with the *Three Virtues of St. Francis* (poverty, chastity, and obedience) and *St. Francis's Triumph*, frescoes attributed to Giotto's followers. In the transept to your left, Pietro Lorenzetti's *Madonna and Child with St. Francis and St. John* sparkles when the sun hits it. Notice Mary's thumb; legend has it Jesus is asking which saint to bless, and Mary is pointing to Francis. Across the way in the right transept, Cimabue's *Madonna Enthroned Among Angels and St. Francis* is a famous portrait of the saint. Surrounding the portrait are painted scenes from the childhood of Christ, done by the assistants of Giotto.

Nearby is a painting of the crucifixion attributed to Giotto himself.

You reach the crypt via stairs midway along the nave—on the crypt's altar, a stone coffin holds the saint's body. Steps up from the transepts lead to the cloister, where there's a gift shop, and the treasury, which contains holy objects.

THE UPPER CHURCH

The St. Francis fresco cycle is the highlight of the Upper Church. (See facing page.) Also worth special note is the 16th-century choir, with its remarkably delicate inlaid wood. When a 1997 earthquake rocked the basilica, the St. Francis cycle sustained little damage, but portions of the ceiling above the entrance and altar collapsed, reducing their frescoes (attributed to Cimabue and Giotto) to rubble. The painstaking restoration is ongoing. ⚠ The dress code is strictly enforced—no bare shoulders or bare knees. Piazza di San Francesco, 075/819001, Lower Church Easter–Oct., Mon.–Sat. 6 AM–6:45 PM, Sun. 6:30 AM–7:15 PM; Nov.–Easter, daily 6:30–6. Upper Church Easter–Oct., Mon.–Sat. 8:30–6:45, Sun. 8:30–7:15; Nov.–Easter, daily 8:30–6.

FRANCIS, ITALY'S PATRON SAINT

PREGANDO ASPETTERO CHE TORNI

St. Francis was born in Assisi in 1181, the son of a noblewoman and a well-to-do merchant. His troubled youth included a year in prison. He planned a military career, but after a long illness Francis heard the voice of God, renounced his father's wealth, and began a life of austerity. His mystical embrace of poverty, asceticism, and the beauty of man and nature struck a responsive chord in the medieval mind; he quickly attracted a vast number of followers. Francis was the first saint to receive the stigmata (wounds in his hands, feet, and side corresponding to those of Christ on the cross). He died on October 4, 1226, in the Porziuncola, the secluded chapel in the woods where he had first preached the virtue of poverty to his disciples. St. Francis was declared patron saint of Italy in 1939, and today the Franciscans make up the largest of the Catholic orders.

THE UPPER CHURCH'S ST. FRANCIS FRESCO CYCLE

The 28 frescoes in the Upper Church depicting the life of St. Francis are the most admired works in the entire basilica. They're also the subject of one of art history's biggest controversies. For centuries they thought to be by Giotto (1267-1337), the great early Renaissance innovator, but inconsistencies in style, both within this series and in comparison to later Giotto works, have thrown their origin into question. Some scholars now say Giotto was the brains behind the cycle, but that assistants helped with the execution; others claim he couldn't have been involved at all.

Two things are certain. First, the style is revolutionary—which argues for Giotto's in-

volvement. The tangible weight of the figures, the emotion they show, and the use of perspective all look familiar to modern eyes, but in the art of the time there was nothing like it. Second, these images have played a major part in shaping how the world sees St. Francis. In that respect, who painted them hardly matters.

Starting in the transept, the frescoes circle the church, showing events in the saint's life (and afterlife). Some of the best are grouped near the church's entrance—look for the nativity at Greccio, the miracle of the spring, the death of the knight at Celano, and, most famously, the sermon to the birds.

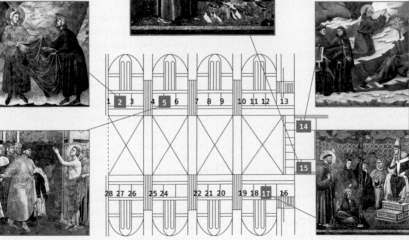

The St. Francis fresco cycle
1. Homage of a simple man
2. Giving cloak to a poor man
3. Dream of the palace
4. Hearing the voice of God
5. Rejection of worldly goods
6. Dream of Innocent III
7. Confirmation of the rules
8. Vision of flaming chariot
9. Vision of celestial thrones
10. Chasing devils from Arezzo
11. Before the sultan
12. Ecstasy of St. Francis
13. Nativity at Greccio
14. Miracle of the spring
15. Sermon to the birds
16. Death of knight at Celano
17. Preaching to Honorius III
18. Apparition at Arles
19. Receiving the stigmata
20. Death of St. Francis
21. Apparition before Bishop Guido and Fra Agostino
22. Verification of the stigmata
23. Mourning of St. Clare
24. Canonization
25. Apparition before Gregory IX
26. Healing of a devotee
27. Confession of a woman
28. Repentant heretic freed

FODOR'S FIRST PERSON

Sister Marcellina,
Order of St. Bridget

Sister Marcellina of the Order of St. Bridget talks about her life in Assisi, where she and 11 other sisters live in a convent and guesthouse on the outskirts of the town:

"Before coming to Assisi, I lived in various countries. I've lived in India, and in England, and been to Holland, to Sweden, and to Finland, as well as lived in Rome. But Assisi is the place that I would never want to change for any other. I don't know, I think there is something very special about this place. I've been here 13 years now, and each year I pray that I won't be sent somewhere else. I'm very happy here.

"I like the atmosphere of Assisi, it's very friendly, and of course with St. Francis and St. Claire, but especially St. Francis, there is a simplicity to life that I like very much. Even though I'm in the Order of St. Bridget, living here I feel very much a part of Franciscan spirituality. There is also a very strong ecumenical feeling to Assisi and this is very nice. There are over 60 different religious communities, with people from all over the world. And even though they come from different religious backgrounds they still feel a part of Assisi. Living here, you don't see the people of Assisi, you see people who have come from all over the world.

"There is something you feel when you come to Assisi, something you feel in your heart that makes you want to come back. And people do return! They feel the peacefulness and tranquility. Not that there aren't other aspects, like the commercialism—but these things happen. People return for the simplicity of this place. People feel attracted to Assisi. There's always something that people feel when they come here—even the hard-hearted ones!"

Asked if she thinks Assisi is changing, Sister Marcellina answers, with laughter in her voice, "When they wanted to make all the changes in the year 2000, the Jubilee Year, our Lord said, 'I must stop everything.' They had lots of projects to build new accommodations to house the people coming for the Jubilee Year, but the Lord said, 'No!'"

$$ UMBRIAN 🍴 **San Francesco.** An excellent view of the Basilica di San Francesco from the covered terrace is just one reason to enjoy the best restaurant in town, where creative Umbrian dishes are made with aromatic locally grown herbs. The seasonal menu might include gnocchi topped with a sauce of wild herbs and *oca stufata di finocchio selvaggio* (goose stuffed with wild fennel). Appetizers and desserts are especially good. [$] *Average meal: €35* ✉ *Via di San Francesco 52* ☎ *075/812329* ⏲ *Closed Wed. and July 15–30.*

WHERE TO STAY

Advance reservations are essential at Assisi's hotels between Easter and October and over Christmas. Latecomers are often forced to stay in the modern town of Santa Maria degli Angeli, 8 km (5 miles) away. As a last-minute option, you can always inquire at restaurants to see if they're renting out rooms.

Until the early 1980s, pilgrim hostels outnumbered ordinary hotels in Assisi, and they present an intriguing and economical alternative to conventional lodgings. They're usually called *conventi* or *ostelli* ("convents" or "hostels") because they're run by convents, churches, or other Catholic organizations. Rooms are spartan but peaceful. Check with the tourist office for a list.

For expanded hotel reviews, visit Fodors.com.

$$ HOTEL Fodor's Choice ★ 🏨 **Castello di Petrata.** Wood beams and sections of exposed medieval stonework add a lot of character to this fortress built in the 14th century, while comfortable couches turn each individually decorated room into a delightful retreat. **Pros:** great views of town and countryside; medieval character; pool. **Cons:** slightly isolated; far from Assisi town center. [$] *Rooms from: €150* ✉ *Via Petrata 25, Località Petrata* ☎ *075/815451* 🌐 *www.castellopetrata.com* 🛏 *16 rooms, 7 suites* ⏲ *Closed Jan.–Mar.* 🍽 *Breakfast.*

$$ HOTEL 🏨 **Hotel Subasio.** The converted monastery is well past its prime, when Marlene Dietrich and Charlie Chaplin were guests, but such vestiges of glamour as Venetian chandeliers remain, as do the splendid views. **Pros:** perfect location next to the basilica; views of the Assisi plain. **Cons:** lobby a bit drab; some small rooms; service can be spotty. [$] *Rooms from: €160* ✉ *Via Frate Elia 2* ☎ *075/812206* 🌐 *www.hotelsubasio.com* 🛏 *54 rooms, 8 suites* 💳 *No credit cards* 🍽 *Breakfast.*

$ HOTEL 🏨 **Hotel Umbra.** Rooms on the upper floors of this charming 16th-century town house near Piazza del Comune look out over the Assisi rooftops to the valley below, as does a sunny terrace. **Pros:** friendly welcome; pleasant small garden. **Cons:** difficult parking; some small rooms. [$] *Rooms from: €100* ✉ *Via degli Archi 6* ☎ *075/812240* 🌐 *www.hotelumbra.it* 🛏 *25 rooms* ⏲ *Closed Dec. and Jan.* 🍽 *Breakfast.*

$$ HOTEL 🏨 **San Francesco.** Rooms and facilities range from simple to dreary, but you can't beat the location—the roof terrace and some of the rooms look out onto the basilica. **Pros:** excellent location; great views and breakfast. **Cons:** simple rooms; sometimes noisy in peak season. [$] *Rooms from: €130* ✉ *Via San Francesco 48* ☎ *075/812281* 🌐 *www.hotelsanfrancescoassisi.it* 🛏 *44 rooms* 🍽 *Breakfast.*

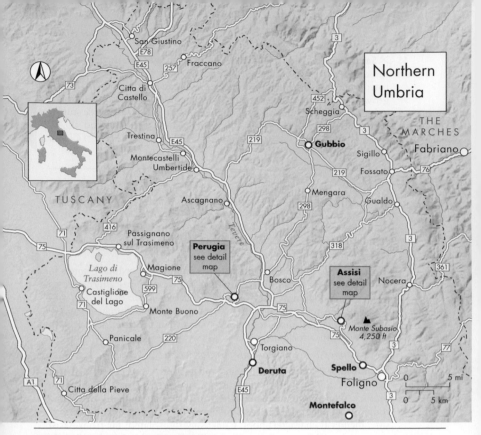

NORTHERN UMBRIA

To the north of Perugia, placid, walled Gubbio watches over green countryside, true to its nickname, City of Silence—except for its fast and furious festivals in May, as lively today as when they began more than 800 years ago. To the south, along the Tiber River valley, are the towns of Deruta and Torgiano, best known for their hand-painted ceramics and wine—as locals say, go to Deruta to buy a pitcher and to Torgiano to fill it.

GUBBIO

35 km (22 miles) southeast of Città di Castello, 39 km (24 miles) northeast of Perugia, 92 km (57 miles) east of Arezzo.

There's something otherworldly about this jewel of a medieval town tucked away in a mountainous corner of Umbria. Even at the height of summer, the cool serenity and quiet of Gubbio's streets remain intact. The town is perched on the slopes of Monte Ingino, meaning the streets are dramatically steep. Gubbio's relative isolation has kept it free of hordes of high-season visitors, and most of the year the city lives up to its Italian nickname, *La Città del Silenzio* (City of Silence). Parking in the central Piazza dei Quaranta Martiri—named for 40 hostages

murdered by the Nazis in 1944—
is easy and secure, and it's wise to
leave your car in the piazza and
explore the narrow streets on foot.
At Christmas, kitsch is king. From
December 7 to January 10, colored
lights are strung down the mountainside in a shape resembling
an evergreen: the world's largest
Christmas tree.

GETTING HERE AND AROUND

The closest train station is Fossato
di Vico, about 20 km (12 miles)
from Gubbio. Ten daily buses con-

12

nect the train station with the city, a 30-minute trip. If you're driving
from Perugia, take the SS298, which rises steeply up toward the Gubbio
hills. The trip will take you one hour. There are also 10 buses a day that
leave from Perugia's Piazza Partigiani, the main Perugia bus terminal.

VISITOR INFORMATION

Gubbio Tourism Office ⊠ *Via della Repubblica 15* ☎ *075/9220693.*

EXPLORING

Basilica di Sant'Ubaldo. Gubbio's famous *ceri*—three 16-foot-tall pillars
crowned with statues of Saints Ubaldo, George, and Anthony—are
housed in this basilica atop Monte Ingino. The pillars are transported
to the Palazzo dei Consoli on the first Sunday of May, in preparation
for the Festa dei Ceri. ⊠ *Monte Ingino* ☎ *075/9273872* ۞ *Daily 8:30–
noon and 4–7.*

Duomo. On a narrow street on the highest tier of the town, the Duomo
dates from the 13th century, with some Baroque additions—in particular, a
lavishly decorated bishop's chapel. ⊠ *Via Ducale* ۞ *Daily 8–12:30 and 3–7.*

Funicular. For a bracing ride to the top of Monte Ingino, hop on the
funicular that climbs the hillside just outside the city walls at the eastern end of town. It's definitely not for those who suffer from vertigo.
⊠ *Follow Corso Garibaldi or Via XX Settembre to end* ☎ *€4, €5 round
trip* ۞ *Sept.–June, daily 10–1:15 and 2:30–6; July and Aug., daily 9–8.*

Palazzo dei Consoli. Gubbio's striking Piazza Grande is dominated by this
medieval palazzo, attributed to a local architect known as Gattapone,
who is still much admired by today's residents (though some scholars
have suggested that the palazzo was in fact the work of another architect, Angelo da Orvieto). In the Middle Ages the Parliament of Gubbio
assembled in the palace, which has become a symbol of the town and
now houses a museum with a collection famous chiefly for the Tavole
Eugubine. These seven bronze tablets are written in the ancient Umbrian
language, employing Etruscan and Latin characters, and provide the
best key to understanding this obscure tongue. Also in the museum is a
fascinating miscellany of rare coins and earthenware pots. A lofty loggia provides exhilarating views over Gubbio's roofscape and beyond.
For a few days at the beginning of May, the palace also displays the

famous *ceri,* the ceremonial wooden pillars at the center of Gubbio's annual festivities. ✉ *Piazza Grande* ☎ *075/9274298* 🌐 *www.comune.gubbio.pg.it* 🎟 *€5* 🕒 *Apr.–Oct., daily 10–1 and 3–6; Nov.–Mar., daily 10–1 and 2:30–5:30.*

Palazzo Ducale. This scaled-down copy of the Palazzo Ducale in Urbino (Gubbio was once the possession of that city's ruling family, the Montefeltro) contains a small museum and a courtyard. Some of the public rooms offer magnificent views. ✉ *Via Ducale* ☎ *075/9275872* 🎟 *€5* 🕒 *Tues.–Sun. 9–7:30.*

WHERE TO EAT

$$ UMBRIAN 🍴 **Grotta dell'Angelo.** The rustic trattoria sits in the lower part of the old town near the main square. The menu features simple local specialties, including *capocollo* (a type of salami), stringozzi, and lasagne *tartufata* (with truffles). The few outdoor tables are in high demand in the summer. The restaurant also offers a few small, basically furnished guest rooms, which should be booked in advance. [$] *Average meal: €28* ✉ *Via Gioia 47* ☎ *075/9271747* ✍ *Reservations essential* 🕒 *Closed Tues. and Jan. 7–Feb. 7.*

$ UMBRIAN Fodor's Choice ★ 🍴 **Taverna del Lupo.** One of the city's most famous taverns gets hectic on weekends and during the high season. Lasagne made in the Gubbian fashion, with ham and truffles, is an unusual indulgence, and the *suprema di faraono* (guinea fowl in a delicately spiced sauce) is a specialty. The restaurant has two fine wine cellars and an extensive wine list. Save room for the excellent desserts. [$] *Average meal: €26* ✉ *Via Ansidei 21* ☎ *075/9274368* 🕒 *Closed Mon. from Oct.–June.*

$$ UMBRIAN 🍴 **Ulisse e Letizia.** A stone-and-wood structure from the 1300s (once an important ceramics factory) is the setting for flavorful seasonal menus. The creative fare might include tagliatelle *al tartuffo* (in a truffle sauce), *gnochetti al finocchio selvatico* (potato dumplings with wild fennel), and *raviolini di faro con asparagi* (tiny ravioli with spelt and asparagus). [$] *Average meal: €30* ✉ *Via Mastro Giorgio 2* ☎ *075/9221970* 🕒 *Closed Mon.*

WHERE TO STAY

For expanded hotel reviews, visit Fodors.com.

$ HOTEL 🏨 **Hotel Bosone Palace.** A former palace is now home an elegant hotel, where elaborate frescoes grace the ceilings of the two enormous suites and delightful breakfast room. **Pros:** friendly welcome; excellent location. **Cons:** some noise in tourist season; simple lobby. [$] *Rooms from: €110* ✉ *Via XX Settembre 22* ☎ *075/9220688* 🌐 *www.hotelbosone.com* 🛏 *28 rooms, 2 suites* 🕒 *Closed 3 wks in Jan.* 🍽 *Breakfast.*

DERUTA

7 km (4½ miles) south of Torgiano, 19 km (11 miles) southeast of Perugia.

This 14th-century medieval hill town is most famous for its ceramics. A drive through the countryside to visit the ceramics workshops is a good way to spend a morning, but be sure to stop in the town itself for a wander through the medieval streets and squares.

GETTING HERE AND AROUND

From Perugia follow the directions for Rome and the E45 highway; Deruta has its own exits. There are also trains from the smaller St. Anna train station in Perugia. Take the train in the direction of Terni, and get off at Deruta.

VISITOR INFORMATION

Deruta Tourism Office ✉ *Piazza dei Consoli 4* ☎ *075/9711559.*

EXPLORING

Museo Regionale della Ceramica (*Regional Ceramics Museum*). It's only fitting that Deruta is home to an impressive ceramics museum, part of which extends into the adjacent 14th-century former convent of San Francesco. The museum tells the history of ceramics, with panels (in Italian and English) explaining artistic techniques and production processes, and also holds the country's largest collection of Italian ceramics—nearly 8,000 pieces are on display. The most notable are the Renaissance vessels using the *lustro* technique, which originated in Arab and Middle Eastern cultures some 500 years before coming into use in Italy in the late 1400s. Lustro, as the name sounds, gives the ceramics a rich finish, which is accomplished with the use of crushed precious materials such as gold and silver. ✉ *Largo San Francesco* ☎ *075/9711000* ⊕ *www.sistemamuseo.it* 💶 *€5, includes admission to Pinoteca Comunale* ☉ *Daily 10:30–1 and 2:30–5.*

SHOPPING

Deruta is home to more than 70 ceramics shops. They offer a range of ceramics, including extra pieces from commissions for well-known British and North American tableware manufacturers. If you ask, most owners will take you to see where they actually throw, bake, and paint their wares. A drive along Via Tiberina Nord takes you past one shop after another.

SPELLO

12 km (7 miles) southeast of Assisi, 33 km (21 miles) north of Spoleto.

Spello is a gastronomic paradise, especially compared to Assisi. Only a few minutes from Assisi by car or train, this hilltop town at the edge of Monte Subasio makes an excellent strategic and culinary base for exploring nearby towns. Its hotels are well appointed and its restaurants serve some of the best cuisine and wines in the region—sophisticated in variety and of excellent quality. Spello's art scene includes first-rate frescoes by Pinturicchio and Perugino and contemporary artists who can be observed at work in studios around town. If antiquity is your passion, the town also has some intriguing Roman ruins. And the warm, rosy-beige tones of the local *pietra rossa* stone on the buildings brighten even cloudy days.

GETTING HERE AND AROUND

Spello is an easy half-hour drive from Perugia. From the E45 highway, take the exit toward Assisi and Foligno. Merge onto the SS75 and take the Spello exit. There are also regular trains on the Perugia–Assisi line. Spello is 1 km (½ mile) from the train station, and buses run every 30 minutes for Porta Consolare. From Porta Consolare continue up the steep main street that begins as Via Consolare and changes names several times as it crosses the little town, following the original Roman road. As it curves around, notice the winding medieval alleyways to the right and the more uniform Roman-era blocks to the left.

VISITOR INFORMATION
Spello Tourism Office ⊠ *Piazza Matteotti 3* ☏ *0742/301009* ⊕ *www.prospello.it* ⊘ *Daily 9:30–12:30 and 3:30–5:30.*

EXPLORING
Santa Maria Maggiore. The two great Umbrian artists hold sway in this 16th-century basilica. Pinturicchio's vivid frescoes in the Cappella Baglioni (1501) are striking for their rich colors, finely dressed figures, and complex symbolism. Among Pinturicchio's finest works are the *Nativity, Christ Among the Doctors* (on the far left side is a portrait of Troilo Baglioni, the prior who commissioned the work), and the *Annunciation* (look for Pinturicchio's self-portrait in the Virgin's room). The artist painted them after he had already won great acclaim for his work in the Palazzi Vaticani in Rome for Borgia Pope Alexander VI. Two pillars on either side of the apse are decorated with frescoes by Perugino (circa 1450–1523). ⊠ *Piazza Matteotti 18* ☏ *0742/301792* ⊘ *Daily 9–12:30 and 3–7.*

WHERE TO EAT
$

UMBRIAN

✕ **Bar Giardino Bonci.** A perfect place for a morning cappuccino also serves delicious lunches, with simple panini and a platter of local cheeses, perhaps buttressed by a glass of local wine. The fine garden in the back has a beguiling view of the valley and beyond. $ *Average meal: €20* ⊠ *Via Garibaldi 10, Spello* ☏ *0742/651397.*

$

UMBRIAN

Fodor's Choice

★

✕ **Il Molino.** A former mill is one of the region's best restaurants. Appetizers are varied, and often highlight foods found only here, like the *risina,* a tiny white bean. The meat is first-rate, either elaborately prepared or grilled and topped with a signature sauce, and for any dish, the type of olive oil and the names of the local farmers who grew the produce are noted on the menu. Service is attentive and the wine list has plenty of local and Italian options, including the pungent Sagrantino di Montefalco and fresh Orvieto whites. Outside seating lets you soak up the passing street scene; inside is a series of impressive 14th-century arches. $ *Average meal: €26* ⊠ *Piazza Matteotti 6/7* ☏ *0742/301021* ⊘ *Closed Tues.*

WHERE TO STAY
$$

HOTEL

▦ **Hotel Palazzo Bocci.** Lovely sitting areas, a reading room, bucolic ceiling and wall frescoes, and a garden terrace all add quiet and elegant charm to this 14th-century building, where several rooms have valley views. **Pros:** central location; splendid views of the valley from public areas and some rooms. **Cons:** noisy in summer months; not all rooms have views. $ *Rooms from: €150* ⊠ *Via Cavour 17* ☏ *0742/301021* ⊕ *www.palazzobocci.com* ⤳ *23 rooms* ⏐◎⏐ *Breakfast.*

$

HOTEL

▦ **La Bastiglia.** Polished wood planks and handwoven rugs have replaced the rustic flooring of a former grain mill, and comfortable sitting rooms and cozy bedrooms are filled with a mix of antique and modern pieces. **Pros:** lovely terrace restaurant; cozy rooms; fine views from top-floor rooms, some with terraces. **Cons:** some shared balconies;

CLOSE UP

The Sagrantino Story

Sagrantino grapes have been used for the production of red wine for centuries. The wine began centuries ago as Sagrantino *passito,* a semisweet version in which the grapes are left to dry for a period after picking to intensify the sugar content.

One theory traces the origin of Sagrantino back to ancient Rome in the works of Pliny the Elder, the author of the *Natural History,* who referred to the Itriola grape that some researchers think may be Sagrantino.

Others believe that in medieval times Franciscan friars returned from Asia Minor with the grape. ("Sagrantino" perhaps derives from *sacramenti,* the religious ceremony in which the wine was used.)

The passito is still produced today, and is preferred by some. But the big change in Sagrantino wine production came in the past decades, when Sagrantino *secco* (dry) came onto the market.

Both passito and secco have a deep ruby-red color that tends toward garnet highlights, with a full body and rich flavor.

For the dry wines, producers not to be missed are Terre di Capitani, Antonelli, Perticaia, and Caprai. Try those labels for the passito as well, in addition to Ruggeri and Scacciadiavoli.

Terre di Capitani is complex, and has vegetable and mineral tones that join tastes of wild berries, cherries, and chocolate—this winemaker hand-pampers his grapes and it shows.

Antonelli is elegant, refined, and rich. The Ruggeri passito is one of the best, so don't be put off by its homespun label.

Caprai is bold and rich in taste, and has the largest market share; much of it goes to the United States.

Perticaia has a full, rounded taste.

Salute!

breakfast is underwhelming; no elevator and plenty of steps, so pack light. [$] *Rooms from: €110* ✉ *Via Salnitraria 15* ☎ *0742/651277* 🌐 *www.labastiglia.com* 🛏 *31 rooms, 2 suites* 🕒 *Closed early Jan.–early Feb.* 🍴 *Breakfast.*

MONTEFALCO

6 km (4 miles) southeast of Bevagna, 34 km (21 miles) south of Assisi.

Nicknamed the "balcony over Umbria" for its high vantage point over the valley that runs from Perugia to Spoleto, Montefalco began as an important Roman settlement situated on the Via Flaminia. The town owes its current name—which means "Falcon's Mount"—to Emperor Frederick II (1194–1250). Obviously a greater fan of falconry than Roman architecture, he destroyed the ancient town, which was then called Coccorone, in 1249, and built in its place what would later become Montefalco. Aside from a few fragments incorporated in a private house just off Borgo Garibaldi, no traces remain of the old Roman center. However, Montefalco has more than its fair share of interesting art and architecture and is well worth the drive up the hill.

GETTING HERE AND AROUND

If you're driving from Perugia, take the E45 toward Rome. Take the Foligno exit, then merge onto the SP445 and follow it into Montefalco. The drive takes around 50 minutes. The nearest train station is in Foligno, about 7 km (4½ miles) away. From there you can take a taxi or a bus into Montefalco.

VISITOR INFORMATION

The staff at this tourist office in the piazza will advise you on selecting a wine, direct you to nearby enoteche for tastings, and give you free maps with which to find your way around the Sagrantino Road and the remarkable wine territory it transverses. They can also book you a room in a hotel, at a vineyard, in a hillside apartment, or at an agriturismo.

Montefalco Tourism Office ⊠ *Piazza del Comune 17* ☎ *0742/378490* ⊕ *www.stradadelsagrantino.it.*

La Strada del Sagrantino. ⊠ *Piazza del Comune 17* ☎ *0742/378490* ⊕ *www.stradadelsagrantino.it.*

WHERE TO EAT AND STAY

For expanded hotel reviews, visit Fodors.com.

Montefalco is a good stop for sustenance: here you need go no farther than the main square to find a restaurant or bar with a hot meal, and most establishments—both simple and sophisticated—offer a splendid combination of history and small-town hospitality.

$ × **L'Alchemista.** "The Alchemist" is an apt name, as the chef's transfor-
WINE BAR mations are magical. Try the *fiore molle della Valnerina*, baked saffron cheese, bacon, and zucchini—served only here. In summer, cold dishes to try are *panzanella*, vegetable salad mixed with bread, or the barley salad tossed with vegetables. The farro soup made with Sagrantino wine is a local specialty. The desserts are delicious: all are made on the premises and not too sweet. $ *Average meal: €25* ⊠ *Piazza del Comune 14* ☎ *0742/378558* ⊙ *Closed Tues. and Jan.–Mar.*

$$ ⚑ **Villa Pambuffetti.** If you want to be pampered in the refined atmosphere
HOTEL   of a private villa, this is the spot, with the warmth of a fireplace in the win-
Fodor's Choice   ter, a pool to cool you down in summer, and cozy reading nooks and guest
★   rooms year-round. **Pros:** peaceful gardens; refined furnishings; excellent dining room. **Cons:** outside the town center; can get crowded on weekends. $ *Rooms from: €160* ⊠ *Viale della Vittoria 20* ☎ *0742/379417* ⊕ *www.villapambuffetti.it* ⇨ *15 rooms, 3 suites* ⊙ *Breakfast.*

SPOLETO

For most of the year, Spoleto is one more in a pleasant succession of sleepy hill towns, resting regally atop a mountain. But for three weeks every summer the town shifts into high gear for a turn in the international spotlight during the Festival dei Due Mondi (Festival of Two Worlds), an extravaganza of theater, opera, music, painting, and sculpture. As the world's top artists vie for honors, throngs of art aficionados vie for hotel rooms. If you plan to spend the night in Spoleto during the festival, make sure you have confirmed reservations, or you may find yourself scrambling at sunset.

Spoleto has plenty to lure you during the rest of the year as well: the final frescoes of Filippo Lippi; beautiful piazzas and streets with Roman and medieval attractions; and superb natural surroundings with rolling hills and a dramatic gorge. Spoleto makes a good base for exploring all of southern Umbria, as Assisi, Orvieto, and the towns in between are all within easy reach.

■**TIP**➔ A €12 combination ticket purchased at the tourist office allows you entry to all the town's museums and galleries.

GETTING HERE AND AROUND

Spoleto is an hour's drive from Perugia. From the E45 highway, take the exit toward Assisi and Foligno, then merge onto the SS75 until you reach the Foligno Est exit. Merge onto the SS3, which leads to Spoleto. There are regular trains on the Perugia–Foligno line. From the train station it's a 15-minute uphill walk to the center, so you'll probably want to take a taxi.

The walled city is set on a slanting hillside, with the most interesting sections clustered toward the upper portion. Parking options inside the walls include Piazza Campello (just below the Rocca) on the southeast end, Via del Trivio to the north, and Piazza San Domenico on the west end. You can also park at Piazza della Vittoria farther north, just outside the walls. There are also several well-marked lots near the train station. Regular bus connections are every 15 to 30 minutes. You can also use the *trenino*, as locals call the shuttle service, from the train station to Piazza della Libertà, near the upper part of the old town, where you'll find the tourist office.

Like most other towns with narrow, winding streets, Spoleto is best explored on foot. Bear in mind that much of the city is on a steep slope, so there are lots of stairs and steep inclines. The well-worn stones can be slippery even when dry; wear rubber-sole shoes for good traction. Several pedestrian walkways cut across Corso Mazzini, which zigzags up the hill.

VISITOR INFORMATION

Spoleto Tourism Office ✉ *Piazza della Libertà 7* ☏ *0743/202027* ⊕ *www.regioneumbria.eu.*

EXPLORING SPOLETO

TOP ATTRACTIONS

Duomo. The 12th-century Romanesque facade received a Renaissance face-lift with the addition of a loggia in a rosy pink stone, creating a stunning contrast in styles. One of the finest cathedrals in the region is lit by eight rose windows that are especially dazzling in the late afternoon sun. The original floor tiles date from an earlier church that was destroyed by Frederick I (circa 1123–90).

Above the church's entrance is Bernini's bust of Pope Urban VIII (1568–1644), who had the church redecorated in 17th-century Baroque; fortunately he didn't touch the 15th-century frescoes painted in the apse by Fra Filippo Lippi (circa 1406–69) between 1466 and 1469. These immaculately restored masterpieces—the *Annunciation, Nativity,* and

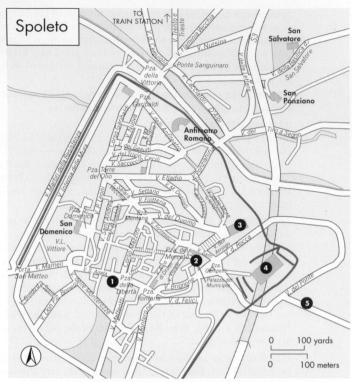

Dormition—tell the story of the life of the Virgin. The *Coronation of the Virgin,* adorning the half dome, is the literal and figurative high point. Portraits of Lippi and his assistants are on the right side of the central panel. The Florentine artist priest "whose colors expressed God's voice" (the words inscribed on his tomb) died shortly after completing the work. His tomb, which you can see in the right transept (note the artist's brushes and tools), was designed by his son, Filippino Lippi (circa 1457–1504).

Another fresco cycle, including work by Pinturicchio, is in the Cappella Eroli, off the right aisle. Note the grotesques in the ornamentation, then very much in vogue with the rediscovery of ancient Roman paintings. The bounty of Umbria is displayed in vivid colors in the abundance of leaves, fruits, and vegetables that adorn the center seams of the cross vault. In the left nave, not far from the entrance, is the well-restored 12th-century crucifix by Alberto Sozio, the earliest known example of this kind of work, with a painting on parchment attached to a wood cross. To the right of the presbytery is the Cappella della Santissima Icona (Chapel of the Most Holy Icon), which contains a small Byzantine painting of a Madonna given to the town by Frederick Barbarossa as a peace offering in 1185, following his destruction of the cathedral and town three decades earlier. ⊠ *Piazza del Duomo* ☎ *0743/231063* ⊙ *Apr.–Oct., daily 8:30–12:30 and 3:30–6:30; Nov.–Mar., daily 8:30–12:30 and 3:30–5.*

Ponte delle Torri (*Bridge of the Towers*). Standing massive and graceful through the deep gorge that separates Spoleto from Monteluco, this 14th-century bridge is one of Umbria's most photographed monuments, and justifiably so. Built over the foundations of a Roman-era aqueduct, it soars 262 feet above the forested gorge— higher than the dome of St. Peter's

12

in Rome. Sweeping views over the valley and a pleasant sense of vertigo make a walk across the bridge a must, particularly on a starry night. ⊠ *Via del Ponte.*

WORTH NOTING

Casa Romana. Spoleto became a Roman colony in the 3rd century BC, but the best excavated remains date from the 1st century AD. Best preserved among them is the Casa Romana. According to an inscription, it belonged to Vespasia Polla, the mother of Emperor Vespasian (one of the builders of the Colosseum and perhaps better known by the Romans for taxing them to install public toilets, later called "Vespasians"). The rooms, arranged around a large central atrium built over an *impluvium* (rain cistern), are decorated with black-and-white geometric mosaics. ⊠ *Palazzo del Municipio, Via Visiale 9* 🕾 *0743/234250* 🖭 *€3, €6 combination ticket includes Pinacoteca Comunale and Galleria d'Arte Moderna* ⊙ *Daily 11–5; closed Tues. and last wk of Dec.*

La Rocca. Built in the mid-14th century for Cardinal Egidio Albornoz, this massive fortress served as a seat for the local pontifical governors, a tangible sign of the restoration of the Church's power in the area when the pope was ruling from Avignon. Several popes spent time here, and one of them, Alexander VI, in 1499 sent his capable teenage daughter Lucrezia Borgia (1480–1519) to serve as governor for three months. The Gubbio-born architect Gattapone (14th century) used the ruins of a Roman acropolis as a foundation and took materials from many Roman-era sites, including the Teatro Romano. La Rocca's plan is long and rectangular, with six towers and two grand courtyards, an upper loggia, and inside some grand reception rooms. In the largest tower, Torre Maestà, you can visit an apartment with some interesting frescoes. A small shuttle bus gives you that last boost up the hill from the ticket booth to the entrance of the fortress. If you phone in advance, you may be able to secure an English-speaking guide. ⊠ *Via del Ponte* 🕾 *0743/223055* 🖭 *€7:50* ⊙ *Tues.–Sun. 9:30–6:30.*

Teatro Romano. The Romans who colonized the city in 241 BC constructed this small theater in the 1st century AD; for centuries afterward it was used as a quarry for building materials. The most intact portion is the hallway that passes under the *cavea* (stands). The rest was heavily restored in the early 1950s and serves as a venue for Spoleto's Festival dei Due Mondi. The theater was the site of a gruesome episode in Spoleto's history: during the medieval struggle between Guelph (papal) and Ghibelline (imperial) forces, Spoleto took the side of the Holy Roman Emperor. Afterward, 400 Guelph supporters were massacred in the theater, their bodies burned in an enormous pyre. In the end, the Guelphs were triumphant, and Spoleto was incorporated into the states of the Church in 1354. Through a door in the west portico of the adjoining building is the **Museo Archeologico,** with assorted artifacts found in excavations primarily around Spoleto and Norcia. The collection contains Bronze Age and Iron Age artifacts from Umbrian and pre-Roman eras. Another section contains black-glaze vases from the Hellenistic period excavated from the necropolis of Saint Scolastica in Norcia. The highlight is the stone tablet inscribed on both sides with the Lex Spoletina (Spoleto Law). Dating from 315 BC, this legal document prohibited the desecration of the woods on the slopes of nearby Monteluco. ✉ *Piazza della Libertà* ☎ *0743/223277* 🎫 *€4* 🕒 *Daily 8:30–7:30.*

WHERE TO EAT

$ UMBRIAN 🍴 **Apollinare.** Low wooden ceilings and flickering candlelight make this monastery from the 10th and 11th centuries Spoleto's most romantic spot. The kitchen serves sophisticated, innovative variations on local dishes. Sauces of cherry tomatoes, mint, and a touch of red pepper, or of porcini mushrooms, top the long, slender strangozzi. The *caramella* (light puff-pastry cylinders filled with local cheese and served with a creamy Parmesan sauce) is popular. In warm weather you can dine under a canopy on the piazza across from the archaeological museum. [$] *Average meal: €25* ✉ *Via Sant'Agata 14* ☎ *0743/223256* 🕒 *Closed Tues.*

$ UMBRIAN 🍴 **Il Tartufo.** As the name indicates, dishes prepared with truffles are the specialty here—don't miss the risotto al tartufo. Incorporating the ruins of a Roman villa, the surroundings are rustic on the ground floor and more modern upstairs. In summer, tables appear outdoors and the traditional fare is spiced up to appeal to the cosmopolitan crowd attending (or performing in) the Festival dei Due Mondi. [$] *Average meal: €25* ✉ *Piazza Garibaldi 24* ☎ *0743/40236* ✍ *Reservations essential* 🕒 *Closed Mon. and last 2 wks in July. No dinner Sun.*

$ UMBRIAN 🍴 **Osteria del Trivio.** Everything is made on the premises and the menu changes daily, depending on what's in season. Dishes might include stuffed artichokes, pasta with local mushrooms, or chicken with artichokes. For dessert, try the homemade biscotti, made for dunking in sweet wine. There's a printed menu, but the owner can explain the dishes in a number of languages. [$] *Average meal: €20* ✉ *Via del Trivio 16* ☎ *0743/44349* 🕒 *Closed Tues.*

$$ UMBRIAN 🍴 **Ristorante Panciolle.** A small garden filled with lemon trees in the heart of Spoleto's medieval quarter provides one of the most appealing settings you could wish for. Dishes change throughout the year, and may include pastas served with asparagus or mushrooms, as well as grilled meats. More expensive dishes prepared with fresh truffles are also available in season. [$] *Average meal: €30* ✉ *Via Duomo 3/5* ☎ *0743/45677* ✍ *Reservations essential* 🕒 *Closed Wed.*

CLOSE UP

A Taste of Truffles

Umbria is rich with truffles—more are found here than anywhere else in Italy—and those not consumed fresh are processed into pastes or flavored oils. The primary truffle areas are around the tiny town of Norcia, which holds a truffle festival every February, and near Spoleto, where signs warn against unlicensed truffle hunting at the base of the Ponte delle Torri.

Although grown locally, the rare delicacy can cost a small fortune, up to $200 for a quarter pound—fortunately, a little goes a long way. At such a price there's great competition among the nearly 10,000 registered truffle hunters in the province, who use specially trained dogs to sniff them out among the roots of several types of trees, including oak and ilex. Despite a few incidents involving inferior tubers imported from China, you can be reasonably assured that the truffle shaved onto your pasta has been unearthed locally. Don't pass up the opportunity to try this delectable treat. The intense aroma of a dish perfumed with truffles is unmistakable and the flavor memorable.

WHERE TO STAY

For expanded hotel reviews, visit Fodors.com.

$$ HOTEL — **Cavaliere Palace Hotel.** A sense of old-world comfort pervades the 17th-century home of an influential cardinal, and many rooms retain their sumptuous frescoed ceilings. **Pros:** quiet elegance; central position. **Cons:** finding parking can be a problem; crowded in summer. [$] *Rooms from: €150* ✉ *Corso Garibaldi 49* ☎ *0743/220350* 🌐 *www.hotelcavaliere.eu* 🛏 *29 rooms, 2 suites* 🍴 *Breakfast.*

$ HOTEL — **Hotel Clitunno.** Cozy guest rooms and intimate public rooms, some with timbered ceilings, give the sense of a traditional Umbrian home—albeit one with a good restaurant. **Pros:** friendly staff; good restaurant. **Cons:** difficult to find a parking space; some small rooms. [$] *Rooms from: €110* ✉ *Piazza Sordini 6* ☎ *0743/223340* 🌐 *www.hotelclitunno.com* 🛏 *45 rooms* 🍴 *Breakfast.*

$$ HOTEL Fodor'sChoice ★ — **Hotel San Luca.** Hand-painted friezes decorate the walls of the spacious guest rooms, and elegant comfort is the gracenote throughout—you can sip afternoon tea in oversize armchairs by the fireplace, or take a walk in the sweet-smelling rose garden. **Pros:** very helpful staff; peaceful location. **Cons:** outside the town center; a long walk to the main sights. [$] *Rooms from: €150* ✉ *Via Interna delle Mura 19* ☎ *0743/223399* 🌐 *www.hotelsanluca.com* 🛏 *33 rooms, 2 suites* 🍴 *Breakfast.*

SOUTHERN UMBRIA

Orvieto, built on a tufa mount, produces one of Italy's favorite white wines and has one of the country's greatest cathedrals and most compelling fresco cycles. Nearby Narni and Todi are pleasant medieval hill towns. The former stands over a steep gorge, its Roman pedigree evident in dark alleyways and winding streets; the latter is a fairy-tale village with incomparable views and one of Italy's most perfect piazzas.

TODI

34 km (22 miles) south of Perugia, 34 km (22 miles) east of Orvieto.

As you stand on Piazza del Popolo, looking out onto the Tiber Valley below, it's easy to see why Todi is often described as Umbria's prettiest hill town. Legend has it that the town was founded by the Umbri, who followed an eagle who had stolen a tablecloth. They liked this lofty perch so much that they settled here for good. The eagle is now perched on the insignia of the medieval palaces in the main piazza.

GETTING HERE AND AROUND

Todi is best reached by car, as the town's two train stations are way down the hill and connected to the center by infrequent bus service. From Perugia, follow the E45 toward Rome. Take the Todi/Orvieto exit, then follow the SS79bis into Todi. The drive takes around 40 minutes.

VISITOR INFORMATION

Todi Tourism Office ⊠ *Piazza del Popolo 38* ☏ *075/8942526* ⊕ *www.regioneumbria.eu.*

EXPLORING

Duomo. One end of the Piazza del Popolo is dominated by this 12th-century Romanesque-Gothic masterpeice, built over the site of a Roman temple. The simple facade is enlivened by a finely carved rose window. Look up at that window as you step inside and you'll notice its peculiarity: each "petal" of the rose has a cherub's face in the stained glass. Also take a close look at the capitals of the double columns with pilasters: perched between the acanthus leaves are charming medieval sculptures of saints—Peter with his keys, George and the dragon, and so on. You can see the rich brown tones of the wooden choir near the altar, but unless you have binoculars or request special permission in advance, you can't get close enough to see all the exquisite detail in this Renaissance masterpiece of woodworking (1521–30). The severe, solid mass of the Duomo is mirrored by the Palazzo dei Priori (1595–97) across the way. ⊠ *Piazza del Popolo* ☏ *075/8943041* ⊙ *Daily 8–1 and 3–6.*

Piazza del Popolo. Built above the Roman Forum, Piazza del Popolo is Todi's high point, a model of spatial harmony with stunning views onto the surrounding countryside. In the best medieval tradition, the square was conceived to house both the temporal and the spiritual centers of power.

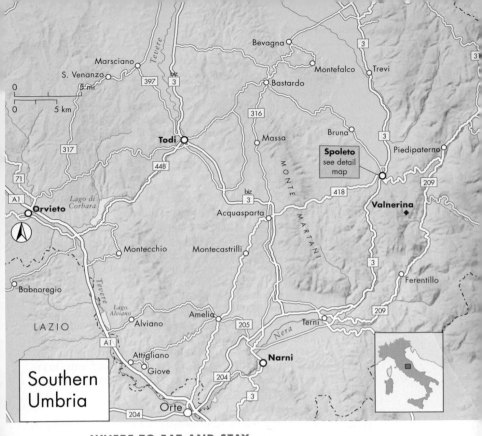

WHERE TO EAT AND STAY

For expanded hotel reviews, visit Fodors.com.

$$ ✕**Ristorante Umbria.** Todi's most popular restaurant for more than four
UMBRIAN decades is reliable for its sturdy country food and the wonderful view
from the terrace. Since it has only 16 tables outside, make sure you
reserve ahead. In winter, try legume soup, homemade pasta with truffles,
or *palombaccio alla ghiotta* (roasted squab). Steaks, accompanied by
a rich dark-brown wine sauce, are good as well. $ *Average meal: €35*
✉ *Via San Bonaventura 13* ☎ *075/8942737* ⊘ *Closed Tues.*

$ ⛺ **San Lorenzo 3.** Surrounded by antique furniture, paintings, and period
HOTEL knickknacks, you will be as charmed by a sense of being in the 19th
century as you are by the magnificent views over valleys and hills. **Pros:**
Old World atmosphere; excellent central location. **Cons:** few modern
amenities; basic furnishings; some shared bathrooms. $ *Rooms from:*
€100 ✉ *Via San Lorenzo 3* ☎ *075/8944555* ⊕ *www.sanlorenzo3.it*
🛏 *6 rooms, 3 with bath* ⊟ *No credit cards* ⊘ *Closed Jan. and Feb.*
🍴 *Breakfast.*

ORVIETO

30 km (19 miles) southwest of Todi, 81 km (51 miles) west of Spoleto.

Carved out of an enormous plateau of volcanic rock high above a green valley, Orvieto has natural defenses that made the high walls seen in many Umbrian towns unnecessary. The Etruscans were the first to settle here, digging a honeycombed network of more than 1,200 wells and storage caves out of the soft stone. The Romans attacked, sacked, and destroyed the city in 283 BC; since then, it has grown up out of the rock into an enchanting maze of alleys and squares. Orvieto was solidly Guelph in the Middle Ages, and for several hundred years popes sought refuge in the city, at times needing protection from their enemies, at times seeking respite from the summer heat of Rome.

When painting his frescoes inside the Duomo, Luca Signorelli asked that part of his contract be paid in Orvietan wine, and he was neither the first nor the last to appreciate the region's popular white. In past times the caves carved underneath the town were used to ferment the Trebbiano grapes used in making Orvieto Classico; now local wine production has moved out to more traditional vineyards, but you can still while away the afternoon in tastings at any number of shops in town.

■TIP→ A Carta Orvieto Unica (single ticket) is expensive but a great deal if you want to visit everything; for €18 you get admission to the three major sights in town—Cappella di San Brizio (at the Duomo), Museo Claudio Faina, and Orvieto Underground—along with entry to the Torre del Moro; with views of Orvieto, plus a combination bus-funicular pass or five hours of free parking.

GETTING HERE AND AROUND

Orvieto is well connected by train to Rome, Florence, and Perugia. From the station, you can make a view-filled ascent up to the town center via funicular. It's also adjacent to the A1 Superstrada that runs between Florence and Rome. Parking areas in the upper town tend to be crowded. A better idea is to follow the signs for the Porta Orvetiana parking lot, then take the funicular that carries people up the hill.

VISITOR INFORMATION

Orvieto Tourism Office ⊠ *Piazza del Duomo 24* ☎ *0763/341772* ⊕ *www.regioneumbria.eu.*

EXPLORING

Fodor's Choice
★

Duomo. Orvieto's stunning cathedral was built to commemorate the Miracle at Bolsena. In 1263 a young priest who questioned the miracle of transubstantiation (in which the Communion bread and wine become the flesh and blood of Christ) was saying mass at nearby Lago di Bolsena. His doubts were put to rest, however, when a wafer he had just blessed suddenly started to drip blood, staining the linen covering the altar. The cloth and the host were taken to the pope, who proclaimed a miracle and a year later provided for a new religious holiday—the Feast of Corpus Domini. Thirty years later, construction began on a duomo in Orvieto to celebrate the miracle and house the stained altar cloth.

It's thought that Arnolfo di Cambio (circa 1245–1302), the famous builder of the Duomo in Florence, was given the initial commission, but the project was soon taken over by Lorenzo Maitani (circa 1275–1330), who consolidated the structure and designed the monumental facade. Maitani also made the bas-relief panels between the doorways, which graphically tell the story of the Creation (on the left) and the Last Judgment (on the right). The lower registers, now protected by Plexiglas, succeed in conveying the horrors of hell as few other works of art manage to do, an effect made all the more powerful by the worn gray marble.

Above, gold mosaics are framed by finely detailed Gothic decoration.

Inside, the cathedral is rather vast and empty; the major works are in the transepts. To the left is the **Cappella del Corporale,** where the square linen cloth (*corporale*) is kept in a golden reliquary that's modeled on the cathedral and inlaid with enamel scenes of the miracle. The cloth is removed for public viewing on Easter and on Corpus Domini (the ninth Sunday after Easter). In the right transept is the **Cappella di San Brizio,** or Cappella Nuova. In this chapel is one of Italy's greatest fresco cycles, notable for its influence on Michelangelo's *Last Judgment,* as well as for the extraordinary beauty of the figuration. In these works, a few by Fra Angelico and the majority by Luca Signorelli, the damned fall to hell, demons breathe fire and blood, and Christians are martyred. Some scenes are heavily influenced by the imagery in Dante's (1265–1321) *Divine Comedy.* ✉ *Piazza del Duomo* ☎ *0763/342477* ✎ *Cappella Nuova €3* ☉ *Mar.–Oct., daily 9:30–7:30; Nov.–Feb., daily 9:30–1 and 2:30–5.*

Museo Archeologico Claudio Faina. This superb private collection, beautifully arranged and presented, goes far beyond the usual museum offerings of a scattering of local remains. The collection is particularly rich in Greek- and Etruscan-era pottery, from large Attic amphorae (6th–4th century BC) to Attic black- and red-figure pieces to Etruscan *bucchero* (dark-reddish clay) vases. Other interesting pieces in the collection include a 6th-century sarcophagus and a substantial display of Roman-era coins. ✉ *Piazza del Duomo 29* ☎ *0763/341511* ⊕ *www.museofaina. it* ✎ *€4.50* ☉ *Apr.–Sept., daily 10–5; Oct.–Mar., Tues.–Sun. 9:30–6.*

Orvieto Underground. More than just about any other town, Orvieto has grown from its own foundations. The Etruscans, the Romans, and those who followed dug into the tufa (the same soft volcanic rock from which catacombs were made) to create more than 1,000 separate cisterns, caves, secret passages, storage areas, and production areas for wine and olive oil. Much of the tufa removed was used as building blocks for the city that exists today, and some was partly ground into *pozzolana,* which was made into mortar. You can see the labyrinth of dugout chambers beneath the city on the **Orvieto Underground tour** (✉ *Orvieto tourism office, Piazza del Duomo 24* ☎ *0763/341772*) run daily at 11, 12:15, 4, and 5:15. Admission for the hour-long English tour is €6. ⊕ *www.orvietounderground.it.*

Pozzo della Cava. If you're short on time but want a quick look at the cisterns and caves beneath the city, head for the Pozzo della Cava, an Etruscan well for spring water. ✉ *Via della Cava 28* ☎ *0763/342373* 🎫 *€3* 🕒 *Tues.–Fri. 9–8*

WHERE TO EAT

The streets around the Duomo are lined with all types of bars and restaurants where you can eat simple or elaborate food and try wines by the glass.

$ UMBRIAN Fodor's Choice ★ 🍴 **Il Giglio D'Oro.** A great view of the Duomo is coupled with superb food. Eggplant is transformed into an elegant custard with black truffles in the *sformatino di melenzane con vellutata al tartuffo nero.* Pastas, like *ombrichelli al pesto umbro,* are traditional, but perhaps with a new twist like fresh coriander leaves instead of the usual basil. Lamb roasted in a crust of bread is delicately seasoned with a tomato cream sauce. The wine cellar includes some rare vintages. [$] *Average meal: €25* ✉ *Piazza Duomo 8* ☎ *0763/341903* 🕒 *Closed Wed.*

$ UMBRIAN 🍴 **Le Grotte del Funaro.** Dine inside tufa caves under central Orvieto, where the two windows afford splendid views of the hilly countryside. The traditional Umbrian food is reliably good, with simple grilled meats and vegetables and pizzas. Oddly, though, the food is outclassed by an extensive wine list, with top local and Italian labels and quite a few rare vintages. [$] *Average meal: €25* ✉ *Via Ripa Serancia 41* ☎ *0763/343276* ✍ *Reservations essential* 🕒 *Closed 1 wk in July.*

$ UMBRIAN 🍴 **Trattoria La Grotta.** Franco, the owner, has been in this location for more than 20 years and has attracted a steady American clientele without losing his local following—or his touch with homemade pasta, perhaps with a duck or wild-boar sauce. Roast lamb, veal, and pork are all good, and the desserts are homemade. Franco knows the local wines well and has a carefully selected list, including some from smaller but excellent wineries, so ask about them. [$] *Average meal: €26* ✉ *Via Luca Signorelli 5* ☎ *0763/341348* 🕒 *Closed Tues.*

WHERE TO STAY

For expanded hotel reviews, visit Fodors.com.

$$ HOTEL 🏨 **Hotel Palazzo Piccolomini.** A 16th-century family palazzo has been beautifully restored, with inviting public spaces and handsome guest quaters where contemporary surroundings are accented with old beams, vaulted ceilings, and other distinctive touches. **Pros:** peaceful atmosphere; efficient staff; good location. **Cons:** slightly overpriced. [$] *Rooms from: €120* ✉ *Piazza Ranieri 36* ☎ *0763/341743* 🌐 *www.palazzopiccolomini.it* 🛏 *28 rooms, 3 suites* 🍽 *Breakfast.*

NARNI

13 km (8 miles) southwest of Terni, 46 km (29 miles) southeast of Orvieto.

Once a bustling and important town at a major crossroads on the Via Flaminia, Narni is now a quiet backwater with only the occasional tourist invading its hilltop streets. Modern development is kept out of sight in the new town of Narni Scalo, below. This means that you'll find the older neighborhood safely preserved behind, and in the case of Narni's subterranean Roman ruins, beneath, the town's sturdy walls.

Hiking the Umbrian Hills

CLOSE UP

Magnificent scenery makes the heart of Italy excellent walking, hiking, and mountaineering country. In Umbria, the area around Spoleto is particularly good; several pleasant, easy, and well-signed trails begin at the far end of the Ponte alle Torri bridge over Monteluco. From Cannara, an easy half-hour walk leads to the fields of Pian d'Arca, the site of Saint Francis's sermon to the birds. For slightly more arduous walks, you can follow the saint's path, uphill from Assisi to the Eremo delle Carceri, and then continue along the trails that crisscross Monte Subasio. At 4,250 feet, the Subasio's treeless summit affords views of Assisi, Perugia, far-off Gubbio, and the distant mountain ranges of Abruzzo.

For even more challenging hiking, the northern reaches of the Valnerina are exceptional; the mountains around Norcia should not be missed. Throughout Umbria and the Marches, you'll find that most recognized walking and hiking trails are marked with the distinctive red-and-white blazes of the Club Alpino Italiano. Tourist offices are a good source for walking and climbing itineraries to suit all ages and levels of ability, while bookstores, *tabacchi* (tobacconists), and *edicole* (newsstands) often have maps and hiking guides. Depending on the length and location of your walk, it can be important that you have comfortable walking shoes or boots, appropriate attire, and plenty of water to drink.

12

GETTING HERE AND AROUND

From Perugia, take the E45 highway toward Rome. Merge onto the SS675, then take the exit to San Gemini and follow signs for Narni Scalo. The drive takes around 1½ hours. There are also regular trains from Perugia.

VISITOR INFORMATION

Terni Tourism Office. Stop here for information about Narni and a number of other smaller towns. ⊠ *Via Cassian Bon 4, Terni* ☎ *0744/423047* ⊕ *www.regioneumbria.eu.*

EXPLORING

Roman Aqueduct. You can take a unique tour of Narni's underground Roman aqueduct—the only one open to the public in all of Italy—but it's not for the claustrophobic. Contact Narni Sotterranea at least ten days ahead to book a visit. ⊠ *Narni Sotterranea, Via San Bernardo 12* ☎ *0744/722292* ⊕ *www.narnisotterranea.it* ⊠ *€20* ⊗ *Apr.–Oct., by appointment.*

WHERE TO EAT

$ ✕ **Il Cavallino.** Run by the third generation of the Bussetti family, this
UMBRIAN trattoria is south of Narni on the Via Flaminia. The most dependable menu selections are the grilled meats. Rabbit roasted with rosemary and sage and juicy grilled T-bone steaks are house favorites; in the winter, phone ahead to request the wild pigeon. The wine list has a limited selection of dependable local varieties. $ *Average meal: €18* ⊠ *Via Flaminia Romana 220, 3 km (2 miles) south of center* ☎ *0744/761020* ⊗ *Closed Tues. and Dec. 20–26.*

VALNERINA

Terni is 13 km (8 miles) northeast of Narni, 27 km (17 miles) southeast of Spoleto.

The Valnerina (the valley of the River Nera, to the east of Spoleto) is the most beautiful of central Italy's many well-kept secrets. The twisting roads that serve the rugged landscape are poor, but the drive is well worth the effort for its forgotten medieval villages and dramatic mountain scenery.

GETTING HERE AND AROUND

You can head into the area from Terni on the S209, or on the SP395bis north of Spoleto, which links the Via Flaminia (S3) with the middle reaches of the Nera Valley through a tunnel.

EXPLORING

Cascata delle Marmore. The road east of Terni (SS Valnerina) leads 10 km (6 miles) to the Cascata delle Marmore (Waterfalls of Marmore), which, at 541 feet, are the highest in Europe. A canal was dug by the Romans in the 3rd century BC to prevent flooding in the nearby agricultural plains. Nowadays the waters are often diverted to provide hydroelectric power for Terni, reducing the roaring falls to an unimpressive trickle, so check with the information office at the falls (there's a timetable on their website) or with Terni's tourist office before heading here. On summer evenings, when the falls are in full spate, the cascading water is floodlit to striking effect. The falls are usually at their most energetic at midday and at around 4 pm. This is a good place for hiking, except in December and January, when most trails may be closed. ⊠ *SP79 10 km (6 miles) east of Terni* ☎ *0744/62982* ⊕ *www.marmorefalls.it* ⧄ *€8* ⊙ *May, weekends noon–1 and 4–5; June–Aug., daily 11–10; mid-Mar.– Apr. and Sept., weekends noon–9; Jan.–mid-Mar., weekends noon–4.*

Norcia. The birthplace of Saint Benedict, Norcia is best known for its Umbrian pork and truffles. Norcia exports truffles to France and hosts a truffle festival, the Sagra del Tartufo, every February. The surrounding mountains provide spectacular hiking. ⊠ *67 km (42 miles) northeast of Terni.*

Piano Grande. A mountain plain 25 km (15 miles) to the northeast of the valley, Piano Grande is a hang glider's paradise and a wonderful place for a picnic or to fly a kite. It's also nationally famous for the quality of the lentils grown here, which are a traditional part of every Italian New Year's feast.

THE MARCHES

An excursion from Umbria into the Marches region allows you to see a part of Italy rarely visited by foreigners. Not as wealthy as Tuscany or Umbria, the Marches does have a diverse landscape of mountains and beaches, and marvelous views. Like that of neighbors to the west, the patchwork of rolling hills of Le Marche (as it's known in Italian) is stitched with grapevines and olive trees, bearing luscious wine and olive oil.

Traveling here isn't as easy as in Umbria or Tuscany. Beyond the narrow coastal plain and away from major towns, the roads are steep and twisting. An efficient bus service connects the coastal town of Pesaro to Urbino. Train travel in the region is slow, however, and stops are limited—although you can reach Ascoli Piceno by rail.

URBINO

75 km (47 miles) north of Gubbio, 116 km (72 miles) northeast of Perugia, 230 km (143 miles) east of Florence.

Majestic Urbino, atop a steep hill with a skyline of towers and domes, is something of a surprise to come upon. Although quite remote, it was once a center of learning and culture almost without rival in Western Europe. The town looks much as it did in the glory days of the 15th century: a cluster of warm brick and pale stone buildings, all topped with russet-color tile roofs. The focal point is the immense and beautiful Palazzo Ducale.

The city is home to the small but prestigious Università di Urbino—one of the oldest in the world—and the streets are usually filled with students. Urbino is very much a college town, with the usual array of bookshops, bars, and coffeehouses. In summer the Italian student population is replaced by foreigners who come to study Italian language and arts at several prestigious private fine-arts academies.

Urbino's fame rests on the reputation of three of its native sons: Duke Federico da Montefeltro (1422–82), the enlightened warrior-patron who built the Palazzo Ducale; Raffaello Sanzio (1483–1520), or Raphael, one of the most influential painters in history and an embodiment of the spirit of the Renaissance; and the architect Donato Bramante (1444–1514), who translated the philosophy of the Renaissance into buildings of grace and beauty. Unfortunately there's little work by either Bramante or Raphael in the city, but the duke's influence can still be felt strongly.

GETTING HERE AND AROUND
Take the SS3bis from Perugia, and follow the directions for Gubbio and Cesena. Exit at Umbertide and take the SS219, then the SS452, and at Calmazzo, the SS73bis to Urbino.

VISITOR INFORMATION
Urbino Tourism Office ⊠ *Piazza de Rinascimento 1* ☏ *0722/2613* ⊕ *www.comune.urbino.ps.it.*

EXPLORING
Casa Natale di Raffaello (*House of Raphael*). This is the house in which the painter was born and where he took his first steps in painting, under the direction of his artist father. There's some debate about the fresco of the Madonna here; some say it's by Raphael, whereas others attribute it to the father—with Raphael's mother and the young painter himself standing in as models for the Madonna and Child. ⊠ *Via Raffaello 57* ☏ *0722/320105* 💶 *€3.50* ⊗ *Mon.–Sat. 9–2, Sun. 10–1.*

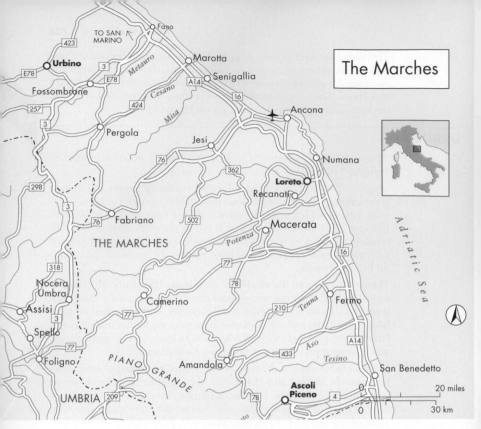

The Marches

Fodor's Choice **Palazzo Ducale** (*Ducal Palace*). The Palazzo Ducale holds a place of
★ honor in the city. If the Renaissance was, ideally, a celebration of
the nobility of man and his works, of the light and purity of the
soul, then there's no place in Italy, the birthplace of the Renaissance,
where these tenets are better illustrated. From the moment you enter
the peaceful courtyard, you know you're in a place of grace and
beauty, the harmony of the building reflecting the high ideals of the
time. Today the palace houses the **Galleria Nazionale delle Marche**
(National Museum of the Marches), with a superb collection of paintings, sculpture, and other objets d'art. Some works were originally
the possessions of the Montefeltro family; others were brought here
from churches and palaces throughout the region. Masterworks in the
collection include Paolo Uccello's *Profanation of the Host,* Titian's
Resurrection and *Last Supper,* and Piero della Francesca's *Madonna
of Senigallia.* But the gallery's highlight is Piero's enigmatic work long
known as *The Flagellation of Christ.* Much has been written about
this painting, and few experts agree on its meaning. Legend had it
that the figures in the foreground represent a murdered member of
the Montefeltro family (the barefoot young man) and his two killers.
However, Sir John Pope-Hennessy—the preeminent scholar of Italian Renaissance art—argues that they represent the arcane subject of
the vision of Saint Lawrence. Academic debates notwithstanding, the

experts agree that the work is one of the painter's masterpieces. Piero himself thought so: it's one of the few works he signed (on the lowest step supporting the throne). ✉ *Piazza Duca Federico* ☎ *0722/322625* 🌐 *www.comune.urbino.ps.it* 🎟 *€5* 🕒 *Mon. 8:30–2, Tues.–Sun. 8:30–7:15; ticket office closes at 6.*

WHERE TO EAT

$ ITALIAN 🍴 **Angolo Divino.** At this osteria in the center of Urbino, tradition reigns supreme: the menu is written in local dialect, flanked by Italian and English translations. Dishes range from the deliciously simple spaghetti *col pane grattugiato* (with bread crumbs) to the temptingly rich *filetto al tartufo* (beef fillet with truffles). [$] *Average meal: €25* ✉ *Via S. Andrea 14* ☎ *0722/327559* 🕒 *Closed Mon. and mid-Oct.–mid-Nov. No dinner Sun.*

$ ITALIAN 🍴 **La Vecchia Fornarina.** Locals often crowd this small, two-room trattoria near the Piazza della Repubblica. The specialty is meaty country fare, such as *coniglio* (rabbit) and *vitello alle noci* (veal cooked with walnuts) or *ai porcini* (with mushrooms). There's also a good selection of pasta dishes. [$] *Average meal: €22* ✉ *Via Mazzini 14* ☎ *0722/320007* ✍ *Reservations essential.*

WHERE TO STAY

For expanded hotel reviews, visit Fodors.com.

$$ HOTEL 🏨 **Hotel Bonconte.** Pleasant rooms just inside the city walls and close to the Palazzo Ducale are decorated with a smattering of antiques, and those in front have views of the valley below Urbino. **Pros:** some nice views; away from the bustle. **Cons:** an uphill walk to town center; service can be sleepy. [$] *Rooms from: €130* ✉ *Via delle Mura 28* ☎ *0722/2463* 🌐 *www.viphotels.it* 🛏 *23 rooms, 2 suites* 🍽 *No meals.*

LORETO

118 km (73 miles) southeast of Urbino.

There's a strong Renaissance feel about this hilltop town, which is home to one of the most important religious sites in Europe, the Sanctuario della Santa Casa (House of the Virgin Mary). Bramante and Sansovino gave the church its Renaissance look, although many other artists helped create its special atmosphere. Today the town revolves around the religious calendar; if you can be here on December 10, you will witness the Feast of the Translation of the Holy House, when huge bonfires are lighted to celebrate the miraculous arrival of the house in 1294.

GETTING HERE AND AROUND

If you're driving from Perugia, take the SS318 and then the SS76 highway to Fabriano and then on to Chiaravalle, where it merges with the A14 autostrada. The drive takes around 2½ hours. Trains also go to Loreto, but the station is about a mile outside the town center. Regular buses leave from the station to the center.

VISITOR INFORMATION

Loreto Tourism Office ✉ *Via Solari 3* ☎ *071/970276* 🌐 *www.turismo.marche.it.*

EXPLORING

Basilica della Santa Casa. Loreto is famous for one of the best-loved shrines in the world, that of the **Santuario della Santa Casa** (House of the Virgin Mary), within the Basilica della Santa Casa. Legend has it that angels moved the house from Nazareth, where the Virgin Mary was living at the time of the Annunciation, to this hilltop in 1295. The reason for this sudden and divinely inspired move was that Nazareth had fallen into the hands of Muslim invaders, whom the angelic hosts viewed as unsuitable keepers of this important shrine. Excavations made at the behest of the Catholic Church have shown that the house did once stand elsewhere and was brought to the hilltop—by either crusaders or a family named Angeli—around the time the angels (*angeli*) are said to have done the job.

The house itself consists of three rough stone walls contained within an elaborate marble tabernacle. Built around this centerpiece is the giant basilica of the Holy House, which dominates the town. Millions of visitors come to the site every year (particularly at Easter and on the December 10 Feast of the Holy House), and the little town of Loreto can become uncomfortably crowded with pilgrims. Many great Italian architects, including Bramante, Antonio da Sangallo the Younger (1483–1546), Giuliano da Sangallo (circa 1445–1516), and Sansovino (1467–1529), contributed to the design of the basilica. It was begun in the Gothic style in 1468 and continued in Renaissance style through the late Renaissance. The bell tower is by Luigi Vanvitelli (1700–73). Inside the church are a great many mediocre 19th- and 20th-century paintings but also some fine works by Renaissance masters such as Luca Signorelli and Melozzo da Forlì (1438–94).

If you're a nervous air traveler, you can take comfort in the fact that the Holy Virgin of Loreto is the patron saint of air travelers and that Pope John Paul II composed a prayer for a safe flight—available here in a half-dozen languages. ⊠ *Piazza della Madonna* ☎ *071/970104* ⊕ *www. santuarioloreto.it* ⊘ *Apr.–Sept., daily 6 am–8 pm; Oct.–Mar., daily 6:15 am–7:45 pm. Santuario della Santa Casa closed daily 12:30–2:30.*

ASCOLI PICENO

88 km (55 miles) south of Loreto, 105 km (65 miles) south of Ancona.

Ascoli Piceno sits in a valley ringed by steep hills and cut by the Tronto River. In Roman times it was one of central Italy's best-known market towns, and today, with almost 60,000 residents, it's a major fruit and olive producer, making it one of the most important towns in the region. Despite growth during the Middle Ages and at other times, the streets in the town center continue to reflect the grid pattern of the ancient Roman city. You'll even find the word *rua,* from the Latin *ruga,* used for "street" instead of the Italian *via.* Now largely closed to traffic, the city center is great to explore on foot.

GETTING HERE AND AROUND

From Perugia take the SS75 to Foligno, then merge onto the SS3 to Norcia. From here take the SS4 to Ascoli Piceno. There are also trains, but the journey would be quite long, taking you from Perugia to Ancona before changing for Ascoli Piceno.

VISITOR INFORMATION

Ascoli Piceno Tourism Office ✉ *Piazza Aringo 7* ☎ *0736/298204* 🌐 *www.comune.ascolipiceno.it.*

EXPLORING

Piazza del Popolo. The heart of the town is the majestic Piazza del Popolo, dominated by the Gothic church of **San Francesco** and the **Palazzo del Popolo,** a 13th-century town hall that contains a graceful Renaissance courtyard. The square functions as the living room of the entire city and at dusk each evening is packed with people strolling and exchanging news and gossip—the sweetly antiquated ritual called the *passeggiata,* performed all over the country.

WHERE TO EAT AND STAY

For expanded hotel reviews, visit Fodors.com.

$ SEAFOOD 🍴 **Il Ristorante del Corso.** This quiet little affair is the place if you want to eat fresh fish from the Adriatic coast. Close to the center, the portions are generous and the service friendly and prompt. [$] *Average meal: €22* ✉ *Via C. Mazzini 277* ☎ *0736/256760.*

$ HOTEL 🏨 **Il Pennile.** A modern, family-run hotel in a quiet residential area outside the old city center is pleasantly set amid a grove of olive trees. **Pros:** peaceful; a good budget option. **Cons:** distance from town center; basic rooms. [$] *Rooms from: €60* ✉ *Via G. Spalvieri* ☎ *0736/41645* 🌐 *www.hotelpennile.it* 🛏 *33 rooms* 🍽 *Breakfast.*

SOUTHERN
ITALY

WHAT'S WHERE

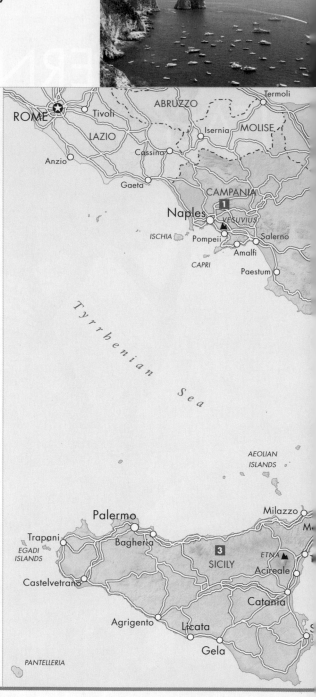

1 Naples and Campania.
Campania is the gateway to
southern Italy—and as far
south as many travelers get.
The region's happy combination of spectacular geology
and rich cultural heritage
makes it a wildly popular
place to unwind. Dream away
two magical weeks on the
pint-size islands of Capri and
Ischia and the fabled resorts—
Positano, Amalfi, Ravello—of
the Amalfi Coast. Or explore
the past at the archaeo-
logical ruins of Pompeii,
Herculaneum, and Paestum.
In the middle of everything is
Naples, a chaotic metropolis
that people love and hate
in nearly equal measure,
though after decades of
urban renewal the lovers now
appear to be in the majority.
On a good day it's Italy's most
fun and operatic city. On a
rare bad one it's a giant traffic
jam, filled with crooked cab-
bies and purse-snatching kids
on scooters.

2 The Southern Peninsula.
The southernmost regions
of the peninsula—Puglia,
Basilicata, and Calabria—are
known for their laid-back
medieval villages, shimmering
seas, and varied landscapes.
The coastline of Puglia, along
the heel of Italy's boot, is
popular with beachgoers, but
for the most part you're off
the beaten path here, with all

the pleasures and challenges that entails. You'll find fewer English-speakers but more genuine warmth from the people you encounter. The most distinctive attractions are the *Sassi* (cave dwellings in the Basilicata village of Matera) and *trulli* (mysterious conical-roof dwellings found in abundance in Puglia's Valle d'Itria). Both are UNESCO World Heritage sites.

3 Sicily. The architecture of Sicily reflects the island's centuries of successive dominion by the Greeks, Romans, Byzantines, Arabs, Normans, Spaniards, and, most recently, Italians. Baroque church–hopping could be a sport in the cacophonous streets of Palermo and seafaring Siracusa. The breezes are sultry, and everyday life is without pretense, as witnessed in the workaday stalls of the fish markets in ports all along the Tyrrhenian and Ionian coasts, bursting with tuna, swordfish, and sardines. Greek ruins stand sentinel in Agrigento's Valley of the Temples, blanketed in almond, oleander, and juniper blossoms. All over the island the ins and outs of life are celebrated each day as they have been for centuries—over a morning coffee, at the family lunch table, and in the evening *passeggiata* (stroll).

SOUTHERN ITALY PLANNER

Speaking the Language

Here, as in much of Italy, when locals talk among themselves, they often revert to dialect that's unintelligible to the student of textbook Italian. Each region has a dialect of its own; Salentinu (spoken in the tip of the heel) and Barese (around Bari) are distinctive enough to be considered separate languages, though they developed in neighboring areas.

Thanks to the education system and the unifying influence of radio and television, pretty much everyone speaks standard Italian as well, so you can still benefit from whatever knowledge you have of the language. English-speakers aren't as prevalent as in points north, but this is the land of creative gesticulation and other improvised nonverbal communication. Chances are, you'll be able to get your message across.

Getting Here

Aeroporto Capodichino (NAP), 8 km (5 miles) outside Naples, serves the Campania region. It handles domestic and international flights, including several flights daily between Naples and Rome (flight time 55 minutes).

The three main airports of the deep south are Bari and Brindisi, in Puglia, and Lamezia Terme, in Calabria. All three have regular flights to and from Rome and Milan. In addition, Reggio di Calabria's airport has flights to and from Rome.

Sicily can be reached from all major international cities on flights connecting through Rome, Milan, or Naples. Planes to Palermo land at **Aeroporto Falcone-Borsellino** (named in memory of two anti-Mafia judges famously assassinated in 1992) in Punta Raisi, 32 km (19 miles) west of town. Catania's **Aeroporto Fontanarossa**, 5 km (3 miles) south of the city center, is the main airport on Sicily's eastern side.

There are direct trains from Milan and Rome to Palermo, Catania, and Siracusa. The Rome-Palermo and Rome-Siracusa trips take around 12 hours. After Naples, the run is mostly along the coast, so try to book a window seat on the right if you're not on an overnight train. At Villa San Giovanni, in Calabria, the train is separated and loaded onto a ferryboat to cross the strait to Messina. Direct trains run from Milan, Rome, and Bologna to Bari and Lecce.

TYPICAL TRAVEL TIMES		
	Hours by Car	Hours by Train
Naples–Rome	2 hrs 30 min	1 hrs 30 min
Bari–Lecce	2 hrs	1 hr 45 min
Naples–Matera	4 hrs	6 hrs
Naples–Cosenza	4 hrs 15 min	4 hrs
Naples–Messina	7 hrs 15 min	5 hrs 30 min
Messina–Palermo	2 hrs 45 min	3 hrs
Messina–Siracusa	2 hrs	2 hrs 45 min
Siracusa–Palermo	3 hrs	4 hrs 15min
Palermo–Agrigento	2 hrs 45 min	2 hrs 05 min

When to Go

Spring: In April, May, and early June southern Italy is at its best. The weather is generally pleasant, and the fields are in full bloom. Easter is a busy time for most tourist destinations—if you're traveling then, you should have lodging reserved well ahead of time. By May the seawater is warm enough for swimming by American standards, but you can often have the beach to yourself, as Italians shy away until at least June.

Summer: Temperatures can be torrid in summer, making it a less than ideal time for a visit to the south. In Campania, Naples can feel like an inferno, the archaeological sites swarm with visitors, and the islands and Amalfi Coast resorts are similarly overrun. Even the otherwise perfect villages of the interior are too dazzlingly white for easy comfort from July to early September. If you seek a beach, whether on the mainland or in Sicily, keep in mind that during August all of Italy flocks to the shores. Even relatively isolated resorts can be overrun.

Fall: Visit the south from late September through early November and you can find gentle, warm weather and acres of beach space; swimming temperatures last through October. Watch the clock, however, as the days get shorter. At most archaeological sites you're rounded up two hours before sunset—but by then most crowds have departed, so late afternoon is still an optimum time to see Pompeii, Herculaneum, or Agrigento in peace and quiet.

Winter: Early winter is relatively mild (bougainvillea and other floral displays can bloom through Christmas), but, particularly later in the season, cold fronts can arrive and stay for days. In resort destinations many hotels, restaurants, and other tourist facilities close down from November until around Easter. Elsewhere, you need to reserve rooms well in advance between Christmas and Epiphany (January 6) and during Agrigento's almond festival in February and the Carnevale in Acireale and Sciacca.

On the Calendar

These are some of the top seasonal events in southern Italy:

From December through June, the **stagione operistica** (opera season) is underway at Teatro San Carlo in Naples.

In early February in Agrigento's Valley of the Temples, **Sagra del Mandorlo in Fiore** (Almond Blossom Festival, ⊕ *www.sagradelmandorlo.net*) is a week of folk music and dancing, with participants from many countries.

The **Settimana Santa** (Holy Week), culminating with Easter, features parades and outdoor events in every city and most small towns. Naples and Trapani have particularly noteworthy festivities.

Twice a year—the first Sunday in May and on September 19—Naples celebrates the **Feast of San Gennaro**. In the Duomo worshippers anxiously await the miraculous liquefaction of a remnant of the saint's blood, after which there's a ceremonial parade.

Maggio dei Monumenti is a cultural initiative in Naples lasting the entire month of May. Special exhibits, palaces, private collections, and churches are open to the public for free or at a discount.

Estate a Napoli (Summer in Naples) is a season-long festival of concerts and performances—a reward for those enduring the Neapolitan heat.

SOUTHERN ITALY
TOP ATTRACTIONS

Underground Naples

(A) In Naples the locals point to the ground and say there's another city underneath. This is *Napoli Sotterranea,* a netherworld of ancient Greek quarries and aqueducts, Roman streets, and World War II bomb shelters. Parts have been cleaned up and made accessible to the public. *(⇨ Chapter 13.)*

The Ruins around Vesuvius

(B) This may be the closest you'll ever get to time travel. Thanks to Vesuvius's blowing its top in AD 79, the towns round its base were carpeted in fallout and preserved for posterity. Allow a good half-day to look around bustling Pompeii or the more compact, less busy, and better preserved Herculaneum. For the best Roman frescoes, head to the Villa Oplontis between the two ancient cities. *(⇨ Chapter 13.)*

The Amalfi Coast

(C) One moment you're gazing out at a luxury sailcraft, the next you're dodging mules on precipitous footpaths. "Comforts of the 21st century in a medieval setting" just about sums up the remarkable Amalfi Coast. *(⇨ Chapter 13.)*

Matera's Sassi

You can see why Matera is a favorite with filmmakers shooting biblical scenes. You get that time-warp feeling especially in early morning or at night among the *Sassi*—buildings seemingly gouged out of the limestone cliffs. *(⇨ Chapter 14.)*

Lecce

(D) With its much-feted Baroque facades and extensive Roman remains in the city center, Lecce has a legitimate claim to being Puglia's fairest city. As an added bonus, nearby are a largely undeveloped coastline and the magical walled town of Otranto. *(⇨ Chapter 14.)*

Bronzi di Riace, Reggio di Calabria

(E) Few bronze statues have survived intact from the ancient Greek world. The presence of not one but two larger-than-life bronzes, restored to almost perfect condition, is reason enough to trek to Reggio di Calabria, on the eastern side of the Strait of Messina. (⇨ *Chapter 14.*)

Mt. Etna

(F) You can take the single-gauge railway around its foothills, splurge on an SUV experience near the summit, or just stroll across old lavafields on its northern flank. Alternatively, go down into the gorge of Alcantara and see what happens when lava flow meets mountain spring water. (⇨ *Chapter 15.*)

Palermo, Monreale, and Cefalù

When it comes to medieval mosaics and Norman cathedrals, Palermo and its environs are the envy of the world. Biblical scenes in the newly restored Palatine Chapel in Palermo shimmer in ripples of gold leaf, and nearby Monreale and Cefalù's cathedrals are replete with heavenly golden mosaics. (⇨ *Chapter 15.*)

Imperial Roman Villa, Piazza Armerina

(G) "Villa" doesn't begin to describe this opulent palace from the latter years of the Roman Empire. The stunning mosaics that fill every room are perhaps the best preserved and certainly the most extensive of the ancient Roman Empire. (⇨ *Chapter 15.*)

Duomo, Siracusa

(H) Few buildings encapsulate history better than the Duomo of Siracusa. The cathedral started life as a temple dedicated to the goddess Athena sometime in the early 5th century BC, as one glance at the majestic fluted columns inside confirms. (⇨ *Chapter 15.*)

TOP EXPERIENCES

Edenic Gardens

"What nature gives you makes you rich," they say in Campania. One look at Capri's perfectly tonsured palm trees, Sorrento's frangipani, and Amalfi's lemon trees laden with fruit, and you know that they mean. So it is not surprising to learn that one of the major joys of this region is the abundance of spectacular gardens. Many of the most celebrated were created by English "green thumbs," such as the Romantic, exotic eden created by Lord Grimthorpe at his Villa Cimbrone or the even larger horticultural extravaganza laid out by Sir Frances Neville Reid at the spectacular Villa Rufolo, both located in Ravello. From the Orto Botanico in Naples to the Villa San Michele in Capri, Campania's gardens are *incomparabilo.*

Pasticceria Siciliana

Cannolo, setteveli, cartoccio, cassata, and diminutive *cassatina*: it sounds like the list of characters from an opera, but these ricotta-filled delights can be found in any self-respecting *pasticceria* (pastry shop) on the island of Sicily. The top performers cluster around Palermo and Catania: Massaro and Cappello, both a short walk from Palermo's Porta Nuova, have been delighting palates for more than a century, while Savia's pedigree in Catania stretches even farther back. The secret lies in the freshness and simplicity of the ricotta made from the whey of ultrafresh sheep or goat's milk, and, depending on the recipe, studded with chocolate chips, liqueur, or candied fruit.

Fiery Landscapes

Volcanoes have long fascinated people on the move. The ancient Greeks—among the first sailors around the central Mediterranean—explained away Etna as the place where the god Hephaestus had his workshop. Millennia later, northern European visitors to Naples in the 18th and 19th centuries would climb the erupting Vesuvius or cross the steaming craters of the Campi Flegrei west of the city. Farther south, in the Aeolian Islands northeast of Sicily, Stromboli performs a lightshow about every 20 minutes, ejecting incandescent cinder, lapilli, and lava bombs high into the air. To add to the fascination, several of the Aeolian Islands rise sheer out of the Mediterranean, and beaches are black with volcanic fallout. Though stripped of their mythology by generations of geologists and deprived by local authorities of even a frisson of risk, Italy's volcanoes are still a terrific crowd-puller.

The Great Summer Performances

Exploiting its Mediterranean climate and atmospheric venues, the south of Italy lays on an impressive range of cultural events during those hot summer months. The ancient theaters of Segesta, Siracusa, and Taormina in Sicily are used for anything from Greek plays to pop concerts, while in Campania the Greek temples at Paestum serve as a scenic backdrop for opera and symphonic music. The 18th-century villas near Herculaneum at the foot of Vesuvius have also joined the musical act in recent years. With time (and money), head across the bay to Capri for a sunset concert at Villa San Michele. For the most gorgeous setting, head to sky-high Ravello, the village on the Amalfi Coast that is nicknamed La Bellissima, "the most beautiful" town in the country. Here, at the Villa Rufolo (immortalized as Klingsor's Garden in Wagner's *Parsifal*) is the Ravello Music Festival (☎ 089/858422 ⊕ *www.ravellofestival.com*), concerts are held on a breathtaking terrace set over a Cinerama vista of the bluer-than-blue Bay of Salerno.

SOUTHERN ITALY TODAY

. . . is losing its distinctive character

First put on the map by 19th-century Grand Tour travelers, the Amalfi Coast has recently come under assault by international hotel chains. One by one, its richly atmospheric hotels, veritable time machines that offer sepia-toned dreams of the past, have given way to grotesque face-lifts, all in the name of progress. This is especially tragic in that last outpost of old-world refinement, Ravello.

First, the Palazzo Sasso was Las Vegasized by Richard Branson with the addition of hot tubs on the roof, glass elevators, and roaring fountains with Playboy Mansion statuary. Then the Orient-Express luxury chain eviscerated the magical Hotel Caruso-Belvedere, trading its antiques and lace-trimmed ambience for dreary rattan sofas seen from Kansas to Katmandu, beige-on-beige cocktail lounges, and, almost prosecutable, destroying the fabled medieval Belvedere Window, seen on 1,001 travel posters, by encasing it alive within a plastic Lucite wall.

Next up was the Hotel Cappuccini Convento in Amalfi, which once delighted Longfellow and Wagner, dukes and duchesses. Now, modern furniture, art, and supermodern facilities have displaced the royal sense of civility this hotel used to have. Happily, however, they have left untouched much of the historic magic of this place.

There may still be some hotels left on the Costiera Divina that retain the patina of the past—but hurry!

. . . has its economic ups and downs

While the north has developed relatively rapidly in the past 50 years, the entrepreneurial spirit in the south struggles to make good. Despite a pool of relatively cheap, willing labor, foreign investment across the entire south is merely one tenth of that going to Lombardy alone. The discrepancy can be attributed in large part to the stifling presence of organized crime. Each major region has its own criminal association: in Naples, it's the Camorra. The system creates add-on costs at many levels, especially in retail.

It's not all bad news though. Southern Italy has woken up to its major asset, its remarkable cultural and natural heritage. UNESCO lists 13 World Heritage Sites in southern Italy alone, while the last decade has seen the creation of several national parks, marine parks, and regional nature preserves. Environmental and cultural associations have mushroomed as locals increasingly perceive the importance of preserving across the generations. In general, the small average farm size in the south has helped preserve a pleasing mosaic of habitats in the interior.

. . . is attracting visitors

Tourism is on the rise in Puglia and Basilicata, while Campania—traditionally the biggest tourist region—has had some adversity, largely due to the black eye of sanitation problems in Naples, now fortunately no longer an issue. Sicily still pulls nature lovers and adventure seekers who cycle or hike its rugged terrain, and Calabria remains largely a beach holiday destination crowded only from mid-July through August. Religious tourism accounts for large visitor flows throughout the year—as many visitors pay their respects to the Madonna di Pompei sanctuary as they do to the archaeological site up the road. In almost every village in southern Italy you're likely to see the bearded statue of Capuchin priest Padre Pio.

A GREAT ITINERARY

Day 1: Naples
Fly into Naples's Aeroporto Capodichino, a scant 8 km (5 miles) from the
city. Naples is rough around the edges and
may be a bit jarring if you're a first-time
visitor, but it's classic Italy, and most visitors end up falling in love with the city's
alluring palazzi and spectacular pizza.

First things first, though: recharge with a
nap and, after that, a good caffè—Naples
has some of the world's best. Revive in
time for an evening stroll down Naples's
wonderful shopping street, Via Toledo, to
Piazza Plebescito, before dinner and bed.

Logistics: Under no circumstances should
you rent a car for Naples. Take a taxi
from the airport—it's not far, or overly
expensive—and you should face few logis-
tical obstacles on your first day in Italy.

Day 2: Naples
Start the day at the Museo Archaeologico Nazionale, budgeting at least two
hours for the collection. Then take Via
Santa Maria di Costantinopoli and grab
a coffee at one of the outdoor cafés in
Piazza Bellini. From here, head down Via
dei Tribunali for a pizza at I Decumani
or Di Matteo. Continue along Tribunali
to Via del Duomo for a visit to the city's
cathedral. From Via del Duomo, turn
right onto Spaccanapoli, turning off for a
brief stop at the Cappella Sansevero for a
look at the pinnacle of Masonic sculpture
before heading to Piazza del Gesù and the
churches of Il Gesù Nuovo and Santa Chiara. Walk downhill, and turn left to follow Via Monteoliveto and Via Medina
to the harbor and the Castel Nuovo;
then head past the Teatro San Carlo to
the enormous Palazzo Reale. Walk 15
minutes south to the Castel dell'Ovo in
the Santa Lucia waterfront area, one of
Naples's most charming neighborhoods.

Then it's back up to Via Caracciolo and
the Villa Comunale, before heading back
to your hotel for a short rest before dinner
and perhaps a night out at one of Naples's
lively bars or clubs.

Logistics: This entire day is easily done on
foot.

Day 3: Pompeii/Sorrento
After breakfast, pack your luggage and
head from Naples to Pompeii, one of the
true archaeological gems of Europe. If it's
summer, be prepared for an onslaught of
sweltering heat as you make your way
through the incredibly preserved ruins of
a city that was devastated by the whims
of Mt. Vesuvius nearly 2,000 years ago.
You'll see the houses of noblemen and
merchants, brothels, political graffiti, and
more. From Pompeii, it's on to Sorrento,
your first taste of the wonderful peninsula
that marks the beginning of the fabled
Amalfi Coast. Sorrento is touristy, but it
may well be the Italian city of your imagination: cliff-hanging, cobblestone-paved,
and graced with an infinite variety of fishing ports and coastal views. There, have
a relaxing dinner of fish and white wine
before calling it a day.

Logistics: Naples to Pompeii by car is all
about the A3: a short 24 km (15 miles)
brings you to this archaeological gem.
From Pompeii it's a short ride back on
the A3 until the exit for Sorrento; from
the exit, you'll take the SS145 to reach
Sorrento. Most people choose the easier
option of the Circumvesuviana, a twice-
hourly train to Sorrento, stopping at Pompeii's Villa dei Misteri.

Day 4: Positano/Ravello
Your stay in Sorrento will be short, as
there's much of the Amalfi Coast still to
see: Positano, your next stop, is a must.
It's one of the most-visited towns in Italy

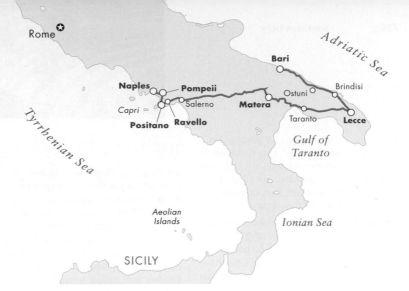

for good reason: its blue-green seas, stairs "as steep as ladders," and white Moorish-style houses make for a truly memorable setting. Walk, gaze, and eat (lunch), before heading on to the less traveled, even loftier town of Ravello, your Amalfi Coast dream come true, an aerie that's "closer to the sky than the sea." Don't miss the Duomo, Villa Rufolo, or Villa Cimbrone before settling in for a dinner in the sky.

Logistics: Sorrento to Positano is a 30-km (19-mile) jaunt, but the winding roads will draw it out for the better part of an hour—a scenic hour. From Positano, Ravello is another slow 18 km (11 miles) to the east, perched high above the rest of the world. The SITA bus is your best option; motorists should be prepared to use low gears if driving a stick shift (as they almost surely will be).

Day 5: Matera

Those with a car will have a bit of a drive to get to Basilicata from the Amalfi Coast; leaving Campania and entering Basilicata is generally a lonely experience. Little-traveled roads, wild hills, and distant farms are the hallmarks of this province, which produces deep, dark aglianico wines and has perfected the art of peasant food. You'll spend a while in your car to make it to Matera, a beautiful,

ancient city full of Paleolithic *Sassi* (cave-like dwellings hewn out of rock)—but it's worth it. Traversing the city is like taking a voyage through time. Spend the afternoon exploring the Sassi, but take care not to miss the new part of the city, too. Then enjoy a relaxing dinner at one of Matera's excellent restaurants.

Logistics: It's a long haul from your starting point, Ravello, to Matera—if using public transportation you may find it easier to return first to Naples—but the effort is worth it, as Basilicata's landscape is so pretty. Once in Matera, if staying in the Sassi, motorists should get extra-detailed driving and parking instructions from the hotel beforehand—navigating through thousand-year-old alleyways can be challenging.

Day 6: Lecce

This drive will take a good 2½ hours, so get an early start. Those without a car should return to Bari, then take the train south. The Baroque city of Lecce will mark your introduction to Puglia, the heel of Italy's boot. It's one of Italy's best-kept secrets, as you'll soon find out upon checking out the spectacular church of Santa Croce, the ornate Duomo, and the harmonious Piazza Sant'Oronzo. The shopping is great, the food is great, and

the evening passeggiata is great. Don't miss the opportunity, if you wind up at a bar or café in the evening, to chat with Lecce's friendly residents—unfazed by tourism, the welcoming Leccesi represent southern Italians at their best.

Logistics: It's not far from Matera to Lecce as the crow flies, but the trip is more involved than you might think; patience is required. The best route is via Taranto—don't make the mistake of going up through Bari.

Day 7: Bari

The trip from Lecce to Bari is a short one. Check into the pleasant Palace Hotel and spend the morning and afternoon wandering through Bari's *centro storico* (historic center). The wide-open doors of the town's humble houses and apartments, with bickering families and grandmothers drying their pasta in the afternoon sun, will give you a taste of the true flavor of Italy's deep south. Don't miss Bari's castle and the walk around the ridge of the ancient city walls, with views of wide-open sea at every turn. Finish the day with a good fish dinner, and celebrate your last night in Italy by checking out one of the city's multitude of lively bars—Bari boasts some of southern Italy's most hopping nightlife.

Logistics: This is one of your most straight-forward, if not quickest, connections: a direct train or the coastal S16 for 154 km (95 miles) until you hit Bari. The road is a two-lane highway, though, so don't be surprised if the trip takes two hours or more. If you get tired, beautiful Ostuni (dubbed the *città bianca*, or the "white city") is a perfect hilltop pit stop half-way there.

TIPS

Alitalia usually doesn't mark up open-jaw trips, but EasyJet (⊕ *www.easyjet.com*) has inexpensive domestic air service and operates Milan (Malpensa)–Naples, London (Gatwick and Stanstead)—Naples, and Bari–Milan (Malpensa) routes. Blu-Express (⊕ *www.blu-express.com*) flies from Rome (Fiumicino) to Palermo, Catania, Reggio Calabria and Lamezia Terme. If you can find a cheap round-trip fare from your home to Milan plus those two flights on low-cost carriers, you might save some money.

Also look at low-cost carriers that shuttle passengers between London and southern Italy; you can often save the most money of all by combining two such one-way fares with a round-trip discount fare to London; however, beware of inconvenient connections in London (Luton, for example).

Day 8: Bari/Departure

Bad news: This is your wake-up-and-leave day. Bari's Aeroporto Palese is small but quite serviceable. Exploit its absence of crowds and easy access and use it as your way out of Italy. Connections through Rome or Milan are more frequent than you might think. Plan on leaving with southern Italy firmly established in your heart as the best way to see the Italy that once was—and be thankful that you were able to see it while it's still like this.

Logistics: Bari hotels offer easy airport transfers; take advantage of them. There are also regular public transportation connections between the central train station and the airport. Return your rental car at the Bari airport; you won't have to arrive at the airport more than an hour or so before your flight.

NAPLES AND CAMPANIA

WELCOME TO NAPLES AND CAMPANIA

TOP REASONS TO GO

★ **Naples, Italy's most operatic city:** Walk through the energy, chaos, and beauty that is Spaccanapoli, the city's historic district, and you'll create an unforgettable memory.

★ **Exploring Pompeii:** The excavated ruins of Pompeii offer a unique, occasionally spooky glimpse into everyday life—and sudden death—in Roman times.

★ **"The Living Room of the World":** Pose oh-so-casually with the beautiful people on La Piazzetta, the central crossroads of Capri—a stage-set square that always seems ready for a gala performance.

★ **Ravishing Ravello:** High above the Amalfi Coast, this place is a contender for the title of most beautiful village in the world.

★ **A world made of stairs:** Built like a vertical amphitheater, Positano may very well be the best triathlon training ground imaginable. The town's only job is to look enchanting—and it does that very well.

1 Naples. Italy's third-largest city is densely packed with people, cafés, pizzerias, and an amazing number of Norman and Baroque churches.

2 Herculaneum, Vesuvius, and Pompeii. Two towns show you through their excavated ruins how ancient Romans lived the good life—until, one day in AD 79, Mt. Vesuvius buried them in volcanic ash and lava.

3 Procida and Ischia. Though they lack Capri's glitz, these two sister islands in the Bay of Naples share a laid-back charm.

4 Capri. The rocky island mixes natural beauty and *dolce vita* glamour.

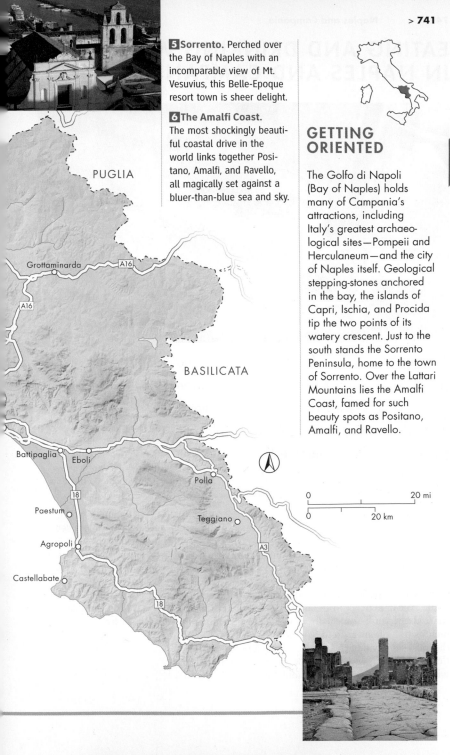

5 **Sorrento.** Perched over the Bay of Naples with an incomparable view of Mt. Vesuvius, this Belle-Epoque resort town is sheer delight.

6 **The Amalfi Coast.** The most shockingly beautiful coastal drive in the world links together Positano, Amalfi, and Ravello, all magically set against a bluer-than-blue sea and sky.

GETTING ORIENTED

13

The Golfo di Napoli (Bay of Naples) holds many of Campania's attractions, including Italy's greatest archaeological sites—Pompeii and Herculaneum—and the city of Naples itself. Geological stepping-stones anchored in the bay, the islands of Capri, Ischia, and Procida tip the two points of its watery crescent. Just to the south stands the Sorrento Peninsula, home to the town of Sorrento. Over the Lattari Mountains lies the Amalfi Coast, famed for such beauty spots as Positano, Amalfi, and Ravello.

PUGLIA

Grottaminarda   A16

A16

BASILICATA

Battipaglia   Eboli

Polla

18

Paestum

Teggiano

Agropoli   A3

Castellabate

18

0   20 mi
0   20 km

EATING AND DRINKING WELL IN NAPLES AND CAMPANIA

A TIPPING TIP

Neapolitans are easily recognized in bars elsewhere in Italy by the tip they leave on the counter when ordering. This habit does not necessarily ensure better service in bars in Naples, notorious for their fairly offhand staff, but you do blend in better with the locals.

In restaurants, a service charge is often included (alternatively 5%–10% is reasonable). In pizzerias, tips are given less often unless you've splurged on side dishes or sweets, or have had particularly good service.

Think of Neapolitan food and you conjure up pasta, pizza, and tomatoes. The stereotype barely scratches the surface of what's available in Naples—to say nothing of the rest of Campania, where the cuisine reflects an enormously diverse landscape.

The region is known for its enclaves of gastronomy, notable among them the tip of the Sorrento Peninsula and the Campi Flegrei, west of Naples. You may well come across *cucina povera,* a cuisine inspired by Campania's *contadino* (peasant) roots, with all the ingredients sourced from a nearby garden. Expect to see roadside stalls selling stellar local produce, including *annurca* apples (near Benevento), giant lemons (Amalfi Coast), roasted chestnuts (especially near Avellino), and watermelons (the plains around Salerno). Try to get to one of the local *sagre* village feasts celebrating a *prodotto tipico* (local specialty), which could be anything from snails to wild boar to cherries to, commonly, wine.

13

PIZZA

Naples is the undisputed homeland of pizza, and you'll usually encounter it here in two classic forms: *margherita* and *marinara*. Given the larger-than-your-plate proportions of standard pizzas some choose to ask for a *mignon* (kids' portion), or even share, divided on two plates. Take-away outlets in most town centers sell pizza by the slice, along with the usual range of fried *arancini* (rice balls) and *crocchè di patate* (potato fritters).

COFFEE

Given the same basic ingredients—coffee grounds, water, a machine—what makes *caffè* taste so much better in Naples than elsewhere remains a mystery. If you find the end product too strong, ask to have it with a dash of milk (*caffè macchiato*) or a little diluted (*caffè lungo*). Many bars serve with sugar already added, so if you want it without, request *senza zucchero* or *amaro*.

BUFFALO

Long feted for the melt-in-your-mouth mozzarella cheese (*pictured at right*) made from its milk, the river buffalo—related to the Asian water buffalo—is also the source of other culinary delights. Throughout the region, look for buffalo ricotta and mascarpone, as well as buffalo *provola* and *scamorza*, which may be lightly smoked (resulting in a golden crust). Caserta has more

mature *nero di bufala* (aged like sheep's cheese), while around Salerno you'll find smoked *caciocavallo* cheese as well as *carne di bufala* (buffalo meat), which can be braised to perfection.

THE ORAL TRADITION

Locals in Campania like to bypass the restaurant menu and ask what the staff recommends. Take this approach and you'll often wind up with a daily special or house specialty. Though you're unlikely to get multilingual staff outside the larger hotels and main tourist areas, the person you talk to will spare no effort to get the message across.

WINE

Wine in Campania has an ancient pedigree. Some say fancifully that Campania's undisputed king of reds, the aglianico varietal, got its name from the word "Hellenic"; and fiano, the primary white grape, closely resembles the Roman variety apianus. Horace, the Latin poet, extolled the virtues of drinking wine from Campania. A century later, Pliny the Elder was harsher in his judgment: wine from Pompeii would give you a hangover until noon the next day, and Sorrento wine tasted of vinegar.

In recent decades though, Campania has gained respect for its boutique reds. Due to the rugged landscape, small farms, and limited mechanization, prices can be relatively high, but the quality is high as well.

Updated
by Fergal
Kavanagh

A kinetic gust of 3-D garlic-and-basil aromatherapy, Campania is a destination that no one ever forgets. More travelers visit this region than any other in Italy's South, and it's no wonder. An area of evocative names—Capri, Sorrento, Pompeii, Positano, Amalfi—Campania conjures up visions of cliff-shaded, sapphire-hue coves, sundappled waters, and mighty ruins.

Home to Vesuvius, the area's unique geology is responsible for Campania's photogenic landscape. A spectacular coastline stretches out along a deep blue sea, punctuated by rocky islands.

Through the ages, the area's temperate climate, warm sea, fertile soil, and natural beauty have attracted Greek colonists, then Roman emperors—who called the region Campania Felix ("the happy land")—and later Saracen raiders and Spanish invaders. The result has been a rich and varied history, reflected in everything from architecture to mythology. The highlights span millennia: the near-intact Roman towns of Pompeii and Herculaneum, the Greek temples in Paestum, the Norman and Baroque churches in Naples, the white-dome fisherman's houses of Positano, the dolce vita resorts of Capri. Campania piles them all onto one mammoth must-see sandwich.

The region's complex identity is most intensely felt in its major metropolis, Naples. Exasperating both critics and defenders, Napoli is lush, chaotic, scary, funny, confounding, intoxicating, and very beautiful. Few who visit remain ambivalent. You needn't participate in the mad whirl of the city, however. The best pastime in Campania is simply finding a spot with a stunning view and indulging in *"il dolce far niente"* ("the sweetness of doing nothing").

NAPLES AND CAMPANIA PLANNER

MAKING THE MOST OF YOUR TIME

In Campania there are three primary travel experiences: Naples, with its restless exuberance; the resorts (Capri, Sorrento, the Amalfi Coast), dedicated to leisure and indulgence; and the archaeological sights (Pompeii, Herculaneum, Paestum), where the ancient world is frozen in time. Each is wonderful in its own way. If you have a week, you can get a good taste of all three. With less time, you're better off choosing between them rather than stretching yourself thin.

Pompeii, being a day trip, is the simplest to plan for. To get a feel for Naples, you should give it a couple of days at a minimum. The train station makes a harsh first impression (a recent overhaul softens the blow), but the city grows on you as you take in the sights and interact with the locals.

That said, many people bypass Naples and head right for the resorts. These places are all about relaxing—you'll miss the point if you're in a rush. Though Sorrento isn't as spectacular as Positano or Capri, it makes a good base because of its central location.

THE CAMPANIA ARTECARD

A big boon for museum lovers, this pass offers free or discounted admission to almost 50 museums and monuments over a three- or seven-consecutive-day period for the city or the whole region, plus discounted services ranging from audio guides to theater tickets and parking lots.

The benefits depend on the pass: a three-day version (€27) gets you free entry to the first two sites you visit, half-price entry for the others, and free transportation—including the Alibus from the airport. The main passes are: Naples historic center, €12 (access to four sites); Naples and Campi Flegrei, €16; Naples and Caserta, €20; and Archeologia del Golfo including Pompeii, Herculaneum, Caserta, and Paestum, €30 (access to 12 sites). In addition, there are generous youth discounts. As sites and discounts are frequently updated, check ⊕ *www. campaniartecard.it* for the latest details. Cards are available at all major participating museums and archaeological sites, at main city hotels, as well as at the airport and train station.

GETTING HERE AND AROUND

BOAT TRAVEL

Several companies offer a variety of fast craft and passenger and car ferries connecting the islands of Capri, Ischia, and Procida with Naples and Pozzuoli year-round. Hydrofoils and other fast craft leave from Naples's Molo Beverello, adjacent to Piazza Municipio, and also from Mergellina, about 1½ km (1 mile) west of Piazza Municipio. Slower car ferries leave from the more inaccessible berths at Calata Porta di Massa, a 10-minute walk east of Molo Beverello.

Information on departures is published every day in the local paper, *Il Mattino*. Alternatively, ask at the tourist office or at the port, or contact these companies directly. Always double-check schedules in stormy weather.

Contacts **Alilauro** ☎ 081/5513236 ⊕ www.alilauro.it. **Caremar**
☎ 081/5513882 ⊕ www.caremar.it. **Navigazione Libera del Golfo** (*NLG*).
☎ 081/5520763 ⊕ www.navlib.it. **SNAV** ☎ 081/4285555 ⊕ www.snav.it.

BUS TRAVEL

Within Campania there's an extensive network of local buses, although finding information about it can be trying.

SITA buses. Buses bound for Salerno leave every 30 minutes between 6 am and 9 pm, Monday through Saturday, from its terminal in the port near the Stazione Marittima. There are also four departures from the airport. There are no services on Sunday. SITA buses also serve the Amalfi Coast, connecting Sorrento with Salerno. ☎ 089/405145 ⊕ www.sitasudtrasporti.it.

CAR TRAVEL

You can get along fine without a car in Campania, and there are plenty of reasons not to have one. Much of Naples is pedestrianized, meaning motorized arteries are often bottlenecked; you can't bring a car to Capri (except in winter, when everything's closed); and parking in the towns of the Amalfi Coast is hard to come by and expensive.

Italy's main north–south route, the A1 (also known as the Autostrada del Sole), connects Rome with Naples and Campania. In good traffic the drive to Naples takes a little more than two hours. Autostrada A3, a somewhat perilous continuation of the A1, runs south from Naples through Campania and into Calabria. Herculaneum (Ercolano) and Pompeii (Pompei) both have marked exits off the A3. For Vesuvius, take the Ercolano exit. For the Sorrento Peninsula and the Amalfi Coast, exit at Castellammare di Stabia. To get to Paestum, take the A3 to the Battipaglia exit and follow the road to Capaccio Scalo–Paestum. Roads on the Sorrento Peninsula and Amalfi Coast are narrow and twisting, but they have outstanding views.

If you come to Naples by car, find a garage, agree on the cost, and leave it there for the duration of your stay. (If you park on the street, you run the risk of theft.)

Contacts **Garage Cava** ✉ Via Mergellina 6, Naples ☎ 081/660023 ⊘ 24 hrs. **Grilli** ✉ Hotel Ramada, Via Ferraris 40, near Stazione Centrale, Naples ☎ 081/264344 ⊘ 6 am–midnight. **Turistico** ✉ Via de Gasperi 14, near port, Naples ☎ 081/5525442 ⊘ 6:30 am–midnight.

TRAIN TRAVEL

There are up to three trains every hour between Rome and Naples. Both the Alta Velocità Freccia Rossa and Italo trains (the fastest types of train service) makes the trip in a little more than an hour, with the Intercity taking two. All trains to Naples stop at the newly refurbished Stazione Centrale.

The efficient (though run-down) suburban Circumvesuviana runs from Naples's Stazione Circumvesuviana and stops at Stazione Centrale before continuing to Herculaneum, Pompeii, and Sorrento. Travel time between Naples and Sorrento on the Circumvesuviana line is about 75 minutes.

For ticketing purposes, the region is divided into travel zones depending on distance from Naples. A Fascia 2 ticket (€2.10 for 120 minutes) takes you to Herculaneum, Fascia 3 (€2.80 for 140 minutes) includes Pompeii, and Fascia 5 (€4 for 180 minutes) covers trips to Sorrento. If you're traveling from Naples to anywhere else in Campania, there's no need to buy a separate ticket for your subway, tram, or bus ride to the train station. Your train ticket covers the whole journey.

Contacts Circumvesuviana ☏ *081/7722444, 800/211388 toll-free* ⊕ *www.vesuviana.it.* **Stazione Centrale** ✉ *Piazza Garibaldi, Naples* ☏ *892021* ⊕ *www.trenitalia.com, www.italotreno.it.*

13

PUBLIC TRANSIT IN NAPLES

Naples's rather old Metropolitana (subway system), also called Linea 2, provides fairly frequent service and can be the fastest way to get across the traffic-clogged city.

The other, continually expanding, urban subway system, Metropolitana Collinare (or Linea 1), links the hill area of the Vomero and beyond with the National Archaeological Museum and Via Toledo. Many of the stations are also mini–art galleries. Trains on both lines run from 6 am until 10:30 pm.

For standard public transit—including the subways, buses, and funiculars—an UnicoNapoli costs €1.30 and is valid for 90 minutes as far as Pozzuoli to the west and Portici to the east; €3.70 buys a *biglietto giornaliero,* good for the whole day (€3.10 on weekends).

Bus travel has become viable over the last few years, especially with the introduction of larger buses on regular routes. Electronic signs display wait times at many stops.

TAXI TRAVEL

When taking a taxi in Naples, make sure that the meter is switched on at the start of your trip. Trips around the city are unlikely to cost less than €6 or more than €20. Set fares for various destinations within the city should be displayed in the taxi—for instance, in accordance with the new taxi tariff, you should pay €6 for travel between the *centro storico* (historic center) and the train station. You need to establish this before the trip begins. Extra charges for things like baggage and night service should also be displayed. For trips outside the city, negotiate your fare before getting in. Watch out for overcharging at three locations: the airport, the railway station, and the hydrofoil marina. And in peak summer weeks, don't forget that many cabs in Naples have no air-conditioning—which the city's buses and metro do have—so you can practically bake if caught in one during a half-hour traffic jam.

RESTAURANTS

Please note that restaurant prices listed as "average meal" include a meal consisting of first course *(primo),* second course *(secondo),* and dessert *(dolce).*

HOTELS

Most parts of Campania have accommodations in all price categories, but they tend to fill up in high season, so reserve well in advance. In summer, on the coast and the islands, hotels that serve meals often require you to take half board.

Hotel reviews have been condensed for this book. Please go to Fodors. com for full reviews of each property.

TOURS

Centro di Accoglienza Turistica Museo Aperto Napoli. A welcome center in the old town, the Centro di Accoglienza Turistica Museo Aperto Napoli, offers €6 audio guides you can listen to as you wander around. It's based in the Museo Diocesano. ✉ *Largo Donnaregina, Naples* ☎ *081/5571365* ⊕ *www.museoapertonapoli.it.*

City Sightseeing. Close to the port, beside the main entrance to Castel Nuovo, is the terminal for double-decker buses belonging to City Sightseeing. For €22 you can take four different excursions, giving you reasonable coverage of the downtown sights and outlying attractions like the Museo di Capodimonte. ✉ *Piazza Municipio, Naples* ☎ *081/5517279* ⊕ *www.napoli.city-sightseeing.it.*

NAPLES

"Built like a great amphitheater around her beautiful bay, Naples is an eternally unfolding play acted by a million of the best actors in the world," Herbert Kubly observed in his *American in Italy.* "The comedy is broad, the tragedy violent. The curtain never rings down." Is it a sense of doom from living in the shadow of Vesuvius that makes some Neapolitans so volatile, so blind to everything but the pain or pleasure of the moment?

A huge zest for living and crowded conditions are the more probable causes. But whatever the reason, Naples remains the most vibrant city in Italy—a steaming, bubbling, reverberating minestrone in which each block is a small village, every street the setting for a Punch-and-Judy show, and everything seems to be a backdrop for an opera not yet composed.

It's said that northern Italians vacation here to remind themselves of the time when Italy was *molto Italiana*—really Italian. In this respect, Naples—Napoli in Italian—doesn't disappoint: Neapolitan rainbows of laundry wave in the wind over alleyways open-windowed with friendliness; mothers caress children; men break out into impromptu arias at sidewalk cafés; and street scenes offer Fellini-esque slices of life. Nowhere is this more apparent than in the Spaccanapoli district, everywhere contrasting elements of faded gilt and romance, rust and calamity, grandeur and squalor form a pageant of pure *Italianità*—Italy at its most Italian.

In most of the city you need a good sense of humor and a firm grip on your pocketbook and camera. Expect to do a lot of walking (take care crossing the chaotic streets); buses are crowded, and taxis often get held up in traffic. Use the funiculars or the metro Line 1 to get up and down the hills, and take the quick—but erratic—metro Line 2 (the city's older subway system) when crossing the city between Piazza Garibaldi and Pozzuoli.

CAMPANIA THROUGH THE AGES

Ancient History. Lying on Mediterranean trade routes plied by several pre-Hellenic civilizations, Campania was settled by the ancient Greeks from approximately 800 BC onward. Here myth and legend blend with historical fact. The town of Herculaneum is said—rather improbably—to have been established by Hercules himself; and Naples in ancient times was called Parthenope, the name attributed to one of the sirens who preyed on hapless sailors in antiquity.

Thanks to archaeological research, some of the layers of myth have been stripped away to reveal a pattern of occupation and settlement well before Rome became established. Greek civilization flourished for hundreds of years all along this coastline, but there was nothing in the way of centralized government until centuries later when the Roman Republic, uniting all Italy for the first time, absorbed the Greek colonies with little opposition. Generally, the peace of Campania was undisturbed during these centuries of Roman rule.

Foreign Influences. Naples and Campania, like Italy in general, decayed with the Roman Empire and collapsed into the abyss of the Middle Ages. Naples itself regained some importance under the rule of the Angevins in the latter part of the 13th century and continued its progress in the 1440s under Aragonese rule. The nobles who served under the Spanish viceroys in the 16th and 17th centuries enjoyed their pleasures, even as Spain milked the area for taxes.

After a short Austrian occupation, Naples became the capital of the Kingdom of the Two Sicilies, which the Bourbon kings established in 1738. Their rule was generally benevolent as far as Campania was concerned, and their support of papal authority in Rome was important in the development of the country as a whole. Their rule was important artistically, too, contributing to the architecture of the region, and attracting great musicians, artists, and writers who were drawn by the easy life at court. Finally, Giuseppe Garibaldi launched his famous expedition, and in 1860 Naples was united with the rest of Italy.

Modern Times. Things were relatively tranquil through the years that followed—with visitors thronging to Capri, Sorrento, Amalfi, and, of course, Naples—until World War II. Allied bombings did considerable damage in and around Naples. At the fall of the fascist government, the sorely tried Neapolitans rose up against Nazi occupation troops and in four days of street fighting drove them out of the city. A monument was raised to the *scugnizzo* (the typical Neapolitan street urchin), celebrating the youngsters who participated in the battle. With the end of the war, artists, tourists, writers, and other lovers of beauty returned to the Campania region.

As time passed, some parts gained increased attention from knowing visitors, while others lost the cachet they once had. Years of misgovernment have left their mark, yet the region's cultural and natural heritage is finally being revalued as local authorities and inhabitants recognize the importance the area's largest industry, tourism.

13

EXPLORING

ROYAL NAPLES

Naples hasn't been a capital for more than 150 years, but it still prides itself on its royal heritage. Most of the modern center of the town owes its look and feel to various members of the Bourbon family, who built their palaces and castles in this area. Allow plenty of time for museum visits; the views of the bay from the Castel dell'Ovo (good at any time) are especially fine at sunset.

TOP ATTRACTIONS

Castel dell'Ovo. Dangling over the Porto Santa Lucia on a thin promontory, this 12th-century fortress built atop the ruins of an ancient Roman villa overlooks the whole harbor—proof, if you need it, that the Romans knew a premium location when they saw one. For the same reason, some of the city's top hotels share this site. Walk up onto the rooftop Sala della Terrazze for a postcard-come-true view of Capri. Then, as the odd car honk drifts across from inland, use the tiled map to identify the sights of the city and maybe plot an itinerary for the rest of the day. It's a peaceful spot for strolling and enjoying the views. ⊠ *Via Partenope, Santa Lucia waterfront* ☎ *081/7956180* ☞ *Free* ⊙ *Mon.– Sat. 9–7:30; Sun. 9–2.*

Castel Nuovo. Known to locals as Maschio Angioino, in reference to its Angevin builders, this imposing castle is now used more for marital than military purposes—a portion of it serves as a government registry office. Its looming Angevin stonework is upstaged by a white four-tiered triumphal entrance arch, ordered by Alfonso of Aragon after he entered the city in 1443 to seize power from the increasingly beleaguered Angevin Giovanna II. At the arch's top, as if justifying Alfonso's claim to the throne, the Archangel Gabriel slays a demon.

Across the courtyard within the castle is the Sala Grande, also known as the Sala dei Baroni, which has a stunning vaulted ceiling 92 feet high. In 1486 local barons hatched a plot against Alfonso's son, King Ferrante, who reacted by inviting them to this hall for a wedding banquet, which promptly turned into a mass arrest. (Ferrante is said to have kept a crocodile in the castle as his special executioner, too.) You can also visit the Sala dell'Armeria, where a glass floor reveals recent excavations of Roman baths from the Augustan period. In the next room on the left, the Cappella Palatina, look on the frescoed walls for Nicolo di Tomaso's painting of Robert Anjou, one of the first realistic portraits ever.

The castle's first floor holds a small gallery that includes a beautiful early Renaissance Adoration of the Magi by Marco Cardisco, with the roles of the three Magi played by the three Aragonese kings: Ferrante I, Ferrante II, and Charles V. ⊠ *Piazza Municipio, Toledo* ☎ *081/7955877* ☞ *€5* ⊙ *Mon.–Sat. 9–7* Ⓜ *Toledo (under construction: Piazza Municipio).*

Gallerie di Palazzo Zevallos Stigliano. Tucked inside this beautifully restored palazzo, which houses the Banca Intesa San Paolo (one of Italy's major banks), is a small museum that's worth seeking out. Enter the bank through Cosimo Fanzago's gargoyled doorway and take the handsome elevator to the upper floor. The first room to the left holds the star attraction, Caravaggio's last work, *The Martyrdom of Saint Ursula.* The saint here is, for dramatic effect, deprived of her usual retinue of a thousand followers. On the left, a face of pure spite, is the king of the Huns, who has just shot Ursula with an arrow after his proposal of marriage has been rejected. Opposite the painting is an elaborate map of the city of Caravaggio's day, not so different from now. Further treasures from the bank's vaults are due to be unveiled in the fall of 2013. ✉ *Via Toledo 185, Piazza Plebiscito* ☎ *800/454229* ⊕ *www.palazzozevallos. com* ✆ €4 ⊘ *Tue.–Fri. and Sun. 10–6, Sat. 10–8* Ⓜ *Toledo.*

13

Fodor'sChoice
★ **Palazzo Reale.** Dominating Piazza del Plebiscito, this huge palace— perhaps best described as overblown imperial—dates from the early 1600s. It was renovated and redecorated by successive rulers, including Napoléon's sister Caroline and her ill-fated husband, Joachim Murat (1767–1815), who reigned briefly in Naples after the French emperor sent the Bourbons packing and before they returned to reclaim their kingdom. Don't miss seeing the **royal apartments,** sumptuously furnished and full of precious paintings, tapestries, porcelains, and other objets d'art. The monumental marble staircase gives you an idea of the scale on which Neapolitan rulers lived. ✉ *Piazza del Plebiscito, Toledo* ☎ *081/5808111, 848/800288 schools and guided tours* ⊕ *www. palazzorealenapoli.it* ✆ €4 ⊘ *Thurs.–Tues. 9–7* Ⓜ *Dante (under construction: Piazza Municipio).*

QUICK BITES
Caffè Gambrinus. Across from the Palazzo Reale, this is the most famous coffeehouse in town. Founded in 1850, this 19th-century jewel once functioned as a brilliant intellectual salon. The glory days are over, but the inside rooms, with amazing mirrored walls and gilded ceilings, make this an essential stop for any visitor to the city. To its credit, the caffè doesn't inflate prices to cash in on its fame. ✉ *Piazza Trieste e Trento, near Piazza del Plebiscito* ☎ *081/417582.*

Teatro San Carlo. This large theater was built in 1737, 40 years earlier than Milan's La Scala—though it was destroyed by fire and rebuilt in 1816. You can visit the interior, decorated in the white-and-gilt stucco of the neoclassical era, as part of a 30-minute guided tour. The space is made for opera on a grand scale: nearly 200 boxes are arranged on six levels, and the huge stage (12,000 square feet) permits productions with horses, camels, and elephants. A removable backdrop can be lifted to reveal the Palazzo Reale Gardens. ✉ *Via San Carlo 101–103, Toledo* ☎ *081/5534565 Mon.–Sat., 081/7972468 Sun.* ⊕ *www.teatrosancarlo. it* ✆ *Tour €5* ⊘ *Tours Mon.–Sat. 10–5:30, Sun. 11–12:30* Ⓜ *Piazza Municipio (under construction).*

WORTH NOTING
Piazza Plebiscito. After spending time as a parking lot, this square was restored in 1994 to one of Napoli Nobilissima's most majestic spaces, with a Doric semicircle of columns resembling Saint Peter's Square in Rome. It was originally built under the Napoleonic rule. When that regime fell, Ferdinand (new king of the Two Sicilies) ordered the addition of the Church of San Francesco di Paola. On the left as you approach the church is a statue of Ferdinand and on the right his father, Charles III,

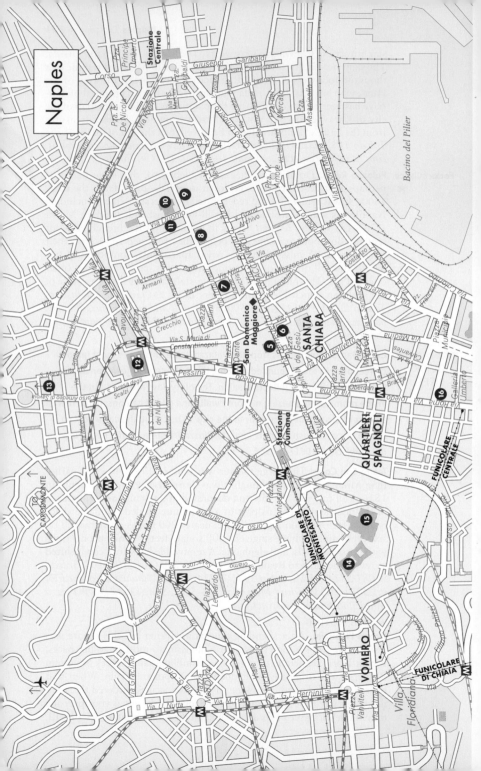

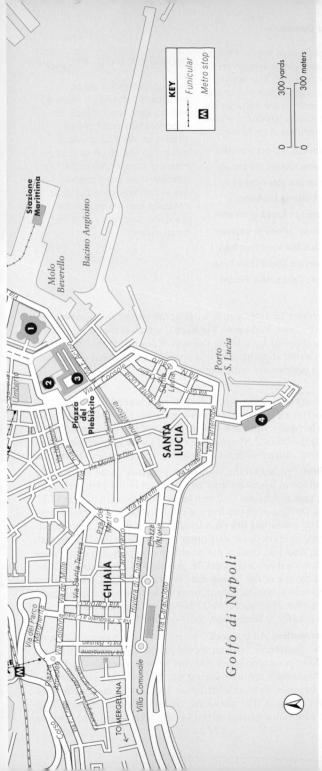

KEY

━━━ Funicular

Ⓜ Metro stop

0 — 300 yards

0 — 300 meters

Stazione Marittima

Molo Beverello

Bacino Angioino

Porto S. Lucia

Piazza del Plebiscito

SANTA LUCIA

CHIAIA

Golfo di Napoli

Via Acton, *Via Console*, *Via Santa Lucia*, *Via Chiatamone*, *Via Partenope*, *Via Cesario Console*, *Via N. Sauro*, *Via Lucilio*, *Via Generale Orsini*, *Via Gennaro Serra*, *Via Monte di Dio*, *Via Chiaia*, *Via G. Martucci*, *Via dei Mille*, *Via Santa Teresa*, *Via Carlo Poerio*, *Riviera di Chiaia*, *Via F. Caracciolo*, *Via Morelli*, *Piazza dei Martiri*, *Piazza Vittoria*, *Via S. Pasquale a Chiaia*, *Via G. Filangieri*, *Via dei Martiri*, *Via Vittoria Colonna*, *Via del Parco Margherita*, *Via 5 Bausan*, *Via Ascensione*, *Piazza Amedeo*, *Corso Vittorio Emanuele*, *Via Chiatamone*, *Via Monte di Dio*, *Via Gennaro Serra*, *Via N. Sauro*, *Via Partenope*

TO MERGELLINA →

Villa Comunale

both clad in Roman togas. Around dusk the floodlights come on creating a magical effect. The square is aired by a delightful sea breeze and on Sunday one corner becomes an improvised soccer stadium where local youth emulate their heroes.

Galleria Umberto. Across from the Teatro San Carlo towers the imposing entrance to the glass-capped neoclassical Galleria Umberto, a late-19th-century shopping arcade where you can sit at one of several cafés and watch the vivacious Neapolitans as they go about their business. ⊠ *Via San Carlo, near Piazza Plebiscito.*

> **WORD OF MOUTH**
>
> "Naples itself should not be overlooked. I particularly enjoyed walking along Spaccanapoli. The integrated bus/tram/funicular ticket is excellent value—allows you to hop on/hop off various means of transport within the city. Although there is not much to see at the castle itself, the views of Naples from the walls make the Castel Sant'Elmo one of my favorite places."
>
> —willit

Via Toledo. Sooner or later you'll wind up at one of the busiest commercial arteries, also known as Via Roma, which is thankfully closed to through traffic—at least along the stretch leading from the Palazzo Reale. Don't avoid dipping into this parade of shops and coffee bars where plump pastries are temptingly arranged.

VOMERO

Heart-stopping views of the Bay of Naples are framed by this gentrified neighborhood on a hill served by the Montesanto, Centrale, and Chiaia funiculars. The upper stations for all three are an easy walk from Piazza Vanvitelli (on the Linea 2 Metro line), a good starting point for exploring this thriving district with no shortage of smart bars and trattorias.

Castel Sant'Elmo. Perched on the Vomero, this massive castle is almost the size of a small town. It was built by the Angevins in the 14th century to dominate the port and the old city; then remodeled by the Spanish in 1537. The parapets, configured in the form of a six-pointed star, provide fabulous views. The whole bay lies on one side; on another, the city spreads out like a map, its every dome and turret clearly visible; and to the east, is slumbering Vesuvius. Once a major military outpost, the castle these days hosts occasional cultural events. Its prison, the Carcere alto di Castel Sant'Elmo, is the site of the **Museo del Novecento Napoli,** which traces Naples's 20th-century artistic output, from the futurist period through the 1980s. ⊠ *Largo San Martino* ☎ *081/2294401* ⊕ *www.polomusealenapoli. beniculturali.it* 🎟 €5 ⊙ *Wed.–Mon. 8:30–6:30* Ⓜ *Vanvitelli.*

Fodor's Choice
★

Certosa di San Martino. Atop a rocky promontory with sweeping views of the city and majestic salons that would please any monarch, the Certosa di San Martino is a religious site that seems more like a palace. A Carthusian monastery restored during the 17th century in exuberant Neapolitan baroque style, this structure has now been transformed into a diverse museum. The gorgeous Chiostro Grande (Great Cloister) and the panoramic garden terraces—strangely quiet, with the city sprawling below—are among the most impressive spots in the city. Popular exhibits include the *presepi* (Christmas crèches) and an anonymous painting that depicts the Naples waterfront in the 15th century and the return of the Aragonese fleet from the Battle of Ischia. Take the funicular from Piazza Montesanto to Vomero. ✉ *Piazzale San Martino 5, Vomero* ☎ *081/2294589* ⊕ *www.polomusealenapoli.beniculturali. it* ☎ *€6* ⊘ *Thurs.–Tues. (Christmas crèches, Thurs.–Mon.) 8:30–6:30. Some rooms are often closed depending on staffing* Ⓜ *Vanvitelli.*

SPACCANAPOLI AND CAPODIMONTE

13

Nowhere embodies the spirit of Naples better than the arrow-straight street informally known as Spaccanapoli (literally, "split Naples"). Gazing down it, you can sense where the name comes from—the street resembles a trench, running from Castel Capuano (until recently the city's courthouse) up to the Vomero hill, retracing one of the main arteries of the ancient Greek, and later Roman, settlements. Along its western section, Spaccanapoli is officially named Via Benedetto Croce, in honor of the illustrious philosopher born here in 1866, in the building at No. 12. Over its course, the street changes its name seven times. But no matter what it's called, a vibrant street culture remains constant.

Capodimonte, to the north, was open countryside until the Bourbon kings built a hunting lodge there, after which it rapidly became part of the city proper. Between the two neighborhoods is the Museo Archeologico, Naples's finest museum. It's best to visit shortly after lunchtime, when the crowds have thinned out. Two hours will be just enough to get your bearings and cover the more important collections. Since the Museo di Capodimonte is well lighted—unlike many of the churches and the archaeological museum—and can be viewed in fading daylight, it's best left until the afternoon (leaving enough time to return to the center of town before sunset).

TOP ATTRACTIONS

Fodor's Choice
★

Museo Cappella Sansevero. Off Vicolo Domenico Maggiore at the beginning of Via Francesco de Sanctis, this chapel/museum has an intriguing sculpture collection. The chapel itself was founded in 1590 by Prince Giovan Francesco di Sangro, fulfilling a vow to the Virgin after recovery from an illness (his statue is on the second niche to the left.) Over the generations the simple sanctuary became a family mausoleum, with statues of the various princes lining the walls.

Most of the building work here is due to restructuring in the mid-18th century under the seventh Sangro di Sansevero prince, Raimondo—a larger-than-life figure, popularly believed to have signed a pact with the devil allowing him to plumb nature's secrets. Prince Raimondo commissioned the young sculptor Giuseppe Sammartino to create numerous works, including the chapel's centerpiece: the remarkable *Veiled Christ*, which has a seemingly transparent marble veil some say was produced using a chemical formula provided by the prince. If you have the stomach for it, take a look in the crypt, where some of the anatomical experiments conducted by the prince are gruesomely displayed. ✉ *Via Francesco de Sanctis 19, Spaccanapoli* ☎ *081/5518470* ⊕ *www.museosansevero.it* ☎ *€7* ⊘ *Mon. and Wed.–Sat. 10–5:40, Sun. 10–1:10* Ⓜ *Dante.*

Duomo. Though the cathedral was established in the 1200s, the building you see was erected a century later and has since undergone radical changes—especially during the baroque period. Inside, 110 ancient columns salvaged from pagan buildings are set into the piers that support the 350-year-old wooden ceiling. Off the left aisle you step down into the 4th-century church of **Santa Restituta,** which was incorporated into the cathedral. Though Santa Restituta was redecorated in the late 1600s in the prevalent Baroque style, a few very old mosaics remain in the **Battistero** (Baptistery).

On the right aisle of the cathedral, in the **Cappella del Tesoro di San Gennaro,** are multicolor marbles and frescoes honoring Saint Januarius, the miracle-working patron saint of Naples, whose altar and relics are encased in silver. Three times a year—on September 19 (his feast day); on the Saturday preceding the first Sunday in May, which commemorates the transfer of his relics to Naples; and on December 16—his dried blood, contained in two sealed vials, is believed to liquefy during rites in his honor. On these days large numbers of devout Neapolitans offer up prayers in his memory. The **Museo del Tesoro di San Gennaro** houses a rich collection of treasures associated with the saint. Paintings by Solimena and Luca Giordano hang alongside statues, busts, candelabras, and tabernacles in gold, silver, and marble by Cosimo Fanzago and other 18th-century Baroque masters. ⊠ *Via Duomo, 149, Spaccanapoli* ☎ *081/449097 Duomo, 081/294980 museum* ⊕ *www.museosangennaro.it* ▨ *€7, €1.50 for Baptistery* ⊙ *Daily 9–6; Baptistery, 8:30–1 and 3:30–6:30.*

Gesù Nuovo. The oddly-faceted stone facade of this elaborate Baroque church dates to the late 16th century. Originally a palace, the building was seized by Pedro of Toledo in 1547 and donated to the Jesuits. Recent research revealed that the symbols on the stones on the front are, in fact, Aramaic musical notes that produce a 45-minute concerto. Be sure not to miss the votive chapel dedicated to recently beatified surgeon Giuseppe Moscato, along with a re-creation of his studio. Here hundreds of tiny silver ex-voto images have been hung on the walls to give thanks to the saint for his assistance in medical matters. On the opposite far left corner a smaller chapel similarly gives thanks to San Ciro (Saint Cyrus). ⊠ *Piazza Gesù Nuovo, Spaccanapoli* ☎ *081/5578111* ⊙ *Daily 7–12:30 and 4–7:30* Ⓜ *Dante.*

Fodor's Choice
★
Museo Archeologico Nazionale (*National Museum of Archaeology*). Those who know and love this legendary museum—now restyled as MANN (Museo Archeologico Nazionale Napoli) although the name has yet to catch on—have the tendency upon hearing it mentioned to heave a sigh: it's famous not only for its unrivaled collections but also for its cordoned-off rooms, missing identification labels, poor lighting, billows of dust, suffocating heat in summer, and indifferent personnel—a state of affairs seen by some critics as an encapsulation of everything that's wrong with southern Italy in general.

Precisely because of this emblematic value, the National Ministry of Culture has decided to lavish attention and funds on the museum in a complete reorganization. This process has been ongoing for some time and looks as if it will continue for a while longer, although improvements are gradually becoming visible: ticketing has been privatized and opening hours extended (for the core "masterpiece" collection, that is; other rooms are subject to staffing shortages and can be closed on a rotating basis). Some of the "newer" rooms, covering archaeological discoveries in the Greco-Roman settlements and necropolises in and around Naples, have helpful informational panels in English. A fascinating free display of the finds unearthed during digs for the Naples metro has been set up in the Museo station close to the museum entrance.

Even if some rooms may be closed, the core of the museum is always available—a nucleus of world-renowned archaeological finds that puts most other museums to shame, with over 13,500 items on display (and a further 300,000 in storage). It includes the legendary Farnese collection of ancient sculpture, together with local sculptural finds, and almost all the good stuff—the best mosaics and paintings—from Pompeii and Herculaneum. The quality of these collections is unmatched and, as far as the mosaic, painting, and bronze sections are concerned, unique in the world. ⊠ *Piazza Museo 19, Spaccanapoli* ☎ *081/440166* ⊕ *sbanap.campaniabeniculturali.it* ⊡ *€6.50, more for special exhibits* ⊗ *Wed.–Mon. 9–7* Ⓜ *Museo.*

QUICK BITES

Timpani e Tempura. A tiny shrine to local culinary culture—though there are only three small tables and a bar-style counter, it's worth the squeeze for the *timballi di maccheroni* (baked pasta cakes) and unique *mangiamaccheroni* (spaghetti in broth with caciocavallo cheese, butter, basil, and pepper). High-quality wines by the glass make this a spot for a swift but excellent lunch. You can also buy cheese and salami to take home with you. ⊠ *Vico della Quercia 17, Spaccanapoli* ☎ *081/5512280* ⊕ *www. timpanietempura.it* ⊗ *Tues.–Sat. 9:30–7:30, Sun. and Mon. 9:30–3:30.*

Museo di Capodimonte. The grandiose 18th-century neoclassical Bourbon royal palace houses an impressive assortment of fine and decorative art. Capodimonte's greatest treasure is the excellent collection of paintings well displayed in the **Galleria Nazionale,** on the palace's first and second floors. Aside from the artworks, part of the royal apartments still has a complement of beautiful antique furniture (most of it on the splashy scale so dear to the Bourbons), and a staggering range of porcelain and majolica from the various royal residences. The walls of the apartments are hung with numerous portraits, providing a close-up of the unmistakable Bourbon features, a challenge to any court painter. Most rooms have fairly comprehensive information cards in English, whereas the audio guide is overly selective and somewhat quirky. The main galleries on the first floor are devoted to work from the 13th to 18th centuries, including many pieces by Dutch and Spanish masters. On the second floor look out for stunning paintings by Simone Martini (circa 1284–1344), Titian (circa 1488/90–1576), and Caravaggio (1573–1610). The palace is situated in the vast Bosco di Capodimonte (Capodimonte Park), which served as the royal hunting preserve and later as the site of the Capodimonte porcelain works. ✉ *Via Miano 2, Porta Piccola, Via Capodimonte, Capodimonte* ☎ *199/199100 for information and tickets for special exhibitions, 081/7499111* ⊕ *museodicapodimonte. campaniabeniculturali.it* 💶 *€7.50* ⊘ *Thurs.–Tues. 8:30–7:30; ticket office closes at 6:30.*

Fodor'sChoice
★
Pio Monte della Misericordia. One of Spaccanapoli's defining sites, this octagonal church was built around the corner from the Duomo for a charitable institution founded in 1601 by seven noblemen. The institution's aim was to carry out acts of Christian charity: feeding the hungry, clothing the poor, nursing the sick, sheltering pilgrims, visiting prisoners, ransoming Christian slaves, and burying the indigent dead—acts immortalized in the history of art by Caravaggio's famous altarpiece depicting the *Sette Opere della Misericordia* (*Seven Acts of Mercy*). In this haunting work the artist has brought the Virgin, borne atop the shoulders of two angels, down into the streets of Spaccanapoli (scholars have suggested a couple of plausible locations) populated by figures in whose spontaneous and passionate movements the people could see themselves. The original church was considered too small and destroyed in 1655 to make way for a new church, designed by Antonio Picchiatti and built between 1658 and 1678. Pride of place is given to the great Caravaggio above the altar, but there are other important Baroque-era paintings on view here: some hang in the church while others are in the adjoining *pinacoteca* (picture gallery). ✉ *Via Tribunali 253, Spaccanapoli* ☎ *081/446973* ⊕ *www. piomontedellamisericordia.it* 💶 *€6, including audio guide* ⊘ *Thurs.–Wed. 9–2* Ⓜ *Piazza Cavour (under construction: Duomo).*

Santa Chiara. This monastery church is a Neapolitan landmark and the subject of a famous old song. It was built in the 1300s in Provençal Gothic style, and it's best known for the quiet charm of its cloister garden, where columns and benches are sheathed in 18th-century ceramic tiles painted with delicate floral motifs and vivid landscapes. An adjoining museum traces the history of the convent; the entrance is off the courtyard at the left of the church. ✉ *Piazza Gesù Nuovo, Spaccanapoli* ☎ *081/5516673* ⊕ *www.monasterodisantachiara.eu* 💶 *Museum and cloister €6* ⊘ *Church: daily 7:30–1 and 4:30–8. Museum and cloister: Mon.–Sat. 9:30–5:30, Sun. 10–2:30* Ⓜ *Dante, Università.*

▌QUICK
BITES

Scaturchio. While you're exploring the old part of town, take a break at what the Neapolitans call "the best pastry shop in Italy"— Scaturchio. Although the coffee is top-of-the-line and the ice cream and pastries quite good (including the specialty, the *ministeriale*, a pert chocolate cake whipped with rum-cream filling), it's the atmosphere that counts here. In the heart of Spaccanapoli, it's where nuns, punks, businesspeople, and housewives come to share the good things they all have in common. ✉ *Piazza San Domenico Maggiore 19, Spaccanapoli* ☎ *081/5516944* ⊕ *www.scaturchio.it* ⊘ *Daily 7:30 am–8:30 pm.*

WORTH NOTING

Quadreria dei Girolamini. Off an improbably quiet cloister enclosing a prolific forest of citrus, fig, and loquat trees, the Girolamini art museum is attached to the restored Girolamini church. Its intimate, high-quality collection of 16th- and 17th-century paintings (one of the city's best-kept secrets) and the newly restored 16th-century libraries are well worth a visit. Opening hours are staggered so plan your visit carefully. ✉ *Via Duomo 142, Spaccanapoli* ☎ *081/294980, 081/3442286* 🔲 *€7* 🕙 *Church: Mon., Tues., Thurs., and Fri. 10–11 and 2:30–3:15, Sat. 10–11, Sun. 9:30–10:15 and 11:30–1. Cloisters: Mon., Tues., Thurs., and Fri. 9:30–5, Sat., Sun. 9:30–1. Museum: Mon., Tues., Thurs., and Fri. 11:15–12:15 and 3:30–4, Sat. 11:15–12:15, Sun. 10–11:15* Ⓜ *Piazza Cavour.*

San Lorenzo Maggiore. It's unusual to find French Gothic style in Naples, but it has survived to great effect in this medieval church, decorated with 14th-century frescoes. Outside the 17th-century cloister is the entrance to an underground archaeological site, revealing what was once part of the Roman forum, and before that the Greek agora. You can walk among the streets, shops, and workshops of the ancient city and see a model of how the Greek Neapolis might have looked. Next door to the church is the four-story **museum,** housed in a 16th-century palazzo and displaying a wealth of archaeological finds and religious art (panels regrettably are only in Italian). ✉ *Via dei Tribunali 316, Spaccanapoli* ☎ *081/2110860* ⊕ *www.sanlorenzomaggiore.na.it* 🔲 *Excavations and museum €9* 🕙 *Museum: Mon.–Sat. 9:30–5:30, Sun. 9:30–1:30. Church: daily 9–1 and 5:30–7. Closed to sightseers during services* Ⓜ *Dante.*

WHERE TO EAT

CHIAIA

$$
SOUTHERN
ITALIAN

✕ **Amici Miei.** A place favored by meat eaters who can't take another bite of sea bass, this small, dark, and cozy den is well loved for specials such as tender carpaccio with fresh artichoke hearts, and a rice-and-arugula dish featuring duck breast. There are also excellent pasta dishes, such as orecchiette with chickpeas or *alla barese* (with chewy green turnips), or that extravaganza, the *carnevale lasagne*, an especially rich concoction relied on to sustain revelers in the build-up before Lent. Everyone finishes with a slice of chocolate and hazelnut cake. $ *Average meal: €35* ✉ *Via Monte di Dio 78, Chiaia* ☎ *081/7646063* ⊕ *www. ristoranteamicimiei.com* 🍴 *Reservations essential* 🕙 *Closed Mon. and June–Aug. No dinner Sun.*

$$$
NEAPOLITAN
Fodor's Choice
★

✕ **Da Dora.** Despite its location up an unpromising-looking *vicolo* (alley) off the Riviera di Chiaia, this small restaurant has achieved cult status for its seafood platters. It's remarkable what owner-chef Giovanni can produce in his tiny kitchen. Start with linguine *alla Dora*, laden with local seafood and fresh tomatoes, and perhaps follow up with grilled *pezzogna* (blue-spotted bream). Like many restaurants on the seafront, Dora has its own guitarist, who is often robustly accompanied by the kitchen staff. $ *Average meal: €60* ✉ *Via Fernando Palasciano 30, Chiaia* ☎ *081/680519* 🍴 *Reservations essential* 🕙 *Closed Sun., 2 wks in Dec., and 2 wks in mid-Aug. No lunch Mon.*

$$$ NEAPOLITAN 🍴 **L'Altro Loco.** This place has taken the Naples dining scene by storm, thanks to the innovative cuisine of master chef Diego Nuzzo, a stylish ambience, and a quiet location off Piazza dei Martiri, 10 minutes by foot from the Palazzo Reale. A bar runs the length of the restaurant where salami and other glorious tidbits are served. But for the real deal take a table and be pampered with subtle dishes like *insalata di aragosta e gamberi alla catalana* (lobster and prawn salad garnished with citrus). Larger groups can book a private room. [$] *Average meal: €52* ✉ *Vicoletto Cappella Vecchia 4, Chiaia* ☎ *081/7641722* 🌐 *www.ristorantelaltroloco.com* 🕒 *Closed 3 wks in Aug. No lunch July–Sept.; no dinner Sun. Feb.–Oct.*

$ ITALIAN 🍴 **L'Ebbrezza di Noè.** A simple enoteca by day, the dining area at the back fills up in the evening. Owner Luca has an enthusiasm for what he does that is quite moving—as you sip a recommended wine you can sense that he hopes you like it as much as he does. The attention paid to the quality of the wine carries over to the food. Here you can taste delicate *carpaccio di chianina* (thinly sliced Tuscan steak), rare cheeses such as the Sicilian *ragusano di razza modicana* and the local *caciocavallo podolico,* plus a daily selection of hot dishes. [$] *Average meal: €25* ✉ *Vico Vetriera a Chiaia 8b/9, Chiaia* ☎ *081/400104* 🌐 *www.lebbrezzadinoe.com* 🕒 *Closed Mon. No lunch.*

$$ NEAPOLITAN 🍴 **Umberto.** Run by the Di Porzio family since 1916, Umberto is one of the city's classic restaurants. It combines the classiness of the Chiaia neighborhood and the friendliness of other parts of Naples. Try the *tubettoni 'do tre dita* ("three-finger" pasta with octopus, tomato, olives and capers); it bears the nickname of the original Umberto, who happened to be short a few digits. Owner Massimo and sisters Lorella and Roberta (Umberto's grandchildren) are all wine experts and oversee a fantastic cellar. Note that Umberto is also one of the few restaurants in the city catering to those who have a gluten allergy. [$] *Average meal: €30* ✉ *Via Alabardieri 30–31, Chiaia* ☎ *081/418555* 🌐 *www.umberto.it* 🕒 *No lunch Mon., and 2 wks in Aug.*

PIAZZA GARIBALDI

$ PIZZA Fodor's Choice ★ 🍴 **Da Michele.** You may recognize this from the movie "Eat, Pray, Love," but for more than 140 years before Julia Roberts arrived this place has been a culinary reference point in Naples. Despite offering only two types of pizza—*marinara* (with tomato, garlic, and oregano) and *margherita* (with tomato, mozzarella, and basil)—plus a small selection of drinks, it still manages to attract long lines. The prices have something to do with it. But the pizza itself suffers no rivals, so even those waiting in line are good-humored: the boisterous, joyous atmosphere wafts out with the smell of yeast and wood smoke onto the street. Step right up to get a number at the door and then hang outside until it's called. Note: The restaurant is off Corso Umberto, between Piazza Garibaldi and Piazza Nicola Amore. [$] *Average meal: €7* ✉ *Via Sersale 1/3, Piazza Garibaldi* ☎ *081/5539204* 🌐 *www.damichele.net* 💳 *No credit cards* 🕒 *Closed 2 wks in Aug. and Sun June–Nov.*

$$ NEAPOLITAN 🍴 **Mimì alla Ferrovia.** Patrons of this Neapolitan institution have included Fellini and that true-Neapolitan comic genius and aristocrat Totò. Mimì cheerfully lives up to its history, serving fine versions of everything from pasta *e fagioli* (with beans) to the sea bass *al presidente,* baked

in a pastry crust and enjoyed by any number of visiting Italian presidents. The owner's son Salvatore is the new chef, working wonders in the kitchen. This is not so much a see-and-be-seen place as common ground for the famous and the unknown to mingle, feast, and be of good cheer. Given the fairly seedy neighborhood, travel there and back by taxi, especially at night. [$] *Average meal: €35* ✉ *Via A. D'Aragona 19/21, Piazza Garibaldi* ☎ *081/5538525* 🌐 *www.mimiallaferrovia.com* 🕒 *Closed Sun. (except Dec.) and last 2 wks in Aug.*

SANTA LUCIA

$$$$ ITALIAN 🍴 **La Terrazza.** The Hotel Excelsior's Terrazza attracts visiting A-list stars with its Pompeian red marble floorings and brown leather furnishings (all aimed at highlighting the gold cutlery, *capisce?*). A breathtaking buffet that counts as an appetizer would be a banquet in itself for mere mortals; while the à la carte menu creates a fusion of Italian regional culinary styles. Dress up, and expect to be impressed. [$] *Average meal: €85* ✉ *Hotel Excelsior, Via Partenope 48, Santa Lucia* ☎ *081/7640111* 🌐 *www.laterrazzaexcelsior.com* 🕒 *Closed Sun.*

SPACCANAPOLI

$ PIZZA 🍴 **Gino Sorbillo.** There are three restaurants called Sorbillo along Via dei Tribunali; this is the one with the crowds waiting outside. Order the same thing the locals come for: a basic Neapolitan pizza (try the unique pizza al pesto or the stunningly simple marinara—just tomatoes and oregano). They're cooked to pe rfection by the third generation of pie makers who run the place. The pizzas are enormous, flopping over the edge of the plate onto the white marble tabletops. [$] *Average meal: €17* ✉ *Via dei Tribunali 32, Spaccanapoli* ☎ *081/446643* 🕒 *Closed Sun. (except Dec.) and 3 wks in Aug.*

$ PIZZA 🍴 **I Decumani.** Every pizzeria along Via dei Tribunali is worth the long wait (all the good ones are jammed packed) but none more so than the Decumani, thanks to the superlative *pizzaioli* (pizza makers)—say hello to Gianni and Enzo for us—at work here. They turn out a wide array of pizzas and do them all to perfection. If you aren't on a diet, try the *frittura* and you'll be pleasantly surprised with this mix of Neapolitan-style tempura: zucchini, eggplants, rice-balls, and many other delicacies. [$] *Average meal: €10* ✉ *Via dei Tribunali 58, Spaccanapoli* ☎ *081/5571309* 🕒 *Closed Mon. (except Dec.).*

$$$ NEAPOLITAN 🍴 **Palazzo Petrucci.** In a 17th-century mansion facing the grand Piazza San Domenico Maggiore, Palazzo Petrucci doesn't lack for dramatic dining options—under the vaulted ceiling of the former stables, in the gallery where a glass partition reveals the kitchen, or in the cozy room overlooking the piazza. Fortify yourself with a complimentary glass of prosecco before agonizing between the à la carte and the tasting menu (€55). A popular starter is a *mille-feuille* of local mozzarella layered with raw prawns and vegetable sauce. The *paccheri all'impiedi* (large tube pasta served standing on end) in a rich ricotta-and-meat sauce is an interesting twist on an old regional favorite. The interior is elegantly minimal; the culinary delights are anything but. [$] *Average meal: €60* ✉ *Piazza San Domenico Maggiore 4, Spaccanapoli* ☎ *081/5524068* 🌐 *www.palazzopetrucci.it* ✍ *Reservations essential* 🕒 *Closed 2 wks in Aug. No dinner Sun., no lunch Mon.*

Continued on page 764

PIZZA: THE CLASSIC MARGHERITA

Locally grown San Marzano tomatoes are a must.

The best pizza should come out with cheese bubbling and be ever-so-slightly charred around its edges.

Only buffalo-milk mozzarella or fior di latte cheese should be used.

The dough has to use the right kind of durum wheat flour and be left to rise for at least six hours.

Be prepared: ranging from the size of a plate to that of a Hummer wheel, Neapolitan pizza is pretty different from anything you might find elsewhere in Italy—not to mention what's served up at American pizza chains. The "purest" form is the marinara, topped with only tomatoes, garlic, oregano, and olive oil.

OTHER FAVORITES ARE . . .

- **CAPRICCIOSA** (the "capricious"), made with whatever the chef has on hand.

- **SICILIANA** with mozzarella and eggplant.

- **DIAVOLA** with spicy salami.

- **QUATTRO STAGIONE** ("four seasons"), made with produce from each one.

- **SALSICCIA E FRIARIELLI** with sausage and a broccoli-like vegetable.

A PIZZA FIT FOR A QUEEN

Legend has it that during the patriotic fervor following Italian unification in the late 19th century, a Neapolitan chef decided to celebrate the arrival in the city of the new Italian queen Margherita by designing a pizza in her—and the country's—honor. He took red tomatoes, white mozzarella cheese, and a few leaves of fresh green basil—reflecting the three colors of the Italian flag—and gave birth to the modern pizza industry.

Margherita of Savoy

ONLY THE BEST

An association of Neapolitan pizza chefs has standardized the ingredients and methods that have to be used to make pizza certified DOC (*denominazione d'origine controllata*) or STG (*specialità tradizionale garantita*). See the illustration on the opposite page for the basic requirements.

Buffalo-milk mozzarella

FIRED UP!

The Neapolitan pizza must be made in a traditional wood-burning oven. Chunks of beech or maple are stacked up against the sides of the huge, tiled ovens, then shoved onto the slate base of the oven where they burn quickly at high temperatures. If you visit Pompeii, you will see how similar the old Roman bread-baking ovens are to the modern pizza oven. The *pizzaiolo* (pizza chef) then uses a long wooden paddle to put the pizza into the oven, where it cooks quickly.

A pizzaiolo at work

PIZZERIE

There are hundreds of restaurants that specialize in pizza in Naples, and the best of these make pizza and nothing else. As befits the original fast food, *pizzerie* tend to be simple, fairly basic places, with limited menu choices, and quick, occasionally brusque service: the less complicated your order, the happier the waiters.

Typical pizzeria in Naples

THE REAL THING

Naples takes its contribution to world cuisine seriously. The Associazione Verace Pizza Napoletana (www.pizzanapoletana.org) was founded in 1984 in order to share expertise, maintain quality levels, and provide courses for aspirant pizza chefs and pizza lovers. They also organize the annual Pizzafest—three days in September, dedicated to the consumption of pizza, when *maestri* from all over the region get together and cook off.

Simple, fresh toppings

TOLEDO

$$ NEAPOLITAN Fodor's Choice ★ 🍴 **Trattoria San Ferdinando.** This cheerful trattoria seems to be run for the sheer pleasure of it. Try the excellent fish or the traditional (but cooked with a lighter modern touch) pasta dishes, especially those with *verdura* (fresh leaf vegetables) or with potatoes and smoked mozzarella (*pasta e patate con la provola*). Close to the San Carlo Theater and aptly decorated with playbills and theatrical memorabilia, both ancient and modern, this is an excellent place to stop after a visit to the opera. Note that it's almost the first doorway on the right as you go up Via Nardones from Piazza Trieste e Trento—ring the bell outside to be let in. [$] *Average meal: €30* ✉ *Via Nardones 117, Toledo* ☎ *081/421964* 🕒 *Closed Sun. No dinner Sat.–Mon.*

WHERE TO STAY

For expanded hotel reviews, visit Fodors.com.

CHIAIA

$ B&B/INN 🏨 **Cappella Vecchia 11.** One of the city's good budget options lies just a stone's throw from the Platinum Card square of Naples, Piazza dei Martiri, now colonized by the likes of Cartier, Ferragamo, and Versace. **Pros:** fabulous location off chic Martiri square; friendly staff. **Cons:** lack of room phones; prefers cash payment. [$] *Rooms from: €85* ✉ *Vicolo Santa Maria a Capella Vecchia 11, Chiaia* ☎ *081/2405117* 🌐 *www.cappellavecchia11.it* 🛏 *6 rooms* 🍽 *Breakfast.*

$ HOTEL 🏨 **Chiaja Hotel de Charme.** No views, but a great location—and there's plenty of atmosphere in the first-floor apartments in this spruce 18th-century palazzo. **Pros:** central location near Piazza Plebiscito, the Royal Palace, and the liveliest nightlife in town; on bustling pedestrians-only street. **Cons:** small rooms get hot in summer (a/c notwithstanding); difficult to reach by car. [$] *Rooms from: €100* ✉ *Via Chiaia 216, Chiaia* ☎ *081/415555* 🌐 *www.hotelchiaia.it* 🛏 *27 rooms* 🍽 *Breakfast.*

$$ HOTEL Fodor's Choice ★ 🏨 **Palazzo Alabardieri.** Just off the chic Piazza dei Martiri, this is the most fashionable choice among the city's growing number of smaller luxury hotels—for some, there is simply no other hotel in Naples. **Pros:** impressive public salons; central yet quiet location (a rare combination); polite, pleasant staff. **Cons:** no sea view; difficult to reach by car. [$] *Rooms from: €150* ✉ *Via Alabardieri 38, Chiaia* ☎ *081/415278* 🌐 *www.palazzoalabardieri.it* 🛏 *36 rooms* 🍽 *Breakfast.*

$$ HOTEL 🏨 **Pinto Storey.** The name juxtaposes a 19th-century Englishman who fell in love with Naples and a certain Signora Pinto; together they went on to establish this hotel, which overflows with warmth and charm. **Pros:** safe neighborhood; near public transit: option of not using a/c with an €8-a-day reduction. **Cons:** not close to major sights; only a few rooms have views. [$] *Rooms from: €180* ✉ *Via G. Martucci 72, Chiaia* ☎ *081/681260* 🌐 *www.pintostorey.it* 🛏 *16 rooms* 🍽 *No meals.*

SANTA LUCIA

$$$ HOTEL Fodor's Choice ★ 🏨 **Grand Hotel Vesuvio.** You'd never guess from the modern exterior that this is the oldest of Naples' great seafront hotels—the place where Enrico Caruso died, Oscar Wilde dallied with lover Lord Alfred Douglas, and Bill Clinton charmed the waitresses. **Pros:** luxurious atmosphere; historic

CLOSE UP

Folk Songs à la Carte

If you want to hear *canzoni napo-letane*—the fabled Neapolitan folk songs—performed live, you can try to catch top city troupes, such as the Cantori di Posillipo and I Virtuosi di San Martino, at venues like the Teatro Trianon. An easier alternative is to head for one of the more traditional restaurants (such as Mimì alla Ferrovia), where most every night you can expect your meal to be interrupted by a *posteggiatore*. These singers aren't employed by the restaurants, but they're encouraged to come in, swan around the tables with a battered old guitar, and belt out classics such as "Santa Lucia," "O' Surdato Innamurate," "Torna a Surriento," and, inevitably, "Funiculì Funiculà."

These songs are the most famous of a vast repertoire that found international fame with the mass exodus of southern Italians to the United States in the early 20th century. "Funiculì Funiculà" was written by Peppino

Turco and Luigi Denza in 1880 to herald the new funicular railway up Vesuvius. "O Sole Mio," by Giovanni Capurro and Eduardo di Capua, has often been mistakenly taken for the Italian national anthem. "Torna a Surriento" was composed by Ernesto di Curtis in 1903 to help remind the current Italian prime minister how wonderful he thought Sorrento was (and how many government subsidies he had promised the township).

Interest in this genre has been rekindled, both locally and internationally, by John Turturro's 2010 film *Passione*, which explores the current and historical music scene. Note that singers are more than happy to do requests, even inserting the name of your *innamorato* or *innamorata* into the song. When they've finished they'll stand discreetly by your table. Give them a few euros and you'll have friends for life (or at least for the night).

13

setting; location directly opposite Borgo Marinaro. **Cons:** spa, pool and Internet cost extra; reception staff can be snooty; not all rooms have great views. [$] *Rooms from: €230* ⊠ *Via Partenope 45, Santa Lucia* ☎ *081/7640044* ⊕ *www.vesuvio.it* ➾ *149 rooms, 21 suites* ⓘⓞⓘ *Breakfast.*

$$ | ⚏ **Hotel Naples.** You can't beat the location of this four-star hotel on the
HOTEL lower edge of the centro storico—it occupies an entire block opposite the imposing facade of the Federico II University, with a metro station almost outside the door. **Pros:** convenient address; fantastic rooftop views. **Cons:** perhaps too close to the action; not all agree it's worthy of four stars, particularly the breakfast. [$] *Rooms from: €140* ⊠ *Corso Umberto I 55, Santa Lucia* ☎ *081/5517055* ⊕ *www.hotelnaples.it* ➾ *80* ⓘⓞⓘ *Breakfast* Ⓜ *Università.*

$$$ | ⚏ **Hotel Santa Lucia.** Neapolitan enchantment can be yours if you stay
HOTEL here—in addition to its luxurious, quietly understated polish, it overlooks the port immortalized in the song "Santa Lucia," bobbing with hundreds of boats, lined with seafood restaurants, and backed by the medieval Castel dell'Ovo. **Pros:** great views from most rooms; proximity to the port is convenient for trips to the islands. **Cons:** rooms disappointingly boxy; the entrance is on the busy Via Partenope. [$] *Rooms from: €220* ⊠ *Via Partenope 46, Santa Lucia* ☎ *081/7640666* ⊕ *www.santalucia.it* ➾ *95 rooms* ⓘⓞⓘ *Breakfast.*

$$ ⊞ **MGallery Palazzo Caracciolo.** Built in the 1200s, this one-time home of
HOTEL   Murat, King of Naples offers royal treatment within walking distance of
Fodor's Choice   the train station and centro storico. **Pros:** a tranquil respite; great value;
★   free shuttle service. **Cons:** not an ideal area for evening strolls; some
guests have complained of unfriendly staff. $ *Rooms from: €130* ⊠ *Via
Carbonara 112, Porta Capuana* ☎ *081/0160111* ⊕ *www.mgallery.com*
⇨ *139* ⫶○⫶ *Breakfast.*

$ ⊞ **Transatlantico Napoli.** Perhaps enjoying Naples's most enchant-
HOTEL   ing setting, at the edge of Borgo Marinaro's toy-sized harbor, in the
shadow of the Castel dell'Ovo, this modestly priced hotel also sits at
the top of most travelers' "dream lodgings" list. **Pros:** fabulous loca-
tion; gentle prices. **Cons:** rather cheap and ugly furniture. $ *Rooms
from: €120* ⊠ *Via Luculliana 15, Santa Lucia* ☎ *081/7648842* ⊕ *www.
transatlanticonapoli.com* ⇨ *8 rooms* ⫶○⫶ *Breakfast.*

SPACCANAPOLI

$$ ⊞ **Costantinopoli 104.** An oasis of what Italians call *stile liberty* (art nou-
HOTEL   veau style), with impressive stained glass fittings and striking artwork,
Fodor's Choice   this calm and elegant hotel is well placed for the Museo Archeologico
★   Nazionale and Spaccanapoli. **Pros:** swimming pool (a rarity in Neapolitan hotels) and garden; pleasant service. **Cons:** pool surrounded
by buildings; can be difficult to find from street (look for the sign saying Villa Spinelli, the name of the original building). $ *Rooms from:
€176* ⊠ *Via Costantinopoli 104, Spaccanapoli* ☎ *081/5571035* ⊕ *www.
costantinopoli104.com* ⇨ *19 rooms* ⫶○⫶ *Breakfast.*

$$ ⊞ **Hotel Palazzo Decumani.** Opened in 2008, this early-20th-century
HOTEL   palazzo is pleasingly contemporary and a welcome addition to the
Fodor's Choice   small list of higher-end hotels in Spaccanapoli. **Pros:** well located for
★   both transportation links and sightseeing; large rooms and bathrooms;
soundproofed windows. **Cons:** the location on a side street can be hard
to find—follow signs from Corso Umberto. $ *Rooms from: €140* ⊠ *Pi-
azzetta Giustino Fortunato 8, Spaccanapoli* ☎ *081/4201379* ⊕ *www.
palazzodecumani.com* ⇨ *28 rooms* ⫶○⫶ *Breakfast.*

TOLEDO

$ ⊞ **Il Convento.** In a 17th-century palazzo, tucked away in the Quart-
HOTEL   ieri Spagnoli, close to Via Toledo, guest rooms are small but elegant,
with original architectural features such as arched or beamed ceilings.
Pros: close to cafés and shops; free Internet access; warm Neapolitan
reception and pleasantly personal touch. **Cons:** locale sometimes dicey;
church bells may wake you in the morning; on a busy street; tiny lobby.
$ *Rooms from: €120* ⊠ *Via Speranzella 137/A, Toledo* ☎ *081/403977*
⊕ *www.hotelilconvento.com* ⇨ *12 rooms, 2 suites* ⫶○⫶ *Breakfast.*

$$ ⊞ **Palazzo Turchini.** Adjacent to the impressive *fontana di Nettuno,*
HOTEL   just a few minutes' walk from the Castel Nuovo, Palazzo Turchini is
one of the more attractive smaller hotels in the city center. **Pros:** good
location for the port; more intimate than neighboring business hotels.
Cons: close to an open building site as construction of the metro drags
on. $ *Rooms from: €160* ⊠ *Via Medina 21, Toledo* ☎ *081/5510606*
⊕ *www.palazzoturchini.it* ⇨ *27 rooms* ⫶○⫶ *Breakfast.*

VOMERO

$$$ ⛄ **Grand Hotel Parker's.** Midway up the Vomero hill, with fine views of
HOTEL the bay and distant Capri, this landmark hotel, first opened in 1870,
continues to serve up a supremely elegant dose of old-style atmosphere
to visiting VIPs, ranging from rock stars to Russian leaders. **Pros:** excel-
lent restaurant; fabulous views. **Cons:** a long walk from the funicular;
a very long walk or taxi ride from city center and seafront; not quite as
grand as it once was. $ *Rooms from: €300* ⊠ *Corso Vittorio Emanu-
ele 135, Vomero* ☎ *081/7612474* ⊕ *www.grandhotelparkers.it* ⇆ *73
rooms, 9 suites* ⦿| *Breakfast.*

13

NIGHTLIFE AND THE ARTS

OPERA

Teatro San Carlo. Opera is a serious business in Naples—not in terms of
the music so much as the costumes, the stage design, the players, and
the politics. What's happening on stage can be secondary to the news of
who's there, who they're with, and what they're wearing. Given the cir-
cumstances, it's hardly surprising that the city's famous San Carlo Com-
pany doesn't offer a particularly innovative repertoire. Nonetheless, the
company is usually of very high quality—and if they're not in form the
audience lets them know it. Performances take place in the historic Teatro
San Carlo, the luxury liner of opera houses in southern Italy. In 2008
the concert hall underwent a massive renovation, with everything from
the seats to the gold inlay on the ceiling frescoes replaced, and the statue
of the mermaid Parthenope (missing since 1969) restored to its place
on the building's facade. ⊠ *Via San Carlo 101–103, Piazza Municipio*
☎ *081/7972331, 081/7972412 box office* ⊕ *www.teatrosancarlo.it.*

NIGHTLIFE

Bars and clubs are found in many areas around Naples. The sophisticated
crowd heads to Posillipo and the Vomero, Via Partenope along the sea-
front, and the Chiaia area (between Piazza dei Martiri and Via dei Mille).
A more bohemian contingent makes for the centro storico and the area
around Piazza Bellini. The scene is relatively relaxed—you might even be
able to sit down at a proper table. Keep in mind that clubs, and their clien-
tele, can change rapidly, so do some investigating before you hit the town.

Caffè Intramoenia. The granddaddy of all the bars in Piazza Bellini was set
up as a bookstore in the late 1980s and still has its own small publishing
house with a variety of attractive titles. Seats in the heated veranda are
at a premium in winter, though many sit outside all year round. ⊠ *Pi-
azza Bellini 70, Spaccanapoli* ☎ *081/290988* ⊕ *www.intramoenia.it.*

Enoteca Belledonne. This place is something of an institution among
inhabitants of the more upscale Chiaia area. Between 8 and 9 in the
evening it seems like the whole neighborhood has descended into the
tiny space for an *aperitivo* (cocktail). The small tables and low stools
are notably uncomfortable, but the cozy atmosphere and the pleasure
of being surrounded by glass-front cabinets full of wine bottles with
beautiful labels more than makes up for it. Excellent local wines are
available by the glass at great prices. ⊠ *Vico Belledonne a Chiaia 18,
Chiaia* ☎ *081/403162* ⊕ *www.enotecabelledonne.com.*

SHOPPING

Leather goods, jewelry, and cameos are some of the best items to buy in Campania. In Naples you can generally find good deals on handbags, shoes, and clothing. Most boutiques and department stores are open Monday 4:30–8; Tuesday–Saturday 9:15–1 and 4:30–8. The larger chains now open on Sunday, too.

SHOPPING DISTRICTS

Most of the luxury shops in Naples are along a crescent that descends the Via Toledo to Piazza Trieste e Trento and then continues along Via Chiaia to Via Filangieri and on to Piazza Amedeo, as well as continuing south toward Piazza dei Martiri and the Riviera di Chiaia. Within this area, the Via Chiaia probably has the greatest concentration and variety of shops (and café–pastry shop Cimmino, on the corner of Via Filangieri and Via Chiaia, makes for an excellent rest stop en route). The area around Piazza Vanvitelli, and Via Scarlatti in particular, in the Vomero also has a nice selection of shops outside the tourist zone. These can be conveniently reached by funiculars from Piazza Amedeo, Via Toledo, or Montesanto or the metro Linea 2. Secondhand book dealers tend to collect in the area between Piazza Dante, Via Port'Alba, and Via Santa Maria di Constantinopoli. Antiques stores can also be found in the latter. The charming shops specializing in Presepi (Nativity scenes) are in Spaccanapoli, on the Via San Gregorio Armeno. Via San Sebastiano, close to the Conservatory, is the kingdom of musical instruments.

SPECIALTY STORES

Ferrigno. Shops selling Nativity scenes cluster along the Via San Gregorio Armeno in Spaccanapoli, and they're all worth a glance. The most famous is Ferrigno: Maestro Giuseppe Ferrigno died in 2008, but the family business continues, still faithfully using 18th-century techniques. ⊠ *Via San Gregorio Armeno 10, Spaccanapoli* ☎ *081/5523148* ⊕ *www. arteferrigno.it.*

Nel Regno di Pulcinella. This is the workshop of Lello Esposito, a Neapolitan artist renowned for his renderings of a popular puppet named Pulcinella. A statue of his creation was recently unveiled in Vico dei Fico al Purgatorio, just off Via dei Tribunali. ⊠ *Vico San Domenico Maggiore 9, Spaccanapoli* ☎ *081/5514171* ⊕ *www.lelloesposito.com.*

FAMILY **Ospedale delle Bambole.** This tiny storefront operation with a laboratory across the street is a world-famous "hospital" for dolls, in business since 1850—it's a wonderful place to take kids. ⊠ *Via San Biagio dei Librai 81, Spaccanapoli* ☎ *339/5872274* ⊕ *www.ospedaledellebambole.it* ☾ *Weekdays 10–3.*

Tramontano. Since 1865 this place has been crafting fine leather luggage, bags, shoes, belts, and wallets. ⊠ *Via Chiaia 142, Chiaia* ☎ *081/414837* ⊕ *www.tramontano.it.*

HERCULANEUM, VESUVIUS, AND POMPEII

Volcanic ash and mud preserved the Roman towns of Herculaneum and Pompeii almost exactly as they were on the day Mt. Vesuvius erupted in AD 79, leaving them not just archaeological ruins but museums of daily life in the ancient world. The two cities and the volcano that buried them can be visited from either Naples or Sorrento, thanks to the Circumvesuviana, the suburban railroad that provides fast, frequent, and economical service.

13

HERCULANEUM

10 km (6 miles) southeast of Naples.

GETTING HERE AND AROUND

Take a train on the Circumvesuviana to Ercolano. From the station, walk across at the nearest traffic circle and head down Via 4 Novembre for 10 minutes. If driving from Naples, take the Ercolano exit from the Napoli–Salerno Autostrada. Follow signs for Scavi di Ercolano.

VISITOR INFORMATION

Ufficio Turistico ⊠ *Via IV Novembre 82, Ercolano* ☎ *081/7881243* ⊙ *Mon.–Sat. 8–6.*

EXPLORING

Fodor's Choice **Herculaneum Ruins.** Lying more than 50 feet below the present-day town ★ of Ercolano, the ruins of Herculaneum are set among the acres of greenhouses that make this area one of Europe's principal flower-growing centers. About 5,000 people lived here when it was destroyed; many of them fishermen, craftsmen, and artists. In AD 79 the gigantic eruption of Vesuvius (which also destroyed Pompeii) buried the town under a tide of volcanic mud. The semiliquid mass seeped into the crevices and niches of every building, covering household objects, enveloping textiles and wood—and sealing all in a compact, airtight tomb.

Excavation began in 1738 under King Charles of Bourbon, using the technique of underground tunneling. Digging was interrupted but recommenced in 1828, continuing until the following century. Today less than half of Herculaneum has been excavated. (With contemporary Ercolano and the unlovely Resina Quarter—famous among bargain hunters for its secondhand-clothing market—sitting on top of the site, progress is limited.) From the ramp leading down to Herculaneum's well-preserved edifices, you get a good overall view of the site, as well as an idea of the amount of volcanic debris that had to be removed to bring it to light.

Though Herculaneum had only one-third the population of Pompeii and has been only partially excavated, what has been found is generally better preserved. In some cases you can even see the original wooden beams, staircases, and furniture. Do not miss the Villa dei Papiri, an excavation in a corner of the site, built by Julius Caesar's father-in-law. The building is named for the 1,800 carbonized papyrus scrolls dug up here in the 18th century, leading scholars to believe that this may have been a study center or library.

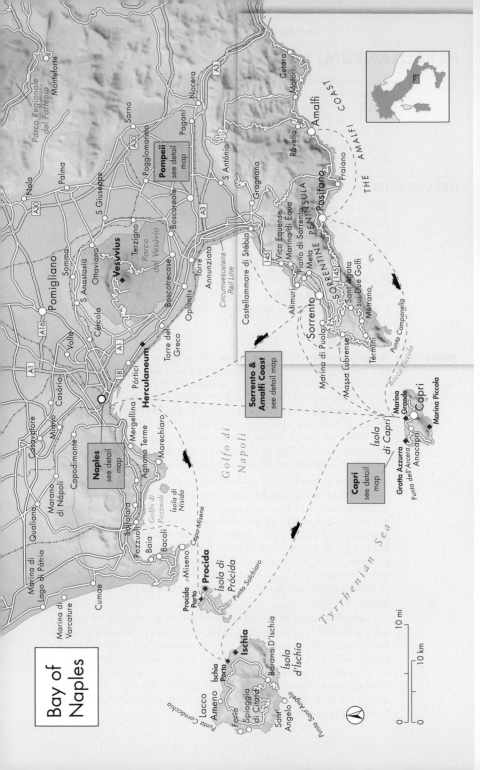

Bay of Naples

Parco Regionale del Partenio

Monteforte

Nola

Palma

A30

Sarno

Nocera

Pagani

S António

A3

S Giuseppe

Somma

S Anastasia

Ottaviano

Terzigno

Parco del Vesúvio

Vesuvius

A30

Poggiomarino

Pompeii
see detail map

Gragnana

Pomigliano

A16

Cercola

Volla

Casória

Marano di Nápoli

Casavatore

Miano

A1

18

Casoria

Capodimonte

Boscoreale

Boscotrecase

Torre del Greco

Oplontis

Torre Annunziata

Castellammare di Stábia

Vico Equense

Marina di Équa

Piano di Sorrento

Meta

SORRENTINE PENINSULA

Alimuri

145

Gragnano

Quagliano

Soccavo

Pozzuoli

Agnano Terme

Mergellina

Pórtici

Herculaneum

Marechiaro

Naples
see detail map

Golfo di Pozzuoli

Isola di Nisida

Golfo di Napoli

Sorrento & Amalfi Coast
see detail map

Marina di Puolo

Marina di Cantone

Sant'Agata sui Due Golfi

Metrano

Massa Lubrense

Sorrento

Vico Equense

145

Ravello

Amalfi

THE AMALFI COAST

Praiano

Positano

Praiano

Cetara

Maiori

Bocca Piccola

Punta Campanella

Marina Grande

Capri
see detail map

Ísola di Capri

Capri

Marina Piccola

Grotta Azzurra

Anacapri

Punta dell'Arcera

Marina di Lago di Pátria

Marina di Varcature

Cumae

Bacoli

Baia

Capo Miseno

Miseno

Procida Porto

Procida

Ísola di Prócida

Punta Solchiaro

Tyrrhenian Sea

Lacco Ameno

Forio

Spiaggia di Citara

Punta Corndchia

Sant' Angelo

Ischia Porto

Barano D'Ischia

Ísola d'Ischia

Ischia

Punta Sân Ângelo

Circumvesuviana Rail Line

10 mi

10 km

0

Pompeii Prep

Pompeii, impressive under any circumstances, comes alive if you do some homework before seeing it in person.

First, read up—there are piles of good books on the subject, including these engaging, jargon-free histories: *Pompeii: The Day a City Died* by Robert Etienne, *Pompeii: Public and Private Life* by Paul Zanker, and *The Lost World of Pompeii* by Colin

Amery. For accurate historical information woven into the pages of a thriller, pick up *Pompeii: A Novel* by Robert Harris.

Second, be sure to visit the Museo Archeologico Nazionale (MANN) in Naples, where most of the finest art from Pompeii now resides. The museum is a remarkable treasure trove—and a rewarding place to visit even if Pompeii isn't in your plans.

13

Be sure to stock up on refreshments beforehand, as there is no food at the archaeological site. At the entrance, pick up a map showing the gridlike layout of the dig. Splurge on an audio guide (€6.50 for one, €10 for two); then head down the tunnel to start the tour at the old shoreline. Recent restoration means most of the houses are open and a fair cross-section of domestic, commercial, and civic buildings can be seen. Decorations are especially delicate in the **Casa del Nettuno ed Anfitrite** (House of Neptune and Amphitrite), named for the subjects of a still-bright mosaic on the wall of the *nymphaeum* (a recessed grotto with a fountain), and in the **Terme Femminili** (Women's Baths), where several delicate black-and-white mosaics embellished the rooms. Annexed to the former house is a remarkably preserved wine shop, where amphorae still rest on carbonized wood shelves. On the other side of the house is the **Casa del Bel Cortile** (House of the Beautiful Courtyard). One of its inner rooms displays a cast taken of three skeletons found in the storerooms down at the old seafront, where almost 300 inhabitants sought refuge from the eruption and were ultimately encapsulated for posterity. The **Casa dei Cervi** (House of the Stags), with an elegant garden open to the sea breezes, evokes a lively, luxurious way of life. The sumptuously decorated **Terme Suburbane** (Suburban Baths) is well worth a visit if it is open. ⊠ *Corso Resina 6, Ercolano* ☎ *081/8575347* ⊕ *www.pompeiisites.org* 🎫 *€11 for Herculaneum only; €20 for biglietto cumulativo ticket to 5 sites (Pompeii, Herculaneum, Boscoreale, Oplontis, and Stabiae) valid for 3 days* ⊘ *Nov.–Mar., daily 8:30–5, ticket office closes at 3:30; Apr.–Oct., daily 8:30–7:30, ticket office closes at 6.*

FAMILY

Fodor'sChoice

★

Museo Archeologico Virtuale (MAV). Dazzling "virtual" versions of Herculaneum's streets and squares, computerized re-creations of the House of the Faun, even a multi-D simulation of Vesuvius erupting: Herculaneum's 1st-century-meets-the-21st-century museum extravaganza has it all. After stopping at the ticket office for the headset audio tour (€3), you descend, as in an excavation, to a floor below. Passing ancient faces that have now been given a name, the *percorso* path inserts you inside a re-creation of Herculaneum's first dig, replete with voices echoing from large terra-cotta vases.

You'll experience Herculaneum's Villa dei Papiri before and—even more dramatically—during the eruption, courtesy of special effects; enter "the burning cloud" of AD 79 (actually vaporized water); then emerge, virtually speaking, inside Pompeii's House of the Faun, which can be seen both as it is and (depending on a mere movement of your feet) as it was for two centuries BC. The next re-creation—complete with rippling grass and moving cart and oxen—is again Villa dei Papirii. Then comes a stellar pre- and post-flooding view of Baia's "Nymphaeum," the now-displaced statues arrayed as they were in the days of Emperor Claudius who commissioned them. Another screen displays Villa Jovis, Tiberius's residence on Capri.

Visitors here are also invited to take a front-row seat for "Day and Night in the Forum of Pompeii," with soldiers, litter-bearing slaves, and toga-clad figures moving spectrally to complete the spell; or to make a vicarious visit to the "Lupari" brothels, their various pleasures illustrated in virtual and graphic frescoes along the walls. There are holograms of jewelry of the earthquake fugitives and a touch-and-browse section of the Papyrii's 1,800 scrolls, too. Recent installations add reconstructions of Herculaneum's theater and baths, and Pompeii's gladiator school. The most spectacular of all, though, is a vivid simulation of the eruption of Vesuvius, with even the floor vibrating to give you an as-close-to-real-as-possible feel for what happened that fateful day. "Wisdom begins in wonder," said Socrates and this museum does a great job in proving the ancient philosopher correct. ⊠ *Via IV Novembre 44, Ercolano* ☏ *081/19806511* ⊕ *www.museomav.it* 🎫*€11.50 (€7.50 museum only, €5 eruption simulation only)* ⊘ *Tues.–Fri. 9:30–5, weekends 9:30–5.*

VESUVIUS

8 km (5 miles) northeast of Herculaneum, 16 km (10 miles) east of Naples.

GETTING HERE AND AROUND

To arrive by car, take the A3 Napoli–Salerno highway exit "Ercolano" or "Torre del Greco" and follow signs for the Parco Nazionale del Vesuvio.

Vesuvio Express. Based at Ercolano Circumvesuviana train station, runs minibuses to the parking lot and the starting point of the path up to the cone's summit (€10 round-trip). There are also services from Pompeii. ☏ *081/7393666* ⊕ *www.vesuvioexpress.info.*

EXPLORING

Mt. Vesuvius. As you tour the cities that it destroyed, you may be overwhelmed by the urge to explore Vesuvius itself. In summer especially, the prospect of rising above the sticky heat of Naples is a heady one. The view when the air is clear is magnificent, with the curve of the coast and the tiny white houses among the orange and lemon blossoms. If the summit is lost in mist you'll be lucky to see your hand in front of your face. When you see the summit clearing—it tends to be clearer in the afternoon—head for it. If possible, see Vesuvius after you've toured the ruins of buried Herculaneum to appreciate the magnitude of the volcano's power.

Continued on page 781

ANCIENT POMPEII
TOMB OF A CIVILIZATION

The site of Pompeii, petrified memorial to Vesuvius's eruption on the morning of August 24, AD 79, is the largest, most accessible, and probably most famous of excavations anywhere.

A busy commercial center with a population of 10,000–20,000, ancient Pompeii covered about 160 acres on the seaward end of the fertile Sarno Plain. Today Pompeii is choked with both the dust of 25 centuries and more than 2 million visitors every year; only by escaping the hordes and lingering along its silent streets can you truly fall under the site's spell. On a quiet backstreet, all you need is a little imagination to sense the shadows palpably filling the dark corners, to hear the ancient pipe's falsetto and the tinny clash of cymbals, to envision a rain of rose petals gently covering a Roman senator's dinner guests. Come in the late afternoon when the site is nearly deserted and you will understand that the true pleasure of Pompeii is not in the seeing but in the feeling.

A FUNNY THING HAPPENS ON THE WAY TO THE FORUM

as you walk through Pompeii. Covered with dust and decay as it is, the city seems to come alive. Perhaps it's the familiar signs of life observed along the ancient streets: bakeries with large ovens just like those for making pizzas, tracks of cart wheels cut into the road surface, graffiti etched onto the plastered surfaces of street walls. Coming upon a *thermopolium* (snack bar), you imagine natives calling out, "Let's move on to the am-phitheater." But a glance up at Vesuvius, still brooding over the scene like an enormous headstone, reminds you that these folks—whether

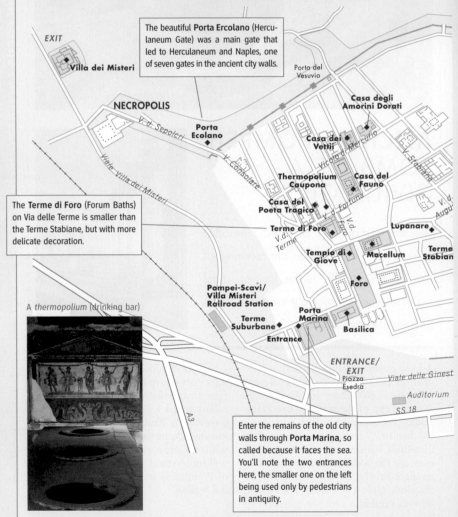

EXIT

Villa dei Misteri

The beautiful **Porta Ercolano** (Herculaneum Gate) was a main gate that led to Herculaneum and Naples, one of seven gates in the ancient city walls.

Porto del Vesuvio

NECROPOLIS

V. d. Sepolcri

Viale Villa dei Misteri

Porta Ecolano

V. Consolare

Casa degli Amorini Dorati

Casa dei Vettii

Vicolo di Mercurio

V. Stabiana

Thermopolium Caupona

Casa del Fauno

The **Terme di Foro** (Forum Baths) on Via delle Terme is smaller than the Terme Stabiane, but with more delicate decoration.

Casa del Poeta Tragico

V. d. Fortuna

V. d. Augu

V. d. Terme

Terme di Foro

V. d. Foro

Lupanare

Tempio di Giove

Macellum

Terme Stabian

Pompei-Scavi/ Villa Misteri Railroad Station

Foro

A *thermopolium* (drinking bar)

Porta Marina

Terme Suburbane

Entrance

Basilica

A3

ENTRANCE/ EXIT Piazza Esedra

Viale delle Ginest

Auditorium

SS 18

Enter the remains of the old city walls through **Porta Marina**, so called because it faces the sea. You'll note the two entrances here, the smaller one on the left being used only by pedestrians in antiquity.

imagined in your head or actually wearing a mantle of lava dust—have not taken a breath for centuries. The town was laid out in a grid pattern, with two main intersecting streets. The wealthiest took a

Pompeii's cemetery, or Necropolis

whole block for themselves; those less fortunate built a house and rented out the front rooms, facing the street, as shops. There were good numbers of *tabernae* (taverns) and *thermopolia* on almost every corner, and frequent shows at the amphitheater.

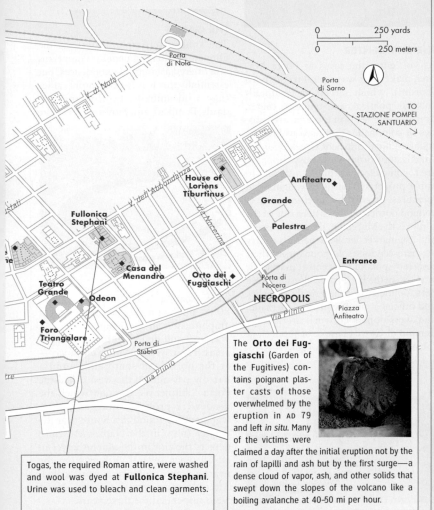

Togas, the required Roman attire, were washed and wool was dyed at **Fullonica Stephani**. Urine was used to bleach and clean garments.

The **Orto dei Fuggiaschi** (Garden of the Fugitives) contains poignant plaster casts of those overwhelmed by the eruption in AD 79 and left *in situ*. Many of the victims were claimed a day after the initial eruption not by the rain of lapilli and ash but by the first surge—a dense cloud of vapor, ash, and other solids that swept down the slopes of the volcano like a boiling avalanche at 40-50 mi per hour.

PUBLIC LIFE IN ANCIENT POMPEII

Forum

THE CITY CENTER

As you enter the ruins at Porta Marina, make your way uphill to the **Foro** (Forum), which served as Pompeii's cultural, political, and religious center. You can still see some of the two stories of colonnades that used to line the square. Like the ancient Greek *agora* in Athens, the Forum was a busy shopping area, complete with public officials to apply proper standards of weights and measures. Fronted by an elegant three-column portico on the eastern side of the forum is the **Macellum**, the covered meat and fish market dating to the 2nd century BC; here vendors sold goods from their reserved spots in the central market. It was also in the Forum that elections were held, politicians let rhetoric fly, speeches and official announcements were made, and worshippers crowded around the **Tempio di Giove** (Temple of Jupiter), at the northern end of the forum.

Basilica

On the southwestern corner is the **Basilica**, the city's law court and the economic center. These rectangular aisled halls were the model for early Christian churches, which had a nave (central aisle) and two side aisles separated by rows of columns. Standing in the Basilica, you can recognize the continuity between Roman and Christian architecture.

THE GAMES

The **Anfiteatro** (Amphitheater) was the ultimate in entertainment for Pompeians and offered a gamut of experiences, but essentially this was for gladiators rather than wild animals. By Roman standards, Pompeii's amphitheater was quite

Amphitheater

small (seating 20,000). Built in about 80 BC, making it the oldest permanent amphitheater in the Roman world, it was oval and divided into four seating areas. There were two main entrances—at the north and south ends—and a narrow passage on the west called the Porta Libitinensis, through which the dead were probably dragged out. A wall painting found in a house near the theater (now in the Naples Museum) depicts the riot in the amphitheater in AD 59 when several citizens from the nearby town of Nocera were killed. After Nocerian appeals to Nero, shows were suspended for three years.

Fresco of Pyramus and Thisbe in the House of Loreius Tiburtinus

BATHS AND BROTHELS

In its day, Pompeii was celebrated as the Côte d'Azur, the seaside Brighton, the Fire Island of the ancient Roman empire. Evidence of a Sybaritic bent is everywhere—in the town's grandest villas, in its baths, and especially in its rowdiest *lupanaria* (brothels), murals still reveal a worship of hedonism. Satyrs, bacchantes, hermaphrodites, and acrobatic couples are pictured indulging in hanky-panky.

The first buildings to the left past the ticket turnstiles are the **Terme Suburbane** (Suburban Baths), built—by all accounts without permission—right up against the city walls. The baths have eyebrow-raising frescoes in the *apodyterium* (changing room) that strongly suggest that more than just bathing and massaging went on here. Reservations are required for entry.

On the walls of **Lupanare** (brothel) are scenes of erotic games in which clients could engage. The **Terme Stabiane** (Stabian Baths) had underground furnaces, the heat from which circulated beneath the floor, rose through flues in the walls, and escaped through chimneys. The water temperature could be set for cold, lukewarm, or hot. Bathers took a lukewarm bath to prepare themselves for the hot room. A tepid bath came next, and then a plunge into cold water to tone up the skin. A vigorous massage with oil was followed by rest, reading, horseplay, and conversation.

GRAFFITI

Thanks to those deep layers of pyroclastic deposits from Vesuvius that protected the site from natural wear and tear over the centuries, graffiti found in Pompeii provide unique insights into the sort of things that the locals found important 2,000 years ago. A good many were personal and lend a human dimension to the disaster that not even the sights can equal.

At the baths: "What is the use of having a Venus if she's made of marble?"

At the entrance to the front lavatory at a private house: "May I always and everywhere be as potent with women as I was here."

On the Viale ai Teatri: "A copper pot went missing from my shop. Anyone who returns it to me will be given 65 bronze coins."

In the Basilica: "A small problem gets larger if you ignore it."

PRIVATE LIFE IN ANCIENT POMPEII

The facades of houses in Pompeii were relatively plain and seldom hinted at the care and attention lavished on the private rooms within. When visitors arrived they passed the shops and entered an open peristyle, from which the occupants received air, sunlight, and rainwater, the latter caught by the *impluvium*, a rectangular-shaped receptacle under the sloped roof. In the back was a receiving room, the *tablinum*, and behind was another open area, the atrium. Life revolved around this uncovered inner courtyard, with rows of columns and perhaps a garden with a fountain. Only good friends ever saw this part of the house, which was surrounded by *cubicula* (bedrooms) and the *triclinium* (dining area). Interior floors and walls usually were covered with colorful marble tiles, mosaics, and frescoes.

Several homes were captured in various states by the eruption of Vesuvius, each representing a different slice of Pompeiian life.

House of Paquius Proculus

The **Casa del Fauno** (House of the Faun) displayed wonderful mosaics, now at the Museo Archeologico Nazionale in Naples. The **Casa del Poeta Tragico** (House of the Tragic Poet) is a typical middle-class house. On the floor is a mosaic of a chained dog and the inscription *cave canem* ("Beware of the dog"). The **Casa degli Amorini Dorati** (House of the Gilded Cupids) is an elegant, well-preserved home with original marble decorations in the garden. Many paintings and mosaics were executed at **Casa del Menandro** (House of Menander), a patrician's villa named for a fresco of the Greek playwright. Two blocks beyond the Stabian Baths you'll notice on the left the current digs at the **Casa dei Casti Amanti** (House of the Chaste Lovers). A team of plasterers and painters were at work here when Vesuvius erupted, redecorating one of the rooms and patching up the cracks in the bread oven near the entrance—possibly caused by tremors a matter of days before.

Small Garden
Triclinium
Owner's Quarters
Kitchen
Servant's Quarters
Secondary Atrium
Entrance
Garden
Main Peristyle
Impluvium
Atrium

CASA DEI VETTII

The **House of the Vettii** is the best example of a house owned by wealthy *mercatores* (merchants). It contains vivid murals—a magnificent *pinacoteca* (picture gallery) within the very heart of Pompeii. The scenes here—except for those in the two wings off the atrium—were all painted after the earthquake of AD 62. Once inside, cast an admiring glance at the delicate frieze around the wall of the *triclinium* (on the right of the peristyle garden as you enter from the atrium), depicting cupids engaged in various activities, such as selling oils and perfumes, working as goldsmiths and metalworkers, acting as wine merchants, or performing in chariot races. Another of the main attractions in the Casa dei Vettii is the small cubicle beyond the kitchen area (to the right of the atrium) with its faded erotic frescoes now protected by Perspex screens.

UNLOCKING THE VILLA DEI MISTERI

Villa dei Misteri

There is no more astounding, magnificently memorable evidence of Pompeii's devotion to the pleasures of the flesh than the frescoes on view at the **Villa dei Misteri** (Villa of the Mysteries), a palatial abode 400 yards outside the city gates, northwest of Porta Ercolano. Unearthed in 1909, this villa had more than 60 rooms painted with frescoes; the finest are in the *triclinium*. Painted in the most glowing Pompeiian reds and oranges, the panels relate the saga of a young bride (Ariadne) and her initiation into the mysteries of the cult of Dionysus, who was a god imported to Italy from Greece and then given the Latin name of Bacchus. The god of wine and debauchery also represented the triumph of the irrational—of all those mysterious forces that no official state religion could fully suppress.

Pompeii's best frescoes, painted in glowing reds and oranges, retain an amazing vibrancy.

The Villa of the Mysteries frescoes were painted circa 50 BC, most art historians believe, and represent the peak of the Second Style of Pompeiian wall painting. The triclinium frescoes are thought to have been painted by a local artist, although the theme may well have been copied from an earlier cycle of paintings from the Hellenistic period. In all there are 10 scenes, depicting children and matrons, musicians and satyrs, phalluses and gods. There are no inscriptions (such as are found on Greek vases), and after 2,000 years historians remain puzzled by many aspects of the triclinium cycle. Scholars endlessly debate the meaning of these frescoes, but anyone can tell they are the most beautiful paintings left to us by antiquity. In several ways, the eruption of Vesuvius was a blessing in disguise, for without it, these masterworks of art would have perished long ago.

PLANNING FOR YOUR DAY IN POMPEII

GETTING THERE

The archaeological site of Pompeii has its own stop (Pompei–Villa dei Misteri) on the Circumvesuviana line to Sorrento, close to the main entrance at the Porta Marina, which is the best place from which to start a tour. If, like many visitors every year, you get the wrong train from Naples (stopping at the other station "Pompei"), all is not lost. There's another entrance to the excavations at the far end of the site, just a seven-minute walk to the Amphitheater.

ADMISSION

Single tickets cost €11 and are valid for one full day. The site is open Apr.–Oct., daily 8:30–7:30 (last admission at 6), and Nov.–Mar., daily 8:30–5 (last admission at 3:30). For more information, call 081/8575347 or visit www.pompeiisites.org.

WHAT TO BRING

The only restaurant inside the site is both overpriced and busy, so it makes sense to bring along water and snacks. If you come so equipped, there are some shady, underused picnic tables outside the Porta di Nola, to the northeast of the site.

MAKING THE MOST OF YOUR TIME

Visiting Pompeii does have its frustrating aspects: many buildings are blocked off by locked gates, and enormous group tours tend to clog up more popular attractions. But the site is so big that it's easy to lose yourself amid the quiet side streets. To really see the site, you'll need four or five hours.

Three buildings within Pompeii—Terme Suburbane, Casa del Menandro, and Casa degli Amorini Dorati—are open for restricted viewing. Reservations must be made on-line at www.arethusa.net, where you can find information on opening times.

TOURS

To get the most out of Pompeii, rent an audio guide (€6.50 for one, €10 for two; you'll need to leave an ID card) and opt for one of the three itineraries (2 hours, 4 hours, or 6 hours). If hiring a guide, make sure the guide is registered for an English tour and standing inside the gate; agree beforehand on the length of the tour and the price, and prepare yourself for soundbites of English mixed with dollops of hearsay. For a higher quality (but more expensive) full-day tour, try Context Travel (⊕ www.contexttravel.com).

MODERN POMPEI

Caught between the hammer and anvil of cultural and religious tourism, the modern town of Pompei (to use the modern-day Italian spelling, not the ancient Latin) is now endeavoring to polish up its act. In attempts to ease congestion and improve air quality at street level, parts of the town have been pedestrianized and parking restrictions tightened. Several hotels have filled the sizable niche in the market for excellent deals at affordable prices. As for recommendable restaurants, if you deviate from the archaeological site and make for the center of town, you will be spoiled for choice.

IF YOU LIKE POMPEII

If you intend to visit other archaeological sites nearby during your trip, you should buy the *biglietto cumulativo* pass, a combination ticket with access to four area sites (Herculaneum, Pompeii, Oplontis, Boscoreale). It costs €20 and is valid for three days. Unlike many archaeological sites in the Mediterranean region, those around Naples are almost all well served by public transport; ask about transportation options at the helpful Porta Marina information kiosk.

Local EAV buses (☎ *081/0141094* ⊕ *www.eavbus.it*) climb the volcano from Pompeii ten times daily (€10 round trip) with two morning connections from Naples. Those who cannot wait for the bus can ride the 10-seat minibus run by Vesuvio Express, leaving from Ercolano train station (☎ *081/7393666* ⊕ *www.vesuvioexpress.it*). This is a quick, painless, and relatively cheap way of getting to the top. The vehicles thread their way rapidly up on back roads, reaching the top in 20 minutes. Allow at least 2½ hours for the journey, including a 30-minute walk to the crater on a soft cinder

WORD OF MOUTH

"My son and I did the Vesuvius trek when he was 18 and just 3 months out of chemo for NHL. The climb was well worth it even though we could not see the crater because when we got up there, we were in a cloud. The path is not too difficult and when we were there, there was an old man renting out walking sticks for one euro. It was a nice thing to have."

—Basingstoke

13

track. The €8 admission to the crater includes a compulsory guide service, usually young geologists with a smattering of English. At the bottom you'll be offered a stout walking stick (a small tip is appreciated on return). The climb can be tiring if you're not used to steep hikes. Because of the volcanic stone you should wear athletic shoes, not sandals. ☎ *081/7775720* 🖃 *€8* ⏱ *Daily 9 am–2 hrs before sunset.*

Osservatorio Vesuviano (*Vesuvius Observatory*). At the observatory—2,000 feet up—you can view instruments used to study the volcano, some dating to the middle of the 19th century. ⊠ *Via Osservatorio, Ercolano* ☎ *081/6108483 booking and information, 081/7777149 museum* ⊕ *www.ov.ingv.it* 🖃 *Free* ⏱ *Weekends 10–2.*

ISCHIA AND PROCIDA

Though Capri gets star billing among the islands that line the Bay of Naples, Ischia and Procida also have their own, lower-key appeal. Ischia is a popular destination on account of its spas, beaches, and hot springs. Procida, long the poor relation of the three and the closest to Naples, is starting to capitalize on its chief natural asset, the unspoiled isle of Vivara. The pastel colors of Procida will be familiar to anyone who has seen the widely acclaimed film *Il Postino*.

PROCIDA

35 mins by hydrofoil, 1 hr by car ferry from Naples.

Lying barely 3 km (2 miles) from the mainland and 10 km (6 miles) from the nearest port of Pozzuoli, Procida is an island of enormous contrasts. It's the most densely populated island in Europe—just more than 10,000 people are crammed into less than 3½ square km (less than 1½ square miles)—and yet there are oases such as Marina Corricella and Vivara that seem to have been bypassed by modern civilization. It's no surprise that picturesque Procida has strong artistic traditions and is widely deemed to be a painters' paradise.

GETTING HERE AND AROUND

Procida's ferry timetable caters to the many daily commuters who live on the island and work in Naples or Pozzuoli. The most frequent—and cheapest—connections are from the Port of Pozzuoli. After stopping at Procida's main port, Marina Grande (also called Sancio Cattolico), many ferries and hydrofoils continue on to Ischia, for which Procida is considered a halfway house.

VISITOR INFORMATION

Procida Tourism Office ✉ *Via Marina* ☎ *081/8101968* 🌐 *www.procida.net.*

EXPLORING

Corricella. This sleepy fishing village, used as the setting for the waterfront scenes in the Oscar-winning film *Il Postino,* has been relatively immune to life in the limelight. Apart from the opening of an extra restaurant and bar, there have been few changes. This is the type of place where even those with failing grades in art class feel like reaching for a paintbrush to record the delicate pink and yellow facades. The **Graziella** bar at the far end of the seafront offers the island's famous lemons squeezed over crushed ice to make an excellent granita.

WHERE TO EAT

$$ SOUTHERN ITALIAN 🍴 **La Conchiglia.** A meal at this beachfront spot really offers an appreciation of the magic of Procida. Beyond the lapping waves, Capri twinkles in the distance. The seafood is divinely fresh and the pasta dishes usually soul-warming. Access here is either on foot down the steps from Via Pizzaco or by boat from the Corricella harborfront—phone owner Gianni if you want the latter to pick you up (it's free for diners). [$] *Average meal: €40* ✉ *Via Pizzaco 10* ☎ *081/8967602* 🌐 *www.laconchigliaristorante.com* ⏲ *Closed mid-Nov.–Mar.*

ISCHIA

45 mins by hydrofoil, 90 mins by car ferry from Naples, 60 mins by ferry from Pozzuoli.

Whereas Capri wows you with its charm and beauty, Ischia takes time to cast its spell. In fact, an overnight stay is probably not long enough for the island to get into your blood. Admittedly there are few signs of antiquity here, the architecture is unremarkable, the traffic can be overwhelming, and hoteliers have yet to achieve a balanced mix of clientele—most are either German (off-season) or Italian (in-season). But Ischia does have its share of vine-growing villages beneath the lush volcanic slopes of Monte Epomeo, and unlike Capri it enjoys a life of its own that survives when the tourists head home. So this is an ideal spot should you want to plunk down in the sun for a few days and tune out the world. When Augustus gave the Neapolitans Ischia for Capri, he knew what he was doing.

The island is volcanic in origin, and from its hidden reservoir of seething molten matter come thermal springs said to cure whatever ails you. As early as 1580 a doctor named Lasolino published a book about the mineral wells at Ischia. "If your eyebrows fall off," he wrote, "go and try the baths at Piaggia Romano. If you know anyone who is getting bald, anyone who suffers from elephantiasis, or another whose wife yearns for a child, take the three of them immediately to the Bagno di Vitara; they will bless you." Today Ischia is covered with thermal baths, often surrounded by tropical gardens.

A good 35-km (22-mile) road makes a circuit of the island; the ride takes most of a day if you stop along the way to enjoy the views and perhaps have lunch. You can also book a boat tour around it at the booths in various ports along the coast; there's a one-hour stop at Sant'Angelo. The information office is at the harbor. You may drive on Ischia year-round. There's fairly good bus service as well, and you'll find plenty of taxis.

13

GETTING HERE AND AROUND
Ischia is well connected with the mainland in all seasons. The last boats leave for Naples and Pozzuoli at about 8 pm (in the very high season there's a midnight sailing), and you should allow plenty of time for getting to the port and buying a ticket. Ischia has three ports—Ischia Porto, Casamicciola, and Forio (hydrofoils only)—so choose your ferry or hydrofoil according to your destination. Cars can be brought to the island relatively freely, though there are restrictions for residents of Naples.

VISITOR INFORMATION
Azienda Autonoma di Cura, Soggiorno e Turismo. The information office is housed in the historic municipal bath building. ✉ *Ufficio Informazioni, Banchina Porto Salvo, Ischia Porto* ☎ *081/5074231* 🖷 *081/5074230* ⊕ *www.infoischiaprocida.it* ☉ *Mon.–Sat. 9.2 and 3–8.*

EXPLORING
Casamicciola. This popular beach resort is 5 km (3 miles) west of Ischia Porto.

Forio. The far-western and southern coasts of Ischia are more rugged and attractive. Forio, at the extreme west, has a waterfront church and is a good spot for lunch or dinner.

Giardini Poseidon Terme (*Poseidon Gardens Spa*). These sybaritic hot pools are on Citara Beach, south of Forio. You can sit like a Roman senator on a stone chair recessed in the rock and let the hot water cascade over you—all very campy, and fun. ✉ *Via Giovanni Mazzella 87, Forio* ☎ *081/9087111* ⊕ *www.giardiniposeidonterme.com* 🖷 *€32 for one day, special deal for two* ☉ *Apr.–Oct., daily 9–7.*

Ischia Ponte. Most of the hotels are along the beach in the part of town called Ischia Ponte, which gets its name from the *ponte* (bridge) built by Alfonso of Aragon in 1438 to link the picturesque castle on a small islet offshore with the town and port. For a while the castle was the home of Vittoria Colonna, poetess, granddaughter of Renaissance Duke Federico da Montefeltro (1422–82), and platonic soul mate of Michelangelo, with whom she carried on a lengthy correspondence. You'll find a typical resort atmosphere: countless cafés, shops, and restaurants, and a 1-km (½-mile) stretch of fine-sand beach. ✉ *Ischia Porto.*

Ischia Porto. Ischia Porto is the largest town on the island and its main port. It's no workaday place, however, but rather a lively resort with plenty of hotels, the island's best shopping area, and low, flat-roof houses on terraced hillsides overlooking the water. Its narrow streets and villas and gardens are framed by pines. ⊠ *Ischia Porto.*

Lacco Ameno. This chic and upscale spot, next to Casamicciola, is distinguished by a mushroom-shape rock offshore and some of the island's best hotels. Here, too, you can enjoy the benefits of Ischia's therapeutic waters. ⊠ *Ischia Porto.*

Monte Epomeo. The inland town of Fontana is the base for excursions to the top of this long-dormant volcano that dominates the island landscape. You can reach its 2,585-foot peak in less than 1½ hours of relatively easy walking.

Sant'Angelo. On the southern coast, this is a charming village with a narrow path leading to its promontory; the road doesn't reach all the way into town, so it's free of traffic. It's a five-minute boat ride from the beach of Maronti, at the foot of cliffs.

WHERE TO EAT

$$

SOUTHERN
ITALIAN

✕ **Da Gennaro.** The oldest restaurant on the island has been a favorite of the stars, including Tom Cruise and Sophia Loren. Family-run, it opened on the seafront overlooking the boats in 1965 and continues to serve excellent fish in a convivial atmosphere. Specialties include risotto *alla pescatore* (with shellfish) and linguine *all'aragosta* (with lobster). In perfect English, friendly owner Gennaro will happily take you through the celebrity-laden wall of photos. $ *Average meal: €40* ⊠ *Via Porto 32, Ischia Porto* ☎ *081/992917* ⊕ *www.ristorantegennaro. it* ⊗ *Closed Nov.–mid-Mar.*

$

SOUTHERN
ITALIAN

✕ **Ristorante Calise Capriccio.** The town's most centrally located restaurant is run by Caffè Calise, which has been in business since 1925. Bang in the middle of the square, this one-time nightclub has a terrace overlooking the busy road and the boats of the tourist marina. Presided over by Giuseppe Marra (who has an impressive international CV), the menu is based on the day's catch with an experimental twist. Starters include fried *calamaretti* (squid) with onion, and swordfish with capers. Local wine accompanies *paccheri con cozze e pecorino*, a bold combination of pasta with mussels sprinkled with cheese. Leave space for the glorious deserts, all from the renowned Calise *pasticceria*—try the yummy Valentina cake (strawberries and cream on a sponge base). $ *Average meal: €25* ⊠ *Piazza Marina, Casamicciola* ☎ *081/994724* ⊗ *Closed Nov.–Mar.*

WHERE TO STAY

For expanded hotel reviews, visit Fodors.com.

$

HOTEL

Fodor'sChoice

★

⊡ **Albergo Il Monastero.** The Castello Aragonese, in a quiet traffic-free area, houses this hotel with a peaceful ambience and rustic rooms that overlook the Mediterranean far below. **Pros:** stunning views; how often do you get to stay in a castle? **Cons:** rather difficult to negotiate the steps before reaching the elevator; some consider it too far from the town's action. $ *Rooms from: €120* ⊠ *Castello Aragonese 3, Ischia Ponte* ☎ *081/992435* ⊕ *www.albergoilmonastero.it* ⇥*21 rooms* ⊗ *Closed Nov.–Mar.* ⦿*Breakfast.*

$$$$ HOTEL Fodor's Choice ★ [H] **Mezzatorre Resort & Spa.** Far from the madding, sunburned crowds that swamp Ischia, this luxurious getaway sits in splendid isolation on the extreme promontory of Punta Cornacchia. **Pros:** tranquil retreat; wonderful views; shuttle provided from Lacco Ameno. **Cons:** very isolated. [$] *Rooms from: €310* ✉ *Via Mezzatorre 23, Forio d'Ischia* ☎ *081/986111* 🌐 *www.mezzatorre.it* 🛏 *57 rooms* ⏲ *Closed Nov.–Apr.* 🍴 *Breakfast.*

$ HOTEL [H] **Villa Antonio.** With a superlative panoramic view over the Bay of Cartaromana, with the Castello Aragonese posing front and center, the Antonio offers a quiet haven five minutes from the crowds. **Pros:** attractive price; lovely seaside location. **Cons:** many steps to negotiate before elevator; guest rooms' small windows don't do justice to the view. [$] *Rooms from: €90* ✉ *Via S. Giuseppe della Croce, Ischia Ponte* ☎ *081/982660* 🌐 *www.villantonio.it* 🛏 *18 rooms* 💳 *No credit cards* ⏲ *Closed Nov.–mid-Mar.* 🍴 *Breakfast.*

13

CAPRI

Once a pleasure dome to Roman emperors and now Italy's most glamorous seaside getaway, Capri (pronounced with an emphasis on the first syllable) is a craggy island at the southern end of the bay, 75 minutes by boat or 40 minutes by hydrofoil from Naples. The boom in cruises to the Naples area (almost 1 million passengers annually) means that Capri is inundated with day-trippers, making seemingly simple excursions (like the funicular ride up from Marina Grande) a nerve-fraying experience. Yet even the crowds are not enough to destroy Capri's special charm. The town is a Moorish opera set of shiny white houses, tiny squares, and narrow medieval alleyways hung with flowers. It rests on top of rugged limestone cliffs hundreds of feet above the sea, and on which herds of *capre* (goats) used to roam—thereby giving Capri its name. Unlike the other islands in the Bay of Naples, this one is not of volcanic origin; it may be a continuation of the limestone Sorrento Peninsula.

Limestone caves on Capri have yielded rich prehistoric and Neolithic finds. The island is thought to have been settled by Greeks from Cumae in the 6th century BC and later by other Greeks from Neapolis, but it was the Romans in the early Imperial period who really left their mark. Emperor Augustus vacationed here; Tiberius built a dozen villas around the island, and, in later years, he refused to return to Rome, even when he was near death. In the 16th century Capri was one of the strongholds of the pirate Barbarossa, who first sacked it and then made it a fortress. In 1806 the British wanted to turn the island into another Gibraltar and were beginning to build fortifications until the French took it away from them in 1808. Over the next century, from the opening of its first hotel in 1826, Capri saw an influx of visitors that reads like a Who's Who of literature and politics, especially in the early decades of the 20th century.

Like much else about Capri, the island's rare and delicious white wine is sensuous and intoxicating. Note, though, that most of the wine passed off as "local" comes from the much more extensive vineyards of Ischia.

GETTING HERE AND AROUND

Capri is well connected with the mainland in all seasons, though there are more sailings between April and October. You can't, however, return to Naples after about 10:20 pm in high season (in low season often 8 pm or even earlier). Hydrofoils, Seacats, and similar vessels leave from Molo Beverello (below Piazza Municipio) in Naples, while ferries leave from Calata Porta di Massa (1,000 yards to the east) and *aliscafi* (hydrofoils) also sail from the small marina of Mergellina, a short distance west of the Villa Comunale in Naples.

VISITOR INFORMATION

Azienda Autonoma di Cura, Soggiorno e Turismo. The tourist office's excellent website has an English-language version. ⊠ *Banchina del Porto, Marina Grande* ☎ *081/8370634* ⊕ *www.capritourism.com* ☉ *Mon.–Sat. 8:30–8:30, Sun. 9–3 in high season; Mon.–Sat. 8:30–2:30 in winter* ⊠ *Piazza Umberto I, Capri Town* ☎ *081/8370686* ⊠ *Via G. Orlandi 59, Anacapri* ☎ *081/8371524.*

EXPLORING
TOP ATTRACTIONS

Fodor's Choice ★ **Grotta Azzurra.** Only when the Grotta Azzurra was "discovered" in 1826 by the Polish poet August Kopisch and Swiss artist Ernest Fries, did Capri become a tourist haven. The watery cave's blue beauty became a symbol of the return to nature and revolt from reason that marked the Romantic era, and it soon became a required stop on the Grand Tour. In reality, the grotto had long been a local landmark. During the Roman era—as testified by the extensive remains, primarily below sea level, and several large statues now at the Certosa di San Giacomo—it had been the elegant, mosaic-decorated nymphaeum of the adjoining villa of Gradola. Historians can't quite agree if it was simply a lovely little pavilion where rich patricians would cool themselves or truly a religious site where sacred mysteries were practiced. The water's extraordinary sapphire color is caused by a hidden opening in the rock that refracts the light. At highest illumination the very air inside seems tinted blue.

The Grotta Azzurra can be reached from Marina Grande or from the small embarkation point below Anacapri on the northwest side of the island, accessible by bus from Anacapri. If you're pressed for time, however, skip this sometimes frustrating and disappointing excursion. You board one boat to get to the grotto, then transfer to a smaller boat that takes you inside. If there's a backup of boats waiting to get in, you'll be given precious little time to enjoy the gorgeous color of the water and its silvery reflections. ⊠ *€25.50 from Marina Grande, €12.50 by rowboat from Grotta Azzurra near Anacapri* ☉ *9–1 hr before sunset; closed if sea is even minimally rough.*

Fodor's Choice ★ **Villa San Michele.** From Anacapri's Piazza Vittoria, picturesque Via Capodimonte leads to Villa San Michele, the charming former home of Swedish doctor and philanthropist Axel Munthe (1857–1949) that Henry James called "the most fantastic beauty, poetry, and inutility that one had ever seen clustered together." At the ancient entranceway to Anacapri at the top of the Scala Fenicia, the villa is set around Roman-style courtyards, marble walkways, and atria. Rooms display the doctor's varied collections, which range from bric-a-brac to antiquities. Medieval choir stalls, Renaissance lecterns, and gilded statues of saints are all part of the setting, with some rooms preserving the doctor's personal memorabilia. A spectacular pergola path overlooking the entire Bay of Naples leads from the villa to the famous Sphinx Parapet, where an ancient Egyptian sphinx looks out toward Sorrento: you cannot see its face—on purpose. It is said that if you touch the sphinx's hindquarters with your left hand while making a wish, it will come true. The parapet is connected to the little Chapel of San Michele, on the grounds of one of Tiberius's villas.

13

Besides hosting summer concerts, the Axel Munthe Foundation has an ecomuseum that fittingly reflects Munthe's fondness for animals. There you can learn about various bird species—accompanied by their songs—found on Capri. Munthe bought up the hillside and made it a sanctuary for birds. ⊠ *Viale Axel Munthe 34, Anacapri* ☎ *081/8371401* ⊕ *www.villasanmichele.eu* ⊠ *€7* ⊘ *Nov.–Feb., daily 9–3:30; Mar., daily 9–4:30; Apr. and Oct., daily 9–5; May–Sept., daily 9–6.*

WORTH NOTING

Anacapri. A tortuous road leads up to Anacapri, the island's "second city," about 3 km (2 miles) from Capri Town. To get here you can take a bus either from Via Roma in Capri Town or from Marina Grande (both €1.80), or a taxi (about €30 one-way; agree on the fare before starting out). Crowds are thick down Via Capodimonte leading to Villa San Michele and around Piazza Vittoria, the square where you catch the chairlift to the top of Monte Solaro. Via Vinestrale leads to the noted **Le Boffe quarter,** centered on the Piazza Ficacciate. Le Boffe owes its name to the distinctive domestic architecture prevalent here, which uses vaults and sculpted groins instead of crossbeams. Elsewhere, Anacapri is quietly appealing. It's a good starting point for walks, such as the 80-minute round-trip journey to the **Migliara Belvedere,** on the island's southern coast.

Capri Town. On arrival at the port, pick up the excellent map (€1) of the island at the tourist office. You may have to wait for the funicular railway (€1.80 one way) to Capri Town, some 450 feet above the harbor. So this might be the time to splurge on an open-top taxi—it could save you an hour in line. From the upper station, walk out into Piazza Umberto I, better known as the Piazzetta, the island's social hub.

Certosa di San Giacomo. You can window-shop in expensive boutiques and browse in souvenir shops along Via Vittorio Emanuele, which leads south toward the many-domed Certosa di San Giacomo. You'll be able to visit the church and cloister of this much-restored monastery and also pause long enough to enjoy the breathtaking sight of Punta Tragara and the Faraglioni, three towering crags, from the viewing point at the edge of the cliff. ⊠ *Via Certosa* ☎ *081/8376218* ⊕ *www.polomusealenapoli. beniculturali.it* ⊠ *Free* ⊘ *Tues.–Sun. 9–2; longer for exhibitions.*

OFF THE
BEATEN
PATH
Villa Jovis. From Capri Town, the hike east to Villa Jovis (the grandest of those built by Tiberius) is strenuous but rewarding. Follow the signs for it, taking Via Le Botteghe from the Piazzetta; then continuing along Via Croce and Via Tiberio. At the end of a lane that climbs the

steep hill, with pretty vistas all the way, you come to the precipice over which the emperor reputedly disposed of the victims of his perverse attentions. From a natural terrace above, near a chapel, are spectacular views of the entire Bay of Naples and, on clear days, part of the Gulf of Salerno. Here starts the footpath around the ruins of Tiberius's palace. Allow 45 minutes each way for the walk alone. ⊠ *Via A. Maiuri* ☎ *€2* ⊙ *11–3; closed 1st 2 Tues. and last 2 Sun. of month.*

Giardini di Augusto (*Gardens of Augustus*). From the terraces of this beautiful public garden, you can see the village of Marina Piccola below—restaurants, cabanas, and swimming platforms huddle among the shoals—and admire the steep, winding Via Krupp, actually a staircase cut into the rock. Friedrich Krupp, the German arms manufacturer, loved Capri and became one of the island's most generous benefactors. If you find the path too challenging you can reach the beach by taking a bus from the Via Roma terminus down to Marina Piccola. ⊠ *Via Matteotti, beyond monastery of San Giacomo* ☎ *€1* ⊙ *Daily dawn–dusk.*

Monte Solaro. An impressive limestone formation and the highest point on Capri (1,932 feet), Monte Solaro affords gasp-inducing views toward the bays of both Naples and Salerno. A 12-minute chairlift ride will take you right to the top (refreshments available at the bar), where you can launch out on a number of scenic trails on the western side of the island. Picnickers should note that even in summer it can get windy at this height, and there are few trees to provide shade or refuge. ⊠ *Piazza Vittoria, Anacapri* ☎ *081/8371428* ☎ *€7.50 one-way, €10 round-trip* ⊙ *Daily 9:30–5. Closed Jan. 7–Feb. 7 and in adverse weather conditions.*

San Michele. In the heart of Anacapri, the octagonal Baroque church of San Michele, finished in 1719, is best known for its exquisite majolica pavement designed by Solimena and executed by the *mastro-riggiolaro* (master tiler) Chiaiese from Abruzzo. A walkway skirts the depiction of Adam and a duly contrite Eve being expelled from the Garden of Eden, but you can get a fine overview from the organ loft, reached by a winding staircase near the ticket booth (a privileged perch you have to pay for). ⊠ *Piazza San Nicola, Anacapri* ☎ *081/8372396* ⊕ *www.chiesa-san-michele.com* ☎ *€2* ⊙ *Apr.–Sept., daily 9–7; Oct.–late Nov. and early Dec.–Mar., daily 10–2.*

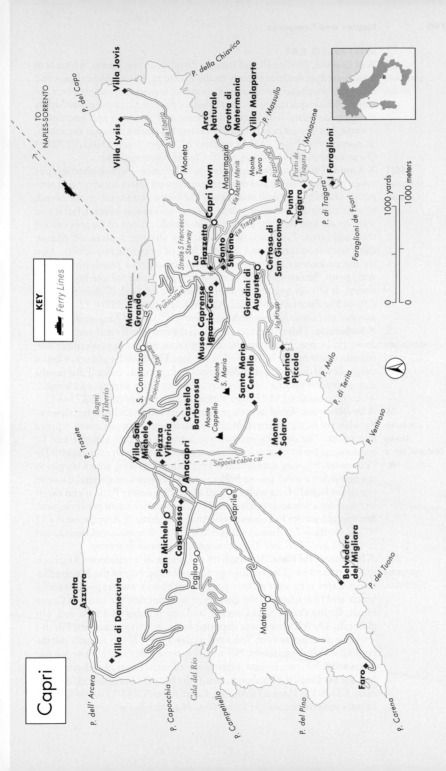

Capri

TO
NAPLES-SORRENTO

P. del Capo

P. della Chiavica

Villa Jovis

Villa Lysis

Arco
Naturale

Grotta di
Matermania

Villa Malaparte

P. Massullo

I Faraglioni

Moneta

Matermania

Via Tiberio

Capri Town

Monte Tuoro

Via Mater Mania

Via Pizzolungo

Porto de
Tragara

Monacone

P. di Tragara

Punta
Tragara

Faraglioni de Fuori

La Piazzetta

Santo
Stefano

Via Tragara

Certosa di
San Giacomo

Strada S Francesco
Stairway

Marina
Grande

Museo Caprense
Ignazio Cerio

Giardini di
Augusto

Funicolare

Via Krupp

S. Constanzo

Bagni
di Tiberio

Phoenician Stairway

Castello
Barbarossa

Santa Maria
a Cetrella

Marina
Piccola

Monte
S. Maria

P. Mulo

P. di Terita

Monte
Cappello

P. Trasele

Villa San
Michele

Piazza
Vittoria

Monte
Solaro

P. Ventroso

Anacapri

Segovia cable car

Caprile

San Michele

Casa Rossa

Pagliaro

Capille

P. dell' Arcera

Grotta
Azzurra

Villa di Damecuta

P. Copocchia

Cala del Rio

Campitello

Materita

Belvedere
del Migliara

P. del Tuono

P. del Pino

Faro

P. Carena

1000 yards

1000 meters

WHERE TO EAT

$$
SOUTHERN
ITALIAN
⚔ **Al Grottino.** This small and friendly family-run restaurant, which is in a 14th-century building handy to the Piazzetta, has arched ceilings and lots of atmosphere; autographed photos of famous customers cover the walls. House specialties are *scialatielli ai fiori di zucchine e gambaretti* (homemade pasta with zucchini flowers and shrimps) and linguine *ai scampi*, but the owner delights in taking his guests through the menu. $ *Average meal: €42* ✉ *Via Longano 27, Capri Town* ☎ *081/8370584* ⊕ *www.ristorantealgrottino.net* ⊗ *Closed Nov.–mid-Mar.*

$$$$
SOUTHERN
ITALIAN
⚔ **Aurora.** Though often frequented by celebrities—whose photographs adorn the walls inside and out—this restaurant offers courtesy and *simpatia* irrespective of your star status. The oldest restaurant on the island, now in its third generation, it has a sleekly minimalist interior, but if you want to see and be seen, book a table outside on one of Capri's chicest thoroughfares. The cognoscenti start by sharing a pizza *all'Acqua*: thin, with mozzarella and a sprinkling of *peperoncino* (chili). Also try the *gnocchetti al pesto con fagiolini croccanti e pinoli* (dumplings with pesto, beans and pine nuts)—but leave room for the homemade sweets. It fills up quickly, so reservations are advised. $ *Average meal: €70* ✉ *Via Fuorlovado 18/22, Capri Town* ☎ *081/8370181* ⊕ *www. auroracapri.com* ⚖ *Reservations essential* ⊗ *Closed Jan.–mid-Mar.*

$
NEAPOLITAN
⚔ **Barbarossa.** This ristorante-pizzeria is the first you'll see if you arrive in Anacapri by bus. Its panoramic covered terrace takes in views of the Barbarossa castle on the hill as well as the sea. The no-frills ambience belies the quality of the cucina: besides pizzas they specialize in local dishes—be sure to try the risotto *con gamberi a limone* (with shrimp and lemon). $ *Average meal: €25* ✉ *Piazza Vittoria 1, Anacapri* ☎ *081/8371483.*

$$
SOUTHERN
ITALIAN
Fodor's Choice
★
⚔ **Da Gelsomina.** Amid its own terraced vineyards with inspiring views to the island of Ischia and beyond, this is much more than just a well-reputed restaurant. The owner's mother was a friend of Axel Munthe and he encouraged her to open a kiosk serving hot food, which evolved into Da Gelsomina. It has an immaculately kept swimming pool, which is open to the public for a small fee—a buffet is served as you lounge here. Close to one of the island's finer walks as well as the Philosophy Park, it's an excellent base for a whole day or longer. There's also a five-room pensione, with free transfer service by request from Anacapri center. $ *Average meal: €32* ✉ *Via Migliara 72, Anacapri* ☎ *081/8371499* ⊕ *www.dagelsomina.com* ⊗ *Closed Jan.–Feb. and Tues. in winter. No dinner in winter.*

$$$
SOUTHERN
ITALIAN
⚔ **La Canzone del Mare.** Although it's not primarily a restaurant, luncheon in the covered pavilion of this legendary bathing lido of the Marina Piccola is Capri at its most picture-perfect. With two seawater pools, a rocky beach, and I Faraglioni in the distance, it was the erstwhile haunt of Gracie Fields, Emilio Pucci, Noël Coward, and any number of 1950s and '60s glitterati. The VIPs may have departed for more private beaches, but this setting is as stellar as ever. You need to pay a fee (€20) to actually use the bathing *stabilimento* (club), but why not make a day of it? There are five suites available, too, in case a day is not enough. Boats also depart from here for Da Luigi, the lido/restaurant at the base of I Fariglioni. $ *Average meal: €55* ✉ *Via Marina Piccola 93, Capri Town* ☎ *081/8370104* ⊕ *www. lacanzonedelmare.com* ⊗ *Closed Oct.–Mar. No dinner.*

$$$ SOUTHERN ITALIAN Fodor's Choice ★ 🍴 **La Capannina.** For decades one of Capri's most celebrity-haunted restaurants, La Capannina is near the busy social hub of the Piazzetta, and the discreet flower-decked covered veranda is ideal for dining by candlelight—or you can join the regulars in the outdoor courtyard. Specialties, aside from an authentic Capri wine with the house label, are ravioli *capresi* and linguine *con lo scorfano* (with scorpion fish), squid stuffed with caciotta cheese and marjoram, and an exquisite *pezzogna* (sea bream cooked whole in a copper casserole, topped with a layer of potatoes). The wine cellar is open for perusal, and their nearby gourmet store ships worldwide. The small late-night bar across the side alleyway is under the same ownership. [$] *Average meal: €50* ✉ *Via Le Botteghe 12b, Capri Town* ☎ *081/8370732* 🌐 *www.capanninacapri.com* ✍ *Reservations essential* ⏲ *Closed Nov.–mid-Mar., and Wed. in Mar. and Oct.*

$$ SOUTHERN ITALIAN 🍴 **La Fontelina.** Given its position right on the water's edge, seafood is almost de rigueur here, but for a slightly different starter, try the *polpette di melanzane* (eggplant fritters); then dip into the vegetable buffet. The house sangria is a highly recommendable, blissful mix of white wine and fresh fruit. La Fontelina also functions as a lido, with steps and ladders into fathoms-deep blue water, and this location—accessible by boat from Marina Piccola or on foot from Punta Tragara (10 minutes)—makes it a good place to spend a delightfully comatose day. Only lunch is served and reservations are recommended during high season. [$] *Average meal: €40* ✉ *At end of Via Tragara, Capri Town* ☎ *081/8370845* ⏲ *Closed mid-Oct.–Easter. No dinner.*

$$ SOUTHERN ITALIAN 🍴 **Le Grottelle.** This extremely informal trattoria enjoys a distinctive setting: it's built up against limestone rocks not far from the Arco Naturale, with a cave at the back doubling as the kitchen and wine cellar. Whether you stumble over it (and are lucky enough to get a table) or make it your destination after an island hike, Le Grottelle will prove memorable, thanks to that ambience and sea views encompassing the Amalfi Coast's Li Galli islands. The food? Oh, that . . . the menu includes ravioli and local rabbit, but go for the seafood, with linguine *con gamberetti e rucola* (with shrimp and arugula) being one of the more interesting specialties. [$] *Average meal: €46* ✉ *Via Arco Naturale 13* ☎ *081/8375719* ✍ *Reservations essential* ⏲ *Closed Nov.–mid-Mar.*

WHERE TO STAY

For expanded hotel reviews, visit Fodors.com.

$$ HOTEL 🏨 **Biancamaria.** This tastefully refurbished hotel with its pleasing facade and whitewashed spreading arches lies in a traffic-free zone close to the heart of Anacapri. **Pros:** friendly staff; Anacapri literally at your doorstep. **Cons:** on the main pedestrian road; no gardens. [$] *Rooms from: €170* ✉ *Via G. Orlandi 54, Anacapri* ☎ *081/8371000* 🌐 *www.hotelbiancamaria.com* 🛏 *25 rooms* ⏲ *Closed mid-Oct.–Easter* 🍽 *Breakfast.*

$$$$ HOTEL Fodor's Choice ★ 🏨 **Capri Tiberio Palace.** Offering comfort, style, luxury, and sigh-inducing views since the 19th century, this hotel is just short walk from the Piazzetta—near the action, but not quite in the thick of it. **Pros:** friendly staff; pure luxury; luggage collected at the port. **Cons:** no port-to-door guest shuttle; some rooms are not as large as expected

in a five-star. $ *Rooms from: €350* ✉ *Via Croce 11–15, Capri Town* ☎ *081/9787111* ⊕ *www.capritiberiopalace.com* ⇆ *38 room, 17 suites* ⊙ *Closed mid-Oct.–mid-Apr.*

$$$$
HOTEL
Fodor's Choice
★

⊡ **J. K. Place.** The most supremely stylish and glamorous hotel in southern Italy, occupying an 1876 villa above Marina Grande harbor, almost makes every other accommodations on Capri seem dowdy and dull. **Pros:** exquisite pool; very close to chic Tiberio beach; free shuttle to town. **Cons:** only for high rollers; pool visible from main road. $ *Rooms from: €700* ✉ *Via Provinciale Marina Grande 225* ☎ *081/8384001* ⊕ *www.jkcapri.com* ⇆ *22 rooms* ⊙ *Closed mid-Oct.– mid-Apr.* �‖ *Breakfast.*

$$
HOTEL

⊡ **La Tosca.** Although it's hard to find in the warren of side streets in Capri Town, La Tosca is worth all the trouble. **Pros:** simple unadorned charm; pleasant owner; free WiFi throughout hotel. **Cons:** a ten-minute walk to the piazzetta; not all rooms have good views. $ *Rooms from: €150* ✉ *Via Birago 5, Capri Town* ☎ *081/8370989* ⊕ *www.latoscahotel. com* ⇆ *10 rooms* ⊙ *Closed Nov.–Feb.* �‖ *Breakfast.*

$$$$
HOTEL
Fodor's Choice
★

⊡ **Punta Tragara.** The most beautiful hotel on Capri—originally a private villa designed by Le Corbusier and site of a secret wartime meeting between Churchill and Eisenhower—was opened in the 1970s by Count Manfredi. **Pros:** a taste of the good life; the entire staff seems to have graduated from the finest finishing schools. **Cons:** a 10-minute walk from the center; some find the style dated, although others find it a plus. $ *Rooms from: €420* ✉ *Via Tragara 57, Capri Town* ☎ *081/8370844* ⊕ *www.hoteltragara.com* ⇆ *23 rooms, 21 suites* ⊙ *Closed mid-Oct.– mid-Apr.* �‖ *Breakfast.*

$$$$
HOTEL
Fodor's Choice
★

⊡ **Quisisana.** Some say there are three villages on Capri: Capri Town, Anacapri, and this celebrated landmark hotel, which looms large in the island's mythology. **Pros:** luxe atmosphere on a large scale. **Cons:** not for all pockets; convention-size and far from cozy. $ *Rooms from: €360* ✉ *Via Camerelle 2, Capri Town* ☎ *081/8370788* ⊕ *www.quisisana.com* ⇆ *148 rooms* ⊙ *Closed Nov.–mid-Mar.* �‖ *Breakfast.*

$$
B&B/INN

⊡ **Villa Krupp.** Occupying a beautiful house overlooking the idyllic Gardens of Augustus, this historic hostelry was once the home of Maxim Gorky, whose guests included Lenin. **Pros:** direct access to the Gardens of Augustus, stunning views. **Cons:** a lot of steps to be negotiated; rooms are simple. $ *Rooms from: €140* ✉ *Viale Matteotti 12, Capri Town* ☎ *081/8370362* ⊕ *www.villakrupp.com* ⇆ *12 rooms* ⊙ *Closed Nov.–Mar.* �‖ *Breakfast.*

$$$
HOTEL

⊡ **Villa Sarah.** Few hotels offer such a quintessentially Caprese spirit as this and, hosted by the De Martino family in one of the island's most pleasant residential quarters, you'll feel like a guest in a private villa. **Pros:** gorgeous pool; lush gardens. **Cons:** a long and steep climb from the Piazzetta; rooms are small. $ *Rooms from: €220* ✉ *Via Tiberio 3/a, Capri Town* ☎ *081/8377817* ⊕ *www.villasarah.it* ⇆ *19 rooms* ⊙ *Closed Nov.–Mar.* �‖ *Breakfast.*

SORRENTO AND THE AMALFI COAST

Sorrento may have become a jumping-off point for visitors to Pompeii, Capri, and Amalfi, but you can find countless reasons to love it for itself. The Sorrentine people are fair-minded and hardworking, bubbling with life and warmth. The tufa cliff on which the town rests is like a great golden pedestal spread over the bay, absorbing the sunlight in deepening shades through the mild days, and orange and lemon trees waft a luscious perfume in spring. In the evening, people fill cafés to nibble, sip, and talk nonstop; then, arms linked, they stroll and browse through the divinely picturesque maze of shop-lined lanes that is the Old Town quarter of Sorrento. Like a Belle Époque stage set—festooned with palazzi, charming streets, and gorgeous landmarks—it is custom-tailored for one of the most enjoyable promenades you will ever take.

It has been this way for centuries, ever since Sorrento became a prescribed stop for Grand Tour travelers, who savored its mild winters while sopping up its culture and history. According to a letter from his traveling companion in 1876, the philosopher Nietzsche, not generally known for effervescence, "laughed with joy" at the thought of going to Sorrento, and French novelist Stendhal called it "the most beautiful place on earth." Many visitors still share his opinion.

SORRENTO

50 km (31 miles) south of Naples.

Winding along a cliff above a small beach and two harbors, Sorrento is split in two by a narrow ravine formed by a former mountain stream. To the east, dozens of hotels line busy Via Correale along the cliff— many have "grand" included in their names, and some indeed still are. To the west, however, is the historic sector, which still enchants—it's a relatively flat area, with winding, stone-paved lanes bordered by balconied buildings, some joined by medieval stone arches. Every corner is another photo-op, the sound of strumming mandolins never far away. The central piazza is named after the poet Torquato Tasso, born here in 1544. This part of town is a delightful place to walk through, especially in the mild evenings, when people are out and about, and everything is open. Craftspeople are often at work in their stalls and shops and are happy to let you watch; in fact, that's the point. You will probably enjoy two or three of the most romantic hours in your life strolling about here. Along the way, be sure to stop in—whether for a drink or meal—at one of the town's unbelievably magical grand hotels, such as the Excelsior-Vittorio or the Bellevue-Syrene.

GETTING HERE AND AROUND

From downtown Naples, take a Circumvesuviana train from Stazione Centrale (Piazza Garibaldi) or hydrofoil from Molo Beverello. If you're coming directly from the airport in Naples, pick up a direct bus to Sorrento. By car, take the A3 Naples–Salerno highway; exiting at Castellammare, follow the signs for Penisola Sorrentina, and then for Sorrento.

Sorrento and Amalfi Coast

VISITOR INFORMATION

Azienda Autonoma di Soggiorno Sorrento-Sant'Agnello. Besides dispensing a wealth of information, the tourist office also has a useful booking service for hotels, B&Bs, and vacation apartments throughout the peninsula. ⊠ *Via L. De Maio 35* ☎ *081/8074033* 🖷 *081/8773397* ⊕ *www.sorrentotourism.com* ☉ *Weekdays 8:30–4:15 (also Sat. 8:30–4:15 in summer).*

EXPLORING

Convento di San Francesco. Near the Villa Comunale gardens and sharing its view over the Bay of Naples, the convent is celebrated for its 14th-century cloister. Filled with greenery and flowers, the Moorish-style cloister has interlaced pointed arches of tufa rock, alternating with octagonal columns topped by elegant capitals, supporting smaller arches. The combination makes a suitably evocative setting for summer concerts and theatrical presentations. The church portal is particularly impressive, with the original 16th-century door featuring intarsia (inlaid) work. The interior's 17th-century decoration includes an altarpiece, by a student of Francesco Solimena, depicting St. Francis receiving the stigmata. The convent is now an art school, where students' works are often exhibited. ⊠ *Piazza S. Francesco* ☎ *081/8781269* 🖅 *Free* ☉ *Daily 8–1:30 and 3:30–8.*

Marina Grande. Via Marina Grande turns into a pedestrian lane, then a stairway leading to Sorrento's only real beach at Marina Grande, where fishermen pull up their boats and some good seafood restaurants are found. A frequent bus also descends to the beach; tickets are sold at the *tabacchi* (tobacconist).

Museo Correale di Terranova. In an 18th-century villa with a lovely garden, on land given to the patrician Correale family by Queen Joan of Aragon in 1428, this museum is a highlight of Sorrento and a must for connoisseurs of the *seicento* (Italian 17th century). It has an eclectic private collection amassed by the count of Terranova and his brother—one of the finest devoted to Neapolitan paintings, decorative arts, and porcelains. Magnificent 18th-century inlaid tables by Giuseppe Gargiulo, Capodimonte porcelains, and rococo portrait miniatures are reminders of the age when pleasure and delight were everything. Also on view are regional Greek and Roman archaeological finds, medieval marble work, glasswork, old-master paintings, 17th-century majolicas—even the poet Tasso's death mask. The building itself is fairly charmless, with few period rooms, but the garden offers an allée of palm trees, citrus groves, floral nurseries, and an esplanade with a panoramic view of the Sorrento coast. ⊠ *Via Correale 50* ☎ *081/8781846* ⊕ *www.museocorreale. it* ⌦ *€7* ⊘ *Tues.–Sat. 9:30–6:30, Sun 9:30–1:30.*

13

Sedile Dominova. Enchanting showpiece of the Largo Dominova—the little square that is the heart of Sorrento's historic quarter—the Sedile Dominova is a picturesque open loggia with expansive arches, balustrades, and a green-and-yellow-tile cupola, originally constructed in the 16th century. The open-air structure is frescoed with 18th-century trompe-l'oeil columns and the family coats of arms, which once belonged to the *sedile* (seat), the town council where nobles met to discuss civic problems as early as the Angevin period. Today Sorrentines still like to congregate around the umbrella-topped tables near the tiny square. ⊠ *Largo Dominova at Via S. Cesareo and Via P.R. Giuliani* ⊘ *Daily 9–1 and 4–8.*

Villa Comunale. The largest public park in Sorrento sits on a clifftop overlooking the entire Bay of Naples. It offers benches, flowers, palms, and people-watching, plus a seamless vista that stretches from Capri to Vesuvius. From here steps lead down to Sorrento's main harbor, the Marina Piccola. ⊠ *Adjoining church of San Francesco.*

WHERE TO EAT

$$$$
SOUTHERN
ITALIAN

✕ **Don Alfonso 1890.** Campania's most heralded restaurant is the domain of Alfonso Iaccarino: *haute*-hungry pilgrims come here to feast on culinary rarities, often centuries-old recipes given a unique spin. The braciola of lamb with pine nuts and raisins is a recipe that dates to the Renaissance, and the cannoli stuffed with foie gras pays homage to the Neapolitan Bourbon court. Nearly everything is homegrown, and the wine cellar ranks among the finest in Europe. Those who want to make a night of it can stay in one of eight suites above the restaurant. $ *Average meal: €110* ⊠ *Corso Sant'Agata 13* ☎ *081/8780026* ⊕ *www.donalfonso.com* ⊘ *Closed Nov.–Mar.; closed Mon. and Tues. in Apr., May, and Oct.; closed Mon. and no lunch June–Sept.*

$ SOUTHERN ITALIAN

🍴 **La Basilica.** Under the same ownership as the Ristorante Museo Caruso, this budget alternative to its famous brother has no cover or service charges, but offers the same wine list (about 1,700 labels) plus a bountiful choice of hearty Italian dishes. In a tiny alley between piazzas Tasso and St. Antonino, its main salon is decorated with modern paintings of an erupting Vesuvius, but for a more romantic setting, the smaller room on the opposite side of the road has a tiny balcony overlooking the tortuous road to the harbor. There is also outside seating. Try the *strozzapreti* ("priest-chokers") pasta with scampi and cherry tomatoes or the fabulous rice cake on zucchini sauce. [$] *Average meal: €25* ✉ *Via S. Antonino 28* ☎ *081/8774790* 🌐 *www.ristorantelabasilica.com.*

$$ SOUTHERN ITALIAN Fodor's Choice ★

🍴 **La Favorita—'o Parrucchiano.** This restaurant is in a sprawling, multilevel, high-ceiling greenhouse and orchard, with tables and chairs set amid enough tropical greenery to fill a Victorian conservatory. The effect is enchantingly 19th century. Opened in 1868 by an ex-priest (*'o parrucchiano* means "the priest's place" in the local dialect), La Favorita continues to serve classic Sorrentine cuisine. The shrimp baked in lemon leaves, cannelloni, homemade Sorrentine pasta, chocolate and hazelnut cake, and lemon profiteroles are all excellent, but they can't compete with the unique interior. [$] *Average meal: €35* ✉ *Corso Italia 71* ☎ *081/8781321* 🌐 *www.parrucchiano.com* ⏲ *Closed Wed. from mid-Nov.–mid-Mar.*

$$$ SOUTHERN ITALIAN Fodor's Choice ★

🍴 **Ristorante Museo Caruso.** It's not surprising that a restaurant named for an internationally acclaimed opera star would carry an international and operatic theme through from *preludio* appetizers, such as shrimp in a limoncello dressing, to *rapsodia delicatesse* desserts, like crêpes suzette. Sorrentine favorites, including ravioli with broccoli sauce and squid with almonds, are also tweaked creatively. The staff is warm and helpful, the singer on the sound system is the long-departed "fourth tenor" himself, and the operatic memorabilia (including posters and old photos of Caruso) is viewed in a flattering blush-pink light. This elegant restaurant deserves its longtime popularity. It is open from noon to midnight and has five-course tasting menus from €40. [$] *Average meal: €50* ✉ *Via S. Antonino 12* ☎ *081/8073156* 🌐 *www.ristorantemuseocaruso.com.*

WHERE TO STAY

For expanded hotel reviews, visit Fodors.com.

$$$$ HOTEL Fodor's Choice ★

🏨 **Bellevue Syrene.** In the late 19th century, Empress Eugénie of France came for a week and stayed three months—you'll understand why if you choose this retreat, magnificently set on a bluff high over the Bay of Naples. **Pros:** impeccable design elements; elegant common areas; half board available. **Cons:** very expensive; parking is €25 a day. [$] *Rooms from: €450* ✉ *Piazza della Vittoria 5* ☎ *081/8781024* 🌐 *www.bellevue.it* 🛏 *49 rooms* ⏲ *Closed Jan.–Mar.* 🍽 *Some meals.*

$$$$ HOTEL Fodor's Choice ★

🏨 **Excelsior Vittoria.** Overlooking the Bay of Naples, this luxurious Belle Époque dream has been in the same family since 1834; they have traded witticisms with Alexandre Dumas and Oscar Wilde, welcomed crowned heads, and comforted the dying Caruso. **Pros:** beyond the protected gates you're in the heart of town; gardens buffer city noise. **Cons:** not all rooms have sea views; some rooms are rather small; front desk can be cold. [$] *Rooms from: €330* ✉ *Piazza Tasso 34* ☎ *081/8071044, 800/980053 in Italy* 🌐 *www.exvitt.it* 🛏 *97 rooms* 🍽 *Breakfast.*

$$$ HOTEL [icon] **Grand Hotel La Favorita.** Sorrento is rightly known for gorgeous and sumptuous hotels, but the traditional choices have had to make room for this glamorous newcomer—a striking beauty that can hold its own against some great hotel names. **Pros:** central location; beautiful terrace; idyllic garden. **Cons:** no views from the guest rooms. [$] *Rooms from: €260* ✉ *Via T. Tasso 61* ☎ *081/8782031* 🌐 *www.hotellafavorita.com* 🛏 *80 rooms, 5 suites* ⏲ *Closed Nov. and Jan.–Mar.* 🍴 *Breakfast.*

$$ B&B/INN [icon] **Relais Palazzo Starace.** There is no lobby and no view, but this B&B does boast a gentle price tag in a central part of town, and that's a winning combo for summertime Sorrento. **Pros:** great location; helpful owner; competitive prices; discounted parking at nearby garage. **Cons:** no views; room with a/c on balcony is noisy. [$] *Rooms from: €60* ✉ *Via Santa Maria della Pietà 9* ☎ *081/8784031* 🌐 *www.palazzostarace.com* 🛏 *5 rooms* ⏲ *Closed Jan. and Feb.* 🍴 *Breakfast.*

13

THE AMALFI COAST

One of the most gigglingly gorgeous places on Earth, this corner of Campania tantalizes, almost beyond bearing, the visitor who can stay but a day or two. Poets and millionaires have long journeyed here to see and sense its legendary sights: perfect, precariously perched Positano (a claim that is more than alliteration); Amalfi, a shimmering medieval city; romantic mountain-high Ravello; and ancient Paestum, with its three legendary Greek temples.

Today, the coast's scenic sorcery makes this a top destination and also a honeymoon Shangri-la—it is arguably the most divinely sensual 48-km (30-mile) stretch of water, land, and habitation on Earth.

By the late 19th century tourism had begun to blossom, giving rise to the creation of the two-lane Amalfi Drive, what has come to be called the "Divina Costiera." A thousand or so gorgeous vistas and a photo-op at nearly every bend appear along these almost 40 km (25 miles), stretching from just outside Sorrento to Vietri, coursing over deep ravines and bays of turquoise-to-sapphire water, spreading past tunnels and timeless villages.

The justly famed jewels along this coastal necklace are Positano, Amalfi, and Ravello, which fill up in high season but in the surrounding countryside not much seems to have changed since the Middle Ages: mountains are still terraced and farmed for citrus, olives, wine, and dairy; and the sea is dotted with the gentle reds, whites, and blues of fishermen's boats. Vertiginously high villages, dominated by the spires of *chiese* (churches), are crammed with houses on, into, above, and below hillsides to the bay; crossed by mule paths; and navigated by flights of steps called *scalinatelle* often leading to outlooks and belvederes that take your breath away—in more ways than one.

Semitough realities lurk behind the scenic splendor of the Divina Costiera, most notably the extremes of driving (potentially dangerous, although accidents are reassuringly rare), the endless steps, and virtually nonexistent parking. Furthermore, it often rains in spring, parts of the hills burn dry in summer, museums are few, and until you adjust, people seem to talk at maximum decibels. So what? For a precious little time, you are in a land of unmarred beauty.

POSITANO

14 km (9 miles) east of Sorrento, 57 km (34 miles) south of Naples.

When John Steinbeck lived here in 1953, he wrote that it was difficult to consider tourism an industry because "there are not enough *tourists.*" It's safe to say that Positano, a village of white Moorish-style houses clinging to slopes around a small sheltered bay, has since been discovered. Another Steinbeck observation still applies, however: "Positano bites deep. It is a dream place that isn't quite real when you are there and becomes beckoningly real after you have gone. . . . The small curving bay of unbelievably blue and green water laps gently on a beach of small pebbles. There is only one narrow street, and it does not come down to the water. Everything else is stairs, some of them as steep as ladders. You do not walk to visit a friend, you either climb or slide."

In the 10th century Positano was part of Amalfi's maritime republic, which rivaled Venice as an important mercantile power. During its 16th-and-17th-century heyday, its ships traded in the Near and Middle East carrying spices, silks, and precious woods. But the coming of the steamship in the mid-19th century led to the town's decline and some three-fourths of its 8,000 citizens emigrated to America.

What had been reduced to a forgotten fishing village is now the number-one attraction on the coast. From here you can take hydrofoils to Capri in summer, escorted bus rides to Ravello, and tours of the Grotta dello Smeraldo. If you're staying in Positano, check whether your hotel has a parking area. If not, you'll have to pay for space in a lot, which is almost impossible to find during the high season, from Easter to September. The best bet for day-trippers is to arrive by bus—there's a regular, if crowded, service from Sorrento—or else get to Positano early enough to find an overpriced parking space.

No matter how much time you spend here, make sure you have some comfortable walking shoes (no heels) and that your back and legs are strong enough to negotiate those daunting *scalinatelle* (little stairways). Alternatively, you can ride the municipal bus, which frequently plies along the one-and-only-one-way Via Pasitea: a hairpin road running from Positano's central Piazza dei Mulini to the mountains and back, making a loop through the town every half hour. Heading down from the Sponda bus stop toward the beach, you pass Le Sirenuse, the hotel where Steinbeck stayed in 1953. Its stepped terraces offer vistas over the town, so you might splurge on lunch or a drink on the pool terrace, a favorite gathering place for Modigliani-sleek jet-setters.

GETTING HERE AND AROUND

SitaSud buses leave from the Circumvesuviana train station in Sorrento. Buses also run from Naples and, in summer, Rome. But June to September your best option is the ferry from Sorrento or Naples.

VISITOR INFORMATION

Azienda Autonoma Soggiorno e Turismo ⊠ *Via del Saracino 4* ☎ *089/875067* ⊕ *www.aziendaturismopositano.it* ⊙ *Oct.–May, Mon.–Sat. 9–4:30; June–Sept., Mon.–Sat. 9–7, Sun. ???.*

EXPLORING

Palazzo Murat. Past a bevy of resort boutiques, head to Via dei Mulini 23 to view the prettiest garden in Positano—the 18th-century courtyard of the Palazzo Murat, named for Joachim Murat, who sensibly chose the palazzo as his summer residence. This was where Murat, designated by his brother-in-law Napoléon as King of Naples in 1808, came to forget the demands of power and lead the simple life. Since Murat was a Continental style setter, it couldn't be *too* simple; he built this grand abode (now a hotel) just steps from the main beach. ⊠ *Via dei Mulini 23* ☏ *089/875177* ⊕ *www.palazzomurat.it.*

13

Santa Maria Assunta. Beyond the Palazzo Murat is the Chiesa Madre, or parish church of Santa Maria Assunta, its green-and-yellow majolica dome topped by a perky cupola visible from just about anywhere in town. Built on the site of the former Benedictine abbey of Saint Vito, the 13th-century Romanesque structure was almost completely rebuilt in 1700. The last piece of the ancient mosaic floor can be seen under glass behind the altar. Note the carved wooden Christ, a masterpiece of devotional religious art, with its bathetic face and bloodied knees, on view before the altar. At the altar is a Byzantine 13th-century painting on wood of Madonna with Child, known popularly as the Black Virgin, carried to the beach every August 15 to celebrate the Feast of the Assumption. Legend claims that the painting was once stolen by Saracen pirates, who, fleeing in a raging storm, heard from a voice on high saying, *"Posa, posa"*—"Put it down, put it down." When they placed the image on the beach near the church, the storm calmed, as did the Saracens. Embedded over the doorway of the church's bell tower, set across the tiny piazza, is a medieval bas-relief of fishes, a fox, and a *pistrice* (the mythical half-dragon, half-dog sea monster). This is one of the few relics of the medieval abbey of Saint Vito. The Oratorio houses historic statues from the Sacristy, while renovations to the Crypt have unearthed 1st-century Roman columns. ⊠ *Piazza Flavio Gioia* ☏ *089/875480* ⊕ *www.chiesapositano.com* 🎟 *Crypt €2* ☉ *Church: daily 9–noon, in summer also 4–9. Crypt: daily 9–1 and 4–7, but may not always be open.*

Spiaggia Grande. The walkway from the Piazza Flavio Gioia leads down to the Spiaggia Grande, or main beach, bordered by an esplanade and some of Positano's best—and priciest—restaurants. Head over to the stone pier to the far right of the beach as you face the water.

QUICK
BITES

Bar-Pasticceria La Zagara. If you want to catch your breath after a bus ride to Positano, take a quick time-out here for an espresso, a slice of *Positanese* (a chocolate cake as delectable as its namesake), or a fresh-fruit iced granita. Deservedly famous for its lemon profiteroles as much as for its tree-lined terrace, suspended on a wooden platform above the Lower Town, Zagara is also ideal for morning coffee, an aperitivo, or digestivo. ⊠ *Via dei Mulini 8* ☏ *089/875964* ⊕ *www.lazagara.com.*

Via Positanesi d'America. A staircase leads to this lovely seaside walkway, and halfway up the path you can find the Torre Trasìta. Now a residence available for summer rental, it's the most distinctive of Positano's three coastline defense towers (once used to warn of pirate raids), which, in various states of repair, define the edges of Positano. Continuing along the Via Positanesi d'America you pass tiny inlets and emerald coves until the large beach, Spiaggia di Fornillo, comes into view.

WHERE TO EAT

$$ SOUTHERN ITALIAN 🍴 **Da Adolfo.** On a little beach where pirates used to build and launch boats, this laid-back trattoria has long been a favorite Positano landmark. The pirates are long gone, but their descendants now operate the free ferry to and from Positano (every half-hour in the morning)—look for the boat with the red fish on the mast named for the restaurant—or make the steep descent from the main coastal road at Laurito. Sit under a straw canopy on the wooden terrace to enjoy *totani con patate* (squid and potatoes with garlic and oil); then sip white wine with peaches until sundown. Some diners even swim—so bathing suits are fine. It gets busy, so ask your hotel to book a table for you: personal reservations are often not honored. [$] *Average meal: €30* ✉ *Spiaggia di Laurito, Via Laurito 40* ☎ *089/875022* 🌐 *www.daadolfo.com* ✍ *Reservations essential* ⏲ *Closed Oct.–Apr.*

$$ SOUTHERN ITALIAN 🍴 **La Pergola.** Occupying a prime location near dead center on Spaggia Grande beach, this arbor-covered seating area offers a fabulous (and festive, due to the happy crowds) setting. Often confused with the equally good Buca di Bacco upstairs, it was a dance club until the 1970s. Dining here is just as seductive, with seafood unsurprisingly being the main fare—be sure to try the *scialatielli ai frutti di mare* (fresh pasta with shellfish) or sea bass in *acqua pazza* (poached in a herb broth). Pizza and chicken breast with fries are also available, if you want to carb up for an afternoon under the beach umbrella. Open until midnight, there's plenty of time to digest before trying the *dolci* (desserts) and ice cream from their own *pasticceria,* Il Vicoletto on Via Sariceno. [$] *Average meal: €35* ✉ *Via del Brigantino 35* ☎ *089/811461* 🌐 *www.bucapositano.it* ⏲ *Closed Nov. and Dec.*

$$ SOUTHERN ITALIAN 🍴 **La Tagliata.** If your enthusiasm for overpriced seafood dishes is waning, La Tagliata has the answer: local produce provide the ingredients for great antipasti, homemade pastas with rich tomato sauce, and meats grilled before your eyes in the dining room. (Ask for a *piccola porzione* unless you are ravenous.) All this comes with endless views of the Amalfi Coast. The prices are reasonable, and include a jug of red wine; however, aficionados will do better choosing their own bottle. Though it lies between Montepertuso and Nocelle, the restaurant will arrange a shuttle to pick you up from your hotel in Positano. [$] *Average meal: €35* ✉ *Via Tagliata 22* ☎ *089/875872* 🌐 *www.latagliata.com* ✍ *Reservations essential* ⏲ *Closed weekdays Dec.–Feb.*

$$ SOUTHERN ITALIAN Fodor's Choice ★ 🍴 **Lo Guarracino.** In a supremely romantic setting, this partly arbor-covered, poised-on-a-cleft aerie is about the most idyllic place to enjoy lemon pasta and glass of vino as you watch the yachts come and go. Set a few steps above Positano's prettiest seaside path, the terrace vista takes in the cliffs, the sea, Li Galli islands, Spiaggia Fornillo, and Torre Clavel. The super-charming backroom arbor, beneath thick, twining vines, where tables are covered in cloths that match the tint of the bay, is *the* place to sit. Fine fish specialties are top delights on the menu. In fact, the day's catch is often cooked, with potatoes, in

the wood-fired pizza oven, which gives it a distinct flavor. [$] *Average meal: €30* ✉ *Via Positanesi d'America 12* ☎ *089/875794* 🌐 *www.loguarracino.net* 🕒 *Closed Jan.–Mar.*

WHERE TO STAY

For expanded hotel reviews, visit Fodors.com.

$$ HOTEL Fodor's Choice ★ 🏨 **La Fenice.** This tiny unpretentious hotel on the outskirts of Positano beckons with bougainvillea-laden views, castaway cottages, and a turquoise seawater pool—all perched over a private beach. **Pros:** paradise; 250 steps to private beach. **Cons:** some rooms overlook noisy road; a 10-minute walk to town. [$] *Rooms from: €155* ✉ *Via G. Marconi 4* ☎ *089/875513* 🌐 *www.lafenicepositano.com* 🛏 *14 rooms* 💳 *No credit cards* 🍴 *Breakfast.*

$$$$ HOTEL 🏨 **Le Sirenuse.** As legendary as its namesake sirens, this 18th-century palazzo has long set the standard for luxury in Italian hotels. **Pros:** unrivalled views; many rooms have whirlpool tubs; close to the bus stop. **Cons:** a bit of a climb from the town center; lower priced rooms are small. [$] *Rooms from: €460* ✉ *Via Cristoforo Colombo 30* ☎ *089/875066* 🌐 *www.sirenuse.it* 🛏 *59 rooms* 🍴 *Breakfast.*

$$$ HOTEL Fodor's Choice ★ 🏨 **Palazzo Murat.** A perfect location in the heart of town above the beachside church of Santa Maria Assunta—and an even more perfect entrance through a bougainvillea-draped patio and garden—help make the Murat a top lodging contender. **Pros:** once a regal residence; stunning surroundings. **Cons:** only five rooms with seaside views; a constant stream of curious day-trippers. [$] *Rooms from: €200* ✉ *Via dei Mulini 23* ☎ *089/875177* 🌐 *www.palazzomurat.it* 🛏 *31 rooms* 🕒 *Closed Nov.–Mar.* 🍴 *Breakfast.*

$ RENTAL 🏨 **Villa Flavio Gioia.** If you are eager to settle in for a while, this villa has bright mini-apartments, each with its own terrace or large balcony, and a cooking area. **Pros:** convenient location; ideal for longer stays. **Cons:** one-week minimum stay in high season; no pool. [$] *Rooms from: €100* ✉ *Piazza Flavio Gioia 2* ☎ *089/875222* 🌐 *www.villaflaviogioia.it* 🛏 *13 rooms* 🕒 *Closed Feb.* 🍴 *No meals.*

GROTTA DELLO SMERALDO

13 km (8 miles) east of Positano, 27 km (17 miles) east of Sorrento.

Grotta dello Smeraldo. A peculiar green light that casts an eerie emerald glow over impressive formations of stalagmites and stalactites, many of them under water, inspired the name of the Grotta dello Smeraldo (Emerald Grotto). You can park at the signposts for the grotto along the coast road and take an elevator down, or you can drive to Amalfi and take a return trip to the grotto by more romantic means—via boat (€10 return from Amalfi, excluding entrance to grotto). ✉ *Beyond Punta Acquafetente by boat, or off Amalfi Dr.* ☎ *089/871107 Amalfi tourist board* 🎫 *€5* 🕒 *Apr.–mid-Oct., daily 9–4; mid-Oct.–Mar., daily 9–3. Closed in adverse weather conditions.*

AMALFI

17 km (11 miles) east of Positano, 35 km (22 miles) east of Sorrento.
"The sun—the moon—the stars—and Amalfi," Amalfitans used to say. During the Middle Ages, Amalfi was an independent maritime state with a population of 50,000. The republic also brought the art of papermaking to Europe from Arabia. Before World War II there were 13 mills making paper by hand in the Valle dei Molini, but now only two remain. The town is romantically situated at the mouth of a deep gorge and has some good hotels and restaurants. It's also a convenient base for excursions to Capri, Positano, and the Grotta dello Smeraldo. The parking problem here, however, is as bad as that in Positano, although a large parking lot has recently opened a 10-minute walk east of the center. The small lot in the center of town fills quickly. Alternatively, if you're willing to pay the steep prices, make a lunch reservation at one of the hotel restaurants and have your car parked for you.

GETTING HERE AND AROUND
From April to October the optimal way to get to Amalfi is by ferry from Salerno. In the summer months you can also arrive from Naples by fast craft. SitaSud buses run from Naples and Sorrento throughout the year.

VISITOR INFORMATION
Amalfi Tourism Office ⊠ *Corso delle Repubbliche Marinare 27* ☎ *089/871107* ⊕ *www.amalfitouristoffice.it.*

EXPLORING
Fodor'sChoice **Duomo di Sant' Andrea.** Amalfi's main historic sight is its cathedral,
★ which shows an interesting mix of Moorish and early Gothic influences. You're channeled first into the adjoining **Chiostro del Paradiso** (Paradise Cloister), built around 1266 as a burial ground for Amalfi's elite and one of the architectural treasures of southern Italy. Its flower-and-palm-filled quadrangle has a series of exceptionally delicate intertwining arches on slender double columns in a combination of Byzantine and Arabian styles. Next stop is the 9th-century basilica, a museum housing sarcophagi, sculpture, Neapolitan gold artifacts, and other treasures from the cathedral complex.

Steps from the basilica lead down into the **Cripta di Sant'Andrea** (Crypt of Saint Andrew). The cathedral above was built in the 13th century to house the saint's bones, which came from Constantinople and supposedly exuded a miraculous liquid believers call the "manna of Saint Andrew." Following the one-way traffic up to the cathedral itself, you finally get to admire the elaborate polychrome marbles and painted, coffered ceilings from its 18th-century restoration. Art historians shake their heads over this renovation, as the original decoration of the apse must have been one of the wonders of the Middle Ages. ⊠ *Piazza Duomo* ☎ *089/871324* ☑ *€3* ⊙ *Mar.–6 Jan. daily 9–7. Closed Jan. 7– Feb. except for daily services.*

Valle dei Mulini (*Valley of the Mills*). Uphill from town, this was for centuries Amalfi's center for papermaking, an ancient trade learned from the Arabs (who learned it from the Chinese). Beginning in the 12th century, former flourmills in the town were converted to produce paper made from cotton and linen, being among the first in Europe to do so. In 1211 Frederick II of Sicily prohibited this lighter, more readable paper for use in the preparation of official documents, favoring traditional sheepskin parchment. But by 1811 more than a dozen mills here, with more along the coast, were humming. Natural waterpower ensured that the handmade paper was cost-effective. Catastrophic flooding in 1954, however, closed most of the mills for good, and many of them have now been converted into private housing. The **Museo della Carta** (Museum of Paper) opened in 1971 in a 15th-century mill: paper samples, tools of the trade, old machinery, and the audiovisual presentation are all enlightening. You can also participate in a papermaking laboratory. ⊠ *Via delle Cartiere 23* ☎ *089/8304561* ⊕ *www.museodellacarta.it* ≊ *€4, laboratory €7* ☉ *Mar.– Oct., daily 10–6:30; Nov.–Feb., Tues, Wed., Fri.–Sun. 10–2:30.*

WORD OF MOUTH

"I love Amalfi so much, we stayed in a beautiful apartment there for two weeks. At night the town is just for the locals and the stay-overs, which makes it so pleasant. I think we tried almost all the restaurants in town, some of them hidden away in the covered alleys."

—SeaUrchin

WHERE TO EAT

$$
SOUTHERN
ITALIAN
✕ **Al Teatro.** Once a children's theater, this informal and charming white-stucco restaurant in the medieval quarter is 50 steps above the main drag. A house specialty is grilled squid and calamari with mint sauce, reflecting its position—suspended between sea and mountains. Try also the *scialatielli al teatro*, with tomatoes and eggplant. The pizzas from their wood oven are terrific. $ *Average meal: €30* ⊠ *Via E. Marini 19* ☎ *089/872473* ☉ *Closed Wed. and Jan.–mid-Feb.*

$
SOUTHERN
ITALIAN
✕ **Il Tari.** Locals highly recommend this little ristorante, named after the ancient coin of the Amalfi Republic, a few minutes' walk north of the Duomo. This used to be a stable, and the space has changed little outwardly since those equine days. But appealing local art, crisp tablecloths, old photos, and tile floors make it cozy enough. The menu is vast: winning dishes include the wood-oven-baked thin-crust pizza with fresh sauces, and the *scialatielli alla Saracena* (long spaghetti-style pasta laden with tasty treats from the sea). The *menu della casa* is a great deal. $ *Average meal: €20* ⊠ *Via P. Capuano 9–11* ☎ *089/871832* ⊕ *www. amalfiristorantetari.it* ☉ *Closed Tues.*

$$$$
SOUTHERN
ITALIAN
Fodor's Choice
★
✕ **La Caravella.** No wonder this is considered the most romantic restaurant in Amalfi, with lace-covered tables, *ciuccio* (donkey) ceramics, tall candles, and fresh floral bouquets in salons graced with frescoes and marble floors. Opened in 1959, it became the first in Southern Italy to earn a Michelin star in 1966, and once drew a gilded guest list that included such fans as Andy Warhol, Agnelli, and Federico Fellini. Now in its third generation, the menu maintains dishes favored 50 years ago: picture slices of fish grilled in lemon leaves marinated with an almond and wild fennel sauce. A tasting menu is available, but don't miss the antipasti. $ *Average meal: €70* ⊠ *Via Matteo Camera 12, near Arsenale* ☎ *089/871029* ⊕ *www.ristorantelacaravella.it* ⌂ *Reservations essential* ☉ *Closed Tues. and Nov.–Feb.*

Amalfi's Luscious Lemons

Lemons as big as oranges (and oranges as big as grapefruits) are cultivated on the seemingly endless net-covered pergolas of the Amalfi Coast. From linguine with lemon at trattorias to lemon soufflés at fancy restaurants, the yellow citrus is everywhere—and all parts are used, as can be seen from the delicious habit of baking raisins, figs, or pieces of cheese wrapped in lemon leaves, bound up with thin red thread.

Not only are lemons a main component of meals and drinks, they're also offered as a remedy for everything from flu to bunions. But the most renowned end product is that local digestif known as limoncello, which captures in a bottle the color, fragrance, and taste of those tart-sweet lemons. Drink it cold in a tiny, frosty glass or after a shot of hot espresso—a golden memory quenched with each sip.

WHERE TO STAY

For expanded hotel reviews, visit Fodors.com.

$

HOTEL

Fodor'sChoice

★

🏨 **Albergo Sant'Andrea.** With everyone gazing at the magnificent steps leading to Amalfi's cathedral, few turn around to notice that this tiny, family-run *pensione* occupies one of the top spots in town. **Pros:** on the main square; divine views of the Duomo; friendly staff. **Cons:** steep flight of steps to entrance; very simple rooms. $ *Rooms from: €100* ⊠ *Piazza Duomo* 🕾 *089/871145* ⊕ *www.albergosantandrea.it* 🛏 *8 rooms* ⊗ *Closed Nov.–Mar.* ⼌ *No meals.*

$$$$

HOTEL

Fodor'sChoice

★

🏨 **Grand Hotel Convento di Amalfi.** This fabled medieval monastery was lauded by such guests as Longfellow and Wagner, and though recent modernization has sacrificed some of its historic charm, it remains an iconic destination. **Pros:** a slice of paradise; iconic Amalfi. **Cons:** traditionalists will miss its old-world charm; a 10-minute walk to town. $ *Rooms from: €360* ⊠ *Via Annunziatella 46* 🕾 *089/8736711* ⊕ *www.ghconventodiamalfi.com* 🛏 *53 rooms* ⊗ *Closed Nov.–Mar.* ⼌ *Breakfast.*

RAVELLO

Fodor'sChoice

★

5 km (3 miles) northeast of Amalfi, 40 km (25 miles) east of Sorrento.

Poised on a ridge high above Amalfi and the neighboring town of Atrani, enchanting Ravello has stupendous views, quiet lanes, two important Romanesque churches, and several irresistibly romantic gardens. Set "closer to the sky than the sea," according to André Gide, the town has been the ultimate aerie ever since it was founded as a smart suburb for the richest families of Amalfi's 12th-century maritime republic. Rediscovered by English aristocrats a century ago, Ravello now hosts one of Italy's most famous music festivals.

GETTING HERE AND AROUND
Buses from Amalfi make the 20-minute trip along white-knuckle roads. From Naples, take the A3 Naples–Salerno motorway; then exit at Angri and follow signs for Ravello. The journey takes about 75 minutes. Save yourself the trouble of driving by hiring a car and driver.

VISITOR INFORMATION
Azienda Autonoma Soggiorno e Turismo ⊠ *Via Roma 18b* ☎ *089/857096* 🖷 *089/857977* ⊕ *www.ravellotime.it* ⏱ *Nov.–Mar., daily 9–6; Apr.–Oct., daily 9–7.*

13

EXPLORING
Auditorium Niemeyer (*Auditorium New Energy*). Crowning Via della Repubblica and the hillside, which overlooks the spectacular Bay of Salerno, Auditorium Niemeyer (now relabeled Auditorium New Energy) is a startling piece of modernist architecture. Designed with a dramatically curved, all-white roof by Brazilian architect Oscar Niemeyer (creator of Brasília), it was conceived as an alternative indoor venue for concerts, including those of the famed town music festival. The subject of much controversy since its first conception back in 2000, it raised the wrath of some locals who denounced such an ambitious modernist building in medieval Ravello. They need not have worried. The result, inaugurated in 2010, is a design masterpiece—a huge, overhanging canopied roof suspended over a 400-seat concert area, with a giant eye-shape window allowing spectators to contemplate the extraordinary bay vista during performances. The terrace's "LifeStyle" Lounge Bar complements the experience. ⊠ *Via della Repubblica* ⊕ *www. auditoriumnewenergy.eu.*

Duomo. Dedicated to patron saint Pantaleone, the cathedral was founded in 1086 by Orso Papiro, the town's first bishop. Rebuilt in the 12th and 17th centuries, it retains traces of medieval frescoes in the transept, an original mullioned window, a marble portal, and a three-story 13th-century bell tower playfully interwoven with mullioned windows and arches. The 12th-century bronze door has 54 embossed panels depicting Christ's life, and saints, prophets, plants, and animals, all narrating biblical lore. The nave's three aisles are divided by ancient columns, and treasures include sarcophagi from Roman times and paintings by southern Renaissance artist Andrea da Salerno. Most impressive are the two medieval pulpits: the earlier one (on your left as you face the altar), used for reading the Epistles, is inset with a mosaic scene of Jonah and the whale, symbolizing death and redemption. The more famous one opposite, used for reading the Gospels, was commissioned by Nicola Rufolo in 1272 and created by Niccolò di Bartolomeo da Foggia. It seems almost Tuscan in style, with exquisite mosaic work and bas-reliefs and six twisting columns sitting on lion pedestals. An eagle grandly tops the inlaid marble lectern.

A chapel to the left of the apse is dedicated to Saint Pantaleone, a physician beheaded in the 3rd century in Nicomedia. Every July 27 devout believers gather in hope of witnessing a miracle (similar to that of San Gennaro in Naples), in which the saint's blood, collected in a vial and set out on an inlaid marble altar, appears to liquefy and come to a boil. In the crypt is the **Museo del Duomo,** which displays treasures from about the 13th century, during the reign of Frederick II of Sicily. ⊠ *Piazza del Duomo* ☎ *089/858311* ⊕ *www.chiesaravello.com* ✉ €3 ⊙ *Sept.–May, daily 9–7; June–Aug., daily 9–9:30; between noon and 5:30 access to church is through museum, to right of steps.*

Villa Cimbrone. From Ravello's main piazza, head west along Via San Francesco and Via Santa Chiara to this medieval-style fantasy poised 1,500 feet above the sea. Created in 1905 by England's Lord Grimthorpe and made famous when Greta Garbo stayed here in 1937, the Gothic castle is set in fragrant rose gardens that lead to the **Belvedere dell'Infinità** (Belvedere of Infinity): a grand stone parapet that overlooks the Gulf of Salerno and frames a panorama that former Ravello resident Gore Vidal called "the most beautiful in the world." The villa itself is now a 5-star hotel. ⊠ *Via S. Chiara 26* ☎ *089/857459* ⊕ *www. villacimbrone.it* ✉ €6 ⊙ *Daily 9–half hr before sunset.*

Villa Rufolo. Directly off Ravello's main piazza is the Villa Rufolo, which—if the master storyteller Boccaccio is to be believed—was built in the 12th century by the Rufolo family, whose immense fortune stemmed from trade with Moors and Saracens. Within the hotel is a scene from the earliest days of the Crusades. Norman and Arab architecture mingle in a welter of color-filled gardens so lush that composer Richard Wagner used them as his inspiration for the home of the Flower Maidens in his opera *Parsifal.* Beyond the Arab-Sicilian cloister and the Norman tower lie the two spectacular terrace gardens. The lower one, the "Wagner Terrace," is often the site for concerts, with the orchestra perched on a precarious-looking platform constructed over the precipice. ⊠ *Piazza Duomo* ☎ *089/857621* ⊕ *www.villarufolo.it* ✉ €5, extra charge for concerts ⊙ Daily 9–8; winter, daily 9–sunset. Closes early for rehearsals.*

WHERE TO EAT

$
SOUTHERN
ITALIAN
Fodor's Choice
★

✕ **Cumpa' Cosimo.** Lustier-looking than most Ravello spots, Cumpa' Cosimo is run devotedly by Netta Bottone, who tours the tables to ensure her clients are content. Her family has owned this cantina for 75 of its 300-plus years, and she has been cooking under the arched ceiling for more than 60 of them. You can't miss with any of the classic Ravellian dishes. A favorite (share it—it's huge) is a *misto* of whatever homemade pasta inspires her, served with a fresh, fragrant pesto. Meats, from Netta's own butcher shop next door, are generally excellent and local wines ease it all down gently. The *funghi porcini* mushroom starter is delicious and the house cheesecake or homemade gelato provide a luscious ending. 💲 *Average meal: €25* ⊠ *Via Roma 46* ☎ *089/857156* ⌂ *Reservations essential* ⊙ *Sometimes closed Mon. in winter.*

$$
PIZZA

✕ **Vittoria.** Between the Duomo and the church of San Francesco, this is a good place for a return to reality and an informal bite. Vittoria's thin-crust pizza with loads of fresh toppings is the star attraction, and locals praise it *molto*—it was a favorite of Gore Vidal. But also try the pasta, maybe fusilli with tomatoes, zucchini, and mozzarella. Vittoria is pretty, too, with arches and tile floors. All this adds up to crowds, so try to arrive on the early side. 💲 *Average meal: €30* ⊠ *Via dei Rufolo 3* ☎ *089/857947* ⊕ *www.ristorantepizzeriavittoria.it* ⊙ *Closed Nov.–Mar.*

WHERE TO STAY

For expanded hotel reviews, visit Fodors.com.

$$$
HOTEL
Fodor'sChoice
★

Palumbo. This is the real deal—the only great hotel left in Ravello that's still a monument to the Grand Tour sensibility that first put the town on the map, and views of the Bay of Salerno are incredible. **Pros:** impossibly romantic; wonderful coastal retreat; rooms in modern annex almost half the cost. **Cons:** with all this finery it can be difficult to relax; restaurant closed November to March. $ *Rooms from: €295* ⊠ *Via S. Giovanni del Toro 16* ☎ *089/857244* ⊕ *www.hotelpalumbo.it* 🛏 *17 rooms* ⊙ *Some meals.*

$$
HOTEL

Parsifal. In 1288 this diminutive property overlooking the coastline housed an order of Augustinian friars; today the intact cloister hosts travelers simply intent on enjoying themselves mightily. **Pros:** staying in a convent in Ravello; charming manager and his family dote on Americans. **Cons:** slightly removed from town; tiny rooms; restoration work ongoing in low season. $ *Rooms from: €130* ⊠ *Viale Gioacchino d'Anna 5* ☎ *089/857144* ⊕ *www.hotelparsifal.com* 🛏 *17 rooms* ⊙ *All meals.*

$
HOTEL

Villa Amore. A 10-minute walk from the Piazza Duomo, this charmingly secluded hotel with a garden is family-run and shares the same exhilarating view of the Bay of Salerno as Ravello's most expensive hotels. **Pros:** wonderful views; onsite restaurant has indoor and terrace seating. **Cons:** rather far from the main drag; basic rooms. $ *Rooms from: €100* ⊠ *Via dei Fusco 5* ☎ *089/857135* ⊕ *www.villaamore.it* 🛏 *10 rooms* ⊙ *All meals.*

$$$$
HOTEL
Fodor'sChoice
★

Villa Cimbrone. Suspended over the azure sea and set amid legendary rose-filled gardens, this Gothic-style castle was once home to Lord Grimthorpe and a hideaway of Greta Garbo. **Pros:** gorgeous pool and grounds; stay where Garbo chose to "be alone." **Cons:** a longish hike from town center (porters can help with luggage); daily arrival of respectful day-trippers. $ *Rooms from: €400* ⊠ *Via Santa Chiara 26* ☎ *089/857459* ⊕ *www.villacimbrone.com* 🛏 *19 rooms* ⊙ *Closed Nov.–Mar.* ⊙ *Breakfast.*

PAESTUM

99 km (62 miles) southeast of Naples.

GETTING HERE AND AROUND

From Naples, follow the A3 motorway to Salerno; continuing south along it, take the Battipaglia exit to SS18 and then exit at Capaccio Scala. Trains to Paestum depart from Stazione Centrale in Naples every hour. The archaeological site is a 10-minute walk from the station.

VISITOR INFORMATION

Paestum Tourism Office ⊠ *Via Magna Grecia 887* ☎ *0828/811016* ⊕ *www.infopaestum.it* ⊙ *Daily 9–1 and 2–4.*

EXPLORING

Greek Temples. One of Italy's most majestic sights lies on the edge of a flat coastal plain: the remarkably preserved Greek temples of Paestum. This is the site of the ancient city of Poseidonia, founded by Greek colonists probably in the 6th century BC. When the Romans took it over in 273 BC, they latinized the name to Paestum and changed the layout of the settlement, adding an amphitheater and a forum. Much of the archaeological material found on the site is displayed in the well-labeled **Museo Nazionale,** and several rooms are devoted to the unique tomb paintings—rare examples of Greek and pre-Roman pictorial art—discovered in the area.

At the northern end of the site opposite the ticket barrier is the **Tempio di Cerere** (Temple of Ceres). Built in about 500 BC, it's now thought to have been originally dedicated to the goddess Athena. Follow the road south past the **Foro Romano** (Roman Forum) to the **Tempio di Nettuno** (Temple of Poseidon), a showstopping Doric edifice with 36 fluted columns and an entablature (the area above the capitals) that rivals those of the finest temples in Greece. Beyond is the so-called **Basilica.** The oldest of Paestum's standing structures, it dates from the early 6th century BC. The name is an 18th-century misnomer, though, since it was, in fact, a temple to Hera, the wife of Zeus. Try to see the temples in the late afternoon, when the light enhances the deep gold of the limestone and tourists have left them almost deserted. ☎ *0828/722654* 🎫 *Site and museum €7, museum only (after site closing time) €4* 🕒 *Excavations daily 8:45–2 hrs before sunset; museum daily 8:30–6:45; museum closed 1st and 3rd Mon. of month.*

WHERE TO STAY

For expanded hotel reviews, visit Fodors.com.

$ B&B/INN 🏨 **Azienda Agrituristica Seliano.** This working-farm-with-a-difference, about 3 km (2 miles) from the temples, consists of a cluster of 19th-century baronial buildings. **Pros:** a great taste of a working farm; a banquet every evening; transfers available from the station. **Cons:** confusing to find; not for non-dog fans. [$] *Rooms from: €120* ✉ *Via Seliano, about 1 km (½ mile) down dirt track west off main road from Capaccio Scalo to Paestum* ☎ *0828/723634* 🌐 *www.agriturismoseliano.it* 🛏 *14 rooms* 🕒 *Closed Nov.–Mar., will open for bookings* 🍴 *All meals.*

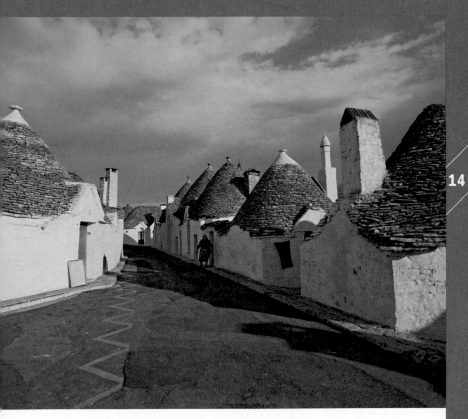

PUGLIA, BASILICATA, AND CALABRIA

WELCOME TO PUGLIA, BASILICATA, AND CALABRIA

TOP REASONS TO GO

★ **A wander through Sassi:** The simple Basilicata town of Matera is endowed with one of the most unusual landscapes in Europe: a complex network of ancient cave dwellings partially hewn from rock, some of which now house chic bars and restaurants.

★ **A trip to peasant-food heaven:** Dine on Puglia's famous puree of fava beans with chicory and olive oil in a humble country restaurant.

★ **Lecce and its Baroque splendors:** The beautiful, friendly city of Lecce might be known for its peculiar brand of fanciful Baroque architecture, but it's not yet famous enough to have lost its Pugliese charm.

★ **The *trulli* of the Valle d'Itria:** Strange, conical houses—many of them still in use—dot the rolling countryside of Puglia, centering around Alberobello, a town still composed almost entirely of these trulli. They must be seen to be believed.

1 Bari. Puglia's biggest city is a lively, quirky, and sometimes seedy port on the Adriatic Coast. It's also home to the region's principal airport.

2 The Trulli District. Named for its mysterious conical houses, the Trulli District is centered on the town of **Alberobello**.

3 Salento and Ports of the Heel. The ports of Puglia include casbahlike fishing villages such as **Gallipoli** and the gritty shipping centers of **Taranto** and **Brindisi**. Italy's heel finally smooths out and terminates in a region of Puglia known as **Salento**, home to **Lecce**, famous for its ornate Baroque architecture.

4 Basilicata. One of Italy's least-visited and most secluded regions is the place to find Matera, whose cave dwellings make the city feel like a Nativity scene.

5 Calabria. The region that makes up Italy's "toe" is a land of dusty hill towns, rows of olive trees, and spicy food. **Cosenza** mixes turn-of-the-20th-century cafés with fascist-era architecture, and Tropea is an enticing seaside getaway.

CAMPANIA

Naples

Salerno

Sorrento

Capri

Salina Island

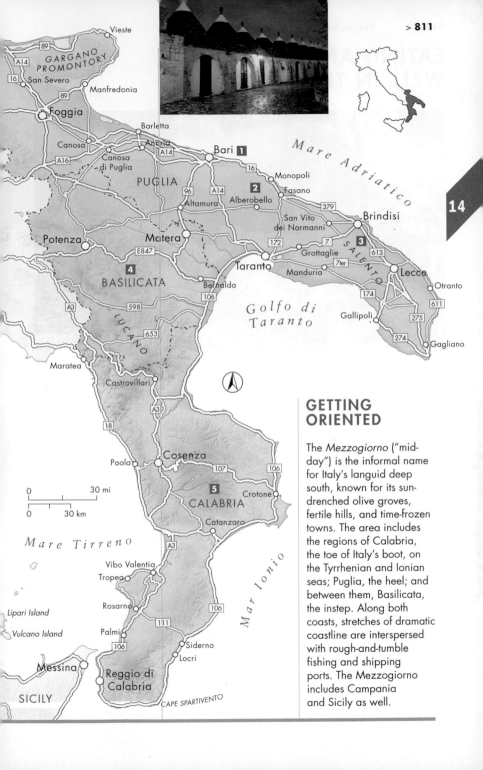

14

GETTING ORIENTED

The *Mezzogiorno* ("midday") is the informal name for Italy's languid deep south, known for its sundrenched olive groves, fertile hills, and time-frozen towns. The area includes the regions of Calabria, the toe of Italy's boot, on the Tyrrhenian and Ionian seas; Puglia, the heel; and between them, Basilicata, the instep. Along both coasts, stretches of dramatic coastline are interspersed with rough-and-tumble fishing and shipping ports. The Mezzogiorno includes Campania and Sicily as well.

EATING AND DRINKING WELL IN THE SOUTH

Southern Italian cuisine is rustic and hearty, featuring homemade pasta and cheese, fresh vegetables, seafood, and olive oil. A defining principle of Italian cooking is to take excellent ingredients and prepare them simply. That philosophy reaches its purest expression here.

The best—and cheapest—meals are often found at a rustic family-run trattoria (sometimes referred to as a *casalinga*), commonly located in the countryside or city outskirts. These bare-bones places often dispense with printed menus, but they manage to create flavors rivaling those of any highbrow restaurant. Assent to the waiter's suggestions with a simple *va bene* (that's fine) or *faccia Lei* (you decide) and leave yourself in the chef's hands.

More upscale establishments turn authentic local ingredients into deliciously inventive dishes. Many such restaurants are set in breathtaking locations, yet prices remain relative bargains compared to similar places farther north. Fish, unsurprisingly, is the star attraction on the coast.

FABULOUS FAVA

Puré di fave e cicorielle, a puree of fava beans topped with sautéed chicory, is unique to Puglia and Basilicata.

The simple recipe has been prepared here for centuries and continues to be a staple of the local diet. The dried favas are soaked overnight, cooked with potatoes, seasoned with salt and olive oil, and served warm with wild green chicory, often with a sprinkling of ground *peperoncino* (chili pepper). Mix it together before eating and wash it down with a glass of primitivo or aglianico.

PASTA

Puglia is the home of orecchiette, *pictured at right*, with *cime di rapa* (broccoli rabe) and olive oil, a melodious dish that's wondrous in its simplicity. Try also *cavatelli* (rolled-up orecchiette) and *strascenate* (rectangles of pasta with one rough side and one smooth side).

MEAT

With cattle grazing on the plains and pigs fed only natural foods, the south is a meat eater's paradise. As well as its excellent beef, Basilicata is known for its *salsicce lucane* (sausages), seasoned with salt, cayenne pepper, and fennel seeds. Enormous grills are a feature of many of the region's restaurants, infusing the dining area with the aroma of freshly cooked meat. Adventurous eaters in Puglia should look for *turcinieddhri* (a blend of lamb's innards) and *pezzetti di cavallo* (braised horse meat).

PEPPERS

Calabria is known for hot peppers—try *peperonata,* a stew of peppers and capers. They also pop up in *nduja* (creamy spicy salami), *sopressata* (dried spicy salami), and *salsiccia piccante* (hot sausage), *pictured at left,* often sold by street vendors on a roll with peppers, onions, french fries, and mayonnaise. Pasta dishes are often seasoned with dried *peperoncini* or *olio piccante* (spicy olive oil). The delicious *peperoni cruschi* or *senesi* are grown in

14

Basilicata—they're used both fresh and dried, and are often powdered for seasoning cheeses and cured meats.

SEAFOOD

With so much coastline, seafood is an essential element of Southern Italian cuisine. Fish can be grilled (*alla griglia*), baked (*al forno*), roasted (*arrosto*), or steamed (*in umido*). Among the highlights are delicate *orata* (sea bream), *pictured below, branzino* (sea bass), *gamberi rossi* (sweet red shrimp), and calamari, while Puglia is the home of *cozze pelose* (a kind of mussel). The *frutti di mare* (shellfish) can be enjoyed as an antipasto, in a *zuppa* (soup), or with homemade linguine.

WINES

Puglia produces around 17% of Italy's wine, more than the whole of Australia. For years, most of it was *vino sfuso* (jug wine), but since the mid-1990s quality has risen. The ancient primitivo grape (an ancestor of California's zinfandel) yields strong, heady wines like Primitivo di Manduria. The negroamaro grape is transformed into palatable *rosato* (rosé), as well as the robust Salice Salentino. Pair a dessert with the sweet red Aleatico di Puglia or Moscato di Trani.

In Basilicata, producers use the aglianico grape variety to outstanding effect in the prestigious Aglianico del Vulture. In Calabria, they've worked wonders with the gaglioppo variety.

Updated
by Fergal
Kavanagh

Making up the heel and toe of Italy's boot, the Puglia, Basilicata, and Calabria regions are the largest part of what is known informally as the *Mezzogiorno,* a name that translates literally as "midday." It's a curiously telling nickname, because midday is when it's quietest here. While the blazing sun bears down, cities, fishing ports, and sleepy hillside villages turn into ghost towns, as residents retreat to their homes for three or more hours.

This is Italy's deep south, where whitewashed buildings stand silently over three turquoise seas, castles guard medieval alleyways, and grandmothers dry their handmade orecchiette, the most Puglian of pastas, in the mid-afternoon heat. The Greek city-states of Magna Graecia (Greater Greece) once ruled here, and ancient names, such as Lucania, are still commonly used.

At every turn, these three regions boast dramatic scenery. Geographical divides have preserved an astonishing cultural and linguistic diversity that's unequaled elsewhere on the Italian mainland. It's here that you'll find long-isolated hill communities where Albanian and Greek are still spoken by the descendants of 16th-century refugees from the Balkans.

Italians and foreign visitors alike return summer after summer to the beaches of the south, where the relative lack of industry ensures good bathing water quality along much of the coastline. One of southern Italy's most popular vacation destinations is the Gargano Promontory, where safe, sandy shores and secluded coves are nestled between whitewashed coastal towns and craggy limestone cliffs. Elsewhere the beach scene is more laid-back. You won't find impeccably manicured sand lined with regiments of sunbathers, but you can pick and choose strands at whim and spread out.

There are cultural gems everywhere, including Valle d'Itria's fairy-tale trulli (curious conical structures, some dating from the 15th century), Matera's *Sassi* (a network of ancient dwellings carved out of rock), and the Baroque churches in the town of Lecce, the jewel of the south. Beyond the cities, seaside resorts, and the few major sights, there's a sparsely populated, sun-baked countryside where road signs are rare and expanses of silvery olive trees, vineyards of primitivo and aglianico grapes, and giant prickly pear cacti fight their way through the rocky soil in defiance of the relentless summer heat. Farmhouses, country trattorias, and weary low-lying factories sit among eternally half-built structures that tell a hard-luck story of economic stagnation. Year after year, even as tourism grows in the region—especially in Salento—economic woes persist. In any case, the region still doesn't make it onto the itineraries of most visitors to Italy. This translates into an unusual opportunity to engage with a rich culture and landscape relatively untouched by international tourism.

14

PUGLIA, BASILICATA, AND CALABRIA PLANNER

MAKING THE MOST OF YOUR TIME

If your priority is relaxing on the beach, plan on a few days at a seaside resort in one of the Gargano Promontory's fishing villages, such as Peschici, Rodi Garganico, and Vieste, and perhaps a further stay at one of the Calabrian coastal resorts, such as Diamante or Tropea, or Maratea in Basilicata.

Otherwise, choose a base like Polignano a Mare or Trani, especially if you land or dock in Bari. Take day trips out to the Valle d'Itria, or to the remarkable octagonal Castel del Monte. Then head east along the Adriatic route (SS16), stopping to see the idyllic hilltop Ostuni before continuing on to Lecce, where you'll want to spend at least two to three nights exploring the city's Baroque wonders and taking a day trip down to Otranto and Gallipoli.

Next, take regional roads and Via Appia (SS7) to reach Matera, whose Sassi cave dwellings are a Southern Italian highlight; allow at least two nights here. Then it's back out to the SS106 to Calabria, along the coast dotted with ancient Greek settlements, as far as Tropea. At this point, cut inland on the SS107 across the Sila Massif, stopping at the hill resort of Camigliatello or carrying on to the more vibrant lowland Cosenza. Reggio Calabria is worthwhile only if you're an archaeology buff and must see the Riace bronzes.

GETTING AROUND
BUS TRAVEL
Direct, if not always frequent, connections operate between most destinations within Calabria, Puglia, and Basilicata. In many cases bus service is the backup when problems with train service arise. Matera is linked with Bari by frequent Ferrovie Appulo–Lucane trains and buses and with Taranto by SITA bus. In Calabria various companies make the north–south run with stops along both coasts. Ferrovie della Calabria operates many of the local routes.

Ferrovie Appulo-Lucane ☎ *199/811811* ⊕ *www.fal-srl.it.*

Ferrovie della Calabria ☎ *0961/896262* ⊕ *www.ferroviedellacalabria.it.*

SITA ☎ *0835/385007* ⊕ *www.sitasudtrasporti.it.*

CAR TRAVEL

Though roads are generally good in the south and major cities are linked by fast *autostrade* or four-lane highways, driving here is a major test of navigation skills. Junctions are poorly signposted—especially in Puglia—and cutting straight through town centers can add considerably to travel time. Seemingly under eternal construction, the toll-free (from Salerno) A3 Napoli–Reggio Calabria links Naples to the south, with major exits at Sicignano (for the interior of Basilicata and Matera), Cosenza (the Sila Massif and Crotone), and Pizzo (for Tropea). Parts of the A3 in northern Calabria cross uplands more than 3,000 feet high, so snow chains may be required during winter months. In the summer and during holiday weekends this is the main north–south route for Italy's sun-seekers, so factor in plenty of time for delays and avoid peak travel times. Take the SS18 for coastal destinations—or for a better view—on the Tyrrhenian side, and likewise the SS106 (which is uncongested and fast) for the Ionian. Given speed detectors and driver-tracking technology, stick to speed limits: You may become unpopular with the traffic behind but you'll be spared an unwelcome ticket when you get home.

Entering the centers of many towns requires a very small car, folding side-view mirrors, and a bit of nerve; tentative drivers should park outside the center and venture in on foot. If you're squeamish about getting lost, don't plan on night driving in the countryside—roads can be confusing without the aid of landmarks or large towns, and GPS is far from infallible. Bari, Brindisi, and Reggio Calabria are notorious for car thefts and break-ins. In these cities, don't leave valuables in the car, and find a guarded parking space if possible.

TRAIN TRAVEL

Trenitalia trains run to Calabria, either following the Ionian Coast as far as Reggio Calabria or swerving inland to Cosenza and the Tyrrhenian Coast.

Ferrovie Appulo–Lucane. This service links Matera to Altamura in Puglia (for connections to Bari) and to Ferrandina (for connections to Potenza). ☎ *199/811811* ⊕ *www.fal-srl.it.*

Ferrovie Sud-Est. The private Ferrovie Sud-Est connects Martina Franca with Bari and Taranto, and the fishing port of Gallipoli with Lecce. ☎ *080/5462111 in Bari, 0832/668111 in Lecce, 800/079090 Mon.–Sat. 7–5* ⊕ *www.fseonline.it.*

Trenitalia. Within Puglia, the Italian national railroad links Bari to Brindisi, Lecce, and Taranto, but smaller destinations can often be reached only by completing the trip by bus. ☎ *892021* ⊕ *www.trenitalia.com.*

RESTAURANTS

Please note that restaurant prices listed as "average meal" include a meal consisting of first course *(primo)*, second course *(secondo)*, and dessert *(dolce)*.

HOTELS

Hotels in the region range from grand, slightly faded resorts to family-run rural *agriturismi* (country inns, often part of farms), which compensate for a lack of amenities with their famous southern hospitality. *Fattorie* and *masserie* (small farms and grander farm estates) offering accommodation are listed at local tourist offices.

In beach areas such as the Gargano Promontory and Salento, campgrounds and bungalow lodgings are ubiquitous and popular with families and budget travelers. Note that many seaside hotels open up just for the summer season, when they often require several-day stays with full or half board. And do remember that in a region like this—blazingly hot in summer and chilly in winter—air-conditioning and central heating can be important.

Hotel reviews have been condensed for this book. Please go to Fodors. com for expanded reviews of each property.

14

BARI AND THE ADRIATIC COAST

The coast of Puglia has a strong flavor of the Norman presence in the south, embodied in the distinctive Apulian-Romanesque churches, the most atmospheric being in Trani. The busy commercial port of Bari offers architectural nuggets in its compact, labyrinthine old quarter abutting the sea, while Polignano a Mare combines accessibility to the major centers with the charm of a medieval town. For a unique excursion, drive inland to the imposing Castel del Monte, an enigmatic 13th-century octagon.

BARI

260 km (162 miles) southeast of Naples, 450 km (281 miles) southeast of Rome.

The biggest city in the region, Bari is a major port and a transit point for travelers catching ferries across the Adriatic to Greece, Croatia, and Albania. It's also a cosmopolitan city with one of the most interesting historic centers in the region. Most of Bari is set out in a logical 19th-century grid, following the designs of Joachim Murat (1767–1815), Napoléon's brother-in-law and King of the Two Sicilies. The heart of the modern town is **Piazza della Libertà,** but just beyond it, across Corso Vittorio Emanuele, is the *città vecchia* (old town). This maze of narrow streets lies on the promontory that juts out between Bari's old and new ports. Circumscribed by Via Venezia, the area offers elevated views of the Adriatic in every direction.

GETTING HERE AND AROUND

By car, take the Bari-Nord exit from the A14. Bari's train station is a hub for Puglia-bound trains. Alitalia, and Ryanair fly to Bari Airport from Rome and Milan,

VISITOR INFORMATION

Bari Tourism Office ⊠ *Piazza Moro 33/a* ☎ *080/9909341* ⊕ *www.infopointbari.com.*

PUGLIA, PAST AND PRESENT

Puglia has long been inhabited, conquered, and visited. On sea voyages to their colonies and trading posts in the west, the ancient Greeks invariably headed for Puglia first—it was the shortest crossing—before filtering southward into Sicily and westward to the Tyrrhenian coast. In turn, the Romans—often bound in the opposite direction—were quick to recognize the strategic importance of the peninsula. Later centuries were to see a procession of other empires raiding or colonizing Puglia: Byzantines, Saracens, Normans, Swabians, Turks, and Spaniards all swept through, each group leaving its mark. Romanesque churches and the powerful castles built by 13th-century Holy Roman Emperor Frederick II (who also served as king of Sicily and Jerusalem) are among the most impressive of the buildings in the region. Frederick II, dubbed *Stupor Mundi* (Wonder of the World) for his wide-ranging interests in literature, science, mathematics, and nature, was one of the foremost personalities of the Middle Ages.

Recent years have brought a huge economic revival after the decades of neglect following World War II. Having benefited from EU funding, state incentive programs, and subsidies for irrigation, Puglia is now Italy's top regional producer of wine, with most of the rest of the land devoted to olives, citrus fruits, and vegetables. The main ports of Bari, Brindisi, and Taranto are thriving centers, though there remain serious problems of unemployment and poverty. However, the much-publicized arrival of thousands of asylum seekers from Eastern Europe and beyond has not significantly destabilized these cities, as had been feared, and the economic and political refugees have dispersed throughout Italy. Today, despite several years of region-wide *recessione*, an air of prosperity still wafts through the streets of Lecce, Trani, and smaller towns like Otranto and Peschici.

EXPLORING

Fodor's Choice ★ **Basilica di San Nicola.** In the città vecchia, overlooking the sea and just off Via Venezia, is the Basilica di San Nicola, built in the 11th century to house the bones of Saint Nicholas, the inspiration for Santa Claus. His remains, buried in the crypt, are said to have been stolen by Bari sailors from Myra, in what is now Turkey, where Saint Nicholas was bishop. The basilica, of solid and powerful construction, was the only building to survive the otherwise wholesale destruction of Bari by the Normans in 1152. ⊠ *Piazza San Nicola* ☎ *080/5737111* ⊕ *www. basilicasannicola.it* ☾ *Daily 7 am–8 pm.*

Castello Svevo. Looming over Bari's cathedral is the huge Castello Svevo. The current building dates from the time of Holy Roman Emperor Frederick II (1194–1250), who rebuilt an existing Norman-Byzantine castle to his own exacting specifications. Designed more for power than beauty, it looks out beyond the cathedral to the small Porto Vecchio (Old Port). Inside, a haphazard collection of medieval Puglian art is frequently enlivened by changing exhibitions featuring local, national, and international artists. ⊠ *Piazza Federico II di Svevia* ☎ *080/5286262* ⊠ *€3* ☾ *Thurs.–Tues. 8:30–7:30; last entrance at 7.*

14

Cattedrale di San Sabino. Bari's 12th-century cathedral is the seat of the local bishop and was the scene of many significant political marriages between important families in the Middle Ages. The cathedral's solid architecture reflects the Romanesque style favored by the Normans of that period. ⊠ *Piazza dell'Odegitria* ☎ *080/5210605* ⊗ *Daily 8–12:30 and 4–8.*

Via Sparano. By day, you can explore the old town's winding alleyways, where Bari's open-door policy offers a glimpse into the daily routine of southern Italy—matrons hand-rolling pasta with their grandchildren home from school for the midday meal, and handymen perched on rickety ladders, patching up centuries-old arches and doorways. Back in the new town, join the evening *passeggiata* (stroll) on pedestrians-only Via Sparano, then, when night falls, saunter amid the outdoor bars and restaurants in Piazza Mercantile, past Piazza Ferrarese at the end of Corso Vittorio Emanuele.

WHERE TO EAT AND STAY

For expanded hotel reviews, visit Fodors.com.

$$$ ✕ **Ristorante al Pescatore.** In the old town, opposite the castle and just
SEAFOOD around the corner from the cathedral, stands one of Bari's best sea-food restaurants. In summer the fish is grilled outdoors, so you can enjoy the delicious aroma as you sit amid a cheerful clamor of quaffing and dining. Try a whole fish accompanied by a crisp salad and a carafe of invigorating local wine. Reservations are essential in July and August. Beware of bag snatchers if you sit outside. Ⓢ *Average meal: €50* ⊠ *Piazza Federico II di Svevia 6/8* ☎ *080/5237039* ⊕ *www. ristorantealpescatorebari.com* ⊗ *Closed 2 wks mid-Jan.*

$$ 🏨 **Palace Hotel.** This downtown landmark is steps away from Corso
HOTEL Vittorio Emanuele in the New City, but is also extremely convenient to the medieval center. **Pros:** convenient location. **Cons:** often very busy; staff can be brusque. Ⓢ *Rooms from: €164* ⊠ *Via Lombardi 13* ☎ *080/5216551* ⊕ *www.palacehotelbari.it* 🛏 *177 rooms, 18 suites* ⦿ *Breakfast.*

TRANI

43 km (27 miles) northwest of Bari.

Trani has a harbor filled with fishing boats and a quaint old town with polished stone streets and medieval churches. The town is also justly famous for its sweet dessert wine, Moscato di Trani. It's smaller than the other ports along this coast.

GETTING HERE AND AROUND

By car, take the Trani exit from the A14 Autostrada. Frequent trains run from Bari.

VISITOR INFORMATION

Trani Tourism Office ⊠ *Piazza Trieste 10* ☎ *0883/588830* ⊕ *www.viaggiareinpuglia.it.*

Puglia

50 miles
75 km

Adriatic Sea

Golfo di Taranto

Golfo di Manfredonia

Golfo di Salerno

ISOLE TREMITI
I Cameroni
ISOLE S. DOMINO
ISOLE S. NICOLA

TO TERMOLI

GARGANO PROMONTORY

Vieste
Peschici
Rodi Garganico
Foresta Umbra
Mattinata
Monte Sant'Angelo
Manfredonia
San Giovanni Rotondo
L'Anfunziata
Zapponeta
Lago di Varano
San Severo
Lucera
Foggia
Cerignola
Barletta
Andria
Corato
Trani
Molfetta
Bari
Castel del Monte
Spinazzola
Gravina in Puglia
Santeramo in Colle
Altamura
Matera
Gioia del Colle
Locorotondo
Alberobello
Grotte di Castellana
Fasano
Polignano a Mare
TRULLI DISTRICT
Ostuni
Ceglie Messapica
Martina Franca
Grottaglie
Massafra
Taranto
Mare Piccolo
Mare Grande
Castellaneta Marina
Lido di Metaponto
Scanzano
Brindisi
Mesagne
Francavilla Fontana
Manduria
Campi
Lecce
Oria
Nardò
Gallipoli
Maglie
Otranto
Santa Cesarea Terme
Castro
Leuca
Capo Santa Maria di Leuca
SALENTO

PUGLIA
CAMPANIA
BASILICATA
LUCANO

Melfi
S. Angelo dei Lombardi
Auletta
Potenza
Eboli
Battipaglia
Salerno

Via Appia
Via Appia

TO NAPLES

Road numbers: 89, 528, 272, 141, 16, A14, 89, 160, 16, 17, 655, 90, A16, 91, 164, A3, 91, 7, 407, 96, 168, 170, 271, 96, A14, E55, 100, 7, 174, 16, 7, 611, 101, 16, 275, 274, 123, 16, 598, 653, 92, 166, 407, 18, A3

EXPLORING

Castello. The boxy, well-preserved castle was built by Frederick II in 1233. ✉ *Piazza Manfredi 16* ☎ *0883/506603* 🌐 *www.castelloditrani.beniculturali.it* 🎟 *€3* 🕓 *Daily 8:30–7:30.*

Cattedrale. The stunning, pinkish-white 11th-century cathedral, considered one of the finest in Puglia, is built on a spit of land jutting into the sea. ✉ *Piazza Duomo* ☎ *0883/494210* 🕓 *Daily 8:30–12:30 and 3:30–6.*

Via Sinagoga (*Synagogue Street*). A Jewish community flourished here in medieval times, and on Via Sinagoga two of the four synagogues still stand. **Scolanova** and **Santa Anna,** both built in the 13th century, are now churches; the latter still bears a Hebrew inscription and houses a **museum of Trani's Jewish history** (*0883/021345*).

14

WHERE TO STAY

For expanded hotel reviews, visit Fodors.com.

$ HOTEL 🏨 **Hotel Trani.** This centrally located hotel has rooms that are pleasant, and it's efficiently and courteously run. **Pros:** close to the train station; within walking distance of the old town; off-street parking at low prices. **Cons:** uninspiring 1960s architecture; basic rooms. [$] *Rooms from: €86* ✉ *Corso Imbriani 137* ☎📠 *0883/588010* 🌐 *www.hoteltrani.it* 🛏 *46 rooms* 🍴 *No meals.*

$$ HOTEL 🏨 **La Regia.** This small hotel-restaurant occupies a 17th-century palazzo superbly positioned in front of the Duomo, on a swath of land jutting out into the sea. **Pros:** great restaurant; hospitable staff; most rooms have sea views. **Cons:** no parking outside hotel; area can be very busy on weekends. [$] *Rooms from: €150* ✉ *Piazza Mons. Addazi 2* ☎📠 *0883/584444* 🌐 *www.hotelregia.it* 🛏 *10 rooms* 🍴 *Breakfast.*

POLIGNANO A MARE

35 km (22 miles) southeast of Bari, 14 km (9 miles) north of Castellana.

With a well-preserved whitewashed old town perched on limestone cliffs overlooking the Adriatic, Polignano a Mare makes an atmospheric base for exploring the surrounding area.

The town is virtually dead all winter, but becomes something of a weekend hot spot for city dwellers in summer. Justin Timberlake and Jessica Beal chose the tiny seaside town of Savelletri di Fasano, 25 km (16 miles) south, for their 2012 wedding.

GETTING HERE AND AROUND

From Bari, take the Polignano exit from the SS16. Frequent trains run from Bari.

WHERE TO STAY

For expanded hotel reviews, visit Fodors.com.

$ HOTEL Fodor's Choice ★ 🏨 **Grotta Palazzese.** Carved out of a cliff opening onto the Adriatic, the Grotta Palazzese inhabits a stunning group of rocks and grottoes that have wowed onlookers for ages. **Pros:** romantic (albeit overpriced) restaurant; great location. **Cons:** a long climb down to the sea. [$] *Rooms from: €120* ✉ *Via Narciso 59* ☎ *080/4240677* 🌐 *www.grottapalazzese.it* 🛏 *23 rooms* 🍴 *Breakfast.*

CASTEL DEL MONTE

56 km (35 miles) southwest of Bari.

GETTING HERE AND AROUND
Take the Andria-Barletta exit from the A14 Autostrada, then follow the SS170d to Castel del Monte. From April through October there's minibus service from Piazza Bersaglieri d'Italia in Andria.

VISITOR INFORMATION
Castel del Monte Tourism Office ⊠ *Via Vespucci 114, Andria* ☎ *0883/592283* ⊕ *www.proloco.andria.ba.it.*

EXPLORING

Fodor'sChoice **Castel del Monte.** Built by Frederick II in the first half of the 13th century,
★ Castel del Monte is an imposing octagonal castle with eight austere towers on an isolated hill. Little is known about the structure, since virtually no records exist. The ground-floor gift shop (closed in winter months) has many books that explore its mysterious past and posit theories based on its dimensions and Federico II's love of mathematics. It has none of the usual defense features associated with medieval castles, so it probably had little military significance. Some theories suggest it might have been built as a hunting lodge or may have served as an astronomical observatory, or even a stop for pilgrims on their quest for the Holy Grail. Most of the helpful information panels in the castle are translated into English and the tourist office organizes guided tours. Note that if coming by car between April and September you have to park in designated areas about a mile away and then get a shuttle bus. ⊠ *On signposted minor road, 18 km (11 miles) south of Andria, Andria* ☎ *0883/569997, 0883/592283 tour reservations* ⊕ *www. casteldelmonte.beniculturali.it* ⊠ *€5* ⊙ *Mar.–Sept., daily 10:15–7:15; Oct.–Feb., daily 9–5. Last entrance ½ hr before closing.*

THE GARGANO PROMONTORY

Forming the spur of Italy's boot, the Gargano Promontory (Promontorio del Gargano) is a striking contrast to the Adriatic's flatter coastline. This is a land of whitewashed coastal towns, wide sandy beaches interspersed with secluded coves, and craggy limestone cliffs topped by deep-green pine and scrubby Mediterranean *maquis* (underbrush). Not surprisingly, it pulls in the crowds in July and August, driving up the prices considerably. Camping is almost always an option, as plentiful and pretty campgrounds dot the Gargano's curvy, cliff-hugging roads. The beaches and the Foresta Umbra national park are great places for kids to let off steam.

VIESTE

93 km (58 miles) northeast of Foggia, 179 km (111 miles) northwest of Bari.

This large, whitewashed town jutting off the tip of the spur of Italy's boot is an attractive place to wander around. Though curvy mountain roads render it slightly less accessible from the autostrade and mainline rail stations than, say, Peschici and Mattinata, the range of accommodations (including camping) makes it a useful base for exploring Gargano. The resort attracts legions of tourists in summer, some bound for the Isole Tremiti, a tiny archipelago connected to Vieste by regular ferries.

GETTING HERE AND AROUND

If you're driving from Foggia, take the winding SS89. Regular buses leave from Foggia's train station.

PESCHICI

22 km (14 miles) northwest of Vieste, 199 km (124 miles) northwest of Bari.

Peschici is a pleasant resort on Gargano's north shore, a cascade of whitewashed houses and streets with a beautiful view over a sweeping cove. Some surrounding areas are particularly popular with campers from northern Europe. Development has not wreaked too much havoc on the town: the mazelike center retains its characteristic low houses topped with little Byzantine cupolas.

GETTING HERE

From Foggia, take the winding S89 road. Regular buses leave from Foggia's train station. Seasonal ferry service leaves from the Trémiti archipelago between June and September.

THE TRULLI DISTRICT

The inland area to the southeast of Bari is one of Italy's oddest enclaves, mostly flat terrain given over to olive cultivation and interspersed with the idiosyncratic habitations that have lent their names to the district. Looking like igloos constructed out of pure stone, the beehive-shape *trulli* have origins that hark to the 15th century and maybe further. The trulli, found nowhere else in the world, are built of local limestone, without mortar, and with a hole in the top for escaping smoke. Some are painted with mystical or religious symbols, some are isolated, and others are joined together with common roofs. Legends of varying credibility surround the trulli (for example, that they were originally built so that residents could quickly take apart their homes when the tax collectors came by). The center of Trulli Country is Alberobello in the enchanting Valle d'Itria: it has the greatest concentration of buildings. You'll spot them all over this region, some in the middle of desolate fields, and many in disrepair, but always adding a quirky charm to the landscape.

ALBEROBELLO

59 km (37 miles) southeast of Bari, 45 km (28 miles) north of Taranto.

Although Alberobello is something of a tourist trap, the amalgamation of more than 1,000 trulli huddled together along steep, narrow streets is nonetheless a striking phenomenon that has been designated a UNESCO World Heritage Site. As one of the most popular destinations in Puglia, Alberobello has spawned some excellent restaurants (and some not-so-excellent trinket shops).

14

GETTING HERE AND AROUND
By car, take the Monopoli exit from the SS16, follow the SP237 to Putignano, then SS172 to Alberobello. Trains run hourly from Bari.

VISITOR INFORMATION
Alberobello Tourism Office ⊠ *Via Monte Nero 1* ☎ *080/4322060* ⊕ *www.viaggiareinpuglia.it.*

EXPLORING
Alberobello–Martina Franca road. The trulli in Alberobello itself are impressive, but the most beautiful concentration of conical trulli is along a stretch of about 15 km (9 miles) on the Alberobello–Martina Franca road. Amid expanses of vineyards, you can see trulli put to all sorts of uses—including as wineries.

Trullo Sovrano. Alberobello's largest trullo, the Trullo Sovrano, is up the hill through the trulli zone (head up Corso Vittorio Emanuele past the obelisk and the basilica). Inside is a fairly conventional domestic dwelling: the real interest is the structure itself.

WHERE TO EAT

$$$
SOUTHERN
ITALIAN
✕ **Il Poeta Contadino.** Proprietor Leonardo Marco serves creative regional cooking in this upscale country restaurant in the heart of the attractive trulli zone. The refined, understated dining room features candles casting shadows on the ancient stone walls. Dishes might include *triglie con vinaigrette alla menta* (red mullet with a mint vinaigrette) or *filetto di maiale in crosta di erbe con salsa agrodolce* (herb-crusted pork fillet with a sweet-and-sour sauce). In season, try anything with white truffles. $ *Average meal: €50* ⊠ *Via Indipendenza 21* ☎ *080/4321917* ⊕ *www.ilpoetacontadino.it* ⚠ *Reservations essential* ⊘ *Closed 3 wks in Jan., and Mon. Oct.–Jun.*

$$
SOUTHERN
ITALIAN
Fodor's Choice
★
✕ **L'Aratro.** This welcoming rustic restaurant set inside adjoining trulli has dark-wood beams, whitewashed walls, and an outdoor patio for summer dining. The *antipasti misti* could stand as a meal in itself, but leave room for country-style dishes using lamb and veal. Among the seasonal specialties are *cavatellucci di terra madre* (tomatoes, onions, and *capocollo*—a cured meat—on a bed of fava beans) and roast lamb with *lampasciuni* (a type of wild onion). $ *Average meal: €35* ⊠ *Via Monte S. Michele 25–29* ☎ *080/4322789* ⊕ *www.ristorantearatro.it* ⚠ *Reservations essential.*

WHERE TO STAY
For expanded hotel reviews, visit Fodors.com.

$
HOTEL
🏨 **Hotel Lanzillotta.** On Alberobello's main piazza, this modern hotel is near one of the two trulli districts. **Pros:** convenient location; helpful staff. **Cons:** lacks charm; lackluster restaurant. $ *Rooms from: €80* ⊠ *Piazza Fernando IV 33* ☎ *080/4321511* ⊕ *www.hotellanzillotta.it* ⇥ *30 rooms* ⦿l *Breakfast.*

OSTUNI

50 km (30 miles) west of Brindisi, 85 km (53 miles) southeast of Bari.

This sun-bleached, medieval town lies on three hills not far from the coast. From a distance, Ostuni is a jumble of blazingly white houses and churches spilling over a hilltop and overlooking the sea—thus earning it the nickname *la Città Bianca* (the White City).

GETTING HERE AND AROUND

By car, take the Ostuni exit from the SS16. Trenitalia (Italy's national railway) runs frequent trains from Bari. The station, however, is 3 miles from the town—there is an almost hourly local bus service.

VISITOR INFORMATION

Ostuni Tourism Office ✉ *Corso Mazzini 8* ☎ *0831/301268* 🌐 *www.viaggiareinpuglia.it.*

EXPLORING

Old Town. On the highest of the hills, the old town has steep cobbled lanes, wrought-iron lanterns, some good restaurants, and stupendous views out over the coast and the surrounding plain.

Piazza Libertà. The city's main square divides the new town to the west and the old town to the east. The triangular piazza contains an obelisk dedicated to Saint Oronzo, patron saint of Ostuni.

WHERE TO EAT

$$ SOUTHERN ITALIAN 🍴 **Osteria del Tempo Perso.** Buried in the side streets of the old town, this laid-back restaurant occupies an actual cave, where ancient rough-hewn stone walls contrast with the elegant table settings and a second room has a plethora of intriguing objects adorning the white walls. Service is friendly, and dishes focus on local cuisine such as delectable eggplant Parmesan, homemade orecchiette *con cime di rapa* (with bitter greens and fried breadcrumbs) and baked sea bass with clams, squid, and tomatoes. Unadventurous diners may want to learn the Italian for donkey meat, but won't be short on alternative choices. [$] *Average meal: €35* ✉ *Via G. Tanzarella Vitale 47* ☎ *0831/304819* 🌐 *www.osteriadeltempoperso.com* ⏲ *Closed Mon. No lunch Tues.–Sat. Apr.–Oct.*

CEGLIE MESSAPICA

11 km (7 miles) southwest of Ostuni, 18 km (11 miles) southwest of Martina Franca.

With its 14th-century Piazza Vecchia, tattered Baroque balconies, and lordly medieval castles, the little whitewashed town of Ceglie Messapica is a jewel. The town, at the center of the triangle formed by Taranto, Brindisi, and Fasano, was once the military capital of the region, and often defended itself against invasions from the Taranto city-state, which wanted to clear a route to the Adriatic. Nowadays, more and more visitors come to Ceglie Messapica for its restaurants alone.

GETTING HERE AND AROUND

By car, take the Ostuni exit from the SS16, and follow SP22 to Ceglie Messapica. Ferrovie del Sud-Est runs frequent trains from Bari.

14

WHERE TO EAT

$$ **✗ Al Fornello Da Ricci.** Any respect-
SOUTHERN able culinary tour of Puglia must
ITALIAN pass through this elegant dining
Fodor's Choice room in the whitewashed town
★ of Ceglie Messapica. The distin-
guished kitchen sends out a long
succession of antipasti, all of them
inspired by ancient Pugliese tra-
ditions—meats, cheeses, perhaps
fried zucchini flowers stuffed with
fresh goat's milk ricotta. Then come
delicate pasta and ambitious meat
dishes. It's an haute Pugliese expe-
rience not to be missed. $ *Average
meal: €55* ✉ *Contrada Montevicoli*
☎ *0831/377104* ⊕ *www.lesoste.
it or www.gra.it* ⟶ *Reservations
essential* ⊘ *Closed Tues., for 10 days in late Feb., and Sept. 10–30.
Closed Mon. and no dinner Sun. Nov.–Feb.*

$$ **✗ Cibus.** Amid the vaulted stone archways of this humble but elegant
SOUTHERN osteria in the old city sit rows of bottles and books devoted to the wor-
ITALIAN ship of food and wine. It's no wonder, then, that the food is so good:
after an *antipasto del territorio* (sampling of local meats, cheeses, and
other delights) comes lasagne *di pasta fresca con cime di rape* (with
bitter greens), and then perhaps an *arrosto misto di capretto, capocollo, e salsiccia* (a mixture of roast meats, including baby goat and
sausage). For the more adventurous: braised horse meat in *ragù* (a
tomato-based meat sauce). $ *Average meal: €40* ✉ *Via Chianche di
Scarano* ☎ *0831/388980* ⊕ *www.ristorantecibus.it* ⊘ *Closed Tues. and
2 wks in late June.*

WORD OF MOUTH

"We fell in love with Puglia. The
Adriatic is so beautiful, the people
so friendly (and curious, as there
aren't a lot of Americans that
travel there), and it is unspoiled.
It has a very different 'look' than
other parts of Italy we have seen
because they have been invaded
so many times. The people are
taller and more angular, and while
I have never been to Greece, it
is a bit of what I imagine Greece
would be like."

—travel52

MARTINA FRANCA

29 km (18 miles) west of Ostuni, 36 km (22 miles) north of Taranto.

Martina Franca is a beguiling town with a dazzling mixture of medieval
and Baroque architecture in the light-color local stone. Ornate balconies
hang above the twisting, narrow streets, with little alleys leading off
into the hills. Martina Franca was developed as a military stronghold
in the 14th century, when a surrounding wall with 24 towers was built,
but now all that remains of the wall are the four gates that had once
been the only entrances to the town. Each July the town holds the Valle
D'Itria music festival (⊕ *www.festivaldellavalleditria.it*).

GETTING HERE AND AROUND

By car, take the Fasano exit from the SS16, then follow the SS172. The
Ferrovie Sud-Est runs frequent trains from Bari and Taranto.

VISITOR INFORMATION

Martina Franca Tourism Office ✉ *Piazza XX Settembre 3* ☎ *080/4805702*
⊕ *www.viaggiareinpuglia.it.*

WHERE TO EAT AND STAY

For expanded hotel reviews, visit Fodors.com.

$$ SOUTHERN ITALIAN 🍴 **Ristorante Sagittario.** Just outside the historical center, in Martina Franca's new town, this restaurant is a favorite with locals. The homemade pastas and pizzas are delicious, but it's the excellent grilled meats (lamb chops and pork shoulder are first-rate) that keep people coming back for more. The atmosphere is warm and convivial. [$] *Average meal: €30* ✉ *Via Quarto 15* ☎ *080/4858982.*

$ HOTEL 🏨 **Park Hotel San Michele.** Built around a 19th-century former winery, this hotel has long been a focal point in the area, hosting visiting dignitaries—including Pope John Paul II, who stopped in for a meal in 1989—and even a "Miss Italia" contest (in 1975). **Pros:** pretty pool area; taxi service to Bari airport on request. **Cons:** old-fashioned handheld showers. [$] *Rooms from: €109* ✉ *Viale Carella 9* ☎ *080/4807053* 🌐 *www.parkhotelsanmichele.it* 🛏 *85 rooms* 🍽 *Breakfast.*

SALENTO AND PORTS OF THE HEEL

This far south, the mountains run out of steam and the land is uniformly flat. The monotony of endless olive trees is redeemed by the region's most dramatic coastline, with sandstone cliffs falling fast toward the sea. Here you can find a handful of small, alluring fishing towns, such as Otranto and Gallipoli. Taranto and Brindisi don't quite fit this description: both are big ports where historical importance is obscured by heavy industry. Nonetheless, Taranto has its archaeological museum, and Brindisi, an important ferry jumping-off point, marks the end of the Appian Way (the "Queen of Roads" built by the Romans). Farther south, Salento (the Salentine Peninsula) is the local name for the part of Puglia that forms the end of the heel. Lecce is an unexpected oasis of grace and sophistication, and its swirling architecture will melt even the most uncompromising critic of the Baroque.

TARANTO

100 km (62 miles) southeast of Bari, 40 km (25 miles) south of Martina Franca.

Taranto (the stress is on the first syllable) was an important port even in Greek times, and it's still Italy's largest naval base. It lies toward the back of the instep of the boot on the broad Mare Grande bay, which is connected to a small internal Mare Piccolo basin by two narrow channels, one artificial and one natural. The old town is a series of palazzi in varying states of decay and narrow cobblestone streets on an island between the larger and smaller bodies of water, linked by causeways; the modern city stretches inward along the mainland. Circumnavigate the old town and take in a dramatic panorama to the north, revealing Italy's shipping industry at its busiest: steelworks, dockyards, a bay dotted with fishing boats, and a fish market teeming with pungent activity along the old town's western edge.

GETTING HERE AND AROUND

By car, the A14 Autostrada takes you almost directly to Taranto. Trenitalia runs frequent trains from Bari and Brindisi.

VISITOR INFORMATION

Taranto Tourism Office ⊠ Corso Umberto 113 ☎ 099/4532392
⊕ www.viaggiareinpuglia.it.

EXPLORING

Museo Nazionale. The large collection of prehistoric, Greek, and Roman artifacts in this museum include many that were discovered in the immediate vicinity—some in Puglian tombs dating from before 1000 BC. The museum is a testament to the importance of this ancient port, which has always taken full advantage of its unique trading position at the end of the Italian peninsula; you'll find it just over the bridge from the old town. ⊠ Via Cavour 10 ☎ 099/4532112 ⊕ www.museotaranto.org ⌨ €5 ☉ Daily 8:30–7:30; last entrance at 7.

San Domenico. A major reminder of Taranto's past is the 14th-century church of San Domenico, jutting into the sea at one end of the island. It occupies the site of an old Greek temple, remains of which are still visible. ⊠ Via Duomo 33 ☎ 099/4707733 ☉ Daily 8:30–noon and 4–7.

LECCE

Fodor's Choice ★ *40 km (25 miles) southeast of Brindisi, 87 km (54 miles) east of Taranto.*

Lecce is the crown jewel of the Mezzogiorno. The city is called "the Florence of the south," but that term doesn't do justice to Lecce's uniqueness in the Italian landscape. Though its pretty boutiques, lively bars, bustling streets, laid-back student cafés, and evening passeggiata draw comparisons to the cultural capitals of the north, Lecce's impossibly intricate Baroque architecture and its hyperanimated crowds are distinctively southern. The city is a cosmopolitan oasis two steps from the idyllic Otranto–Brindisi coastline and a hop from the olive-grove countryside of Puglia. Relatively undiscovered by foreign tourists, Lecce exudes an optimism and youthful joie de vivre unparalleled in any other Baroque showcase.

Summer is a great time to visit. In July courtyards and piazzas throughout the city are the settings for dramatic productions. Autumn has its charms as well. A Baroque music festival is held in churches throughout the city in September and October.

GETTING HERE AND AROUND

By car from Bari, take the main toll-free coast road via Brindisi and continue along the SS613 to Lecce. Frequent trains run along the coast from Bari and beyond. The closest airport is in Brindisi.

VISITOR INFORMATION

Lecce Tourism Office ⊠ Corso Vittorio Emanuele 24 ☎ 0832/332463
⊕ www.viaggiareinpuglia.it.

EXPLORING

Duomo. Lecce's ornate Duomo, first built in 1114 but reconstructed in Baroque style from 1659 to 1670, is uncharacteristically set in a solitary lateral square off a main street, rather than at a crossroads of pedestrian traffic. To the left of the Duomo, the more austere **bell tower,** reconstructed by master architect Giuseppe Zimbalo in the 17th century, takes on a surreal golden hue at dusk. The facades of the adjoining 18th-century **Palazzo Vescovile** (Bishops' Palace), farther past the right side of the Duomo, and the **Seminario** on the piazza's right edge complement the rich ornamentation of the Duomo to create an effect almost as splendid as that of the town's church of Santa Croce. The Seminario's tranquil **cloister** is also worth a visit. ⊠ *Piazza Duomo, off Corso Vittorio Emanuele* ☎ *0832/308557* ⊙ *Daily 8:30–12:30 and 4–6:30.*

14

Piazza Sant'Oronzo. In the middle of the city's putative center, surrounded by cafés, pastry shops, and newsstands, is a Roman column that once stood at the end of the Appian Way in Brindisi. This war trophy, carried off in 1660, is imaginatively surmounted by an 18th-century statue of the city's patron saint, Orontius. Next to the column, the shallow rows of seats in the **Anfiteatro Romano** suggest Verona's arena or a small-scale Roman Colosseum.

Fodor'sChoice ★ **Santa Croce.** Although Lecce was founded before the time of the ancient Greeks, it's often associated with the term *Barocco leccese,* the result of a citywide impulse in the 17th century to redo the town in an exuberant fashion. But this was Baroque with a difference. Such architecture is often heavy and monumental, but here it took on a lighter, more fanciful air, and the church of Santa Croce is a fine example, along with the adjoining **Palazzo della Prefettura.** Although every column, window, pediment, and balcony is given a curling baroque touch—and then an extra one for good measure—the overall effect is lighthearted. The buildings' proportions are unintimidating, and the local stone is a glowing honey color: it couldn't look menacing if it tried. ⊠ *Via Umberto I 3* ☎ *0832/241957* ⊕ *www.basilicasantacroce.eu* ⊙ *Daily 9–noon and 5–8.*

WHERE TO EAT

$
SOUTHERN
ITALIAN

✕ **Alle Due Corti.** Renowned local culinary expert Rosalba De Carlo runs this traditional trattoria, where the long tradition and culture of Salentine cuisine is treated with both respect and originality. The menu is printed in the Leccese dialect; the adventurous can try country dishes like *pezzetti te cavallu* (spicy horse meat in tomato sauce) or *turcineddhi* (roasted baby goat entrails)—a crisp, fully flavored delight. The white-wall interior is stark, but character comes from the red-and-white checked tablecloths and the gregarious local families and groups of friends that inevitably fill the place. $ *Average meal: €23* ✉ *Corte dei Giugni 1* ☎ *0832/242223* ⊕ *www.alleduecorti.com* ⊘ *Closed Sun.*

$$ ✗ **Corte dei Pandolfi.** Here you can choose from a vast list of Salen-
SOUTHERN to's best wines and feast on an unparalleled spread of artisanal *salumi*
ITALIAN (cured meats) and local cheeses, accompanied by delicious local honey and *mostarda* (preserved fruit). Traditional primi and secondi are also served, as well as vegetarian specialties, with the menu changing with the season's fresh produce—fresh fish is a staple in the summer months. The location is on a little piazza just off Via degli Ammirati, which starts at the back of the Duomo. $ *Average meal: €30* ✉ *Piazzetta Orsini* ☎ *0832/332309* ⊕ *www.cortedeipandolfi.com* ⊘ No lunch Mon.–Sat. Closed 1 wk in Nov.

$$ ✗ **Le Zie.** This is an excellent place to try traditional Pugliese cooking in
SOUTHERN a warm, casual setting of white walls and loud chatter. Don't expect a
ITALIAN menu; choose from the daily specials, which might include homemade
Fodor's Choice whole-wheat pasta served with a delicate sauce of tomato and sharp,
★ aged ricotta *scanta*. The rustic *purè di fave e cicoria* (bean purée with wild chicory) is topped with local olive oil and hot peppers; mix it together before eating. Service is informal and welcoming. $ *Average meal: €30* ✉ *Via Costadura 19* ☎ *0832/245178* ⊘ *Closed Mon., 1 wk at Easter, last wk in Aug., 1st wk in Sept., last wk in Dec., and 1st wk in Jan. No dinner Sun.*

WHERE TO STAY

For expanded hotel reviews, visit Fodors.com.

$$ 🛏 **Patria Palace.** It's a happy coincidence that the best hotel in Lecce hap-
HOTEL pens to be in one of the best possible locations: a few steps from all the
Fodor's Choice action. **Pros:** luxurious rooms; ideal location. **Cons:** not all rooms have
★ great views. $ *Rooms from: €157* ✉ *Piazzetta Riccardi 13* ☎ *0832/245111* ⊕ *www.patriapalacelecce.com* ⇆ *67 rooms* ❙O❙ *Breakfast.*

$ 🛏 **President.** Rub elbows with visiting dignitaries at this business hotel
HOTEL and conference center near Piazza Mazzini. **Pros:** comfortable rooms; convenient location; low-season bargains. **Cons:** more for business than pleasure; a bit dated. $ *Rooms from: €86* ✉ *Via Salandra 6* ☎ *0832/456111* ⊕ *www.hotelpresidentlecce.it* ⇆ *150 rooms, 3 suites* ❙O❙ *Breakfast.*

OTRANTO

36 km (22 miles) southeast of Lecce, 188 km (117 miles) southeast of Bari.

In one of the first great Gothic novels, Horace Walpole's 1764 *The Castle of Otranto*, the English writer immortalized this city and its mysterious medieval fortress. Otranto (the stress is on the first syllable) has had more than its share of dark thrills. As the easternmost point in Italy—and therefore closest to the Balkan Peninsula—it's often borne the brunt of foreign invasions. A flourishing port from ancient Greek times, Otranto (Hydruntum to the Romans) has a history like most of southern Italy: after the fall of the western Roman Empire, centuries of Byzantine rule interspersed with Saracen incursions, followed by the arrival of the Normans. Modern Otranto's dank cobblestone alleyways alternatively reveal dusty, forgotten doorways and storefronts for modern Italian fashion chains; the spooky castle still looms above, between city and sea. On a clear day you can see across to Albania.

GETTING HERE AND AROUND

By car from Lecce, take the southbound SS16 and exit at Maglie. To follow the coast, take the SS53 from Lecce, then follow SS611 south. There's regular train service from Lecce on Ferrovia del Sud-Est.

VISITOR INFORMATION

Otranto Tourism Office ✉ *Piazza Castello* ☎ *0836/801436* 🌐 *www.comune.otranto.le.it.*

EXPLORING

Castello Aragonese. Surrounding and within the historic city center are impressive city walls and bastions, dominated by this famous castle, which is attributed to the Spanish of the 16th century. ✉ *Piazza Castello* ☎ *0836/424282* 🌐 *www.castelloaragoneseotranto.it* 🎟 *€2, more for exhibitions* ⏲ *Oct.–May, daily 10–1 and 3–7; June and Sept., daily 10–1 and 3–11; July and Aug., daily 10–1 and 3–midnight.*

Cattedrale. The best sight in Otranto is the Cattedrale, originally begun by the Normans and conserving an extraordinary 12th-century mosaic pavement in the nave and aisles. ✉ *Piaza Basilica* ☎ *0836/802720* ⏲ *Daily 7:30–noon and 3–5, later in summer.*

WHERE TO STAY

For expanded hotel reviews, visit Fodors.com.

$$$ B&B/INN Fodor's Choice ★

🏨 **Masseria Montelauro.** Beautifully restored, with stylish designer interiors, this interesting 19th-century former *masseria* (traditional farmhouse for communal living) is an oasis of comfort just a short drive from lovely Otranto. **Pros:** interesting building; lovely interior; friendly, helpful service; great food. **Cons:** car is absolutely necessary; food is pricey. [$] *Rooms from: €255* ✉ *Strada Provinciale Otranto–Uggiano, Località Montelauro* ☎ *0836/806203* 🌐 *www.masseriamontelauro.it* 🛏 *26 rooms, 3 suites* ⏲ *Closed Nov.–Apr.* 🍴 *Breakfast.*

GALLIPOLI

37 km (23 miles) south of Lecce, 190 km (118 miles) southeast of Bari.

The fishing port of Gallipoli, on the eastern tip of the Golfo di Taranto, is divided between a new town, on the mainland, and a beautiful fortified town, across a 17th-century bridge, crowded onto its own small island in the gulf. The Greeks called it Kallipolis ("the fair city"), the Romans Anxa. Like the infamous Turkish town of the same name on the Dardanelles, the Italian Gallipoli occupies a strategic location and thus was repeatedly attacked through the centuries—by the Normans in 1071, the Venetians in 1484, and the British in 1809. Today life in Gallipoli revolves around its fishing trade. Fishing boats in primary colors breeze in and out of the bay during the day, and Gallipoli's fish market, below the bridge, throbs with activity all morning.

GETTING HERE AND AROUND

From Lecce, take the SS101. From Taranto, follow the coastal SS174. Frequent trains run from Lecce.

VISITOR INFORMATION

Gallipoli Tourism Office ✉ *Via Antonietta de Pace 86* ☎ *0833/262529.*

EXPLORING

Castello Aragonese. Gallipoli's historic quarter, a mix of narrow alleys and squares, is guarded by the Castello Aragonese, a massive fortification that grew out of an earlier Byzantine fortress you can still see at the southeast corner. Closed for renovation in recent years, it is due to reopen in 2014.

Duomo. Gallipoli's Duomo is a notable Baroque cathedral from the late 17th century. Built in local limestone, the ornate facade is matched by an equally elaborate interior featuring fine polychrome marble by Cosimo Fanzago and paintings by Luca Gordano, both leading *maestri* at the time. Particularly interesting are the stone carvings that depict episodes from the city's history. ✉ *Via Antonietta de Pace* ☎ *0833/261987* 🌐 *www.cattedralegallipoli.it* 🕒 *Daily 8–noon and 3:30–7.*

La Purità. The stuccoed interior of this church is as elaborate as a wedding cake, with an especially noteworthy tile floor. ✉ *Riviera Nazario Sauro* ☎ *0833/261699.*

WHERE TO EAT AND STAY

For expanded hotel reviews, visit Fodors.com.

$$ SEAFOOD 🍴 **Marechiaro.** Unless you arrive by boat—as many do—you will cross a little bridge to reach this simple waterfront restaurant, not far from the town's historic center. It's built out onto the sea, with wood paneling, flowers, and terraces, with panoramic coastal views. Try the renowned *zuppa di pesce alla gallipolina* (a stew of fish, local red shrimp, clams, and mussels) and linguine with seafood. [$] *Average meal: €40* ✉ *Lungomare Marconi* ☎ *0833/266143.*

$$$$ HOTEL 🏨 **Costa Brada.** A stunning location on a private beach and rooms that all have a sea-view terrace are among the good reasons to stay at this classic Mediterranean beach hotel. **Pros:** lovely views; peaceful setting. **Cons:** meal plans required in summer; very expensive. [$] *Rooms from: €440* ✉ *Litoranea Santa Maria di Leuca, Baia Verde* ☎ *0833/202551* 🌐 *www.grandhotelcostabrada.it* 🛏 *80 rooms* 🍽 *Some meals.*

SPORTS AND THE OUTDOORS

BEACHES

FAMILY **Beaches.** Ample swimming and clean, fine sand make Gallipoli's beaches a good choice for families. The 5-km (3-mile) expanse of sand sweeping south from town has both public and private beaches, the latter equipped with changing rooms, sun beds, and umbrellas. Water-sports equipment can be bought or rented at the waterfront shops in town.

BASILICATA

Occupying the instep of Italy's boot, Basilicata formed part of Magna Graecia, the loose collection of colonies founded along the coast of southern Italy whose wealth and military prowess rivaled those of the city-states of Greece itself. More recently it was made famous by Carlo Levi (1902–75) in his *Christ Stopped at Eboli*, a book that underscored the poverty of the region. (The title comes from a local saying that implied that progress had stopped at Eboli, some 60 miles to the west, near the coast, and that Bascilicata had "been bypassed by Christianity, by morality, by history itself—that they have somehow been excluded from the full human experience.")

Basilicata is no longer so desolate, as it draws travelers in search of bucolic settings, great food, and archaeological treasures. The city of Matera, the region's true highlight, is built on the side of an impressive ravine that's honeycombed with Sassi, rock-hewn dwellings, some of them still occupied, forming a separate enclave that contrasts vividly with the attractive Baroque town above.

14

MATERA

62 km (39 miles) south of Bari.

Matera is one of southern Italy's most unusual towns. On their own, the elegant Baroque churches, palazzi, and broad piazzas—filled to bursting during the evening passeggiata, when the locals turn out to stroll the streets—would make Matera stand out in Basilicata's rugged landscape. But what really sets this town apart are the Sassi.

GETTING HERE AND AROUND
From Bari, take the SS96 to Altamura, then the SS99 to Matera. Roughly one train per hour (Ferrovie Appulo Lucane) leaves Bari Centrale for Matera.

VISITOR INFORMATION
Matera Tourism Office ⊠ *Via De Viti De Marco 9* ☎ *0835/331983* ⊕ *www.aptbasilicata.it.*

EXPLORING
Duomo. Matera's cathedral was built in the late 13th century and occupies a prominent position between the two Sassi. It has a pungent Apulian-Romanesque flavor; inside, there's a recovered fresco, probably painted in the 14th century, showing scenes from the *Last Judgment*. On the Duomo's facade the figures of saints Peter and Paul stand on either side of a sculpture of Matera's patron, the Madonna della Bruna. At the time of writing, the Duomo was closed for a long-term restoration. ⊠ *Piazza Duomo* ☎ *0835/332908.*

Museo Archaeologico Nazionale Domenico Ridola. Housed in the former monastery of Santa Chiara, Matera's archaeological museum illustrates the history of the area. Its collection includes an extensive selection of prehistoric and classical finds, notably Bronze Age weaponry and beautifully decorated red-figure pottery from Greece. ⊠ *Via Ridola 24* ☎ *0835/310058* ⊡ *€2.50* ☉ *Mon. 2–8, Tues.–Sun. 9–8.*

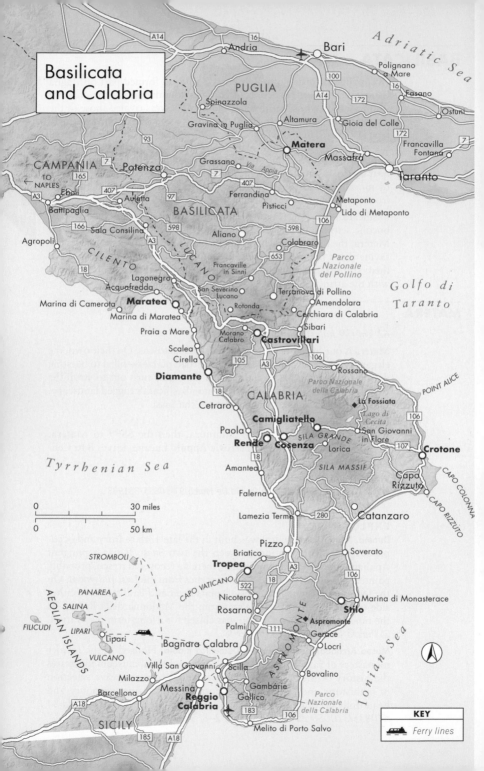

San Giovanni Battista. The 13th-century Romanesque church of San Giovanni Battista was restored to its pre-Baroque simplicity in 1926. As you go in through a side door—the original end door and facade were incorporated into later buildings—note the interesting sculpted decorations in the porch. The interior still maintains its original cross vaulting, ogival arches, and curious capitals. ⊠ *Via San Biagio* ⊙ *Daily 8–12:30 and 3:30–7.*

Fodor'sChoice
★
Sassi. Matera's Sassi are rock-hewn dwellings piled chaotically atop one another, strewn across the sides of a steep ravine. Some date from Paleolithic times, when they were truly just caves. In the years that followed, the grottoes were slowly adapted as houses only slightly more modern, with their exterior walls closed off and canals regulating rainwater and sewage. Until relatively recently, these troglodytic abodes presented a Dante-esque vision of squalor and poverty, which is graphically described in Carlo Levi's 1945 memoir, *Christ Stopped at Eboli.* In the 1960s, however most of them were emptied of their inhabitants, who were largely consigned to the ugly apartment blocks seen on the way into town. Today, having been designated a World Heritage Site, the area has been cleaned up and is gradually being populated once again—and even gentrified, as evidenced by the bars and restaurants that have moved in. (The filming here of Mel Gibson's 2004 film *The Passion of the Christ* also raised the area's profile.) The wide Strada Panoramica leads you safely through this desolate region, which still retains its eerie atmosphere and panoramic views.

14

There are two areas of Sassi, the **Sasso Caveoso** and the **Sasso Barisano,** and both can be seen from vantage points in the upper town. Follow the Strada Panoramica down into the Sassi and feel free to ramble among the strange structures, which, in the words of H. V. Morton in his *A Traveller in Southern Italy,* "resemble the work of termites rather than of man." Among them you can find several *chiese rupestri,* or rock-hewn churches, some of which have medieval frescoes, notably **Santa Maria de Idris,** right on the edge of the Sasso Caveoso, near the ravine. Guided tours can be arranged through the tourist office.

WHERE TO EAT

$$
SOUTHERN
ITALIAN
✕ **Le Botteghe.** A pleasingly restored building in the Sassi, with rough white walls and arched ceilings, contains this stylish restaurant. One standout on the menu is the charcoal-grilled steak, especially selected by a local butcher and cooked wonderfully rare—this is one of the finest pieces of meat in the region. It's best washed down with local Aglianico del Vulture red wine. Solid renditions of local pasta dishes are also available. There's outdoor seating in summer. Ⓢ *Average meal: €35* ⊠ *Piazza San Pietro Barisano 22* ☎ *0835/344072* ⊕ *www.hotelamatera. it* ⊙ *Closed Wed. No lunch Tues.–Thurs. Oct.–Mar.*

$$
SOUTHERN
ITALIAN
Fodor'sChoice
★
✕ **Lucanerie.** On the edge of Sasso Barisano, this restaurant bases its menu on seasonal ingredients from around Matera, some of which are gathered by the owner himself. The *cavatelli con peperoni cruschi* (with local peppers) is dusted with breadcrumbs and full of flavor. The grilled *bistecca* (steak) is from the native Podolico cattle breed that grazes in upland areas around Matera and has a tenderness all its own. Top off your meal with a slice of homemade goat-cheesecake. Ⓢ *Average meal: €40* ⊠ *Via Santo Stefano 61* ☎ *0835/332133* ⊙ *Closed Mon. No dinner Sun.*

WHERE TO STAY

For expanded hotel reviews, visit Fodors.com.

$$$
HOTEL
Fodor'sChoice
★
🛌 **Hotel Sant'Angelo.** What better way to get close to Matera's trogloditic Sassi than to stay in a hotel that actually incorporates some of the caves as highly upgraded guest rooms. **Pros:** unrivaled views; atmospheric rooms. **Cons:** no elevator and many steps to climb. $ *Rooms from: €226* ⊠ *Piazza San Pietro Caveoso* 🕾 *0835/314010* ⊕ *www. hotelsantangelosassi.it* ⇘ *23 rooms* ❍I *Breakfast.*

$
HOTEL
Fodor'sChoice
★
🛌 **Locanda di San Martino.** Combining good taste, agreeable surroundings, and excellent value, the Locanda is a prime place to stay among Matera's Sassi. **Pros:** convenient location; comfortable rooms; no traffic noise. **Cons:** rooms are reached via outdoor walkway; limited parking nearby. $ *Rooms from: €109* ⊠ *Via Fiorentini 71* 🕾 *0835/256600* ⊕ *www.locandadisanmartino.it* ⇘ *32 rooms* ❍I *Breakfast.*

$$$$
HOTEL
Fodor'sChoice
★
🛌 **Palazzo Margherita.** This is Francis Ford Coppola's Xanadu—a large and luxurious palazzo in the town of his ancestors and now, thanks to the guiding hand of French designer Jacques Grange, Basilicata's top lodging. **Pros:** professional, courteous staff; a garden pool; spacious rooms with lots of high-tech gadgetry. **Cons:** very expensive; private transport needed; not much to do in Bernalda. $ *Rooms from: €500* ⊠ *Corso Umberto 64, Bernalda, Matera* ⊕ *A 40-minute drive south of Matera: take SS7 out of Matera heading for Potenza and then join SS407 for Metaponto and Taranto. Look for turnoff to Bernalda after 25 km (16 miles)* 🕾 *0835/549060* ⊕ *www.palazzomargherita.com* ⇘ *9 suites* ❍I *Breakfast.*

MARATEA

217 km (135 miles) south of Naples.

When encountering Maratea for the first time, you can be forgiven for thinking you've somehow arrived at the French Riviera. The high, twisty road comes complete with glimpses of a turquoise sea below and is divided by the craggy rocks into various separate localities—Maratea, Maratea Porto, Marina di Maratea, Fiumicello, and Cersuta. Maratea is the name given to this cluster of towns, as well as to the main inland village, a tumble of cobblestone streets where the ruins of a much older settlement (Maratea Antica) can be seen. At the summit of the hill stands the gigantic Cristo Redentore, a massive statue of Christ reminiscent of the one in Rio de Janeiro. There's no shortage of secluded sandy strips in between the rocky headlands, which can get crowded in August. A summer minibus service connects all the different points once or twice an hour.

GETTING HERE AND AROUND

By car, take the Lagonegro exit from the A3 Autostrada and continue along the SS585. Intercity and regional trains from Reggio Calabria and Naples stop at Maratea. In the summer months there's a bus linking the train station to the upper town 4 km (2½ miles) away.

VISITOR INFORMATION

Maratea Tourism Office ⊠ *Piazza del Gesù 32, Località Fiumicello* 🕾 *0973/876908* ⊕ *www.aptbasilicata.it.*

WHERE TO EAT

$$
SOUTHERN
ITALIAN

✕ **Da Cesare.** With an open kitchen so you can watch the chef and a veranda overlooking the azure waters of the Golfo di Policastro, there's always something to see at this family-run seafood restaurant. Even better, it serves some of the freshest catch in town. The only drawback may be that the portions are very large, so you might not want every course from antipasto to dolce. Try the linguine *al nero di seppie* (with cuttlefish ink) and *grigliata mista* (mixed grilled fish and seafood). $ *Average meal: €35* ✉ *Strada Statale 18, Località Cersuta* ⚓ *Da Cesare is on the main SS18 coast road in the village of Cersuta, about 5 km (3 miles) north of Maratea and 3 km (2 miles) south of Acquafredda.* ☎ *0973/871840* ⊗ *Closed Thurs. Nov.–Mar.*

WHERE TO STAY

For expanded hotel reviews, visit Fodors.com.

$$
HOTEL

☷ **Villa Cheta Elite.** Immersed in Mediterranean greenery with glorious sea views, this elegant and historic villa is in the seaside village of Acquafredda, just north of Maratea. **Pros:** surrounded by lush vegetation; beautiful views of the coast and mountains; lovely art nouveau building. **Cons:** on a busy road; no pool; steps to climb. $ *Rooms from: €262* ✉ *Via Timpone 46, Località Acquafredda* ☎ *0973/878134* ⊕ *www.villacheta.it* ⇆ *23 rooms* ⊗ *Closed Nov.–Mar.* ⦿ *Breakfast.*

CALABRIA

Italy's southernmost mainland region may be poor, but it also claims more than its share of fantastic scenery and great beaches. The accent here is on the landscape, the sea, and the constantly changing dialogue between the two. Don't expect much in the way of big-city sophistication in this least trodden of regions, but instead remain open to the simple pleasures to be found—the country food, the friendliness, the disarming hospitality of the people. Aside from coast and culture, there are also some destinations worth going out of your way for, from the vividly colored murals of Diamante to the hiking trails of the Pollino and Sila national parks.

The drive on the southbound A3 Autostrada alone is a breathtaking experience, the more so as you approach Sicily, whose image grows tantalizingly nearer as the road wraps around the coastline once challenged by Odysseus. The road has been under reconstruction since his time, with little sign of completion.

DIAMANTE

51 km (32 miles) south of Maratea, 225 km (140 miles) south of Naples.

One of the most fashionable of the string of small resorts lining Calabria's north Tyrrhenian Coast, Diamante makes a good stop for its whitewashed maze of narrow alleys, brightly adorned with a startling variety of large-scale murals. The work of local and international artists, the murals—which range from cartoons to poems to serious portraits, and from beautiful to downright ugly—give a sense of wandering through a huge open-air art gallery. Flanking the broad, palm-lined seaside promenade are sparkling beaches to the north and south.

GETTING HERE AND AROUND

Driving from Maratea, take the SS18; from Cosenza, take the SS107 to Paola, then the SS18. Regional trains leave from Naples four times a day, with regular service from Paola.

WHERE TO STAY

For expanded hotel reviews, visit Fodors.com.

$$$ HOTEL **Grand Hotel San Michele.** A survivor from a vanishing age, the San Michele occupies a Belle Époque–style villa atop a cliff near the village of Cetraro, 20 km (12 miles) south of Diamante on the SS18. **Pros:** lovely views; nice gardens; comfortable accommodations. **Cons:** a bit pricey. [$] *Rooms from: €220* ✉ *Località Bosco 8/9, Cetraro* ☎ *0982/91012* 🌐 *www.sanmichele.it* *78 rooms, 6 suites, 22 apartments* ⏲ *Closed Nov.–Mar.* 🍴 *Breakfast.*

CASTROVILLARI

68 km (43 miles) east of Diamante, 75 km (48 miles) north of Cosenza.

Accent the first "i" when you pronounce the name of this provincial Calabrian city, notable for its Aragonese castle, synagogue, and 16th-century San Giuliano church. It's also a great jumping-off point for the Albanian-speaking village of Cìvita and the Pollino National Park, farther afield. Castrovillari's world-class restaurant-inn, La Locanda di Alia, has made the city something of a gastronomical destination.

GETTING HERE AND AROUND

By car, take the A3 Autostrada and exit at Frascineto-Castrovillari. Ferrovie della Calabria runs buses from Cosenza, but service is irregular.

VISITOR INFORMATION

Castrovillari tourism office ✉ *Corso Garibaldi 160* ☎ *0981/209595* 🌐 *www.prolococastrovillari.it.*

WHERE TO EAT

$$$ MODERN ITALIAN Fodor's Choice ★ **La Locanda di Alia.** It's hard to say what's more surprising about this inn and restaurant: its improbable location in Castrovillari, or the fact that it's been here since 1952. Chef Gaetano Alia's menu swerves from the unique (beef with a delicious strawberry-and-onion sauce) to the dangerously spicy (*candele,* like rigatoni without the ridges, in a pecorino-cheese sauce). If you like it so much you want to stay, more than a dozen guest rooms are available. Surrounded by plenty of greenery, they're decorated in bright colors with frescoes from local artists. Rounding off the experience in summer months is a small but enticing swimming pool. [$] *Average meal: €50* ✉ *Via Ietticelli 55* ☎ *0981/46370* 🌐 *www.alia.it* *Reservations essential* ⏲ *No dinner Sun.*

COSENZA

75 km (48 miles) south of Diamante, 185 km (115 miles) north of Reggio Calabria.

Cosenza has a steep, stair-filled centro storico that truly hails from another age. Wrought-iron balconies overlook narrow alleyways with old-fashioned storefronts and bars that have barely been touched by centuries of development. Flung haphazardly—and beautifully—across the top and side of a steep hill ringed by mountains, and watched over by a great, crumbling medieval castle, Cosenza also provides the best gateway for the Sila, whose steep walls rear up to the town's eastern side. Though Cosenza's outskirts are largely modern and ugly, culinary gems and picturesque views await in the rolling farmland nearby and the mountains to the east.

GETTING HERE AND AROUND

By car, take the Cosenza exit from the A3 Autostrada. By train, change at Paola on the main Rome–Reggio Calabria line. Regional trains run from Naples. Ferrovie della Calabria runs buses from Spezzano della Sila, Castrovillari, and Camigliatello.

EXPLORING

Castello Svevo. Crowning the Pancrazio hill above the old city, with views across to the Sila mountains, Castello Svevo is largely in ruins, having suffered successive earthquakes and a lightning strike that ignited gunpowder stored within. The castle takes its name from the great Swabian emperor Frederick II (1194–1250), who added two octagonal towers, though it dates originally to the Normans, who fortified the hill against their Saracen foes. Occasional exhibitions and concerts are staged here in summer, and any time of year it's fun to check out the old ramparts and take in the views of the old and new cities—a shocking study in contrast. It's currently undergoing extensive restoration. ⊠ *Colle Pancrazio* 🖃 *Free* 🕙 *Daily 8–8.*

Duomo. Cosenza's original Duomo, probably built in the middle of the 11th century, was destroyed by an earthquake in 1184. A new cathedral was consecrated in the presence of Emperor Frederick II in 1222. After many baroque additions, later alterations have restored some of the Provençal Gothic style. Inside, look for the lovely monument to Isabella of Aragon, who died after falling from her horse en route to France in 1271. ⊠ *Piazza del Duomo 1* 🕾 *0984/77864* 🕙 *May–Oct., daily 8–noon and 4:30–8; Nov.–Apr., daily 8–noon and 3:30–7.*

Piazza XV Marzo. Cosenza's noblest square, Piazza XV Marzo (commonly called Piazza della Prefettura), houses government buildings as well as the elegant **Teatro Rendano.** From the square, the **Villa Comunale** (public garden) provides plenty of shaded benches for a rest.

WHERE TO EAT AND STAY

For expanded hotel reviews, visit Fodors.com.

$ ✕ **Osteria dell'Arenella.** On the banks of the river, this grilled-meat spe-
SOUTHERN cialist caters to the local bourgeoisie with a comfortable, friendly set
ITALIAN of rooms under old archways. Go for the grigliata mista and enjoy the wonderful meatiness of local grass-fed beef. The wine list, too,

14

is excellent and the local wine made with the gaglioppo grape pairs nicely with meat, sausage, and aged cheeses. [$] *Average meal: €30* ✉ *Via Arenella 12* ☎ *0984/76573* 🌐 *www.ristoranteosteriadellarenella.com* 🕒 *Closed Mon. Oct.–May. No lunch Tues.–Sat.*

$ HOTEL 🏨 **Royal Hotel.** Decent accommodations are hard to come by in Cosenza, which makes this hotel in the new center quite a find. **Pros:** one of the town's best lodgings; close to pedestrian-only shopping area; free parking. **Cons:** not close to Cosenza's main attractions. [$] *Rooms from: €100* ✉ *Via Molinella 24/e* ☎ *0984/412165* 🌐 *www.hotelroyalsas.it* 🛏 *80 rooms* 🍴 *Breakfast.*

RENDE

13 km (8 miles) northwest of Cosenza.

Rende is a pleasing stop on the way to or from Cosenza. Leave your car in the parking lot at the base of a long and bizarre series of escalators and staircases, which will whisk you off to this pristine, cobbleston hilltop town, whose winding streets and turrets preside over idyllic countryside views.

GETTING HERE AND AROUND

By car, take the A3 Autostrada and exit at Cosenza-Rende. Local buses make the trip from nearby Cosenza.

WHERE TO EAT

$$ SEAFOOD 🍴 **Pantagruel.** You're completely in the hands of the chef at this temple to seafood. They're good hands indeed, which is why Pantagruel is one of the most respected restaurants in Calabria. The prix-fixe menu (the only option) depends on the day's catch, but you'll surely encounter something memorable: for instance, a salad of octopus so thinly sliced and delicate that it's reminiscent of carpaccio, or a tender whole *orata* (sea bream) with fava beans. Pantagruel is set in an elegant old house with sweeping views of hills dotted with little towns. [$] *Average meal: €35* ✉ *Via Pittore Santanna 2* ☎ *0984/443508* 🌐 *www.pantagruelilristorante.it* 🕒 *Closed 1 wk in late Dec. and 1 wk in Sept. No dinner Sun.*

CAMIGLIATELLO

30 km (19 miles) east of Cosenza.

Lined with chalets, Camigliatello is one of the Sila Massif's major resort towns. Most of the Sila isn't mountainous at all; it is, rather, an extensive, sparsely populated plateau with areas of thick forest. Unfortunately, there's been considerable deforestation. However, since 1968, when the area was designated a national park called Parco Nazionale della Sila, strict rules have limited the felling of timber, and forests are now regenerating. There are well-marked trails through pine and beech woods, and ample opportunities for horseback riding. Fall and winter see droves of locals hunting mushrooms and gathering chestnuts, while ski slopes near Camigliatello draw crowds.

GETTING HERE AND AROUND

By car, take the Cosenza Nord exit from the A3, then follow the SS107.

VISITOR INFORMATION
Camigliatello Tourism Office ✉ *Via Roma 5* ☎ *0984/578159*
⊕ *www.camigliatellosilano.eu.*

EXPLORING
La Fossiata. A couple of miles east of town, Lago Cecita makes a good starting point for exploring La Fossiata, a lovely wooded conservation area within the park. The forestry commission office in nearby Cupone can provide maps and arrange guides. ✉ *Cupone Frazione, Spezzano della Sila* ☎ *0984/537109 tourist office* ⊕ *www.parcosila.it.*

WHERE TO STAY
For expanded hotel reviews, visit Fodors.com.

$ 🏨 **Tasso.** On the edge of Camigliatello, less than 1 km (½ mile) from the
HOTEL ski slopes, this hotel is in a peaceful, picturesque location. **Pros:** beauti-
FAMILY ful surroundings; lively. **Cons:** dated architecture. $ *Rooms from: €80*
✉ *Via degli Impianti Sportivi, Spezzano della Sila* ☎☎ *0984/578113*
⊕ *www.hoteltasso.it* ⌁*82 rooms* ☉ *Closed Apr.–May and Nov.*
†⊙*Breakfast.*

CROTONE

105 km (65 miles) east of Cosenza, 150 km (94 miles) northeast of Locri.

GETTING HERE AND AROUND
By car, take the Cosenza Nord exit from the A3, then follow the SS107. There are regular trains from Sibari.

VISITOR INFORMATION
Crotone Tourism Office ✉ *Via Manna Giacomo 25* ☎ *0962/26700*
⊕ *www.crotoneturismo.it.*

EXPLORING
Museo Archeologico Nazionale. Close to the seafront castle in Cro-tone, this museum displays the treasure from the Santuario di Hera Lacinia, which includes Hera's gold crown with intertwined fig and myrtle leaves. ✉ *Via Risorgimento 120, Crotone* ☎ *0962/23082* ⌁*€2* ☉ *Tues.–Sun. 9–7.*

Fodor's Choice **Santuario di Hera Lacinia.** Occupying the main bulge along Calabria's
★ Ionian coastline, Crotone was founded by Achaeans from the Greek Peloponnese in about 708 BC and soon became one of the great cities in Magna Graecia. A drab modern town has obliterated most of the ancient settlement; the main attraction now is a remarkable gold hoard, found in 1987 at the Santuario di Hera Lacinia on a promontory 11 km (7 miles) to the south, known as Capo Colonna for the single remain-ing column from a temple dedicated to Hera. It's well worth a visit, especially in April and May, when the area is awash with wildflow-ers. An on-site archaeology museum provides some key background information for the site and has an interesting display of underwater finds from the area. ✉ *Via per Capo Colonna, Crotone* ☎ *0962/934814* ⌁*Free* ☉ *Sanctuary: Tues.–Sun. 9–1 and 3:30–7. Park: daily 8–1 hr before sunset.*

14

WHERE TO STAY

For expanded hotel reviews, visit Fodors.com.

$$ HOTEL **Hotel Helios.** The functional Helios may not be the Ritz, but it's got what you need: it's in a quiet part of town, it's open year-round, and it's handily located on the coast road to Capo Colonna. **Pros:** bright, airy rooms; efficient courteous staff; on bus route into town. **Cons:** uninspiring architecture; skimpy breakfasts. [$] *Rooms from: €150* ✉ *Via Makalla 2, Crotone* ☎ *0962/901291* 🌐 *www.helioshotels.it* 🛏 *42 rooms* 🍴 *Breakfast.*

WORD OF MOUTH

"In America one of your most famous trips is 'coast to coast.' Well, also in Calabria, it is possible the coast-to-coast trip: from Tyrrhenian sea to the Ionian sea. One of the little differences is the distance: 6,600 kilometers in USA and 100 kilometers in Calabria!!! That's my suggestion, take a coast to coast trip in Cosenza province."
—vincenzod

TROPEA

120 km (75 miles) south of Cosenza, 107 km (66 miles) north of Reggio.

Ringed by cliffs and wonderful sandy beaches, the Tropea Promontory is still mostly undiscovered by foreign tourists. The main town of Tropea, its old palazzi built in simple golden stone, easily wins the contest for prettiest town on Calabria's Tyrrhenian coast. On a clear day the seaward views from the waterfront promenade take in Stromboli's cone and at least four of the other Aeolians. You can visit the islands by motorboats that depart daily in summer. Accommodations are good, and beach addicts won't be disappointed by the choice of magnificent sandy bays within easy reach. Two of the best are south at Capo Vaticano and north at Briatico.

GETTING HERE AND AROUND

By car, exit the A3 Autostrada at Pizzo and follow the southbound SP6/SS522. Eleven trains depart daily from Lamezia Terme.

VISITOR INFORMATION

Tropea Tourism Office ✉ *Piazza Ercole* ☎ *0963/61475* 🌐 *www.prolocotropea.eu.*

EXPLORING

Cattedrale. In Tropea's harmonious warren of lanes, seek out the old Norman Cattedrale, whose interior displays a couple of unexploded U.S. bombs from World War II, with a grateful prayer to the Madonna attached to each. Note that the hours below don't necessarily guarantee that the church will be open. ✉ *Largo Duomo* ☎ *0963/61034* 🕓 *Daily 7:30–noon and 4–7.*

Santa Maria dell'Isola. From the belvedere at the bottom of the main square, Piazza Ercole, the church and Benedictine monastery of Santa Maria dell'Isola glisten on a rocky promontory above an aquamarine sea. The path out to the church is lined with fishermen's caves. Dating to medieval times, the church was remodeled in the Gothic style, then given another face-lift after an earthquake in 1905. At this writing, access to the promontory has been improved, but the site is temporarily closed until renovation of the church is completed. The interior has an 18th-century Nativity and fragments of medieval tombs. ⊠ *Lungomare A Sorrentino* ☎ *0963/61475.*

WHERE TO EAT AND STAY

For expanded hotel reviews, visit Fodors.com.

$$ × **Pimm's.** Since its glory days in the 1960s, this basement restaurant
SOUTHERN in Tropea's historic center has offered the town's top dining experi-
ITALIAN ence. Seafood is the best choice, with such specialties as pasta with sea urchins, smoked swordfish, and prawns served on a bed of red Tropea onions. The splendid sea views from the rear windows are a surpris-ing—and substantial—reason to head here. They also five rooms for overnight guests. $ *Average meal: €35* ⊠ *Corso Vittorio Emanuele 2* ☎ *0963/666105* ⊕ *www.ristorantepimmstropea.com* ☾ *Closed Mon. Oct.–May.*

$$ ⊡ **Villa Antica.** In a fin-de-siècle villa just a stone's throw from Tropea's
HOTEL main square, Piazza Vittorio Veneto, this hotel is within walking dis-tance (downhill) from the train station. **Pros:** open all year; attentive staff; good location. **Cons:** some rooms need renovation; noise from street; no parking available at the hotel. $ *Rooms from: €130* ⊠ *Via Ruffo di Calabria 37* ☎ *0963/607176* ⊕ *www.villaanticatropea.it* ↝ *28 rooms* ⦿ *Breakfast.*

REGGIO CALABRIA

115 km (71 miles) south of Tropea, 499 km (311 miles) south of Naples.

Reggio Calabria, on the tip of Italy's toe, was laid low by the same catastrophic earthquake that struck Messina in 1908. This raw city is one of Italy's busiest ports, where you can find every type of container ship and smokestack. Hydrofoils for Sicily depart from here—vehicle-carrying ferries depart from Villa San Giovanni 13 km (8 miles) north.

GETTING HERE AND AROUND

The A3 Autostrada runs directly to Reggio Calabria. Eight trains depart from Naples and Rome daily. There are daily flights from Rome, Milan, Turin, and Venice.

VISITOR INFORMATION

Reggio Calabria Tourism Office ⊠ *Via Venezia 1a* ☎ *0965/21010* ⊕ *www.prolocoreggiocalabria.it.*

EXPLORING

Museo Nazionale della Magna Grecia. Reggio has one of southern Italy's most important archaeological museums, its prize exhibit being two statues, known as the **Bronzi di Riace,** that were discovered by an ama-teur deep-sea diver off Calabria's Ionian Coast in 1972. Flaunting phy-siques gym enthusiasts would die for, they are thought to date from the 5th century BC and have been attributed to both Pheidias and Polyklei-tos. It's possible they were taken by the Romans as trophies from the site of Delphi and then shipwrecked on the trip to Italy. At the time of writing the museum is undergoing extensive renovations so the bronzes and main exhibits are on display every day from 9 to 7 at Palazzo

Campanella (✉ *Via Cardinale Portanova* ☎ *0965/812255* 🎟 *Free*). If you're making a special trip to see them, call the tourist office, the museum, or the Palazzo to ascertain their current whereabouts. ✉ *Piazza De Nava 26* ☎ *0965/812255* 🌐 *www.museonazionalerc.it.*

WHERE TO STAY

For expanded hotel reviews, visit Fodors.com.

$$ HOTEL 🏨 **E'Hotel.** On the seafront beside the Lido Comunale, this sleek modern hotel has great views and one of the best locations in town. **Pros:** great location; unbeatable views; luxurious rooms. **Cons:** can be busy during conferences. [$] *Rooms from: €190* ✉ *Via Giunchi 6* ☎ *0965/893000* 🌐 *www.ehotelreggiocalabria.it* 🛏 *48 rooms, 4 suites* 🍴 *Breakfast.*

STILO

50 km (31 miles) north of Locri, 138 km (86 miles) northeast of Reggio Calabria.

Grandly positioned on the side of the rugged Monte Consolino, the village of Stilo is known for being the birthplace and home of the philosopher Tommaso Campanella (1568–1639), whose magnum opus was the socialistic *La Città del Sole* (*The City of the Sun*, 1602)—for which he spent 26 years as a prisoner of the Spanish Inquisition.

GETTING HERE AND AROUND

From Reggio Calabria, follow the Ionian coastal SS106 and exit at Stilo. Regular trains run from Lamezia Terme.

SICILY

WELCOME TO SICILY

TOP REASONS TO GO

★ **Taormina—Sicily's most beautiful resort:** The view of the sea and Mt. Etna from its jagged cactus-covered cliffs is as close to perfection as a panorama can get.

★ **A walk on Siracusa's Ortygia Island:** Classical ruins rub elbows with faded seaside palaces and fish markets in Sicily's most striking port city, where the Duomo is literally built atop an ancient Greek temple.

★ **Palermo's palaces, churches, and crypts:** Virtually every great European empire ruled Sicily's strategically positioned capital at some point, and it shows most of all in the diverse architecture, from Roman to Byzantine to Arab-Norman.

★ **Valley of the Temples, Agrigento:** This stunning set of ruins is proudly perched above the sea in a grove full of almond trees; not even in Athens will you find Greek temples this finely preserved.

1 The Ionian Coast. For many, the Ionian Coast is all about touristy **Taormina**, spectacularly poised on a cliff near **Mount Etna**; but don't overlook lively **Catania**, Sicily's modern nerve center.

2 Siracusa. This was one of the great powers of the classical world. Today, full of fresh fish and remarkable ruins, it's content to be one of Italy's most charming cities.

3 The Interior. In hill towns such as **Enna**, the interior of Sicily exhibits a slower pace of life than in the frenetic coastal cities. **Piazza Armerina** features the Villa Casale and its ancient Roman mosaics.

4 Western Sicily. Following the island's northern edge west of Palermo, this coast meanders past **Monreale** and its mosaics, **Segesta** with its temple, and the fairy-tale town of **Erice**.

Greek ruins stand sentinel in **Agrigento** at the **Valley of the Temples**, blanketed in almond blossoms. Nearly as impressive is **Selinunte**, rising above rubble and overlooking the sea.

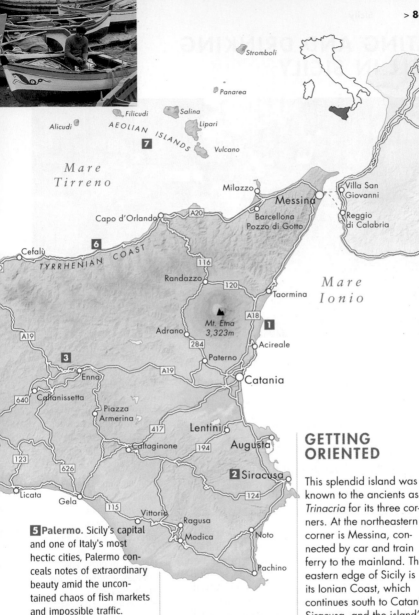

15

GETTING ORIENTED

This splendid island was known to the ancients as *Trinacria* for its three corners. At the northeastern corner is Messina, connected by car and train ferry to the mainland. The eastern edge of Sicily is its Ionian Coast, which continues south to Catania, Siracusa, and the island's southeastern corner. Sicily's northern edge is the Tyrrhenian Coast, which includes Palermo and extends out to the island's third (western) corner.

5 **Palermo.** Sicily's capital and one of Italy's most hectic cities, Palermo conceals notes of extraordinary beauty amid the uncontained chaos of fish markets and impossible traffic.

6 **Tyrrhenian Coast.** Filled with summer beachgoers, the **Tyrrhenian Coast** also has several quaint villages, including **Cefalù**, with its famous cathedral.

7 **Aeolian Islands.** You may know these tranquil windswept islands from the *Odyssey*, and some of them seem to have changed little since Homer's time.

EATING AND DRINKING WELL IN SICILY

Sicilian cuisine is one of the oldest in existence, with records of cooking competitions dating to 600 BC. Food in Sicily today reflects the island's unique cultural mix, imaginatively combining fish, fruits, vegetables, and nuts with Italian pastas and Arab and North African elements—*cous cous* is a staple in Palermo.

It's hard to eat badly here. From the lowliest of trattorias to the most highfalutin' ristorante, you'll find the classic dishes that have been the staples of the family dinner table for years—basically pasta and seafood. A more sophisticated place may introduce a few adventurous items onto the menu, but the main difference between the cheapest and the most expensive restaurants will be the level of service and the accoutrements: in more formal ones you'll find greater attention to detail and a more respectful atmosphere, while less pretentious trattorias tend to be family-run affairs, often without even a menu to guide you. However, in this most gregarious of regions in the most convivial of countries, you can expect a lively dining experience wherever you choose to eat.

SICILIAN MARKETS

Sicily's natural fecundity is evident wherever you look, from the prickly pears sprouting on roadsides to the slopes of vine and citrus groves covering the inland to the ranks of fishing boats moored in every harbor.

You can come face-to-face with this bounty in the clamorous street markets of Palermo (*pictured above*) and Catania. Here, you'll encounter teetering piles of olives and oranges, enticing displays of cheeses and meats, plus pastries and sweets of every description. The effect is heady and sensuous. Immerse yourself in the hustle and bustle of the Sicilian souk, and you'll emerge enriched.

DELICIOUS FISH

In Sicily, naturally, you can find some of the freshest seafood in all of Italy. Pasta *con le sarde,* an emblematic dish that goes back to the Saracen conquerors, with fresh sardines (*pictured at right*), olive oil, raisins, pine nuts, and wild fennel, gets a different treatment at every restaurant. Grilled *tonno* (tuna) and *orata* (daurade) are coastal staples, while delicate *ricci* (sea urchins) are a specialty. King, however, is *pesce spada* (swordfish), best enjoyed *marinato* (marinated), *affumicato* (smoked), or as the traditional *involtini di pesce spada* (roulades).

SNACKS

Sicily offers a profusion of toothsome snacks, two prime examples being *arancini* ("little oranges"—rice croquettes with a cheese or meat filling; *pictured below*), and *panelle* (seasoned chickpea flour boiled to a paste, cooled, sliced, and fried), normally bought from street vendors. Other tidbits to look out for include special foods associated with festivals, often pastries and sweets, such as the ominously named *ossa dei morti* ("dead men's bones," rolled almond cookies). But the most eye-catching of all are the *frutta martorana,* also known as *pasta reale*—sweet marzipan confections shaped to resemble fruits, temptingly arrayed in bars and *pasticcerie* (pastry shops).

LOCAL SPECIALTIES

Many ingredients and recipes are unique to particular Sicilian towns and regions. In Catania, for example, you'll be offered *caserecci alla Norma* (a short pasta with a sauce of tomato, eggplant, ricotta, and basil), named after an opera by Bellini (a Catania native). The *mandorla* (bitter almond), the pride of Agrigento, plays into everything from risotto *alle mandorle* (with almonds, butter, Grana cheese, and parsley) to incomparable almond granita—an absolute must in summer. Pistachios produced around Bronte, on the lower slopes of Etna, go into pasta sauces as well as ice cream and granita, while capers from the Aeolian Islands add zest to salads and fish sauces. Anyone with a sweet tooth will find nirvana in the *cannoli* and *cassata,* fresh ricotta-based delights.

WINES

Sicilian wines are up-and-coming; they're also among Italy's best bargains. The earthy nero d'avola grape bolsters many of Sicily's traditionally sunny, expansive reds, but now it's often softened with cabernet or merlot. Sicily produces crisp white varieties, too, such as catarratto bianco, inzolia, and grillo that marry delightfully with the island's seafood. When it comes to sweet accompaniments, the small island of Pantelleria produces the smooth dessert wines Zibibbo and Passito.

15

Updated
by Fergal
Kavanagh

Sicily has beckoned seafaring wanderers since the trials of Odysseus were first sung in Homer's *Odyssey*—perhaps the world's first travel guide. Strategically poised between Europe and Africa, this mystical land of three corners and a fiery volcano once hosted two of the most enlightened capitals of the West—one Greek, in Siracusa, and one Arab-Norman, in Palermo.

The island has been a melting pot of every great civilization on the Mediterranean: Greek and Roman; then Arab and Norman; and finally French, Spanish, and Italian. Today the ancient ports of call peacefully fuse the remains of sackings past: graceful Byzantine mosaics stand adjacent to Greek temples, Roman amphitheaters, Romanesque cathedrals, and Baroque flights of fancy.

The invaders through the ages weren't just attracted by the strategic location, however; they recognized a paradise in Sicily's deep blue skies and temperate climate, its lush vegetation, and rich marine life—all of which prevail to this day. Factor in Sicily's unique cuisine—another harmony of elements, mingling Arab and Greek spices, Spanish and French techniques, and some of the world's finest seafood, all accompanied by big, fruity wines—and you can understand why visitors continue to be drawn here, and often find it hard to leave.

In modern times the traditional graciousness and nobility of the Sicilian people have survived side by side with the destructive influences of the Mafia under Sicily's semiautonomous government. Alongside some of the most exquisite architecture in the world lie the shabby, half-built results of some of the worst speculation imaginable. In recent years coastal Sicily, like much of the Mediterranean Coast, has experienced a surge in condominium development and tourism. The island has emerged as something of an international travel hot spot, drawing increasing numbers of visitors. Astronomical prices in northern Italy have contributed to the boom in Sicily, where tourism doesn't seem to be leveling off as it has elsewhere in the country. Brits and

Germans flock in ever-growing numbers to Agrigento and Siracusa, and in high season Japanese tour groups seem to outnumber the locals in Taormina. And yet, in Sicily's windswept heartland (a region that tourists have barely begun to explore) vineyards, olive groves, and lovingly kept dirt roads leading to family farmhouses still tie Sicilians to the land and to tradition, forming a happy connectedness that can't be defined by economic measures.

SICILY PLANNER

MAKING THE MOST OF YOUR TIME

You should plan a visit to Sicily around Palermo, Taormina, Siracusa, and Agrigento, four don't-miss destinations. The best way to see them all is to travel in a circle. Start your circuit in the northeast in Taormina, worth at least a night or two. If you have time, stay also in Catania, a lively, fascinating city that's often overlooked. From there, connect to the Catania–Ragusa toll-free *autostrada* (four-lane highway) and head toward the spectacular ancient Greek port of Siracusa, which merits at least two nights.

Next, backtrack north on the same highway, and take the A19 toward Palermo. Piazza Armerina's impressive mosaics and Enna, a sleepy mountaintop city, are worthwhile stops in the interior. Take the SS640 to the Greek temples of Agrigento. Stay here for a night before driving west along the coastal SS115, checking out Selinunte's ruins before reaching magical Erice, a good base for one night. You're now near some of Sicily's best beaches at San Vito Lo Capo. Take the A19 to Palermo, the chaotic and wonderful capital city, to wrap up your Sicilian experience. Give yourself at least two days here—or, ideally, four or five.

GETTING HERE AND AROUND
BUS TRAVEL

Air-conditioned coaches connect major and minor cities and are often faster and more convenient than local trains—still single-track on many stretches—but also slightly more expensive. Various companies serve the different routes. SAIS runs frequently between Palermo and Catania, Messina, and Siracusa, in each case arriving at and departing from near the train stations.

Contacts Cuffaro. A service between Palermo and Agrigento. ☎ *091/6161510* ⊕ *www.cuffaro.info.* **Interbus/Etna Trasporti.** This company operates between Catania, Caltagirone, Piazza Armerina, Taormina, Messina, and Siracusa. ☎ *095/532716* ⊕ *www.interbus.it.* **SAIS.** On the south and east coasts and in the interior, SAIS connects the main centers, including Catania, Agrigento, Enna, Taormina, and Siracusa. ☎ *800/211020 toll-free* ⊕ *www.saisautolinee.it.*

CAR TRAVEL

This is the ideal way to explore Sicily. Modern highways circle and bisect the island, making all main cities easily reachable. A20 connects Messina and Palermo; Messina and Catania are linked by A18; running through the interior, from Catania to west of Cefalù, is A19; threading west from Palermo, A29 runs to Trapani and the airport, with a leg stretching down to Mazara del Vallo. The south side of the island is less well served, though stretches of the SS115 west of Agrigento are relatively fast and traffic-free.

You'll likely hear stories about the dangers of driving in Sicily. In the big cities—especially Palermo, Catania, and Messina—streets are a honking mess, with lane markings and stop signs taken as mere suggestions; you can avoid the chaos by driving through at off-peak times or on weekends. However, once outside the urban areas and resort towns, the highways and regional state roads are a driving enthusiast's dream—they're winding, sparsely populated, well maintained, and around most bends there's a striking new view. Obviously, don't leave valuables your car, and make sure baggage is stowed out of sight—in some cities it may be wise to keep the doors locked while in traffic. If leaving the car overnight, splurge on a garage.

TRAIN TRAVEL

There are direct express trains from Rome to Palermo, Catania, and Siracusa. The Rome–Palermo and Rome–Siracusa trips take at least 10 hours. After Naples, the run is mostly along the coast, so try to book a window seat on the right if you're not on an overnight train. At Villa San Giovanni, in Calabria, the train is separated and loaded onto a ferryboat to cross the strait to Messina—kids will love it!

Within Sicily, main lines connect Messina, Taormina, Siracusa, and Palermo. Secondary lines are generally very slow and unreliable. The Messina–Palermo run, along the northern coast, is especially scenic. For schedules, check the website of the Italian state railway.

Contact **FS** ☎ *892021 in Italy* ⊕ *www.trenitalia.com.*

RESTAURANTS

Please note that restaurant prices listed as "average meal" include a meal consisting of first course *(primo)*, second course *(secondo)*, and dessert *(dolce)*.

HOTELS

The high-quality hotels tend to be limited to the major cities and resorts of Palermo, Catania, Taormina, Siracusa, and Agrigento, along with the odd beach resort.

However, there's recently been an explosion in the development of *agriturismo* lodgings (rural bed-and-breakfasts), many of them quite basic but others providing the same facilities found in hotels. These country houses also offer all-inclusive, inexpensive full-board plans that can make for some of Sicily's most memorable meals.

Hotel reviews have been condensed for this book. Please go to Fodors. com for expanded reviews of each property.

THE IONIAN COAST

On the northern stretch of Sicily's eastern coast, Messina commands an unparalleled position across the Ionian Sea from Calabria, the mountainous tip of mainland Italy's boot. Halfway down the coast, Catania has the vivacity of Palermo, if not the artistic wealth; the city makes a good base for exploring lofty Mount Etna, as does Taormina.

MESSINA

8 km (5 miles) by ferry from Villa San Giovanni, 94 km (59 miles) northeast of Catania, 237 km (149 miles) east of Palermo.

Messina's ancient history lists a series of disasters, but the city nevertheless managed to develop a fine university and a thriving cultural environment. At 5:20 am on December 28, 1908, Messina changed from a flourishing metropolis of 120,000 to a heap of rubble, shaken to pieces by an earthquake that turned into a tidal wave: 80,000 people died as a result and the city was almost completely leveled. As you approach by ferry, you won't notice any outward indication of the disaster, except for the modern countenance of a 3,000-year-old city. The somewhat flat look is a precaution of seismic planning: tall buildings aren't permitted.

GETTING HERE AND AROUND

Frequent hydrofoils and ferries carry passengers and trains across the Straits of Messina from Villa San Giovanni, from just below the train station. There are also regular departures for foot passengers from Reggio Calabria.

VISITOR INFORMATION

Messina Tourism Office ✉ *Via dei Mille 270* ☎ *090/2935292* 🌐 *www.regione.sicilia.it/turismo.*

EXPLORING

Duomo. The reconstruction of Messina's Norman and Romanesque Duomo, originally built by the Norman king Roger II and consecrated in 1197, has retained much of the original plan—including a handsome crown of Norman battlements, an enormous apse, and a splendid wood-beam ceiling. The adjoining bell tower contains one of the largest and most complex mechanical clocks in the world: constructed in 1933, it has a host of gilded automatons (a roaring lion among them), that spring into action every day at the stroke of noon. ✉ *Piazza del Duomo* ☎ *090/774895* 🕒 *Daily 9–1 and 4–7, closed during services.*

WHERE TO EAT AND STAY

For expanded hotel reviews, visit Fodors.com.

$ SICILIAN 🍴 **Al Padrino.** The jovial owner of this stripped-down trattoria keeps everything running smoothly. Meat and fish dishes are served with equal verve in the white-wall dining room. Start with antipasti like eggplant stuffed with ricotta; then move on to supremely Sicilian dishes such as pasta with chickpeas or *polpette di alalunga* (albacore croquettes). [$] *Average meal: €22* ✉ *Via Santa Cecilia 56* ☎ *090/2921000* 🌐 *www.alpadrino.it* 🕒 *Closed Sun. and Aug. No dinner Sat.*

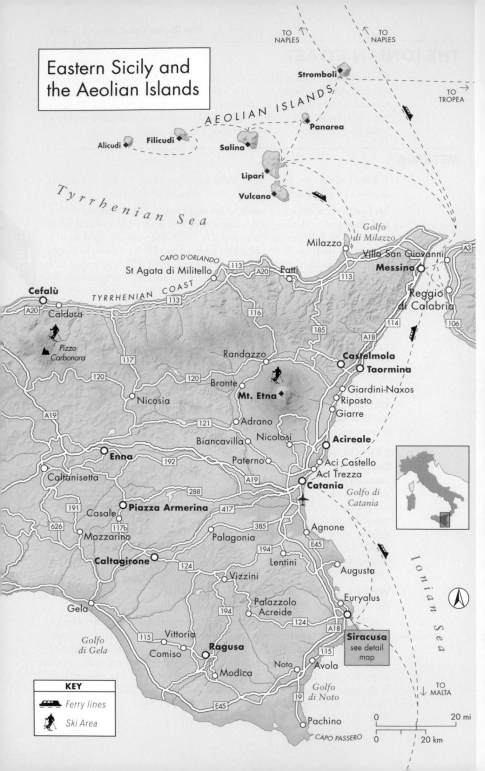

Eastern Sicily and the Aeolian Islands

AEOLIAN ISLANDS

TO NAPLES

TO NAPLES

TO TROPEA

Stromboli

Panarea

Alicudi **Filicudi**

Salina

Lipari

Vulcano

Tyrrhenian Sea

Golfo di Milazzo

Milazzo

Villa San Giovanni

Messina

CAPO D'ORLANDO

St Agata di Militello

Patti

113

A20

A3

Cefalù

Caldura

TYRRHENIAN COAST

113

116

185

113

Reggio di Calabria

106

A20

Pizzo Carbonara

117

120

Randazzo

120

Bronte

Mt. Etna

114

A18

Castelmola

Taormina

Nicosia

121

Adrano

Biancavilla

Nicolosi

Giardini-Naxos

Riposto

Giarre

Acireale

A19

Enna

192

Paternò

Aci Castello

Aci Trezza

Catania

Golfo di Catania

Caltanissetta

A19

191

Casale

288

Piazza Armerina

417

Agnone

626

Mazzarino

117b

Palagonia

385

E45

Caltagirone

124

Vizzini

194

Lentini

Augusta

Euryalus

Gela

194

Palazzolo Acreide

124

A18

Golfo di Gela

115

Vittoria

Comiso

Ragusa

Modica

Noto

Avola

115

Siracusa
see detail map

Ionian Sea

TO MALTA

Golfo di Noto

19

E45

Pachino

CAPO PASSERO

0   20 mi

0   20 km

$ HOTEL **NH Liberty** (*Grand Hotel Liberty*). In the heart of the city, across from the train station, this hotel is a haven from the hustle and bustle of the surrounding streets. **Pros:** close to bus and train stations; plush public rooms. **Cons:** carpets a bit threadbare; poor views from most rooms. [$] *Rooms from: €110* ✉ *Via I Settembre 15* ☎ *090/6409436* 🌐 *www.nh-hotels.com* *48 rooms, 3 junior suites* ⏲ *Closed 2 wks in Dec. and 6 wks in summer.* 🍴 *Breakfast.*

TAORMINA

43 km (27 miles) southwest of Messina.

Fodor's Choice ★ The medieval cliff-hanging town of Taormina is overrun with tourists, yet its natural beauty is still hard to dispute. The view of the sea and Mt. Etna from its jagged cactus-covered cliffs is as close to perfection as a panorama can get—especially on clear days, when the snowcapped volcano's white puffs of smoke rise against the blue sky. Writers have extolled Taormina's beauty almost since it was founded in the 6th century BC by Greeks from nearby Naxos; Goethe and D. H. Lawrence were among its well-known enthusiasts. The town's boutique-lined main streets get old pretty quickly, but the many hiking paths that wind through the beautiful hills surrounding Taormina promise a timeless alternative. A trip up to stunning Castelmola (whether on foot or by car) should also be on your itinerary.

15

GETTING HERE AND AROUND

Buses from Messina or Catania arrive near the center of Taormina, while trains from these towns pull in at the station at the bottom of the hill. Local buses bring you the rest of the way. A cable car takes passengers up the hill from a parking lot about 2 km (1 mile) north of the train station.

VISITOR INFORMATION

Taormina Tourism Office ✉ *Palazzo Corvaja, Largo Santa Caterina* ☎ *0942/23243* 🌐 *gate2taormina.ns0.it.*

EXPLORING

TOP ATTRACTIONS

Fodor's Choice ★ **Villa Comunale.** Stroll down Via Bagnoli Croce from the main Corso Umberto to the Villa Comunale. Also known as the Parco Duca di Cesarò, the lovely public gardens were designed by Florence Trevelyan Cacciola, a Scottish lady "invited" to leave England following a romantic liaison with the future Edward VII (1841–1910). Arriving in Taormina in 1889, she married a local professor and devoted herself to the gardens, filling them with native Mediterranean and exotic plants, ornamental pavilions (known as the beehives), and fountains. Stop by the panoramic bar, which has stunning views. ✉ *Via Bagnoli Croce* ⏲ *Daily 9 am–sunset.*

WORTH NOTING

Castello Saraceno. An unrelenting 20-minute walk up the Via Crucis footpath takes you to the church of the Madonna della Rocca, hollowed out of the limestone rock. Above it towers the medieval Castello Saraceno. Though the gate to the castle has been locked for decades, it's worth the climb just for the panoramic views. ✉ *Monte Tauro.*

Funivia. Taormina Mare is accessible by a *funivia*, or suspended cable car, that glides past incredible views on its way down. It departs every 15 minutes. In June, July, and August, the normal hours are extended until midnight or later. ⊠ *Down hill from town center* ☎ *0942/23906* 🖪 *€3 one way* ☉ *Daily 7:45 am–8 pm.*

Palazzo Corvaja. Many of Taormina's 14th- and 15th-century palaces have been carefully preserved. Especially beautiful is the Palazzo Corvaja, with characteristic black-lava and white-limestone inlays. Today it houses the tourist office and the **Museo di Arte e Tradizioni Popolari,** which has a collection of puppets and folk art, carts, and crèches. ⊠ *Largo Santa Caterina* ☎ *0942/23243* 🖪 *Museum €2.60* ☉ *Museum Tues.–Sun. 9–1 and 4–8.*

Taormina Mare. Below the main city of Taormina is Taormina Mare, where summertime beachgoers jostle for space on a pebble beach against the scenic backdrop of the aptly-named island of Isolabella.

Teatro Greco. The Greeks put a premium on finding impressive locations to stage their dramas, such as Taormina's hillside Teatro Greco. Beyond the columns you can see the town's rooftops spilling down the hillside, the arc of the coastline, and Mount Etna in the distance. The theater was built during the 3rd century BC and rebuilt by the Romans during the 2nd century AD. Its acoustics are exceptional: even today a stage whisper can be heard in the last rows. In summer Taormina hosts an arts festival of music and dance events and a film festival; many performances are held in the Teatro Greco. ⊠ *Via Teatro Greco* ☎ *0942/620198* 🖪 *€8* ☉ *Daily 9–1 hr before sunset.*

QUICK BITES

Pasticceria Etna. No marzipan devotee should leave Taormina without trying one of the almond sweets—maybe in the guise of the ubiquitous *fico d'India* (prickly pear) or in more unusual shapes—at Pasticceria Etna. A block of almond paste makes a good souvenir—you can bring it home to make an almond latte or granita. ⊠ *Corso Umberto 112* ☎ *0942/24735.*

WHERE TO EAT

$

SICILIAN

✕ **Bella Blu.** If you fancy a meal with a view but don't want to spend a lot, it would be hard to do much better than to come here for the decent €20 three-course prix-fixe meal. Seafood is the specialty; try the spaghetti with fresh clams and mussels. You can also opt for the €10 pizza and drink menu. Through giant picture windows you can watch the gondola fly up and down from the beach, with the coastline in the distance. There is free Wi-Fi, a special children's area, and a pianist performs on Saturday night in winter. 🖫 *Average meal: €20* ⊠ *Via Pirandello 28* ☎ *0942/24239* ⊕ *www.bellablu.it* ☉ *Closed weekdays Oct.–Mar.*

$$$$

SICILIAN

✕ **La Giara.** This restaurant, named after a giant vase unearthed under the bar, is famous for being one of Taormina's oldest restaurants. The food's not bad, either. The kitchen blends upscale modern techniques with the simple flavors of traditional specialties. It specializes in everything fish: one spectacular dish is the fish *cartoccio* (wrapped in paper and baked). You can also extend your evening at the popular, if touristy, piano bar, or at the dance club that operates here on Saturday night (and every night in August). There's a terrace with stunning views, too. $ *Average meal: €70* ⊠ *Vico La Floresta 1* ☎ *0942/23360* ⊕ *www.lagiara-taormina.com* ⊗ *Closed mid-Nov.– mid-Mar. No lunch.*

$$ ✕ **La Piazzetta.** Sheltered from the city's hustle and bustle, this elegant
SEAFOOD little eatery exudes a mood of relaxed sophistication. Classic dishes such as risotto *alla marinara* (with seafood) are competently prepared, the grilled fish is extremely fresh, and the service is informal and friendly. The modest room has simple white walls—you're not paying for a view. $ *Average meal: €32* ⊠ *Vico Francesco Paladini, off Corso Umberto* ☎ *0942/626317* ⊗ *Closed Nov., and 2 wks in Feb. No lunch Mon.– Thurs., June –Sept.*

$$ ✕ **L'Arco dei Cappuccini.** Just off Via Costantino Patricio lies this diminu-
SEAFOOD tive restaurant. Outdoor seating and an upstairs kitchen help make room for a few extra tables—a necessity, as locals are well aware that neither the price nor the quality is equaled elsewhere in town. Indulge in the spaghetti with sea urchin, fresh pasta with swordfish and fennel, or hand-made fettuccini with red mullet and fava beans. Reservations are usually essential for more than two people. $ *Average meal: €45* ⊠ *Via Cappuccini 5A, off Via Costantino Patricio* ☎ *0942/24893* ⊗ *Closed Wed., Feb., and 1 wk in Nov.*

$ ✕ **Vecchia Taormina.** Warm, inviting, and unassuming, Taormina's best
PIZZA pizzeria produces deliciously seared crusts topped with fresh, well-balanced ingredients. Try the pizza *alla Norma,* featuring the classic Sicilian combination of eggplant and ricotta—here, in the province of Messina, it's made with ricotta *al forno* (cooked ricotta), while in the province of Catania, it's made with ricotta *salata* (uncooked, salted ricotta). The restaurant also offers fresh fish in summer, and there's a good list of Sicilian wines. Choose between small tables on two levels or on a terrace. $ *Average meal: €25* ⊠ *Vico Ebrei 3* ☎ *0942/625589* ⊗ *Closed Wed. and Nov.–Feb.*

WHERE TO STAY

For expanded hotel reviews, visit Fodors.com.

$$$$ ⊞ **Grand Hotel Timeo.** On a princely perch overlooking the town, the
HOTEL Greek theater, and the bay, this truly grand hotel wears a graceful patina
FodorsChoice that suggests la dolce vita. **Pros:** feeling of indulgence; central location;
★ quiet setting. **Cons:** very expensive; some rooms are small; staff can be scarce. $ *Rooms from: €580* ⊠ *Via Teatro Greco 59* ☎ *0942/23801* ⊕ *www.grandhoteltimeo.com* ⤴ *70 rooms, 13 suites* ⦿ *Some meals.*

$$$ ⊞ **Hotel Villa Paradiso.** On the edge of the old quarter, overlooking the
HOTEL lovely public gardens and facing the sea, this hotel is not as well known as some of its neighbors, despite its 100 year history. **Pros:** friendly service; good value; great rooftop views, wonderful beach. **Cons:** only three free parking spaces; not all rooms have views. $ *Rooms from: €200* ⊠ *Via Roma 2* ☎ *0942/23921* ⊕ *www.hotelvillaparadisotaormina.com* ⤴ *20 rooms, 17 junior suites* ⦿ *Breakfast.*

$$$ ⊞ **San Domenico Palace.** Sweeping views of the castle, the sea, and Mount
HOTEL Etna from this converted 15th-century Dominican monastery linger in your mind, along with equally memorable levels of luxury and wonderful food. **Pros:** stellar restaurant; attentive service; quiet and restful.

15

Cons: expensive; dull corridors; some small rooms. *Rooms from: €300 Piazza San Domenico 5 0942/613111 www.amthotels.it/sandomenico 87 rooms, 15 suites Breakfast.*

$$$ HOTEL **Villa Ducale.** The former summer residence of a local aristocrat has been converted into a luxurious hotel where each room has a balcony with a view. **Pros:** away from the hubbub; camera-ready views. **Cons:** A 10- to 15-minute walk to the center of Taormina; the restaurant menu can be limited. *Rooms from: €250 Via Leonardo da Vinci 60 0942/28153 www.villaducale.com 11 rooms, 6 suites Closed Dec.–Feb. 20 Breakfast.*

$$ HOTEL **Villa Fiorita.** Near the historic center and the cable-car station, this converted private house has excellent north-coast views from nearly every room. **Pros:** good rates; pretty rooms. **Cons:** service can be slack; you have to climb 65 steps to get to the elevator. *Rooms from: €125 Via Pirandello 39 0942/24122 0942/625967 www.villafioritahotel.com 24 rooms, 2 suites Breakfast.*

NIGHTLIFE AND THE ARTS

Taoarte. The Teatro Greco and the Palazzo dei Congressi, near the entrance to the theater, are the main venues for the summer festival dubbed Taoarte, held each year between June and August. Performances encompass classical music, ballet, and theater. *0942/21142 www.taormina-arte.com.*

Taormina Film Festival. This famous festival takes place in June. *06/486808 www.taorminafilmfest.it.*

Teatro dei Due Mari. This company stages Greek tragedy at the Teatro Greco, usually in May. *Via Teatro Greco 0941/240912 www.teatrodeiduemari.net.*

EN ROUTE The 50-km (30-mile) stretch of road between Taormina and Messina is flanked by lush vegetation and seascapes. Inlets are punctuated by gigantic, oddly shaped rocks.

CASTELMOLA

5 km (3 miles) west of Taormina.

Although many believe that Taormina has the most spectacular views, tiny Castelmola, floating 1,800 feet above sea level, takes the word "scenic" to a whole new level—literally. Along the cobblestone streets within the ancient walls the 360-degree panoramas of mountain, sea, and sky are so ubiquitous that you almost get used to them (but not quite). Collect yourself with a sip of the sweet almond wine (best served cold) made in the local bars, or with lunch at one of the humble pizzerias or *panino* (sandwich) shops.

A 10-minute drive on a winding but well-paved road leads from Taormina to Castelmola; you must park in one of the public lots below the village and walk up to the center. On a nice day hikers are in for a treat if they make the trip on foot rather than drive. It's a serious uphill climb, but the 1½-km (¾-mile) path offers breathtaking views, which compensate for the somewhat poor maintenance of the path itself. You'll begin at Porta Catania in Taormina, with a walk along Via Apollo Arcageta past the Chiesa di San Francesco di Paola on the left. The Strada Comunale della Chiusa then leads past Piazza Andromaco, revealing good views of the jagged promontory of Cocolanazzo di Mola to the north. Allow around an hour for the ascent, a half hour for the descent. There's another, slightly longer—2-km (1-mile)—path that heads up from Porta Messina past the Roman aqueduct, Convento dei Cappuccini, and the northeastern side of Monte Tauro. You could take one up and the other down. In any case, avoid the midday sun, wear comfortable shoes, and carry plenty of water with you.

GETTING HERE AND AROUND

Regular buses bound for Castelmola leave from two locations in Taormina: the bus station on Via Pirandello and Piazza San Pancrazio.

EXPLORING

Fodor'sChoice
★ **Castello Normanno.** The best place to savor Castelmola's views is from the castle ruins, reached by a set of steep staircases rising out of the town center. In all of Sicily there may be no spot more scenic than atop Castello Normanno: you can gaze upon two coastlines, smoking Mount Etna, and the town spilling down the mountainside. Come during daylight hours to take full advantage of the vista.

WHERE TO EAT AND STAY

For expanded hotel reviews, visit Fodors.com.

$ ✕ **Il Vicolo.** Along a side street, this is one of the simpler dining choices in
SICILIAN town, and also one of the better ones. It might not have the views you'll find elsewhere, but a pleasant rustic ambience plus a great selection of handmade pasta and, in the evening, *forno a legna* (wood-fired-oven) pizzas make up for that shortcoming. (In winter, pizzas are served weekends only.) Friendly staff serves the food in a pleasing little room. Ⓢ *Average meal: €27* ✉ *Via Pio IX 26* ☎ *0942/28481, 331/9094077* ⊕ *www.trattoriailvicolo. com* ⊘ *Closed Tues. Sept.–June, and 2 wks late Jan.–early Feb.*

$$ 🏨 **Villa Sonia.** All the rooms at Castelmola's best hotel have private terraces
HOTEL with gorgeous grab-the-camera views of Etna. **Pros:** far from the madding crowds; onsite sauna and pool. **Cons:** some accommodations are far from the main building; not much to do in the evening. Ⓢ *Rooms from: €140* ✉ *Via Porta Mola 9* ☎ *0942/28082* ⊕ *www.hotelvillasonia.com* ⇆ *42 rooms, 2 suites* ⊘ *Closed Nov.–Dec. 20 and Jan. 8–Mar. 15* ⦿| *Breakfast.*

NIGHTLIFE

Bar San Giorgio. This place has lorded over Castelmola's town square since 1907. The interior of the bar is filled with knickknacks that tell a fascinating history of the tiny town. Try the *vino de mandorle* (almond wine) from a recipe produced by the original owner more than a century ago. ✉ *Piazza Sant'Antonino* ☎ *0942/28228.*

Bar Turrisi. Truly one of the most unusual places to have a drink in all of Italy, this famous bar has cozy nooks and crannies on three levels—all decked out with phallic images of every size, shape, and color imaginable, from bathroom wall murals inspired by the brothels of ancient Greece to giant wooden carvings honoring Dionysus. The roof terrace has extraordinary views of Taormina and the coast, while a limited selection of hearty pasta dishes are served inside. ✉ *Piazza del Duomo 19* ☎ *0942/28181* ⊕ *www.turrisibar.it.*

15

MOUNT ETNA

64 km (40 miles) southwest of Taormina, 30 km (19 miles) north of Catania.

GETTING HERE AND AROUND

Reaching the lower slopes of Mount Etna is easy, either by driving yourself or taking a bus from Catania. Getting to the more interesting higher levels requires taking one of the stout four-wheel-drive minibuses that leave from Piano Provenzana on the north side and Rifugio Sapienza on the south side. A cable car from Rifugio Sapienza takes you part of the way.

VISITOR INFORMATION

Nicolosi Tourism Office ⊠ *Piazza Vittorio Emanuele 32/33, Nicolosi* ☎ *095/914488.*

Funivia dell'Etna ⊠ *Rifugio Sapienza* ☎ *095/914141, 095/914142* ⊕ *www.funiviaetna.com* 🎟 *€28.75* ⊗ *Daily 9–4, longer in the summer.*

EXPLORING

Circumetnea. Instead of climbing up Mount Etna, you can circle it on the Circumetnea, which runs near the volcano's base. The private railroad almost circles the volcano, running 114 km (71 miles) between Catania and Riposto—the towns are just 30 km (19 miles) apart by the coast road. The line is small, slow, and only single-track, but has some dramatic vistas of the volcano and goes through lava fields. The one-way trip takes about three and a half hours, with departures every 90 mins or so. After you've made the trip, you can get back to where you started from on the much quicker, but less scenic, conventional state rail service between Riposto and Catania. ⊠ *Via Caronda 352, Catania* ☎ *095/541250* ⊕ *www.circumetnea.it* 🎟 *€7.25 one way* ⊗ *Mon.–Sat. 6 am–9 pm.*

Club Alpino Italiano. A great resource for Mount Etna climbing and hiking guides. If you have some experience and don't like a lot of hand-holding, these are the guides for you. ⊠ *Via Messina 593/a, Catania* ☎ *095/7153515* ✉ *giorgiopace@katamail.com* ⊕ *www.caicatania.it.*

Gruppo Guide Etna Nord. If you're a novice climber, call this company to arrange for a guide. Their service is a little more personalized—and expensive—than others. Reserve ahead. ⊠ *Piazza Attilio Castrogiovanni 19, Linguaglossa* ☎ *095/7774502, 348/0125167* ⊕ *www. guidetnanord.com.*

Fodor's Choice ★ **Mount Etna.** One of the world's major active volcanoes, Etna is the largest and highest in Europe—the cone of the crater rises to 10,902 feet above sea level. Plato sailed in just to catch a glimpse in 387 BC; in the 9th century AD the oldest gelato of all was shaved off its snowy slopes; and in the 21st century the volcano still claims annual headlines. Etna has erupted a dozen times in the past 30 or so years, most spectacularly in 1971, 1983, 2001, 2002, and 2005. There were also a pair of medium-size eruptions in 2008, one in 2009, and fairly constant eruptive activity during the summer of 2011. Travel in the proximity of the crater depends on Mount Etna's temperament, but you can walk up and down the enormous lava dunes and wander over its moonlike surface of dead craters. The rings of vegetation change markedly as you rise, with vineyards and pine trees gradually giving way to growths of broom and lichen.

OFF THE BEATEN PATH

The villages that surround Mt. Etna offer much more than pretty views of the smoldering giant. They're charming and full of character in their own right, and make good bases for visiting nearby cities such as Catania, Acireale, and Taormina. **Zafferana Etnea** is famous for its orange-blossom honey; **Nicolosi,** at nearly 3,000 feet, is known as La Porta dell'Etna (The Door to Etna); **Trecastagni** (The Three Chestnut Trees) has one of Sicily's most beautiful Renaissance churches; **Randazzo,** the largest of the surrounding towns, is the site of a popular Sunday-morning wood, textile, and metalwork market; and **Bronte** is Italy's center of pistachio cultivation. The bars there offer various pistachio delicacies such as nougat, *colomba* (Easter sponge cake), panettone, and ice cream.

15

WHERE TO STAY

For expanded hotel reviews, visit Fodors.com.

$$ HOTEL **Hotel Villa Paradiso dell'Etna.** A painstaking renovation has returned this 1920s villa to its former elegance, complete with mementoes of its illustrious past, and there are breathtaking views of Mount Etna. **Pros:** beautiful furnishings; delightful gardens; excellent food; low-season bargains. **Cons:** difficult to find; not much to do in the area. [$] *Rooms from: €160* ✉ *Via per Viagrande 37, 10 km (6 miles) northeast of Catania; exit A18 ME-CT toward San Gregorio, or A19 PA-CT toward Paesi Etnei, San Giovanni La Punta* ☎ *095/7512409* 🌐 *www.paradisoetna.it* 🛏 *29 rooms, 4 suites* 🍴 *Breakfast.*

ACIREALE

40 km (25 miles) south of Taormina, 16 km (10 miles) north of Catania.

Acireale sits amid a clutter of rocky pinnacles and lush lemon groves. The craggy coast is known as the Riviera dei Ciclopi, after the legend narrated in the *Odyssey* in which the blinded Cyclops Polyphemus hurled boulders at the retreating Ulysses, thus creating spires of rock, or *faraglioni* (pillars of rock rising dramatically out of the sea). Tourism has barely taken off here, so it's a good destination if you feel the need to put some distance between yourself and the busloads of tourists in Taormina. And though the beaches are rocky, there's good swimming here, too.

The Carnival celebrations, held the two weeks before Lent, are considered the best in Sicily. The streets are jammed with thousands of revelers. Acireale is an easy day trip from Catania.

GETTING HERE AND AROUND

Buses arrive frequently from Taormina and Catania. Acireale is on the main coastal train route, though the station is a long walk south of the center. Local buses pass every 20 minutes or so.

VISITOR INFORMATION

Acireale Tourism Office ✉ *Via Oreste Scionti 15* ☎ *095/891999* 🌐 *www.acirealeturismo.it.*

EXPLORING

Belvedere di Santa Caterina. Lord Byron (1788–1824) visited the Belvedere di Santa Caterina to look out over the Ionian Sea during his Italian wanderings. The viewing point is south of the old town, near the Terme di Acireale, off SS114.

Duomo. With its cupola and twin turrets, Acireale's Duomo is an extravagant Baroque construction dating to the 17th century. In the chapel to the right of the altar, look for the 17th-century silver statue of Santa Venera (patron saint of Acireale) made by Mario D'Angelo, and the early-18th-century frescoes by Antonio Filocamo. ✉ *Piazza del Duomo* ☎ *095/601797* 🕒 *Daily 9–noon and 4–7:30.*

QUICK BITES

El Dorado. Delicious ice creams—and the *granita di mandorla* (almond granita), available in summer—invite a firsthand acquaintance. It's closed on Tuesday between September and June. ✉ ***Corso Umberto 5*** ☎ ***095/601464.***

Villa Belvedere. Begin your visit to Acireale with a stroll down to the public gardens, Villa Belvedere, at the end of the main Corso Umberto. It promises superb coastal views. Restoration work is underway, and the gardens may be temporarily closed.

WHERE TO EAT

$$ SEAFOOD 🍴 **La Grotta.** A dining room within a cave, with part of the cave wall exposed, is a feature of this rustic trattoria above the harbor of Santa Maria La Scala. Try the *insalata di mare* (a selection of delicately boiled fish served with lemon and olive oil), pasta with clams or cuttlefish ink, or fish grilled over charcoal. Chef Rosario Strano's menu is small, but there isn't a dud among the selections. [$] *Average meal: €35* ✉ *Via Scalo Grande 46* ☎ *095/7648153* ✍ *Reservations essential* 🕒 *Closed Tues. and mid-Oct.–mid-Nov.*

NIGHTLIFE AND THE ARTS

FAMILY **Teatro dell'Opera dei Pupi.** Although it has died out in most other parts of the island, the puppet-theater tradition carries on in Acireale. The Teatro dell'Opera dei Pupi has a puppet exhibit and puppet shows every Sunday (at 5:30 in the Summer, 6:30 in the Winter). ✉ *Via Alessi 11* ☎ *095/606272* 🌐 *www.teatropupimacri.it.*

SHOPPING

Acireale is renowned in Sicily for its marzipan, made into fruit shapes and delicious cookies available at many pasticcerie around town.

Pasticceria Castorina. A unique creation here is the "nucatole," a large cookie made with heaping quantities of chocolate, Nutella, nuts, and other wholesome ingredients. ✉ *Corso Savoia 109* ☎ *095/601547.*

EN ROUTE

Aci Castello and Aci Trezza. These two gems on the coastline between Acireale and Catania—the Riviera dei Ciclopi (Cyclops Riviera)—fill with city dwellers in the summer months, but even in colder weather their beauty is hard to fault. Heading south from Acireale on the *litoranea* (coastal) road, you'll first reach Aci Trezza, said to be the land of the one-eyed Cyclops in Homer's *Odyssey.* Less developed than Aci Trezza, Aci Castello has its own fish houses plus the imposing Castello

Sweet Sicily

Sicily is famous for its desserts, none more than the wonderful cannoli (*cannolo* is the singular), whose delicate pastry shell and just-sweet-enough ricotta filling barely resemble their foreign impostors. They come in all sizes, from pinkie-size bites to holiday cannoli the size of a coffee table. Even your everyday bar will display a window piled high with dozens of varieties of ricotta-based desserts, including delicious fried balls of dough. The traditional cake of Sicily is the *cassata siciliana,* a rich chilled sponge cake with sheep's-milk ricotta and candied fruit. Often brightly colored,

it's the most popular dessert at many Sicilian restaurants, and you shouldn't miss it. From behind bakery windows and glass cases beam tiny marzipan sweets fashioned into brightly colored apples, cherries, and even hamburgers and prosciutto.

If it's summer, do as the locals do and dip your morning brioche—the best in Italy—into a cup of brilliantly refreshing coffee- or almond-flavored granita. The world's first ice cream is said to have been made by the Romans from the snow on the slopes of Mount Etna. Top-quality gelato is also prevalent throughout the island.

15

Normanno (Norman Castle), which sits right on the water. The castle was built in the 11th century with volcanic rock from Mount Etna—the same rock that forms the coastal cliffs.

Trattoria da Federico. It should be easy to satisfy your literal (rather than literary) hunger at Aci Trezza's Trattoria da Federico, which lays out a sprawling antipasto buffet featuring delectable marinated anchovies and eggplant parmigiana. ⊠ *Via Provinciale 115, Aci Trezza* ☎ *095/276364* ⊘ *Closed Mon.*

CATANIA

16 km (10 miles) south of Acireale, 94 km (59 miles) south of Messina, 60 km (37 miles) north of Siracusa.

The chief wonder of Catania, Sicily's second city, is that it's there at all. Its successive populations were deported by one Greek tyrant, sold into slavery by another, and driven out by the Carthaginians. Every time the city got back on its feet it was struck by a new calamity: plague decimated the population in the Middle Ages, a mile-wide stream of lava from Mt. Etna swallowed part of it in 1669, and 25 years later a disastrous earthquake forced the Catanesi to begin again.

Today Catania is completing yet another resurrection—this time from crime, filth, and urban decay. Although the city remains loud and full of traffic, signs of gentrification are everywhere. The elimination of vehicles from the Piazza del Duomo and the main artery of Via Etnea, and the scrubbing of many of the historic buildings have added to its newfound charm. Home to what is arguably Sicily's best university, Catania is full of exuberant youth, and it shows in the chic *osterie* (taverns) that serve wine, the designer bistros, and the trendy ethnic boutiques that have popped up all over town. Even more impressive is the vibrant cultural life.

GETTING HERE AND AROUND

Catania is well connected by bus and train with Messina, Taormina, Siracusa, Enna, and Palermo. The airport of Fontanarossa serves as a transportation hub for the eastern side of the island. From here you can get buses to most major destinations without going into the city center.

VISITOR INFORMATION

Catania Tourism Office ⊠ *Via Vittorio Emanuele 172* ☎ *800/841042, 095/7425573* ⊕ *www.comune.catania.it/turismo.*

EXPLORING

Agorà Youth Hostel. An underground river, the Amenano, flows through much of Catania. You can glimpse it at the Fontana dell'Amenano, but the best place to experience the river is at the bar-restaurant of the Agorà Youth Hostel. Here you can sit at an underground table as swirls of water rush by. If you're not there when the bar is open, someone at the reception desk can let you in. ⊠ *Piazza Currò 6* ☎ *095/7233010* ⊕ *www.agorahostel.com.*

Cattedrale di Sant'Agata (Duomo). The Giovanni Vaccarini-designed facade of the cathedral dominates the Piazza del Duomo. Inside the church, composer Vincenzo Bellini is buried. Also of note are the three apses of lava that survive from the original Norman structure and a fresco from 1675 in the sacristy that portrays Catania's submission to Etna's attack. A guided tour of the museum is available with a reservation. Across from the Cattedrale are underground ruins of Greco-Roman baths. ⊠ *Piazza del Duomo, bottom end of Via Etnea* ☎ *095/281635* ⊕ *www. museodiocesicatania.it* ✍ *Museum €7, baths €5, combined ticket €10* ⊙ *Weekdays 9–2, Sat. 9–1, Sun. by appointment only.*

Centro Storico. Many of the town's buildings were constructed three centuries ago using lava; the black buildings combine with Baroque architecture to give the city a singular appearance. Nowhere is this clearer than in the centro storico. Don't miss the stunning **Piazza Università**, a nerve center made interesting by the facade of a majestic old university building, and the nearby Castello Ursino.

Festa di Sant'Agata. Each February 3–5, the Festa di Sant'Agata honors Catania's patron saint with one of Italy's biggest religious festivals. A staggering number of people crowd the streets and piazzas for several processions, music, dancing, art, theater, and all-out street partying.

Museo Belliniano. Catania's greatest native son was the composer Vincenzo Bellini (1801–35), whose operas have thrilled audiences since their premieres in Naples and Milan. His home, now the Museo Belliniano, preserves memorabilia of the man and his work. ⊠ *Piazza San Francesco 3* ☎ *095/7150535* ✍ *€5* ⊙ *Daily 9–1.*

Piazza del Duomo. Shining from a 21st-century renovation, this piazza, which is closed to traffic, has at its heart an elephant carved out of lava, balancing an Egyptian obelisk. This is the city's informal mascot, called "u Liotru," the Sicilian pronunciation of Heliodorus, an 8th-century sorcerer tied by legend to the origins of the statue. From here you can look way down the long, straight Via Garibaldi to see a black-and-white-striped fortress and entrance to the city, the Porta Garibaldi.

Via Etnea. Lined with cafés and stores selling jewelry, clothing, and shoes, this street is host to one of Sicily's most enthusiastic passeggiate, in which Catanese of all ages take part. It is closed to automobile traffic until 10 pm during the week and all day on weekends.

QUICK BITES

Pasticceria Savia. The lively Pasticceria Savia makes superlative arancini with *ragù* (a slow-cooked, tomato-based meat sauce). Or you could choose cannoli or other snacks to munch on while you rest. It's closed Monday.
✉ Via Etnea 302–304 and Via Umberto 2, near Villa Bellini ☎ 095/322335 🌐 www.savia.it.

WHERE TO EAT

$$ SEAFOOD 🍴 **Ambasciata del Mare.** When a seafood restaurant sits next door to a fish market, it bodes well for the food's freshness. Choose swordfish or *gamberoni* (large shrimp) from a display case in the front of the restaurant; then enjoy it simply grilled with oil and lemon. This basic, bright, and cozy place couldn't be friendlier or more easily accessed—it's right on the corner of Piazza del Duomo by the fountain. Book early. *[$] Average meal: €45 ✉ Piazza del Duomo 6/7 ☎ 095/341003 🌐 www.ambasciatadelmare.it ✍ Reservations essential.*

$$ SICILIAN Fodor's Choice ★ 🍴 **La Siciliana.** Brothers Salvo and Vito La Rosa serve memorable seafood and meat dishes, exquisite homemade desserts, and a choice of more than 220 wines. The restaurant specializes in the ancient dish *ripiddu nivicatu* (risotto with cuttlefish ink and fresh ricotta cheese), as well as *sarde a beccafico* (stuffed sardines) and calamari *ripieni alla griglia* (stuffed and grilled squid). A meal at this fine eatery more than justifies the short taxi ride 3 km (2 miles) north of the city center. *[$] Average meal: €40 ✉ Viale Marco Polo 52a ☎ 095/376400 🌐 www.lasiciliana.it ⏲ Closed Mon. No dinner Sun.*

$$ SICILIAN 🍴 **Sicilia in Bocca alla Marina.** Behind historic stone walls near the marina, this bright, bustling seafood restaurant is a Catania institution, much favored by locals for its faithful renditions of traditional cusine. The well-thought-out wine list includes more than 200 Sicilian wines. *[$] Average meal: €45 ✉ Via Dusmet 35 ☎ 095/2500208 🌐 www.siciliainbocca.it ⏲ No lunch Mon.*

WHERE TO STAY

For expanded hotel reviews, visit Fodors.com.

$$ HOTEL 🏨 **Excelsior Grand Hotel.** Large and modern, with a restrained atmosphere and impeccably designed rooms, this hotel sits in a quiet part of downtown Catania. **Pros:** efficient staff; modern facilities; clean rooms. **Cons:** chain hotel lacking personality; can get overrun with groups; a longish walk from the main sights. *[$] Rooms from: €200 ✉ Piazza Verga 39 ☎ 095/7476111 🌐 www.hotelexcelsiorcatania.it 🛏 176 rooms 🍽 Breakfast.*

SHOPPING

Catania is justly famous for its candies and bar snacks.

Café del Duomo. Sample the hustle and bustle of Catania at Café del Duomo, which has handmade cookies and cakes and a great local atmosphere. ⊠ *Piazza Duomo 11–13* ☎ *095/7150556.*

I Dolci di Nonna Vincenza. The selection of almond-based delights here may be small, but everything is fresh and phenomenally good. International shipping is available. ⊠ *Palazzo Biscari, Piazza San Placido 7* ☎ *095/7151844* ⊕ *www.dolcinonnavincenza.it* ⊠ *Aeroporto Fontanarossa* ☎ *095/7234522.*

Outdoor Fish and Food Market. Beginning on Via Zappala Gemelli and emanating in every direction from Piazza di Benedetto, this is one of Italy's most memorable markets. It's a feast for the senses, with thousands of just-caught fish (some still wriggling), endless varieties of meats, ricotta, and fresh produce, plus a symphony of vendor shouts to fill the ears. Open Monday–Saturday, the market is at its best in the early morning.

SIRACUSA

Siracusa, known to English speakers as Syracuse, is a wonder to behold. One of the great ancient capitals of Western civilization, the city was founded in 734 BC by Greek colonists from Corinth and soon grew to rival, and even surpass, Athens in splendor and power. It became the largest, wealthiest city-state in the West and a bulwark of Greek civilization. Although Siracusa lived under tyranny, rulers such as Dionysius filled their courts with Greeks of the highest cultural stature—among them the playwrights Aeschylus and Euripides, and the philosopher Plato. The Athenians, who didn't welcome Siracusa's rise, set out to conquer Sicily, but the natives outsmarted them in what was one of the greatest military campaigns in ancient history (413 BC). The city continued to prosper until it was conquered two centuries later by the Romans.

Present-day Siracusa still has some of the finest examples of Baroque art and architecture; dramatic Greek and Roman ruins; and a Duomo that's the stuff of legend—a microcosm of the city's entire history in one building. The modern city also has a wonderful lively Baroque old town worthy of extensive exploration, as well as pleasant piazzas, outdoor cafés and bars, and a wide assortment of excellent seafood. There are essentially two areas to explore in Siracusa: the Parco Archeologico, on the mainland; and the island of Ortygia, the ancient city first inhabited by the Greeks, which juts out into the Ionian Sea and is connected to the mainland by two small bridges. Ortygia is becoming increasingly popular with tourists, and is starting to lose its old-fashioned charm in favor of modern boutiques.

Siracusa's old nucleus of Ortygia, a compact area, is a pleasure to amble around without getting unduly tired. In contrast, mainland Siracusa is a grid of wider avenues. At the northern end of Corso Gelone, above Viale Paolo Orsi, the orderly grid gives way to the ancient quarter of Neapolis, where the sprawling Parco Archeologico is accessible from

Viale Teracati (an extension of Corso Gelone). East of Viale Teracati, about a 10-minute walk from the Parco Archeologico, the district of Tyche holds the archaeological museum and the church and catacombs of San Giovanni, both off Viale Teocrito (drive or take a taxi or city bus from Ortygia). Coming from the train station, it's a 15-minute trudge to Ortygia along Via Francesco Crispi and Corso Umberto. If you're not up for that, take one of the free electric buses leaving every 10 minutes from the bus station around the corner.

GETTING HERE AND AROUND

On the main train line from Messina and Catania, Siracusa is also linked to Catania by frequent buses.

VISITOR INFORMATION

Siracusa Tourism Office ⊠ *Via Maestranza 33, Ortygia* ☎ *0931/1756232 Chamber of commerce, 0931/464255 Regione* ⊕ *www.siracusaturismo.net.*

EXPLORING

15

ARCHAEOLOGICAL ZONE

TOP ATTRACTIONS

Fodor's Choice
★
Parco Archeologico. Siracusa is most famous for its dramatic set of Greek and Roman ruins. Though the various ruins can be visited separately, see them all, along with the Museo Archeologico. If the park is closed, go up Viale G. Rizzo from Viale Teracati to the belvedere overlooking the ruins, which are floodlighted at night.

Before the park's ticket booth is the gigantic **Ara di Ierone** (Altar of Hieron), which was once used by the Greeks for spectacular sacrifices involving hundreds of animals. The first attraction in the park is the **Latomia del Paradiso** (Quarry of Paradise), a lush tropical garden full of palm and citrus trees. This series of quarries served as prisons for the defeated Athenians, who were enslaved; the quarries once rang with the sound of their chisels and hammers. At one end is the famous **Orecchio di Dionisio** (Ear of Dionysius), with an ear-shape entrance and unusual acoustics inside, as you'll hear if you clap your hands. The legend is that Dionysius used to listen in at the top of the quarry to hear what the slaves were plotting below.

The **Teatro Greco** is the chief monument in the Archaeological Park. Indeed it's one of Sicily's greatest classical sites and the most complete Greek theater surviving from antiquity. Climb to the top of the seating area (which could accommodate 15,000) for a fine view: all the seats converge upon a single point—the stage—which has the natural scenery and the sky as its background. Hewn out of the hillside rock in the 5th century BC, the theater saw the premieres of the plays of Aeschylus. Greek tragedies are still performed here every year in May and June. Above and behind the theater runs the Via dei Sepulcri, in which streams of running water flow through a series of Greek sepulchres.

The well-preserved and striking **Anfiteatro Romano** (Roman Amphitheater) reveals much about the differences between the Greek and Roman personalities. Where drama in the Greek theater was a kind of religious ritual, the Roman amphitheater emphasized the spectacle of combative sports and the circus. This arena is one of the largest of its kind and was built around the 2nd century AD. The corridor where gladiators and beasts entered the ring is still intact, and the seats (some of which still bear the occupants' names) were hauled in and constructed on the site from huge slabs of limestone. ⊠ *Viale Teocrito (entrance on Via Agnello), Archaeological Zone* ☎ *0931/65068* 🖾 *€10, combined ticket with Museo Archeologico €13.50* ⊙ *9–1 hr before sunset; last entrance 1 hr before closing.*

QUICK BITES

Leonardi. On your way to the Archaeological Park, stop in at this bar-cum-pasticceria for some great Sicilian cakes and ice cream. It's popular with the locals, so you may have to line up for your cakes during holiday times. It's closed Wednesday. ⊠ *Viale Teocrito 123, Archaeological Zone* ☎ *0931/61411.*

WORTH NOTING

Catacomba di San Giovanni. Not far from the Archaeological Park, off Viale Teocrito, the catacombs below the church of San Giovanni are one of the earliest-known Christian sites in the city. Inside the crypt of San Marciano is an altar where Saint Paul preached on his way through Sicily to Rome. The frescoes in this small chapel are mostly bright and fresh, though some dating from the 4th century AD show their age. ⊠ *Piazza San Giovanni, Tyche* ☎ *0931/64694* 🖾 *€6* ⊙ *Daily 9:30–12:30 and 2:30–5:30 (may be extended in summer); evening visits are also arranged. Closed Mon. in winter.*

Museo Archeologico. The impressive collection of Siracusa's splendid archaeological museum is organized by region around a central atrium and ranges from Neolithic pottery to fine Greek statues and vases. Compare the *Landolina Venus*—a headless goddess of love who rises out of the sea in measured modesty (a 1st-century-AD Roman copy of the Greek original)—with the much earlier (300 BC) elegant Greek statue of Hercules in Section C. Of a completely different style is a marvelous fanged Gorgon, its tongue sticking out, that once adorned the cornice of the Temple of Athena to ward off evildoers. ⊠ *Viale Teocrito 66, Tyche* ☎ *0931/464022* 🖾 *€8, combined ticket with Parco Archeologico €13.50* ⊙ *Tues.–Sat. 9–7, Sun. 9–2; last entry 1 hr before closing.*

ORTYGIA ISLAND
TOP ATTRACTIONS

Fodor's Choice
★

Duomo. Siracusa's Duomo is an archive of island history: the bottom-most excavations have unearthed remnants of Sicily's distant past, when the Siculi inhabitants worshipped their deities here. During the 5th century BC (the same time as Agrigento's Temple of Concord was built), the Greeks erected a temple to Athena over it, and in the 7th century Siracusa's first Christian cathedral was built on top of the Greek structure. The massive columns of the original Greek temple were incorporated into the present structure and are clearly visible, embedded in the exterior wall along Via Minerva. The Greek columns were also used to dramatic advantage inside, where on one side they form chapels connected by elegant wrought-iron gates. The Baroque facade, added in the 18th century, displays a harmonious rhythm of concaves and convexes. In front, the piazza is encircled by pink and white oleanders and elegant buildings ornamented with filigree grillwork. ⊠ *Piazza del Duomo, Ortygia* ☎ *0931/65328* ⊙ *Daily 7:30–7, longer in summer.*

Fonte Aretusa. A freshwater spring, the Fountain of Arethusa, sits next to the sea, studded with Egyptian papyrus that's reportedly natural. This anomaly is explained by a Greek legend that tells how the nymph Arethusa was changed into a fountain by the goddess Artemis (Diana) when she tried to escape the advances of the river god Alpheus. She fled from Greece, into the sea, with Alpheus in close pursuit, and emerged in Sicily at this spring. It's said if you throw a cup into the Alpheus River in Greece it will emerge here at this fountain, which is home to a few tired ducks and some faded carp—but no cups. If you want to stand right by the fountain, you need to gain admission through the aquarium; otherwise look down on it from Largo Aretusa. ⊠ *Off promenade along harbor, Ortygia.*

Museo del Papiro. Housed in the 16th-century ex-convent of Sant'Agostino, the Papyrus Museum demonstrates how papyri are prepared from reeds and then painted—an ancient tradition in the city. Siracusa, it seems, has the only climate outside the Nile Valley in which the papyrus plant—from which the word "paper" comes—thrives. ⊠ *Via Nizza 14, Ortygia* ☎ *0931/22100* ⊕ *www.museodelpapiro.it* 🎟 *€2* ⊙ *Tues.–Sun. 9–2; last entry 1 hr before closing.*

Piazza Archimede. The center of this piazza has a baroque fountain, the *Fontana di Diana,* festooned with fainting sea nymphs and dancing jets of water. Look for the Chiaramonte-style **Palazzo Montalto,** an arched-window gem just off the piazza on Via Montalto.

Piazza del Duomo. In the heart of Ortygia, this ranks as one of Italy's most beautiful piazzas. Its elongated space is lined with Sicilian Baroque treasures and outdoor cafés. Check with the tourist office for guided tours of the underground tunnels.

Tempio di Apollo. Scattered through the piazza just across the bridge to Ortygia are the ruins of a temple dedicated to Apollo, a model of which is in the Museo Archeologico. In fact, little of this noble Doric temple remains except for some crumbled walls and shattered columns; the window in the south wall belongs to a Norman church that was built much later on the same spot. ⊠ *Piazza Pancali, Ortygia.*

WORTH NOTING

Castello Maniace. The southern tip of Ortygia island is occupied by this castle built by Frederick II (1194–1250), until recently an army barracks, from which there are fine sea views. 🎟 *€4* ⊙ *Daily 9–1.*

Museo Bellomo. Siracusa's principal museum of art is inside a lovely Catalan Gothic palazzo with mullioned windows and an elegant exterior staircase. Among the paintings is the *Annunciation* by 15th-century maestro Antonello da Messina, newly restored to its original brilliance. There are also exhibits of Sicilian nativity figures, silver, furniture, ceramics, and religious vestments. ⊠ *Palazzo Bellomo, Via Capodieci 14/16, Ortygia* ☎ *0931/69511* 🎟 *€8* ⊙ *Tues.–Sat. 9–7, Sun. 9–1; last entry ½ hr before closing.*

15

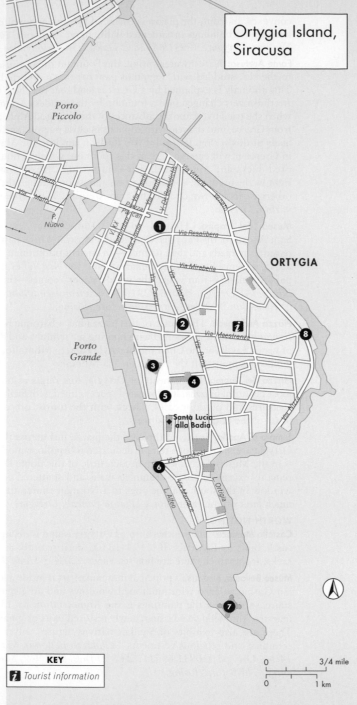

Ortygia Island, Siracusa

Porto
Piccolo

Porto
Grande

ORTYGIA

Santa Lucia
alla Badia

KEY

i *Tourist information*

0   3/4 mile

0   1 km

Palazzo Beneventano del Bosco. At one end of Piazza del Duomo, this elegant palazzo is a private residence, but you can take a peek at the impressive interior courtyard with its central staircase. ⊠ *Piazza del Duomo, Ortygia.*

OFF THE BEATEN PATH

If Siracusa's Baroque beauties whet your appetite for that over-the-top style, head 32 km (19 miles) southwest to Noto. Lying about 40 minutes away on the A18—and connected to Siracusa by both train and bus—the city is doable as a day trip. Having been decimated by an earthquake in 1693 and rebuilt in the prevailing fashion of the day, Noto has remarkable architectural integrity. A prime example of design from the island's Baroque heyday, it presents a pleasing ensemble of honey-color buildings, strikingly uniform in style but never dull. The domed Cattedrale di San Niccolò (divine in more ways than one) is an undisputed highlight of the extraordinary Baroque architecture for which the town is world famous. The recently restored Palazzo Nicolaci, which offers a rare insight into the lifestyle of social climbers in the 18th century, is another must-see. But simply walking the pedestrianized main street qualifies as an aesthetic experience. When you need a break from the architectural eye candy, indulge in an edible sweet (and a restorative coffee or granita) at a wondrous cake shop, the Caffè Sicilia, located at Corso Vittorio Emanuele 125.

15

WHERE TO EAT

$

PIZZA

✕ **Archimede.** Considered the best pizzeria in Ortygia, this place offers pizzas (evenings only) with classical names. Witness the Polifema, with sliced tomatoes, mozzarella, speck, and corn; or the Teocrite, topped with fresh tomato, mozzarella, garlic, onion, and basil. For those who can't face the full-size offerings, minipizzas are also available. The calzone *del ciclope* (literally "of the Cyclops") is stuffed with tomato, mozzarella, ham, and egg. One of the good selection of bottled beers makes a perfect accompaniment. Ⓢ *Average meal: €18* ⊠ *Via Gemmellaro 8, Ortygia* ☎ *0931/69701* ⊘ *Closed Sun. Sept.–May.*

$$$

SICILIAN

Fodor's Choice

★

✕ **Don Camillo.** A gracious series of delicately-arched rooms, lined with wine bottles and sepia-tone images of Old Siracusa, overflows with locals in the know. Preparations bring together fresh seafood and inspired creativity: taste, for instance, the sublime spaghetti *delle Sirene* (with sea urchin and shrimp in butter) or gamberoni prepared, unexpectedly (and wonderfully), in pork fat. The wine list is, in a word, extraordinary. Ⓢ *Average meal: €50* ⊠ *Via Maestranza 96, Ortygia* ☎ *0931/67133* ⊕ *www.ristorantedoncamillosiracusa.it* ⊘ *Closed Sun. and 2 wks in July.*

$$

MODERN ITALIAN

✕ **Oinos.** This restaurant–wine bar's ambitious food represents the most modern face of Siracusa. The dining rooms are stark but inviting, carefully balancing style consciousness with restrained refinement. Surrender to the sensational antipasto *sformatino di patate, cavolo capuccio, scamorza e braduro,* a molded potato tart with cabbage and rich, creamy cheeses. In season, special dishes spotlight white truffles from Alba priced by the gram (as is customary) and worth every penny. Ⓢ *Average meal: €35* ⊠ *Via della Giudecca 69/75, Ortygia* ☎ *0931/464900* ⊘ *Closed Mon. and Jan.–Feb. No dinner Sun. in winter.*

$ × Taverna Sveva. Once you've actually found this traditional osteria
SICILIAN   down the maze of streets behind the Castello Maniace, you can sit
back and enjoy both land-based and seafood dishes. The surroundings
are studiously minimalist (no tablecloths, leather mats) and dishes are
served on hand-painted ceramic ware. A major plus is that you can
order half portions of several pasta dishes. As a secondo, try the unusual
pesce in crosta di patate (grilled fish in a potato crust), but leave space
for the special tiramisù *agli agrumi* (with citrus fruit). $ *Average meal:*
€25 ⊠ Piazza Federico di Svevia 1, Ortygia ☎ 0931/24663 ⊙ Closed
Jan. and Wed. Sept. 15–Jun. No lunch Jun.–Sept.

WHERE TO STAY
For expanded hotel reviews, visit Fodors.com.

$$ ⊡ Domus Mariae. On Ortygia's eastern shore, this hotel, in an unusual
HOTEL   twist, is owned by Ursuline nuns, who help to make the mood placid
and peaceful—but the elegant accommodations are far from monastic.
Pros: nice breakfast room; gorgeous sea views; enthusiastic staff. **Cons:**
stairs to climb. $ *Rooms from: €145 ⊠ Via Vittorio Veneto 76, Ortygia*
☎ 0931/24854, 0931/24858 ⊕ www.siracusahoteldomusmariae.com
↪ 12 rooms ⎮⦶⎮ Breakfast.

$$$ ⊡ Grand Hotel Ortigia. An elegant, fantasy-inspired design prevails at this
HOTEL   venerable institution, which has enjoyed a prime position on the Porto
Grande at the base of Ortygia since 1890. **Pros:** wonderful views from
the restaurant; attentive service. **Cons:** back rooms have no view; small
bathrooms; Wi-Fi weak in some rooms. $ *Rooms from: €280 ⊠ Viale*
Mazzini 12, Ortygia ☎ 0931/464600 ⊕ www.grandhotelortigia.it ↪ 41
rooms, 17 suites ⎮⦶⎮ Breakfast.

$ ⊡ Hotel Aurora. In a pretty old palazzo, this bare-bones inn caters mostly
B&B/INN   to backpackers and those who have the stamina to brave the four-
story climb. **Pros:** good value; full of character. **Cons:** breakfast is not
always served on the premises; some rooms are poorly furnished; lots
of stairs to climb. $ *Rooms from: €60 ⊠ Via Maestranza 111, Orty-*
gia ☎ 0931/69475 ⊕ www.siracusahotel.com ↪ 9 rooms, 5 with bath
⎮⦶⎮ Breakfast.

$$ ⊡ Hotel des Étrangers et Miramare. This stylish hotel is one of the city's top
HOTEL   addresses for visiting dignitaries and tourists seeking luxury, high lev-
Fodor'sChoice   els of service, and good views. **Pros:** well-maintained facility; attentive
★   service; central location. **Cons:** some bathrooms are poorly designed;
no parking. $ *Rooms from: €145 ⊠ Passeggio Adorno 10/12, Ortygia*
☎ 0931/319100 ⊕ www.hotel-desetrangers.it ↪ 65 rooms, 11 junior
suites ⎮⦶⎮ Breakfast.

$ ⊡ Mercure Siracusa Prometeo. Offering excellent value for money, the
HOTEL   Mercure occupies a brand new building along the busy Viale Teracati
and, like most other hotels in the same chain, it's a slick operation with
first-rate facilities. **Pros:** a two-minute walk from the archaeological
site of Neapolis; easy to find; good parking facilities. **Cons:** restaurant
closed weekends; a long way from the island of Ortygia. $ *Rooms from:*
€120 ⊠ Viale Teracati 20, Tyche ☎ 0931/464646 ⊕ www.mercure.com
↪ 93 ⎮⦶⎮ Some meals.

NIGHTLIFE AND THE ARTS

Santa Lucia alla Badia. The feast of the city's patron, Santa Lucia, is held on December 13 and 20 at Santa Lucia alla Badia. A splendid silver statue of the saint is carried from the church to the Duomo; a torchlight procession and band music accompany the bearers, while local families watch from their balconies. ⊠ *Piazza del Duomo, near Catacombs of San Giovanni, Ortygia.*

Teatro Greco (*Greek Theater*). From mid-May to late June, Siracusa's Teatro Greco stages performances of classical tragedy and comedy. Tickets run €32 to €64, with a small discount if you buy the ticket in person. ⊠ *Archaeological Zone* ☎ *0931/487248, 800/542644 toll-free in Italy* ⊕ *www.indafondazione.org.*

THE INTERIOR

15

Sicily's interior is for the most part untrammeled, though the Imperial Roman Villa at Casale, outside Piazza Armerina, gives precious evidence from an epoch gone by. Don't miss windy mountaintop Enna, dubbed the "Navel of Sicily," or Caltagirone, a renowned ceramics center.

RAGUSA

90 km (56 miles) southwest of Siracusa.

Ragusa and Modica are the two chief cities in Sicily's smallest and sleepiest province, and the centers of a region known as Iblea. The dry, rocky, gentle countryside filled with canyons and grassy knolls is a unique landscape in Sicily. Iblea's trademark dry-stone walls divide swaths of land in a manner reminiscent of the high English countryside—but summers are decidedly Sicilian, with dry heat so intense that life grinds to a standstill for several hours each day. This remote province hums along to its own tune, clinging to local customs, cuisines, and traditions in aloof disregard even for the rest of Sicily. Ragusa, a modern city with a beautiful historic core, is known for some great local red wines and its wonderful cheese—a creamy, doughy, flavorful version of *caciocavallo*, made by hand every step of the way.

GETTING HERE AND AROUND

Trains and buses leave from Siracusa four or five times daily.

VISITOR INFORMATION

Ragusa Tourism Office ⊠ *Piazza San Giovanni* ☎ *0932/684780* ⊕ *www.comune.ragusa.it.*

EXPLORING

Basilica di San Giorgio. Designed by Rosario Gagliardi in 1738, this is a fine example of Sicilian Baroque. ☉ *10–noon and 4–6, until 7 in summer. Closed Tues. morning.*

Ibla. The lovely historic center of Ragusa, known as Ibla, was completely rebuilt after the devastating earthquake of 1693. A tumble of buildings perched on a hilltop and suspended between a deep ravine and a sloping valley, it's tiny squares and narrow lanes make for pleasant meandering.

CALTAGIRONE

66 km (41 miles) northwest of Ragusa.

Built over three hills, this charming Baroque town is a center of Sicily's ceramics industry. Here you can find majolica balustrades, tile-decorated windowsills, and the monumental Scala Santa Maria del Monte.

GETTING HERE AND AROUND

Buses and trains from Catania stop in the lower town, a pleasant stroll from the center and also well connected by local buses and taxis. Connections with Ragusa, Enna, and Piazza Armerina are less frequent.

VISITOR INFORMATION

Caltagirone Tourism Office ⊠ *Galleria Luigi Sturzo, Piazza Municipio 10* ☎ *0933/41365* ⊕ *www.comune.caltagirone.ct.it.*

EXPLORING

Museo della Ceramica. Caltagirone was declared a UNESCO World Heritage Site for its ceramics as well as for its numerous Baroque churches. One of Sicily's most extensive pottery collections, ranging from neolithic finds to red-figure ware from 5th century BC Athens and 18th-century terra-cotta nativity figures, is on display here. ⊠ *Via Roma, inside Giardini Pubblici* ☎ *0933/58418, 0933/58423* ⊠ *€4* ☉ *Daily 9–6:30.*

Scala Santa Maria del Monte. Exactly 142 individually-decorated tile steps lead up to the neglected Santa Maria del Monte church. On July 24 (the feast of San Giacomo, the city's patron saint) and again on August 15 (the feast of the Assumption) this staircase is illuminated with candles that form a tapestry design. Months of work go into preparing the 4,000 *coppi,* or cylinders of colored paper, that hold oil lamps—then, at 9:30 pm on the nights of July 24, July 25, August 14, and August 15, a squad of hundreds of youngsters (tourists are welcome to participate) springs into action to light the lamps, so that the staircase flares up all at once. ⊠ *Begins at Piazza Municipio.*

PIAZZA ARMERINA

30 km (18 miles) northwest of Caltagirone.

A quick look around the fanciful town of Piazza Armerina is rewarding—it has a provincial warmth, and the crumbling yellow-stone architecture with Sicily's trademark bulbous balconies creates quite an effect. The greatest draw, however, lies just down the road.

GETTING HERE AND AROUND

Piazza Armerina is linked to Caltagirone, Catania, Enna, and Palermo by regular buses. There's no train station.

VISITOR INFORMATION

Piazza Armerina Tourism Office ⊠ *Via Generale Muscará 47/A* ☎ *0935/680201* ⊕ *www.comune.piazzaarmerina.en.it.*

EXPLORING

Fodor'sChoice
★
Imperial Roman Villa. The exceptionally well-preserved Imperial Roman Villa is thought to have been a hunting lodge of the emperor Maximian (3rd–4th century AD). The excavations were not begun until 1950,

and most of the wall decorations and vaulting have been lost. However, some of the best mosaics of the Roman world cover more than 12,000 square feet under a shelter that hints at the layout of the original buildings. The mosaics were probably made by North African artisans; they're similar to those in the Tunis Bardo Museum, in Tunisia. The entrance was through a triumphal arch that led into an atrium surrounded by a portico of columns, after which the *thermae,* or bathhouse, is reached. It's colorfully decorated with mosaic nymphs, a Neptune, and slaves massaging bathers. The peristyle leads to the main villa, where in the Salone del Circo you look down on recently restored mosaics illustrating scenes from the Circus Maximus in Rome. A theme running through many of the mosaics, especially the long hall flanking the whole of one side of the peristyle courtyard, is the capturing and shipping of wild animals, which may have been a major source of the master's wealth. Yet the most famous mosaic is the floor depicting ten girls wearing the ancient equivalent of bikinis, going through what looks like a fairly rigorous set of training exercises. ✉ *SP15, Contrada Casale, 4 km (2½ miles) southwest of Piazza Armerina* ☎ *0935/680036* 🌐 *www.villaromanadelcasale.it* 🎫 *€10* 🕓 *Daily 9–7 in the summer, 9–5 in winter. Last entrance 1 hr before closing.*

WORD OF MOUTH

"If you like hand-painted pottery, Caltigirone is worth a few hours, just for the amazing tiled stairs and pistachio pesto!"

—swalter518

WHERE TO EAT

$$ MODERN ITALIAN Fodor's Choice ★

🍴 **Al Fogher.** A beacon of culinary light shines in Sicily's interior, a region generally filled with good, but basic, places to eat. Ambitious—and successful—dishes here combine traditional ingredients with the creative flair of chef Angelo Treno. Try the tuna tartare with orange essence, or the fillet of baby pig served with a sauce made from *bottarga* (cured tuna roe), green olives and crushed pistachio nuts. The wine list includes nearly 500 labels, and there's even a water list featuring more than a dozen kinds of mineral water. The dining room is unassuming and elegant, but the terrace is the place to be in summer. From town, follow Viale Ciancio and Viale Gaeta about 1 km (½ mile) north of Piazza Cascino. [$] *Average meal: €35* ✉ *Contrada Bellia, near SS117bis, Aidone exit* ☎ *0935/684123* 🌐 *www.alfogher.net* 🕓 *Closed Mon. No dinner Sun.*

ENNA

33 km (20 miles) northwest of Piazza Armerina, 136 km (85 miles) southeast of Palermo.

Deep in Sicily's interior, the fortress city of Enna (altitude 2,844 feet) commands exceptional views of the surrounding rolling plains, and, in the distance, Mt. Etna. It's the highest provincial capital in Italy and, thanks to its central location, is nicknamed the "Navel of Sicily." Virtually unknown by tourists and relatively untouched by industrialization, this sleepy town charms and prospers in a distinctly old-fashioned, Sicilian way. Enna makes a good stopover for the night or just for lunch, as it's right along the autostrada between Palermo and Catania (and thus Siracusa).

GETTING HERE AND AROUND

Just off the A19 Autostrada, Enna is easily accessible by car. With the train station 5 km (3 miles) below the upper town, the most practical public transportation is by bus from Palermo or Catania.

EXPLORING

Castello di Lombardia. The narrow, winding streets are dominated at one end by the impressive cliff-hanging Castello di Lombardia, built by Frederick II, and easily visible as you approach town. Inside the castle, you can climb up the tower for great views from the dead center of the island—on a very clear day, you can see to all three coasts. Immediately to the south you see Lake Pergusa (dried out in late summer), now almost swallowed by Enna's sprawling suburbs and the racetrack around its perimeter. According to Greek mythology, this was where Persephone was abducted by Hades. While a prisoner in his underworld realm she ate six pomegranate seeds, and was therefore doomed to spend half of each year there. For the ancients, she emerged at springtime, triggering a display of wild flowers that can still be admired all over Sicily. ✉ *Piazza di Castello di Lombardia* 🎫 *Free* 🕒 *Daily 9–1 hr before sunset.*

Piazza Vittorio Emanuele. In town, head straight for Via Roma, which leads to Piazza Vittorio Emanuele—the center of Enna's shopping scene and evening passeggiata. The attached **Piazza Crispi,** dominated by the shell of the grand old Hotel Belvedere, affords breathtaking panoramas of the hillside and smoking Etna looming in the distance. The bronze fountain in the middle of the piazza is a reproduction of Gian Lorenzo Bernini's famous 17th-century sculpture *The Rape of Persephone,* a depiction of Hades abducting Persephone.

Rocca di Cerere (*Rock of Demeter*). The Greek cult of Demeter, goddess of the harvest, was said to have centered on Enna. It's not hard to see why its adherents would have worshipped at the Rocca di Cerere, protruding out on one end of town next to the Castello di Lombardia. The spot enjoys spectacular views of the expansive countryside and windswept Sicilian interior.

Torre di Federico II. This mysterious octagonal tower—of unknown purpose—stands above the lower part of town. It has been celebrated for millennia as marking the exact geometric center of the island—thus the tower's, and city's, nickname, Umbilicus Siciliae (Navel of Sicily). The interior is not open to the public, but the surrounding park is.

WHERE TO EAT AND STAY

For expanded hotel reviews, visit Fodors.com.

$ SICILIAN

🍴 **Centrale.** Housed in an old palazzo, this casual place has served meals since 1889. One entire wall is covered with a vast mirror, the others are adorned with Sicilian pottery, and an outdoor terrace soothes diners in summer. The seasonal menu includes local preparations such as *coppole di cacchio* (peppers stuffed with spaghetti, potato, and basil), grilled pork chops, and a 15th-century specialty called *controfiletto di vitello all'annese*—a veal filet with onions, artichokes, pig jowel, and white wine. Choose from a decent selection of Sicilian wines to accompany your meal. [$] *Average meal: €20* ✉ *Piazza VI Dicembre 9* ☎ *0935/500963* 🌐 *www.ristorantecentrale.net* 🕒 *No lunch Sat. (with some exceptions).*

$ **Hotel Sicilia.** Sicily's interior has few decent accommodations, and
HOTEL   of Enna's two hotels, this one has more character. **Pros:** central location; friendly staff; good breakfast. **Cons:** a bit dated; some rooms
can be noisy. *$ Rooms from: €75 ✉ Piazza Napoleone Colajanni 7
☎ 0935/500850 ⊕ www.hotelsiciliaenna.it ⟲ 60 rooms ⦿ Breakfast.*

AGRIGENTO AND WESTERN SICILY

The crowning glory of western Sicily is the concentration of Greek
temples at Agrigento, on a height between the modern city and the
sea. The mark of ancient Greek culture also lingers in the cluster of
ruined cliffside temples at Selinunte and at the splendidly isolated site
of Segesta. Traces of the North African culture that for centuries exerted
a strong influence on this end of the island are tangible in the coastal
town of Marsala. In contrast, the cobblestone streets of hilltop Erice,
retain a strong medieval complexion, giving the quiet town the air of a
last outpost on the edge of the Mediterranean. On the northern coast,
not far outside Palermo, Monreale's cathedral glitters with mosaics that
are among the finest in Italy.

15

AGRIGENTO

95 km (59 miles) southwest of Enna.

Agrigento owes its fame almost exclusively to its ancient Greek temples—though it was also the birthplace of playwright Luigi Pirandello
(1867–1936).

GETTING HERE AND AROUND
Driving from Enna, take the A19 Autostrada 35 km (21 miles) southwest to Caltanissetta; then follow the SS640 to Agrigento. Motorists
can also access the town easily via the coastal SS115 and, from Palermo,
by the SS189. Buses and trains run from Enna, Palermo, and Catania;
both bus and train stations are centrally located.

VISITOR INFORMATION
Agrigento Tourism Office ✉ *Via Empedocle 73* ☎ *0922/20391.*

EXPLORING
Monastero di Santo Spirito. There are a few other things to do and see in
the area. Along the coast, around 12 km (7 miles) to the west of Agrigento near the town of Realmonte, you can view the Scala dei Turchi
(Stairs of the Turks), which are natural white cliffs eroded into unusual
shapes. By visiting the beaches closest to the temples, near the town of
San Leone, you can sunbathe beside the locals. If, instead, you head
up the hill from the Valle dei Templi to the modern city you'll have
the opportunity to try a local treat or stay at an inexpensive lodging.
Need another reason to go there? Just ring the doorbell at the **Monastero di Santo Spirito** and try the *kus-kus* (sweet cake), made of pistachio nuts, almonds, and chocolate, that the nuns prepare. The clositers
and courtyard of the church are open to the public. ✉ *Salita di Santo
Spirito, off Via Porcello, cortile Santo Spirito 8* ☎ *0922/20664* ⊕ *www.
monasterosantospiritoag.it* ☉ *Weekdays, irregular hrs.*

Continued on page 882

VALLE DEI TEMPLI

Built on a broad open field that slopes gently to the sun-simmered Mediterranean, Akragas (ancient Agrigento's Greek name) was a showpiece of temples erected to flaunt a victory over Carthage. Despite a later sack by the Carthaginians, mishandling by the Romans, and neglect by the Christians and Muslims, the eight or so monuments in the Valle dei Templi are considered to be, along with the Acropolis in Athens, the finest Greek ruins in all the world.

 TIMING TIP

The temples are at their very best in May, when the weather is warm but the summer tourist crowds haven't yet arrived.

Whether you first come upon the Valle dei Templi in the early morning light, or bathed by golden floodlights at night, it's easy to see why Akragas was celebrated by the Greek poet Pindar as "the most beautiful city built by mortal men."

MAKING THE MOST OF YOUR VISIT

GETTING AROUND

Though getting to, from, and around the dusty ruins of the Valle dei Templi is no great hassle, this important archaeological zone deserves several hours. The site, which opens at 8:30 AM, is divided into western and eastern sections. For instant aesthetic gratification, walk through the eastern zone; for a more comprehensive tour, start way out at the western end and work your way back uphill.

The temples are a bit spread out, but the valley is all completely walkable and generally toured on foot. However, note that there is only one hotel (Villa Athena) that is close enough to walk to the ruins, so you will most likely have to drive to reach the site; parking is at the entrance to the temple area.

WHAT TO BRING

It's a good idea to pack your own snacks and drinks. There are two snack shops with limited selections within the site, and the handful of high-priced bars around the site cater to tourists.

In summer the site can get extremely hot, so wear light clothing, a hat, and sun protection if possible.

A BRIEF HISTORY OF AGRIGENTO

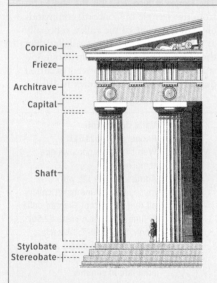

Cornice
Frieze
Architrave
Capital
Shaft
Stylobate
Stereobate

KEY DATES	
750 BC	Greek city-states begin to colonize Sicily and southern Italy.
734 BC	Neighboring Siracusa founded.
582 BC	Akragas settled. The city grows wealthy through trade with Carthage, just across the Mediterranean.
ca. 450 BC–350 BC	Temples at Akragas erected over a period of about 100 years to celebrate the city's prosperity.
413 BC	Battle of Siracusa vs. Athens.
406 BC	Fire from Carthaginian attack destroys much of Akragas. Despite this and future attacks, the city and its temples survive through the Roman era, the Middle Ages, and into the modern age.

The natural defenses of ancient Akragas depended on its secure and quite lovely position between two rivers on a floodplain a short distance from the sea. In Agrigento you will be treated to what many experts consider the world's best-preserved remains of classical Greece. All of the temples in the Valle dei Templi are examples of Doric architecture, the earliest and simplest of the Greek architectural orders (the others are Ionic and Corinthian). Some retain capitals in addition to their columns, while others are reduced to nothing more than fragments of stylobate.

THE TEMPLES

TEMPIO DI ERCOLE

The eight pillars of the **Temple of Hercules**, down the hill from the Temple of Concord, make up Agrigento's oldest temple complex (dating from the 6th century BC), dedicated to the favorite god of the often-warring citizens of Akragas. Partially reconstructed in 1922, it reveals the remains of a large Doric temple that originally had 38 columns. Like all the area temples, it faces east. The nearby Museo Archeologico Regionale contains some of the marble warrior figures that once decorated the temple's pediment.

Tempio di Ercole

TEMPIO DELLA CONCORDIA

The beautiful **Temple of Concord** is perhaps *the* best-preserved Greek temple in existence. The structure dates from about 430 BC, and owes its exceptional state of preservation to the fact that it was converted into a Christian church in the 6th century and was extensively restored in the 18th century. Thirty-two Doric columns surround its large interior, and everything but the roof and treasury are still standing. For preservation, this temple is blocked off to the public, but you can still get close enough to appreciate how well it's withstood the past 2,400 years.

TEMPIO DI GIUNONE

The **Temple of Juno**, east on the Via Sacra from the Temple of Concord, commands an exquisite view of the valley, especially at sunset. It's similar to but smaller than the Concordia and dates from about 450 BC. Traces of a fire that probably occurred during the Carthaginian attack in 406 BC,

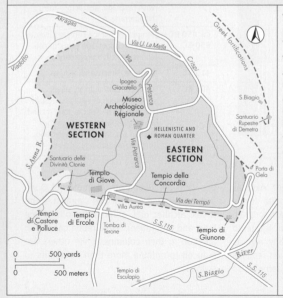

Valle dei Templi
Phone: 0922/621611
Web site: www.parcovalledetempi.net
Admission: Site €8, with museum €10. One ticket covers all temples except Giardini della Kolimbetra (which costs €2.50). Open daily 8:30–7; Nov.–Mar., western section closes at 5; the eastern section is usually open until late in summer.

Museo Archeologico Regionale
Contrada San Nicola, 12
Phone: 0922/401565
Admission: €8, with temples site €10
Open Tues.–Sat. 9–7, Sun.–Mon. 9–1.

which destroyed the ancient town, can be seen on the walls of the cellar. Thirty of the original 34 columns still stand, of which 16 have retained their capitals.

TEMPIO DI GIOVE

Though never completed, the **Temple of Jupiter** was considered the eighth wonder of the world. With a length of more than 330 feet, it was once the biggest of the Akragas temples and one of the largest temples in the Greek world. The temple was probably built in gratitude for victory over Carthage and was constructed by prisoners captured in that war. Basically Doric in style, it did not have the usual colonnade of freestanding columns but rather a series of half columns attached to a solid wall. This design is unique among known Doric temples—alas, only the stereobate was left behind. Inside the excavation you can see a cast (not the original) of one of the 38 colossal Atlas-like figures, or telamones, that supported the temple's massive roof.

Tempio di Giove

TEMPIO DI CASTORE E POLLUCE

The **Temple of Castor and Pollux** is a troublesome reconstruction of a 5th-century BC temple. It was pieced together by some enthusiastic if misguided 19th-century romantics who, in 1836, haphazardly put together elements from diverse buildings. Ironically, the four gently crumbling columns supporting part of an entablature of the temple have become emblematic of Agrigento.

15

IN FOCUS VALLE DEI TEMPLI

OTHER SITES OF INTEREST

To the left of the Temple of Concord is a Paleochristian **necropolis**. Early Christian tombs were both cut into the rock and dug into underground catacombs.

Right opposite the Temple of Castor and Pollux, facing north, the **Santuario delle Divinità Ctonie** (Sanctuary of the Chthonic Divinities) has cultic altars and eight small temples dedicated to Demeter, Persephone, and other Underworld deities. In the vicinity are two columns of a temple dedicated to Hephaestus (Vulcan).

At the end of Via dei Templi, where it turns left and becomes Via Petrarca, stands the **Museo Archeologico Regionale**. An impressive collection of antiquities from the site includes vases, votives, everyday objects,

weapons, statues (including one of the surviving original telamones from the Temple of Jupiter), and models of the temples.

The **Hellenistic and Roman Quarter**, across the road from the archaeological museum, consists of four parallel streets, running north–south, that have been uncovered, along with the foundations of some houses from the Roman settlement (2nd century BC). Some of these streets still have their original mosaic pavements, and the complex system of sidewalks and gutters is easy to make out—reminding you that the ancient world wasn't all temples and togas.

WHERE TO EAT

$$ ✕ **Leon d'Oro.** In the community of San Leone di Agrigento, lying
SICILIAN between the temples and the seaside, this restaurant is run by a pair
of local food and wine personalities, brothers Totó and Vittorio Col-
lura, who make adventurous use of traditional ingredients. Their sea-
sonal menu is full of pleasant surprises. Try the pasta with sardines,
accented with traditional Agrigento spices; or one of the dishes inspired
by the *Commissario Montalbano* detective series set nearby. The wine
list is playful, organized with an opera theme and featuring frowning
faces when a certain label is temporarily out of stock. $ *Average meal:*
€30 ✉ *Viale Emporium 102, San Leone di Agrigento* ☎ *0922/414400*
⊘ *Closed Mon.*

$$ ✕ **Trattoria dei Templi.** Along a road on the way up to Agrigento proper
SICILIAN from the temple area, this family-run vaulted restaurant serves up some
Fodor's Choice of the best food in the area. The menu includes five different homemade
★ pastas each day as well as plenty of fresh fish dishes, all prepared with
Sicilian flair. The antipasti, such as the carpaccio of *cernia* (grouper),
are exceptional, and the ample wine list has many Sicilian choices. The
best bet is to ask for the advice of brothers Giuseppe and Simone, the
owners and chief orchestrators in the restaurant. Reservations are recommended in the high season, as things get busy after it becomes too
dark for temple exploration. $ *Average meal: €30* ✉ *Via Panoramica*
dei Templi 15 ☎ *0922/403110* ⊕ *www.trattoriadeitempli.com* ⊘ *Closed*
Sun. Jun.–Oct.

WHERE TO STAY

For expanded hotel reviews, visit Fodors.com.

$ ⛭ **Foresteria Baglio della Luna.** Fiery sunsets and moonlight cast a glow
HOTEL over the ancient tower at the center of this farmhouse-hotel complex,
in the valley below the temples. **Pros:** quiet location; serene environment. **Cons:** difficult to reach from the temples and the city (buses run
hourly); service can be slipshod; guests have complained about lighting
and heating. $ *Rooms from: €99* ✉ *Via Serafino Amabile Guastella*
1, Contrada Maddalusa ☎ *0922/511061* ⊕ *www.bagliodellaluna.com*
⇱ *21 rooms, 2 suites* ⌹ *Breakfast.*

$ ⛭ **Tre Torri.** If you're an outdoors enthusiast bent on exploring the
HOTEL countryside around Agrigento, this is a smart choice because bicycle
tours and nature walks can be arranged. **Pros:** good facilities; socia-
ble atmosphere; multilingual staff. **Cons:** a little run-down; busy with
tour groups; a bit far from the temples and the city. $ *Rooms from:*
€100 ✉ *Viale Cannatelo 7, Villaggio Mosè* ☎ *0922/606733* ⊕ *www.*
hoteltretorri.eu ⇱ *118 rooms* ⌹ *Breakfast.*

NIGHTLIFE AND THE ARTS

Festa delle Mandorle (*Almond Blossom Festival*). During the first half
of February, when most of the almond trees are in blossom, Agrigento hosts a Festa delle Mandorle, with international folk dances,
a costumed parade, and the sale of marzipan and other sweets made
from almonds.

SELINUNTE

100 km (62 miles) northwest of Agrigento, 114 km (71 miles) south of Palermo.

GETTING HERE AND AROUND

You can get here by bus or car via the town of Castelvetrano, 11 km (7 miles) north, which is itself accessible from Palermo by car on the A29 Autostrada, as well as by bus and train.

VISITOR INFORMATION

Selinunte Tourism Office ✉ *Piazzale Bovio Marconi* ☎ *0924/46251.*

EXPLORING

Fodor's Choice ★ **Greek Temple Ruins.** Near the town of Castelvetrano, numerous Greek temple ruins perch on a plateau overlooking an expanse of the Mediterranean at Selinunte (or Selinus). The city was one of the most superb colonies of ancient Greece. Founded in the 7th century BC, Selinunte became the rich and prosperous rival of Segesta, which in 409 BC turned to the Carthaginians for help. The Carthaginians, in turn, sent an army to destroy the city. The temples were demolished, the city was razed, and 16,000 of Selinunte's inhabitants were slaughtered. The remains of Selinunte are in many ways unchanged from the day of its sacking—burn marks still scar the Greek columns, and much of the site still lies in rubble at its exact position of collapse. The original complex held seven temples scattered over two sites separated by a harbor. Of the seven, only one—reconstructed in 1958—is whole. ■ **TIP→ This is a large archaeological site, so you might make use of the private *navetta* (shuttle) to save a bit of walking. Alternatively, if you have a car, you can visit the first temples close to the ticket office on foot and then drive westward to the farther site. Be prepared to show your ticket at various stages.**

Selinunte is named after a local variety of wild parsley (*Apium graveolens* or *petroselinum*) that in spring grows in profusion among the ruined columns and overturned capitals. Although there are a few places to stay right around Selinunte, many people see it as an easy—and richly rewarding—stopover along the road to or from Agrigento. It takes only an hour or two to see. ✉ *SS115, 13 km (8 miles) southeast of Castelvetrano* ☎ *0924/46277* 🎟 *€6* ⏲ *Apr.–Oct., Mon.–Sat. 9–6, Sun. 9–1; Nov.–Mar., Mon.–Sat. 9–4.*

$ SICILIAN 🍴 **Lido Zabbara.** Known to the locals as Da Yoyo—the owner is constantly getting up and down to attend to his customers—this is really no more than a glorified salad bar right on the beach at Selinunte. Pick up a plate and serve yourself from the various delicacies laid out on the center spread. Wine comes by the carafe and is surprisingly drinkable. As an added plus there are sunbeds and umbrellas at reasonable prices if you want to unwind before the next archaeological bonanza. [$] *Average meal: €20* ✉ *Via Pigafetta, Marinella* ☎ *0924/46194* 💳 *No credit cards* ⏲ *Closed Nov.–Mar.*

15

MARSALA

88 km (55 miles) northwest of Selinunte.

The quiet seaside town of Marsala, together with the nearby island of Mozia, were once the main Carthaginian bases in Sicily: from them Carthage fought for supremacy over the island against Greece and Rome. But nowadays Marsala is more readily associated with the world-famous, richly colored fortified wine named after it. In 1773 a British merchant named John Woodhouse happened upon the town and discovered that the wine here was as good as the port the British had long imported from Portugal. Two other wine merchants, Whitaker and Ingram, rushed in, and by 1800 Marsala was exporting its wine all over the British Empire.

GETTING HERE AND AROUND
Buses and trains from Palermo, Trapani, and Castelvetrano stop in Marsala. Drivers can take the coastal SS115.

15

VISITOR INFORMATION
Marsala Tourism Office ⊠ *Via XI Maggio 100* ☎ *0923/714097* ⊕ *www.comune.marsala.tp.it.*

EXPLORING
Donnafugata Winery. One of Sicily's foremost wine producers, the 160-year-old Donnafugata Winery, is open for tours of its *cantina* (wine cellar); reservations are required. It's an interesting look at the winemaking process in Sicily, and it ends with a tasting of several whites and reds and a chance to buy; don't miss the delicious, full-bodied red Mille e Una Notte, and the famous Ben Ryè Passito di Pantelleria, a sweet dessert wine made from dried grapes. ⊠ *Via Lipari 18* ☎ *0923/724245* ⊕ *www.donnafugata.it* 🎫 *€7 (visit and tasting 3 wines) or €10 (visit and tasting 6 wines)* ⊙ *Tours: weekdays 10, 11:30, 3, and 5; Sat. 10, 11:30, and 3. Shop: weekdays 9–1 and 3–6:30, Sat. 9–5.*

Museo Archeologico Baglio Anselmi. A sense of Marsala's past as a Carthaginian stronghold is captured by the well-preserved Punic warship displayed in the town's Museo Archeologico Baglio Anselmi, along with some of the amphoras and other artifacts recovered from the wreck. The vessel, which was probably sunk during the great sea battle that ended the First Punic War in 241 BC, was dredged up from the mud near the Egadi Islands in the 1970s. There's also a good display of maritime and archaeological finds. ⊠ *Lungomare Boéo 2* ☎ *0923/952535* 🎫 *€4* ⊙ *Mon. 9–1, Tues.–Sun. 9–7.*

ERICE

45 km (28 miles) northeast of Marsala, 15 km (9 miles) northeast of Trapani.

Perched 2,450 feet above sea level, Erice is an enchanting medieval mountaintop aerie of palaces, fountains, and cobblestone streets. Shaped like an equilateral triangle, the town was the ancient landmark Eryx, dedicated to Aphrodite (Venus). When the Normans arrived they built a castle on Monte San Giuliano, where today there's a lovely public park with benches and belvederes offering striking views of Trapani, the Egadi Islands offshore, and, on a *very* clear day, Cape Bon and the Tunisian coast. Because of Erice's elevation, clouds conceal much of the view for most of winter. Sturdy shoes (for the cobbles) and something warm to wear are recommended.

GETTING HERE AND AROUND

Make your approach via Trapani, which is on the A29 Autostrada and well connected by bus and train with Marsala and Palermo. Mid-March to December a funivia runs from the outskirts of Trapani to Erice Monday 2 pm to 8:30 pm, Tuesday to Friday 7:30 am to 8:30 pm, and weekends 9:45 am to midnight. Going by car or bus from Trapani takes around 40 minutes.

VISITOR INFORMATION

Erice Tourism Office ✉ *Palazzo Municipale, Piazza Loggia 3.*

EXPLORING

Capo San Vito. The cape has a long sandy beach on a promontory overlooking a bay in the Gulf of Castellammare. The town here, San Vito Lo Capo, is famous for its North African couscous, made with fish instead of meat. In late September it hosts the five-day **Cous Cous Fest,** a serious international couscous competition and festival with live music and plenty of free tastings. San Vito is also one of the bases for exploring the **Riserva dello Zingaro**: this nature preserve—one of the few stretches of coastline in Sicily, which is not built-up—is at its best in late spring, when both wildflowers and birds are plentiful. ✉ *40 km (25 miles) north of Erice.*

Pasticceria del Convento. Here, Maria Grammatico's sister sells similar delectable treats. The shop is open from March through November. ✉ *Via Guarnotti 1* ☎ *0923/869777.*

Pasticceria Grammatico. Fans of Sicilian sweets make a beeline for this place, run by Maria Grammatico, a former nun who gained international fame with *Bitter Almonds,* her life story cowritten with Mary Taylor Simeti. Her almond-paste creations are works of art, molded into striking shapes, including dolls and animals. There are a few tables and a tiny balcony with wonderful views. ✉ *Via Vittorio Emanuele 14* ☎ *0923/869390.*

WHERE TO EAT AND STAY

For expanded hotel reviews, visit Fodors.com.

$ SICILIAN 🍴 **Elimo.** On Erice's main cobblestone street, Carmelo Tilotta's restaurant offers superb views of passersby through large picture windows. But your eyes will be on the food, made with fresh local ingredients. The pasta *all'ericina* (with basil, garlic, tomatoes, and almonds) is alone worth the trip. Tables spread onto the terrace in summer. There are also spacious and sometimes quirky rooms if you want to stay over. [$] *Average meal: €25* ✉ *Via Vittorio Emanuele 75* ☎ *0923/869377* 🌐 *www.hotelelimo.it* 🕒 *Closed Jan. and Feb.*

$$ SICILIAN 🍴 **Monte San Giuliano.** At this traditional restaurant, you can sit out on the tree-lined patio or in the white-walled dining room and munch on free *panelle* (chickpea fritters), which are delicate and judiciously seasoned. Follow them up with citrusy *sarde a beccafico* (sardines, arranged in the shape of a bird) and exemplary ravioli in cuttlefish ink. Or order the seafood couscous—it's served with a bowl of fish broth on the side so you can add as much as you wish. The restaurant, near the main piazza, is hidden within the labyrinth of lanes that makes up Erice. [$] *Average meal: €30* ✉ *Vicolo San Rocco 7* ☎ *0923/869595* ⏲ *Closed Mon., 2 wks in mid-Jan., and 1st 2 wks in Nov.*

$ HOTEL 🏨 **Moderno.** This delightful hotel has a creaky old feel to it, but that's part of the charm—the lobby area, scattered with books, magazines, and knickknacks, calls to mind your aunt's living room. **Pros:** central location; great rooftop terrace. **Cons:** very modest rooms; street-facing rooms can be noisy. [$] *Rooms from: €100* ✉ *Via Vittorio Emanuele 67* ☎ *0923/869300* 🌐 *www.hotelmodernoerice.it* 🛏 *40 rooms* 🍽 *Breakfast.*

15

SEGESTA

35 km (22 miles) east of Erice, 85 km (53 miles) southwest of Palermo.

GETTING HERE AND AROUND

Three or four daily buses travel from Trapani to Segesta. About as many trains from Palermo and Trapani stop at Segesta-Tempio station, a 20-minute uphill walk from Segesta. The site is easily reached via the A29 Autostrada.

EXPLORING

Fodor's Choice ★ **Tempio Dorico** (*Doric Temple*). Segesta is the site of one of Sicily's most impressive temples, constructed on the side of a windswept barren hill overlooking a valley of giant fennel. Virtually intact today, the temple is considered by some to be finer in its proportions and setting than any other Doric temple left standing. It was actually started in the 5th century BC by the Elymian people, who may have been refugees from Troy. At the very least, evidence—they often sided with the Carthaginians, for example—indicates that they were non-Greeks. However, the style is in many ways Greek. The temple was never finished; the walls and roof never materialized, and the columns were never fluted. A little more than 1 km (½ mile) away, near the top of the hill (a shuttle bus leaves every 30 minutes, €1.50 round trip), are the remains of a fine **theater** with impressive views, especially at sunset, of the plains and the Bay of Castellammare. Concerts and plays are staged here in summer. ✉ *Calatafimi-Segesta* ☎ *0924/952356* 🎫 *€6* ⏲ *May–Sept., daily 9–7; Oct.–Apr., daily 9–5. Last entry 1 hr before closing.*

MONREALE

59 km (37 miles) northeast of Segesta, 10 km (6 miles) southwest of Palermo.

GETTING HERE AND AROUND

You can reach Monreale on the frequent buses that depart from Palermo's Piazza dell'Indipendenza. From Palermo, drivers can follow Corso Calatafimi west, though the going can be slow.

EXPLORING

Cloister. The lovely cloister of the abbey adjacent to the Duomo was built at the same time as the church but enlarged in the 14th century. The beautiful enclosure is surrounded by 216 intricately carved double columns, every other one decorated in a unique glass mosaic pattern. Afterward, don't forget to walk behind the cloister to the belvedere, with stunning panoramic views over the Conca d'Oro (Golden Conch) valley toward Palermo. ✉ *Piazza del Duomo* ☎ *091/6404403* 🎟 *€6* ⏲ *Tues.–Sat. 9–6:30, Mon. and Sun. 9–1; last entry ½ hr before closing.*

Fodor's Choice ★ **Duomo.** Monreale's splendid cathedral is lavishly executed with mosaics depicting events from the Old and New Testaments. After the Norman conquest of Sicily the new princes showcased their ambitions through monumental building projects. William II (1154–89) built the church complex with a cloister and palace between 1174 and 1185, employing Byzantine craftsmen. The result was a glorious fusion of Eastern and Western influences, widely regarded as the finest example of Norman architecture in Sicily.

The major attraction is the 68,220 square feet of glittering gold mosaics decorating the cathedral interior. *Christ Pantocrator* dominates the apse area; the nave contains narratives of the Creation; and scenes from the life of Christ adorn the walls of the aisles and the transept. The painted wooden ceiling dates from 1816–37. The roof commands a great view (a reward for climbing 172 stairs).

Bonnano Pisano's bronze doors, completed in 1186, depict 42 biblical scenes and are considered among the most important of medieval artifacts. Barisano da Trani's 42 panels on the north door, dating from 1179, present saints and evangelists. ✉ *Piazza del Duomo* ☎ *091/6404413, 347/3510886* ⏲ *Daily 8–1:30 and 4:30–6.*

WHERE TO EAT

$$ SICILIAN 🍴 **La Botte 1962.** It's worth the short drive or inexpensive taxi fare from Monreale to reach this restaurant, which is famous for well-prepared local specialties. Dine alfresco on seafood dishes such as *bavette don Carmelo,* a narrow version of tagliatelle with a sauce of swordfish, squid, shrimp, and pine nuts. Other regular favorites include *involtini alla siciliana* (meat roulades stuffed with salami and cheese). Local wines are a good accompaniment. The restaurant is open only on Saturday for dinner and on Sunday for lunch, or for reservations of at least 20 people. [$] *Average meal: €40* ✉ *Contrada Lenzitti 20, SS186 Km 10* ☎ *091/414051* 🌐 *www.mauriziocascino.it* ✍ *Reservations essential* ⏲ *Closed weekdays except by reservation, and July–mid-Sept. No lunch Sat. and no dinner Sun.*

PALERMO

Once the intellectual capital of southern Europe, Palermo has always been at the crossroads of civilization. Favorably situated on a crescent bay at the foot of Monte Pellegrino, it's attracted almost every culture touching the Mediterranean world. To Palermo's credit, it's absorbed these diverse cultures into a unique personality that's at once Arab and Christian, Byzantine and Roman, Norman and Italian. The city's heritage encompasses all of Sicily's varied ages, but its distinctive aspect is its Arab-Norman identity, an improbable marriage that, mixed in with Byzantine and Jewish elements, created some resplendent works of art. These are most notable in the churches, from small jewels such as San Giovanni degli Eremiti to larger-scale works such as the cathedral. No less noteworthy than the architecture is Palermo's chaotic vitality, on display at some of Italy's most vibrant outdoor markets, public squares, street bazaars, and food vendors, and, above all, in its grand, discordant symphony of motorists, motorcyclists, and pedestrians that triumphantly climaxes in the new town center each evening with Italy's most spectacular passeggiata.

> **WORD OF MOUTH**
>
> "If you plan to visit the western part of the island anyway, Palermo would be a very worthwhile visit. The mosaics are incredible . . . the restaurants are amazing and full of real local people. . . . Since it's a real city it can be more challenging than a small town, but if you're relatively fit you can practically walk across the entire tourist area. If anything frightened me about the place it was the tremendous density of things to see!"
>
> —abbydog

15

GETTING HERE AND AROUND

Palermo is well connected by road and rail; its airport links it to other cities in Italy, as well as around Europe.

VISITOR INFORMATION

Palermo Tourism Office ✉ *Via Belmonte 92* ☎ *091/585172* 🖷 *091/586338* ⊕ *www.provincia.palermo.it/turismo* ✉ *Aeroporto di Palermo* ☎ *091/591698.*

EXPLORING

Sicily's capital is a multilayered, vigorous metropolis with a strong historical profile; approach it with an open mind. You're likely to encounter some frustrating instances of inefficiency and, depending on the season, stifling heat. If you have a car, park it in a garage as soon as you can, and don't take it out until you're ready to depart.

Palermo is easily explored on foot, but you may choose to spend a morning taking a bus tour to help you get oriented. The Quattro Canti, or Four Corners, is the hub that separates the four sections of the old city: La Kalsa (the old Arab section) to the southeast, Albergheria to the southwest, Capo to the northwest, and Vucciria to the northeast. Each of these is a tumult of activity during the day, though at night the narrow alleys empty out and are best avoided in favor of the more animated avenues of the new city north of Teatro Massimo. Sights to see by day are scattered along three major streets: Corso Vittorio Emanuele, Via Maqueda, and Via Roma. The tourist information office in Piazza Castelnuovo will give you a map and a valuable handout that lists opening and closing times, which sometimes change with the seasons.

TOP ATTRACTIONS

Fodor's Choice **Cattedrale.** This church is a lesson in Palermitan eclecticism—originally
★   Norman (1182), then Catalan Gothic (14th to 15th century), then fitted out with a Baroque and Neoclassical interior (18th century). Its turrets, towers, dome, and arches come together in the kind of meeting of diverse elements that King Roger II (1095–1154), whose tomb is inside along with that of Frederick II, fostered during his reign. The back of the apse is gracefully decorated with interlacing Arab arches inlaid with limestone and black volcanic tufa. ⊠ *Corso Vittorio Emanuele, Capo* ☎ *091/334373* 🎟 *Free, €3 for treasury, crypt and royal tombs* ⊙ *Mon.–Sat. 7–7, Sun. 7–1 and 4–7.*

La Martorana. Distinguished by an elegant Norman campanile, this church was erected in 1143 but had its interior altered considerably during the Baroque period. High along the western wall, however, is some of the oldest and best-preserved mosaic artwork of the Norman period. Near the entrance is an interesting mosaic of King Roger II being crowned by Christ. In it Roger is dressed in a bejeweled Byzantine stole, reflecting the Norman court's penchant for all things Byzantine. Archangels along the ceiling wear the same stole wrapped around their shoulders and arms. The much plainer San Cataldo is next door. At the time of writing the interior is closed for restoration. ⊠ *Piazza Bellini 3, Quattro Canti* ☎ *091/6161692* ⊙ *Mon.–Sat. 8:30–1 and 3:30–5:30, Sun. 8:30–1.*

Museo Archeologico Regionale Salinas (*Salinas Regional Museum of Archaeology*). Especially interesting pieces in this small but excellent collection are the examples of prehistoric cave drawings and a marvelously reconstructed Doric frieze from the Greek temple at Selinunte, which reveals the high level of artistic culture attained by the Greek colonists in Sicily some 2,500 years ago. (To enter, use the door around the corner on Via Roma.) Extensive renovations at the museum are ongoing, so—if making a special journey from outside town—phone the museum or the tourist information office to check whether it's open. ⊠ *Piazza Olivella 24, Via Roma, Olivella* ☎ *091/6116806* 🎟 *€4, subject to increase when museum reopens* ⊙ *Closed at time of writing; regular hours when open: Tues.–Fri. 8:30–1:30 and 2:30–6:30, weekends 8:30–1; last entry ½ hr before closing.*

Palazzo Reale (*Royal Palace*). This historic palace, also called Palazzo dei Normanni (Norman Palace), was the seat of Sicily's semiautonomous rulers for centuries. The building is a fascinating mesh of abutting 10th-century Norman and 17th-century Spanish structures. Because it now houses the Sicilian Parliament, parts of the palace are closed to the public from Tuesday to Thursday when the regional parliament is sitting. The **Cappella Palatina** (Palatine Chapel) remains open. Built by Roger II in 1132, it's a dazzling example of the harmony of artistic elements

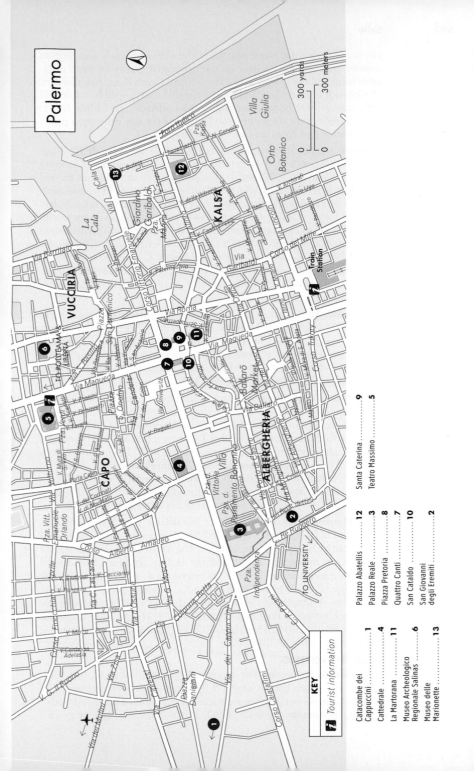

Palermo

KALSA

VUCCIRIA

CAPO

ALBERGHERIA

La Cala

Villa Giulia

Orto Botanico

Train Station

TO POLITEAMA & LIBERTÀ

TO UNIVERSITY

0   300 yards
0   300 meters

produced under the Normans. Here the skill of French and Sicilian masons was brought to bear on the decorative purity of Arab ornamentation and the splendor of 11th-century Greek Byzantine mosaics. The interior is covered with glittering mosaics and capped by a splendid 10th-century Arab honeycomb stalactite wooden ceiling. Biblical stories blend happily with scenes of Arab life—look for one showing a picnic in a harem—and Norman court pageantry.

Upstairs are the royal apartments, including the **Sala di Re Ruggero** (King Roger's Hall), decorated with medieval murals of hunting scenes—an earlier (1120) secular counterpoint to the religious themes seen elsewhere. French, Latin, and Arabic were spoken here, and Arab astronomers and poets exchanged ideas with Latin and Greek scholars in one of the most interesting marriages of culture in the Western world. The Sala is always included with entry to the palace or chapel. ⊠ *Piazza Indipendenza, Albergheria* ☎ *091/6262833* ⊕ *www.federicosecondo. org* ✎ *Palazzo Reale or Cappella Palatina €7, entry to both €8.50* ☯ *Palazzo Reale: Mon.–Sat. 8:15–5:40, Sun. 8:15–1. Cappella Palatina: Fri., Sat., and Mon. 8:15–5:40, Sun. 8:15–9:45 and 11:15–1. Last entry 40 mins before closing.*

San Cataldo. Three striking Saracenic scarlet domes mark this church, built in 1154 during the Norman occupation of Palermo. The church now belongs to the Knights of the Holy Sepulchre and has a spare but intense stone interior. If closed, inquire next door at La Martorana. ⊠ *Piazza Bellini 3, Kalsa* ☎ *091/6161692* ✎ *€2.50* ☯ *Nov.–Feb., daily 9–2.; Mar.–Oct., Mon.–Sat. 9–2 and 3:30–7, Sun. 9–2.*

San Giovanni degli Eremiti. Distinguished by its five reddish-orange domes and stripped-clean interior, this 12th-century church was built by the Normans on the site of an earlier mosque—one of 200 that once stood in Palermo. The emirs ruled Palermo for nearly two centuries and brought to it their passion for lush gardens and fountains. One is reminded of this while sitting in San Giovanni's delightful cloister of twin half-columns, surrounded by palm trees, jasmine, oleander, and citrus trees. ⊠ *Via dei Benedettini 14, Albergheria* ☎ *091/6515019* ✎ *€6* ☯ *Tues.–Sat. 9–7, Mon. and Sun. 9–1:30; last entry ½ hr before closing.*

Teatro Massimo. Construction of this formidable Neoclassical theater, the largest in Italy, was started in 1875 by Giovanni Battista Basile and completed by his son Ernesto in 1897. A reconstruction project started in 1974 ran into gross delays, and the facility remained closed until just before its centenary in 1997. Its interior is as glorious as ever. *The Godfather: Part III* ended with a famous shooting scene on the theater's steps. Visits, by 25-minute guided tour only, are available in five languages, including English. ⊠ *Piazza Verdi 9, at top of Via Maqueda, Olivella* ☎ *091/6053267* 🖷 *091/6053342* ⊕ *www.teatromassimo.it* ✎ *€8* ☯ *Tues.–Sun. 9:30–4:30.*

WORTH NOTING

Catacombe dei Cappuccini. The spookiest sight in all of Sicily, this 16th-century catacomb houses nearly 9,000 corpses of men, women, and young children—some in tombs but many mummified and preserved—hanging in rows on the walls, divided by social caste, age, or gender.

PALERMO'S MULTICULTURAL PEDIGREE

Palermo was first colonized by Phoenician traders in the 6th century BC, but it was their descendants, the Carthaginians, who built the important fortress here that caught the covetous eye of the Romans. After the First Punic War the Romans took control of the city in the 3rd century BC. Following several invasions by the Vandals, Sicily was settled by Arabs, who made the country an emirate and established Palermo as a showpiece capital that rivaled both Córdoba and Cairo in the splendor of its architecture. Nestled in the fertile Conca d'Oro (Golden Conch) plain, full of orange, lemon, and carob groves and enclosed by limestone hills, Palermo became a magical world of palaces and mosques, minarets, and palm trees.

It was so attractive and sophisticated a city that the Norman ruler Roger de Hauteville (1031–1101) decided to conquer it and make it his capital (1072). The Norman occupation of Sicily resulted in Palermo's golden age (1072–1194), a remarkable period of enlightenment and learning in which the arts flourished. The city of Palermo, which in the 11th century counted more than 300,000 inhabitants, became the European center for the Norman court and one of the most important ports for trade between the East and West. Eventually the Normans were replaced by the Swabian ruler Frederick II (1194–1250), the Holy Roman Emperor, and incorporated into the Kingdom of the Two Sicilies. You'll also see plenty of evidence in Palermo of the Baroque art and architecture of the long Spanish rule. The Aragonese viceroys also brought the Spanish Inquisition to Palermo, which some historians believe helped foster the protective secret societies that evolved into today's Mafia.

15

Most wear signs indicating their names and the years they lived. The Capuchins were founders and proprietors of the bizarre establishment (many of the corpses are Capuchin friars) from 1599 to 1911, and it's still under the auspices of the nearby Capuchin church. It was closed when an adjacent cemetery was opened, making the catacombs redundant. Although memorable, this is not a spot for the faint of heart; children might be frightened or disturbed. ⊠ *Piazza Cappuccini 1, off Via Cappuccini, near Palazzo Reale* ☎ *091/6524156* ⊠ *€3* ⊙ *Mon.–Sat. 9–1 and 3–6, Sun. 9–1.*

FAMILY **Museo Internazionale delle Marionette Antonio Pasqualino.** With a collection of more than 4,000 pieces showcasing the traditional Sicilian, and farther afield, *Opera dei Pupi* (puppet shows) these masterpieces with their glittering armor and fierce expressions will delight visitors of all ages. Plots of performances center on the chivalric legends of troubadours of bygone times, in regular episodes to keep you coming back for more. The museum can be hard to find: look for the small alley just off Piazzetta Antonio Pasqualino 5. ⊠ *Piazzetta Antonio Pasqualino 5, near Via Butera, Kalsa* ☎ *091/328060* ⊕ *www.museomarionettepalermo.it* ⊠ *€5* ⊙ *Mon.–Sat. 9–1 and 2:30–6:30, Sun. 10–1. Performances generally Oct.–June, Mon. and Fri. at 5:30 pm.*

Palazzo Abatellis. Housed in this late-15th-century Catalan Gothic palace with Renaissance elements is the **Galleria Regionale.** Among its treasures are the *Annunciation* (1474), a painting by Sicily's prominent Renaissance master Antonello da Messina (1430–79), and an arresting fresco by an unknown 15th-century painter, titled *The Triumph of Death*, a macabre depiction of the plague years. ✉ *Via Alloro 4, Kalsa* ☎ *091/6230011* 🎫 *€8* 🕓 *Tues.–Sat. 9–6, Sun. 9–1.*

Piazza Pretoria. The square's centerpiece, a lavishly decorated fountain with 500 separate pieces of sculpture and an abundance of nude figures, so shocked some Palermitans when it was unveiled in 1575 that it got the nickname "Fountain of Shame." It's even more of a sight when illuminated at night.

Quattro Canti. The Four Corners is the intersection of Corso Vittorio Emanuele and Via Maqueda. Four rather exhaust-blackened Baroque palaces from Spanish rule meet at concave corners, each with its own fountain and representations of a Spanish ruler, patron saint, and one of the four seasons.

Santa Caterina. The walls of this splendid Baroque church (1596) in Piazza Bellini are covered with decorative 17th-century inlays of precious marble. ✉ *Piazza Bellini, Quattro Canti* ☎ *3384512011* 🕓 *Apr.–Sept., daily 9:30–1 and 3–7; Oct.–Mar., daily 9:30–1.*

WHERE TO EAT

$ SICILIAN 🍴 **Antica Focacceria San Francesco.** Turn-of-the-20th-century wooden cabinets, marble-top tables, and cast-iron ovens characterize this neighborhood bakery. Come here for the locally beloved snacks that can be combined to make an inexpensive meal. The big pot on the counter holds the delicious regional specialty *pani ca meusa* (boiled calf's spleen with caciocavallo cheese and salt). The squeamish can opt for some chickpea fritters, an enormous arancino, or the outstanding cannoli. [$] *Average meal: €20* ✉ *Via A.Paternostro 58, Kalsa* ☎ *091/320264* 🕓 *Closed Tues. Oct.–May and 2 wks mid-Jan.*

$$ SICILIAN 🍴 **Casa del Brodo.** On the edge of the Vucciria is a restaurant that dates to 1890, one of Palermo's oldest. In winter its namesake dish, tortellini *in brodo* (in beef broth), is the specialty of the house. There's an extensive antipasto buffet, and you can't go wrong with the *fritella di fave, piselli, carciofi, e ricotta* (fried fava beans, peas, artichokes, and ricotta). Most days they offer a fixed-price meat menu (€19) and a fish menu (€21). A mix of tourists and locals crowds the three small rooms. [$] *Average meal: €30* ✉ *Corso Vittorio Emanuele 175, Vucciria* ☎ *091/321655* 🌐 *www.casadelbrodo.it* 🕓 *Closed Tues. Oct.–May and Sun. Jun.–Sept.*

$$$ SICILIAN Fodor's Choice ★ 🍴 **Osteria dei Vespri.** This foodie paradise occupies a cozy-but-elegant space on an unheralded piazza in the historic city center. Local seafood is a big draw here, so try the superb antipasto *cinque variazioni di crudo dal mare* (five variations of raw delicacies from the sea). Alternately, you can order the ravioli *pieni di ricotta al forno con aroma di cedro* (ricotta ravioli with a citrus fruit aroma)—sheep's-milk cheese ravioli with basil, fresh tomato, eggplant, and crispy onions

adds creative depth to traditional preparation. The wine list is also one of the best in Palermo. The winter menu is traditional fare, but in the summer months the sommelier and chef collaborate to make a special tasting menu (€75) built around Sicilian wines. $ *Average meal: €60* ✉ *Piazza Croce dei Vespri 6, Kalsa* ☎ *091/6171631* ⊕ *www. osteriadeivespri.it* ☉ *Closed Sun.*

$ ✕ **Pani Ca Meusa.** A civic institution facing Palermo's old fishing port,
SICILIAN this joint has been serving its titular calf's spleen sandwich for more than 70 years. The original owner's grandsons produce this local specialty sprinkled with a bit of salt and some lemon and served with or without cheese to a buzzing crowd of Palermo's well-weathered elders. New to the menu are the *panino con panelle* (sandwich with fried chick peas) and potato crocche. In our book, the sandwich (and the overall menu) here beats the Antica Focacceria San Francesco's for the title of best in town. There's no seating, though—only counters. $ *Average meal: €2* ✉ *Via Cala 62, Porta Carbone, Kalsa* ☎ *091/323433* ◿ *Reservations not accepted* ▭ *No credit cards* ☉ *Closed Sun.*

$$ ✕ **Piccolo Napoli.** Founded in 1951, this is one of Old Palermo's most
SICILIAN esteemed seafood eateries. Locals come at midday to feast on the
Fodor's Choice freshest of fish. You can begin with a memorable buffet featuring
★ baby octopus, raw *neonata* (tiny fish resembling sardines but with a milder flavor), and chickpea fritters. Next tuck into spaghetti with sea urchin or *casarecce* (partially rolled pasta) with swordfish and mint; then finish with glorious fresh fish or shellfish, roasted or grilled. Depending on what you select, the bill can creep up on you, but it's worth every cent. $ *Average meal: €40* ✉ *Piazzetta Mulino a Vento 4, Borgo Vecchio* ☎ *091/320431* ☉ *Closed Sun. and last 2 wks in Aug. No dinner Mon.*

$ ✕ **Pizzeria Ai Comparucci.** One of Palermo's best pizzerias serves delicious
PIZZA Neapolitan pies from a big oven in the open kitchen—the genius is in the crust, which is seared in a matter of seconds. The owners make their money on a quick turnover (so don't expect a long, leisurely meal). But the pizza is delicious, and the place often serves until midnight—later than almost any other restaurant in the neighborhood. $ *Average meal: €12* ✉ *Via Messina 36/A, Libertà* ☎ *091/6090467* ☉ *Closed Mon. No lunch.*

$ ✕ **Trattoria Altri Tempi.** This small and friendly "retro" restaurant is a
SICILIAN favorite among locals who pine for the rustic dishes served by their ancestors. A meal begins when the server plunks down a carafe of the house red and a superb spread of traditional antipasti on your table. Dishes have old-fashioned names: *fave a cunigghiu* is fava beans prepared with olive oil, garlic, and remarkably flavorful oregano; and *pasta al'anciova* with a concentrated sauce of tomatoes and anchovies. The meal ends well, too, with free house-made herb or fruit liquors and excellent cannoli. $ *Average meal: €25* ✉ *Via Sammartino 65/67, Libertà* ☎ *091/323480* ☉ *Closed 2 wks late Aug., and Sun. June–Aug.*

$$ ✕ **Trattoria Biondo.** It would be hard to argue that the *lasagne al forno* at
SICILIAN this traditional local restaurant, on a convenient block near Politeama, is anything less than the best in Sicily. The baked lasagna is made with

15

perfectly al dente noodles, a wonderfully seasoned ragù, a silky bécha-mel, and ham for good measure. Another traditional pasta specialty is hand-made *busati* garnished with prawns and pesto made with pista-chio nuts. None of the dining rooms is bigger than an oversize pantry, making for a cozy atmosphere. $ *Average meal: €37* ⊠ *Via Giosué Carducci 15, Libertà* ☎ *091/583662* ☉ *Closed Wed. and Aug.*

WHERE TO STAY

For expanded hotel reviews, visit Fodors.com.

$$
HOTEL
Centrale Palace Hotel. A stone's throw from Palermo's main historic sites, the Centrale Palace is the only hotel in the heart of the centro storico that was once a stately private palace. **Pros:** sparkling clean; good bathrooms; convenient garage parking. **Cons:** traffic noise; some rooms have no view. $ *Rooms from: €180* ⊠ *Corso Vittorio Emanu-ele 327, Vucciria* ☎ *091/336666* ⊕ *www.centralepalacehotel.it* ⇆ *88 rooms, 16 suites* ❙❂❙ *Breakfast.*

$$$
HOTEL
Hotel Principe di Villafranca. Fine Sicilian antiques, imperial striped silks, creamy marble floors, and vaulted ceilings evoke a luxurious pri-vate home in the heart of Palermo's glitzy shopping district. **Pros:** help-ful staff; well-maintained building; safe neighborhood. **Cons:** breakable knick-knacks make it unsuitable for small children; bathrooms are on the small side. $ *Rooms from: €230* ⊠ *Via G. Turrisi Colonna 4, Lib-ertà* ☎ *091/6118523* ⊕ *www.principedivillafranca.it* ⇆ *29 rooms, 3 junior suites* ❙❂❙ *Breakfast.*

$
B&B/INN
Le Terrazze. Though it's just steps from the bustling streets around the Cattedrale, complete calm envelops this small, beautifully restored B&B, named for its five roof terraces, all with sublime views of Palermo's skyline. **Pros:** convenient location; in summer, breakfast is served on the glorious rooftop. **Cons:** parking can be difficult; books up quickly. $ *Rooms from: €110* ⊠ *Via Pietro Novelli 14, Capo* ☎ *091/6520866, 320/4328567* ⊕ *www.leterrazzebb.it* ⇆ *2 rooms* ▤ *No credit cards* ☉ *Closed Nov. and Feb.* ❙❂❙ *Breakfast.*

$$
HOTEL
Massimo Plaza Hotel. Small and select, this hotel enjoys one of Pal-ermo's best locations—opposite the renovated Teatro Massimo, on the border of the old and new towns. **Pros:** central location; low-season bargains; airport taxi service. **Cons:** plain interiors; some noisy rooms. $ *Rooms from: €180* ⊠ *Via Maqueda 437, Vucciria* ☎ *091/325657* ⊕ *www.massimoplazahotel.com* ⇆ *15 rooms* ❙❂❙ *Breakfast.*

$$$
HOTEL
Villa Igiea. This grand dame, a local landmark for a century, is an oasis of luxury and comfort set in a private tropical garden at the edge of the bay. **Pros:** secluded setting; historic building with lots of style; free shuttle to city center in the summer. **Cons:** noise and fumes from nearby marina; service is hit or miss. $ *Rooms from: €230* ⊠ *Salita Belmonte 42, 3 km (2 miles) north of Palermo, Acquasanta* ☎ *091/6312111* ⊕ *www.amthotels.it* ⇆ *110 rooms, 6 suites* ❙❂❙ *Breakfast.*

NIGHTLIFE AND THE ARTS

THE ARTS

CONCERTS AND OPERA

Teatro Massimo. Teatro Massimo is truly larger than life—it's the biggest theater in Italy. Concerts and operas are presented throughout the year, though in summer concerts are usually held outdoors. An opera at the Massimo is an unforgettable Sicilian experience. ⊠ *Piazza Verdi, at top of Via Maqueda, Capo* ☎ *091/6053580, 06/48078400* 🖷 *091/6053391* ⊕ *www.teatromassimo.it* 🎫 *Tours €8, performances €15–€125* ⊙ *Tours: Tues.–Sun. 9:30–5; Box office: Tues.–Sun. 10–3.*

Teatro Politeama Garibaldi. The shamelessly grandiose Neoclassical Teatro Politeama Garibaldi stages a season of opera and orchestral works from November through May. ⊠ *Piazza Ruggero Settimo, Libertà* ☎ *091/6072532.*

PUPPET SHOWS

FAMILY **Figli d'Arte Cuticchio Association.** Palermo's tradition of puppet theater holds an appeal for children and adults alike, and street artists often perform outside the Teatro Massimo in summer. The Figli d'Arte Cuticchio Association hosts performances most weekends (6:30 pm) from September to June. ⊠ *Via Bara all'Olivella 95, Kalsa* ☎ *091/323400* ⊕ *www.figlidartecuticchio.com* 🎫 *€8.*

NIGHTLIFE

Each night between 6 and 9, Palermo's youth gather to shop, socialize, flirt, and plan the evening's affairs in an epic passeggiata along Via Ruggero Settimo (a northern extension of Via Maqueda) and filling Piazza Ruggero Settimo in front of Teatro Politeama. Some trendy bars also line Via Principe del Belmonte, intersecting with Via Roma and Via Ruggero Settimo.

BARS AND CAFÉS

Kursaal Kalhesa. Truly representative of the New Palermo, this is one of the most fascinating places to drink or socialize. Down by the port and the Porta Felice, it attracts an energetic, eclectic crowd of Palermitan youth for lively jazz, coffee, and drinks inside an ancient city wall with spectacular 100-foot ceilings and an idyllic courtyard. Interesting, if pricey, Sicilian food with an Arab touch is served in the adjacent restaurant. ⊠ *Foro Umberto I 21, Kalsa* ☎ *091/6162111* ⊕ *www. kursaalkalhesa.it* ⊙ *Closed Mon.*

Santa Monica. Immensely popular with the twenty- and thirtysomething crowd, who belly up to the bar for pizza, bruschetta, and, of course, excellent German-style draft beer, this pub is also a good place to watch televized soccer. ⊠ *Via E. Parisi 7, Libertà* ☎ *091/324735* ⊕ *www.santamonicapub.it.*

SHOPPING

North of Piazza Castelnuovo, Via della Libertà and the surrounding streets represent the luxury end of the shopping scale. A second nerve center for shoppers is the pair of parallel streets connecting modern

15

Palermo with the train station, Via Roma and Via Maqueda, where boutiques and shoe shops become increasingly upscale as you move from the Quattro Canti past Teatro Massimo to Via Ruggero Settimo.

Most shops are open 9–1 and 4 or 4:30–7:30 or 8 and closed Sunday and on Monday morning; in addition, most food shops are closed on Wednesday afternoon.

FOOD AND WINE

Enoteca Picone. The best wine shop in town has a fantastic selection of Sicilian and national wines. Though the service can be curt, you can taste a selection of wines by the glass in the front of the store. There are tables in the back, where meats and cheeses are also served. ⊠ *Via Marconi 36, Libertà* ☎ *091/331300* ⊕ *www.enotecapicone.it* ⊘ *Closed Sun.*

I Peccatucci di Mamma Andrea. With a name that means "Mamma Andrea's small sins," this charming store sells a plethora of mouth-watering original creations, including jams, preserves, and Sicilian treats like the superb marzipan *frutta di Martorana.* ⊠ *Via Principe di Scordia 67, near Piazza Florio, Vucciria* ☎ *091/334835* ⊕ *www. mammaandrea.it.*

Pasticceria Alba. One of the most famous sweets shops in Italy, this is the place to find favorite pastries such as cannoli and cassata siciliana. ⊠ *Piazza Don Bosco 7/C, off Via della Libertà near La Favorita Park, Libertà* ☎ *091/309016* ⊕ *www.pasticeriaalba.it.*

MARKETS

Ballarò Market. Wind your way through the Albergheria district and this historic market, where the Saracens did their shopping in the 11th century—joined by the Normans in the 12th. The market remains faithful to seasonal change as well as the original Arab commerce of fruit, vegetables, and grain. Go early; the action dies out by 4 pm most days.

Bancherelle (*market stalls*). If you're interested in truly connecting with local life while searching for souvenirs, a visit to one of Palermo's many bustling markets is essential. Between Via Roma and Via Maqueda, the many bancherelle on Via Bandiera sell everything from socks to imitation designer handbags.

Vucciria Market. It's easy to see how this market got its name—*vucciria* translates to "voices" or "hubbub. Palermo's most established outdoor market, in the heart of the centro storico, is a maze of side streets around Piazza San Domenico, where hawkers deliver incessant chants from behind stands brimming with mounds of olives, blood oranges, fennel, and long-stem artichokes. One hawker will be going at the trunk of a swordfish with a cleaver while across the way another holds up a giant squid or dangles an octopus. Morning is the best time to see the market in full swing.

THE TYRRHENIAN COAST

Sicily's northern shore, the Tyrrhenian Coast, is mostly a succession of small holiday towns interspersed with stretches of sand. It's often difficult to find a calm spot among the thousands of tourists and locals in high summer, though the scene quiets down considerably after August. The biggest attraction is the old town of Cefalù, with one of Sicily's most remarkable medieval cathedrals, encrusted with mosaics. The coast on either side is dotted with ancient archaeological remains and Arab-Norman buildings.

Some 48 km (30 miles) south of Cefalù, Pizzo Carbonara (6,500 feet) is the highest peak in Sicily after Mount Etna. Piano della Battaglia has a fully equipped ski resort with lifts. The area has a very un-Sicilian aspect, with Swiss-type chalets, hiking paths, and even Alpine churches.

15

CEFALÙ

70 km (43 miles) east of Palermo, 161 km (100 miles) west of Messina.

The coast between Palermo and Messina is dotted with charming villages. Tindari (which dates back to the early Christian era) and Laghetti di Maranello are two that are worth a stop, but it's Cefalù, a classically appealing Sicilian old town built on a spur jutting out into the sea, that's the jewel of the coast.

GETTING HERE AND AROUND

Trains and buses run between Palermo and Messina. Drivers can take the A20 Autostrada.

VISITOR INFORMATION

Cefalù Tourism Office ⊠ *Corso Ruggero 77* ☎ *0921/421050.*

EXPLORING

Duomo. Cefalù is dominated by a massive headland—*la rocca*—and a 12th-century Romanesque Duomo, which is one of the finest Norman cathedrals in Italy. Roger II began the church in 1131 as an offering of thanks for having been saved here from a shipwreck. Its mosaics rival those of Monreale. (Whereas Monreale's Byzantine Christ figure is an austere and powerful image, emphasizing Christ's divinity, the Cefalù Christ is softer, more compassionate, and more human.) The traffic going in and out of Cefalù town can be heavy in summer, so you may want to take the 50-minute train ride from Palermo instead of driving. At the Duomo you must be suitably attired—no shorts or beachwear are permitted. ⊠ *Piazza Duomo* ☎ *0921/922021* ⊙ *Oct.–Apr., daily 8–noon and 3:30–5; May–Sept., daily 8–6; hours may be subject to change, so check before visiting.*

WHERE TO EAT

$$ ✕ **Al Porticciolo.** Nicola Mendolia runs two restaurants, 50 feet apart,
SICILIAN both comfortable, casual, and faithfully focused on food. You might start with the *calamaretti piccoli fritti* (fried baby squid and octopus) and then follow with one of the chef's specials, which change weekly. Regardless, a refreshing *sgroppino* (whipped lemon sorbet with

spumante) should end the meal. Dark, heavy, wooden tables create a comfortable environment filled with a mix of jovial locals and businesspeople. $ *Average meal: €45* ✉ *Via C. Ortolani di Bordonaro 66 and 86* ☎ *0921/921981* 🕒 *Closed Wed. Nov.–Apr.*

THE AEOLIAN ISLANDS

Off Sicily's northeast coast lies an archipelago of seven spectacular islands of volcanic origin. The Isole Eolie (Aeolian Islands), also known as the Isole Lipari (Lipari Islands), were named after Aeolus, the Greek god of the winds, who is said to keep all the Earth's winds stuffed in a bag in his cave here.

The Aeolians are a world of grottoes and clear-water caves carved by waves through the centuries. Superb snorkeling and scuba diving abound in the clearest and cleanest of Italy's waters. The beautiful people of high society discovered the archipelago years ago—here Roberto Rossellini courted his future wife, Ingrid Bergman, in 1950—so you shouldn't expect complete isolation, at least on the main islands. August, in particular, can get unpleasantly overcrowded, and lodging and travel should always be booked as early as possible.

Lipari provides the widest range of accommodations and is a good jumping-off point for day trips to the other islands. Most exclusive are Vulcano and Panarea: the former is noted for its black sands and stupendous sunsets, as well as the acrid smell of its sulfur emissions, whereas the latter is, according to some, the prettiest. Most remarkable is Stromboli (pronounced with the accent on the first syllable) with its constant eruptions, while the greenest island—and the one with the best hiking trails—is Salina. The remotest are Filicudi and Alicudi, where electricity was introduced only in the 1980s, and broadband internet connections are still the stuff of pipedreams.

The bars in the Aeolian Islands, and especially those on Lipari, are known for their granitas of fresh strawberries, melon, peaches, and other fruits. Many Sicilians on the Aeolians (and in Messina, Taormina, and Catania) begin the hot summer days with a granita *di caffè* (a coffee ice topped with whipped cream), into which they dunk their breakfast rolls. You can get one any time of day.

GETTING HERE AND AROUND

Car ferries and much faster hydrofoils carry passengers to and between the islands. They depart from Milazzo and Messina (on Sicily), and from Reggio di Calabria (on the mainland), with the majority stopping at Lipari before continuing on to other islands in the chain. Service is most frequent in summer. May to September, a few car ferries a week also provide overnight service to and from Naples; during that same period hydrofoils run to and from Naples, Cefalù, and Palermo. Operators' websites are the best source of information regarding schedules and fares.

Ferry and Hydrofoil Contacts N.G.I ☎ *090/9283415, 800/250000* 🌐 *www.ngi-spa.it* 💳 *No credit cards.* **SNAV** ☎ *081/4285555* 🌐 *www.snav.it* 💳 *No credit cards.* **Siremar** ☎ *095/7493315* 🌐 *www.siremar.it* 💳 *No credit cards.* **Ustica Lines** ☎ *0923/873813* 🌐 *www.usticalines.it* 💳 *No credit cards.*

LIPARI

2 hrs and 10 mins from Milazzo by ferry, 1 hr by hydrofoil; 60–75 mins from Reggio di Calabria and Messina by ferry.

The largest and most developed of the Aeolians, Lipari welcomes you with distinctive pastel-color houses. Fields of spiky agaves dot the northernmost tip of the island, Acquacalda, indented with pumice and obsidian quarries. In the west is San Calogero, where you can explore hot springs and mud baths. From the red-lava base of the island rises a plateau crowned with a 16th-century castle and a 17th-century cathedral.

GETTING HERE AND AROUND

Ferries and hydrofoils from Milazzo, which is 41 km (25 miles) west of Messina, stop here. There's also ferry service from Reggio di Calabria and Messina.

VISITOR INFORMATION

15

Lipari Tourism Office. The office is scheduled to relocate; call, or check the website before visiting. ⊠ *Corso Vittorio Emanuele 202* ☎ *090/9880095.*

EXPLORING

Fodor's Choice ★ **Museo Archeologico Eoliano.** The vast, multibuilding Museo Archeologico Eoliano is a terrific museum, with an intelligently arranged collection of prehistoric finds—some dating as far back as 4000 BC—from various sites in the archipelago. ⊠ *Via Castello 2* ☎ *090/9880174* ⊕ *www. regione.sicilia.it/beniculturali/museolipari* ⊠ *€6* ☉ *Mon.–Sat. 9–1.30 and 3–7, Sun. 9–1:30; last entry 1 hr before closing.*

Fodor's Choice ★ **Vulcano.** A popular day-trip from Lipari is to visit the most notorious of the Aeolian Islands: Vulcano. True to its name—and the origin of the term—Vulcano has a profusion of fumeroles sending up jets of hot vapor, though the volcano here has long been dormant. This is an island most travelers wish to visit, perhaps to soak in the strong-smelling sulphur springs, but not to stay on: when the wind is right, the odors greet you long before you disembark. The island has some of the archipelago's best beaches, though the volcanic black sand can be off-putting at first glance. Ascend to the crater (1,266 feet above sea level) on muleback for eye-popping views or take a boat ride into the grottoes around the base. From Capo Grillo you can see all the Aeolians. **Ustica Lines** (☎ *0923/873813* ⊕ *www.usticalines.it*) has high-speed passenger vessels that make the crossing from Lipari in 10 minutes. Frequent daily departures are offered year-round, with round-trip tickets priced at €11.

WHERE TO EAT AND STAY

For expanded hotel reviews, visit Fodors.com.

$$ SICILIAN Fodor's Choice ★ ✕ **Filippino.** The views from this upper-town restaurant's outdoor terrace are a fitting complement to the superb fare featured on its menu. Founded in 1910, Filippino is rightly rated as one of the archipelago's best dining venues—you'll understand why when you sample the seafood. *Zuppa di pesce* (fish soup) and the antipasto platter of smoked and marinated fish are absolute musts. Just leave some room for the local version of cassata siciliana, accompanied by sweet Malvasia

wine from Salina. $ *Average meal: €40* ⊠ *Piazza Mazzini Lipari* ☎ *090/9811002* ⊕ *www.eolieexperience.it* ⊘ *Closed mid-Nov.–late Dec., and Mon. Oct.–Mar.*

$$$
HOTEL
▦ **Gattopardo Park Hotel.** Bright bougainvillea and fiery hibiscus set the tone at this grand villa, and its restaurant has sweeping views of the sea. **Pros:** friendly staff; good recreational facilities; large pool. **Cons:** a bit removed from the port; staff doesn't speak English. $ *Rooms from: €220* ⊠ *Viale Diana* ☎ *090/9811035* ⊕ *www.gattopardoparkhotel.it* ⇆ *47 rooms* ⊘ *Closed Nov.–Mar.* ⦿I *Some meals.*

SALINA

50 mins from Lipari by ferry, 20 mins by hydrofoil.

The second largest of the Aeolians, Salina is also the most fertile—which accounts for its excellent Malvasia dessert wine. Salina is the archipelago's lushest and highest island, too (Mt. Fossa delle Felci rises to more than 3,000 feet), and the vineyards and fishing villages along its slopes add to its allure. Pollara, in the west of the island, has capitalized on its fame as one of the locations in the 1990s cult movie, *Il Postino* (*The Postman*), and is an ideal location for an evening passeggiata on well-maintained paths along the volcanic terrain.

GETTING HERE AND AROUND
Ferries and hydrofoils arrive here from Lipari.

WHERE TO STAY
For expanded hotel reviews, visit Fodors.com.

$$
HOTEL
▦ **Hotel Solemar.** In a valley between Salina's two mountains, this hotel has most of the hallmarks of Mediterranean charm—large terraces for contemplation, a location in a sleepy town, and pleasing food served on summer evenings in the restaurant. **Pros:** relaxed atmosphere; helpful staff; terrific views. **Cons:** no pool; hit-and-miss Wi-Fi in public areas; a 15-minute taxi ride from Salina's main port. $ *Rooms from: €180* ⊠ *Via Roma 8, Leni* ☎ *090/9809445* ⊕ *www.salinasolemarhotel. it* ⇆ *13* ⊘ *Closed Nov.–Mar.*

PANAREA

2 hrs from Lipari by ferry, 25–50 mins by hydrofoil; 7–9 hrs from Naples by ferry.

Panarea has some of the most dramatic scenery of the islands: wild caves carved out of the rock and dazzling flora. The exceptionally clear water and the richness of life on the sea floor make Panarea especially suitable for underwater exploration, though there's little in the way of beaches. The outlying rocks and islets make a gorgeous sight, and you can enjoy the panorama on an easy excursion to the small Bronze Age village at Capo Milazzese.

GETTING HERE AND AROUND
Ferries and hydrofoils arrive here from Lipari and Naples.

WHERE TO STAY

For expanded hotel reviews, visit Fodors.com.

$$$$
HOTEL

🖼 **Il Raya.** Discreet, expensive, looking out over the sea toward Stromboli, Il Raya is perfectly in keeping with the elite style of Panarea, most exclusive of the Aeolian Islands. **Pros:** great views of Stromboli; fashionable ambience; well-known dance club on the premises. **Cons:** snooty staff; uphill trudge to rooms; mediocre food; dance club means noise after dark. $ *Rooms from: €420* ⊠ *San Pietro* 🖃 *090/983013* ⊕ *www.hotelraya.it* 🛏 *36 rooms* ☉ *Closed mid-Oct.–mid-Apr.* ⦿ *Breakfast.*

15

STROMBOLI

3 hrs and 45 mins from Lipari by ferry, 65–90 mins by hydrofoil; 9 hrs from Naples by ferry, 5 hrs by hydrofoil.

This northernmost of the Aeolians consists entirely of the cone of an active volcano. The view from the sea—especially at night, as an endless stream of glowing red-hot lava flows into the water—is unforgettable. Stromboli is in a constant state of mild dissatisfaction, and every now and then its anger flares up, so authorities insist that you climb to the top (about 3,031 feet above sea level) only with a guide. The round-trip—climb, pause, and descent—usually starting around 6 pm, takes about six hours; the lava is much more impressive after dark. Some choose to camp overnight atop the volcano—again, a guide is essential. The main town has a small selection of reasonably priced hotels and restaurants and a choice of lively clubs and cafés for the younger set. In addition to the island tour, excursions might include boat trips around the naturally battlemented isle of Strombolicchio.

GETTING HERE AND AROUND

Ferries and hydrofoils arrive here from Lipari and Naples.

EXPLORING

Pippo Navigazione. Numerous tour operators have guides that can lead you up Stromboli or take you round in a boat, among them Pippo Navigazione. Rates are around €25 per person for three hours. A €20 night tour explores where the lava reaches the sea. 🖃 *090/986135, 338/9857883.*

FILICUDI

30–60 mins from Salina and Lipari by hydrofoil; 2 hrs from Cefalù and Palermo, 2 hrs from Milazzo, and 10 hrs from Naples by ferry.

Just a dot in the sea, Filicudi is famous for its unusual volcanic rock formations and the enchanting Grotta del Bue Marino (Grotto of the Sea Ox). The crumbled remains of a prehistoric village are at Capo Graziano. The island, which is spectacular for walking and hiking and is still a truly undiscovered, restful haven, has a handful of hotels and pensions, and some families put up guests. Car ferries are available only in summer.

GETTING HERE AND AROUND

Ferries and hydrofoils arrive throughout the year from Salina and Lipari, and also in summer from Palermo, Cefalù, Milazzo, and Naples.

WHERE TO STAY

For expanded hotel reviews, visit Fodors.com.

$$ La Canna. It's wonderful to wake up to the utter tranquility that
HOTEL   characterizes a stay on Filicudi—especially if you happen to be greeting the day at this hotel, set above the tiny port. **Pros:** relaxed setting; family-friendly atmosphere; great views. **Cons:** an uphill climb from the port; half or full board required in peak season. $ *Rooms from: €150* ⊠ *Via Rosa 43* ☎ *090/9889956* 🖨 *090/2509929* ⊕ *www.lacannahotel. it* ⌁ *14 rooms* ⊙ *Closed Nov.–Mar.* �101 *Some meals.*

SARDINIA

WELCOME TO SARDINIA

TOP REASONS TO GO

★ **Relax on idyllic beaches:** Covering more than 1,200 miles of coastline, Sardinia's beaches beckon with their turquoise waters, white sand, and rippled dunes.

★ **Discover natural beauty:** A network of trails explores Sardinia's resplendent mountains, deep gorges, lush forests, and cascading waterfalls.

★ **Explore charming towns and villages:** From coastal towns to rural villages, the island is dotted with a variety of settlements that take pride in their history and tradition. Each has its own culture, cuisine, and unique way of life.

★ **Dive or snorkel the outer reefs:** Crystalline waters, warm weather and outer reefs make Sardinia a paradise for underwater adventurers. Sunken ships and marine reserves provide the ideal place to discover marine life.

★ **Savor Sardinian delicacies:** From pasta and prosciutto to lamb and cheese, the island's cuisine is sure to satisfy any appetite.

1 Cagliari and the Southern Coast. The gateway to Sardinia's spectacular coastline, Cagliari bustles with modern commercial activity while preserving ancient history as the island's capital. Along the southern coast, rural coastal villages stretch along idyllic waters, and archaeological ruins enrich the breathtaking natural beauty of the dramatic mountain peaks, and rugged promontories. Pristine white sand beaches are set against flawless sapphire seas.

2 Su Nuraxi to the Costa Smeralda. From the UNESCO World Heritage Site of Su Nuraxi—a mysterious complex of bee-hive stone structures near the town of Barumini—to the remote beaches, secluded coves, enchanting enclaves, posh towns, and luxury resorts along the northern coast, this region is a summer playground for the world's rich and famous. Iconic Porto Cervo serves as the hedonistic heart, where superyachts moor after sun-drenched days in Romazzino, Liscia Ruia, Capriccioli, Rena Bianca, and Del Principe. The Emerald Coast's unparalleled beauty stretches into the archipelago of La Maddalena, site of one of the world's most important marine wildlife reserves.

GETTING ORIENTED

The soul of Sardinia lies in its spectacular natural beauty and historical roots dating back to the Bronze Age. With Europe's highest dunes in the southwest, deepest canyons in the mountainous center, and best beaches on eastern and western coastlines, Sardinia enchants with fortified towns, open air museums, stunning vistas, and crystalline coastal waters from north to south.

16

By Victoria
Tang

The second largest island in the Mediterranean, Sardinia
remains unique and enigmatic with its stretches of rugged
coastline and white-sand beaches, dramatic granite cliffs
and mountainous inlands, and modern provinces and
medieval villages.

Would-be conquerors from all directions—Phoenicians, Carthaginians, Romans, Catalans, Pisans, Piemontese—have left their traces,
but no single outside culture has had a dominant impact. Pockets
of foreign influence persist along the coasts (for example, the walled
Catalan city of Alghero), but inland, a proud Sardinian culture and
language flourish.

As a travel destination, Sardinia's identity is split: the island has some of
Europe's most expensive resorts, but it's also home to untamed naturally
pristine areas, untouched by commercial development. Fine sand and
clean waters draw summer sun-worshippers to beaches, unquestionably
among the best in the Mediterranean. Most famous are those along the
Costa Smeralda (Emerald Coast), where the über-rich have anchored
their yachts since the 1960s. Less-exclusive beach holidays can be found
elsewhere on the island at La Maddalena, Villasimius, and Pula. There
are also wonderfully intact medieval towns—Cagliari, Oristano, Sassari—on or near the water.

Apart from the glamorous shores and upscale locales found in the east,
most of Sardinia's coast is rugged and unreachable, a jagged series of
wildly beautiful inlets accessible only by sea. Inland, Sardinia remains
shepherd's country, silent and stark. Against this landscape are the striking and mysterious stone *nuraghi* (ancient defensive structures) that
provide clues to the island's ancient culture. Found only on Sardinia,
these sites have been included on the UNESCO World Heritage List in
what is considered "the finest and most complete example of a remarkable form of prehistoric architecture."

SARDINIA PLANNER

GETTING HERE AND AROUND

AIR TRAVEL

Flying is by far the fastest and easiest way to get to the island. Sardinia's major airport, Aeroporto di Elmas, is in Cagliari, with smaller ones at Alghero (Aeroporto Fertilia) and Olbia (Aeroporto Costa Smeralda).

Airport Contacts Aeroporto Alghero-Fertilia (AHO). ⊠ *Regione Nuraghe Biancu* ☎ *079/935282* ⊕ *www.aeroportodialghero.it.* **Aeroporto Cagliari-Elmas** (CAG). ⊠ *Via dei Trasvolatori* ☎ *070/211211* 🖷 *070/241013* ⊕ *www.sogaer.it.* **Aeroporto Oblia Costa Smeralda** (OLB). ⊠ *Regione Aeroporto Costa Smeralda* ☎ *0789/563444* ⊕ *www.geasar.it/it.*

BUS TRAVEL

Cagliari is linked with the other towns of Sardinia by a network of buses. All major cities and most local destinations are served by ARST. The heart of the Sardinian bus system is the Stazione Autolinee, across the square from the main tourist office in Cagliari. City buses in Cagliari and Sassari operate on the same system as those on the mainland: buy your ticket first, at a tobacco shop or machine, and punch it in the machine on the bus.

16

Contacts ARST. ⊠ *Sede territoriale di Cagliari, Piazza Matteotti 9, Cagliari* ☎ *800/865 042 in Italy* ☉ *Mon.–Sat.7–2,* ☎ *070/4098324 abroad* ⊕ *www.arst.sardegna.it.* **Stazione Autolinee.** ⊠ *Via F. Domiziano 9, Roma* ☎ *39/0514210530* ⊕ *www.ibus.it.*

CAR TRAVEL

Sardinia is about 260 km (162 miles) long from north to south and takes three to four hours to drive on the main roads; it's roughly 120 km (75 miles) across. Cars may be taken on board most of the ferry lines connecting Sardinia with the mainland.

Roads are generally in good condition with clear signage pointing you in the right direction. "Superstrade" double lane routes are well developed. Expect winding inland mountain and coastal roads with hairpin turns. Gas stations are closed on Sunday and roadside facilities are infrequent, especially in the east. Try to avoid driving at night, when mountain roads are particularly hazardous and dark. Fog is an issue in winter.

TRAIN TRAVEL

The Stazione Centrale in Cagliari is next to the bus station on Piazza Matteotti. There are fairly good connections between Olbia, Cagliari, Sassari, and Oristano. Service on the few other local lines is infrequent and slow. The fastest train between Olbia and Cagliari takes more than four hours. Local trains connect Golfo Aranci, the Ferrovie dello Stato (Italian State Railways, or Trenitalia) port for the train ferry, with Olbia (20 minutes), and Sassari with Alghero (35 minutes).

Contacts Ferrovie dello Stato. ☎ *892021* ⊕ *www.fsitaliane.it.* **Trenino Verde della Sardegna.** ☎ *070/580 246 in Italy, 39 070/40981 abroad* ⊕ *www.treninoverde.com* ☉ *June–mid-Sept.*

WHEN TO GO

The best time to visit Sardinia is May through September. European vacationers flock to the island for sunshine in July and August. Expect to pay the highest rates during these two peak summer months, when roads, tourist sites, and beaches are most crowded. From September to early October, when accommodations start to shut down for the year, you'll find end-of-season deals and fewer tourists. Any other time of year, expect near–ghost towns of closed restaurants, hotels and shops.

RESTAURANTS

Sardinia is a gastronomic paradise. Feast on mouthwatering local cuisine in a wide selection of restaurants highlighting regional ingredients and cooking techniques that draw out incredible flavors. With its culinary history rooted in both fertile sea and land, Sardinia's best foods include fresh fish and crustaceans, *su porchedddu* (spit-roasted suckling pig), pasta *con carciofi e bottarga* (with artichokes and fresh mullet roe), burrida (dogfish), culurgiones (stuffed ravioli), and flakey *panada* (meat pie). Although wood-oven pizzas of every kind are ubiquitous, opt for antipasti and platti di mare or terra to savor authentic Sardinian cuisine at its finest.

Please note that restaurant prices listed as "average meal" include a meal consisteing of first course (primo), second course (secondo), and dessert (dolce).

HOTELS

In Sardinia, there are numerous luxury resorts with stunning beachfront vistas, B&B inns in medieval villages, private villas tucked away on lush hills, modern hotels in the trendy capital, and farmhouses on tranquil mountainsides. During summer months, the most popular destination on the island is the Costa Smeralda in the east. High demand during July and August raises nightly rates to an astronomical range above €1,500 for the most deluxe accommodations. Find more reasonable hotel rates in other parts of the island, equally breathtaking and less crowded. Plan dates well in advance as many hotels close at the end of September until the following April or May.

Prices in the hotel reviews are the lowest cost of a standard double room in high season, excluding taxes, service charges, and meal plans (except at all-inclusives). Prices for rentals are the lowest per-night cost for a one-bedroom unit in high season.

TOURS

Cagliari-based travel agency, Viaggi Orrù, conducts tours of Sardinia. The Associazione Nazionale di Turismo Equestre can provide information on horseback riding tours for individuals or groups along the coast and inland. The Centro Vacanze Ala Birdi organizes riding vacations that showcase horsemanship and the historic relationship of equines and Sardinia culture.

Contacts Associazione Nazionale di Turismo Equestre ✉ *Via Carso 35/a, Sassari* ☎ *070/305816 Cagliari, 0783/71586 Oristano, 079/299889 Sassari.* **Viaggi Orrù** ✉ *Via Pola 41, Cagliari* ☎ *070/659858* ⊕ *www.viaggiorru.com.* **Centro Vacanze Ala Birdi** ✉ *Strada Ventiquattresima Ovest 27, near Oristano, Arborea* ☎ *0783 805 00, 0783 801 083* ⊕ *www.horsecountry.it.*

CAGLIARI AND THE SOUTHERN COAST

Cagliari (pronounced *Cahl*-yah-ree) is Sardinia's capital and largest city; it contains the island's principal art and archaeology museums as well as an old cathedral and medieval towers that have lofty views of the surrounding sea, lagoons, and mountains. East of Cagliari the coast is no less scenic, but it's more developed; though blissfully uncommercialized for the most part in the old town up on the hill, the coast, port area, and surrounding regions toward the airport have pockets of development and industrial zones that have sprouted. To the southwest, Pula is an inland town within easy reach of both good beaches and the excavated ruins at Nora.

CAGLIARI

268 km (166 miles) south of Olbia.

Known in Sardinia as Casteddu, the island's capital of nearly 160,000 inhabitants has steep streets and impressive Italianate architecture in styles ranging from modern to medieval. Cagliari is characterized by a busy commercial center and waterfront with broad avenues and arched arcades, as well as by the typically narrow streets of the old hilltop citadel (called, simply, *Castello*). A visit to the city is not complete without seeing the imposing Bastion of Saint Remy and strolling through Mercato di San Benedetto, considered to be one of the best fish markets in Italy.

GETTING HERE AND AROUND

The easiest way to arrive in Cagliari is by plane or boat. From the airport, it's easy to get into the city center by bus or taxi. You can also rent a car at the airport; pre-booking before arrival is highly recommended. If you arrive by boat, travel from Trapani or Palermo (Sicily), Civitavecchia (Rome), or Naples. The port is located steps away from the city center.

ESSENTIALS

Cagliari ⊠ *Piazza Matteotti 9, Cagliari* ☎ *070/669255* ⊠ *Tourism Office at SEARCH (Municipal Building), Largo Carlo Felice 2* ☎ *39 070/6777187* ⊕ *www.cagliariturismo.it* ⊗ *Daily 8–8.*

EXPLORING

Castello. On the narrow streets of this hillside quarter perched over the vast expanse of Cagliari and its port, discover ancient monuments and piazzi amidst sidewalk cafés and humble dwellings with wash hung out to dry on elaborate wrought-iron balconies. Enter through the commanding medieval archway of the Bastione San Remy on the Piazza Costituzione and climb up to the Piazza Palazzo to view the Cagliari Cathedral, the 13th-century limestone Saint Pancras, and Elephant Towers. An impressive panorama of the cityscape and Gulf of Cagliari is best seen from Piazza Indepenza. ⊕ *www.comune.cagliari.it.*

Duomo. Cattedrale di Santa Maria, also known as the Duomo, was begun in the 12th century, but major renovation in the 17th century and reconstruction during the mid-1930s have left little of the original medieval church. The tiers of columns on the facade resemble those

16

of medieval Pisan Romanesque churches, but only sections of the central portal, the bell tower, and the two side entrances are from the 13th century. Look for one of the most memorable features inside—the oversized marble pulpit sculpted in the 1300's and divided in half to fit into the church nave. ✉ *Piazza Palazzo off Via Martini* ☏ *070/663837* ⊕ *www.duomodicagliari.it* ⊙ *Daily 7:30–noon and 4–8; hrs vary during holidays.*

Museo Archeologico. Begin your visit to Cagliari at the archaeological museum within the walls of a castle erected by Pisans in the early 1300s to ward off the Aragonese and Catalans (attacking from what is now Spain). Among the intriguing artifacts are bronze statuettes from the tombs and dwellings of Sardinia's earliest inhabitants, who remain a prehistoric enigma. Ancient writers called them the "nuraghic people" from the name of their curious stone dwellings, the *nuraghi,* which are unique to Sardinia. Archaeologists date most of the nuraghi to about 1300–1200 BC, the same time the ancient Israelites were establishing themselves in Canaan. The museum is the world's foremost authority on this particular ancient civilization. Of special interest are the pearl-laden Phoenician faience necklace, medieval gold coins, and remnants of the Nora and Tuvixeddu necropolis. ✉ *Cittadella dei Musei, Piazza Arsenale* ☏ *070/684800, 070/070655911* ⊕ *www.comune.cagliari.it* ▭ *€3* ⊙ *Tues.–Sun. 9–8; ticket office closes at 7:15.*

<table>
<tr><td>OFF THE
BEATEN
PATH</td><td>

San Sperate. Considered a *paese museo,* literally "museum country," the walls of houses throughout this small town 20 km (12 miles) northwest of Cagliari have been brightened with *murales* (murals) by local artists and some well-known Italian painters. The murals were begun in the 1960s and continue to be expanded, transforming the entire town into an open-air art gallery with its series of colorful trompe l'oeils and artistic renderings of daily life. Look for suggestive stone and bronze sculptures by world-renowned Pinoccio Sciola that also pay tribute to the region's ancient history. ✉ *Via Sassari and adjoining streets throughout commune* ☏ *070/9601434* ⊕ *www.sansperate.net.*

</td></tr>
</table>

Torre di San Pancrazio. The 1305 tower of the imposing medieval Pisan defenses is just outside Cagliari's archaeological museum and marks the edge of the Castello district. You can climb up the limestone tower for a fabulous panorama of the city and its surroundings. Curiously enough, the tower's back wall is missing, which allows you to see the series of wooden stairs and landings inside the cross-section without climbing a step. ✉ *Piazza Indipendenza* ☏ *070/6776400* ⊕ *www.camuweb.it* ▭ *€4* ⊙ *May–Oct., Tues.–Sun. 9–1 and 3:30–7:30; Nov.–April 9–4:30.*

WHERE TO EAT

$$$ ✗ **Antico Caffè.** The gilded Antico Caffè is Sardinia's version of the Café
ITALIAN de Flore in Paris, an intellectual haunt for famous writers like D. H. Lawrence and Grazia Deledda. With its streetfront terrace and polished wood and brass interior, it has anchored the base of Terrazza Umberto I since 1855, serving as a social center from breakfast until well after midnight. A daily set menu (€35) features local fish and meat specialties. The pastas and salads are reliable à la carte choices made from fresh local ingredients. Desserts are the real attraction here: try the

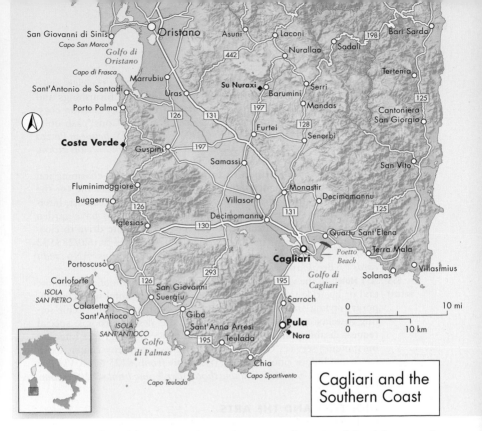

Cagliari and the Southern Coast

flavorful *crema catalana* (crème caramel) or one of the elaborate artisanal gelato *coupe* concoctions. A sublime *granita di caffe con panna* refreshes on a hot summer afternoon. $ *Average meal: €20* ⊠ *Piazza Costituzione 10/11* ☎ *070/658206* ⊕ *www.anticocaffe1855.it* ⊙ *7:30 am–2 am* ⊙ *Closed Tues.*

$$$$

ITALIAN

✕ **Dal Corsaro.** This elegant restaurant near the port is one of the island's most recommended with a strong reputation for fine Italian haute cuisine, so make reservations. The interior is refined with fine antiques and silver cutlery; the service, cordial and accommodating. A menu using local organic ingredients includes fish and meat, with popular dishes such as seafood antipasto, squid tagliatelle, and porcheddu. Regional and international wines, selected by professional sommelier Giuseppina Pilloni (the owner's wife), are perfectly matched with each course including a variety of island cheeses and honey. At various unpredictable times each year—always including August—the restaurant opens a branch at the seaside. Watch for special fixed price menus (€60) that include outstanding wine pairings. $ *Average meal: €30* ⊠ *Viale Regina Margherita 28* ☎ *070/664318* 🖷 *070/653439* ⊕ *www. dalcorsaro.com* ᐦ *Reservations essential Jacket required* ⊙ *Closed Sun. and Jan. 1–15. No lunch.*

WHERE TO STAY

For expanded hotel reviews, visit Fodors.com.

$ HOTEL **AeR Bundes Jack Vittoria.** Welcoming mostly foreign travelers since 1938, the courtyard-facing rooms and period-style furnishings and flooring make this central *secondo piano* (third-floor) pension cozy. **Pros:** clean rooms; central location near port; a/c. **Cons:** cash only; limited amenities. [$] *Rooms from: €60* ✉ *Via Roma 75, between Piazza Matteotti and Port Authorities* ☎ *070/657970* 🌐 *wwww.hotelbjvittoria.it* 🛏 *18 rooms* 💳 *No credit cards* 🍴 *Breakfast.*

$$ B&B/INN **Residenza Donna Pomptilla.** A former farmhouse, this charming inn is named for a Roman noblewoman who sacrificed her life for the love of her husband. **Pros:** Great location; impressive breakfast; Internet; wheelchair accessible rooms **Cons:** Not all rooms have garden views; airplane noise from nearby airport; 20-minute drive to closest beach. [$] *Rooms from: €100* ✉ *Viale Trento 124* ☎ *070/283532* 📠 *070/2085288* 🌐 *www.donnapomptilla.com* 🛏 *4 rooms* 💳 *No credit cards* 🍴 *Breakfast.*

$$$ RESORT **T Hotel.** In the vicinity of Parco di Monte Claro, about a 15-minute taxi or bus ride into Cagliari's center, this trendy hotel with contemporary styling and outstanding service offers the city's most chic setting to relax and rejuvenate. **Pros:** spacious designer rooms; special request disability and "dust-free" rooms; free parking; free Internet; outstanding service. **Cons:** 4 km (2½ miles) from city center; extra fee to use indoor pool and spa. [$] *Rooms from: €125* ✉ *66 Via Dei Giudicata* ☎ *070/47400* 🌐 *www.thotel.it/en/home.html* 🛏 *207 rooms* 🍴 *Breakfast.*

NIGHTLIFE AND THE ARTS

Cagliari's university stages concerts with local and well-known European artists throughout the academic year. Contact the tourist office for information.

FESTIVALS

Fodor's Choice ★ **Festa di Sant'Efisio.** From May 1 to 4, thousands of costumed villagers parade through town during Sardinia's greatest annual festival, the Festa di Sant'Efisio, named after the martyred saint who saved the city from the plague in the 17th century. The festival is part of a four-day procession from Cagliari to Nuoro and back again. Search for the saint's statue being passed along in flower-lined streets. The festival is one of the world's most renowned religious celebrations and the island's most significant event of traditional culture. 🌐 *www.santefisio.com.*

CAFÉS

Caffè de Candia. Relax in the atmospheric interior or casual terrace of De Candia, built directly into the castle walls near Terrazzo Umberto I. It's a great place to enjoy a cappucino or glass of vermentino after exploring the Castello quarter. ✉ *Bastione de Saint Remy, Via Maria de Candia 3* ☎ *070/655884* ⏲ *Mon.–Sun. 7 am–2 am.*

Librarium Nostrum. The Librarium Nostrum ranks as one of the coolest café-bars in Sardinia: its a dim, bohemian haunt full of wooden beams and brick-lined nooks and crannies that gets pumping with occasional live music. The real draw, however, is upstairs, where the outdoor terrace features a panoramic view and lounging sofas on which to enjoy cocktails and people-watching high atop Cagliari's medieval ramparts. ⊠ *Bastioni di Santa Croce 33/35* ☎ *346/5220212* ⊕ *www.caffelibarium. com* ☻ *Tues.–Sun. 7:30 am–2 am.*

Ritual's Cafe. Contemporary art, house music, and a kitchen open until midnight attract university students to Ritual's Cafe, located in a large grotto that originally served as a stable and gunpowder depot. At night, the club scene takes over, with DJ sets and live local bands. ⊠ *Via Università 33* ☎ *070/652071.*

Sesto Senso Cafe & Lounge Bar. On the summit of Mount Urpinu, a rustic wood-and-stone café and lounge with an excellent panoramic view of the city is a popular meeting place for young Sardinians. During the day, breakfast and lunch offer a copious choice of fresh menu items and beverages. ⊠ *Belvedere Monte Urpinu, Viale Europa* ☎ *329/1091302.*

SHOPPING

Cagliari's two best shopping streets, full of boutiques and specialty shops for clothes, shoes, bags, and jewelry are Via Manno and Via Garibaldi, just up from the port.

ISOLA. The Istituto Sardo Organizzazione Lavoro Artigiano is a government-sponsored cooperative of artisans with a comprehensive website describing fabrication techniques and typical products. Look for handmade ceramics, woven and wooden goods, baskets, metalwork, and beautiful gold filigree or precious stone jewelry at two locations. ⊠ *Via Bacaredda 184* ☎ *070/404791* ⊕ *www.regione.sardegna.it/isola* ⊠ *Via Santa Croce 37/41* ☎ *070/651488.*

SPORTS AND THE OUTDOORS

BEACHES

FAMILY
Fodor'sChoice
★

Poetto Beach. Only a few miles from the city center and easily accessible by a quick bus ride, Poetto Beach with its shallow and clean turquoise waters is considered one of the hottest spots to relax in summer for both locals and tourists alike. It stretches from Cagliari to Quartu Sant'Elena and is lined with cafés, restaurants, shops, snackstands, and parks. Beach lounging chairs and umbrellas are available for rent from a variety of vendors for about €10–€12. From the large sandy shores, you can admire the red flamingos that nest in the marshy reeds of the nearby Molentargius pond. Visiting Cagliari, this postcard setting is a must. **Best for:** families with small children; picnics; inexpensive dining. **Amenities:** public toilets; pedal boats; cafés; bars; refreshment stands. ⊠ *Take Viale Diaz from Cagliari to Viale Poetto.*

BOATING AND SAILING

Lega Navale Italiana. The Lega Navale Italiana, a public state-sponsored organization, has information on the island's sailing facilities, as well as everything associated with maritime activity. ⊠ *Marina Piccola* ☎ *070/300240* ⊕ *www.leganavale.it.*

16

DID YOU KNOW?

The gorgeous Costa Smeralda was a luxury hideaway in the 1960s for celebrities; these days the area is more accessible, with an airport in Olbia and some budget dining and lodging options.

WINDSURFING

FAMILY **Windsurfing Club Cagliari.** Sardinia has some of the best windsurfing spots in Europe throughout the year; the Windsurfing Club Cagliari can provide advice for beginner to expert levels. ⊠ *Viale Marina Piccola* ☎ *070/372694* ⊕ *www.windsurfingclubcagliari.it* ☉ *Daily 10:30–7.*

EN ROUTE Driving east from Cagliari takes you through some dismal industrial suburbs on the road that leads to the scenic coast and beaches of Capo Boi and Capo Carbonara. **Villasimius,** 50 km (31 miles) east of Cagliari, is the chief resort here; the beautiful beaches lie a couple of miles north of the town center, on the golden sands of the Costa Rei.

PULA

29 km (18 miles) southwest of Cagliari, 314 km (195 miles) southwest of Olbia.

Resort villages sprawl along the coast southwest of the capital, which has its share of fine scenery and good beaches. On the marshy shoreline between Cagliari's Aeroporto di Elmas and Pula, huge flocks of flamingos are a common sight. Home to one of Sardinia's most magnificent stretches of coastline, Pula offers white-sand beaches, turquoise waters, placid coves, and powdery dunes. Beaches and lodging catering to summer crowds are concentrated 4 km (2½ miles) south of Pula, a little more than 1½ km (1 mile) south of Nora, in a conglomeration that makes up the town of Santa Margherita di Pula.

16

GETTING HERE AND AROUND

From Cagliari, drive approximately 40 km on the SS 195. Follow directions for Pula/Chia.

From Olbia, take SS 131 direction Cagliari-Sassari. Follow SS 554 towards Pula/Chia. The journey is approximately 350 km.

EXPLORING

Fodor's Choice ★ **Nora.** Considered the oldest town in Sardinia, the narrow promontory outside Pula was the site of a Phoenician, Carthaginian, and then, later, Roman settlement. Nora was a prime location as a stronghold and important trading town—Phoenician settlers scouted for good harbors, cliffs to shelter their craft from the wind, and an elevation from which they could defend themselves against attack. An old Roman paved road passes the temple ruins that include baths, a Roman theater, and an amphitheater now reserved for summer music festivals. Extensive excavations have shed light on life in this ancient city more than 1,500 years old. Make out the channels through which hot air rose to warm the Roman baths. Note the difference between the Carthaginians' simple mosaic pavements and the Romans' more elaborate designs in well-preserved multicolored tiles. If the Mediterranean is calm, look under clear waters along the shore for more ruins of the ancient city, slowly submerging due to rising seas, earthquakes, and erosion. Guided tours of this open-air museum begin on the hour. ⊠ *3 km (2 mile) south of Pula* ☎ *070/9209138* ⊕ *www.sardegnacultura.it* ☜ *€5.50, including Museo Archeologico Comunale* ☉ *Daily 9–dusk; last entrance ½ hr before closing.*

EATING WELL IN SARDINIA

Sardinian cuisine is sharply divided between hearty, meat-based dishes from the interior and Mediterranean seafood fare with Catalan and North African influences along the coast. Meat dishes are most commonly veal, roast *agnello* (lamb) and *agnellino* (an even younger lamb), or *porcheddu* (roast suckling pig, most often available at Easter). *Cavallo*, or *carne equino* (horse meat), is also a common specialty of Sardinia; it's generally served in the form of a *bistecca* (thin steak), which can be a bit chewy, but when properly grilled, also intensely flavored and delicious. Homemade pastas might be topped with a wild-boar sauce. Finally, Italy's original and best, pecorino cheese, made from sheep's milk, comes from the rugged slopes of the interior.

Langouste or *aragosta* (lobster) is a seafood specialty of the northern coast that can get expensive. Looking for the unusual? Try the *ricci* (sea urchins), which, unlike the Japanese *uni*, are served atop pasta.

Bottarga, another prized Sardinian product, is a dried, cured tuna roe that's best when shaved off a block directly onto spaghetti or with butter on *crostini* (thin slices of toasted bread). Foreign conquerors left their legacies of bouillabaisse (known here as *zimino*), paella, and *cus cus* (couscous), also called *cashkà*.

Native pastas include *malloreddus* (small shells of bran pasta sometimes flavored with saffron), *culurgiones* (the Sardinian version of ravioli), and *maccarones de busa* (thick pasta twists). And crispy bread called *pane carasau* (*carta di musica* in Italian) is typical island fare. Prized around Italy and around the world is Sardinia's *amaro di corbezzolo*, a honey with a slightly bitter and dazzlingly complex bouquet and taste. It's made by bees that suck nectar from a plant known as *arbutus*, the tree strawberry. A popular after-dinner drink, the traditional liqueur *mirto*, is made from wild myrtle berries found only in Sardinia.

FAMILY **Tharros.** Past the large stone walls of Su Muru Mannu on the Sinis peninsula, ancient traces of the first Nuraghic village from the Bronze Age are part of the open-air museum situated on a hilly cliff topped with the San Giovanni fortress tower. Put on your walking shoes to tour and understand Phoenician-Punic city planning that includes sophisticated water channeling and masonry foundations. Meander through the well-marked wooden walkways to see the largest bath, Terme di Convento Vecchio, then head towards the sea, where emblematic temple columns still stand as testament to the site's Roman history. ⊠ *Area Archeologica di Tharros c/o San Giovanni di Sinis, near Pula* ☎ *0783/370019, 0783/3971* ⊕ *www.comunedicabras.it* ☉ *Apr.–Sep., 9–1 and 4–8; Oct.–Mar., 9–1 and 3–6.*

WHERE TO STAY

For expanded hotel reviews, visit Fodors.com.

$$ 🔲 **Is Molas Hotel and Golf Course.** If you love golf and stargazing, then
HOTEL the place to stay in southern Sardinia is this peaceful hotel with 80
FAMILY Mediterranean-style rooms and an 18-hole golf course that has won tributes from Tom Watson and Jack Nicklaus. **Pros:** immediate access to golf course; large freshwater pool; very tranquil setting with countryside

views **Cons:** isolated location with poor Internet connection; inconsistent food and bar service hours; must have car to visit local beaches and villages. [$] *Rooms from: €112* ✉ *Off SS195, Santa Margherita di Pula* ☎ *070/9241006* 🌐 *www.ismolas.it* 🛏 *80 rooms and 1 suite* 🕒 *Closed Nov.–Feb.* 🍴 *Multiple meal plans.*

$$$$ RESORT FAMILY 🏨 **Is Morus Relais.** A luxurious enclave hidden in a large palm-filled garden with undulating paths, the Is Morus sits on a sandy cove and has all the amenities of a fine beach resort. **Pros:** lovely grounds; large pool and poolside grill restaurant; free Wi-Fi in main lobby and public areas. **Cons:** restaurant/bar service slow; bathrooms need updating; very thin walls; very expensive room rates. [$] *Rooms from: €415* ✉ *SS195, Km 37.4, Santa Margherita di Pula* ☎ *070/921171* 🌐 *www.ismorus.com* 🛏 *55 rooms,18 villas* 🕒 *Closed Nov.–Apr.* 🍴 *Some meals.*

COSTA VERDE

80 km (50 miles) northwest of Cagliari.

If you've come to Sardinia in search of untrammeled wilderness and sweeping sands as far as the eye can see, this deserted coast is the place to find them. Hidden away in the forgotten southwest corner of Cagliari province, the Costa Verde, or Green Coast, is accessible only by a bumpy, unpaved track. The effort is worth it. The dune-backed sands shelter rare grasses and birdlife, and the area offers magnificent swimming in stretches of beach that seem endless.

GETTING HERE AND AROUND

The best way to access the Green Coast is by car, though roads can be dangerously steep and winding. Take precautions and drive during daytime, also because roads and exits are poorly lit. SS-marked roads are developed freeways with fast-flowing traffic. You can approach the coast either from the town of Guspini, on the straggling S126, or from a turnoff a couple of miles farther south, which leads through the abandoned mining town of Ingurtosu. It's a strange, ghostly cluster of chimneys and workers' dwellings, forlorn amid the encroaching scrubland. Drive down the dirt track another 10 km (6 miles) or so, through woods of juniper, to reach the sea.

SU NURAXI TO THE COSTA SMERALDA

A more traditional—and wild—Sardinia awaits the traveler who ventures into the island's mountainous interior. Inland Sardinians are hardy souls, used to living in a climate that is as unforgiving in winter as it is intolerable in summer. Old traditions, including the *vendetta* (a claim to personal revenge, against another family or individual, that may sometimes endure from generation to generation), are softening with time but are still firmly rooted in the social fabric.

The land is hilly, barren, and beautiful. Here, rare species of wildlife share the rocky uplands with sturdy medieval churches and the mysterious nuraghi left by prehistoric people. The nuraghi were built beginning in the 16th century BC, and they vary from single beehive-shaped defensive towers to multi-tower complexes sheltering whole communities—prehistoric versions of medieval walled towns. As you move northward, the timeless beauty of the landscape begins to show greater signs of 20th-century development. The sunny resort of Alghero, the Spanish-influenced port on the west coast, is one of the island's premier holiday spots. Costa Smeralda, the luxury resort complex on the northeast corner of Sardinia, is considered one of the most prestigious summer destinations for Europeans and continues to attract international celebrities and the wealthy jet-set crowd.

> ### WORD OF MOUTH
>
> "Unfortunately, too many travelers make the mistake of focusing on the Costa Smeralda area, which is *least* representative of Sardinia. By contrast, there are numerous interesting towns in the hinterland which are worth visiting, lovely medieval basilicas scattered about the lonely countryside, as well as beautiful Roman ruins along the coasts."
>
> —gac

SU NURAXI (BARUMINI)

Barumini is 65 km (40 miles) north of Cagliari.

It's definitely worth a detour to see the extraordinary stone village-fortress of Su Nuraxi, in the quiet town of Barumini.

GETTING HERE AND AROUND

The best way to reach Su Nuraxi is by car. From the capital, follow SS131 to SS197. There are no direct buses to the site.

EXPLORING

FAMILY
Fodor'sChoice
★

Su Nuraxi. The most extensive of Sardinia's 7,000 discovered nuraghi, Su Nuraxi's significance merits its inclusion on the UNESCO World Heritage List. Concentric rings of thick stone walls conceal dark chambers and narrow passages in a central, beehive-shape tower. The excellent guided tour (which, depending on the nature of the group and language abilities of the guide, may be available in English) allows you to explore the interior. In the ruins of the surrounding village there are benches, ovens, wells, and other Bronze Age remnants.

The specific functions of individual nuraghi remain a mystery, largely because their construction predates written or pictorial history. Though this particular type of construction is unique to Sardinia in Italy, similar buildings dating from the same era are found in other parts of the Mediterranean, such as Cyprus and the Balearic islands off Spain. If driving from SS131, don't be misled by other, lesser nuraghi—follow signs all the way to Barumini. All visits are accompanied by a local guide, start every 30 minutes, and last for approximately 45 minutes. ⊠ *SP Barumini-Tuilli, 1 km (½ mile) west of Barumini* ☏ *070/9368128, 39/070–9364277 Guided tours* ⊕ *www.comunebarumini.it* ☑ *€9* ⊗ *Daily, 9—one hour before sunset.*

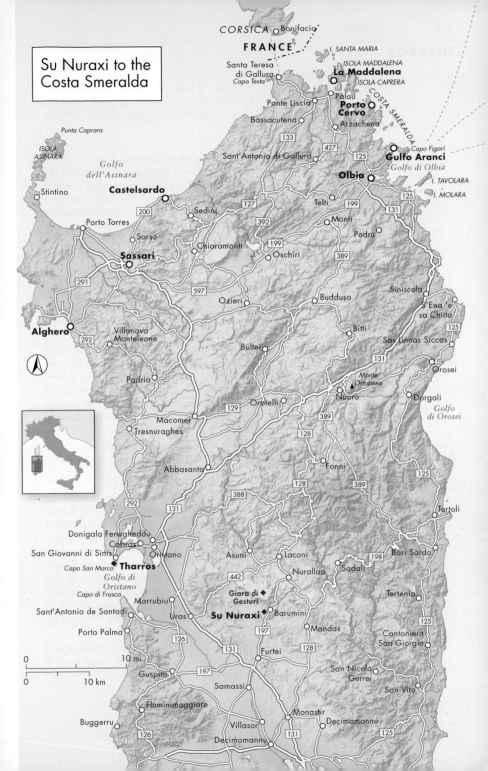

Su Nuraxi to the Costa Smeralda

CORSICA · Bonifacio
FRANCE

I. SANTA MARIA
Santa Teresa di Gallura
Capo Testa
ISOLA MADDALENA
La Maddalena
ISOLA CAPRERA
Ponte Liscia
Palau
Porto Cervo
Bassacutena
Arzachena
COSTA SMERALDA

Punta Caprara
ISOLA ASINARA
Golfo dell'Asinara
133
427
125
Capo Figari
Gulfo Aranci
Golfo di Olbia
Sant'Antonio di Gallura
Olbia
125
I. TAVOLARA
I. MOLARA

Stintino
Castelsardo
200
Sedini
127
Telti
199
131
Monti
Porto Torres
Sorso
392
Sassari
Chiaramonti
199
Monti
Padru
291
Oschiri
389
597
125
Ozieri
Budduso
Siniscola
Alghero
292
Bitti
S'Ena 'e sa Chitta
Villanova Monteleone
Bultei
Sas Linnas Siccas
125
131
Orosei
Padria
129
Orotelli
Monte Ortobene
Nuoro
Dorgali
Golfo di Orosei
Macomer
Tresnuraghes
389
128
Abbasanta
128
Fonni
389
125
Tortoli
388
Donigala Fenughedu
Cabras
Oristano
Asuni
Laconi
Bari Sardo
San Giovanni di Sinis
Tharros
Nurallao
198
Capo San Marco
Golfo di Oristano
Sadali
Capo di Frasca
442
Giara di Gesturi
Tertenia
Marrubiu
Su Nuraxi
Barumini
Sant'Antonio de Santadi
Uras
197
Mandas
125
Porto Palma
126
Furtei
128
Cantoniera San Giorgio
131
0   10 mi
0   10 km
Guspini
197
Samassi
San Nicolo Gerrei
Fluminimaggiore
Villasor
Monastir
Decimomannu
San Vito
Buggerru
126
Decimomannu
131
125

THARROS

GETTING HERE AND AROUND

Whether you're heading to Tharros from the north or south, follow the SS131 to Oristano. From the south, drive through Oristano towards Donigala Fenugheddu/Cabras/San Giovanni di Sinis. Follow SP6 toward Capo San Marco.

EXPLORING

FAMILY **Tharros.** The spectacular site of the Carthaginian and Roman city of Tharros, like Nora to the south, was chosen because it commanded the best views of the harbor and could provide an easy escape route if inland tribes threatened. Climb up the steep hill to reach the ruins and get a scenic view over the Sinis Peninsula. Two towering Corinthian columns still stand near the cliff edge, and there are baths visible and mosaic fragments from the Roman city. Look for the Cardo Maximo, the main road of the city built to last for centuries. As at Nora, many more ruins are submerged under water. A small souvenir shop and attached cafe serving snacks and beverages completes a visit to this open-air museum. ✉ *20 km (12 miles) west of Oristano, 113 km (70 miles) northwest of Cagliari, Cabras, San Giovanni di Sinis* ☎ *0783/370019* ⊕ *www. penisoladelsinis.it* 🎟 *€7 including Museo Civico di Cabras* ☉ *May– Sept., daily 9–8; Oct.–Apr., daily 9–6.*

EN ROUTE

On the way to the archaeological ruins in Tharros you pass the ghost town of **San Salvatore,** revived briefly in the 1960s as a locale for spaghetti Westerns and since abandoned, save local residents. The saloon from the movie set still stands. Among the dunes past San Salvatore are large rush huts formerly used by fishermen and now much in demand as back-to-nature vacation homes. The 5th-century church of **San Giovanni in Sinis,** on the Sinis Peninsula, is the oldest Christian church in Sardinia.

ALGHERO

137 km (85 miles) southwest of Olbia.

A tourist-friendly town of about 45,000 inhabitants with a distinctly Spanish flavor, Alghero is also known as "Barcelonetta" (little Barcelona). Rich wrought-iron scrollwork decorates balconies and screened windows; a Spanish motif appears in stone portals and bell towers. The town was built and inhabited in the 14th century by the Aragonese and Catalans, who constructed seaside ramparts and sturdy towers encompassing an inviting nucleus of narrow, winding streets with whitewashed palazzi. The native language spoken here is a version of Catalan, not Italian, although you probably have to attend one of the Masses conducted in Algherese (or listen in on stories swapped by older fishermen) to hear it.

Besides its historic architectural gems such as the Alghero Cathedral and Palazzo d'Albis, the fortified city is well worth a visit to simply stroll and discover local culture on narrow cobblestone streets. The city also has a reputation to serve great food at reasonable prices.

GETTING HERE AND AROUND

Alghero International Airport is just 15 km (9 miles) from the city center. The short distance is accessible by car, taxi, or public transport. Regional buses connect the city with the capital of Cagliari and other major towns and local villages. The closest passenger port to Alghero is in Porto Torres (approx. 40 km away).

ESSENTIALS

Alghero ⊠ *Comune di Alghero, Via Sant'Anna 38, Sassari* ☎ *079/997 800* ⊕ *www.comune.alghero.ss.it.*

EXPLORING

Capo Caccia. Head northwest of Alghero for broad sandy beaches and the spectacular heights of an imposing limestone headland. The rugged promontory, blanketed by lush maquis, is close to the Porto Ferro marina, popular Lampianu beach, and remote coves and caves such as the Grotte di Nettuno.

FAMILY
Fodor's Choice
★

Grotta di Nettuno (*Neptune's Caves*). At the base of a sheer cliff, the pounding sea has carved an entrance to the vast fantastic cavern filled with stunning water pools, stalactites, and stalagmites. You must visit with a guide; tours start on the hour. It's possible to reach the caves by boat or by land. Boat trips depart at regular intervals from the port of Alghero for €10 (price of admission to Grotto extra). The dramatic cave and coves, discovered by fishermen in the 18th century, are considered one of the most popular tourist attractions on the island for their sheer natural beauty. ⊠ *13 km (8 miles) west of Alghero* ☎ *079/946540* ⓔ *€12* ⓒ *Apr.–Sept., daily 9–7; Oct., daily 9–5; Nov.–Mar., daily 9–4.*

16

Escala del Cabirol (*Mountain Goat's Stairway*). By land, you can reach the entrance to the Grotta di Nettuno by descending the 654 dizzying "goat steps" of the aptly named zig-zagging stairway cut into the steep cliff. By public bus, the trip to the top of the stairway takes about 50 minutes. Allow 15 minutes for the descent by foot. ⊠ *Via Catalogna* ☎ *079/950179* ⓔ *€12 round-trip* ⓒ *From Alghero: 9:15 year-round and 3:10 and 5:10 June–Sept. From Capo Caccia: noon year-round and 4:05 and 6:05 June–Sept.*

Torre San Giovanni. This old stone tower fortress can be climbed for good views from the terrace. Stop at the interesting city history display on the computer terminals inside the tower. There's also a rotating set of exhibits and a miniature model of Alghero's Old Town. ⊠ *Via Mateotti 12* ☎ *079/9731605* ⓔ *€2* ⓒ *Apr.–Jun., Tue.–Sun. 10–1 and 5–8; Jul.–Aug., Tue.–Sat. 10–1 and 6:30–10, Sun.–Mon. 6:30–10.*

WHERE TO EAT

$$$$
ITALIAN

✕ **Andreini.** Traverse the loftiest heights of Sardinian elegance at an expensive, opulent, ambitious—yet somehow cozy—restaurant operated by talented chef Cristiano Andreini. The cavernous place is set to the nines: votive candles, linen tablecloths, chill-out music and stylish waiters abound; the service and wine list are adequate. The food is equally romantic: a great tasting menu highlights the artful use of local ingredients like pecorino cheese, wild fennel, and bottarga with special attention for the blending of textures and flavors. Creations might include homemade cuttlefish-ink tagliatelle with asparagus or wild boar with Cannonau wine sauce. The weekday three-course "business lunch" is a good value. $ *Average meal: €60* ⊠ *Via Ardoini 45* ☎ *079/982098* ⊕ *www.ristoranteandreini.it* ⌖ *Reservations essential* ☉ *Closed Mon. Oct.–Mar.*

$$$
SEAFOOD
✕ **La Lepanto.** A covered veranda by the seafront marks out Alghero's top seafood restaurant, an expansive and sunny room complete with crustacean-filled aquarium usually crowded with both locals and tourists in summer and evenings. The specialty is *aragosta* (lobster) cooked different ways, including *alla catalana* (with tomato and onions)—or try it with ricotta foam, parsley, basil, and tomato. For starters, try risotto *nero di seppia* (with cuttlefish ink). $ *Average meal: €70* ⊠ *Via Carlo Alberto 35, Sassari* ☎ *079/979116* ⊕ *www.lalepanto.com* ☉ *Closed Mon. Oct.–Mar.*

$$
ITALIAN
✕ **Il Pavone.** Located on the active Piazza Sulis, this delightful eatery has been serving locals good Sardinian fare since 1979. Fresh flowers on white linen tablecloths add color to the bright dining area encased in glass. Oversized wine bottles capped in wax add Italian charm and there are gold-framed paintings covering every inch of the back wall. Although the menu changes seasonally, you're likely to find a large selection of pasta and seafood dishes like tagliatelle with shrimp, or octopus with pesto. The three-course menu for two includes an appetizer, pasta and traditional dessert. For a caffeine boost, head next door to the restaurant's small café for their signature Dado coffee, an espresso made with chili peppers and honey. $ *Average meal: €40* ⊠ *Piazza Sulis 3, Sassari* ☎ *079/979584* ⌖ *Reservations essential* ☉ *Closed Sun. Oct.–Mar.*

WHERE TO STAY
For expanded hotel reviews, visit Fodors.com.

$$$$
HOTEL
▦ **Iberostar Carlos V.** On the shore boulevard opposite the Villa Las Tronas and 10 minutes from the airport, this thoroughly modern hotel (pronounced Carlos Quinto) has an array of gardens and terraces, and a huge pool overlooking the sea. **Pros:** Rental cars available onsite; spacious rooms; comfortable beds. **Cons:** Centrally controlled air conditioning; expensive rates; large hotel atmosphere $ *Rooms from: €245* ⊠ *Lungomare Valencia 24* ☎ *079/9720600* ⊕ *www.gioricohotels.it* ⇆ *173 rooms, 6 suites* ⦿︎ *Breakfast.*

$$$$
HOTEL
Fodor's Choice
★
▦ **Villa Las Tronas.** Privacy. Elegance. Charm. Gardens surround a narrow drive that separates this hotel's little island from the road, imparting a regal sense of seclusion to what was once a royal mansion. **Pros:** regal setting; incredible service; exceptional views. **Cons:** very expensive; rocky beach $ *Rooms from: €420* ⊠ *Lungomare Valencia 1* ☎ *079/981818* ⊕ *www.hotelvillalastronas.it* ⇆ *22 rooms, 3 suites* ⦿︎ *Some meals.*

$
B&B/INN
▦ **San Francesco.** The Gothic–late Renaissance convent that was once attached to the church of San Francesco has been reinvented as a hotel. **Pros:** historic location; easy to walk to village; very tranquil with lots of character **Cons:** low-light spaces; somber rooms; not good for kids $ *Rooms from: €101* ⊠ *Via Machin 2* ☎ *079/980330* ⊕ *www.sanfrancescohotel.com* ⇆ *20 rooms* ☉ *Closed Nov.–mid-Dec.* ⦿︎ *Breakfast.*

NIGHTLIFE

Baraonda. Baraonda, a marvelous local wine bar, also carries specialty liqueurs and grappas from all over Sardinia. ✉ *Piazza della Misericordia* ☎ *079/975922.*

Caffè Costantino. The elegant and historic Caffè Costantino continues to attract tourists and locals alike to its tables on the pretty square. Inside, yellow flowered walls, chandeliers, classical music, and a warm crowd of distinguished, well-dressed Algherese maintain its authenticity and popularity. Stop in for a glass of local wine or macchiato; it's open until midnight. ✉ *Piazza Civica 30* ☎ *079/976154 .*

SASSARI

34 km (21 miles) northeast of Alghero, 212 km (132 miles) north of Cagliari.

The island's second largest city and relatively chaotic with cars, Sassari is an important university town and administrative center, notable for its history of intellectualism and bohemian student culture, an ornate old cathedral, and a good archaeological museum. Look for downtown vendors of *fainè,* a pizzalike chickpea-flour pancake glistening with olive oil, which is a Genoese and Sassarese specialty. Sassari is the hub of several highways and secondary roads leading to various coastal resorts, among them Stintino and Castelsardo.

16

GETTING HERE AND AROUND

Sassari can be reached by plane, ferry, train, bus, or car. The nearest airport is Alghero-Fertilia, located about 30 km (19 miles) from Sassari. From the airport there is an inexpensive bus service to the center of Sassari. The closest port is Porto Torres, about 20 km (12½ miles) from Sassari. Ferries connect Genoa and Civitavecchia (Rome). Frequent bus service operates between Sassari and Cagliari, Olbia, and Arbatax.

ESSENTIALS

Sassari ✉ *Via Sebastiano Satta 13, Sassari* ☎ *079/2008072* ⊕ *www.comune.sassari.it.*

EXPLORING

Duomo. A must-see in Sassari, the elegant stone structure of the city's Duomo dedicated to Saint Nicolas of Bari took just under 600 years to build. The foundations were laid in the 12th century and the facade, in Spanish colonial style, was finished in the 18th. Of particular interest in the interior are the ribbed Gothic vaults, the 14th-century painting of the Maddona del Bosco on the high alter, and the early-19th-century tomb of Placido Benedetto di Savoia, the uncle of united Italy's first king. ✉ *Piazza Duomo 3* ☎ *079/233185* ⊕ *www.ilportalesardo.it* ✑ *Free* ☉ *Apr.–Oct., daily 9–noon and 5–7; Nov.–Mar., daily 9–12:30 and 4–6.*

FAMILY **Museo Sanna.** Sassari's excellent cultural museum has the best archaeological collection outside Cagliari, spanning nuraghic, Carthaginian, and Roman histories, including well-preserved bronze statues and household objects from the 2nd millennium BC. Summer hours vary from year to year. ✉ *Via Roma 64* ☎ *079/272203* ⊕ *www.museosannasassari. it* ✑ *€4* ☉ *Tue.–Sun. 9–8.*

WHERE TO EAT

> **WORD OF MOUTH**
>
> "I love the Costa Smeralda, the ultimate Italian island experience."
> —m kingdom

$ ITALIAN 🍴 **L'Assassino.** Get a true taste of great local Sassarese cooking—and many of the other obscure Sardinian specialties for which you may be searching—in a cozy vaulted room with terracotta tiling. Horse, donkey, and roast pig figure prominently on the menu; best of all is a *cena sarda,* a 10-dish tasting menu with *porcetto*—roast suckling pig—also spelled porcheddu. The service is friendly, and the room is warm and cozy. Food is served throughout the afternoon. [$] *Average meal: €25* ✉ *Via Pettenadu 19* ☎ *079/235041* 🌐 *www.trattorialassassino.it* 🕓 *Closed Sun.*

CASTELSARDO

32 km (20 miles) northeast of Sassari.

The walled seaside citadel of Castelsardo is a delight for craft lovers, with tiny shops crammed with all kinds of souvenirs, particularly woven baskets. The appropriately shaped **Roccia dell'Elefante** (Elephant Rock) on the road into Castelsardo was hollowed out by primitive man to become a *domus de janas* (literally, "fairy house," in fact a Neolithic burial chamber).

GETTING HERE AND AROUND

In summer, a daily bus runs between Alghero Airport and Castelsardo. Tickets can be purchased directly from the driver. Check the ARST bus service timetable from Sassari, which operates a route with stops in Castelsardo. The trip takes about an hour. The main bus stop in Castelsardo is located in the central Piazza Pianedda. The second stop is on a seafront front by the beach.

By car, access from Alghero, heading toward Porto Torres. Follow signs for Sassari onto the SS200, merging onto the SS134. Follow signs for S. Teresa di Gallura that takes you along the beautiful coastline.

LA MADDALENA

45 km (20 miles) northwest of Olbia.

From the port of Palau you can visit the archipelago of La Maddalena, seven granite islands embellished with lush green scrub and wind-bent pines that belong to the Olbia-Tempio province. Car ferries make the 3-km (2-mile) trip about every half hour. A handful of sites to see include ancient Roman ruins and squares. Explore the village then head to one of several picture-postcard coves, the perfect spot to pack a picnic and rejuvenate after your journey to the region.

GETTING HERE AND AROUND

The only way to access this small island is by boat or ferry. From Olbia, take a bus or drive to Palau, then catch the ferry to La Maddalena. During the day, ferries operate every 15 minutes. Upon reaching the dock, the city center is a 10 minute walk. On the island, there are local buses that access the major beach, although the island is best explored by foot.

EXPLORING

Tomb of Giuseppe Garibaldi's. Pilgrims pay homage to the 19th century national hero and military leader who is buried on the grounds of his farm on Isola Caprera. The patriot, who laid the groundwork for the first unification of Italy, lived from 1807 to 1882, and at one point owned half of Isola Caprera. Take the ferry to Isola Maddalena and then the bridge to Isola Caprera. Currently the site is closed to the public. In 2012, upon the request of descendants, authorities are currently exhuming the body and conducting DNA tests to verify the body's authenticity. Garibaldi continues to make history. ⊠ *7 km (4½ miles) east of Isola Maddalena* ☎ *0789/727162* ⊕ *www. compendiogaribaldino.it* ⊡ *€4* ⊙ *Oct.–Apr., Tues.–Sun. 9–1:30; May– Sept., Tues.–Sun. 9–6:30.*

PORTO CERVO

35 km (22 miles) southeast of La Maddalena, 30 km (19 miles) north of Olbia.

Sardinia's northeastern coast is fringed with low cliffs, inlets, and small bays. This has become an upscale vacationland, with glossy resorts such as Baia Sardinia and Porto Rotondo just outside the confines of the famed Costa Smeralda. Italy's most expensive hotels are here, and the world's most magnificent yachts anchor in the waters of Porto Cervo. Golf courses, yacht clubs, and numerous alfresco restaurants and bars cater to those who want to see and be seen.

All along the coast, carefully tended lush vegetation surrounds vacation villages and discreet villas that have sprung up over the past decade in spurious architectural styles best described as "bogus Mediterranean." The trend has been to keep this an enclave of the very rich. Outside the peak season, however, prices plunge and the majesty of the natural surroundings shines through, justifying all the hype and the Emerald Coast's fame as one of the truly romantic corners of the Mediterranean.

GETTING HERE AND AROUND

Porto Cervo is accessible by boat, car, taxi, train, bus, and ferry. Regional buses and trains run regularly from major Sardinian towns. Boats and ferries from numerous connecting cities in Corsica and Italy are available.

Whichever airport or port of entry into Sardinia you choose, head to Olbia. By car, follow SS 125 north towards Arzachena Costa Smeralda. After 10 km, turn right onto SP 73 towards Porto Rotondo/Port Cervo. Continue on SP 94 and turn onto SP 59 to Port Cervo. The trip takes about 30 minutes.

16

WHERE TO STAY

For expanded hotel reviews, visit Fodors.com.

$$$$ RESORT Fodor's Choice ★ **Cala di Volpe.** Long a magnet for the beautiful people, this hyper-glamorous establishment attracting jetsetters and wannabes (now owned by the Starwood Luxury Collection) was built to resemble an ancient Sardinian fishing village with its own covered wooden bridge. **Pros:** Stunning pool area; incredible food; kind staff. **Cons:** Crowded golf course in summer; astronomical prices for rooms; extra amenites and drinks equally expensive. [$] *Rooms from: €1500* ✉ *Cala di Volpe* ☎ *0789/976111* 🌐 *www.luxurycollection.com/caladivolpe* 🛏 *123 rooms, 1 suite* 🕐 *Closed mid-Oct.–mid-Apr.* 🍴 *Some meals.*

$$$ HOTEL **Nibaru.** Pinkish-red brick buildings with tiled roofs stand on a secluded inlet amid lush gardens provide a small resort feel. **Pros:** Courteous staff; nice pool; relatively low-key ambience **Cons:** Need a car to reach neighboring restaurants; basic decor and furnishings; crowded in summer. [$] *Rooms from: €200* ✉ *Località Cala di Volpe* ☎ *0789/96038* 🌐 *www.hotelnibaru.it* 🛏 *50 rooms, 2 suites* 🕐 *Closed mid-Oct.–Apr.* 🍴 *Breakfast.*

SPORTS AND THE OUTDOORS

BEACHES

The beaches around the Costa Smeralda are some of the most exclusive in Europe, but they don't disappoint, with fine golden sand sheltered by red cliffs and fronting azure waters. Most can only be reached by boat, and there are regular small ferries from Porto Cervo. Rentals of sun beds and towels are reassuringly expensive.

BOATING AND SAILING

Yacht Club Costa Smeralda. The Yacht Club Costa Smeralda was founded in 1967 by H. H. the Aga Khan, Andrè Ardoin, Giuseppe Kerry Mentasti, and Luigi Vietti as a non-profit making sporting association for fellow sailing enthusiasts and with a view to promoting related activities. The club provides use of its pool, restaurant, bar, and guest rooms to those with memberships at other yacht clubs. Watch for club-sponsored regattas and check out the sailing academy. The YCCS Sailing school has been organizing courses on dinghies and cabin cruisers for the past 30 years and is recognized by the *Federazione Italiana Vela* (Italian national sailing federation). ✉ *Via della Marina, Port Cervo* ☎ *0789/902200* 🌐 *www.yccs.it.*

GOLF

Pevero Golf Course. Opened in 1972 and considered one of Europe's most beautiful fairways, Pevero is a world-class, 18-hole, Par 72 golf course designed by Robert Trent Jones. It stretches nearly 4 miles and promises challenging playing conditions with 70 bunkers, several rocks, and vegetation. As a result of its exclusive location, technical design, and stunning landscaping, Pevero ranks in the world's top fifty best places to play golf. Green fees run €125 in high season. Expect formal dress codes in the upscale Club House that attracts a jetset crowd regularly. ✉ *Bay of Pevero, Cala di Volpe* ☎ *0789/958000 abroad* 🌐 *www.golfclubpevero.com.*

OLBIA

30 km (19 miles) south of Porto Cervo.

Amid the resorts of Sardinia's northeastern coast, Olbia, a town of about 60,000, is a lively little seaport and port of call for mainland ferries at the head of a long, wide bay.

GETTING HERE AND AROUND

The main airport Olbia-Costa Smeralda is only one mile from the town center. Inexpensive airport shuttles and taxis are available outside the terminal. Trains operate between Olbia and Cagliari and take about 4 hours. If driving, main roads are clearly marked to reach the city center, outlying areas, and other major towns.

The Olbia-Isola Bianca harbor provides daily connections with the Italian mainland, less than 300 km away. Regular ferries arrive from Genoa, Civitavecchia, and Livorno. Fast and modern, ferry rides last approximately 5 hours.

ESSENTIALS

Olbia ✉ *Via Catello Piro 1* ☎ *0789/21453* 📠 *0789/22221* 🌐 *www.olbiatempioturismo.it* ✉ *Aeroporto Costa Smeralda, Olbia* ☎ *0789/563444* 🌐 *www.ciaosardinia.com.*

WHERE TO EAT

$$$ ITALIAN 🍴 **Ristorante Barbagia.** Traditional dishes from Sardinia's wild interior fuse with local ingredients here. Antipasti might be a refreshing salad of sliced tomato and fresh cheese (called *sa t'amata chi sa frughe*) with carasau flatbread. Try maccarones de busa with a wild-boar (*cinghiale*) sauce; you might also find roast lamb and suckling pig in season. A good selection of pizza, fresh pasta, and wine is available. A simple array of tables and outdoor seating facing the busy center street draws visitors and locals alike. [$] *Average meal: €50* ✉ *Via Galvani 94* ☎ *0789/51640* 🌐 *www.ristorantebarbagia.it* ⏲ *Closed Wed. Oct.–June, and Jan. 2–31.*

WHERE TO STAY

For expanded hotel reviews, visit Fodors.com.

$$ HOTEL 🏨 **Hotel Martini.** Modern and businesslike, the Hotel Martini occupies an eye-catching site on the shore of a lagoon north of town. **Pros:** lovely restaurant; friendly staff; central location **Cons:** No room service; small showers; expensive Wi-Fi; a/c breakdowns [$] *Rooms from: €150* ✉ *Via Gabriele D'Annunzio 21* ☎ *0789/26066* 🌐 *www.hotelmartiniolbia.com* 🛏 *66 rooms* 🍽 *Breakfast.*

$$$$ HOTEL 🏨 **Petra Segreta Resort and Spa.** A stylish stone farmhouse perched on a hilltop hamlet blanketed by junipers, olive trees, and white granite boulders sets the scene for a romantic retreat close to Olbia's beaches. **Pros:** tranquil mountainside setting with spectacular views; blend of traditional setting and modern amenities; spacious rooms. **Cons:** inconvenient to beach; not suitable for families; very expensive. [$] *Rooms from: €388* ✉ *130 Strada Di Buddeu, Frazione San Pantaleo* 🌐 *www.petrasegretaresort.com* 🛏 *17 rooms* ⏲ *Closed Nov.–Apr.* 🍽 *Breakfast.*

GOLFO ARANCI

19 km (12 miles) northeast of Olbia.

At the mouth of the Gulf of Olbia, Golfo Aranci is a small-scale resort and major arrival point for ferries from the mainland. Tour the village to relax on an outdoor terrace or shop in one of many quaint shops. There is a large selection of restaurants, cafés, and bars. On August 15, the annual fish festival promises excellent seafood. The craggy headland west of town has been left undeveloped as a nature reserve. Drive a few miles along the panoramic road to Olbia. You will reach the enchanting waters of Cala Moresca, Cala Greca, Cala Sabina and White Beach, perfect for swimming, diving, and any other water sport imaginable.

GETTING HERE AND AROUND

The airport Olbia–Costa Smeralda is located about 24 km from Golfo Aranci. The resort is the terminus of the railway line Dorsale Sarda (Cagliari–Golfo Aranci), the largest of Sardinia. To reach Golfo Aranci by car, there are connections with the city of Olbia on SP82, and Porto Rotondo (about 11 km [7 miles] by car on SP16). Golfo Aranci is connected to Italy by ferry from Livorno; the trip takes 6 hours 25 minutes.

ESSENTIALS

Golfo Aranci ✉ *Via Liberta 59* ☎ *393/0213994* ⊕ *www.visitgolfoaranci.it.*

ITALIAN VOCABULARY

	ENGLISH	ITALIAN	PRONOUNCIATION
BASICS			
	Yes/no	Sí/no	see/no
	Please	Per favore	pear fa-**vo**-ray
	Yes, please	Sí grazie	see **grah**-tsee-ay
	Thank you	Grazie	**grah**-tsee-ay
	You're welcome	Prego	**pray**-go
	Excuse me, sorry	Scusi	**skoo**-zee
	Sorry!	Mi dispiace!	mee dis-spee-**ah**-chay
	Good morning/ afternoon	Buongiorno	bwohn-**jor**-no
	Good evening	Buona sera	**bwoh**-na **say**-ra
	Good-bye	Arrivederci	a-ree-vah-**dare**-chee
	Mr. (Sir)	Signore	see-**nyo**-ray
	Mrs. (Ma'am)	Signora	see-**nyo**-ra
	Miss	Signorina	see-nyo-**ree**-na
	Pleased to meet you	Piacere	pee-ah-**chair**-ray
	How are you?	Come sta?	**ko**-may **stah**
	Very well, thanks	Bene, grazie	**ben**-ay **grah**-tsee-ay
	Hello (phone)	Pronto?	**proan**-to
NUMBERS			
	one	uno	**oo**-no
	two	due	**doo**-ay
	three	tre	tray
	four	quattro	**kwah**-tro
	five	cinque	**cheen**-kway
	six	sei	say
	seven	sette	**set**-ay
	eight	otto	**oh**-to
	nine	nove	**no**-vay
	ten	dieci	dee-**eh**-chee
	twenty	venti	**vain**-tee

ENGLISH	ITALIAN	PRONOUNCIATION
thirty	trenta	**train**-ta
forty	quaranta	kwa-**rahn**-ta
fifty	cinquanta	cheen-**kwahn**-ta
sixty	sessanta	seh-**sahn**-ta
seventy	settanta	seh-**tahn**-ta
eighty	ottanta	o-**tahn**-ta
ninety	novanta	no-**vahn**-ta
one hundred	cento	**chen**-to
one thousand	mille	**mee**-lay
ten thousand	diecimila	dee-eh-chee-**mee**-la

USEFUL PHRASES

Do you speak English?	Parla inglese?	**par**-la een-**glay**-zay
I don't speak Italian	Non parlo italiano	non **par**-lo ee-tal-**yah**-no
I don't understand	Non capisco	non ka-**peess**-ko
Can you please repeat?	Può ripetere?	pwo ree-**pet**-ay-ray
Slowly!	Lentamente!	**len**-ta-men-tay
I don't know	Non lo so	non lo **so**
I'm American	Sono americano(a)	**so**-no a-may-ree-**kah**-no(a)
I'm British	Sono inglese	so-no een-**glay**-zay
What's your name?	Come si chiama?	**ko**-may see kee-**ah**-ma
My name is . . .	Mi chiamo . . .	mee kee-**ah**-mo
What time is it?	Che ore sono?	kay **o**-ray **so**-no
How?	Come?	**ko**-may
When?	Quando?	**kwan**-doe
Yesterday/today/tomorrow	Ieri/oggi/domani	**yer**-ee/**o**-jee/do-**mah**-nee
This morning	Stamattina	sta-ma-**tee**-na
This afternoon	Oggi pomeriggio	**o**-jee po-mer-**ee**-jo
Tonight	Stasera	sta-**ser**-a

ENGLISH	ITALIAN	PRONOUNCIATION
What?	Che cosa?	kay **ko**-za
What is it?	Chee cos'é?	kay ko-**zay**
Why?	Perché?	pear-**kay**
Who?	Chi?	kee
Where is . . .	Dov'è . . .	doe-**veh**
the bus stop?	la fermata dell'autobus?	la fer-**mah**-tadel ow-toe-**booss**
the train station?	la stazione?	la sta-tsee-**oh**-nay
the subway	la metropolitana?	la may-tro-po-lee-**tah**-na
the terminal?	il terminale?	eel ter-mee-**nah**-lay
the post office?	l'ufficio postale?	loo-**fee**-cho po-**stah**-lay
the bank?	la banca?	la **bahn**-ka
the . . . hotel?	l'hotel . . . ?	lo-**tel**
the store?	il negozio?	eel nay-**go**-tsee-o
the cashier?	la cassa?	la **kah**-sa
the . . . museum?	il museo . . . ?	eel moo-**zay**-o
the hospital?	l'ospedale?	lo-spay-**dah**-lay
the first-aid station?	il pronto soccorso?	Eel **pron**-to so-**kor**-so
the elevator?	l'ascensore?	la-shen-**so**-ray
a telephone?	un telefono?	oon tay-**lay**-fo-no
the restrooms?	il bagno?	eel **bahn**-yo
Here/there	Qui/là	kwee/la
Left/right	A sinistra/a destra	a see-**neess**-tra/a **des**-tra
Straight ahead	Avanti dritto	a-**vahn**-tee **dree**-to
Is it near/far?	È vicino/lontano?	ay vee-**chee**-no/ lon-**tah**-no
I'd like . . .	Vorrei . . .	vo-**ray**
a room	una camera	**oo**-na **kah**-may-ra
the key	la chiave	la kee-**ah**-vay
a newspaper	un giornale	oon jor-**nah**-lay
a stamp	un francobollo	oon frahn-ko-**bo**-lo

ENGLISH	ITALIAN	PRONOUNCIATION
I'd like to buy . . .	Vorrei comprare . . .	vo-**ray** kom-**prah**-ray
How much is it?	Quanto costa?	**kwahn**-toe **coast**-a
It's expensive/cheap	È caro/economico	ay **car**-o/ ay-ko-**no**-mee-ko
A little/a lot	Poco/tanto	**po**-ko/**tahn**-to
More/less	Più/meno	pee-**oo**/**may**-no
Enough/too (much)	Abbastanza/troppo	a-bas-**tahn**-sa/**tro**-po
I am sick	Sto male	sto **mah**-lay
Call a doctor	Chiama un dottore	kee-**ah**-mah oon doe-**toe**-ray
Help!	Aiuto!	a-**yoo**-toe
Stop!	Alt!	ahlt
Fire!	Al fuoco!	ahl **fwo**-ko
Caution/Look out!	Attenzione!	a-ten-**syon**-ay

DINING OUT

A bottle of . . .	Una bottiglia di . . .	**oo**-na bo-**tee**-lee-ahdee
A cup of . . .	Una tazza di . . .	**oo**-na **tah**-tsa dee
A glass of . . .	Un bicchiere di . . .	oon bee-key-**air**-ay dee
Bill/check	Il conto	eel **cone**-toe
Bread	Il pane	eel **pah**-nay
Breakfast	La prima colazione	la **pree**-ma ko-la-**tsee**-oh-nay
Cocktail/aperitif	L'aperitivo	la-pay-ree-**tee**-vo
Dinner	La cena	la **chen**-a
Fixed-price menu	Menù a prezzo fisso	may-**noo** a **pret**-so **fee**-so
Fork	La forchetta	la for-**ket**-a
I am diabetic	Ho il diabete	o eel dee-a-**bay**-tay
I am vegetarian	Sono vegetariano/a	**so**-no vay-jay-ta-ree-**ah**-no/a
I'd like . . .	Vorrei . . .	vo-**ray**
I'd like to order	Vorrei ordinare	vo-**ray** or-dee-**nah**-ray
Is service included?	Il servizio è incluso?	eel ser-**vee**-tzee-o ay een-**kloo**-zo

ENGLISH	ITALIAN	PRONOUNCIATION
It's good/bad	È buono/cattivo	ay **bwo**-no/ka-**tee**-vo
It's hot/cold	È caldo/freddo	ay **kahl**-doe/**fred**-o
Knife	Il coltello	eel kol-**tel**-o
Lunch	Il pranzo	eel **prahnt**-so
Menu	Il menù	eel may-**noo**
Napkin	Il tovagliolo	eel toe-va-lee-**oh**-lo
Please give me . . .	Mi dia . . .	mee **dee**-a
Salt	Il sale	eel **sah**-lay
Spoon	Il cucchiaio	eel koo-kee-**ah**-yo
Sugar	Lo zucchero	lo **tsoo**-ker-o
Waiter/waitress	Cameriere/ cameriera	ka-mare-**yer**-ay/ ka-mare-**yer**-a
Wine list	La lista dei vini	la **lee**-sta **day**-ee **vee**-nee

TRAVEL SMART ITALY

GETTING HERE AND AROUND

▌ AIR TRAVEL

Most nonstop flights between North America and Italy serve Rome and Milan, though the airports in Venice and Pisa also accommodate nonstop flights from the U.S. Many travelers find it more convenient to connect via a European hub to Florence, Bologna, or another smaller Italian airport.

Flying time to Milan or Rome is approximately 8–8½ hours from New York, 10–11 hours from Chicago, and 11½ hours from Los Angeles.

Labor strikes are not as frequent in Italy as they were some years ago, but when they do occur they can affect not only air travel, but also local public transit that serves airports. Your airline will have usually have details about strikes affecting its flight schedules.

Airline Security Issues Transportation Security Administration (*TSA*). The agency has answers for almost every security question that might come up. ⊕ *www.tsa.gov*.

Contact A helpful website for information (location, phone numbers, local transportation, etc.) about all of the airports in Italy is ⊕ *www.italianairportguide.com*.

AIRPORTS

The major gateways to Italy include Rome's Aeroporto Leonardo da Vinci (FCO), better known as Fiumicino, and Milan's Aeroporto Malpensa (MXP). Most flights to Venice, Florence, and Pisa make connections at Fiumicino and Malpensa or another European airport hub. You can take the FS airport train or bus to Rome's Termini station or to Milan's central train station (Centrale); then catch a train to any other location in Italy. It'll take about 30 minutes to get from Fiumicino to Roma Termini, less than an hour to Milano Centrale.

Many carriers fly into the smaller airports. Milan also has Linate airport (LIN) and

Rome has Ciampino (CIA). Venice is served by Aeroporto di Venezia Marco Polo (VCE), Naples by Aeroporto Internazionale di Napoli Capodichino (NAP), and Palermo by Aeroporto di Palermo (PMO). Florence is serviced by Aeroporto di Firenze (FLR) and by Aeroporto di Pisa (PSA), which is about 2 km (1 mile) outside the center of Pisa and about one hour from Florence. The train to Florence stops within 100 feet of the entrance to the Pisa airport terminal. Aeroporto de Bologna (BLQ) is a 20-minute direct Aerobus-ride away from Bologna Centrale, which is less than 30 minutes from Florence by high-speed train.

Many Italian airports have undergone renovations in recent years and have been ramping up security measures, which include random baggage inspection and bomb-detection dogs. All airports have restaurants, snack bars, shopping, and Wi-Fi access. Each also has at least one nearby hotel. In the case of Milan Linate, Florence, Pisa, Naples and Bologna, the city centers are less than a 15-minute taxi or bus ride away—so if you encounter a long delay, spend it in town.

When you take a connecting flight from a European airline hub (Frankfurt or Paris, for example) to a local Italian airport (Florence or Venice), be aware that your luggage might not make it onto the second plane with you. The airlines' lost-luggage service is efficient, however, and your delayed luggage is usually delivered to your hotel or holiday rental within 12 to 24 hours.

Airport Information Aeroporto di Bologna (*BLQ, also called Guglielmo Marconi*). ⊠ *6 km [4 miles] northwest of Bologna* ☎ *051/6479615* ⊕ *www.bologna-airport. it.* **Aeroporto di Firenze** (*FLR, also called Amerigo Vespucci and Peretola*). ⊠ *6 km [4 miles] northwest of Florence* ☎ *055/3061300* ⊕ *www.aeroporto.firenze.it.* **Aeroporto di Milan Linate** (*LIN*). ⊠ *8 km (5 miles) southeast*

of Milan ☎ 02/23223 ⊕ www.milanolinate.
eu. **Aeroporto di Palermo** (PMO, also
called Falcone e Borsellino and Punta Raisi).
✉ 32 km [19 miles] northwest of Palermo
☎ 091/7020111, 800/541880 in Italy (toll
free) ⊕ www.gesap.it. **Aeroporto di Pisa** (PSA,
also called Aeroporto Galileo Galilei). ✉ 2 km
[1 mile] south of Pisa, 80 km [50 miles] west
of Florence ☎ 050/849300 ⊕ www.pisa-
airport.com. **Aeroporto di Roma Ciampino**
(CIA). ✉ 15 km (9 miles) southwest of Rome
☎ 06/65951 ⊕ www.adr.it. **Aeroporto di
Venezia** (VCE, also called Marco Polo). ✉ 6 km
[4 miles] north of Venice ☎ 041/2609260
⊕ www.veniceairport.com.**Aeroporto Fiumicino** (FCO, also called Leonardo da Vinci).
✉ 35 km [20 miles] southwest of Rome
☎ 06/65951 ⊕ www.adr.it. **Aeroporto Internazionale di Napoli** (NAP, also called Capodichino). ✉ 7 km [4 miles] northeast of Naples
☎ 081/7896111 weekdays 8–4, 848/888777
for flight info ⊕ www.naples-airport.com.
Aeroporto Malpensa (MXP). ✉ 45 km [28
miles] north of Milan ☎ 02/232323
⊕ www.airportmalpensa.com.

FLIGHTS

From the United States, Alitalia and Delta
Air Lines serve Rome, Milan, Pisa, and
Venice. The major international hubs in
Italy (Milan and Rome) are also served
by United Airlines and American Airlines;
US Airways serves Rome as well. From
June through October, the Italy-based
Meridiana fly has nonstop flights from
New York to Naples and Palermo.

Alitalia has direct flights from London
to Milan and Rome, while British Airways and smaller budget carriers provide
services between Great Britain and other
locations in Italy. EasyJet connects London's Gatwick and Stansted airports with
12 Italian destinations, Ryanair, departing from Stansted, flies to 17 airports.
Meridiana fly has flights between Gatwick and Olbia on Sardinia in summer.
For flights within Italy, check Alitalia
and smaller airlines, such as Air One,
blu-express, and Meridiana fly. Since
tickets are frequently sold at discounted
prices, it's wise to investigate the cost of

flying—even one-way—as an alternative
to train travel.

Airline Contacts Alitalia ☎ 800/223–5730
in U.S., 892/010 in Italy, 06/65649 Rome
office ⊕ www.alitalia.it. **American Airlines** ☎ 800/433–7300, 199/257300 in
Italy ⊕ www.aa.com. **British Airways**
☎ 800/247–9297 in U.S., 02/69633602 in Italy
⊕ www.britishairways.com. **Delta Air Lines**
☎ 800/241–4141 for international reservations, 02/3859 1451 in Italy ⊕ www.delta.
com. **EasyJet** ☎ +44843/104 5454 from
outside U.K., 199/201 840 in Italy (toll free),
0843/104 5000 from inside U.K. ⊕ www.
easyjet.com. **Ryanair** ☎ 0871/246 0002 in
U.K., 899/552589 in Italy (toll number) ⊕ www.
ryanair.com. **United Airlines** ☎ 800/864–8331
in U.S., 02/6963 3256 in Italy ⊕ www.united.
com. **US Airways** ☎ 800/428–4322 for U.S.
reservations, 848/813177 in Italy ⊕ www.
usairways.com.

Domestic Carriers Air One ☎ 091/2551047
outside Italy, 892/444 in Italy ⊕ www.flyairone.
it. **blu-express** ☎ 06/989 56666 ⊕ www.blu-
express.com. **Meridiana fly** ☎ 866/387–6359
in U.S., 892928 in Italy, 0871/222 9319 U.K.
call center ⊕ www.euroflyusa.com.

∎ BUS TRAVEL

Italy's far-reaching regional bus network,
often operated by private companies, is
not as attractive an option as in other
European countries, partly due to convenient train travel. Schedules are often
drawn up with commuters and students
in mind and may be sketchy on weekends.
But, car travel aside, regional bus companies often provide the only means of getting to out-of-the-way places. Even when
this isn't the case, buses can be faster and
more direct than local trains, so it's a good
idea to compare bus and train schedules.
Lazzi operates in Tuscany and central
Italy; while BusItalia–Sita Nord covers
Tuscany and Veneto. SitaSud caters to
travelers in Puglia, Foggia, Matera, Basilicata, and Campania. Dolomiti Bus serves
the Dolomites.

All major cities in Italy have urban bus services. It's inexpensive, and tickets should be purchased from newsstands or tobacconists and validated on board (some city buses have ticket machines on the buses themselves). Buses can become jammed during busy travel periods and rush hours.

Smoking is not permitted on Italian buses. All, even those on long-distance routes, offer a single class of service. Cleanliness and comfort levels are high on private motor coaches, which have plenty of legroom, sizable seats, and luggage storage, but do not often have toilets. Private bus lines usually have a ticket office in town or allow you to pay when you board.

Bus Information ATAC ✉ *Rome* ☎ *06/57003* ⊕ *www.atac.roma.it.* **ATAF** ✉ *Stazione Centrale di Santa Maria Novella, Florence* ☎ *800/424500, 199/104245 from mobile phone* ⊕ *www.ataf.net.* **BusItalia–Sita Nord** ✉ *Viale dei Cadorna, 105, Florence* ☎ *055/47821* ⊕ *www.fsbusitalia. it.* **Dolomiti Bus** ✉ *Via Col da Ren 14, Belluno* ☎ *0437/217111* ⊕ *www.dolomitibus. it.* **Lazzi** ✉ *Via Mercadante 2, Florence* ☎ *0573/1937900* ⊕ *www.lazzi.it.* **SitaSud** ✉ *Putignano, Bari* ☎ *080/4052245* ⊕ *www.sitasudtrasporti.it.*

▌ CAR TRAVEL

Italy has an extensive network of *autostrade* (toll highways), complemented by equally well maintained but free *superstrade* (expressways). Save the ticket you're issued at an autostrada entrance, as you need it to exit; on some shorter autostrade you pay the toll when you enter. Viacards, on sale for €25 and up at many autostrada locations, let you pay for tolls in advance, exiting at special lanes where you simply slip the card into a designated slot. There is no need to purchase this, as the toll booths also accept Visa and Mastercards.

An *uscita* is an "exit." A *raccordo annulare* is a ring road surrounding a city; a *tangenziale* bypasses a city entirely. *Strade statale, strade regionale,* and *strade provinciale* (regional and provincial highways, denoted by *S, SS, SR,* or *SP* numbers) may be two lanes, as are all secondary roads; directions and turnoffs aren't always clearly marked.

GASOLINE

You'll find gas stations on most main highways. Those on autostrade are open 24 hours. Otherwise, gas stations are generally open Monday–Saturday 7–7, with a break at lunchtime. At self-service stations the pumps are operated by a central machine for payment, which often doesn't take credit cards: it accepts bills in denominations of 5, 10, 20, and 50 euros, and doesn't give change. Stations with attendants accept cash and credit cards. It's not customary to tip the attendant.

At this writing, gasoline (*benzina*) costs about €1.82 per liter and is available in unleaded (*verde*) and superunleaded (*super*). Many rental cars in Italy use diesel (*gasolio*), which costs about €1.72 per liter (remember to confirm the fuel type your car requires before leaving the agency).

DRIVING IN *CENTRI STORICI* (HISTORIC CENTERS)

To avoid hefty fines (which you may not be notified of until months after your departure from Italy), make sure you know the rules governing where you can and can't drive in historic city centers. You must have a permit to enter many towns, and Florence, for example, is very strict in enforcement. Check with your lodging or car-rental company to find out about acquiring permits for access.

PARKING

Parking is at a premium in most towns, especially in historic centers. Fines for parking violations are high, and towing is common. Don't think about tearing up a ticket, as car-rental companies can use your credit card to be reimbursed for any fines incurred. It's a good idea to park in a designated (and preferably attended) lot; even small towns often have a large lot at the edge of historic centers.

In congested cities indoor parking costs €25–€30 for 12–24 hours; outdoor parking costs about €10–€20. Parking in an area signposted *zona disco* (disk zone) is allowed for short periods (from 30 minutes to two hours or more—the time is posted); if you don't have an appropriate cardboard disk (check in the glove box of your rental car) to show what time you parked, you can write your arrival time on a piece of paper. In most metropolitan areas you can find curbside *parcometro* machines; once you insert cash or a credit/debit card, it prints a ticket that you then leave on your dashboard.

RENTALS

Fiats, Fords, and Alfa Romeos in a variety of sizes are the most typical rental cars. Note that most Italian cars have standard transmission—if you need an automatic, specify one when you make your reservation. Significantly higher rates will apply.

Most American chains have affiliates in Italy, but costs are usually lower if you book a car before leaving home. Rentals at airports usually cost less than city pickups (and airport offices are open later). An auto broker such as ⊕ *www.rent.it* lets you compare rates among companies while guaranteeing the lowest price.

Most rental companies won't rent to someone under age 21. Most also refuse to rent any model larger than an economy or subcompact to anyone under 23, and, further, require customers under that age to pay by credit card. There are no special restrictions on senior citizen drivers. Any additional drivers must be identified in the contract and qualify with the age limits. There's also a supplementary daily fee for additional drivers. Expect to pay extra for add-on features, too. A car seat (required for children under age three) will cost about €36 for the duration of the rental and should be booked in advance. In some areas snow chains are compulsory in winter months and can be rented from €30 to €60—it may be cheaper to buy your own at the first open garage. Upon rental, all companies require credit cards as a warranty; to rent bigger cars (2,000 cc or more), you may be required to show two credit cards.

Hiring a car with a driver can simplify matters, particularly if you plan to indulge in wine tastings or explore the distractingly scenic Amalfi Coast. Search online (the travel forums at ⊕ *fodors.com* are a good resource) or ask at your hotel for recommendations. Drivers are paid by the day, and are usually rewarded with a tip of about 15% upon completion of the journey.

All rental agencies operating in Italy require you to buy a collision-damage waiver (CDW) and a theft-protection policy, but those costs should already be included in the rates you're quoted. Verify this, along with any deductible, which can vary greatly depending on the company and type of car. Be aware that coverage may be denied if the named driver on the rental contract isn't the driver at the time of an accident. In Sicily there are some roads for which rental agencies deny coverage; ask in advance if you plan to travel in remote regions. Also ask your rental company about other included coverage when you reserve the car and/or pick it up. Finally, try not to leave valuables in your car, because thieves often target rental vehicles. If you can't avoid doing so—for instance, if you want to stop to see a sight while traveling between cities—park in an attended lot.

ROAD CONDITIONS

Autostrade are well maintained, as are most interregional highways. Typically autostrade have two lanes in both directions; the left lane is used only for passing. Italians drive fast and are impatient with those who don't. Tailgating (and flashing with bright beams to signal intent to pass) is the norm if you dawdle in the left lane—the only way to avoid it is to stay to the right.

The condition of provincial (county) roads varies, but road maintenance at this level is generally good in Italy. In many small hill towns the streets are winding and extremely narrow, so try to park at the edge of town and explore on foot.

Driving on back roads isn't difficult as long as you're on the alert for bicycles and passing cars. In addition, street and road signs are often missing or placed in awkward spots; a good map or GPS is essential. If you feel pressure from a string of cars in your rearview mirror but don't feel comfortable speeding up, pull off to the right, and let them pass.

Be aware that some maps may not use the SR or SP (*strade regionale* and *strade provinciale*) highway designations, which took the place of the old SS designations in 2004. They may use the old SS designation or no numbering at all.

ROADSIDE EMERGENCIES

Automobile Club Italiano offers 24-hour road service (dial ☎ *803116*); English-speaking operators are available. Your rental-car company may also have an emergency tow service with a toll-free phone number: keep it handy. Be prepared to report which road you're on, the *verso* (direction) you're headed, and your *targa* (license plate number). Also, in an emergency, call the police (☎ *113*).

When you're on the road, always carry a good road map and a flashlight—a reflective vest should be provided with the car. A cell phone is highly recommended, though there are emergency phones on the autostrade and superstrade. To locate them, look on the pavement for painted arrows and the term "SOS."

Emergency Services Automobile Club Italiano (ACI). ☎ *803/116 emergency service* ⊕ *www.aci.it.*

RULES OF THE ROAD

Driving is on the right. Speed limits are 130 kph (80 mph) on autostrade, reduced to 110 kph (70 mph) when it rains, and 90 kph (55 mph) on state and provincial roads, unless otherwise marked. In towns the speed limit is 50 kph (30 mph), which may drop as low as 10 kph (6 mph) near schools, hospitals, and other designated areas. Note that right turns on red lights are forbidden. Headlights are required to be on while driving on all roads (large

or small) outside of municipalities. You must wear seat belts and strap young children under 1.5 meters (4.9 feet) into car seats at all times. Using handheld mobile phones while driving is illegal—and fines can exceed €100. In most Italian towns the use of the horn is forbidden in many areas. A large sign, *zona di silenzio,* indicates a no-honking zone.

In Italy you must be 18 years old to drive a car. A U.S. driver's license is acceptable to rent a car, but by law Italy also requires non-Europeans to carry an International Driver's Permit (IDP), which essentially translates your license into Italian (and a dozen other languages). In practice, it depends on the police officer who pulls you over whether you'll be penalized for not carrying it. The IDP costs only $15, and obtaining one is easy: see the AAA website ⊕ *www.aaa.com* for more information.

The blood-alcohol content limit for driving is 0.05% (stricter than in the U.S.). Surpass it and you'll face fines up to €5,000 and the possibility of six months' imprisonment. Although enforcement of laws varies depending on the region, fines for speeding are uniformly stiff: 10 kph over the speed limit can warrant a fine of up to €500; greater than 10 kph, and your license could be taken away. The police have the power to levy on-the-spot fines.

▌ TRAIN TRAVEL

Traveling by train in Italy is simple and efficient. Service between major cities is frequent, and trains usually arrive on schedule. The fastest trains on the Trenitalia Ferrovie dello Stato (FS)—the Italian State Railways—are Freccie Rosse Alta Velocità. Ferrari mogul Montezemolo launched the competing Italo high-speed service in 2012. Bullet trains on both services run between all major cities from Venice, Milan, and Turin down through Florence and Rome to Naples and Salerno. Seat reservations are mandatory, and you'll be assigned a specific seat; to avoid having to squeeze through narrow aisles, board only at your designated coach (the number on your ticket matches the one near the door of each coach). Reservations are also required for Eurostar and the slower Intercity (IC) trains, tickets for the latter are about half the price of the faster trains. If you miss your reserved train, go to the ticket counter within the hour and you may be able to move your reservation to a later one (this depends on the type of reservation, so check rules when booking). Note that you'll still need to reserve seats in advance if you're using a rail pass.

Note that there are often significant discounts when you book well in advance. On the websites, you'll be presented with available promotional fares, such a Trenitalia's "Mini" (up to 60% off), "Famiglia" (a 20% discount for one adult and at least one child), and "A/R" (a round trip in a day). Italo offers "Low Cost" and "Economy." The caveat is that the discounts come with restrictions on changes and cancellations; make sure you understand them before booking.

Reservations are not available on Interregionale trains, which are slower, make more stops, and are less expensive than high-speed and Intercity trains. Regionale and Espresso trains stop most frequently and are the most economical (many serve commuters). There are refreshments on long-distance trains, purchased from a mobile cart or a dining car, but not on the commuter trains.

All but commuter trains have first and second classes. On local trains a first-class fare ensures you a little more space; on long-distance trains you also get wider seats (three across as opposed to four) and a bit more legroom, but the difference is minimal. At peak travel times a first-class fare may be worth the additional cost, as the coaches may be less crowded. In Italian, *prima classe* is first class; second is *seconda classe*.

Many cities—Milan, Turin, Genoa, Naples, Florence, Rome, and even Verona included—have more than one train station, **so be sure you get off at the right station.** When buying tickets be particularly aware that in Rome and Florence some trains don't stop at all of the cities' stations and may not stop at the main, central station. When scheduling train travel online or through a travel agent, request to arrive at the station closest to your destination in Rome and Florence.

Except for Pisa, Milan, and Rome, none of the major cities have trains that go directly to the airports, but airport shuttle buses connect train stations and airports.

You can purchase train tickets and review schedules online, at travel agencies, at train station ticket counters, and at automatic ticketing machines located in all but the smallest stations. If you'd like to board a train and don't have a ticket, seek out the conductor prior to getting on; he or she will tell you whether you may buy a ticket onboard and what the surcharge will be (usually €8). Fines for attempting to ride a train without a ticket are €50 plus the price of the ticket.

For trains without a reservation **you must validate your ticket before boarding** by punching it at wall- or pillar-mounted yellow or green boxes in train stations or at the track entrances of larger stations. If you forget, find a conductor immediately to avoid a hefty fine.

Train strikes of various kinds are not uncommon, so it's wise to ensure that your train is actually running. During a strike minimum service is guaranteed (especially for distance trains); ask at the station or search online to find out about your particular reservation.

Traveling by night can be a good deal—and somewhat of an adventure—because you'll pass a night without having to have a hotel room. Comfortable trains run on the longer routes (Sicily–Rome, Sicily–Milan, Rome–Turin, Lecce–Milan); request the good-value T3 (three single

Travel Times by Train

TO AUSTRIA & EAST EUROPE
TARVISIO

TO AUSTRIA & GERMANY
BRENNERO

TO SLOVENIA & CROATIA

TO SWITZERLAND
DOMODOSSOLA

CHIASSO

MODANE
TO FRANCE

VENTIMIGLIA
TO FRANCE & CÔTE D'AZUR

Trieste

Udine

< 1hr 45mn >

Venezia

Belluno

Treviso 40mn >

< 2hr

Padova

Vicenza

< 1hr 45mn >

Ferrara

Trento

< 2hrs

Bolzano/Bozen

Sondrio

Lecco

Bergamo

Brescia

< 1hr

< 30mn >

Verona

< 1hr 30mn >

Mantova

Piacenza

< 1hr

Parma

< 40mn >

Modena

Bologna

< 1hr

Forlì

Rimini

< 1hr 45mn >

Ancona

< 1hr 20mn >

Pescara

L'Aquila

Ascoli

Teramo

Terni

Perugia

< 3hrs

< 15mn >

Arezzo

< 1hr 45mn >

Viterbo

Firenze

< 1hr >

Pistoia

Siena

Lucca

Livorno

Grosseto

< 20mn >

< 3hrs

Pisa

< 2hrs >

La Spezia

Genova

30mn >

Milano

< 1hr

< 1hr 20mn >

Pavia

Novara

Vercelli

< 1hr 30mn >

Alessandria

Asti

Savona

Imperia

Torino

Cuneo

Aosta

VENEZIA - POLA - CROATIA 3HRS

ANCONA - ZADAR - CROATIA 4HRS

SPLIT - CROATIA 5HRS

TO GREECE

TO GREECE

PESCARA

TO GREECE

5HRS

GENOVA - PALERMO 20HRS

GENOVA - PORTO TORRES 13HRS

10 HRS

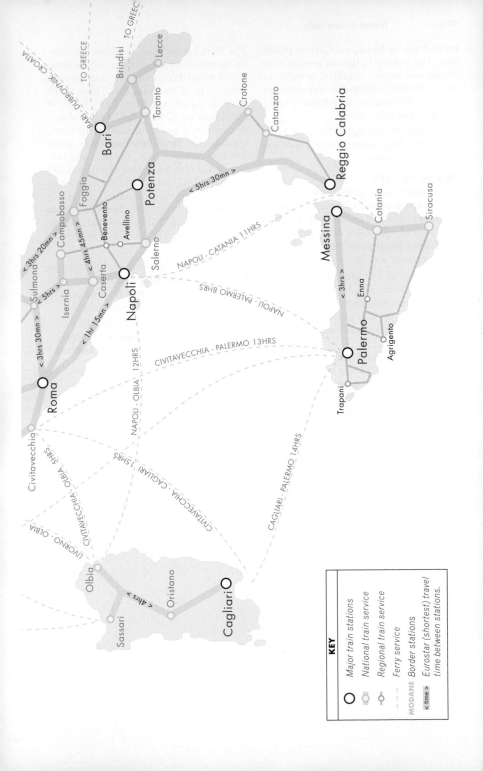

KEY

⭕	Major train stations
	National train service
	Regional train service
------	Ferry service
⭕	Border stations
MODANE	Border stations
< time >	Eurostar (shortest) travel time between stations.

beds), Intercity Notte, and Carrozza Comfort. The Vagone Letto has private bathrooms and single-, double-, or twin-bed suites. Overnight trains also travel to international destinations like Paris, Vienna, Munich, and other cities.

Information FS–Trenitalia ☎ *06/6847 5475 from outside Italy (English), 892021 inside Italy* ⊕ *www.trenitalia.com.*

TRAIN PASSES

Rail passes promise savings on train travel. But compare prices with actual fares to determine whether a pass will truly pay off. Generally, the more often you plan to travel long distances on high-speed trains, the more sense a rail pass makes.

Italy is one of 24 countries that accept the Eurail Pass, which provides unlimited first- and second-class travel. If you plan to rack up miles across the Continent, get a Global Eurail Pass (covering all participating nations). The Eurail Select Pass allows for travel in three to five contiguous countries. Other options are the Eurail Youth Pass (for those under 26), the Eurail Flexipass (valid for a certain number of travel days within a set period), and the Eurail Saver (aimed at two to five people traveling together).

The Eurail Italy Pass, available for non-European residents, allows a certain number of travel days within the country over the course of two months. Three to 10 days of travel cost from $295 to $539 (1st class) or $240 to $439 (2nd class). If you're in a group of more than three, consider the **Eurail Italy Pass Saver**: good for 3 to 10 travel days, the price per person is $251 to $459 (1st class) or $205 to $374 (2nd class); family passes offer further discounts for children under 12; kids under 4 travel free. **Eurail Italy Youth** (for those under 26) is second-class only and costs from $195 to $357 for one to 10 days of travel.

All passes must be purchased before you leave for Europe. Keep in mind that even with a rail pass you still need to reserve seats on the trains that require them.

Contacts Italia Rail ☎ *877/375–7245 in U.S.* ⊕ *www.italiarail.com.* **Rail Europe** ☎ *800/622–8600 in U.S.* ⊕ *www.raileurope.com.* **RailPass** ⊕ *www.railpass.com.*

ESSENTIALS

■ ACCOMMODATIONS

Hotels in Italy are becoming increasingly distinctive. Palazzi, villas, and monasteries have been restored as luxurious lodgings, while retaining their original atmosphere, and small hotels are revamping historic buildings with contemporary decor. The famed Italian wineries are offering rooms and apartments for three-day to weeklong stays.

The lodgings we list are the cream of the crop in each price category. Properties are assigned price categories based on the rate for two people sharing a standard double room in high season, including tax and service.

APARTMENT AND HOUSE RENTALS

Renting a vacation property can be economical depending on your budget and the number of people in your group. Most are owned by individuals and managed by rental agents who advertise online; and because many properties are represented by multiple agents, one may appear on different sites under different names (hence "Chianti Bella Vista," "Tuscan Sun Home," and "Casa Toscana Sole" could all refer to the same villa). In some cases rental agents handle only the online reservation and financial arrangements; in others, the agent and/or owner may meet you at the property for the initial check-in.

Issues to keep in mind when renting an apartment in a city or town are the neighborhood (street noise and ambience), the availability of an elevator or number of stairs, the furnishings (including pots and linens), what's supplied on arrival (dishwashing liquid, coffee or tea), and the cost of utilities (are all covered by the rental rate?). Inquiries about countryside properties should also include how isolated the property is (do you have to drive 45 minutes to reach the nearest

town?). If you're arriving too late in the day to grocery shop, request that provisions for the next day's breakfast be supplied.

Contacts At Home Abroad ☎ 212/421–9165 ⊕ www.athomeabroadinc.com. **Barclay International Group** ☎ 800/845–6636, 516/364–0064 ⊕ www.barclayweb.com. **Doorways, Ltd.** ☎ 610/520–0806, 800/261–4460 ⊕ www.villavacations.com. **Drawbridge to Europe** ☎ 888/268–1148, 541/482–7778 ⊕ www.drawbridgetoeurope.com. **Hosted Villas** ☎ 800/374–6637, 416/920–1873 ⊕ www.hostedvillas.com. **Italy Rents** ☎ 202/821–4273, 06/39728556 in Italy ⊕ www.italyrents.com. **Rent A Villa** ☎ 877/250–4366, 206/417–3444 ⊕ www.rentavilla.com. **Suzanne B. Cohen & Associates** ☎ 207/622–0743 ⊕ www.villaeurope.com. **Tuscan House** ☎ 800/844–6939 ⊕ www.tuscanhouse.com. **Vacation Rentals by Owner** ☎ 877/228–0710 ⊕ www.vrbo.com. **Villas & Apartments Abroad** ☎ 212/213–6435 ⊕ www.vaanyc.com. **Villas International** ☎ 800/221–2260, 415/499–9490 ⊕ www.villasintl.com. **Villas of Distinction** ☎ 800/289–0900 ⊕ www.villasofdistinction.com. **Wimco** ☎ 800/449–1553 ⊕ www.wimco.com.

CONVENTS AND MONASTERIES

Throughout Italy tourists can find reasonably priced lodging at convents, monasteries, and religious houses. Religious orders commonly charge about €30 to €60 per person per night for rooms that are clean, comfortable, and convenient. Many have private bathrooms; spacious lounge areas and secluded gardens or terraces are standard features. A continental breakfast ordinarily comes with the room, but be sure to ask. Sometimes, for an extra fee, family-style lunches and dinners are provided, too.

Be aware of three issues when considering a convent or monastery stay: many have a curfew of 11 pm or midnight; you need to book in advance because they fill up quickly; and your best means of booking is usually email or fax—the person answering the phone may not speak English.

Contact Hospites.it. Info and listings for religious housing facilities throughout Italy are provided. ⊕ www.hospites.it.

FARM HOLIDAYS AND AGRITOURISM

Rural accommodations in the agriturismo category are growing in popularity among both Italians and visitors; you may have to look a little hard, though, to find an actual working farm or vineyard. Accommodations vary in size and range from luxury apartments, farmhouses, and villas to basic facilities. Agriturist has compiled *Agriturism,* which is available only in Italian, but includes more than 1,450 farms in Italy; pictures and the use of international symbols to describe facilities make the guide a good tool. Local APT tourist offices also have information.

Information Agriturismo.com ☎ 0575/1645101 ⊕ www.agriturismo.com. **Agriturismo.net** ☎ 050/8665377 ⊕ www.agriturismo.net. **Agriturist** ☎ 06/6852342 ⊕ www.agriturist.it.

HOME EXCHANGES

With a direct home exchange you stay in someone else's home while they stay in yours. Some outfits also deal with vacation homes, so you're not really occupying someone's full-time residence, just their vacant weekend place.

Italians have historically not been as enthusiastic about home exchanges as others; however, there are many great villas and apartments in Italy owned by foreigners (Americans, English, etc.) who use the home-exchange services.

Exchange Clubs Home Exchange.com. Membership is $9.95 monthly or $15.95 for three months. ☎ 800/877–8723, 310/798–3864 ⊕ www.homeexchange.com. **HomeLink International.** Membership is $95 for one year, $152 for two; additional listings are $25. ☎ 800/638–3841, 954/566–2687

⊕ www.homelink.org. **Intervac Home Exchange.** One-year membership is $99.99. ☎ 800/756–4663 ⊕ www.intervac-homeexchange.com.

■ COMMUNICATIONS

INTERNET

Getting online in Italian cities isn't difficult: public Internet stations and Internet cafés, some open 24 hours, are fairly common, and Wi-Fi is widely available. Most hotels have Wi-Fi and/or a computer for guests to use. Many business-oriented hotels also offer in-room broadband, though some (ironically, often the more expensive ones) charge for broadband and Wi-Fi access. Note that chargers and power supplies may need plug adapters to fit European-style electric sockets (a converter probably won't be necessary).

Italy is also looking to improve city Wi-Fi access; Rome and Venice are continuing to develop and expand services, some free for now, some at a daily or weekly rate for temporary access.

Paid and free Wi-Fi hot spots can be found in major airports and train stations, and shopping centers; they're most likely be free in bars or cafés that want your business.

Contact Provincia Wi-Fi. For use with Italian cell phones only, this service offers the ability to surf the internet free (for now) with a daily limit of 300MB of total traffic. Users must register online at any hotspot. ☎ 06/4040 9434 ⊕ www.provincia.roma.it/percorsitematici/ innovazione-tecnologica.

PHONES

With the advent of mobile phones, public pay phones are becoming increasingly scarce in Italy, but they can be found at train and subway stations, main post offices, and in some bars. In rural areas, town squares usually have a pay phone. These require a *scheda telefonica* (⇨ *Calling Cards*).

LOCAL DO'S AND TABOOS

GREETINGS

Upon meeting and leave-taking, both friends and strangers wish each other good day or good evening (*buongiorno, buona sera*); *ciao* isn't used between strangers. Italians who are friends greet each other with a kiss, usually first on the left cheek, then on the right. When you meet a new person, shake hands and give your name.

SIGHTSEEING

Italy's churches house significant works of art, too, but they're also places of worship, so remember to dress appropriately.

Shorts, tank tops, and sleeveless garments are taboo in most churches throughout the country. To avoid being denied entrance, carry a shawl or other item of clothing to cover bare shoulders.

You should never bring food into a church, and don't sip from your water bottle inside. If you have a cell phone, turn it off before entering. Ask whether photographs are allowed—and *never use flash*. Never enter a church when a service is in progress either, especially if it's a private affair such as a wedding, funeral, or baptism.

OUT ON THE TOWN

Table manners in Italy are formal; rarely do Italians share food from their plates. In a restaurant, be reserved and polite with your waiter—no calling across the room for attention.

When you've finished your meal and are ready to go, ask for the check (*il conto*); unless it's well past closing time, it is unlikely a waiter will put a bill on your table until you've requested it.

Italians don't have a culture of sipping cocktails or chugging pitchers of beer. Wine, beer, and other alcoholic drinks are usually consumed only as part of a meal. Public drunkenness is abhorred.

Smoking has been banned in all public establishments, much as in the United States.

DOING BUSINESS

Showing up on time for business appointments is the norm and expected in Italy. There are more business lunches than business dinners, and even business lunches aren't common, as Italians view mealtimes as periods of pleasure and relaxation.

Business cards (*biglietto da visita*) are used throughout Italy, and business attire is the norm for both men and women. To be on the safe side, it's best not to use first names or a familiar form of address until invited to do so.

Business gifts aren't the norm, but if one is given it's usually small and symbolic of your home location or type of business.

LANGUAGE

One of the best ways to connect with Italians is to learn a little of the local language. You need not strive for fluency; just mastering a few basic words and terms is bound to make interactions more rewarding.

"Please" is *per favore*, "thank you" is *grazie*, "you're welcome" is *prego*, and "excuse me" is *scusi (or "permesso" when you need to move past someone, as on a bus)*.

In larger cities like Venice, Rome, and Florence, language isn't a big problem. Most hotels have English-speakers at their reception desks, and if not, they can always find someone who speaks at least a little English. You may have trouble communicating in the countryside, but expressive gestures and a good phrase book—like *Fodor's Italian for Travelers* (available at bookstores everywhere)—will go a long way. Need audio assistance? Click ⊕ *www.fodors.com/language/italian* to hear more than 150 essential phrases.

CALLING ITALY FROM ABROAD

When telephoning Italy from North America, dial 011 (to get an international line), followed by Italy's country code, 39, and the phone number, including any leading 0. Note that Italian cell numbers have 10 digits and always begin with a 3; Italian landline numbers will contain from 4 to 10 digits and always begin with a 0. So, for example, when calling Rome, where local numbers start with 06, dial 011 + 39 + 06 + phone number; for a cell phone, dial 011 + 39 + cell number.

CALLING WITHIN ITALY

For all calls within Italy, whether local or long-distance, you'll dial the entire phone number that starts with 0, or 3 for cell phone numbers. Rates from landlines vary according to the time of day; it's cheaper to call before 9 am and after 7 or 8 pm; calling a cell phone will cost significantly more, depending on the calling plan. Italy uses the prefix "800" for toll-free or *numero verde* (green) numbers.

MAKING INTERNATIONAL CALLS

Rates to the United States and Canada are lowest on Sunday around the clock and between 10 pm and 8 am (Italian time) on weekdays and Saturday. The country code for the U.S. and Canada is 1 (dial 00 + 1 + area code and number).

Because of the high rates charged by most hotels for long-distance and international calls, you're better off making such calls from public phones or your mobile phone and/or using an international calling card (⇨ *Calling Cards*).

Although not advised because of the exorbitant cost, you can place international calls or collect calls through an operator by dialing 170.

CALLING CARDS

Prepaid *schede telefoniche* (phone cards) are available throughout Italy for use in pay phones. Cards in different denominations are sold at post offices, newsstands, tobacco shops, and some bars. Before the first use, break off the corner of the card; then, to make a call, insert it into the phone's slot and dial. The card's credit will be displayed in the window as you chat. After you hang up, be sure not to walk off without retrieving the card.

International calling cards are different; you call a toll-free number from any phone, entering the access code found on the back of the card followed by the destination number. With calling cards offered by AT&T, MCI, and Sprint, instructions and operator assistance are in English, avoiding language difficulties, and the charges appear on your phone bill. A reliable prepaid card for calling North America and elsewhere in Europe is the TIM Welcome card, which comes in two denominations, €5 for 500 minutes and €10 for 1,000 minutes and is available at tobacco shops and newsstands. When purchasing, specify your calling destination (the United States, or the country you prefer).

Access Codes AT&T Direct ☎ *800/172-444.* **MCI WorldPhone** ☎ *800/90-5825.* **Sprint International Access** ☎ *800/172-405.*

MOBILE PHONES

If you have a multiband phone (Europe and North America use different calling frequencies) and your service provider uses the world-standard GSM network (as do T-Mobile, AT&T, and Verizon), you can probably use your own phone and provider abroad. But roaming fees can be steep—99¢ a minute is considered quite low—and overseas you'll normally pay toll charges for incoming calls, too.

■**TIP➜ If you're carrying a laptop, tablet, or smartphone, investigate apps and services such as Skype, Viber, and Whatsapp, which offer free or low-cost calling and texting services.**

To keep calling expenses to a minimum, consider purchasing an Italian SIM card—these can be purchased for as little as €5, depending on the provider (make sure your home service provider first unlocks your phone for use with a different SIM) and choose a prepaid service plan, topping off the credit as you go. You then have a local number and can make calls at local rates (about €.15 per minute, and only for ones made, not received), or send text messages for a reasonable fee (12¢ per message or less). Have the service provider enable international calling; use an international calling card with your cell for even more savings.

■**TIP→** If you're a frequent international traveler, save your old mobile phone (ask your cell phone company to unlock it for you) or buy an unlocked, multiband phone online. Use it as a travel phone, buying a new SIM card with pay-as-you-go service in each destination.

The cost of cell phones is dropping: you can purchase a dual band (Europe only) cell phone in Italy with a prepaid calling credit for as little as €40. Alternatively, you can buy a multiband phone that will also function in North America (European phones aren't "locked" to their provider's SIM, which is why they cost more). That means you can use it with your own service provider once you return home. You'll find dedicated cell phone stores in all but the smallest towns. Service providers include TIM, Tre, Vodafone, and Wind; stop by a multivendor shop to compare offers, or check their websites. Note that you'll need to present your passport to purchase any SIM card.

Rental cell phones are available online prior to departure and in Italy's cities and larger towns. Many Internet cafés offer them as well. Shop around for the best deal. Most rental contracts require a refundable deposit that covers the cost of the cell phone (€75–€150) and then set up a monthly service plan that's automatically charged to your credit card. Frequently, rental cell phones will be triple band with a plan that allows you to call North America. You should check the rate schedule, however, to avoid a nasty surprise on your credit-card bill two or three months later. Often the local purchase with a prepaid plan will be the more cost-effective one.

■**TIP→** Beware of cell phone (and PDA) thieves. Use your device's security code option. Keep your phone or PDA in a secure pocket or purse. Don't lay it on the bar when you stop for an espresso. Don't zip it into the outside pocket of your backpack in crowded cities. Don't leave it in your hotel room. Notify your provider immediately if it's lost or stolen; providers can disable your SIM and give you a new one, copying the original's number and contents.

Contacts Cellular Abroad. This is a good source for SIM cards that work in many countries; travel-friendly phones can also be purchased or rented. ☎ *800/287–5072* ⊕ *www.cellularabroad.com.* **Mobal.** GSM phones that will operate in 190 countries are available for purchase (starting at $49) and rent. Per-call rates in Italy are $1.25 per minute; sending a text costs $.80. ☎ *888/888– 9162, 212/785–5800 for support* ⊕ *www.mobal.com.* **Planet Fone.** Rental cell phones, with per-minute rates costing $.99– $1.98, are available. ☎ *888/988–4777* ⊕ *www.planetfone.com.*

▮ CUSTOMS AND DUTIES

Travelers from the United States should experience little difficulty clearing customs at any Italian airport. It may be more difficult to clear customs when returning to the United States, where residents are normally entitled to a duty-free exemption of $800 on items accompanying them. You'll have to pay a tax (most often a flat percentage) on the value of everything beyond that limit. When you shop in Italy, keep all your receipts handy, as customs inspectors may ask to see them as well as the items you purchased.

Although there's no problem with aged cheese (vacuum-sealed works best), you cannot bring back any of that delicious prosciutto, salami, or any other meat product. Fresh mushrooms, truffles, or fresh fruits and vegetables are also forbidden. There are restrictions on the amount of alcohol allowed in duty-free, too. Generally, you can bring in one liter of wine, beer, or other alcohol without paying a customs duty; visit the travel area of the Customs and Border Patrol Travel website for complete information.

Italy requires documentation regarding the background of all antiques and antiquities before these items are taken out of the country. Under Italian law, all antiquities found on Italian soil are considered state property, and there are other restrictions on antique artwork. Even if purchased from a business in Italy, legal ownership of artifacts may be in question if brought into the United States. Therefore, although they don't necessarily confer ownership, documents such as export permits and receipts are required when importing such items into the United States.

Information in Italy Dogana Sezione Viaggiatori ☎ 06/50241 ⊕ www.agenziadogane.it.

U.S. Information U.S. Customs and Border Protection ☎ 877/227–5511 ⊕ www.cbp.gov.

▌EATING OUT

Italian cuisine is still largely regional. Ask what the specialties are—and, by all means, try spaghetti *alla carbonara* (with bacon and egg) in Rome, pizza in Naples, *bistecca alla fiorentina* (steak) in Florence, *cinghiale* (wild boar) in Tuscany, truffles in Piedmont, *la frittura* (fish fry) in Venice, and risotto alla milanese in Milan. Although most restaurants in Italy serve local dishes, you can find Asian and Middle Eastern alternatives in Rome, Venice, and other cities. The restaurants we list are the cream of the crop in each price category.

MEALS AND MEALTIMES

What's the difference between a *ristorante* and a *trattoria*? Can you order food at an *enoteca* (wine bar)? Can you go to a restaurant just for a snack or order only salad at a pizzeria? The following definitions should help.

Not long ago, *ristoranti* tended to be more elegant and expensive than *trattorie*,

(which serve traditional, home-style fare in an atmosphere to match) or *osterie* (which serve local wines and simple, regional dishes). But the distinction has blurred considerably, and an osteria in the center of town might now be far fancier (and pricier) than a ristorante across the street. In any sit-down establishment, however, you're generally expected to order at least a two-course meal, such as: a *primo* (first course) and a *secondo* (main course) or a *contorno* (vegetable side dish); an *antipasto* (starter) followed by either a primo or secondo; or a secondo and a *dolce* (dessert).

If you'd prefer to eat less, best head to an enoteca or pizzeria, where it's more common to order a single dish. An enoteca menu is often limited to a selection of cheese, cured meats, salads, and desserts, but if there's a kitchen you can also find soups, pastas, and main courses. The typical pizzeria serves *affettati misti* (a selection of cured pork), simple salads, various kinds of bruschetta, *crostini* (similar to bruschetta, with a variety of toppings) and, in Rome, *fritti* (deep-fried finger food) such as *olive ascolane* (green olives with a meat stuffing) and *suppli* (rice balls stuffed with mozzarella).

The most convenient and least expensive places for a quick snack between sights are probably bars, cafés, and pizza *al taglio* (by the slice) spots. Pizza al taglio shops are easy to negotiate, but few have seats. They sell pizza by weight: just point out which kind you want and how much. Note that in Italy it's considered rude to walk and eat.

Bars in Italy resemble what we think of as cafés, and are primarily places to get a coffee and a bite to eat, rather than drinking establishments. Expect a selection of panini warmed up on the griddle (*piastra*) and *tramezzini* (sandwiches made of untoasted white bread triangles). In larger cities, bars also serve vegetable and fruit salads, cold pasta dishes, and gelato. Most offer beer and a variety of alcohol, as well as wines by the glass (sometimes good but more often mediocre). A café is like a bar but typically has more tables. Pizza at a café should be avoided—it's usually heated in a microwave.

If you place your order at the counter, ask whether you can sit down. Some places charge for table service (especially in tourist centers); others don't. In self-service bars and cafés it's good manners to clean your table before you leave. Be aware that in certain spots (such as train stations and stops along the highway) you first pay a cashier; then show your *scontrino* (receipt) at the counter to place your order. Menus are posted outside most restaurants (in English in tourist areas). If not, you might step inside and ask to take a look at the menu, but don't ask for a table unless you intend to stay.

Italians take their food as it's listed on the menu, seldom if ever making special requests such as "dressing on the side" or "hold the olive oil." If you have special dietary needs, however, make them known; they can usually be accommodated. Although mineral water makes its way to almost every table, you can order a carafe of tap water (*acqua di rubinetto* or *acqua semplice*) instead—just keep in mind that such water can be highly chlorinated.

An Italian would never ask for olive oil to dip bread in, and don't be surprised if there's no butter to spread on it either. Wiping your bowl clean with a (small) piece of bread is usually considered a sign of appreciation, not bad manners. Spaghetti should be eaten with a fork only, although a little help from a spoon won't horrify locals the way cutting spaghetti into little pieces might. Order your *caffè* (Italians drink cappuccino only in the morning) after dessert, not with it. As for doggy bags, Italians would never ask for one, though eateries popular with tourists are becoming more accustomed to travelers who do.

Breakfast (*la colazione*) is usually served from 7 to 10:30, lunch (*il pranzo*) from 12:30 to 2:30, and dinner (*la cena*) from 7:30 to 10, later in the south; outside those hours, best head for a bar. Peak times are usually 1:30 for lunch and 9 for dinner. Enoteche and Venetian *bacari* (wine bars) are also open in the morning and late afternoon for *cicchetti* (finger foods) at the counter. Most pizzerias open at 8 pm and close around midnight—later in summer and on weekends. Bars and cafés are open from 7 am until 8 or 9 pm; a few stay open until midnight.

Unless otherwise noted, the restaurants listed in this guide are open for lunch and dinner, closing one or two days a week.

PAYING

Most restaurants have a cover charge per person, usually listed at the top of the check as *coperto* or *pane e coperto*. It should be a modest (€1–€2.50 per person) except at the most expensive restaurants. Whenever in doubt, ask before you order to avoid unpleasant discussions later. It's customary to leave a small cash tip (between 5% and 10%) in appreciation of good service: you will usually see a *servizio* charge included at the bottom of the check, but the server will not likely receive it.

The price of fish dishes is often given by weight (before cooking), so the price quoted on the menu is for 100 grams of fish, not for the whole dish. (An average fish portion is about 350 grams.) In Tuscany, bistecca alla fiorentina is also often priced by weight (about €4 for 100 grams or $18 per pound).

Major credit cards are widely accepted in Italy; however, cash is always preferred. More restaurants take Visa and MasterCard than American Express or Diners Club.

When you leave a dining establishment, take your meal bill or receipt with you. Although not a common experience, the Italian finance (tax) police can approach you within 100 yards of the establishment at which you've eaten and ask for a receipt; if you don't have one, they can fine you and will fine the business owner for not providing it. The practice is intended to prevent tax evasion; it's not necessary to show receipts when leaving Italy.

RESERVATIONS AND DRESS

Although we only mention reservations specifically when they're essential (there's no other way you'll ever get a table) or when they're not accepted, it's always safest to make one for dinner. For popular restaurants, book as far ahead as you can (two to three weeks), and reconfirm as soon as you arrive. Large parties should always call ahead to check the reservations policy. If you change your mind, be sure to cancel, even at the last minute.

We mention dress only when men are required to wear a jacket or a jacket and tie. But unless they're dining outside or at a seafront resort, Italian men never wear shorts or running shoes in a restaurant. The same applies to women: no casual shorts, running shoes, or rubber sandals when going out to dinner. Shorts are acceptable in pizzerias and cafés.

WINES, BEER, AND SPIRITS

The grape has been cultivated in Italy since the time of the Etruscans, and Italians justifiably take pride in their local varieties, which are numerous. Though almost every region produces good-quality wine, Tuscany, Piedmont, the Veneto, Puglia, Calabria, and Sicily are some of the more renowned areas, with Marches and Umbria being well reputed as well. Wine in Italy is less expensive than almost anywhere else, so it's often affordable to order a bottle of wine at a restaurant rather than sticking with the house wine (which is usually good but quite simple). Many bars have their own *aperitivo della casa* (house aperitif); Italians are imaginative with their mixed drinks, so you may want to try one.

You can purchase beer, wine, and spirits in any bar, grocery store, or enoteca, any day of the week, any time of the day. Italian and German beer is readily available, but it can be more expensive than wine. Some excellent microbreweries are beginning to dot the Italian beer horizon, so ask if there's a local brew available to sample.

There's no minimum drinking age in Italy. Italian children begin drinking wine mixed with water at mealtimes when they're teens (or thereabouts). Italians are rarely seen drunk in public, and public drinking, except in a bar or eating establishment, isn't considered acceptable behavior. Bars usually close by 9 pm; hotel and restaurant bars stay open until midnight. Brewpubs and discos serve until about 2 am.

▌ ELECTRICITY

The electrical current in Italy is 220 volts, 50 cycles alternating current (AC); wall outlets accept continental-type plugs, with two or three round prongs.

You may purchase a universal adapter, which has several types of plugs in one lightweight, compact unit, at travel specialty stores, electronics stores, and online. You can also pick up plug adapters in Italy in any electric supply store for about €2 each. You'll likely not need a voltage converter, though. Most portable devices are dual voltage (i.e., they operate equally well on 110 and 220 volts); just check label specifications and manufacturer instructions to be sure. Don't use 110-volt outlets marked "for shavers only" for high-wattage appliances such as hair dryers.

Contacts Global Electric and Phone Directory. This site has information on electrical and telephone plugs around the world as well as details on international telephone calls. ⊕ *www.kropla.com.*

▌ EMERGENCIES

No matter where you are in Italy, you can dial ☎ *113* in case of emergency: the call will be directed to the local police. Not all 113 operators speak English, so you may want to ask a local person to place the call. Asking the operator for *"pronto soc-corso"* (first aid and also the emergency room of a hospital) should get you an *ambulanza* (ambulance). If you just need a doctor, ask for *"un medico."*

Italy has the *carabinieri* (national police force, their emergency number is ☎ *112* from anywhere in Italy) as well as the *polizia* (local police force). Both are armed and have the power to arrest and investigate crimes. Always report the loss of your passport to the caribinieri as well as to your embassy. When reporting a crime, you'll be asked to fill out *una denuncia* (official report); keep a copy for your insurance company. You should also contact the police any time you have a car accident of any sort.

Local traffic officers, known as *vigili*, are responsible for, among other things, giving out parking tickets. They wear white (in summer), navy, or black uniforms. Should you find yourself involved in a minor car accident in town, contact the vigili.

Pharmacies are generally open weekdays 8:30–1 and 4–8, and Saturday 9–1. Local pharmacies rotate covering the off-hours in shifts: on the door of every pharmacy is a list of which pharmacies in the vicinity will be open late.

Foreign Embassies U.S. Consulate Florence ✉ *Via Lungarno Vespucci 38, Florence* ☎ *055/266951* ⊕ *florence.usconsulate. gov.* **U.S. Consulate Milan** ✉ *Via Principe Amedeo 2/10, Milan* ☎ *02/290351* ⊕ *milan. usconsulate.gov.* **U.S. Consulate Naples** ✉ *Piazza della Repubblica, Naples* ☎ *081/5838111* ⊕ *naples.usconsulate.gov.* **U.S. Embassy** ✉ *Via Vittorio Veneto 121, Rome* ☎ *06/46741* ⊕ *italy.usembassy.gov.*

General Emergency Contacts Emergencies ☎ *115 Fire, 118 Ambulance.* **National and State Police** ☎ *112 Polizia (National Police), 113 Carabinieri (State Police).*

▌ HOURS OF OPERATION

Religious and civic holidays are frequent in Italy. Depending on the holiday's local importance, businesses may close for the day. Businesses don't close Friday or Monday when the holiday falls on the weekend, though the Monday following Easter is a holiday.

Banks are open weekdays 8:30–1:30 and for one or two hours in the afternoon, depending on the bank. Most post offices are open Monday–Saturday 9–1:30, some until 2; central post offices are open 9–6:30 weekdays, 9–12:30 or 9–6:30 on Saturday.

Most churches are open from early morning until noon or 12:30, when they close for three hours or more; they open again in the afternoon, closing at about 6. A few major churches, such as St. Peter's in Rome and San Marco in Venice, remain open all day. Walking around during services is discouraged. Many museums are closed one day a week, often Monday or Tuesday. During low season museums often close early; during high season many stay open until late at night.

Most shops are open Monday–Saturday 9–1 and 3:30 or 4–7:30. Clothing shops are generally closed Monday mornings. Barbers and hairdressers, with certain exceptions, are closed Sunday and Monday. Some bookstores and fashion- or tourist-oriented shops in places such as Rome and Venice are open all day, as well as Sunday. Many branches of large chain supermarkets such as Standa, COOP, and Esselunga don't close for lunch and are usually open Sunday; smaller *alimentari* (delicatessens) and other food shops are usually closed one evening during the week (it varies according to the town) and are almost always closed Sunday.

HOLIDAYS

Traveling through Italy in August can be an odd experience. Although there are some deals to be had, the heat can be oppressive, and much of the population is on vacation. Most cities are deserted (except for foreign tourists) and privately run restaurants and shops are closed. The national holidays in 2014 include January 1 (New Year's Day); January 6 (Epiphany); April 20 and 21 (Easter Sunday and Monday); April 25 (Liberation Day); May 1 (Labor Day or May Day); June 2 (Festival of the Republic); August 15 (Ferragosto); November 1 (All Saints' Day); December 8 (Immaculate Conception); and December 25 and 26 (Christmas Day and the Feast of Saint Stephen).

In addition, feast days of patron saints are observed locally. Many businesses and shops may be closed in Florence, Genoa, and Turin on June 24 (Saint John the Baptist); in Rome on June 29 (Saints Peter and Paul); in Palermo on July 15 (Santa Rosalia); in Naples on September 19 (San Gennaro); in Bologna on October 4 (San Petronio); in Trieste on November 3 (San Giusto); and in Milan on December 7 (Saint Ambrose). Venice's feast of Saint Mark is April 25, the same as Liberation Day, so the Madonna della Salute on November 21 makes up for the lost holiday.

▌ MAIL

The Italian mail system has a bad reputation but has become noticeably more efficient in recent times with some privatization. Allow from 7 to 15 days for mail to get to the United States. Receiving mail in Italy, especially packages, can take weeks, usually due to customs (not postal) delays.

Most post offices are open Monday–Saturday 9–1:30; central post offices are open weekdays 9–6:30, Saturday 9–12:30 (some until 6:30). You can buy stamps at tobacco shops as well as post offices.

Posta Prioritaria (for regular letters and packages) is the name for standard postage. It guarantees delivery within Italy in three to five business days and abroad in five to six working days. The more expensive express delivery, *Postacelere* (for larger letters and packages), guarantees one-day delivery to most places in Italy and three- to five-day delivery abroad. Note that the postal service has no control over customs, however, which makes international delivery estimates meaningless. Mail sent as Posta Prioritaria Internazionale to the United States costs €2 for up to 20 grams, €3.50 for 21–50 grams, and €4.50 for 51–100 grams. Mail sent as Postacelere to the United States costs €56.70 for up to 500 grams.

Reliable two-day international mail is generally available during the week in all major cities and at popular resorts via UPS and Federal Express—but again, customs delays can slow down "express" service.

SHIPPING SERVICES

Sending a letter or small package to the United States via Federal Express takes at least two days and costs about €45. Other package services to check are Quick Pack Europe (for delivery within Europe) and Express Mail Service (a global three- to five-day service for letters and packages). Compare prices with those of Postacelere to determine the cheapest option.

If your hotel can't assist you with shipping, try an Internet café; many offer two-day mail services using major carriers.

If you've purchased antiques, ceramics, or other fragile objects, ask if the vendor will do the shipping for you. In most cases this is possible, and preferable, because many merchants have experience with these kinds of shipments. If so, ask whether the article will be insured against breakage.

▌ MONEY

Prices vary from region to region and are substantially lower in the country than in urban centers. Of Italy's major cities, Milan is by far the most expensive. Resort areas such as Amalfi, Portofino, and Cortina d'Ampezzo cater to wealthy vacationers and charge top prices. Good values can be had in the scenic Trentino–Alto Adige region of the Dolomites and in Umbria and the Marches. With a few exceptions, southern Italy and Sicily also offer bargains for those who do their homework before they leave home.

ITEM AVERAGE COST	
Cup of Coffee	€0.80–€1.50
Soft drink (glass/can/bottle)	€2–€3
Glass of Beer	€2–€4.50
Sandwich	€2–€4
2-km (1-mile) Taxi Ride in Rome	€8.50

Prices throughout this guide are given for adults. Substantially reduced fees are almost always available for children, students, and senior citizens from the EU; citizens of non-EU countries rarely get discounts, but inquire before you purchase tickets, as this situation is constantly changing.

■TIP➜ U.S. banks do not keep every foreign currency on hand, and it may take as long as a week to order. If you're planning to exchange funds before leaving home, don't wait until the last minute.

ATMS AND BANKS

An ATM (*bancomat* in Italian) is the easiest way to get euros in Italy. There are numerous ATMs in large cities and small towns, as well as in airports and train stations. Be sure to **memorize your PIN in numbers,** as ATM keypads in Italy won't always display letters. Check with your bank to confirm that you have an international PIN (*codice segreto*) that will be recognized in the countries you're visiting; to raise your maximum daily withdrawal allowance; and to learn what your bank's fee is for withdrawing money (Italian banks don't charge withdrawal fees). ■TIP➜ Be aware that PINs beginning with a 0 (zero) tend to be rejected in Italy.

Your own bank may charge a fee for using ATMs abroad and/or for the cost of conversion from euros to dollars. Nevertheless, you can usually get a better rate of exchange at an ATM than you will at a currency-exchange office or even when changing money inside a bank with a teller, the next best option. Whatever the method, extracting funds as you need them is safer than carrying around a large amount of cash. Finally, it's advisable to carry more than one card that can be used for cash withdrawal, in case something happens to your main one.

CREDIT CARDS

It's a good idea to **inform your credit-card company before you travel,** especially if you're going abroad and don't travel internationally often. Otherwise, the credit-card company might put a hold on your card owing to unusual activity—not a welcome occurrence halfway through your trip. Record all your credit-card numbers—as well as the phone numbers to call if your cards are lost or stolen. Keep these in a safe place, so you're prepared should something go wrong. MasterCard and Visa have general numbers you can call (collect if you're abroad) if your card is lost. But you're better off calling the number of your issuing bank, because MasterCard and Visa generally just transfer you there; your bank's number is usually printed on your card.

■TIP➜ North American toll-free numbers aren't available from abroad, so be sure to obtain a local number with area code for any business you may need to contact.

Although it's usually cheaper (and safer) to use a credit card abroad for large purchases (so you can cancel payments or be reimbursed if there's a problem), note that some credit-card companies *and* the banks that issue them add substantial percentages to all foreign transactions, whether they're in a foreign currency or not. Check on these fees before leaving home, so there won't be any surprises when you get the bill. Because of these fees, avoid using your credit card for ATM withdrawals or cash advances (use a debit or cash card instead).

■TIP→ Before you charge something, ask the merchant whether he or she plans to do a dynamic currency conversion (DCC). In such a transaction the credit-card processor (shop, restaurant, or hotel, not Visa or MasterCard) converts the currency and charges you in dollars. In most cases you'll pay the merchant a 3% fee for this service in addition to any credit-card company and issuing-bank foreign-transaction surcharges.

Merchants who participate in dynamic currency conversion programs are supposed to ask whether you want to be charged in dollars or the local currency, but they don't always do so. And even if they do offer you a choice, they may well avoid mentioning the additional surcharges. The good news is that you *do* have a choice—you can simply say no. If this practice really gets your goat, you can avoid it entirely by using American Express; with its cards, DCC simply isn't an option.

Italian merchants prefer MasterCard and Visa, but American Express is usually accepted in popular tourist destinations. Credit cards aren't accepted everywhere, though; if you want to pay with a credit card in a small shop, hotel, or restaurant, it's a good idea to make your intentions known early on.

Reporting Lost Cards
American Express ☎ *800/528–4800 in U.S., 905/474–0870 collect from abroad* ⊕ *www.americanexpress.com.* **Diners Club** ☎ *800/234–6377 in U.S., 514/881–3735 collect from abroad, 800/393939 in Italy* ⊕ *www.dinersclub.com.* **MasterCard** ☎ *800/627–8372 in U.S., 636/722–7111 collect from abroad, 800/151616 in Italy* ⊕ *www.mastercard.us.* **Visa** ☎ *800/847–2911 in U.S., 303/967–1096 from abroad, 800/819014 in Italy* ⊕ *usa.visa.com.*

CURRENCY AND EXCHANGE
The euro is the main unit of currency in Italy. Under the euro system there are 100 *centesimi* (cents) to the euro. There are coins valued at 1, 2, 5, 10, 20, and 50

centesimi as well as 1 and 2 euros. There are seven notes: 5, 10, 20, 50, 100, 200, and 500 euros.At this writing, 1 euro was worth was about 1.29 U.S. dollars.

Post offices exchange currency at good rates, but employees speak limited English, so be prepared. (Writing your request can help in these cases.)
■TIP→ Even if a currency-exchange booth has a sign promising no commission, rest assured that there's some kind of huge, hidden fee. You're almost always better off getting foreign currency at an ATM or exchanging money at a bank or post office.

▌ PASSPORTS AND VISAS
U.S. citizens need only a valid passport to enter Italy for stays of up to 90 days.

PASSPORTS
Although somewhat costly, a U.S. passport is relatively simple to obtain and is valid for 10 years. You must apply in person if you're getting a passport for the first time; if your previous passport was lost, stolen, or damaged; or if it has expired and was issued more than 15 years ago or when you were under 16. All children under 18 must appear in person to apply for or renew a passport. Both parents must accompany any child under 14 (or send a notarized statement with their permission) and provide proof of their relationship to the child.

There are 25 regional passport offices as well as 7,000 passport acceptance facilities in post offices, public libraries, and other governmental offices. If you're renewing a passport, you may do so by mail; forms are available at passport acceptance facilities and online, where you trace the application's progress.

The cost of a new passport is $135 for adults, $105 for children under 16; renewals are $110 for adults, $105 for children under 16 plus. Allow four to six weeks for processing, both for first-time passports and renewals. For an expediting fee of $60 you can reduce this time to two to three weeks. If your trip is less than two weeks away, you can get a passport even more rapidly by going to a passport office with the necessary documentation. Private expediters can get things done in as little as 48 hours, but charge hefty fees for their services.

■TIP→ Before your trip, make two copies of your passport's data page (one for someone at home and another for you to carry separately). Or scan the page and email it to someone at home and/or yourself.

GENERAL REQUIREMENTS FOR ITALY	
Passport	Must be valid for 6 months after date of arrival.
Visa	Tourist visas aren't needed for stays of 90 days or less by U.S. citizens.
Vaccinations	None
Driving	International driver's license required. CDW is compulsory on car rentals and will be included in the quoted price.

VISAS

When staying for 90 days or less, U.S. citizens aren't required to obtain a visa prior to traveling to Italy. A recent law requires that you fill in a declaration of presence within eight days of your arrival—the stamp on your passport at airport arrivals substitutes for this. If you plan to travel or live in Italy or the European Union for longer than 90 days, you must acquire a valid visa from the Italian consulate serving your state *before you leave the United States*. Plan ahead, because the process of obtaining a visa will take at least 30 days, and the Italian government doesn't accept visa applications submitted by visa expediters.

U.S. Passport Information U.S. Department of State ☎ 877/487–2778 ⊕ *www.travel.state. gov/passport.*

U.S. Passport Expediters A. Briggs Passport & Visa Expeditors ☎ *800/806–0581, 202/338–0111* ⊕ *www.abriggs.com.* **American Passport Express** ☎ *800/455–5166* ⊕ *www. americanpassport.com.* **Passport Express** ☎ *800/362–8196* ⊕ *www.passportexpress.com.* **Travel Document Systems** ☎ *800/874–5100* ⊕ *www.traveldocs.com.* **Travel the World Visas** ☎ *866/886–8472, 202/223–8822* ⊕ *www.world-visa.com.*

■ TAXES

A 10% V.A.T. (value-added tax) is included in the rate at all hotels except those at the upper end of the range.

No tax is added to the bill in restaurants. A service charge of approximately 10%–15% is often added to your check; in some cases a service charge is included in the prices.

The V.A.T. is 22% on clothing, wine, and luxury goods. On consumer goods it's already included in the amount shown on the price tag (look for the phrase "IVA *inclusa*"), whereas on services it may not be. If you're not a European citizen and if your purchases in a single day total more than €154.94, you may be entitled to a refund of the V.A.T.

When making a purchase, ask whether the merchant gives refunds—not all do, nor are they required to. If they do, they'll help you fill out the V.A.T. refund form, which you then submit to a company that will issue you the refund in the form of cash, check, or credit-card adjustment.

Alternatively, as you leave the country (or, if you're visiting several European Union countries, on leaving the EU), present your merchandise and the form to customs officials, who will stamp it. Once through passport control, take the stamped form to a refund-service counter for an on-the-spot refund (the quickest and easiest option). You may also mail it to the address on the form (or on the envelope with it) after you arrive home, but processing time can be long, especially if you request a credit-card adjustment.

Note that in larger cities the cash refund can be obtained at in-town offices prior to departure; just ask the merchant or check the envelope for local office addresses.

Global Blue is the largest V.A.T.-refund service with 225,000 affiliated stores and more than 700 refund counters at major airports and border crossings. Its refund form, called a Tax Free Check, is the most common across the European continent. Premier Tax Free is another company that represents more than 70,000 merchants worldwide; look for their logos in store windows.

V.A.T. Refunds Global Blue ☎ 866/7066090 *in North America, 421/232 111111 from abroad* ⊕ *www.global-blue.com.* **Premier Tax Free** ☎ *905/542-1710 from U.S., 06/699-23383 from Italy* ⊕ *www.premiertaxfree.com.*

TIME

Italy is in the Central European Time Zone (CET). From March to October it institutes Daylight Saving Time. Italy is 6 hours ahead of U.S. Eastern Standard Time, 1 hour ahead of Great Britain, 10 hours behind Sydney, and 12 hours behind Auckland. Like the rest of Europe, Italy uses the 24-hour (or "military") clock, which means that after noon you continue counting forward: 13:00 is 1 pm, 23:30 is 11:30 pm.

TIPPING

In restaurants a service charge of 10% to 15% may appear on your check, but it's not a given that your server will receive this; so you may want to consider leaving a tip of 5% to 10% (in cash) for good service. Tip checkroom attendants €1 per person and restroom attendants €0.50 (more in expensive hotels and restaurants). In major cities, tip €0.50 or more for table service in cafés. At a hotel bar, tip €1 and up for a round or two of drinks.

Italians rarely tip taxi drivers, which isn't to say that you shouldn't. A euro or two is appreciated, particularly if the driver helps with luggage. Service-station attendants are tipped only for special services; give them €1 for checking your tires. Railway and airport porters charge a fixed rate per bag. Tip an additional €0.25 per person, more if the porter is helpful. Give a barber €1–€1.50 and a hairdresser's assistant €1.50–€4 for a shampoo or cut, depending on the type of establishment.

On sightseeing tours, tip guides about €1.50 per person for a half-day group tour, more if they're especially knowledgeable. In monasteries and other sights where admission is free, a contribution (€0.50–€1) is expected.

In hotels, give the *portiere* (concierge) about 10% of the bill for services, or €2.50–€5 for help with dinner reservations and such. Leave the chambermaid about €0.75 per day, or about €4.50–€5 a week in a moderately priced hotel; tip a minimum of €1 for valet or room service. In an expensive hotel, double these amounts; tip doormen €0.50 for calling a cab and €1.50 for carrying bags to the check-in desk, and tip bellhops €1.50–€2.50 for carrying your bags to the room.

TOURS

Guided tours are a good option when you don't want to do it all yourself. You travel along with a group (sometimes large, sometimes small), stay in pre-booked hotels, often eat with your fellow travelers (the cost of meals may or may not be included in the price of your tour), and follow a set schedule. Not all guided tours are an if-it's-Tuesday-this-must-be-Belgium experience, however. A knowledgeable guide can take you places that you might never discover on your own, give you a richer context, and lead you to a more in-depth experience than you would have otherwise. They may be just the thing if you don't have the time or inclination to make travel arrangements on your own.

Whenever you book a guided tour, find out what's included and what isn't. A "land-only" tour includes all your travel (by bus, in most cases) in the destination, but not necessarily your flights to and from or even within it. Also, in most cases prices in tour promotions don't include fees and taxes. You'll also want to review how much free time you'll have, and see if that meets with your personal preferences. Remember, too, that you'll be expected to tip your guide (in cash) at the end of the tour.

Even when planning independent travel, keep in mind that every province and city in Italy has tour guides licensed by the government. Some are eminently qualified in relevant fields such as architecture and art history and are a pleasure to spend time with. Lots of private guides have websites, and you can check the travel forums at fodors.com for recommendations (it's best to book before you leave home, especially for major destinations, as popular guides and tours are in demand). Once in Italy, tourist offices and hotel concierges can also provide the names of knowledgeable local guides and the rates for certain services. When hiring on the spot, ask about their background and qualifications—and make sure you can understand each other. Tipping is always appreciated, but never obligatory, for local guides.

Recommended Generalists
Abercrombie & Kent ☎ 800/554-7016 ⊕ www.abercrombiekent.com. **Maupin Tour** ☎ 800/255-4266, 954/653-3820 ⊕ www.maupintour.com. **Perillo Tours** ☎ 800/431-1515 ⊕ www.perillotours.com. **Travcoa** ☎ 800/992-2003, 310/649-7104 ⊕ www.travcoa.com.

Biking and Hiking Tour Contacts
Backroads ☎ 800/462-2848, 510/527-1555 ⊕ www.backroads.com. **Butterfield & Robinson** ☎ 866/551-9090, 416/864-1354 ⊕ www.butterfield.com. **Ciclismo Classico** ☎ 800/866-7314, 781/646-3377 ⊕ www.ciclismoclassico.com. **Genius Loci Travel** ☎ 089/791896 ⊕ www.genius-loci.it. **Italian Connection** ☎ 800/462-7911, 780/438-5712 ⊕ www.italian-connection.com.

Culinary Tour Contact Epiculinary
☎ 707/815-1415 ⊕ www.epiculinary.com.

Educational Programs Road Scholar
☎ 800/454-5768, 978/323-4141
⊕ www.roadscholar.org.

Golf Tour Contact Golf Italy ☎ 051/266277
⊕ www.golfitaly.com.

Wine Tour Contacts Cellar Tours
☎ 310/496-8061 ⊕ www.cellartours.com.
Food and Wine Trails ☎ 800/367-5348
⊕ www.foodandwinetrails.com.

∎ TRIP INSURANCE

Comprehensive trip insurance is valuable if you're booking an expensive or complicated trip (particularly to an isolated region) or if you're booking far in advance. Comprehensive policies typically cover trip cancellation and interruption, letting you cancel or cut your trip short because of illness (yours or that of someone back home), or, in some cases, acts of terrorism in your destination. Such policies usually also cover evacuation and medical care. (For trips abroad you should have at least medical and medical evacuation coverage. With a few exceptions, Medicare doesn't provide coverage abroad, nor does regular health insurance.) Some also cover you for trip delays because of bad weather or mechanical problems as well as for lost or delayed luggage.

Another type of coverage to consider is financial default—that is, when your trip is disrupted because a tour operator, airline, or cruise line goes out of business. Generally you must buy this when you book your trip or shortly thereafter, and it's available to you only if your operator isn't on a list of excluded companies.

Many travel insurance policies have exclusions for preexisting conditions as a cause for cancellation. Most companies waive those exclusions, however, if you take out your policy within a short period (which varies by company) after the first payment toward your trip.

Always read the fine print of your policy to make sure that you're covered for the risks that most concern you. Compare several policies to be sure you're getting the best price and range of coverage available.

Comprehensive Insurers

Allianz ☎ 866/884–3556 ⊕ www. allianztravelinsurance.com. **CSA Travel Protection** ☎ 877/243–4135, 240/330–1529 ⊕ www.csatravelprotection.com. **HTH Worldwide** ☎ 610/254–8700 ⊕ www.hthworldwide. com. **Travel Guard** ☎ 800/826–1300, 715/345–0505 collect ⊕ www.travelguard. com. **Travel Insured International** ☎ 800/243–3174, 603/328–1707 collect ⊕ www.travelinsured.com.**Travelex Insurance** ☎ 800/228–9792, 603/328–1739 collect ⊕ www.travelex-insurance.com.

Insurance Comparison Info

Insure My Trip ☎ 800/487–4722, 401/773–9300 ⊕ www.insuremytrip.com. **Square Mouth** ☎ 800/240–0369, 727/564–9203 ⊕ www.squaremouth.com.

INDEX

PHOTO CREDITS

Front cover: Travel Pictures Ltd/SuperStock [Description: Ravello, Campania]. 1, Paul D'Innocenzo. 2-3, PCL/Alamy. 5, Javier Larrea/age fotostock. Experience Italy: 10-11, Paul D'Innocenzo. 12, Albo/Shutterstock. 13 (left), Antonio Petrone/Shutterstock. 13 (right), Agência Brasil, via Wikimedia Commons [Creative Commons License Attribution 3.0 Brazil]. 14, Thomas Barrat/Shutterstock. 15 (left and right), Ackab Photography/Shutterstock. 16 (top), Peter Clark/Shutterstock. 16 (bottom), Alfi o Ferlito/Shutterstock. 17, Olav Wildermann/Shutterstock. 18, Ant Clausen/Shutterstock. 20 (left), Ronald Sumners/Shutterstock. 20 (top center), Victoria German/Shutterstock. 20 (top right), Knud Nielsen/Shutterstock. 20 (bottom right), pxlar8/Shutterstock. 21 (left), Casper Voogt/Shutterstock, 21 (top center), John Lumb/Shutterstock. 21 (top right), Ivonne Wierink/Shutterstock. 21 (bottom right), Alfi o Ferlito/Shutterstock. 22, italianestro/Shutterstock. 23 (left), Thomas M Perkins/Shutterstock. 23 (right), Yanta/Shutterstock. 24, Eric Gevaert/Shutterstock. 25, Stefano Cellai/age fotostock. 26, Gina Sanders/Shutterstock. Part I: Rome and Environs: 30-31, Luciano Mortula/Shutterstock.com. 32, Paul D'Innocenzo. 33 (left), Angelo Campus. 33 (right), Paul D'Innocenzo. 36 (left), Angelo Campus. 36 (top center), Paul D'Innocenzo. 36 (top right), Angelo Campus. 36 (bottom right), Angelo Campus. 37 (top left), Paul D'Innocenzo. 37 (right), Public Domain. 37 (bottom left), Angelo Campus. 38, Angelo Campus. 39 (left), Angelo Campus. 39 (right), Paul D'Innocenzo. 41 (left and right), Angelo Campus. 42, Angelo Campus. 43 (left and right), Angelo Campus. 44, Jono Pandolfi . 45 (top), Angelo Campus. 45 (bottom), Jono Pandolfi . 46, Paul D'Innocenzo. Chapter 1: Rome: 47, Angelo Campus. 48, Paul D'Innocenzo. 51 (left), Justin D. Paola. 51 (right), Edis Jurcys/age fotostock. 52-53 (bottom), Justin D. Paola. 53 (top left), Renata Sedmakova/Shutterstock. 53 (top right), (c) Mrallen | Dreamstime.com. 54-55 (bottom), Justin D. Paola. 55 (top left), Rome Tourist Board. 55 (top right), Atlantide S.N.C./age fotostock. 57 (left), Chie Ushio. 57 (right), Dan Radmacher/iStockphoto/Thinkstock. 59 (left), Chie Ushio. 59 (right), Corbis. 84-85, SuperStock. 84 (bottom), Public Domain. 86, Russell Mountford/age fotostock. 88-91, Dave Drapak. Chapter 2: Side Trips from Rome:145, dave tonkin/iStockPhoto. 146 (top), Maurizio Farnetti/Shutterstock. 146 (bottom), Vito Arcomano/Fototeca ENIT. 148, avatra images/Alamy. Part II: Northern Italy. 168-169, Peter Adams/Agency Jon Arnold Images/age fotostock. 170, Steven Lee/Shutterstock. 171 (left), silvano audisio/Shutterstock. 171 (right), Patricia Hofmeester/Shutterstock. 174 (left), Paul Reid/Shutterstock. 174 (top center), Thomas M Perkins/Shutterstock. 174 (right), Public Domain. 174 (bottom), Rostislav Glinsky/Shutterstock. 175 (left), Public Domain. 175 (top center), Giovanni/Shutterstock. 175 (right), Public Domain. 175 (bottom), RookCreations/Shutterstock. 176, Izmael/Shutterstock. 177, Alfonso 'Agostino/Shutterstock. 178, Ljupco Smokovski/Shutterstock.180, Seet/Shutterstock. Chapter 3: Venice: 181, Paul D'Innocenzo. 182 (top), Nicole Vogels, Fodors.com member 182 (bottom), John Fasciani, Fodors.com member. 183, J.J. Burns, Fodors.com member. 184, Paul D'Innocenzo. 185 (top), Bon Appetit / Alamy. 185 (bottom), Robert Milek/Shutterstock. 186, S. Greg Panosian/iStockphoto. 191, Sailorr/Shutterstock. 192, Alexey Arkhipov/Shutterstock. 193 (left), Guido Alberto Rossi / age fotostock. 193 (right), Paul D'Innocenzo. 194, Javier Larrea/age fotostock. 195 (left), Steve Allen/Brand X Pictures. 195 (right), Doug Scott/age fotostock. 196, Bruno Morandi/age fotostock. 197 (left), Corbis. 197 (right), Sergio Pitamitz/age fotostock. Chapter 4: The Veneto and Friuli–Venezia Giulia: 255, Wojtek Buss/age fotostock. 256 (top), wikipedia.org. 256 (bottom) and 257, Vito Arcomano/Fototeca ENIT, 258, Francesco Majo/age fotostock, 259 (bottom), Michele Bella/age fotostock. 259 (top), Danilo Donadoni/age fotostock. 260, vesilvio/iStockphoto. 275 and 276 (top), from Quattro Libri by Andrea Palladio. 276 (bottom), Classic Vision/age fotostock. 277, By Hans A. Rosbach (Own work) [CC-BY-SA-3.0]. 278 (left), Vito Arcomano/Fototeca ENIT. 278 (right), Wojtek Buss/age fotostock 279, Wojtek Buss/age fotostock. Chapter 5: The Dolomites: 305, Angelani/fototeca Trentino. 306 (top), gpatchet, Fodors.com member. 306 (bottom), Angelani/fototeca Trentino. 307 (top and bottom), Vito Arcomano/Fototeca ENIT. 308, Danilo Donadoni/age fotostock. 309 (bottom), CuboImages srl / Alamy. 309 (top), franco pizzochero/age fotostock. 310, MartinDry/Shutterstock. 332, APT Dolomiti di Brenta/Fototeca ENIT. Chapter 6: Milan, Lombardy, and the Lakes: 339, Worldscapes/age fotostock. 340, Corbis. 341 (left), RookCreations/Shutterstock. 341 (right), APT del Comasco. 342, Danilo Donadoni/age fotostock. 343 (top), ubik/age fotostock. 343 (bottom), g.lancia/Shutterstock. 344, Public domain. 369, Stefano Politi Markovina / Alamy. Chapter 7: Piedmont and Valle d'Aosta: 399, (c) Paroli Galpertii. 400 (top), Krom/Shutterstock. 400 (bottom), Giuseppe Bressi/Fototeca ENIT. 401 (top), Roberto Borgo/Turismo Torino. 401 (bottom), Vito Arcomano/Fototeca ENIT. 402, CuboImages srl / Alamy. 403 (bottom), Piga & Catalano/age fotostock. 403 (top), Danilo Donadoni/age fotostock. 404, Dario Egidi/Stockphoto. 421 (top), Targa/age fotostock. 421 (bottom), FoodPhotography Eising / age fotostock. 422, alberto gagna/iStockphoto. 423 (top and bottom), Targa/age fotostock. Chapter 8: The Italian Riviera: 437, silvano audisio/Shutterstock. 438 (left), Vincent Thompson, Fodors.com member. 438 (right), Kelli Glaser, Fodors.com member. 439 (top), luri/Shutterstock. 439 (bottom Left), skyfi sh/Shutterstock. 439 (bottom right), Tifonimages/Shutterstock. 440, PCL / Alamy. 441 (top), ubik/age fotostock. 441 (bottom), Bon Appetit / Alamy. 442, laura rizzi/Stockphoto. 451, Oana Dragan/iStockphoto. 452 (top left), Peter Phipp/age fotostock. 452 (top center), Borut Trdina/iStockphoto. 452 (top right), Loren Irving/age fotostock. 452 (bottom), Carson Ganci/age fotostock. 453 (left), Angelo Cavalli/age fotostock. 453 (center), Cornelia Doerr/age fotostock. 453 (right), Bruno Morandi/age fotostock. 455 (top), Siepmann / age fotostock. 455 (bottom), Rechitan Sorin/Shutterstock. 456, Corbis. Chapter 9: Emilia–Romagna: 487, Atlantide S.N.C./age fotostock. 488 (top), Atlantide S.N.C./age fotostock. 488 (bottom), Javier Larrea/age fotostock. 489, FSG/age fotostock. 490 and 491 (top), Matz Sjöberg/age fotostock. 491 (bottom), franco pizzochero/age fotostock. 492, maria luisa berti/iStockphoto/Thinkstock. 505, John A. Rizzo/age fotostock. 506 (top), piccerella/iStockphoto. 506 (2nd from top), marco vacca / age fotostock. 506 (center), Consorzio del Prosciutto di Parma. 506 (4th from top), Parma 040 by http://www.fl ickr.com/photos/ nordelch/6198040562/ Attribution-ShareAlike License. 506 (bottom), Grischa Georgiew/iStockphoto/ Thinkstock. 507 (top two), Consorzio del Formaggio Parmigiano- Reggiano. 507 (3rd from top), Hermes Images / age fotostock. 507 (4th from top), Roberto A Sanchez/iStockphoto. 507 (bottom), Vito Arcomano/Fototeca ENIT. 508 (top and bottom), Hermes Images / age fotostock. 509 (top two), John A. Rizzo/age fotostock. 509 (center), Atlantide S.N.C./age fotostock. 509 (4th from top), Archivio Fotografi co Di Bologna Turismo. 509 (bottom), Claudio Baldini/Shutterstock. Part III: Central Italy: 534-35, SIME s.a.s / eStock Photo. 536, Susan Hurlburt, Fodors.com member. 537 (left), Patrick S. Golden, Fodors.com member. 537 (right), esamberg50, Fodors.com member. 539, JAX9000, Fodors. com member. 540 (left), Gijs van Ouwerkerk/Shutterstock. 540 (top center), Anja Peternelj/Shutterstock. 540 (top right), Knud Nielsen/Shutterstock. 540 (bottom right), Paul Merrett/Shutterstock. 541 (left), Danilo Ascione/Shutterstock. 541 (top center), Franco Deriu/iStockPhoto. 541 (top right), Ivonne Wierink/Shutterstock. 541 (bottom right), John Henshall/Alamy. 542, Jeremy R. Smith Sr./Shutterstock. 543, Tamara Kenyon Photography, Fodors.com member. 544, fpmassa, Fodors.com member. 546, bruno pagnanelli/Shutterstock Chapter 10: Florence: 547, alysta/Shutterstock. 548 (top), Ronald Sumners/Shutterstock. 548 (bottom), PhotoDisc. 549, Bertrand Collet/Shutterstock. 550, Cubo-Images srl / Alamy. 551 (top), Paolo Gallo / Alamy. 551(bottom), Sue Wilson / Alamy. 552, Luboslav Tiles/Shutterstock. 564-65, Wojtek Buss/age fotostock. 566 (all), Public domain. 567 (top), eye35.com/ Alamy. 567 (inset), Jessmine/Shutterstock. 567 (bottom), Rough Guides / Alamy. 568 (top left), Mary Evans Picture Library / Alamy. 568 (top right), Library of Congress Prints and Photographs Division (LCUSZ62-105343). 568 (bottom), Bruno Morandi/age fotostock. 587 (left), Classic Vision/age fotostock. 587 (center), SuperStock/age fotostock. 587 (right), Classic Vision/age fotostock. 588 (left) Chie Ushio. 588 (right), Planet Art. 589 (top), Classic Vision/age fotostock. 589 (center), SuperStock/Super Stock/age fotostock. 589 (bottom right), Corbis. 589 (bottom left), Wojtek Buss/age fotostock. 590 (left), Public Domain. 590 (center), SuperStock/age fotostock. 590 (right), Bruno Morandi/age fotostock. 591 (left), SuperStock/age fotostock. 591 (center), Public Domain via Wikimedia Commons. 591 (right), PTE/age fotostock. 592 (all), Planet Art. Chapter 11: Tuscany: 619, Cornelia Doerr/age fotostock. 620 (top), CarlB9090, Fodors.com member. 620 (bottom), Maugli/Shutterstock. 621, Julius Honnor. 622, Bon Appetit / Alamy. 623 (top), marco scataglini/age fotostock. 623 (bottom), nico tondini/age fotostock. 624, javarman/Shutterstock. 639 (left), Black Rooster Consortium. 639 (top right), Cephas Picture Library /Alamy. 639 (center right), Juergen Richter / age fotostock. 639 (bottom right), Cephas Picture Library /Alamy. 640, Cephas Picture Library / Alamy. 641 (left), Chuck Pefl ey / Alamy. 641 (right), Jon Arnold Images / Alamy. 642 (top left), CuboImages srl / Alamy. 642 (right), Cephas Picture Library / Alamy. 642 (bottom left), Black Rooster Consortium. 644 (left), Steve Dunwell/age fotostock. 644 (top right), IML Image Group Ltd / Alamy. 644 (bottom right), www.stradavinonobile. it. 660, Javier Larrea/age fotostock. 660 (inset), Photodisc. 662 (top left and right), M. Rohana / Shutterstock.com. 662 (bottom left), Bruno Morandi/age fotostock. Chapter 12: Umbria and the Marches: 679, Atlantide S.N.C./age fotostock. 680, magicinfoto/Shutterstock 681, sano7/Shutterstock. 682, B&Y Photography/Alamy. 683 (top), MEHMET OZCAN/iStockphoto 683 (bottom), Doco Dalfi ano/ age fotostock. 684, Ale_s/Shutterstock. 697, Atlantide S.N.C./age fotostock. 698, Picture Finders/age fotostock. 699 (all), Fototeca ENIT. 700, Atlantide S.N.C./age fotostock. Part IV: Southern Italy 726-27, Chris Sargent/Shutterstock. 728, Yanta/Shutterstock. 729 (left), cristina ferrari/Shutterstock. 729 (right), Bensliman/Shutterstock. 730, ollirg/Shutterstock. 731, Ivan Cholakov/Shutterstock. 732 (left), Valeria73/Shutterstock. 732 (top center), John Lumb/Shutterstock. 732 (top right), wikipedia.org. 732 (bottom right), Alfi o Ferlito/Shutterstock. 733 (left), Ventura/Shutterstock. 733 (top center), wikipedia. org. 733 (top right), Danilo Donadoni/age fotostock. 733 (bottom right), ollirg/Shutterstock. 734, akva/Shutterstock. 735, fl abobcat, Fodors.com member. 736, Danilo Ascione/Shutterstock. 738, Mario Savoia/Shutterstock Chapter 13: Naples and Campania: 739, Stephen Miller, Fodors.com member. 740,

NOTES

NOTES

NOTES

NOTES